Sociology

Sociology

Fourth Edition

James Fulcher and John Scott

OXFORD
UNIVERSITY PRESS

OXFORD

UNIVERSITY PRESS

Great Clarendon Street, Oxford OX2 6DP

Oxford University Press is a department of the University of Oxford.
It furthers the University's objective of excellence in research, scholarship,
and education by publishing worldwide in
Oxford   New York

Auckland Bangkok Buenos Aires Cape Town Chennai
Dar es Salaam Delhi Hong Kong Istanbul Karachi Kolkata
Kuala Lumpur Madrid Melbourne Mexico City Mumbai Nairobi
Sao Paulo Shanghai Singapore Taipei Tokyo Toronto

and an associated company in Berlin

Oxford is a registered trade mark of Oxford University Press
in the UK and in certain other countries

Published in the United States
by Oxford University Press Inc., New York

© James Fulcher and John Scott 2011

British Library Cataloguing in Publication Data
Data available

Library of Congress Cataloging in Publication Data

Typeset by Techset Compostion Ltd, Salisbury, UK

Printed and bound in China
on acid-free paper by C&C Offset Printing Co Ltd.

ISBN 978-0-19-956375-3

10 9 8 7 6 5 4 3 2 1

To all students of sociology, whoever they
are and wherever they may be.

Brief Contents

Detailed Contents

About the Authors

James Fulcher teaches sociology at the University of Leicester and has long experience as the course leader of an introductory sociology course. His main interests have been in the comparative study of the historical development of different societies. He has carried out research into the distinctive features of the social democratic model of society and has written a comparative study of the development of employment relations in Britain and Sweden, *Labour Movements, Employers, and the State: Conflict and Cooperation in Britain and Sweden* (1991). He has also been particularly interested in the distinctive features of Japanese society and the intriguing question of how the Japanese were able to beat the West at its own game by escaping colonial domination and becoming first a military and then an economic superpower. Interest in these societies led him to explore the issue of whether globalization was leading to the convergence of all societies towards a common model of capitalism or whether they were maintaining their historic distinctiveness. He discusses this and takes up many related issues, such as the origins of capitalism, its stages of development, its global spread, and its crisis tendencies in *Capitalism: A Very Short Introduction* (2003). He believes that sociology provides not only the best way to approach these very important questions but also the only way in which we can make sense of the world we live in, grasp our place within it, and ultimately understand ourselves.

John Scott teaches sociology at the University of Plymouth and was formerly Professor of Sociology at the Universities of Essex and Leicester. His interests in introductory sociology derive from his long involvement as editor of the student magazine *Sociology Review*. His main research interests cover the areas of economic and political sociology, social stratification, and social theory. He has undertaken comparative studies of business organization and capitalist class formation, most especially concentrating on Britain, the United States, and Japan. His principal publications in this area include *Capitalist Property and Financial Power* (1986) and *Corporate Business and Capitalist Classes* (1997). He has also undertaken detailed studies of the formation and current structure of the British upper class and the relationship between wealth and poverty. The major publications in this area include *Who Rules Britain?* (1991) and *Poverty and Wealth* (1994). His larger theoretical ideas on theories of power and class have been discussed in *Stratification and Power* (1996) and *Power* (2001). He has developed a view of social theory as a continuing area of intellectual debate that lies at the heart of the sociological enterprise, emphasizing the continuing importance of the formative ideas of the 'classical' writers as well as contemporary contributions. These arguments have been set out in *Sociological Theory* (1995) and *Social Theory* (2006). These empirical and theoretical interests have led to a long engagement with issues of research methodology, with major contributions to discussions of documentary research (*A Matter of Record*, 1990) and social network analysis (*Social Network Analysis: A Handbook*, 1992 and 2000).

About the Book

We enjoyed writing and revising this book, and we hope that you will enjoy reading it. Our aim has been to write a book that is comprehensive and interesting, but also easy to read. We have included many special textbook features to help you find your way through what is a complex subject, and these are listed in the 'How to use this book' section.

In this fourth edition we have maintained the same broad approach to sociology that has worked well in previous editions but, in addition to generally updating and revising the text, we have made important changes to reflect areas of growing interest, and to extend and improve the book's special features.

New to this edition

- A 'Concepts and theories' section in each chapter.
- Greater coverage of feminist theories and post-modern theories.
- More attention to global perspectives.
- Improved coverage of online identities, cyber ethnography, and the digital world.
- Discussion of the relationship between social networking sites and the media.
- Greater coverage of Scotland, Ireland, and Wales, taking account of devolution.
- A discussion of *sharia* law.
- Analysis of the current crisis of capitalism and the state's response to it.
- New material on sex work and AIDS.
- New material on the sociology of sport.

Still here from the previous edition

- 'Workshops' that consolidate the end-of-chapter material.
- 'Media watch' stories that examine articles from the media and relate them back to the core chapter issues.
- Useful hints and cross-references to help you build connections.

Focus of the book

This book is mainly focused on contemporary British society, but it is important to set this in its historical and global perspective. Many of the most strongly held ideas found in Britain today, such as beliefs about 'sex' and 'race', which we explore in Chapters 5 and 6, originated in the nineteenth century or earlier. Recent and far-reaching changes in the relationship between the state and society, which we examine in Chapter 15, attempted to reverse a century of expansion in the role of the state and return to an earlier age when market forces ruled. You will find that in all of our substantive chapters we set recent changes in the context of the longer-term development of society.

It is important also to take account of the experience of other societies, and you will find that we often discuss particular questions from a comparative point of view. For example, we make comparisons with many other countries when we discuss recent changes in the British welfare state in Chapter 15. We refer to the Japanese case when we examine changes in education in Chapter 9 and changes in work organization and work relationships in Chapters 14 and 17. We look at changes in patterns of political power in Russia when we explore elite theories in Chapter 20.

With globalization, it is, anyway, no longer sensible to separate one society sharply from another. What happens in one society is often very closely related to what happens in another. Indeed, some would say that we now live in a 'global society' where the boundaries between countries no longer matter, an issue that we discuss in Chapter 16, which is devoted to globalization. We consider it so important to take account of globalization that we have also included either a section or a box on globalization in every chapter.

The structure of the book

Part One is concerned with the broad areas of ***Theories and Methods***. Its chapters provide a general discussion of sociology and many of the theories and methods that you will come across in other chapters. You may indeed find it useful to treat these Part One chapters as reference sources to turn to when you wish to explore a theoretical question further or consider the issues raised by use of a particular method. You do not have to read the Part One chapters first and you should certainly not feel that you have to understand everything in Part One before you go further into the book.

Part Two examines the construction of ***Social Identities***. We begin in Chapter 4 by considering the process of socialization, the formation of social identities, and the way people present themselves to others. We highlight issues of role learning and changes occurring across the life course. Then, in Chapters 5 and 6, we explore two fundamental aspects of identity: gender and ethnicity. In Chapter 7 we consider how people acquire deviant identities. In Chapter 8 we examine the bodily aspects of identity, discussing here the medicalization of mental illness, and the significance of conceptions of the body for views of disability, cosmetic surgery, and eating disorders.

Part Three deals with ***Culture, Knowledge, and Belief***. In Chapter 9 we examine the acquisition of culture and knowledge through education, and its significance for inequality and economic success. In Chapter 10 we consider the communication of ideas and images through the media, and their influence on the way that people feel, think, and behave. In Chapter 11 we examine religious belief, its decline through processes of secularization and its revival in recent times, with the rise of new religions and the growth of fundamentalist movements in religion.

Part Four covers ***Social Organization and Control***. We examine here the main levels of social organization, beginning with the family in Chapter 12, before moving to larger structures with city and community in Chapter 13 and organizations in Chapter 14. In Chapter 15 we examine the development of the nation state and its transformation since the 1970s. Then in Chapter 16 we consider the impact of globalization on the nation state, and examine global movements of capital and people, before discussing whether we now live in a global society.

Part Five deals with ***Production, Inequalities, and Social Divisions***. We begin by examining production, through the topics of work, employment and leisure, in Chapter 17. Many social inequalities are grounded in work and employment relationships, and we move on to analyse inequality, poverty, and wealth in Chapter 18. In the Chapter 19 discussion of stratification we examine the organization of inequalities into hierarchies of class and status. Finally, in Chapter 20, we consider the relationship between class and power, before discussing whether class divisions have now been displaced by new social divisions and social movements.

There are many connections between these parts, and between various chapters. For example, while gender, ethnicity, and class are most fully discussed in Chapters 5, 6, and 19 respectively, every chapter in this book refers to them. Thus, the relationship between all three and educational achievement is discussed in Chapter 9, while their media representation is examined in Chapter 10. We draw attention to the more important of these links through our 'Connections' boxes, but we also cross-reference many others in the text.

The chapters of Parts Two, Three, Four, and Five have a common organization. Each begins with a 'Concepts and theories' section, in which we review the principal theoretical debates and the main concepts that are relevant to the subject of the chapter. The sections that follow look in detail at the studies and research carried out in the area and consider how they relate to the theoretical debates. After examining longer-term tendencies, often going back into the nineteenth century or earlier, we concentrate in the later sections of each chapter on recent changes and contemporary issues.

We are keen to hear your ideas about this new edition. Visit our website at www. oxfordtextbooks.co.uk/orc/fulcher4e/ or send us your feedback at fulcherandscott.uk@oup.com and let us know what you think of it!

James Fulcher and John Scott
2010

How to Use This Book

Chapter-opening vignettes

Each chapter begins with a short story drawn from the mass media, to illustrate a key issue covered in the chapter you are about to read and show its relevance to everyday life.

Race and racism

'On current demographic trends, we,
in our own country within sixty years
British people retain their homeland
immigration, the immediate deporta
introduction of a system of voluntary

Concepts and theories

Michel Foucault described in some detail the role of the state in controlling the bodies of its members. He related the development of the medical profession and modern forms of medical practice to the transformation of modern states and their growing capacity to exercise powers of surveillance over their populations.

Concepts and theories

This section introduces you to the concepts and theories which are explored fully in the chapter and help you understand the key issues.

'Global focus' boxes

No society can be understood in isolation. 'Global focus' boxes have been included throughout the chapter text to place the topics under discussion into an international context, and to compare social identities and structures across a number of different cultures.

Global focus Education and globalization

Growing state intervention in education has been, partly at least, a response to globalization. Global economic integration, the mobility of capital, and neo-liberal policies have reduced the capacity of governments to protect industries against foreign competition or direct the development of national economies. One of the few ways in which international competitiveness can be increased is through investment in human capital by putting resources into education and training.

All this
well. Acco
production
educated
neers, and
global de
related to
Data fro

'Controversy and debate' boxes

It is important that you are aware of the lively debates that are going on within sociology and their relevance to controversial issues in wider society. 'Controversy and debate' boxes aim to make you think about the contested nature of sociological ideas and become critical thinkers.

Controversy and debate Academies

City academies were launched in 2000 to replace failing secondary schools. It was claimed they would be innovative schools that would raise standards by bringing in business skills and enterprise. In 2008 the Labour government announced an increased target of 400 such schools. By May 2010, out of 3,100 secondary schools, 203 were academies.

spon
unive
Af
Demo
exter
be al
be se

Frontiers Internet democracy

Can the Internet solve the problems faced by democracy? It h been claimed that it provides a 'technology of democracy' making information freely available, facilitating communicatio and enabling organization by opposition or campaign groups. has also been argued that it can counteract declining popul participation and involvement in the political process.

'Frontiers' boxes

'Frontiers' boxes take you to the edge of the subject and give you a taste of the more innovative and ground-breaking research that is taking place within the discipline, to keep you abreast of important developments and complement the core ideas in the textbook.

'New technology' boxes

We live in a world of rapid and transforming technological change! These boxes focus on the impact of such changes on the way we live and the character of our society, and provide examples of the effect of the Internet and new forms of communication on societal groups.

New technology Mobiles in Africa

Fixed telephone lines are scarce in Africa, but mobile ownership has been increasing rapidly, and by the end of 2007 there were 280 million mobile subscribers, a penetration rate of 30 per cent. In Kenya the number of mobiles rose from 1 million to 5 million in five years, while the number of landlines has stayed at 300,000, most of which are in government offices.

THEORY AND METHODS

Marx and the social survey

In 1880 Karl Marx drew up a questionnaire that was to be distributed to readers of the *Revue Socialiste*, and to workers' societies, socialist societies, and anyone else who requested a copy. The purpose of the questionnaire was to explore the condition of the working class. Twenty-five thousand copies of the questionnaire were distributed, but very few replies were

'Theory and methods' boxes

Questions of theory and method are absolutely central to sociology and so these boxes have been included throughout the chapter to highlight research tools, techniques or problems and draw your attention to particular theoretical issues.

'Briefing' boxes

'Briefing' boxes have been included throughout the chapter text to showcase a miscellany of interesting and relevant examples, questions, and issues, to help expand your general knowledge of sociology and the arguments presented in each chapter.

Briefing: what is an individual? 4.2

Social identity is a person's sense of the type of person that he or she is: man, woman, black, white, tinker, tailor, soldier, sailor. Personal identity, on the other hand, is a person's sense of his or her own individuality and uniqueness and is marked by a name, personal appearance, identification numbers, and so on. A sense of self is the particular image that is associated with a personal identity, the defining characteristic of individuality. It is how people see themselves and how others see them.

Many countries already issue identity cards with unique identification numbers and credit card-style identity cards that ensure entitlements to welfare

➔ Connections

You may find it helpful to refer here to our detailed discussion of role-learning and socialization theories in Chapter 4, pp. 120–2.

➜ 'Connections' feature

There are many important links betweenchapters and so our 'Connections' featuresuggests ways in which you can follow upon a point and link it to related discussions-elsewhere in the book.

Key concepts and glossary

Key concepts are highlighted and explained when they are introduced to give the text a strong theoretical and analytical foundation. These concepts are also listed at the end of each chapter and included in the glossary at the end of the book.

World economy Used by Immanuel Wallerstein to refer to a *world system* that has multiple political centres but is integrated economically.

World empire Used by Immanuel Wallerstein to refer to a *world system* that has a single political centre and is integrated by a bureaucratic structure.

World system Used by Immanuel Wallerstein to refer to a social unit that includes a complete range of specialized activities in a *division of labour*.

World-accommodating religion A religion that adopts an attitude of mild disapproval or of acceptance of the world as it is.

Stop and reflect

In this section we have looked at professional and career crimes and at the relationships between gender, class, and crime. We started out by showing that not all deviation from legal norms is criminal activity. Criminal actions involve deviation from the criminal law. In considering theft and career crime, we showed

'Stop and reflect' summaries

At the end of each main section of a chapter you will find 'Stop and reflect' summaries that remind you of the points that have been made and suggest things that you should think about before you move on to the next main section, to aid your revision.

End-of-chapter workshop

At the end of every chapter you will find a 'Workshop' that comprises a series of case studies and exercises for revision and debate, to help you develop skills in critical analysis and apply your learning to new situations.

Case studies

Each case study focuses on an important piece of sociological research to help you to keep up to date with the latest thinking and help you to understand the implications of these research findings for the world around you.

Workshop 15

Study 15 A privatized NHS?

In April 2000 the Labour government unveiled its plan for transforming the NHS through a massive increase in its resources. There were to be over 100 new hospitals by 2010 and 7,500 new consultants, while waiting times for hospital treatment would be

'Media watch' stories

'Media watch' stories examine contemporary articles from the local media and relate them back to the key issues raised in the chapter, to help you think about the relevance of sociology in modern society.

Media watch 12 The family

There has been much concern in the media and amongst politicians about the consequences of the changes in the family that we have examined in this chapter. The bad behaviour of children is seen as a growing problem, which is commonly attributed to poor parenting, which is in turn blamed on the decline of m

Discussion points

Discussion points have been included to allow you to focus on important sociological issues raised in the chapter in greater detail, and develop strong skills in sociological argument.

Discussion points

Community

Before discussing this, read the sections on 'Urban society', 'Community', 'Changing communities', and Media watch 13.

● What are the key features of a community?

'Explore further' section

Further reading lists and web links have been provided to help you locate supplementary sources of information that will aid your revision and coursework.

Explore further

A clear and very readable introduction to gender theory, the history of gender, and its comparative study can be found in:

Holmes, M. (2009), *Gender and Everyday Life* (London: Routledg

Online resources

Suggested websites at the end of each chapter direct you towards valuable sources of information to help you broaden your knowledge of the topics covered in the chapter.

Online resources

Visit the Online Resource Centre that accompanies this book to access more learning resources and other interesting material on inequality, poverty, and wealth at:
www.oxfordtextbooks.co.uk/orc/fulcher4e/

The Joseph Rowntree Foundation provides reports on its monitoring of poverty at:

Online Resource Centre

www.oxfordtextbooks.co.uk/orc/fulcher4e/

The Online Resource Centre that accompanies this book provides students and instructors with ready-to-use teaching and learning materials. These resources are free of charge and designed to maximize the learning experience.

For students

Case studies

Sometimes the best way to understand sociological ideas is through a story: as such, each chapter is supplemented by a case study online which draws on recent sociological research and news from the popular media, to help you grasp core concepts and strengthen your skills in case analysis.

Case Study: Shyness

At Cardiff University, Susie Scott has been conducting a doctoral research project on the *sociology of shyness*, an innovative topic for the sociological imagination. The study involved in-depth interviews and an email discussion group, both with people who saw themselves as shy. Some of the questions Scott has been exploring are: What exactly is shyness, and how does it affect everyday interaction? Why is shyness seen as a problem, and why are individuals pressurised to overcome it? How does being seen as 'shy' affect a person's self-identity? These issues reflect many of the ideas from the Symbolic Interactionist tradition: the data from the project showed how shyness as a social identity is created in everyday situations and becomes real to the actors involved. When somebody is recognised by others as shy, this is because of the impressions they have given off through their body, gestures and language: it is a definition of reality that emerges from the interaction. It can often be seen as a form of deviance, because shy behaviour breaks some of the unspoken rules about 'pulling your weight' in a

Information and advice on careers

Provides guidance on careers available to students of sociology and links to valuable sources of information to make you aware of opportunities in this field.

Multiple-choice questions

The best way to reinforce your understanding of sociology is through frequent and cumulative revision. Each chapter is accompanied by multiple-choice questions you can complete online. These self-marking questions include instant feedback on your answers and cross references back to the textbook, to assist with independent study.

Instructions

Choose your answers from a-d by clicking the radio button next to each choice and then press 'Submit' to get your score.

Question 1

Socialization is:

- a) the formation of an attachment bond between an infant and its carer
- b) a tendency of social theorists to explain everything in terms of social causes
- c) the process of becoming part of a society by learning its norms and values
- d) the historical process by which societies change from traditional to modern

Question 2

Role-learning theory suggests that...

- a) we internalise and take on social roles from a pre-existing framework
- b) we create and negotiate our roles through interaction with others
- c) social roles are not fixed or stable but fluid and pluralistic
- d) roles have to be learned to suppress unconscious motivations

Revision activities

A suite of interactive revision activities have been prepared to help you think like a sociologist and apply your learning to new situations. Activities include questions about key sociology concepts; simply click a button to access detailed feedback on your answers.

Q.1 Distinguish between crime and deviance and say why the distinction matters.

Answer*:

Crime and deviance are distinct categories and it is mistaken to conflate them. Deviance contravenes norms while crime breaks laws. Not all deviance is illegal. Lemert (1967) suggests that 'primary deviance' as non-conformity to wider social norms may sometimes be 'normalized' within particular groups (swearing, spitting, late coming, for example). 'Secondary deviance' refers mainly to lifestyles and behaviours firmly rejected as 'abnormal' and sanctioned by official authorities or public opinion. People can 'drift' (Matza 1964) between delinquency and deviance without settling into criminal 'careers' (McIntosh 1975) or 'identities' (Goffman 1963).

Crime, whether 'petty' (Downes 1966) or 'serious' (Hobbs 1994), 'amateur' (Maguire and Bennett 1982) or 'professional' (Sutherland 1937), has overwhelmingly negative connotations, except, perhaps, within 'gangland' (Morton 1992) 'underworlds' (Chesney 1968), such as the Mafia (Gambetta 1993) or *Yakuza* (Hill 2003). It risks state-sanctioned punishments from fines to imprisonment and, in extreme instances, legal executions. Crime has specific relevance to the operations of the criminal justice

Web links

A series of annotated web links organized by chapter, direct you towards important associations, articles, reports, research papers and other sources of relevant sociological information. These links will keep you informed of the latest developments in the field.

Qualidata

http://www.qualidata.essex.ac.uk

Based at the University of Essex and funded by the ESRC, this archive collects and disseminates *qualitative* data from a wide range of research projects. You can use the 'Qualicat' catalogue to search for data on a particular topic, or locate datasets from some of the classic studies in sociology. Well worth exploring on a wet and windy afternoon!

The ESRC Data Archive

http://www.data-archive.ac.uk/

Also housed at the University of Essex, this archive contains a wider selection of *quantitative* data from social science research. You can browse the catalogue to find abstracts and methodological details of each study, and registered users can order a copy of the original data sets. There is also a bank of data from the major national surveys, including the British Crime Survey and the Social Attitudes Survey.

Sociological Research Online

http://www.socresonline.org.uk/

This is a journal about research methods that is published online. You can search the catalogue for articles on any aspect of research design and methodology, and read them on the web pages. The journal is published quarterly every year and it is a good way of keeping up to date with current trends in social research.

For lecturers

Case studies

A further collection of relevant and engaging case studies has been provided for use in group tutorial work and assignments. These cases have high student relevance and appeal, focus on new and emerging themes of sociology, and are accompanied by critical thinking questions for students.

Case Study:

Manchester is a British city with a unique identity. In the nineteenth century, it was dominated by the heavy industries and factory work, which gave it a distinct appearance and shaped the lives of many of its inhabitants. Since the decline of these traditional industries, however, the city has been transformed into a thriving metropolis, home to thousands of students, young professionals and a whole set of new 'de-masculinised' cultural industries. Nicola Richards and Katie Milestone (2000) conducted a study of women's participation in one of these industries, the local music scene. Manchester is the birthplace of many figureheads of late twentieth century pop music: bands like The Smiths, Joy Division/New Order, Oasis and The Stone Roses identified strongly with the city's image as a gritty, down to earth, straight-talking place in which high rates of unemployment and crime coexisted with a strong sense of community.

This in turn has led to the emergence of distinct youth subcultures and new patterns of consumption. Richards & Milestone argue that Manchester's music scene is sustained not only by the mainstream record industry but also by networks of 'micro-businesses' that reflect innovation and entrepreneurship alongside creative freedom. They interviewed twenty-seven women who worked as DJs, nightclub owners, musicians, music journalists and venue managers, and considered the ways in which these women struggled to gain

Essay and short answer questions

A bank of diverse and challenging essay and short answer questions has been provided to enrich the assessment program. Each question is designed to encourage students to synthesise their cumulative knowledge of chapter concepts and demonstrate the linkages between them.

Essay Questions

*These suggested **essay questions** are intended to encourage students to synthesise their cumulative knowledge of chapter concepts and demonstrate the linkages between them, and to solicit a 1,500 word written response.*

Q. 1 In what respects are sociological approaches to deviance more scientific that biological approaches?

Q. 2 Discuss the view that we are made, not born, members of deviant groups.

Q. 3 Is there evidence of the increase of deviance in modern society?

Q. 4 How would you seek to counteract the effects of negative labelling?

Q. 5 What might be the challenges of rehabilitation faced by an ex-criminal offender?

Q. 6 Does the phrase 'lock them up and throw away the key' make sociological sense?

Guide to discussion points in the book

This guidance to the discussion points at the end of each chapter highlights key points that students could consider in their answers to help with your seminar preparation.

Instructor's manual

A practically-focused and comprehensive Instructor's manual has been provided for new and experienced lecturers, and includes lecture outlines, guidance notes on how the textbook features may be used in class, and teaching activities for tutorials and seminars.

 Lecture outline

UNDERSTANDING SOCIAL INEQUALITY

Social inequalities comprise patterns of advantaged and disadvantaged life-chances: opportunities to acquire income, education, housing, health, and other valued resources. It is difficult to separate 'natural' from 'artificial' aspects of social inequalities. Debate: Is it possible to distinguish a genetic from an environmental aspect in measured intelligence.

Equality and Inequality
Citizenship and Equality
Equality:
- Considered as an ideal.
- Theme: all citizens should enjoy similar life chances linked to the 'Third Way' (Giddens).
- Critics of equality: New Right – it is inevitable and morally acceptable.
- Meaning of equality highly contested.
- Linked to citizenship, i.e. full citizenship = rights and obligations. Civil, social, and political rights. Social citizenship (Marshall, 1949) – welfare state.
- Three different conceptions of equality: opportunity, outset (starting at the same point, necessary condition for equality, social reform required), and outcome (radical position that all should enjoy same standard of living and life chances).

Equality of Opportunity
- Access to all social positions should be governed by universalistic criteria.
- On basis of merit.
- Achievement not ascription.
- Individual merit and social achievement – meritocracy.

PowerPoint slides

A suite of customizable PowerPoint slides has been included for use in lecture presentations. Arranged by chapter theme the slides may also be used in hand-outs in class.

Ethnicity and Education
- Children from ethnic minorities appear to underachieve
- due to in-school factors?
  - teacher expectations affect subject choice, performance and careers (CRE 1992)
  - ethnocentric contents of curriculum
  - institutional racism in the classroom
- but important differences in values and achievement *between* ethnic minorities
- intersects with class and gender inequalities

Authored by Susie Scott

© OXFORD UNIVERSITY PRESS

Acknowledgements

We have many people to thank for their contribution to the long and complex process of producing this fourth and extensively revised edition and its accompanying website.

We are most grateful to the Oxford editorial team, to Nicki Sneath, Claire Brewer, and Kirsty Reade (Commissioning Editors), Joanna Hardern (Production Editor), Hilary Walford (Copy Editor), Simon Witter (Designer), Fiona Barry, Vanessa Plaistir (Proofreaders). The book builds heavily on the previous editions and we would like to acknowledge the important contributions made by these by Angela Griffin, Tim Barton, Angela Adams, and Jane Clayton. Many thanks to Denny Einav for her picture research and to Alice Chadwick, Lucy Dawkins, Alan Felstead, and Hymers College (Hull) for their imaginative photography.

We would like to thank the many reviewers for the detailed and very helpful comments they have given us at various stages in the process of writing and rewriting this edition.

Last, but not least, we wish to thank Jonathan Clark who compiled the online resources, based upon original material supplied by Susie Scott. Will Keenan and ShaminderTakhar also contributed to the extensive online materials.

PART ONE

THINKING SOCIOLOGICALLY:
THEORIES AND METHODS

What is Sociology?

Contents

01

We introduce you to sociology in this chapter. We begin by explaining why we think that you should study sociology, and by telling you what you can get out of it and what you can use it for. We go on to tackle two fundamental questions. Sociologists study society but what do we mean by this term? How do sociologists study society—is sociology a science?

Why study sociology?

Sociology enables us to understand the world we live in but also understand ourselves, for we are the products of that world. This understanding can help us to gain more control over our lives but it can also be put to many more practical uses as well.

Understanding our world

We live in a world of extraordinary choice. Our choice of food to eat, holiday destinations to visit, and television channels to watch seems almost limitless. We can to some extent choose our own identity, by constructing a lifestyle that suits us or creating a new persona in a virtual community on the Net. We can select the body shape that we want and, through a combination of diet, exercise, and cosmetic surgery, at least try to change our body accordingly. The provision of greater choice, whether in education or in health care, has become one of the main priorities of government policy.

Although we have a strong sense of choice, we are also subject to social pressures that seem often to make these choices for us. We are under pressure to conform to other people's ideas of how we should look and how we should live. While we may think that we choose certain products or decide to hold certain views, we are manipulated by advertisers, media moguls, and spin doctors. Many people anyway feel that work pressures and shortage of time leave them with very little opportunity to do anything but get up in the morning, work all day, and do the housework or look after the children when they get home at night.

We also live in a world where the ability to choose varies enormously between people. In Britain the poor, the unemployed, the single parent, the refugee, all have less choice than others. In many African, Asian, or Latin American countries, many people just struggle to survive from day to day. Choice is, therefore, unequally distributed and has become steadily more so, as inequality has increased—not only within our own society but also in the world as a whole, for the gap between rich and poor countries has been widening as well.

How are we to understand and explain this strange world we live in, a world that gives us choice but also takes it away, that provides some with enormous choice but others with very little, that makes people think that they have choice when they often have hardly any? It is, above all, sociology that has tackled these issues, and you will find that they come up again and again in this book, when we examine the way that beliefs, values, and identities are shaped and created; or analyse inequalities of class, gender, and ethnicity; or discuss the influence of the mass media on the way that we think and behave; or consider the conflicting pressures of work demands and household obligations.

Understanding our place in the world

Sociology enables us to understand not only the world around us, but also our place within it. This is not just a matter of where we live, important as this is, but of where we are located within social structures and the changes taking place in these structures.

Sociologists use the term **social structure** to refer to any relatively stable pattern of relationships between people. In Box 1.1 (p. 6), C. Wright Mills refers to the structure of 'society as a whole', but any social group, however big or small, from a family to a political party, has a social structure. So does any organization, such as a university, a business corporation, or a hospital. There are also the wider structures of class, gender, and ethnicity that stretch across a whole society and, indeed, beyond it. Some organizations, such as transnational corporations, cross national boundaries, and national societies themselves exist within a global structure of international relationships.

By describing such structures, sociology provides us with a map of society within which we can locate ourselves, so that we can begin to understand the social forces that act upon us. These structures are, however, constantly changing, and one of the main tasks of sociology is to understand and explain social change and the impact that it has on people. You will find that most of our chapters are centrally concerned with processes of social change.

Some recent changes that have in one way or another impacted on all of us are:

- advances in communications that have made it possible to transfer huge quantities of information and money instantly across the world, and have enabled the emergence of an electronic world of cyberculture, virtual communities, and anonymous identities;

- the decentralization of cities, as superstores, hospitals, hotels, and leisure complexes have moved from the centre to the edge of the city, and the transformation of city centres by a rapidly expanding night-time world of pubs and clubs where bouncers rule;

- changes in family life, as more people have decided to live on their own, more couples have cohabited without marriage, women have increasingly found employment in paid work, divorce rates have risen, and the number of single-parent families has increased;

- the transformation of work, with the decline of old industries and the expansion of service occupations requiring emotional labour, while more flexible and less secure forms of part-time and temporary work have spread, and more employees now telework from home;

- increasing inequality, as more people have experienced poverty and exclusion, and the gap has widened not only between the rich and the poor within societies but also between rich and poor countries.

You will find that we discuss all these changes and many others in this book. Each may seem to be quite distinctive in character, but they have many processes in common and are interconnected in various ways. Globalization, for example, is involved in all of them and connects one process of change with another. It is sociology that has the concepts that enable us to comprehend these processes of change and grasp the connections between them.

Understanding ourselves

Above all, sociology enables us to understand ourselves. The way that we think, behave, and feel, indeed our

How has city life been changed by the growth of superstores?
© Lucy Dawkins

identity, is socially produced. It is only through a knowledge and understanding of the social processes that make us the people we are that we can truly understand ourselves.

Socialization is the general term that sociologists use for this process. We use this term because it is a process that makes us into social and cultural beings, that turns an individual into a member of society. It begins with upbringing and continues through education but does not stop there, for it goes on throughout our lives. Every time that we join a new group, perhaps of first years at university or colleagues at work, a process of socialization starts. Whenever we enter a new stage in life, we learn to take on certain roles—for example, the role of a parent, later of a grandparent. Socialization is so fundamental to

understanding how a society works that we discuss it at length in Chapter 4.

Socialization also provides us with an identity. Our sense of **personal identity** seems so strong and so individual that we tend to think it results from some process going on mysteriously inside us that makes us who we *really* are. Sociology shows, however, that identities are social. Even such basic personal characteristics as sex, race, and age are socially not biologically constructed, for the categories that we use are sociological, not biological.

Although the categories we place ourselves in, as 'men' or 'women', 'blacks' or 'whites', 'young' or 'old', 'healthy' or 'sick', refer to physical characteristics, they are, nonetheless, social categories that reflect certain culturally specific ways of thinking about people. For example, the notion

---

THEORY AND METHODS　　　　　　　　　　　　　　　　　　　　　1.1

Sociologists reflect on their subject

C. Wright Mills
'The sociological imagination enables its possessor to understand the larger historical scene in terms of its meaning for the inner life and the external career of a variety of individuals. . . . The sociological imagination enables us to grasp history and biography and the relations between the two within society. That is its task and its promise. . . . those who have been imaginatively aware of the promise of their work have consistently asked three sorts of questions:

1　What is the structure of this particular society as a whole? What are its essential components, and how are they related to one another? How does it differ from other varieties of social order? Within it, what is the meaning of any particular feature for its continuance and for its change?

2　Where does this society stand in human history? What are the mechanics by which it is changing? What is its place within and its meaning for the development of humanity as a whole? How does any particular feature we are examining affect, and how is it affected by, the historical period in which it moves?. . .

3　What varieties of men and women now prevail in this society and in this period? And what varieties are coming to prevail? In what ways are they selected and formed, liberated and repressed, made sensitive and blunted?'

Source: Mills (1959: 5–7)

C. Wright Mills (1916–62) was an American sociologist well known for his criticism of abstract approaches in sociology, and his belief that sociology should relate the 'personal troubles' of the individual to the 'public issues' of social structure. Apart from

The Sociological Imagination (1959), he is most well known for *White Collar: The American Middle Classes* (New York: Oxford University Press,, 1951); and *The Power Elite* (New York: Oxford University Press, 1956).

Peter Berger
'A more adequate representation of social reality now would be the puppet theatre, with the curtain rising on the little puppets jumping about on the ends of their invisible strings, cheerfully acting out the little parts that have been assigned to them in the tragi-comedy to be enacted. . . . We see the puppets dancing on their miniature stage, moving up and down as the strings pull them around, following the prescribed course of their various little parts. We learn to understand the logic of this theatre and we find ourselves in its motions. We locate ourselves in society and thus recognize our own position as we hang from its subtle strings. For a moment we see ourselves as puppets indeed. But then we grasp a decisive difference between the puppet theatre and our own drama. Unlike the puppets, we have the possibility of stopping in our movements, looking up and perceiving the machinery by which we have been moved. In this act lies the first step towards freedom.'

Source: Berger (1963: 140, 199).

Peter Berger (1929–) is an American sociologist, who (with Thomas Luckmann) wrote *The Social Construction of Reality: A Treatise in the Sociology of Knowledge* (New York: Doubleday, 1966). Two other well-known books by him are *The Sacred Canopy: Elements of a Sociological Theory of Religion* (New York: Doubleday, 1967; published in 1969 in the UK as *The Social Reality of Religion*), and *The Capitalist Revolution: Fifty Propositions about Prosperity, Equality, and Liberty* (Aldershot: Wildwood House, 1987).

that there are two sexes may appear self-evident, but it emerged quite recently in European history (see Chapter 5, p. 165). The same applies to the categorization of people as belonging to distinct races (see Chapter 6, pp. 191–2). What happens is that we learn these categories through socialization and then see ourselves as having the characteristics that these categories specify.

Freeing ourselves

A knowledge of the social structures that constrain us, and the social processes that give us identities, does not, however, condemn us to passivity. Indeed, the reverse is the case, for, by making us aware of the forces acting upon us, sociology also enables us to see them for what they are,

resist them if we wish to, and, to some (but only some) extent, free ourselves from them. This point is made well by Peter Berger and Zygmunt Bauman.

Berger (see Box 1.1) uses the metaphor of the puppet theatre to represent 'social reality'. He suggests that, as in a puppet theatre, people act out certain parts that are prescribed for them, and are pulled this way and that by the 'invisible strings' of society. Through sociology, they can, however, see the strings that pull them and the social machinery that operates the strings. Once they do this they are no longer puppets and have taken 'the first step towards freedom'.

Bauman (see Box 1.2) similarly points out that through sociology we can become aware of, and can then explore, the previously invisible social context of our lives. This means that we become aware of the social forces that

---

THEORY AND METHODS 1.2

Sociologists reflect on their subject

Zygmunt Bauman

'One could say that the main service the art of thinking sociologically may render to each and every one of us is to make us more *sensitive*; it may sharpen up our senses, open our eyes wider so that we can explore human conditions which thus far had remained all but invisible. Once we understand better how the apparently natural, inevitable, immutable, eternal aspects of our lives have been brought into being through the exercise of human power and human resources, we will find it hard to accept once more that they are immune and impenetrable to human action—our own action included. Sociological thinking is, one might say, a power in its own right, an *anti-fixating* power. It renders flexible again the world hitherto oppressive in its apparent fixity; it shows it as a world which could be different from what it is now. It can be argued that the art of sociological thinking tends to widen the scope, the daring and the practical effectiveness of your and my *freedom*. Once the art has been learned and mastered, the individual may well become just a bit less manipulable, more resilient to oppression and regulation from outside, more likely to resist being fixed by forces that claim to be irresistible.'

Source: Bauman (1990: 16).

Zygmunt Bauman (1925–) has been Professor of Sociology at the Universities of Leeds and Warsaw. Among his many reflections on sociological theory and contemporary society are *Modernity and the Holocaust* (Cambridge: Polity Press, 1989); *Globalization: The Human Consequences* (Cambridge: Polity Press, 1998); and *Liquid Modernity* (Cambridge: Polity Press, 2000). A second edition of *Thinking Sociologically* (written with Tim May) was published in 2001.

Steve Bruce

'To summarize, whatever reservations we may have about how closely actual scientists conform to the high standards set in their programmatic statements about what they do and why it works, we need not doubt that the natural sciences offer the best available template for acquiring knowledge about the material world. Critical reasoning, honest and diligent accumulation of evidence, subjecting ideas to test for internal consistency and for fit with the best available evidence, seeking evidence that refutes rather than supports an argument, engaging in open exchanges of ideas and data unconstrained by ideological commitments: all of those can be profitably adopted by the social sciences. However, we need to appreciate the differences between the subject matter of the natural and the human sciences. People think. They act as they do, not because they are bound to follow unvarying rules but because they have beliefs, values, interests, and intentions. That simple fact means that, while some forms of sociological research look rather like the work of chemists or physicists, for the sociologist there is always a further step to take. Our notion of explanation does not stop at identifying regular patterns in social action. It requires that we understand.'

Source: Bruce (1999*b*: 18–19).

Steve Bruce (1954–) has been Professor of Sociology at the University of Aberdeen since 1991. He is the author of *The Edge of the Union: The Ulster Loyalist Political Vision* (Oxford: Oxford University Press, 1994); *Religion in Modern Britain* (Oxford: Oxford University Press, 1995); *Choice and Religion: A Critique of Rational Choice Theory* (Oxford: Oxford University Press, 1999*a*); and many other publications in the sociology of religion.

shape our lives. It also means that we discover that what seemed natural or inevitable is actually the result of human actions. To return to Berger's metaphor, we find out that it is in fact people who are pulling the puppets' strings. Once we realize this, we understand that things do not have to be the way they are. If human actions make the world the way it is, then the world can be changed. If the way we live is not the fixed result of human nature, then we can live differently.

People have, for example, often thought that patterns of behaviour are biologically determined when they are not. It has been widely believed that the different roles performed by men and women are biologically prescribed. This can lead to the false idea that for biological reasons men are not fitted to be, say, nurses and women to be, say, pilots. In Britain, beliefs of this sort became established in the nineteenth century as men sought to exclude women from many occupations and confine them to domestic and caring roles. Knowledge of the way this

idea became established and the socializing processes that maintain it help us to understand that gender role differences are socially constructed (we discuss this in Chapter 5). This awareness makes it possible to challenge them and change them, as has clearly happened, for there are now many male nurses and female pilots.

Applying sociology

You may reasonably say that this is all very well but what is sociology useful for? Sociology may provide plenty of knowledge and understanding but what else can it do?

Sociological knowledge has important applications in many areas of work. It has made major contributions to the study of social problems and the work of those seeking to deal with them. Thus, sociologists have carried out research into drug use, crime, violence, industrial disputes, family problems, and mental illness, to name

A female RAF pilot: gender role expectations can be challenged and changed.
© Crown/RAF

some of the more well-known problems of society. Indeed, no investigation of the causes and consequences of these social problems would be complete without an input from sociology.

Sociologists have not only, however, been concerned with explaining why some people behave in problematic ways. They are also interested in the deeper sources of such behaviour in, say, the patterns of family relationships, the structure of organizations, or the distribution of resources. They are concerned, too, with the processes that lead to the treatment of certain actions as problematic, as deviant or criminal behaviour. Why, for example, are poor people prosecuted for failing to pay council taxes, when the rich are allowed to avoid paying income tax by shifting their money into tax havens?

Sociology has made a central contribution to the study of management and the training of managers. Sociologists have researched the structures that enable organizations to function productively and efficiently. They have asked what kinds of structure and what styles of management facilitate creativity and innovation. One of the most important contributions of sociologists here has been to penetrate beneath the surface of things. They have shown how apparently well-designed organizations are disrupted by internal conflicts. They have revealed the unintended consequences of rules and regulations (see Chapter 14, p. 519).

Those sociologists working in this area, however, have not just focused on issues of organizational efficiency. They are also concerned with the perspectives of those who work for organizations. How meaningful do employees find the work that they do? How do they meet the requirements of the employer but continue carrying out their work in a professional way and protect themselves against exploitation? One of the current frontiers here (see Chapter 4, pp. 141–3, and Chapter 17, pp. 660–1) is the struggle between managers and employees over the 'emotional labour' of customer-service work in call centres.

Arguably, sociology should perform a critical function, exposing exploitation and revealing the structures and processes that lie behind it. Advocates of 'public sociology' go further and hold that sociology should not only be critical but should move out of the academic world and engage much more with the world outside, taking part in policy debates and social movements. Michael Burawoy, a British sociologist who became President of the American Sociological Association in 2004, called for sociology to carry out such a mission.

As mirror and conscience of society, sociology must define, promote and inform public debate about deepening class and racial inequalities, new gender regimes, environmental degradation, market fundamentalism, state and non-state violence. I believe that the world needs public sociology—a sociology that transcends the academy—more than ever. Our potential publics are multiple, ranging from media audiences to policy makers, from silenced minorities to social movements. . . . Teaching is equally central to public sociology: students are our first public for they carry sociology into all walks of life.

Burawoy 2004.

In the application of sociology, there is a constant tension between those who seek to use it to deal with organizational and social problems by making social control more effective and those who want to deploy it against exploitation, domination, and manipulation.

Careers in sociology

What can *you* do with sociology? How can sociology help you in finding a career?

One possible career is to become a professional sociologist, carrying out sociological research and communicating its results. This might be in a university but not necessarily, as there are many other organizations, such as specialized research institutes and think tanks, that employ professional sociologists. Sociology is an exceptionally rewarding area in which to do research. It is an enormously diverse and dynamic field, with frontiers opening up in all directions, as our Frontiers boxes and end-of-chapter Studies will show. The range of methods involved, which stretch from large-scale quantitative surveys to intensive observational studies of the social life of small groups, provides scope for many different skills and inclinations. Research is, furthermore, not just a matter of acquiring knowledge, but also of developing the ideas, concepts, and methods of sociology itself.

As a subject to teach, it has a lot to offer, as it deals all the time with topics and issues that are central to the lives of those being taught. As you teach sociology, you can draw on the experiences of those you are teaching, using their daily lives to illustrate sociological theories and concepts, while using sociology to provide them with a greater understanding of their situation in the world, the forces acting upon them, and the sources of their own beliefs and identities. Those who teach in schools and colleges can play their part in developing the subject by contributing articles to such publications as the *Sociology Review* or writing pieces for sociology websites.

Most sociology graduates will probably not, however, go into teaching or research careers. What other things can sociologists do? Sociology is not a vocational subject, in the sense of providing a training for a specific occupation. It is, however, relevant to a very wide range of occupations, and this broad range of occupational destinations makes sociology a good choice for those who have not decided what career they wish to pursue or simply want to keep their options open. You *can* be sure that a subject that gives you a greater understanding of social situations, social interaction, and human behaviour in general will provide you with insights that will come in useful whoever employs you and whatever you do.

The skills and knowledge of the sociologist also become increasingly relevant as information about people becomes more and more central to the functioning of the society we live in. Most expanding occupations, in such areas as marketing, public relations, opinion formation, the media, human resource management, education, research, and social policy, depend on the collection, analysis, and communication of information about people, and this is, after all, what sociologists do.

If you want to find out more about careers for sociologists, visit our Online Resource Centre, where you will find more detailed information and links you can follow up.

What is society?

Most would agree that sociologists study **society**, but what do we mean by this term?

It is used in many different ways in sociology but most commonly to refer to a national unit, as in British society. This is, however, quite problematic, given devolution, on the one hand, and the European Union, on the other. Some would argue anyway, that we now live in a global society. We particularly address the issues of devolution in Chapter 15 (see pp. 586–7) and global society in Chapter 16 (see pp. 602–5).

The easiest way to get a sense of what we mean by 'society' is to examine its main aspects in turn. These are also the main lines of enquiry along which sociology has developed.

A complex of institutions

Institutions are the established practices that regulate the various activities that make up social life. Some examples of institutions are marriages, markets, educational curricula, religious rituals, and laws, which in their different ways all give order to different aspects of the way that we live. In contemporary societies, these institutions, and also the organizations associated with them, are highly specialized. Thus, the educational, economic, political, military, and religious activities of society each have specialized institutions and organizations.

We speak of a complex of institutions, because these specialized institutions are closely interrelated with each other. Consider, for example, educational institutions and their organizations. In Britain, public-sector schools, colleges, and universities are dependent on political institutions for their funding, and it is ultimately the government that decides how much money to distribute to them. Governments are themselves dependent on the economy. The amount of money that the government has to spend on education depends on how much it can raise in taxes. While this is partly a political question, it also depends on the state of the economy. This itself depends, however, on education, for it is education that supplies the economy with skilled labour. This has been an important issue in Britain since the 1970s, for it has been claimed that education has not been giving people the skills that the economy needs (see Chapter 9, pp. 317–18).

These interrelationships mean that institutions should not be studied in isolation from each other. Sociologists cannot, of course, study everything simultaneously and they tend to specialize in the study of particular areas, such as the family or religion or the media. Most of this book is divided into chapters that specialize in distinct areas of this sort. To achieve a complete understanding of what is going on in any one of these areas, you must always, however, bear in mind its links with others. In this book we have indicated what we see as the more important links through cross-references and Connections boxes.

It is one of the distinctive features of sociology that it is concerned with whole societies. As C. Wright Mills put it (see p. 6), sociologists should ask: 'What is the structure of this particular society as a whole?' Sociology is the only subject that sees societies as 'wholes' in this way. This distinctive perspective means that it overlaps with many other fields of specialized enquiry. Economics and politics, for example, are subjects in their own right, which explore in detail the workings of the areas concerned and the issues specific to them. Economic and political institutions are, however, crucial to the functioning of any society, and there is also, therefore, a sociology of economic life and a sociology of politics, which address the relationships between these areas and the wider society.

Figure 1.1 Institutional interdependence

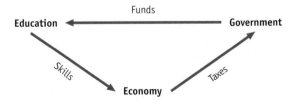

Sociology's concern with whole societies and all activities that occur within them means that any aspect of social life can become a field within sociology. Indeed, one of the exciting and dynamic things about the subject is the way that new specialities are constantly opening up within it, as sociologists begin to explore new areas of activity that have not been studied before or have newly emerged through social change. Examples of new fields are the sociology of tourism and the sociology of the body.

A multi-level structure

In discussing society as a complex of institutions, we have been operating at one particular level, the national level, of society. People do commonly see themselves as members of national societies. If someone asks you which society you belong to, you will probably reply that you live in, say, British or American or Indian society. If you live in Britain, you might, of course, prefer to say that you live in Scottish or Welsh or even English society, for nationality is a contentious matter, which we discuss in Chapter 16, pp. 598–600. The point that we are making, here, however, is that the national level is one level of social organization but only one level.

Another level is that of interpersonal, face-to-face interactions in small-group situations. During their daily lives people interact with each other in patterned ways. They will usually be members of small groups, such as a **family** or **household** unit (see Chapter 12), but also of work groups and friendship circles, perhaps of gangs or sports teams,

and you can no doubt think of other small groups that are important in your life. People also interact with others on a more transitory basis. Indeed, urban sociologists have argued that city life is a 'world of strangers', where people interact with others that they know very little about (see Chapter 13, p. 478). Some sociologists have been primarily interested in these small groups and interpersonal interactions (see Chapter 2, pp. 48–52), and the study of such interactions is indeed an essential part of sociology. These interactions are, however, structured by larger social units, and interpersonal behaviour cannot be explained solely in terms of face-to-face interaction patterns.

One such larger social unit is the **organization** (see Chapter 14, p. 518). Business corporations, churches, hospitals, and schools are all examples of organizations. Organizations are designed to carry out a particular social activity and will usually have a clearly stated and specific goal. They will also have a defined membership and will generally require their members to follow certain rules of behaviour. Whether their members actually do so is another matter and one that has preoccupied the sociology of organizations. All such organizations do, however, have a definite authority structure that controls the membership but also generates opposition and creates internal conflict.

Another larger and less formal social unit is the **community**. Two centuries or so ago most people lived in small, relatively self-sufficient and self-contained communities in villages or small towns, where everyone knew everyone else. Industrialization and urbanization disrupted communities of this sort and brought large numbers of people who did not know each other together.

Education and politics: why are politicians so interested in education?

©Getty Images/Matt Cardy

As we show in Chapter 13, pp. 498–9, new kinds of community have, however, established themselves within cities. Furthermore, the Internet has made possible the emergence of virtual communities, which we discuss on pp. 499–500. Many people still see themselves as members of communities of one kind or another.

Whether or not people feel that they are members of a community, they are inevitably members of a larger social unit, the **nation state** which, during the nineteenth and twentieth centuries became steadily more important in people's lives. With the development of the nation state, national institutions emerged. At its centre is the state apparatus itself, but there are also national educational systems, national health services, national armies, and national churches, to name some of the more obvious examples. As members of a nation state, people have the rights and responsibilities of citizens of that state, and a sense of national identity, though these may not neatly overlap, and strains between national state structures and sub-nationalities are commonly found. We examine the development of nations and nation states in Chapter 16, pp. 606–7, and we consider devolution to sub-national units in Chapter 15, pp. 586–7.

Nation states are far from self-sufficient, much as they would like to be, for they are interlinked with each other and interdependent in complex ways. These links developed particularly strongly with industrialization, which made national economies highly dependent on one another through an international division of labour. The industrial societies specialized in producing manufactured goods for the world as a whole, while other parts of the world specialized in producing food for the workers, and raw materials for the factories, of the industrial societies.

National societies have become more closely interlinked through a process known as **globalization**, which we discuss at length in Chapter 16. The world—the globe— has become a 'smaller' place, as a result of improvements in communication, which make possible travel to most places within a day or so, while information can be transmitted instantly to almost any part of the globe. Nowadays, some companies are global corporations operating in large numbers of countries on every continent. There are also global political organizations, such as the United Nations, and global movements, such as Greenpeace. As well as being citizens of national societies, people are also arguably members of a global society.

As society has developed, social units have become steadily larger in their scale. Thus, communities became parts of national societies and national societies have become parts of a global society. This raises the issue of how smaller-scale units relate to larger ones. Do larger-scale units supersede smaller ones? There are literatures on the decline of the family (see Chapter 12, pp. 435–6), the decline of community (see Chapter 13, pp. 477–9), and, more recently, the decline of the nation state (see Chapter 16, pp. 604–5). Arguably, smaller-scale units have, however, not so much disappeared as survived and changed, as society has become multi-level in character. There are many important questions here for sociologists as they examine the relationships between the overlapping units that make up human society.

A structure of inequality and domination

In our discussion of society as a complex of institutions, we emphasized the way in which each organized a particular activity for the society as a whole. Some groups benefit more, however, from these activities than others and seek to maintain or increase their advantages. Societies are characterized by inequality between dominant and dominated groups. Structures of inequality may stretch right across a society, indeed across the whole world, as a dominant group tries to gain control of all areas of activity and secure benefits in all aspects of life. We particularly address the issues raised by inequality in Chapters 18 and 19, but you will find them cropping up throughout the book.

There are various dimensions of inequality within national societies. There are class inequalities between, say, aristocracies and commoners or employers and workers. There are ethnic inequalities between, say, whites, Asians, and African Caribbeans. There are gender inequalities between men and women. In some societies, religion or nationality has become a major line of division. There are also inequalities between national societies, for increasing global integration has not resulted in greater international equality, as we show in Chapter 16.

The study of inequality and its consequences brings up a number of important issues that have been much

Figure 1.2 Society as a multi-level structure

International/transnational organizations
Global society

Nation states
National societies

Nation states
National societies

Organizations
Communities

Organizations
Communities

Small groups
Interactions

Small groups
Interactions

discussed in sociology. These can be grouped under three headings:

- social stratification;
- social control;
- social conflict.

Social stratification. **Social stratification** is concerned with the way in which a structure of layers, or strata, emerges within society. Typically there is a top layer of the rich and powerful, a bottom layer of the poor and powerless, and various other layers in between. Important questions that are raised are the number of layers that exist in a society, where the boundaries between them should be drawn, the ease with which people can move between them (social mobility), and the way in which the layers persist and change from one generation to the next.

Social control. This raises the question of how inequality is maintained. How do the upper layers dominate and exploit those below them and maintain their various

Figure 1.3 Social stratification by class

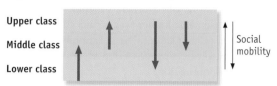

advantages? One way is through control of the use of force—typically through control of the military and police forces of a society. Sociologists generally emphasize, however, that there are more subtle means of control that operate by influencing beliefs and attitudes. Thus, it has been variously argued that people are controlled through education, religion, the mass media, or social policy, and we discuss these arguments in the chapters on these areas.

Social conflict. Here the issue is whether and under what conditions inequality generates conflict. Do the mechanisms of social control break down? Do those in the lower layers organize themselves to improve their situation and

Are communities alive and well in the contemporary city?
© Lucy Dawkins

challenge those with wealth and power? Under what conditions, for example, can workers organize themselves collectively to demand higher wages and challenge the power of the employer? Under what conditions do women organize themselves through feminist movements to challenge male domination?

The study of inequality is linked to the study of institutions and their interrelationships, for the rich and powerful maintain their wealth and power by controlling institutions. Similarly, those who challenge their position have to contest their control of these institutions. Thus, the study of this aspect of society is closely related to the issues we raised in our discussion of institutions.

Structure and culture

We have been making much reference to structures, but there are aspects of a society that sociologists treat as its cultural rather than structural features. A society not only has an institutional structure and a structure of inequality; it also has ideas and beliefs. These, together with their symbolic representation through communicative and creative activities, are described as its **culture**. A symbol is simply a representation, such as a word or an image or a gesture, that embodies and communicates an idea. Indeed, beliefs and ideas cannot exist without symbolic representation. It is hard to see how belief in a god can exist without the word 'god' and without representations of a god. Symbols also convey feelings, as when a representation of a god, say a painting or a sculpture, expresses feelings of religious devotion.

Beliefs are concerned with both ideas about the way things *are* and ideas about how they *ought* to be. Ideas about how things are include beliefs about the nature of things—the physical world, human nature, and the character of society. Ideas about how things ought to be are embodied in values and norms:

- **Values** specify what people ought to do. Thus, the belief that people should accumulate wealth or the belief that they should live in harmony with the natural environment both express values, though rather different ones.

- **Norms** are rules of behaviour that regulate how people behave. A typical norm, for example, is the rule that people should not accumulate wealth by stealing from each other. Such norms are often embodied in laws.

Beliefs about the way that the world *is* and the way that it *ought to be* are commonly linked together by religion and politics. Thus, Christianity contains ideas about God's creation of the world and the belief that human beings are naturally sinful. Christianity also emphasizes certain values, such as love and charity, and provides a set of norms,

such as the prohibition of sexual behaviour outside marriage. Political beliefs, such as socialism or liberalism, similarly link together ideas about the nature of society and distinctive visions of what a society should be like.

As we argued above, the term 'culture' also refers to the communicative and creative activities that express ideas and feelings. It is often used to refer to the *high* culture of a society, its collections of paintings, its opera houses, and its great works of literature. But there is also its *popular* culture, and this has become an area of growing interest in sociology, which we discuss in Chapter 10. Cinema, popular music, magazines, and soap operas are part of our popular culture. Ordinary activities as various as gardening, craftwork, dressing, cooking, and talking are all creative activities that can be considered part of culture.

Indeed, the term 'culture' is often used in a very broad way to refer to the general customs and way of life of a society or a group within it, as in references, say, to American culture or to working-class culture. Culture in this sense includes the way that people meet and greet each other, the way they behave towards each other at work and at leisure, their sporting and religious activities, and so on. Indeed, all social activity has a cultural aspect, for all social actions have meaning and therefore express the ideas of a culture.

The question then arises of the relationship between social structure and culture, a much debated issue in sociology. Some sociologists, such as C. Wright Mills, see sociology's task as the explanation of a person's situation by reference to the wider social structure that constrains and shapes the circumstances of that person's life (see p. 6). Others, notably some post-modern theorists (see pp. 61–3), claim that cultural representations are the only social reality. There are no external structures and the only reality is what people believe about the world. This leads them to a cultural relativism where all beliefs are equally valid and scientific investigation is impossible.

Most sociologists would argue that neither structural determinism nor cultural relativism enables us properly to explain and to understand social life. To do this we do need to refer to the relationships, organizations, and institutions that can best be thought of as structures external to the individual. We need also to refer to the cultural beliefs and ideas that people hold about the world, which give their actions meaning.

Structure and culture are not, however, independent of each other. The beliefs that people hold are, for example, shaped through the institutional and organizational structures of education, the media, and religion. These institutions may in turn be created or reformed because of the ideas and beliefs of those who control them. Statements of this kind can be made only if we distinguish between structure and culture, give both some explanatory weight, and examine the relationship between them.

Is sociology a science?

In the previous section we discussed what sociologists mean by society. Here we take up issues raised by the way in which they study it. The question of whether sociology should be considered a science has been hotly debated both inside and outside the subject. It is an interesting and important question that enables us to explore the nature of the subject, its distinctiveness, and its relationships with other subjects. Before discussing it, we must first consider, however, what is meant by science.

What is science?

It is commonly thought that scientists are simply engaged in the discovery and collection of facts. Scientists do not, however, just look around to see what they can discover, for scientific enquiry is directed by the theoretical concerns of scientists. Scientific *ideas* lie behind the design of experiments or the search for data.

The search for 'dark matter' by astronomers provides a good example. 'Dark matter', together with 'dark energy', is considered to account for most of the matter in the universe, but it is not visible by its very nature. Astronomers 'discovered' it, not because they came across it but because their theories indicated that there had to be far more matter in the universe than could be accounted for by its visible material. The existence of dark matter was first predicted in 1933, but there is still no direct evidence of it, and it is still therefore not known what most of the universe consists of.

The conventional idea of a fact is of something that is observed existing 'out there'. The discovery of facts does certainly require some kind of observation, but they do not speak for themselves. They must be interpreted and made sense of *before* they can become facts. Interpretation always involves explanatory ideas and this returns us again to the importance of theories.

Science is both an *empirical* and a *theoretical* enterprise. In saying that it is empirical, we mean that it is based on observations. The word *empirical* is derived from the Greek word for experience and refers to the observational work that provides us with experience of the world. In saying that science is theoretical we mean that it also involves systematic thought about the world. A *theory* is a logically connected set of ideas. Theories guide empirical work and are used to interpret and explain its observations, which may or may not fit existing theories. If they do not fit it, a theory needs at least to be revised and may have to be abandoned. Science advances through the constant interplay of theoretical and empirical work.

While it is important to be clear about the logic of scientific activity, it is also important to bear in mind the scientific spirit. By this we mean the set of ideals that motivate and guide scientific work. Science is both *rational* and *critical*. It is rational in that it rejects explanations of the world that are based on religious beliefs or mysterious forces, rather than reasoned thought. It is critical, as it questions received ideas and accepted beliefs. It is concerned with establishing the truth about how the world is and how things actually work, rather than how they ought to be or how they are supposed to be.

This does not mean that scientists lack values and beliefs. Like anyone else, they hold values and beliefs, which may well influence what they do. For example, scientists concerned about the state of the natural environment might well carry out research into global warming. Values and beliefs should not, however, influence the scientist's investigation or interpretation of observations. Thus, however concerned such a scientist might be about this issue, if the observations did not support the theory of global warming, the scientist would be expected to say so.

We have in some ways presented an idealized picture of science. Most scientific enquiry is driven by the requirements of industry or government rather than the pursuit of knowledge. Scientists sometimes suppress results that do not fit their theories or might damage their careers, because they conflict with their employer's interest in a particular policy or product. Research results are faked by some researchers, who are more concerned to achieve publications and advance their careers than advance knowledge. At the heart of science there is, nonetheless, an ideal of disinterested enquiry into the nature of things, and it is against this ideal that the work of scientists is judged.

Is sociology a natural science?

The first sciences to develop were the natural sciences, and they therefore became the model for scientific activity. Some sociologists adopted this model and tried to develop a natural science of human behaviour. Most contemporary sociologists would, however, argue that society cannot be studied in this way. Social behaviour is in important respects quite different from natural behaviour.

Human actions are meaningful, for whatever human beings do means something to them. They act in the context of beliefs and purposes that give their actions meaning and shape the way that they behave. If sociologists are to understand and explain human behaviour, they have to take account of the meanings that people give to their actions.

Thus, no universal statements can be made about human behaviour, for the same behaviour means different things in different societies. Let us take eating practices as a simple example. The eating of roast beef has been traditional in England and regarded as one of the distinctive features of English life. In India, however, cows are considered sacred by Hindus and may not be killed, let alone eaten. On the other hand, while the eating of dogs in the Far East is commonplace, it is quite abhorrent to most British people. Behaviour considered quite normal in one society is unacceptable in another. No general statements can therefore be made about human eating behaviour in the way that they can about the eating behaviour of animals.

Human behaviour is also different because people think about what they are doing. They are at least partly aware of the forces acting upon them and can resist these forces and act differently. Thus, while the eating of snails and frogs' legs is not a normal feature of the British diet and is generally viewed in Britain with some disgust, some British people may consider that there is no good reason for rejecting these foods. They may decide that it must be possible to enjoy them, if the French eat them with such relish, and may then try them out. Similarly vegetarians may reject traditional British beef-eating practices. Behaviour is not therefore entirely culture-bound, because people can break out of their culture and, indeed, change it. However, whether they do so is not simply a matter of choice, for those who break away from established patterns will themselves be distinctive in certain ways. They may, for example, be more educated.

> ⊃ *Connections*
> Weber particularly emphasized the importance to sociological explanation of understanding the meaning of human action. See Chapter 2, pp. 39–40.

Given this cultural content of social behaviour, we cannot just observe it. If they are to be explained, human actions have to be understood. This special requirement of sociology comes out clearly in the reflections of the sociologists in Boxes 1.1 and 1.2 (see pp. 6 and 7). Thus, after arguing that many of the features of natural science should be adopted by the sociologist, Steve Bruce insists that the sociologist must go further. As he puts it: 'Our notion of explanation does not stop at identifying regular patterns in social action. It requires that we understand.'

Is sociology a science at all?

Some have, however, questioned whether there can be a science of society at all. If sociology has to understand what people do, is there any real difference between sociology and ordinary common sense?

The answer to this question is a resounding yes.

The problem with common sense is that in their everyday lives people are too involved in what is going on around them to have any detachment from it. They are immersed in their own situations, their own families, their own work relationships, their own friendship and leisure patterns. These colour their view of the world. Their knowledge of the world is limited to the situations that they have experienced. They generally interpret their own and other people's behaviour in terms of preconceived ideas and beliefs. In doing so they make little distinction between the way the world is and the way they think it ought to be. Their experience is fitted into these ideas and beliefs, which are important to their sense of identity, and they are therefore usually very reluctant to alter them.

The sociologist's knowledge of the world is very different. Sociology builds up a knowledge of society that is not based upon the experience of one individual but accumulated from the research of large numbers of sociologists. This is knowledge of many different aspects of many different societies at many different times. It is a cumulative knowledge that is constantly increasing through further research. This bank of knowledge means that the experience of large numbers of people in many very different situations and from very different cultures is available to the sociologist.

Sociologists are trained to develop their ideas in a logical, disciplined, and explicit way by constructing theories, which are quite unlike the everyday beliefs of common sense. These ideas are made explicit, because their assumptions have been brought into the open, thought about, and justified. Logical connections are made between the various ideas that make up a theory so that its train of thought can be followed. Theories are also subject to the scrutiny of other sociologists, who will critically examine their assumptions and check the logic of their arguments.

Sociology was, indeed, characterized from its beginning by a debate between different theoretical perspectives, which first became established in the nineteenth century. These perspectives are particularly associated with the work of Karl Marx, Emile Durkheim, and Max Weber. We examine their approaches in Chapter 2 and often refer to them in the 'Concepts and theories' sections that you will find in our substantive chapters. These and other early sociologists originated many of the key concepts of the subject, concepts that are still widely used today, and their work is full of insights that help us to understand the society that we live in.

As we argue in Chapter 2 (see p. 22), these different perspectives should not, however, be seen as *alternative* approaches to the subject, for each has made a vital contribution to its development. Each makes particular assumptions about the nature of society and the process of social change, and it is important to be aware of these assumptions, but theories should not be judged on this basis alone, for what ultimately matters is their capacity to explain and make sense of the world. You should approach the various perspectives in an open-minded way to discover what each contributes to our knowledge and understanding of the world we live in.

This is where the methods used by sociologists come in. Sociologists do not assume that they know the answers, that their theory is right. They have to test their ideas by collecting appropriate information, using a wide variety of methods to do this. These range from large-scale surveys to the small-scale, in-depth, participant observation of particular situations. Sociologists draw on many different sources of material, from documents to census data or interview responses. As we show in Chapter 3, pp. 73–4, different methods are appropriate to different issues and different situations but can also be used to complement and check upon each other. As with their theories, their methods and the way that they interpret their data are open to the scrutiny of other sociologists.

Sociology is, then, a science. It has explicit theories and collects data in an objective and systematic way, in order to check those theories and revise them if they are found wanting. As we showed above, it is not a natural science, because there are important differences between the social and natural worlds as objects of study, differences that actually require sociologists to go beyond the methods of the natural sciences. It is a social science, not a natural science, but a science nonetheless.

The sociological imagination

Sociologists have, however, argued strongly that a scientific approach is insufficient on its own. C. Wright Mills famously insisted that the mechanical application of the rules of scientific method was not enough, that the understanding of social structures required a special quality of mind, the **sociological imagination** (Mills 1959, 2000). In Box 1.1 (p. 6) we have quoted some of his words on this.

Anthony Giddens has taken up this idea in his 'brief but critical introduction' to sociology. As Giddens (1986: 13) puts it: 'The practice of sociology . . . demands invoking what C. Wright Mills has aptly called the "sociological

imagination".' Giddens takes this to mean that there are 'several related forms of sensibility indispensable to sociological analysis'. These are:

- historical sensibility;
- anthropological insight;
- critical sensitivity.

Historical sensibility enables us to understand the distinctiveness of the society we live in. This is a society that has been transformed by industrialization and the rise of the nation state. It is a society where there is a very high rate of technological change. Yet all this has happened quite recently, and during most of human history people lived very differently in small, self-sufficient, and traditionally minded communities. To appreciate what is distinctive about our world, we have to compare it with past worlds, and you will find that we do this in most of our chapters.

Anthropological insight is necessary to enable us to appreciate the diversity of human society. Giddens here refers to the work of social anthropologists, who provided us with a knowledge and understanding of the functioning, the beliefs, and the way of life of non-industrial societies that are very different from our own. Apart from enabling us to comprehend human diversity, this knowledge helps us to combat an ethnocentrism that judges other societies from the standpoint of our own. This ethnocentrism has typically considered our own society to be superior and therefore justified in 'the greedy engulfing of other modes of life by industrial capitalism' (Giddens 1986: 20).

The exercise of these two sensibilities makes possible the third, *critical* sensitivity. Through the *historical* and *anthropological* sensibilities we can escape the 'straitjacket' of the society that we live in and discover that very different societies, with other ways of organizing life, other institutions, and other beliefs, have existed and continue to exist. This enables us to examine critically our own society and consider alternative ways of living and thinking, alternative organizations and institutions.

Why, one may ask, does all this require *imagination*? An effort of imagination is required because, to acquire these sensibilities, sociologists have to go beyond their immediate day-to-day experience of the world. They have to grasp quite abstract concepts of structure and process that enable them to make sense of the workings of the wider society and its historical development. They have to make an imaginative leap to understand ways of living and organizing that are very different from the ones that they know. They have to get 'inside the heads' of other people so that they can understand their actions and the meanings they attach to them. As you read this book you will find that you have to develop and exercise your sociological imagination in all these ways.

Key concepts

Workshop 1

Discussion points

Sociology and science

- What do you consider to be the key features of a science?
- Do scientists simply carry out observations that discover facts?
- What do you think facts are?
- How well does sociology fit your definition of science?

- Is there any reason to suppose that sociology is not a science?
- Should one distinguish between natural and social sciences?
- What do we mean by 'common sense'?
- Is sociology different from common sense?
- Should sociology be considered superior to common sense?

Explore further

The following references, some of which we have quoted in Boxes 1.1 and 1.2 on pp. 6–7, all provide interesting and perceptive discussions of the nature of sociology:

Bauman, Z., and May, T. (2001), *Thinking Sociologically* (2nd edn, Oxford: Basil Blackwell).

Berger, P. L. (1963), *Invitation to Sociology: A Humanistic Perspective* (Harmondsworth: Penguin).

Bruce, S. (1999), *Sociology: A Very Short Introduction* (Oxford: Oxford University Press).

Hamilton, P., and Thompson K. (2002) (eds), *The Uses of Sociology* (Oxford: Blackwell).

Jenkins, R. (2002), *Foundations of Sociology* (Basingstoke: Palgrave Macmillan).

Mills, C. W. (1959), *The Sociological Imagination* (2nd edn, New York: Oxford University Press, 2000).

Urry, J. (2000), *Sociology beyond Societies* (London: Routledge).

Online resources

Visit the Online Resource Centre that accompanies this book to access more learning resources and other interesting material on what sociology is about at:
www.oxfordtextbooks.co.uk/orc/fulcher4e/

The website of the British Sociological Association, where you can find general information about the subject, including another answer to the question 'What is sociology?', and advice about career opportunities and postgraduate courses for sociologists, is at:
www.britsoc.co.uk

For a comprehensive but carefully selected list of sociology web links, with very helpful descriptions of what can be found at each one, visit:
www.intute.ac.uk/socialsciences

Theories and Theorizing

Contents

'That's all very well in theory'

How often have you heard someone say 'That's all very well in theory' or 'Well, I know how it ought to work in theory'? The implication is that 'theory', no matter how logical or clear-cut, can never grasp the realities of a situation and so is a poor guide to action. Theory is seen as abstract and irrelevant, perhaps produced by those who live in 'ivory towers' and do not understand the 'real world'. Theory is sometimes seen as evaluative or ideological, contrasting with a sombre reliance on 'the facts'. This view is particularly strong in popular discussions of the social world. Sociologists are criticized for theorizing, rather than getting on with more important things—much as Nero was supposed to have fiddled while Rome burned. This view often goes hand in hand with the assertion that sociological theory is, in any case, mere jargon: commonplace ideas are dressed up in scientific mumbo-jumbo language. According to these critics, theory is simply the spinning-out of long but essentially meaningless words. The jargon is a smokescreen for ignorance or platitudes. The implication is clear: sociological theorizing is not the kind of thing that any self-respecting person need be concerned with.

Popular criticisms of theory misunderstand what theory is all about. Theory is—or should be—an attempt to describe and explain the real world. It is impossible to know anything about the real world without drawing on some kind of theoretical ideas. Sociological theories are attempts to highlight interesting aspects of social situations by drawing out their general features. They abstract from the particular and unique features of events and situations in order to isolate what they have in common and what can, therefore, guide us in understanding events and situations that we have not yet encountered.

It is undoubtedly true that sociologists can be as susceptible to prejudice and jargon as anybody else. They have sometimes adopted cumbersome terminology in a misguided attempt to justify their claims to scientific status in the face of exactly these kinds of objections. However, any scientific activity must employ specialized technical terms in its theories, and these terms will not always be comprehensible to the person in the street. Similarly, many sociological concepts originate in everyday terms and must be given a more precise and technical meaning if they are not to be misunderstood.

Theory lies at the heart of sociology. It enables us to understand and explain the social world. Many sociological theories concern specific social phenomena or social processes such as crime, health, education, politics, deviance, socialization, or stratification. You will encounter many such theories in the various chapters of this book.

> ## ➲ Connections
>
> Theory can be difficult and demanding. You will not necessarily understand all that we say in this chapter the first time that you read it. However, you should not worry about this. It is not your fault. The problem lies with the complexity of the theories and—it has to be said—with the failure of certain theorists to present their ideas clearly. You will find it best to skim through the chapter as a whole, not worrying too much about the detail. You can spend more time on the parts that you find easiest to handle. Treat the whole chapter as a reference source, as something to come back to as and when you read the various sections of the book. Theory is best handled in the context of particular empirical issues.

These specialized theories are often connected into larger theoretical frameworks that try to grasp the most general features of social life as a whole. It is these theories that we will look at in this chapter. We will outline the key ideas of the main theorists, and we will show how their ideas are related to the issues raised in the other chapters of the book.

There is no single theory to which all sociologists subscribe. There are, instead, a number of different theories, each of which has its advocates and its detractors. These theories are sometimes seen as mutually opposed and as defining rival positions among which sociologists must choose. It is sometimes thought that adherents of one theory have nothing to learn from any of the others. Some textbooks, for example, present their readers with a range of different theoretical positions on each topic and imply that all are equally valid. It is as if you enter the sociological supermarket and see, laid out on the shelves in front of you, 'Marxism', 'functionalism', 'feminism', 'interactionism', and so on. You walk down the aisles, picking up those theories that appeal to you or that have the best packaging. Having made your choice, you return home to use your new theories.

Theoretical choice is not like this. The choice between theories is not made on the basis of individual preference ('I just don't like functionalism') or political standpoint ('I'm working class, so I'm a Marxist'). Preferences and politics do, of course, enter into sociology, but they do not determine the merits of particular theories. The choices that we must make among theoretical positions are shaped, above all, by empirical considerations. When judging a theory, what really matters is its capacity to explain what is happening in the real world. Theories must always be tested through empirical research. As we show in this and the next chapter, the 'facts' are not quite as straightforward as this statement suggests. However, the point still remains. Theories are attempts to describe and explain the social world. Their merits and limitations depend, ultimately, on their ability to cope with what we know about that world.

We will show that the leading sociological theorists have attempted, in their different ways, to understand the modern world. They have each, however, concentrated on particular aspects of that world. None has given a full and complete picture. The least satisfactory theories are, in fact, those that have tried, prematurely, to give a very general and comprehensive picture. The most powerful theories are those that have emphasized a particular aspect of the social world and have concentrated their attention on understanding that aspect. In doing so, these theories have neglected or put to one side the very processes that other theories have taken as their particular concern. Even in such a well-developed field as physics, there are numerous partial theories that have not yet been synthesized into a larger and more comprehensive theory.

If it is ever possible to produce a comprehensive understanding of the social world, this is likely to result from the slow synthesis of these partial viewpoints. Because the social world is constantly changing, any such synthesis would not last long before it needed to be revised. For this reason, theoretical change and the development of new theories are constant features of scientific activity.

For the present, then, different theories must be seen, in principle, as complementary to one another. We are not proposing that all theories are of equal value, or that they can simply be hashed together in some unwieldy mixture. Some are bad theories that have received no support from empirical research. Even the useful theories have their particular strengths and, of course, their particular weaknesses. Each theory must be assessed against the facts relevant to its particular concerns, not against those more relevant to some other theory. By the end of this chapter you should have some appreciation of how the various sociological theories do, indeed, complement one another. You should begin to see how, collectively, they provide a picture of the social world that is far better than any of them can provide alone.

This chapter looks at sociological theory from the point of view of its historical development. The reason for this is not simply that we want you to acquire a knowledge of the history of sociology—though that is important. The theories that we discuss are still relevant today and are not to be abandoned simply because they are 'old'. Theories constructed over 100 years ago are, of course, likely to have been superseded, in many respects, by more recent theories. However, many of these new developments build on the theories of the past. Contemporary theories have added to the theories of the past and are not simply replacements for them. It is possible to gain a better understanding of contemporary ideas only if their connections to longer-established ideas is known. A common mistake to make is to think that a theory can be judged by the date it was written. In fact, a theory can be judged only by whether or not it helps us to understand and explain the social world.

We begin with an overview of the earliest attempts to establish a science of sociology and to show that these were the basis from which the classical statements of sociology were produced around the turn of the twentieth century. The section on 'Sociology established' looks at the three main theoretical traditions of the twentieth century—structural-functionalist theories, interaction theories, and conflict theories—and shows that these ideas provide the core elements in a sociological understanding of the world. We conclude the chapter with a discussion of the feminist and post-modernist theorists whose arguments have broadened our sociological imagination, and we indicate some of the implications of globalization for social theorizing. We consider these arguments at greater length in the later chapters of the book. In this chapter and throughout the book you will find that we consider both classic and contemporary theorists, treating them as participants in the same great intellectual enterprise that is sociology.

The beginning of sociology

For as long as humans have existed, they have tried to understand their societies and have constructed theories about them. For much of human history, however, these attempts have looked very different from what is currently meant by sociology. Early attempts at social understanding took the form of myths or poetry and they were often religious or highly speculative. The building of a distinctively scientific approach to social understanding is a very recent thing. While the philosophers of ancient Greece developed many ideas about social and political life, it is only since the seventeenth century, and then mainly in Europe, that there has been anything that could truly be called a science of society.

The origins of this *scientific* perspective on social life can be found in the European Enlightenment of the seventeenth and eighteenth centuries. The Enlightenment marked a fundamental change in the cultural outlook of European intellectuals. Rational and critical methods were adopted in one field after another, and religious viewpoints were squeezed out by scientific ones.

Great advances were made in the philosophy of Descartes and the physics of Newton in the middle decades of the sixteenth century. Descartes set out a view of intellectual enquiry as the attempt to achieve absolutely certain knowledge of the world, using only rational and critical methods. He argued that science is the attempt to construct theories that can be assessed against the evidence of the human senses. Observation and direct experience of the world provide the raw materials for scientific work, and the rational and critical faculties of the scientist guide the way these are accounted for. Newton's use of this method in physics produced elegant mathematical theories that related the behaviour of physical objects to their mass, volume, and density, and to the forces of gravity and magnetism. This model of science was extended with the development of chemistry, biology, and geology. Not until the nineteenth century was the same method advocated as the basis of a scientific sociology.

Early social theories tended to be individualistic, seeing social life as resulting from the rational, calculating activities of individuals motivated only by a desire to increase their own happiness and satisfaction. Societies were seen as collections of individuals. These theorists had not grasped what most people now take for granted: that individuals cannot be understood in isolation from the social relations into which they are born and without which their lives have no meaning.

A more properly *social* perspective gradually developed during the eighteenth and nineteenth centuries as a response, in particular to the beginnings of industrialization. The development of industrial production and the corresponding growth of industrial cities brought together ever larger numbers of people. The urban, industrial classes became the major economic and political force, resulting in economic and social problems of poverty and conflict and forcing states to accommodate to their populist and democratic pressures. Sociological theories developed as reflections on these social changes. British theorists stressed economic activities and relations and took a **materialist** view of social life. For a materialist, social life is organized around the struggle over economic resources and the inequalities and social divisions to which this gives rise. Many French and German writers, on the other hand, highlighted the part played in social life by moral values and ideas, and they have been described as **idealist** theorists. They saw societies as having a cultural spirit that was the basis of their national customs and practices.

Development and change

The first systematic theories of social life to have a major influence were those of Georg Hegel and Auguste Comte. Hegel built a comprehensive idealist theory of society and history. Similar concerns are apparent in the work of Comte, though he was a more self-consciously scientific writer who owed a great deal to the economic analyses of the earlier materialists. Where Hegel remained satisfied with a very general account of the social character of human life, Comte tried to analyse this into its constituent elements. These were, he said, aspects of the structure of social systems. Both writers identified long-term processes of social change that they described as processes of social development. Herbert Spencer, writing later in the nineteenth century, carried all these themes forward. He saw society as a social organism that develops over time through a process of social evolution.

Hegel: society as spirit

The inspiration behind Hegel's ideas was the philosophy of Immanuel Kant, the next great landmark in philosophical thought after Descartes. Kant's central argument was that scientific knowledge had to be seen as an active and creative production of the human mind. All observations, Kant argued, depend upon the particular ways in which experiences are interpreted in relation to current cultural concerns. According to Hegel, the interpretation of experience reflects the 'spirit' of the culture. This term was taken from Montesquieu (1748) and refers to the general principles and ideas that lay behind the particular customs and practices of a society and motivated its members. The spirit of a culture shapes the subjective ideas and meanings on which individuals act, and so Hegel saw individuals as the mere embodiments of a cultural spirit. There is, then, a one-to-one relationship between cultural spirit, social institutions, and social actions, and Hegel saw actions and institutions as simply the means through which cultural ideas and values are formed into a social reality.

> **◒ Connections**
> Hegel's ideas are complex and his works are difficult to read. At this stage, you should not try to track down his books. If you ever do feel able to tackle him, you should start with his *Philosophy of Right* (1821). Do not expect an easy ride!

History, for Hegel, involves a gradual shift from local to more global social institutions. Family and kinship obligations contained people's lives within localized communities with tight communal bonds. These communal forms of social life were followed by societies in which the division of labour and market relations tied people into larger societies marked by deep divisions into unequal social classes and driven by the commercial spirit of property-owners and merchants. A new stage of social development saw the nation state as the key social institution in contemporary societies. The state embodies the spirit of the people as a whole and not just the spirit of a particular class or kinship group. As national societies become more integrated through transnational links, the *world spirit*, an all-embracing cultural spirit, gives way to a cosmopolitan world spirit.

Hegel's work, while pioneering, was not yet sociology. He saw history as the automatic and inevitable expression of an abstract spirit into the world, with spirit itself being the active, moving force in social life. He personified spirit, seeing it as some kind of active and creative force, and he discovered God as the holy spirit behind the human spirit and, therefore, social development.

The religious character of Hegel's work meant that he had few direct followers. Some aspects of his thought were taken ahead, in a very different direction, by Karl Marx, as we will shortly show. Idealism had its greatest impact on the development of sociology in France. The key writer here was Comte, who was the first to set out a comprehensive, if flawed, account of a theoretical science of society.

Comte and positivism

It is thanks to Comte that the science of society is called 'sociology', as he invented the word in 1839 to describe his system of ideas. He drew on the ideas of his teacher and first employer, Saint-Simon, though a disagreement led Comte to exaggerate the originality of his own work.

Saint-Simon had popularized the idea of what he called *positive science*. The term 'positive' means definite and unquestionable, and Saint-Simon saw this as characteristic of the precise or exact sciences based on observation and mathematics. This led him to advocate a positive 'science of man', a psychological and social science of the human mind. This would be the basis on which the various positive sciences could be unified into a single 'positive philosophy' that could provide a complete knowledge of everything that exists. Comte took on the task of systematizing Saint-Simon's work into his own positive philosophy and positive science of society.

A positive science of society

Comte (see Box 2.1) held that sociology could advance human understanding only if it emulated the other positive sciences. This did not mean that sociology had slavishly to follow the natural sciences. Each major discipline had its own distinctive subject matter, which had to be studied in its own right and so could not be reduced to the subject matter of any other science. Comte's point was simply that there was only one way of being scientific, whatever the subject matter of the science.

Comte's **positivism** saw science as the study of observable phenomena. The scientist must directly observe things, examining their similarities and differences and investigating the order in which they occurred. These observations had then to be explained by theoretical laws that state causal relationships between observed events and so allow the prediction of future events. A law stating that intellectual unrest is a cause of political instability, for example, would lead us to predict a period of political instability if intellectual unrest is observed. The task of the scientist is to produce theories that are able to arrive at just these kinds of laws. Positivism is discussed in Box 2.2.

While many of the details of Comte's sociology are no longer accepted by sociologists, his main principles have largely been accepted and now form a part of the mainstream of the subject. His key insight was that societies had to be understood as complex *systems*. They are organic wholes that have a unity similar to that of biological organisms. The human body, for example, is a biological system of parts that are connected together into a living whole. Similarly, a society may be seen as a cohesive and integrated whole. The parts of a society are not simply individuals, but social institutions. A society consists of family and kinship institutions, political institutions, economic institutions, religious institutions, and so on. These do not exist in isolation but are interdependent parts of the whole social system. Change in any one institution is likely to have consequences for the other institutions to which it is connected.

Comte identified two ways in which social systems could be studied:

- *social statics*: study of the coexistence of institutions in a system and of their structures and their functions;
- *social dynamics*: study of change in institutions and systems over time and of their development and progress.

THEORY AND METHODS   2.1

Auguste Comte

Inventor of the word 'sociology'.

© Bibliothèque Nationale, Paris/The Bridgeman Art Library

Isidore Auguste Marie François Xavier Comte (1798–1857) was born in Montpellier. After an unspectacular education, during which his political interests led him into conflict with the authorities, he settled in Paris. He was a dogmatic and self-important individual, whose arrogance made it difficult for him to establish secure relationships. His intellectual relationship to Saint-Simon was stormy, and ended a year before the death of Saint-Simon in 1825. His personal life was equally unstable. Comte's early life was marked by periods of depression and paranoia, and his marriage broke down because of his extreme jealousy.

Comte decided on the plan for his life work while still working for Saint-Simon. He planned a *Course in Positive Philosophy*, which he delivered in public lectures and published in serial form between 1830 and 1842. The *Course* eventually ran to six volumes, covering the whole of what he took to be established knowledge in mathematics, astronomy, physics, chemistry, biology, and sociology. The section on sociology (which he originally called 'social physics') was its centrepiece and took up three of the six volumes.

Having completed this task, Comte went on to write the *System of Positive Polity*, which he considered to be even more important. This, too, was a multi-volume work and was completed in 1854, just three years before his death. The *System* set out a summary of his position and his programme for the social reconstruction of European society. This reconstruction involved the establishment of a 'Religion of Humanity', a religion that abandoned dogma and faith and was itself constructed on a scientific basis. Sociology was to be the core of this religion, with sociologists replacing priests as the expert teachers and policy-makers.

Comte's works are difficult to get hold of in English editions, but you might like to scan some of the extracts reprinted in K. Thompson (1976).

The study of social statics is similar to the study of organization or anatomy in biology. It looks at the **social structure** of a social system, at the way in which the institutions that make up the system are actually connected to each other. Comte argues that the aim of social statics is to produce *laws of coexistence*, principles concerning the interdependence of social institutions.

The main elements of a society, according to Comte, are its division of labour, its language, and its religion. It is through a division of labour—a socially organized distribution of productive tasks—that people are able to satisfy their material needs. Through their language they communicate with each other and pass on the knowledge and values that they have learned. Through their religion, they can achieve a sense of common purpose and of working towards a common goal. These elements are all cemented together into the overall social structure.

The connections between the parts of a social system are their **functions**. In general terms, however, Comte used the term 'function' to refer to the contribution that particular institutions or practices make to the rest of the society, the part they play in reproducing or maintaining its existence by contributing to its solidarity or coherence. Comte saw a coherent society as a 'healthy' society. Those systems that show a high level of solidarity, consensus, or coherence are integrated and work more smoothly. They are more likely to persist than those with only a low level of integration. Integrated societies are in a healthy state of balance or equilibrium, with all their parts working effectively together. As with other organisms, however, some societies may be in a 'pathological' condition of imminent breakdown or collapse. If their parts are not functioning

THEORY AND METHODS   2.2

Positivism

For Comte, the positivist approach in science simply involves an emphasis on rational, critical thought and the use of evidence. In many contemporary discussions, however, it is presented as a much narrower and more restricted idea. 'Positivist' is sometimes used as a term of abuse, applied to those who use mathematics or social surveys. This kind of distortion is not helpful. You will find it much easier to handle sociological debates if you avoid trying to label people as positivists and non-positivists. If you must use the word, try to use it as Comte intended. Bear in mind, however, that Comte tied positive science to positive politics and his religion of humanity.

correctly, they will not have the integration they need to survive.

Social dynamics concerns the flow of energy and information around a social system and, therefore, the ways that societies may change their structures. Structural change is what Comte calls development or progress. The aim of social dynamics is to produce *laws of succession* that specify the various stages of structural development through which a particular social system changes.

Comte saw the development of positive science as something that could be explained by the most important law of succession. This was the law of the three stages, according to which cultural ideas pass through three successive stages and particular types of social institution correspond to each of them. These three stages are the theological, the metaphysical, and the positive. In the theological stage, people think in exclusively supernatural terms, seeing human affairs as resulting from the actions of gods and other supernatural beings. In the metaphysical stage, these ideas are abandoned and people begin to think in terms of more abstract spiritual forces such as 'nature'. Finally, the positive stage is one in which these abstractions give way to scientific observation and the construction of empirical laws.

In Europe, Comte saw the theological stage as having persisted from the simplest tribal societies to the more complex kingdoms of the fourteenth century. The metaphysical stage lasted from the fourteenth century until about 1800, and Comte saw its development as having been closely linked with the rise of Protestantism. Societies in the metaphysical stage were militaristic and feudal societies that depended on a vast agricultural base. The positive stage began early in the nineteenth century and corresponds to what Comte called **industrial society**. This term, now so taken for granted, was first used by Saint-Simon and was taken up by Comte to describe the type of society that was gradually maturing in the Europe of his day. Industrial societies were contrasted with earlier 'militaristic' societies, suggesting that social life had become organized around the peaceful pursuit of economic welfare rather than preparation for war. More specifically, an industrial society is organized around the achievement of material well-being through an expanding division of labour and new technologies of production. This kind of society is headed by the entrepreneurs, directors, and managers, who are the technical experts of the new industrial technology.

As they developed, however, industrial societies created great inequalities of income. The resentment that the poor felt towards the wealthy produced a pathological state of unrest and social crisis. The only long-term solution to this, Comte argued, was for a renewed moral regulation of society through the establishment of a new, rational system of religion and education. This would establish the moral consensus that would encourage people to accept the inevitable inequalities of industrialism.

Comte's political aspirations were unfulfilled, and his religion of humanity inspired only small and eccentric groups of thinkers. His view of the need for a critical and empirical science of society, however, was massively influential and secured the claims of his sociology to a central place in intellectual discussions. His particular view of the development of modern industrial society rested on a rather inadequate historical understanding of pre-modern societies, but he accurately identified many of its most important characteristics. His concept of the industrial society has continued to inform debates about the future development of modern societies.

Spencer and social evolution

The materialist tradition in Britain had its major impact on the growth of economic theory (usually termed political economy), where a long line of theorists attempted to uncover the way in which the production of goods is shaped by the forces of supply and demand. In the work of Herbert Spencer this was combined with ideas drawn from the work of Comte to form a broader sociological theory. Many see Spencer as the direct heir to Comte, though this was certainly not how he saw himself. Although he gave far less attention to religious and intellectual factors than did Comte, there is, nevertheless, a great similarity in their views. It is also true to say, however, that Spencer remained very close to the British tradition in giving a great emphasis to individual action. Spencer took forward Comte's idea that societies were organic systems, but he also emphasized that they must be seen as produced by individuals and their actions (see Box 2.3)

Spencer adopted Comte's distinction between social statics and social dynamics as the two main branches of his sociology. His social statics stressed the idea of society as an organism. Each part in a society is specialized around a particular function and so makes its own distinctive contribution to the whole. A society is an integrated and regulated system of interdependent parts. Spencer's sociology attempted to describe these interdependencies in general terms and as they are found in actual societies.

His most distinctive contribution to sociology, however, was his emphasis on the dynamic principle of **evolution**. Evolutionary ideas achieved a great popularity in Victorian Britain following the publication of Darwin's *On the Origin of Species* in 1859. The debate over Darwin's work made widely known the idea that biological species evolve through a constant struggle for existence in which only the fittest can survive. Those species that are best adapted to the environment under which they live are more likely to survive than those that are only weakly adapted or not

THEORY AND METHODS   2.3

Herbert Spencer

Herbert Spencer (1820–1903) was born in Derby and was privately educated in mathematics and physics. He started work in the new railway industry, and became a successful railway engineer. His intellectual interests in geology and biology, and his interest in political issues, led him to publish a number of articles, and in 1848 he decided to move into journalism. His first book was *Social Statics*. This and a series of papers on population and evolution were followed by a major work that was to take the whole of the rest of his life to complete. Like Comte, he aimed at an encyclopaedic summary of human knowledge; a 'synthetic philosophy'. He published this work in his *Principles of Biology*, *Principles of Psychology*, *Principles of Sociology*, and *Principles of Ethics*.

Spencer's sociological works are difficult to get hold of and it is probably better to approach him through the extracts reprinted in Andreski (1976).

adapted at all. In fact, the phrase 'survival of the fittest' had been introduced by Spencer some years before Darwin published his work, and both Darwin and Spencer acknowledged that the idea of a struggle for existence came from Malthus's work (1798) on population.

Spencer's great contribution to the debate over evolution, however, was his advocacy of the principle of *social* evolution. This consisted of two processes:

- structural differentiation;
- functional adaptation.

Structural differentiation is a process through which simple societies develop into more complex ones. This idea was modelled on the biological process through which, as Spencer saw it, advanced organisms had more differentiated and specialized parts than less advanced ones. In all spheres of existence, he held, there is an evolution from the simple to the complex. In the social world, structural differentiation involves the proliferation of specialized social institutions.

Simple societies are organized around family and kinship relations, and achieve their material needs through hunting and gathering. Few aspects of social life are specialized, and almost everything is organized through kinship. Gradually, however, separate governmental and economic institutions are formed and systems of communication are established. Many activities previously organized through the family come to be organized through these specialized institutions. As a result, the family loses some of its functions, which are 'differentiated' into the specialized

institutions. Over time, the specialized institutions are themselves subject to structural differentiation. Governmental institutions, for example, become differentiated into separate political, legal, and military institutions.

The reason for structural differentiation, Spencer held, is that it allows societies to cope better with the problems and difficulties that they face in their material environment (physical conditions, climate, natural resources) and their relations to other societies. This coping is what Spencer called *functional adaptation*. Structural differentiation allows societies to become better adapted, and so a changing environment tends to be associated with increasing structural differentiation.

Spencer saw the nineteenth century as the period in which industrial societies were beginning to evolve. These societies were well adapted to the conditions under which people then lived. They were highly differentiated social systems with only a very loose degree of overall regulation, and individuals had considerable intellectual, economic, and political freedom. Adam Smith had argued that the economic market operates as a 'hidden hand' to ensure that the greatest level of economic happiness results from individually selfish behaviour. Spencer extended this argument and held that all the structurally differentiated institutions of contemporary societies could be seen as working, generally in unintended ways, to produce the greatest collective advantages. There is a natural harmony or coherence that results only from the rational, self-interested actions of free individuals. Spencer was, therefore, opposed to state intervention of any kind, whether in the sphere of education, health, or the economy. Individuals had to be left to struggle for existence with each other. The fittest would survive, and this was, he argued, in the best interest of society as a whole.

Karl Marx: social conflict

Despite the differences in their views, Comte and Spencer produced pioneering versions of a science of sociology and were engaged in a common intellectual exercise. Karl Marx too aspired to build a science of society, but he was on the margins of the intellectual world and did not describe himself as a sociologist. To the extent that he took any account of the work of the sociologists, he was critical of it. Marx's rejection of sociology reflects the fact that the word was still very new and, for many people, it described only the specific doctrines of Comte and Spencer. As we will see in 'The formative period of sociology', pp. 31–41, it was only in the next generation of social theorists that Marx's ideas began to receive any proper recognition as a part of the same *sociological* enterprise as the works of Comte and Spencer.

The inspiration for Marx's work was provided by the growth of the European labour movement and socialist ideas, and he tied his philosophical and scientific interests to the needs of this labour movement. Marx was trained in Hegel's philosophy, studying at Berlin just a few years after Hegel's death, but he was also influenced by the British materialist tradition. He saw writers such as Ferguson and Millar as having provided the basis for an understanding of the power and significance of the labour movement, but only if combined with the historical perspective of Hegel (see Box 2.4).

Marx's model of society

The central idea in Marx's early work was **alienation**. This occurred when the way in which the economic relations under which people work changed their labour from a creative act into a distorted and dehumanized activity. Alienated people do not enjoy their work or find any satisfaction in it. They see it merely as a means to provide themselves with the wage that will ensure their survival and therefore their ability to turn up the next week to work once more. Work and its products become separate or 'alien' things that dominate and oppress people.

The economy, Marx held, is central to the understanding of human life, and alienation was seen as a result of particular property relations and divisions of labour. Private property divides people into **social classes**, creating a division between property-owners and propertyless workers. Classes are categories of people with a specific position in the division of labour, a particular standard of living, and a distinct way of life. While the existence of classes and of social inequality was first highlighted by the British materialists, Marx saw his own contribution as showing how and why these classes are inevitably drawn into conflict with each other. This he did in his later work for *Capital* (1867). The property-owning class, he argued, is an exploiting class that benefits at the expense of the propertyless. This exploitation leads the classes into a struggle over the distribution of economic resources.

Marx saw societies as social systems that could be divided into two quite distinct parts: the **base** and the **superstructure**. The economy and class relations comprise what he called the material base or substructure of society. The base always involves a particular **mode of production**: the technical and human resources of production that comprise specific 'forces of production' and the particular property relations and division of labour (the 'relations of production') under which these resources are used. This economic base is the foundation upon which a superstructure of political, legal, and customary social institutions is built. It is also the basis of various forms of consciousness and knowledge. The ideas that people form, Marx said, are shaped by the material conditions under which they live. They must be regarded as what he called **ideologies**.

In its most general sense, the division of the social system into a base and a superstructure involves the claim that only those societies that are able to ensure their material survival, through an efficiently organized system of production, will be able to sustain any other social activities. People must eat and have adequate clothing and shelter before they can stand for parliament, write poetry, or engage in sociology. Some Marxists saw this as an economic determinism and allowed no autonomy at all for politics and culture, which they saw as mere reflections of economic divisions and struggles. Marx was too sophisticated to accept such a deterministic position, and the claims made by some of his followers led him to remark 'I am not a Marxist'.

Comte and Spencer saw social systems, in their normal states, as characterized by harmony and cohesion. Marx's view, on the other hand, recognized conflict and division as normal features of all societies. There are divisions not only within the economic base (between classes), but also between base and superstructure. While a superstructure normally reinforces and supports the economic base, it can frequently come into contradiction with it. Marx meant that the superstructure obstructs the further development of the mode of production, and, if production is to expand any further, the superstructure must be transformed.

Historical materialism

Marx's materialism was a specifically **historical materialism**, because he saw social systems developing over time as a result of their economic contradictions. Historical materialism is a theory of the transitions from one mode of production to another.

The simplest, least-developed forms of society were those in which the mode of production took the form of *primitive communism*. Property is owned by the community as a whole, and the community is organized around bonds of kinship. As technology develops and production expands, so property relations must change. If they do not, then societies will not be able to continue to develop their powers of production. Systems with private property and more complex divisions of labour therefore tend to evolve out of the simple form of primitive communism. These complex societies have distinct political institutions and, in many cases, centralized states.

Marx traced the evolutionary line in Western Europe from the primitive communism of the Germanic and Celtic tribes, through the slave-owning systems of ancient Greece and Rome, and on to the feudal states of the medieval period. Feudal societies centred on the division between the landowners and the unfree labourers who must work for them. Eastern Europe and the Near East followed a similar path, but passed through an 'Asiatic' stage instead of a feudal one. The form of society that was emerging in Western Europe at the time that Marx was

Karl Marx

Voted the greatest ever philosopher.

© Getty Images/Hulton Archive

Karl Marx (1818–83) was born in Trier, Germany. He studied law at Bonn and Berlin. His radical political views led him into a journalistic career, but this was cut short by the suppression of the various journals for which he wrote. He fled to Paris in 1843, to Brussels in 1845, and, finally, to London in 1848. It was in London that he spent the rest of his life. His massive tomb can still be seen in Highgate cemetery.

Marx began work on a series of philosophical and economic books while in Paris, and he spent the rest of his life studying, engaging in radical politics, and writing articles for newspapers and periodicals. He was able to spend his time in this way only because of the financial support from his friend and collaborator Friedrich Engels.

Engels (1820–95) was the son of a wealthy cotton manufacturer. Like Marx, he was involved in radical politics and intellectual work, but was sent to Manchester by his father to manage the English branch of the family firm. This gave him the financial independence to support both himself and Marx. Engels wrote an important study of poverty, *The Condition of the Working Class in*

England in 1844 (1845), and he collaborated with Marx on a number of works, including *The Communist Manifesto* (1848).

Marx found it difficult to complete books. A number of his most important studies were published long after his death, thanks to the editorial work of Engels and others. The most important of his early works, where he set out a theory of alienation, was the *Economic and Philosophical Manuscripts* (1844), published only in 1932. After *The Communist Manifesto*, he went on to produce a series of massive drafts for *Capital*, a critical study of economic theory and the economic basis of society. Only volume one (Marx 1867) was published in his lifetime.

There is some controversy about the relationship between the works of the older, mature Marx of the 1860s and those of the youthful Marx of the 1840s. For some commentators, the early works on alienation were immature exercises that he later abandoned. For others, however, exploitation and alienation are closely related ideas. A close reading of Marx's texts shows that there is a great deal of continuity and that the so-called *Grundrisse* (1858) is a key link between the two phases of his work.

Marx's central idea of the organization of a society into a base and a superstructure (discussed more fully in the text) drew a comparison with architecture. If the superstructure of a building (its walls and roof and the internal layout of the rooms) is to remain solid and not fall down, then it must stand on solid foundations that run deep into the ground. Marx saw kinship, politics, and ideology as the various levels of the social superstructure, and he saw these standing on the firm foundations of an economic base comprising the forces and relations of production. The superstructure is the most obvious and visible aspect of the social structure, but the base is the essential—if hidden—support for it.

Ideology and forms of consciousness	
Politics and the state	Superstructure
Family and kinship	
Relations of production	Base or foundation
Forces of production	

Marx remains an influential theorist. In a poll carried out for a BBC radio programme in 2005, Marx was voted the greatest ever philosopher—he received 28 per cent of the 30,000 votes cast.

Useful discussions of Marx's ideas can be found in Giddens (1971) and Craib (1997). There is more detail in McLellan (1971), which contains some extracts from Marx's own work. A good biography is McLellan's *Karl Marx: His Life and Thought* (1973). If you want to try to understand Marx's economic theory, you should try Mandel's *The Formation of the Economic Thought of Karl Marx* (1967).

A good collection of electronic texts by Marx can be found at
http://eserver.org:16080/marx
Links to the ideas of Marx and other Marxists can be found at
www.marxists.org
A useful biographical overview is at
www.historyguide.org/intellect/marx. html

➔ The details of Marx's work are discussed in various parts of this book. You will find them in the following chapters:

- alienation and the nature of work *Chapter 17*
- poverty *Chapter 18*
- class relations and class polarization *Chapter 19*
- labour organization, ruling class, politics, and the state *Chapters 14, 20*
- religion and ideology *Chapter 11*.

writing was not simply an industrial society (as Comte had argued) but a specifically **capitalist society**. Capitalist societies developed only in those societies in which feudalism had prepared the way.

Beginning in the towns and commercial centres of the feudal world, a class of private property-owners had become, from the sixteenth century, the most important economic force. These capitalist entrepreneurs had built plants, workshops, and factories in which they employed large numbers of workers, and they generated profits for themselves through market exchange and the employment of wage labour. These capitalists eventually became the **ruling classes** of their societies, displacing the old feudal landowners through often violent revolutions.

Capitalism had a limited life span, Marx argued. As capitalist societies developed, exploitation increased and the superstructures became an obstacle to further economic growth. This meant that property relations and the whole superstructure had to be swept away in a revolution. This time, however, it would be a revolution of the workers, who would displace the capitalist ruling class. Workers would become more conscious of their alienation and of the need to change the conditions that produced it. They would form radical political parties and, in due course, would overthrow the capitalist system. A workers' revolution, Marx rather optimistically thought, would abolish alienation, exploitation, and oppression, and it would establish a new and more advanced form of communist production (see Box 2.5).

A theory of knowledge

Marx accepted that the natural sciences could produce objective and certain knowledge of the physical world, but he did not think this was possible in the social sciences. The social world could only ever be known from the class standpoints of particular observers. Members of a dominant class see the social world differently from those below them.

Social knowledge, then, is relative to the class position of the knower and so must be judged as ideological. Because there is no standpoint outside the class structure, there can be no impartial or objective knowledge. Social knowledge—and therefore social science—must reflect a political alignment with one side or another in the class struggle.

Marx held that his own theories were relative to the standpoint of the **proletariat**, the subordinate class of the capitalist system to which he had aligned himself. Classical economics and the sociologies of Comte and Spencer were, for Marx, uncritical expressions of the capitalist or **bourgeois** world-view. The standpoint of this

---

THEORY AND METHODS 2.5

Modes of production

Marx recognized six main modes of production, each defined by a particular type of property ownership and labour:

- primitive communism—relatively egalitarian, communal property;
- ancient—slave-owning systems;
- Asiatic—despotic and bureaucratic control;
- feudalism—serfdom, combined with urban commercial centres;
- capitalism—wage labour and private property;
- advanced communism—re-establishes communal property.

In each of these modes of production, the productive forces are developed to a different level. Before the stage of advanced communism they are also marked by growing levels of exploitation and alienation.

Do not worry about the details of this scheme. We will introduce some of these, where relevant, in other chapters. You might like to compare Marx's scheme with the stages of development identified by Hegel, Comte, and Spencer.

---

subordinate class gave access to a deeper and more adequate understanding of society than that possible from the standpoint of the ruling class. Marx presented his core ideas in a political manifesto for the communist movement (Marx and Engels 1848).

Marx's work provides a powerful challenge to the ideas of Comte and Spencer. Where the latter saw modern societies as *industrial societies* ruled by benign industrialists, Marx saw them as *capitalist societies* ruled by oppressive capitalists. Marx also differed in his stress on conflict and struggle rather than coherence and integration. Taken together, these theories highlighted the various factors relevant to understanding social life.

⊃ *Connections*

Marx saw social knowledge as relative to the class standpoint of the observer. What social divisions, other than class, could be seen as providing distinctive standpoints on the social world? Do you agree with Marx's rejection of the possibility of 'objectivity'? Come back and consider this question again when you have read our discussions of Max Weber and of feminist theories.

Stop and reflect

This section has traced the early stages of scientific sociology up to the pioneering statements of Comte, Spencer, and Marx. Although you are not expected to understand or recall everything that we have written about them, you should try to make sure that you have some familiarity with their key ideas.

- The idea of a *science* of society was a product of the European Enlightenment of the seventeenth and eighteenth centuries.

- Only gradually was an understanding of the distinctively *social* features of human life separated from an understanding of *individuals*.

- Why do you think that these early social theories differed so much in their main themes and ideas?

The pioneering statements of a specifically sociological approach are found in the works of Comte and Spencer. An alternative approach—that of Marx—broadened out this emerging form of social thought.

Comte established the idea of sociology as a *positive science* that explained empirical observations through causal laws.

- Both Comte and Spencer drew a distinction between social statics and social dynamics. Social statics is concerned with the structure and functioning of social systems. Social dynamics is concerned with their development over time.

- Spencer saw social development as a process of structural differentiation, shaped by functional adaptation.

- How useful do you think it is to make a distinction between 'industrial' societies and the 'militant' societies of the past?

While Marx also saw societies as systems that could be studied in terms of their structures and development over time, he placed more emphasis on the part played by conflict and struggle in social development.

- Marx saw economic activity as fundamental to social life. Work, property, and the division of labour form the economic base of society, its mode of production. They are the basis of class divisions that result in the alienation and exploitation of labour.

- Social development has followed a sequence of modes of production from primitive communism through feudalism to contemporary capitalist societies.

- Political and legal institutions, together with cultural values and ideologies, form the superstructure of society and are shaped by the economic base.

- Was Marx correct to see class conflict as the means through which the base and the superstructure of a capitalist society can be transformed and a new society created?

The formative period of sociology

Sociology began to be established as a scientific discipline between the 1880s and the 1920s. Increasing numbers of professors in the universities of Europe and North America began to call themselves sociologists or to take sociological ideas seriously. Their work is often referred to as 'classical sociology'. Both Spencer and Marx had their heirs and followers. In Britain, Spencer's ideas were developed in a more flexible way by Leonard Hobhouse, the first person to hold a sociology professorship in a British university. In the United States, William Sumner developed versions of Spencer's ideas that had a considerable influence, and Lester Ward developed a sociology that owed rather more to Comte.

Marx's ideas were taken up in the leading Communist parties of Europe and, even before his death, they began to be codified into 'Marxism'. Those who regarded themselves as Marxists shared his identification with the proletariat. The country in which Marxism had the greatest impact was Russia, where the revolution of 1917 led to the dominance of the Communist Party and the enshrinement of Marxism as the official ideology of the Soviet Union. The political content of Marxism limited its influence in academic sociology. While there was some attempt to grapple with his ideas—especially in Germany—Marxism was a neglected tradition of thought until the 1960s.

Sociology thrived most strongly in France and Germany, where a number of important theorists began to construct more disciplined and focused theoretical frameworks that could be used in detailed empirical investigations. In France, there was the work of Le Play, Tarde, and, above all, Durkheim. In Germany, the leading theorists were Tönnies, Simmel, and Weber. In terms of their impact on the later development of sociology, it is Durkheim and Weber who must be seen as the key figures.

Émile Durkheim: social structure

Émile Durkheim saw his principal task as the construction of a philosophical basis for a *science* of sociology. He wanted to show that sociology could be a rigorous scientific discipline worthy of a place in the university system. This was the basis of the distinctive view of sociology that he developed on the basis set out by Comte.

The nature of social facts

Durkheim saw the subject matter of sociology as a distinctive set of **social facts**. These are specific phenomena that can be sharply distinguished from the facts studied by other scientists. They are, in particular, distinct from the facts of individual consciousness studied by psychology and the organic facts of individual bodies studied by biology. They are the things that define the specific intellectual concerns of sociology (see Box 2.6).

Durkheim characterizes social facts as ways of acting, thinking, or feeling that are collective, rather than individual, in origin. Social facts have a reality *sui generis*. This is a Latin phrase that means 'of its own type' or 'distinctive to itself'. Because this was a difficult idea for others to understand—and it is still not completely understood by many critics of sociology—he set out his views at some length.

As an example of a social fact Durkheim gave what later writers would call a role. There are certain established ways of acting, thinking, or feeling as a brother, a husband, a citizen, and so on. They are, in the most general sense, expected, required, or imposed ways of acting, thinking, or feeling for those who occupy these positions and may be established in custom or law.

Social facts are not invented by the individuals who conform to them. They are general patterns that have been acquired through learning and training. Individuals learn what is expected of them quite early in life, and these expectations become part of their own personality. They are passed from generation to generation and are received by particular individuals in a more or less complete form. It is for this reason that they often involve a sense of obligation. Even when people feel that they are acting through choice or free will, they are likely to be following a socially shared pattern of expectations. Social facts are the

---

THEORY AND METHODS   **2.6**

Émile Durkheim

The study of social facts.

© Bibliothèque Nationale de France

Émile Durkheim (1858–1917) was born in Épinal, France. He studied social and political philosophy at the École Normale Supérieure in Paris, reading the works of Montesquieu and Rousseau. He studied for a year in Germany and then taught educational theory at Bordeaux from 1887 to 1902, after which he moved to a professorship at the Sorbonne in Paris. He made a close but critical study of the work of Comte, and produced a number of exemplary sociological studies. In 1913, only four years before his death, he was allowed to call himself Professor of Sociology.

Durkheim's key works appeared regularly and became the basis of a distinctive school of sociology. His major writings were *The Division of Labour in Society* (1893), *The Rules of the Sociological Method* (1895), *Suicide: A Study in Sociology* (1897), and *The Elementary Forms of the Religious Life* (1912). He founded a journal (the *Année Sociologique*) that became a focus for his work. One of his principal followers was his nephew, Marcel Mauss, who produced some important work himself (Durkheim and Mauss 1903; Mauss 1925).

The texts by Giddens (1971) and Craib (1997) give useful discussions of Durkheim. More detail and a biographical account can be found in Lukes (1973). A good brief introduction is K. Thompson (1982). Useful attempts to set up Durkheim home pages are **www.relst.uiuc.edu/durkheim** and **www.emile-durkheim.com** You will find extracts from some of Durkheim's books at: **http://durkheim.itgo.com/main.html**

➔ You will find more detailed discussions of Durkheim's principal ideas in various parts of this book:

- religion *Chapter 11*
- education *Chapter 9*
- anomie and the division of labour *Chapter 17*.

collective products of a society as a whole or of particular social groups.

Because they are matters of expectation, obligation, or deep commitment, social facts also have a 'compelling and coercive power', which Durkheim summarizes by the term 'constraint'. This constraint takes various forms: punishment, disapproval, rejection, or simply the failure of an action to achieve its goal. Someone who breaks the law by killing another person is likely to face arrest, trial, and imprisonment or execution. On the other hand, someone who misuses language is simply likely to be misunderstood. A French citizen is not forced to speak French, nor is he punished if he does not, but he will be understood by his compatriots only if he uses the rules and conventions of French vocabulary and grammar (see Box 2.7).

Social facts are very difficult to observe, and are often apparent only through their effects. The role of husband, for example, cannot be observed: only particular individuals acting as husbands can be seen. Similarly, the grammar of a language cannot be observed, only the speech of particular individuals. Because they are invisible and intangible, their properties have to be discovered indirectly. By observing the actions of large numbers of people who act in similar ways, for example, it is possible to infer the existence of the role of husband. By observing a large number of conversations, it is possible to infer the existence of particular rules of grammar.

Social facts may be more directly observable if they are codified in laws, summarized in proverbs, set down in religious texts, or laid down in books of grammar. These laws, proverbs, texts, and books are not themselves the social facts. They are simply the attempts that individuals have made to bring social facts to consciousness and to make them explicit. These formulations can, nevertheless, be useful evidence on social facts and can be used alongside the direct observation of actions in an investigation into social facts.

Studying social facts

Durkheim's approach owes a great deal to Comte's positivism and was set out as a set of rules or principles that Durkheim thought should guide the scientific sociologist.

The first of these rules draws on Comte's contrast between metaphysical thought and positive science, and simply says 'consider social facts as things'. Durkheim meant that all preconceived ideas must be abandoned if things are to be studied as they really are. This is the only way to be objective and of practical value. Sociologists must abandon the common-sense preconceptions that they rely on in their everyday lives and must make direct observations of phenomena. Sociology, Durkheim argued, must treat its objects—social facts—as 'things'.

Everyday ideas about the state, the family, work, crime, and so on embody religious, political, and personal prejudices that are mistakenly treated as if they are objective facts. Adopting the scientific attitude means abandoning the accepted ideas of your social group and attempting to construct new concepts that directly grasp the real nature of things. Scientific concepts must be produced from within scientific practice itself.

While Durkheim correctly identified the need to avoid the prejudice and distortion that often results from preconceived ideas, he was mistaken in his belief that it was possible to observe things independently of *all* concepts. Nevertheless, his core idea that sociology must collect evidence through the direct observation of social facts remains a valuable insight.

Durkheim identified two complementary aspects of sociological explanation: **causal explanation** and **functional analysis**. Causal explanation is the more fundamental of the two. A causal explanation accounts for the origins of a social fact in relation to the other social facts that brought it into being. If the punishment attached to a crime expresses an intense collective sentiment of disapproval, then the collective sentiment is a cause of the punishment: if the sentiment did not exist, the punishment would not occur.

THEORY AND METHODS   **2.7**
....

Social facts

Social facts 'consist of manners of acting, thinking and feeling external to the individual, which are vested with a coercive power by virtue of which they exercise control over him' (Durkheim 1895: 52). Social facts are characterized by:

- externality;
- constraint.

Some social facts are collective representations: shared ways of thinking about a group and its relations to the things that affect it. Examples of collective representations are myths, legends, and religious ideas. Others are institutions. These are modes of behaviour that are long established in a society or social group.

⤷ Connections

Showing causal relationships is not quite as straightforward as Durkheim implied. The fact that variations in *A* are followed by variations in *B* may not indicate that *B* is caused by *A*. The variations could indicate that both *A* and *B* are caused by some other, as yet unknown, third factor. We look at this problem in Chapter 18, pp. 718–19, where we consider it in relation to occupational achievement.

Functional analysis is concerned with the *effects* rather than the causes of a social fact. It looks at the part that a social fact plays in relation to the *needs* of a society or social group. The term 'need' refers simply to those things that must be done if a society is to survive. More generally, the function of something is the part that it plays in the **adaptation** of a society to changing circumstances.

A simplified functional analysis of religion is shown in Figure 2.1. Durkheim argued that religion helps to meet a society's need for social solidarity. High levels of religious observance tie people together and so increase the level of social solidarity; low levels of religious observance reduce the level of social solidarity. This is matched by the effects of social solidarity on religion. If the level of social solidarity is too low, then individualistic impulses may threaten the survival of the society. Stability can be maintained only if religious observance increases and a higher level of social solidarity is re-established. If, on the other hand, the level of social solidarity becomes too high, individual creativity may be stifled and a reduction in the level of religious observance may be required. Religion and social solidarity are, then, interdependent.

Much in this view of functional analysis remains unclear. In particular, it does not show what mechanisms actually ensure that increases or reductions in religious observance take place. Durkheim minimized this problem by equating need with 'goal' or 'purpose'. He assumed that people consciously and deliberately act to meet social needs. Most later writers have rejected this view and have tried to show that the meeting of needs is often an unintended and unrecognized consequence of social action. Durkheim's rules of sociological method are summarized in Box 2.8.

Social differentiation and social solidarity

Durkheim applied his scientific method in a great book on the development of modern society (Durkheim 1893) in

---

THEORY AND METHODS   **2.8**

Rules of the Sociological Method

Durkheim (1895) set out a number of rules or principles. We have considered only the most important of these. A simplified and slightly shortened version of his list is:

- consider social facts as things;
- cause and function must be investigated separately;
- a particular effect always follows from the same cause;
- a full explanation of a social fact involves looking at its development through all the stages of its history;
- social facts must be classified according to their degree of organization;
- a social fact is normal for a given type of society when it is found in the average example of the type;
- a social fact is normal when it is related to the general conditions of collective life in a type of society.

Reread the discussion of Durkheim's philosophy and identify the paragraphs in which we discuss each of these rules.

In the title of his book *Rules of the Sociological Method*, Durkheim used the word 'method' in the sense of a philosophy of science or 'methodology' of science. He was not talking about the specific research methods that we discuss in Chapter 3.

---

which he criticized and extended the ideas of Spencer. This book, the first that he wrote, was an attempt to examine **social differentiation**, the specialization of activities into a complex structure of occupations. Durkheim called this the **division of labour**, using this term to refer not only to the differentiation of economic activities, but also to the

Figure 2.1 Functional analysis

This model is based on Durkheim's account of suicide, which we discuss on pp. 35–7 below, and the view of social solidarity that we set out on pp. 34–5. You might find it useful to come back to this diagram after you have read our account of social differentiation and social solidarity.

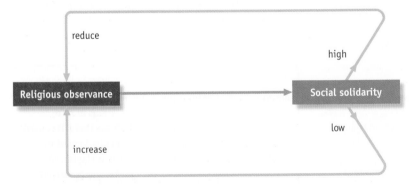

specialization of political, administrative, legal, scientific, and other tasks. The division of labour was a key concept for economists, but Durkheim showed that their understanding was too limited. The division of labour, which had achieved an unprecedented scale in modern society, is not simply an economic matter, but is central to the cohesion and integration of modern societies.

Durkheim's book is divided into two parts: the first gives a causal explanation of the division of labour and the second a functional analysis. He argued that a division of labour occurs only when communal societies give way to more organized societies. Communal societies are divided into 'segments' (families, clans, local villages) and have little or no division of labour. Each segment is self-sufficient. As segments break down, individuals are brought into more intimate contact with each other. This expanded scale of social interaction depends on increasing population density and on the emergence of cities and commercial centres, which bring about an increase in **dynamic density**. This refers to an increase in the number of social relationships and therefore in the amount of communication and interaction between the members of a society.

Growing population density leads to more and more people carrying out the same activities and so results in increased competition and an ever more intensive struggle for survival. Competition can be reduced only by people becoming more specialized in their activities. For example, self-sufficient households may become specialized in farming, milling, brewing, weaving, and other tasks and so begin to form a division of labour. The division of labour, Durkheim argued, develops directly with the dynamic density: as the dynamic density of a society increases, so the division of labour becomes more marked. Hence, a growth in the scale of societies over time produces ever more complex and differentiated societies.

Durkheim's functional analysis showed that the division of labour creates not simply exchange relationships in a market system, but a feeling of **solidarity** that becomes an essential factor in the integration of the society as a whole. Social solidarity involves the *integration* of individuals into social groups and their *regulation* by shared norms.

Durkheim argued that the most important external indicator of social solidarity is the system of law. In societies with an extensive division of labour, he argued, the law tends to be restitutive rather than repressive. Legal procedures attempt to restore things to the way that they were before a crime occurred. Punishment for its own sake is less important. This, he said, indicates a sense of solidarity that is tied to cooperation and reciprocity. Durkheim called this **organic solidarity**. People are tied together through relations of trust and reciprocity that correspond to their economic interdependence, and each sphere of activity is regulated through specific types of norms.

The organized, organic solidarity produced by the division of labour is contrasted with the **mechanical solidarity** of traditional, communal societies. In these undifferentiated societies characteristic of the pre-modern, pre-industrial world, social solidarity revolves around a sense of similarity and a consciousness of unity and community. Conformity in such a society is maintained through the repressive force of a strong system of shared beliefs.

Organic solidarity is a normal or integral feature of modern society, but it may fail to develop in some. In the early stages of the transition from pre-industrial to industrial society, Durkheim argued, there is a particular danger that abnormal forms of the division of labour will develop. The normal condition of organic solidarity encourages a high level of individual freedom, controlling this through the normative systems that Durkheim called moral individualism. The abnormal forms of the division of labour, however, lack this moral framework, and individual actions are left uncontrolled.

The two abnormal situations that he describes are egoism and **anomie**. *Egoism* is that situation where individuals are not properly integrated into the social groups of which they are members. *Anomie* is the situation where individual actions are not properly regulated by shared norms. Durkheim saw anomie and egoism as responsible for the economic crises, extremes of social inequality, and class conflict of his day. As we show below, he also saw them as responsible for high rates of suicide. All these problems, he held, would be reduced when the division of labour was properly established and organic solidarity instituted in its normal form.

Suicide and social solidarity

Durkheim's best-known book is his study of suicide (Durkheim 1897). His aim in this book was not only to provide an account of suicide but also to illustrate how his methodology could be applied to even the most individual of acts. The book was intended to serve as a model of sociological explanation. He showed that the taking of one's own life, apparently the most individual and personal of acts, was patterned by social forces that constrain individuals from outside. Suicide rates are therefore social facts, which Durkheim demonstrated by showing how suicide rates varied from one group to another and from one social situation to another. Some of the main variations that he identified were as follows:

- *Religion.* Protestants are more likely to commit suicide than Catholics. The suicide rate is much higher in Protestant than Catholic countries and regions.

- *Family relationships.* The married are less likely to commit suicide than the single, widowed, or divorced.

- *War and peace*. The suicide rate drops in time of war, in both victorious and defeated countries.
- *Economic crisis*. Suicide rates rise at times of economic crisis and sudden changes in economic conditions, whether towards recession or prosperity.

Durkheim's demonstration of systematic variations in the suicide rate showed that suicide cannot be explained solely in terms of the psychology of the individual but requires sociological explanation. His sociological theory of suicide is based on the idea that the degree of social solidarity explains variations in suicide rates. A person who is only loosely connected into a society or social group is more likely to commit suicide, but, if the level of solidarity is too strong, then this, too, can lead to a higher suicide rate.

His theory distinguished two aspects of social connection, which he called *integration* and *regulation*. Integration refers to the strength of the individual's attachment to social groups. Regulation refers to the control of individual desires and aspirations by group norms or rules of behaviour. This led him to identify four types of suicide, which correspond to low and high states of integration and regulation (see Figure 2.2):

- egoistic suicide;
- anomic suicide;
- altruistic suicide;
- fatalistic suicide.

Egoistic suicide results from 'egoism', the weak social integration of the individual who is excessively focused on the self or ego. Protestantism is a less integrative religion than Catholicism, for it places less emphasis on collective rituals and emphasizes the individual's direct relationship with God. Protestants are, therefore, more prone to suicide. Those who are single or widowed or childless are also weakly integrated and therefore more prone to suicide. War, on the other hand, tends to integrate people into society and therefore reduces the suicide rate.

Anomic suicide results from anomie. This means normlessness, lacking any regulation by shared norms.

Regulation and control of needs and passions keep desires and circumstances in balance with each other. Changes in the situation, such as those brought about by economic change or divorce, could upset this balance. In these circumstances, the normal regulation of people's lives breaks down and they find themselves in a state of anomie.

Altruistic suicide is the opposite of egoistic suicide. In this case, social bonds are too strong. People may set little value on themselves as individuals, or they may obediently sacrifice themselves to the requirements of the group. This form of suicide is characteristic of primitive societies, though it is also found among the military, where there is a strong emphasis on the importance of loyalty to the group. Durkheim used the term 'altruistic' to convey the idea that the individual self is totally subordinated to others.

Fatalistic suicide is the opposite of anomic suicide and results from an oppression of the individual by excessively high regulation. Durkheim gives as an example the suicide of slaves, but he considered this type to be of little contemporary significance and he limited his discussion of it to a footnote.

Egoism and anomie are often found together, as, for example, when a divorce occurs. This both isolates people and leaves their lives in an unregulated state. He was, however, careful to distinguish between the social processes involved in egoism and anomie, on the one hand, and the states of mind that each produced, on the other hand. One of the most notable features of Durkheim's theory of suicide, and one that is often overlooked by commentators, is that he shows the consequences of social conditions for an individual's psychological state. He demonstrated not only that the behaviour of the individual was social but also that the individual's internal world of feelings and mental states was socially produced.

Thus, Durkheim argued that the social isolation characteristic of egoistic suicide results in apathy or depression. Anomic suicide is associated with a much more restless condition of irritation, disappointment, or frustration. When lack of regulation leads desires and

Figure 2.2 Durkheim's typology of suicide

There has been much discussion in the media about the motives of suicide bombers. How do you think that Durkheim would classify these suicides?

Type	Degree of solidarity	Social situation	Psychological state	Examples
Egoistic	Low	Lack of integration	Apathy, depression	Suicides of protestants and single people
Anomic	Low	Lack of regulation	Irritation, frustration	Suicides during economic crisis
Altruistic	High	Excessive integration	Energy and passion	Suicides in primitive societies; military suicides
Fatalistic	High	Excessive regulation	Acceptance and resignation	The suicide of slaves

ambitions to get out of control, people become upset and frustrated by their inability to achieve them. Altruistic suicide is generally accompanied by an energy and passion quite opposite to the apathy of egoism. Durkheim did not discuss the psychological state characteristic of fatalistic suicide, but it would seem to involve a mood of acceptance and resignation.

Since Durkheim, the study of suicide has moved on, and later sociologists have pointed to problems with the methods that he used. The main problem was that the suicide rates on which he based his study were calculated from official statistics. These depended on coroners' decisions on the classification of deaths as suicides, and it has been shown that their practices vary (Douglas 1967; J. M. Atkinson 1978). For a death to be suicide, it must be intentional, and the assessment of intention is difficult, particularly if no suicide note is left. This leaves a lot of room for interpretation and considerable scope for others, such as friends and relatives of the dead person, to influence coroners' decisions. The existence of social variations in suicide rates cannot, however, be denied, and Durkheim's

fundamental point, that the apparently most individual of acts requires sociological explanation, stands.

> **Connections**
> We discuss many of the general problems that arise with the use of official statistics in Chapter 3, pp. 99–103.

Max Weber: social action

Max Weber worked with other social scientists in Germany to develop a distinctively sociological perspective, but his approach to sociology was very different from Durkheim's. Weber argued that sociology had to start out from people's actions not from structures, initiating a division between a sociology of structure and a sociology of action that marked the whole subsequent development of sociology. He took on Hegel's idea that social life was an expression of 'spirit' or culture, but saw this as something that is expressed in individual subjectivity and action. An overview of Weber can be found in Box 2.9.

THEORY AND METHODS   2.9
....

Max Weber

The study of social action.

© Bildarchiv Preussischer Kulturbesitz

Max Weber (1864–1920) was born in Erfurt, Germany, but spent most of his early life in Berlin. He studied law at the University of Heidelberg—his father was a lawyer. He was particularly

interested in Roman law and agrarian relations, and undertook many studies in economic history. He became Professor of Economics at Freiburg in 1893, and in 1896 moved to Heidelberg. After a dispute with his father, he suffered a mental breakdown and gave up his teaching post the following year. He was later able to continue with research and writing, but he did not return to university teaching until he was appointed to a professorship at Munich in 1917. Weber was active in liberal politics, and was a member of the German delegation to the Versailles peace conference after the First World War.

Much of Weber's work appeared as essays and was published in book form only later in his life or after his death. His most influential work was a study of Protestantism and the rise of capitalism (Max Weber 1904–5), and he produced related studies of religion in China (1915) and India (1916). His key works on economic and political sociology were not completed in his lifetime and were brought together for publication after his

death (Max Weber 1914, 1920).

Giddens (1971) and Craib (1997) both provide very useful accounts of Weber's work. The standard biography was written by his wife (Marianne Weber 1926), but a new biography has recently appeared (Radkau 2009). Parkin (1982) gives a good, brief introduction. You can find attempts to set up home pages for Weber at
www.faculty.rsu.edu/~felwell/Theorists/Weber/Whome.htm
and
www.sociosite.net/topics/weber.php
the latter containing many online texts.

> You will find detailed discussions of Weber's main ideas in the following chapters:

- religion and rationality *Chapter 11*
- social stratification *Chapter 19*
- bureaucracy *Chapter 14*
- authority and the state *Chapter 15*

Concepts, values, and science

Durkheim's view was that sociology must consider social facts as things and disregard all preconceptions. Weber's position was more complex. He argued that observation was impossible without concepts, but saw this as perfectly compatible with the production of objective scientific knowledge (Max Weber 1904).

Weber argued that there can be no knowledge of things as they actually exist, independently of thought. To have knowledge is to give meaning to the world by interpreting it. The world does not simply present itself to our senses but must be given significance by the observer. An area of land, for example, may be of significance as a place for physical exercise, an environment for flora and fauna, a beautiful landscape, or the site of a historical ruin. All observers, scientists included, carve out particular aspects of reality and give them meaning and significance.

The concepts through which meaning is given to the world are based in cultural **values**. Concepts are 'value relevant': they are relative to particular cultural values. It is our values that tell us which aspects of reality are significant and which are insignificant. Those who subscribe to feminist values are likely to be interested in the relationships between men and women and to form concepts such as patriarchy to describe male domination of women. Those with communist values, on the other hand, will focus on the relationships between workers and property-owners and will use concepts such as exploitation to describe them. As there are a large number of possible value standpoints, reality can only ever be known from particular value-relevant points of view.

Weber did not think this meant that all knowledge is arbitrary or subjective. Scientific knowledge can be objective, despite being value-relevant. The sociologist must adopt strict and disciplined methods of investigation, must be critical in his or her use of concepts and evidence, and must follow strict logical principles of reasoning. It must be possible for any other sociologist to replicate and test results. Feminist and communist sociologists may disagree over which concepts are most useful for studying the modern world, but they should each be able to see whether the other has been honest, rational, and critical in carrying out his or her research.

Weber also distinguished between *factual judgements* and *value judgements*. Sociologists, like all scientists, make objective factual judgements about happenings in the world. They may also make subjective value judgements about things of which they approve or disapprove, but these value judgements are no part of science. Subjective disapproval of inequality has no bearing on the question of how much inequality there is in any particular society. The latter is a purely empirical matter, a matter of fact. When a scientist makes a value judgement, he or she is making an ethical or political statement, not a scientific statement. Weber held that those who allowed value judgements to interfere with scientific activities were abandoning the principles of science and the pursuit of objective knowledge.

> ⟶ *Connections*
> Weber's argument is very difficult to follow, so do not worry if you have problems with it at first. It is probably one of the most difficult things that you will come across in sociology. The important point is that Weber rejected the idea that we all experience the world in exactly the same way. He concluded that there can be a number of equally legitimate ways of doing sociology. Come back to Weber's argument after you have completed the rest of this chapter.

The final element in Weber's scientific method is what he called the **ideal type**. The concepts used by social scientists are logical, idealized constructions from one-sided, value-relevant standpoints. Aspects of reality that are of interest are pulled together and forged into an idealized model. Ideal types are idealizations because they are analytical or conceptual and do not actually exist in reality. Ideal types of capitalism, the nation state, and bureaucracy are analytical devices constructed by social scientists in order to understand a very complex reality.

This is also true in the natural sciences. The concept of H_2O, for example, is an idealization. Actual samples of water contain impurities and additives of all kinds, and it is only under highly artificial, laboratory conditions that it is possible to isolate pure H_2O. In the social sciences, laboratory experimentation is not usually possible, and so sociologists are never likely to observe things that correspond precisely to their ideal types. Class and gender relations, for example, only ever exist in combination and alongside many other factors.

Understanding social actions

The most important ideal types for sociology are, according to Weber, types of social action, and the more complex ideal types are nothing but intricate patterns of action. A typology of action provides the building blocks for sociological investigations. Weber did not see social structures as external to or independent of individuals. All social structures were seen as complex, interweaving patterns of action. They exist as social facts only when individuals define them as 'things' with a separate existence. For example, a state exists only if particular forms of administration and decision-making have been reified—defined as things—by the people involved in them.

Weber identified four ideal types of action as the fundamental building blocks for sociology:

- instrumentally rational action;
- value-rational action;

- traditional action;
- affectual action.

People action in an *instrumentally rational* way when they adopt purely technical means to their goals. This action involves a clear goal or purpose, and the best or most efficient means of achieving it are chosen. Weber argued that much of the economic, political, and scientific action that involves rational choice and decision-making approximates to this type of action. A capitalist entrepreneur calculates the most efficient and economic means for attaining maximum profit from a line of business. A party leader calculates the combination of policy proposals that will maximize the party's vote in forthcoming elections.

Value-rational action, on the other hand, is action that is rational in relation to an irrational or arbitrarily chosen value. The religious believer who prays and gives alms to the poor may be acting value-rationally if he or she is acting this way for its own sake and as an absolute duty, with no account taken of instrumental or technical considerations. This type of action involves no easily identifiable goal, even if the believer hopes that he or she might achieve salvation. Value-rational action is rational in relation to the expression of value commitments.

Traditional action is unreflective and habitual, barely involving any rationality at all. It is undertaken as a matter of routine and with little or no conscious deliberation, and is characteristic of many everyday actions. People act in the ways that they always have done in the past. Finally, *affectual* action is a direct expression of emotion without any reflection on its relation to specific goals or values. Angry outbursts of violence, for example, would be seen as affectual.

These four types of action are ideal types and do not exist in reality. Concrete patterns of action combine them in various ways. The manager of a large business enterprise who sets a wage level for employees may instrumentally calculate the financial consequences of different rates of pay, but may also rule out extremely low pay and certain forms of coercion as they conflict with his or her values. The manager may respond unreflectively to wage negotiations, treating trade-union proposals in the way that they have always been handled in the past, and a breakdown in negotiations may lead to angry recriminations as one side or the other storms away from the bargaining table.

Weber used a particular technique to uncover the relation between a course of action and his ideal types. This is the technique of **understanding** (*Verstehen* in German). Social science must use the ideal types to understand the meanings that people give to their actions. These meanings include their intentions and motives, their expectations about the behaviour of others, and their perceptions of the situations in which they find themselves. These meanings must be inferred from the observation of actions.

To explain serial murder, for example, it is necessary to get close enough to serial murderers to see the world as they see it. The sociologist must try to identify with them up to the point at which the reasons for their actions can be comprehended. However, this empathy does not mean that the sociologist must sympathize with them or condone their actions. To move from empathy to sympathy is to make the same mistake as those who move from factual judgements to value judgements.

Traditionalism and rationality

Weber's methodology led him to reject all determinism. Causal explanations in sociology must be rooted in an interpretative understanding of the subjective meanings that individuals give to their actions. Individuals have the power to act freely and not simply as the occupants of class positions or social roles. For this reason, the future is open and undetermined and cannot be predicted. Weber therefore took a different view of modern industrial capitalism and its future from the predictions made by Marx and Durkheim.

The transition from feudal, pre-industrial societies to modern industrial capitalism in Europe was seen by Weber in terms of a change in the typical meanings that individuals give to their actions. There had been a process of **rationalization** in which these meanings had changed from value rational to instrumentally rational. In medieval societies, people's actions had been oriented to absolute religious and political values, while in modern societies they involved a rational calculation of the likely effects of different courses of action. Political authority in modern society, for example, is based on formal, legal procedures, rather than ultimate religious values such as the divine right of kings.

In medieval societies, furthermore, a great deal of everyday action was not rational at all but was traditional. Tradition itself was treated as an absolute value in many situations. In modern societies, on the other hand, more and more areas of social life have been opened up to rational, reflective considerations. Economic actions, for example, have come to be based on market calculations and contractual relations, rather than on fixed ways of living rooted in traditional styles of life.

Much everyday action in modern societies, of course, remains traditional in character. It continues unreflectively and routinely, with little concern for immediate ends or ultimate values. Traditional forms of action may even acquire a new importance in modern societies. Weber held, for example, that religious values motivated the actions of the first generations of calculating capitalist entrepreneurs, but later generations were more likely to continue in business because it had become a matter of routine. They had become mere cogs in huge bureaucratic machines and their work had become a 'dull compulsion' in which they had no real choice. Formally, they remain free, but in practice they are tightly constrained.

⊃ Connections

You will understand more about Weber's views on rational economic action when you have read our discussion of *The Protestant Ethic and the Spirit of Capitalism* (1904–5) in Chapter 11, pp. 397–8. You may like to read that discussion now.

Stop and reflect

In this section we have looked at the two leading figures of the classical period of sociology, Durkheim and Weber. Durkheim was the principal French sociologist and founder of an approach that emphasized social structures as the fundamental social facts. He set this out in an account of the basic principles of sociology.

- Social facts are ways of acting, thinking, or feeling that are both external and constraining. They are collective products, and individuals experience them as coercive or obligatory.

- Social facts are to be studied as things, through observation rather than on the basis of prejudice and preconception. Although they cannot always be observed directly, social facts can be observed indirectly through their effects on individual actions.

- Do you agree with Durkheim's view that even such an individual act as taking one's own life is socially patterned and can be explained sociologically?

- Durkheim said that in causal explanation social facts are accounted for in terms of the other social facts that brought them into being; in functional analysis social facts are examined in relation to the part that they play in relation to the survival or adaptation of other social facts. How useful is it to make this distinction?

Durkheim applied this sociological approach in a number of substantive studies of the division of labour, suicide, education, and religion. We discuss a number of these studies in other chapters. These were seen as aspects of a general account of social development.

- Social solidarity comprises the integration of individuals into social groups and their regulation by shared norms. Durkheim contrasted the mechanical solidarity of traditional societies with the organic solidarity of modern societies.

- One of the central problems of contemporary society was the pathological state of individualism that Durkheim described as involving egoism and anomie. Egoism and anomie are associated with particular psychological conditions and rates of suicide.

- How did Durkheim understand the relationship between social differentiation and social solidarity?

Weber, as one of a number of important German sociologists, tried to build a sociology of social action that was sensitive to the meanings and motives that shaped people's behaviour.

- Social reality can only ever be studied through the use of concepts that reflect cultural values. Knowledge of social reality is objective only if it results from the rational and critical use of these concepts in a scientifically disciplined way.

- While all concepts are value relevant, Weber emphasizes the need to distinguish clearly factual judgements from value judgements.

- Sociological concepts are ideal types and do not correspond to things that actually exist in reality. They are the basic building blocks of sociological analysis and grasp particular aspects of reality.

- Is Weber's typology of action—instrumentally rational action, value-rational action, traditional action, and affectual action—a useful way of approaching the study of social interaction?

- How easy is it to understand social actions by empathizing with those who are studied?

Weber rejected all forms of structural determinism, emphasizing the open-ended character of social life. He did, however, undertake a number of studies of social development, including the important study of religion that we look at in Chapter 11.

- Western societies had experienced a process of rationalization. This was a growth in the significance of rational motivations and a shift from value-rational to instrumentally rational considerations.

- In modern, capitalist societies, market calculation and contractual relations have achieved a central significance.

- Although capitalist economic actions originated in religiously motivated actions, they had come to be a mere matter of routine and dull compulsion.

- Can the growth of standardized production and distribution—a process often referred to as 'McDonaldization'—be seen as an example of the rationalization that Weber described?

Sociology established

Sociology was firmly established as a university discipline by the first decades of the twentieth century. This was the achievement of Durkheim, Weber, and their contemporaries. There were still few professors of sociology—and sociology was barely taught in schools—but a sociological perspective had been established in history, law, politics, education, religion, and elsewhere.

There were, of course, great differences in the theoretical positions put forward by those who called themselves 'sociologists'. Durkheim and his followers stressed the importance of structure and saw societies as systems of structured relationships. Weber and other German sociologists tended to emphasize action and held that all social structures were, ultimately, to be seen as the outcome of human actions.

In the early days of academic sociology it was easy for Durkheim and Weber each to believe that his particular theory was uniquely correct. Some writers today still suggest that there is a great gulf between structure and action perspectives and that only one of them can be correct. These positions are not stark alternatives. Two different statements about the same thing are not necessarily contradictory: a ball may be both round and red, just as a social phenomenon may be both structured and the outcome of action. As soon as one tries to do any sociological work, it becomes clear that the structure and action approaches are complementary.

Durkheim and Weber, then, emphasized different aspects of a highly complex reality; social life involves *both* structure and action. Some sociologists have tried to combine both aspects in the same theory, but these have not been particularly successful. There may one day be a single, all-encompassing theory, but it is probably a long way from completion (but see Giddens 1976). The point is that sociologists need to develop a theoretical understanding of both the structural aspects of social life and their shaping by social actions. Distinct theoretical traditions may continue to exist, but they must cooperate in studies of particular phenomena.

In the generation that followed Durkheim and Weber, their leading ideas were consolidated and further developed, though there were no major advances for some time. The mainstream of academic sociology in Europe and America owed most to the ideas of Durkheim. Sociology and intellectual life generally were suppressed in Germany during the 1930s and 1940s, and this limited the wider impact of the ideas of Weber and his contemporaries.

In Britain and the United States, Durkheim's ideas were welded into a theoretical framework that came to be described as 'structural functionalism', or simply 'functionalism'. Much of this theoretical work was undertaken in the study of small-scale, tribal societies of the kind that Durkheim (1912) had studied for his own investigations into religion, and many functionalists called themselves anthropologists rather than sociologists (see Box 2.10, p. 42).

Much of the sociological research that was undertaken in the first thirty years or so of the twentieth century ignored theoretical issues. Work by Booth, Rowntree, and others in localities and communities across Britain, for example, investigated poverty and inequality with little concern for how these could be explained in relation to the overall structure of British society. The principal exception to this neglect of theory was to be found in the United States, where the new Department of Sociology at Chicago—the first full department in the world—was associated with a large number of local studies that drew explicitly on European traditions of theory.

Like the British anthropologists, the Chicago sociologists made a major contribution to fieldwork methods, but they did so from very different theoretical traditions. They paid little attention to Durkheim, finding their main inspiration in German sociology and, in particular, in Weber's friend Simmel. The Chicago sociologists took up the emphasis on action and interaction and combined this with an awareness of the importance of group conflict. Their main studies concerned the city of Chicago itself (Park and Burgess 1925), and they began to develop theoretical ideas that achieved their fullest recognition only after the Second World War.

Figure 2.3 (p. 42) shows how these ideas relate to the wider development of sociological theory. From the 1940s, and for at least a generation, sociological theorists continued to build on these foundations. By the 1950s, when sociology had begun to break out of its national boundaries, the theoretical landscape had been transformed. Theoretical debates crystallized into a smaller number of separate positions,

Social anthropology

Social anthropology is the term often used to describe the work of those sociologists who specialize in the study of small-scale, pre-industrial societies.

Most influential among the early followers of Durkheim was Alfred Radcliffe-Brown, a Cambridge-trained anthropologist who carried out fieldwork in Australia and in the Andaman Islands of the Indian Ocean. His work (Radcliffe-Brown 1922, 1930) reported on religious ritual and kinship in tribal societies, and he drew out some general conclusions in a series of essays (Radcliffe-Brown 1952). Radcliffe-Brown inspired the work of Lloyd Warner, an American who undertook investigations in Australian tribal societies and small American towns during the 1930s and 1940s (Warner and Lunt 1941). Radcliffe-Brown added little to Durkheim's own ideas, but he popularized the idea that theories had to be applied in detailed fieldwork studies.

Bronislaw Malinowski developed this fieldwork tradition in Britain. He carried out some early research on native Australian kinship, but his most important work was undertaken in the Trobriand Islands of the Pacific. His main books (Malinowski 1922, 1929, 1935) emphasized the need to study all social phenomena in terms of their functions in relation to other social phenomena and in relation to the structure of the society as a whole. He further emphasized that this kind of research could most easily be undertaken by living in a society and trying to grasp its whole way of life.

Franz Boas followed a similar fieldwork method in the United States, though his work owed a great deal to Hegel as well as to Durkheim. Boas (1911) emphasized the importance of culture and the need to grasp the inner spirit of the culture as a whole. He and his many students carried out a series of studies of native American tribes and small communities in the Pacific. While Malinowski saw functional analysis in relation to material and environmental factors, Boas set out a more cultural or idealist theory.

---

each of which had a far more international character than before. Three principal traditions of thought dominated sociological debate: structural functionalism, symbolic interactionism, and a number of conflict theories.

Structural theories

Structural functionalism had its roots in the sociology of Durkheim and the social anthropology that followed him. Its leading figure, Talcott Parsons, was an American who trained in economics and studied in Britain and Germany (see Box 2.11). Influenced by some early work by Robert Merton (1936, 1949), Parsons allied himself with sociology and began to construct a structural-functional theory of the social system. This theory had a great influence on the development of sociology and is currently being developed as a system theory.

The action frame of reference

In *The Structure of Social Action* (Parsons 1937), Parsons aimed to synthesize the main insights of Durkheim and

Figure 2.3 The development of sociology up to the 1940s

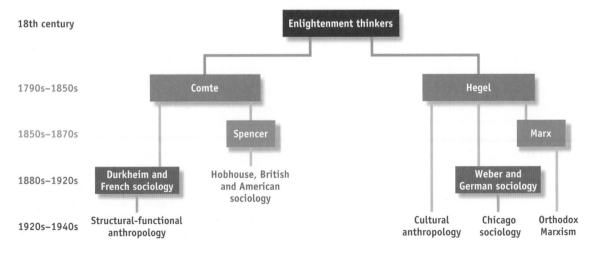

THEORY AND METHODS   2.11

Talcott Parsons

Talcott Parsons (1902–79) was the son of a clergyman. He studied economics at Amherst, and then undertook postgraduate research at the London School of Economics and at Heidelberg. He taught economics from 1926 to 1931, when he switched to sociology at Harvard University. His early works were concerned with the relationship between economics and sociology, as this had been seen by Weber, Pareto, and the British economist Alfred Marshall. Under the influence of the biologist L. J. Henderson, Parsons began to take Durkheim's work more seriously and in 1937 he produced his first book, *The Structure of Social Action*. Parsons remained at Harvard throughout his academic career.

Parsons has a reputation for his impenetrable prose style and the large number of new, long words that he invented. His work is certainly difficult. Do try to read Parsons's work, but do not expect to understand it all at a first reading.

After his first book, his most important works were the massive *Social System* (1951), a book on the family (Parsons and Bales 1956), one on the economy (Parsons and Smelser 1956), and two shorter volumes on social development (Parsons 1966b, 1971). Some of his more accessible work has been reprinted in a collection of essays (Parsons 1954). A valuable and brief introduction to his work is Hamilton (1983).

➜ You will find more detailed discussions of Parsons's work in the following chapters:

- socialization and social roles *Chapter 4*
- family and kinship *Chapter 12*
- health and illness *Chapter 8*
- social stratification *Chapter 19*.

Weber. He called his synthesis of the two positions **analytical realism**. It was analytical in that, like Weber, he recognized that all observations were dependent on concepts. But it was also realist in that, like Durkheim, he saw these observations telling us something about what the world was actually like (Scott 1995). He argued that we must use concepts to make observations, but we must check our observations against evidence.

The particular concepts needed in sociology, Parsons said, comprise an **action frame of reference**. This is a set of concepts that allow sociologists to talk about social action rather than about physical events or biological behaviour. This frame of reference had begun to emerge in the work of the classical sociologists. Each started from his own distinctive theoretical position, but they had gradually and unconsciously begun to move towards a similar framework. This was the action frame of reference.

> ➜ *Connections*
>
> If you are interested in philosophical issues, you should look back at our discussion of Durkheim on social facts and Weber on value relevance before continuing. We do not intend to go very far into these issues. You may prefer to look further at them when you have studied more sociology. Once you have tackled a few substantive topics, you may find it easier to struggle with some philosophy! For those who do want to read further, some good discussions are Keat and Urry (1975) and Williams and May (1996).

According to the action frame of reference, any action involves five basic elements:

- *actors*: the people who actually carry out the actions;
- *ends*: the goals that these people pursue;
- *means*: the resources that are available to achieve these ends;
- *conditions*: the particular circumstances in which actions are carried out;
- *norms*: the standards in relation to which people choose their ends and means.

Parsons holds that sociologists must construct models of action using these elements. To do this, they must try to understand things and events as they appear to the actors involved. The various ideal types and general concepts used in sociological explanation must be compatible with the basic principles of the action frame of reference. You will probably recognize how much Parsons owed to Weber here.

This action frame of reference became the basis of the structural functionalism of Parsons, Merton, and others. In undertaking this task, they drew heavily on the ideas of Durkheim. They developed concepts to describe the *structural* features of social life and to ground these in the *action* frame of reference. Societies, and social groups of all kinds, were seen as *social systems* consisting of mutually dependent parts such as roles, institutions, and organizations. These parts together formed the social structure. Sociological analysis had to identify these parts and show the functions they fulfil in the system as a whole.

Social structure

Structural functionalists see the structure of a society as a framework of norms that define the expectations and obligations that govern people's actions and so shape their social relations. At the heart of this normative framework are definitions of the various social positions that together form a complex social division of labour. These are family positions such as husband, wife, and child, economic and professional positions such as teacher, miller, doctor, and banker, and such other positions as student, priest, politician, and so on.

Those who occupy social positions are expected by others to behave in certain ways. These expectations define the social **roles** that are attached to the positions. A role is a cluster of normative expectations that sets out a script for those in particular social positions. It defines standards of appropriate and inappropriate behaviour, telling people what is 'normal' or expected behaviour in different situations. A teacher, for example, knows how he or she ought to behave in relation to pupils, parents, head teachers, governors, and others who play their parts in the same school and in the wider educational system (Merton 1957; Gross *et al.* 1958).

Many norms are quite specific and concern just one role. Others, however, may be very general in their scope. These generalized norms, rooted in widely shared cultural values, are 'social institutions'. These are established and solidified sets of norms that cross-cut social roles and tie them together. The institutions of property, contract, and the market, for example, define a large number of economic and occupational roles. Similarly, the institutions of kinship and marriage regulate a range of family roles, and the institutions of bureaucratic administration and democratic leadership regulate many political roles. Structural functionalists recognize a tendency for positions, roles, and institutions to cluster together into more or less distinct subsystems. A society may, for example, consist of an economic system, a political system, an educational system, a system of social stratification, and so on. At its most general, then, the structure of a social system might be described in terms of the connections between such subsystems. A simplified structural-functionalist model is shown in Figure 2.4.

The key to the stability and cohesion of a social structure, argue structural functionalists, is **socialization**. During infancy and childhood, as well as in later life, individuals learn the norms of their society. They come to learn what is expected of them and of those with whom they are likely to come into contact. They learn, in short,

Figure 2.4 A model of social structure

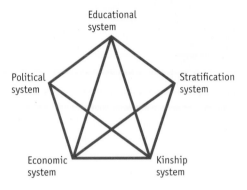

how to be a socially acceptable member of their society. Many structural functionalists assume the existence of a wide social consensus, an agreement over the basic principles that will regulate social life. This means that all socialized members of a society will share a broad commitment to the same values, beliefs, and ideas.

Merton (1938*b*), however, has recognized that this consensus may be far from complete. Individuals may be committed to some aspects of their culture, while rejecting or remaining neutral about others. He used this insight to develop a very important theory of anomie. The starting point for this theory is Merton's discussion of culture. The culture of a society, he holds, specifies the *ends* or goals that people should pursue and the *means* that they are expected to follow in achieving them. People's goals include such things as promotion at work, pleasing a husband or wife, learning to drive a car, writing a book, passing an examination, and so on. Means are those things that help to achieve these goals: working hard, money, physical skills, power, and so on. When people are fully socialized into their culture, they are committed to both the ends and the means that are attached to their social positions. They will be conformists, who follow only culturally approved goals and use only culturally approved means. For example, a person who desires a pleasant and well-decorated home will work hard to earn the money required. A conformist would not even consider stealing the money. If a culture emphasizes ends much more than means, leaving the means only loosely regulated, people's commitment to the approved means —and therefore their conformity to social norms—may be eroded. This is especially likely where the material structure of opportunities available to people makes it difficult for them to achieve the approved ends. They may lack the resources needed for the means to which they are supposed to be committed. It is the rift between culturally approved ends and means that Merton calls anomie. In a situation of anomie, conformity is far from automatic.

⊃ Connections

Merton's concept of anomie is not exactly the same as Durkheim's, although they are closely related. Whenever you come across the word 'anomie', make sure that you know how it is being used.

In Chapter 4, pp. 120–2, you will find a full discussion of the structural-functionalist view of socialization on which Merton relies.

Merton suggests that his model is particularly applicable to a modern society such as the United States, where financial success in an occupation is a central social value. Contemporary culture, he says, places great emphasis on the need to maximize income. It also requires that individuals pursue this end through occupational achievement: they should work diligently and efficiently in order to be promoted to a higher salary. The distribution of resources, however, makes it difficult for people to compete on an equal basis in this race for financial success. Not all people have the same opportunities to enter well-paid employment, as divisions of class, gender, and ethnicity set limits on the chances they are able to enjoy. Their commitment to the prescribed means may be weakened, especially if these are given less cultural emphasis than the overriding goal of success.

Merton identified four possible responses to this anomie, as shown in Figure 2.5. First is *innovation*, where a person responds to cultural strains by rejecting the legitimate means and employing illegitimate ones. Criminal activities aimed at financial gain are typical innovative acts. This is most common, Merton argued, among the poor, who have fewest opportunities. He recognized this also as the response of those who are relatively successful, but who are willing to 'bend the rules' and engage in fraud and embezzlement to increase their income.

Figure 2.5 Conformity and response to anomie

Robert Merton was born in 1910 and died in 2003. He studied under Talcott Parsons and published important papers on roles, anomie, and functional analysis. You will find applications of his model of anomie to the rise of new religions in Chapter 11, pp. 415–18, and to drug use in Chapter 7, pp. 249–51. A useful introduction to his thought is Crothers (1987). Check the Merton home page at **www.faculty.rsu.edu/~felwell/Theorists/Merton**.

	Ends	Means
Conformity	+	+
Innovation	+	−
Ritualism	−	+
Retreatism	−	−
Rebellion	±	±

+ acceptance
− rejection
± rejection of dominant values and acceptance of alternative values

Ritualism is another response to anomie and occurs where people decide they have little chance of any significant success and so reject this goal. However, they remain loosely committed to the conventional means but simply go through the motions in a ritualistic way, as they have little or no commitment to the approved goal. The time-serving bureaucrat who rigidly follows rules and procedures, regardless of the consequences, is a typical ritualist. Such a person, if challenged about the consequences of his or her actions, is likely to respond that 'I'm only doing my job'. Ritualistic bureaucrats are likely to be fatalistic, resigned to their lot. They feel that they have no control over their lives.

A third response to anomie is *retreatism*. The retreatist rejects both the means and the ends prescribed by the culture. This is the response of the drop-out, of whom Merton sees the hobo or vagrant as the typical example. Others have suggested that persistent deviant drug use may be the action of a retreatist. Merton's analysis of retreatism, however, fails to recognize that many of those who drop out of conventional society establish new conventions for themselves in deviant subcultures. This is the case for many drug users and vagrants.

The retreatist response, therefore, is difficult to distinguish from *rebellion*, where the legitimate ends and means are rejected but are replaced by alternative ends and means that may challenge conventional values. Radical political action, aimed at altering the distribution of resources or the political system, is, for Merton, the typical response of the rebel. This claim can be seen as Merton's reformulation of Durkheim's idea that organized class conflict is a consequence of anomie.

Functional analysis

Structural functionalists have developed and clarified the method of functional analysis outlined by Durkheim, making it the centrepiece of their work. Both Spencer and Durkheim, like many of their contemporaries, had seen parallels between societies and biological organisms. Spencer saw societies as 'social organisms' to be studied by the same scientific methods as biological organisms. The most important part of any scientific investigation, he held, is to uncover the functions carried out by the various structures of the organism. The function of the heart in the human body, for example, is to maintain the circulation of the blood. In sociology, Spencer suggested, we must investigate such things as the functions of government and ritual. In Durkheim's work, functional analysis was drawn out more clearly and set alongside causal explanation at the heart of sociological explanation.

The functional method has been much misunderstood. Some critics of structural functionalism have claimed that it involves the idea that societies literally are the same as biological organisms, or that social facts can be reduced to biological facts. These misunderstandings are, in part, the result of the misleading language used by many functionalists. Nevertheless, functional analysis is an important aspect of any sociological investigation, and its core ideas are straightforward. The functionalist method sees any system having *needs* or requirements, and, if a system is to survive and to continue in more or less its current form, then these needs must be met. The function of a structure is the contribution that it makes to meeting a need, and a functional analysis consists in identifying the processes through which these needs are met.

The idea of a need is quite simple. A human body needs food if it is to survive; it will die without this food. However, it is important to recognize that needs are not automatically met. The need for food does not, in itself, cause food to become available, and many people across the world do, in fact, starve to death. It is for this reason that Durkheim tried to separate cause from function.

Parsons followed Spencer in seeing a gradual differentiation of social activities into structurally distinct roles, institutions, and subsystems or a response to attempts to meet functional needs. The first step in a functional analysis of a society is to identify its needs. As a relatively self-contained unit and well-bounded system, a society has many internal needs. These include the biological and psychological needs of its members (for example, their needs for food and company) and the need to maintain its boundaries and identity. Some of these needs can be met, in whole or in part, from internal resources. The need to socialize infants, for example, can be met through the educational efforts of already socialized members such as the infant's parents.

However, many needs can be met only by drawing on resources from the external environment. This comprises the natural world that surrounds the society, together with the other societies and social groups with which it has contacts. A society must adapt itself to its environment, and the environment must be adapted to its needs. For example, if a large society is to feed its members, then crops must be planted and harvested, soil must be improved and irrigated, commodities must be imported, minerals must be mined and converted into ploughs and tractors, and so on. To achieve this kind of environmental adaptation, a society needs to restructure itself by establishing ways of handling its external relations and, perhaps, altering its own boundaries.

Restructuring may lead to new internal needs. For example, if a system of food production is established, then a society must ensure that the pace and level of production are, in some degree, coordinated with its actual food requirements and that the resources given over to this production do not prevent it from meeting any of its other needs. Social systems, then, are dynamic systems, constantly altering their structures with changes in the ways in which they meet, or fail to meet, their needs.

It is important to remember that needs will not be inevitably or automatically met, though some functionalists have tended to assume that they will. The needs of a social system are simply the conditions necessary for its survival in its current form. These conditions will be met only if, for whatever reason, people carry out the actions that meet them. The need does not itself cause the action that meets it.

A number of theorists have attempted to compile lists of the needs or functional requirements of a social system (Aberle *et al.* 1950; Levy 1966). The most influential was that of Parsons himself, though this was not without its critics. Parsons arrived at a classification of functional needs by looking at two aspects or dimensions of them:

- whether they are *internal* or *external* to the system;
- whether they involve the *ends* or the *means* of action.

Parsons defines internal needs as those that concern the integrity and cohesion of a social system. External needs, on the other hand, concern the facilities and resources that must be generated from its environment. Whether they are internal or external, needs may be relevant to either the means or the ends of action. In the former case, they are concerned with the production and accumulation of human and physical resources for use in the future, while in the latter they involve the immediate use and consumption of resources in current actions.

A model of a social system can be constructed by cross-classifying the two dimensions, as shown in Figure 2.6. According to this model, any social system has four functional needs, and its structures can be classified according to which of the four functions they are mainly concerned with. This model lies at the heart of Parsons's work, and

Figure 2.6 The Parsonian social system

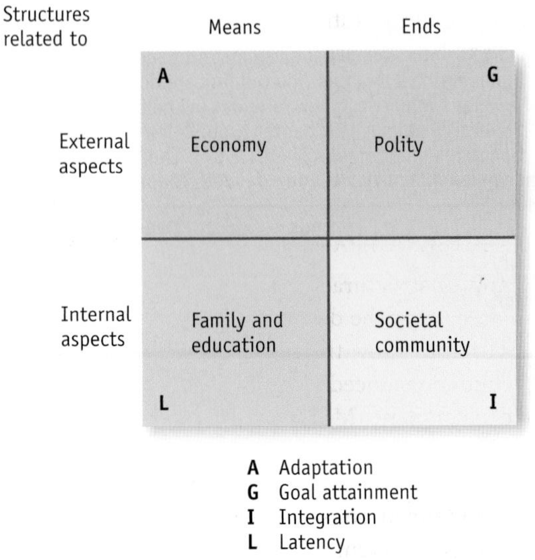

A Adaptation
G Goal attainment
I Integration
L Latency

versions of it can be found throughout his books. It has come to be known as the Parsonian boxes.

The four functions shown in Figure 2.6 are adaptation, **goal attainment**, integration, and latency. Adaptation is the need to accumulate and control resources from the environment so that they are available for future actions. This need is met through economic structures of production, distribution, and exchange. Goal attainment is the need to mobilize existing resources in relation to individual and collective goals. This can be met through political structures of decision-making and executive control. **Integration** is the need to ensure the cohesion and solidarity of the social system itself. Parsons introduced the term societal community to refer to the structures concerned with this function. It refers not only to localized community structures of kinship and neighbourhood, but also to the larger bonds of national and ethnic community and of social stratification. Finally, **latency** (or 'pattern maintenance') is the need to build up a store of motivation and commitment that can be used, when required, for all the various activities of the society. Institutions such as the family and education, where people are socialized into the values and norms of their society, are the main structures concerned with this need. These structures are much less likely to become differentiated than are other structures, and they remain closely tied to the structures of the societal community.

Parsons's language sometimes gives the impression that needs are automatically met, and perhaps he did, on occasion, believe this. He maintained, however, that structural functionalism was rooted in the action frame of reference, according to which functions will be met only if people act in ways that actually do meet these needs. This was clarified by Merton (1949), who showed that functions are generally met, if at all, as the unintended consequences of human action. One of the strongest criticisms of Parsons has been that he failed to analyse action as thoroughly as structure and function. Although he claimed to base his arguments on the action frame of reference, action played only a minor part in his work. A structural-functionalist model that focuses on the structural level of analysis must still be complemented by an analysis of action.

The evolution of modern society

A main aim of structural-functionalist theorists was to build an account of the development of modern society, and they tried to show that it was the need to adapt to changing functional needs that determined the direction of this development. Modern societies, then, are the results of long processes of structural differentiation shaped by the need to adapt to changing environments and the unintended consequences of the responses to this need. This argument has been most clearly stated by Parsons, who placed it in the context of a larger theory of social evolution.

The starting point for social evolution, according to Parsons (1966b), is the structure of the 'primitive' hunting and gathering societies. In these relatively undifferentiated societies, the societal community is formed from a network of kinship relations that extends across the whole society, and there are no functionally specialized structures. Each society is integrated through its shared religious beliefs, which provide an all-embracing cultural framework for people's actions. As these societies increase in size and become more involved in settled agriculture, so structures of private property and social stratification begin to develop to organize the new systems of production. When societies achieve this level of complexity, they may require systems of chiefhood or kingship to coordinate them.

Across the world, tribes and chiefdoms prevailed for thousands of years. In certain circumstances, however, development to even more complex forms of social organization occurred. In Egypt and Mesopotamia, more complex forms of agriculture were associated with the building of large systems of irrigation. Social stratification became sharper, religion came under the control of a specialized priesthood, and political control became stronger. By the third millennium BC, these societies had evolved into *advanced intermediate* societies that had both a historic religion and an imperial political system. Similar developments occurred somewhat later in China, India, and the Roman world. Following Comte, Parsons sees their religions becoming more philosophical and metaphysical in character.

The breakthrough to modern forms of society, Parsons said, occurred in medieval Europe in the centuries following the collapse of the Roman Empire and the gradual rebuilding of royal structures. Though no one intended it to occur, traditional agricultural societies underwent a process of *modernization* that brought into being the new social institutions of modernity. Political and scientific spheres of action were differentiated from the previously all-encompassing religious structures, and a separate sphere of economic action also appeared. Private property, the market, and the division of labour expanded, forming specialized elements in the economies of the European societies. From the eighteenth century, industrialism and democracy transformed the ways in which the **adaptation** and **goal attainment** functions were met, and more fully modern societies were formed. Nation states and industrial technologies were the characteristic institutions of these modern societies, which were characterized by the spread of bureaucracy and market relations. Modern social institutions developed especially rapidly in the United States, where pre-modern survivals were very much weaker, and it became the key modern society.

System theory

Structural functionalism came under heavy criticism from those who stressed interaction and conflict, and whose views we consider below. It was argued that structural functionalism overemphasized value consensus and socialization into these values. A number of recent structural functionalists have attempted to come to terms with these criticisms and developed a form of structural functionalism that takes this conflict of values more seriously. They have generally defined their position as neofunctionalism or simply system theory. Jeffrey Alexander (1985, 1988) in the United States and Niklas Luhmann (1982, 1984) in Germany have been the key figures.

Neofunctionalism and system theory hold that social systems may not be perfectly integrated and coherent and can show numerous contradictions and strains among their various parts. Luhmann saw these as the driving forces in structural differentiation, as they are likely to generate tendencies towards change in the structure. Early forms of society, he argued, are organized around core institutions of kinship and religion, but, over time, distinct spheres of action and structure split off from these core social institutions. Specialized economic, political, legal, scientific, educational, and other social systems are, therefore, differentiated from each other and may come to operate according to different values and norms.

The arguments of the neofunctionalists and system theorists do not mark a fundamental change from the earlier structural functionalism. What they show, rather, is how to use structural-functionalist ideas in a more flexible way and how to build theoretical explanations that are more sensitive to the conflict and change that is such an obvious feature of social life.

Action theories

Structural functionalism provided the mainstream of sociological thought from the 1940s until at least the 1970s, and it remains an important part of contemporary sociology. With its roots in Comte, Spencer, and Durkheim, it is at the heart of the sociological tradition. However, it was never unchallenged. Many critics pointed out that, despite its advocacy of an action frame of reference, structural functionalism did not really take sufficient account of action. In providing a comprehensive theory of social structures and their functions, it minimized the active and creative part played by social action. This concern for social action has a long history in the work of Weber and his contemporaries in Germany and in the early Chicago sociologists. However, it was a subordinate trend until the 1960s, when those critical of structural functionalism returned to the founding statements in attempt to construct a full-blown sociology of action.

In this section, we will look at two related theories of action: the symbolic interactionism of the Chicago school and the phenomenological theories that reconsidered Weber's typology of action.

Symbolic interactionism

Symbolic interactionism was nurtured in the Department of Sociology at Chicago from the 1920s to the 1950s. However, it originated outside Chicago and it has, since the 1950s, spread far beyond it. The core of the sociological work carried out at Chicago was a series of empirical studies in the city itself. The theoretical framework behind these studies stressed the struggles of social groups for resources and their competition over the use of space in the city. Group behaviour was explored through a theory of action that originated in the philosophical and psychological studies that William James carried out at Harvard towards the end of the nineteenth century. James, brother of the novelist Henry James, nurtured the brilliant work of the eccentric Charles Peirce, and the works of James and Peirce together produced the philosophy called pragmatism. It was this approach to knowledge and meaning that was transformed into symbolic interactionism.

Pragmatism holds that ideas are produced and used in practical situations. The knowledge that people acquire is not a mental copy, like a photograph, of things that actually exist in reality. It is, rather, an attempt to understand the world well enough to make practical sense of it and to act effectively. James held that knowledge is 'true' if it helps us to get by in our practical actions. Peirce developed this into a theory of *meaning* according to which the meaning of a concept is given by the way in which that concept is used in practical situations. What we mean by a 'chair' is something to sit on when we wish to relax, and many different physical objects can meet this need. Similarly, one of the things that we mean by a mother is someone who looks after children. There can be no abstract definitions of these concepts that identify essential characteristics of what chairs or mothers 'really' are. They simply mean whatever they are used to refer to in practical everyday situations.

These arguments were developed—and made much clearer—in the works of Dewey, Cooley, Thomas, and George Mead. It was Thomas and Mead, after they joined the staff at Chicago, who began to convert pragmatist ideas into a sociological theory of action. Mead was by far the more sophisticated writer of the two. He had undertaken his postgraduate studies in Germany, and he found many congenial ideas in the German philosophical and sociological tradition. Weber was, of course, an influence on him, but the most important of the German theorists in shaping Mead's position was Simmel. Work by Simmel was translated and published in the *American Journal of Sociology*, the journal of the Chicago Department, and through these translations Simmel had a major impact on the new theory (see Box 2.12).

Mead argued that individuals give meaning to the world by defining and interpreting it in certain ways. The world is never experienced directly, but always through the ideas that we hold about it. The meaning of reality is, in a fundamental sense, the meaning that we *choose* to give to it. Thomas summarized this point of view in the statement that 'When men define situations as real, they are real in their consequences.' What he meant by this is that the actions of men (and women) depend far more on how they define a situation than on the situation itself. People define situations and act upon those definitions. As a pragmatist, however, Thomas stressed that these definitions were not simply arbitrary and artificial constructions. Only those definitions that are useful in practical actions are likely to persist in use for any time.

This argument becomes clearer if we consider the example of a bus. A bus exists as a purely physical object, an assemblage of metal, plastic, rubber, fabric, and so on. Its meaning for us, however, depends on how we choose to define it. In calling it a bus, we define it as something that will follow a particular route, stop at particular places, and pick up people who pay to take a journey. Redundant buses, however, have been defined and used as social centres, caravans, chicken coops, and works of art. Each of these definitions—and many others—is compatible with the particular physical object that, in other circumstances, we define as a bus. What makes its definition as a bus

appropriate is our practical success in being able to use it to travel to our destination. What is true of the bus is true of all social objects. It is possible to define things in any of a number of different ways, and the effective definition is simply the one that works when people come to act on their definitions.

These definitions cannot be unique to particular individuals, or they will not work. The concept of a bus, for example, is one that is useful only because it is widely shared. It is a concept shared by all those interested in its operations: passengers, drivers, conductors, inspectors, traffic police, ministers of transport, and so on. Many of these people acquire their identities from the idea of the bus. It is, for example, impossible to have bus drivers unless we have the concept of a bus. It is usually possible to rely on a bus service because there are widely shared definitions and conventions concerning timetabling, queuing, and fare-paying. A widely shared meaning, communicated to us by others, has a greater reality than does an idiosyncratic one, and it is more likely to be useful in practical situations.

The definitions that people use are constructed from the *symbols* (the names and labels for objects) that are available to them in their culture. Spoken and written words, together with pictures, images, and other conventional signs, convey information and are used by people to give meaning to the situations in which they find themselves. It is through these means that the world in which we live and the objects we encounter are socially constructed (see Box 2.13, p. 50). These symbols used in social construction are learned and communicated through interaction with others. This is why the theoretical position has come to be called **symbolic interactionism**.

This name was coined by Herbert Blumer (1966), who also did much to popularize it and to mark out its distinctiveness from mainstream structural-functionalist sociology. According to Blumer, societies are not fixed and objective structures. What we call 'society' is the set of fluid and flexible networks of interaction within which we act. To describe these overlapping networks of interaction as 'structures', Blumer held, is to reify them and to distort the part that individuals play in creating and altering them through action. This led Blumer to reject all talk of structures, systems, and functional needs. There are simply actions, interactions, and their consequences for individuals.

Others in the symbolic interactionist tradition have been less extreme in their opposition to mainstream sociology. They have seen symbolic interactionism as concerned merely with those aspects of action and interaction that have not been given their due attention in structural functionalism. This is, for example, the case with Erving Goffman, whose work owes as much to Durkheim as it does to Mead (Collins 1994: 218).

THEORY AND METHODS　　　　2.12

Georg Simmel

Georg Simmel (1858–1917) was born in Berlin, Germany. He spent most of his academic career at the University of Berlin. He studied philosophy, but he taught and wrote on both philosophy and sociology. During his lifetime he was probably better known than Weber among other sociologists.

Simmel stressed the need to study the *forms* of social relationships, rather than their content. He explored such things as the relations of insiders to outsiders, relations of domination and subordination, relations of conflict, and the significance of the size of groups. His ideas were developed in a book called *Sociology* (Simmel 1908), most of which has been translated in K. H. Wolff (1950). Simmel was particularly concerned with uncovering the distinctive features of contemporary urban life, and he set out these ideas in an essay on the metropolis and a book called *The Philosophy of Money* (Simmel 1900). A good home page for Simmel is **http://socio.ch/sim/index_sim.htm**, though some parts of this are in German.

Controversy and debate Social construction   2.13

The idea of social construction has been derided by many opponents of sociology, who see the things we encounter in our everyday lives as 'obvious' and unproblematic. All social phenomena, however, involve a degree of social construction. The case of a bus—discussed in the text—is typical of all social definitions, which is why we have discussed it at such length. Whenever we employ words to refer to objects in our social world, we are, quite literally, *constructing* them as meaningful social objects that we can take account of in our actions.

Try to think about the implications of attempting to redefine some common social objects. What would happen if you defined a table as a chair? What consequences would follow if you defined newly washed curtains as paint covers? (Don't try this one at home!) When you have considered these relatively simple cases, you might think about the consequences of defining an unmarried man as a gay man, rather than as a bachelor—and the implications of the now outmoded term 'bachelor gay'.

> **➲ Connections**
>
> The arguments of Mead, Goffman, and other symbolic interactionists figure prominently in this book. You will find substantial discussions of their core ideas in the following chapters:
> - self, roles, identity *Chapter 4*
> - deviance and social reaction *Chapter 7*
> - social construction of health *Chapter 8*
> - organizations *Chapter 14*

Goffman's work, undertaken between the 1950s and the 1970s, gave particular attention to face-to-face interaction and small-scale social contexts. He called his approach *dramaturgical* (Goffman 1959). By this he meant that it was a theory of action that uses the metaphor of drama in a theatre to examine people's abilities to present particular images of themselves in their interactions with others. Goffman used such terms as actor, audience, and, of course, role in his theory. Actors play their parts in interaction, and they attempt to give their audiences convincing performances.

In their interactions, Goffman said, people aim to create a particular impression or image of themselves in the eyes of others. Goffman calls this image the **self**. People present this image to others through using techniques of impression management that help them to control the performances they give. The image they present varies according to the expectations of the audience. The self presented to friends at a club on a Friday night is likely to be very different from that presented to a bank manager in an interview about an overdrawn account. The self presented to parents at home is likely to be different again. Whenever we wish others to think of us as a particular kind of person, we try to present exactly that image to them.

Goffman has emphasized the ability that people have to manipulate the images that they present to others.

However, symbolic interactionism also shows that images and conceptions of self can be imposed on people by their audiences. The social process is an interplay of action and reaction, an interplay in which each actor interprets and responds to all others. Interaction involves a reciprocal and continuous negotiation over how situations are to be defined. A definition of the situation is the joint construction of the participants in interaction. Consensus exists only when this definition has been established and agreed by all involved. Though often implicit, this negotiation is necessary because any definition can be contested by others. What we call reality is constructed through social interaction; it is a socially constructed reality. Where there is disagreement, and dissension, the individual or group that is most powerful may be able to impose a definition of the situation on all others. They have the power to ensure that their views prevail.

This point of view became the cornerstone of the trends in the sociology of deviance that powerfully enlarged symbolic interactionism during the 1960s and 1970s (Becker 1963). This work stressed the way in which the *labels* used to define behaviour by those with the power to enforce them could influence the actions of those who were labelled. The use of such labels as 'criminal', 'junkie', 'queer', and so on defines behaviour as deviant by identifying it as a departure from social norms and attributing certain characteristics to the person labelled. Through their reactions to a person's behaviour, then, an audience of labellers may cause her or him to take on the image that is held out.

Phenomenological approaches to interaction

While symbolic interactionism mounted an increasingly successful challenge to the excessive claims made by some structural functionalists, it, too, was challenged in the 1960s by what claimed to be a more radical perspective on interaction. This was the approach of **phenomenology**, which originated in the philosophy of Husserl. During the

1920s and 1930s, Husserl began to produce what he saw as the fundamental basis for all knowledge, his aim being to describe the contents of people's experiences of their world. Husserl's work inspired Schütz, who saw his task as that of uncovering the content and form of everyday interpersonal experiences of the social world. Schütz took as his fundamental question how Weber's typology of action is possible. He asked how the types of action could be justified, on philosophical grounds, as the necessary basis for sociological research.

This work appeared rather idiosyncratic, and it was not until the 1960s that it really began to inspire sociological work. Berger and Luckman (1966) and Douglas (1967) used phenomenological ideas to investigate the taken-for-granted reality that people construct in response to the reactions of others. They stressed the way in which an everyday world comes to be seen as natural, inevitable, and taken for granted. People are born into a prestructured and meaningful world that they rarely question in later life. This taken-for-granted reality is objective as well as subjective and has the character of a Durkheimian social fact.

The everyday world is a product of human subjectivity, and action is *reified*—made into a thing—whenever people forget that it is a human product and begin to take it for granted. Language is the principal means through which social reality is reified. An example might be the very use of the terms symbolic interactionism and phenomenological sociology as names for loose and diverse collections of writers. Use of these particular labels gives the impression that these approaches have more unity and reality than is, in fact, the case. Repetition of the words in textbooks, essays, and examination questions reinforces the taken-for-granted assumption that they exist as sharply defined schools of thought. When we give a name to something, we make it appear as something that is separate from us, external to us, and that is solid and substantial. Berger and Luckman show how this creates the apparent solidity of 'the family', while Douglas argues that suicide is a similarly reified term.

These phenomenological approaches began to rediscover some of the themes raised in classical German sociology and to translate them into contemporary concerns. They stressed, as Weber had done, that all social realities have to be studied from the standpoint of the subjective meanings given to them by individual actors. As they were being developed, however, an important extension of the phenomenological approach was being developed from Schütz's work. This was the ethnomethodology of Harold Garfinkel and Aaron Cicourel. Ethnomethodology originated in papers written by Garfinkel in the 1950s (see the essays collected in Garfinkel 1967 and see Box 2.14), and it was taken up by others in the 1960s and 1970s.

Garfinkel criticizes Parsons and other structural functionalists for treating people as what he calls *cultural*

THEORY AND METHODS   2.14

Ethnomethodology

Sociology is often criticized for using too many big words and phrases. Our use of phenomenology and ethnomethodology might have convinced you that these critics are right. Don't panic! Many professional sociologists still find it difficult to pronounce the words, let alone spell them. Concentrate on the ideas and do not get caught up on the words themselves. To help you along, however, the word 'ethnomethodology' has two elements in it: *ethno*, meaning 'people', and *methodology*, meaning 'how things are done'. So ethnomethodology simply means 'how people do things'.

If you find that you struggle to keep clear the meanings of sociology's specialized words, you should try regularly consulting a good sociological dictionary or encyclopaedia, such as *The Oxford Dictionary of Sociology* (3rd edn, 2005).

---

dopes. Structural functionalists tend to assume that people are simply socialized into a cultural consensus and so have no real freedom of action. They act in their roles as if they are puppets, controlled by the social system. In place of this point of view, Garfinkel stresses individual autonomy. He holds that the objective reality of everyday life is something that people struggle to achieve in their practical actions: it is, he says, a 'practical accomplishment'.

In accounting for their actions and for the actions of others, people continually create and re-create their social world. Their accounts, however, are never complete, but always leave something implicit or taken for granted. People rely on their audiences sharing a background of assumptions that allow them to fill in the gaps for themselves and so to understand what is being said. Organizational accounts, such as police records, medical records, and personnel files, contain gaps and incomplete information that can be filled in by their readers. They are descriptions of actions and interactions that are seen as meaningful by those involved and that provide a satisfactory basis for action. They are not, however, so easily readable by non-participants, who are less likely to share the background knowledge and assumptions employed by those in the organization.

An important part of this taken-for-granted background is a sense of social structure that people use to interpret and account for the actions of others. People explain actions by showing that they are exactly the kinds of things that people in that situation would do. They see it as a part of their role, for example. These interpretative processes are not normally visible, and ethnomethodology assigns itself the special task of uncovering them in order to demonstrate what is really going on in the routine activities of everyday life. They believe that this can be achieved through experimental interventions in social life. Taken-for-granted realities have to be disrupted or challenged so that people are forced to reflect on what they are doing. Only in this way can the ethnomethodologist obtain any proper knowledge about these processes. Garfinkel suggested, for example, that his students should react to their parents as they would if they were merely a lodger. This forced parents to bring out into the open the normally taken-for-granted assumptions about how children ought to behave in relation to their parents.

Rational-choice theory

A final approach to action and interaction focuses not on interpretative processes and the construction of meaning, but on rational choices and calculative decision-making. This theory of action draws heavily on the models of action used by economists to explain producer and consumer choices in markets, but its advocates argue that such models can be applied to actions in the political, religious, familial, ethnic, and other spheres, as well as to the economic sphere. One of the most important formulations of rational-choice theory was given by George Homans (1961), but it has also been developed by Peter Blau (1964), James Coleman (1990), and Jon Elster (1989).

What these theories have in common is the view that all actions are oriented towards goals and that people choose those means that are likely to be most effective in attaining them. They choose from a range of alternative courses of action by calculating the chances they have of achieving their goals. In doing so, they consider the rewards and costs attached to each alternative. Some of these rewards and costs will be monetary, but many are not. Choosing whether to earn money from employment or to obtain it through theft, for example, involves a calculation of the obvious monetary rewards but also involves considering the time costs involved, the amount of effort, the hardship that will be caused, the social approval or disapproval that will be experienced, and so on. Similarly, the choice between voting or staying at home on an election day involves considering the time and effort required and the strength of commitment to the democratic process. While some of these rewards and costs are tangible material factors and others are less tangible symbolic and emotional factors, all are seen as equally subject to rational calculation. People must find a way of comparing very different rewards and costs and deciding what course of action is, overall, most rewarding or least costly to them.

This kind of theory is often described as game theory, as the emphasis on rational and strategic calculation is comparable with that required by the rules of games such as poker and chess. People are seen as acting exclusively on the basis of simple strategic principles in pursuit of a series of 'moves' that will ensure they 'win' their various social encounters.

Homans and Blau described their approach as 'exchange theory' in order to emphasize that they were dealing especially with interaction rather than with isolated rational actions. When people encounter one another, each tries to maximize their profit—or minimize their loss—by gaining rewards and avoiding costs. Any interaction, therefore, involves an exchange of some kind: there may be an exchange of goods for money, as in an economic transaction, an exchange of love for financial support, an exchange of loyalty for political support, and so on. In successful, ongoing interactions, each participant will tend to have ensured that the overall reward that they earn is greater than could be earned for any other interaction: if this were not the case, they would have abandoned the interaction in favour of that other alternative.

Blau argues, however, that many interactions may involve unbalanced exchange: one person will be gaining more than the other. People may, for example, undertake a course of action that is costly to them if they think that, in the long term, they will benefit in some way. On the other hand, people may continue with an unprofitable relationship simply because other possibilities have been shut off from them. A married woman, for example, may remain with a violent husband because she has no realistic possibility of finding employment or housing on her own.

Larger claims have been made for rational-choice theory (Downs 1957; G. Becker 1976, 1981), and it has proved to give valuable insights into many aspects of social life. Its fundamental limitation, however, is that it cannot properly take account of precisely those features that are central to symbolic interactionism. In order to apply a rational-choice model of action, it is necessary to draw on other action theories to show how people are able to construct a definition of the situation and how their norms and values influence the decisions that they make.

Theories of action prospered because of the failure of structural functionalists to pay serious attention to action and interaction. They promised a sociology that properly considered the creative element that human beings bring to their social relations. Symbolic interactionists, phenomenologists, and ethnomethodologists, in their various ways, aimed to uncover the processes of communication and interaction that allowed people to make sense of their social worlds and to construct the structures that structural functionalists treated simply as social facts. Many advocates of these theories, however, claimed that the matters that concerned structural functionalists could safely be forgotten. In saying this, they overstated their case. Action and structure are not alternative explanatory principles but complementary ones (see Box 2.15).

Controversy and debate Action and system   2.15

The opposition between structural-functionalist theories and interactionist theories can usefully be seen in terms of their central concepts of system and action. Where the concept of action points to issues of *agency* and will, the concept of system points to issues of *structure* and determinism. The contrast should not be taken too far, but it highlights a real difference in focus.

Action

- The actions of individuals are the basic elements in social life. They are the building blocks of sociology.
- Individuals define situations and construct social reality.
- Sociologists must understand actions in terms of their subjective meanings.
- Individuals improvise and create their own roles on the basis of what they learn during their socialization.

System

- Social structures are the basic elements in social life. They have a reality over and above individuals.
- Social reality is external to individuals and constrains their actions.
- Sociologists must look at the functional connections among the structural parts of social systems.
- Individuals conform to the role expectations that they learn during their socialization.

Conflict theories

The analysis of conflict has a long history, yet structural functionalism developed as an approach that placed far more emphasis on consensus and cohesion. This was one of the reasons why Marx—who saw conflict as playing a central part in social life—refused to identify himself as a sociologist. While some sociologists recognized the importance of conflict, they had little impact on the mainstream of academic sociology. Marxism was a major influence on the work of Weber and other German sociologists, but this tradition itself was of secondary importance until after the Second World War. The growing dissatisfaction with structural functionalism as a complete and all-embracing theory of social life was associated not only with a growing interest in theories of interaction but also with attempts to recover an awareness of conflict.

Those who saw structural functionalism as paying too much attention to consensus looked to conflict theories for an expansion of the intellectual tools available to them. They highlighted, instead, the part played by divisions, power, force, and struggle. They looked at the ways in which groups came to be organized for collective action, entered into conflict with one another, and established relations of domination and control. No single theory of conflict has dominated the field, but a great many views of conflict have been put forward. We will look at four of the most influential arguments—those of Ralf Dahrendorf, John Rex, C. Wright Mills, and Jürgen Habermas.

Authority, resources, and conflict

In the section on 'Action theories' we showed that Weber had an important influence on some of the American symbolic interactionists. His major impact, however, has been on conflict theorists. Weber's discussion of social action has been a particularly fruitful source of ideas, and the most important writers to develop this into conflict theories were Dahrendorf (1957), Rex (1961), and Mills (1959). Dahrendorf argues that structural functionalists presented, in effect, a consensus theory. They looked at only one side of reality, ignoring the existence of conflict and division. The theory of consensus, *then, needed to be complemented by a theory of conflict. Dahrendorf wanted to use ideas from Weber and Marx to build a theory of conflict. He did not, however, see any need to bring consensus and conflict theories together into a new synthesis. Each theory had something separate to offer. Consensus theory illuminated some aspects of reality, while a conflict theory would be better able to illuminate others.

At the heart of Dahrendorf's theory of conflict is **authority**. In all organizations an unequal distribution of authority creates a division between the dominant and the subordinate, between those who rule and those who are ruled. In a business organization, for example, there is a division between managers and workers, in a state there is a division between the elite and the mass of citizens, and in a church there is a division between clergy and laity.

Where consensus theorists focus on the normative expectations attached to social positions, Dahrendorf looks at their **interests**. A person's interests are those things that are advantageous or disadvantageous, given his or her position in society. Those in ruling positions have an interest in keeping the structure of authority as it is and so will act to maintain it. Those they rule, on the other hand, have an interest in altering the distribution of authority and will try to change so as to improve their positions. Individuals may not always be aware of their own interests, as they rarely have a complete and perfect knowledge of the circumstances they face, and this lack of knowledge may often lead people to act in ways that disadvantage them. Because of these differences in interest and outlook, rulers and ruled will tend to be formed into what Dahrendorf calls social classes. These are the bases from which trade unions, political parties, and other associations are recruited. These **interest groups** come into conflict with one another and are the actual driving forces in social change.

Rex focuses on social divisions that originate in the distribution of economic, political, and cultural resources, rather than the distribution of authority. He sees economic resources as fundamental, and draws on a number of ideas from Marx to explore the conflicts that result from the unequal distribution of economic resources. He shows that classes are formed around differences of property and market situation and that they struggle with each other over this distribution. Agricultural land, company shares, factories, and houses, for example, are sources of power for their owners, who tend to come into conflict with those who lack these resources and seek to alter their distribution. Similar divisions are produced around political and cultural resources, and there is a close correspondence between the various distributions. Whole societies tend to be divided into sharply defined classes, and these become organized for conflict through the kinds of interest groups described by Dahrendorf.

Collective action by conflict groups establishes what Rex calls a *balance of power*. In some situations, a powerful group may be able to impose its ideas and values on others, establishing a dominant ideology. In other situations, however, the conflicting groups may be more equally balanced, and so the institutions of the society will reflect a compromise between the values of the two groups. Occasionally, the members of a subordinate group may be able to carry through revolutionary actions aimed at transforming their society.

Mills drew heavily on symbolic interactionist ideas to provide a social psychological basis for his arguments, but his core ideas focused on the class divisions of societies and the ways that these organized political power and cultural processes. His particular concern was to explore the ways in which personal experiences and problems were linked to possible issues of structural change. Individual

biographies, he said, must be related to the historical development of social structures.

> **⮂ Connections**
>
> Dahrendorf, Rex, and Mills talk about the division of societies into conflicting classes. However, they mean different things by this. For Dahrendorf, classes are defined by authority relations, while Rex and Mills see them as defined by economic and other resources, but Mills gives particular attention to their participation in political and military power. You will find a discussion of these issues in 'Class and status', Chapter 19, pp. 746–9, and 'Elites and power', Chapter 20, pp. 791–2.

Social structures, according to Mills, must be explored by uncovering the processes through which they are integrated. Social systems may be integrated through consensus and the 'correspondence' among their social institutions, but also through processes of 'coordination' that reflect the society's conflicts and tensions. In a situation of coordination, one or more institutional orders predominates over others and regulates their relations with each other (Gerth and Mills 1953: ch. 12). The clearest examples of this are provided by totalitarian societies in which political institutions are dominant and which are organized into single-party states. Even in the United States and similar capitalist societies, however, Mills (1956) saw a close association between the political, economic, and military institutions, and an overlapping of power relations among them. Ordinary people, as a result, have become increasingly powerless and feel that they can do little to influence the decisions that shape their lives. The United States has become a 'mass society', divided between the powerful elite and the powerless masses. The task for sociology is to uncover and explore this link between historical trends and individual experiences (Mills 1959: ch. 1).

> **⮂ Connections**
>
> This might be a useful point at which to review Marx's main ideas, as you will find they will help you to understand the following section on 'Critical theory'. Look back at our whole discussion of Marx on pp. 27–30.

Critical theory

Dahrendorf, Rex, and Mills made use of ideas from Marx and Weber. Marx's recognition of conflict, however, was kept alive even more strongly in Marxist political parties and in the works of a number of Marxist theorists. Of most importance in developing Marx's ideas were the so-called critical theorists. They have suggested that a renewed understanding of Marx's ideas will allow sociologists to advance beyond its conventional concerns and, indeed, beyond Marxism itself.

The idea of critique was, in many ways, a part of the Marxist tradition from its beginnings. This was certainly the way that Marx saw his own work. In the Marxism of the Russian, German, and other European Communist parties, however, Marx's thought was transformed into an uncritical and dogmatic system of theory. This began to change in the 1920s, when a number of independent thinkers started to develop a critique of established Marxism. Antonio Gramsci in Italy and Karl Korsch and Gyorgy Lukács in Germany were the pioneers in developing a form of Marxism that broke with dogmatic styles of thought and also took the political and cultural spheres more seriously than earlier Marxists (see Lukács 1923). Many of these ideas were taken up by Marxists such as Theodor Adorno and Max Horkheimer in Frankfurt and the United States during the 1930s and 1940s. Although these ideas had little impact outside Marxist circles, they helped to change the direction of Marxist thought, and their ideas were taken up by radical writers in the 1960s

and 1970s. Prominent among these has been Jürgen Habermas (see Box 2.16).

Some of Habermas's most important work has concerned issues of scientific method, where he has tried to clarify the nature of a truly critical theory. All knowledge, he argues, develops in relation to what he calls the **cognitive interests** of social groups. These are the particular social interests that shape people's needs for knowledge. There are three of these cognitive interests, each associated with a particular kind of knowledge:

- an interest in technical control;
- an interest in practical understanding;
- an interest in emancipation.

An interest in *technical control* is inherent in the whole way in which human labour is organized for productive purposes. Labour involves an attempt to use and to transform the resources provided by the natural environment, and it stimulates people to acquire the kind of knowledge that will help them to control the natural world. The natural sciences and industrial technology are based on what

THEORY AND METHODS 2.16

Jürgen Habermas

A critical theory of society.

© Getty Images/Darren McCollester

Jürgen Habermas (1929–) studied under Theodor Adorno, a leading figure in

critical theory, at Frankfurt. It is here that he has spent most of his academic career. He produced a number of essays on philosophy and scientific method in the 1960s (Habermas 1967, 1968), and he began to engage with the radical student movement. His initial attempt to construct a sociological account of this new movement (Habermas 1968–9) owed as much to Weber as it did to Marx.

Habermas set out the basis of a critical theory of modern society, along with a research programme to study it, in *Legitimation Crisis* (1973). Through the 1970s he worked on the more general theoretical principles underlying this, publishing the results in his *Theory of Communicative Action* (1981*a*, 1981*b*). Since completing this, he has concentrated rather more on philosophical issues and on engaging with his political and philosophical critics.

Critical theorists' views on the mass media are discussed in Chapter 10.

A good account of Habermas's early work can be found in McCarthy (1978), and a brief overview of his whole output can be found in Pusey (1987). The best accounts of the wider context of critical theory are Jay (1973) and Held (1980). General websites on critical theorists can be found at **www.uta.edu/huma/illuminations/** and **http://home.cwru.edu/~ngb2/Pages/Intro.html**

➲ You can find more on the applications of Habermas's theory in other parts of this book:

- state and crisis *Chapter 15*
- social movements *Chapter 20*.

Habermas calls empirical–analytical knowledge of the kind produced in the positive sciences. This knowledge, he says, provides the kind of objective information that can be used to make explanations and predictions that will help to ensure the technical success of our actions.

An interest in *practical understanding*, on the other hand, is fundamental to human communication and interaction in everyday settings. In their interactions, people need to attain an understanding of one another. They must build up a degree of consensus and shared understanding if their actions are not to collapse into mutual incomprehension and conflict. The cultural disciplines, concerned with understanding texts, are based on what Habermas calls historical–hermeneutic knowledge. (You need not worry about the precise meaning of all the long words that he uses.) This knowledge provides the interpretations and meanings that make practical understanding possible.

Habermas sees approaches to the social world as having tended towards one or the other of these two types of knowledge. The positivism of Comte, Durkheim, and structural functionalism has largely followed the natural-science model and has aimed at producing empirical–analytical knowledge for a positive science of society. The interpretative work of Weber and the interactionist theorists, on the other hand, has been closer to cultural studies and has aimed at producing historical–hermeneutic knowledge.

Both forms of knowledge have their uses, but Habermas sees neither of them as giving a satisfactory base for social theory. Both the main traditions of sociological thought are partial and one-sided. They are limited and distorted by the underlying cognitive interests around which they are organized. Only an emancipatory interest, he holds, can produce the kind of knowledge that can synthesize these two partial perspectives.

An interest in *emancipation* is what is required if distorted forms of knowledge and action are to be overcome. Habermas holds that people can be liberated from ideology and error only through what he calls critical–dialectical thought. Once liberated, they can go on to achieve the kind of autonomy and self-determination that Marx saw as the ultimate goal of human history. An interest in emancipation develops along with the evolution of human society, and Marx was the first to construct a properly critical theory appropriate to this interest.

This is how Habermas locates his own work, along with that of the earlier critical theorists. An interest in human emancipation, he argues, requires that all knowledge is subjected to criticism. To be true to the interest that motivated Marx's work, it is necessary to go beyond it and to reconstruct it continually in the light of changing circumstances. Societies have changed since Marx's death, and a critical theory must reflect these changes. In contemporary societies there are new sources of division, unforeseen by Marx. It is no longer possible to see the working class as the sole agents of revolutionary change. A challenge to the system may come from any of its many oppressed social groups. For some time, critical theorists saw the radical student movement as the group most likely to initiate social change, but they now recognize a great variety of groups from the women's movement to environmental and anti-militarist movements.

Habermas's critical theory, then, is critical of contemporary social theories for their distorted views of social reality, but it is also self-critical. Critical theory must continually reassess its own foundations and the specific theories that it builds on them. Habermas's own major work (1981*a*, 1981*b*) was cast in exactly this spirit. It is an attempt at a comprehensive reconstruction of Marx's social theory, but it makes this reconstruction by critically reconsidering also the work of structural functionalists and interaction theorists. All these strands are synthesized by Habermas.

With structural functionalism and systems theory, Habermas emphasizes the importance of systems and structures, seeing these concepts as especially applicable to the economic and political systems of modern societies. However, he builds an awareness of conflict and social division into his account of these social systems. With interaction theories, on the other hand, he recognizes the importance of communication and meaning, which he sees as essential for understanding face-to-face encounters in everyday life. These face-to-face situations comprise what he calls the *lifeworld* through which people's experiences are formed into human communities. This argument allows him to combine a concern for conflict with one for consensus (see Box 2.17).

These two traditions of theory, Habermas says, highlight different aspects of social reality. Modern societies, for example, are organized around the separation of systems of economic and political relations from a communal lifeworld of interpersonal interactions. The systems are concerned with the integration of actions and relations into more or less coherent and coordinated wholes. They are studied by tracing the functional connections among the structures and the parts that they play in the maintenance of the system as a whole. Habermas, like Marx, stresses that it is important to look at contradictions within these systems as well as at their coherence. The lifeworld is concerned with the harmonization of the meanings given to actions in the communal life of social groups. It is studied by examining the shared ideas and values that form the taken-for-granted cultural framework for interaction.

Controversy and debate Consensus and conflict   2.17

While the opposition between consensus and conflict perspectives can be exaggerated, there are real differences that it is important to recognize. The approaches can be contrasted in terms of their main concepts and themes.

Consensus

- Norms and values are the basic elements of social life. There is a consensus over them.
- People conform because they are committed to their societies and their rules.
- Social life depends on cohesion and solidarity.
- People tend to cooperate with one another.

Conflict

- Interests are the basic elements of social life. They are the sources of conflict.
- People react to one another on the basis of inducement and coercion.
- Social life involves division and exclusion.
- People tend to struggle with one another.

Source: Adapted from Craib (1984: 60).

➔ You might like to consider whether Habermas adequately combines consensus and conflict themes in his work.

Stop and reflect

In this section we have identified three broad approaches to sociological theory, and have argued that they have to be seen as grasping different aspects of a complex reality. They are, therefore, complementary rather than alternative approaches. These three approaches are structural-functionalist theories, interaction theories, and conflict theories.

The main source of inspiration for structural-functionalist theories was the work of Durkheim, who laid its foundations in the classical period. You might like to remind yourself about his key ideas.

- The key figure in the construction of structural functionalist ideas was Talcott Parsons, who saw his task as that of synthesizing the ideas inherited from the classical writers. He set out the basis for this in his action frame of reference, according to which the basic elements in any course of action are actors, ends, means, conditions, and norms.

- The structure of a society is the normative framework that defines its social positions and their social relations in a division of labour. The normative expectations attached to social positions define the roles to be played by their occupants.

- Dislocations between culturally approved ends and structurally available means establish conditions of anomie.

Individuals respond to anomie through innovation, ritualism, retreatism, or rebellion.

- The function of any structure is its contribution to meeting the needs of the system of which it is a part. At the most general level, needs include the internal needs of the system and its adaptation to its external environment. Parsons recognized four fundamental needs: adaptation, goal attainment, integration, and latency.

- Neofunctionalism and systems theory try to retain an emphasis on structure and system, but they combine this with a sensitivity to conflict and change.

- Is it accurate to describe Parsons as a 'consensus' theorist?

- Does Parsons's account of social life involve a conservative bias?

A diverse range of interaction theories have attempted to provide the analysis of action that tends to get lost in the work of the structural functionalists. We considered symbolic interactionism, phenomenological approaches, ethnomethodology, and rational-choice theory.

- Symbolic interactionism originated in pragmatist philosophy, which held that the truth of theories and concepts depends on their value in practical actions.

- Central to symbolic interactionism is the idea of the definition of the situation. By acting in terms of their definition of the situation, people construct and make meaningful the objects of their social world. Definitions are built in interaction through processes of self-presentation, labelling, and negotiation.

- Are symbolic interactionists correct to claim that their approach provides a more subtle and flexible approach to that of Parsons?

- Phenomenological approaches focus their attention on the taken-for-granted contents of everyday consciousness. Ethnomethodology, originating in the work of Garfinkel, takes this one step further and examines the processes through which people sustain a taken-for-granted sense of reality in their everyday encounters.

- Rational-choice theory, using an economic model of action, sees people as making rational calculations about the rewards and costs involved in their interactions with others.

- Why do these various interaction theories make such different assumptions about the nature of social action?

The works of Weber and Marx inspired a number of theories that put conflict at the centre of their attention. These theorists criticized the structural-functionalist mainstream for its overemphasis on consensus.

- Dahrendorf saw conflict as originating in the distribution of authority, while Rex saw it as originating in the distribution of resources. Both writers saw interest groups as recruited from classes and as engaged in struggles that lead to social change.

- Mills emphasized the emergence of a power elite as the central element in contemporary class structure.

- Why have these conflict theories been seen as posing such a challenge to the sociology of theorists such as Parsons?

- Critical theory aimed at a reconstruction of Marxism so as to combine its recognition of social divisions and social conflict with an awareness of how societies had changed since the death of Marx.

- Habermas placed his analysis of conflict and collective action in the context of a theory of the relationship between economic and political systems, on the one hand, and a communal lifeworld, on the other.

- Is Habermas correct to see a strong relationship between knowledge and interests in science?

New directions for a new century

Structural, action, and conflict theories continue to provide a core of theoretical ideas for contemporary sociology, but they have not gone unchallenged. The rise of a strong and powerful women's movement in the 1970s led many women to challenge not only the male domination of senior positions in sociology but also the intellectual content of sociology itself. A number of influential *feminist theories* saw male bias in the leading approaches to social theory. They argued that these have ignored women and failed to consider issues of gender. While feminists found much to value in existing social theory, they suggested that a comprehensive reconstruction was needed to overcome this bias.

A further challenge to the established theories has come from *theorists of the post-modern*, who have argued that crucial features of contemporary societies cannot be grasped by existing intellectual tools. Established theories, including most feminist theories, are seen as built around concepts that are specific to modern societies. They must be complemented—and some have said replaced—by new forms of theorizing that are better able to grasp the *post-modern* condition.

A final group of theoretical ideas has a long history but has received far greater attention in recent years. These theories of global systems and **globalization** have rejected the focus on national societies and nation states, arguing that the contemporary world is characterized by a growth of transnational linkages and an increased importance of global flows and structures.

We will look at each of these theoretical approaches. Our discussions of particular topics in Part Two of this book draw on these theories as well as the established theories. Indeed, the shift from modern forms of regulated, centralized, and organized social life to post-modern flexible, pluralistic, and globalized forms is one of the principal ideas that we explore. While we are critical of the idea that we now live in a post-modern society, you will find that the chapters in this book treat contemporary social changes as features of the development of a post-modern condition.

Feminist theories

Feminist writers have posed a fundamental and comprehensive challenge to all existing social theories and to their attempts to inform and interpret empirical research. They have attempted nothing less than a long-overdue reformulation of the way in which sociologists—and other social scientists—have tried to understand modern societies. This transformation of theories and research is still underway, and it has not gone unchallenged by those who cling to existing styles of work. We look at the impact of these arguments in the various chapters that follow, and particularly in Chapter 5, where we look at the central issue of gender divisions and gender identities.

Feminist knowledge and the feminist standpoint

Feminist theory and theorizing about gender has a long history, though for much of this time it has been a rather marginal part of the sociological tradition, ignored by the mainstream of established—generally male—theorists. It is sometimes claimed that the study of theory is the study of 'dead white males', and this claim carries a great deal of truth. However, it is a truth about the way that theory is taught rather than a truth about theory itself. In this section we look at a number of important women who contributed theoretical ideas in the early period of sociology's history but whose work has achieved a wider impact only recently. We also consider how that work has engaged with work by and on people of colour to produce novel strands in sociological theorizing.

Mary Wollstonecraft (1792) was the first person seriously to challenge the view that the 'individuals' studied by social theorists could be studied without regard for their sex. The attempt to describe the characteristics of individuals in general, she argued, had treated all individuals, implicitly, as male. Male scientists and social theorists, with their stress on scientific rationality, saw men as the only people capable of rational thought. They saw women as irrational and emotional by nature and so as not fully civilized members of society. In their view, women are incapable of effective participation in the public world of political and economic life. Wollstonecraft, however, argued that differences between men and women were largely cultural and could be altered by appropriate forms of education. Her daughter, Mary Shelley, developed her critique of male scientific activity in her novel *Frankenstein* (1818).

Harriet Martineau (1837), who can lay claim to being the first woman empirical sociologist, undertook a study of American society in which she showed that women, like black Americans, were structurally disadvantaged by a male-dominated society. These views were strongly developed by Gilman (1898, 1911) in the United States and Schreiner (1899, 1911) in Britain. Gilman argued that women had been confined to motherhood, domesticity, and an economic dependence on men. This reflected the long historical formation of men and women by cultural processes that shaped and rigidified biological differences of sex. Men and women occupied different social worlds and so had different outlooks on social life. Schreiner shared this view and stressed that male–female differences reflected a 'sex parasitism' through which women were restricted to household work and certain forms of 'female' employment.

These arguments were important influences on the women's suffrage movement in the early years of the twentieth century, but they had little impact on the development of sociological theory. Although Simone de Beauvoir (1949) explored the construction of male and female identities in interaction and showed the ways in which male-dominated thought treated women as 'alien', as 'other', it was not until the 1970s that there was any significant revival in feminist theory. Underlying this renewal in feminist theory was a critique of the overly strong claims made for the absolute objectivity of scientific thought.

We showed on p. 30 that Marx saw all social knowledge as related to the class position of the observer or theorist. This view was echoed by Lukács, an early influence on critical theory, who held that the standpoint of the proletariat—the working class—was the only one that allowed its occupants to grasp the real nature of their society as a whole. One of the most important and far-reaching developments in contemporary sociology has been the way in which these arguments have been taken up and extended by feminist writers. The main thrust of feminist thought has been the claim that knowledge is related not so much to class as to divisions of sex and gender. Put simply, men and women have different experiences and so have different standpoints from which they construct their knowledge. All social knowledge is related to the gender of the observer or theorist.

Marxists and feminists agree that aspects of social position and social action determine what people can know about their world. Conventional, mainstream theories are seen, variously, as based on bourgeois or male standpoints. Despite their claimed objectivity, they are one-sided and biased. Those who occupy dominant and privileged positions in society are tied closely to the system from which they benefit; their ideas tend to legitimate and reinforce existing social relations. Liberating and critical theories, therefore, can be built from the subordinate positions of proletarian or female standpoints. Those who occupy subordinate or oppressed social positions are uniquely able to challenge the social order and to produce knowledge that is critical of it.

Feminists suggest that mainstream theory must be seen as *malestream* theory. It is rooted in patriarchal relations that embody male power over women and that establish the male standpoint on knowledge. The technical character of scientific knowledge and its emphasis on objectivity reflects a male way of seeing the world. This **gendering** of knowledge is denied, ignored, or unacknowledged by mainstream theorists, virtually all of whom have been male. Women, it is claimed, are invisible in social theory and in social research. Studies of people are, in reality, studies of men. Gendered knowledge, feminists argue, must be challenged by theorizing and research conducted from a female or feminist standpoint.

> **⊃ Connections**
>
> Gender differences are those differences of masculine and feminine identity that are linked to biological differences of sex. We discuss these issues at length in Chapter 5, pp. 154–9, where various strands in feminist thought are identified.
>
> Knowledge is said to be gendered when its content and its structure express specifically masculine or feminine characteristics. Look back over this chapter and see how few female theorists have been mentioned: can you find any? Is this simply bias on the part of two male authors, or is something deeper involved? When you have read more widely into sociological theory, you might like to see if you can find any female theorists who could have been mentioned in our sections on 'The beginning of sociology' and 'The formative period of sociology'.

A feminist standpoint is seen as providing knowledge that is radically different from malestream knowledge (Hartsock 1983; Harding 1986). The human mind, feminists argue, does not acquire knowledge in abstraction and detachment from the world. It is only through the senses and through bodily involvement in real situations that knowledge is possible. Differences of sex and gender, it is held, lead men and women to have quite different patterns of bodily involvement and experience, and so knowledge is necessarily *embodied*. Women have had primary responsibility for childbirth, mothering, and domestic labour, and they have learned to behave in distinctly female ways. They have quite different ways of being and acting in the world, and their lives are characterized by a much greater intensity of feeling and emotion

than is typical for men. Through 'patriarchal' structures and processes they are excluded from or marginalized in their participation in many areas of public political and economic life. The public world of patriarchal, malestream ideas and institutions comprises the 'relations of ruling' through which men dominate women (D. E. Smith 1987).

Knowledge acquired from a feminist standpoint, then, is deeply marked by this subjectivity. Feminists do not, of course, see this as a failing, though this is how subjectivity has often been seen in mainstream theory. According to feminists, their standpoint gives women distinct advantages in the pursuit of knowledge. They have access to whole areas of social life that are inaccessible or unavailable to men (see Box 2.18).

Feminist writers have raised crucial issues about the gendered character of scientific methodology and empirical research. They have also suggested that sociological theory itself is gendered. Their argument suggests that such concepts as structure, system, and action may themselves be part of the malestream world-view. This is a difficult position to uphold, as feminists have developed their criticisms by drawing on precisely these concepts. There are, for example, structural feminists, interactionist feminists, and feminists who draw on Marxist ideas about conflict. It seems that these most general concepts of sociological theory are not intrinsically gendered, although they have often been *used* in gendered ways. That is, arguments about structure, action, and conflict are not, in themselves, malestream discussions. They become part of the malestream when they are discussed exclusively in terms of the world of male experience and involvement. For example, theories of class structure have tended to

---

Controversy and debate Knowledge and standpoints   2.18

There are many different feminist approaches, and not all accept this particularly strong version of the argument for the feminist standpoint. There is, however, a broad agreement about the features that are supposed to characterize malestream and feminist knowledge. These are set out below. While malestream writers place a positive value on the things listed on the left-hand list, feminists see these in a negative light and stress the importance of things on the right-hand list.

Malestream	Feminist	Malestream	Feminist
• rationality	• emotion	• detachment	• embodied
• facts	• experiences	• public	• private
• objectivity	• subjectivity	• culture	• nature
• neutral	• personal		

You might have noticed an interesting ambiguity in these arguments. It is the distinctive standpoint of women that has been identified, yet the theory describes itself as a 'feminist-standpoint' theory rather than a female-standpoint or feminine-standpoint theory. Is it valid to equate a female standpoint with a specifically feminist consciousness?

focus on men's class position and have either ignored women or derived their class positions from those of their husbands, partners, and fathers.

Feminist critics of the malestream have correctly identified, in particular, the gaps and the absences that have characterized substantive sociological work. This substantive work has, for example, tended to emphasize class as the overriding social division. Until feminist critics raised the problem, little or no attention was given to the significance of gender divisions or to the theorization of the body and the emotions (Shilling 1993; B. Turner 1996).

However, in showing that knowledge is gendered and in promoting the claims of the feminist standpoint over malestream knowledge, feminist writers tend to accept many of the characteristics and consequences of contemporary gender differences. They argue that women have a distinctive standpoint because of their oppression, and they go on to advocate the cultivation of this standpoint. A truly critical and radical position would challenge this very differentiation of male and female and would try to overcome the oppression that it produces.

Feminist standpoint theorists have, of course, realized this problem, and they have made some attempts to overcome it. Harding (1986), for example, has tried to explore the ways in which feminist knowledge can be enlarged into knowledge that is not gendered at all. Current feminist standpoints are seen as transitional and as destined to be transformed in the future into a broader form of knowledge that is neither male nor female in character. Butler (1993) has argued for the need to reject all taken-for-granted ideas about fixed gender divisions. Gendered identities are constructed through interaction and are inherently flexible and malleable. It is for this reason that Butler advocates 'gender-bending' actions that challenge established identities and open up new possibilities.

The original formulations of feminist standpoint theories were based on the idea that the specific experiences of women were common to *all* women. A number of writers have reminded us, however, that women's experiences are shaped, also, by ethnicity and sexual orientation, as well as by such factors as class, age, and disability. Black feminist writers, for example, have challenged mainstream white feminists, on the grounds that they ignore the distinct experiences of women of colour (Hill Collins 1990).

A recognition of such diversity poses a number of challenges for sociological theory. Because they are factors that also divide men, the simple dichotomy of male and female must be abandoned. Middle-class women and middle-class men, for example, may have more in common with each other than do middle-class women and working-class women. More importantly, these divisions cross-cut each other and prevent the construction of any single female standpoint. There is no single category of 'woman': there are black middle-class women, Asian working-class women, white gay women, and so on.

Theorizing sex and gender

The main focus of feminist theory has been on the theorization of sex and gender. Although we discuss this fully in Chapter 5, it is important to outline the basic position here. The predominant position within feminist social theory starts out from a fundamental distinction between biological sex and socially constructed gender. This allows them to recognize the wide range of variation in cultural definitions of male and female characteristics and to argue that the particular gender identities prevailing in contemporary Western societies should not be seen as universal or 'natural'. Children are socialized into particular gender roles on the basis of their perceived sex. By the time they are adults they have been confirmed in their given identities. These learned representations of masculinity and femininity are the basis on which extensive inequalities can be built and perpetuated. Inequalities at work and in politics, divisions within the family, and patterns of violence can all be seen in relation to the socially variable patterns of gender. The conclusion drawn by feminists, however, is that gender divisions and inequalities can be changed through political action.

> ⇨ *Connections*
>
> We have simply outlined the feminist position here and have not looked at the important range of arguments within contemporary feminism. Those arguments are reviewed at length in 'Concepts and theories' in Chapter 5, pp. 151–63. You should look quickly at that section now and return to it when you look in more detail at sex and gender.

The feminist criticism of sociological thought has opened up possibilities for other critiques of the mainstream: black and anti-racist perspectives, 'queer theories', post-colonial theories, and many others have all been proposed. The end result of the critique of the mainstream seems to be a proliferation of competing perspectives. This proliferation has been encouraged and welcomed by the contemporary theoretical approach that we consider in the next section.

Post-modernism and theory

Post-modern theories are very diverse but are united by the view that scientists have made over-inflated claims for the certainty of their knowledge. The world is changing so rapidly, post-modern theorists argue, that existing concepts can no longer grasp the features of contemporary society. In the contemporary world, all is rapid flux and new concepts that reflect this plasticity must be used.

These arguments have their roots in the work of those who have stressed the relativity of all knowledge. This relativism is something that we have shown in both Marxism and feminism, but the argument goes much deeper. The leading figure in popularizing this relativism was Thomas Kuhn, who stressed that science did not deal with *given* facts but *created* its facts. Scientists, he argued, worked within communities of theorists and researchers who share certain basic concepts and methods. Without these shared preconceptions, no factual knowledge is possible. Scientists employ what Kuhn (1962) called *paradigms* of knowledge that tell them what to look for in their experiments and that help them to explain away observations that do not fit their preconceived theories.

Eventually, Kuhn said, the sheer bulk of the observations that had been ignored would become so great that support for a paradigm might begin to crumble. Younger scientists might begin to use a new one that is better able to handle these observations. The history of science is a sequence of theoretical revolutions in which paradigms replace one another periodically. It is impossible, said Kuhn, to describe this in terms of scientific *progress* or the *advance* of knowledge, as there is no way of comparing the results produced by scientists using different paradigms. Each paradigm creates its own facts, and there are no theory-neutral facts that we can use to decide among them. The paradigm that survives is one that is able to attract the largest number of new recruits and the highest levels of research funding. As so often in the political world, might makes right. Theoretical approaches are, therefore, *different* from each other, but it is much more difficult to say whether any one is *better* or more truthful than another. Scientific activity is necessarily pluralistic (Friedrichs 1970). Many people concluded that we merely have to *choose* a theoretical position that appeals. In the world of science, anything goes and there can be as many alternative positions as our imaginations can produce.

These arguments were echoed and elaborated in the works of two French writers who have been central to the development of post-modern theory. These are Michel Foucault (1971) and Jean-François Lyotard (1979). Both highlighted the plurality and diversity of scientific knowledge, but Lyotard argued that this reflected the *post-modern condition* that contemporary societies were entering (see Box 2.19). It is simply no longer possible to use such terms as truth and objectivity. Under post-modern conditions, all thought has to be seen as relative, partial, and limited. No standpoint is fixed or absolute.

The post-modern condition

Lyotard's argument concerned the nature of science and technical knowledge, but he was identifying a wider cultural phenomenon. Cultural activities of all kinds are seen as having become more important in the second half of the

---

THEORY AND METHODS 2.19

Post-structuralism and post-modernism

Foucault's work is often described as 'post-structuralist', as he developed it in response to certain structuralist writers in the Marxist tradition (see Althusser 1965). We discuss his extremely important ideas at many places in this book, but particularly in Chapter 8. Foucault's work is often linked with that of Lyotard, though they differ in many ways. What they have in common is their rejection of the idea that there are overarching structures in social life, and their recognition of fragmentation and diversity in cultural and social life. Lyotard saw himself as setting out a theory of the post-modern condition, and he is generally seen as a 'post-modernist'. This position has been most forcibly developed by Baudrillard (1977).

You will find that some writers use a hyphen in post-modernism, but others prefer it without. In fact, the dictionary definition of 'postmodernism' (without a hyphen) refers to a movement of thought in art and architecture. This idea inspired contemporary writings, but the term has now acquired a different meaning. It is used in its hyphenated form to show this difference in meaning: a post-modern condition is one that goes beyond the modern condition.

---

twentieth century. In modern societies, cultural institutions are embedded in other social institutions that shape people's cultural life. Marx's model of the economic base and the cultural and political superstructure was simply the most extreme formulation of this. As these modern societies have entered the post-modern condition, however, the autonomy of the cultural sphere has grown to the point that it has become the most important aspect of social life.

Some theorists of the post-modern condition have seen this as resulting from changes in economic and political structures themselves. These changes are seen as having lead from modern industrial capitalism to late capitalism (Jameson 1984), late modernity (Giddens 1990), or even post-industrialism and post-capitalism (Bell 1979). These writers point to such things as the development of more flexible and globalized systems of production in which marketing, advertising, and consumerism play a more central part. The cultural sphere becomes extended and enlarged, and through the mass media it comes to stress diversity and choice in all matters. We discuss this further in Chapter 10, pp. 373–6. In the post-modern condition, the idea of absolute and universal standards loses its meaning (see also Lash and Urry 1987).

More radical theorists have argued that these changes are so fundamental that completely new forms of theory—post-modern theories—are required. The most important of these theorists is Baudrillard, who held that it is no longer valid to search for economic and political realities beyond our cultural images of them. According to this **post-modernism**, the contemporary condition of life is one in which there is nothing for us to do except produce and consume cultural images. Baudrillard (1981) argued that the cultural products of the mass media define reality for people. We live in a media-saturated world and can no longer draw sharp lines between fact and fiction, between news and entertainment.

This led Baudrillard to abandon the idea of building scientific theories to explain the world. Sociology, for Baudrillard, is no different from any other cultural activity: there is no real difference between building a theory, writing a poem, and composing an advertising jingle. Post-modern theorists enthusiastically accept the complete relativity of knowledge and the abandonment of the Enlightenment idea of scientific knowledge.

These ideas have had a massive impact on recent work, not only in sociology but also in literature, cultural studies, and many other disciplines. There are signs that some of the excessive claims made by post-modernists have begun to wane, and a more reasoned consideration of diversity and difference is beginning to take place. It is too early yet to say what the final outcome of this will be. We hope that your engagement with some of the implications of their work while you read the rest of this book will stimulate you to make your own contribution to this debate over the future of sociology and science.

Globalization and social theory

Many of the theories that we have considered have, implicitly or explicitly, taken the nation state as their basic point of reference. Societies have been seen as contained within the territorial boundaries of nation states, and the processes that sociologists study have been seen as largely confined to such societies. Thus, much sociology refers to British society, German society, American society, and so on. As we show in Chapter 16, in particular, this has always been an unreal approach, and the growth in connections between national societies has made their boundaries even more artificial than before. We live in an increasingly globalized world, and the proper objects of sociological explanation are transnational organizations and global structures themselves.

An awareness of the importance of transnational linkages and the global integration of the world was importantly developed in the world-system theory of Immanuel Wallerstein (1974). Writing in the 1970s, and drawing on arguments from the sociology of development, Wallerstein set out a form of Marxism that saw capitalism as developing within world systems rather than nation states and national societies. A world system is a large social system that contains many states and cultural regions and that is integrated through an extensive division of labour. The modern world system—rooted in a capitalist world economy—came into being in sixteenth-century Europe and was the context within which classical sociology arose.

Robertson (1992) proposed a powerful framework that brings many of these arguments together. He argues that the long-standing interest in economic and political relations has to be complemented by an awareness of the crucial importance of cultural globalization. Cultural globalization has resulted in fundamental changes in world view and outlook in contemporary societies. It has resulted in a 'compression' of the world, as the possibility of immediate communication becomes easier, and an 'intensification of consciousness of the world as a whole' (Robertson 1992: 8). Though the world has become more pluralistic in cultural terms, people have become more cosmopolitan in outlook.

To understand this change Robertson returned to the idea of the world system as a totality but reconstructed it as a concept of the *global field*, aiming to see the interrelations between national societies and global systems of societies. National societies undergo a process of differentiation in which it is the various specialized institutions that are integrated at the global level and not whole societies. Thus, economic systems, educational systems, religious institutions, and so on are each tied separately into global structures and processes (Urry 2000). A growing number of international agencies and transnational organizations and movements become increasingly important actors in the global system. Albrow (1996) argues that the years since 1945 were marked by the growth of the women's, peace, and green movements, each of which was involved in a global agenda. This argument has most recently been formulated by Castells (1996), who has traced the implications of the growing global network of economic and political linkages for the collective identities of social movements.

In this global age, people identify less and less with nations and local communities. One particularly important feature is the global extension of national citizenship into larger concerns for universal human rights that enable radical challenges to national political regimes in the name of 'humankind'. The universal society of humankind exists only as a diverse and chaotic system of often contradictory structures, limiting the development of the global consciousness implied in the cosmopolitanism of human rights.

The global field is characterized by great complexity. National societies become fragmented and 'disorganized' (Lash and Urry 1987) and global systems become pluralistic and decentred. There is a growing dependence of local conditions on global processes, such that people's local attachments and consciousness reflect their awareness of these global processes. Robertson has described this complex interdependence as 'glocalization'. One feature of this is the resistance to globalization apparent in the political activity of organizations and movements opposed to the effects of globalization on traditional social structures.

These theories are taken up in all the various chapters of this book, where we try to highlight the shift towards more global forms of social life. You will find a useful discussion of many of these issues in Urry's *Sociology beyond Societies* (2001).

Stop and reflect

In this section we have sketched out the contemporary criticisms of the mainstream theories that we looked at in 'Sociology established'. These criticisms are explored at greater length in our discussions of particular topics in the later parts of this book.

- Feminist writers have criticized mainstream sociology for its malestream characteristics, arguing that a concern for rationality and objectivity can often mask the adoption of a male standpoint. A feminist standpoint, reflecting the distinct position and experiences of women, is seen as offering a different and more adequate basis for knowledge.

- Are feminists correct to see knowledge as gendered in this way?

- Black feminists and others have pointed to the need to abandon the single category of woman and to recognize the diversity of female experiences.

- Post-modern theorists embrace a complete relativism in knowledge and reject the very ideas of rationality, objectivity, and scientific certainty. Is this embrace of relativism a helpful advance in sociological analysis?

When discussing post-modern theorists and globalization theorists, we showed that their ideas were part of a wider movement of thought that suggested fundamental changes in the structure of modern societies.

- The modern structures of industrialism and capitalism, described by structural functionalists and Marxists, have developed into more flexible and fragmented structures that create the post-modern condition.

- In the post-modern condition, cultural activities of all kinds acquire a greater autonomy and significance in social life.

- Contemporary societies are integrated at the global level through transnational economic, political, and cultural relations and processes.

- There is a growing tension between processes of globalization and the formation of local identities and commitments

We stressed, however, that the claims made by the more radical post-modern theorists have themselves been challenged and that there is a need to explore the implications of their work in relation to specific substantive topics.

Key concepts

- action frame of reference 43
- adaptation 34
- alienation 28
- analytical realism 43
- anomie 35
- authority 53
- base 28
- bourgeois 30
- capitalist society 36
- causal explanation 33
- cognitive interests 55

- division of labour 34
- dynamic density 35
- evolution 26
- function 25
- functional analysis 33
- gendering 59
- goal attainment 47
- globalization 58
- historical materialism 28
- idealist 23
- ideal type 38

- ideologies 28
- industrial society 26
- integration 47
- interest group 54
- interests 54
- latency 47
- materialist 23
- mechanical solidarity 35
- mode of production 28
- organic solidarity 35
- phenomenology 50

Workshop 2

Study 2   How to theorize

Very few sociologists have written about how actually to theorize. Sociological theory is usually presented as an abstract body of ideas, and it is often difficult to see how it can be applied or used in practice. Howard Becker is one of the few exceptions to pay attention to the *processes* through which theories are developed and applied. In his book *Tricks of the Trade* (1998), Becker takes a number of central ideas and shows how students and professional sociologists can actually use these concepts in their research. He does this through a number of 'tricks' that people can use to develop their own theoretical skills.

Becker notes a fundamental problem in teaching students how to use theoretical concepts. Students sent out to observe delinquency and deviant behaviour in the town or city will come back to their class and say, for example, that they could not see the relevance of Durkheim's ideas (or Parsons's, or Merton's), because they could not see any anomie. Becker notes that this involves a failure to appreciate that anomie—like all sociological concepts—is something that is inferred from observations, it is not something that is directly observed itself. This is the question of *generalization*. Observations are specific, but concepts are general. Sociological theorizing involves making a leap from the specific to the general.

How, then, do sociologists generalize? How do they move, say, from observations of drinking behaviour to statements about identities and self-conceptions? To students and outsiders it appears to be a magical leap of imagination. Becker argues, however, that it involves a trick that, once learnt, becomes second nature as a professional skill: it might appear to be magical to outsiders, but it is actually a form of learned behaviour. The key trick he identifies in developing the skill of generalization is the progressive redescription of observations.

This trick involves describing findings without using any of the identifying characteristics of the actual case. Becker

illustrates this from his own work on the careers of Chicago school teachers, among whom he had carried out a series of interviews and observations. When first attempting to describe his findings he would disregard all the personal details of the individuals (names, addresses, ages, and so on) and would come up with a summary such as:

> These teachers make their careers by moving from school to school within the Chicago school system, rather than trying to rise to higher, better paid positions, or moving to other systems in other cities, and their moves between positions in the school system can be understood as trying to find a school in which the people they interacted with—students, parents, principals, other teachers—would act more or less the way the teachers expected them to. (Becker 1998: 126)

This redescription is a basic summary that remains fairly close to the observations, but contains no personal or idiosyncratic detail. Most people can manage to produce such an account from their observations fairly easily. The second step in theorizing is to redescribe the research without using any of the remaining identifiers and specifically avoiding words such as 'teacher', 'school', 'pupil', 'Chicago', and so on. This might seem odd, but most people would be able to take this second step. Becker presents the following redescription:

> people in bureaucratic systems choose between potential positions by assessing the way all the other participants will treat them and choosing places where the balance will be best, given whatever they are trying to maximize. (Becker 1998: 127)

This is immediately much more theoretical than the initial descriptions of observations. It is now very easy to see links between the observations and such fully theoretical concepts as rational choice and career commitment. The jump has been made by making progressively more general redescriptions of the observations. Practice makes perfect, and Becker holds that continued use of such a technique results in the researcher being able to move back and forth between concepts and data, almost without thought—it has become second nature.

Many of you will be undertaking small-scale projects. Try to apply this trick in your research and see if it helps you to discover the relevance of the sociological theories that we have discussed in this chapter. Becker's book is full of similar tricks, many of which are aimed at the integration of theory with research methods, and you will find it useful to read the whole book.

Media watch 2 Values and family breakdown

Writing in the *Daily Mail*, journalist Melanie Phillips presented the case of Julie Atkins, a divorced mother of three girls who are themselves mothers. The girls are aged 14, 15, and 18, and two of the fathers of their children are in their teens. Melanie Phillips's diagnosis of this 'baby factory' is that Julie is 'guilty of the most reckless neglect' and has failed to take responsibility for her own family. She relies on the support provided by the welfare system. This is a symptom of the 'collapse of civilized values' in contemporary Britain that has resulted in a 'culture of disrespect'. Phillips argues that fatherless children are being reared by feckless mothers, producing a 'yob' culture and the breakdown of civility and order. We live in a 'fractured and brutish society' that contrasts markedly with the cohesive and well-integrated society of the past in which people took individual responsibility for their own actions and subscribed to a common set of values:

> There was a time when standards of behaviour were upheld to which all would aspire and by which they would be judged. Sobriety, sexual restraint, hard work and abiding by the law were all held to be vital for civilising the masses. These virtues were policed by a combination of laws and informal sanctions such as shame or stigma.

The collapse in social values, Phillips argues, has produced a divided society. There is a division between those who subscribe to 'basic civilised codes which everyone acknowledges' and those who are 'disconnected from mainstream life and its values'. The remedy for this, she concludes, is the rebuilding of respect for established values through education and through encouraging the better parenting skills that will ensure the socialization of the next generation into these values. She seeks to 'provide children for whom all the codes of civilised life are absent with the security of absolutely rigid discipline and educational structure'.

Melanie Phillips is implicitly drawing on the kinds of consensus ideas set out by Talcott Parsons. For Parsons, societies were held together by shared cultural values, and social problems were a result of what Durkheim called anomie—the breakdown of all commitment to social values. Try to collect some articles from other newspapers that show this same point of view. How many discussions of 'anti-social behaviour' and social problems ascribe this to a breakdown in values and social cohesion?

When you have considered this question you should try to evaluate the argument. What evidence is produced in support of the claims? More importantly, what evidence can you find that raises problems for the theory?

Some counter-evidence was presented in an article by Anastasia de Waal in the *Guardian*. She, too, looked at the decline of personal responsibility in families and the position of single-parent, female-headed households. She, however, highlights the increasing pressures on these women to hold down a job and manage their family without the material and financial support of a partner. The link between lone motherhood and welfare dependency, decried by Phillips, is more often a result of a failure of the fathers to pay their child maintenance in full. Both men and women are locked into a structure of limited employment opportunities, low pay, and poor working conditions that make it economically difficult for them to meet their responsibilities.

De Waal makes little reference to values. Instead, she emphasizes economic resources, interests, and opportunities. Read back over our discussion of Marxist theory and see if you think that arguments from Marx might be brought to bear on this. Try to construct a Marxist explanation of the causes and consequences of family breakdown.

We have encouraged you to consider two different ways of explaining a social issue from the mass media: a Parsonian explanation and a Marxist explanation. Summarize each of these theories in a table. How would you go about choosing between them? Indeed, how far should we regard them as competing theories and how far as complementary ones?

Source: M. Phillips (2005); de Waal (2005).

Discussion points

Look back over the 'Stop and reflect' points at the end of each section of this chapter and make sure that you understand the issues that have been highlighted. The most general issues running through the chapter can be covered by considering four questions:

- What do you understand by materialist, idealist, and positivist views of knowledge?
- What is meant by gendered knowledge, and in what sense can it be said that sociological theory is malestream theory?
- What intellectual problems, if any, can you identify in the post-modern theorists' defence of relativism and feminist views of knowledge standpoints?
- Should we abandon the idea of a social *science* and its search for objectivity? If we do abandon objectivity and impartiality, what distinguishes sociological argument from an argument in the pub?

Theories of structure

- Consider how you would use such concepts as structure, structural differentiation, and social role in the analysis of a work situation.
- How would you characterize the social solidarity of a society, and how useful are Durkheim's concepts of mechanical solidarity and organic solidarity?
- How did Merton's concept of anomie differ from that of Durkheim? Try to think of some examples of the responses to anomie that Merton identified.
- Contemporary societies are often referred to as 'industrial societies'. What is meant by this, and what is meant by the claim that they have entered a post-industrial or post-modern condition?

Theories of interaction

- How did Weber construct his ideal types of action? What did he mean by describing them as 'ideal' types?
- What is meant by the ideas of social construction and the definition of the situation? How might these be used in a study of a school, college, or university?

- What does it mean to describe a theory of action as phenomenological? How does this relate to Weber's idea of 'understanding'?
- Why do you think we have argued that it is appropriate to consider Weber under the headings of both 'interaction theories' and 'conflict theories'?

Theories of conflict

- What does it mean to describe Marx's historical materialism, and his concepts of base and superstructure, as involving an economic determinism? Is this a valid criticism of Marx?
- How might a Marxist look for evidence of alienation, class relations, and ideology in contemporary societies?
- Has the break-up of the Soviet Union and the other Communist states of Eastern and Central Europe finally undermined the intellectual claims of Marxism?
- To what extent can the theories of Dahrendorf and Rex be seen as improving on Marx's ideas on class and conflict?
- Can Habermas appropriately be called a Marxist? To what extent does his introduction of the concept of the lifeworld involve a significant departure from Marxist ideas?

Contemporary theories

- What are the key ideas in a distinctively feminist approach to sociology?
- Can there be a feminist theory that ignores issues of ethnicity and sexuality that divide women from each other? What are the implications of this for the women's movement?
- Does it make sense to describe the contemporary world as 'post' modern? Can contemporary theoretical approaches be characterized as 'post' structural?
- How valid is it to see transnational social movements and international agencies as the key actors in the contemporary world?
- Can the idea of a growing cosmopolitanism and a strengthening of universal human rights be reconciled with the growing signs of ethnic conflict within and between nations?

Explore further

Useful overviews of the main trends in sociological theory can be found in:

Craib, I. (1997), *Classical Social Theory* (Oxford: Oxford University Press). *An excellent and very readable introduction to the ideas of Marx, Weber, Durkheim, and Simmel.*

Giddens, A. (1971), *Capitalism and Modern Social Theory* (Cambridge: Cambridge University Press). *Gives an excellent account of Marx, Weber, and Durkheim, but also puts them into the historical context of the development of European society.*

Scott, J. (1995), *Sociological Theory: Contemporary Debates* (Cheltenham: Edward Elgar). *Looks in detail at Parsons and at the various strands of theory that developed in relation to his work, including interaction theories and conflict theories.*

Scott, J. (2006), *Social Theory: Central Issues in Sociology* (London: Sage). *Takes a thematic approach to the development of theoretical ideas and includes discussions of a large number of theorists in relation to these themes.*

More detailed discussions can be found in:

Berger, P. L., and Luckmann, T. (1966), *The Social Construction of Reality: A Treatise in the Sociology of Knowledge* (New York: Doubleday; repr. Harmondsworth: Allen Lane, 1971). *An important and influential statement of the phenomenological point of view.*

Dahrendorf, R. (1957), *Class and Class Conflict in an Industrial Society* (London: Routledge & Kegan Paul, 1959). *A readable statement of the need for a conflict perspective that goes beyond the ideas of Marx.*

Goffman, E. (1959), *The Presentation of Self in Everyday Life* (Harmondsworth: Penguin). *Gives a powerful extension of the symbolic interactionist position. We look at his work in more detail in Chapter 4, pp. 124–5 and Chapter 8, pp. 292–3.*

You will find short summaries of all the major theorists considered, and many more, in:

Scott, J. (2006b), *Fifty Key Sociologists: The Formative Theorists* (London: Routledge).

Scott, J. (2006c), *Fifty Key Sociologists: The Contemporary Theorists* (London: Routledge).

You should try to read at least one of the works of each of the leading classical theorists. The best starting points might be:

Durkheim, E. (1897), *Suicide: A Study in Sociology* (London: Routledge & Kegan Paul, 1952).

Marx, K., and Engels, F. (1848), *The Communist Manifesto* (Harmondsworth: Penguin, 1967).

Weber, Max (1904–5), *The Protestant Ethic and the Spirit of Capitalism* (Oxford: Basil Blackwell, 2002).

Online resources

Visit the Online Resource Centre that accompanies this book to access more learning resources and other interesting material on theories and theorizing at:
www.oxfordtextbooks.co.uk/orc/fulcher4e/

The views of all the principal sociologists can be assessed through the comprehensive pages set up at the 'Dead Sociologists' Society:
http://media.pfeiffer.edu/lridener/DSS/DEADSOC.HTML

Important sites for studying Marx, Durkheim, and Weber can be found in the boxes dedicated to these writers earlier in this chapter.

Symbolic interactionism can be pursued through the Society for the Study of Symbolic Interactionism's own page:
www.espach.salford.ac.uk/sssi/index.php

Feminist thought is well represented by the Feminist Majority Foundation at:
www.feminist.org

Many of Baudrillard's works on post-modernism are covered at:
www.uta.edu/english/archives/apt/collab/baudweb.html

Methods and Research

Contents

Statistics show that . . .

'Figures released today from the British Crime Survey (BCS), compiled using interviews with the public, showed overall crime down a record 10%. Statistics published by the police, based on recorded offences, showed crime down 9%. . . . Police recorded 22,151 offences involving knives last year in England and Wales, including grievous bodily harm, attempted murder, woundings and robbery. . . . That is 25% down on last year, when the figure stood just shy of 173,000, and well under half the 1995 peak of 340,000. . . . Other figures published recently suggest knife crime may be on the increase. Department of Health statistics show that almost 14,000 people were treated in hospital for stab wounds last year (446 of them aged 14 and under)—an increase of nearly 20% in five years. . . . So what is the truth? Has the impact of headlines about the horrific death of teenagers caused us to lose sight of an overall reduction in knife crime? Or is the BCS fatally flawed and painting a positive picture that is alien to you?'

Source: Guardian News Blog (2008).

George Canning, the nineteenth-century British Prime Minister, famously said: 'I can prove anything by statistics except the truth.' A later Prime Minister, Benjamin Disraeli, was even more forceful, holding that 'there are three kinds of lies: lies, damned lies, and statistics'. Yet people still like to quote statistics in support of their arguments. As Homer Simpson once said: 'Oh, people can come up with statistics to prove anything. 14% of people know that.' The claim that 'you can prove anything with statistics' is often produced as an argument against the scientific pretensions of sociologists. How valid is this judgement? Is the sociologist simply a scientific charlatan whose methods leave much to be desired?

We have already shown in Chapter 1, pp. 15–17, that a scientific method is essential in scientific research. Any scientist must be careful and critical of the evidence used to build and test theories. Handled properly, statistical sources are an essential part of the sociological enterprise. It is their *misuse*, not their *use*, that can mislead people. Darrell Huff, author of *How to Lie with Statistics*, recognized the need for statistical data and argued that, 'without writers who use the words with honesty and understanding and readers who know what they mean, the results can only be semantic nonsense' (Huff 1954: 8). In this chapter

we will look at the ways in which this kind of evidence can be collected and used in sociological research and how it can help to inform public debates.

Not all sociological evidence is statistical. The image of the sociologist as a survey researcher processing large numbers of statistics with a computer is only a part of the truth. In fact, sociologists use a variety of methods to collect their evidence. They carry out observations and interviews, and they examine historical and contemporary documents. Our aim in this chapter is to give you an overview of the range of sociological methods and the kinds of evidence used in sociological work. In the section on 'Research design and methodology' we look at the main forms of sociological research and how they complement each other in the sociological toolbox. In 'Surveys, ethnography, and documents' we look at the variety of data sources and their analysis. The section on 'Displaying and using data' helps you to read the tables and charts produced by other researchers and gives you some guidance on how to produce your own. Finally, 'The ethics of social research' looks at the effects of research on the people studied and on the sociologist him- or herself. It asks 'What are the ethical responsibilities of the sociologist?'

Research design and methodology

The studies you will come across in this book and in your wider reading have used a great variety of research methods to collect their information. If you are to approach these studies critically, you need to know something about the advantages and disadvantages of the various methods used. Our aim in this section is to outline the basic ideas about research methods that will enable you to do this.

Some of you may be carrying out a small project of your own as a part of your studies and we hope that this section will give enough information for you to make an informed choice about the kinds of research methods you want to use. When you begin your research, you will find that you need to go beyond what we tell you and consult some of the many specialist books that give detailed guidance on the techniques and skills of sociological research (see O'Connell Davidson, and Layder 1994; May 2001; Bryman 2008). Our discussion will, we hope, convey the flavour of social research, but it cannot provide you with the full recipe!

Research design

Research does not simply happen. It has to be planned in advance. This planning is called **research design**. Designing a research project involves translating general ideas and concerns into specific and researchable topics. You may start out with a general interest in, say, deviance, work, or health, but this must be made more specific before you can start to design a project. The focus of interest must be narrowed down to something that can actually be investigated in an empirical study. Instead of a general wish to investigate deviance, a researcher might finally decide to look at violent street crime in urban areas, especially as this affects women. This topic is specific enough to suggest particular theoretical questions and practical issues to examine and therefore will point to the kinds of research methods that might be used.

Varieties of research

Research design involves decisions about four different aspects of the research process. The researcher must be clear about the *purposes* of the research, the *methods* that will be used, the ways in which these methods are combined into a particular *style* of research, and the *strategy* through which these will be tied together into a coherent project.

There are many *purposes* for which research might be carried out. A researcher may be trying to please an employer, complete a Ph.D., advance the sum of human knowledge, and so on. We are focusing here, however, on

the scientific purposes of a project. Robson (1993: 42) has usefully suggested that three broad scientific purposes can be identified:

- exploration;
- description;
- explanation.

A project concerned with *exploration* is one in which the researcher seeks to find out something in a new or under-researched area. The project seeks to map out the area in order to generate ideas and further questions to examine. An exploratory study asks 'What is going on here?' A researcher may, for example, try to find out how many families are living in poverty in a particular city, or where the main areas of urban deprivation are to be found.

A project with a *descriptive* purpose, on the other hand, is one where the researcher tries to construct a clearer and more comprehensive picture of something in relation to the theoretical questions from which the research began. The research will build on existing bodies of knowledge and fill in further details in order to arrive at a rounded picture of the extent or significance of something. A descriptive project might try to show how poverty, health, and diet are related together as aspects of working-class life in a particular city. Both exploration and description are concerned with reporting the facts, and they are distinguished from one another only in terms of how well defined an area is already.

When a project has an *explanatory* purpose, it seeks to go beyond reporting the facts to seek out the causes and influences at work. It asks 'Why is this happening?' or 'What is the most important factor in producing this?' The theory that the researcher uses will suggest certain factors to study, or these may be drawn from previous exploratory and descriptive research. An explanatory study might try to see whether low pay, unemployment, or bad housekeeping is the most important cause of poverty.

When the most important causal factors have been identified, they may be combined into a **model** of the causal influences. A model is a simplified picture of a situation or process that tries to show how its various elements are connected to each other. A model can often be suggested by the particular theory that informs the research. Projects informed by structural-functionalist theories, for example, are likely to construct models of the functional connections among the things studied. A model may suggest one or more hypotheses that can be examined in further research. A **hypothesis** is a suggested relationship between two or more factors that can be tested against evidence. A model that links poverty to low pay, for example, may suggest the hypothesis that increasing the legal minimum rate of pay will reduce the level of poverty. A researcher whose model links poverty to unemployment, however, may draw the hypothesis that a higher rate of pay, by increasing business costs, would increase the level of unemployment and, therefore, the level of poverty.

Once the purpose of the research has been clarified, it is possible to choose the particular *methods* to use. A research method is a particular technique for collecting or analysing evidence, and the kinds of research methods used by sociologists include questionnaires, participant observation, interviewing, the interpretation of documents, content analysis, and many others. We will look at a number of these methods in this chapter and in other parts of this book. It is important that the methods chosen relate closely to the purposes of the research and the topics being examined. An attempt to explain the causes of poverty in contemporary Britain, for example, might seem to require a standardized method, such as a questionnaire that can easily be administered to a large number of people. An exploratory study of the consequences of poverty for lone-parent households, on the other hand, might seem to require more informal interview techniques.

The particular methods chosen and combined by a researcher will often be associated with a distinctive *style* of research. A style of research comprises methods that fit well together and that tend to be associated with particular theoretical approaches and philosophical assumptions. In this chapter, we will discuss three principal styles of research:

- survey research;
- ethnographic research;
- documentary research.

Survey research involves formal and standardized methods for asking questions that, it is hoped, those being studied will answer. Survey research is often, though not always, a quantitative form of research. In *ethnographic research*, on the other hand, observational and conversational methods are used, as these help to highlight the qualitative aspects of the social world. Finally, *documentary research* involves the use of written texts of all kinds, from government reports to mass-media broadcasts. This is often, though not always, concerned with historical investigations.

Survey research has often been linked with structural-functionalist theories, while ethnographic research has been seen as more closely linked with interaction theories. These links are, however, far from rigid, and there are many exceptions. Symbolic interactionists, for example, have used questionnaires, while structural functionalists have used participant observation. Similarly, it is not only

Marxists and other conflict theorists who have relied on documentary research: documentary methods have been used by both structural functionalists and interactionists, and conflict theorists have undertaken both surveys and ethnographies.

It is not possible, then, to draw a rigid connection between particular theories and methods. More typically, researchers choose the particular style of research that seems appropriate for their purposes and that they feel match their particular skills. Many researchers, for example, do not feel comfortable with ethnographic methods, because they feel that they do not have the particular interpersonal skills required. Others are unhappy about the more mathematical aspects of much survey research. All researchers have particular skills and personal characteristics that make them more likely to choose, and to use successfully, a particular style of research. This personal element is an important feature of all social research.

The final decisions about research design are those concerning the research *strategy* that ties together the various methods chosen. A research strategy defines a logic of investigation or enquiry that specifies the way in which the researcher uses his or her subject matter. In formulating a research strategy, two decisions must be made. First, a decision must be made between a *case study* and a *comparative* strategy. Secondly, it is necessary to choose between a *longitudinal* and a *cross-sectional* strategy.

In a *case-study strategy*, the researcher looks in detail at one particular case (Yin 2003). This may be one individual, one organization, or one society. The aim is to carry out a detailed exploration or description of that case or to explain how things work in that case. Street violence, for example, might be examined in one particular inner-city district in order to produce the maximum amount of detailed knowledge. A case to study must be chosen with care if generalizations are to be made to some larger category. The researcher must know, for example, in what respects it is valid to generalize from the situation in, say, Chicago to that in other large cities.

In a *comparative strategy*, on the other hand, a researcher chooses two or more cases to investigate in order to examine their similarities and differences. This is particularly helpful when testing hypotheses or producing classifications. Durkheim's research on suicide (1897), for example, compared rates of suicide in different countries and among different social groups in order to uncover the factors responsible for high and low levels of suicide. He did this by classifying suicides into a number of different types.

A *longitudinal strategy* investigates changes over time. This may involve taking a historical approach to a society, a biographical or life-history approach to an individual, or it may involve following a particular group of individuals over a period. Longitudinal research can be combined with either a case study or a comparative strategy. Max Weber

THEORY AND METHODS 3.1

Issues of research design

Research design involves making decisions in relation to each of four issues: research purposes, research methods, research styles, and research strategies. These can be summarized as follows:

Research purposes	Research methods	Research styles	Strategies
• exploration	• questionnaires	• survey research	• case study or comparative
• description	• observation	• ethnographic research	• longitudinal or cross-sectional
• explanation	• interviews	• documentary research	
	• documents, etc.		

Researchers must make decisions under each of the four headings, though their projects will often involve the triangulation of different forms of research.

(1904–5) undertook a longitudinal case study when he looked at the historical relationship between the Protestant religion and capitalist economic activity in Western Europe. However, Weber went on to combine this with comparative investigations into the development of religion and economic activity in China and India.

In a *cross-sectional strategy*, the researcher ignores change and produces a single picture of how things are at one particular date. Durkheim's study of suicide consisted mainly of cross-sectional comparisons, though he did make some use of longitudinal evidence. The cross-sectional case study is, perhaps, one of the most widely used research strategies. Many social surveys aim to collect information about a population at a particular date. A survey may, for example, collect information about poverty in Britain in 1966, or domestic violence in the United States in 1922. These issues of research design are summarized in Box 3.1.

Multiple methods

It is sometimes assumed that a particular research project must rigorously follow a single method. This is, of course, sometimes the case. More typically, however, a project will find it useful to combine methods so that the strengths of one can compensate for the weaknesses of another. Bringing together different methods enriches the research by highlighting different facets of the situation being studied. This combination of methods is called **triangulation**. The term 'triangulation' comes from geographical surveying, where it refers to a geometrical technique for working out unknown measures from two known measures. In social research, however, it refers to the use of two (or more) separate methods to illuminate what is being studied from different angles. Quantitative and qualitative methods might be combined, official statistics might be supplemented by information from a questionnaire, and so on.

Two approaches can often complement each other or can facilitate or support each other. This form of triangulation is important in many projects. It is particularly likely to occur in team-based projects, where specialists in survey research, ethnographic research, and documentary research can be brought together in a scientific division of labour. A team can often investigate a problem more effectively than can a lone researcher. This simple idea is shown in Figure 3.1.

The use of multiple methods is nowhere more important than in the issue of quantitative *versus* qualitative sources of data. Many discussions of research methods are organized around a differentiation between quantitative and qualitative approaches. Quantitative approaches are usually seen as those that use structured interviews, questionnaires, content analysis, and official statistics, and subject these to analysis through numerical and statistical techniques. Qualitative approaches, on the other hand, are usually seen as involving participant observation, focus groups, and the reading of documents in order to arrive at interpretations of the subjective meanings and perspectives of individuals and groups. There are, of course, important differences in techniques, but the contrast is often overdrawn. In the following section we show that

Figure 3.1 Triangulation in social research

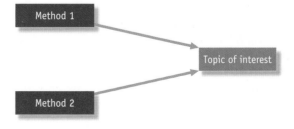

there is far more commonality among sources and methods than this contrast implies.

Quantitative research is generally very useful in drawing out the broad features of a problem, in highlighting its extent and significance, and in showing the typicality, or otherwise, of particular individuals or social groups. Combining such results with qualitative material on the subjective orientations of particular individuals, however, gives far greater depth to the conclusions drawn. Issues that cannot be uncovered through a large survey, for example, may more easily be uncovered in in-depth interviews with a small number of people. The converse is also true. Large surveys can uncover evidence on the extent and range of attitudes and opinions that simply would not be apparent from an individual interview or from participant observation. See the discussion of quantitative and qualitative data in Box 3.2.

The variety of research purposes, methods, and styles are the individual tools that fill the sociological toolbox, and nothing can be worse than going out into the field without the whole tool box. When in the field, it is a matter of choosing the appropriate tool for the particular task at hand. Sociologists should not regard themselves as simply survey researchers or qualitative researchers, but should be alive to the possibilities of a variety of methods and of combining them in fruitful and powerful ways.

 Controversy and debate Quality and quantity   3.2

The distinction between qualitative and quantitative data should not be drawn too sharply. Quantitative data are those that involve the use of numbers to measure the extent of social characteristics and their trends over time. Qualitative data, on the other hand, are those that refer far more directly to the meanings that actions have for people. The distinction is related to that between Durkheim's emphasis on *social facts* and Weber's emphasis on *social actions*, but both writers were more subtle than this implies and tried to combine quantitative and qualitative approaches in their work. The quantitative cannot easily be separated from the qualitative: numbers must be interpreted to uncover their meanings, and meanings make sense only if we know how frequently they occur. These are complementary, not alternative, forms of data.

 Stop and reflect

In this section we have looked at a number of aspects of research design and methodology.

- Research design is the whole process of planning a project that relates to theoretical concerns and is easily researchable. It involves issues relating to purposes, methods, styles, and strategies of research.

- Is it useful to see research sources and methods as involving a fundamental contrast between the quantitative and the qualitative?

- Triangulation is a fundamental feature of social research. It involves combining different methods so that the strengths of one complement the weaknesses of another.

Surveys, ethnography, and documents

Whatever research design is used, research will, if properly carried out, be a difficult but rewarding process. This is something you will discover if you undertake a project of your own. In the next three sections, we will illustrate some of the issues that arise in research practice by considering the three styles of research identified. We look first at survey research, then at ethnographic research, and finally at documentary research. You should remember, however, that these are often combined in particular studies (see Box 3.3).

Survey research

Most people nowadays are familiar with surveys. The person with the clipboard is almost a fixed feature in high

THEORY AND METHODS 3.3

Some important studies and their methods

Survey research

- Young and Willmott (1957)
- Goldthorpe *et al.* (1969)
- Townsend (1979)
- Wellings *et al.* (1994)

Ethnographic research

- Festinger *et al.* (1956)
- Humphreys (1970)
- Wallis (1976)
- Bourgois (2003)

Documentary research

- Durkheim (1897)
- Weber (1904–5)
- Glasgow University Media Group (1976)
- McRobbie (1991)

streets across the country. Thanks to opinion polls and market research, almost everyone is likely to have been stopped in the street or approached at home and asked if they can 'spare a few minutes to answer a few questions'. These surveys ask about such things as voting intentions, coffee preferences, purchases of washing powder, and television-viewing. Survey research in sociology has much in common with these commercial surveys and polls.

To survey something is to carry out a systematic overview in order to produce data for a comprehensive general report (see Box 3.4, p. 76). The term came into sociology from geography, where it refers to the mapping of the boundaries and landscape of an area. Early urban sociologists extended this idea to the study of social areas and promoted social surveys of living conditions in town and country. The term soon came to mean the systematic collection of standardized information

'Can you spare a few minutes to answer some questions?'
© Alice Chadwick

THEORY AND METHODS   3.4
....

Data

Data are the items of information produced through research. In survey research, the data are the answers given to particular questions by each individual. The word comes from the Latin for 'given'. It is a plural word (an individual item of information is a *datum*), and this means that you should only ever say 'The data show . . .', and not 'The data shows . . .'.

about a population through the use of comprehensive lists of questions. Although this kind of research had a much longer history, the idea of the social survey helped to fix it as a distinct style of sociological research.

Many social surveys are purely exploratory or descriptive. They collect information on such things as the extent of poverty, the level of divorce, experiences of crime, and so on. Of great importance in this kind of research is the collection of data on attitudes, rather than simply on behaviour. There have, for example, been many studies of attitudes towards political parties and their leaders, work and employment, churches and religious beliefs, and so on. Other surveys are explanatory, going beyond description to search for the factors that might account for attitudes and behaviour. This involves the more explicit incorporation of theoretical ideas into the design of the survey, and surveys often attempt to test which of two or more rival theories is better able to explain what is being studied.

The growth of survey research was closely linked to the development of new techniques of statistical sampling that allowed conclusions to be drawn about large populations from investigations of relatively small numbers of people. These techniques developed rapidly during the first three decades of the twentieth century. A little later, ways of asking questions were themselves given more precision, and survey practice became far more rigorous.

Many commercial surveys have been designed and carried out with great technical sophistication. Indeed, it is probably true to say that many sociological surveys have been unable to match this level of sophistication. The reason for this difference between commercial and sociological research is their funding. Commercial surveys are funded by television companies, newspapers, political parties, and business enterprises. Their resources are generally far in excess of those available for sociological research, which usually relies on public funding. Commercial surveys can hire and train large numbers of interviewers, they can question large numbers of people, and they can employ the staff needed to analyse the results.

There are, of course, exceptions to this generalization. There are large private-sector research organizations that carry out excellent sociological research, and there are a number of public-sector research organizations (in government departments and in universities) that have carried out sophisticated large-scale survey research. It is undoubtedly the case, however, that far more good-quality survey research could be undertaken by sociologists if improved levels of funding were available.

The common element in all social surveys is the asking of questions in a more or less formal and standardized way. Information is sought on a number of matters through asking the same questions to large numbers of people and then collating the answers in order to produce a general picture. The printed list of questions used in a survey is called a **questionnaire**; the person who responds to the questions is called the **respondent**. Surveys differ in terms of the kind of questionnaire used and the way that respondents are approached. Three types of social survey are in common use:

- The *interview survey*. This is a door-to-door or street-based survey where a trained interviewer asks questions and records the answers. A questionnaire used by an interviewer is often called a schedule.

- The *postal survey*. This involves sending a questionnaire through the post to chosen addresses. This is said to be a self-administered or self-completion questionnaire, as respondents write in the answers themselves. A variation on this that is sometimes used is the online survey, in which answers to questions are submitted electronically through a web page.

- The *telephone survey*. This is a more recent variation on the interview survey, the interview being carried out over the telephone, rather than face to face.

In the following sections, we will look at the two main ways in which social surveys, of whatever type, differ.

Asking questions and getting answers

The design of a questionnaire is not easy, though people often think it is. Deciding on the topics and themes to be covered can be quite straightforward, but converting these into precise and unambiguous questions that can be used to produce sociological data involves a number of steps. Unless a question is carefully worded, there will be scope for ambiguity and misunderstanding on the part of the respondents and the answers they give may be difficult to interpret. To deal with this problem, professional questionnaires go through a long and complicated process of drafting and evaluation of surveys before they are used in an actual survey. Even the small-scale questionnaires used in student project work need to be carefully worked out. An example of a badly designed survey is discussed in Box 3.5. The whole process of questionnaire design is shown in Figure 3.2 on p. 78.

THEORY AND METHODS 3.5

Marx and the social survey

In 1880 Karl Marx drew up a questionnaire that was to be distributed to readers of the *Revue Socialiste*, and to workers' societies, socialist societies, and anyone else who requested a copy. The purpose of the questionnaire was to explore the condition of the working class. Twenty-five thousand copies of the questionnaire were distributed, but very few replies were received. No results were ever published.

What do you think went wrong with Marx's research design? Would he have produced useful results if he had used a different sampling method? Why did he not do this?

The questionnaire contained 101 questions. Have a look at some of these, shown below, and see if you can identify any problems with the ways that they are worded. Which questions do you think might have worked?

1 What is your occupation?

3 State the number of persons employed in your workshop.

12 Is your work done by hand or with the aid of machinery?

13 Give details of the division of labour in your industry.

56 If you are paid piece rates, how are the rates fixed? If you are employed in an industry in which the work performed is measured by quality or weight, as is the case in the mines, does your employer or his representative resort to trickery in order to defraud you of a part of your earnings?

The initial stage, of course, is to decide on the specific topics to be investigated in the survey. These will often have been decided, in general terms, in the initial phases of research design, but it is important that they are clarified before any attempt is made to draw up specific questions. This is usually done by building a checklist of topics that can be broken down and combined until they form a reasonably coherent and manageable list. This list is usually kept as short as possible. A questionnaire takes time to complete, and if unnecessary topics are covered, there will be less time for the respondents to provide the more important information. This means, in practice, that information that is easily available elsewhere (for example, from other surveys or from published sources) should not usually be sought.

Once a brief and workable checklist of topics has been completed, it is possible to begin to turn these topics into specific questions. When all topics have been converted into questions, a questionnaire has been produced. The most important considerations are to make the wording of the various questions as clear as possible and to decide on the order in which they should be asked. We will look at these matters in some detail later in the section. In the initial phase of questionnaire design, the aim is to produce fairly good, workable questions, but not the final, polished questions that will actually be used in the survey. Many alterations will later need to be made to the questions, and detailed polishing of grammar and vocabulary would be a waste of time in the early phases.

The draft questions must go through a process of evaluation. In the first phase of questionnaire design this is often called a *pre-test*. This involves a general assessment of the questions by asking friends and colleagues to have a look at them and see if they can identify any obvious problems. Even experienced groups of professional survey researchers find it useful to get the opinions of professional colleagues. It is all too easy to miss problems in your own questions. Written comments on the questions, including suggestions for improvement, are usually obtained in the pre-test.

The draft questionnaire must be revised at the end of the pre-test to take account of the suggestions received. This involves reconsidering many of the same issues that arose in the first phase of question definition. In some cases, where the subject matter is complex or sensitive, this reconstruction may be quite substantial. Even if the outcome of the pre-test is positive and the draft questions all seem acceptable, it will be necessary to begin producing instructions for the interviewers or written instructions for the respondents. A questionnaire will, for example, need to have instructions added that tell the respondent 'Please tick the appropriate box' or 'Please go to question 8'.

Similarly, an interviewer needs written instructions about exactly how much more information to give the respondent when asking a question. An interviewer may, for example, need to probe further in relation to a respondent's answer by saying 'What exactly do you mean by . . . ?', 'Could you say a little more about . . . ?', or even just remaining silent until the respondent offers more information. If the questionnaire is to be standardized, it is essential that all interviewers respond in similar ways to each respondent. The written instructions are an attempt to ensure that this happens. Some questions may require that a number of *prompts* be given to the respondent. A list of possible answers may need to be read out to them in a particular order, or they may have to be shown to the respondent on prompt cards. All these matters need to be set down as a part of the questionnaire in order to ensure that each response is as standardized as possible.

Once the questionnaire has been reviewed, it must again be evaluated. In the second phase of questionnaire design this is often called a *test*. In a test there will be a trial of the full questionnaire under near-normal survey conditions. This may involve a small number of respondents similar to those who will eventually be approached in the full survey, but far less attention is usually given to the details of who is and who is not selected for interview. The test will seek comments on the questionnaire from interviewers and, very often, from respondents. These comments will, again, feed into the next revision of the questionnaire. In some

Figure 3.2 Questionnaire design

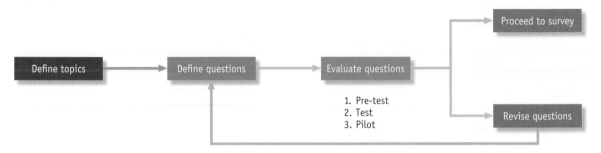

small surveys, a pre-test and test will be sufficient to resolve most problems and to allow the survey to proceed. With very large surveys, however, a third evaluation may be carried out in a *pilot* survey. This is, in effect, a full dress rehearsal for the actual survey, but using a much smaller sample. Following the test or pilot survey, the final version of the questionnaire will be produced, and, if interviewers are to be used, they can be trained to carry it out.

In practice, of course, questionnaire design is rarely as clear-cut as this discussion implies. The distinction between a test and a pilot survey, as we have noted, is not always drawn, and some poorly thought-out surveys may dispense with formal testing altogether. In good surveys, however, proper testing of the questionnaire will be of great importance, and full attention will be given to all the issues discussed, even if some of the stages are compressed into one another. Similarly, it must not be assumed that there will be a neat arrangement of the various phases over time. Training of interviewers, for example, begins at an early stage in the planning of the survey. In some surveys that use people who have not previously worked as interviewers on sociological projects, the test and pilot surveys may be used as means of training. Similarly, the writing of instructions for interviewers and respondents will be undertaken in parallel with the defining of the questions.

We have, so far, talked about the drafting and redrafting of questions in very general terms. It is now necessary to look at this in a little more detail. The most important consideration is to make the individual questions as short, clear, and unambiguous as possible. It is important, for example, that the terms used in questions should be meaningful to the respondents. Questions that ask 'Have you ever experienced anomie?' or 'Do you occupy a contradictory class location?' are unlikely to get meaningful answers from respondents, unless they happen to be sociology graduates. Similarly, questions that ask about eligibility rules for social-security entitlements will be misunderstood by all except the most knowledgeable respondents.

Even if obscure and technical terms are avoided, the actual wording of the questions may be ambiguous. A question that asks 'How often have you been to the cinema?'

is not likely to produce useful information as it does not make it clear what is meant by 'often' and what time period is to be considered. It is far more useful to ask 'How often have you visited the cinema to see a film in the last year?' and then to offer a choice of, say, 'once a month', 'once every two months', 'once every three months', 'less than once every three months', and 'not at all'.

This example also illustrates the difference between 'open-ended' and 'fixed-choice' questions. In a fixed-choice question, the respondent must choose one of the alternative answers provided on the questionnaire. This has the advantage that the results of the survey can easily be totalled up. Where the respondents are allowed to reply in their own words, they have more flexibility about how they answer. In these circumstances, however, the researcher may find it more difficult to quantify the results.

One of the most important considerations in wording a question is to avoid what have been called leading questions. These are questions that lead the respondent to a particular kind of response because of the way in which they have been worded. An example of a leading question is 'Why do you think Barak Obama makes a good president?' This question makes it difficult for people to reply that they do not think that he is a good president. They may simply follow the lead of the interviewer and give a reason, particularly if they are offered a fixed number of choices.

The things to consider when drawing up topics and forming them into questions are numerous, and many complex issues arise. The most useful discussions of these can be found in Moser and Kalton (1979), A. N. Oppenheim (1966), and de Vaus (1991). From these and other sources we have constructed a checklist of major issues. There are ten key points to remember when constructing a questionnaire (see Box 3.6).

The first is to make the task as easy as possible for the respondent. The questions on a questionnaire must always be kept as easy and as straightforward as possible, but it is sometimes necessary to include complex questions or even questions that may appear threatening or upsetting. Many people, for example, do not like to tell strangers details about their income, and most people would feel uneasy

THEORY AND METHODS   3.6

A checklist for questionnaire construction: ten key points

1 *Easy*: start with straightforward and non-threatening questions.
2 *Writing*: put questions that require a lot of writing towards the end.
3 *Funnel*: questions should move from the more general to the more specific.
4 *Biography*: use the respondent's own biography to organize the questions.
5 *Transition*: when switching topics, make this as smooth as possible.
6 *Variety*: try to include a wide range of question types.
7 *Short*: keep the questionnaire as brief as possible.
8 *Attractive*: make the questionnaire as neat and well designed as possible.
9 *Code*: classify responses in advance, wherever possible.
10 *Confidentiality*: offer and maintain promises of confidentiality and anonymity wherever appropriate.

answering questions about their involvement in criminal activities. For this reason, it is generally a good idea to begin the questionnaire with the relatively easy and non-threatening questions that respondents will be happiest to answer. If a questionnaire begins with difficult and threatening questions, respondents are less likely to cooperate or to complete it.

For the same reason, it is always a good idea to have lengthy questions that require a lot of writing towards the end of the questionnaire. If a respondent must, from the beginning, write long responses on the questionnaire, she or he is far less likely to complete the task. Where an interviewer is asking the questions, the amount of writing should, in any case, be kept to an absolute minimum. If the interviewer has to write down a great deal, mistakes may occur and the respondent is left to sit idly while the interviewer writes.

Funnelling is a useful principle in questionnaire design. It involves starting out with the more general questions on a topic and gradually making them more specific. If the amount of detail required at the beginning of a questionnaire is too great, the cooperation of the respondents is put under great strain. Respondents are more likely to give the details required if they have been led to them by more general questions.

Using the respondent's biography to organize questions is something that, where it can be done, gives a logic and coherence to a questionnaire. If the purpose of a questionnaire is to explore work careers, then it will usually be sensible to begin with questions about the first job and then to follow through any job changes in sequence. Similarly, it is

sensible to put any questions about education before those on work. Using this kind of chronological or biographical framework makes it far easier for people to organize their responses and makes it less likely that they will forget important events and information.

The first four of our key points suggest that, in general, a questionnaire should begin with easy, brief, and general questions and move gradually towards more difficult, lengthy, and specific questions. If appropriate, it should also have a biographical structure. For short questionnaires, these principles can usually be applied quite consistently. In larger questionnaires, however, a number of separate topics may be covered and a more modular approach will be needed. If a questionnaire covers, for example, both work career and political activities, then these would usually be treated as separate sections or modules of the questionnaire. Each module might be structured in terms of the principles that we have discussed, but the overall structure of the questionnaire will be more complex.

Our next key point concerns the transition from one part of a questionnaire to another. Where there are two or more sections, the transition from one to another must be as smooth as possible. It is important to avoid a sudden switch of topic that leaves the respondent confused. When changing topic, the interviewer might say something like 'I would now like to ask you a few questions about . . .'. In a postal questionnaire, such phrases can be printed before each batch of questions begins.

The next three key points in questionnaire construction relate rather more to the appearance and feel of the questionnaire than to its content. While the subject matter or purpose of a survey may often help to ensure that respondents cooperate, this is not always the case. A subject that is of great interest to the researcher may appear unimportant or baffling to the respondent. In these circumstances, the actual appearance of the questionnaire or the manner of its implementation may be critical.

Having a variety of question formats will help to retain the interest of respondents and prevent them from getting too bored. A mixture of open-ended and fixed-choice questions, for example, prevents the responses from becoming too mechanical. If the questionnaire is kept as short as possible, this will also help to retain the cooperation of the respondent. Survey researchers need to remember that respondents are giving up their time, and it is important that this is kept to a minimum. In postal surveys an attractively presented questionnaire can help to ensure that people complete it, especially if it is quite long. A questionnaire that is simply a dense list of single-spaced questions is unlikely to show a good response. Major surveys employ professional designers and specialist software packages to produce neat and attractive questions.

The coding of a questionnaire—the ninth key point on the checklist—is something of particular relevance to the person analysing the results. Coding is the process through which individual responses are converted into categories and classifications for use in the research. Sex, for example, may be coded as 'female' or 'male', and occupations may be coded into one of a set of class categories. In order to process the data more effectively, by computer, these categories are given numbers. This may be 1 for female and 2 for male, or classes numbered from 1 to 7. These numbers are generally quite arbitrary and are used simply as labels that a computer can handle more easily. Coding is often used in studies of attitudes (see Box 3.7).

Where fixed-choice questions are used, it is very easy to *pre-code* the responses by printing the numbers beneath them or down the side of the questionnaire. Similarly, the scale points used in attitude scaling can be used as codes. Wherever pre-coding is possible, it can save a great deal of time. If pre-coding is not possible, as in the case of open-ended questions, the researcher must look at a selection of responses after the survey has been completed and try to distinguish different types of answer. Only then is it possible to use these as codes to be applied to all completed questionnaires. The advantages and disadvantages of questionnaires are summarized in Box 3.8.

The final key point on our checklist relates to matters that we will discuss more fully in 'The ethics of social research', pp. 103–5. In order to gain the cooperation of respondents, it will often be necessary to guarantee the privacy of their responses. They must feel that no one except those on the research team will read the questionnaires. This guarantee is usually given in a covering letter sent with the postal questionnaire or verbally by the interviewer, right at the beginning of the interview. It should go without saying, of course, that a researcher should give only those guarantees that can actually be kept. If the questionnaires are to be stored in an archive or made available to other researchers, full confidentiality may not be possible. A related issue concerns the privacy of the interview itself. If a person is interviewed in the presence of other people who can overhear what is said, this may affect her or his willingness to be completely open in answering the questions.

Ethnographic research

Ethnography simply means 'writing about people', but it has come to be used in a more specific sense to describe forms of research that try to get close to how people actually feel and experience social life. Ethnographic methods aim to understand the meanings people give to their actions. They often involve research in which the researcher actually participates in some way in the situation being studied. This kind of research may involve observing what people are doing, engaging them in conversations and

THEORY AND METHODS 3.7

Attitude scaling

Many surveys ask people for their attitudes and opinions. You will find that these kinds of questions tend to have a particular format. Surveys sometimes ask attitude questions in a normal question format: 'Do you agree with the view that the monarchy is out of touch with ordinary people?' More typically, however, they involve an attempt to measure—or *scale*—the strength of an attitude.

The most common way of doing this uses a so-called *Likert scale*, named after its originator. People are given a phrase and are asked to circle a number from 1 to 5, labelled to show the strength and direction of their attitude. For example:

Some people say that the unemployed should help themselves and not be dependent on welfare benefits. Do you

1	2	3	4	5
strongly agree	agree	neither agree nor disagree	disagree	strongly disagree?

If items are labelled consistently across questions, it is possible to add up scores and get an assessment of the overall strength of a person's attitudes on a particular set of issues.

This method is similar to the way that magazine quizzes claim to measure such things as 'How sexy are you?' from scored responses to questions. This was not exactly what Likert intended the method to be used for.

informal interviews, or some mixture of the two. This is easiest in small-scale, face-to-face settings, though ethnographies of large organizations and communities have been carried out.

Ethnographic participation may be overt or covert. **Overt research** occurs when researchers are open about the fact that research is being undertaken and that they are trying to collect information. **Covert research**, on the other hand, involves keeping the research secret and trying to appear to others as just ordinary participants.

Some see ethnography as including only participant observation and informal conversations, but this is rather restrictive. Long, informal interviews, for example, have played an important part in ethnographic studies. While these have some similarities with the questionnaire-based interviews of the survey method, they have far more in common with participant observation. This kind of interviewing has often been combined with observation and the use of personal documents. The advantage of this rather broader view of ethnography is that it highlights its most distinctive feature: to explore the *qualitative* and more intimate aspects of social life. While survey research is not exclusively *quantitative*, it is far more suited to the production of quantitative data.

Controversy and debate Advantages and disadvantages of using questionnaires 3.8

Advantages

- Information is standardized and can be easily processed. This is especially useful for quantitative data.
- It is possible to collect information on a large number of people and so allow more valid generalizations to be made.
- Reliability is high: all respondents answer exactly the same questions in near-identical situations. Differences in response can be assumed to reflect real differences among the respondents.
- Postal questionnaires are often the easiest and most efficient way of reaching large numbers of people.
- Postal questionnaires give great anonymity to respondents, encouraging honesty and openness.

Disadvantages

- Respondents may misrepresent or distort their views.
- Respondents may not remember relevant information.
- Large surveys can be very costly.
- Interviewers may antagonize respondents or cause biased responses if they are not properly trained.
- People may refuse to be interviewed or to complete a postal questionnaire, creating a non-response problem.
- Postal questionnaires may not be completed by the person they are addressed to, and they may not be taken seriously.

Ethnographic methods were developed in the field-work techniques of the structural-functionalist anthropologists discussed in Chapter 2. Anthropologists such as Malinowski lived among the peoples they studied, learning their language and trying to understand their culture. This research was, out of necessity, overt research, as there was no way in which a white anthropologist could simply pass as a member of the black societies being studied. The purposes of the research were not, of course, fully disclosed to the subjects, who had little or no conception of what research was and probably identified the anthropologist with the colonial authorities.

Similar techniques were developed in the work of the Chicago sociologists, though these involved far more covert research. This is easier when the subjects of the research are ethnically similar to the researcher. The research carried out in Chicago combined observation and conversation with more systematic interviewing and the collection of personal data. In such classic studies as those of the hobo (N. Anderson 1923), the gang (Thrasher 1927), and the jack roller (Shaw 1930), powerful techniques of ethnographic investigation were developed.

> **➲ *Connections***
>
> We briefly discuss the background to the Chicago school of sociology in Chapter 2, pp. 48–50, and you might find it useful to look at that now. Goffman's work is an important example of ethnographic research that draws on this tradition. You will find a discussion of the use of life-history interviews by the Chicago sociologists in Chapter 7, p. 238, where we look at Sutherland's work on the professional thief.

Making observations

Observation is, of course, one of the principal ways in which sociologists can collect their data. In many everyday situations, we can watch people and see what they do; we can listen to what they say and see who they speak to. However, sociological observation involves more than this. It is necessary to decide when and where to observe, how to ensure observation of exactly those things that are of interest, and how to make sociological use of the observations. The ways in which these issues are handled depend upon the particular research role taken. Sociological observers have typically chosen one of three research roles:

- the complete participant;
- the participant-as-observer;
- the complete observer (Schwartz and Schwartz 1955; Gold 1958).

In the role of the *complete participant*, observers take a highly active and involved stance towards those being observed. They aim to become a member of a group or to enter an organization in order to appear to others as an ordinary participant. The researcher may, for example, take employment in a factory or hospital in order to observe fellow workers. Researchers have increasingly taken advantage of the Internet to engage in 'cyber ethnography'—for example, by joining chat rooms or discussion groups in order to study other participants. Research as a complete participant is covert, as those being studied do not know that they are being observed for research purposes. This role has often been adopted in social research. In his study of a secretive religious group, Wallis (1976) joined in its

Ethnographic researchers can sometimes find it difficult to be unobtrusive: Edward Evans-Pritchard and the Azande.
© Pitt Rivers Museum

activities as if he were an ordinary recruit. Another example is a study of homosexual activities in toilets, where Humphreys (1970) got to know the men and acted as a voyeur and look-out. Through participation, a researcher can observe people in many off-guard situations that would not really be open to an outsider. Where entry to the group or organization is possible, this kind of research can be highly effective and allows the sociologist to understand activities from the standpoint of the actors concerned.

A major practical difficulty in complete participant observation is that it is difficult to ask questions or raise issues that would make it obvious that the researcher is not merely a participant. The researcher must always act in role and cannot step outside it. This may lead to such involvement in the life of the group or organization that it is impossible to maintain the distance required by the research. A particular problem is the difficulty of recording observations. A complete participant may observe a great deal, but may not have the opportunity to write this down without arousing suspicion. In their study of a religious group, Festinger and his colleagues (1956) found that they had to make frequent trips to the lavatory in order to write up their field notes in secret. If this kind of subterfuge is not possible, observations will have to be written down many hours, and perhaps days, later, making errors and omissions very likely.

When studying some online communities, it may be possible to participate in the community electronically. The ethnographer may join a group or discussion forum and participate in its deliberations, using his or her own contributions to elicit comments from other members. This approach avoids many of the problems of maintaining cover that exist in face-to-face situations, but it has its own problems. The researcher in an online discussion has far less evidence available on which to judge the authenticity and representativeness of the other participants, especially where pseudonyms or avatars are used to hide personal identities.

The role of the *participant-as-observer* resolves some of these problems. In this role, the researcher's purposes are overt and the actors know that research is being undertaken. This gives a researcher access to the situation to be studied, but it also allows questions to be asked and notes to be made. Research by Hargreaves (1967) and Lacey (1970) on schools used this method, as does much anthropological fieldwork. The main disadvantage of this research role is that it may be more difficult to gain entry to a group when its members know that they are going to be observed.

Even if access is gained, people may be more guarded in what they say and do in the presence of the researcher.

The third observation role is that of the *complete observer*, who engages in no interaction with those being studied. The thinking behind this is that any involvement through participation will affect the very situation being studied. The participant observer cannot help but affect what is happening. By avoiding any interaction, the complete observer hopes to avoid any influence on what is being observed. R. King (1978), in his study of classroom behaviour, adopted this role. He sat at the back of a classroom and refused to be involved in any way, even if spoken to.

It can be argued, of course, that the very presence of an observer—particularly an impassive and mute observer—will have just as much influence on people's actions as a participant-as-observer. In a famous set of experiments carried out at the Hawthorne electrical works in Chicago, researchers observed the behaviour of workers who were wiring electrical components (Roethlisberger and Dickson 1939). It was found that the mere presence of an observer affected the productivity of the workers. This effect of the observer on the observed has, since then, been called the *Hawthorne effect*.

> **⟳ Connections**
> You will find a discussion of the Hawthorne researches in Chapter 14, pp. 539–40.

The only way in which the complete observer can truly avoid having any influence is by staying out of sight and becoming a covert observer. This is very difficult to arrange in real-life situations. The nearest approximations are the observations made by Bales (1950) of small-group behaviour. By using a one-way mirror, Bales was able to observe without being observed, albeit in a rather artificial laboratory setting.

The influence of the observer on the observed is a critical matter in ethnographic research (see Box 3.9, p. 84). Survey interviewers can also influence the responses of their respondents if they do not behave in a standardized way, and there is some evidence that female interviewers generally achieve a better rapport, and therefore better results, than do male interviewers. The possibility of such influence in participant observation, however, is far greater. It is clear, of course, that women would make more obtrusive observers than men in a study of male gang delinquency. Women are likely to find it especially hard to gain any kind of access to such a gang and could certainly not undertake covert research as a gang member. However, things are not always this clear-cut. Warren and Rasmussen (1977) report that in an observation study of

Unobtrusive observation.

© Alice Chadwick

a nude beach in California a male researcher experienced difficulties studying men, while a female researcher had difficulties with women. Warren, the female researcher, also found that she had certain advantages when studying gay men. Similarly, C. Alexander (1996) has claimed that her study of black male youths was enhanced by the fact that she was a young woman and by the fact that she, too, was from an ethnic minority.

Using conversations

Conversation is an essential part of ethnographic research. Even when a researcher adopts the role of the complete observer, he or she is able to hear the conversations of others. The participant observer is able to engage people in a dialogue to ask questions that will help in understanding how they see their world and the meanings they give to their actions. This can be taken further if the ethnographer can interview the subjects. Collecting natural conversations as they occur and continuing conversations in the form of interviews are fundamental forms of data collection in social research.

Systematic collections of natural conversations can uncover the accounts people produce to explain and justify their actions. Conversations are fundamental to the building of a sense of social order, as it is through their talk that people persuade each other of the reality of their social world. Many sociologists have investigated this, using techniques of **conversation analysis**. This involves examining the structure of natural conversations in order to investigate such things as the rules and procedures used in turn-taking, interrupting, and accounting for actions (Sacks 1965–72).

Interviews involve a more deliberate use of conversation. Beatrice and Sidney Webb described the interview as 'conversation with a purpose' (Webb and Webb 1932). They were referring to what are now called **semi-structured interviews**, and not to the more formal, questionnaire-based interviews that we looked at in the section on 'Survey research'. This has, typically, involved face-to-face interviewing, but the growth of the Internet has made it possible to interview people by e-mail in a form of cyber ethnography. In a cyber ethnography, online methods are used to investigate actual or online communities. Ward

---

THEORY AND METHODS 3.9

The observer and the observed

We have suggested that the personal characteristics of researchers can influence their ability to carry out the research. Try to think how the gender of the researcher might affect each of the following participant observation projects:

- a study of a male street-corner gang;

- a study of domestic work in a convent;

- a study of classroom interaction in a mixed-sex secondary school.

❓ How might the age, class, and ethnicity of the researcher have an effect in each of these projects?

(1999*a*, *b*), for example, used interactive websites to study two online feminist communities.

In a semi-structured interview, face-to-face or virtual, the interviewer has a checklist of topics and questions to be explored, but the way in which they are approached and the order in which they are asked depends on the flow of the conversation with each individual. The interviewer can, therefore, take conversational opportunities as they arise in order to explore matters more fully or to pursue relevant issues not explicitly covered in the checklist.

This does not mean that the interviewer simply responds to the lines along which the subject takes the conversation. An effective interviewer must steer the conversation in those directions most relevant to the research. This requires great conversational skills. The interviewer must know when to keep silent, when to nod or smile, when to intervene, and even when to argue with the interviewee. The aim is always to establish the kind of rapport that will allow the research to be carried out as effectively and as efficiently as possible. Such rapport may be far more difficult to achieve in an e-mail or other cyber interview, as the normal visual cues of conversation are not available to the interviewer.

Research may often be carried out on subjects with whom the interviewer has little personal sympathy, but personal feelings must not be allowed to interfere with the research process. A sociologist who interviews rapists or serial killers must establish the same kind of rapport and shared understanding as the sociologist who interviews nuns or nurses. This does not mean that their behaviour must be condoned or given implicit approval. Researchers must, however, put their personal feelings to one side and concentrate on trying to understand the way their subjects actually see the world. Difficult as this may be, an understanding of why people engage in serial killing may do more to help reduce the murder rate than any amount of moral condemnation.

On the other hand, interviewers must avoid too close an identification with their subjects. Some research concerns intimate and highly personal matters that are of great significance to the subject, and a sympathetic and encouraging researcher runs the risk of becoming, in effect, a therapist. Most sociologists are not trained for this role. Furthermore, the overly sympathetic interviewer, like the observer who identifies with the observed, is unlikely to achieve the detachment necessary for effective research.

Topics covered in a semi-structured interview can range across all the areas covered in surveys. They are generally used, however, to get more detailed, in-depth information. This may concern attitudes and values or the knowledge that people have. A particularly common format is for the interview to follow a biographical pattern, building up a person's **life history** in so far as it is relevant to the research. The aim of such an interview is to uncover the development of a person's values and knowledge and to explore the causative influences on them, in so far as they are perceived and interpreted by the subject him- or herself. In some cases, particular individuals have been taken as exemplary illustrations of specific social types and whole projects have been organized around them. Classic examples of this are the famous Chicago studies of a juvenile delinquent (Shaw 1930) and a professional thief (Sutherland 1937).

Another important style of interviewing is the **oral history** interview, in which the aim is to uncover people's knowledge about the events through which they have lived and to construct a picture of their shared memories of the past (P. Thompson 1978). In some cases, this type of research involves an attempt to recapture the past from contemporary memories, while in other cases the focus is on the memories themselves. In the latter case, researchers are interested in the ways in which memories—real or false—become myths that justify and legitimate actions in the present.

The use of **focus groups** has become an important feature of ethnographic research in recent years. A focus group is a group of people brought together by the researcher to be interviewed as a group. The advantage of this technique is that it allows a more open and free-ranging discussion, with the various individuals challenging or agreeing with each other and so providing insights into the strength of opinions and the processes through which judgements are made. A focus group usually comprises at least four individuals, chosen by the researcher in order to highlight the ways in which individuals discuss matters as members of a group. The researcher must become a moderator or facilitator of group discussion, rather than simply asking a sequence of questions. It is central to the sociological perspective that people's views are influenced by the groups of which they are members, and the focus group method is a means through which this can be directly explored. Focus groups are, however, artificial groups—they have been created by the researcher for the purposes of the research—and it is important to be aware that people may not behave in precisely the same ways that they may in the real social groups of which they are members. People may feel they are 'on show' in a focus group and must put on a convincing display of their opinions and arguments. In everyday life they may be far less reflective and may not be forced to consider the alternatives raised in the focus-group discussion. The technique does, however, allow researchers to gauge how people come to form opinions and how they respond to challenges from others.

Observational and conversational data are often supplemented by data from personal documents. We will consider the whole question of documentary research on pp. 86–90, but these particular types of document are so widely used in ethnographic research that they need to be mentioned here. Personal documents include such things as letters and diaries produced by people in their everyday lives, but that may be made available to researchers. A classic study by Thomas and Znaniecki (1918–19) used letters written by Polish migrants to supplement life-history data obtained from interviews. (See Plummer 2001 for a discussion of this use of personal documents.)

The most important use of documents in ethnographic research, however, is where a document is produced explicitly for the researcher. An ethnographer may, for example, ask people to write accounts of their life or to keep a diary for a particular period. In these cases, the researcher does not rely on existing documents but gives detailed and explicit instructions to subjects about how they are to write them. Such diaries will often have to be kept in special booklets, issued by the researcher, so as to ensure a degree of standardization. This kind of diary can be considered as, in effect, a series of open-ended questions that are to be used in an observational or interview study. These documents can provide important information for the researcher and may later be used as the basis of an interview (Burgess 1984: ch: 6). The Mass Observation organization collected a lot of data of this kind in the 1930s and 1940s (Broad and Fleming 1981; Mass Observation 1943; Cross 1990).

In survey research the interviewer can record responses on the questionnaire for later analysis. In ethnographic research, observations and conversations have to be recorded in less formal ways. It may sometimes be possible to use pen and paper to note down what is said, but this is a very slow process, and it is difficult to produce complete, verbatim reports on what is said. It is crucial that interview notes remain as close to the actual words of the subject as possible. It is generally much easier to use a tape recorder, though some subjects may object to this or may be inhibited by it. Where conversations are tape-recorded, they must later be transcribed, converting them into a written text. This is a lengthy and time-consuming process, but can be a useful way of consolidating the information collected.

Transcriptions can be analysed in the same way as any other text. They may often be used alongside written records of observations and, perhaps, with diaries and other personal documents produced by the subjects. Some textual analysis can be automated through specialized software packages that allow text to be indexed, sorted, and retrieved. There is, however, no substitute for reading and rereading ethnographic field notes. Only in this way can the researcher gain the level of familiarity needed for a proper interpretation of the data.

Ethnographic researchers must ensure that the situation and people chosen for study are appropriate for the purposes for which the research was designed (Burgess 1984). Sampling is an issue for ethnographers as well as survey researchers. In many cases, a representative group may be sought. A researcher studying teacher behaviour in classrooms, for example, might wish to investigate representative teachers in representative schools, so that the research has something to say about the educational system as a whole. In other situations, however, the researcher may deliberately search out places of research that are unrepresentative. A study of industrial change, for example, might choose to look at workers in workplaces that are at the forefront of technical advance. These are situations that may be untypical now, but are expected to be representative of work in the future.

Techniques of sampling in ethnography are not so straightforward and well defined as those used in survey research. Most ethnography might be said to use methods of non-probability sampling. Much of this kind of research relies on purposive or snowball sampling, and most studies make only impressionistic judgements about the appropriateness of the sample (see, e.g., Becker 1953; Polsby 1969). Margaret Mead (1953) noted that the representativeness of an ethnographic sample depends not simply on the number of subjects but on whether the human properties of the subjects are representative of the wider social category with which the research is concerned. Thus, the life history of a professional thief may be treated as representative of professional thieves in general.

In some cases, of course, probability sampling may be possible, especially where interviews are carried out. A random sample of individuals for interview can be drawn in exactly the same way as in survey research, with the individuals being given semi-structured interviews rather than questionnaire-based interviews. The length of a typical semi-structured interview, however, means that the total sample size will usually need to be much smaller than in a survey.

Documentary research

The third type of research that we have distinguished is documentary research, where the sources of data are published and unpublished documents. A **document**, in its broadest sense, is an object that contains a text. A handwritten or printed text on paper, such as a letter or a government report, is the clearest example of a document, but there are many others. A text can be inscribed on clay, stone, parchment, film, or a liquid crystal display, and it can be produced with a pen, a pencil, a chisel, a printing machine, or a computer. Documents that can be used by sociologists include newspapers, diaries, stamps, directories, handbills, maps, photographs, paintings, gravestones, television broadcasts, and computer files.

Documents are often seen as the particular concern of the historian, but they have a wide relevance across the social sciences. The three leading sociologists of the formative period made far greater use of documentary sources than any other research method. Marx's *Capital* (1867) relied on his heavy use of official publications produced by the factory inspectors and other government agencies. Max Weber's *Protestant Ethic and the Spirit of Capitalism* (1904–5) used religious tracts and pamphlets to explore seventeenth- and eighteenth-century beliefs and practices. Durkheim's *Suicide* (1897), perhaps the best known of all sociological studies, drew on a variety of official statistics on rates of suicide in European countries.

Classifying documents

The range of documents is immense, and it is important to have some understanding of the types of document that can be used in research. Documents differ in terms of their *origin*s and the conditions under which researchers can have *access* to them. An important distinction is that between the personal and the official. Personal documents, as we showed in the section on 'Ethnographic research', originate in households, being produced mainly for domestic purposes. Official or public documents, on the other hand, are produced in administrative situations. Some are produced in state bureaucracies and others in private bureaucracies, such as business enterprises and churches.

The issue of access concerns whether documents are made available to people other than their authors. Access ranges from completely closed access, where documents are available only to a very limited group of people, to completely open access through publication. Between these two extremes of closed and open access are the restricted documents available quite widely, but under tight and limited conditions.

Figure 3.3 classifies documents by origins and access to produce a typology of twelve different kinds. Closed personal documents (type 1) include letters, diaries, household account books, and other domestic items. These are normally available only to the individuals who own them or to their immediate households. Sometimes they may become available more widely through storage in public records offices (type 3) or through publication (type 4). Diaries, for example, are normally closed documents, although they are often produced with the intention that they should eventually be made available to a wider readership. This is the case with the diaries of many politicians. The records of many landed and wealthy families originate in the personal sphere, but may be deposited in public archives and so become more easily accessible to researchers. Many personal documents remain in private hands and can be seen only if their owners give specific permission (type 2).

Official documents are produced by businesses, schools, hospitals, churches, and other private-sector organizations. Confidential organizational documents (type 5) include medical records, school records, and company personnel files. These can usually be seen only by those who have an administrative or professional responsibility within the organization. Documents of type 6 include share registers and lists of borrowers held by businesses and made available only to specified researchers when they are no longer of any current relevance to the business. Some of these, however, are periodically deposited in public archives, becoming documents of type 7. Share registers of companies in England and Wales, for example, have to be sent to the Companies Registration Office, where there is public access to them. Documents of type 8 include timetables, directories, newspapers, and the various other products of the mass media.

Official documents of local and national governments are, probably, the single biggest type of document available to social researchers. Those subject to closed access (type 9) include criminal records and security reports, local-authority housing records, and current taxation records. Many of these are covered by official secrecy laws that prevent unauthorized disclosure of them to people outside the department responsible for them. Some secret documents remain closed permanently, but some are made available on restricted access (type 10), while others are eventually made available in public archives (type 11). State documents are often put into public archives only when they are no longer seen as confidential or sensitive. For example, Cabinet papers are made available for consultation after 30 years and census returns after about 100 years. Many state documents are produced explicitly for publication (type 12). This includes Acts of Parliament, Reports of Royal Commissions, statistical reports, and research reports. These state publications are among the most important sources of information for sociological research (see Box 3.10, p. 88).

Using documents

It might seem as if documents are very straightforward sources of data: they can be read and the data simply extracted. However, many texts are extremely difficult to understand. It is also necessary to consider many of the same issues of sampling and representativeness that we looked at when considering survey and ethnographic

Figure 3.3 Types of document

Access	Origins		
	Personal	Official	
		Private	State
Closed	1	5	9
Restricted	2	6	10
Open archival	3	7	11
Open published	4	8	12

THEORY AND METHODS   **3.10**

Official statistics

The statistics produced by governments are one of the most important sources of data available to sociologists. They cover population, crime, health, employment, and a whole range of other issues. You will find a full discussion of them in 'Using official statistics', pp. 99–100. You might want to look at that discussion when you have finished this section. Try to apply the criteria of authenticity, credibility, representativeness, and meaning while you read what we say about crime and other statistics.

➲ To get some idea of the kinds of statistics produced in Britain, look at a recent issue of *Social Trends*.

research. It has been suggested (J. Scott 1990) that, if a document is to be used in sociology, it must be assessed in terms of four criteria:

- *authenticity*: is it genuine?
- *credibility*: is it true?
- *representativeness*: is it typical?
- *meaning*: is it comprehensible?

The question of *authenticity* concerns the soundness and authorship of documents. A sound document is an original or a reliable copy, and a first step in assessing a document must be to find out whether it is an original or a copy. The process of copying, whether by handwriting, typing, filming, or photocopying, can result in missing or unreadable text. Even originals can be incomplete if they have deteriorated over the years. An 'unsound' document is one that is not close enough to its original form because it has been corrupted in some way. Researchers must try to reconstruct sound versions of their documents by trying to discover what is missing. The more corrupted a document has become, the more difficult this will be. In extreme cases, it may not be possible to reconstruct a sound version at all, and adequate research may be impossible.

A genuine document is not only sound, but also of known authorship. Even when authorship seems straightforward, the possibility of forgery or fraud must be considered. It is important to know, for example, whether diaries attributed to particular individuals were actually written by them. In many cases the authorship of a document may not be clear. Official documents, even when issued in the name of a particular minister, are produced by a complex administrative apparatus. In the same way, books and newspapers are the products of a division of labour in which the work of named writers is processed and reprocessed by copy-editors, subeditors, and editors.

In these cases, it might be quite inappropriate to see a particular named individual as the author of a document.

Assessing the *credibility* of a document involves looking at its sincerity and accuracy. All documents are, to a greater or lesser extent, selective or distorted, as it is impossible to construct accounts independently of particular points of view. Nevertheless, they can be more or less credible as accounts, depending on whether an observer is sincere in the choice of a point of view from which to write and whether the account gives an accurate report from that starting point.

The sincerity of authors is related to their motives. Some people may be motivated to report on events with as much objectivity as possible. Others, however, may write to justify their own actions, to make propaganda, to deceive others, or for financial gain. The motivation is not always clear. Official documents may present themselves as factual information, but they may actually be attempts to persuade people towards a particular position or course of action. More obviously, newspapers are produced by journalists who are paid to write marketable material and who may be subject to political pressure from a proprietor.

➲ **Connections**
At this point you might like to consider some of the issues that we look at in Chapter 10, 'Communication and the Media'. Look, in particular, at 'Ownership and control', pp. 376–8, and 'The commercialization of the media', pp. 378–9.

Even when an author has acted sincerely, the credibility of a document is affected by its accuracy. The accuracy of a report depends on the conditions under which it was compiled and how close the author was to the events reported. Historians have generally preferred to use what they call primary sources (see Box 3.11). These are first-hand accounts of events, and it is felt that they minimize any loss of accuracy that is due to lapses of memory and inadequate records. However, even first-hand observers may have difficulties in recording their observations in such a way that they can be used to construct accurate reports. As we noted in connection with interviews and observations, it is generally very difficult to record what is seen and heard with complete accuracy. Shorthand was invented only in the seventeenth century, and tape recorders were not available until well into the twentieth century. Accuracy of recall is, therefore, a problem even with primary sources.

The *representativeness* of a document is determined by its survival and availability. We discuss the issue of sampling in the following section. A representative sample of relevant documents will not always be needed, but it is important to know whether the chosen documents are, in fact, representative. Most documents are produced some

Documenting
women's lives?

© Lucy Dawkins

time before they are used in research, and their users will need to know what proportion of the relevant documents have actually survived and whether they are all available for research purposes.

If documents are to survive, they must be stored in some way. This may simply involve dumping them in a cardboard box, as happens with many personal documents, or it may involve storage in a proper archive. Many public and private documents are destroyed soon after their production, while others are stored for a period and destroyed at a later date. Household receipts and many letters, for example, are often not retained at all. Because of the massive number of documents produced by modern bureaucratic organizations, it is impossible for them to retain more than a small portion. These official documents are stored while in current use and may then be 'weeded' for destruction before the remainder are transferred to an archive. In many private organizations, however, there is no archive and all non-current documents are destroyed.

Even when documents are stored, the number that survive may decrease over time through deterioration and decay or through periodic clear-outs. The introduction of computer technology has resolved some of the problems of paper storage, as large amounts of data can be stored on a single computer disk. However, computerized records are continually updated by overwriting existing files, which means that historical records may be lost. The survival of computerized records is further threatened by the rapid pace of change in software and hardware, which can make files unreadable.

THEORY AND METHODS 3.11

Primary and secondary sources

A distinction is often made between primary and secondary sources, though there is some confusion over this. For most historians, a primary source is a first-hand account produced by a participant. It involves little or no intervention by the historian. Diaries, autobiographies, letters, and many administrative documents are primary sources. Secondary sources, on the other hand, are those that have been produced by historians or others, using primary sources, and which are therefore second-hand accounts. When a historian relies on the work of other historians or commentators, instead of going to new primary sources, he or she is said to be using secondary sources.

Some sociologists have defined primary sources as consisting of data collected by researchers themselves, and secondary sources as comprising data that already exist. This means that the fieldwork data of a participant observer is correctly recognized as a primary source, but it is rather misleading to see letters and diaries as 'secondary' sources. This confusion seems to result from different concerns: historians are generally concerned with whether accounts are first-hand (participant) or second-hand; sociologists are more concerned with whether accounts are produced by a professional sociologist or by people in their everyday lives. Both points of view are important, but you may conclude that the attempt to see them in terms of a simple distinction between primary and secondary sources should be abandoned.

Not all documents that survive will be available for research purposes. Considerations of confidentiality and official secrecy limit access to state documents, and access to private documents may be even more difficult. State documents often enter the public sphere after a particular period of time has lapsed, this period ranging from 30 years to 150 years, but some documents may be permanently closed. Problems can be even greater in the private sphere. Researchers will often be refused access to household documents such as diaries and letters, for obvious reasons. Unless they are stored in family archives—which is unusual, except among very wealthy families—personal documents tend to be neither available nor catalogued.

The final consideration is the *meaning* of the documents that the researcher wishes to use. This involves both the literal meaning of the document and its interpretation. The literal meaning of a document is its surface or word-for-word meaning. To produce this, the researcher must be able to read the language in which it is written, know the accepted definitions of the words used, and be able to understand any dating systems or shorthand conventions. In the case of hand-written documents, of course, the handwriting must be legible if it is to be read at all.

Once a literal reading has been produced, the researcher can go on to the far more complex task of interpretation. This is achieved by grasping the underlying selective point of view from which the individual concepts in a text acquire their meaning. Methods of interpretation are considered more fully in other parts of this book (see especially 'Approaches to media research', Chapter 10, pp. 358–9). The two principal methods are quantitative **content analysis** and qualitative **textual analysis**. Content analysis involves counting the number of times that particular words or images appear, while textual analysis concentrates on grasping the qualitative significance of these words and images.

Selection and sampling

It is rarely possible to study all of the people or documents you are interested in. This means that you will have to rely on a small selection or 'sample' from those available. Sampling issues are usually mentioned only in relation to survey methods, but they are, in fact, applicable to all forms of research. Even where a small number of cases are investigated for qualitative purposes, the researcher must still give some consideration to whether these cases are typical or untypical. Some of the implications of this for documentary research have already been discussed.

Unless a very small social group is being surveyed, it is not usually possible to include a whole population in the study. There are practical limits to the number of people who can be observed, interviewed, telephoned, or sent postal questionnaires. It may be possible to interview a few thousand people, but it is simply not possible to interview all the hundreds of thousands who live in even a small city. The only large-scale studies that do aim to cover a whole population today are the national censuses. These are carried out in Britain just once every ten years and use a very short postal questionnaire. Even this limited task is possible only because the government employs large numbers of full-time and temporary staff to collect and process the data.

> **⊃ Connections**
> We discuss the development of the census and government surveys in Chapter 8, pp. 270–2. You may find it useful to return to this discussion of sampling after you have read that chapter.

In almost all research, then, it is necessary to use a **sample**. A sample is a selection drawn from the population being studied. The intention behind sampling is to draw a sample that will allow the researcher to generalize about the population as a whole. Sampling is a relatively recent innovation that resulted from mathematical advances made early in the twentieth century. However, you do not need to understand very much of the mathematics in order to understand the general principles of sampling.

Sampling rests on a particular branch of statistics called the theory of probability. Mathematical theories of probability concern the calculation of such things as the likelihood that a tossed coin will come up 'heads' or that you will win the national lottery. Sampling is possible when the probability that any sample will be *representative* of the population as a whole can be calculated. If the probability of drawing a representative sample is the same as the probability of winning the lottery (about one in fourteen million in the case of the British lottery), then sampling would not be a very good idea. Fortunately, there are ways of ensuring that the probability of a representative sample is quite high. There will always be a slight chance that the particular sample drawn will give inaccurate results, but it is possible to calculate the likelihood of this and to try to keep it as low as possible.

That is almost all that you need to know about the mathematics of probability theory. All the basic principles of sampling follow from these points. The basic principle is that getting a representative sample depends on whether it is possible to calculate the probabilities involved. When this is possible, the method of sampling is called **probability sampling** (see Box 3.12). When these kinds of calculation are not possible, other methods of sampling can be used, but these cannot be relied on to the same extent as a probability sample. They may produce perfectly valid results, but it is always difficult to know how confident we can be in them. We will try to explain these ideas a little further.

THEORY AND METHODS   3.12

Sampling

There are two types of sampling: probability sampling (where the mathematical properties of the population are known) and non-probability sampling (where these mathematical properties are unknown). The 'population' referred to is a technical term that refers to all the units of interest, not just the population of a country. The population may be a collection of organizations or countries, or any subgroup within a country. Statisticians sometimes refer to the population as the *universe*. The main types of sampling you will encounter are listed below. They are discussed briefly in the text.

Probability samples	Non-probability samples
• simple random	• convenience
• systematic random	• purposive
• stratified random	• snowball
• cluster	• quota
• multi-stage	

The basic form of probability sample is the *simple random* sample. In this, respondents or subjects are drawn at random from a complete list of all those in the population. Technically, the list is called a *sampling frame*, and it might be an electoral register, a telephone book, an attendance register, and so on. The basic requirement is that it must be a complete list, though few are perfectly complete. A telephone directory would be an acceptable sampling frame for a survey of telephone subscribers, but it would be little use for a survey of the poor (who tend not to have telephones). In many surveys today, the official postcode address file is used to generate samples of addresses.

The word 'random' does not mean haphazard, though many non-statisticians use it this way. A sample is drawn at random when every member of the population has an equal chance of being selected. This is the same principle involved in drawing a playing card from a well-shuffled deck: if the deck is complete (containing fifty-two cards) and has been properly shuffled, then every card has a one in fifty-two chance of being selected. Similarly, the selection of winning numbers in the lottery is a random process, as every numbered ball has the same chance of being drawn. Simple random samples are often drawn for sociological surveys by using printed tables of random numbers. These are generated by computer and are printed in books of statistical tables. If each person in the population is assigned a number, then the lists of random numbers allow the researcher to draw a simple random sample of people. Similar considerations apply in documentary research wherever there is a comprehensive list of the relevant documents to be studied. In research on women's magazines, for example, a simple random sample can be drawn by selecting random dates and using the copies of the magazines published on those dates.

A variation on simple random sampling occurs where it is not possible or is impractical to number people or to use random numbers. The so-called *systematic random* sample involves making *one* random choice of starting point in the list and then selecting occurrences on a systematic basis: say, every 10th, 50th, or 100th person. If the population contains 10,000 people, a sample of 100 could be drawn by choosing every 100th person on the list. It is crucial that the list itself should not be organized in any way relevant to the topic of the research. An alphabetical list, for example, would be useful for most purposes.

A more complex form of probability sample is the *stratified random* sample. This term is a little confusing, as it has nothing at all to do with the social stratification that we discuss in Chapter 19. In sampling theory, a stratum is simply a group or category that has particular characteristics in common. A population may be stratified into its male and female members, into age groups, or, of course, into social classes. Whatever criterion is used, a stratified random sample involves drawing separate random samples from each of the categories into which the population has been divided. The sampling method is usually devised so that the numbers in each category are reflected in the sample. For example, if there are equal numbers of men and women in the population, there should also be equal numbers in the sample. In some cases, however, extra numbers may be drawn from very small categories. This is most likely if the number that would otherwise appear in the sample is too small to allow any reliable conclusions to be drawn. In general, however, stratified random samples are used to ensure that the sample matches the population in all crucial respects.

In some studies, practical needs lead researchers to adapt these strict procedures. A sample of engineering workers, for example, might be drawn by making a random sample of engineering factories and then choosing all the workers in those factories. This would ensure that the sample is not too geographically dispersed, but it does involve a departure from strict probability principles. The technical term for such a method is *cluster* sampling. This form of sampling is particularly appropriate for ethnographic observation, where a researcher may, for example, make a random selection of organizations or departments and then undertake systematic participant observation of workers in each of the places selected. When this method of cluster sampling is further adapted (for example, by taking a random sample of workers in each factory), the sampling is said to be *multi-stage* sampling.

In many research situations, there is no obvious sampling frame that can be used or compiled. This means that it is not possible to draw random samples. In these circumstances, sociologists must resort to non-probability sampling. In these types of survey, the researcher tries to produce a representative sample but cannot be certain how representative it really is.

One of the most commonly used and, unfortunately, least useful non-probability sampling methods in smaller studies is to build a *convenience* sample. This involves building a sample almost by accident from those who are most conveniently to hand. Interviewing friends and neighbours or standing on a street corner and stopping passers-by are examples. Much ethnographic observation that relies on participant observation is, of necessity, of this type. The participant observer may have to take whatever opportunities there are to carry out the study and may have little chance of making an ideal selection. This method leaves the researcher open to all sorts of bias in the selection of respondents. It is, for example, all too easy to study only those people who look as if they might be helpful or cooperative, and there is no likelihood that they will be at all representative of the target population. This is, in general, a method to avoid, unless there is some way in which the representativeness of a sample can be assessed after the data have been collected. It may, for example, be possible to compare data collected with already known data about the population.

A great improvement is the adoption of *purposive* sampling. Here the researcher deliberately seeks out those who meet the needs of the project. An investigation into student attitudes may involve seeking out students in areas where they are known to live in large numbers. This kind of sampling is often associated with so-called *snowballing* techniques, in which those in an initial sample are asked to name others who might be willing to be approached. The full sample grows with each round of interviews or observations. This type of sampling has been used in studies of deviant or closed groups, where the names of members can be discovered only from those who might help in making contact.

Neither purposive nor snowball samples are useful in most large-scale surveys, and a method that tries to approximate to random sampling is most often used. This is the method of the *quota* sample. This is superficially similar to stratified random sampling, but it does not involve any statistically random procedures. In quota sampling the population is divided into categories that are known to be important and for which it is possible to get some basic information. A population might be divided by age and sex, for example, making it possible to construct a grid, as shown in Figure 3.4.

Using data from a census or a similar source, it is possible to work out how the whole population is distributed across the cells in the grid. In 2000, for example, males aged 16–29 comprised 9.2 per cent of the population of the

Figure 3.4 A grid for a quota sample

United Kingdom, while females aged 16–29 comprised 8.7 per cent. A researcher seeking a representative sample would try to ensure that 9.2 per cent of the sample were young men and 8.7 per cent were young women. If a sample of 5,000 was to be drawn, it would need to contain 460 young men and 435 young women. These target numbers are the quotas that need to be filled, and the total quota is divided up into separate quotas for each interviewer. In such a survey, interviewers are given strict instructions that they must stop people in the street or call at houses until they achieve their particular quota.

The method of quota sampling is very widely used in large-scale surveys, as it is an economical and efficient way of achieving a sample that matches the broad and known features of a population. The actual individuals chosen, however, are not randomly selected and so it is not strictly legitimate to apply certain statistical measures to the results.

The aim of any method of sampling is to achieve a representative sample. It may fail to achieve this for two reasons. First, the sample itself may not be drawn at random. This is termed *sampling bias*. Secondly, a random sample may differ, by chance, from a truly representative sample. This is termed *sampling error*. This distinction is very important. Sampling error declines as the size of a sample increases, but this is not true of sampling bias. No matter how large a sample may be, if it has not been drawn at random it may be biased. The advantage of using a probability sample is that, if properly random methods are used, bias can be ignored and its representativeness can accurately be measured by the sampling error alone. These calculations are quite complex, and are purely technical. As a general rule, it has been found that increases in sample size above about 2,500 have little effect on the sampling error, regardless of the size of the population. For this reason, even national population samples rarely need to go above this level.

Statistics defines the ideal qualities that a sample should possess. In practice, it is difficult to meet these criteria. In actual research projects, corners have to be cut and ad hoc adjustments need to be made if any research at all is to be possible. Statistical purism would make research impossible. For this reason, it is important to be suspicious whenever a great battery of statistical tests and measures is reported. In some cases these may be precise reports on surveys using probability sampling, but in many other cases they are, at best, a rough-and-ready guide to how much reliance can be placed on the data. Many large-scale quota surveys, for example, cite measures of sampling error that should not, strictly, be taken seriously.

> **⊋ Connections**
>
> The implications of measuring sampling error are considered in relation to opinion polls on voting intentions in Box 20.9, p. 812.

The basic problem with any sampling procedure is the problem of non-response. As we have shown, a sample has a **bias** if it is not truly representative of the population. The aim of probability sampling, and of quota sampling, is to minimize the bias in the sample. This assumes, however, that all those who are drawn in the sample will actually cooperate. In fact, a great many of those who are selected refuse to cooperate with the survey. The proportion of the sample who respond is called the **response rate**. Non-response can result from direct refusals and because people are away from home or cannot be contacted.

A certain level of non-response is acceptable and need not mean that the remaining sample will be biased. In practice, it is very difficult to achieve more than a 75 per cent response rate, meaning that virtually all surveys will involve a degree of bias. If the response rate falls below 60 per cent (that is, more than 40 per cent of the sample are non-responders), the results cannot usually be relied on with any certainty.

It is important to note that a representative sample may often not be possible to secure. In the case of much documentary research, for example, the researcher must study those documents that happen to have survived and are available for study. This does not necessarily reduce the value of the research. What is important is that the unrepresentative character of the documents be realized and taken into account in the analysis of the results. Knowing how unrepresentative or untypical your sample is becomes the first step towards a realistic assessment of its value for your research purposes.

Stop and reflect

In this section we have looked at the issues that arise in survey research, ethnographic research, and documentary research. We have also considered the issues of sampling that are common to all of these forms of research.

Survey research involves the use of a questionnaire to study the behaviour, attitudes, or opinions of a sample of respondents. Distinctions can be made between interview surveys, postal surveys, and telephone surveys.

- Questionnaire design involves a complex process of evaluation in which questions are drafted and modified in the light of practical tests.
- How many of the ten key points for good questionnaire design can you recall? (Check your answers on p. 79.)

Ethnographic research involves observations and conversations aimed at understanding the meanings of social actions and social situations.

- Ethnographic observation may be overt or covert and observers can take one of three research roles: complete participant, participant-as-observer, and complete observer.

- Ethnographic interviewing is semi-structured, rather than questionnaire-based. Effective interviewing relies on good interpersonal skills.
- Are ethnography and survey research completely opposed approaches to sociological investigation?

Documentary research is based on the use of written texts of all kinds.

- Documents may be personal or public documents, and the researcher may be granted varying degrees of access.
- Documents must be assessed in relation to the criteria of authenticity, credibility, representativeness, and meaning.
- Why do sociologists make so much use of documents in their research?

Whichever of these three forms of research is pursued, a number of issues in sampling must be considered.

- It is rarely possible to study all the individuals, locations, or documents that interest you. It will always be necessary to select, or to sample, in some way.

- A sample is drawn from a larger population, of which it is supposed to be representative. The most important distinction is that between probability and non-probability sampling methods.

- Within each of the methods of sampling there is a number of different types of sample: the simple random sample, the systematic random sample, the stratified random sample, the cluster and multi-stage sample, the convenience sample, the purposive sample, and the quota sample.

- Is it ever possible to disregard issues of sampling in social research?

Displaying and using data

We have shown that research design involves constructing a researchable project from theoretical ideas. Theories are systems of concepts that are connected together through logical reasoning and that may be translatable into models and hypotheses. If models and hypotheses are to guide empirical research, the concepts must be converted into *variables*. That is, a concept must be turned into something that is measurable. This is generally seen as a process of **operationalization**, of specifying the operations needed to produce evidence relevant to the concept. A concept that is successfully operationalized, then, is specified in terms of a number of quite specific empirical indicators and measures.

Anomie, for example, was a central concept for both Durkheim and Merton. But how do we know when we have observed a situation of anomie? Unless specific indicators of anomie are set out, we cannot do so. It was for this reason that Durkheim defined anomie as an absence of normative regulation, but took such things as a lack of religious affiliation and being unmarried as indicators of this.

When a concept has been defined in terms of a set of indicators that can be used in empirical research, it is said to have been transformed into a variable. A variable consists of a concept and its indicator(s). The concept is the idea, and the indicator is the item or items on which relevant empirical data can be collected. An example of this, which we look at more fully in 'Technology and the meaning of work', Chapter 17, pp. 656–8, is the Marxist concept of alienation. Seeman (1959) took Marx's ideas about alienation and developed them into a set of measurable indicators that Blauner (1964) went on to explore in his study of work relations (see the criticism of this in Lukes 1967).

The two fundamental issues that arise in the operationalization of concepts are validity and reliability. When an indicator has been devised that gives a theoretically acceptable measure of a concept, the indicator is said to be *valid*. When the indicator can be used to generate reproducible results, it is said to be *reliable*. Blauner (1964) claimed to have produced a reliable indicator of alienation, but his Marxist critics claimed that he had failed to produce a valid one. No matter how reliable an indicator may be, if it does not relate properly to the concept that it is supposed to measure it will be of little use. Blauner produced some valuable information about work satisfaction and work attitudes, but he did not really address the theoretical issues that Marx referred to in his discussion of alienation.

Operationalization has led to the construction of relatively uncontentious indicators of such things as urban and rural contexts, employment and self-employment, church membership, voting intention, and many other concrete concepts. It is far more difficult, however, to operationalize the more basic sociological concepts. Lukes (1974) has suggested that it is difficult to arrive at an operationalization of a concept such as power, because there are so many different views of what power is. Similar problems arise with such concepts as class, patriarchy, and ethnicity. As we show in Chapter 8, even such concepts as health, illness, and mental health are difficult to define in uncontentious ways.

The difficulty in producing valid and reliable indicators of sociological concepts has been taken by some philosophers as a sign that sociology is not scientific. If Marx's concepts, for example, cannot be given operational definitions, then Marxism cannot be a scientific theory (Popper 1959). Countering this view, Marxists and others have decried what they have called the positivist view of science. By this, they mean an approach that seeks to reduce all theoretical and conceptual issues to measurable and, perhaps, quantifiable indicators (Adorno *et al.* 1969).

However, a positive science—in the sense in which this term was used by Comte and Durkheim—need not be as narrowly quantitative as this implies. It is important to recognize that conceptual differences are an essential feature of social life. This is true for all the concepts and variables that we use. Much research, for example, makes use of the concept of sex, and we show in Chapter 5 that there are important theoretical issues surrounding the study of sex. The use of categories of ethnic origin, even if they are not presented as 'racial' categories, involve many similar issues (Burgess 1986). Even the category of age—used almost as widely in official statistics as sex—is far from straightforward, as chronologically defined categories rarely correspond to socially constructed concepts of age (Pilcher 1995).

One of the most problematic, and most widely discussed, concepts is social class. This has been used in official statistics as a routine way of summarizing occupational and employment data so that their effects on fertility, mortality, and health can be assessed. It has also been used as a fundamental concept in sociological studies on education, religion, family relations, crime, media viewing, language, and so on. The official categories of social class, though frequently used in sociological work, do not correspond in any straightforward way to any of the theoretically sophisticated concepts of social class that are current in sociology. This raises important questions about their validity and about the operationalization of sociological concepts in general. In Chapter 19, pp. 752–7, we will illustrate this through a detailed consideration of the operationalization of class and its use as a key variable in the analysis of sociological data. In the remainder of this chapter we will look at some of the practicalities of using sociological classifications and presenting sociological data. Finally, we will consider how, in the light of all this, it is possible to make use of official statistics.

Presenting data

Through the conversion of concepts into variables, sociologists are able to collect the data that they need for their research. Once these data have been collected, however, they must be organized and presented in ways that highlight their relevance for the theoretical interests that inform the research design. We are not able to look at the many specialist techniques available to sociologists for doing this. We can, however, look at some of the procedures most relevant to you when you try to understand the results of sociological research. We will look, in particular, at the ways in which data can be presented in tables and in charts, two different ways of trying to summarize sociological data. We will also, but very briefly, consider some of the statistical measures that you may come across.

Reading a table

The best way to approach the question of how to construct a table is to consider how to read one. Tables can be quite daunting, as many people are—quite unnecessarily—frightened by numbers. There is no need for this. A table can be read in exactly the same way as a piece of prose. You simply need to know where to start.

Look at Figure 3.5 on p. 96 for a few moments. Where did you look first? The chances are that you glanced down the left-hand side and then across some of the numbers. This is the wrong thing to do. The first thing that you should do when reading any table is to *read the title*. This is obvious when you think about it, but people tend to ignore the obvious when it comes to tables.

The title of this table is 'A table to read', but below this you will see the original title as it appeared in *Social Trends*. This tells you that it concerns 'AIDS cases' and 'HIV-1-infected persons' and that it looks at these in relation to 'probable exposure' and 'gender'. It also tells you that the data refer to 1995. We already know quite a lot about the table, just from its title. If you are not familiar with any of the terms used in a title, you should check back through the text or consult other sources to check them out. For example, in this case you would need to know, in general terms, what AIDS is, what HIV is, and how exposure and gender are likely to be relevant. In most cases, this will be obvious to you from the content of the book or article that you are reading. In the case of this example table, of course, this may not be the case, as we have introduced it out of its original context.

The next thing that you should do is look for any notes about the table. These are usually underneath it. In this case, you will see that one of the notes relates specifically to the title. This note clarifies something about the date to which the information relates. A second note merely clarifies one of the headings in the table, so we do not need to worry about this for the moment. The final note is one that gives the original source of the data (ignore our own 'Source' reference to *Social Trends* 1996). This is often a very useful piece of information. The original source information in this table tells you that the data were produced by a centre that monitors 'communicable diseases', another term that you will need to understand. (PHLS is the Public Health Laboratory Service, though the table does not actually tell you this.) In many cases, these notes will give you some useful definitions or may give you details of any sampling method.

You can now turn to the main body of the table: but do not look at any numbers yet. Look at the headings along the top and down the left-hand side of the table. Immediately under the title you are told that the data relate to the 'United Kingdom' (not England, not Scotland, not even Great Britain, but the United Kingdom as a whole). You are also told that they are 'numbers'. It might seem obvious that the data are numbers, but this is stated in order to make it clear that you are being given the actual numbers and not percentage figures.

Figure 3.5 A table to read

Further information can be found by searching for 'Sexual health' at http://webarchive.nationalarchives.gov.uk.

AIDS cases and related deaths and reports of HIV-1-infected persons: by probable exposure category and gender, to end June 1995[1]

United Kingdom	Numbers					
	AIDS				Reports of HIV-1-infected persons[2]	
	Cases		Related deaths			
	Males	Females	Males	Females	Males	Females
Probable HIV exposure category						
Sexual intercourse						
Between men	8,101		5,725		15,001	
Between men and women	782	627	433	333	2,000	2,280
Injecting drug use (IDU)	449	202	292	118	1,885	859
Blood						
Blood factor (e.g. haemophilia)	493	6	424	5	1,218	11
Blood/tissue transfer (e.g. transfusion)	39	71	26	48	77	85
Mother to child	81	82	42	40	152	149
Other/undetermined	100	18	76	9	621	115
All categories	10,045	1,006	7,018	553	20,954	3,499

[1] Cumulative reported cases and deaths up to the end of June 1995.

[2] Includes 49 reports where the gender was not stated; also includes those individuals who progressed to AIDS.

Source: PHLS Communicable Disease Surveillance Centre.

Source: Social Trends (1996: table 7.10).

Along the top is given a breakdown of the columns showing the AIDS and HIV-1 categories mentioned in the title. The AIDS category is broken down into 'cases' and 'related deaths', while the HIV-1 category refers only to 'infected persons'. Each of these is further subdivided into 'males' and 'females', something else that you were told about in the title. On the left-hand side of the table there is a general heading referring to 'exposure category'. So far, then, the title has given you a very good idea about the whole structure of the table. It is going to compare AIDS cases, AIDS-related deaths, and HIV-1 infection in men and women, and it is going to look at the causes of their exposure to the virus. To find out more about the table, you need to look at the row headings down the left-hand side.

The headings down the left-hand side show five main categories, followed by a total for 'All categories'. The categories are 'exposure categories': sex, drugs, blood, mother to child (during pregnancy), and 'other/undetermined'. Two of these categories are subdivided: 'Sexual intercourse' is subdivided by type of sex, while 'Blood' is subdivided by the type of blood exposure.

By now you should have a very clear idea about the kinds of things that the table is trying to show you, even before you have looked at a single number. By far the best approach to the actual numbers in a table is to use the method called eyeballing. Simply cast your eyes down and across the table, looking for the biggest numbers. In this table, the columns are the important things, as all the numbers are totalled at the bottom. (Do you remember that the 'All categories' heading is down there?) Do not worry about the details of the numbers at this stage. If there are any decimal figures, just ignore them and concentrate on the very broad patterns.

This table shows that the biggest numbers are in the column for males and that the category for sexual intercourse between men is the largest. Ignoring the odd hundreds, there were 8,000 cases, 5,000 related deaths, and 15,000 infected persons. These are the most striking results in the table. Only under 'infected persons', where the total numbers are much bigger, did any other figure approach these levels.

Eyeballing is a very useful technique for summarizing a table. Ignoring numbers after a decimal point, ignoring odd hundreds, and so on allow you to scan the table and immediately identify its most significant features. The largest and smallest figures stand out from all the others. Can you see where the smallest figures are in the table?

In many cases, this is all that you will need to do. You may want to go on to conclude that 'nearly all' cases of AIDS in males were due to exposure in homosexual intercourse or that 'about three-quarters' of all reports of infected persons involved exposure to the same risk, but you will not often need to be more precise than this. If you do need greater precision for any reason, then you should by now have enough knowledge and confidence about the table to extract these without any difficulty.

Constructing a table

Once you have mastered the techniques for reading a table, you should be able to make critical assessments of other people's data. You will be able to do this more effectively, however, if you know a little more about how to construct tables. This is also useful knowledge for whenever you come to present data of your own in essays or research projects. Many of the skills necessary to construct a table are, of course, simply the opposite of those involved in reading one, but they are worth looking at in a little more detail. When you come to read tables (including some in this book), you will find that people often break the rules of table construction and make the tables unnecessarily complex.

The most useful overview of this whole question is an official handbook called *Plain Figures* (Chapman and Wykes 1996), which gives an introduction to the dos and don'ts of table construction. The authors distinguish between tables for demonstration and tables for reference. The former are tables that aim to communicate a message and to show relationships, while the latter are the more comprehensive compilations found in many reports on official statistics. For many purposes, demonstration tables are quite sufficient, and they are what you will usually come across in books and newspapers. A good understanding of them will allow you to tackle more complex tables at a later stage in your career.

Chapman and Wykes give seven rules for the construction of demonstration tables:

- round all numbers to two effective digits wherever possible;
- put the numbers to be most often compared with each other in columns, rather than rows;
- arrange columns and rows in some natural order or in size order;
- where possible, put big numbers at the top of the table;
- give column and row averages or totals as a focus;
- use layout to guide the eye;
- give a verbal summary of the main points in the table.

Effective digits are those that vary and have the greatest significance. In a sequence of three-digit numbers, for example, it is usually the first two digits (the hundreds and the tens) that are the most significant, as the third digit (the units) is a very small part of the overall total. Rounding numbers to two effective digits simplifies matters by concentrating on the most important things. So, the sequence of numbers 152, 271, 384, 623, can usefully be simplified into the sequence 150, 270, 380, 620. This conveys the broad pattern more clearly, without any serious loss in detail.

The purpose of this rounding is to make it easier for people to eyeball the resulting table. Although there are many exceptions, and the rule must be used with care, it is generally a very effective technique to use. Whenever the data are to be used for reference purposes, however, the full numbers are likely to be important and rounding will not be appropriate.

The second rule that Chapman and Wykes give is to put the numbers to be compared in columns, not rows. It is far easier to eyeball a column than a row, especially when you need to do some arithmetic. It may be necessary, for example, to subtract a number from the overall total or to add up entries to produce a subtotal. We all learn to do our sums at school in columns, and it remains the most efficient way to do mental arithmetic for most people. In constructing a table, then, the researcher must decide which is the most important set of figures to compare and must use these as the columns.

The next two rules concern the order of the columns and rows. Nothing is more confusing than to have them listed in haphazard order. Chapman and Wykes suggest that, if there is a natural order of size, then this should be used and that the largest should be put at the top of the column. This, again, makes the data very easy to inspect. Where data are organized by date (as in, for example, a year-by-year table), it is usually best to put the data for the earliest date at the top or at the left of the table so that the information appears to run logically down or across the table.

All columns and rows should, where appropriate, have average or total figures as a focus. These appear in the margins of the table (at the bottom and the right), and they are often referred to as the *marginals*. This can save the reader a lot of work and can, again, bring out any patterns that the data show.

The rule that the layout should be a guide to the eye is really a summary of all the previous rules. It should be obvious to the reader what the table is trying to show, even before the detailed numbers are considered. One aspect of this rule is to give proper headings to all columns and rows and to title the table appropriately. You should give as much attention to the construction of the table as you do to the grammar of your text. A reader can read your table, as described in the previous section, if you follow the rules of layout when you construct it.

The final rule is simply that you should never just insert a table without any comment. In some situations it may be useful to provide people with illustrative tables, but it is generally important to tie them into your text in some way. If they are to function as *evidence*, rather than illustrations, there must be some kind of verbal summary of the key points and their significance. It is not necessary to summarize everything in the table, as that would make the table unnecessary, but the main points should be covered. This normally means highlighting patterns or trends.

Chapman and Wykes add a final point that charts are often more useful when data are to be displayed for demonstration only, and we will look at the use of charts in the following section.

Drawing charts

If the actual numbers are not important and you simply wish to convey the broad patterns and trends, a chart is often useful. You will find a number of examples of charts in this book. These include maps and diagrams of various kinds, as well as graphs of numerical data. It is graphs that we will look at in this section. It is not necessary that you understand all the mathematics behind the graphs. You simply need to have some idea about how they are constructed. The three types of graph that we will consider (shown in Figure 3.6) are:

- line charts;
- bar charts;
- pie charts.

The **line chart** or line graph is especially useful for showing trends and patterns over time. If time is shown along the bottom of the graph, the particular variable that is of interest can be shown along the left-hand axis. This

Figure 3.6 Types of graph

The information in these figures is artificial and is used simply to illustrate the three types of graph. For this reason, we have not included all the titles and labels that you would find on an actual graph.

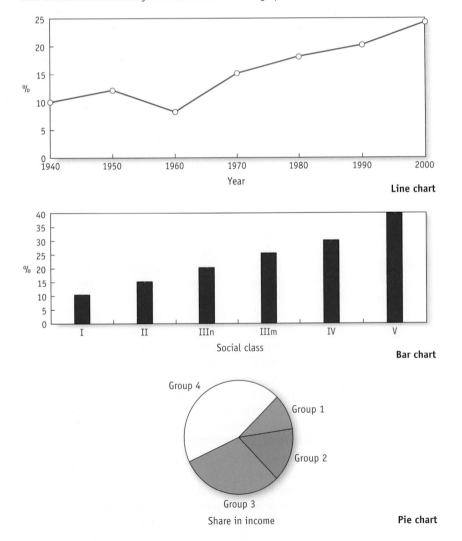

might be the percentage of the population unemployed, the percentage committing suicide, and so on. The percentage level for each time period is marked with a diamond, a cross, or some other symbol, and the points can be connected with a line that shows the trend. If there are separate data for men and women, for different age groups, or for different social classes, then these can each be plotted separately and a line drawn for each group. This kind of line chart allows the trends for the different groups to be compared.

Care must be taken in drawing a line graph, as the vertical scale (the scale for the variable along the left-hand side) can exaggerate a trend. If a change of 5 per cent in the crime rate is represented by 5 centimetres on a graph, then this will look far more significant than if it is represented by 5 millimetres. This gives great scope for misleading people, as it allows the unscrupulous researcher or politician to produce the gee-whizz graph (Huff 1954: 60). An example of this is shown in Figure 3.7.

A **bar chart** represents variables as horizontal or vertical bars. The lengths of the bars correspond to the totals shown in the columns or rows of a table. Separate bars can, then, be drawn for each social group or category in the original table. We might, for example, draw bars for each social class in the population, the length of each bar showing the percentage that go to church, the percentage convicted of offences, the percentage with substantial savings, and so on. When a bar chart is drawn with data measured in terms of a continuous variable (such as age or income), it is technically termed a *histogram*. Although this has certain distinct statistical properties, it is not necessary for you to worry about this.

The final type of chart that we will look at is the **pie chart**. This is a circular graph that, like a pie, can be divided into separate slices. If the area of the whole circle is made to represent a total figure, then the area of each slice represents the share of the total belonging to a particular social group or category. A population divided into six social classes, for example, could be represented as six slices of the overall circle, the size of each slice representing, say, its share in total national income.

A pie chart is a very useful visual representation of some kinds of data, but it requires just a little more skill to draw it. These skills are those of school geometry. While a line or bar chart has a vertical scale running along the left-hand side, the scale of a pie chart is, in effect, the circumference of the circle. The chart is constructed by making the overall total of the variable measured equal to the 360 degrees that define the circle. A group that has, say, 25 per cent of the total would be represented by a slice that describes an angle of 90 degrees (a quarter of 360 degrees).

Certain skills are needed to construct charts by hand, but this is not always necessary. Many word-processing programs now contain built-in routines for producing tables and for converting them, instantly, to line charts, bar charts, and pie charts, as do all spreadsheets. Researchers who use survey analysis and statistical packages will have even more facilities available to them. So long as the general principles are understood, the computer takes care of the details.

What is true for charts is also true for the various statistics that sociologists formerly calculated by hand. If you can handle basic addition and subtraction, and if you can use a pocket calculator when necessary, you will be able to read and produce most basic tables. With just a few more skills, charts and diagrams can be produced, and with access to a computer numerous advanced statistical procedures are at hand.

Figure 3.7 The gee-whizz graph

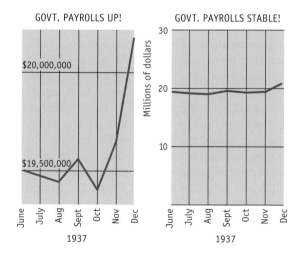

Source: Huff (1954: 65).

Using official statistics

Official statistics are among the most important sources of data available to sociologists. They have been produced for administrative and political purposes and reflect the needs and concerns of politicians and civil servants, rather than those of academic sociologists. They remain, however, a fundamental source of information on most of the topics with which sociologists deal and they are essential to the overall picture they try to construct. Official statistics are a relatively cheap and plentiful source of data. They are constructed in ways that, in general, make it possible to assess their reliability and validity, and they are often available on a regular basis over long periods of time. For all of these reasons, sociologists have made a great deal of use of them.

⊙ Connections

In other parts of this book you will find discussions of how to calculate and use averages, correlation coefficients, and various other statistical measures. You are unlikely, at this stage in your career, to need much more. If you want to learn about significance tests, standard deviations, variance, and chi-squared, you should look at a text such as Hinton (1995). The use of computers to produce these statistics is covered in Rose and Sullivan (1993). You should not try to learn any of these measures, but you might want to refer to the books if you come across research reports that use them.

There has, however, been much discussion of the very serious problems that they involve. Criminal statistics, for example, are held to underestimate the real level of crime, unemployment statistics to underestimate the actual number of people who are out of work, and so on. For some, these problems are so great that the whole idea of using statistics to study real social processes has been rejected. Indeed, some interactionists and ethnomethodologists claim that there is no such thing as a real rate of crime, unemployment, or suicide. They argue that all rates depend on definitions that are socially constructed. If this is so, the idea of using official statistics to measure them cannot make sense (Cicourel 1964; Douglas 1967; from a different theoretical perspective, see the similar point made in Hindess 1973).

These critics undoubtedly have some important arguments on their side. Suicide statistics, for example, depend on the ways in which coroners, police, and others classify deaths. This does not, however, mean that rates cannot be constructed or used. What it does mean is that whenever we use such a rate it is vital to be clear about the definitions used in its construction. Differences in rates still require explanation, and the different definitions that have been used may provide a part of that explanation. It is also possible to control, at least in part, for differences of definition. This is how Durkheim examined not only differences between countries but also differences between areas within countries. Important questions still arise, however, about how these rates might be explained. We might ask, for example, whether the particular conclusions of Durkheim (1897) were valid, but the reality of suicide cannot seriously be questioned (J. M. Atkinson 1978).

Despite the problems involved in the use of official statistics, we will try to show that they remain an essential part of the sociological toolbox. So long as we are *aware* of their limitations, we can try to overcome them or, at least, be honest about the limits on the conclusions that we draw from the statistics. The problems of official statistics are, in fact, no greater than the problems of using participant

observation or historical documents. One of the most valuable things that a sociologist can do is to *combine* various types of data in a single piece of research. The limitations of any one source would, wherever possible, be compensated by the advantages of another.

⊙ Connections

If the word 'triangulation' did not spring to your mind at this point, read our discussion of combining research methods on p. 73.

Official statistics of crime

The limitations of official statistics have been most comprehensively explored in relation to statistics on crime. It does make sense to talk about rates of crime—the numbers of rapes, murders, or burglaries—and it is important to try to measure these rates. However, the available criminal statistics provide wholly inadequate measures of these rates. The criminal statistics include only those offences that are 'known to the police'. Many offences are simply not reported to the police and so do not appear in the statistics.

The rate of reporting varies quite considerably from one type of crime to another. Offences that are seen as relatively minor, such as dropping litter in a public place, may be regarded as annoying, but they are not seen as worth reporting to the police. Most murders, on the other hand, are likely to be reported, as it is an offence that is generally regarded as serious, and, in any case, it is difficult to conceal a dead body for any period of time. Rape is far less likely to be reported. While it is undoubtedly regarded as a serious crime, many women victims of rape prefer not to face police questioning. The prospect of an interrogation in court, particularly when the likelihood of a successful prosecution is seen as fairly low, discourages many from reporting their rapes.

These remarks bring out the fact that victims and others make assessments of the likely consequences of reporting crimes. They try to judge whether the police will take the report seriously, or will simply file it away and get on with other business. Similarly, they try to assess the chances that the police will solve the crime and bring the offender to book. Detection rates for many crimes are very low, and victims may simply not think it worth reporting them. Burglaries, for example, have a low detection rate, and it is largely because of pressure from insurance companies that people report burglaries and theft. Insurance companies will not consider a claim for any burglary that has not been reported, and so those who wish to claim on their home insurance policy must report it, no matter how unlikely they think it is that the offender will be apprehended. Where householders have not insured their property, reporting rates for burglary are low.

Victims and others also take account of whether detected offenders are likely to be charged, rather than given a warning, and, if charged, whether they are likely to be convicted in court. Where these probabilities are seen to be low, as they are for many kinds of crime, reporting is also likely to be low.

Considerations such as these lead many people to talk about the 'hidden figure' or **dark figure** of crime. Crimes known to the police are merely the tip of an iceberg (see Figure 3.8), and an unknown amount of unreported crime remains invisible in official statistics. The size of the dark figure varies from one kind of crime to another. In the case of murder, for example, it is likely to be very small, while in the case of traffic speeding it is likely to be very high. One of the major problems in research on crime is the unknown size of the dark figure. It is also very difficult to assess whether those crimes that are reported to the police are a representative sample of all crimes. If they are, then it is possible to discover some important characteristics of crime and criminals from the criminal statistics. If we do not know whether they are a representative sample, then any conclusions drawn from the criminal statistics may be unfounded.

This problem has been addressed in the sociology of crime through self-report and victim studies. In self-report studies, people are asked whether they have ever committed particular offences. In victim studies, they are asked whether they have ever been the victims of particular kinds of crime. Such studies have helped to quantify the dark figure and to show how crime statistics can be used. Recent research has suggested that, overall, only 47 per cent of all offences are reported to the police, and only 27 per cent are recorded by them. Just 2 per cent of all offences result in the conviction of an offender. However, the broad *trends* in crime rates are, for the most part, accurately reflected in the statistics.

On this basis, Lea and Young (1984: 15) have concluded that criminal statistics 'have to be interpreted with extreme caution. It is not that they are meaningless; they do reflect public, police and court definitions of crime, the disposal of limited resources and the extent of infractions thus defined; but what they do not do is tell about an independent entity called "crime".' If the limitations of the criminal statistics are fully recognized, this helps us to make a proper and sensitive use of them (Maguire 1994).

Statistics of employment and health

What holds for criminal statistics also holds for other official statistics. For example, the newspapers and television regularly report the current unemployment rate. In Britain, this figure is calculated and published by the Department for Employment and Learning. Since 1982, the department has regarded someone as 'unemployed' if he or she is registered for unemployment benefit, since 1996 the Jobseeker's Allowance. These are people officially seen as both available for work and actively seeking employment. The official rate of unemployment is simply the number claiming welfare benefits on the grounds of unemployment (Jobseeker's Allowance, Income Support, and all their predecessors).

This might seem a plausible measure of unemployment, and this is the way it has been treated by governments and the mass media. However, things are not that simple. Not everyone who would like to be employed is entitled to receive benefit. Many married women, for example, do not have a record of national insurance contributions that would entitle them to a benefit and so are not counted as unemployed in the official statistics.

Figure 3.8 Reported and unreported crimes

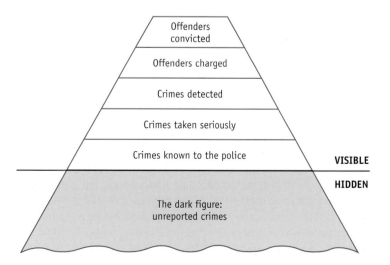

Offenders convicted

Offenders charged

Crimes detected

Crimes taken seriously

Crimes known to the police

VISIBLE

HIDDEN

The dark figure: unreported crimes

Greater problems arise if trends over time are examined. Prior to 1982, welfare entitlement and registration as unemployed were not so closely tied. The official rate of unemployment was a measure of those on the register, whether or not they were entitled to benefit. The administrative change to a count of benefit claimants removed 200,000 people from the unemployed count almost overnight. Over the course of the recession of the 1980s and 1990s, Conservative governments sought to contain the welfare bill by changing criteria of eligibility for various benefits and so taking people off the registers. In all, thirty different changes were made to the rules for registration as unemployed between 1979 and 1989. In 1998 the Labour government moved back to a measure closer to that used before 1979. The rate of 'unemployment' can alter purely because of administrative changes, and not because there has been a change in the real rate of employment (Levitas 1996). There is, then, a 'dark figure' of hidden unemployment.

Attempts to arrive at a more accurate measure of unemployment, avoiding the problem of the dark figure, have been made using data from the Labour Force Survey (LFS). As this is a sample survey, it is not affected by administrative changes to eligibility rules, but it does have problems of its own. The LFS uses an internationally agreed definition of unemployment that is, however, far from perfect. This counts as unemployed those without a job who were available to start work in the two weeks following the survey and who had either looked for work in the four weeks before the interview or were waiting to start a job they had already obtained. Those who do *any* part-time work, no matter how little and how low paid, are not counted as unemployed. The numbers lost in this way are more or less balanced by the numbers of non-claimants counted as unemployed. As a result, the LFS measure does not differ significantly from the official rate. The nearest to a measure that avoids these problems comes from the 1991 Census, when people were asked (for the first time in a census) to identify themselves as employed or unemployed. The figure of 2,485,000 found in the April 1991 Census compares with a figure of 2,302,000 recorded by the LFS (just over 8 per cent of the labour force) in the same month (Levitas 1996: 58). This is further discussed in Box 3.14.

The problem of the dark figure is far less of a difficulty for the main demographic statistics produced from the Census and the registration of births, deaths, and marriages. Because compliance with the Census and registration is a legal requirement, these are generally regarded as complete and, therefore, very accurate. Nevertheless, concern over the possible use of census data to register people for the so-called poll tax (the Community Charge) led many people to boycott the 1991 Census. It has been estimated that the Census may have involved an under-count of as many as two million people. Subsequent survey findings, on which this estimate is based, suggest that the

---

THEORY AND METHODS 3.14

Calculating unemployment

Figures from the 2001 Census have been available since the middle of 2003. Consult the National Statistics website (**www.statistics.gov.uk**) and find the Census tables and the LFS tables. Use these tables to discover estimates of the level of unemployment in April 2001. What is the relationship between the two figures? Does the Census still report a higher level of unemployment?

Look at the questions asked in the Census (you can see a copy of the questionnaire on the website). Which approach—the Census or the LFS—gives the best measure of unemployment? Why do you think this?

The LFS carries out interviews in about 60,000 households, using a systematic random sample. The Census is not a sample survey but collects information from the whole population. These two types of investigation are discussed in Chapter 8, pp. 270–2.

⮕ Look at the officially recorded level of unemployment today: is this a valid measure? Try to find official measures of unemployment in other countries: can any reliable conclusions be drawn from international comparisons?

'hidden population' consisted mainly of young males living in inner-city areas who were not listed on the electoral register and did not complete census forms, and there have been suggestions that the 2001 Census failed to record many of the homeless.

More significant problems have always existed for health statistics derived from general practitioners and hospitals (H. Roberts 1990). Not all illnesses are reported to doctors, especially when people believe there is nothing that doctors can do to help them and when no medical certificate is required for absence from work. Colds, influenza, and other minor ailments may, therefore, be significantly underrepresented in the official statistics. The real rates of such illnesses are unknown (Stacey 1987: 213–14). Serious illnesses, on the other hand, are much more likely to be reported, as this is the only way in which it is possible to get medical treatment. Self-report studies—asking people about their illnesses—can help to resolve the problems of the dark figure of illness, but people cannot always recall all the minor ailments they had during the survey period. In addition, they may not always be aware of the fact that they have had certain diseases if they had them in a particularly mild form. It is, for example, possible to have very mild and virtually symptomless forms of such diseases as rubella.

Just as the users of the criminal statistics must know what is meant, in legal discourse, by 'summary offence', 'theft', and 'notifiable offence', so the user of mortality statistics must have some understanding of 'malignant neoplasm', 'respiratory disease', and so on. These problems are, in some respects, purely technical matters that can be resolved by checking the appropriate medical definition. We show in Chapter 8, however, that medical diagnoses are socially constructed and that diagnostic categories cannot be regarded as technically neutral devices.

Demographic statistics from official sources, such as crime statistics, emerged with the transformation of nation states in the eighteenth and nineteenth centuries. They continue to show the signs not only of their historical origin, but also of the contemporary administrative purposes to which they are geared. They involve many technical and conceptual problems (J. Scott 1990: ch. 5). They are, however, the only sources we have on many matters, and a proper understanding of their construction allows us to overcome many of their limitations. If they cannot be accepted at face value, they can, nevertheless, be used, with care, for a great many sociological purposes. They are an invaluable tool of sociological analysis.

 Stop and reflect

In this section we have looked at a number of issues concerned with classifying and using data. We looked, in particular, at the use of official statistics.

- Official statistics are to be treated critically and with care, though they are essential sources of information in many areas of sociology.

- The problem of the dark figure in official statistics can be partly overcome through the use of such sources as victim surveys, self-report surveys, and other types of survey data.

- Why have sociologists been so critical of official statistics?

This section has also been concerned with the principles involved in constructing and reading tables and charts.

- When reading a table, begin with the title, notes, and headings. Finally, eyeball the table to uncover its broad patterns.

- When constructing a table, follow the seven rules set out in Chapman and Wykes (1996) (see above, p. 97).

- The most important charts for sociologists to use and to understand are line charts, bar charts, and pie charts. Can you write a brief description of each of these?

The ethics of social research

Social research does not occur in a moral or political vacuum. Questions of confidentiality and anonymity in all styles of research are fundamental to the ways in which the research is undertaken and the uses to which its results are put. Once research results have been published, they can have unforeseen consequences for the groups studied, and the sociologist cannot stand aside from these. In many cases, the ethical and political issues that must be considered are general questions of human responsibility for other human beings. These are, of course, massive questions, on which there are no easy answers. As sociologists, we cannot avoid them, but nor do we have any particular right to pontificate on them.

The detailed implementation of certain research procedures, however, does raise quite specific questions about how these general considerations are to be translated into specific rules of research practice. While these ethical issues cannot be resolved in any clear-cut way, it is important that they be aired and that various alternative answers be considered. We will illustrate these issues from ethnographic research involving participant observation, though similar issues arise in other forms of social research.

We first of all look at how these have been raised in debates around particular observational studies. We then go on to look at the response of the British Sociological Association (BSA) and the American Sociological Association (ASA) and the guidance they give to members. You will find the whole of the BSA's Statement of Ethical Practice on the Internet at www.britsoc.co.uk/equality/Statement+Ethical+Practice.htm and the ASA code at **www.asanet.org/cs/root/leftnav/ethics/ethics**. We suggest that you read these or similar professional documents before you undertake any research of your own.

Ethics of covert research

Covert observation is the research method of the hidden observer or the complete participant. In these situations, people are not aware that they are being observed for research purposes. They believe that they are merely going about their ordinary lives.

The main objection to covert participant observation is that it is unethical for sociologists to misrepresent their identity just in order to undertake research. To do this is to make an unwarranted intrusion into people's lives. Covert participant observation involves lies, fraud, and deceit on the part of the sociologist, and many people see this as an inappropriate way to behave. This is often justified by sociologists, however, on the grounds that any harm done is outweighed by the benefits of the research. These claims and counterclaims can be seen in a number of actual cases.

Simon Holdaway (1983) conducted covert participant observation on the British police during the 1970s. Holdaway had been a police officer for many years and had been seconded to university to study sociology. He decided to undertake a sociological research project on the force, but kept this secret from his superiors and colleagues. While he was apparently working as an ordinary police officer, he actually spent two years studying the occupational culture of the police. He felt that overt research would not be possible or would lead people to modify their behaviour and that the benefits that would flow from his study outweighed the implications of the secrecy he adopted.

Having completed the research and left the police, Holdaway faced the further ethical problem of whether to publish his results, which had been undertaken for a Ph.D. His own professional interests as a sociologist and his desire to make his work known had to be balanced against the rights of his subjects and the fact that publication would bring his deception into the open. To protect particular individuals from any recriminations, Holdaway changed their names and obscured the places where the research had been carried out, aiming to give people a degree of anonymity. His justification for the research and its publication was that his concern was with the *structure* of policing and the ways in which it constrains individuals. He was not trying to blame particular individuals for their actions (Holdaway 1982).

Similar issues arose in Nigel Fielding's study (1981) of the National Front (now the British National Party), a racist political party of which he was not a member and of which he strongly disapproved. To begin the research he had to approach a party branch as a potential member, and this involved him claiming to have racist views to which he did not actually subscribe. By appearing to be sympathetic, he was able to obtain access to party situations and could observe meetings and talk to people freely. The ethical problem for Fielding was that he was not only *concealing* his intentions; he was actually *lying* and so misleading those he was studying.

Fielding's research also involved some overt interviewing, in different situations, and the research developed as a mixture of covert and overt methods. When it was completed, Fielding published his book but decided to retain the original names of all those that he had studied. He felt no obligation to protect the identities of his subjects, but he engaged a lawyer to read through the book to search for anything that might have left him open to legal action. Fielding faced fewer problems than Holdaway, because of his lack of sympathy with the National Front, but he still had to protect his own personal and professional situation (Fielding 1982).

It could be argued that, in these cases, the ends justified the means. Disclosing the causes of racism, for example, whether in the police or the National Front, might be seen as something that justifies any deception of the subjects. Not all would accept this justification, however; some would never see this kind of deception as acceptable. Before we can consider this view, however, it is worth considering another case where the justification was used. This is a famous study by Laud Humphreys (1970) where the benefit claimed was that to the subjects themselves.

Humphreys studied male homosexual activities in public toilets. One of the accepted activities in these settings is that of the 'watch queen', who gets a voyeuristic excitement from watching homosexual sex but also acts as a look-out for any police activity in the area. It was this role that Humphreys adopted, and it allowed him to gain a great deal of information about the men that he studied. This argument was not accepted by his Head of Department, Alvin Gouldner, who physically attacked him in the university.

Humphreys was able to use information on car number plates to get addresses from the police computer, pretending to the police that he was doing market research. He then approached the men and requested interviews. This was, of course, a further invasion of their privacy, but Humphreys argues that it could be justified if it led to a better understanding of homosexuality and, therefore, to an improvement in the social situation of the gay men that he studied.

Some sociologists have gone even further than Holdaway, Fielding, and Humphreys, claiming that no justification is necessary for deception. Lies, fraud, and deceit are part and parcel of everyday life in any case, it has been argued, and there is no reason to expect sociological research to be any different. We all keep things secret in our interactions with others (Goffman 1959). If we are constantly manipulating and misleading one another, why should the sociologist not do the same thing? Complete openness is, in any case, impossible to achieve in any social relationship. The very distinction between covert and overt observation cannot be drawn so sharply as some discussions imply. The overt researcher, for example, will rarely give a full explanation of the nature of the research, and most people who agree to be studied would not be interested in the full account. A simple statement about 'doing research' or 'writing a book' is generally enough to persuade people to cooperate, and any further explanation of the research is kept as simple as possible in order to avoid technical language and to avoid having too much influence on what the researcher hopes to observe.

We live in a world in which there are few moral certainties, and there can be no clear-cut ethical standards. Bulmer has suggested, however, that the principle of *informed consent*, now accepted as the basis of medical experimentation, should be observed whenever possible. People have a right, in all circumstances, to be fully informed about those things that affect them, and they must freely consent to their involvement in any course of action. Medical doctors testing new drugs must inform patients that they will be part of a medical trial, and the patients must have the right to refuse and to continue with conventional treatment. In the same way, Bulmer argues, people must be informed that they may be involved in sociological research, and they must have the right to refuse any involvement. While it may be impossible to give people full knowledge of the nature and purpose of the research, he argues, the kind of deception involved in covert participant observation is clearly a denial of individual rights to informed consent. Even if there are great public benefits from a piece of research, these can never override individual rights to privacy. (There is a useful discussion in Homan and Bulmer 1982.)

> ### ⊃ *Connections*
> You might like to discuss some of these ethical issues with other people before reading much further. Imagine you are going to carry out research into drug-trafficking in an inner-city district. Would it be justifiable to use covert participant observation to study those involved? Would any study be possible if you did not use covert participant observation?

Decisions about the ethics of particular research methods will always involve balancing competing ethical demands and moral principles. To help in handling these issues, professional bodies of sociologists in the United States and Britain have set up guidelines on ethical practice that set out the things that researchers must take into account in coming to their decisions. Many universities have ethics committees to consider research projects, including those of undergraduate students.

 Stop and reflect

Ethical issues are fundamental to social research. Like ethical problems in general, they cannot be resolved in any clear-cut or consensual way. No abstract principles can be applied under all circumstances.

* Covert research has often been justified in terms of the benefits of the research to the wider society or to the subjects themselves. This use of deception has to be offset against the need to ensure the informed consent of those who are the subjects of research.

* Professional associations have established guidelines that social researchers are expected to follow in their projects.

* Do you think that covert research can ever be justified?

 Key concepts

* bar chart 99
* bias 93
* content analysis 90
* conversation analysis 84
* covert research 80
* dark figure 101
* documents 86
* focus group 85
* hypothesis 71

* life history 85
* line chart 98
* model 71
* observation 81
* operationalization 94
* oral history 85
* overt research 80
* pie chart 99
* probability sampling 90

* questionnaire 76
* research design 71
* respondent 76
* response rate 93
* sample 90
* semi-structured interviews 84
* textual analysis 90
* triangulation 73

Workshop 3

Study 3 Learning to labour

We have covered a number of issues in research methodology in this chapter. If you look at published sociological studies, you will find that they are not always as clear as they might be about the sources and methods used. A useful exercise is to look at a major and important study and consider it from the standpoint of its methodology.

A classic study in the sociology of education, discussed in Chapter 9, p. 317 below, is *Learning to Labour* by Paul Willis (1977). Willis studied a group of boys in a West Midlands city, examining their attitudes to school and their orientations to work. He traced the development of anti-school subcultural views among the boys and saw this as reflecting the class culture they brought to their schooling. Working-class boys did not subscribe to the values held up by the school and did not aspire to high-paid or fulfilling jobs. Instead, they 'learned to labour'— they left school with a commitment to the same kinds of working-class jobs as their parents. The schools, Willis concludes, were failing the 'lads'.

Look at Willis's book and try to find answers to the following questions:

- Where was the study carried out?
- How did Willis decide in which school to study?
- How did he choose the particular lads for interview?
- How would you describe this sampling method?
- How did Willis collect his data from the lads? Was it through a survey, through observation, from interviews, or in some other way?
- Was this the most appropriate method to follow? Could he have learned more if he had used multiple methods and a strategy of triangulation?

You should write up your conclusions as a critical assessment of the study and then see what this suggests about our reliance on Willis's findings.

It is important to be critical, but not over-critical. We have not chosen Willis's book for study because it is bad. Quite the opposite: it is one of the best ethnographies carried out and it came to extremely important conclusions. However, we can often learn more from criticizing the good than we can from criticizing the poor.

Media watch 3 A survey has shown . . .

If you read the papers, watch television, or surf the news pages on the Internet, you will frequently come across the phrase 'a survey has shown'. News reports are often based around published surveys or use surveys to justify particular policy proposals or changes. How often, however, do they provide you with the evidence that you need in order to assess how valid and reliable the survey results are?

Here is an example from a local newspaper. This paper reported that 'A survey in North Lincolnshire has given the thumbs-up to the *Scunthorpe Telegraph* with nine out of ten people saying they use the paper to find out about their local council.' It adds: 'The survey showed 86 per cent of the 1,106 people surveyed had got information about the council from the *Telegraph* in the past 12 months, with 47 per cent of them saying it was their main source.' The paper's editor was, understandably 'delighted but not surprised with the result of this survey' (*Scunthorpe Telegraph*, 19 December 2000).

How critical would you be of such claims? The article does not say who carried out the survey, what sampling methods were used, or how good the response rate was. Nor is there any indication of exactly how the question was worded. It is impossible to know what reliance to put on the results quoted to such editorial approval.

Consider another example, this time from the BBC. The BBC website suggests that 'Clubbers are more likely to show signs of a psychiatric illness, a survey has shown.' It reports that 'A survey of readers of *Mixmag* found they were twice as likely to score highly on a standard test to measure mental health' (**http://news.bbc.co.uk/1/hi/health/1759777.stm**, 14 January 2002). This report does, at least, tell us that the survey was 'carried out by researchers at the National Addiction Centre at the Institute of Psychiatry, South London and the Maudsley Trust and the University of Kent', which ought to give us some grounds for accepting the conclusions, but no further details are given. Indeed, we are given some reasons for suspecting that the sample was rather biased, as the report adds that 'the survey was a self-selection questionnaire, and . . . those who take the trouble to complete the form are likely to be more drug-involved in some way'.

Does the information in this report give us more reason to believe or to question the survey results? Finally, consider the claim that 'Nearly half of Britons would help a terminally-ill relative commit suicide, a survey has shown' (**www.guardian. co.uk/society/2004/sep/09/health.medicineandhealth**). Striking evidence, perhaps: but the report shows that the survey was carried out for The Voluntary Euthanasia Society. Do you think that this might have affected the results?

CNN reported that 'America is a less Christian nation than it was 20 years ago, and Christianity is not losing out to other religions, but primarily to a rejection of religion altogether, a survey published Monday found. Survey finds percentage of Americans identifying themselves as Christian has fallen over two decades' (**http://edition.cnn.com/2009/LIVING/wayof-life/03/09/us.religion.less.christian/index.html**).

What further information would you need to assess this claim?

Look through a local or national newspaper and find a report that is based on what 'a survey has shown'. See if you can find out the following information:

- Who carried out the survey?
- What sampling methods were used?
- How many people responded? (And what response rate does this represent?)
- How were the questions actually worded?

What conclusions would you draw about the reliability of newspaper reports?

 Discussion points

Look back over the 'Stop and reflect' points at the end of each section and make sure that you appreciate the general issues raised:

- How would you distinguish between the ideas of exploration, description, and explanation?
- Make sure that you understand the main differences between a case study, a comparative study, a longitudinal study, and a cross-sectional study.

Survey research, sampling, and statistics

- What do you consider to be the main advantages and disadvantages of each of the following: an interview survey, a postal survey, and a telephone survey?
- Try to explain, in non-technical terms, the differences between probability and non-probability sampling.
- People often talk about a random sample when they really mean a haphazard or arbitrary selection. How would you try to tell if a sample is genuinely random?
- Test your presentation skills by taking the data in Figure 3.5 to draw a pie chart showing the various exposure categories for AIDS cases among males.

Ethnographic research and research ethics

- Consider the ethical implications of covert research. To what extent is it ever justified to mislead the subjects of research or to study them without their knowledge? We have discussed research by Holdaway and Fielding in this chapter. Using this book and any other sources available to you, identify any other study that has used covert observation methods.
- How might it be possible to assess whether an ethnographic study has used a representative sample? What kind of information would you need?
- Compile a list of the advantages and disadvantages of participant observation studies. Consider both covert and overt approaches.

Documentary research and official sources

- Choose a document such as a newspaper, a personal letter, or a government report and consider the issues of authenticity, credibility, representativeness, and meaning that would arise in using it as a source in a sociological study.
- We have questioned the conventional distinction between primary and secondary sources, and we have pointed to the differing ways in which these have been defined. Do you think that the distinction is a helpful way of identifying forms of social research?
- Go to the website of the Office of National Statistics and find some up-to-date official statistics on crime, health, or employment. How do the issues that we raise in relation to official statistics in this chapter help you to assess what the statistics tell us about trends in crime, health, or employment?

Explore further

You will find a comprehensive coverage of many of the issues covered in this chapter in:

May, T. (2001), *Social Research: Issues, Methods and Processes* (3rd edn, Buckingham: Open University Press).

O'Connell Davidson, J., and Layder, D. (1994), *Methods, Sex and Madness* (London: Routledge).

The most comprehensive overview, however, is:

Bryman, A. (2008), *Social Research Methods* (3rd edn, Oxford: Oxford University Press).

Basic styles of research and handling data are covered in:

de Vaus, G. (1991), *Surveys in Social Research* (London: UCL Press). *A useful compilation of principles and issues for survey research.*

Burgess, R. G. (1984), *In the Field: An Introduction to Field Research* (London: George Allen & Unwin). *Gives a good coverage of issues of ethnographic research.*

Brewer, J. D. (2000) *Ethnography* (Buckingham: Open University Press). *A recent text on ethnography that gives particular attention to ethical issues and the study of dangerous and sensitive situations.*

Scott, J. (1990), *A Matter of Record: Documentary Sources in Social Research* (Cambridge: Polity Press). *A systematic overview of the history and use of official and administrative documents, together with a discussion of the principles of documentary research.*

Chapman, M., and Wykes, C. (1986), *Plain Figures* (2nd edn, London: HMSO). *An excellent set of guidelines for the construction and use of tables and charts.*

Issues of research methodology are taken further in:

Burgess, R. G. (1986) (ed.), *Key Variables in Social Research* (London: Routledge & Kegan Paul). *A collection of discussions that cover the construction of basic sociological variables.*

Hinton, P. R. (1995), *Statistics Explained* (London: Routledge). *A good introduction to statistical measures. One of many similar books.*

Huff, D. (1954), *How to Lie with Statistics* (London: Victor Gollancz). *A classic, if a little dated, example of how statistics can mislead the unwary reader.*

Levitas, R., and Guy, W. (1996) (eds), *Interpreting Official Statistics* (London: Routledge). *A useful collection that discusses the use of a wide range of official statistics.*

Moser, C., and Kalton, G. (1979), *Survey Methods in Social Investigation* (London: Heinemann Educational Books). *Probably the standard source on all aspects of sampling, questionnaire design, and interviewing.*

Oppenheim, A. N. (1966), *Questionnaire Design and Attitude Measurement* (London: Heinemann Educational Books). *A more detailed consideration of issues covered in Moser and Kalton.*

An interesting video dramatization of observational and documentary data can be found in:

Housewife, 49. *A TV dramatization of the Mass Observation diaries of Nella Last, starring Victoria Wood* (ITV DVD, 2007).

Online resources

Visit the Online Resource Centre that accompanies this book to access more learning resources and other interesting material on methods and research at:
www.oxfordtextbooks.co.uk/orc/fulcher4e/

The Office of National Statistics website is:
www.statistics.gov.uk

Here you will find key statistical data on a vast range of subjects, especially through the 'virtual bookshelf' at:
www.statistics.gov.uk/onlineproducts/default.asp

The most accessible way to find this is through the summary tables in *Social Trends*, which is published in paper form or can be downloaded from:
www.statistics.gov.uk/StatBase/Product.asp?vlnk=5748

Many countries produce similar publications. For example, the Australian *Social Trends* can be found at:
http://www.abs.gov.au/ausstats/abs@.nsf/mf/4102.0

Results from major sociological surveys can be found at:
www.data-archive.ac.uk
(the home of the UK Data Archive at Essex University).

An excellent source of information on qualitative data and methods is maintained by Judy Norris at the University of Georgia:
www.qualitativeresearch.uga.edu/QualPage

PART TWO

SOCIAL IDENTITIES

Socialization, Identity, and Interaction

Contents

Attachment disorder

When he was 5 years old, Mike was adopted by a couple who already had children of their own. His adoptive parents loved him and looked after him along with their other children, and he seemed to settle in well to family life and to school. However, his parents and teachers began to notice worrying things about his behaviour, though they tried to see these as 'normal' and as just part of growing up: he talked constantly about TV programmes, he told lies, he hurt the family pet, he did not like family members showing affection to one another but not to him, he found it difficult to make friends, he stole from his mother's purse, and he acquired the belongings of other children. By the time he was 12 his parents were so concerned that they took him to a child psychiatrist, but no problems were discovered. Then, when he was 14, he was found to have been sexually abusing his younger sister and was referred for social work assessment. His social workers discovered that he, too, had been sexually abused in a children's home before he was adopted, and they classed him as a low risk of re-offending. Problems continued and eventually Mike was diagnosed as having an attachment disorder. His psychiatrist said that Mike's relationship to his birth mother had been weak and inadequate. As a result, Mike engaged in behaviour that he thought would bring him some attention from those around him. His adoptive parents could find no treatment for him that they could afford, and they feared he would end up in prison.

Source: Guardian, 17 April 2002.

How important are early family attachments in ensuring that children grow up to become acceptable and well-integrated members of their society, and how typical is Mike of those who are deprived of these close relationships? These questions depend on an understanding of the processes of socialization through which people learn what those in their society expect of them and how to act in autonomous ways. In this chapter, we look at socialization, identity formation, and interaction. We show these to be central not only to understanding problems of 'attachment disorder' but also to *all* the actions and experiences through which people's lives are organized. Family life, education, and work all depend upon particular patterns of socialization through which people build a picture of their social world and of their own place within it.

Concepts and theories

One of the striking things about human behaviour is that most of the things we do are learned. While much that an animal does is determined by its biology, very little human behaviour is instinctive or fixed in this way. Children come into the world as helpless infants, and they develop into slightly less helpless adults only because they learn from their parents and from other adults how to speak, study, work, marry, vote, pray, steal, and do all the many other things with which people fill their time. All these activities must be learned.

Animals do, of course, learn as well. Birds, for example, must learn how to fly. Many animals can even be trained by human beings to do things that are not 'natural' to them—dogs can be house trained and they can also be taught to sit up and beg for food. The dependence of human beings on learned behaviour, however, is fundamentally different from anything else found in the animal kingdom. While some aspects of human behaviour do have similarities with animal behaviour—particularly with that of monkeys and the higher primates—most is qualitatively distinct from all other animal behaviour. Human beings learn to be conscious agents, capable of reflecting upon their own behaviour and of modifying it in the light of their experiences. It is this conscious, subjective element in human conduct that makes it more appropriate to describe it as 'action' than as mere 'behaviour'. Action is behaviour to which a subjective meaning has been attached and that can, therefore, be reflexively monitored by a human actor. To be a person is to *act*, not simply to behave.

This point is not always fully appreciated, and many non-sociologists have held that human behaviour can be explained in purely biological terms. As a result, the relative merits of biology and sociology have been hotly debated, though often with considerable misunderstanding on each side of the argument.

The relationship between biology and culture has been a matter of much contention, with advocates of the most extreme positions tending to dominate the debates. Through the nineteenth century and well into the twentieth, advocates of **biological determinism** held sway. Biological determinists hold that all aspects of human behaviour can be explained in terms of the universal and innate characteristics that people have in common as human beings. These claims have been further developed in recent years because of advances in the understanding of genetics. Biological determinism has once more been forcefully promoted, most notably in the new scientific specialisms of sociobiology and evolutionary psychology.

The fundamental limitation to biological explanations of human conduct is that, as action, it is meaningful, and not simply instinctive or reactive. Social life involves interactions through which people take account of each other's behaviour in determining their own behaviour. Biological predispositions may create behavioural tendencies, but humans engage in a conscious reflection on the meaning of the other's behaviour and on the significance of this for their own future actions. Georg Simmel referred to interaction as 'sociation', emphasizing that it is the means through which all social phenomena are produced. In sociation we try to understand the actions of others, and they try to understand ours. Interaction, then, involves the establishment of mutual knowledge that allows us to predict with a greater or lesser degree of accuracy what is likely to happen in any particular situation.

This mutual knowledge comprises expectations about the kinds of things that others will or ought to do: it consists of *norms* of behaviour. A norm is a more or less conscious expectation that someone will 'normally' act in one way or another. It is a rule of behaviour that may exist as a formal prescription such as a law or moral principle or a more informal expectation about what is typically likely to occur.

Norms and the larger systems of ideas and symbols that people use to understand their own and other people's behaviour comprise the **culture** of a society. Culture is learned and is quite variable from one society to another. To know how to behave in any particular society, people must be socialized into its culture. They must learn how to understand the other people that they will encounter and, in particular, they must learn the norms that prevail and that must shape their interactions.

The importance of culture in human life led some sociologists and anthropologists to a position of **cultural determinism** as a counter-doctrine to biological determinism. A central figure in the promotion of cultural determinism was Margaret Mead, an anthropologist whose views we will look at later in this chapter. She undertook a series of studies that seemed to show the infinite variability of human behaviour from one culture to another and that were therefore taken as firmly establishing the claims of cultural determinism. Recently, however, some of the key elements in her account have been questioned. The way has been opened for a more sophisticated understanding of the interdependence of culture and biology, an understanding that avoids the extreme deterministic theories that have been advocated on both sides of the debate.

Identity and socialization

Human beings are social animals, and the process through which someone learns how to be a member of a particular society is termed **socialization**. It is through socialization that people acquire their culture, their specific skills and abilities, and a knowledge of what kinds of people they are. People continue to learn throughout their lives, but the first few years of life are critical. Through their interactions with others, infants gradually become aware of themselves as 'individuals'. They come to see themselves as conscious and reflective entities—agents or subjects—capable of independent and autonomous action. Central to this growing awareness is a child's conception of him or herself as a person. Without close social relationships with other people during these early years, children will fail to learn how to interact and to communicate. For ethical reasons, it is impossible to produce direct evidence for this claim by depriving human infants of social experience in an experiment. Nevertheless, evidence from observations of those children who have, for one reason or another, been brought up in isolation from normal human contact shows this to be the case. Such children may, in later life, learn basic table manners and toilet behaviour, but they have no real ability to use or to understand normal language, and they have only a very limited ability to engage in normal social interaction.

A distinction can be made between primary socialization and secondary socialization. **Primary socialization** takes place in infancy and childhood, typically within a family or a small household of carers. This early socialization provides the foundation for all later learning. Through their interaction with parents or carers, children are able to learn a great deal about what it is to be a member of their particular society. They also learn such specific skills as the ability to speak their own language and to interact and communicate with others (see Box 4.1).

Secondary socialization begins in later childhood, when children begin to interact more frequently outside the household and with people other than their parents. Interacting with other children and with teachers at school, they begin to learn a broader range of social skills and to acquire a more detailed knowledge of roles outside the family. As they get older, much of this interaction takes place beyond the direct control of their parents. During adolescence, the peer group of other adolescents becomes a particularly important agency of socialization. Secondary socialization runs parallel with formal education in contemporary societies, but much socialization takes place outside the school—for example, in clubs and on the street corner—and it continues into adult life. In a very real sense,

human beings are still being socialized into their society, learning new things about it, until the very moment of their death.

Self and society

It is through socialization that a person acquires a sense of social identity and an image of his or herself as a person. People attribute personality characteristics of all sorts to themselves, and those with whom they interact also define their characters and their actions in various ways. When someone is defined, or labelled, as a specific *type* of person, it can be said that a **social identity** has been attributed to him or her. A social identity, then, is a particular label that has been applied in order to indicate the type of person that someone is. As a result of the label, that person may take on the description and so interact with others in terms of that identity. They may even come to feel that they *are* that kind of person.

Social identities do not refer to specific, discrete personality characteristics (such as cleverness, honesty, or reliability), though any of these may be involved in an identity. They are, rather, clusters of personality characteristics and attributes that are linked to particular social roles, categories, or groups. Examples of commonly identified and labelled social identities in contemporary societies include woman, child, father, Asian, Jew, doctor, teacher, clerk, mechanic, lesbian, druggie, criminal, and so on. Some of these identities are based around clearly defined occupational roles, some relate to more general social positions, and others correspond more to stereotypes than to actual roles. Nevertheless, each designates a particular type of real or imagined person, to whom particular moral characteristics and social abilities are imputed, and with whom people may identify or be identified by others.

Someone identifies with a particular social type—or is identified in this way by others—when there is a feeling that the type adequately describes certain enduring features of his or her life. A social identity is regarded as somehow fundamental to a person's whole way of being: it is what the person *is*, above all else. It should not be assumed, however, that people can identify themselves in only one way. In contemporary societies, in particular, people are likely to identify themselves in a number of ways and can be said to have multiple identities. Because of the various roles or positions that she has, for example, a woman may see herself as a woman, an Asian, *and* a doctor. Multiple identification has become more common. Instead of identifying exclusively with one particular type of person—a worker, for example—people are now more likely to identify with a variety of social types. They may shift from one identity to another according to the situation or context in which they are acting and the roles that they take on. For example, a

---

⦿ Briefing: wild children   4.1

Kamala (about 8 years old) and Amala (about 1½) were discovered in India in 1920, living as part of a pack of wolves. After their rescue they were seen to walk on all fours, and to eat and drink with their mouths, directly from the plate, and at night they howled. No one knows how they came to live with wolves rather than in a human group. Amala did not survive the discovery for long. She died within a year. Kamala, however, lived to be 18. By the time that he died, he had learned to walk upright and to wear clothes, but he had learned to speak only a few words.

A boy called Ramu, also discovered living with wolves, was taken to an orphanage run by Mother Theresa. He continued to hunt chickens at night, but, although he learned to dress, he never learned to speak before he died, aged 10, in 1985.

The truth of these accounts of 'wild children' has been questioned, but evidence from the case of Genie, an American child, supports the general position. Genie was systematically abused by her parents and was kept away from any social contact until the age of 13. Despite being taken into care and given physical attention and social support, Genie has never learned to speak and lives in a residential home.

Source: Gleiman (1995: 73–80).

man may regard himself as being a teacher when he is at work, a father when he is at home, and a Labour activist when he is involved in local politics.

We will often refer to social identity simply as identity, but this is a little ambiguous. The word 'identity' is widely used to refer both to what we call social identity and to the related idea of personal identity. A social identity marks people out as, in certain respects, *the same as* others. A **personal identity** marks someone out as a *unique* and quite distinct individual. Central to a personal identity is a personal name. Personal names are attempts to individualize and so distinguish a person from all other people with whom he or she may share one or more social identities. It is, for most people, the most immediate and important marker of personal identity.

Having a personal name marks out our individuality as a unique person. In fact, of course, few names are actually unique, as even a cursory examination of any telephone directory will show. Nevertheless, even those with quite common names regard them as being their personal property, and they can be quite disconcerted to come across other people with the same name. People feel, in the words of the football chant, that 'there's only one …'. A name is closely tied to other markers of individuality: signature, fingerprints, photograph, address, birth certificate, and various official identification numbers (R. Jenkins 1996: ch. 7). Where names are shared within a family or group, pet names or nicknames are often used to differentiate people and to emphasize their individuality.

The growth in online banking and retailing has created huge new problems of 'identity theft'. When someone can obtain the name, date of birth, and other items of personal information relating to another, he or she may be able to use this information to pose as the other and fraudulently to obtain bank loans or consumer goods. They are able to do this because identity claims in online transactions do not involve the face-to-face encounters through which people normally gain information to validate or invalidate personal and social identities.

Personal identity is the link between the concepts of social identity and self. Social identities are, in principle, *shared* with others. There are, for example, large numbers of people who might identify themselves as men, as English, or as engineers. The word **self**, on the other hand, is used to distinguish a person's sense of her or his own uniqueness or individuality. A sense of self is built up when people reflect on their personal history and construct a biography of how they came to be the people they are. They grasp their various social identities and characteristics and unify them into a conception of what is particular or peculiar about them as an individual (Strauss 1959: 144–7). Only in very extreme situations where a person has a single, all-encompassing identity might a social identity and a sense of self coincide (see Box 4.2).

 ### Briefing: what is an individual? 4.2

Social identity is a person's sense of the type of person that he or she is: man, woman, black, white, tinker, tailor, soldier, sailor. Personal identity, on the other hand, is a person's sense of his or her own individuality and uniqueness and is marked by a name, personal appearance, identification numbers, and so on. A sense of self is the particular image that is associated with a personal identity, the defining characteristic of individuality. It is how people see themselves and how others see them.

Many countries already issue identity cards with unique identification numbers and credit card-style identity cards that ensure entitlements to welfare benefits and hospital treatment. Supporters of civil liberties see this as a fundamental threat to freedom and individuality, and a sociological study has highlighted its costs (**http://is.lse.ac.uk/idcard/ identityreport.pdf**).

This kind of threat has often been explored in popular television programmes. The cult 1960s television series *The Prisoner* depicted the attempt by an all-pervasive power to subject the prisoner, 'Number Six' (played by Patrick McGoohan), to its control. The Prisoner was confined to a self-contained village from which escape seemed impossible. Control was exercised by a constantly changing 'Number Two', subject to an unseen 'Number One'. The prisoner's constant response to attempts to control him is 'I am not a number, I am an individual.'

The more recent television series *Star Trek: Voyager* explored this theme through the character 'Seven of Nine' (played by Jeri Ryan). Originally a member of the Borg collective, where individuality does not exist, this 'drone' was designated simply as the seventh of nine members in a particular work group—her full Borg designation was 'Seven of Nine, Tertiary Adjunct of Unimatrix Zero One'. Liberated from the collective by the *Voyager* crew, Seven of Nine was given a crash course of secondary socialization into the nature of individuality and her Borg designation was transformed into a personal name: her familiar name among the crew became simply 'Seven'.

❓ *Why are numbers seen as more anonymous and less individual than names?*

➔ *You will find a cultural analysis of the* Star Trek *series in Barrett and Barrett (2001).*

The sense of individuality that is central to the idea of the self is obvious from the importance attached to markers of personal identity in modern societies. This highlights a very significant social change. In many pre-modern societies, identities were collective and corporate. People had little sense of their own individuality. They had *public* social identities—as citizens, peasants, and lords, for example—but they had no real sense of a *private self* that was separate from these social identities. Their whole existence was tied up in the collective life they shared with others around them. This identification with the group is fundamental to what Durkheim called mechanical solidarity.

As societies have become more complex and diversified, so a greater sense of individuality has emerged. Durkheim (1893) saw this growth of individualism as a central feature of the spread of modernity. In societies with a growing sense of individuality, there is a greater tendency to use the idea of the self. Personal names become more important as ways of distinguishing among different individuals. The development of individual names, then, is a comparatively recent feature of human history. In England, for example, it was not until the twelfth or thirteenth centuries that surnames came into use for the majority of the population.

Primary and secondary identities

The moment of birth is, in contemporary societies, the point at which social identities are first ascribed to

individuals. The period of preparation for birth may, of course, involve some anticipation of the child's identity: bedrooms may be decorated, clothes bought, and so on. Not until birth, however, can a true identity be given to the child. A newborn infant is immediately identified as being a boy or a girl and, soon afterwards, is given a name. The baby's sex and name, together with the names of his or her parents, are officially recorded by a government official, and they are often announced and affirmed in a religious service. Infants are not, of course, in a position to respond to these imputed social and personal identities—certainly not in any conscious or reflexive way—and will have little choice about them. Both the given identity and the official record are likely to remain with them throughout their life. A married woman who adopts her husband's name does so only by convention and custom, and only her 'maiden name' is shown on the marriage certificate.

> **⊃ Connections**
>
> The sexual identification of a newborn infant is not always straightforward, as we show in the opening section of Chapter 5, p. 150, where a case of intersexual identity is considered. Running through Chapter 5 is a discussion of the relationship between sex and gender identity.

Through the period of primary socialization, in infancy and childhood, the core social identities are added to. Children gradually take a more active part in the construction of their social identities. It is through these processes of primary socialization that **primary identities** of personhood, gender, and, perhaps, ethnicity are built up (R. Jenkins 1996: 62).

Personhood is a sense of selfhood and human-ness. It is something that develops quite early in infancy, but it does so only very gradually. The newborn child's first active role in determining its own identity comes as it develops a conception of its own personhood. An infant only gradually learns that it exists as something separate from its surroundings. Similarly, it slowly learns that it is capable of making things happen, that it is capable of being an agent. This involves learning a sense of difference.

The child learns that it is different from its cot and its toys, and that it is different from its parents. It also learns, however, that it shares certain characteristics with its parents. These shared characteristics separate the child not only from inanimate objects but also from the family pet and from other animals. In these ways, the infant begins to learn an initial sense of self and of its own human status: it learns that it is a person. This begins to develop prior to the acquisition of any language, and it seems to be a crucial precondition for developing a linguistic competence. It is, however, massively extended once a language is acquired. The sense of personhood develops rapidly as a child's language abilities expand during the second year of its life.

Gender and ethnicity interact in social identity.
© Alice Chadwick

When a child becomes aware that it is a person, its parents or carers can begin to solidify those other social identities that they have made and recorded for it. These identities are those that the parents regard as being important defining characteristics of their own identities and circumstances. Most important among these is a gender identity—being masculine or feminine. This gender identity shapes the ways in which parents act towards their children. Clothes, toys, and the use of language, for example, are all differentiated by gender from the very earliest hours of a child's life. In due course, gender also shapes the way that a child will act him or herself.

Closely linked to gender identity is a child's identity within its family or household. When learning that it is a boy or a girl, it typically learns that it is a child and, moreover, that it is the child of a particular mother and father. Through its parents, it may learn that it is a brother or sister, that it is a grandchild, a nephew, and so on. All these aspects of its gendered kinship identity define it genealogically within a particular family.

An ethnic identity—membership in a particular cultural group defined by 'race', religion, or language—is likely to be ascribed to a child in its early years whenever ethnicity is salient to its parents and those with whom they interact. In contemporary Britain, for example, being black is highly salient for most people of African or African-Caribbean background. It is something that their children learn very early on. Being white, on the other hand, is not so salient to members of the majority ethnic group. It is not widely employed by them as a personal marker, and many white children do not learn to see themselves as being white. Where ethnicity is salient, an ethnic identity is learned as an integral part of a gendered family identity. In these circumstances, it might be said, ethnicity is an aspect of genealogy.

> **⊃ Connections**
> We discuss gender identity in greater detail in Chapter 5. Racial and ethnic identity is covered in Chapter 6, pp. 194–5. You will find our discussion of these topics very relevant to the general argument of this chapter.

Primary identities are far more stable than those acquired later in life. As Richard Jenkins (1996: 62) argues:

> Identities entered into early in life are encountered as more authoritative than those acquired subsequently. At most, a child can only muster a weak response of internal definition to modify or customise them. Taken on during the most foundational learning period, they become part of the individual's axiomatic cognitive furniture, 'the way things are'. Very young children lack the competence to counter successfully their external identification by others. They have limited reserves of experience and culture with which to question or resist, even were they disposed to. And they may not: during and before the process of language acquisition the human learning predisposition leaves the individual open to forceful and consequential definition by others.

As the child grows up, it usually comes to think of its primary, ascribed identities as being fixed and all but unalterable. Some aspects of personal identity can be altered: given names may be shortened or modified into nicknames, and people have a certain degree of freedom to modify their name in relation to what they perceive to be its image or connotation. A man may, for example, prefer to be known as James rather than Jim, or Mick rather than Michael. This freedom rarely stretches to a complete change of name, though the law generally permits this. Parenthood and sex, however, are much more likely to be treated as permanent and unchangeable. They are seen as natural and normal features of the way the world is. Changes in these matters are likely to be seen as unthinkable or as extremely difficult, if not impossible. Despite some widely publicized court cases, it is difficult for a child to 'divorce' his or her parents, though disowning parents is slightly more common. Only a very few individuals ever reconsider their gender identity, and few of these go so far as to seek medical treatment to change or correct their sexual characteristics. Those who do will often experience great difficulties in convincing others of their new social identity, and they may face very great difficulties in altering some aspects of their personal identity. It may be very difficult—often impossible—for example, to change the details that are recorded on a birth certificate. John Smith, who has sex-correction surgery and becomes Joan Smith, is likely to encounter resistance from others who refuse to accept that she is really female. Legislation is beginning to alter this situation. In Britain, the Gender Recognition Act of 2004 allows transsexuals, under certain circumstances, to acquire a birth certificate issued in their new name and gender.

Secondary identities, acquired during secondary socialization, are built onto a foundation provided by primary identities. The most important secondary identity that most people acquire in modern societies is an occupational identity. Through entering the labour market and a particular type of work, they come to see themselves as the type of person who fills that occupational role. They describe themselves and are described by others as an engineer, a baker, a doctor, or a sociologist. Other secondary identities are also important, and some of these have gradually become more important than occupational identity. Leisure- and consumption-related identities, for example, have become particularly important. People may define themselves as antiques collectors, football fans, opera buffs, horse enthusiasts, and so on.

A sense of national identity has also been sharpened for many people. In Britain and the United States, for example, nationality is an important secondary identity for many members of the white majority populations. For members of their ethnic minorities, on the other hand, their primary identities as black or Asian remain highly salient and these identities are reinforced by the actions of those who exclude and oppress them. The persistence of these ethnic identities may often run counter to governmental attempts to foster a common sense of national citizenship. We will return to secondary identities later in the chapter. We discuss them more fully in various parts of this book.

Narratives of identity

It is important not to treat identities as completely fixed or essential attributes of individuals. The identities that people see as salient vary according to the particular situations in which they find themselves. People can present themselves to one another in varying ways as they pass from one situation to another. They have a stock of identities on which they can draw as seems appropriate, much as they have a stock of clothes from which they can select according to the occasion. Identities are multiple, diverse, and constantly shifting. Of course, not all aspects of identity are completely unanchored. Primary identities are relatively stable and underpin the more shifting and transient secondary identities, and some secondary identities may be particularly salient and will shape the ways in which individuals present themselves in a range of situations. Nevertheless, the fundamental flexibility of identities must be recognized.

For many commentators, this flexibility is something that has increased in contemporary societies. The plurality and diversity of the social situations in which people find themselves in these highly differentiated societies gives a far greater scope for the deployment of multiple, but transient, self-presentations. People are no longer bound so deeply into the tight and enclosed communities that formerly sustained their unified and relatively fixed identities. These days, people have a far greater choice as to how they identify themselves to each other.

A recognition of this growing flexibility of identities has been particularly closely associated with post-modern theory (see our discussion in Chapter 2, pp. 61–3) and with those theorists who see the plurality and diversity of identities as a central feature of a post-modern condition. Identities, they argue, are not essences that lie behind forms of self-expression and self-presentation: they *are* these presentations. It is acts of self-presentation, then, that produce or 'perform' identity (Butler 1990). Identities become stabilized and relatively enduring only when continued and repeated performance fixes them in the minds of the performers and their audiences.

Zygmunt Bauman (1995), for example, has argued that the problem of identity in the past has been the problem of how to build an identity and to keep it solid and stable. In the contemporary world, on the other hand, the problem is that of avoiding complete fixity and maintaining a range of choices as to what kind of person to be. People today, Bauman argues, seek to keep their options open and pursue flexibility in the ways they are seen by others and, therefore, in their own life experiences. They no longer want to be tied down to the communal and organizational contexts that, for much of the modern period, have defined shared and fixed identities.

A particularly important strand in recent work is the argument that the production of identities must be seen in relation to the **narratives** that people construct to account for their actions. People account for their actions and offer explanations of them, and, as they do so, they construct and reconstruct their own biographies, drawing selectively on their memories (Gergen and Gergen 1983; Gergen 1994). In producing these accounts, they also draw on a cultural stock of acceptable explanations, and these tend to have a standardized form. The more acceptable motivational narratives that there are, the more likely are identities to be plural and transitory.

In any society, then, there are typical, recurrent accounts that can be used to explain actions. The culture of a society comprises a number of available character types and patterns of motivation that allow people to construct stories with characteristic plots that the others with whom they interact are likely to see as acceptable accounts of their behaviour. These narratives shape their future actions and the likely reactions of others, and the available cultural stock of narratives is an outcome of the interaction, dialogue, and negotiation that makes up the social process. Narratives are, in part, self-conscious attempts to create continuity and coherence in personal experiences, but they also shift in response to the varying situations in which people find themselves. This underlines the fact that there is no 'real' identity. When people do succeed in producing a coherent account of their 'true' identity, this is a consequence of their narrative success and their ability to persuade themselves and others of this 'truth'.

The possibilities people have to present themselves in varying ways through the appropriate use of narratives have increased with the growth of the Internet. Any form of communication at a distance—by letter, by telephone, and by e-mail—allows people to escape some of the constraints of face-to-face encounters and to present themselves in alternative ways: it is possible, for example, to say things in writing that it would be very difficult to say in person. With Internet-based communication, however, this has increased greatly. Virtual communities can be built through discussion groups, bulletin boards, and chat rooms. And contacts may be followed up through individual e-mail. This opens up new possibilities of self-presentation:

> Since participants cannot see each other, and are not obliged to reveal their names or physical location, there is considerable scope for people to reveal secrets, discuss problems, or even enact whole 'identities' which they would never do in the real world. . . . These secrets or identities may, of course, be 'real', or might be completely made up. In cyberspace, as the saying goes, no one can tell if you're talking complete garbage.

Gauntlett 2000a

People on the Net engage in 'identity play', and this may often allow them to try out an identity before presenting it in face-to-face situations. They can try out their biographical narratives in a situation from which they can easily withdraw, testing its acceptability to other people (Turkle 1997). In some cases, of course, identities may be cynically presented in order to make sexual contacts with those who may not be aware of the identity 'play' that is going on: there has been evidence, for example, of paedophiles using chat rooms to make apparently innocent contact with young children.

Internet sites such as Facebook (www.facebook.com), You Tube (www.youtube.com), Bebo (www.bebo.com), My Space (www.myspace.com), Twitter (http://twitter.com/), and other social-networking sites have become increasingly important means of self-presentation, allowing people to display images of themselves and to construct narratives in support of their proclaimed identities (see Box 4.3). They are able to construct an image or representation of themselves and to build networks of Internet 'friends' with whom they can interact.

In the rest of this chapter, we will review the main theoretical perspectives on socialization and the formation of social identity. We will show how identities are related to the shared construction of social realities, and we will look at how emotions are socially shaped in different societies.

Theories of socialization, identity, and interaction

Three theoretical approaches to socialization and social identity can be considered: role-learning theory, symbolic interactionism, and psychoanalytic theory. Although often seen as rival theories, they actually contribute different components to an understanding of socialization. There are, of course, many points on which they disagree, but their central insights are complementary viewpoints on a highly complex phenomenon.

The first approach that we consider is role-learning theory. This stresses the importance of role behaviour in social life and, therefore, the need to learn the norms that make up role expectations. People are seen as learning about various social roles and then reproducing what they have learned in their own behaviour. Symbolic interactionism, on the other hand, gives more attention to the formation of the self through social interaction. It sees role-playing as a *creative* process, not simply as the replaying of things learned during socialization. Psychoanalytic theory, the third theory that we will look at, gives particular attention to the unconscious aspects of the mind and to the ways in which emotional forces drive people towards particular patterns of action throughout their lives. The sense of self built up during socialization is seen as reflecting the ways in which people come to terms with these unconscious emotional forces.

Role-learning theory

Role-learning theory has been developed mainly by writers associated with the structural-functionalist approach to sociology. However, it is not only functionalists who have used it. It is a much broader approach towards the learning of social behaviour. The theory starts out from the rejection of biological reductionism that we have already looked at. The biological attributes with which infants are born give only the *potential* for social action, and these have to be developed through socialization into

---

New technology Home pages   4.3

One way in which people present themselves on the Internet is through the construction of home pages, where narrative accounts of lives and careers are presented for all who care to consult the page.

Log onto the Internet and visit some personal home pages: just type a personal name into a search engine (such as www.google.co.uk) and you will discover a number of home pages.

What identities are presented on these pages, and how would you try to judge their truthfulness?

How many social networking sites can you find on the Internet? How do they differ from each other? What restrictions and controls is it legitimate for governments and ISPs to impose on self-presentations and interaction on social networking sites?

Cheung (2000) contains a useful discussion of these issues.

the normative expectations that define their social roles. People become social by learning social roles.

Social roles are treated as *social facts*: they are seen as institutionalized social relationships that are matters of constraint rather than choice. People are not free to renegotiate what it is to be a doctor, a teacher, or a mother. They must largely accept the ways in which these have come to be defined within their culture. Someone employed as a teacher, for example, is seen as having very little freedom of choice about how to act when carrying out that role. Social roles are blueprints or templates for action, and people must follow the specific requirements and obligations that define the role. They provide people with examples or illustrations of how to behave, and these can be directly copied in their own behaviour (H. M. Johnson 1961: 135–6). Socialization is, above all, the process through which individuals learn how to perform social roles.

Conformity to learned role expectations is seen, in part, as resulting from external pressure through the rewards and punishments that people apply to each other's behaviour. Role partners reward conformity and punish deviation, so bringing role performance into line with their expectations. A child seen as naughty, for example, may be smacked or offered an inducement—perhaps sweets or an extra hour of television viewing—if he or she will behave as the parents expect. In the same way, a teacher thought of as poor may suffer the rejection or disapproval of children, parents, and other teachers, and may be denied promotion opportunities by his or her head teacher. A teacher felt to be good, on the other hand, may be awarded a higher salary, popularity from pupils, and high status from colleagues. In these ways, role performance and role expectations are kept in line.

Role-learning theory holds, however, that this kind of external coercion and constraint is insufficient on its own. If conformity to role expectations is to continue, there must be a process of **internalization**. People must internalize their roles, making them a part of their self, and so become committed to them (Parsons 1951; Parsons and Bales 1956). They must not only learn the expectations that define particular roles; they must also come to see these as requirements, as obligations. They must become integral elements in their own personality and motivation. People must *want* to act in the way that they are expected to act. These ways of acting must come to seem natural or normal to them because they are morally committed to them.

According to this point of view, a good mother does not remain good because of public approval or financial inducement—although these are, of course, seen as important. Rather, the good mother is committed to doing the best for her children simply because she loves them and knows no other way of being a mother. Ideas about what makes a good mother may vary quite widely from one culture to another, and the good mother is someone who

has internalized the particular expectations of her own culture. Socially approved patterns of behaviour are so deeply ingrained in her personality that she no longer recognizes that they have their origin outside her in cultural expectations. She has truly internalized them.

Role-learning theory sees primary socialization within the family as laying the foundation for all later social learning. It is from their parents that children learn their culture and the basic roles of their society (see Box 4.4). Children internalize a large number of common social roles during their primary socialization. As well as learning the roles that become part of their own social identity, they build up an image of the basic roles of their society. They construct a mental map of its many social positions.

At the same time, people build up emotional attitudes towards these internalized representations. They can be recalled to memory and so become the objects of thought and of sentiments of approval or disapproval, desire, or aversion. Children can, for example, imagine particular social positions and the roles associated with them, and they can think and feel what it would be like to be that kind of person.

The first roles that children are likely to learn are the immediate family roles of mother, father, brother, and sister, and their own role as a child. They may also learn wider family and friendship roles (aunt, uncle, cousin, friend) and, through their play, some basic occupational roles (train driver, postal worker, police officer, and so on). Secondary socialization begins when children enter schools and other groups and organizations to learn specific skills. Schools, for example, are more formal means of

Briefing: is a family necessary for socialization?   4.4

Some proponents of role-learning theory write as if everybody is born into the same kind of family—the conventional nuclear family that we discuss in Chapter 12. The theory is, however, quite compatible with a recognition of a much wider range of family and household patterns. The key point is that primary socialization is seen as occurring in small social groups that are organized around face-to-face interaction, and that variations in the type and composition of this social group will result in variant patterns of socialization. Role-learning theory sees the potential for 'failures' of socialization to occur wherever this kind of small-group interaction does not exist or is weakened.

For most people today, this social group remains the two-parent or lone-parent family household. If you want to pursue this further, look at our discussion of family and household in Chapter 12.

training and instruction into specific skills and bodies of knowledge, but they also deepen and enlarge a knowledge of social roles. Indeed, socialization is a lifelong process, as individuals continue to acquire role-specific knowledge through their interactions with others in the local community, at work, and in the political sphere. In all these ways, socialization gives people a knowledge of the particular cluster of roles that define them as an individual and that give them their identities.

While stressing the process of socialization, role-learning theory itself offers no specific theory of the actual mechanisms of learning that are involved. Its major contribution has been to emphasize the link between roles and socialization. The accounts offered of how socialization actually takes place tend to draw on one or other of the two theories that we will consider later in this chapter—symbolic interactionism and psychoanalysis.

Role-learning theory emphasizes a process of **role-taking**. It sees people as taking on culturally given roles and acting them out in a rather mechanical way. People's actions are seen as almost completely determined by the cultural definitions and expectations that they have learned during their socialization. This deterministic view of social behaviour has been criticized for its 'over-socialized' view of action (Wrong 1961). From this point of view, individuals are rather misleadingly seen as the mere puppets of their culture, as having no real freedom of action in the face of the institutionalized social facts. Role-learning theory, then, overemphasizes the degree of internalization and commitment that is normally achieved through socialization.

R. Turner (1962) has shown that individuals do, in fact, have considerable freedom in almost all situations to decide how they will act out their roles. Social roles are not tightly specified and compulsory blueprints for action, but are loose frameworks within which people must *improvise* their actions. Roles invariably allow people a degree of latitude in deciding how to conform and whether to disregard or to bend certain of the expectations placed on them. Indeed, it can be said that role-learning theory overstates the degree of consensus that exists over role expectations. There may often be quite contrary views of how the occupants of particular roles should behave, and role-learning theory has taken over the strong consensus model that is found in much structural-functionalist theory.

> ⮞ *Connections*
>
> You might find it useful to return quickly to our discussion of structural-functionalist theory in Chapter 2, pp. 42–8.
> There you will find a discussion and criticism of the idea that all societies rest upon a consensus of opinion and values.

The freedom available to people in their roles is especially apparent where—as is typically the case—people have to play two or more conflicting roles at the same time. A woman in paid employment as a teacher who also has childcare responsibilities as a mother will often have to juggle the expectations attached to the two roles of teacher and mother. She must construct a course of action that will, she hopes, meet at least the more pressing demands of both work and home. This is likely to involve her disregarding many other expectations and acting in ways that have not been explicitly scripted in the cultural definition of the role.

It is important to recognize, then, that people create and modify the roles they play. Socialization does not program people in the same way that a computer can be programmed to behave (Giddens 1976: 160–1). People are active, not passive: they *make* roles, rather than simply *take* them. In order to develop this point of view, it is necessary to draw on the work of George Mead and the symbolic interactionists.

Symbolic interactionism

We showed in Chapter 2 that the key figures in the development of symbolic interactionism were George Mead and

The games children play help them to learn about social identities.

© Alice Chadwick

Erving Goffman. It was Mead's ideas on the social construction of the self that were later developed by Goffman (1959) and extended into a theory of the social *presentation* of the self. These general ideas are discussed in Box 4.5; Goffman is discussed in Box 4.6, p. 124.

Mead held that sociological analysis must always start out from the meanings that objects have for individuals. These meanings are not 'given' in the nature of the objects themselves. A meaning is a social construction. It is a definition that is decided through communication and negotiation and in relation to shared interests and concerns. The social construction of meaning is a process that depends upon the communication of meanings within and between social groups.

The social process is a complex pattern of socially constructed meanings, both other people and social objects depending on the social context for their meanings. A man identifies the particular other people with whom he interacts as, for example, his wife, his boss, his friend, his bus driver, and so on. These people, in turn, define him as a husband, subordinate, friend, or passenger. A central tenet of symbolic interactionism is that the way in which a person is labelled is highly fateful. A child who is called a thief when taking something that belongs to someone else may eventually come to see him or herself as having the character of thief if the accusation is repeated often enough.

Similarly, the various objects used in interactions—houses, offices, buses, pubs, beds, desks, coins, and glasses—are also socially constructed. They have no intrinsic meaning as physical objects. A limestone cave in Somerset, for example, may be a dwelling place, a storage area for cheese, or a tourist attraction, depending on whether it is being used by a Neolithic hunter-gatherer, a nineteenth-century dairy farmer, or a twenty-first-century entrepreneur in the leisure industry. A particular knife can be defined as a cooking implement, a letter opener, or a means of suicide. Objects are, of course, produced with their social meanings in mind, but they are never completely predefined, and depend on usage for their social meaning. Social interaction is a process in which these constructions and definitions are used and built up.

Mead argued that the creation and use of meanings depends upon individuals consciously monitoring their own actions. It is only when they have developed a sense of their own self that this is possible. A self is constructed through a process of socialization in which children, and adults, must continually come to terms with the reactions of others to their actions. Mead saw play activities as the means through which young children initially develop into social beings. In their games, children imitate what they have seen their mothers, fathers, and other adults doing. By playing 'house' or 'mothers and fathers', for example, they gradually begin to learn how it might feel to *be* a mother or father. Mere imitation is unreflective copying. Mead saw this as characteristic only of very young infants who had not developed a symbolic capacity. Once they have learned to understand and manipulate symbols and have, in particular, acquired an image of their self and of others, they will always interpret and reflect upon what they see others do. They imagine alternatives and assess these alternatives in relation to the likely reactions of others.

Mead called this process taking the role of the other. The role of the mother, for example, is taken on and explored by a young girl in her games, as the mother is typically the most salient person in her life. She is a **significant other**, an interaction partner who is especially important in an emotional sense. In her play, however, the child does not simply copy her own particular mother. She improvises motherly behaviour from her rudimentary understanding of the role expectations attached to motherhood. As the child's play becomes more complex, particularly through play with siblings and other children, so her understanding of these role expectations becomes gradually more refined.

By acting out the role of a parent towards a child, Mead argued, the child also comes to acquire a conception of self, an idea of 'me' as someone who can be the object of other people's attention. In Mead's terminology, there are two aspects to the self: the 'I' and the 'me'. The I is the source of action, but other people observe and react towards the me. The me is the social self, constructed through interactions with others and reflecting the attitudes that they adopt. The me has been termed the 'reflected' or 'looking-glass self' (Cooley 1902) because it is a reflection of the attitudes of others.

The social self is seen as having developed by about the age of 4 or 5. At about 8 or 9, children's play activities become more detached from the roles of particular others (their mother or their father) and they begin to take on the

---

THEORY AND METHODS   4.5

The symbolic interactionist approach

Originating in the social psychology of William James, and developed in the early work of Cooley and Dewey, symbolic interactionism received its classic formulation by George Mead at the University of Chicago. The key ideas were set out in an influential set of lectures (1927) that he delivered. Mead's ideas were developed by his student, Herbert Blumer, and then, more radically, by writers such as Everett Hughes and Howard Becker. Goffman took up central themes from Mead's work to develop a powerful theory of social action as 'performance'. If you are unclear about the general framework of symbolic interactionism, reread the discussion of this in Chapter 2, pp. 48–50.

Self-presentation depends on the use of appropriate props and scenery.

© John Scott

THEORY AND METHODS 4.6

Erving Goffman

Erving Goffman (1922–82) was born in Alberta, Canada. After graduating from the University of Toronto in 1945 he began his graduate work in sociology and social anthropology at the University of Chicago. Although he cannot be unambiguously regarded as a symbolic interactionist—he owed at least as much to the structural functionalism of Durkheim—he was firmly grounded in the traditions of Chicago ethnography. His theory is sometimes described as a 'dramaturgical' theory, because it sees social life as being like a drama or theatre play. He undertook fieldwork in the Shetland Islands for his Ph.D., producing the data on social interactions that became the basis of his famous book on *The Presentation of Self in Everyday Life* (1959). In the middle of the 1950s he carried out participant observation in mental hospitals that he later published in *Asylums* (1961*b*). His first teaching post, in 1957, was at the University of California, Berkeley, where Herbert Blumer—the systematizer of symbolic interactionism—also taught. During the 1960s and 1970s Goffman undertook a long series of studies in such areas as disability, advertising, and gambling. His best-known books include *Relations in Public* (1963*a*), *Stigma* (1963*b*), and *Gender Advertisements* (1979).

attitude of what Mead calls the **generalized other**. They begin to infer the common or widely held values of their society by generalizing from particular adults to society in general. They begin to consider how other people in general within their society might react to particular kinds of actions, and they may also begin to objectify these attitudes as norms and standards of conduct that have a *moral* authority. The attitudes of the generalized other become the voice of their moral conscience. Through constructing a sense of self and moral conscience, children become properly socialized members of their society, and they can begin to broaden their experience of the world through their secondary socialization.

Play involves pretending to be something other than what one really is: the child pretends to be a mummy or a teacher. Goffman (1959) has argued that, in important respects, people continue to play with one another when they interact in adult life. When they take on a particular role, they must interpret it creatively in their actions. As we have seen, roles are not fixed blueprints, but loose guides to action. People must play their social roles in the same way that professional actors play theatrical roles. Goffman holds that people are like actors on the stage, and they employ props and scenery in their interactions in order to try to convince others that they really are what they claim to be. Their aim is to give a convincing dramatic performance in front of their audience.

A man who is employed as a hospital doctor, for example, might typically wear a white coat or hang a stethoscope around his neck in order to symbolize his medical competence. As technical instruments of medical investigation, they are constructed as objects that symbolize the professional status of the doctor and the special social position that he or she occupies. The scenery against which the doctor acts will typically include a couch, screen, sink, table, cabinets, and the particular coloured paintwork that define the room as a surgery rather than a kitchen, bedroom, or office. Many of the props and much of the scenery, of course, have a technical purpose, but Goffman argues that they also have a symbolic purpose that allows the doctor to persuade his or her patients that it really is all right to take their clothes off, swallow a pill, or allow a scalpel to be inserted into their bodies. Without these props, patients may find it difficult to accept that person as a doctor. To sustain this acceptance, doctors must also give a convincing performance through their actions: they must try to convey an air of competence, even if secretly they have to resort to a textbook or ask the advice of nurses.

Goffman's argument, then, is that social interaction is a process of **self-presentation**. We are always presenting ourselves for others to observe, and we have a considerable amount of discretion as to exactly *how* we present ourselves. People cannot usually check out all the claims made by those with whom they interact, and much must be taken on trust. This is why it is so easy for the confidence trickster and the fraudster to gain at the expense of others. More generally, however, we are all engaged in a more or less cynical manipulation of the others with whom we interact. We constantly try to present ourselves in the best possible light by 'bending' the truth, obscuring conflicting evidence, and employing the appropriate props.

Theatre actors can retreat backstage and avoid the gaze of their audience, and Goffman argues that social actors also rely on **back regions**. Much social interaction occurs in front regions, where people are on stage and acting out their roles in public. Offices, hospitals, factories, and schools are all, for most of their participants, public front regions. The back regions are those places to which people can withdraw and relax, abandoning some of the pressures of public performance. In the back regions, people can say and do things that are incompatible with the self-image they are trying to present in public. The front region of the hospital ward, for example, may have its back-region kitchen, where nurses can get away from their patients. Similarly, the school has its staff room and common rooms, the office block has its private office areas, and so on.

For many people, their home is the ultimate back region, a private haven for relaxation away from the public world. The distinction between back region and front region is maintained within the home, however. The hall and lounge, for example, may be treated as front regions where visitors can be entertained, while the kitchen and back sitting room may be a back region that only the family can enter. Even in private family settings, however, people must still present a self to other family members. Members of the family may, therefore, defend their own bedrooms as back regions to which they can escape from the rest of the family and 'really be themselves' (Lincoln 2004).

This highlights the important ways in which Goffman has developed the concept of the self. This is no longer seen as an internal cause of action, but as an external product of action. Personal and social identities, then, need not be seen as completely fixed by an automatic process of socialization. They are presentations or performances through which people actively seek to identify themselves, in varying ways, in the eyes of others. The self that is presented in interaction is something that an individual works to produce and that depends, in large part, on the ability or willingness of others to cooperate in this:

A correctly shaped and performed scene leads the audience to impute a self to a performed character, but this imputa-tion—this self—is a *product* of a scene that comes off, and is not a *cause* of it. The self, then, as a performed character, is not an organic thing that has a specific location, whose fundamental fate is to be born, to mature, and to die; it is a dramatic effect arising diffusely from a scene that is presented, and the characteristic issue, the crucial concern, is whether it will be credited or discredited.

Goffman 1959: 223

Our ability to act out multiple identities—and therefore to present different selves—is made possible by the segregation of different types of activity. We can behave as one kind of person at work, another at home, and yet another at a party because we interact with different people in each of these settings. In each setting, we present a self that conforms to the expectations of the particular audience and of which we think the audience will approve. By segregating activities in this way, we can try to ensure that those who see us in one situation will not see us in any other. Problems of self-presentation arise, however, if there is any seepage between different settings. When parents turn up at university at the beginning or end of term, for example, students may not only find the parents' behaviour excruciatingly embarrassing, but will also experience a conflict between acting in the way that they usually act with friends at university and acting in the way that they usually act at home.

Psychoanalytic theory

Where interactionism has focused on cognitive meanings, psychoanalysis focuses more directly on *emotional* meanings. At the heart of this theory is the idea that human behaviour can be explained in terms of the relationship between the conscious and **unconscious** elements of the mind. People are seen as being motivated by unconscious drives. These are emotions of which they are unaware or that they experience only in a distorted form. Their conscious lives are dominated by the attempt to control the expression of these drives. Psychoanalysis, then, looks at the relationship between the surface structure of consciousness and the deeper structure of the unconscious.

Much early psychoanalytical theory has emphasized the biological basis of the emotions and, therefore, the ways in which people learn to try to control their 'natural' tendencies and drives. A failure to control successfully the unconscious is seen as the source of mental disorder and of mental illness. Later psychoanalysts have broadened this out and have recognized the cultural formation of these unconscious drives.

The main theorist of unconscious mental processes was Sigmund Freud, who saw them as rooted in people's biological drives (see Box 4.7, p. 126). Freud (1900, 1901, 1915–17) held that the biology of the human body generated unconscious drives and desires, in particular the

THEORY AND METHODS   4.7

Freud and psychoanalysis

Sigmund Freud (1856–1939) was born in Vienna and trained in medicine, specializing in nervous disorders and the use of hypnosis. From his clinical conversations with his patients, he developed his method of interpreting dreams and conscious processes in terms of deeper unconscious forces. Freud is, perhaps, best known for his emphasis on the centrality of sex in human life. As a Jew, he was forced to leave Austria when the Nazis seized power, and he spent the rest of his life in London. His key ideas were developed by his daughter, Anna Freud (1895–1982), and, above all, by Melanie Klein (1882–1960).

Later psychoanalysts, who built a firm awareness of cultural diversity into Freudian theory and who departed from some of the ideas of the Freudian orthodoxy, were Alfred Adler (1870–1937), Karen Horney (1885–1962), and Harry Stack Sullivan (1892–1949).

A number of writers attempted to synthesize aspects of psychoanalysis with Marxism, most notably Erich Fromm (1900–80) and Herbert Marcuse (1898–1979). More radical and controversial forms of psychoanalysis were produced by Carl Jung (1875–1961), who formulated theories of inherited unconscious symbolism, and Wilhelm Reich (1897–1957), who developed theories of the orgasm and authoritarianism.

drive for pleasurable experiences that satisfy bodily needs. The conscious mind—which Freud called the 'ego'—had to come to terms with these forces. Human action is shaped by the continuing struggle between unconscious, instinctive drives and the conscious, rational control exercised by the ego.

Freud recognized many sources of bodily pleasure that could motivate people in diverse ways—the pleasures of eating, drinking, urination, and defecation, for example, all play an important part in human motivation. It is, for example, pleasurable to eat food that satisfies a feeling of hunger. These pleasures are experienced through the senses, and Freud saw sensual pleasure as culminating in the pleasures of genital sex. For this reason, Freud virtually equated the sensual with the sexual, and he described all pleasure-seeking as having a sexual character (Freud 1905). It is undoubtedly true that he seriously overstated the significance of sexuality, and also that he tended to see this in deterministic, biological terms (Webster 1995). Nevertheless, the broader implications of his thought, as explored by later writers, concern the need to explore human bodily pleasures in the broadest sense.

In his later work, Freud added an account of a drive towards aggression that operated alongside the drive towards pleasure, although he never properly spelled out the biological basis of this aggressive drive. Later psychoanalysts, as we will show, have explained this drive in cultural terms, just as they have also given greater attention to the cultural shaping of the drive towards pleasure.

The conscious ego is seen by Freud as responding to emotional drives on a practical, rational basis. It learns to control the ways in which they are expressed, forming them into habitual, recurrent patterns of behaviour that can be undertaken with little or no conscious deliberation. This control may involve deferring desires until they can be safely and properly expressed, but they may often be denied expression altogether. Those emotions that are denied are pushed back to form the unconscious part of the mind that Freud called the 'id'.

The id was seen as a seething mass of forces formed from biological drives and from their repression by the conscious mind. Through repression, these drives can be converted ('sublimated') into socially acceptable forms of behaviour. This denial of the drives, however, can mean that they return to consciousness in distorted forms. Repressed sexual desires, for example, can make themselves felt as slips of the tongue—so-called Freudian slips. They may also appear in a disguised form while dreaming, or as anxiety, hysteria, and more serious forms of mental disorder. It was this dynamic relationship between the conscious and the unconscious that Freud saw as being both a creative force and a destructive or pathological force in human action. Repression does not only produce the energy that makes social life possible; it also produces forms of mental illness.

Freud argued that the core elements of the personality are formed during childhood. It is through infants' interaction with their parents and other members of their immediate family household that their drives are satisfied or frustrated. A baby attempts to discover how to achieve satisfaction rather than frustration. It learns, for example, that a particular behaviour, such as a sound (a cry or, later, a word), is likely to be an effective way of influencing the carer. It is through their experiences of satisfaction and frustration that infants gradually become aware of themselves as individuals with a capacity for self-reflection and conscious thought. The conscious ego, like the unconscious id, is a product of the social interactions through which children learn how to respond to satisfaction and frustration. This is the source of the key emotions identified by psychoanalysis. Adult responses are uncertain, and infants develop a sense of *anxiety* about the reactions of their carers. Later on, they develop a sense of *guilt* about those behaviours that meet with disapproval. It is the handling of anxiety and guilt, and their consequences, that psychoanalysts have seen as the critical element in personality development.

It is in the first few years of life that this sense of self and of conscious orientation to the world develops. At this same time, a sense of morality develops. Parents place prohibitions on a child's behaviour by punishing it and saying such things as 'Don't do that, it's not right.' These parental prohibitions are gradually internalized by the child as its own sense of right and wrong, as a conscience. They become that part of the child's conscious mind that Freud called the **superego**. It is the superego that provides the standards in relation to which the demands of the id are assessed by the ego (Freud 1923). Particular kinds of sexual experience, for example, come to be judged as bad, and therefore as things that cannot be expressed in action. Mental illness results from states of anxiety or guilt that are caused by the conflict between the moral demands of the superego and the unconscious urges of the id. The relations between Freudian concepts and Mead's ideas are discussed in Box 4.8.

Freud stressed the biological basis of people's unconscious desires, but he gradually came to give more

attention to the cultural desires that they derived from their social experiences. This broadened understanding of the relationship between the biological and the cultural was taken further by a number of later psychoanalytical writers, who also moved away from Freud's overemphasis on childhood sexuality. Alfred Adler (1928), for example, held that people are motivated by a striving for power and for recognition (a sense of belonging or acceptance). They seek to be superior to others in these respects and to avoid any experience of inferiority. Feelings of inferiority are, however, inescapable, as superiority and inferiority are necessary consequences of social inequality. Adler, therefore, saw people as developing a sense of their self in relation to their perceived successes and failures. It was when people consistently felt inferior that they showed symptoms of the mental disorder that he called an **inferiority complex**.

Karen Horney (1937, 1946) opened up psychoanalysis even more. She argued that what is regarded as 'normal' varies from one culture to another, and that what is normal in one society may be regarded as neurotic in another (see also Fromm 1942; Riessman 1961). Nevertheless, Horney did still recognize that particular forms of socialization were essential for the formation of a coherent sense of self. Children who do not receive warmth or affection from their parents, Horney argued, will grow up with a deep-seated and generalized sense of anxiety. They will be unable to achieve a mental balance. Horney saw neurotic behaviours as the results of attempts to escape this 'basic anxiety'.

This move towards a proper recognition of cultural variability in socialization, and so towards a fully sociological form of psychoanalysis, culminated in the work of Harry Stack Sullivan (1939), according to whom anxiety results from a failure to realize biological and socialized needs in culturally appropriate ways. His understanding of this process has striking parallels with the arguments of the symbolic interactionists. While accepting that a drive for recognition and a sense of acceptance or of belonging was of fundamental importance in human life, Sullivan held that people are motivated to seek this from others by sustaining a particular image or *self-conception* that they believe will be valued by others. In Sullivan, then, the Freudian analysis of the unconscious—the hallmark of psychoanalysis—is united with an interactionist view of the self and self-presentation.

The three theories that we have considered in this section have been used, separately and together, to build understandings of the development of social identities. Whatever insights have been generated by each theory, a more powerful understanding can be achieved if they are used as complementary approaches to socialization.

THEORY AND METHODS   4.8

Freud and Mead

The relationships between the psychoanalytic categories of id, ego, and superego, on the one hand, and the interactionist categories of I, me, and generalized other, on the other hand, are interesting, but far from straightforward. Mead had no real understanding of the unconscious, while Freud gave little attention to the situational presentation of self. The two approaches are, however, complementary.

The ego is the term that Freud used for the conscious mind in its broadest sense. It is similar to Mead's self, of which the I and the me are aspects. It is the interplay of the id and the ego that produces the impulsive, but reflexive, driving force that Mead termed the I. The me, on the other hand, is the 'looking-glass self', the image of how I appear to others. Where Freud gave greatest attention to the interplay of the id and the ego, Mead gave greatest attention to the 'internal conversation'—within the conscious ego—between the I and the me.

The generalized other and the superego have, perhaps, the most direct relationship to each other. They are terms for the internalized responses of others that are constructed into a supervising and controlling conscience.

Stop and reflect

In this section we have discussed the relationship between cultural and biological factors in socialization and identity. We have shown that:

- Human behaviour, unlike most animal behaviour, is learned. However, neither biological determinism nor cultural determinism gives an adequate picture of social behaviour.
- Human learning involves processes of primary socialization and secondary socialization.
- People acquire social identities through their socialization. People today have multiple identities.
- Primary identities develop during primary socialization. These primary identities are those of personhood, gender, and ethnicity.
- How useful is it to distinguish between primary and secondary socialization?

We reviewed the three major theories of socialization and identity, and we have argued that they must be seen as complementary rather than competing theories. We first of all looked at role-learning theory.

- Role-learning theory stresses the importance of learning role expectations. Roles are social facts that constrain people.

- Conformity to role expectations depends upon commitment as well as rewards and punishments.
- Do you agree that role-learning theory tends to have a rather over-socialized view of action?

  Next we examined the symbolic interactionist theory.

- Symbolic interactionism stresses the construction of the self in social interaction. The self is a looking-glass self that reflects the attitudes of others.
- Social actors, like theatrical actors, play roles and act out their parts in public performances. This is how people 'present' their self to others.
- How realistic is it to make parallels between social interaction and acting in a theatre?

The last theoretical framework that we looked at was that of psychoanalysis.

- Psychoanalytic theory places great emphasis on the role of unconscious emotional factors in primary socialization.
- Freud stressed the role of sexuality and, more generally, sensual factors in socialization. Later psychoanalysts have placed more emphasis on cultural factors in the formation of personality.
- Was Freud correct to see sexuality as such an important factor in human life?

Socialization and family relations

We have shown that socialization can be considered as having primary and secondary phases. Primary socialization occurs in infancy and childhood, largely within the family, while secondary socialization involves the later learning that takes place outside the family household. We discuss some aspects of secondary socialization more fully in Chapter 9 and in 'Building social worlds', pp. 136–41 below. In this section, we look a little more closely at the processes of primary socialization through which a basic sense of personal and gender identity is developed. We focus on early childhood and adolescence and highlight the significance of parental roles in socialization and the relationship between culture and biology.

It is conventional to distinguish between infancy, childhood, adolescence, youth, adulthood, maturity, and old age, all understood as stages of life between the ultimate stages of birth and death. The number and length of these stages is culturally and historically variable, and it is clear that we are dealing with socially constructed categories and not biological stages. The idea of childhood, for example, is a relatively recent construction in Western culture (Ariès 1962). The idea of the **life course** brings these stages together, pointing to similarities of experience for all those growing up in a particular society. Fundamental aspects of social identity are those that people share with others as an **age cohort**. An age cohort is a category of people who are born at the same or similar time and who, therefore, undergo life-course transitions at the same time. As a 'generation', they also have definite historical experiences in common that may have a major impact on their outlook on life (K. Mannheim 1927).

Childhood, ageing, and the life course

The implications of ageing for a sense of identity have been explored in works on personality development. Piaget (1924, 1932, 1936; see also Kohlberg 1981) looked at the way in which the biological maturity of children is a pre-condition for them to engage with, and learn from, the world around them. Their sense of space, time, and number, of the nature of the physical world, and of the moral implications of their behaviour develop and are transformed through the specific kinds of 'operations' that they perform on the world as they explore it in their infancy and in formal education. The ways in which they physically operate on the world—handling objects and manipulating them—is itself a social process, made possible by the kinds of social situation in which children are placed. It is this combination of biological maturation and social interaction that results in their move from one stage of personality development to the next. Jerome Bruner (1966) has shown how teachers can draw on this understanding of child development to devise more effective systems of learning in the school.

Noam Chomsky (1965) took a similar approach to the development of language, arguing that the acquisition of language depends upon the innate 'linguistic competence' of human beings, stressing that this can give rise to an understanding and development of language only if children are exposed to language users at an appropriate age. If they do not interact linguistically with their parents and others in the critical early years of life—around the age of 2—they will never be able to develop any sense of language or any linguistic facility. It has also been suggested that the ability to learn additional languages is greatly diminished after the age of 13, when the biological capacity for language acquisition is 'switched off' with bodily maturation.

The work of Lev Vygotsky (1934) has been especially important in stressing that the learning process identified by Piaget depends not only on physical engagement with the world but also on social interaction. For Piaget this was largely taken for granted, but Vygotsky highlights the varying ways in which social conditions can establish opportunities and constraints for children. Their ability to learn from their actions depends upon their social location. This argument is relevant also to that of Chomsky, as it highlights the social shaping of language learning. These ideas were also explored in some of the work on schooling and language acquisition undertaken by Basil Bernstein (1962).

One of the most important contributions to an understanding of personality development has come from the psychoanalytical work of Erik Erikson (1950), who is firmly rooted in the more cultural approach of writers such as Horney. Erikson argues that people go through eight stages of personality development in the course of their lives, thus adding an important account of later adult personality development through social encounters.

The first four stages identified by Erikson are those of infancy (up to age 1), the toddler (from age 1 to 2), early childhood (from 2 to 6), and the early school years (from 6 to 12). These are closely related to what Freud had called the oral, anal, phallic, and latency stages of sexual development, but Erikson emphasizes the specific identity problems that arise at each stage. The first stage is one in which the child can achieve a 'basic trust' in others if its needs are met by the adults (its parents) on whom it depends completely. In the second stage, children begin to do things for themselves and acquire greater autonomy in their behaviour. The third stage is one in which children are able to engage in social interaction with other children and, through play activities, learn to deal with feelings of shame and guilt and begin to take responsibility for their own actions. Finally, through their early schooling they begin to interact with more people outside their own family and can acquire a sense of intellectual competence in their own skills. Development from each stage to the next is not inevitable, but depends upon the cultural context and the social opportunities created by the adults on whom the child depends.

Between the ages of 12 and 18, children are in the stage of adolescence or youth, when their lives are dominated by their developing sexuality. It is in this stage, Erikson argued, that young people are concerned with issues of personal identity. They are concerned with knowing who they are and how they fit in; they build a meaningful self-image. People who fail to resolve this 'identity crisis' will enter adulthood with a sense of uncertainty about their role in life and their sexuality. The young adult stage runs from the age of 18 to the late twenties and is the period when people are concerned with establishing intimacy with others through secure emotional relationships. This is possible, Erikson argues, only if they have successfully resolved the prior identity crisis. By the time a person enters the adulthood of their late twenties or early thirties they will, if they have resolved the 'crisis of intimacy', become concerned with 'generativity', with having and rearing children and, at the same time, building their careers. They seek to establish a home and family as a secure basis for those close to them. Finally, around the age of 50, people enter 'maturity' or the beginnings of 'old age', in which they turn from family building to their own gradual withdrawal from social life. Their children leave home and begin their own young adulthood, and people have to plan for the approach of retirement from work. Ultimately, they must face the approach of their own death, and the whole period is marked by concern and constant 'despair' about 'time running out'. Successful handling of this problem, Erikson claimed, involves the achievement of 'wisdom' and fulfilment.

Erikson certainly does not see any inevitability in the passage through these life-course stages. Each is marked by problems and anxieties that result from the failure to resolve the characteristic crises thrown up by changing social circumstances and bodily abilities. The resolution of each successive crisis is made easy, difficult, or impossible by the resolutions achieved in earlier crises, and the mature personality is a complex sedimentation of all these stages. It is the changing social circumstances of individuals that comprise the driving force in the crises they face and the resolutions they achieve, and societies differ in the demands that they place on individuals and the opportunities that they offer for them to cope with them. The movement from one stage to the next is often marked by rituals and ceremonies that make the transition easier: a marriage ceremony, for example, is a public marker of the transition to adulthood. The socially structured ceremonials, then, are cultural markers on the life course (see Box 4.9).

THEORY AND METHODS 4.9

Rite of passage

A rite of passage is a ritual or ceremonial activity through which a person passes from one social role to another. Such rites are typically linked to phases in the life course, and they are the means through which people can demonstrate that they have made this particular passage in their life, and through which other members of society come to accept them in their new roles. An example of a rite of passage would be a christening ceremony—can you think of other examples?

Mothers, fathers, and children

All three of the theories that we have looked at saw family relations as central to primary socialization. A helpless newborn child requires the care and support of its parents for its physical survival and security. Through this relationship to its parents, the infant also acquires its social skills, social knowledge, and sense of self. All three theories see effective socialization as involving this continuing family support. An important question, therefore, is whether primary socialization is most effective when it takes place in a conventional two-parent household with a close and intimate relationship between, in particular, the mother and child. Not all families are of this conventional form, and not all family households can provide the kind of care that the theories see as being important for normal development. The growing importance of employment outside the household and the increasing number of single-parent households have raised the question of whether primary socialization is adversely affected by changing family relations.

Childhood and parental deprivation

It is psychoanalysis, in particular, that sees early socialization within the family as holding the key to adult emotional development. The relationship between a baby and its adult carer is the critical factor in the development of its personality. For the satisfaction of most of their needs, young children are dependent on an adult to care for them. The baby comes to perceive the carer as the source of its pleasure, as it is only through the carer's actions that its needs can be satisfied. Bonds of attachment are made with a carer who can satisfy the baby's needs and bring it pleasure. Psychoanalysts hold that the mother is central to this. Her pregnancy—so it is argued—will normally have led her to develop strong feelings of affection towards her baby and a willingness to provide continuing care for it.

This emphasis on the role of the mother in psychoanalysis is one of the most contentious areas in psychoanalytic theory, because of the assumptions it makes about female involvement in early socialization. The theory holds that children who are deprived of the close and sustained attention of their mother will be inadequately socialized and will experience serious psychological problems in later life. The chief advocate of this view of maternal deprivation was John Bowlby, who held that what is 'essential for mental health is that an infant and young child should experience a warm, intimate and continuous relationship with his mother' (Bowlby 1965: 13; see also Winnicott 1965). Because of its stress on the importance of attachment to the mother, and on the negative consequences of absence, Bowlby's argument has been described as 'attachment theory'.

A close relationship between mother and child, Bowlby argued, is very weak when the child is looked after by a childminder. It is completely absent when the mother has died or has rejected the baby, and where the child, therefore, has to be brought up in residential care, an orphanage, or a hospital. Part way between these two situations, Bowlby suggested, is the experience of those children who come from so-called broken homes, where contact with their mother is limited or irregular. Most controversially, Bowlby's conclusions have sometimes been extended to the cases of children whose mothers are involved in full-time paid employment outside the household. In all these situations, it is held, the child is deprived of the kind of close and continuing maternal attachment that is required for proper socialization.

Bowlby's evidence showed that maternal deprivation in early life can lead to anxiety in a child, expressed in a growing depression and withdrawal from social contact. This can result in serious physical, intellectual, and social problems in a child's later life, Bowlby said, and in extreme cases it can result in physical or mental illness. The effects of protracted early separation continue into adult life, when they are difficult to reverse or to overcome. Parallels with the experiences of 'wild children' and children such as Genie have often been drawn.

The most crucial period for child development, Bowlby held, is when an infant is aged between 6 months and 1 year. Separation before this time has little psychological effect, so long as maternal care is re-established by 6 months of age. After the end of the first year, the effects of separation are, again, less stark, though Bowlby argued that serious long-term problems can occur as a result of any prolonged separation during the first three years of life. After age 3, problems of separation become less marked, and after 5 there are few significant problems for children.

A great deal of empirical evidence was produced by Bowlby to support his case—though he had no direct evidence on either lone parents or on mothers in paid employment. Nevertheless, his research has been criticized for appearing to place all the responsibility for children's psychological problems onto their mothers. In fact, Bowlby was careful not to do this. Although he held that, at the time he was writing, the nuclear family provided the most usual context for primary socialization and that in most families mothers took the main responsibility for the care of their children, he felt that 'mothering' was an activity that could be provided by what he called a 'permanent mother-substitute'. It is the activity of mothering that is important, not the social position of the person who performs it. A 'mother-substitute' could be an aunt or grandmother providing informal help, or it could be a paid nanny. As a Kleinian psychoanalyst, however, Bowlby did see the gender of the carer as being important. He held that the mother–child relationship was a gendered relationship. Others, however, have suggested that a male carer, such as the father, could provide all the mothering that a child needs. There is nothing in the broader thesis of maternal deprivation that requires that the principal carer should be a woman (Rutter 1972). The crucial finding highlighted by Bowlby's research was that the establishment of a close, intimate, and enduring relationship with the mother or a mother-substitute in the critical period of infancy and early childhood was necessary for effective socialization.

> ⊃ *Connections*
>
> We look at the issue of gender identities in Chapter 5, pp. 154–6, where we also consider the psychoanalytic explanation offered by Chodorow. You might find it useful to review some of that argument now. What are the implications of the view that fathers can 'mother' a child? Evidence on variations in family form are considered in Chapter 12, 'Sex, Marriage, and Divorce', pp. 448–56.

Narratives of motherhood

Mothering, therefore, is not a 'natural' or biologically fixed activity. It is not simply an instinctive nurturing provided to a child by its biological mother. Mothering is a social activity in which both the needs of the dependent child and the responses of the person who mothers are socially constructed. They are shaped by prevailing cultural ideas, and so the forms of mothering can be quite variable from one society to another.

While we have shown that the evidence from attachment theory does not require that this mothering be provided by the biological mother, or even by a woman, mothering is, in contemporary Western societies, a gendered task. It is a task whose social construction is inextricably tied to the social construction of the woman and of femininity and to such related social constructions as wife. These 'feminine' roles and norms form part of a larger system of cultural meanings. They are involved in such constructions as family and kinship, and through these mothering is also linked to ideas of fathering. Fatherhood and fathering are socially constructed as male tasks, linked to the ideas of manhood, masculinity, and the husband. This cluster of social meanings around parenting is the crucial element in the cognitive mappings through which people organize the upbringing of children.

The gendered character of the activity of mothering has been explored by Lawler (2000) in an empirical study of mothers and daughters. She looks, in particular, at the narratives produced by mothers to account for the ways in which they carry out their role and, in particular, to explain how they depart from the cultural idea of the 'good' mother. The mothers that she interviewed held to the idea that a child's character, its fundamental sense of identity, is inborn. They believed that children are destined by nature to be a particular kind of person and that the task of the mother is to allow this essential character to express itself. The nurturing activities of mothers are geared to providing the conditions under which the child can 'be herself'. Their daughters' adult characteristics were seen as the products of their childhood selves, so that they, too, were largely products of nature. Mothers did not, therefore, claim any responsibility for the positive achievements of their daughters: children are destined from birth to develop in certain ways, and it is felt that there is little that mothers can do to change their character or temperament. They did, however, take some responsibility for what they saw as their daughters' failings. These they saw as the results of their own failure to provide proper nurturing. In particular, they felt that they had passed on negative traits of their own to their daughters.

Lawler also examined the accounts of their upbringing produced by the grown-up daughters themselves, and she found echoes of this same narrative. There was a common feeling that their mothers had been too restrictive and had not allowed them enough independence for them to 'be themselves'. Adolescence was seen as the key period in life when conflicts with their mothers had become apparent. Their own desire for autonomy had begun to express itself at this time, and there was considerable conflict between mothers and daughters over how their independence was to be exercised. The daughters, then, felt that they had had to overcome some of the failings that they identified in their mothers, and they claimed that they would not make the same mistakes with their own daughters.

Growing up

It seems that motherhood and growing up, in contemporary Western societies, draw on cultural ideas that deny or ignore their own character as social constructions. Like all social definitions, however, they are real in their consequences for the behaviour of those who act upon them and those who are affected by this behaviour. Adolescence, in particular, becomes a battleground between parents and their children. There has been much work on this generational conflict (Pilcher 1995), and we look at some of the consequences of this for the formation of oppositional youth subcultures in Chapter 7, pp. 249–50. In this section, we turn to some of the consequences of generational conflict for the self-formation of adolescents and the impact of this on their adult lives. We look, in particular, at the work of R. D. Laing and his associates, who have provided vivid examples of the most extreme forms of breakdown in socialization. The generational conflict over autonomy that lies at the heart of the Western family, they argue, can produce serious problems of mental health. These problems, however, are to be seen as problems of the family as a whole, and not just problems for the particular member who comes to be labelled as mentally ill.

It is also important to consider the extent to which this intergenerational conflict is built into Western culture rather than being, as Lawler's mothers believed, rooted in biological universals. If adolescent conflict is not an inevitable feature of family relations, then alternative, and equally effective, patterns of socialization might be possible. A belief that adolescent conflict was not universal lay behind a classic comparative study by Margaret Mead, which tied this to a larger account of cultural determinism. This important work, though flawed, provides important insights into the cultural variability of parent–child relations.

Sanity, madness, and the family

Laing and Esterson (1964) were medically trained psychiatrists who became very critical of the biomedical assumptions behind much psychiatry. They recognized the crucial importance of social factors in the production of mental illness, but they also rejected those views that saw this mental illness as simply an individual pathology, whether psychological, genetic, or constitutional. Echoing the arguments of Szasz (1962), they held that the diagnosed patient has to be seen simply as someone who has strange experiences and behaves in strange ways, as judged by the others with whom the patient interacts. What psychiatrists describe as mental illness is generated within families, and it is the family as a whole that should be seen as having the problem. In particular, they argue that the apparently bizarre behaviour of psychiatric patients makes perfect sense as a rational and comprehensible form of behaviour if seen in the context of the behaviour of the other members of their families.

This opposition to psychiatric approaches to mental illness earned Laing and Esterson the label 'antipsychiatrists', a label that they took on with pride to mark the distinctiveness of their social approach to mental health. The theoretical basis of their work (Laing 1960, 1961) is that of existential phenomenology, a position that shares much with cultural approaches in psychoanalysis and with symbolic interactionism. They applied this theoretical approach to the formation of the particular mental and behavioural patterns commonly diagnosed as schizophrenia. The exercise of autonomy and independence on the part of a child as it grows up is often experienced as threatening and worrying by its parents, who are used to controlling its behaviour closely. When parents expect that their child will continue to conform in all respects as it grows up, they may interpret its individuality and difference as worrying signs that something is 'wrong' with the child. Normal childhood and teen behaviour comes to be seen as a sign of disturbance or of illness. Laing and Esterson explored how the dynamics of family relations produced a concern for the mental health of one of its members and how medical interventions led to formal psychiatric diagnosis.

Schizophrenia is a diagnosis that gets applied to women far more often than it does to men, and it is a diagnosis that often has its roots in adolescent behaviour. In order to explore the family dynamics that lie behind this, Laing and Esterson studied a number of families of hospitalized females diagnosed as schizophrenic. Through interviews and observations, they attempted to uncover the patient's own perspective on the situation and the views and behaviour of the other family members. Their argument is built up through a number of biographical accounts of patients and their families, of which the case of Maya Abbott is typical.

> ⮑ *Connections*
>
> You will find a longer discussion of the debate over mental illness, and how sociologists have tried to understand mental disorders in Chapter 8, pp. 291–6. You might find it useful to read that discussion now.

Interviews with Maya's parents and observations of the family together showed that she had consistently been seen as an isolated, apathetic, and withdrawn child. Maya's parents had found it difficult to allow their daughter to do anything of her own choice, unless it was under their supervision. The more independently that Maya acted, the more disturbed she was felt to be. Maya herself denied this interpretation of her behaviour. She felt that she was not treated as a 'person' in her own right and that her ideas and comments were not taken seriously. She claimed that her parents had never shown her any real emotion or ever allowed her to express her own emotions spontaneously. However, Maya's only point of reference for judging her own behaviour was the attitude of her parents. As she grew up, she, in turn, became increasingly anxious about her own thoughts and came to feel that they might, indeed, be unusual or unnatural.

Maya's parents felt that she told them nothing about herself and was not interested in them, but they interpreted this as a sign that she possessed exceptional powers of mind reading: she did not need to communicate verbally because she could read their minds directly. They began to experiment in their relations with her, trying to catch her out in her mind reading. The things that she said or did were interpreted as signs that confirmed their belief in her strange mental powers. However, the various signals that the parents exchanged with each other as they carried out these experiments (nods, winks, smiles, and so on) were interpreted by Maya as signs that *they* were trying to influence *her* through the power of their minds. Not wanting to admit to experimenting on their daughter, her parents denied that they were signalling to each other, and Maya found it increasingly difficult to know if she was perceiving or imagining the signals. Parent and child, then, became locked into a cycle of misinterpretation and misunderstanding in which the distinction between what was 'real' and what was 'imagined' became more and more difficult to make.

Maya's confusions, as the youngest and weakest member of the family were the 'symptoms' that resulted in her diagnosis as a schizophrenic. She was taken to her doctor and referred to psychiatrists, who diagnosed her as suffering from 'ideas of influence'. The symptom of her schizophrenia was that she felt that she 'influenced' other people and that they 'influenced' her. Laing and Esterson argue, however, that these apparent delusions of influence made complete sense if they were seen in the context of the interpersonal relations of her family: 'Much of what could be taken to be paranoid about Maya arose because she mistrusted her own mistrust. She could not really believe that what she thought was going on was going on' (Laing and Esterson 1964: 40).

Thus, Maya's confusion, anxiety, and withdrawal were a rational and comprehensible response to her experiences in her interaction with her parents. They appeared to be irrational and bizarre to her parents, because they were unaware of their own anxieties and confusions and the effects that these had on their daughter. Maya's behaviour appeared as symptomatic of schizophrenia to her doctors, because they were unaware of the family interactions that gave them their meaning. What psychiatrists and others treated as individual 'illness' became perfectly understandable behaviour when seen in its interpersonal context.

Laing and Esterson concluded that the problems of living that Maya and others like her experience are wrongly and unhelpfully seen as organic, psychiatric illnesses. Treatment based on such diagnoses, they argue, cannot alleviate the problems. Such women could be helped only by bringing the whole family to an understanding of their situation and of the interpersonal spiral of misunderstanding into which they had locked themselves. The interpersonal knots must be unravelled through therapeutic work with the whole family. While the validity of their argument as a complete explanation of schizophrenia has been disputed, they provide a compelling account of how behaviour that appears bizarre or irrational can be understood in terms of the family dynamics involved in socialization.

Adolescence in its cultural context

Franz Boas was the leading American anthropologist of the 1920s and a firm advocate of cultural determinism. He expected to find that non-Western societies such as the Pacific territory of Samoa would show a completely different approach to adolescence from that found in the United States and in Europe. Differences of culture, he argued, would result in different experiences of growing up. If people of the same physiological age could behave in radically different ways, then the problems faced by adolescents in the United States had to be explained in cultural terms. They could not be explained simply in terms of the biological aspects of puberty and adolescence. To explore and, he hoped, establish this idea, he sent a young graduate student, Margaret Mead (see Box 4.10, p. 134), to undertake some fieldwork.

Margaret Mead

Margaret Mead (1901–78) was no relation to George Mead. She studied anthropology at Columbia University, and it was her Samoan fieldwork that made her name and became the most influential anthropological work of all time. This was published as *Coming of Age in Samoa* (1928). A few years later, she carried out some related work into adolescence in the Admiralty Islands, producing *Growing up in New Guinea* (1930). Pursuing her interest in cultural variation, she later carried out work, also in the Pacific, on sex and gender roles for her books *Sex and Temperament in Three Primitive Societies* (1935) and *Male and Female* (1950). She felt very marginal to the male academic world and followed a career as Curator of the American Museum of Natural History in New York. Her work on culture closely paralleled the influential ideas of Ruth Benedict on native Americans (1934) and on Japan (1946).

Mead's study (1928) was undertaken in the small island of Ta'u, part of the Samoan group of islands. Samoa was an American colony and naval base, and Ta'u itself was heavily dependent on its trading relations with the United States navy. Although it was still a tribal society, its chiefs were highly Westernized. Mead concentrated her attention on a sample of twenty-five local girls, who ranged in age from 14 to 20. She lived in a house belonging to the only white family on the island and, working from the house—and using the school building during the holidays—she talked with the girls and began to collect much information about their lives. She claimed that, by contrast with adolescent girls in the United States, those in Samoa had a very easy and stress-free life. This, she thought, reflected the overall balance and moderation of Samoan culture.

Life in Samoa, Mead held, was easy and relaxed, with little or no conflict. Its inhabitants lacked any deep feelings, and they had no strong passions. As they did not get worked up about day-to-day matters, they were rarely drawn into stressful or hostile relationships. Children grew up in large extended families and had no strong attachment to their individual parents. They were, instead, embedded in diffuse, warm relationships with large numbers of adults. They learned, early on, not to act impulsively. Samoa, then, was a very harmonious society. Its people, Mead claimed, were happy and well adjusted.

In this idyllic society, adolescence was the age of maximum ease and freedom. When they entered adolescence, Samoans were free to engage in sexual activity promiscuously. Mead claimed that this reflected the adult view of sex in Samoa: it was an enjoyable and playful activity that should not be taken too seriously.

The girls that Mead studied grew up with a great deal of sexual knowledge. This was unavoidable when large extended families lived in single-room houses with little or no privacy. They began to masturbate in early childhood, generally at 6 or 7, and homosexual relationships were not uncommon during puberty. Adolescence was a time for erotic dancing and singing, and playful heterosexual relations emerged naturally out of this sexual experimentation.

As a result of this, Mead argues,

> . . . adolescence represented no period of crisis or stress, it was instead an orderly developing of a set of slowly maturing interests and activities. The girls' minds were perplexed by no conflicts, troubled by no philosophical queries, beset by no remote ambitions. To live as a girl with many lovers as long as possible and then to marry in one's own village, near one's own relatives, and to have many children, these were uniform and satisfying ambitions.

M. Mead 1928: 129

Mead contrasted this with the typical adolescent experience in the United States. Adolescence there was widely seen as a period of great emotional turmoil. Conflict between parents and their children was rife. Because the ease and balance of Samoan adolescence could be related to the central features of Samoan culture, Mead argued that adolescence in the United States must be seen as reflecting the peculiarities of its culture. The biological universals of puberty and biological maturation, she claimed, have little or no direct impact on people's actions and relationships. Behaviour is shaped, above all else, by the culture into which people are born and socialized.

Mead's study became widely accepted as an exemplary proof of cultural determinism and as a final repudiation of biological determinism. By the 1960s it had become the most widely read of any anthropology book and it was a popular best-seller. Mead's reputation was confirmed by her studies in New Guinea (1930, 1935), where she explored the extent of cultural variation in gender relations. The three societies that she studied—those of the Arapesh, the Mundugumor, and the Tchambuli—appeared to show all possible permutations of masculinity and femininity. Taken together, they further reinforced the claims of cultural determinism.

In Arapesh society, both men and women were gentle, caring, and passive, while in Mundugumor society both were assertive and sexually aggressive. By contrast with the United States and other Western societies, then, neither of these societies showed any significant gender differentiation. They varied considerably, however, in the type of personality that they valued most highly. Arapesh personality was similar to Western femininity, while Mundugumor personality was similar to Western masculinity. In the third society that she studied, the Tchambuli, Mead identified a sharp differentiation of gender roles, and she claimed that these varied in the opposite direction from the United States. Tchambuli men decorated themselves and gossiped with each other, while Tchambuli women were assertive and competent in practical affairs.

Mead's study, then, showed that the situations described by Laing and Esterson (1964) were culturally specific. Laing and Esterson were correct to look at the social factors and to reject biological explanations of schizophrenia, as the adolescent conflicts they described simply did not occur in Samoa. However, while the general thrust of Laing and Esterson's argument is now accepted, some of Mead's conclusions have been challenged. Culture, as we have shown, is an important determinant of human behaviour, but it is not the only determinant and it is not so all-pervasive as Mead had argued. Mead believed that she had conclusively refuted the thesis of biological determinism. The single study of Samoa seemed sufficient to show that there were no universal biologically determined stages of social development. The New Guinea studies simply added more weight to her argument for cultural determinism. These conclusions have been questioned.

The limits to culture

This challenge to cultural determinism was clarified in a systematic criticism of Margaret Mead's research (Freeman 1984). Freeman argued that Mead had been seriously misled in her Samoan studies. She had undertaken only very limited fieldwork, and she had a rather poor understanding of the language. In fact, she had got it all wrong. Drawing on a wide range of less well-known anthropological studies and on his own period of more than five years of detailed fieldwork, Freeman conveys a very different picture of Samoa and of its adolescents. Samoan society, he says, is highly competitive and beset by conflict. Far from being the stable, peaceful, and cohesive society that Mead had claimed, it has much aggression, violence, and rape. Child-rearing is far from being the open and flexible system that Mead had described. It centres on firm parental authority and harsh discipline.

Above all, however, Freeman rejects Mead's account of adolescent sexual behaviour. He shows that virginity at marriage is held in extremely high esteem. A central aspect of marriage ceremonies throughout Western Polynesia is the ritual deflowering of the young bride in public by her husband to-be. Through this violent and humiliating ritual assault, the girl's virginity is publicly demonstrated by a flow of blood. Mead had reported such occasions, but had claimed them to be empty rituals that could easily be avoided and were of no significance. In fact, they have been central to Samoan culture. Given the great importance

attached to virginity, it is unlikely that adolescent promiscuity would be at all widespread. Young girls have always, in fact, been tightly controlled by their parents and by other members of their kinship group. They would themselves ensure that they maintained their purity—whether out of moral commitment or fear of public shame—until their marriages.

Why, then, does Freeman think that Mead could have got things so wrong? When she began to speak to the girls about their sexual behaviour, her lack of fluency in their language meant that she was unaware of the subtle nuances of speech and of the emotional state of her interviewees. Freeman met one of the girls in 1987, by which time she was a rather elderly lady. She told him that she and the other girls had been so embarrassed by the questions that Mead had asked them that they had playfully lied to her. They created a picture of promiscuity and sexual freedom that accorded so well with what Mead had hoped to discover that she had not questioned its truth. The difficulty of studying these issues through participant observation are discussed in Box 4.11.

Mead's views have, however, been supported by other studies, and her wider conclusions are still accepted as valid (Orans 1996). The criticisms of her Samoan study, however, suggest that there are greater similarities with patterns of growing up in the United States than she had wanted to find. To this extent, biological maturation and

---

THEORY AND METHODS   4.11

Problems of participant observation

Mead's difficulties highlight important methodological problems in participant observation. The usual method in anthropological fieldwork is for the researcher to live as a participant in the society that is being studied for a period of one or more years. The fieldworker must learn the language and talk to the locals in order to try to understand their culture from within. Margaret Mead spent only two months studying the Samoan language, and she completed her fieldwork in just five months. In this time, she lived with a white, American family, not with a Samoan family, and she relied on rather formal and uncomfortable interviews. She reports very few of her own observations in the book. Instead of a close ethnographic encounter, Mead relied upon hearsay and on observation at a distance. In these circumstances, she had little or no way of checking the narratives produced by the girls with whom she spoke.

➲ Look at 'Ethnographic research', Chapter 3, pp. 80–6. What lessons do you think that other ethnographers can learn from Mead's study?

its consequences for adolescent behaviour cannot be ignored. Cultural variation may not be quite as extreme as she thought. Nevertheless, it is clear from her work that patterns of socialization and their outcomes are shaped by the cultural context of the societies in which they take place.

Stop and reflect

This section has looked at primary socialization within families. We first looked at a number of issues concerning personality development.

- A child's intellectual, linguistic, and moral development depends upon both biological maturation and interaction with the world. Social interaction is a crucial aspect of the latter.
- The human life course involves the complex negotiation of a series of 'stages' of development, each marked by characteristic social constraints and involving specific subjective responses.
- Should the sociologist accept that biology sets the conditions under which human behaviour and personality can be shaped by culture and social relations?

We then looked at issues related to mothering and motherhood:

- The attachment of a child to its carer is important for the development of its sense of self and its later psychological health. This attachment is built up through the carer's 'mothering' of a child.
- The task of mothering a child can be undertaken by a carer, who need not be the biological mother and who may be a mother-substitute.
- Is mothering an instinctive, biological response or a socially constructed activity?

When we turned to look at adolescence and its shaping by family relations we showed that:

- Adolescence in contemporary Western societies is a period of conflict between parents and children over a child's exercise of its growing independence.
- In certain situations this conflict over independence and autonomy can result in the child being labelled as 'troubled' or, in extreme cases, mentally ill.
- What limits might there be to the cultural determination of adolescent behaviour?

Building social worlds

Secondary socialization builds on the foundations of primary socialization. It allows people to build the social worlds in which they live and into which the next generation will be born. Central to this world-building activity is the playing of social roles. People learn the social roles that comprise their society and they play these roles out in their interactions with others. They do not, however, mechanically act out tightly defined roles. We showed in our discussion of role-learning theory that people do not simply 'take' roles: they 'make' them. That is, they learn merely the outlines or general patterns that define roles, acquiring this knowledge from their observations of large numbers of individuals, as well as from formal learning. When they come to act in a role themselves, they must improvise their actions on the basis of these learned patterns. In doing so, they contribute to the reproduction and, perhaps, the transformation of these roles.

As we showed in Chapter 2, Berger and Luckman drew on phenomenological ideas to show that the social structures that surround and constrain us must be seen as socially constructed realities. Individuals encounter one another with their varying, and perhaps conflicting, views about the nature of the situation in which they find themselves. They negotiate an agreed meaning—a definition of the situation—which then becomes the reality to which they orient themselves. It becomes, over time, taken for granted, and those involved may forget that they built it. When they pass on their knowledge to their children and to younger members of their society, it may be acquired by these others as a fixed and completely given reality that is beyond question and unchangeable. Most social realities are perceived as somewhere between these two extremes: neither unchangeable nor easily renegotiable but capable of change, through individual or collective action, given the appropriate time, effort, and inclination.

Role-playing and the building of social worlds is not a purely calculative activity. People have emotional commitments to the norms and ideas they have learned. This emotional aspect to socialization has been particularly emphasized by psychoanalysts, though Freudian theory has tended to see the emotions as fixed biological drives. An implication of all that we have looked at so far, however, is that emotions must be seen as socially constructed and, therefore, as culturally variable. There is a biological basis to emotions, but the ways in which these are shaped and expressed reflects cultural factors. Work based on this important idea has shown that many roles involve the performance of 'emotional labour' and that contemporary societies have generated high levels of emotional anxiety that are difficult to handle.

Constructing realities

The argument that secondary socialization is central to the building of social worlds can be illustrated from a number of areas, and we take two examples of the general processes involved. We look first at the marital roles of husband and wife in order to consider how these roles are creatively performed, on the basis of outline cultural 'scripts', by those who marry. Marital partners build a family world into which their own children are born and in which these children will, in turn, learn how they, in due course, may produce themselves as husbands and wives. We then look at this same process of world building in occupational roles, taking hospital nursing as our example. Any occupational role is performed by those who have learned the basics of the role before they enter it, but who must learn—and create—its details at the same time that they play it.

Once they are constructed, social realities must be maintained. Because social roles are only partially defined in the culture and so are creatively performed by their occupants, there is a constant risk of disruption by those whose definitions of the situation differ or who have been less well socialized. Taking the example of medical investigations, we show how the various participants must cooperate to minimize the effects of these disruptions.

Constructing a marriage

The roles played by men and women in their marital relationships—the roles of husband and wife—are learned as very general cultural typifications or templates. These predefined typifications of what it is to be a husband or wife give only a very general guidance on how to act in these domestic roles. They are outline scripts whose details are produced and reproduced in the negotiated interactions of the marital partners.

It is within the private sphere of the household that all family relations have their focus (Berger and Kellner 1970). Each family is felt by its members to be a sub-world, an area of interaction segregated from more public spheres of interaction and within which people generally feel free to express themselves as individuals and to produce the kind of world in which they can feel comfortable and relaxed. It is there that the most basic meanings and identities that people live by can be produced.

The starting point for constructing a family and its small-scale sub-world is the construction of the marital roles of husband and wife. Berger and Kellner see this as a new stage of socialization, following on from socialization in childhood and adolescence. The wedding ceremony itself is the crucial rite of passage that marks the entry of the marital partners into a new household and a new stage of life.

In forming a marital partnership, those who are still relative strangers to one another gradually come to know each other better and, at the same time, they construct, through their actions, their own particular performances as husband and wife. They bring to their marital interactions the highly generalized cultural typifications learned through observing their own parents and others in marital relationships, and through reading and watching television. They also draw on those wider cultural themes that run through these typifications: such themes as romantic love, sexual fulfilment, self-realization through love, family relationships, and so on. It is in these general and very abstract scripts that people acquire the means through which they can extend and enlarge on what is expected of them and can invent new forms of husbandly and wifely behaviour:

> Their society has provided them with a taken-for-granted image of marriage and has socialized them into an anticipation of stepping into the taken-for-granted roles of marriage. All the same, these relatively empty projections now have to be actualised, lived through, and filled with experiential content by the protagonists. This will require a dramatic change in their definitions of reality and of themselves.
>
> *Berger and Kellner 1970: 58*

The first step is coming to be seen as a unit—a 'couple' or an 'item'—rather than two completely separate individuals. They must convince themselves, as well as others, that this is the way in which they should be seen. Each partner's identity must be reconstructed as the partners come to be seen—by those outside the relationship and by the partners themselves—as conjoined: they are seen, and they see themselves, as a unit. Each partner must align his or her definitions of situations with those of their partner. Only in this way can their actions within the marital relationship be coordinated.

Each husband is expected to be the most significant other to the wife, and vice versa. People enter this process, however, with only a partial awareness of what they are doing. They generally believe that they remain largely unchanged within their new relationship. They believe that they have a fixed social identity, rooted in their experiences of developing as a child and a youth. For this reason, they typically believe that their fundamental identity remains culturally invariant. They experience their change of identity on marriage as a series of encounters with particular others who now define them, in important respects, differently. In responding to these definitions, however, they construct themselves as a husband or a wife and their identity is slowly and inexorably transformed: old friends are dropped and old relationships transformed, new joint friendships are formed, and new, shared experiences are built up.

A new shared definition of reality is constructed and is constantly redefined through conversation and interaction and through encounters with those outside the marital relationship. When children are born, their existence strengthens the identity of the marital relationship. The children refer to the partners as 'Mummy' and 'Daddy', reinforcing their identity as parents as well as husband and wife.

> **Connections**
> The Berger and Kellner argument focuses on the conventional marriage relationship and the conventional family. They tend to give a rather idealized view of the family. How well do you think the argument applies to non-marital partnerships and the cohabitation of men and women? How much of their argument do you think applies to same-sex partnerships and 'marriages'?

Being a nurse

The improvised construction of roles also occurs in the world of employment, where much secondary socialization takes place. The nature of this role behaviour is particularly well illustrated in a study of nursing carried out by Davina Allen (2001). Allen focused on nursing as a gendered occupational role, a specific occupational position in the division of labour that is disproportionately filled by women. Like many 'caring' occupations, nursing originated in the voluntary work undertaken by many women as an extension of their domestic role, as wife and mother, within the family. Although now organized in hospitals and medical practices and undertaken as paid employment, nursing is still influenced by its origins.

Allen shows that contemporary nursing has come to be shaped by two competing ideas of work organization: 'professionalism' and 'managerialism'. The idea of professionalism sees nursing as organized around a moral obligation to provide care as autonomous and trained experts. The idea of managerialism, on the other hand, depicts the nurse as an employee at a particular career grade in a bureaucratic organization and as subject to the authority of supervisors (Dingwall *et al.* 1988; Witz 1992). The larger context for these rival ideas was a complex of changes in health policy and nurse education during the 1990s. The introduction of the internal market, accountability, and managerialism to the health service had an impact on many occupations, including nursing. At the same time, however, nurse education came to emphasize greater professionalism through degree-level training. In particular, Project 2000 emphasized the autonomy of clinical nursing and the need for a 'holistic' approach to patient care.

> **Connections**
> You will find a discussion of wider changes in working practices in Chapter 17, pp. 680–4, and Chapter 14, pp. 539–45. Policy changes are considered in Chapter 15, pp. 576–82.

These changes resulted in much debate over the nature of the nursing role, and to greater uncertainty for nurses as to how the role should actually be performed on the wards and in surgeries. Nurses come to their training with only a general idea of what it is to be a nurse, and their training and the reorganization of nursing and health care have meant that their concrete formal knowledge about the role—as against their purely technical, medical knowledge—was ambiguous and uncertain. The reforms reshaped the cultural templates of the nursing role, making them even less certain than before. The meaning of the role had to be reconstructed and renegotiated in the day-to-day interactions of those who were actually undertaking the task of nursing in hospitals and medical units.

Allen focuses on the issues of role conflict that arise within the role-set of the nurse. Merton's contribution (1957) to structural functionalism and role-learning theory had been to introduce this idea of the role-set to describe all those pairs of roles that are regularly involved in structured relationships with each other. Thus, Allen identifies role relations among nurses of various grades as well as role relations between nurses and support workers, management, doctors, and patients. Each of the relations in this role-set is an area of negotiation and has the potential for conflict. The boundaries and the links that make up the role-set are contested and subject to constant negotiation.

Allen's study involved observations and interviews in two hospitals in the Midlands. Her focus was on the ward nurses and the ways in which they organized their work. In particular, she was concerned with how they organized the teamwork required by the new nursing practices.

In wards dominated by managerialist ideas, conflict between junior and senior nurses was especially marked. The junior nurses claimed that senior staff did not devolve responsible jobs to them but retained control over them in order to boost their own status in the ward hierarchy. The junior nurses saw the senior nurses as too bureaucratic and regulatory, and they opposed this in the name of what they saw as their own—professional—'patient-centredness'.

Doctors, nurses, and other medical staff spend more time in managerial work.
© Getty Images/Nicholas Russell.

In units dominated by ideas of professionalism, on the other hand, senior nurses saw themselves as coordinating rather than controlling. As a result, there was less conflict over work allocation. However, the senior staff in these units were less happy with the situation. The senior nurses felt that their job had little real content to it: much primary nursing care was devolved to the junior nurses, and the senior nurses were left with more paperwork and administration.

Thus, staff experienced role strains, expressed as boundary disputes over participation in patient care. These strains reflected the role realignment that had been required by Project 2000, though the ways in which they were worked out depended upon the particular negotiated interactions of nurses in the various kinds of ward and medical unit: 'Nurses are subject to conflict and ambiguous ideologies. The professional rhetoric of "new nursing" emphasizes their status as autonomous practitioners but as employees in a managed organization they are expected to render

obedience to superiors and conform to formal rules and regulations' (Allen 2001: 75).

These strains deeply affected their sense of professional identity: what did it now mean to identify oneself as a 'nurse'? The general public may have images of nurses drawn from accounts of Florence Nightingale and television programmes such as *Casualty*, *The Royal*, *Scrubs*, or *House MD*, but nurses themselves had a far less clear idea of what nursing means in practice and how their work relates to the larger division of labour in health care.

These ambiguities were also apparent in concerns over the demarcation between nursing work and the work undertaken by unqualified support staff. Project 2000 reforms had introduced the new occupation of health-care assistant, and there was much ambiguity over the boundaries between this and professional nursing. Where the organization of ward-level care put great emphasis on the work of the ward team as a whole, the boundary was very blurred, especially in the non-technical areas of work.

Allen notes that there were also implications for the nurse–patient boundary, as patients themselves had become more actively involved in routine care tasks such as the keeping of records, maintaining fluid balances, and making some technical measurements and adjustments to equipment.

It was in relation to management, however, that conflict was especially marked. Nurses recognized the gendered character of both nursing and management, routinely referring to managers as 'the men in suits'. The relation between managers and nurses was a gendered power relationship: men holding authority over the women who were undertaking the caring work. Many nurses felt that the increased paperwork they were expected to do undermined their ability to participate fully in professional patient care and involved them in tasks that were properly the sphere of management. Those employed in the grade of 'nurse manager' were pulled in both directions and tended to see themselves playing an intermediary role, as translating central requirements into more professional and collegial forms whenever possible. However, they tended to be seen as outsiders by both the managers and other nurses.

Nurses followed flexible working practices that led them into areas that were often regarded as the province of junior doctors—it was often easier to make a decision on the spot than it was to consult a doctor. This gave the nurses greater autonomy, but was a source of conflict with doctors.

The boundaries of nursing work are produced in particular practical situations where nurses come into contact with patients, other professionals, and managers. The ways in which these boundaries are produced, however, are constrained by the general institutional context and the combination of competing managerial and professional ideas. They are further constrained by consumerist ideas that try to give patients rights as 'customers' of the healthcare system. This led to conflicts with the more traditional 'service' orientation that nurses had long held to.

Changes in the organization of health care make it more than ever impossible for nurses to undertake their work immediately on the basis of their generic training and its induction of them into the nursing role. They cannot simply 'take' a pre-existing nurse role and play it out. They must 'make' this role for themselves through their conflict and negotiation with others involved in the provision and receipt of health care.

Sustaining medical definitions

In interaction, people build and sustain shared definitions of reality that define the various situations they enter. It is rarely the case that there is a single, consensual definition of reality—as some forms of structural functionalism have argued. There are usually 'counter-realities' or, at the very least, counter-themes that oppose or qualify any dominant definition. A dominant definition is likely to be the outcome of complex negotiations among a group of actors. For this reason, the participants must work hard to maintain the dominance of their preferred reality, and their ability to sustain it depends on their power, on the resources that they can bring to bear on the situation.

Joan Emerson illustrates these processes through her investigation in a gynaecological clinic. Like any medical examination, a gynaecological examination involves sustaining a medical definition of reality that justifies forms of intrusion that are not normally permissible in interpersonal encounters: doctors must be able to ask highly personal questions and to interfere with another person's body, and this is possible only if the participants agree to maintain a medical definition of reality. In a gynaecological examination, however, these problems are especially acute because the personal intrusions concern the genitals: 'Since a woman's genitals are commonly accessible only in a sexual context, sexual connotations come readily to mind. While most people realize that sexual responses are inappropriate in this situation, they may be unable to dismiss the sexual reaction' (Emerson 1970: 76).

Thus, the medical definition is countered by a sexual definition of reality that continually threatens to undermine the medical definition and so make medical intervention impossible. Doctors and medical staff must work hard to prevent the patients from seeing the examination in sexual terms. The medical definition gives staff the right to carry out their work, and it minimizes any threat to the dignity of the patient.

A medical definition is sustained through the adoption of a matter-of-fact stance, implying that 'this happens all the time' and 'nothing unusual is going on'. Staff make it clear that they are not interested in the aesthetics of the patient's body and that 'their gaze takes in only medically pertinent facts' (Emerson 1970: 78). The aim is to convey the idea that the patient is regarded as a technical object—they are concerned with the biological body and not with the self that inhabits it. Of course, there may be occasions on which doctors really do take a sexual interest in their patients and use the medical definition of reality to mask their deviance (see Box 4.12). At the same time as adopting a technical stance, a doctor must also acknowledge the patient as a person, as without this there will not be the necessary cooperation. Some of the counter-themes, then, must be recognized and brought into play alongside the medical definition of reality.

The complexity of the medical encounter results from the need to balance these contradictory elements. Various routine ways of doing this are established:

- Props and scenery are utilized to emphasize the clinic as a 'medical space': decoration, equipment, titles, nameplates, uniforms, and announcements all work to this end.

Briefing: medical assaults   4.12

Newspapers regularly report cases of doctors who sexually assault their female patients. The power inherent in the doctor–patient relationship makes it difficult for women, in vulnerable situations and seeking medical help, to resist such assaults. It can be very difficult for them to prove their cases against the doctor.

❓ *What does Emerson's argument suggest about the causes of such behaviour by doctors? Are they, too, less well socialized into the norms of medical investigations, or is their commitment to these norms overridden by stronger motivations?*

➲ *You might like to look at newspaper archives, surfing the Internet, to collect reports from recent cases and see if you can come up with any evidence on this.*

- Rituals of respect are employed. For example, the patient's body is covered so that only the part to be examined is visible, and a female nurse may act as 'chaperone' to a male doctor.

- The use of technical language and impersonal forms to refer to the patient's genitals helps to depersonalize and desexualize the conversation: medical staff refer to 'the vagina', not 'your vagina'. Similarly, they may use oblique terms when addressing the patient, such as referring to problems 'down below'.

- A nonchalant demeanour.

A crucial problem, however, is that patients are less well socialized into these norms and routines, and so there is the ever-present possibility that they may do or say things that disrupt the medical definition of reality. They may show signs of embarrassment, such as blushing, which emphasize the sexual aspects of the situation and make it more difficult for medical staff to adopt an impersonal and technical orientation. Similarly, displays of modesty or of concern over the aesthetics of the body show that the patient has not fully accepted the requirements of the medical definition of reality.

Where such things occur, doctors and nurses adopt strategies to neutralize the disruptions. One strategy is to continue to maintain a nonchalant demeanour, not acknowledging the patient's disruptive actions and hoping that a medical definition will re-establish itself. Often it may be necessary to redefine behaviour: signs of embarrassment, for example, may be defined as signs of 'pain', so reasserting a medical interpretation of the behaviour. Humour may also be used to acknowledge but defuse

disruptions by channelling them away from the doctor–patient encounter. Conversations with nurses, for example, are safe ways in which patients' fears and concerns can be addressed before they meet the doctor.

Emotions and reflexivity

We have looked at the construction of social realities through interaction, exploring the cognitive images of social life and the normative expectations that people build up to shape their actions towards each other. In this section we look at the idea that human emotions can also be seen as socially constructed. The part played by emotions in social life was particularly stressed by psychoanalytical writers, but many of them—and most notably Freud himself—saw these emotions as natural, biological factors that are a fixed and universal element in human motivation. Those who incorporated a cultural dimension into psychoanalysis were particularly concerned to emphasize the interdependence of culture and biology: culture shapes, or constructs, not only the ways in which emotions are expressed, but also the very emotions themselves. This is not to deny the biological, bodily aspects of emotion—this cannot be ignored. However, the meaning and experience of anxiety, love, fear, and so on are culturally variable.

In this section we will look at the social construction of emotions through an important study by Arlie Hochschild, who examined this through an investigation into the organization of particular kinds of work and their implications for self and identity. Hochschild draws on the work of symbolic interactionists—and on Goffman, in particular—to complement the insights of psychoanalysis. We also look at the argument of those writers who have seen contemporary societies as particularly likely to develop high levels of anxiety because they are structured around a growing awareness of the risks inherent in modern social life.

Emotional presentations

Hochschild sees an emotion as a socially constructed mode of response that links bodily feelings to specific objects and circumstances. Bodily feelings sensitize us to certain objects or aspects of our environment, and it is our cultural definition of the situation that picks out or identifies these objects and aspects and so makes them meaningful in relation to our feelings. We can call up particular emotions by imagining situations that would evoke them, or we can suppress an emotion by suppressing the images that would evoke it. The whole social setting in which someone lives and works (as Emerson showed for the medical context) may be constructed in order to ensure that a particular emotional feeling occurs among the participants.

These ideas are applied to work contexts through the concept of **emotional labour**. Any concrete form of labour,

Hochschild argues, has physical, mental, and emotional aspects to it. It involves the physical coordination of the body, the mental planning of actions, and the emotional inducement or suppression of feelings. Hochschild defines emotional labour as the use of techniques of emotion management, or 'emotion work', to control the emotions that must be expressed as an integral part of a particular process of labour. Emotional labour, she holds, is undertaken whenever a job 'requires one to induce or suppress feeling in order to sustain the outward countenance that produces the proper state of mind in others' (Hochschild 1983: 7).

Emotion work involves the application of norms that Hochschild (1983: 18) calls 'feeling rules'. These are the cultural norms that shape emotions and determine how they are presented or performed in interaction. The ways in which actors perform their particular emotions may be more or less consciously managed. The cultural control of emotions may typically be a matter of routine, giving the appearance of spontaneous or uncontrolled emotion, but it may also be subject to conscious control in the same way as any other aspect of self-presentation.

All occupations involve emotional labour, to a greater or lesser extent. In some, however, the presentation of positive emotions is more obvious. This is the case, for example, of the nurses discussed in an earlier section, where 'caring' involves an emotional element as well as a purely technical element. Similar considerations apply to many occupations in the service sector, where the ways in which a worker relates to others is central to the work itself. In these cases, specific feeling rules may be imposed by employing organizations in order to ensure the public display of feeling. This results in a 'transmutation' of private acts of feeling: people try to feel what they ought to feel and what they are obliged to display in their public acts.

Hochschild looks at situations where the norms that shape emotions are set by the managers of an organization, who require their employees to exercise emotion management in ways they might not otherwise have chosen. Particular forms of emotional expression are required as an integral feature of the performance of particular kinds of labour. In this situation, specific kinds of display are required—smiling, being polite, saying 'Have a nice day', and so on—so that customers or clients of the organization will believe that the worker actually feels concern for their pleasure or well-being.

She looked at this through the case of airline cabin crew in the American company Delta Airlines. Flight attendants—stewards, stewardesses, pursers, and so on—are the most visible part of an airline, and the growth of commercial competition from the 1930s led airline companies to focus on the flight attendant in their advertising. The high point of this was the 1950s and 1960s. Delta Airlines chose an image of the ideal flight attendant to represent the company as a whole, and as a southern

company they chose a southern image: 'The image they chose . . . was that of a beautiful and smartly dressed Southern white woman, the supposed epitome of gracious manners and warm personal service' (Hochschild 1983: 93).

The company developed systems of staff selection and training aimed at producing flight attendants who conformed to this ideal. They also used advertising slogans and images that sexualized the attendant. All this meant that the attendant's work had to express emotions that were appropriate to this imagery. The successful candidates in the selection process were those who were aware of the feeling rules that had to be applied and who were willing to take them seriously. Interview manuals stressed sincerity, a friendly smile, enthusiasm, vivaciousness, and similar qualities, and they emphasized the importance of using the right body language (such as maintaining eye contact). Applicants were screened for an 'outgoing middle-class sociability' (Hochschild 1983: 97).

During training it was made clear that cabin-crew members would keep their jobs only so long as they lived and worked as a particular type of person. They had to maintain the correct physical appearance (make-up, clothing, weight), personal behaviour (smoking, drinking, hours of sleep), and, above all, emotion management. Flight attendants were expected to show particular kinds of feelings and were trained in the techniques that would achieve this. Attendants were told to regard the plane as their home and to treat passengers as if they were guests. Imagining the plane in this way helped to evoke the emotions of care and hospitality that the airline required.

In the case of angry or troublesome passengers, attendants were taught to treat them in the same way as they would treat naughty children. They must maintain a good-humoured but firm approach and not react with anger themselves. Again, conjuring up the image of dealing with children allowed the attendant to evoke the appropriate emotional response towards the unruly passenger.

It was emphasized by the trainers that the emotional presentation had to be 'sincere': attendants had to act from the heart, rather than acting in an obviously unnatural way. That is, they were required, through their displays, actually to produce the emotion in themselves. Everything that the attendants do in their job, then, involves them in emotion work.

The airline industry changed rapidly from the 1970s. Larger and faster planes were introduced, and journey times became shorter. Discount fares, family travel, and greater competition meant that passengers were no longer simply the affluent business travellers. These changes make it more difficult for cabin crew to perform their emotional labour effectively. Attendants must give greater priority to safety and to other technical skills, leaving less time and energy for emotion work. As a result, Hochschild argues, attendants have reasserted a claim to their own emotions and to a greater autonomy in deciding their appearance. They display positive emotions by acting superficially rather than from the heart. This brings them into greater conflict with the airline company managers. The managers, in response, have attempted to recruit lower-paid and more submissive ethnic-minority employees in an attempt to build a workforce that can be drilled into the 'proper' performance of emotional labour.

> **⊃ Connections**
> Try to think of other examples of work that involves high levels of emotional labour. How do selection and training processes bring this about?

Anxiety and risk

Psychoanalytical writers, and Adler in particular, stressed the part played by anxiety in human life. Anxiety was seen as resulting from the cultural demands placed upon the impulses of the id, and Adler saw it as the root of the inferiority complex. The question of anxiety has recently been taken up by a number of writers, who see it as having an increased importance in contemporary Western societies because of the fundamental social changes that they have experienced (I. Wilkinson 2001). In particular, it is argued that the increasing risks faced by people in their everyday lives generate high levels of anxiety.

Among the earliest writers to point in this direction were David Riesman (1961) and C. Wright Mills (1959). Riesman recognized what he called a 'diffuse anxiety' as a characteristic personality feature in America, while Mills identified economic dislocations, military conflicts, urban disorganization, and family breakdown as the structural conditions responsible for this growing anxiety. According to some, this anxiety is a fundamental social malaise that produces a deep cultural pessimism (Bailey 1988).

At the heart of the contemporary discussions of anxiety is the idea of the **risk society**, postulated by Beck (1992). Beck argues that the increase in technologically and socially generated dangers—as against purely natural disasters—in modern societies has encouraged the growth of a 'risk consciousness'. This is a predisposition to express anxieties about these dangers in the language of risk.

The risks that concern people are what Giddens (1990) has called 'manufactured risks'. These are risks that result from the effects of human actions on the world, through technologies of production and the other social practices people are involved in. The whole of nature has been transformed by human activity, and there are few parts of the global human environment that have not been affected by this. Ostensibly 'natural' disasters, such as famines and floods, are increasingly the results of environmental changes brought about by industrial and urban life. Strikingly, these risks are overwhelmingly produced in the advanced societies of the

West, but they are overwhelmingly experienced in the poor countries of the world. There is a global distribution of risk. Within the advanced societies themselves, there is not only a perception of this globalization of risk, but also an awareness of the internal risks that the advanced societies face. There is less certainty concerning both the personal relations of intimacy, marriage, and family, and the public relations of work, employment, and politics.

In the contemporary world, Beck argues, there is an increasing awareness of the dangers that face whole populations and that, indeed, operate on a global scale. This awareness is overwhelmingly derived from the output of the mass media. The hazards that can result from genetically modified foodstuffs, reproductive technologies, ecological change, and so on, are reported and discussed in the newspapers and on television, and the ways in which these reports are constructed shapes people's perceptions of the risks involved in them. A shared sense of crisis or catastrophe may be generated among readers and viewers, and people tend to become very anxious about their own fate and their particular circumstances. They perceive the world as a dangerous world, a runaway world (Giddens 1999) over which they have little or no control. Such a consciousness evokes feelings of anxiety that are attached to the world in general, rather than to specific dangers or problems. This is Riesman's diffuse anxiety.

Scientific knowledge and scientific experts are of little help in reducing this anxiety. They may be seen as

Briefing: to vaccinate or not to vaccinate?   4.13

There has been much anxiety among parents in Britain over the possible risks to children of the MMR triple vaccine for measles, mumps, and rubella. Reports of differences of opinion among medical experts, and uncertainty within the government meant that many parents preferred to face the risk that their children would catch one of the diseases rather than the risk of damage from a side-effect of the vaccine. The British government commissioned a full investigation, which came up with a clear statement that there was no significant risk attached to the vaccination, but many parents saw this as simply another opinion and remained very confused and anxious about what course of action to take. The US and British medical services have set up websites to present a medical view of the risks of immunization: see **www.cdc.gov/vaccines/vpd-vac/mumps/default. htm** and **www.dh.gov.uk/en/Publichealth/ Immunisation/index.htm**. A map of countries using the triple vaccine can be found at www.immunisation. nhs.uk/Vaccines/MMR/World_Map.

responsible for the technologically induced risks, and a growth in knowledge that people have about the risks they face may simply serve to increase their level of anxiety. Scientific experts will often disagree among themselves over the likely consequences of particular actions, and people become critical of science and scientists and feel that they must come to their own conclusions (see Box 4.13, p.143).

Giddens has seen this growth in anxiety in terms of the implications of modernity for the formation of identities. He holds that people seek to cope with everyday life by 'bracketing-off', or disregarding, the uncertainties and dangers of the world. They try to build everyday social realities that cocoon them from these dangers and allow them to get on with the routines of daily life.

In pre-modern societies, this framework of routine was provided by tradition and custom: people had to make few decisions or choices and could simply rely on the ways that things had always been done. Their fates and destinies in life were fixed, and they had to play a largely passive part in the world. In modern societies, with their high degree of individualism and the disappearance of traditional ideas in the face of critical, rational reflection, this is no longer the case, as people must make individual decisions for themselves.

Modern societies, Giddens argues, rest upon a culture of 'reflexivity', a cultural requirement to constantly monitor, assess, and modify one's own actions in the light of their likely consequences. The self is a 'reflexive project' (Giddens 1991: 32), a constantly reconstructed identity that is legitimated through the production of appropriate narratives. People are compelled to take responsibility for deciding and building their own identities and for constructing a constantly changing 'narrative of the self'. They become what Bauman (1995) has called 'pilgrims': they travel through their lives towards a chosen destination

Global focus Tourism and identity   4.14

Most secondary identities—identities of occupation, class, politics, and religion—have been tied to the boundaries of nation states. This is at its clearest in a person's 'national' identity as British, French, German, American, and so on. But does this still apply in an era of globalization? John Urry (2002) has explored this through an investigation into the ideas of travel and tourism. What does it mean when a person identifies him or herself as a 'tourist': is he or she a 'national' citizen in a 'foreign' country, or is the tourist a distinctively transnational or global identity?

Tourism is a specifically modern phenomenon that arose with the creation of a distinction between 'work' and 'leisure' in modern societies. In pre-modern societies there was no distinction between paid work and unpaid leisure, and so there was no possibility of travelling for leisure. The journey and the stay that make up a tour or holiday are to places other than the normal places of residence and work, for purposes not directly connected with work, and for a specified period of time. The person who travels in this way adopts a specific identity: that of the tourist. According to Urry, the tourist identity involves the adoption of what he calls the tourist gaze. That is, the tourist is someone who looks on things and places in a particular and distinct way that is not that of the local resident or worker. The tourist gazes on 'sights', recording them in photographs and postcards in order to be able to re-create them in memory at a later date. What the tourist sees, however, is not the 'real' place (whatever that may be), but the image of that place that has been constructed through the various tourist professionals that have arisen around the holiday and travel industries of the modern world.

Tourism initially involved travel within one's own country, except for the very rich. The typical holiday into the first half of the twentieth century was a short break at a seaside resort. As air travel became cheaper in the second half of the twentieth century, foreign holidays became more usual, and foreign travel has increasingly involved travelling great distances and to a greater variety of places.

More than ever before, tourist venues are specifically constructed for the tourist gaze: the clearest examples of this are, perhaps, the various Disneyland resorts. A tourist is separated from his or her normal routines and places of work and residence, and is, at the same time, not a part of the place that he or she visits. The tourist, then, is a detached figure, a cultural nomad in a simulated reality.

The global growth of tourism has meant that the immense international flows of people are, for the most part, flows of tourists. Global realities are constructed through the images present in the tourist gazes. Constructions of nationhood are, increasingly, constructions by and for tourists from outside the nation. People's own sense of national identity reflects the constructions of the global tourist industry, and nations must compete to present themselves in images and as spectacles that will appeal to a large number of visitors. National identity is no longer so closely linked to a sense of territory, but is more closely related to a sense of the image of a particular place. Britain, for example, projects an international image of its history and national heritage. At the same time, the very idea of travel and mobility becomes central to people's identities. They no longer define themselves simply by the places where they live and work; they also define themselves by the places to which they can travel and, therefore, by the very idea of travel and movement.

forming and reforming their identities as they travel (see also Bauman 1993). Even successfully socialized individuals, Giddens argues, can face anxieties that swamp these efforts and impel individuals into a state of constant diffuse anxiety over their own identity and their place in the world. These issues have been explored in relation to the global growth of tourism (see Box 4.14).

The growth of risk society and its risk consciousness, then, generates the kinds of concerns that make it impossible for individuals to ignore the dangers they face. The emergence of the reflexive project of building the self and the expansion of risk consciousness means that these modern societies have seen a growth in expert systems that are aimed at helping individuals to live with their anxieties. The growth of academic sociology and psychology are examples of this, but it is manifested, in particular, in the massive growth of therapy and counselling in all areas of life.

 # Stop and reflect

We have looked at a number of aspects of the construction of social reality and the operation of secondary socialization.

- Social realities are actively constructed by the participants and must be maintained and sustained in their interactions.
- A person's identity is reconstructed as his or her social relationships develop and are transformed.
- Does an emphasis on social construction imply that all human behaviour is culturally determined? How adequate would such a view be?

These processes occur in many work situations, where secondary socialization takes place:

- Occupational roles often involve conflicting demands that have to be met. Staff respond to these strains by reconstructing and redefining their roles.

- The emergence of counter-realities has to be prevented in order to sustain dominant definitions of reality.
- Can you think of examples of the ways in which the maintenance of definitions of reality involves the use of specific routines and practices?

Finally, we looked at a number of aspects of the emotional dimension to social interaction:

- Many work tasks involve people in the performance of much emotional labour, and work organizations may require particular forms of emotional display.
- The growth of a risk consciousness has resulted in high levels of anxiety over the nature of these risks and their consequences.
- What is meant by the claim that the reflexive reconsideration of identity has become a central feature of contemporary social life?

 # Key concepts

- age cohort 128
- back regions 125
- biological determinism 113
- cultural determinism 113
- culture 113
- emotional labour 141
- generalized other 124
- inferiority complex 127
- internalization 121

- life course 128
- narratives 119
- personal identity 115
- primary identities 116
- primary socialization 114
- risk society 143
- role-taking 122
- secondary identities 118
- secondary socialization 114

- self 115
- self-presentation 124
- significant other 123
- social identity 114
- socialization 113
- superego 127
- unconscious 125

Workshop 4

Study 4　Negotiating shyness

A recent study has explored the presentation of self among those who regard themselves, and are regarded by others, as 'shy'. Susie Scott (2005, 2007) examines shyness in terms of concepts drawn from the work of George Mead and Goffman. She sees shyness as a social role that has to be negotiated in everyday life through presentational strategies in which those who regard themselves as shy attempt to conceal this discrediting identity from others and to create an illusion of competence.

Shyness is often seen in individualistic terms as a psychological 'problem', but Scott interprets the subjectivity of shy persons rather differently. Anxiety about interactional encounters with others is normal and widespread, but some individuals may experience extreme and uncontrollable attacks of anxiety about social encounters that inhibit them from full participation and lead them to withdraw from or avoid front-stage situations. Such individuals, when they have to enter social situations, tend to blush, stammer, or exhibit other behavioural responses that betray their anxiety to the others with whom they interact. These others act towards them on the basis of cultural stereotypes of shyness and, through their stigmatizing and discrediting responses, they lead the socially anxious to come to perceive themselves as shy. Their image of self derives from the reactions of others, and they perceive a 'shy me'—the shy self perceived by others. In taking on the social expectations about shyness, they come to play the shy role.

Those who take on the shy role as an aspect of their social identity come to see themselves as relatively incompetent: they regard themselves as lacking in the social skills that others possess, and their perceived lack of social skills leads to further avoidance of interaction or to discrediting performances. They act in terms of an image of the generalized other as

a 'competent other': other people are able to handle public, front-stage encounters with ease because they have none of the anxieties or inadequacies possessed by the shy person. Others are socially competent extroverts, whereas the shy person feels a socially incompetent introvert. The adoption of the shy role has led to an internalization of shyness that makes it appear as an individual psychological problem rather than a socially generated condition.

Scott suggests that anxiety is far more widespread than commonly assumed. Those whom the shy person regards as socially competent may also experience anxiety about personal encounters but may be better able to handle them without succumbing to the shy role. The shy can, on occasion, pass as normal or competent. If they are able to learn the techniques that they observe in others, they may be able to give a convincing display of competence in social interaction and so may be less likely to be treated as shy. The fact that others do not define them in terms of their shyness allows them to begin to break with the shy role, despite their continuing anxiety. One such technique is to deflect attention from oneself. Asking a question that encourages others to talk, for example, means that one's own quietness becomes less apparent.

You might like to consider how best to undertake sociological studies of shyness. How can a sociologist go about interviewing or observing people who avoid social encounters? Look at Scott's study and see how she resolved this methodological problem. You can hear the author discussing her work at **www.bbc.co.uk/ radio4/factual/thinkingallowed_20040526.shtml**

If you were to observe social encounters in a public place, how would you know whether you are observing the actions of competent persons or the actions of shy persons who are passing as competent?

Media watch 4　What is a mother?

When Bob Geldof said that there was no significant difference in what a mother or a father could give a child, many disagreed. The *Guardian*'s 'parents' page' decided to explore the range of views on this and invited six people—three men and three women—to set out their thoughts (*Guardian*, 10 May 2002).

Dina Rabinovitch, a writer, based her views on the biology of motherhood. The fact that it is women who get pregnant and give birth, she argues, creates an intense bond—the child grows inside its mother's body, each adapting to the bodily rhythms of the other, and this physical tie creates a unique emotional tie.

She concludes that fathers cannot provide the kind of immediate and intense emotional support that comes 'naturally' to the mother. Although mothers and fathers are complementary in socialization, the mother relationship is primary. The author Kate Figes also sees fathers and mothers as complementary, but she rejects any idea that pregnancy and childbirth create an 'instinctive' bond between mother and child. Parenting is learned, she says, through trial and error, and what matters is not the sex of the parent but whether he or she quickly learns to be a 'good' parent.

Peter Howarth, a magazine editor, took a very different view. Recognizing that mothers and fathers are complementary and that there is a 'powerful maternal bond', he stresses the particular importance of fathering. He grew up without a father, and it was while bringing up his own child that he began to realize what he had lost when he was a child. Richard Reeves, a business consultant for organizations wanting to set up 'father-friendly' workplaces, supported this view and believed that work must be reorganized to allow both parents to participate equally in a child's upbringing. Rather than stressing the complementarity of mothers and fathers, Richard holds that they are virtually interchangeable. The one thing that men cannot do, he argues, is breastfeed, but they can do everything else just as well as women. The only reason that women tend to be better at parenting is that they have had more opportunity to develop the skills. If work was organized differently, men could also develop those skills.

Jack O'Sullivan, founder of a fathers' pressure group, points to medical studies that show that fathers can do just as well in feeding and nurturing their children, and he argues that there is a long history of the part played by men in bringing up their children. Maureen Freely, however, contrasts today with the 1950s, when, she argues, the assumption was that 'real men didn't waste time on their children'. She points out that her own father, though involved in full-time employment, was very involved in her upbringing. The contribution of fathers, she argues, is invisible; because it does not square with the image of the real man, and because father's contribution is invisible, it is seen as dispensable. The task for parents in families, she argues, is to negotiate ways in which they can each put their children before their jobs.

- Look back at our discussion of maternal deprivation and attachment theory and see how these various views relate to the theoretical debates that we considered. Do any of the contributors question the gendered character of mothering? How many of them recognize that not all children are born into conventional nuclear families?

- Carry out some brief interviews with members of your own family—male and female—and see if their views are similar to those reported in the *Guardian*. Do you expect to come up with any different views?

Discussion points

'Look back over the 'Stop and reflect' points at the end of each section of this chapter and make sure that you understand the points that have been highlighted.

Socialization, personhood, and identity

In 'Concepts and theories', we considered a number of conceptual and theoretical ideas in learning a sense of self and social identity, and we compared and contrasted the main concepts used by symbolic interactionists and psychoanalysts:

- What is meant by primary and secondary identities?
- How would you distinguish between primary socialization and secondary socialization?
- How do psychoanalysts understand personality in terms of the superego, sexuality, and guilt?

Childhood, parenthood, and life course

In the section on 'Socialization and family relations' we looked at a number of issues related to motherhood, fatherhood, and childhood, and we saw these as socially constructed roles that correspond to particular stages in the life course.

- Consider the arguments from attachment theory about the significance of mothering. What are the problems with the idea of 'maternal deprivation'?
- How useful is it to see individual personalities as developing according to a particular sequence of developmental stages?

The social construction of reality

'Building social worlds' looked at the construction of social realities and at their cognitive, normative, and emotional dimensions.

- What do you understand by the term 'social construction'? How is this related to the ideas of self-presentation and role-playing?
- What does it mean to talk about role-making rather than role-taking?

Explore further

Good general reading on the issues discussed in this chapter can be found in:

Goffman, E. (1959), *Presentation of Self in Everyday Life* (Harmondsworth: Penguin). *A highly readable and illuminating account of everyday interaction. A sociological classic.*

Jenkins, R. (1996), *Social Identities* (London: Routledge). *A useful overview of debates in the area.*

Strauss, A. L. (1959), *Mirrors and Masks: The Search for Identity* (London: Martin Robertson, 1977). *A useful and well-written statement of the social-constructionist position.*

Becker, H., *et al.* (1961), *Boys in White* (New York: John Wiley; New Brunswick, NJ: Transaction, 1977). *An important study of the secondary socialization of trainee doctors in a medical school.*

Parsons, T., and Bales, R. (1956), *Family, Socialization and Interaction Process* (London: Routledge & Kegan Paul). *A useful but badly written statement of role-learning theory that tries to integrate it with psychoanalytic ideas.*

Hochschild, A. (1983), *The Managed Heart: Commercialization of Human Feeling* (Berkeley and Los Angeles: University of California Press). *An important and influential study of the social construction of emotions.*

Giddens, A. (1991), *Modernity and Self-Identity* (Cambridge: Polity Press). *Looks at the relationship between large-scale processes of modernization and the formation of a sense of self and individuality.*

Online resources

Visit the Online Resource Centre that accompanies this book to access more learning resources and other interesting material on socialization, identity, and interaction at:
www.oxfordtextbooks.co.uk/orc/fulcher4e/

On social interactionism, see the Society for the Study of Symbolic Interactionism at:
www.espach.salford.ac.uk/sssi/index.php

More specifically on G. H. Mead is the Mead Project at:
www.brocku.ca/MeadProject/

Psychoanalytic theory can be approached through Freud at:
http://users.rcn.com/brill/freudarc.html

(where many sources, including excerpts from his major works, are to be found).

The anti-psychiatry of R. D. Laing is well covered at:
http://lainginstitut.ch

The so-called attachment disorder is discussed at:
www.attachmentdisorder.net

Susie Scott's Shyness website can be found at:
www.sussex.ac.uk/profiles/171734

Sex, Gender, and Sexuality

Contents

05

Intersex

In 2009 the 18-year-old South African athlete Caster Semenya won the gold medal in the women's 800 metres at the world athletics championships. Her physical appearance then led to doubts being raised about her sex. The sport's governing body responded by initiating sex testing procedures.

It was later revealed that Semenya had already undergone tests in South Africa before the world championships. These had reportedly shown some internal male organs and very high levels of testosterone for a woman. The team doctor recommended that she be withdrawn from the event but was overruled.

Sex testing began at major international sporting events in the 1960s. It was abandoned by the International Olympic Committee in 1999, after criticism that testing was humiliating, insensitive, and scientifically dubious. Other competitions continued to test, however, and in 2006 the Indian competitor Santhi Soundarajan had her 800 metres silver medal at the Doha Asian Games withdrawn.

According to the Gender Trust, as many as 4 per cent of people, which would mean well over two million of those living in Britain, are born without a clear male or female identity. There is a range of Intersex conditions that in various ways combine the physical characteristics of men and women in the same person.

Sources: Randall and Momberg (2009); 'Intersex Conditions', *The Gender Trust,* http://www.gendertrust.org.uk

People take it for granted that we are born male or female, that our biology determines which sex we are. Some are, however, born with a mixture of male and female characteristics that is labelled 'intersex'. In some cultures intersex children have been treated as special and unique creations that are highly valued, but in contemporary Western societies they are generally forced into one sex or the other. They are categorized as either male or female and their bodies are then required to fit these categories.

This is a particular example of the more general process through which people are made to fit sex categories, as specified by the society in which they live. This generally starts at birth when they are given male or female names, which identify their sex. They are then brought up to be male or female. Throughout their lives they will be expected to behave in the ways considered appropriate to either men or women.

In this chapter we explore the social processes that make us men or women. We investigate the origins of contemporary beliefs about sex, gender, and sexuality, and their significance for the way that people think, feel, and behave.

We also examine the relationships of power and inequality between men and women, and discuss whether these have changed.

The central theme of the chapter is a shift from the separation of identities to their convergence. In the nineteenth century, male and female spheres of activity, male and female behaviour, and different sexualities became sharply separated. Our notions of the different roles that men and women perform, their contrasting characters and distinctive sexualities, as well as the distinction between heterosexuality and homosexuality were established at this time.

These ideas and the categories of thought associated with them are still with us and powerfully influence what people think and do, but more recently they have been challenged. Identities have converged as the barriers between male and female spheres have been broken down, men and women have started to behave in increasingly similar ways, and sexual behaviour has been at least partially liberated from nineteenth-century constraints.

Concepts and theories

In this section we consider the basic concepts used in studying the differences between men and women, theories of the inequalities between them, and the relationship between sex and sexuality.

Sex, gender, and sexuality

In understanding the differences between men and women, we must first make a basic distinction between sex and gender. The term **sex** refers to the physical and anatomical characteristics considered to distinguish *male* and *female* bodies from each other. These include differences in their chromosomes, reproductive organs, hormones, and physical appearance. It has been argued that there is now clear evidence that male and female brains are different as well (Hoag 2008). **Gender** refers to differences in the way that men and women in a particular society are expected to feel, think, and behave. Thus, males are typically expected to feel, think, and behave in a *masculine* way, and females in a *feminine* way.

It was thought at one time that sex determined gender, that differences in the way that men and women behave are biologically rooted in their sex. Thus, differences in their occupations were seen as resulting from differences in their biological make-up that fitted them for very different kinds of work. Nurses were women because women were naturally more caring than men, while soldiers were men because they were naturally more aggressive.

While some people still hold these views, they cannot explain the different occupations of men and women. Many occupations that were once regarded as a male or female preserve have been opened up to the other sex. If women can become competent members of the armed forces and men can become competent nurses, the fact that nurses are predominantly women and soldiers are mainly men cannot have a biological explanation. Gender must therefore be distinguished from sex.

Sexuality too must be separated from sex. The word 'sex' is commonly used to describe sexual behaviour, as in the phrase 'having sex'. We must, however, clearly distinguish between sex, as referring to the physical and anatomical characteristics of men and women, and sexual behaviour, which refers to the activities that they find physically arousing. These activities are extremely diverse and are clearly not simply the result of their sex.

A person's sexuality is not just a description of his or her sexual practices. A person's sexuality refers also to those aspects of identity, lifestyle, and community associated with these activities. Furthermore, these aspects of sexuality are not just the result of particular kinds of sexual behaviour but also shape that behaviour, for the adoption of a lifestyle or identity itself influences sexual behaviour. Sociologists argue that sexuality is not biologically given but is socially constructed.

Semenya wins gold: should athletes ever undergo sex-testing procedures?

Fabrice Coffrini/AFP/Getty Images

Sex

A person's sex might seem to be a simple biological matter. Are we not born male or female? Does not our biology give us either a male or a female body? The distinction between male and female bodies is a much more complex matter that involves social processes and requires sociological as well as biological explanation.

Determining sex

The basic biological difference between men and women is that a man has one X and one Y chromosome, while a woman has two X chromosomes. These chromosomal differences are responsible for primary sexual characteristics—that is, for the reproductive organs that develop in a particular individual, and the hormones that circulate around their bodies.

As our opening piece shows, some people cannot, however, be classified biologically as male or female and are called **intersex**. This may be because they have extra chromosomes or lack one chromosome. In other cases, the chromosomes do not produce clearly male or female bodies for genetic or hormonal reasons. Indeed, Fausto-Sterling (2000) has claimed that five different sexes can be biologically distinguished. Medical interventions have commonly occurred to turn intersex babies into males or females, though recently there has been a greater willingness to leave intersex people to decide their own destinies. The United Kingdom Intersex Association campaigns against the idea that intersexed people should be forced to conform to the two-sex social norm.

There are also some people who fit perfectly well the biological requirements of one sex but consider that they belong elsewhere. This occurs when a person who appears biologically male or female identifies with the other sex. Such people typically feel that they are 'trapped in the wrong body' or 'born with the wrong sex'. They may well seek hormonal treatment or reconstructive surgery to give them the biological characteristics of the sex they believe they should be. These *transsexuals* should not be confused with *transvestites*, who do not believe that their sex should be different but adopt the dress of the other sex because they find it pleasurable to do so.

There is considerable variation in secondary sexual characteristics, such as body size. On average men are taller than women, but this does not mean that all women are shorter than all men. The two distributions overlap. There is, however, a cultural expectation that men will be taller. If a tall woman marries a short man and the difference cannot be remedied by heel sizes, the man may well have to stand on a box for wedding photographs! Other characteristics can be more easily changed. Weight and body shape can be altered by exercise and dieting, cosmetic surgery and

---

THEORY AND METHODS   **5.1**

Gendering sex

Judith Butler reversed the notion that sex determines gender by arguing in her influential book *Gender Trouble* (1990) that gender shapes sex. She rejected essentialist ideas that treat men and women as having a fixed and opposite character, ideas that were bound up with a 'stable and oppositional heterosexuality' (1990: 30). She is here very critical of those feminists who think that all women have the same underlying character and share a common identity. Indeed, Butler was opposed to the whole notion that there is some inner male or female self that makes us think and behave in male and female ways.

Butler argued that sex is shaped by gender discourses, which prescribe male and female ways of behaving by providing 'scripts' that people then perform. It is the repeated *performance* of actions according to these scripts that makes bodies male and female. She developed the concept of **performativity** to describe the formation of the character of men and women through these repeated performances.

For example, dominant conceptions of masculinity provide a male script, emphasizing physical toughness, which men are expected to display. This leads men to develop their muscles and engage in physical aggression, by, say, using their fists to resolve conflicts. These 'performances' result in men appearing more muscular and physically aggressive than women, and this is then seen as an external manifestation of their nature. Physical toughness comes to be regarded as a biological characteristic of the male sex, but it is the result of a repeated acting-out of beliefs about how men should be.

Butler considered that gendered ideas about the nature of men and women could be subverted by transgressive acts that cross the boundaries set up by gender scripts. Drag and cross-dressing show that men and women can challenge these scripts by adopting the appearance of the other sex. But are these acts really subversive, since they perpetuate the association of maleness and femaleness with opposite ways of dressing and behaving? Do they not reinforce gender scripts? Can you think of changes in dress that are more subversive?

---

hormonal treatments. The physical differences between male and female bodies are not just an outcome of their biology.

While sex and gender must be conceptually distinguished, sex characteristics should not be seen as independent of gender identities, for these identities specify the characteristics that the bodies of men and women should have (see Box 5.1). Gendered conceptions of maleness and

A drag queen prepares for a night out. Is this a subversive act?
© Alice Chadwick

femaleness that require men and women to have different bodies have led to the widespread adoption of dieting and exercise regimes, cosmetic surgery and, in intersex cases, more dramatic medical and surgical interventions, which exaggerate the biological differences between men and women.

Sexes

The physical differences between the sexes should not then be seen as biologically determined. This is not just, however, a matter of how the body is shaped to fit gendered conceptions of the two sexes. The whole idea that there are two sexes is itself a particular way of thinking about the differences between men and women.

According to Thomas Laqueur (1990), this is, historically speaking, quite a recent way of thinking. For two millennia, from the time of the ancient Greeks to the eighteenth century, a 'one-sex model' dominated ways of thinking about men and women. People were, of course, aware of differences between men and women but did not think of them as two different sexes. Women were regarded as a less developed version of men. The 'two-sex model' that is now dominant came into existence only during the eighteenth and nineteenth centuries (we examine its emergence and consequences later in this chapter, on pp. 165–6).

The importance of this change in the way that the differences between men and women were seen can hardly be exaggerated. The whole idea that men and women have contrasting bodily characters, that 'men are from Mars and women are from Venus', stems from the two-sex model. This model has had enormous implications for sexual categories and sexual identities, as the section on 'Sexuality' will show. It also assisted the emergence of a feminist movement by freeing women from the notion that they were merely an inferior version of men.

We have now moved a long way from the idea that the physical differences between male and female bodies are the result of biological differences alone. Our actual bodies are to a considerable extent shaped by gendered beliefs about these differences and the practices associated with these beliefs. The whole notion that men and women are two different sexes that are opposite in character is itself cultural, not biological. Sex cannot just be left to biologists and is part of the subject matter of sociology as well.

Gender

The rejection of biological explanations of gender differences resulted in their explanation by reference to **gender-roles** that specify the ways in which men and women are expected to feel, think, and behave. These prescribe not only the kinds of work that men and women are expected to do but the feelings they can express and everyday aspects of their behaviour, such as the way they speak and dress. The term '**sex-roles**' has been widely used to express the same idea, but we refer to gender-roles because the behaviour of men and women is shaped by beliefs about gender.

Gender socialization

These gender-roles are learned through the process of socialization, which begins in the family and continues through education and indeed throughout life, for agencies of socialization, such as the media, continue to shape people's behaviour long after they have become adults.

> **◆ Connections**
> You may find it helpful to refer here to our detailed discussion of role-learning and socialization theories in Chapter 4, pp. 120–2.

There is plenty of evidence to support this account of gender differences. It has been shown that boys and girls are brought up differently from the moment they are born.

Like mother, like daughter: learning gender-roles.
© Alice Chadwick

In Britain they are, for example, commonly dressed in different colours, blue for a boy and pink for a girl. This may seem a trivial observation, but these differences in clothing elicit powerful differentiating responses from adults. In one experiment, reported in Brewer (2001), the same baby was first dressed in pink and then in blue. Adults immediately assumed that pink meant female and blue meant male. The child was then handled and spoken to quite differently. When in pink the baby was described as beautiful, when in blue as strong. Different futures were imagined and projected on to the child, according to the presumed sex.

It is through such processes that boys and girls learn that they are different and acquire gendered identities. Children know whether they are boys or girls as soon as they can talk. By the time that they are three or four years old they see these differences as biological and permanent. They then begin to inhabit different worlds in which each plays only with children of its own sex and avoids contact with the other, thereby reinforcing gender divergence (Brewer 2001).

Behaviourist approaches argue that all this occurs simply through reward and punishment. When boys and girls act in the ways that are prescribed by gender-roles, they are rewarded. When they act in other ways, they are punished. Rewards and punishments involve subtle forms of social approval and disapproval, as well as material rewards or physical punishment. Children themselves reinforce the process by ridiculing behaviour that violates gender norms. The playground and the street are important sites of socialization. Socialization into gender-roles does clearly involve mechanisms of reward and punishment, but are these sufficient to explain the differentiation of male and female identities?

Those working within the Freudian tradition (see Chapter 4, pp. 125–7) provide a very different account that emphasizes the dynamics of personality formation, the significance of emotion, and the intimate relationships of parents and children. Nancy Chodorow (1978) argued that all infants have a close attachment to their mothers. Because mothers have the main responsibility for child-rearing, children tend to identify with them. Soon, however, they come to conform to gendered expectations of their behaviour. Boys and girls are dressed differently, spoken to in different ways, given different kinds of toys and different amounts of attention and encouragement.

Boys are encouraged to achieve their distinct 'masculine' identity by breaking their close attachment to their mothers and stopping 'feminine' behaviour. They acquire values of independence and achievement, and find it more difficult to express their emotions in close relationships. Girls are encouraged to retain a strong identification with their mothers and copy their behaviour. Through this identification they grow up with a more emotional and sensitive outlook. Distinct masculine and feminine personalities are reinforced in school, by the mass media, and at work.

In her focus on early years, personality formation, and emotional relationships between parents and children, Chodorow provides an understanding of the gendering of personality and an explanation of the contrast between female sensitivity and male assertiveness. Her approach has, however, been criticized for perpetuating male and female stereotypes at a time when male and female identities are changing, when men are becoming more sensitive and women more assertive. It has also been seen as a rather culture-bound theory based on the experience of a small number of middle-class, white, and two-parent families.

A knowledge of socialization processes is indispensable to an account of the mechanisms that produce gender differences, but socialization theory faces two major problems:

- social change;
- individual choice.

First, there is its inability to accommodate social change. Changes in male and female behaviour and identity suggest that early socialization is less than permanent in its effects. Arguably, this is because socialization is a lifelong process that involves periodic resocializations, so that changes in society feed through to the way that men and women feel and behave through such agencies as the mass media. Furthermore, different agencies of socialization may come into conflict by promoting alternative ways of living. For example, commercially driven changes in media representations and styles may conflict with those instilled by families and schools. These more complex views of the socialization process do, at the very least, call into question both the emphasis in much of the socialization literature on early experiences and the idea of fixed gender-roles and identities.

Secondly, socialization theory leaves little room for choice, or for people's activity and creativity in shaping their own lives. A more post-modern approach to the formation of identity would see it as constructed through choice of lifestyle and emphasize the part played by consumption in this. People can create (and re-create) their identities through the objects and experiences they buy. They can experiment with the wide range of lifestyles made available through the media and the marketplace. If taken too far, the individualism of this approach can, however, neglect the power of stereotypes in shaping lifestyles and the commercial forces that drive their creation.

The concepts of socialization and gender-role rescued the study of the differences between men and women from biological determinism. They provided a convincing account of the ways in which gender differences in role and personality are acquired, reinforced, and perpetuated. The problem is that they became somewhat determinist themselves and left little room for human agency, for change or choice. Post-modern approaches have then gone to the other extreme and made it appear as though identities could be adopted and created more or less at will. To understand gender we need to take a balanced view, which accepts human agency but recognizes that this operates within the constraints of powerful socializing institutions, from the family to the mass media.

Patriarchy

Although socialization could explain the persistence of gender differences, once they had come into existence, it could not account for the inequalities between men and women. The concept of patriarchy emerged in the feminist literature to describe and explain these inequalities. Here we consider the meaning of patriarchy, different approaches to it, and the criticisms that have been made of it.

Patriarchy originally meant domination by the father and was used by social anthropologists to describe family structures where the father rather than the mother ruled. In the feminist literature it came to mean male domination in general, and this is now the main way that it is used in sociology. Within the feminist literature there are a number of different approaches to patriarchy.

Marxist feminists have emphasized the interconnections between capitalism and patriarchy. They have argued that the subordination of women in the household benefits the capitalist employer by providing free domestic labour. There is a domestic division of labour between the male 'breadwinner', who takes paid employment, and the housewife, who looks after the household and brings up the children. The wife's domestic labour is essential to the capitalist economy, both because it meets the home needs of the male wage-earner, enabling him to work long hours, and brings up the next generation of workers. This essential work is, however, unpaid labour that costs the employer nothing at all.

> ⮎ *Connections*
>
> The domestic division of labour is discussed in detail in Chapter 12, pp. 441–2.

According to radical feminists, such as Kate Millett (1970) and Shulamith Firestone (1971), patriarchy is not, however, specifically associated with capitalism but is found in all known societies. Some indeed argue that men and women comprise 'sex classes'. Men, as the dominant class, oppress women and exploit them economically, politically, and sexually. This domination has its clearest expression in the intimate personal relationships of love, sex, and marriage, which are claimed to be subject to the constant threat of male violence. Millett famously argued that the 'personal is political', for men use their personal relationships with women, especially their sexual relations, to dominate and control them. These two perspectives were combined by some feminists, such as Heidi Hartmann (1981) and Sylvia Walby (1986), in a 'dual systems' approach that saw women as exploited both by men and by capital.

Some feminists have seen family relationships as the main site of patriarchy. Christine Delphy (1977) argued

---

Controversy and debate Feminisms   5.2

There have always been different positions within the feminist movement. Three broad positions of **feminism** can be identified and are briefly outlined here.

Liberal feminism has been concerned primarily with equal rights for women. Key issues have been the right to vote, the ending of discrimination against women, and equal opportunities for women. Liberal feminism has not tried to transform society but to establish equality with men within the existing social order. Legislation was the main means of achieving this. Because of its emphasis on equality, liberal feminism saw men and women as essentially the same in character.

Socialist feminism combined feminism with the Marxist critique of capitalism and its liberal politics, seeing patriarchal relations as being inextricably tied to capitalist relations of production. Key issues were domestic labour and female wage labour, the role of the family in the reproduction of male labour, and the role of the state in the reproduction of the family.

Radical feminism rejected the liberal programme of legislative reform and instead engaged in direct action and political opposition, aimed at challenging the basis of the social and political order. Patriarchy was not specific to capitalism but a universal feature of human society. Particular attention was given to love, sex, and reproduction, which were seen as closely linked to male domination and to violence towards women. This was often a 'difference' feminism that considered women to be different from men and superior to them.

⮎ Note that we discuss feminist theory in more detail in Chapter 2, pp. 58–61.

that these were central to the oppression of women, since they enabled men to exploit the unpaid labour of their wives or partners. She referred to the household as 'the domestic mode of production', in order to emphasize that productive work went on in the home as well as the workplace. Housework was, in her view, as productive and important as any other kind of work. Within the domestic mode of production, men held a superior position and controlled the distribution of money and goods within the family. The family was, therefore, the main institution for the exploitation of women by men.

According to Walby (1990), however, there are multiple patriarchal structures that cumulatively produce male domination. She identified six such structures:

- household production;
- employment relations;
- the state;
- male violence;
- sexual relations;
- cultural institutions.

She argued that there are two main forms of patriarchy, *private* and *public* (see Figure 5.1). Patriarchy in the nineteenth century took a mainly *private* form, with individual males exploiting women's labour in the household and excluding women from public life. Household production was its dominant structure. The private form continued to exist in the twentieth century, but by then, as a result of feminist organization, women had forced their way into the public sphere. This was only a limited success, for women were now subject to the *public* form of patriarchy, in which the state and employment relations were the dominant structures and patriarchy operated in a more collective way. Women were no longer excluded from work but they were still segregated in lower-grade and lower-paid work.

Figure 5.1 Private and public patriarchy

Form of patriarchy	Private	Public
Dominant structure	Household production	Employment/State
Wider patriarchal structures	Employment/State	Household production
	Sexuality	Sexuality
	Violence	Violence
	Culture	Culture
Period	Nineteenth century	Twentieth century
Mode of expropriation	Individual	Collective
Patriarchal strategy	Exclusionary	Segregationist

Source: Walby (1990: 23, table 1.1).

This debate over patriarchy has focused on the development of patriarchal institutions in industrial societies, but religions too are a major source of patriarchal beliefs. There has been much recent concern with the assertive patriarchy of Islamic fundamentalism (see Box 5.3, p. 158), though other major religions—Christianity, Confucianism, Hinduism, and Judaism—contain patriarchal beliefs and practices. In Christianity, for example, God is generally represented as a male authority figure, while all the apostles were male, and priests have until recently been exclusively male and in its Roman Catholic branch still are. In her book *Gyn/Ecology*, Mary Daly (1978) provides many examples of religious practices that subordinate women.

The concept of patriarchy enabled sociology to move beyond sex-roles and examine the power differences between men and women, but in recent years it has been strongly criticized (see Acker 1989; Bradley 1989; Pollert 1996).

First, there is the problem of its explanatory value. If patriarchy is a universal feature of human society, it cannot help us understand the evident differences between societies in the relationships between men and women. Similarly, it cannot account for changes in these relationships. To explain variations or changes we have to go outside the concept of patriarchy.

Secondly, there is the problem of how patriarchy itself is to be explained. If it is universal, it is hard to avoid ending up with some kind of biological determinism. Some feminists have explained its universality by reference to the relations of dependence at the heart of human reproduction. Women are dependent on men for their material needs while they are involved in the long human process of child-rearing. Patriarchy is, therefore, ultimately explained by the biology of reproduction, which produces human infants dependent on parental care for a long time. Biological determinism has been rejected on principle by Walby and many other feminists, but without it patriarchy appears to hang in the air without any explanation of why it should exist.

There is, thirdly, the problem of structural determinism. Patriarchy often appears to be a simple monolithic structure of domination that somehow exists 'behind the scenes'. The analysis is of institutions rather than social practices. There is little sense of the way that institutions have to be maintained through people's actions or of the ways that they can resist, subvert, and change them.

There is, fourthly, the problem of treating men and women as if each was a homogeneous category. The early radical feminists minimized differences between women by emphasizing their common reproductive experiences and, therefore, their common fate. This has been one of the cornerstones of feminist politics, involving as it does the idea that there is a specifically female way of seeing and feeling, a distinctive 'standpoint' from which women view

Controversy and debate Islam and women   5.3

The relationship between Islam and patriarchy has become an issue of contemporary debate. Extreme examples of the subordination and exclusion of women can certainly be found in Islamic countries and communities. In Afghanistan the Taliban excluded women from employment, education, hospital care, and political life. In Saudi Arabia, they are not allowed to vote or even drive cars. In some Islamic communities women are forbidden to show their faces in public and have to cover themselves head-to-toe in the *burka*. In others, women have their clitorises surgically mutilated to prevent them experiencing sexual pleasure. Under some applications of sharia law women may find themselves punished, even stoned to death, if they become pregnant out of wedlock, even if this has resulted from rape. These practices have been justified by reference to the Qu'ran and other teachings of the founder of Islam, the prophet Muhammad.

Haifaa Jawad (1998) has claimed, however, that these interpretations of the holy writings of Islam are quite wrong. According to the Qu'ran and other holy texts, a woman has the following rights:

- to own and manage money and property;
- to marry whom she pleases and initiate divorce;
- to become educated;
- to keep her family name;
- to have sexual pleasure within marriage;

- to inherit from her parents and family;
- to participate actively in politics and decision-making;
- to be regarded as equal to men.

Jawad argues that the position of women in Arabia actually improved greatly with the advent of Islam, but then deteriorated after the death of Muhammad, as their rights were taken away and they were increasingly excluded from public life. The contemporary position of women in Islamic communities is the result of cultural and social practices that are nothing to do with Islam itself. Fundamentalists who oppress women have not returned to the original texts, as they claim, but offer only 'a distorted image of Islam'.

Jawad does not, however, believe that the best way forward for Muslim women is to adopt Western values, as some elite women in Islamic countries and some Muslim women in Western countries have done. She argues that this approach alienates the broad mass of Muslims from the women's movement. Muslim women should instead seek to achieve equality in an 'authentic Islamic way' by basing their demands on the original teachings of Islam.

In 2005, at a meeting in Spain, Muslim feminists launched what they hoped would be a global movement to liberate Muslim women, under the banner of a 'gender jihad'. This was described by one of the organizers as 'a struggle against male chauvinist, homophobic or sexist readings of the Islamic sacred texts' (*Guardian*, 31 October 2005).

the world (see Chapter 2, p. 60). This standpoint has been seen as the basis of a feminist consciousness expressed and nurtured in the organizations and practices of the women's movement.

Many recent feminist writers have criticized the idea that there is some essential female experience that divides *all* women from *all* men. These critics point to the diversity of female experience and, by implication, of male experience too. Black feminists, for example, have argued that feminism is simply the outlook of white, middle-class women and that it fails to recognize the distinctiveness of black women's experiences. Sarah Delamont (2001: 111) has argued that 'class differences between women are more powerful than any gender-based similarities'.

The work of those who have used the concept of patriarchy should not, however, be dismissed because of these criticisms. To start with, there are many differences in the way that it is used by different theorists, and particular criticisms are more relevant to some than others. The analysis of patriarchy has anyway generated an immense amount of knowledge and understanding of how institutions

constrain the relationships between men and women. What should be abandoned, however, is any notion that the concept of patriarchy can provide some simple and all-embracing explanation of these relationships.

The gender order

An alternative and influential way of analysing the relationship between gender and power has been presented by Robert Connell. While Connell was concerned with the same central issue as feminist writers—the description, analysis, and explanation of male domination—his work reflected the growing interest in masculinity and what is happening to men. His first book, *Gender and Power* (1987), developed a framework for the analysis of gender, and this was followed by *Masculinities* (1995).

Social practices are at the heart of his conception of gender. Gender is not ultimately a matter of institutions but of practices, of what people actually do. They can resist and subvert structures, and, within an overall pattern of male domination, there are areas where women dominate. Structures can be maintained only through the policing of practices, and this, importantly, means the practices of both men and women.

A society has what he called an overall **gender order**, which consists of a hierarchy of masculinities and femininities. At the top of this hierarchy is **hegemonic masculinity**, a dominant set of ideas that establish the superiority of the male. Heterosexuality is at the core of hegemonic masculinity, but this also involves the valuation of toughness, physical strength, authority, and aggression. Film characters and sporting heroes provide models of masculinity. Most men cannot live up to this masculine ideal but engage in a 'complicit masculinity', as they benefit from the male domination provided by the hegemonic version. Other forms of 'subordinated masculinity' exist, notably 'homosexual masculinity', which is stigmatized and subordinated by practices of exclusion, abuse, violence, and discrimination. Heterosexual men who do not live up to the masculine model are also subjected to some of these practices.

> ⊃ *Connections*
>
> Hegemony is a widely used concept in sociology, which we discuss in Chapter 10, p. 352 and Chapter 20, pp. 790–1.

There is also a hierarchy of femininities, though this is less pronounced. There is no hegemonic femininity, because femininity is subordinate to masculinity, and cannot therefore be hegemonic. **Emphasized femininity** is at the top of the hierarchy of femininities. Connell (1987: 187) described this as involving:

> . . . the display of sociability rather than technical competence, fragility in mating scenes, compliance with men's desire for titillation and ego-stroking in office relationships, acceptance of marriage and childcare as a response to labour-market discrimination against women.

Arguably, just as most men have difficulty living up to images of the 'real man', most women have difficulty living up to the idealized images of 'emphasized femininity'. There are also other femininities that resist or reject emphasized femininity, but these are not so vigorously subordinated as the masculinities that challenge hegemonic masculinity. Instead they are marginalized, through a cultural exclusion that hides them from view.

Connell's awareness of gender diversity and concern with actual practices leads him to highlight crisis tendencies in the gender order, the conflicts of sexual politics, and alternative futures. The family, sexuality, and work are the key arenas in which these crisis tendencies and conflicts are played out. Connell considered whether the actual abolition of gender would be a feasible project but thought that this would lead to cultural impoverishment, as gender has been so central to art and, indeed, everyday life, to both eroticism and imagination. He proposed

The gender order in a shooting gallery?
© Alice Chadwick

instead a restructuring of gender that would permit greater gender diversity and remove inequalities between men and women.

The key contributions Connell has made to the study of patriarchy are:

● an analysis of gender as *practice*;

● a much more differentiated view of gender.

The diversity of both masculinities and femininities is central to his view of gender, as are the relationships between different masculinities and different femininities. Patriarchy is a matter not just of the domination of women by men but also of the domination of some men by other men and some women by other women.

Sexuality

We argued earlier that sexuality is socially constructed, not biologically determined. This is, however, a much debated question, and some still hold an 'essentialist' view that sees a person's sexual preferences as fixed at birth. According to this view, whether a person is, for example, homosexual or heterosexual is to do with their inborn nature and cannot be changed. This notion has received a recent revival with the idea that homosexuality is genetically determined. We begin this section by discussing this issue before going on to examine the main categories of sexuality and their significance.

Becoming homosexual

A few scientific studies have claimed they have discovered genetic differences between heterosexual and homosexual men. These studies do not, however, show that homosexuality is genetically determined, for the most that they claim is the existence of an inherited *disposition* or *tendency* towards homosexual behaviour, not a biological *determination* of it. The scientific credentials of the studies have, anyway, been heavily criticized by other scientists, and there is currently no general acceptance among biologists of the existence of a genetic disposition of this kind.

Whatever the status of these studies, whether a person is 'gay' or not cannot result simply from his or her biology. Being 'gay' refers not just to sexual practices but to the assumption of a sexual identity that is social in character. Some genetic disposition to sexual preferences may be discovered, but the meanings that are attributed to these preferences and the ways in which they are expressed in behaviour are not themselves matters of biology.

Homosexual activities conventionally labelled as deviant have been seen as perfectly normal in many societies, including ancient Greece and traditional Japan. Whether an activity is treated as deviant or normal is a matter of social definition, and social definitions vary from one society to another. These social definitions are transmitted and adopted through socialization.

The work of Ken Plummer (1975) has shown very clearly that sexual deviance—specifically, male homosexuality—can best be understood if it is seen as a process of social learning. Plummer argues that sexual socialization involves learning to define oneself as a sexual being and

---

THEORY AND METHODS   **5.4**

Telling sexual stories

We live in a world in which 'it's good to talk' and people are encouraged to verbalize their feelings. Plummer (1995) has explored the ways in which sexual identities of all kinds are explored and reconstructed through the production of narrative accounts of personal biography.

Plummer saw the collection of these narratives as an important way of understanding the changing meanings of sexuality. Some are published in books, magazines, or broadcasts, but he also wanted to collect the private 'stories' recounted only among small circles of friends or, perhaps, only to oneself. A sexual story is a reconstruction of a person's sexual biography from the standpoint of his or her current situation. It is a genuine attempt to make sense of the person's experiences and moral career.

Plummer shows that the sexual narratives of those who came out as gay during the 1960s and 1970s have a common pattern in which sexual suffering is survived and then overcome. The most significant act is 'coming out' and announcing one's gayness to others. The

telling of sexual stories in a gay club, for example, helps to reinforce the storytellers' identities through shared experiences and creates a sense of solidarity that can sustain them in the future.

Gay and lesbian accounts of coming out tend to follow a common storyline. This begins with a frustrated or stigmatized erotic desire for someone of one's own sex. It moves on to explorations of childhood and youth in an attempt to uncover 'motives' and 'memories', feelings of unhappiness and difference, that would 'explain' this desire. It then proceeds to a crisis or turning point— perhaps a 'discovery'—that leads to a complete reconsideration of the past and the building of a new identity, often with the help of others in the same situation. A sense of identity and community is established. Subcultures of homosexuality—gay social worlds—are crucial conditions for the production of these accounts.

Plummer suggests that a similar pattern is found in other sexual stories— of sexual abuse, sex addiction, pornography, fetishism, and rape experiences. In the case of rape, for

example, he suggests that from the 1960s and 1970s there was a recasting of women's narratives of rape in the same 'suffering, surviving, and surpassing' structure that has just been described.

These sexual stories, as they become public, enter into a new politics of what Plummer calls 'intimate citizenship'. They contribute to a broadening of cultural self-understanding. The dominance of the expert or the authority figure—the doctor, the psychologist, and even the sociologist —is broken, and participants are able to make their own views known and can begin to shape a more autonomous cultural and political agenda.

➲ In addition to published sources, Plummer used a range of personal contacts to encourage people to write down their sexual stories or to provide them in interviews.

➲ Look at our discussion of documentary research in Chapter 3, pp. 86–90, and see what problems you can identify in this research design. You might like to look at Plummer's own methodological discussion in his book *Documents of Life* (Plummer 2001).

then managing that definition and its consequences for other aspects of one's life. People gradually become committed to a particular sexual identity and the sexual practices associated with it.

The period of adolescence is critical for adult sexual identity. At a time when the biological changes of puberty are occurring, sexual identity becomes crystallized. It is in the peer group, rather than the family, that this adolescent sexual socialization takes place. This is a time when boys tend to enter into casual exploratory sexual encounters with other boys. Mutual masturbation, for example, has been especially common at single-sex boys' schools.

In most cases, these are transient encounters, but in some circumstances boys may come to see them as signs of homosexual inclinations. This is likely if they have other reasons for feeling different from other boys. A boy may, for example, be more interested in art, literature, or hairstyles than in football or aggressive sports, and may be seen as a 'sissy'. Feelings of cultural and sexual difference may be reinforced by parents, teachers, or other boys making remarks about a boy's 'effeminacy'.

A self-identification as 'homosexual' may then be reinforced by social isolation. Feelings of guilt or shame aroused by the negative image of homosexuality in the wider culture may contribute to this isolation. A boy may keep his feelings about his identity secret and become increasingly solitary. Solitude will in turn strengthen his sexual identity because it cuts him off from the possibility of heterosexual experiences.

Some may remain solitary and keep their identity secret for the whole of their lives, passing as heterosexual. Others, however, 'come out' as homosexuals (see Box 5.4). Coming out is an open avowal of homosexuality that allows greater, and more open, contact with others perceived to be similar. By meeting those who share their identity and with whom they can feel at ease, they come into contact with alternative, more positive, views of homosexuality, and are able to reconstruct their sense of self in more positive terms. They fully enter the homosexual role and become committed to a 'gay' identity. Through contacts with other homosexuals they are drawn into a subculture of homosexuality that provides both opportunities for meeting sexual partners and meanings that legitimate their new sexual identity.

Sexualities

The above discussion presumes the existence of distinct sexual identities. It is indeed commonly taken for granted that people are heterosexual, homosexual, or possibly bisexual, that everyone (except the disabled—see Box 5.5 on p. 162) can be placed in one of these categories. The categories themselves are, however, social in origin and reflect a particular way of thinking about sex and sexuality.

They came into use as a means of classifying people in the nineteenth century, when a new language of sexuality derived from the two-sex model (see the section on 'Sexes' above) spread. It was this model that made possible such categories as **heterosexuality**, **homosexuality**, and **bisexuality**, which all depend on the notion of two sexes and are inconceivable without it.

The important point to grasp here is that terms like 'heterosexual' and 'homosexual' (and 'lesbian') are not simply words that describe particular kinds of sexual behaviour. They carry with them all sorts of assumptions about it that derive from nineteenth-century ways of thinking. The classification of people into these categories implies that only certain kinds of people engage in particular sexual practices. The term 'homosexual', for example, implies that sexual acts between men (and between women) occur only within a distinct group called homosexuals. Both men and women had engaged in sexual acts with people of the same sex before the nineteenth century but had not been treated as a distinct kind of person.

Out and about. What is the sociological significance of 'coming out'?
© Alice Chadwick

According to the dominant discourse of the nineteenth century, heterosexuality was the only normal sexuality, and this belief has been so strong that the term 'compulsory heterosexuality' has been used to convey its force (Rich 1980). In more recent years, those engaging in same-sex relationships have rejected the negative valuation of homosexuality by adopting the new, and more positive-sounding 'gay' label. In doing this, they have also, however, perpetuated the distinction between different sexualities. Indeed, some gays have seized hold of the notion of a 'gay gene' in order to argue that being gay is as natural as being heterosexual. Bisexuals challenged nineteenth-century categories more fundamentally by crossing the boundary between heterosexuality and homosexuality, though the very term 'bisexual' showed that a two-sex model still underlay their thinking.

It was **queer theory**, which emerged in the United States during the 1980s, that mounted a thoroughgoing intellectual challenge to nineteenth-century categories. Queer theory not only opposed the idea that heterosexuality was the only normal and natural sexuality, but also rejected the notion of homosexuality as a distinct category of people and behaviour. It rejected all 'binary divides' that separated sexes and sexualities. The theoretical basis for rejecting existing categories was the argument that these did not reflect real differences, biological or otherwise, but a particular *discourse* (see Chapter 6, p. 196, for a discussion of this concept). These categories were part of the language of heterosexual dominance (Stein and Plummer 1994).

Queer theory threw out the notion of distinct sexual identities. It shared with post-modern theorizing a much looser and more decentred conception of identity, recognizing that there are many strands to any one person's identity. Furthermore, individuals could construct and reconstruct themselves through their choice of lifestyles, moving across categories and boundaries as they pleased (Epstein 1994).

The message of queer theory is that the sexual categories that people customarily use are socially produced and not biological in origin. These categories have powerfully constrained people's beliefs, identities, and behaviour, but when they understand that the categories are social in origin, they can challenge them, liberate themselves from them, and then freely choose how they live.

Queer theory is not only a sociological analysis of the origins and significance of social categories but also a political project (we examine the queer movement on p. 183). Some have found this perspective personally liberating, but its whole argument that sexual categories have no real existence outside a particular discourse is open to sociological criticism. It neglects the power of the socialization process, the strength of gender-roles, the creation of distinct identities, and the solidarity of communities based upon them.

Controversy and debate   Disability and sexuality   5.5

This head waiter that I knew well . . . came up to me and said, 'You can't can you . . .?' I said, 'Can't what?' . . . I knew what he meant. I thought, I'll drag this out a bit, and he said, 'Well, you can't have sex, can you?' And I said, 'Why ever not?' And he said, 'Well, you can't walk . . .' And I said, 'You walk while you're having sex? I haven't seen that in the Kama Sutra!' (Paula, quoted by Shakespeare 2003: 144)

Disabled people commonly report that they are treated by the non-disabled as though lacking both sex and sexuality. They are, however, disabled not by their bodies, which have desires and are capable of sexual activity, but by society. Shakespeare (2003: 148) rejects the medicalization of the disabled and claims that, 'in general, the problems of disabled sexuality are not caused by the impairment itself, but by the way people with that particular impairment are viewed and treated in society'. He also argues that, while some disabled people, particularly those in residential institutions, find that their sexuality is denied and others have experienced sexual abuse, they should not be treated as victims. Some of the disabled people that he studied had found their disability sexually liberating, because it freed them from both sexual norms and the pressure to perform, and encouraged them to experiment and explore their sexual potential. Shakespeare concludes that the social barriers to disabled sexuality should be removed by educating those who work with them to recognize their sexual rights and needs, but notions of 'normal sex' should not be imposed on them.

→ What social processes lead to the treatment of the disabled as non-sexual beings?

→ What problems might be raised by facilitating normal sexual behaviour by the disabled?

Stop and reflect

We began this section by distinguishing between the concepts of sex, gender, and sexuality. Make sure that you are clear about the distinctive meanings of these terms and the relationships between them.

- Some people believe that differences in the behaviour of men and women are biologically determined. Why do sociologists reject this idea?

We then examined 'sex'.

- The term 'sex' refers to the biological and physical differences between men and women.
- Is the notion that there are two sexes simply a reflection of human biology?

We moved on to consider 'gender' and 'patriarchy'.

- We argued that socialization can account for the persistence of gender differences but cannot explain them.

- Theories of patriarchy try to provide possible explanations of gender differences, but the concept of patriarchy is problematic.
- Consider whether Connell's approach is an advance on earlier theories of patriarchy.

Finally in this section we discussed 'sexuality'.

- A person's sexuality refers not only to the practices they find sexually stimulating but also to related aspects of identity, lifestyle, and community.
- Why should sociologists be sceptical of the notion of a 'gay gene'?
- Our conventional categories of sexuality are derived from the 'two-sex model' established in the nineteenth century.
- Consider whether the terms 'heterosexual' and 'homosexual' are simply a description of sexual practices.

Separating identities

In this section we examine the processes through which the identities of men and women were created in nineteenth-century Britain. The idea that men and women were different did not originate then, but what are now thought of as their 'traditional' identities did become firmly established. These identities are closely linked to the power relations between men and women, and we examine the interconnections between gender identities, patriarchy, and feminism. We then go on to consider the interaction between identity formation and the emergence of distinct sexualities, for it was also at this time that heterosexuality and homosexuality were first sharply differentiated from each other.

Separating spheres

The separation of male and female spheres was central to the separation of identities. By the separation of spheres we mean that different areas of social life become exclusively male or female. The world of public affairs, of politics and work, became increasingly a male sphere, while the home became a female sphere. This separation was closely connected with the growing separation of home and work but it was also a patriarchal process, for men excluded women from the public world and confined them in the home. Separation and exclusion also generated, however, the first

organized feminist movement, which began to challenge patriarchy in the second half of the nineteenth century.

Patriarchal exclusion

The development of industrial capitalism concentrated paid work in factories and offices away from the home. Workplace and home also became spatially separated, particularly for the middle class. Residential areas, such as Edgbaston in Birmingham, or Islington in London, were built well away from the business and industrial parts of these cities. Home and work were separated further by the growth of suburbs, from which people commuted by rail to work.

The separation of home from work provided the conditions in which a clear separation of male and female spheres could take place. In the middle class, the world of business outside the home became seen as a male sphere and the private world of home and children a female one. Thus, Catherine Hall (1982*b*) has pointed out that informal business partnerships between husbands and wives gave way to formal business partnerships between men. The woman's business was now to look after home and children, with the assistance of servants. Women were excluded from male professions, as is well shown by changes in medicine at this time (see Box 5.6 on p. 164).

An ideology of female domesticity legitimated this separation of spheres. The notion that women's primary responsibility lay in the home was not new but it was given

Briefing: gender and medicine   5.6

In the early nineteenth century, women were excluded from medical practice. Previously health care had been provided by travelling and community-based healers, many of whom had been women.

> By the mid-nineteenth century … medical diagnosis and treatment had become the exclusive prerogative of medical men, and women had become restricted to the care of the sick, as nurses, and to the attendance of women during natural labour, as midwives. (Witz 1992: 75)

Exclusion occurred when the market provision of medical care was expanding and new forms of organizational control were being established. These involved the state registration of medical practitioners after 1858 and the regulation of entry to the medical professions by teaching hospitals and Royal Colleges, which were controlled by men.

Women responded by seeking to gain entry to medical education in order to gain the qualifications required for medical practice. When their first attempts to do this through existing institutions were frustrated, another and more successful strategy was pursued through the opening in 1874 of a new medical school, the London School of Medicine for Women.

❓ *Can the nineteenth-century exclusion of women from medicine be explained by reference to patriarchy? When thinking about this, read our discussion of patriarchy on pp. 156–8.*

Figure 5.2 Spheres and identities

	Male	Female
Spheres	Work/politics	Home
	Public	Private
Identities	Active	Passive
	Rational	Emotional
	Independent	Dependent

factories but women and children too, for they provided employers with cheaper labour. There was, however, a reaction against the employment of women, in part because of the growing strength of the ideology of domesticity but also because it threatened the interests of men. Male-dominated trade unions kept women out of the more skilled and better-paid trades, while they were also excluded from some occupations by legislation (Walby 1986).

Women were not wholly excluded from paid work. Large numbers of them were employed as servants, though this was an extension of their domestic roles. Many also still worked in factories, particularly in the textiles industry, or carried out 'homework' for employers in their own houses. Later, in the twentieth century, the expansion of white-collar work led to the recruitment of women to white-collar jobs. Women's paid work was, however, generally considered secondary to their domestic work and men were seen as the breadwinners who earned a 'family wage' to provide for the needs of the whole family.

➡ *Connections*
We discuss the employment of women in Chapter 17, pp. 663–4.

A separation of spheres had then occurred in both the middle and the working classes, though they were less sharply defined in the working class. Ideological, economic, and residential changes created the conditions in which this separation could occur, but it was a process of patriarchal exclusion. With the separation of spheres, the identities of men and women became more sharply differentiated.

Challenging patriarchy

The separation of spheres excluded women but also stimulated and enabled the growth of organized feminism.

What came, much later, to be called first-wave feminism emerged in the nineteenth century. Feminist ideas were not new—they had first appeared during the eighteenth-century Enlightenment—but it was in 1856 that the first British feminist organization, the 'Ladies of Langham

much greater moral force in the early nineteenth century. Religion contributed significantly to this ideology through the evangelical movement in the Anglican Church, which spread a 'religion of the household' that sharply separated the moral life of the home from the evils of public life, treating the home as a female sphere and public life as a male sphere (C. Hall 1998).

The separation of spheres was linked to the construction of contrasting gender identities. Women were expected to be passive, dependent, and caring, while men were required to be strong, protective, and active. Women were seen as sensitive, emotional creatures, men as rational and calculating. These conceptions of masculine and feminine character strengthened patriarchal ideology and practice by making it appear as though the different roles of men and women expressed differences in their nature (Davidoff 1990).

In the working class, the situation was initially different. Industrialization separated the home from production, but this did not automatically exclude women from paid work. It was not only men who were employed in the new

Place', was founded. In 1859 the Langham Place group launched a Society for Promoting the Employment of Women, which set up an employment exchange to find work for women. They also sought to gain property rights for women and in the 1860s began the campaign for women's right to vote.

It was the separation of spheres that actually enabled women to organize. Their confinement in the home provided middle-class women, who could afford servants to do the domestic work, with the time to meet and organize. As the name of this first organization suggests, it was indeed middle-class women who led and dominated the early feminist movement (Banks 1981).

The separatism that excluded women became the basis of the feminist counter-attack. Access to medical education was a key battleground, and a separate medical school was set up for women in London (see Box 5.6). A separatist strategy was pursued more widely within education, with the establishment of schools for girls in which they would be taught by women (see Chapter 9, p. 327). As Anne Witz (1992: 195) has put it, there was a 'widespread adoption of separatist methods by middle-class women as they forged spaces within which they could participate in the public sphere'. Charities, the care of the sick and the poor were other areas that women came to dominate, indeed to monopolize.

In the working class, the situation was, as we have just shown, rather different, for, although processes of exclusion had operated there too, many women were employed in paid work. Most trade unions excluded women, however, and in the last quarter of the nineteenth century women formed their own union organizations, such as the Women's Trade Union League and the National Federation of Women Workers (Walby 1986). A separatist strategy was pursued here too.

There were, however, limits to such a strategy. While it enabled women to escape domesticity at least partially and to establish a certain independence, it did not directly challenge male control of the central organizations and institutions of British society. Women had made some significant inroads into public affairs but, as Walby has argued, a private patriarchy that sought to confine them in the home had been replaced by a public patriarchy. Men used their control of public organizations and institutions to keep women in a subordinate position.

Separating sexes

The separation of spheres distinguished the roles and activities of men and women, who were now seen as fundamentally different in character. We now look at the grounding of these character differences in the quite new belief that men and women were biologically different sexes.

The two-sex model

We argued earlier that the idea that men and women are different sexes is a comparatively recent idea (see p. 154). Indeed, according to Thomas Laqueur (1990: 149), men and women were not thought of as separate sexes until, 'sometime in the eighteenth century, sex as we know it was invented'.

Before this time, when anatomists examined male and female bodies, they did not see them as having different organs. The vagina was considered an interior penis, another tube through which sperm passed. Ovaries were internal testicles. Women's organs were simply less developed versions of men's. It was thought that they were less developed because women were 'cooler and moister beings', which also meant that they were less active than men and their mental capacities less developed.

The replacement of the 'one-sex' by the 'two-sex' model was the result not of greater knowledge or the advance of science but of new ways of thinking. A new view of men and women as separate sexes can be found in the ideas of both French and Scottish thinkers during the period of the Enlightenment. Old ways of thinking were then demolished by the revolutionary changes and political struggles that followed during the later eighteenth and the nineteenth centuries.

In the nineteenth century, the new 'two-sex' model was *biologized*. It was given a biological content, which not only distinguished between the organs of men and women but also provided a biological account of the presumed differences in their character and behaviour. The growth of biological science in the nineteenth century led to a biological determinism, a general tendency to explain human differences in biological terms. It was also at this time that biological ideas of race and racial differences became established.

So the now familiar idea that biological differences explain differences in the way that men and women behave was in fact a product of new ways of thinking about sex that were established in the nineteenth century.

Female superiority?

By claiming that the differences between men and women were rooted in their natures, the 'two-sex' model gave male domination a biological justification, but it also helped women to challenge male dominance. This model freed women from the earlier one-sex view of them as less-developed versions of men. Indeed, the belief that women were fundamentally different made it possible to argue that they were more virtuous than men, that they were morally superior.

By the end of the nineteenth century, the feminist movement was based not so much on the doctrine of male and female equality as on a notion of female superiority that was accepted not only by women but by many of their male supporters.

Banks 1981: 84

Thus, the campaign for women to have the vote was based not only on the idea that women should be equal to men but also on their moral superiority. Their participation in politics would enable them to improve the world, through, for example, welfare legislation.

The assertion of female superiority clearly played an important part in first-wave feminism, but the belief that the sexes were different by their very nature was something of a two-edged sword. While the notion of the special virtues of women helped to justify their greater participation in public affairs, the claim that women had distinctive qualities, that, for example, they had a 'maternal instinct', trapped them in caring and child-focused occupations such as nursing, teaching, and social work. It also justified the domestic division of labour, since it could be argued that women were better than men at caring for children and attending to the needs of the family.

We showed above that the separation of spheres subordinated women but then enabled the development of a separatist feminism. In a parallel way, the idea of separate sexes could be used to justify male domination but also

made feminism possible and even enabled women to argue that they were naturally superior. A separatist feminism of this kind did, however, make it difficult for women to challenge the argument that their abilities were limited because they had a different nature.

Separating sexualities

The two-sex model also had profound consequences for the way in which people thought about sexual behaviour and the categories of sexuality they used, categories that are still with us today and still deeply influence people's lives.

Male and female sexuality

The two-sex model emphasized male–female differences and was associated with changes in beliefs about sexuality. Just as men were seen as active in public affairs and women as private and passive beings, so men were now regarded as sexually active and women as sexually passive. The old idea that women initiated sex, because their cool bodies sought male heat, gave way to the belief that men should take the lead, as they were 'naturally' the active sex.

The active male penetration of the passive female vagina was considered the natural and only acceptable sexual practice. The male-on-top 'missionary position' apparently became the norm at this time. Mutual sexual fondling, which treated men's and women's sexual desires as essentially the same, was now considered improper. Masturbation, particularly male masturbation, was condemned as unnatural, and doctors warned that dire consequences would follow indulgence in it (Shoemaker 1998).

It is difficult to know how much change there was in what men and women actually did together. Changed conceptions of sexuality did, however, have important implications for male and female identities. Thus, the notion that men were sexually active and women sexually passive reinforced the idea that men should be active in the world, while women should wait patiently at home for them to return.

Heterosexuality and homosexuality

Heterosexuality actually means sexual behaviour between different sexes, and it was, therefore, inconceivable until a two-sex model had come into existence. In the nineteenth century, 'compulsory heterosexuality' became, in the view of many radical feminists, notably Rich (1980), a patriarchal institution. They saw it as the means through which men dominated women and suppressed women's sexuality.

There had long been a religious disapproval of sex between men, but this was, it seems, primarily because it was non-reproductive sex, which meant that it was considered no worse than non-reproductive sex acts between

Briefing: sexology   **5.7**

These new ways of thinking about sex interacted with the nineteenth-century development of science to produce 'sexology'. The development of science was associated with the detailed classification of the natural and social worlds, a search for the biological basis of human differences (see our discussion of the concept of 'race' in Chapter 6, p. 191, and the formulation of the laws considered to govern natural and social behaviour (see our discussion of Comte's laws in Chapter 2, p. 26). A huge amount of work went into attempts to classify different kinds of sexual activity and explain them biologically. Sexology emerged in the late nineteenth century and eventually gave rise to the well-known works of Kinsey, and Masters and Johnson, which have greatly influenced contemporary ideas about sexual behaviour.

This 'science of sex' sought to provide not only scientific explanations of sexual behaviour but also an understanding of the natural forces that made men and women different. 'Sexology came to mean therefore both the study of the sexual impulse and of relations between the sexes, for ultimately they were seen as the same: sex, gender, sexuality were locked together as the biological imperative' (Weeks 1985: 69).

men and women. The fact that it was between men does not seem to have been a source of much concern, as the one-sex model did not sharply distinguish between men and women. Punishment for non-reproductive acts could, however, be severe, for buggery, whether between men and men or men and women, was punishable by the death penalty until 1861 (Weeks 1989).

As the two-sex model became established, sexual activity between members of the same sex threatened the new sexual identities. Men who engaged in sexual acts with other men were stigmatized as 'mollies', a term that implied that they were behaving as women rather than men. Indeed, in England the fear of appearing a 'molly' resulted in men increasingly avoiding ordinary physical contact with each other. By the end of the eighteenth century heterosexual men no longer kissed other men, and male visitors from the Continent were warned that in England they should greet other men only by shaking hands or bowing (Trumbach 1998).

In the nineteenth century the term homosexual began increasingly to be used specifically for men who engaged in sexual activity with other men, though the word actually meant sexual behaviour between members of the same sex, male or female. Homosexuality also came to refer not to the *action* of engaging in sexual activity with other men but to a *distinct group* of men who were considered homosexual by nature. The term 'homosexual' was applied not only to an act but to a person. It was assumed that anyone who engaged in a homosexual act was a homosexual.

Furthermore, homosexuals were treated as deviants who had something wrong with them. Male homosexuality was pathologized and medicalized. There were many different theories of its origins, and some thought it was genetic, while others thought it was a disease, mental or physical in origin (see Box 5.7). Some thought it curable, others incurable (Weeks 1989).

Similar processes occurred, to a lesser extent, with sex between women. The label 'sapphist' or 'tommy' came into use for women who were sexually attracted to other women. While there is some evidence of a growing intolerance of sex between women, this was not a big issue at the time and did not lead to prosecutions (Shoemaker 1998). This difference in attitudes was embodied in laws that criminalized sexual acts between men but not those between women.

Why has there been less tolerance of sex between men than sex between women? According to Jeffrey Weeks, the fragility of male identity made sexuality more important to the male identity and same-sex male activity more threatening:

Masculinity or the male identity is achieved by the constant process of warding off threats to it. It is precariously achieved by the rejection of femininity and of homosexuality. Male violence against women, and the taboo against male homosexuality may both be understood as effects of this fragile sense of identity . . .

Weeks 1985: 190

Connell (1987) has argued rather differently that the hegemonic character of masculinity means that subordinate masculinities are more threatening than subordinate femininities to the gender order (see p. 159). Homosexuality among men presents a more serious challenge to this order, because the assertion of a heterosexual masculinity is central to male dominance.

One may note that, while homosexuality was considered pathological by the dominant discourse of the time, the idea that it was in some sense 'natural' did provide the basis for what Foucault has called a 'reverse discourse' (see Box 5.8). If it was natural for some people to be homosexual, they could not be held responsible for their sexuality or judged as immoral in their behaviour. The notion of a 'gay gene' has recently been used in this way to defend 'gay' sexual practices.

Thus, in the nineteenth century sexuality became central to the identities of men and women. Heterosexuality had become a defining feature of the hegemonic masculinity of nineteenth-century Britain. Those who engaged in same-sex practices were now treated as a quite distinct group of 'homosexuals'. Changes in discourse were quite fundamental to these new distinctions, which can be traced back to the emergence of the two-sex model, for this made it possible to distinguish between heterosexuality and homosexuality.

Deviant identities

While the category 'homosexual' emerged from the dominant discourse of the time, a distinct homosexual identity

---

THEORY AND METHODS   **5.8**

Foucault on homosexuality

'There is no question that the appearance in nineteenth-century psychiatry, jurisprudence, and literature of a whole series of discourses on the species and subspecies of homosexuality, inversion, pederasty, and "psychic hermaphrodism" made possible a strong advance of social controls into this area of "perversity"; but it also made possible the formation of a "reverse" discourse: homosexuality began to speak on its own behalf, to demand that its legitimacy or "naturality" be acknowledged, often in the same vocabulary, using the same categories by which it was radically disqualified.' (Foucault 1976: 101)

➲ We discuss Foucault's concept of discourse on p. 196.

resulted from the formation of sexual subcultures. These raised the distinctiveness of deviant groups, enabled their members to provide mutual support, to resist and challenge negative images, and develop their own more positive view of themselves.

In England signs of a 'homosexual' subculture first emerged in London during the late seventeenth and eighteenth centuries. This had 'its own network of meeting houses and distinctive gestures, language, dress, and pick-up signals' (Shoemaker 1998: 83). It was also characterized by the growth of effeminacy, with its 'mollies' adopting the dress, appearance, and behaviour of women. But the only regular members of the subculture were, it seems, the 'professionals', who sold their sexual services, while many others from varied social backgrounds participated occasionally (Weeks 1989: 110).

According to Weeks (1985: 192), it was not until the later nineteenth century that a separate homosexual community and identity became established.

> Between the 1850s and the 1930s a complex sexual community had developed in many American as well as European cities, which crossed class, racial, gender and age boundaries, and which offered a focus for identity development.

It was also during this period that organized movements of male homosexuals appeared. These organizations assisted those in trouble with the law and sought reform of the various laws that criminalized homosexual acts.

A female homosexual subculture was much slower to emerge. By the end of the nineteenth century the term 'lesbian' had come into use and there were lesbian meeting-places, but there is little evidence of a subculture as such. The roles assigned to women, beliefs about female sexuality, and women's lack of independence made it difficult for a distinctive lesbian identity to emerge. It was in the 1920s that such an identity first became clearly visible and also at that time that **lesbianism** became a social issue and attempts were made to criminalize it (Weeks 1989).

It is important to be clear that the idea that *all* men or women who engage in same-sex sexual activities are 'homosexuals' or 'lesbians' involves very particular beliefs about sexuality. They were treated as such by the dominant ideology, while the formation of a distinctive subculture and identity has meant that some have come to see themselves in this way. It is well known, however, that much same-sex activity, for example in schools, the armed forces, and prisons, is situational in character and does not involve the assumption of a homosexual identity. Furthermore, many people outside these situations who have same-sex experiences do not participate in homosexual subcultures or do so only occasionally. Some who have same-sex experiences see themselves as bisexual or indeed heterosexual rather than homosexual, and do not identify with homosexual groups at all.

 Stop and reflect

In this section we have analysed the separating out of distinct male and female identities in the nineteenth century.

We began by examining the emergence of distinct male and female spheres.

- Domestic life became a female sphere and public life a male sphere.
- Distinct gender identities became associated with these spheres.
- Consider the implications of this separation for gender power relationships.
- What was the significance of separation for the rise of feminism?

By the nineteenth century men and women were seen as different sexes.

- Make sure that you understand what is meant by the idea that sex was 'invented' in the eighteenth century.
- What is meant by the 'biologization' of the 'two-sex' model?
- What were the implications of this model for the power relationships between men and women?

The separation of sexes also led to the separation of sexualities.

- The two-sex model made possible the distinction between 'heterosexuality' and 'homosexuality'.
- Male homosexuality has been treated with less tolerance than female homosexuality. Why do you think this has happened?
- If people engage in sexual activity with people of the same sex, does this mean that they are 'homosexuals'?

Converging identities

The separation of people into categories is one of the most important ways in which one group asserts and maintains its dominance over another. It provides a basis for systematic discrimination and exclusion, and enables those who are dominant to treat those they dominate as different and inferior by nature. As we have shown, separation and exclusion can also create the conditions that enable those who are dominated to organize themselves and establish their own identity. They can then challenge the categories created by the dominant group and seek to end domination by it. In this section we again examine spheres, sexes, and sexualities but this time looking at recent changes to see whether the separateness of the nineteenth century has been broken down.

> ⊃ *Connections*
>
> You can follow up on many of the issues raised in this section by going to other chapters:
> - On women in employment, see Chapter 17, pp. 681–4.
> - On girls' increasing success in education, see Chapter 9, pp. 328–9.
> - On changes in the domestic division of labour, see Chapter 12, pp. 458–60.
> - On divorce, see Chapter 12, pp. 448–51.

Spheres?

The confinement of women in the home was the central feature of the separation of male and female spheres in the nineteenth century, but in recent times far more women have entered paid work and participated in politics. New waves of feminism have challenged male domination. Has the separation of the spheres broken down?

Women in employment

Between 1851 and 1951 there was little change in the proportion of women entering paid work, and their participation rate was roughly half that of men. Since then there has been a big increase in women's participation and the gender gap in employment rates has now almost disappeared. While this is mainly due to the growing employment of women, it is also substantially due to the declining employment of men. The recession of 2008–9 was indeed labelled a 'mancession', as men's private-sector and blue-collar jobs were lost more quickly than the white-collar and public-sector jobs dominated by women. Whether this will continue to be the case when the inevitable public-sector cuts take place remains to be seen.

As women's participation in the labour market has increased, so has their participation in trade unions. These previously highly patriarchal organizations have been significantly feminized (Rees 1992). In the UK, the union density of male workers has fallen from 35 per cent in 1995 to 26 per cent in 2007, while the union density of female workers has remained relatively stable, between 28 and 30 per cent (*Social Trends* 2009: 60).

If women are doing more paid work, does this mean that men are doing more work in the domestic sphere? Although mechanization of housework may have reduced the time that has to be spent on it, someone has to do it. One solution has been the employment of other people to do it, and there is evidence that this has been increasing, though in many households this is not financially possible. As we show in Chapter 12, pp. 459–60, there is some evidence

Is the public sphere still a man's world?
© Alice Chadwick

Figure 5.3 Male and female intake into UK medical schools, 1960–2007

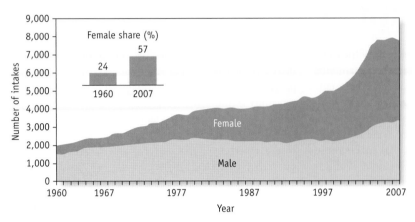

Source: Royal College of Physicians (2009: 3).

of greater male participation in housework, but it is still disproportionately done by women.

As housework and childcare still fall disproportionately on women, they still affect women's access to paid work, earnings, and careers. About 90 per cent of part-time work is done by women, largely because of their domestic responsibilities, and part-time work is paid at lower rates. Gregory and Connolly (2008) found that a third of female corporate managers had to move down the career ladder after the birth of their first child. Some women can do only poorly paid homework because of their childcare responsibilities.

Occupations remain highly gendered. Indeed, one of the main reasons for the narrowing of the gap between male and female rates of employment is the decline of men's occupations, such as mining and other forms of heavy manual work, and the growth of women's service occupations, such as cleaning and catering. Women's occupations are still largely extensions of their 'traditional' domestic roles. Unfortunately for them, it is these occupations that are the lowest paid. In 2002 the ten lowest-paid occupations were in catering, caring, and cleaning, and 80 per cent of the workers who did these jobs were women (Toynbee 2002).

It is not only that particular occupations tend to recruit either men or women. There are also barriers to those who seek to enter occupations considered inappropriate to their sex. In Britain, equal opportunities legislation bans open discrimination, but occupational cultures can isolate or ridicule those who seek to cross gender boundaries. One form that ridicule can take is a questioning of the sexuality of someone of the 'wrong' sex. Men who work in caring occupations may be labelled 'gay', while women employed in manual work in garages or building sites may be called 'dykes' (Charles 2002).

In some occupations women have broken through gender barriers. This is particularly the case in the professions. There were few women in financial services, law,

and medicine in the 1960s but now there are many (see Figure 5.3 and Box 5.9). Women have also made considerable inroads into the armed forces (see Box 5.10) and the police (see Study 5 at the end of this chapter). This is not, however, to say that women have achieved equality with men in these occupations. There is still a tendency to sideline them into the particular jobs they are considered best suited for, and there are still glass ceilings. Professional bodies are still largely controlled by men. The control of business is still largely a male preserve, with women comprising only around one-in-ten of the directors of the top 100 British companies (Equal Opportunities Commission 2006).

The growing employment of women has at least reduced the separation of spheres, particularly in the middle class. There has been less change in the working class, partly because there always was less separation there (see p. 164). Delamont (2001: 03) has indeed fairly recently claimed that 'the mass of women are working as they did in 1893'.

Women in politics

After a long campaign, all adult women finally received the vote in 1928. In 1979 Margaret Thatcher became Britain's first woman prime minister, but there were still only nineteen women MPs. Have women truly entered the public sphere of politics?

The representation of women did increase considerably in the 1987 election (41 MPs), the 1992 election (60), and above all the 1997 election (120). It was claimed that in 1997, with 18 per cent of MPs, women had become a 'critical mass', with the potential to 'initiate changes in organizational structures, gender relations and political agendas' (Puwar 1997: 3). It was also crucial that women occupied ministerial positions and in 1997 five obtained Cabinet office. Since 1997 the representation of women has remained around the same level. After the 2010 election it was 143, with 4 who obtained Cabinet office.

Briefing 'Women are "Taking over the Health Service"' 5.9

There are fears that the feminization of medicine will result in a labour shortage and a crisis of leadership. A working group chaired by Professor Jane Dacre was set up by the Royal College of Physicians to explore this issue and reported in 2009 that:

- there are more female than male students in medical school;
- while 44 per cent of general practitioners are currently women, they will be in a majority by 2013;
- although only 28 per cent of consultants overall are women, they amount to 47 per cent of early appointed UK-trained consultants aged 30–34;
- as early as 2017 a majority of doctors could be women.

There are fears of a future labour shortage, since women tend to opt for part-time employment. When career breaks and part-time work are taken into account, women provide 60 per cent of a full-time equivalent, as compared with an 80 per cent figure for men. Women tend to go into specialist fields involving more interaction with patients and allowing regular hours of work, rather than, say, surgery. Women are also not finding their way into senior positions on NHS Trust boards, Primary Care Trusts, and in Medical Schools.

Does this mean that there are too many women entering medicine? Or is it more a problem to do with equal opportunities, the provision of childcare, and the under-representation of women in senior positions?

Sources: Laurance (2009); Royal College of Physicians (2009).

Puwar (1997) reported that, although their numbers had substantially increased, women faced many problems in parliament. As transgressing interlopers, women MPs had to prove themselves before they were taken seriously. Many found that media interest was primarily in them as women—in their appearance, their families, or their sex life—and they were not taken seriously as political figures. Male colleagues often treated them in the same way, and opponents used sexist language when attacking them, while the House of Commons was historically very much a 'male space', with procedures designed for men. The women MPs had certainly challenged male practices, but they were still a minority facing an uphill struggle (see Box 5.11 on p. 172).

Even though women were heavily underrepresented at the time, there have been important legislative changes in their favour. These were the Equal Pay Act of 1970, the Sex Discrimination Act of 1975, and the Equal Value Amendment of 1984, which widened pay comparisons under the Equal Pay Act to include men and women doing work of equal value. Then the 1994 extension of many of the rights of full-time workers to part-time workers particularly benefited women because so many of them were in part-time work. This legislation has not made women equal but it has had a considerable impact on women's pay, helped women to challenge and remove open discriminatory practices, and put equal opportunities firmly on the agenda of

Controversy and debate Fighting women? 5.10

'For reasons of combat effectiveness', the British army bans women from units that are 'deliberately required to close with and kill the enemy face-to-face'. They are not allowed to serve in either the infantry or the Royal Armoured Corps. It is, however, increasingly difficult to draw a line between combat units and other military occupations in which women serve.

Women have been serving as pilots involved in combat operations. In March 2008 Flight Lieutenant Michelle Goodman was awarded a Distinguished Flying Cross for flying a helicopter into Basra under heavy fire to rescue a wounded soldier.

In Afghanistan in 2008 one in five of British troops was a woman. Women served in front-line operations as medics,

signallers, interpreters, dog handlers, drivers, and in bomb disposal. If attacked, they had to defend themselves. They had to be prepared to kill and be killed. Between 2003 and 2008 seven women died on operations.

The ban on serving in combat units has reportedly come under scrutiny in the army itself, where senior generals have been considering whether it should continue.

Is there any reason why women should be excluded from employment in any military units?

Source: Rayment (2008).

A 'businessman's lunch'. Is this phrase now out of date?

© Alice Chadwick

employers in particular and organizations in general (Walby 1997).

The presence of women in parliament actually had little to do with this legislation. As Walby (1997) has shown, it was the European Union that played the key role in forcing a reluctant British state to make these changes. They were also a response to feminist demands backed by the labour movement. Arguably, women have had a greater political impact through feminism than through participation in formal political institutions.

New/old feminisms

It is no coincidence that the key legislation in the 1970s followed a period of renewed growth and radicalism in the feminist movement. After the 1920s victory of the campaign for the vote, the feminist movement had entered a period of relative weakness and division until the emergence of the second-wave feminism of the Women's Liberation Movement in the 1960s (Banks 1981; Pilcher 1999).

Second-wave feminism was itself far from unified, but its various parts combined to produce the major impact that it had on Western societies in the 1970s. In line with our distinctions between different strands of feminism in Box 5.2 on p. 156, three main branches of second-wave feminism can be identified.

The *liberal* 'equal rights' strand can be traced back to the eighteenth-century Enlightenment and had earlier culminated in the campaign for the vote. The revival of equal rights demands led directly to the call for equal pay and the ending of discrimination.

Radical feminists did not believe that legislation would achieve anything and called for the liberation of women rather than equality with men. There were many threads within this loosely organized strand of feminism but it broadly emphasized the differences between men and women. Some pursued a separatist strategy of 'life without men' and set up women's communes or advocated a militant lesbianism. Radical feminism did frontally attack patriarchy and therefore posed a more direct and general challenge to male domination than liberal feminism had done.

The *socialist* strand allied feminism with the labour movement. This had historically been a patriarchal organization that excluded women, but in the 1960s radicals in sympathy with feminism became more influential and the unions supported equal-rights demands. The labour move-

---

Controversy and debate Women's political dilemma   5.11

If they overcome their many political differences to act as women in the interests of women, they exclude themselves from the main political arena and are unlikely to secure ministerial positions. If they operate primarily as members of a political party and rise up the political hierarchy, they become successful politicians but lose their capacity to act as women in the interests of women. Simply being a woman in a position of power may make little difference to the position of women in general, as was shown by the career of Margaret Thatcher, who 'repeatedly denied the gender significance of her achievements'. (Pilcher 1999: 151)

❷ Which Cabinet offices are currently filled by women?

❷ Do you think that these ministers are doing anything to improve the position of women in British society?

Global focus International differences in gender inequality 5.12

The World Economic Forum (WEF) publishes a league table of countries according to the size of their gender gap. Countries are ranked by the extent to which they have reduced the inequality between men and women.

Top ten		Bottom ten	
1	Sweden	119	Oman
2	Norway	120	Egypt
3	Finland	121	Turkey
4	Iceland	122	Morocco
5	New Zealand	123	Benin
6	Philippines	124	Saudi Arabia
7	Germany	125	Nepal
8	Denmark	126	Pakistan
9	Ireland	127	Chad
10	Spain	128	Yemen

The overall gender gap combines four equally weighted sub-indexes:

1 *economic participation and opportunity;*

2 *educational attainment;*

3 *political empowerment;*

4 *health and survival.*

While the overall position of countries is interesting, the combination of different measures presents problems. A high position on some dimensions combined with a low position on others may result in a middle overall position that does not mean very much. Differences in the position of a given country on the various measures are themselves of considerable interest. The United Kingdom, falling just outside the top 10 at number 11, was ranked at the top on educational attainment (1), and high on political empowerment (12), but much lower on economic participation (32), and health and well-being (67).

Source: World Economic Forum (2007).

❷ Can you see any common features in the top ten and the bottom ten?

❷ Why do you think that the United Kingdom scores so differently on the various dimensions?

❷ How useful is an index of this kind?

---

ment was at the peak of its strength in the 1960s and 1970s. Its adoption of the demand for equal pay and an end to discrimination added industrial muscle to the feminist movement. The labour movement could supply the organizational resources other strands rather lacked.

The feminist movement played a crucial part in bringing about changes improving the position of women, but these were not just the result of feminist organization and activity. Broad changes in the economy and in education were also crucial. We showed above that occupational changes led to the growing employment of women. The post-Fordist shift to more flexible patterns of employment was also very important, as it led to more part-time employment, which helped women to take up paid work. Employment then gave them greater independence at home and made it easier to end marriages they found unsatisfactory. Education too played a key part, for it was the growing educational success of girls that enabled them to acquire the qualifications they needed to enter the professions.

Legislation, occupational changes, and access to education provided opportunities but women had to seize them. That they did so was because women themselves were changing. We will next examine changes in the character of men and women, and the relationship between them.

Sexes?

We argued earlier (see p. 165) that the concept of two distinct sexes emerged in the eighteenth century and was hardened in the nineteenth by the belief that their differences were essentially biological. The growth of feminism, the increasing employment of women, and the rise of sociology have chipped away at this biological essentialism. Have we now returned to a 'one-sex' view of men and women? It can certainly be argued that the behaviour of men and women has converged in recent years. In this section we consider whether women have become more like men and whether men have become more like women.

Changing women

Women in Western societies have become focused less on domestic life and more on paid work, which is nowadays a normal and continuing feature of most women's lives. In Britain most women used to give up work when they married, but by the 1960s they were working until they had their first child and then returning to work once childcare responsibilities had diminished. The amount of time spent out of work because of childcare responsibilities has

Frontiers Where is feminism now?   5.13

Do we live in a 'post-feminist' world where feminism has largely achieved its goals or does it still have a mission? Two feminists agree that there is still much to achieve but disagree on the direction feminism should take.

In *The New Feminism* (1998), Natasha Walter argued that there was still plenty of discrimination against women. They still needed to pursue financial, educational, and legal equality with men. To be successful in achieving equality, feminists should, however, stop focusing on women's private lives and should abandon the slogan that 'the personal is political'. This was distracting attention from the campaign for equal rights and alienating many women who rejected a 'man-hating' feminism. The achievement of equality would bring sexism to an end. More recently, in *Living Dolls: The Return of Sexism* (2010), she has argued very differently that the campaign for equal rights has not ended sexism. In popular culture, sexist imagery, attitudes, and behaviour have actually grown stronger, as has the biological determinist belief that men and women are fundamentally different, and need to be confronted directly.

In *The Whole Woman* (1999), Germaine Greer reacted against Natasha Walter's book and rejected equal-rights feminism to argue that women do not so much need equality with men as liberation from them. Equal-rights legislation had not removed male domination, and women were still seeking to mould themselves into bodies and lives shaped by male conceptions of what women should be like. She claimed that the campaign for equality with men accepted male definitions of the world and sought to turn women into men. Women should instead assert their distinctive qualities and make their own world. This approach belongs to the radical 'difference strand' of feminism that emerged in the 1960s, but can be traced back to the nineteenth-century feminist belief that women were different and superior (see our discussion of this on p. 165).

Post-feminism is discussed in Pilcher (1999: 3). Recent feminist work is examined in Jowett (2001). For some present-day reflections, see Boycott and Margolis (2010).

❓ Do you think that feminism has achieved so many of its goals that women no longer need it?

❓ Are women still dominated by male conceptions of how they should look and behave?

steadily declined, in part because women have had fewer children but also because they have resumed work sooner. Indeed, women with dependent children have increasingly combined childcare with not only part-time but also full-time work (Pilcher 1999).

There is evidence too that the aspirations of girls have changed. Sue Sharpe (1994) compared the expectations of a group of girls in the 1970s and 1990s. She found that the 1970s group looked for love, marriage, and children. The 1990s group were primarily concerned with jobs and careers. Jane Pilcher (1999) has claimed that it is these changed expectations that probably account for the growing success of girls in school. Educational success then facilitates career success and successful women act as role models, which raises girls' expectations further.

There can also be little doubt that since the 1960s women in Western societies have become more independent. Their growing employment was crucial to this, as it reduced their economic dependence on the breadwinning male. In 1960s Britain there were two other key changes:

- divorce law reform;
- oral contraception.

Marriage was one of the central institutions of patriarchy, and greater ease of divorce helped women to escape marital constraints, though it also helped men avoid family responsibilities. The availability of the contraceptive pill meant that women could reliably control when and whether they had children. These changes resulted in the higher divorce rates and childless career women that are characteristic of contemporary British society and sharply distinguish it from the society of the first half of the twentieth century.

Increased employment, higher educational qualifications, greater interest in careers, and more independence have all resulted in women behaving more like men. Another arena in which this has occurred is sport, with women engaging increasingly in what was previously considered to be a male preserve (see Box 5.15, on p. 176). The convergence of behaviour is associated with a unisex convergence of dress and appearance.

The lives of women have changed, but does this mean that ideas of what it means to be a woman have changed as well?

There is certainly evidence of a change in femininities, particularly in media representations of them. Angela McRobbie's research showed that, in magazines for girls and young women, older, more romantic, notions of what it means to be a woman have been increasingly mocked, while their content has focused on sexuality rather than love. McRobbie (1996: 178) suggested that this has 'extended the possibilities of what it is to be a woman'.

Controversy and debate A global revolution?   5.14

Is globalization revolutionizing the position of women? In his BBC Radio 4 Reith Lectures of 1999, Anthony Giddens suggested that it is:

> Traditional family systems are becoming transformed, or are under strain, in many parts of the world, particularly as women stake claim to greater equality. There has never before been a society, so far as we know from the historical record, in which women have been even approximately equal to men. This is a truly global revolution in everyday life, whose consequences are being felt around the world in spheres from work to politics.

Globalization has in various ways resulted in a worldwide increase in the employment of women. Transnational corporations, such as Gap and Nike, employ young women as cheap factory labour in such countries as Cambodia and Indonesia. Global communications make it possible for European and American companies to employ teleworking women in secretarial and clerical work in the West Indies or the Philippines. The growth of global tourism has provided work for women in hotels, catering, tour organization, and the sex industry all over the world. There has been an extensive international migration of women from poor countries to meet the increasing demand for their labour in rich countries.

But does this growing employment give women greater equality? Employment can provide the basis for greater independence, but whether this follows depends on the context in which it occurs. If women are simply cheap or degraded labour, controlled and exploited by men both at work and at home, it is hard to see how this improves their position. This is not just a matter of how patriarchal a particular society may be but of a woman's class (and ethnic) position in that society. Educated middle-class women with jobs in the professions or media careers are in a very

different position from women working in the fields or sweatshops or bars.

Globalization is not just, however, an economic process, and its political aspects have made possible the growth of global women's movements and organizations. Feminist movements now have a global reach. The United Nations has sponsored a series of World Conferences on Women and has provided the framework for many regional women's conferences and meetings. The International Labour Organization has worked to establish worldwide standards for the employment of homeworkers, who are mainly female.

Global communications have also enabled women suffering oppression in highly patriarchal societies to make their situation known to the outside world and seek its support. The Revolutionary Association of the Women of Afghanistan (RAWA) used the Internet to generate international awareness of their treatment by the Taliban and build a network of support. Its website is listed at the end of this chapter.

In some societies globalization has stimulated a patriarchal reaction. This has particularly occurred where traditional values and relationships have been threatened by Western ideas and patterns of consumption. Some fundamentalist religious movements are trying to force women back into traditional roles, modes of dress, and behaviour. In considering the significance of globalization, one must take into account not only the globalizing processes themselves but also responses to them.

Sources: Giddens (1999); Cohen and Kennedy (2000*b*); Ehrenreich and Hochschild (2003).

❷ Do you think that we can speak of a 'global revolution' taking place in the position of women?

A different indication of how women view themselves is the way that they see their bodies. This is particularly significant because of the rapidly expanding possibilities of body modification, which enable women (and men) to reconstruct themselves in an attempt to match reality to image. Dieting, exercise regimes, cosmetic surgery, and hormonal therapy have all become commonplace and highly commercialized activities. While all these ways of changing the body are to some extent a matter of individual choice, they are, like any other form of consumption, subject to commercial pressures and constrained by gendered beliefs about the female body.

Overwhelmingly, body modification is used to make women slimmer, younger in appearance, and sexually

> **⮕ Connections**
> Femininities are discussed on p. 159 of this chapter.
>   Media representations of women are discussed in more detail in Chapter 10, pp. 367–9.
>   You can follow the issue of body modification by referring to our discussion of anorexia in Chapter 8, pp. 301–2.

attractive to men. Unisex has its limits! Styles may change, but there seems little recent change in the kind of body that most women seek to have and keep. The availability of new technologies has, it seems, put pressure on women to conform all the more to male conceptions of women. As

Frontiers Women's football: catching up with men? 5.15

Although a women's football match took place in 1895 and there was an international match between English and French teams in 1920, the Football Association (FA) banned women from playing on Football League grounds in 1921, declaring that 'the game of football is quite unsuitable for females and ought not to be encouraged'.

Things have moved on considerably since then. In 1969 the Women's FA was created and in 1971 the ban on women playing on League grounds was lifted. By 1993 there were 10,400 women players in FA competitions and by 2009 there were 150,000. The FA has trained coaches and referees, and set up Centres of Excellence for 'talented girls'. In 2008 the FA announced plans for a Summer Super League to be launched in 2010 and central con-

tracts for England players. There will be an England women's team at the London Olympics in 2012.

But how far have they moved? In 2009 the FA decided to save money by postponing the start of the Summer Super League (promised since 2000) until 2011. The central contracts would pay women players only £16,000 a year. Women's football in England has lagged far behind its development in other countries, such as Sweden and the United States, where clubs have been threatening to poach the best English players.

Sources: The FA.com; Kessel (2008); Leighton (2009).

❓ What does the development of women's football tell us about changes in gender relationships?

Pilcher (1999: 106) has put it: 'Therefore whilst for individual women these techniques have advantages, for women as a whole they can be argued to represent a cumulative narrowing of the range of valuable femininities within a masculine-dominated culture.'

Do women change their bodies just to please men?
© Alice Chadwick

Changes in women's behaviour, expectations, and appearance show them becoming in some ways more like men. Conceptions of the female body, and the time and money expended on body modification, tell, however, a different story. This is the age-old story of women emphasizing their difference and making themselves attractive to men by conforming to male conceptions of how their bodies should look.

Changing men

Women have been changing. What about men?

Notions of a general male superiority have come under attack as individual women have demonstrated that they can be as successful as men in business, the media, and politics. This is not to argue that women have become equal with men in any of these fields. Individual women have, however, broken through exclusive barriers, and this is of great symbolic importance. If a woman can be prime minister or head of the British intelligence service or a chief constable or a barrister or a newscaster or a chief executive, this refutes the idea that only men are able to do these things.

Changes in employment patterns have undermined traditional notions of the male role. The idea of the male as breadwinner has been weakened by the equalizing of economic activity rates, because of the decline of male, as well as the rise of female, employment. Job expectations have changed too, and men have found themselves called upon to show more feminine skills, to be more flexible, more accommodating, and more responsive to clients and

Has femininity changed?
© Alice Chadwick

Controversy and debate Is women's liberation a danger to their health? 5.16

Voices in the media have claimed that women's health has been damaged by women's liberation.

Women have long had a greater life expectancy than men, but the gap between them has been closing since around 1980. Between 1980 and 2002 it fell from 6.0 years to 4.7 in the UK, in Sweden from 6.0 years to 4.4, in the US from 7.4 years to 5.4. While men's health has been improving, women's health has been declining. Trends in cigarette smoking and lung cancer suggest that, while men have been giving up unhealthy habits, women have been taking them up.

Should women's declining health be seen as a consequence of their liberation? Ellen Annandale argues that the media have been too ready to blame this simply on women's lifestyle choices. They should look instead at the 'contradictory demands that society makes of women'. Women face higher levels of stress, because they are expected to go out and work but still carry out their traditional domestic roles. The media bombard them with conflicting messages, targeting them with alcohol and cigarette products as symbols of liberation, while criticizing them for behaving more like men.

There is some evidence of a deterioration in women's mental health because of stress. The proportion of women (aged 16 to 64) suffering from a common mental disorder—typically depression or anxiety—increased from 19.1 per cent in 1993 to 21.5 per cent in 2007, while the men's rate did not change significantly (NHS Information Centre 2009).

On this topic, see also Media watch 5 at the end of this chapter.

Sources: Annandale, E. (2008); NHS Information Centre (2009).

---

customers (see our discussion of customer service work in Chapter 17, pp. 659–61).

As male employment has declined and women have gone out to work, men have come under pressure to do domestic and childcare work. If in a particular household men are unemployed and women are earning money, there are good reasons for maintaining a domestic division of labour but reversing the sex roles. There is some evidence of this taking place, as we show in Chapter 12, p. 459. There is also considerable evidence of the persistence of traditional roles, but it is significant that these roles have lost some of their previous legitimacy. Men are increasingly expected to do housework and care for children.

Masculinity itself has been assailed. Frank Mort (1996) claimed that there had been a radical change in male identity with the emergence of the 'new man'. A new image of man that feminized male identity was projected in the media during the 1980s. This presented men as caring and cooperative, abandoning masculine aggressiveness and competitiveness. The 'new man' was more sensitive and more emotional, more concerned with appearance, more interested in cosmetics and style. The male body became sexualized in much the same way as the female body had long been.

While Mort saw this as a broad change in culture, Tim Edwards (1997) argued that it is a more limited phenomenon associated with marketing and advertising. It is a result not so much of some male identity crisis caused by changing employment patterns and feminism as of the expanding market for male fashion. This was generated by the individualist consumerism of the 1980s and the high purchasing power of young men in growing occupations, such as financial services, advertising, and marketing. Demographic changes meant that there were more single men and childless couples, with money to spend on fashion products. The 'new man' was largely restricted to these particular social groups. Furthermore, Edwards argues that many traditional images of masculinity can still be found in the men's magazines that appealed to these groups.

Indeed, evidence can be found of the reassertion of traditional masculinities. Connell (1995) showed this occurring within 'masculinity therapy'. This grew up in the 1960s in response to the feminist challenge to traditional gender-roles and was initially concerned with 'curing' men of the 'disease' of masculinity. In the 1980s, however, masculinity therapy completely changed its character and became concerned with the restoration of a traditional masculinity. Men went off to 'bush camps', where they engaged in drumming, hunting, and warrior activities in search of the 'deep masculine' within them.

Masculinity was asserted in other ways, such as the emergence, particularly in the United States, of movements celebrating the gun and defending the right to carry it. Another example was 'gay-bashing', for the coming-out of gays threatened the heterosexual component of traditional masculine identity. Yet another was the reassertion of patriarchal authority by religious movements.

Connell also argued that the questioning of male identity should not lead us to suppose that men are losing their grip, for they have continued to dominate industry, the military, politics, and the media. As he put it, the defence

The 'new man': myth or reality?

© Alice Chadwick

of hegemonic masculinity has 'formidable resources' and has been 'impressively successful' (Connell 1995: 216).

In a study of a secondary school, Jeffrey Smith (2007) found that hegemonic masculinity continued to influence many working-class boys' attitudes. Doing schoolwork was considered feminine, while sporting and sexual prowess were highly valued. Boys who engaged in what were seen as 'feminine' activities were stigmatized as 'gay'. Powerful peer group mechanisms maintained these attitudes, but Smith also found that some teachers acted as 'cultural accomplices', reinforcing and naturalizing these attitudes in order to engage with the boys and 'win them over'. This was not, however, just a strategy adopted by some teachers; it was inherent in the school's authoritarian disciplinary regime and a product of managerial pressures to improve performance. Hegemonic masculinity was embedded in the institution.

We may conclude that in some ways the two sexes have converged, for the work and home lives of men and women have become more similar. Unisex in fashion and the idea of the 'new man' are symptomatic of this. The 'two-sex' model has not, however, disappeared, and the belief that

there are fundamental biological differences between the two sexes seems as strong as ever, while contrasting notions of femininity and masculinity continue to keep the sexes apart. Natasha Walter claims that sexism has actually increased (see Box 5.13 on p. 174). Indeed, the challenge to men has arguably stimulated them to reassert a hegemonic masculinity, while many women still identify with, in Connell's words (see p. 159), a 'subordinated femininity'.

Sexualities?

In this section we consider the impact of changes in relationships between the sexes on sexuality. If the lives of men and women have become more similar, does this mean that the same thing has happened to their sexual behaviour? Have the boundaries between different sexualities weakened?

Sexual revolution

In the nineteenth century male and female sexuality had been sharply differentiated (see p. 166). The sexual behaviour of women in particular was dominated by marriage and child-bearing. Premarital sex had been increasing during the twentieth century, but when it resulted in pregnancy was rapidly followed by marriage (or illegal abortion). Rates of illegitimacy fell from the 1870s until the 1940s (L. Hall 1991; see also T. Harrison 1949).

In the 1960s, however, what has often been called the 'sexual revolution' began to separate sexuality from marriage. The availability of the contraceptive pill played a major part in this, though it also reflected important changes in attitudes and the growth of a women's liberation movement. In the UK, the Abortion Act of 1967 made it much easier to deal legally with unwanted pregnancies. For many women, sex was now no longer something that happened only in marriage in order to produce children but an activity in its own right. Sexual satisfaction became a need and an expectation.

This was, arguably, particularly liberating for women, who had been more constrained than men by the sex-within-marriage norm that had earlier prevailed. The 'double standard' had turned a blind eye to the sexual escapades of men but not those of women. Furthermore, survey evidence from the 1940s suggests that women were more likely than men to be dissatisfied with marital sex (Charles 2002).

Women's sexual needs were now recognized and commercialized. Women were no longer expected to be sexually inactive. In the age of *Cosmopolitan*, their magazines no longer just provided information about cooking, homecare, and family problems but also gave sexual information and advice. Pornography specifically for women became more available, while male strip shows for women appeared long before *The Full Monty*.

But was this a liberation? Some have argued that it was the very reverse of this. Sexual liberation made women more available to men and less able to resist their demands. Women also became more vulnerable to male exploitation in the sex industry with the growth of pornography, which exploits women to meet, mainly, the sexual needs of men. Some feminists here converged with 'new right' moralists in their condemnation of the sexual revolution. A similar debate has taken place over the interpretation of 'raunch' culture, with some feminist writers arguing that this is not sexual liberation so much as a commercialized pandering to male desires.

The double standard of sexual inequality has not disappeared. Social surveys have reported that men continue to have more partners than women. If men sleep around, they are still considered to be demonstrating their virility, but, if women do the same, they are still called 'slags'. Men still discard women when they become older and seek younger female partners, but women who seek younger male partners meet with social disapproval (Pilcher 1999).

National survey material suggests that the sexual behaviour of British women has been converging with that of men, though major differences persist (see Figure 5.4). Thus, according to the 2000 survey, women in Britain as a whole reported nearly twice as many 'lifetime' heterosexual partners as those interviewed in 1990 but still only about half the number of partners reported by the men. Similarly, a substantially higher proportion of women were having two or more relationships at the same time, but this was still more common among men. In at least one respect, however, women had caught up with men. In the 2000 survey the same proportions of men and women reported having same-sex partnerships during the past five years. There is also evidence in the 2000 survey for a convergence of the ages at which boys and girls have their first sexual intercourse (Wellings *et al.* 2001).

This is shown by a comparison of older and younger age groups. There was a big difference in the proportions of men and women aged 40–44 who had had their first sexual intercourse before the age of 16 (27 per cent of males and 17 per cent of females). But for those aged 20–24, women were actually more likely than men to have had their first intercourse before 16 (26 per cent of males and 28 per cent of females). In the youngest age group, those aged 16–19, boys were ahead but not by much (30 per cent of males and 26 per cent of females). Not too much should be made of small variations, but the contrast between those over 40 and those under 25 is clear. One should, however, be wary of over-generalizing, for a later article has shown considerable variation by ethnicity in the proportions of both men and women having their first intercourse before age 16 (Fenton *et al.* 2005).

Elizabeth Bernstein (2007) argues that much of the literature on sexuality treats it as something natural that is either constrained or liberated. The changes we have examined above should not, in her view, be seen simply as a gradual liberation of women from previous constraints. It is not that a suppressed sexuality has come to the surface, but rather that a detached 'recreational sexuality' has emerged from broader social changes, especially changes in the economy and the family.

In a 'post-industrial' service economy, multiple specialized services are available on the market. Many people live alone, and unstable families are 'recombinant' and composed of 'isolable' individuals. Increasingly, sexual needs are not met within stable relationships but individually serviced from the marketplace, in the same way as other needs. Sexuality has accordingly changed its character, now taking the form of 'bounded authenticity'. People seek not only physical sensation but also authentic but limited relationships. Sex workers provide their clients not just with physical excitement and release but a genuine, if short-lived, intimacy, as in the example of sex workers advertising themselves as 'girlfriends for hire'.

Figure 5.4 Changes in sexual behaviour, Britain, 1990–2000[a]

	Men		Women	
	1990	2000	1990	2000
Average number of heterosexual partners during lifetime	8.6	12.7	3.7	6.5
Average number of heterosexual partners during previous five years	3.0	3.8	1.7	2.4
Ever had homosexual partners	3.6%	5.4%	1.8%	4.9%
Percentage with homosexual partners during previous five years	1.5%	2.6%	0.8%	2.6%
Percentage with concurrent partners during previous year[b]	11.4%	14.6%	5.4%	9.0%

[a]The data come from randomly selected respondents at stratified samples of addresses in Britain. The same questions were used in 1990 and 2000.
[b]Partnerships are defined as concurrent if the first sexual act with the more recent partner preceded the last act with the previous partner.

Source: A. Johnson *et al.* (2001).

Women's sexual needs recognized and commercialized.
© Alice Chadwick

> **➲ Connections**
> Sex work is also discussed in Chapter 13, p. 495, and
> Chapter 17, pp. 661–2.

Bernstein emphasizes, however, that this new sexuality coexists with sexualities from earlier periods. The early modern 'procreative' sexuality focused on reproduction, and the modern 'companionate' sexuality embedded in relationships, exist alongside 'recreational' sexuality, not only within society but within individual people. Thus, if we are to properly understand contemporary sexualities we must know not only about the latest form that sexuality has taken but also the still living forms inherited from earlier times.

Heterosexuality and homosexuality

Nickie Charles argues that, although women behave sexually more like men, this convergence has not diminished the force of compulsory heterosexuality or, therefore, the male domination associated with it.

> Although attitudes towards sexual behaviour may have become more liberal, there is evidence that the linkage of sex with male-dominated heterosexuality is as strong at the beginning of the 21st century as it was in the immediate post-war years and that changes in sexual behaviour have resulted in women being able to behave more like men but in male-dominated ways. Thus they can engage in sexual activity and demand more and better orgasms, but the sexuality they engage in is overwhelmingly on men's terms.

Charles 2002: 149

The survey results shown in Figure 5.4 indicate that heterosexuality is still overwhelmingly dominant. Two qualifications must be made to this, however. First, these figures suggest that during the 1990s same-sex relationships increased considerably, even though from a low base. Secondly, the figures produced by the same survey for Greater London show that a much higher percentage of people living there have at some time had same-sex partnerships than in the rest of Britain. According to the 2000 survey, one in ten Greater London men and one in fifteen Greater London women had had same-sex partnerships at some time in their lives.

While those who had experienced same-sex *relationships* were still only a small minority in 2000, evidence from the British Social Attitudes survey suggests that *attitudes* towards gay sex have been transformed since the early 1980s. In the 1980s around two-thirds of respondents thought that sex between same-sex adults was 'always or mostly wrong', but by 2006 only a third did so. In the 1980s under a fifth considered that it was 'rarely or never wrong', but by 2006 around half did. Most respondents agreed that same-sex couples could be as committed to each other as heterosexual couples, though only a third or so thought they could be as good parents (Duncan and Phillips 2008).

The most significant change in homosexuality is the emergence of strong and open 'gay' identities since the 1960s. The very term 'gay' was created to value positively a same-sex subculture and to distance same-sex relationships from the negative associations carried by the term 'homosexuality'. An important feature of this new culture has been its rejection of the notion that same-sex activity violates male and female identities. As Weeks (1985: 191) has put it: '*Sexual* identity, at least in the lesbian or gay subcultures of the west, has broken free from *gender* identity. You can now be gay and a 'real man', lesbian and a true (or even better) woman' (emphasis in original).

It is important, however, to emphasize again that only some of those who engage in same-sex activity participate in or identify with these subcultures, while some of those who participate in them are not sexually active. This point has been made particularly with reference to lesbianism, where solidarity between members of a sisterhood rather than a common sexuality has been considered by some to be the true basis of a lesbian subculture (Rich 1980).

The emergence of openly gay subcultures has been interconnected with the decriminalization of homosexuality and the acceptance of gay lifestyles. Homosexuality was substantially, if not completely, decriminalized in Britain by the 1967 Sexual Offences Act. Toleration of gay lifestyles has increased, notably with the emergence of gay villages in some cities (see Chapter 13, pp. 498–9). The campaigning organization Stonewall was founded in 1989 by gays who had 'come out'. Eventually, under the 1997 Labour government, the age of consent for homosexuality was reduced to 16, the same as for heterosexuality, and the bans on homosexuals serving in the armed forces and gay couples adopting were lifted. Significantly, gay couples have increasingly laid claim to the same legal status as married couples, and in December 2005 they were allowed to register civil partnerships (see Chapter 12, pp. 451–2).

Liberalization has not been unopposed, for the new permissiveness of the 1960s provoked a 'new moralism'. The rise of the New Right, in combination with the spread of AIDS, seen by some as clear proof of the dangers of sexual liberation, led to a growing political conflict between liberationists and moralists during the 1980s. This is reflected in some evidence of increasing intolerance during the 1980s in the British Social Attitudes survey, referred to above. The Local Government Act of 1988, later repealed by Labour, introduced a clause that in effect prevented discussion of homosexuality in schools, and triggered the founding of Stonewall. This conflict has intensified with the rise of fundamentalist groups claiming that religious texts prohibit homosexuality.

Homophobia is still common in schools. Jeffrey Smith (2007) found a 'compulsory heterosexism' amongst many of the working-class boys he studied and a frequent use of the word 'gay' to ridicule boys behaving in ways considered unmasculine. This was reinforced by the cultural complicity of some teachers. According to a YouGov survey commissioned by Stonewall (2009), homophobic bullying is widespread in schools.

- Sixty-five per cent of lesbian, gay, and bisexual pupils have experienced bullying, this figure rising to 75 per cent in faith schools.

- Abusive homophobic language is commonplace, with 97 per cent of pupils hearing insulting remarks such as 'poof', 'dyke', and 'queer'.

- Teachers say the problem is widespread, with 90 per cent saying that young people, regardless of their sexual orientation, experience homophobic bullying.

- Teachers are 'under-equipped' to deal with this problem, since 90 per cent have not received training on how to prevent or respond to homophobic bullying.

The assertion of gay cultures has been something of a two-edged sword. It has given gays a voice, an identity, a positive image, and a collective organization that could provide mutual support and campaign on their behalf to demand an end to discrimination against them. It can also, as Weeks (1985) has pointed out, lead to 'ghettoization', providing a target for gay-bashing and stimulating a backlash against homosexuality. Furthermore, the claim that gays are naturally different maintains the nineteenth-century distinction between the heterosexuality of the majority and the homosexuality of a minority. Nineteenth-century categories are in this way not so much challenged

Are openly gay couples now tolerated?
© Alice Chadwick

or subverted as perpetuated. A hegemonic masculinity centred on heterosexuality may be defied, but the consequence may be that it is also reinforced.

Bisexuality and queerness

As we suggested earlier (see p. 162), it is bisexuality and, above all, the queer movement that have really challenged the categories of the nineteenth century and the cultures and identities derived from them.

The very term 'bisexuality' preserves the notion of two different sexes, but it also transgresses sexual boundaries and provokes not only heterosexual but homosexual condemnation. Some defenders of heterosexuality have considered bisexuality more depraved than homosexuality, while gays and lesbians have attacked it as compromising gay identities and undermining the gay movement. Bisexuals have counterattacked by arguing that everyone is naturally bisexual. Although homosexuality and heterosexuality might have seemed the most obvious opponents in battles over sexual identity, they could coexist as separate worlds, while bisexuality crossed boundaries and threatened both (Weeks 1985).

A bisexual subculture exists, but, given its lack of clear boundaries, it has been less militant and less organized than gay and lesbian groups. There are, nonetheless, many local bisexual groups, national and international bisexual organizations, and websites that enable bisexuals to meet, maintain contact, support each other, exchange information, and promote their cause. The World Wide Web is a valuable resource for a loose network of this kind, which is not centred in defined communities with a bounded sexual identity.

The queer movement is broader still and includes a wide range of 'deviant' sexual groups. It originated with the emergence of a group of activists calling themselves the Queer Nation in a number of cities in the United States during the 1980s. 'Queer' was originally a term of abuse directed at 'abnormal' homosexuals, but it became a rallying cry for radical lesbians and gays who proclaimed their queerness and revelled in it. As Steven Epstein (1994: 195) has put it: 'the invocation of the "Q-word" is an act of linguistic reclamation, in which a pejorative term is appropriated by the stigmatized group so as to negate the term's power to wound'. The movement was intellectually highly self-conscious and was associated with the development of 'queer theory', which we discussed on p. 162.

The queer movement did not seek toleration or acceptance by heterosexuals or their recognition of the minority rights of gays. It directly challenged the whole idea that heterosexuality was normal and natural. It was associated with a confrontational politics, and its members engaged in many provocative actions, such as same-sex 'kiss-ins' in 'straight' bars.

It also rejected the internal divisions of sexual deviance. In its new meaning, the term 'queer' was stretched to include not only gays and lesbians but also bisexuals and all those, such as transvestites and transsexuals, who crossed sex and gender boundaries and in any way subverted heterosexual normality. In its rejection of categories and identities, it meshed with contemporary tendencies to see sexual behaviour as purely a matter of lifestyle choice, like any other aspect of life. The Internet's anonymity has made possible the ultimate separation of body and lifestyle (see Box 5.17).

In spite of this challenge, the heterosexuality/homosexuality discourse has remained dominant in most people's ways of thinking and talking. As we argued earlier in our discussion of queer theory, the capacity of the dominant ideology and the socialization process to perpetuate the 'h' categories should not be underestimated. Furthermore, as we noted above, by proclaiming their difference, 'orthodox' gay cultures and communities have themselves reinforced the 'h' discourse.

New technology Identity play on the Internet   5.17

The Internet has provided new opportunities for experimentation with sexual identities. Participants in chat rooms and bulletin boards cannot see each other and do not have to disclose their real names or their location. They can assume identities that social constraints would normally prevent them adopting. They can allow their imaginations to run riot in experimental acts of cybersex. Webcams do, of course, mean that they can see each other if they wish to, but the freedom of anonymous interaction has become more available than ever before. As Gauntlett (2000*b*: 15) has put it:

> Because the internet breaks the connection between outward expressions of identity and the physical body which (in the real world) makes those expressions, it can be seen as a space where queer theory's approach to identity can really come to life.

For a more detailed discussion of Internet identities, see Chapter 4, pp. 119–20.

Stop and reflect

In this section we have been considering whether the identities separated in the nineteenth century have in recent times converged.

We first looked at male and female spheres.

- There is some evidence of the decline of separate spheres in employment, but occupations are still in many ways gendered.
- Consider how important feminism has been in breaking down this separation. What other social changes have been involved?

We then discussed whether the differences between the sexes had diminished.

- List ways in which men and women have become more similar.
- List ways in which their attitudes, behaviours, and identities still appear to be distinctive.
- List ways in which male and female bodies are becoming more alike or more different.

In the final section we returned to sexualities. We considered whether sexualities have been losing their distinctiveness.

- Male and female sexual behaviour has converged, though significant differences remain and there is still a 'double standard'.
- Has sexuality become simply a matter of lifestyle choice?

Key concepts

- bisexuality 161
- emphasized femininity 159
- feminism 156
- gender 151
- gender order 159
- gender-role 154

- hegemonic masculinity 159
- heterosexuality 161
- homosexuality 161
- intersex 152
- lesbianism 168
- patriarchy 156

- performativity 152
- queer theory 162
- sex 151
- sex-role 154
- sexuality 151

Workshop 5

Study 5 Gender and policing

In *Gender and Policing: Sex, Power and Police Culture*, Louise Westmarland (2001) reports on an ethnographic study of police work. This was a three-year study of two police forces, one in a rural, one in an urban area. The main method used was observation of the police on patrol, though Westmarland tried to make herself an 'informed stranger' by carrying out interviews and focus-group discussions before making her observations.

The police force has become an important area of research in the study of gender, because it is a traditionally male area of work that has increasingly recruited women and has been forced by legislation to integrate them by abolishing their segregation in a separate force. By the year 2000 women comprised 17 per cent of police officers in England and Wales. Although women are disproportionately in the lower ranks, they were promoted at a higher rate in the 1990s, and by 2000 there were twelve women assistant chief constables (8 per cent of the total) and three women chief constables (6 per cent). It is, nonetheless, one of the few remaining occupations where the masculine virtues of toughness and physical strength are still valued, where 'men can still act as men'.

Does the recruitment and promotion of women mean that police work is no longer gendered? It has been claimed that women are segregated in low-status work dealing with women and children. Segregation results from assumptions made about 'embodied expertise'. Women are considered better at caring for children, because of childbirth, and men better at tasks that may involve fighting, because of their physical strength. Westmarland did find evidence for this kind of segregation. In one child and family protection unit, there were fourteen women officers and only three men, while in the other there were seventeen women and fifteen men. The senior positions in both units were filled by men.

She cautions us against the assumption that all the women involved were forced into this work by men. In focus-group discussions many women said that they preferred it, had chosen it, and did not consider it of low status. Some simply regarded it as a step on the way to a higher rank or other duties, which they could move on to when opportunities arose. It was also not always assumed that women were best at dealing with children. After one male officer stated in a focus group that 'a woman is naturally less intimidating to a child', another disagreed and declared that 'I could speak to a child a hell of a lot better than a policewoman who hasn't had children. I've got three children of my own' (Westmarland 2001: 74).

The allocation of work was, anyway, different out on patrol, and this is where Westmarland's observational approach has enabled her to correct misconceptions of the *actual* work done by women officers. When women officers were on patrol, they were not deployed according to the character of the incident. Bureaucratic procedures meant that they were called to deal with incidents according to priorities and dispatch systems, not according to whether they involved women or children.

Where this did not apply was in incidents involving child sexual abuse. This is partly explained by the legal requirement that women officers must be present. There was also a belief among both men and women that women were better at handling the emotional side of these cases. This reflects the much wider and well-established practice of women being responsible for 'emotional labour' (see our discussion on this in Chapter 4, pp. 141–3).

When out on patrol, women officers achieved the same percentage of arrests as men. Indeed, this study actually found the women making more arrests for crimes, such as aggravated house burglary and car crime, that involved physical force. Westmarland (2001: 185) declares that 'the traditional image of the high adrenalin, "macho cop" arrest being made only by men now seems unsupportable'.

There was, nonetheless, still a strong culture of masculinity in the police force. Women officers might make as many arrests as men, but the men did not consider it was right to expose them to violence in this way. There was a 'van culture' of sexual bragging and sexist comments about passing women. An exaggerated masculinity was particularly manifest in some departments, notably those concerned with 'cars, guns, and horses'—that is, the elite traffic department with its fast cars, the firearms departments, and the mounted branch. These were a refuge for men who did not like working with women or carrying out 'female' tasks that might involve caring.

This study shows that police work is still highly gendered. Its ethnographic methods have, however, demonstrated the complexity and limits of the gendering process. It shows that women police officers are not just pushed around by men but are actively involved in choosing work and pursuing their careers. It also shows that out on patrol women can act as men, that, to quote Westmarland (2001: 188), there is an 'equality of opportunity on the streets'.

This case study illustrates many of the concepts and processes examined in this chapter. Try answering the following questions:

❓ What evidence does this study provide of the gendering of occupations?

❓ Does it suggest that this gendering is diminishing?

❓ Does this study show that the police force is a patriarchal organization?

❓ What evidence can you find here of hegemonic masculinity?

Compare this ethnographic account with the portrayal of the police in a television police drama (record one so that you can analyse it more carefully).

❓ What points of similarity and points of difference can you identify?

❓ How do you think the requirements of a drama affect the representation of men and women in the police force?

---

power-hungry
and/or moral
(Jackson and

Sources: ESPAD
Independent, 15
The Oxford Engli
Tinkler (2007).

This mate
behaviour, cl
perceptions
tions:

Patriarchy

How useful i
stand and e
'Patriarchy' a
the meaning
been used.

● What has
● What prob
● Has Robe
    of gender

Identities

How differe
the chapter

● What wer
    ties estab

A clear and
history of g
Holmes, M.

A wide-ran
and politic
institution
Richardson,
    and Wom

The followi
women in l

of 'germ matter'—now termed 'genes'—that determined their biological characteristics. He showed that offspring inherited genes from each parent and that their own biological characteristics depended on the particular ways in which this genetic material was combined at the moment of conception. In particular, he showed that offspring inherited genetic characteristics and possibilities that may not be apparent in their own features but may be passed on to their offspring and find their expression in them.

The child of brown-eyed and blue-eyed parents, for example, will have brown eyes. However, the child will also inherit the gene for blue eyes, though this remains inactive. If, however, he or she reproduces with a brown-eyed person who also had a blue-eyed parent, then their children may be born with blue eyes. Mendel and later genetic researchers have shown how such patterns of inheritance can be explained and predicted for many observable biological traits.

The idea that racial traits are fixed and inherited led many people to consider policies of selective breeding. If one race is culturally superior to another, it was held, then governments should prevent any breeding between the two races, which could result only in a decline in the cultural standard of the superior race. Whites, for example, should not marry or have children with blacks if they want to maintain the intelligence and cultural superiority of their race. The problems with this view are discussed in Box 6.1. Advocacy of the complete biological segregation of the races was given its strongest expression in the racial thought of the Nazis in Germany during the 1930s and 1940s. Nazi thought contrasted the superior characteristics of the white 'Aryan' race with the 'inferior' characteristics of the Jews, and, under the leadership of Adolf Hitler, Nazis attempted to bring about the complete physical elimination of the Jews from Europe (see Box 6.2).

In reaction to the political racism of the Second World War, the United Nations sponsored a scientific dialogue on race between biologists and social scientists. This resulted in a joint statement—called the Moscow Declaration—in 1964. This statement concluded that there was no scientific basis for conventionally identified race categories, and it effectively discouraged scientists from using the term to describe human biological variations. Those variations in biological traits that do exist within and between human populations can be explained by the inheritance of genes, but they do not constitute discrete 'racial' categories. All human populations can interbreed without problem, and so there is a single human species with no obvious way of delineating any 'subspecies' or races. 'Race', the Moscow Declaration concluded, is simply an outdated term, a hangover from unscientific ways of thinking. This view has been reinforced by later scientific work.

 ## Briefing: who is black and who is white?   6.1

It is difficult to relate skin colour directly to genetic inheritance. Dennis Barber, a white bank manager from Staffordshire, discovered that he is the direct descendant of a black African slave who was brought to England in the eighteenth century. Despite his white appearance, Dennis carries genes that could result in his own descendants being born with dark features. It has been estimated that the number of slaves and other black people that lived in Britain in the eighteenth century means that one in five white British people has a direct black ancestor.

Recent research has suggested that 30 per cent of 'white' Americans have some black parentage in their family history, and roughly 18 per cent of 'black' Americans have white ancestry. About 10 per cent of African Americans are 50 per cent white by ancestry.

Source: Sunday Telegraph (1999).

Is it all in the genes?

Genetic accounts of human differentiation have shown clearly that variations and differences in genetic structure from one individual to another are not obviously expressed in simple differences in, say, skin colour. Skin colour is not determined by any major genetic difference, but by a combination of relatively minor ones. These genetic differences are, in any case, the results of differences in climate and other environmental factors operating over many generations. Differences in skin colour are also not directly associated with any of the vastly more extensive genetic differences that produce other physical differences.

One such genetic trait is the blood group. But even this does not support the idea of racial difference. People can be classified as type A, B, AB, or O and according to the rhesus factor, and the pattern of distribution of blood types has been shown to be quite distinct from one human population to another. Attempts to produce discrete racial categories based on externally observable characteristics have proved unsuccessful, as the overlap between populations is too great. Although advances in genetics have led scientists to recognize the important causal effect that genes can have on human behaviour, biology has also shown that separate human populations do not have the degree of genetic uniformity required for a scientific description of them as races. The observable characteristics linked to the use of the term 'race' (skin colour, hair type, facial form, and so on) are the outcome of a whole cluster of genetic

Briefing: Adolf Hitler 6.2

Adolf Hitler (1889–1945) was born in Austria. He dropped out of school, intending to follow an artistic career, but he failed to gain entry to the Vienna Academy. He dodged military service and moved to Germany, where he volunteered for army service during the First World War. After the war he spied on political parties as a paid informer of the authorities, but he gradually became drawn into open political action. He joined a small party, transforming it into the National Socialist German Workers' Party and forming a paramilitary 'brown-shirt' movement.

The Nazis—as they became known—took an extreme right-wing and anti-Jewish position. Hitler was imprisoned after an attempt to overthrow the Bavarian government in 1923. After his release, he cultivated the support of big business and the established political parties, and became German Chancellor (prime minister) in 1933. He immediately set up a framework of terror and abandoned constitutional restraints. Hitler built up the German army, invaded Austria and Czechoslovakia, and, following his invasion of Poland, he found himself embroiled in war against Britain and France in 1939.

One of the principal elements in Hitler's outlook was his anti-Semitism—anti-Jewish sentiment—which he built into an ideology that justified the exclusion of Jews from most forms of employment, the confiscation of their property, and their wholesale persecution. His ideas were set out in the book that he wrote while in prison, *Mein Kampf* (1925), and they were implemented in the 'final solution'. This was a policy to remove Jews and other 'degenerates' (such as gypsies and homosexuals) from German territory to concentration and extermination camps such as Belsen, Dachau, and Auschwitz. More than six million people were murdered by the Nazis in the gas chambers at these camps.

determinant of male sex characteristics. As it appears only in males, it can be used to trace genetic inheritance through the male line. Biologists have found that variations in the genetic patterns on the Y chromosome are related to the degree of biological separation: the longer that two populations have been separate and distinct from each other, the more different are the Y chromosomes carried by their men. This research showed the common African origin of all human populations, but it brought out some striking patterns of similarity and difference. The genetic similarities between Chinese and native Australians, for example, are greater than those between either group and Europeans. The Europeans, however, have close genetic similarities with South Asians. The sharpest genetic differences distinguish African populations from *all* other human populations, although the variation within each group is vast.

Individual differences in detailed genetic characteristics (so-called within-group differences) are much greater than population differences (between-group differences) and they vastly outweigh any differences among conventionally defined skin-colour categories. Two randomly chosen English men, for example, may differ far more genetically from one another than do a typical English and Nigerian man. Similarly, the 'Black' and the 'White' populations in the United States are both internally quite diverse in their genes. Compared with other animal species, human beings are, overall, extremely homogeneous in genetic terms. There are no identifiable sub-species. There is no scientific basis for the identification of biological races in human populations.

The social construction of race

If human populations are not to be called 'races', is there any role for the word in sociological analysis? This is a very contentious question, as the word carries strong moral and political connotations. For many sociologists, as we will show, there is, indeed, a useful role for a properly theorized concept of race. According to this point of view, a human grouping is a 'race' not because of their biological characteristics but because they are socially constructed as a race. If they and others construct their personal and cultural characteristics in terms of a presumed biological or genetic descent, then they can be called a race. In using the word 'race' to describe such a group, the sociologist is simply recognizing the ways in which people themselves use the term to describe one another. The sociologist is not describing the group as a biological race—we have shown that such an idea cannot be sustained—but is recognizing an important element in social consciousness. When people identify themselves as a race, or are identified in this way by others, their actions are shaped by the specifically racial discourse built up since the eighteenth century, and sociological analysis has to be sensitive to this and to its consequences.

and other biological factors operating under particular environmental conditions. While certain natural clusterings of genetic differences can be found in different human populations, these are the results of normal reproduction within those populations as they have developed over time. These patterns of biological difference change as the boundaries of the populations change. They do not correspond to any lines of racial division.

Genes are stored in chromosomes, twenty-three pairs of them in each cell. One chromosome—the so-called Y chromosome—is specific to human beings and is the

Biological race cannot be regarded as a serious scientific concept. Nevertheless, it remains an important term in political debate. It is a central term in those political beliefs that draw on now discredited biological ideas to define social differences and so to justify the oppression and exclusion of those from particular social groups, who are deemed to be naturally inferior. Much prejudice and discrimination against cultural minorities continues to be justified in racial terms.

The use of the term 'race', then, rests on beliefs in the significance of supposed biological differences that are seen as determining social differences. **Race** is a purely social construct, based on the observed physical and cultural characteristics of individuals and on discredited racial theories (Banton 1987). To understand how this is possible, it is necessary to examine the relationship between race and ethnicity.

Ethnic identities and racialization

Ethnicity is a general category for describing collective identities. Ethnic groups are defined by their sense of sharing a distinct culture that can be traced back to the historical or territorial origins of the group. Ethnic groups build an 'imagined community' (B. Anderson 1991), an image of themselves as a collectivity. The solidarity and group consciousness of an ethnic group are organized around this idea of origin and cultural history (A. Smith 1986). Hall (1989) has stressed that ethnicity can also be rooted in a history of common experiences such as those of the exclusion and discrimination experienced by minority groups at the hands of a majority.

Ethnicity, then, involves defining groups by a shared history or culture, a common geographical origin, a common language or religion, or a common set of experiences. Ethnic identifiers based on common history, language, or religion include Asian, Black, Muslim, Scottish, Jewish, Basque, Kurd, Slav, and British. Ethnicity is often expressed in a common language, though merely having a common language does not necessarily confer ethnicity. Hebrew and Arabic are the basis of distinct ethnic identities, while the English language is now a global language spoken by people of many ethnicities, and those who identify themselves as 'Asian' may speak Punjabi, Gujarati, Urdu, Bengali, or Pashto. The same is true of religion: Judaism is strongly associated with Jewish ethnicity, Christianity is a religious system common to those of many ethnicities, and Asians may be Hindu, Sikh, Jain, Buddhist, or Muslim. Nationalism, such as that of the Scots and the Palestinians, is a form of ethnic identity based on attachment to a particular territory and to claims for a political sovereign state to promote and defend national interests (A. Smith 1991). The colonial and post-colonial experience, for example, has shaped and transformed ethnic and racial identities in both the former imperial powers and their ex-colonies. The racial exclusion that has shaped the experience of many migrant groups in Britain is the basis of their identification of themselves as 'Black' British, though this is a precarious sense of identity, and the cultural differences that distinguish the various minorities lead them to fragment into their constituent ethnicities: into Asian and African-Caribbean ethnicities, for example. Most recently in Britain, the sharing of an Islamic heritage and the experience of oppression and exclusion has led many otherwise diverse groups to identify themselves as 'Muslims'. Many ethnic groups have constructed an identity and sense of community for themselves, despite the fact that they have been widely dispersed across the world. Transnational Jewish and Chinese identities, for example, have been built in the face of long histories of **diaspora**—of global dispersion from their original homelands.

While having a specifically cultural identity, ethnic groups are not purely cultural phenomena. In any concrete situation, these cultural representations are entwined with class and political divisions that determine the power and resources available to the ethnic groups (Anthias 1992: 28–9). This means that ethnic groups can be classified in objective terms and not simply on the basis of their more transient and variable subjective identities.

Ethnic origin and ethnic identity

Ethnic classification involves a distinction between *ethnic origin* and *ethnic identity*. While subjective identification with a particular ethnic category is an important element in ethnicity, ethnicity cannot be reduced to this sense of identity. Ethnic origins can be traced in commonalities of religion, language, history, and so on, even if those who originate in these groups do not make their origins a central element in their social identity (Berthoud 1998; Platt 2005b). Ethnic group membership is both normative and relational. Groups with common origins must have some collective awareness of their origins and some shared ideas and norms if they are to count as an ethnic group; however, this does not require a complete consensus of individual members over any particular label of identity. Similarly, an ethnic group is not simply a collection of self-identifying members. It rests on the recognition and acceptance by other members of the group and involvement in social relations and everyday interactions. Identities contribute to a common ethnic origin when they are sustained and reproduced over many generations within a particular population, but origin and identity may differ in the short run.

Objective categories of ethnic-group membership are what government censuses have tried to measure when asking questions about ethnic origin, and sociological surveys have found that people themselves recognize and use similar categories to those of the census (Modood *et al.* 1997). In Britain, such categories as Pakistani, Indian, Bangladeshi, and African Caribbean are the principal ethnic groups classified by ethnic origin. In the United States, the census recognizes many distinct 'European' ethnicities (German, Italian, Irish, Polish, Dutch, and so on), various 'native American' and 'Hispanic' (Mexican, Puerto Rican, Cuban), 'African', and numerous 'Asian' (Chinese, Japanese, Filipino, Korean, and so on) categories. In both societies, the specific labels that individuals adopt to identify themselves ethnically are diverse and vary over time, and the crucial issue for sociological investigation is to examine the changing relationship between ethnic origin and ethnic identity.

While it is notoriously difficult to formulate survey questions that will accurately uncover people's felt sense of ethnic identity, some indications of this ethnic diversity can be found in the recent censuses and some surveys. Since 1991, people have been asked an open question about how they would define their own ethnicity, with the results shown in Figure 6.1.

Just over three million people in England and Wales (7.2 per cent of the population) identified themselves as members of a non-white ethnic group. Almost a half of these people claimed a broadly Asian identity, identifying themselves as Indian, Pakistani, or Bangladeshi, and about a third defined themselves as black.

Racialization and racial discourse

A race-relations situation exists wherever ethnic relations have been racialized. This **racialization** occurs whenever ethnic identities and group boundaries are defined in specifically racial terms—that is, in terms of colour and biological difference (Miles 1989; Anthias and Yuval-Davis 1993). Racialization often involves the imposition of racial identity on a minority by a powerful majority, but this is not always the case.

The use of the language of race divides populations from each other on the basis of assumed biological differences, supposedly reflected in their 'stock' or their collective inheritance of biological traits. As such, racial language transforms ethnic differences that are, in reality, in constant flux into absolute and fixed categorizations. It builds separate and distinct social groups out of permeable and overlapping human differences (Gilroy 1987).

> **⊃ Connections**
> Issues of nationhood and nationalism are discussed at greater length in 'Nation states, nations, and nationalism', in Chapter 16, pp. 598–600. You will find it useful to think about that discussion in the light of what we say here about ethnicity and the language of race.

Race, then, must not be seen as a scientific concept. It is a social construct used by people in their everyday discussions and encounters, and that figures in political debates. When sociologists use the word, they use it to reflect the ways that people have racialized their relations with each other. While the term has often been used by dominant groups to reinforce their dominance over subordinate ethnic groups, it has also been taken over by subordinate groups themselves as the basis of an identity that would enhance their resistance to their social exclusion and subordination. The emergence of a Black Power movement in the United States during the 1960s and its promotion of the slogan 'Black is Beautiful', for example, involved a positive assertion of collective racial identity by African-Americans.

The idea of race is popularized through **racist discourse**. The concept of discourse is discussed in Box 6.3 on p. 196. A racist discourse is a set of ideas, meanings, and representations that structures people's communication and encounters with each other and that serves to advantage some 'races' and to disadvantage others. A racist discourse has its greatest social impact when it informs significant social actions and practices and becomes embodied in social institutions. These social institutions therefore come to discriminate against certain racially defined ethnic groups. The term **racism** has been used to describe those structures and processes of disadvantage and inequality that are built around a racist discourse.

Despite this close relationship between racism and racist discourse, racism can exist even where there is no explicit use of racial concepts by those involved. The term **institutional racism** has been used to describe those situations where a racialized ethnic group is systematically

Figure 6.1 Ethnic composition of the population, England and Wales, 1991 and 2001

Ethnic identity	%	
	1991	2001
White	94.5	92.1
Black Caribbean	0.9	1.0
Black African	0.4	0.8
Black other	0.3	0.2
Indian	1.5	1.8
Pakistani	0.9	1.3
Bangladeshi	0.3	0.5
Chinese	0.3	0.4
Other	0.9	2.0

Source: Mason (2000: table 4.1); www.statistics.gov.uk/cci/nugget.asp?id=273. See also Joshi (1989: 183) and Skellington (1992).

This idea that there is a cultural conflict at the heart of American race relations was taken further in an important study by the Swedish sociologist Gunnar Myrdal (1944). Myrdal described the dominant or core social values as the 'American creed'. This is central to American nationalism and gives Americans their ideas about America's historical mission or destiny as a society. The creed is taught in schools and churches, enunciated in courts, and espoused in the mass media. It is embodied in ideas of equality, liberty, and citizenship, and it defines the principles that most Americans claim ought to apply in their dealings with each other.

Myrdal argued that American society is marked, nevertheless, by major discrepancies between the ideals of the creed and the actual practices engaged in. The gap between ideal and practice is particularly great in the case of black Americans. The exclusion faced by black Americans is rooted in the fact that, unlike other ethnic minorities, they are 'coloured' and are accorded an inferior social status. As Warner argued, they form a subordinate caste whose attitudes and outlook (including, in particular, their relative lack of self-respect and self-confidence) are the result of their social exclusion. African Americans have not had the opportunities to exercise in full the civil, political, and economic rights of citizenship formally accorded to them in the American creed. They are second-class citizens.

The cultural contradiction between the American creed and the assumption of caste inferiority generates disadvantages for black Americans that reinforce their purely economic disadvantages. There is a double confounding of economic disadvantage and caste exclusion:

> When we say that Negroes form a lower caste in America, we mean that they are subject to certain disabilities solely because they are 'Negroes' in the rigid American definition and not because they are poor and ill-educated. It is true, of course, that their caste position keeps them poor and ill-educated on the average, and that there is a complex circle of causation, but in any concrete instance at any given time there is little difficulty in deciding whether a certain disability or discrimination is due to a Negro's poverty or lack of education, on the one hand, or his caste position, on the other hand.

Myrdal 1944: 669

Initially developed as an account of black–white relations in the United States in the 1930s and 1940s, this theoretical approach has been very influential, and it has also been taken up in Britain. In a landmark study of the emerging pattern of race relations during the 1960s, Rose *et al.* (1969) followed Myrdal's argument and held that Britain, too, showed a clash between citizenship rights, on the one hand, and discrimination on the grounds of colour, on the other. This discrimination rests on prejudiced and stereotyped views that originate in the imperial dominance of Britain over the colonies from which migrants arrived. Black migrants to Britain from the West Indies and Africa were prevented from enjoying the full rights of citizenship. They were excluded from full membership in British society.

> **⊃ Connections**
> In Chapter 18, pp. 697–9 and 703, we review the legislation that has shaped the ability of ethnic minorities in Britain to exercise their citizenship rights. You will also find a fuller discussion of the idea of citizenship, and we relate this idea to wider patterns of inequality.

Optimistic versions of this theory, in both Britain and the United States, have seen the denial of full citizenship as something bound to be rectified in due course. Social exclusion persists because of the incomplete modernization of cultural values and social institutions. With the further development of modern social institutions, the values of the old south and the imperial state would become unsustainable, and full citizenship would eventually be achieved (Parsons 1966*a*). The failure to achieve full citizenship is a symptom of a 'cultural lag' in the process of modernization.

Theories of race and colonialism

The second strand of theory that we will consider places imperialism and the colonial encounter of black and white at the centre of attention. Writers in this tradition agree with Warner that race attributions are a matter of culture and status, but they argue that these arise only under certain very specific structural conditions. For this reason, a race-relations situation cannot be analysed in terms of culture and values alone. It has also to be seen in terms of the structure of group relations brought into being. These theorists ask why it is that some group differences are translated into the language of colour and biology—expressed as 'race' relations—while others are not. Warner wrote as a structural functionalist and emphasized the role of values, but we are here concerned with theorists who stress power and conflict.

One of the earliest writers to adopt this approach was Cox, a black American sociologist at the University of Chicago. Cox took a Marxist approach and argued that racial thinking was tied to group relations that arise with the expansion of capitalism and colonialism. Racial thinking is an ideology that promotes the transformation of labour into a commodity and justifies, where necessary,

> **⊃ Connections**
> You might like to review our discussion of conflict theories in Chapter 2, pp. 53–4, looking particularly at the discussion of John Rex's work.

the use of coercion to control this labour (Cox 1948). By creating a division between black and white workers, racial thinking can prevent the development of a strong and oppositional working-class consciousness. Race, therefore, contributes to the 'false consciousness' through which a dominant class justifies its power and control over a subordinate class.

Racial categorization, however, is not a feature of every class-divided society, and those who have followed Cox's lead have tried to specify the conditions under which white workers might be distinguished from black workers, with only the latter being subjected to racial stigmatization. Particularly important in the development of this theory has been John Rex.

Rex (1970) argues that racial ideas have become popular whenever groups come together through conquest into a 'colonial' structure of coercive power with an unequal distribution of political rights and economic resources, and where it is possible to distinguish among the dominant and subordinate groups on the basis of their physical appearance and their culture. Conquest can take many different forms. It might, for example, involve settlement of a territory by economically superior groups or militaristic domination by an imperial state. Conquest brings different cultures into contact and, when the members of these cultures are physically different from one another, the physical differences have been taken as markers of cultural differences. It is the value system of the colonizers—the dominant social group—that shapes the whole of the colonial society. The racial ideas that developed in European science in the eighteenth and nineteenth centuries were especially important contributions to colonial racism.

Conquest and colonization have a long history and occur in many societies. Rex gives particular attention to those forms of conquest involved in the building of the modern world. The growth of the modern world system (see Chapter 16, p. 607) occurred through the building of large political and economic empires by the European nations—initially Spain and Portugal, then Britain, France, the Netherlands, and Germany. Imperial expansion required the establishment of coercive forms of control over the labour of subordinate populations in the colonized territories. The most notable of these coercive forms, of course, was the slave system of the Americas, but Rex highlights also the use of indentured, legally tied labour and the physical confinement of workers to closed compounds.

The racial divisions of the colonies have an impact on the home society of the colonial power itself. The racial thinking that informs official and popular attitudes towards those who live in the colonies also influences attitudes within the metropolitan centres. This is most apparent where members of the colonized society migrate to the imperial society in search of work and economic improvement.

Rights of entry for colonial subjects vary from one imperial society to another, but the second half of the twentieth century—a period of decolonization—involved large numbers of migrant workers and long-term immigrants making the journey from the former colonies to the European metropolises. The entry of economic migrants into the labour market and the wider institutions of the imperial societies were shaped by the values and attitudes towards them that prevailed in the colonial context itself. In the early stages of migration in particular, public and official attitudes towards 'immigrants' are shaped not so much by direct knowledge—people in the metropolitan centres had little of this—but by second-hand evidence from friends, relatives, and colleagues with experience of the colonial situation. The racial ideas and stereotypes of the colony, therefore, are translated into the new metropolitan situation:

> What seems to happen is that colour is taken as an indication that a man [or woman] is only entitled to colonial status, and this means that he [or she] has to be placed outside the normal stratification system. The stratification system thus becomes extended to take account of additional social positions marked by a degree of rightlessness not to be found amongst the incorporated workers.
>
> *Rex 1970: 108*

'Coloured' immigrants, then, are confined to low-paid jobs and face limited opportunities for improvement. They do not find the opportunities for which they migrated. They are likely to experience persistent poverty and disadvantage, and they become the objects of prejudice and discrimination. Miles (1984, 1989) has argued that migration from former colonies results in the formation of 'racialized fractions' within the metropolitan classes.

Rex argues that his theoretical approach throws additional light on the racism experienced by African American migrants from the deep south of the United States to the metropolitan cities of the north. The denial of full citizenship highlighted by Warner and Myrdal is not simply the result of a cultural conflict. It also reflects a structural conflict between groups in a quasi-colonial encounter. Cultural differences rest on power differences.

Theories of racialized discourse

The third type of theory to be considered here focuses neither on values nor on group structure. It focuses on the content and character of racial discourse itself. It looks at the ways in which the idea of race is constructed in the ideologies of different groups. The approach has much in common with the Marxist-inspired arguments of Cox and Rex, but it shifts attention from the power relations to the cultural construction of identities.

Representations of race in the mass media.

© Alice Chadwick

The key arguments in the development of this point of view come from Hall (Centre for Contemporary Cultural Studies 1982) and Gilroy (1987), though echoes of it can be found in earlier writers such as Du Bois (1903) (see Box 6.4). For these writers, race is a social construct that enters into the formation of collective identities. It is a product of specific forms of discourse and of the struggles involved in establishing the dominance of one form of discourse over another. The kinds of accounts and narratives that people produce define themselves and others as specific types of people with particular characteristics, and it is through such discourse that diverse and heterogeneous individuals can be forged into a collectivity. What people have in common does not pre-exist their identity, as some kind of primitive or primordial ethnicity, but results from the very processes through which an identity is constructed. There is no objective basis to race; there are simply historically diverse racialized identities, which are constantly being formed and re-formed.

Initially stressing the racial construction of political and party identities, these writers have increasingly moved in a more cultural direction to explore the language through which race is constructed. They examine the racial constructions built in literature and the mass media in order to examine the particular representations of race and racial identity that they embody and perpetuate. Their argument is that we live in a pluralistic world of competing constructions and that any individual or group identity will be syncretic, combining elements from all the culturally

> ### ➲ Connections
>
> We consider some studies of mass media representations of racial groups in Chapter 10, pp. 69–70. Look at that discussion and then return to consider the specific arguments discussed here.

available constructions. Identities, they argue, are 'hybrid' (Bhaba 1994).

Hybridity has become an important way of understanding the construction of identities from the diverse and contradictory cultural sources available in any society. It is an idea that is particularly compatible with the post-modern theories that we discuss in Chapter 2 (pp. 61–3). Post-modern theory stresses the diversity and plurality of cultural ideas and representations and the need to be aware of this diversity. There is a constant translation, negotiation, and reconstruction of identities, and collective identities often try to combine things that are logically incompatible. A social identity must be seen as an unstable synthesis of diverse ideas that can be sustained only through rhetorical and textual devices aimed at the accounts and practices through which discourses are reproduced.

There are, then, a multiplicity of racisms and racial identities, and there are diverse connections to the cultural construction of the related ideas of 'nation' and 'country'. It is this cultural complexity that leads to the opposing of 'blackness' to 'Englishness' or of 'black' to 'Asian'.

Du Bois

William Edward Burghardt Du Bois was born in 1868 in Massachusetts. He was descended from slaves on both his father's and his mother's side. He graduated from Fisk University and then studied philosophy with William James at Harvard. He was awarded a postgraduate fellowship in history to study the African slave trade. While studying for this in Germany, he attended Weber's lectures. In 1894, Du Bois was appointed as professor at a university run by the African Methodist Church and argued for the introduction of sociology to the syllabus.

Pursuing his interests in sociology, he carried out a sociological survey of a black district in Philadelphia (Du Bois 1899). His model for this work was the London investigation undertaken by Charles Booth (see Chapter 19, p. 714), and Du Bois produced a detailed study of

occupational and family structure, drawing on interviews, personal observations, and official documents. He showed that the social problems of the black population were not a consequence of their biological characteristics but of the economic conditions under which they lived and their experience of segregation, prejudice, and exclusion. The real social problem was racism. Later work in this tradition, though developing both the theory and the methods, is that of Frazier (1932) and Wilson (1987).

Du Bois was clear that the idea of race had to be seen as a social construction that was imposed on individuals and determined their identity in the eyes of others. Those designated as being of the same race share a sense of identity as part of a community, but their shared cultural traits are a product of their shared

history—in the case of African Americans this was a history of slavery, prejudice, and disadvantage. Du Bois developed the concept of 'double consciousness': African Americans had a consciousness of themselves as both 'coloured' and 'American'.

Du Bois became heavily involved in black politics and the civil-rights struggle, publishing an important series of essays (Du Bois 1903). He was critical of Booker T. Washington's conservative position, standing firmly on the left in the black struggles. He became a Director of the National Association for the Advancement of Colored People in 1910, advocating the separate development and self-reliance of black communities. He was very influential in international debates over civil rights and in 1961 he moved to Ghana and renounced his US citizenship. He died in 1963.

 Stop and reflect

In this section we have looked at the relationship between cultural and biological factors in the formation of racial and ethnic identities. Our discussion of race and ethnicity showed that:

- There is no scientific basis to the biological concept of race.
- The use of the term 'race' in political debates involves a racialization of ethnic differences that hardens and sharpens them.
- Do you think that a sociologist should ever use the word 'race'?

Our consideration of the major theories in this area showed that:

- Theories of race and citizenship emphasize a cultural contradiction between a dominant, liberal creed and conservative racial ideas.
- Theories of race and colonialism look at the interdependence of power and cultural construction, relating these to the colonial and post-colonial experience.
- Theories of racialized discourse look at the representations of race that figure in cultural discourses and they examine their role in the formation of identities. Such discursively formed identities are syncretic or hybrid.

Assimilation, incorporation, and segregation

The expansion of the modern world system involved a European colonization of the 'new world' of the Americas and of Africa and of other distant parts of the globe. Central to this expansion was a slave trade through which people were taken from Africa by the colonial powers and sold in the Caribbean and North America to work on plantations set up by the European settlers. Slavery was, by the sixteenth century, already well established in Africa, where slaves were taken in warfare and sold by Arab and African slave traders. As Europeans began to settle and subject Africa, they also began to trade with the slave traders and transported the people that they bought across the Atlantic to the Americas. Slaves and captives were sold in open markets and kept in their slavery through force and coercion. It was through the system of slavery that the tobacco, sugar, and cotton industries of North America were built (Paterson 1967, 1982).

Rigid slave systems were established across the Americas and persisted until the abolition of the slave trade and slavery. This was abolished within the British Empire in 1833 and in the United States in 1865. The end of slavery marked the beginning of a migration of ex-slaves from the rural areas of the southern United States to the northern industrializing centres. Somewhat later, ex-slaves from the British colonies of the Caribbean began to migrate from their poor rural homes to the cities and towns of Britain. Similar migrations occurred from the colonial territories of the other European powers to their imperial centres.

This migration of ex-slave populations brought black and white groups together in the expanding cities of Europe and North America. The resulting pattern of 'race relations' was seen by policy-makers in the imperial centres as foreshadowing a process of acculturation or **assimilation**. It was assumed that the dominant and primordial culture of the metropolitan societies was carried and sustained by their white populations. The black ex-slaves, of a different ethnic background, were seen as destined to be assimilated into this dominant cultural tradition. The ethnic minorities, as 'strangers', would familiarize themselves with the new metropolitan culture and would willingly embrace it, abandoning their own 'archaic' culture. Ethnic differences would disappear and the migrants would become culturally indistinguishable from members of the majority society.

This assumption shaped perceptions of the race-relations situations in the metropolitan cities. The persistence of racial conflict and inequality was seen to be a result of a racial prejudice on the part of the ethnic majority that would eventually disappear through legislative changes and a growing familiarity with members of the ethnic minorities.

Where the black experience in the United States was rooted in slavery, that in Britain was rooted in colonialism.

These two histories were not, of course, separate. The slave trade with the Americas had been operated by British merchants, and the territory that became the United States was a British colony until 1776. Slavery was also established in the British colonies of the Caribbean and persisted well into the eighteenth century. Britain, however, also expanded its power into Africa itself, into the Indian subcontinent, and into many other parts of the world. The building of the British Empire was an integral feature of the emergence of the modern world system that we discuss in Chapter 16, p. 607.

British settlement and conquest led to the establishment of a variety of forms of labour in the different colonies, and in areas such as Canada and Australia the number of white settlers vastly outnumbered the indigenous populations. This shaped the timing and character of migration into Britain. Migration has generally had only a relatively small effect on overall population trends in Britain, as the numbers involved have been so small in relation to the total numbers of births and deaths. Migrants arrived in Britain from its colonies in relatively small numbers until the second half of the twentieth century. Chinese seamen with the East India Company had moved into the dockland districts of London and some other port cities by the end of the eighteenth century, and a few Indians and African Caribbeans, mainly the servants of returning colonists, had also begun to settle in Britain.

The largest group of early migrants was the Irish. As a result of migration from Ireland to the British mainland, especially after the Great Famine of the 1840s, the Irish accounted for 2.9 per cent of the population of England and Wales and almost 5 per cent of the population of London by 1851. Their descendants, together with more recent Irish migrants, are estimated to account for up to 10 per cent of the mainland British population today. A second major wave of migration, however, had little directly to do with British colonialism. Ashkenazi Jewish migrants from Germany and Eastern Europe, driven out by anti-Semitic pogroms, began to arrive in Britain in the 1880s, and they continued to arrive until the early part of the twentieth century. They settled in large numbers in the East End of London and in other major urban centres.

For the first thirty years of the twentieth century, Britain experienced a net loss of population through migration (emigration was greater than immigration). The reason for this was that large numbers of Britons were migrating to Canada, Australia, South Africa, and other parts of the Empire. Despite this movement of population, migration had little effect on the overall composition of the British population. Certain ethnic enclaves were formed, but they were a marginal feature of British society, which remained an ethnically homogeneous society through the first half of the twentieth century. For this reason, 'race relations' were not a significant feature of British society, and racial divisions were largely confined to the colonies themselves.

From the delta to the melting pot

In the United States, the situation was very different, as slavery had established a race-relations situation in the heart of the country. Slavery in the United States was concentrated in the southern states, and stable patterns of race relations were built across the whole of the 'Deep South'. Even after the abolition of slavery, black–white relations were sharply segregated and African Americans were systematically excluded from many areas of life. In the towns and cities of the south, the race-relations pattern was similar to that described by Warner in his model of 'caste'. The growing urbanization of American society and the consequent migration of rural blacks to the cities of the north led many observers in the 1930s and 1940s to endorse the assimilationist expectations of the race and citizenship theorists. The expanding cities, they argued, were 'melting pots' in which race relations would be forged into a new and more equal pattern.

Slave society

Slavery is a system of social stratification in which differences of status define some as free and others as unfree. Slaves lack freedom because they are owned by others. As the objects of property relations, slaves have none of the rights of full membership in their society: they can be bought and sold and have no say in their own fate. Slaves occupy a subordinate social position and must carry out their assigned role of serving the free citizens of their society. Slavery is an ascribed status enforced through compulsion. The children of slaves, for example, have no choice about their status: they are born into slavery and can do nothing to alter the situation.

American slavery was closely linked with the rise of racial thinking in Western culture. Differences of colour between European colonists and African slaves became markers of racialized ethnic differences. Slaves were at the bottom of a system of social stratification headed by the white settlers and their descendants. At the top of the system was an upper stratum of plantation-owners with economic and political powers as well as the highest status. The middle levels of the system consisted of small independent farmers, officials, and other white groups. Some sociologists produced justifications of slavery, as shown in Box 6.5.

THEORY AND METHODS   **6.5**

Sociology for the South

Two of the earliest books to use the word 'sociology' in their titles were produced in the southern states of the United States as justifications for its system of slavery. The racist ideas documented by Warner's fieldworkers in the 1930s and 1940s showed that many of the arguments made in these books almost one hundred years before were still an important element in southern thinking.

In 1854, George Fitzhugh published *Sociology for the South* and Henry Hughes published his *Treatise on Sociology*. These writers saw sociology as informing their criticisms of liberalism and the 'free society'. While much social thought had been socialist in character, Hughes and Fitzhugh aimed to construct a conservative and paternalistic social theory that would justify the anti-liberal principles and practices of slavery. Blacks and whites, they argued, differ in their personal, moral, and intellectual characteristics, and the childlike character of blacks makes it inappropriate to give them the same rights and freedoms as whites. Their ignorance and improvidence would simply result in social conditions worse than those in Africa. On this basis, they saw the white 'master' as the only person able to act in what is the best interest of blacks. The slave system of the Deep South, they argued, is the perfect form of social life, producing the essential conditions of life for all.

❷ How does this argument relate to the often-voiced claim that sociology shows a left-wing bias?

Slavery was legally abolished within the United States in 1865, following a civil war between the southern Confederate states and the northern Unionist states. Despite abolition, the racialized status of African Americans continued to disadvantage them. Although they were formally free, ex-slaves had few real options in life. Many continued to work on the plantations, and their masters simply became their employers. Others became sharecroppers—tenant farmers who paid a part of their crop as rent—and they were as exploited as they had been under slavery. Nevertheless, African Americans did acquire a legal freedom of movement and access to public places during the era of 'Reconstruction' at the end of the nineteenth century, and this raised hopes for their full participation in US society.

Large numbers of ex-slaves moved to the cities of the north in search of work and a better way of life. An urban way of life, however, did not resolve their problems. Migrants to Chicago, Detroit, Philadelphia, New York, and other urban centres found themselves facing poor housing and job opportunities. They lived in ghetto conditions and endured long periods of unemployment.

Migrants from the West Indies arrived in Britain in large numbers from the 1940s to the 1960s.
© Getty Images/Haywood Magee

The greater freedom experienced by African Americans was felt as a threat by many white Americans, who had previously been able to keep a social distance between themselves and African Americans. This fear caused many states to pass laws that restricted the rights of African Americans, the high point of this legislation being between 1890 and the First World War. These laws limited African American voting rights, prevented them from using the same railway carriages, bus seats, toilets, hotels, and eating places as whites, and limited them to certain schools. Social segregation was reasserted, especially in the southern states, where the system came to be known as 'Jim Crow'. This segregation was justified on the grounds that it provided 'separate-but-equal' facilities for blacks and whites, and a structure of racial segregation remained intact in many parts of the south until the 1960s, despite a growth of political radicalism among African Americans.

The Deep South

Warner used race and citizenship theory to organize and interpret the results of a fieldwork study of black–white relations in the southern states of the United States. The states of the Deep South—most especially Georgia, the Carolinas, Mississippi, Louisiana, Alabama, and Arkansas—lay at the heart of southern slave society, and it was here that the old racial divide persisted in its sharpest form. Warner sought out a typical southern city to investigate, hoping to compare it with a typical northern city that he was studying. The northern, New England city of Newburyport—to which Warner had given the pseudonym 'Yankee City' (Warner and Lunt 1941)—had a relatively open and flexible pattern of ethnic relations that Warner felt contrasted sharply with the situation found in the Deep South.

For the southern study, he settled on the city of Natchez, given the pseudonym 'Old City' in his research team's publication (Davis 1941). This was a small city of about 10,000 people and was the principal cotton-trading centre for the plantations of the surrounding Mississippi Delta region, a role it had established for itself in the days of slavery. At the time of the study, Natchez showed a sharp split between a white caste and a black caste. The authors argued that the social system of caste and class had evolved from the destruction of the slave system. It started as a sharp horizontal caste divide between an internally differentiated white group and the predominantly black labourers. The white caste was the dominant group and the black caste was the subordinate group. Gradually, the 'colour line' had tilted upwards slightly, as black society had become more differentiated and those at its top had improved their economic position.

This system was sustained by ideas of the status superiority of whites and the inferiority of blacks, and these ideas were underpinned by the beliefs and sentiments concerning race that united each caste. These racialized attitudes were at the heart of their prejudices towards each other and were rooted in economic differences and differentials of power. Patterns of circulation and association within each caste crystallized into relatively well-defined internal social-class boundaries, but there was no circulation or association across the colour line. There was a sharp spatial separation of the two castes: schools, cinemas, churches, jails, and public transport were all segregated, and blacks always had the least desirable facilities.

> **⊃ Connections**
>
> The idea of social stratification and the role of circulation and association in defining social-class boundaries is discussed in Chapter 19, pp. 744–5. If you feel unsure about the claims that are being made here, you might like to look at that now. You will find a model of a caste-like structural division in Figure 19.1, p. 744. Caste is discussed more fully on p. 752.

The white caste was internally divided into three major social classes, and each of these classes showed a differentiation into more or less distinct upper and lower segments. At the top of this hierarchy was the aristocracy of 'Society' families, the old established families whose wealth originated in the cotton plantations. In the middle were the managers, professionals, and small business families, and at the bottom were the ordinary working families. Those at the bottom had a relatively low standard of living and were referred to as the 'poor whites' by their fellow caste members. The middle and lower classes deferred to aristocratic families who dominated all the major social institutions of the city.

While there were also upper, middle, and lower levels within the black caste, these were not the same as the white social classes, and there were, of course, no significant connections between them and the white classes. The upper levels of black society comprised a very small class of professionals, such as doctors and lawyers, mainly dependent on black clients, and the middle levels comprised skilled and clerical workers. The great bulk of the black population, however, formed a lower social class of porters, drivers, barbers, labourers, and tenant farmers. This class had the lowest standard of living in the city.

African American and white societies, therefore, coexisted. Each had its own culture and social institutions. Their internal social divisions were overridden and obscured by the fundamental social gulf created by the colour line. While the relatively wealthy black professionals who stood at the top of the black caste were much better off than the poor whites, they were still regarded as social inferiors and were denied the full rights enjoyed by all whites.

According to Warner's researchers, the belief system that underpinned the idea of racial superiority in the southern states could be summarized in terms of four core ideas:

- The inherent inferiority of blacks was seen as sanctioned by God. Racial differences were seen as rooted in 'immutable, inevitable and everlasting' biological differences that made 'Negroes' primitive and animal-like. These racial differences were seen as

Briefing: the Ku Klux Klan   6.6

The Ku Klux Klan was originally formed in 1866 by opponents of Reconstruction who wanted to retain a system of white supremacy. Its members posed as the spirits of the Confederate dead who had returned to protect Confederate principles. They covered themselves and their horses in white robes, and they covered their faces with white masks to emphasize this. They intimidated the black population of their localities through public torchlight displays and bonfires, and through the routine use of whippings and lynchings.

The organization was revived in 1915 with wider aims, and drew on anti-Semitic ideas as well as white supremacist ones. It was a powerful political force during the 1920s, when it had between four and five million members. Legal action against the Klan and the economic problems of the 1930s, however, led to a decline in its membership. Although support for the Klan grew again during the civil-rights struggles of the 1960s, it never regained its former strength. Many Klan organizations, nevertheless, still exist in the southern states.

Useful sources are Chalmers (1987) and Dobratz (2000).

Hooded Klansmen salute a burning cross.

© Getty Images/William F. Campbell

willed by God, who had put the races in their separate places in the first place and so was happy with their continued segregation.

- It was believed that contact between races was to be avoided because of its contaminating consequences for whites. Whites believed that they would suffer through any direct contact with black people, and they saw any physical contact as bringing them into dangerous relations with those who were 'unclean', both physically and morally. Eating or drinking from the same tableware, for example, was to be avoided, as was the use of the same chairs, tables, and rooms.

- 'Negroes' were held to be unsocialized and childlike beings, lacking all normal social restraints and obligations. They were seen as lazy and as lacking in ambition, as having to be compelled to work, and as lacking proper respect for property and conventional sexual morality. They were naturally childlike, and could never be expected to become fully socialized members of society.

- White people claimed they had a responsibility to protect blacks from their own failings and weaknesses. They should not put temptations in their way, and they needed to force them to do what was right or in their own best interest. These matters could not be left to their own choice, as such primitive people were incapable of properly exercising their choice (Davis 1941: 15–20).

These beliefs were the basis of exclusionary practices and symbols of subordination that established and justified white superiority. In addition to the spatial segregation of blacks and whites into distinct neighbourhoods, blacks were expected to behave in specific ways in all their interpersonal relationships with whites. They were, for example, expected to show 'respect' by touching their hat and using titles such as 'Boss' and 'Sir' when talking to a white man. Whites, for their part, would call a black man 'boy'. This was, however, modified by social class: lower-class whites showed the same kind of deference towards upper-class whites, and they were sometimes on relatively friendly terms with the blacks who lived close to them. Sexual relations were rigidly controlled. No black American could marry a white person, as this was prohibited by law in the southern states. Non-marital sex across the colour line was also disapproved of, though white men often regarded black women as legitimate objects of coercive sexual relations or of prostitution.

The colour line that divided white from black society was reflected in the explicit use of colour as a criterion of social differentiation among African Americans them-

selves: light-skinned African Americans had taken over some of the negative views that whites held about the black population. The light-skinned professionals distinguished themselves from the dark-skinned lower class, and they often used the language of colour when they disparaged their fellow blacks as 'boisterous' or 'stupid'. 'Blackness', then, was a master symbol that marked someone out as an object of disgust and contempt. The black lower class, in turn, saw the black professionals as 'uppity' or pushy, and as denying their roots.

The American creed was weak in the south and clashed with strongly entrenched assumptions of white racial supremacy. There was no popular drive to implement the recognition of equal rights for all that was emphasized in the American creed. The subordination of African Americans was maintained by local laws and by custom and habit, and these legal exclusions and sanctions were supplemented by the unofficial but publicly tolerated use of direct physical punishment. The social control exercised over African Americans involved individual violence, collectively sanctioned beatings and whippings, and the lynch mob.

The ethnic melting pot and the ghetto

Alongside the study of Natchez, Warner's research group undertook a study of Chicago (Drake and Cayton 1945). Their aim was to explore what was happening in one of the major northern cities to which African Americans had migrated from the Deep South.

Chicago had been a city of migrants from its earliest days. From the second half of the nineteenth century through to the First World War, successive waves of Germans, Irish, Scandinavians, Poles, East European Jews, Italians, and Greeks had arrived in the city. Black migration from the south became a significant factor after the ending of slavery, but rates of black migration were particularly high during the 'Great Migration' of 1916–19, when the growing demand for labour attracted many more rural blacks to work in the city. Migration continued at high levels through the 1920s and 1930s, and by 1944 almost one in five of the population was European born and one in ten was an African American.

Chicago was a new, expanding city, full of opportunities, and its openness meant that its successive waves of migrants felt sure that, in time, they would secure the kinds of advantages and opportunities enjoyed by those who had already established themselves there. A person's ethnic origin posed few long-term problems in what rapidly came to be seen as an ethnic melting pot: a city whose vibrancy and interpersonal familiarity dissolved ethnic boundaries and forged all together into a distinctively 'American' identity (see Box 6.7, p. 208).

Initially, each migrant group would settle in a particular neighbourhood, but groups would soon spread out across

THEORY AND METHODS   6.7

Assimilation

The idea of the ethnic melting pot rests on a model of assimilation. This is the process through which an ethnic minority takes on the values, norms, and ways of behaving of the dominant, mainstream group and is accepted by the latter as a full member of their society.

The problem with the idea of assimilation is that it assumes that there is a social and cultural mainstream and so rests on the idea that the 'host' society is characterized by a value consensus. This may not be the case. It also assumes that there is only one way in which majority and minority groups can coexist—through the disappearance of the minority culture. In the following section we will look at an alternative idea that stresses multiculturalism.

> **⊃ Connections**
>
> The City of Chicago was an important sociological base for the studies undertaken by the so-called Chicago school of sociology. Their theoretical ideas are discussed in Chapter 2, p. 41, and their model of the city is discussed in Chapter 13, pp. 484–7. Look at the plan in Figure 13.8 and find the Black Belt on it.

the city into ethnically mixed neighbourhoods. Where areas of ethnic concentration did persist, they changed their character. Areas of high German and Italian settlement, for example, might persist, but these did not remain areas of concentrated disadvantage. To a considerable degree, people *chose* to continue living there.

Warner's researchers showed that, however idealized the image of the ethnic melting pot might be, there was a considerable amount of truth in it. For one group, however, it just did not apply. African American neighbourhoods had solidified and formed a significant part of Chicago's social structure. The 'Black Metropolis', or 'Black Belt', at the heart of the city was a ghetto settlement, similar to the Harlem district in New York. Over 90 per cent of blacks in Chicago were living in the ghetto during the 1940s.

Despite the relative strength in Chicago of the American creed of citizenship equality, the persistence of racial values meant that black Americans were excluded from the full citizenship that had been gained by other ethnic minorities. Although the colour line was not as sharp as it was in the Deep South, it still existed, and it divided the two societies from each other. The relative freedom and impersonality of the city allowed a certain degree of movement across the line to occur, but the colour line remained an important aspect of the African American experience in Chicago.

The colour line defined the subordination of blacks to whites in employment and their segregation in housing. African Americans had limited opportunities for occupational mobility and did not compete on equal terms with white Americans. They were largely restricted to low-paid and menial work and were always the first to lose their jobs in times of depression. After the Second World War, they began to enter more skilled and clerical jobs, producing an expansion in the black middle class, but a clear job ceiling remained to limit African American opportunities. They were also limited to poor-quality housing, concentrated in the ghetto. This housing segregation determined the educational and recreational facilities available to black Americans. The ghetto had the highest proportion of welfare recipients and low-income earners in the city, as well as the highest rates of illegitimate births, juvenile delinquency, tuberculosis, and mental illness.

The researchers characterized this as a 'social disorganization', symptomatic of its 'slum' character and the low level of cohesion among its residents. The regulatory norms that would normally commit people to the conformist behaviour of the mainstream of American society were absent, and ghetto residents lived in a state of anomie. Those norms and values that did exist simply reflected and sustained the deviant character of ghetto life.

There were, however, some relatively affluent areas within the ghetto, especially around the Washington Park district. This was the area where could be found the homes of the emerging black middle class of doctors, teachers, lawyers, shopkeepers, and insurance sellers, all of whom depended on their fellow ghetto residents. These and other 'respectable' members of ghetto society were organized around the clubs and churches and were able to generate a degree of collective solidarity and mutual support that sustained their sense of community and a distinctiveness from other ghetto residents. Excluded from many areas of white society, they nevertheless followed many of its values and aspired to join it. Their search for respectability and assimilation led them to distinguish themselves particularly sharply from the 'shadies' of the underworld, who were concentrated in the lower class and were the core of the 'disorganized' element of the community.

Stop and reflect

In this section we have looked at the impact of colonialism and slavery on race relations in the advanced capitalist societies.

- Britain was, until the middle of the twentieth century, an ethnically homogeneous society and had few significant problems of race relations.

- The United States had a clear racialization of group relations because of the persistence of ideas and practices from the slave period.

We gave particular attention to the American situation, exploring race relations in both the Deep South and Chicago.

- A sharp racial divide existed in the Deep South, with black and white groups forming distinct 'castes' or sub-societies. These social differences were rooted in differences of economic resources and power.

- Migration to the big cities was associated with a process of assimilation for European migrants, but persistent exclusion for African American migrants.

- How important is it to know the history of slavery if we are to understand contemporary ethnic relations in the United States?

Diversity, racism, and multiculturalism

The failure of the melting pot to work in favour of African Americans meant that divisions around the colour line grew sharper during the second half of the twentieth century. The ghettos of the large American cities continued to attract migrants from southern rural districts, but there were few opportunities for the existing residents of the ghettos to leave them. Struggles over civil rights and the social exclusion of African Americans grew through the 1960s, and conflict became a central feature of racialized ethnic relations in the United States. At the same time, new waves of migrants from Puerto Rico found that they, too, were unable to take advantage of the melting-pot mechanism. The ethnic division between a white mainstream society and the black and Hispanic ghettos became a central feature of American life.

Rates of colonial immigration into Britain increased through the late 1940s, and from the middle of the 1950s into the early 1960s there was a net gain in population from migration. Large numbers of people from the Commonwealth (as the Empire had become) were being recruited into the expanding industries and public services to meet post-war labour shortages. These migrants were overwhelmingly drawn into low-paid work. People from the former British colonies of the Caribbean, India, and Pakistan increased the ethnic diversity of the British population. Most of the early migrants were from Jamaica and the islands in the east of the Caribbean. Their cultures combined their British, French, and Spanish colonial inheritance with some African elements that had survived through the slave period. The predominant feature of their culture, however, was its 'British' character. Their schools had used English textbooks and taught British history, as if it was their own, and they were brought up to define themselves as British. Increasing numbers came from India and

Pakistan, mainly from Pakistan itself, from the Gujarat and Punjab districts of India that bordered Pakistan, and from the eastern part of Pakistan that later became Bangladesh. These Asian migrants were very diverse in their culture: Sikhs came from the Punjab, Muslims from Pakistan and Bangladesh, and Hindus from Gujarat. The character of British colonialism in India meant that there had been far less of a 'British' element in their education, and their religious differences set them apart.

Britain became less ethnically homogeneous. Migrants and their descendants settled in large numbers in London, in Birmingham, and in many other parts of the Midlands and the north. This growing ethnic diversity was associated with a growth in racialized attitudes in many sections of the white population, and 'race' became an important element in British politics and policy from the 1960s.

The numbers of both Asian and Caribbean immigrants to Britain declined from the mid-1960s, partly because of legal restrictions on immigration, and the immigrants that have arrived since then have mainly been the dependants of those who had already settled. During the 1960s there were about a quarter of a million immigrants to Britain each year, but in every year until the middle of the 1980s they were more than balanced by an even larger number of emigrants. Almost a half of all immigrants in this period came from Australia, New Zealand, and Canada (the 'Old Commonwealth' in the official terminology), the United States, or the European Community. These numbers were counterbalanced by the return of short-term migrants to the same areas and by the emigration of Britons to join relatives in the 'Old Commonwealth' or to work in other parts of Europe. Immigrants to Britain from India, Pakistan, and the Caribbean were generally long-term or

London, the second biggest concentration being in Birmingham. Other concentrations of the non-white population can be found in West Yorkshire (Bradford and Leeds), Greater Manchester, and Leicester.

Migration and racism

The pattern of race relations in Britain in its first phase has been clearly documented in classic studies by Sheila Patterson (1963) in London and by John Rex and Robert Moore (1967) in Birmingham. Patterson's study of Brixton was shaped by her expectation that assimilation would be the eventual outcome of the emerging pattern of race relations, but she shows clearly the obstacles to this. The Rex and Moore study of Sparkbrook drew on the race and colonialism theory and the arguments of the Chicago school of sociology, and they gave much more attention to the deep sources of conflict that characterized British race relations.

Separation, exclusion, and conflict are also apparent in work on the United States. Earlier work had been documented by the assumption of assimilation and the metaphor of the melting pot. Later work showed that assimilation was by no means automatic, especially for African Americans, and that the structural separation of a black 'underclass' from the mainstream of white society was as sharp, if not sharper, than ever before.

Settlement and housing

Brixton is in central Lambeth, bordering on Battersea, Wandsworth, and Camberwell. It has been a predominantly working-class district from the middle of the nineteenth century. At the time of the survey it was largely a dormitory area, with few local industries, and was attractive to migrants because of the relatively large numbers of boarding houses and bed-sit housing. Significant levels of immigration from the West Indies began in 1948. As people arrived and settled in the area, news and information were passed back to friends and relatives, who were also likely to aim for Brixton when they, too, migrated.

Patterson (1963) saw the situation in Brixton as typical of that in many other British towns and cities, and she interpreted it as an 'immigration' situation complicated by the fact of racial difference. Conflict and lack of understanding result from unfamiliarity, and the settlement of colonial migrants in relatively large numbers in Brixton has brought together groups of 'strangers' who must learn to live with each other. This unfamiliarity is sharpened, however, by the sense of racial difference that marks both groups. Patterson minimized the extent of any racism in the indigenous 'host' community, and gave far more importance to the colour-consciousness of the migrants themselves. The African Caribbean residents of Brixton at the time of her study were

Why do immigrants often end up in poorly paid work?

© Alice Chadwick

permanent migrants, but they were very few in number: in the middle of the 1980s there were 21,000 migrants from the Indian subcontinent, 11,000 from African Commonwealth countries, and 3,000 from the Caribbean. Only since the middle of the 1980s has there again been a net balance of immigrants over emigrants.

Migrants and their descendants now form a significant element in the British population, and they are increasing at a much faster rate than the majority population. The ethnic minority population has increased by around fifteen times as much as the white population since 2000, and ethnic minorities now account for over 7 per cent of the British population. It has been estimated that a half of the British ethnic minority population was born in the United Kingdom, showing the inadequacy of the common popular designation of them as 'immigrants'. Recent patterns of migration, however, have produced a situation where there are now more German and American migrants living in Britain than there are Bangladeshi migrants. The fastest-growing groups of migrants have been those born in Albania and former Yugoslavia (see Box 6.8). Almost a half of the total ethnic minority population lives in Greater

Global focus Ethnicity, Refugees, and Asylum-Seekers   6.8

National disasters, military action, and political repression have always produced large-scale movements of population, as displaced groups seek new homes. Those displaced for military or political reasons have often sought a right to asylum under a state that will protect them or guarantee their freedom. In the first half of the twentieth century, large numbers of refugees fled or were expelled from Nazi Germany, Palestine, and the Soviet bloc, and in 1951 a legal definition of refugee was created under the Geneva Convention. It is from the second half of the twentieth century, however, that international conflict and tension created ever greater numbers of refugees seeking asylum in a more secure home. This has been driven, in large part, by the ethnic basis of much military and political conflict, which has meant that whole populations have been forced to seek refuge.

The collapse of the Soviet bloc and the dismantling of repressive border controls freed many in Central and Eastern Europe to move westwards in search of work and better living conditions. Ethnic conflict in former Soviet areas, such as Yugoslavia and the Balkans, has displaced large numbers of Bosnians, Albanians, and Kosovans. Famine and war in Africa and Asia have led to large-scale population movements in Sudan, Angola, Afghanistan, and elsewhere.

Refugees seeking asylum and work in the more affluent countries have often encountered difficulties. Countries that have previously accepted refugees, who arrived in relatively small numbers, have increasingly claimed that the large numbers of people involved make this policy more difficult to sustain. Opposition to the entry of large numbers of 'asylum-seekers' and economic migrants, like opposition to large-scale immigration, is often driven by racialized ethnic differences.

Large numbers of asylum-seekers in Europe are kept in camps and detention centres—now renamed removal centres—while their fates are determined by the European immigration authorities. It can take many months to come to a decision on individual cases, and many refugees see this as no different from imprisonment. In Britain, asylum-seekers typically wait for up to a year for an initial decision on their case, and financial support has recently been reduced for those who have been waiting for more than a year.

The largest immigration removal centre in Europe is Yarl's Wood, near Bedford, run by SERCO. Those who are felt to be likely to evade controls may be held in jails. At its peak, the Kosovo crisis produced 71,000 asylum applications. The United Nations High Commission for Refugees estimated that in 2001 there were 169,354 refugees living in Britain. These numbers are increased by illegal entrants who arrive hidden in freight lorries. A national asylum support service undertakes the 'dispersal' of refugees while their claims are decided, offering them accommodation in specific towns and cities to prevent any concentration of large numbers of refugees in any one place.

Hostility to 'asylum-seekers', like opposition to 'immigrants', has been strong in the Conservative Party and has been fuelled by the racism of groups such as the British National Party and its counterparts in other European countries.

Information on the global scale and consequences of the refugee phenomenon can be found at www.unhcr.org/cgi-bin/texis/vtx/home.

---

first generation and they were still oriented towards their home society, to which most of them hoped to return.

The West Indian population amounted to about 5,000 by 1955 and approximately 10,000 by the early 1960s. These migrants had been attracted by job opportunities, but a national decline in employment opportunities between 1956 and 1959 made itself felt in Brixton, and levels of unemployment among recent migrants increased substantially. Poor economic opportunities among the black and white populations led those who felt themselves to be 'different' from one another to come into conflict over economic resources.

The main area of competition and conflict between black and white residents was housing. Because of the wartime destruction of much local housing and later slum-clearance programmes, there was a general shortage of housing in the area. Sellers and landlords charged West Indian purchasers and tenants more than they did white families, but few West Indians made official complaints about their treatment. They recognized that going to a rent tribunal, for example, was likely to be a difficult experience for them and would only create longer-term problems with their landlord.

As a result, African Caribbean migrants were concentrated in the worst—and relatively expensive—housing. Many were crowded into boarding and lodging houses. This housing situation did not improve as African Caribbeans began to buy property. Those who were able to build up some resources bought run-down properties on short leases and sub-let rooms to other West Indian families. Most of these families lived in overcrowded conditions, often one family to a single room. Although their own rooms were kept very clean, shared areas—toilets, kitchens, and hallways—were dirty, damp, and badly maintained. Overcrowding in houses owned by African Caribbean landlords persisted, because the landlords needed to let out as much of their property as possible in order to meet their own mortgage payments on the house.

them. Disputes between white and black men at the ballroom led its owners to formulate a national policy that West Indian men could not be admitted to rock-and-roll nights unless accompanied by a partner. (This was at a time before such policies were made illegal.) When going out for a drink, both blacks and whites tended to establish their own local pubs or sections of pubs.

Patterson argued that this resulted in an 'accommodation' between immigrant and host societies, a limited acceptance and tolerance, rather than full assimilation. Their perception as 'strangers' by members of white society limits the degree to which they are offered acceptance. Patterson saw no inevitability in the move from accommodation to assimilation: whether blacks are assimilated as British citizens, she argued, depended on the attitudes of second-generation migrants and later generations of the host society.

The Rex and Moore (1967) study drew out the implications that this had for politics. Politically, Sparkbrook had shifted from a safe Conservative area to a safe Labour one, represented at the time by Roy (now Lord) Hattersley. The mainstay activists of the Labour Party were Irish, but few other immigrants were involved in its political or social activities. A significant number of the white working class supported the Conservative Party, which espoused the need for immigration controls, and there was some anti-black feeling among Labour supporters. However, there was little support for overtly racist parties in either national or local elections. Few West Indian or Asian migrants were involved in politics, but those few who voted in elections tended to vote Labour.

Beyond the melting pot

Ethnic divisions in the United States were stronger and more entrenched than in Britain. African Americans seemed to have become fixed at the bottom of the social hierarchy, and many observers began to question the assumption of inevitable assimilation and the whole idea of the melting pot. An important study by Glazer and Moynihan (1963, 1970) showed that ethnicity remained a crucial element in social difference and social division, even in a city as large and cosmopolitan as New York.

Glazer and Moynihan argue that mass migration had not culminated in the merging of black Americans into a uniform American national identity. Indeed, American ethnic identities are generally very diverse. The Irish, Italians, and Poles share a common Catholic outlook that combines with their American outlook and, in the case of Irish Americans, shapes their view of the political conflicts in Northern Ireland. American Jews, on the other hand, have been significantly influenced by the Nazi persecutions of the 1930s and 1940s, and the founding of the state of Israel has remained an important part of their political outlook. These 'assimilated' groups have not abandoned their sense of national identity in favour of a simple 'American' one. They have forged a distinctive sense of collective identity that reflects both their national heritage and their distinctive experiences within the United States.

African Americans are also likely to retain such hybrid identities, but their experience of American society is that of disadvantage and social exclusion. They remain concentrated in low-paid jobs and poor housing, and their identity is shaped by their continuing structural exclusion from the mainstream of American society. Despite a relative improvement in the economic circumstances of the black population, their sense of deprivation and exclusion remains. The ethnic division between black and white is the overriding division in American life.

Glazer and Moynihan saw assimilation as unlikely for black Americans, who they held are likely to develop an increasingly strong sense of their separate identity, even if their economic situation continues to improve. They share their depressed condition with the more recent Puerto Rican migrants, but there is a sharp ethnic divide between the two groups. Some black Americans, however, have come to see themselves as part of a larger deprived group of people of colour (black, yellow, and red, combining African American, Hispanic, Asian, and native American).

Moynihan's earlier work (1965) had highlighted what he saw as a breakdown in the fabric of black urban society in America. The accumulated disadvantages and social exclusion of African Americans had produced a growing divide between a relatively stable middle-class group and a disorganized and demoralized lower-class group. The black middle class had not been assimilated into mainstream American society, but it had become separated from the inner-city ghetto poor who came to form what Myrdal (1962) called an 'underclass'.

> ### ➔ Connections
> We critically discuss the idea of an underclass in Chapter 18, pp. 704–6. You will find that discussion a particularly useful background to what we say here.

Moynihan traced many of the disadvantages of African Americans to the breakdown of the lower-class family as a result of an increase in divorce and illegitimacy. This was manifest in the large number of female, single parents dependent on welfare benefits and a whole generation of children who were unable to take advantage of what few opportunities were available to them. Moynihan, it is important to point out, was not seeing family breakdown as the crucial causal factor in producing disadvantage. Rather, he saw exclusion and deprivation in employment and housing, and the continued undermining of black civil rights, as having produced fertile conditions for family breakdown and, therefore, for the perpetuation of disadvantage.

This argument was taken further by Wilson (1987), who established very clearly the structural basis of racial disadvantage in US cities. He argues that the black ghettos of New York, Chicago, and other major cities in the 1930s had been organized around a strong sense of community and collective solidarity that tied all their residents together, whatever their economic position. Middle-class, working-class, and poor African Americans lived together and supported one another in the face of their shared exclusion from white society (see Box 6.9). By the 1960s, the black middle and working classes had moved out to the suburbs, leaving the poor blacks (and the Hispanics) in the ghettos. This broke down the relations of mutual support that had previously integrated them into a larger community. These 'truly disadvantaged' formed an economic underclass that found it ever more difficult to escape its disadvantaged conditions. Unlike

Conservative commentators, however, Wilson saw the black underclass as a product of racialized social exclusion and not as a product of any lack of morality. They are victims of a vicious circle of exclusion and disadvantage.

Hybrid identities and multiculturalism

We have shown that, through most of the twentieth century, ethnic minority relations, in both Britain and the United States, have been shaped by a clash between the liberal idea of equal citizenship and conservative racial thinking. Official policies in both countries have stressed the need to assimilate ethnic minorities into an all-embracing mainstream culture. The ways in which these policies have been implemented have shown that these liberal assumptions have not gone unchallenged. Many members of the ethnic majority, including many of those in the legislative, executive, and administrative branches of the state, hold to racial ideas and values that undermine the liberal ideal and have prevented its implementation. State policies in Britain and other parts of Europe have, from the 1960s, became more restrictive about immigration as racial thinking became a more marked feature of official thinking.

At the same time, ethnic minorities have become less willing to accept the goal of assimilation. They have felt more strongly that their particular experiences and values should be remembered and valued. Their identities draw on shared memories of their ethnic background and of their experiences in the society to which they have migrated. Such identities are not simple expressions of a single cultural origin, but are hybrid, composed of diverse cultural elements.

A study of black and ethnic-minority people in 2005 reported that the majority considered themselves to be fully or mainly British, though still considering their ethnic origin quite or very important to them. Twenty-two per cent of black people said that they did not feel at all British. High levels of prejudice were reported. Sixty per cent of black and 54 per cent of Asian respondents had experienced name-calling or verbal abuse, and 24 per cent of black and 18 per cent of Asian respondents had experienced physical attack or harassment. Over a quarter of those in all categories felt that Britain had become more racist in the previous ten years, and many had considered leaving Britain as a result: 24 per cent of black and 18 per cent of Asian respondents said that they had considered leaving the country because of their experiences of racial intolerance (ICM Research, reported in *Guardian*, 21 March 2005; www.guardian.co.uk/politics/2005/mar/21/race.polls).

This has encouraged new political practices aimed at sustaining collective identities rooted in a shared sense of difference from the white, mainstream culture. Ideas of

Britain's ethnic-minority groups are concentrated in certain inner-city areas, such as Brick Lane in the East End of London.

© Lucy Dawkins

difference have sometimes been more formally articulated as **multiculturalism**, the demand that the diversity of ethnic cultures within a society should be respected and equally valued in official policy and in everyday life. This has been described as 'cultural citizenship' (Pakulski 1997). Where the civil, political, and social rights of citizenship stress equality and ignore or minimize differences, the idea of cultural citizenship involves an explicit recognition of the legitimacy of cultural differences and stresses the need to establish equal rights to express these differences. This includes the right to express one's own identity. Unlike the idea of assimilation, the idea of cultural citizenship does not aim at merging differences into a single cultural framework. It seeks to establish cultural values that recognize and legitimate difference.

A sense of ethnic difference, however, is not expressed only in multiculturalism. Differences within and among ethnic minorities can undermine any common orientation, and a growing conflict between the various minority groups is also apparent. These differing forms of consciousness are rooted in the structural differences between an advantaged majority and various disadvantaged minority groups, and their development has been tied to political conflicts over inequalities of power and resources. The growth of multiculturalist ideas and of autonomous and assertive ethnic minority communities has reinforced the tendency towards racial thinking that has been apparent in majority communities, especially in those that have been most affected by social and economic change. For many white people facing poverty, unemployment, and poor housing, 'immigrants' and racial minorities have been an easy target to blame for these problems: 'they' are taking 'our' jobs and 'our' houses. Social conditions that were actually a consequence of large-scale social changes in work and community relations that were operating at a global level were seen simply as the effects of immigration.

> ⮑ *Connections*
> We discuss some aspects of these larger changes in Chapter 13, pp. 496–7, Chapter 17, pp. 669–70, and Chapter 19, pp. 762–4 and 774–8.

The migrants and their descendants become the scapegoats for social problems and, therefore, the targets of hostility and, increasingly, of violence. The first significant signs of racial conflict in Britain were the Notting Hill riots of 1958, when white residents took to the streets in protest against black settlers who had moved into the area. This marked and reinforced the change in attitudes that was taking place among both black and white groups. Maverick politicians gave voice to these shifts in public opinion during the 1960s, as it became more acceptable to openly express racist ideas and opposition to black immigration. The Conservative candidate in a by-election in the Smethwick district of Birmingham achieved much notoriety when his supporters circulated leaflets proclaiming 'If you want a nigger neighbour, vote Labour'. This climate of hostility culminated in a speech by a former Conservative government minister, Enoch Powell, in 1968. In this speech, Powell spoke of British culture and society being 'swamped' by the growing number of immigrants and their families. He predicted—and, some said, encouraged—a growth in racial conflict, claiming that the rivers of Britain would soon be 'flowing with blood' as levels of racial violence increased.

By the 1970s, the character of official discourse itself was deeply marked by racial ideas and racial hostility, and this lay behind a series of restrictions on the rights of legal entry to Britain that had formerly been open to Commonwealth residents (see Box 18.4, p. 703). In a landmark report on race relations in Britain, Rose *et al.* (1969) showed that policies concerned with the welfare of migrants, which had prevailed from 1948 until the mid-1950s, had progressively given way to policies that were aimed at the control and regulation of the entry of migrants into British society. Both main political parties were more concerned with control than with welfare. This has continued into the new millennium, with ongoing debates over the rights of Muslims and other ethnic minorities to pursue separate and segregated educational practices in 'faith schools' and over the entry of 'asylum-seekers'. Such opposition has occurred across Europe and was also found in the United States. Riots in the Watts district of Los Angeles in the 1960s ignited a long series of urban riots and conflict between black and white. Such riots became a recurrent feature of race relations in Britain and the United States.

> ⮑ *Connections*
> In Chapter 13, pp. 503–5, we look at more recent urban riots involving conflict between ethnic groups. You might find it useful to review that discussion before returning to this chapter.

Racialized politics and the new racism

Martin Barker (1981) has argued that the 1970s saw the emergence of a 'new racism'. The old racism of biological superiority and inferiority, he argues, has given way to a cultural racism that appears, on the surface, to be more benign. Feelings of difference and hostility between ethnic groups are seen as natural responses to the presence of

The Anti-Nazi League challenges racism.
© Alice Chadwick

Barker argues, a more subtle form of racism in which perceived biological differences predispose people to hostility.

The new racism of the British majority population links 'British character' and 'British culture' as central elements in defining a whole way of life. This rests on an image of a cohesive, homogeneous, and solidaristic national society whose shared and 'traditional' way of life is threatened by outsiders and by those who have refused to accept and to be assimilated into this way of life. A national home is felt to be a natural place to be, and the desire to preserve a national identity is seen as equally natural. People's feelings and their culture, traditions, and way of life are the bases of their fear of outsiders; they fear that a cherished way of life, however fictional, will be lost. Those members of the majority culture who feel this way do not see themselves as racist. In fact, they see the outsiders as the racists: it is they who have rejected the way of life of the 'host' society on racial grounds. Members of the majority, then, can claim the moral high ground: they are not racist but are simply striving to maintain a way of life that has existed for many generations. They are not rejecting or decrying the migrants' way of life, but are simply saying that they should pursue this in their home country or accept the way of life of the country to which they or their parents have migrated.

A growth of racial antagonism is apparent in the emergence of new racist political movements of a neo-fascist character from the 1970s. Examples are the Fronte Nationale in France, the National Front and British National Party in Britain, various Neo-Nazi groups in Germany, and the KKK in the United States (Solomos and Back 1996). The growth of such groups has been partly countered by the British Anti-Nazi League, Anti-Racist Alliance, and similar groups. The level of political violence is apparent in such events as the assassination of the Dutch racist politician (and ex-sociologist) Pim Fortuyn in 2002.

other populations. These feelings are not typically formulated in full-blown theories and so do not appear to be racist. They are, however, based on an underlying **xenophobia**, a fear of those who are culturally different. This is,

---

 Briefing: an oath of allegiance?   6.10

Riots by Asian residents on depressed estates in Bradford and Oldham during the summer of 2001 and the terrorist attacks in New York later that year led to much adverse comment about the loyalty of Muslims to the British state. The then Home Secretary responded to such criticisms with the suggestion that those seeking British citizenship should undergo citizenship education and should swear allegiance to Britain. After some discussion an oath and pledge were introduced. The words of these are:

> I . . . do solemnly and sincerely affirm that on becoming a British citizen, I will be faithful and bear true allegiance to Her Majesty Queen Elizabeth the Second, her Heirs and Successors, according to law.

I will give my loyalty to the United Kingdom and respect its rights and freedoms. I will uphold its democratic values. I will observe its laws faithfully and fulfil my duties and obligations as a British citizen.

For many radicals and liberals, the adoption of an oath of allegiance was an expression of the new racism described by Barker: those who refused to swear allegiance would be seen by the authorities as rejecting the British way of life and as threatening national solidarity. For many conservatives, it is a desirable affirmation of loyalty. Indeed, one Conservative Party politician argued that the loyalty of Caribbean and Asian residents in Britain could be tested by which side they cheered for in cricket test matches.

Hate crimes

Violent crimes by white men against black and Asian men are widespread, and they have increasingly come to be defined as hate crimes. They may be expressions of racialized hatred, even where an instrumental crime such as theft is involved. Street attacks, often described as 'Paki bashing', involve the targeting of individuals simply because of their ethnic background. Many racial hate crimes involve repeated harassment of individuals or families. Typical is the case of Sanjay, who was confronted by a group of white teenagers on the front lawn of his Greenwich home. The youths were throwing stones and shouting such chants as 'Go back to your own country'. Many victims of such attacks are, of course, already in their 'own country'. They were born in Britain and regard it as their home. All that marks them off as outsiders is the colour of their skin. In 1993, Stephen Lawrence was murdered in Greenwich by a group of white youths. In 2005, Anthony Walker was murdered with an axe on the streets of a prosperous Liverpool suburb following taunts and racial abuse, and Mohammed al-Majed died after a fracas involving racial abuse in Sussex.

Not all racial hate crimes take place between black and white, and there appears to be a hostility between different ethnic minorities. The killings of black Dexter Coleman by Asians in Bradford and of Abdul Bhatti by African Caribbean men in Notting Hill during 2000 highlighted this issue (*Independent*, 13 September 2000), which was raised again in media discussions of the murder of Damilola Taylor, a 10-year-old Nigerian, who was reported in some newspapers as having been killed by West Indian youths as part of a campaign of harassment. The particular youths accused were initially cleared of the attack, but were eventually convicted in 2006, six years after his death (www.timesonline.co.uk/tol/news/uk/crime/article604421.ece).

The theoretical and policy implications of hate crimes have been well explored in Iganski (2002).

➔ You can follow up on hate crimes at **www.homeoffice.gov.uk/crime-victims/reducing-crime/hate-crime/**. and **www.statistics.gov.uk/cci/nugget.asp?id=267**.

➔ The Stephen Lawrence case and its implications are discussed at **http://news.bbc.co.uk/1hi/english/special_report/1999/02/99/stephen_lawrence/281141.stm.**

Violence against ethnic minorities by racists is a form of hate crime—crime carried out by those whose motivation is hatred of those in a particular social group (see Box 6.11). Racist organizations and parties that foster racial hatred encourage such hate crimes. Hostility towards Asian Muslims, in particular, has increased since the terrorist attacks on the World Trade Center in New York in 2001, the Madrid train bombings in 2004, the London underground bombings of July 2005, and the Glasgow airport bombing of 2007. 'Muslim' and 'terrorist' have become almost interchangeable terms, so far as many people are concerned. Racist organizations are able to use this suspicion of Muslims to justify hate crimes against Asians. The response of the British government to this has been to propose new legislation that would extend existing legislation and make incitement to religious hatred into a crime. At the same time, however, new official policies have targeted Muslim communities and individuals as 'problems', requiring discriminatory practices such as the stopping and searching of Asians on the street and at railway stations.

Antagonism and violence reflect the persistence of segregation in housing and employment, and political mobilization within ethnic minority communities has been associated with a growth in both residential and educational segregation.

Members of ethnic minorities are heavily represented in marginal, insecure, and low-paid jobs, and their rates of unemployment are especially high. This is especially marked for those of African, Pakistani, and Bangladeshi origin, though much less so for the Chinese, and especially Chinese women (Mason 2000: Table 5.4). Their difficulties in entering the mainstream of the labour market have led them to take up forms of self-employment in great numbers. The most significant area of self-employment has been the involvement of large numbers of South Asian families in retailing, catering, and hotels. Research has shown, however, that these businesses find it more difficult to raise capital and are less profitable than comparable white businesses.

> ➔ *Connections*
> We review the wider issues of ethnic inequality and division in Chapter 9 on education, Chapter 17 on work, and Chapter 18 on inequality. A very useful summary can be found in Mason (2000: chs. 5 and 6).

These economic disadvantages are reflected in the relatively great educational disadvantages of ethnic minorities. It is true that ethnic minorities have a higher participation rate in education after the age of 16, and that young Chinese, East African Asians, and Indians have particularly high levels of qualification, but this is not the case for all ethnic minorities. There is much evidence that these findings do not hold for the parental generation, while research on the schooling of those below the age of 16 has shown the considerable underachievement of most ethnic minorities. This underachievement reflects, in part, their social-class background (Troyna and Carrington 1990). However, it is also due to stereotyping by their (white) teachers, whose expectations about the relative performance of white and ethnic-minority pupils tend to produce the very results they anticipate. Even where, as is generally the case, teachers are liberal in their attitudes and show no intention to discriminate, the judgements they make about the likely performance of different groups of students have a major impact on their actual performance.

This is one of the reasons for the growing tendency towards educational segregation. Dissatisfaction with the schooling of their children has led many ethnic-minority parents to support the establishment of evening and Saturday schools and of separate 'faith' day schools. Some Muslim groups, for example, have exercised their right to 'opt out' of local-authority schools and to set up grant-maintained schools along the lines of the long-established Catholic schools. As a result, many neighbourhood schools are dominated by particular ethnic minorities.

As well as a segregation of white and ethnic-minority housing, there is a degree of segregation among the ethnic minorities themselves. For example, Bangladeshis predominate in Spitalfields, East London, while Mirpuris from Kashmir predominate in Bradford. Segregation by school is also shaped by the housing patterns found among ethnic minorities. As we have shown, ethnic-minority settlement has been concentrated in particular localities. In Bradford, where many schools are almost 100 per cent Asian and others are exclusively white, the first voluntary-aided Muslim school for girls has been established. A number of private Muslim schools have been opened in Paris since 1994, reflecting the concentration of Arab families in the north-eastern suburbs of Seine-Saint-Denis.

Racial antagonism and segregation do not mean that there is no communication or sharing of concerns. The essence of hybridity is that identities are constructed from a variety of often contradictory sources. In a study of Deptford, South London, Les Back (1996) has shown this in the construction of white identity. Deptford is a riverside district where residents have long relied on the dock trades and metal working for employment. It sustained the class consciousness of a cohesive working-class community into the 1950s, after which this was undermined by economic decline. Like Brixton, it was an area of migrant settlement for people from the West Indies, who were attracted by its relatively cheap housing. The white residents of the predominantly white estate studied by Back were very hostile towards the black tenants, whom they

---

Global focus Racism   6.12

We have concentrated on describing patterns of ethnic disadvantage and racialization in the United States and Britain, but these patterns actually vary from society to society. White discrimination on the grounds of ethnicity is almost universal, but its extent and its consequences differ.

In France, colonialism has had a major influence. The French state sought to integrate its colonial territories into a single political system, giving colonial populations full citizenship status in France itself. Nevertheless, the common framework of European racism had an influence, and French writers, such as Gobineau, were central to the construction of racial theories. Today, skin colour and national origin still divide people, despite their formal equality of citizenship. High levels of immigration have led to a situation where around a quarter of the French population has origins overseas. Many of these migrants came from North Africa and the Middle East, making Islam the country's second biggest religion, and there is a high level of racist feeling among the white population, as there had been against the Jews in the past. The French government has sought to minimize the visibility of ethnic minorities by banning the wearing of religious symbols, such as the Muslim headscarf, in schools,

but this has fuelled fears that the state itself is pursuing racist policies.

It might be expected that this would be different in the former colonies themselves. Brazil—formerly a colony of Portugal—has a highly diverse population and appears to be highly egalitarian. There is, nevertheless, prejudice and discrimination against those of African origin, whose ancestors arrived in the country as slaves. The inheritance from the slave period remains strong, despite the myth of racial equality. In many situations there is a fine shading of distinction according to the shading of skin colour. South Africa—colonized by the Dutch and the British—had an entrenched system of apartheid (we discuss this in Chapter 19, p. XXX). Under the new multiracial state established initially under the presidency of Nelson Mandela, the political and economic rights of blacks have improved, and there has been little racism of blacks against the white former rulers. A Peace and Reconciliation Commission was established in South Africa as a way of bringing the violence and aggression of apartheid into the open, but in a non-confrontational and non-punitive context.

➲ For further information, see Fagin and Batur (2004).

saw as being responsible for a decline and loss of community. This hostility was expressed in a growth in right-wing racism and electoral support for the National Front.

Among the young white people studied by Back, however, there was a great enthusiasm for many aspects of black culture. Features of black music, masculinity, and 'hardness' were all taken up by the white lads. Reggae, hip hop, and rap music, for example, became important elements in their musical culture. At the same time, however, white lads were involved in a national discourse in which racialized images of black criminals and problem families figured prominently, creating an ambiguity and ambivalence over their own cultural borrowings. Everyday language and culture, Back argues, is necessarily syncretic, as people always forge new symbolic systems out of old and inconsistent elements:

> ... a syncretic working-class youth culture develops that is neither black nor white but somehow a celebration of shared experience. This constitutes a volatile working-class ethnicity that draws on a rich mixture of South London, African-American and Caribbean symbols.

Back 1996: 98

This hybrid sense of identity allows great flexibility about who can be included and who excluded. The boundaries of racial inclusion are constantly shifting, depending on the particular situation and the perceived salience of particular cultural elements. In some situations, collective identities will include both black and white together, while in other situations black youths will be excluded.

The hybridity of ethnic identities emphasizes the need to avoid any *essentialist* concept of ethnic identity. It is not only such all-embracing categories as 'black' and 'white' that imply a fixed and essential identity: all descriptions of identity, if taken as anything other than situationally specific descriptions, invoke an unchanging and inflexible essence. People will describe themselves as 'Asian', 'Muslim', or 'Bangladeshi', depending on the situation they are in and the purposes for which they are describing themselves. No person is 'really' and only 'Bangladeshi', for example. Apparently fixed identities are products of specific narratives of identity and are often tied to particular political projects and patterns of alliance. In the contemporary world, such narratives are difficult to maintain. The differences that separate groups must be constantly addressed if a common identity is to be sustained, and the cultural elements that they must combine and recombine may be incompatible. Thus, a collective identity is always in process of formation and is never finally formed (S. Hall 1992).

The challenge to institutional racism

We have looked a great deal at how racist attitudes have grown and have generated many of the patterns of

disadvantage and exclusion described. However, it is not simply a question of attitudes and ideas. Systematic disadvantage can occur as a result of the ways in which institutions operate. Institutions may operate through routines and practices quite different from the attitudes and preferences of those who occupy positions within them. Discriminating practices may result from prejudiced attitudes, but they may also result from institutional processes overseen by people who espouse tolerant and unbiased ideas. This is the central insight behind the concept of institutional racism that we discussed earlier (p. 215).

Institutional racism has come to the fore in Britain as a result of the Macpherson Report on the handling of a controversial murder case by the Metropolitan Police. In his report, Sir William Macpherson (1999: 6.34) argues that institutional racism is:

> ... the collective failure of an organization to provide an appropriate and professional service to people because of their colour, culture, or ethnic origin. It can be seen or detected through unwitting prejudice, ignorance, thoughtlessness and racist stereotyping which disadvantage minority ethnic people.

Is everyone in Britain racist?

© Alice Chadwick

Macpherson's inquiry was set up by the government in response to criticisms of the ways the criminal justice system responded to the murder of Stephen Lawrence, a young black man. In April 1993, Stephen was assaulted and then murdered by a gang of white youths at a south London bus stop. The police were on the scene within five minutes, and they received a number of tip-offs about who was responsible. There was little momentum to the police enquiries, however, and charges against two youths were dropped for lack of sufficient evidence. Stephen's parents launched a private prosecution a year later, frustrated at the response of the police. After two years, however, the private prosecution had to be withdrawn when identification evidence was ruled inadmissible. It seemed as if the investigation had got nowhere, though many people believed that they knew who was responsible. In February 1997, therefore, the *Daily Mail* carried front-page photographs of five young men that it labelled as 'murderers'. As of 2010, there had still been no convictions in the case.

Public outcry at the handling of the case—even the Head of the Metropolitan Police Murder Squad eventually admitted that he did not know the law relating to his own powers of arrest—led the Police Complaints Authority to set up an internal investigation, while the government asked Sir William Macpherson to carry out an independent, external inquiry. The Police Complaints Authority report was published first in December 1997, and concluded that the police operation had been well organized and that there was no evidence of any racist conduct on the part of police officers. The Macpherson inquiry, however, took almost two years, publishing its final report in 1999. Prior to the publication of the report, senior police officers were aware of what was going to be recommended and they followed a public-relations strategy aimed at countering its central tenets. The Assistant Police Commissioner for London apologized to the Lawrence family in mid-1998, while the Commissioner himself also acknowledged 'our failure' to respond properly.

There has, clearly, been much dispute over the politics of institutional racism, but the sociological importance of the concept is undeniable. Sociological analysis shows that social institutions are major determinants of people's actions and that these actions cannot be explained in terms of individual attributes alone—no matter how widely shared. The importance of the concept of institutional racism, like any other process of institutional constraint, is that it shows that social exclusion and disadvantage cannot be changed by policies that are concerned with prejudice alone: direct institutional reforms are needed as well.

Macpherson's specific point was that the normal operating procedures of the police force systematically worked against the interests of non-whites and that this sustained and reinforced the overt racism that was also present in the police. The force must, therefore, reform its practices as well as attack racism and prejudice. A particular practice highlighted in the report was stop-and-search, where black people are far more likely to be singled out for investigation, but other areas included the recruitment and promotion policies that result in small numbers of black and Asian police officers, especially at senior levels.

As a result of the report, the Race Relations Act was extended to the whole of the public sector, which had previously been exempt from parts of the Act. This highlighted the fact that institutional racism is not confined to the police but is a feature of many of the central institutions, public and private, in contemporary societies. It has been argued, for example, that Home Office immigration procedures and the arrangements for dealing with asylum-seekers have racist consequences. It has been shown that ethnic-minority doctors are less likely to get promoted to consultant grade in hospitals, and they are likely to work in less popular specialisms and badly funded hospitals. Similar issues arise over the appointment and promotion of teachers in schools and universities. Institutional racism in schools, it has been claimed, is responsible for the poor performance of many ethnic-minority children. Policies aimed at racial-awareness training and equal-opportunities training have been introduced in many public-sector, and some private-sector, organizations in an attempt to counter this institutional racism.

 Stop and reflect

In this section we have looked at the patterns of community relations that followed from colonial migration to Britain.

- Colonial migrants have been forced to live in poor, overcrowded housing in declining areas.
- Housing segregation produces misunderstanding and is the basis for hostility and conflict.

We also reviewed trends in ethnic relations in the United States:

- White migrants have not abandoned their sense of national identity when adopting an American one.
- African Americans have continued to be excluded from full participation in American society, and the racialized division between black and white has sharpened.

- The movement of relatively affluent African Americans to the suburbs has left a poor and heavily disadvantaged section in the ghettos.

- Do you think it is useful to talk about heavily disadvantaged African Americans as an 'underclass'?

In the sphere of race policy we have identified the importance of a clash between the liberal idea of equal citizenship and conservative racism:

- Official policy in Britain and the United States has emphasized the ideal of the assimilation of ethnic minorities into mainstream culture.

- There has been a growth of racism since the 1960s, undermining the model of the ethnic melting pot.

- Is it correct to see racialized disadvantage as reflecting institutional racism as well as overt prejudice?

Key concepts

- assimilation 202
- diaspora 194
- ethnicity 194
- hybridity 200

- institutional racism 195
- melting pot 197
- multiculturalism 217
- race 194

- racialization 195
- racism 195
- racist discourse 195
- xenophobia 218

Workshop 6

Study 6 The art of being black

In *The Art of Being Black* (1996), Claire Alexander explored the ways in which young black Britons construct their cultural identities. She recognized that common cultural representations of black youths saw them in stereotypical terms drawn from cultural imagery of the black mugger, the Rastafarian drug dealer, and the rioter. Such labelling of them as 'problems' led to their high levels of alienation from mainstream white society. Her particular concern was to highlight the strengths and the ambiguities that are generated in black youth as they interpret their lived experiences in terms of specific representations of community, class, masculinity, and leisure. Black youths are affected by the labels imposed on them, they draw on their own cultural inheritance, and they interpret all these through their own lived experience of disadvantage and oppression to produce their characteristic outlook on life and sense of identity. Her particular concern was how terms of identity articulated with conceptions of masculinity that were sustained through peer groups and involved distinctive attitudes towards women.

Alexander sees ethnic identity not simply as a label, but as a mode of being. People perform or present their identities through the particular and distinctive ways in which they act. Ethnic identities, therefore, are fluid and shifting, varying according to the particular situations in which people find themselves.

The method that Alexander employed was twelve months of participant observation among groups of young black Londoners in east, north-west, and west London. She studied them at home, at work, and during their leisure-time activities. Her aim was to act, as far as possible, as 'one of the boys'. You might spot some immediate problems in this research strategy: Alexander is a young woman of British Asian descent studying African Caribbean young men through participant observation. Look back at our discussion of participant observation in Chapter 3, pp. 81–4, and see if you can identify the particular problems that she might have faced. Look at Alexander's own account and see how she addresses these issues.

Alexander's account provides a useful way of approaching the issues that we ask you to consider in Media watch 6. In particular she asks questions about being both 'black' and 'British'. What does her approach tell us about the imposition of official categories in censuses and surveys?

Media watch 6 Black and white answers

In the summer of 2005, some Asian community leaders asked the government to introduce US-style hyphenated terms of ethnic identity, such as Asian-British or Indian-British, for official purposes. This, it was held, would help to recognize the complexity of ethnic identity. The political commentator Yasmin Alibhai-Brown supported this idea, saying that it would allow people to show pride in their ethnic roots and in their status as a Briton. The Conservative home affairs spokesman countered that Asian British people in his constituency regarded themselves as British and that 'they don't need a government minister to tell them how to describe themselves' (http://news.bbc.co.uk/1/hi/uk/4130594.stm). This debate followed hard on the London tube and bus bombings of July 2005, which fed a growing climate of concern over 'Muslim' or 'Islamic' terrorists and their supposed links with the British Asian communities. The then-leader of the Conservative Party, Michael Howard, held that the bombings had fundamentally changed the context in which issues of identity and multiculturalism had to be discussed. He argued, however, that 'most people in this country want to share a strong sense of British identity while recognising that this is not incompatible with a continuing attachment to other traditions' (*Guardian*, 17 August 2005).

Any term of ethnic identity is likely to be open to dispute. This problem is especially marked when observers and participants try to use an inclusive label referring to all or a large number of separate ethnic minorities. This is most obvious with the derogatory terms used by members of a majority to describe a minority, and many terms eventually acquire derogatory overtones. This is the case, for example, with 'Negro', which was once used, in both the United States and Britain, as a neutral, descriptive term. The London bombings gave the term 'Muslim' new, and negative, meanings among many members of the white majority. Deciding on an appropriate category is particularly problematic when labels are politically contested. Many African, Caribbean, and Asian people in Britain, for example, have used the word 'black' to describe themselves as a single, racialized category. Other members of the ethnic minorities, however, challenge this usage on the grounds of the political and cultural differences that are felt to distinguish them from each other. In the United States, the term 'black' was perceived as having many negative connotations, and the term 'of colour' was preferred as a generic label for non-white minorities, though this, too, has been challenged from within the minority communities.

This same problem applies to majority groups as well. The term 'white', for example, is not routinely employed by all members of the ethnic majority in Britain and the United States, and it is a term that may be embraced by some ethnic minorities who seek to align themselves with the majority rather than a minority.

- In this book, we have tried to use the most appropriate term for the contexts and situations that we are dealing with, though it is unlikely that we have ever been able to use completely neutral terms. Turn to our discussion of Weber's ideas on value relevance and value freedom (Chapter 2, p. 38) and see what this suggests about the possibility of objective and neutral descriptions.

- You might find it informative to discuss this issue of ethnic identity with friends to see if their preferred labels of identity correspond to those that you would have predicted.

Discussion points

Discourse, science, and ideology

We have looked at a number of issues around the construction of racial ideas and their legitimation through science. While there is no basis to conventional ideas of race, racial thought has often sought a scientific grounding.

- Make sure that you understand the differences between the ideas of ethnic identity and ethnic origin. Which is the most useful in sociological analysis?

- Search the Web for information about the following and their race policies: British National Party, National Socialism, Nation of Islam, Ku Klux Klan, Conservative Party, Anti-Nazi League, Anti-Racist Alliance.

- Is there any acceptable biological meaning that can be given to the concept of race?

Racism, citizenship, and exclusion

Policy and political practices have been shaped by liberal ideas of citizenship and contradictory racist ideas. Patterns of inclusion and exclusion reflect the clash between these two sets of ideas.

- Make sure that you are clear about the meaning of prejudice, discrimination, and disadvantage as they apply in the field of ethnic relations. How would you distinguish between racism and institutional racism?

- Ethnic relations used to be seen in terms of a model of the 'assimilation' of minorities into a majority society. How do contemporary ideas of 'multiculturalism' differ from this?

Colonialism, migration, and conflict

The global context of race and ethnic relations is critically important. We looked at the impact of colonial structures on slavery and on migration from colonial to imperial centres. The historical inheritance is a major influence on contemporary patterns of power and conflict.

- How useful is it to see contemporary patterns of migration in terms of the claims of 'asylum-seekers'? Is this an advance over earlier views of them as 'immigrants'?
- To what extent do contemporary ethnic-relations issues result from the experience of colonialism and empire?

Explore further

Banton, M., and Harwood, J. (1975), *The Race Concept* (Newton Abbott: David and Charles). *A very useful overview of the history of racial ideas. Now partly superseded by the second edition of Banton's* Racial Theories (Cambridge: Cambridge University Press, 2000).

Mason, D. (2000), *Race and Ethnicity in Modern Britain* (2nd edn., Oxford: Oxford University Press). *A very useful and well-written general text.*

Modood, T., Berthoud, R., Lakey, J., Nazroo, J., Smith, P., Virdee, S., and Beishan, S. (1997), *Ethnic Minorities in Britain: Diversity and Disadvantage* (London: Policy Studies Institute). *A classic empirical study with much useful information.*

Schaefer, R. T. (2008) (ed.), *Encyclopedia of Race, Ethnicity, and Society* (New York: Sage). *A useful general source.*

Online resources

Visit the Online Resource Centre that accompanies this book to access more learning resources and other interesting material on racial and ethnic identities at:
www.oxfordtextbooks.co.uk/orc/fulcher4e/

Useful overview sites for these issues are the government's Equality and Human Rights Commission at:
www.equalityhumanrights.com

and the privately financed Runnymede Trust at:
www.runnymedetrust.org

The major academic point of reference for race and ethnic relations research is the website of the Centre for Research in Ethnic Relations at Warwick University:
www.warwick.ac.uk/fac/soc/CRER_RC

The global flow of refugees can be tracked through the United States State Department site:
www.state.gov/g/prm

However, you should also consult Human Rights Watch for impartial reporting on repression and rights problems at:
www.hrw.org

Crime and Deviance

Contents

Mobile crime

Mobile phone theft increased into the early years of the century, but is now claimed to be decreasing. The increase occurred because phones are small and easily portable, they are much in demand, and so could easily be sold on at a considerable profit. Around three-quarters of a million mobile phones were stolen each year and mobile phone theft accounted for 45 per cent of all crime on the London Underground. Two-thirds of the stolen phones were taken from young people aged between 11 and 15. Almost 12 per cent of young people in Britain's inner cities were likely to be victims of such crimes, most of which were also committed by young people. Police statistics suggested that the typical offender was aged 14–17 and was male, black, and worked as part of a gang.

At the end of 2003 the Home Office launched a new National Mobile Phone Crime Unit specifically to counter the growth in this crime. New security measures were introduced to make it far more difficult to re-program stolen phones, and the government announced that the level of phone theft had fallen dramatically. However, research shows that theft of MP3 players—increasingly integrated with phones—has meant that theft figures have continued to rise. Innovations in design and technology have fuelled demand and, therefore, crime.

Sources: http://rds.homeoffice.gov.uk/rds/pdfs/hors235.pdf; *Social Trends* (2008: figure 9.4). See also www.telegraph.co.uk, 24 January 2009; search for 'Children fall victim to phone theft'.

Many are likely to be victims of crime at some time in their lives: phone theft, car theft, domestic burglary, or, in extreme cases, a rape or murder. Many who do not become victims—and some who do—will be the perpetrators of crime. Some crime seems to be carried out as part of a long-term profession of crime. Much crime recently seems to have been motivated by drug use and the need to purchase illegal drugs. At the same time, growing numbers of people, including many young people, are likely to be involved in fairly regular drug use, even if they do not commit other types of offence.

How can this growth in criminality and deviance be understood, and is it possible to explain how some people identify with their deviant acts and see themselves and are seen by others as criminals, drug-users, and so on? In this chapter we look at various forms of deviant behaviour and how they are shaped by the criminal law and informal social relations. We ask how reliable the evidence on deviance can be when it is produced by these very forces of social control: to what extent, for example, can we put our trust in the apparent facts about mobile phone theft reported above?

Concepts and theories

Deviance is nonconformity with social norms or expectations. The word 'deviance' is often used only in relation to moral, religious, or political norms. The 'deviant' is seen as someone whose behaviour departs from normal moral standards (for example, those concerned with sexual behaviour), or who deviates from a political or religious orthodoxy. The sociological concept of deviance, however, takes a broader point of view and recognizes deviation from social norms of all kinds.

Along with sexual deviants, political deviants, and religious deviants must be counted those whose behaviour runs counter to legal or customary norms more generally—criminals, the mentally ill, alcoholics, and many others. What makes these people deviant is not

necessary to take account of processes of socialization. The second level of explanation concerns the variation in norms between social groups, as manifested particularly in cultural and subcultural differences. Socialization takes place within particular social groups, and it is the norms of these groups that provide the standards for identifying particular kinds of behaviour as deviant. The third, and final, level of explanation concerns the ways in which particular individuals are identified as deviants by others and so come to develop a deviant identity. This is a matter of social reaction and control.

In the rest of this section we will outline some of the general processes involved in deviance and control and the processes common to a range of deviant and conformist identities. You may like to read this through fairly quickly, not worrying about all the details, and then go on to our discussion of specific forms of deviance in the following sections. When you have read one or two of these sections, return to this general discussion of deviance and control and try to work through its details.

Primary and secondary deviation

Two key concepts in the study of deviance are primary deviation and secondary deviation, first systematized by Lemert (1967). **Primary deviation** is the object of the first two levels of explanation identified above. It is behaviour that runs counter to the normative expectations of a group, and is recognized as deviant behaviour by its members, but that is 'normalized' by them. That is to say, it is tolerated or indulged as an allowable or permissible departure from what is normally expected. It is ignored or treated in a low-key way that defines it as an exceptional, atypical, or insignificant aberration on the part of an otherwise normal person.

This **normalization** of deviant behaviour defines it as something marginal to the identity of the deviator. Many justifications for the normalization of deviant behaviour may be employed: a man is aggressive because he is 'under stress' at work, a woman behaves oddly because it is 'that time of the month', a child is naughty because he or she is 'overtired', an elderly woman steals from a supermarket because she is 'confused', a middle-aged man exposes himself in public because he has a 'blackout' and 'did not know what came over him', and so on.

What Lemert calls **secondary deviation**, or deviance proper, is the object of our third level of explanation. It arises when the perceived deviation is no longer normalized and is, instead, stigmatized or punished in some way. The social reaction and its consequences become central features of the deviator's day-to-day experiences and so shape future actions. When public opinion, law-enforcement agencies (police, courts, and tribunals), or administrative controls exercised by the welfare and other official agencies react in an overt and punitive way, their reaction

labels the person as a deviant of some kind (a thief, a welfare fraudster, a junkie, and so on). This labelling stigmatizes the behaviour and the person, who must now try to cope with the consequences of the stigma (see Box 7.2).

Stigmatization may involve the rejection, degradation, exclusion, incarceration, or coercion of the deviant, who becomes the object of treatment, punishment, or conversion (Schur 1971). Those who are stigmatized find that their lives and identities come to be organized around their deviance. They may even come to see themselves as a deviant—as a 'thief', as 'mentally ill', and so on—taking on many of the stigmatizing attributes of the popular and official imagery. Even if the deviator rejects this identity, the fact that he or she is identified in this way by others becomes an important factor in determining future behaviour.

The development of secondary deviation may, initially, involve an acceptance of the negative, stigmatizing stereotypes that others hold of the deviant. However, deviants may often be able to construct a more positive image of their deviance and build an identity around a rejection of the stigma. They accept the label, but, instead of merely reflecting back the public stereotype, they construct an alternative view that reflects their own experiences and those of people like them. They construct accounts—narratives—of their coming to be the kind of people they are, and these narratives become central features of the construction and reconstruction of their identity (Plummer 1995: ch. 2). In much the same way that the Black Power movement constructed more positive images of black identity, so such movements as Gay Pride have led to the construction of positive images of homosexuality.

Not all deviance results from the conversion of primary deviation into secondary deviation through an external social reaction. Deviators may, for example, escape the attention of those who might label them, remaining 'secret deviants'. Such people may, nevertheless, move into secondary deviation precisely because of their attempts to keep their deviant behaviour secret. By *anticipating* the reactions of others, they begin to act towards themselves in terms of the stigmatized deviant identity, even if they do not embrace this identity themselves. A gay man who fears possible negative reaction from others may become drawn into closer association with other gay people because the risks of his inadvertent exposure as gay in other social situations are too great.

There is also the possibility of false accusation. Someone who has not violated expectations may, nevertheless, be labelled as a deviant and processed accordingly. Such people will experience many of the same consequences as those who have been correctly labelled. Although they may feel a sense of injustice about their wrongful accusation, they may, as a result of their experience of stigmatization, come to act in ways that are quite indistinguishable from other deviants. Such highly publicized cases of wrongful imprisonment for terrorist bombings as those of the Birmingham Six and the Guildford Four highlight the more general situation of false accusation that is apparent in, for example, the child who is wrongly punished by a teacher for cheating or the political dissidents in the Soviet Union who were officially designated as mentally ill.

Primary deviation that is not normalized does not always result in secondary deviation or commitment to a deviant identity. Many people **drift** in and out of deviant behaviour without being committed to it at all (Matza 1964). Because they are not committed to their deviant acts—they do not see them as a fundamental expression of their identity—they are able to abandon them whenever they choose, or when the circumstances are not right. Conversely, of course, they may feel able—though not required—to deviate whenever the opportunity and the inclination are present. Drift, then, is an important aspect of the structuring of deviant behaviour. Matza suggests, for example, that juvenile delinquency rarely becomes a matter of secondary deviation, precisely because juveniles drift back and forth between deviant and conformist behaviour without ever becoming committed to delinquency as a way of life.

Many of those who become involved in crime do not embrace a deviant identity—they do not see themselves as criminals, burglars, or housebreakers. Rather, they see their involvement in criminal activities as an aspect of the larger social situation in which they find themselves. They may, for example, be long-term unemployed, in serious financial hardship, and faced with the opportunity of illegal gain. Such people drift into crime for situational reasons, and become secondary deviants only if they are unable to drift out again. Certain opportunities may be denied to them, while other courses of action become easier. They become secondary deviants if the whole structure of interests within which they act—the advantages and disadvantages, rewards and punishments—tend to force

them into continued deviance. Those who have been imprisoned for theft or burglary, for example, may experience restricted employment and promotion opportunities in the outside world that make it difficult for them to abandon their criminal life and to enter or re-enter conventional occupations.

Where people do take on a deviant identity, however, their behaviour will be shaped by commitment as well as constraint. Those who have become committed to a deviant identity will be committed to a whole range of behaviours associated with that identity. These ways of behaving will seem more 'natural' to them than any others, and they will identify with the behaviours as much as with the label itself. Commitment and constraint generally operate together: a firmly committed deviant is more likely to face disadvantaged opportunities, and a tightly constrained deviant is more likely to feel a sense of difference from others. If their circumstances change, and these constraints alter, they may find it possible to drift out of crime once more.

Deviant roles and careers

Where deviance becomes a central feature of a person's identity and way of life, it may take the form of role deviance. This occurs if a person's activities become organized into a distinct and recognizable social role to which particular normative expectations are attached. The deviant is expected to act in deviant ways: conformity to these role expectations confirms the person's deviant identity! For example, male homosexuals were in the recent past widely expected to behave in 'effeminate' ways, and one who conformed to these expectations had thereby adopted the public, stereotyped, homosexual role.

Deviant roles, like conformist roles, often have a career structure. This is most likely where the role is defined within a group of deviants, rather than by public stereotypes alone. Where the deviant role involves a particular sequence of events and experiences that are common for all its occupants, role deviance becomes what has been called **career deviance**. This may be highly formalized, paralleling the kinds of career structures found in conventional occupations. Full-time thieves, for example, may be members of teams that make their living from their deviance and have their own internal structures of leadership, reward, and promotion (Sutherland 1937).

When organized as career deviance, the deviant role is likely also to involve what Goffman (1961b) has called a moral career. This term describes the internal or personal aspects of a career, the specific sequence of learning experiences and changes in conceptions of self and identity that occur as people follow their deviant career. It is a process through which people come to terms with their stigma and their commitment to a deviant identity. With each phase of the public career associated with the role, its occupants must reconsider their past in an attempt to make sense of their new experiences. They single out and elaborate, with the benefit of hindsight, those experiences they believe can account for and legitimate their present situation. This is a continuous process in which their personal biography—their life story—is constantly constructed and reconstructed in the light of their changing circumstances.

Deviant groups and communities

Career deviants are likely to become involved with groups that support and sustain their identities and help them to come to terms with the constrained opportunities they face. Gangs and cliques are formed, clubs and pubs are colonized as meeting places, and organizations and agencies are set up to promote shared interests or political goals. With advances in technology, new forms of support and communication become possible. The spread of the telephone allowed people to maintain distant communication far more effectively than was possible through writing letters, and computer technology now allows global communication through e-mail and social networking websites. Those who are involved in two or more of these groups will tie them into larger social networks that bond the groups into cohesive and solidaristic communities with a shared sense of identity.

Criminal gangs, for example, may be involved in localized networks of recruitment and mutual support, to which individual criminals and juvenile gangs may also be attached. These networks form subcultures of crime that comprise an underworld. The subcultures are means through which skills and techniques can be learned and in which criminals can obtain a degree of acceptance and recognition that is denied to them by conventional groups.

Goffman (1963*b*) has argued that the groups of 'sympathetic others' that form the supportive subcultures of deviance comprise two distinct types of people: the own and the wise. The **own** are those who share the deviant identity. They have a common understanding of stigmatization from their personal experiences, and they may be able to help in acquiring the tricks of the trade that allow a deviant to operate more effectively, as well as by providing emotional support and company in which a deviant can feel at home. The own help people to organize a life around their deviance and to cope with many of the disadvantages that they experience.

The **wise**, on the other hand, are 'normals' who have a particular reason for being in the know about the secret life of the deviants and for being sympathetic towards it. They are accepted by the deviants and are allowed a kind of associate membership in their activities. They are those for whom the deviants do not feel the need to put on a show of normality or deviance disavowal: they can safely engage in back-region activities with them. The wise may include family members and friends, employees, and even some control agents (such as nurses or police) who have day-to-day contact with them. The own and the wise together form a network of contacts and connections that support deviants in the construction of their narratives of identity.

Some of the wise may actively support deviants in sustaining their deviance, though there are limits to the willingness of people to become too closely involved in activities where the stigma of deviance is likely to 'rub off' on them. Active support, then, is most likely to come from the own, and this is particularly true where there is a need for representatives to speak or act for their interests and concerns in public. Such representatives may sometimes become very active and make a living—and a new identity—out of their role as spokespersons for particular deviant groups. They make a 'profession' of their deviance in quite a novel way, perhaps appearing in the press and on

Figure 7.1 The deviant career

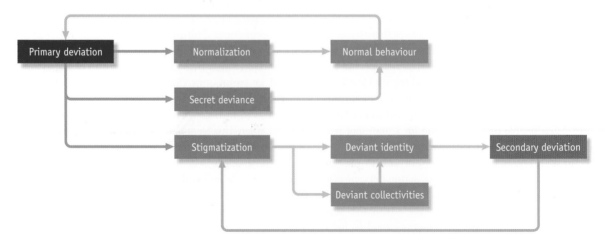

Embracing alternative identities at Gay Pride.

© Getty Images/Joe Raedle

> **➲ Connections**
>
> Look back at our discussion of Goffman's work on self-presentation in 'Symbolic interactionism', Chapter 4, pp. 122–5. You might check, in particular, our discussion of what he called 'front regions' and 'back regions'.

radio and television whenever issues of concern are discussed. There are, of course, limits to this. Only certain forms of deviance are allowed to have the legitimacy of their stigmatization debated in public. Gays and the mentally ill, for example, have active and important organizations that can lobby for their interests, while thieves and burglars do not. Pressure groups on behalf of those involved in serious crime are, for the most part, limited to campaigns for prison reform and are led by the wise and by reformed offenders.

The general account of deviance and control that we have presented (summarized in Figure 7.1) must be treated with caution, as all its elements will not apply equally to every case of deviance and stigmatized identity. It is a general framework that provides the concepts that can sensitize researchers to the specific issues that occur in particular cases. We will illustrate this by considering a number of forms of criminal behaviour. In the following chapter we will show that certain aspects of illness can also be understood as forms of deviance.

Stop and reflect

In this section we have looked at the relationship between biological and social factors in the explanation of deviance and the formation of deviant identities. In reviewing our discussion of biology and deviance, you may like to look back to our discussion of the biology of race in Chapter 6, pp. 199–200. The main points we made in this section were:

- Early approaches to deviance drew on now-discredited evolutionary ideas. Lombroso, for example, saw 'born criminals' as 'atavistic' evolutionary forms.

- Deviance is never a purely biological fact. It depends on an act of social definition, of labelling.

- Does the labelling argument imply that biological conditions—such as genetic inheritance—are never relevant to criminality?

In considering the nature of the social reaction to deviance and its consequences, we showed that:

- It is important to distinguish between primary and secondary deviation.

- Many people drift in and out of deviance without becoming committed to it.

- Much deviation is normalized, but some is stigmatized. Stigmatized secondary deviation may involve role deviance and a deviant career.

- How useful is it to think of deviance as a 'career'?

- Deviant groups and communities are important in supporting and sustaining role deviance.

Crime and legal control

Crime is the form of deviance that involves an infraction of the criminal law. Not all laws are 'criminal'. Lawyers recognize civil law, constitutional law, and various other categories of legal norm.

Civil law, for example, concerns relations among private individuals, such as the contractual relations involved in employment and consumer purchasing. A person who breaks a contract by, say, unfairly dismissing someone from her or his job or failing to supply goods that are 'fit for their purpose' has infringed the civil law, and action can be taken only by the particular individual affected (the dismissed person or the unhappy consumer). The police have no right to become involved, and a completely separate system of courts is involved in hearing any civil case. The outcome of a successful civil case is some kind of 'restitution', such as financial compensation or 'damages'.

The criminal law, by contrast, consists of legal norms that have been established by the state as a *public* responsibility, and that the police and the criminal courts have been designated to enforce. Someone who infringes the criminal law can be arrested, charged, and tried at public expense and, if found guilty, will be subject to repressive or punitive penalties such as a fine or imprisonment.

The criminal law can cover a wide range of actions. It may cover such acts as driving above the legal speed limit, stealing a car, breaking into a house, possessing certain drugs, forging a signature on a cheque, murdering someone, and arson. Penalties attached to these offences range from small fines for speeding to life imprisonment for murder, and, in Britain until 1998, execution for treason. The most visible crimes and those perceived to be the most threatening do not necessarily have the greatest impact in real terms. In practice, many minor crimes are normalized: few people report cases of speeding or dropping litter, and the police may often choose to disregard such offences.

Figure 7.2 shows the main types of serious offence (officially termed 'notifiable offences') recorded in the criminal statistics for England and Wales. The official statistics for an earlier period show that recorded crime had risen between 1981 and 2001, but rates then fell between 2002 and 2009. Car crime, robberies, and burglaries all fell sharply between 2008 and 2009. The murder rate for England and Wales fell to its lowest level since the end of the 1980s.

Further evidence on the extent of crime can be drawn from the British Crime Survey (see Box 7.3), which collects evidence from a sample survey of the general public. This annual survey of victims and potential victims has shown a fall in the amount of crime since 1995. Both vehicle crime and burglary have fallen by over a half, while violent crime has fallen by 43 per cent. The chances of being a victim of crime has fallen by 40 per cent since 1995 to reach the lowest levels in 2010 since 1981. Young men, however, are far

Figure 7.2 Recorded crime in England and Wales, 2002–2009

Offence	2002/3	2008/9
Theft	1,336,924	1,080,655
Burglary	890,099	581,397
Criminal damage	1,120,610	936,729
Violence against the person	845,078	903,993
Fraud and forgery	331,098	163,283
Robbery	110,271	80,104
Sexual offences	58,890	51,488
Drug offences	143,320	242,907
Offences against vehicles	1,074,659	592,117
Criminal damage	1,120,610	936,729
Miscellaneous	64,011	71,141
Total	5,974,960	4,702,468

Source: www.homeoffice.gov.uk/rds/recordedcrime1.html.

more likely to be a victim of crime, while relatively few of those aged over 65 have been victims. People's attitudes, however, reflected the official statistics and their reporting in the media, with 61 per cent of people believing that crime had risen in the country as a whole.

Government policy on minor crime and delinquency in Britain has recently centred around the issue of 'anti-social behaviour' and a 'respect' agenda. This is based on the idea that the low-level criminality and nuisance behaviour that upsets people on a day-to-day basis—petty vandalism, rudeness, drunkenness—should be dealt with through local communities themselves, by inculcating a climate of respect towards other people's property. Improving discipline in schools, for example, is seen as a way of

THEORY AND METHODS   **7.3**
· ·

The British Crime Survey

The British Crime Survey is an annual survey carried out, since 1982, by academic researchers, but financed by the government. It is a survey involving 50,000 interviewees in England and Wales. Preliminary results are published using about a quarter of the interviews, and the full results are published a year later. You will find the British Crime Survey at: www.homeoffice.gov.uk/rds/ bcs1.html.

❷ Why do you think that there is such a big difference between the findings of the British Crime Survey and the statistics on recorded crime? You will find a full discussion of this in 'Using official statistics', Chapter 3, pp. 99–103.

establishing such control. This is seen as an extension of an earlier policy of controlling more serious petty criminality through the issuing of Anti-Social Behaviour Orders (ASBOs). These are orders issued by a civil court, rather than a criminal court, prohibiting a person from specific acts of concern to complainants. Although these are civil court orders, a breach of an ASBO is a criminal offence and can bring the offender under tight legal control.

Public concern over crime relates mainly to theft and violence, which are seen as serious enough to warrant sustained attention from the police. This concern, reflected in periodic moral panics, tends to ensure that many of those involved in theft and criminal violence do so as a form of secondary deviation. As a result, many of them develop a criminal identity. In this section we will look at forms of professional and career crime and at those normalized forms of crime commonly called white-collar crime. We will also look at the gendered nature of criminal activity, in relation both to the undertaking of criminal acts and to becoming the victim of crime.

Professional and career crime

Theft—stealing property belonging to another person— is one of the few forms of crime to be highly organized and to offer the chance of a career or profession to those engaged in it. Theft includes burglary (theft from houses), robbery (theft with violence), forgery, confidence tricks, pickpocketing, and numerous other fraudulent activities. Not all these are organized as career crime, of course, and not all those who drift into theft even make the transition from primary deviation to secondary deviation. School children who steal from shops, for example, rarely continue into a career of thieving. Nevertheless, theft is, indeed, one of the most organized forms of crime.

Career crime is nothing new. Mary McIntosh (1975) traces it back to the actions of pirates, bandits, brigands, and moral outlaws who often combined criminal with political aims. If the Robin Hood image of the rural outlaw is a rather idealized fiction, it nevertheless grasps an important element in pre-modern theft (Hobsbawm 1969). With the growth of towns in the early modern period, opportunities for street and house crime became much greater, and there was a growth in the amount of what McIntosh calls **craft crime**. This is the small-scale, skilled theft engaged in by pickpockets, cutpurses, and confidence tricksters. These forms of career crime proliferated through the eighteenth and nineteenth centuries and remain an important part of everyday crime. McIntosh traces the origins of what she calls **project crime** to a later period. This is large-scale robbery and fraud, and became fully established only in the

Briefing: serious crime 7.4

The kinds of crime that typically hit the newspaper headlines are burglary, robbery, and murder, which are almost universally seen as 'serious'. Other, less visible forms of crime may, however, be equally serious when all their implications are considered. This is particularly true of crime in rural areas, which can have a major financial impact on farming.

Sheep-rustling costs moorland farmers millions of pounds a year. In Dartmoor and the surrounding parts of the south-west, around 10,000 sheep, valued at over £1 million, are stolen each year. The total cost of rustling is more than £7 million a year. When the theft of farm machinery, tools, and equipment is added to this, farm crime amounts to more than £85 million in a year. There had been a sharp rise in sheep-rustling and the sale of illegally butchered meat by late 2008.

A growing form of farm crime is the stealing of Christmas trees. Organized groups drive to isolated plantations and, within minutes, cut down Christmas trees and load them into their truck. A full lorry load of stolen trees could be worth £20,000. Growers have

estimated that up to 10 per cent of their trees are stolen each year—perhaps around 70,000 of the seven million trees sold each year in shops and markets across the country. Big supermarket chains such as Tesco are now the major growers of trees and they employ ex-soldiers to act as private security staff to protect their investment.

The recession of 2008–10 has led to an increase in the reporting of Christmas tree theft in the United States, where it is reported that Garden Centres are also reporting an increase in the theft of Christmas tree decorations.

Source: Guardian, 26 June 1997; 17 December 2001; *The Times*, 8 November, 2008; *Fortune*, 18 December 2008.

> ➔ Consider why it is that rural, farm crime is not usually highlighted in mass-media discussions of the crime problem.

> ➔ Look at the Scottish Farm Crime Survey (www.scotland.gov.uk/cru/resfinds/raf01-00b.htm) for a general discussion of these issues.

early years of the twentieth century. It has become the predominant form of theft only since the 1950s.

Crime and the underworld

Rural bandits and outlaws were enmeshed in the surrounding social life of the rural communities from which they were drawn. Urban craft crime, however, tended to be based in a distinct criminal **underworld**. The growth of such criminal areas was first reported in the sixteenth century, but it was in the eighteenth and nineteenth centuries that they achieved their fullest development. The criminal underworld of a city such as London comprised various 'rookeries' that were the dwelling places and meeting places of craft criminals of all kinds. Segregated from the rest of society, the underworlds provided for the security, safety, shared interests, and concerns of the craft thieves. The underworlds were rooted in the surrounding slum districts of the poor working class. Poverty, unemployment, overcrowding in poor physical conditions, and a lack of leisure opportunities other than the pub were the conditions under which many people drifted into crime and some became confirmed in a criminal career (T. Morris 1957; John Mack 1964; see also M. Kerr 1958).

An urban underworld formed an occupational community with a subculture that established norms of criminal behaviour, a slang and argot, and an *esprit de corps* that sustained the shared identity of the thieves. Central to the underworld code was the injunction not to 'squeal', 'squawk', 'grass', or inform on others. Association with other thieves, and a lack of association with the targets of their theft, inhibited any concern for the feelings of the victims of crime. It also meant that thieves could learn from other thieves the techniques and skills that would help them in their own crimes. In addition, their leisure-time associates formed a pool of partners in crime. They were able to find markets for their stolen goods, and they could attain a degree of protection and insulation from detection and law enforcement (Chesney 1968; McIntosh 1975: 24).

Underworld life, however, has been fundamentally altered by the urban redevelopment of the inner-city areas and the dispersal of population to the suburbs. The London underworld was for long based in the Spitalfields and Cable Street districts of the East End, where there has been much redevelopment. While certain central pubs and clubs remain important venues for career criminals, much activity is now more dispersed through the city, and the underworld forms an extended social network, rather than being confined to a particular physical locale. Even in the 1960s, however, a tradition of craft crime still survived in Spitalfields, and the surrounding district had high levels of crime: there were especially high levels of burglary, violence against the person, gambling, and prostitution. Much crime, however, was 'petty, unsophisticated, unorganized and largely unprofitable—if often squalid and brutal' (Downes 1966: 150).

A subculture of crime continues to sustain career crime, which has, however, changed its character. Alongside older forms of craft crime, project crime has become more significant, and this has also helped to transform the structure of the underworld. Where craft theft involved the stealing of small amounts of money from large numbers of people, project crime involves a much smaller number of large thefts. Growing affluence and, in particular, the increasing scale of business activity have meant that the potential targets of theft have become much bigger. As a result, criminals have had to organize themselves more effectively and on a larger scale if they are to be successful against these targets. Improved safes, alarm systems, and security vans can be handled only by organized teams of specialists: safe-breakers, drivers, gunmen, and so on. Such crimes, organized as

one-off projects, require advanced planning and a much higher level of cooperation than is typical for craft crime.

Teams for particular projects are recruited through the cliques and connections of the underworld, and these may sometimes be organized on a semi-permanent basis. The criminal underworld that existed in the East End of London from the Second World War until the 1960s, for example, contained numerous competing gangs that were held together largely by the violent hegemony of the Kray twins and their associates. The east London gangs engaged in violent feuds with their counterparts (the Richardsons) from the south London underworld, and the leading members of the East End and south London gangs occasionally met on the neutral ground of the West End (Morton 1992; Hobbs 1994).

It is through the subculture of crime that people are socialized into criminal identities, whether as a craft thief or a project thief. The professional thief, like the professional doctor, lawyer, or bricklayer, must develop many technical abilities and skills. He (the thief is generally male)

Gangsters participate in a subculture of crime.

© Getty Images/Ron Gerelli

must know how to plan and execute crimes, how to dispose of stolen goods, how to 'fix' the police and the courts, and so on. These skills must be acquired through long education and training, and it is through his involvement in the underworld that the thief can acquire them most effectively.

Based on his detailed study of a professional thief, Sutherland (1937) showed how the person who successfully learns and applies these techniques earns high status within the underworld. The beginning thief, if successful, is gradually admitted into closer and closer contact with other thieves. It is they who can offer him 'better' work and from whom he can learn more advanced skills. Once successful, the thief dresses and behaves in distinct ways and proudly adopts the label 'thief' in order to distinguish himself from a mere 'amateur', small-time criminal. As well as gaining respect within the underworld, he may also gain a degree of recognition and respect from police, lawyers, and newspaper crime writers. These people are aware of his activities and have often accommodated themselves to professional crime: apart from the corruption that sometimes occurs, there may also be shared interests in not reacting immediately and punitively towards all crime.

Burglary as a way of life

One of the few contemporary investigations of career theft in Britain is an investigation of domestic burglaries (Maguire and Bennett 1982). Burglary is illegal entry into a building with the intent to steal. Domestic burglary was, for a long time, subject to the death penalty, and from 1861 to 1968 it carried a maximum sentence of life imprisonment. Following the Theft Act of 1968, the maximum penalty has been fourteen years' imprisonment. In practice, only just under a half of convicted burglars have been given custodial sentences.

Recognizing the problems involved in assessing rates of crime, Maguire and Bennett concluded that about 60 per cent of all burglaries were committed by a relatively small number of persistent, career criminals. The remaining 40 per cent were committed by juveniles who had drifted into delinquency and would, for the most part, drift out of it again.

Maguire and Bennett interviewed a number of persistent burglars, most of whom were committed to their criminal careers. They had, typically, carried out between 100 and 500 break-ins during their careers. They combined this with involvement in car theft, burglary from commercial premises, and cheque forgery. They were mainly young, single, and with no dependants. The men described themselves as 'thieves', or simply as 'villains', and they described their crimes as 'work' from which they could earn a living and from which they would eventually retire. Maguire and Bennett, however, are more critical of this self-image than Sutherland. In particular, they highlight a

number of ways in which the thieves sought to neutralize the moral implications of their actions through self-serving rationalizations.

Thieves claimed, for example, that any distress suffered by the victims was no concern of theirs. They were simply doing a job, carrying on their trade, and this distress was an unavoidable consequence of their routine, professional activities. This claim was further bolstered by the claim that, in any case, they stole only from the well-to-do, who could easily afford it and who were well insured (Maguire and Bennett 1982: 61). In fact, many of their victims were relatively poor council-house residents who could ill afford to be burgled.

Briefing: the professional thief   7.5

In 1930 Edwin Sutherland, a sociologist at the University of Chicago, carried out lengthy research with Chic Conwell, a man involved full-time in theft between 1905 and 1925. Using the life-history method pioneered at the university, Sutherland (1937) obtained a biographical account of Conwell's life, which he used as the basis for his interpretation of thieving.

Conwell was born in the 1880s and, after a short period of theatre work, got involved in the use of drugs and became a pimp. Through his pimping, he acquired a knowledge of other forms of crime, and he worked in Chicago as a pickpocket, a shoplifter, and a confidence trickster. He spent a number of periods in prison, though only one of his sentences was for theft. He gave up both thieving and drug use after release from prison in 1925 and worked regularly until his death in 1933.

Sutherland specialized in the study of crime. He developed a view that stressed differential association: people learn criminal behaviour by coming into contact with others who define criminality in positive ways. In addition to his study of professional theft, he pioneered the study of white-collar crime (Sutherland 1949).

Sutherland's position on the professional thief was that

> . . . a person can be a professional thief only if he is recognized and received as such by other professional thieves. Professional theft is a group-way of life. One can get into the group and remain in it only by the consent of those previously in the group. Recognition as a professional thief by other professional thieves is the absolutely necessary, universal, and definitive characteristic of the professional thief. . . . A professional thief is a person who has the status of a professional thief in the differential association of professional thieves. (Sutherland 1937: 211)

Similarly, the thieves sought to boost their own status by disparaging the amateurism of the majority of 'losers', 'wankers', 'idiots', and 'cowboys' who carried out unsuccessful thefts. Maguire and Bennett argue, however, that it is more accurate to see the persistent career thieves as divided into low-level, middle-level, and high-level categories on the basis of the scale of their crimes. Thieves move up and down this hierarchy a great deal over the course of their careers.

High-level burglaries are undertaken by thieves who are members of small networks of committed criminals who keep themselves separate from other, small-time criminals. Sometimes they work alone, and sometimes in pairs, but always they keep their principal criminal contacts within their network. Middle-level burglaries are carried out by those who are involved in larger and less exclusive networks of thieves with varying abilities and degrees of commitment. There is less consistent adherence to the code of mutual support, and less effective contacts with receivers of stolen goods and with other specialist criminals. Finally, low-level burglaries are undertaken by individual thieves with only loose connections to one another and who are indiscriminate in both their criminal connections and their choice of crimes.

It is at the lower level that people first enter burglary, as the loose social networks are closely embedded in the surrounding structure of the local community. In most cases, this is a process of drift by those previously involved in juvenile delinquencies. When describing their careers, however, the thieves minimized the element of drift and presented a self-image of themselves as people who had chosen to enter careers of crime. Those who drift into lower-level burglary and become at all successful may graduate, in due course, to middle-level or high-level burglary through the contacts and connections that they make.

Those in the networks carrying out the high-level burglaries are, in a sense, at the pinnacle of the career hierarchy, though Maguire and Bennett show that they are unlikely to be at all involved in large-scale project crimes undertaken by the London gangs. Their activities are confined to housebreaking, shop-breaking, car theft, shoplifting, and cheque forgery. They have little or no involvement in such specialist crimes as hijacking lorries, bank raids, or embezzlement.

Very few burglars—even those at the high level—make a major financial success of their chosen careers, and most spend at least one period in prison. Imprisonment is not, however, a purely negative experience, as it gives the burglar an opportunity to 'widen his circle of criminal acquaintances, learn new techniques and be encouraged to try his hand at more lucrative offences' (Maguire and Bennett 1982: 67). Nevertheless, few burglars continued with burglary beyond their thirties or forties. Most drifted into what they hoped would be safer forms of work. Entry into legal employment is difficult for someone with a criminal record, and few make the transition successfully. Walsh (1986: 58–9) has shown that some burglars are able to combine career crime with a continuing involvement in legitimate employment—typically short-term jobs in the building and construction industry or in other casual work such as catering and cleaning. It seems likely that some who retire from burglary may be able to continue or to re-enter such casual and temporary work.

Career crime has probably never been a completely self-contained, full-time activity. Even in the heyday of the Victorian underworld of the East End, criminal activities were combined with casual labour and street trading, one type of work supplementing the earnings from the other (Mayhew 1861*b*). Hobbs (1988) has shown how the East End has long been organized around an entrepreneurial culture of wheeling and dealing, trading and fixing, that makes no sharp distinction between legal and illegal activities. Shover (1996; see also Shover and Decket 1996) has documented the nature of career thieving and burglary in the United States.

Theft may, indeed, be career crime, a way of life, but it does not take up all of a thief's time and cannot usually provide him with a regular or substantial income. Those involved in thieving, then, must combine it with other ways of gaining an income. Casual labour is combined with their own thieving and the performance of the occasional criminal task for other, more successful thieves. Those who are themselves more successful may be involved as much in trading and dealing as in thieving, and their entrepreneurial activities are likely to range from the legitimate, through various 'shady' deals, to the criminal. The full-time criminal is not a full-time thief, even if he stresses this aspect of his life in constructing his own identity. Much thieving is undertaken by those who are in low-paid or semi-legitimate work or who are unemployed (see Figure 7.3).

There is considerable evidence that the growth of the drugs market in the 1980s has sharpened a distinction between the full-time criminal and the mass of ordinary thieves. The establishment of a large and extensive market in drugs has connected together the criminal networks of London, Manchester, Birmingham, Glasgow, and other large cities. This has allowed a greater degree of organization to be achieved in the project crimes that sustain drug-trafficking. Those who are involved in this organized crime, however, have highly specialized skills—for example, in relation to VAT fraud—and are very different from those who steal hi-fis and videos from domestic premises. The significance of the drug market for ordinary thieves, as we show later in this chapter, is that it offers possibilities for casual and occasional trading in small quantities of drugs that supplement their more established sources of income (Hobbs 1994: 449, 453–4).

Figure 7.3 Unemployment and crime

In periods of growing unemployment during the 1990s and since 2008, there has been much discussion about the link between unemployment and crime. What conclusions would you draw about crime from the two graphs below? Take a few minutes to think about this. Look at our discussion of unemployment measures and the crime statistics in Chapter 3, pp. 101–3, and see if you would want to change any of your conclusions. You might like to try to find figures for unemployment and recorded crime over the period 1994–2008 to see what trend is shown for that period.

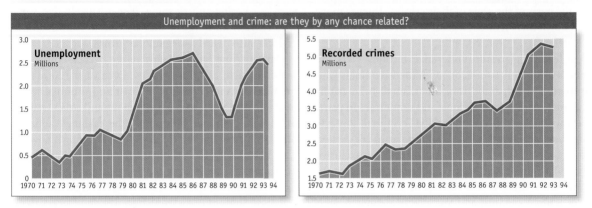

Sources: *Independent on Sunday*, 4 June 1995; Carmichael and Ward (2001).

Gender, ethnicity, class, and crime

Public perceptions of crime focus on robbery, burglary, theft, mugging, rape, and other crimes of theft and violence. This is seen as male, working-class activity. Professional crime is seen as the work of adult males and as expressing conventional notions of masculinity.

This point of view does get some support from the criminal statistics, which seem to show the very small number of women who are convicted of criminal offences (see Figure 7.4). Five times as many men as women are found guilty of or are cautioned for a notifiable offence. It also appears that the kinds of crimes committed by women are less 'serious' than those committed by men. Figures for all parts of Britain show that women have very little involvement as offenders in domestic or commercial theft, vehicle theft, or street violence, though they are often, of course, involved in these as victims. They are, however, more heavily involved in shoplifting than are men, prostitution is an almost exclusively female crime, and only women can be convicted of infanticide. There is some evidence, however, that the number and types of crime committed by women may have altered since the 1960s (Heidensohn 1985).

In a similar way to the crimes of women, many middle-class crimes are not generally regarded as 'real' crimes. While there is a great public fear of street violence and domestic burglary, there is relatively little concern about fraudulent business practices, violations of safety legislation, or tax evasion. While such offences, arguably, have much greater impact on people's lives than does the relatively small risk of theft or violence, they are either invisible to public opinion or are not seen as proper 'crimes'.

There is growing evidence that members of ethnic minorities in Britain have become more heavily involved with the legal system since the 1960s. They are now especially likely to appear as offenders and, more particularly, as victims of crime and as police suspects. Housebreakings and other household offences show little variation among the various ethnic groups, about one-third of all households being victims of such crime.

African Caribbeans, however, are almost twice as likely as whites to be the victims of personal attacks. This is, in

Figure 7.4 Indictable offences by gender, England and Wales, 2006 (000s)

Offence	Males	Females
Theft and handling stolen goods	121.3	50.2
Drug offences	68.2	8.8
Burglary	28.6	2.0
Violence against the person	81.3	17.9
Criminal damage	18.8	2.9
Sexual offences	6.7	0.2
Robbery	7.8	1.0
Other indictable offences	74.5	17.3
Total	407.2	100.3

Source: *Social Trends* (2008: fig. 9.13).

part, a consequence of the fact that African Caribbeans live, disproportionately, in inner-city areas where such crimes are particularly likely to take place. However, their experiences also have a racially motivated character. The growing victimization of black and Asian people reflects a real growth in racial violence and racist attacks by members of the white population. While criminal acts carried out during the urban riots of the 1980s (see Chapter 13, pp. 503–5) often had a racial aspect to them, blacks and Asians are far more likely to be the targets of racial crimes than they are to commit them. There has, nevertheless, been a growing involvement of young African Caribbeans in many kinds of street crime.

The police hold to a widely shared assumption that African Caribbeans, in particular, are heavily involved in crime and that special efforts need to be taken to control them. Many studies have shown the racism inherent in police actions that stop black people in the street and subject them to closer scrutiny than other members of the population (Hall *et al.* 1978; Gelsthorpe 1993). African Caribbeans are more likely than whites, and members of other ethnic minorities, to be approached by the police on suspicion, to be prosecuted, and to be sentenced. This is reflected in a growing hostility of ethnic minorities towards the police, who are often seen as racists rather than as neutral defenders of law and order.

Women and crime

The kinds of crimes committed by women, like those committed by men, reflect the gender-defined social roles available to them. Both men and women are involved in shoplifting, for example, but women are more likely to steal clothes, food, or low-value items. Men are more likely to steal books, electrical goods, or high-value items. This reflects the conventional domestic expectations that tie women to shopping for basic household goods in supermarkets, while men are able to shop for luxuries and extras. Put simply, both men and women tend to steal the same kinds of items that they buy (Smart 1977: 9–10). Similarly, men (especially young men) are heavily involved in vehicle crimes, including car theft, while women are heavily involved in prostitution. This involvement in prostitution can be seen as an extension of a normal feminine role that allows implicit or explicit bargaining over sex.

This connection between crime and conventional gender roles is particularly clear in the patterns of formal involvement in offences related to children. Those who are most responsible for childcare are, other things being equal, more likely to be involved in cruelty to children, abandoning children, kidnapping, procuring illegal abortions, and social-security frauds. Although child sexual abuse is often seen as a crime perpetrated by men, many women are also involved in such crimes (Turton 2008). Theft by women generally involves theft from an employer by those involved in domestic work or shop work. Even when involved in large-scale theft, women are likely to be acting in association with male family members and to be involved as receivers of stolen goods rather than as thieves.

There are, of course, problems in estimating the actual number of offences from the official statistics (as we show in Chapter 3, pp. 100–1), but the overall pattern is clear. Because women are less likely to be arrested and convicted for certain offences—something that we look at below—the difference between male and female involvement in crime is exaggerated by the official figures. The differing patterns of offence do, however, exist. Only in the case of sexual offences is the pattern for male and female involvement more equal, the apparent predominance of women resulting from the fact that their sexual behaviour is more likely to be treated in ways that result in conviction. The sexual double standard means that the authorities normalize much male sexual delinquency, but express moral

Suspicion: young, black, working-class boys are often stopped on 'suspicion', yet young black African Caribbeans are actually the most likely to be victims of crime.
© Alice Chadwick

outrage at female sexual delinquency. As Smart (1977: 15–16) argues:

> None of these types of offences requires particularly 'masculine' attributes. Strength and force are unnecessary and there is only a low level of skill or expertise required. The women involved have not required training in violence, weapons or tools, or in specialised tasks like safe breaking. On the contrary the skills required can be learnt in everyday experience, and socialisation into a delinquent subculture or a sophisticated criminal organisation is entirely unnecessary.

The relatively low representation of women in recorded crime is the main reason why female criminality has been so little researched. Lombroso and Ferrero (1895) set out a deterministic theory, based on the claimed peculiarities of female biology, which still has some influence. They held that women were less highly evolved than men and so were relatively 'primitive' in character. They were less involved in crime, however, because their biology predisposed them to a passive and more conservative way of life. They were, however, weak-willed, and Lombroso and Ferrero saw the involvement of many women in crime as resulting from their having been led on by others. The female drift into crime was a consequence of their weak and fickle character.

The extreme position set out by Lombroso and Ferrero has long been abandoned, but many criminologists do still resort to biological assumptions when trying to explain female criminality. Pollak (1950), for example, held that women are naturally manipulative and deceitful, instigating crimes that men undertake. What such theories fail to consider is that, if women do indeed have lower rates of criminality, this may more usefully and accurately be explained in terms of the cultural influences that shape sex–gender roles and the differing opportunities available to men and to women.

This implies that patterns of conformity among the affluent and the deprived, among men and among women, are to be understood in the context of their wider role commitments and the interactions in which they are involved with their role partners. Those who are predisposed to see criminal actions as appropriate will, if the structure of opportunities allows it, drift into crime. There is no need to assume that women are fundamentally different from men, or that the working classes are fundamentally different from the middle classes.

It appears, then, that women, like men, drift into criminal actions whenever the structure of opportunities makes it seem a reasonable response to their situation. The particular situations in which they find themselves are determined by the ways in which sex–gender identities are institutionalized, and so patterns of criminality are gendered. Cultural stereotypes about men and women, as we will show, are also a major influence on the nature of the social reaction to female criminality. The absence of strong punitive responses to most forms of female crime means that the progression from primary to secondary deviation is less likely to occur. Women may drift into crime, but they only rarely pursue criminal careers.

The principal exception to this rule is prostitution. In law, a prostitute is someone who sells sex, and this is almost invariably seen as a female offence. Men involved in prostitution, other than as clients, tend to be seen as engaged in acts of 'indecency' rather than of 'soliciting' for prostitution. Under British law, a woman who has been arrested and convicted for soliciting is officially termed a 'common prostitute' and is liable to re-arrest simply for loitering in a public place. As most prostitution is arranged in public, on the streets, it is difficult for women so labelled to avoid the occasional spell in custody. They may also find it difficult to live a normal life off the streets:

> It is virtually impossible for them to live with a man or even another woman as it is immediately assumed that such people are living off immoral earnings, thereby making themselves vulnerable to a criminal charge. Also, the legal definition of a brothel, as a dwelling containing two or more prostitutes, has made it difficult for two women to live together even where only one is a prostitute.

Smart 1977: 114; see also O'Connell Davidson 1998

In 2004 the government in Britain floated the idea of changing the law to allow up to three prostitutes to work together without their place of work being defined as a brothel. This idea was abandoned in 2006 in favour of increasing greater restrictions on the purchase and sale of sex.

The reaction of the police is critical in determining whether a woman who breaks the law is defined as a criminal. Police work is structured around the cop culture (Reiner 1992), a culture that strongly emphasizes masculinity and that underpins the harassment and abuse of female police officers and the derogation of many female offenders.

Prostitutes, for example, are often seen as flouting the domesticity of the conventional female role and have been subject to harassment and entrapment. Nevertheless, prostitutes are often able to establish a mutual accommodation with the police, an arrangement in which each can get on with their job with the minimum of interference from the other. When there is pressure on the police to take action, however, such arrangements break down. In these circumstances, prostitutes are highly vulnerable and can be quite susceptible to police persuasion and suggestion. On the other hand, women who conform to conventional role expectations are seen as in need of protection, and

> **⮕ Connections**
>
> You might like to consider street prostitution in relation to our discussion of the gendering of space in Chapter 13, pp. 487 and 495–6. A good discussion can be found in McKeganey and Barnard (1996). While you are looking at the gendering of space in the city, you might also think about the way in which urban space is used by various ethnic groups (see p. 486 in the same chapter).

cautioning is more widely used for female offenders than it is for males (S. Edwards 1984: 16–19).

There is some evidence that this differential treatment of male and female offenders also occurs in the courts. Sexist assumptions in court practices have led some to suggest that women experience greater leniency than men (Mannheim 1940: 343). Others, however, have suggested that greater harshness is more likely (A. Campbell 1981). Heidensohn (1985) correctly points out that this may simply reflect the well-known lack of consistency in sentencing, though she reports evidence that supports the view that women are treated more harshly (Farrington and Morris 1983).

Indeed, S. Edwards (1984) has suggested that women are subjected to much closer scrutiny in courts precisely because the female offender is seen as unusual or unnatural. Women are on trial not only for their offence but for their deviation from conventional femininity. Their punishment or treatment is intended to ensure that they adjust themselves back to what is seen as a natural feminine role.

Very few convicted women are given custodial sentences. Men are two or three times more likely to be imprisoned for an offence than are women, and their sentences tend to be longer. Imprisoned women are mainly those convicted of such things as theft, fraud, forgery, or violence. Prisons do make some attempt to recognize that women's domestic commitments are different from those of men, and a number of mother-and-baby units have been set up. Some well-publicized cases have been reported, however, of pregnant prison inmates being forced to give birth while manacled to a prison officer. Studies of female prisons in the United States have shown them to be important sources of emotional and practical support for their inmates (Giallombardo 1966), often involving the establishment of lesbian family relationships. This appears to be less marked in Britain.

Crimes of the affluent

Offences carried out by men (and women) from the middle classes are generally described as **white-collar crime** (Sutherland 1949; Croal 1992). This term originally referred to crimes and civil-law infractions committed by those in non-manual employment as part of their work. It is now used a little more broadly to refer to three categories of offence:

- *Occupational crimes* of the affluent: offences committed by the relatively affluent and prosperous in the course of their legitimate business or profession. Examples are theft from an employer, financial frauds, and insider dealing in investment companies.
- *Organizational crimes*: offences committed by organizations and businesses themselves—that is, by employees acting in their official capacities on behalf of the organization. Examples are non-payment or under-payment of VAT or Corporation Tax, and infringements of health and safety legislation leading to accidents or pollution.
- Any other crimes committed by the relatively affluent that tend to be treated differently from those of the less affluent. An example is tax evasion, which is treated differently from social-security fraud (Nelken 1994: 362–3).

The concept of white-collar crime, then, is far from clear-cut. It does, however, help to highlight the class basis of much crime. The number of people involved in white-collar crimes is barely apparent from the official statistics, as many go unrecorded. Its status as hidden crime, however, is paradoxical in view of its financial significance. It was estimated that the total cost of reported fraud alone in 1985 was £2,113 million, twice the amount accounted for by reported theft, burglary, and robbery (Levi 1987; see also M. Clarke 1990). Official estimates suggest that the actual cost of all fraud in Britain increased massively after 2000, rising to £40 billion in 2006.

Like the crimes of women, the crimes of the affluent have been little researched. Early discussions of white-collar crime were intended as criticisms of the orthodox assumption that criminality was caused by poverty or deprivation. Those who carried out thefts as part of a successful business career, Sutherland (1949) argued, could not be seen as acting out of economic necessity. Sutherland's own account stressed that white-collar crime was *learned* behaviour and that, in this respect, it was no different from other forms of criminality. All crime, he held, resulted from the effects of 'differential association' on learning: those who interact more frequently with others whose attitudes are favourable to criminal actions are themselves more likely to engage in criminal acts.

The crimes of the affluent, the prosperous, and the powerful can be explained in terms of the same motives as any other criminal act. They differ from 'ordinary' theft and burglary only in terms of their social organization and the social reaction to them. The character and motivation of those involved are no more, and no less, pathological than those of any others who drift into crime. White-collar crimes, however, are much less likely to result in full-time criminal careers. The nature of the social reaction makes the development into secondary deviation much less likely.

Much corporate and occupational crime takes place in the financial services industry, where changing patterns of regulation have created greater opportunities for illicit activities. The British financial system was, for much of the nineteenth and twentieth centuries, regulated in a highly informal way. Recruitment to banks, insurance companies, and other financial enterprises took place through an old-boy network centred on the public schools and the Oxford and Cambridge colleges. The Stock Exchange, as the central institution in the financial system, was at the heart of this system of informal regulation. The system rested on trust and loyalty: those who had been to school together and shared a similar social background felt that they could trust one another in their business dealings. The motto of the Stock Exchange was 'My word is my bond', and many deals were sealed on the shake of hands rather than with a written contract (Lisle-Williams 1984; M. Clarke 1986).

During the 1970s the government introduced a number of changes to this system of regulation in response to the growing internationalization of the money markets. This culminated in the so-called Big Bang of October 1986, when the Stock Exchange was finally opened up to foreign competition. New codes of practice were introduced to reflect the more diverse social backgrounds of those involved in the buying and selling of currency, shares, and commodities. The old system of trust could no longer be relied on, and more formal mechanisms were required. The Bank of England was given greater powers of control and supervision, and a new Securities and Investment Board to regulate the whole system. The offences with which the new system of regulation has had to deal are those made possible by the changing structure of the financial system. The new offshore investment funds to provide high returns to wealthy clients

> **◒ Connections**
>
> Recruitment to the boards of the financial enterprises that make up the City of London financial system is one aspect of the recruitment to elites and top positions in British society. You might like to look at our discussion of elites and the ruling class in Chapter 20, pp. 800–2, where we look in more detail at the part played by schooling and informal social networks.

Is white-collar crime really victimless crime?

© Alice Chadwick

wanting to minimize their tax bills have allowed directors to benefit at the expense of the investors (M. Clarke 1990: 167–70). These financial crimes are discussed in Box 7.6.

Much white-collar crime is low in visibility. It tends to occur in the context of normal business routines, and is less likely to be noticed, even by its victims. Fiddling business expenses, for example, is almost undetectable, and many employers treat it as a source of tax-free perks for their employees (Mars 1982). Large-scale fraud, when discovered, is more likely to result in an official reaction, though it will often be hushed up if it might suggest a failure of supervision or control by senior managers.

Crimes of the affluent are far more likely to be regulated by specialized enforcement agencies than by the police, and this has important consequences for the nature of the social reaction. These agencies—the Health and Safety Executive, the Factory Inspectorate, the Inland Revenue, and so on—generally have a remit to maintain and promote high standards of business and trading, and the enforcement of the criminal law is only one part of this remit (Croal 1992: ch. 5). Their officials, therefore, develop 'compliance strategies' that stress persuasion and administrative sanctions aimed at crime prevention, rather than the detection and punishment of offences. The level of prosecutions is, therefore, very low. Few cases go to court, and very few result in imprisonment. In these ways, the transition to secondary deviation is avoided.

 ## Briefing: financial crimes 7.6

The financial centres of the world economy offer great opportunities for people to make money from illegal financial activity.

During the 1990s, Baring's Bank experienced massive losses and was forced into bankruptcy when one of its employees, Nick Leeson, defrauded the Singapore branch of the bank to the sum of £830 million. Leeson was sentenced to six years in prison, but his story attracted so much attention that he was able to negotiate a book and film deal (for *Rogue Trader*) valued at more than £3 million. Early in 2002, Allied Irish Bank suspended one of its New York traders, John Rusnack, following the discovery of losses of £485 million. It was suspected that a number of currency traders had cooperated in a long-term fraud. In 2009, Bernie Madoff was convicted of the largest investment fraud in US history. Over more than twenty years, $65 billion disappeared from client accounts in his investment funds; 71-year-old Madoff was sentenced to 150 years' imprisonment and forfeited $170 billion in assets.

The big growth area for financial fraud in recent years has been online fraud, involving fraudulent access to bank accounts and credit cards, and often involving 'identity fraud'. E-mail scams and illegal card readers have enabled people to make withdrawals from bank accounts and purchase goods without the permission or knowledge of the account holder. In an attempt to reduce the amount of credit-card fraud, banks introduced new 'chip and pin' cards that are claimed to be more secure. It has been suggested, however, that this has helped to increase the amount of Internet-based credit-card fraud. While card fraud losses fell by 13 per cent in the first half of 2005, online card fraud has increased by 29 per cent over the same period. It is estimated that bank and credit-card fraud amounted to £609.9 million in 2008.

Sources: *Guardian*, 21 February 2002; *Guardian*, 8 March 2005 and 8 November 2005; http://news.bbc.co.uk/1/hi/business/ 3707290.stm.

 Carry out some searches in local and national newspapers to discover evidence on the penalties attached to different kinds of crime. (Don't forget to check the business pages as well as the general news pages.) Can you find any association between the size of any financial loss and the severity of the penalty? Which kinds of serious offence receive the lowest penalties, and which receive the highest?

Stop and reflect

In this section we have looked at professional and career crimes and at the relationships between gender, class, and crime. We started out by showing that not all deviation from legal norms is criminal activity. Criminal actions involve deviation from the criminal law. In considering theft and career crime, we showed that:

- Theft has undergone a series of transformations as the wider society has changed.
- Much theft has been organized in relation to an extensive underworld, a subculture of crime that supports and sustains criminal activities.
- Is there still a criminal underworld in the major cities today?
- Career thieves adopt an identity as professional thieves, though their involvement in theft is quite variable.
- Much burglary is combined with low-paid, semi-legal, and casual work, or is carried out by those who are unemployed.

We explored the popular viewpoint that crime is a male, working-class phenomenon. Looking at gender, ethnicity, class, and crime, we showed that:

- Patterns of male and female crime differ, and they reflect differences in conventional sex–gender roles. Female

criminality, for example, reflects cultural conceptions of femininity and the structure of opportunities open to women.

- There are significant variations in the attitudes of police and the courts to men and to women.
- Why does so much popular discussion explain female criminality in terms of female biology?
- African Caribbeans are twice as likely as whites to experience personal attacks. Many of these crimes are racially motivated.
- Members of ethnic minorities are more likely than whites to be stopped by the police and prosecuted in court.
- White-collar crime includes a diverse range of crimes of the affluent. Its economic impact is far more extensive than is often assumed.
- Trends in white-collar crime are related to changes in the structure of the financial system and the wider economy.
- Why are crimes of the affluent more likely to be normalized or to be regulated by bodies other than the police and the criminal courts?

Drugs and drug abuse

The abuse of drugs is one of the most widely discussed forms of deviance. In its most general meaning, a drug is any chemical that can have an effect on the human body and, perhaps, a physical effect on the mind. Some drugs occur quite naturally in many widely used drinks and foods. Caffeine, for example, is found in both coffee and tea, alcohol is the basis of beer, wine, and spirits, and vitamins are found in fresh fruit and vegetables. Many drugs are used as medicines, usually under the control of doctors. Morphine, penicillin, and steroids, for example, are used very widely and under a variety of commercial trade names in hospitals, clinics, and surgeries. Many other medical drugs are freely available for purchase without prescription: aspirin, codeine, ibuprofen, and numerous other analgesic (pain-killing) drugs can be bought in any high-street pharmacy and in many supermarkets.

This broad, dictionary definition of 'drugs', however, is not what newspaper columnists, politicians, and social commentators mean when they use the word. These people generally use the word in a much narrower sense to refer

to the non-medical use of drugs. This is the deliberate use of chemical substances to achieve particular physiological changes, simply for the pleasure or other non-medical effects they produce. It is in this sense, for example, that many parents and teachers rail against the use of drugs by children and young people. The non-medical use of drugs in the twentieth century has, indeed, been largely an activity of the young. Drug use, then, is seen as a deviant activity, as non-medical drug *abuse*. It becomes, therefore, a matter for social control. For this reason, the non-medical use or possession of many drugs has been made illegal.

There is a great deal of ambiguity over how widely this meaning of the word 'drug' is to be taken, and whether all non-medical drug use is to be regarded as a deviant activity. Many freely available products have the same characteristics as illicit drugs. Tobacco, for example, can be freely bought in shops and it is a major source of tax revenue for the government. At the same time, however, it contains nicotine, an addictive stimulant to the nervous system that is a major health hazard both to those who smoke and to

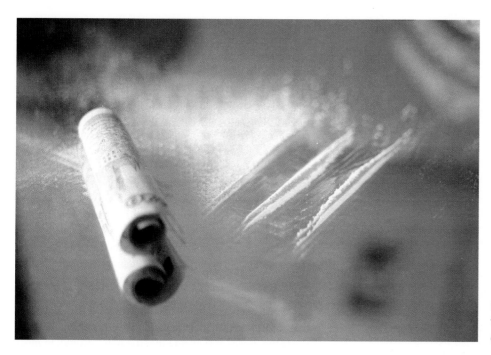

Cocaine is a widely used
illegal substance.
© Alice Chadwick

those around them. Similarly, alcoholic drinks, which can have serious physiological and psychological effects if taken in large quantities, are an accepted and even encouraged part of a normal social life for most people. Like tobacco, alcohol is available in shops and supermarkets, it is a multi-million pound industry, in which many people find legitimate employment, and—unlike cigarettes—it can be advertised freely on television.

Some chemicals with domestic or industrial uses, but which can also be used to produce 'high' feelings, can be purchased quite legitimately and with even fewer restrictions. Recent research has suggested that chocolate may operate in the same way as heroin, nicotine, and cannabis, by its effect on the limbic system in the brain. Eating chocolate can produce a 'rush' or high feeling because it affects the brain in the same way as the active ingredient in cannabis. Glues and solvents, which are used as stimulants and hallucinogenics (mood-changers) by many young people, can be purchased in hardware and do-it-yourself shops. The use of heroin (a morphine derivative), cocaine, or Ecstasy (MDMA), on the other hand, is widely disapproved of, and their use is surrounded by numerous legal restrictions over their acquisition and sale. Many such drugs are the objects of advertising campaigns aimed at discouraging their use by encouraging people to 'say no' if offered them. They can usually be obtained only from illegal sources. Medical trials have been set up in Britain, however, to investigate the part that might be played by cannabis, on prescription, in the treatment of multiple

sclerosis and as a pain-killer. Morphine has long been available in pharmacies in Codeine and similar analgesic tablets, and both cocaine and morphine could be bought over the counter in British high streets until 1916. In 2002 it was announced that heroin would be made available to addicts on prescription.

The different social reaction to alcohol, chocolate, glue, and heroin cannot be explained simply in terms of the medical dangers involved in using any specific stimulant. If the potential danger was the principal determinant of the social reaction, alcohol and tobacco would have been criminalized many years ago.

Learning drug use

The idea of **addiction** to drugs is central to discussions of their non-medical uses. Addiction is seen as occurring where people have become physiologically dependent on the use of a particular drug and suffer serious and persistent withdrawal symptoms when its use is stopped. However, dependence is as much a psychological as a physiological fact and, as such, it is shaped by social factors. People must learn how to use particular drugs, and they become committed to their use only through complex social processes from which physiological dependence cannot be isolated. 'Addiction' is a medically constructed label and a social role that combines elements of the sick role and, in some cases, the criminal role.

⊃ *Connections*

We look at the idea of the sick role in Chapter 8, pp. 286–8. You may want to read our discussion now.

Drugs do, of course, have specific physiological effects: alcohol and barbiturates depress mental activity, cocaine and caffeine stimulate it, and LSD distorts experiences and perception. Their full effects, however, depend upon the social context in which they are used. Individuals who use drugs learn from one another not only the techniques necessary for their use, but also how to shape and experience the kinds of effects they produce. The non-medical use of drugs, then, is a deviant activity that, like all forms of deviance, is surrounded by normative frameworks that structure the lives of users and lead them to experience particular deviant careers and associated moral careers. 'Drug addiction' is a deviant identity that reflects a specific deviant career.

Becoming a cannabis user

In an influential study of deviant activity, Becker (1953) documented the career stages involved in becoming a marijuana (cannabis) user. He showed that people drift into cannabis use for a variety of reasons. Once they begin its use, however, they will—if they persist—follow a particular sequence of stages. Becker called these stages the 'beginner', the 'occasional user', and the 'regular user'. As users follow this career sequence, cannabis-smoking becomes an ever more important part of their identity. Becker shows, however, that cannabis use rarely involves full-blown secondary deviation, despite the fact that its use is illegal. Cannabis use is a low-visibility activity that rarely comes to the attention of those who might publicly stigmatize users, and so these users are less likely to progress to secondary deviation. Becker's career and work are discussed in Box 7.7.

THEORY AND METHODS   **7.7**

Howard Becker

Howard Becker was born in 1928 and was trained at the University of Chicago. His work draws heavily on symbolic interactionism, but he places this in the larger context of power struggles and conflict among social groups. His early work on drug use was followed by work on student doctors (Becker *et al.* 1961), education (Becker *et al.* 1968), and artistic production (Becker 1982). He has also published a number of important methodological essays (Becker 1970). His work on drug use was republished in the early 1960s (Becker 1963), when it made a major contribution to the labelling theory of deviance.

Becker's research was undertaken in Chicago in the late 1940s and early 1950s, and public attitudes have altered somewhat since then. There was a huge increase in cannabis use in both the United States and Britain during the 1960s, and it has, since then, become accepted or tolerated in many situations. In California in 1996, for example, legal restrictions were relaxed in order to allow for its medical use in the treatment of certain cancer patients. Indeed, it has been suggested that cannabis use has become normalized for many people. Research shows that about a quarter of 16–24-year-olds in Britain in 2000 had tried cannabis during the previous year. Most of these users regard their use in the same way that most adults regard alcohol and tobacco use.

In 2004, legislation came into effect in Britain that partly decriminalizes the possession of cannabis by altering its classification to that of a 'Class C' drug (the same legal status as anabolic steroids and growth hormone). This meant that possession of cannabis no longer resulted in automatic prosecution but could be dealt with through an official warning. It was anticipated that the police would, in most situations, pay little attention to those who merely possess cannabis for their own use. In 2009, however, it was once again reclassified into the more serious Class B.

When Becker undertook his research, cannabis use was both illegal and surrounded by social meanings that associated it with irresponsibility, immorality, and addiction. Becker showed that, while the drug is not physically addictive, its image and its illegality led to specific patterns of use. Unlike cigarettes, cannabis cannot be bought at the local newsagent or the supermarket—though it can be obtained in this way in the Netherlands. Most people, therefore, had neither the opportunity nor the inclination to smoke it. Those who were most likely to begin to use the drug, Becker argued, were those involved in social groups where there was already a degree of cannabis use. It was here that there were likely to be opportunities for new users.

The typical locales for exploratory drug use in Chicago were organized around values and activities that oppose or run counter to the mainstream values of the larger society. When Becker undertook his research, these were focused on social groups around jazz and popular music, and on students and 'bohemians'. These groups tended to have a more critical and oppositional stance towards conventional social standards. Participants were likely to see many others using the drug, and their own first use was likely to become a real possibility if an opportunity presented itself. Today, when marijuana use has become more generalized among young people, exposure to its use in peer groups is likely to be the initial introduction for many young people. Someone enters the *beginner* stage in the use of cannabis when he or she is offered the opportunity to smoke it in a social situation where others are smoking, where there is a degree of social pressure to conform to group norms, and where the group itself provides a relatively safe and secluded locale away from the immediate possibility of public censure.

Becker shows that people who move from the stage of the beginner to that of the *occasional user* must learn a number of skills and abilities associated with the use of the drug. Someone willing to use the drug may know that it causes a 'high' feeling, but they are unlikely to know exactly how to produce this. The principal skill that must be learned, then, is the actual technique for smoking canna-bis. This is different from that used in tobacco smoking. Only if the smoke is inhaled in the correct way, with an appropriate amount of air, can cannabis have any signifi-cant effect on a person's body and mind. Group member-ship is essential for the easy learning of this skill, as the new user is surrounded by those who can demonstrate it in their own smoking. Those who fail to learn the proper technique will never experience the physical effects of can-nabis and so are unlikely to persist in using the drug.

A user must also acquire the ability to perceive the effects of the drug and, therefore, must learn what it is to be high or stoned. This is not as strange as it may seem. Users may have experiences that they fail to recognize as effects of the drug, but that others recognize as central features of their high state. Through interaction with others, new users begin to learn what signs and symptoms to look out for and what, therefore, can be taken as indicating that they have successfully learned the smoking technique. Last, but not least, they must learn to enjoy the effects of cannabis. They must learn to treat dizziness, tingling, and distortions of time and space as pleasurable experiences, rather than as unpleasant and undesirable disturbances to their normal physical and mental state. Only those who successfully acquire these skills and abilities—the smoking technique, the ability to perceive the effects, and enjoyment of the effects—will persist as cannabis users.

As occasional users, cannabis smokers acquire further justifications and rationalizations for its use, and these reinforce its continued use. The subculture of the group provides ready-made answers to many of the conventional objections to cannabis use that may be raised in their minds. Users may claim, for example, that cannabis is less dangerous than the alcohol that is tolerated and encour-aged by conventional opinion. They are also likely to hold that cannabis smokers are in complete control of when and where they choose to use the drug; that the drug is not in control of them.

The regular user of cannabis can neutralize any conven-tional or official labels that may be applied to them by non-users. People who lack the support of other users are less likely to become regular users if they accept the stereo-type of addiction or the idea that they are likely to escalate towards the use of hard drugs. If ideas of addiction,

escalation, and mental weakness cannot be neutralized, smokers may revert to occasional use, rather than becom-ing committed, regular users.

To protect themselves from stigmatization, regular users try to learn how to control the effects of the drug, inhibit-ing its effects at will, so that they are able to pass as normal in front of non-users or the police. They must, neverthe-less, run certain risks of detection, as regular use requires access to illegal dealers whose criminal activities may bring the user to the attention of the police. In order to minimize their chances of discovery as users, they are likely to spend more and more of their time in the company of their own, the other regular users who can provide a supportive and relatively safe environment in which to smoke.

Patterns of drug use

People learn how to use drugs in particular social contexts. Becker's work explored cannabis use in the specific context of post-war America, though his conclusions have a much wider application. In this section we will look at the chang-ing context of drug use in Britain. We look first at an account of deviant drug use in the 1970s, and then we turn to the contemporary, normalized use of drugs by young people.

Deviant drug use

Although it was developed in the 1950s, Becker's argument retains much of its relevance for contemporary patterns of cannabis use, and it has much to say about the use of other drugs. This was first confirmed in a study undertaken by Jock Young (1971) in London. Young's primary concern, however, was the origins of the negative social reaction to cannabis use. Why is it, he asks, that there is no similar social reaction to the use of tobacco? He holds that the rea-son is to be found not in the drug, but in the motivation that people are seen as having for using it. Drugs that are seen as being used to aid productivity are likely to be toler-ated, while those that have a purely hedonistic (pleasure-seeking) purpose are seen as 'drug abuse'.

European and North American societies tolerate or even encourage the drinking of coffee and tea, and the smoking of tobacco when working under pressure or as a 'release' from the pressure of a heavy work schedule. The worker 'earns' the right to 'relax with a smoke and a drink' after work, and people may be allowed smoking breaks at work if it 'helps them to concentrate'. Alcohol is widely used and tolerated as a way in which people may, periodically, ease the transition from work to leisure. It is culturally normal-ized. It is only when alcohol is used to excess and interferes with normal, everyday activities that its use is defined as deviant. No such tolerance is allowed for the user of cannabis, which is not seen as linked in any way to work productivity. Young also points out that there can be cultural variations in response to the same drug. Andean peasants use cocaine (in the form of coca leaves) as an aid to work, and it is a normalized feature of their society. In Britain and the United States, however, cocaine is regarded very differently.

Young has shown that these variations in response to drugs can be explained in terms of the relationship between a dominant set of social values and a secondary *subterranean* set of values (Matza 1964). The dominant values of contemporary societies stress work and everyday routines, but they coexist with other values that stress the need for excitement, leisure, and pleasure. These hedonistic, or pleasure-oriented, values are subterranean because they concern experiences that can be pursued only when the demands of employment and family life have been met. It is through their work—paid employment and unpaid work in the household—that people acquire the 'right' to freely enjoy their leisure activities and to pursue the subterranean values. Young sees this as involving a socialized conflict between the desire for pleasure and the repression of this desire as people engage in their everyday activities (Marcuse 1956). Through their socialization, he argues, adults acquire guilt feelings about any expression of these hedonistic values that has not been earned through hard work. Subterranean values can be exercised only with restraint and only so long as they do not undermine the normal everyday realities of work and family life.

The drugs that have come to be seen as problematic in contemporary societies are those that are used to induce an escape from everyday realities into an alternative world where hedonistic values alone prevail. They are seen to be associated with subcultures that disdain the work ethic and enjoy pleasures that have not been earned through work: 'It is drug use of this kind that is most actively repressed by the forces of social order. For it is not drug-taking *per se* but the culture of drug-takers which is reacted against: not the notion of changing consciousness but the type of consciousness that is socially generated' (J. Young 1971: 137). In contemporary societies, Young argues, this kind of drug use is to be found in the inner-city subcultures and many youth subcultures.

Young found an overwhelming emphasis on drug use in the 'Bohemian youth culture' of the hippies of the 1960s. The use of mind-altering drugs was raised to a paramount position as one of the fundamental organizing principles for the identities of its members. This subculture—primarily a subculture of middle-class, student youth—was organized around spontaneity and expressivity and a rejection of work. It was in hippie culture that the main structural supports for cannabis use were found, and in the late 1960s Young documented its increasing emphasis also on the strong hallucinogenic drug LSD. What he called the delinquent youth culture, on the other hand, was more

characteristic of some working-class areas. Young saw this as generating an ambivalent attitude towards drug use. While the delinquent subculture was organized around its strong emphasis on subterranean values, drug use was merely tolerated or allowed—it was not required.

Normalized drug use

Young's work was undertaken in a period of full employment and relative affluence. The period since he wrote has seen the emergence of mass unemployment and economic insecurity, exacerbated by a global recession. Despite some improvement, employment remains insecure or uncertain for many young people. Illegal drug use today is not so much focused on hippie youth who reject the work ethic. It is now more strongly emphasized by the inner-city unemployed who have little experience of or prospect for secure and regular paid employment. Some glimpses of this were apparent in Young's references to the subculture of inner-city black Americans, as it had developed from the 1920s. He saw this as strongly supportive of cannabis use and as a principal source of heroin use. Their poverty and inferior status forced them into a rejection of conventional values and an embrace of subterranean values (Finestone 1964). Indeed, this was one of the principal contexts of drug use studied by Becker. This group has recently been identified as the core of a so-called underclass—an idea that we examine in Chapters 18 and 19.

In the 1970s, 'conformist youth culture' could still be seen as fully embracing conventional culture and its conditional commitment to hedonistic values. Its members were committed to work and to family, and their leisuretime activities posed no challenge to the dominance of the conventional values. Young saw this culture as having little significance for deviant drug-taking, holding that conformist youth simply made illicit use of alcohol (which they were not supposed to buy until aged 18) for the same purposes as their parents. It is clear today, however, that cannabis use has become common within this culture since the 1980s and that there was a growth in the use of Ecstasy in the 1990s. Declining employment opportunities in a period of recession broke the link between conventional work values and hedonistic values for many young people. Where there was little or no employment, the question of 'earning' pleasure simply did not arise.

As a result, drug use has increased among all sections of youth. Almost half (47 per cent) of 16-year-olds in Manchester in 1992 were reported to have used an illegal drug, generally cannabis, and just under three-quarters (71 per cent) had been in situations where drugs were available and on offer. In a national survey of 15–16-year-olds in 1996, 42 per cent had used an illegal drug (Parker and Measham 1994). The British Crime Survey for 2000 found that a quarter of those aged 16–19 and over a quarter of those aged 20–24 had used cannabis during the previous twelve months. A survey in 2004 of 16–24 year olds found that 39 per cent reported that they had used illegal drugs. Cannabis was the most commonly used drug, with 30 per cent of the young adults having used it. Use of Ecstasy, cocaine, or amphetamines was much lower, at about 4–7 per cent of 16–24-year-olds (*Social Trends* 2005: table 7.11). Heroin use, however, has been increasing in Britain, and the average age at which heroin users had first begun to experiment with the drug is 15. Three-quarters of the young people in inner-city areas are reported to have tried crack cocaine (a mixture of cocaine and baking soda). Class and gender show little association with drug availability and take-up, but ethnicity does. Black youths are rather more likely to come into contact with drugs than are white youths, as suggested in an earlier study by Pryce (1986), and Asians are far less likely to do so: only 32 per cent of young Asians in Manchester in 1992 reported having been offered drugs.

The ease of access to drugs such as cannabis—44 per cent of boys and 38 per cent of girls in 1996 had used it—shows that Becker's view of the importance of subcultures to occasional users must now be qualified. Changes in the urban and class conditions that sustained 'delinquent' subcultures in the past, combined with a more commercialized structure of illegal drug-trading, have resulted in a wider availability of drugs.

Drug use is now an integral, normalized part of a generalized youth culture, and not of specific class-based or deviant subcultures. Even the police are tolerant towards its use and generally caution those cannabis users who come their way. Along with music, clothes, magazines, and a love of fast cars, drugs and alcohol are a part of the everyday, pleasure-seeking experience of virtually all young people. The counter-cultural Bohemian and hippie orientations that Young identified in the 1960s are no longer an important part of this youth subculture, which is now a consumerist and leisure-oriented subculture organized around the pursuit of pleasure that is disconnected from the requirement to 'earn' it through productive work.

Despite its high profile in the news media, Ecstasy (MDMA) is far less widely used than cannabis. In a national survey in 1996, 9 per cent of boys and 7 per cent of girls reported having taken Ecstasy. Amphetamines (such as speed and whizz), LSD ('acid'), and solvents are all more widely used than Ecstasy: 20 per cent of boys and 21 per cent of girls had used solvents. Ecstasy, amphetamines, and LSD were all associated with regular involvement in dance clubs and raves, but in these venues cannabis remains the most widely used illegal drug. Indeed, alcohol—consumed under age—was even more widespread: 94 per cent of 15–16-year-olds in a national survey reported that they had consumed alcohol, generally on a regular basis. Over one-third were tobacco smokers, the rate of use and the rate of growth in use being higher among girls than among boys (Ettorre 1992; Oakley *et al.* 1992). These findings support the claim that there is now a 'poly-drug' culture in which users are not confined to the use of any one drug. Cannabis remains the drug of preference, but it is taken alongside other drugs. The latest figures from the British Crime Survey show increased use of Class A drugs among the population as a whole in the period 1996–2009, though a decline in certain specific drugs (see Figure 7.5).

Not all drugs used by young people are normalized features of the conformist youth culture. Heroin use, for example, is found among less than 2 per cent of young people, and these generally have little involvement in consumerism and conventional family life. Indeed, 'conformist' drug-users tend to regard heroin as a drug that would undermine their lifestyle. It is something to be avoided in favour of the more 'pleasure-oriented' drugs (M. Collison 1994). Auld *et al.* (1986) show that there is a characteristic *episodic user* of heroin: neither the occasional nor the regular user, but someone who has periods of sustained heroin use, followed by periods 'coming off' (see also Dorn and South 1987).

Retreatism and withdrawal from what is perceived as a hostile world are principal motives for those who have experienced a lifetime of emotional and physical abuse in broken families and poor districts (Ruggiero and South 1995: 116 ff.). Such users find it difficult to band together for mutual support in the deprived city areas where the homeless congregate, and their lifestyle forces them into close association with a vast criminal underworld of dealers and organized crime (Dorn *et al.* 1992). In these circumstances, heroin users are very likely to make the transition from primary to secondary deviation.

In the inner-city areas, the growth of an informal economy has been associated with the expansion of an extensive fringe of irregular activities—street-level thieving,

Figure 7.5 Trends in previous year drug use among 16–59-year-olds, 1996–2008/9

Increase	Decrease	Stable
• Any Class A drug	• Any drug	• Any stimulant drug
• Any cocaine	• Hallucinogens	• Opiates
• Cocaine powder	• LSD	• Crack cocaine
• Tranquillizers	• Amphetamines	• Ecstasy
	• Anabolic steroids	• Magic mushrooms
	• Cannabis	• Heroin
		• Methadone
		• Amyl nitrite
		• Glues

Source: Home Office (2009: box 2.1); http://rds.homeoffice.gov.uk/rds/pdfs09/hosb1209.pdf.

dealing and exchange of stolen and illicit goods of all kinds (Auld *et al.* 1986). The unemployed residents of these areas seek to make more than the bare public assistance level of income through involvement in these activities. Cannabis has, since the 1960s, become more closely tied to professional drug-dealing and, along with hard drugs such as heroin and cocaine, is traded on the streets. It has been estimated that, by 1997, the number of drug deals in London alone had reached an annual total of 30 million, with a total value of £600 million. Only around one in 4,000 street deals results in an arrest.

Through their involvement in this irregular economy, the unemployed can easily become involved in drug-dealing, and the opportunities for use are great. Small-scale users and others become drawn into large networks of organized drug crime. There is a hierarchical division of labour in the supply of drugs, and the largest rewards tend to go to those who are furthest removed from street-level dealing.

There has been a huge growth in the production and distribution of illegal drugs, and these activities have become entangled in other forms of crime, as well as in conforming and law-abiding behaviour such as money-dealing, commodity-trading, and political activity. The raw materials required for producing many drugs come from countries that are geographically distinct from their main users, and there has been a growing globalization of the drug trade.

Drug crops are fundamental to the agriculture of many of the world's poorest countries. Coca leaves for the production of cocaine are produced in Bolivia and Columbia, opium poppies for the production of heroin are grown in Nepal and Afghanistan, and marijuana is a cash crop in Jamaica. The consumption of these drugs, however, is concentrated in the advanced economies of Europe and the United States, and these crops are attractive to Third World farmers because of the secure and growing market available in those countries.

Local drug-dealers, who buy the crops from the producers, are often involved in other, legitimate, businesses and have strong financial and political connections to the local leaders. These countries allow the dealers to sell the drugs onwards and to launder the proceeds through their other business activities. A case in London in 2002 showed that proceeds from cocaine sales were processed through corrupt *bureaux de change* and through electronic money transfers involving banks in Britain, the Isle of Man, the United States, and Colombia (*Guardian*, 18 June 2002). There are sometimes loose global networks of gangs and dealers, as was reported to be the case with the Chinese

Briefing: drug arrests 7.8

Large sums can be made by those in the major European and American centres who buy Third World drugs in bulk. The British Customs and Excise ran its largest ever drugs investigation, Operation Stealer, in 1997, arresting forty-four people and seizing £65 million worth of drugs from an operation that involved dealers in three continents. Those who run the biggest risks, however, are the small-scale smugglers and street dealers who handle relatively small quantities of drugs. In the same month as Operation Stealer, a young woman in Colchester was found guilty for having nineteen small packets of heroin, some heroin stuffed in a teddy bear, and some cannabis inside her bra. She was sent to jail for three years.

In 2009, someone was arrested every second in the United States for a drug offence. These generally involved relatively minor offences, with only a very few relating directly to large-scale organized dealing.

Sources: *Guardian*, 1 July 1997; *Essex County Standard*, 18 July 1997; *Huffington Post*, 21 October 2009.

triads that dominated the nineteenth-century opium trade. Despite the claims of the US Food and Drug Administration Agency, there is no international cartel behind the Colombian cocaine trade, but there is an extensive and well-connected network of entrepreneurs, brokers, and minor dealers (see Box 7.8).

Opium production was a major element in the Afghanistan conflicts. When the Taliban leadership came to power they allowed the farming and sale of opium, but they outlawed it in 2000. As the Taliban had earned a considerable amount of money from heroin, it was suspected that this was a ploy to reduce supply and increase the price for the opium stockpiled in previous years. The ending of the Taliban regime in the Afghan war meant that many farmers began to plant poppies again, and output of heroin increased. The new government offered Afghan farmers $500 per acre to destroy their fields, but drug-traffickers made a counter offer of $6,400 per acre to grow opium poppies. A United Nations investigation estimated that by 2005, half a million people in Afghanistan were involved in the trafficking chain, and that the crop had an estimated annual value of $25 billion (**www.washingtonpost.com/wp-dyn/content/article/2005/07/14/AR2005071401913.html**).

Stop and reflect

In this section we have looked at how people learn to obtain and to use drugs for pleasure, and we traced the growing normalization of certain types of drug use.

- Is it possible to distinguish between the medical and the non-medical uses of drugs?

- People drift into drug use for a whole variety of reasons, and not all enter a career of persistent drug use. Persistent drug-users pass through a series of stages in which their experiences and identities alter.

- How useful is it to see drug use as the result of a learning process of the kind described by Becker?

- The use of drugs is closely involved with ideas of work, leisure, and pleasure. The use of certain drugs has been normalized in youth culture, and rates of use are now very high.

- The use of drugs and trading in them on the streets and in clubs is closely tied into large international networks of drug-trafficking and organized crime.

Organized crime, international crime, and terrorism

Crime is often seen in highly individual and informal terms, though we have tried to emphasize the ways in which it is generated in and through cultural and subcultural forms of social organization related to class, gender, and ethnic differences. It is also important, however, to recognize that much criminality is professionally organized, and we have, again, tried to indicate some of the ways in which this is socially organized. In this section, we turn to an examination of these issues of the formal social organization of crime in much greater detail. We look, in particular, at crime as a business, organized nationally and internationally in ways that challenge conventional businesses in the scale of their activities. We trace how processes of globalization have produced extensive transnational criminal organizations. We look also at the growing significance of international terrorism—the use of criminal acts for political purposes—and trace some of the parallels and connections between terrorism and organized crime.

Organized crime

Although we have looked at certain forms of professional and career crime, we have not discussed what is commonly referred to as 'organized crime'. This can be defined as a form of criminal activity organized as a business enterprise through the systematic use of administrative mechanisms, formal coordination, alliances, and joint ventures, and does so in relation to a range of markets for goods and services. Organized crime is criminal activity that goes beyond the relatively small-scale professional and gang activity considered so far. Like these, it has its roots in the

specific subcultures of criminality that comprise the underworld, but it also has quite distinctive causes and conditions. Where organized crime exists, it affects the whole pattern of crime within a society. In this section we will look at the common characteristics of organized crime in the United States, Russia, Japan, and Hong Kong, commonly seen as the foci of 'Mafia'-style criminality in the world today.

Mafia and *Cosa Nostra*

Public recognition of something called the Mafia or *Cosa Nostra* in the United States dates largely from the 1950s and 1960s, when a series of Senate hearings brought the activities of a number of leading Italian–American criminals to public attention. The most influential report on 'Mafia' organization was produced by Donald Cressey (1969) for a Presidential Task Force on organized crime (see also Albini 1971; Ianni and Reuss-Ianni 1972). Cressey showed the existence of a huge national confederation involved in fraud, drugs, prostitution, corruption, gambling, and violence, but also using its funds in conventional business operations such as property, finance, clubs, and restaurants. Its methods had come to parallel those of other business enterprises and it was impossible to disentangle illegal from legal activities and profits. This type of organized crime may never have been quite as tight and centralized as it seemed to the public and as it was portrayed in such films as *The Godfather*, but it was, in many ways, a distinctive form of criminal activity.

This kind of organized crime became a prominent feature of major American cities in the 1920s and 1930s. It is often seen as a direct outgrowth of the rural networks of support and control that proliferated in Sicily and other isolated parts of Italian society in the nineteenth century and that were transplanted to the United States by migrants from these areas. These were loose networks of friends and relations, rather than secret societies, and were organized around the 'honour' of family and locality and were involved in a wide range of neighbourhood and regional activities (Blok 1974; Boissevain 1974; Gambetta 1993).

However, the true origins of organized crime are more recent and more complex. It arose in its contemporary form following the great waves of European migration to New York, Chicago, and other American cities and was an outgrowth of the very specific urban conditions of the 1920s and 1930s. The city slums gave rise to many loosely organized groups rooted in their distinctive subcultures. We have already shown how similar gangs also emerged in districts of London. The emergence of such gangs can be explained by the distinctive subcultures found in lower-class areas of large cities and the differential association in which this results (Sutherland 1939). It depends also, however, on the attractiveness of an 'innovative' response to the anomie of such areas (Merton 1938b).

The gangs of the major US cities became heavily involved in the production and sale of 'bootleg' alcohol, made profitable by the 'Prohibition' legislation that made the manufacture and sale of alcohol illegal. The principal bootleggers of whisky were European immigrants and the descendants of immigrants, both Italians and Sicilians being especially prominent. They were actively involved in a range of criminal activities within their neighbourhoods and became drawn into intensive conflict for customers. An alliance of Sicilian and Italian gangs was forged in 1930–1 and came to be known by outsiders as the Mafia. Far from being a direct descendant of the rural neighbourhood networks, then, the gang grouping of the 1930s was a new phenomenon and a distinctive product of American society. It is true, nevertheless, that many of the leading figures in the emerging criminal gangs were recent migrants who had fled the clampdown on the Italian mafia by Mussolini's Fascist regime in the late 1920s. For all these reasons, Cressey rejected the 'mafia' label, holding that it is inaccurate and was not used by the participants themselves. Those in the gangs preferred to refer to themselves with such impersonal terms as the 'organization', 'business', or 'firm', and sometimes *Cosa Nostra* ('our thing').

This organization existed, Cressey argued, as a federation of separate and autonomous family-based gangs, each of which defended its particular territory and depended on the support of its local population. In acting 'honourably'

> **➲ Connections**
>
> At this point you might like to review our discussion of Merton's account of anomie in Chapter 2, pp. 44–5.

towards 'their' people, providing them with the political influence and personal welfare they were denied by the city and national authorities, the gangs earned the respect of those living in their neighbourhoods. This support was reinforced through coercion aimed at ensuring that no one in the locality would challenge the right of the gang to monopolize its profitable ventures. Typical of such territorial groups was the Capone Mob of 1930s Chicago.

By the 1960s, Cressey argued, there were over thirty such family mobs. Each family boss—or 'Don'—held absolute authority in his territory. Through a series of cross-cutting alliances designed to protect the territorial claims of each of the gangs, a vast national organization had been built. The Organization itself had no single leader, but was run by a committee of major mobsters known as the 'Commission'. Cressey held that, by the late 1960s, the Organization was dominated by nine powerful families: three from New York, three in the surrounding cities of Buffalo, Newark, and Boston, and one each in Philadelphia, Detroit, and Chicago. The various families recognized the role of the Commission in resolving disputes and coordinating activities at a national level.

The criminal activities of a family gang were typically organized through a hierarchy of executive positions, running from the Don through his deputy and advisers to the 'Buffer', who acted as the interface or intermediary between senior family members and the lower-level operatives. The Buffer had various 'Lieutenants' responsible for particular operating units, each of which had its Section Chief to liaise with the 'Soldiers', who actually operated particular activities—money-lending, lotteries, vending-machine rackets, protection, and so on. Beyond the level of the Soldiers, many non-Italians were employed or contracted for specific purposes at street level to take bets, answer telephones, sell drugs, collect protection money, and so on.

Cressey further claimed that the Organization and its families operated according to a strict code of behaviour that governs all their activities. This code comprises five principles:

1 *Loyalty*. This is the basic injunction to respect the interests of other families and to keep silent about family activities.

2 *Rationality*. This is the requirement to act coolly and calmly in pursuit of the family's business: not to take drugs, not to get into fights, and to follow orders as a good team player.

3 *Honour*. This is tied to ideas of masculinity and patriarchalism, involving respect for women and for the senior members of the family.

4 *Courage*. Family members are to withstand pressure and punishment without complaint. This is, again, tied to a strong ethos of masculinity.

5 *Commitment*. Family members are to uphold their way of life without being drawn into the conventions of regular employment or social conformism.

Joseph Albini has stressed that the Organization must not be thought of as a bureaucratic enterprise. It is, rather, a loose-knit system of patron–client or network relationships (Albini 1988). As such, its structure is constantly in flux, and no rigid model can describe its shape at any particular time. It is clear, nevertheless, that Cressey highlighted the ways in which such a loose-knit structure can coordinate and control the actions of its constituent gangs through both formal and informal mechanisms. Some questions about sources on organized crime can be found in Box 7.9.

Other organized crime

Much discussion of organized crime in the United States has been concerned with that of Italian Americans, but a number of sociologists have pointed to the existence of many other forms of organized crime. Robert Davidson (1992) has documented the rise of Asian-American gangs in Chicago and other American cities. Those from China, the Philippines, India, Korea, and other parts of Asia now form a significant section of the US population. A number of areas of Asian settlement have shown a growth of criminal involvement in drug-trafficking, especially the trade in heroin from South East Asia. Organized gangs in American cities use their connections with Chinese triads operating from Hong Kong to obtain heroin for resale in the United States. Actual sales to users are handled by street gangs, but the bulk trade itself is a highly organized business.

Outside the United States, evidence for strong organized criminal gangs has been found in Japan, Russia, and parts of Eastern Europe. Organized crime had begun to develop in the final twenty years of Communism in Russia, when corrupt and self-serving politicians used illegal means to further their own interests, but it was the collapse of Communism that really stimulated its growth. The disappearance of the strong, totalitarian state in Russia and the consequent privatization of state economic assets allowed many private individuals to amass considerable wealth through dealing in state assets. Many former Communist politicians were able to use their knowledge and connections to build up personal fortunes themselves and to join this emerging Russian 'mafia'. Organized crime has proliferated because of the economic dislocation that followed the ending of Communism, as this allowed the criminal syndicates to obtain and monopolize scarce resources from which they could benefit.

Russian organized crime, like its American counterpart, is organized through loose 'syndicates' that operate on the basis of patron–client relationships. In these relationships, a person of power or wealth helps or protects specific others (the clients), who, in return, perform services for their patron. The relationship is not a contractual, employment relationship but rests on informal patterns of trust and obligation. Hierarchies of patron–client relationships form networks of reciprocity and obligation centred on the most powerful individuals. Those involved in these networks are engaged in a range of illegal activities. Although Russia has virtually no bank robberies, bank fraud is rife and banks pay high levels of protection money to avoid becoming the targets of robberies. Forging of documents is widespread, as is illegal arms-trading, including dealing in nuclear materials, prostitution, drug-smuggling, money-laundering, and illegal imports. Crime is so closely integrated with conventional business that it has been argued that there is a 'shadow economy' of marginal and unregulated business with its 'black market' for distributing goods. There are high levels of political corruption, giving the criminal syndicates considerable influence over the state (Albini *et al.* 1997; Varese 2001).

Organized crime in Hong Kong and mainland China originated in the 'triad' secret societies, though it now reaches beyond them. Triads are a long-standing feature of traditional Chinese society and prospered in Hong Kong during its separation from the rest of China. A triad is a family- and neighbourhood-based grouping that provides support and services for its members and organizes its activities on the basis of secrecy and elaborate rituals of membership. Acting outside, and often against, the central state, triads became involved in a range of legal and illegal activities. Triad activity in Hong Kong grew after the Communist revolution in China, when many prominent leaders were expelled from the mainland. The economic success of Hong Kong since the 1960s provided many opportunities for triads to expand their involvement in prostitution, gambling, and drugs.

While there is continuity between the traditional triads and those of today, systematic involvement in organized crime is a recent and more specific phenomenon. Triads tend to be organized as loose networks of independent gangs that see themselves as part of a larger 'family' or clan with a decentralized structure of command. The various gangs are loosely ranked as 'Red Pole', 'Blue Lantern', and ordinary. Although they cooperate for common purposes, they are also involved in recurrent and intense conflict over the pursuit of their interests.

Organized crime in Japan originated in gambling groups and itinerant dealers who banded together for mutual protection and were given official encouragement to organize markets at shrines and temples and to regulate the supply of labour for public works construction. By the early twentieth century, they were a strongly entrenched feature of Japanese society and had come to be known as *Yakuza* (Hill 2003). They were used as government tools for strike-breaking and for fighting left-wing political groups, and they had strong links with right-wing political leaders. The *Yakuza* took their present form, however, after the Second World War. Industrial reconstruction and slow political liberalization created opportunities for profitable enterprise in the black markets and in the supply of labour for construction and dock work. They moved into the growing entertainment industry of bars, prostitution, and *pachinko* (pin ball), and they extended their protection and extortion activities. Intense conflict among *Yakuza* led to the emergence of a small number of major syndicates, paralleling the structure of business groups that had developed in the conventional economy. Despite a police clampdown in the 1960s, organized crime in Japan remains highly concentrated.

Hill (2003) established that there were about 90,000 men involved in organized crime in Japan and that about 40 per cent were involved in gangs affiliated to one of the three big syndicates: *Yamaguchi-gumi*, *Iwagawa-kai*, and *Sumiyoshi-kai*. The syndicates have great similarities to Cressey's model of the *Cosa Nostra* and are organized in ways that draw on the idea of the traditional family household, with its paternalistic and authoritarian patterns of control by the 'father' over junior members. Formal administrative mechanisms are also used, however, and the syndicates are organized into series of ranks such as 'boss', executive, soldier, and trainee. A *Yakuza* syndicate and its affiliated groupings are organized in relation to a tight discipline and obedience, embodied in a strict code of behaviour that is enforced, when necessary, through violence. *Yakuza* are currently involved in protection rackets, the supply of drugs, gambling, the sale of festival trinkets, prostitution, debt collection, loan-sharking, rent collection, and the supply of labour through subcontractors. In many of these areas they act under commission from conventional businesses and public authorities, which rely on the ability of the *Yakuza* to manage and manipulate their employees, shareholders, and voters through blackmail and coercion.

International crime

Organized crime, we have suggested, has certain similarities with conventional business activity. Like many businesses, those involved in organized crime have expanded their activities to an international level. Organized criminal gangs in the United States, China, Russia, and elsewhere have been involved in extensive international transactions and have increasingly begun to organize their activities on a global scale.

> **⊙ Connections**
>
> Try to think about organized crime in relation to the general issue of globalization that we discuss in Chapter 16. You may like to have a quick look at pp. 623–5 now.

State borders have always provided opportunities for, as well as barriers to, criminal activity. Within the United States, organized crime has been able to operate under different state jurisdictions, as laws vary from one part of the country to another, and it has been only a small step further to operate across international state borders. Providing goods and services that are legal in one state but illegal in another provides great opportunities for such operations. The smuggling of alcohol and tobacco, because of variations in tax levels, is one example of such international crime that has existed for a very long time. The growing complexity of legal regulations and of the economic and political interdependence of nation states has created immense opportunities that organized crime groups have been able to exploit. It has been argued that the globalization of the political economy has resulted in a globalization of crime (Ruggiero *et al.* 1998; Findlay 1999).

Causes and consequences

The most obvious and important criminal activity is smuggling, and this has always existed alongside and interdependently of legal international trade. The liberalization of international trade, creating global markets and encouraging business enterprises to operate freely and without regard for national borders has created a situation in which smuggling operations come to be seen, almost, as forms of 'free-trade' activity. International smugglers can present themselves as providing commodities that market restrictions prevent from flowing freely across the world. Although smuggling is often thought of in terms of a tourist carrying a few hundred cigarettes or a bottle of whisky, the scale of smuggling is immense and is highly organized. It has been estimated that smuggling is a major global business, valued at more than $600 billion a year, especially through money-laundering operations closely tied to established banking and financial activities.

The transformation of the transport industry with the rise of large container ships and juggernaut lorries has transformed methods of smuggling. Previously, drugs such as cannabis and cocaine were smuggled into the United States in small planes and speedboats, but organized criminal groups are now transporting larger consignments in sealed containers alongside conventional cargos. Containers and sealed lorries are also used to smuggle migrants across national borders. These mechanisms are anonymous and impersonal, making it more difficult for states to trace those responsible. The flow of goods from Mexico to the United States, for example, combines both legal and illegal commodities. Drug-traffickers have established factories and distribution centres in northern Mexico and have taken advantage of the deregulated trucking industry to transport their drugs into the United States alongside legitimate trade in fruit and vegetables. Within the European Union, the opening-up of national borders has made it easier for lorries to transport economic migrants, asylum-seekers, and drugs into Germany, France, and Britain (Andreas 2002).

The liberalization of financial markets was intended to promote the transnational flow of capital, but it has also promoted a huge growth in money-laundering. This is the process through which the proceeds from illegal activities can be converted into legal—and untraceable—financial assets through the use of multiple international bank accounts and investments in tax havens and other financial centres (Sikka 2003). This has been particularly important for organized criminal groups from Russia and Colombia.

The transformation of the international financial system has also created opportunities for new forms of crime. The almost exclusive reliance on credit cards for consumer purchases has made the copying of credit cards and the 'skimming' of credit details from them into a major criminal activity. Information from cards skimmed in a London restaurant can be used to produce cards that can, within hours, be used to make purchases in New York, Athens, or Rome. The technology required makes this an obvious area for the involvement of organized criminal groups, which have increased their level of investment in technologies for fraud in the face of the growth in international credit-card trading (see Box 7.10).

Criminal organizations

The actors involved in international crime are many and diverse. Organized crime groups vary from one country to another, and even within countries. They are not organized in precisely the same way as large-scale business enterprises engaged in conventional activities, but they do have certain common characteristics as international actors and they use many of the same mechanisms as those conventional businesses.

Criminal groups from numerous countries extend their international scope and combine with other criminal groups in a number of ways. At its loosest, there may be a recognition of the respective spheres of influence and territories of each group, but these easily give way to mutual supplier relationships that may persist over time (P. Williams 2002). Colombian drug-producers, for example, have established stable supply linkages with Italian organized criminal groups, and the latter are given exclusive rights to redistribute the drugs across Western Europe. The Russian organized crime groups have established links with organized criminal groups in the Netherlands and Japan for supplying women from Eastern Europe for prostitution. Such supply relations may involve barter rather than money transactions: guns may be exchanged for drugs, for example.

Stronger forms of transnational organization occur when groups form what Williams (2002) has called tactical and strategic alliances. Short-term tactical cooperation may lead to longer-term strategic alliances that allow systematic and extensive cooperation. Drug-trafficking into the United States, for example, has involved the

 New technology Internet crime 7.10

The Internet makes it very easy for organized criminal groups to steal credit details—and even whole identities—through intercepting insecure credit-card transactions. Major Internet providers and dealers, such as Microsoft and e-bay, have sought to increase the security of their systems in the face of technologies of both crime and control.

E-mail has also made new forms of crime possible. A widespread financial scam is the sending of 'spam' messages claiming to be from a deposed politician—generally in Nigeria—who is looking for a bank account in which to lodge millions of pounds. In return for allowing the use of an account, the e-mail user is told that he or she will receive many thousands of pounds in commission. This is, of course, merely another way of persuading people to pass on details about their bank account, which can rapidly be emptied or used for illegal purposes.

There has been a huge growth in the creation of authentic-looking e-mails and websites that appear to be those of legitimate businesses such as banks and payment operations. In a 'spamming' operation, e-mails are sent to millions of Internet users in the hope that just a handful will believe the message to be genuine and will log on to the fraudulent website and enter their account details.

establishment of strong strategic linkages between Colombian producers and dealers in the Dominican Republic, these links being built as their earlier reliance on Mexican intermediaries became less profitable. Most recently, the Colombian dealers have built strategic alliances with Russian groups to handle distribution through Eastern and Central Europe.

If there are no transnational bureaucratic criminal organizations, the loose networks do, nevertheless, have certain formal mechanisms of cooperation. It has been reported that summit meetings of major criminal groups have been used to regulate spheres of influence and to plan joint ventures. Although the participants are not, in any sense, representatives or leaders of whole national criminal gangs, the meetings do bring together many of the important criminal groups and bring some stability to international criminal activity. These meetings are complemented by bilateral meetings and by continued contacts through intermediaries. Some criminal groups, it has been suggested, have made such mediation and courier business their main activity.

Much discussion has focused on the idea that the Chinese triads of Hong Kong have expanded through the overseas Chinese communities to establish transnational triad organizations. Hong Kong has been seen as the directing centre for such global criminal activities, and the drive to globalization has been strengthened since the 1997 return of Hong Kong to rule—and strong political control—from Beijing. While Chinese organized criminal groups have certainly established strong links across national borders, there is no global triad structure. Chinese communities are diverse in their ethnicity and there is little basis for dominance by Hong Kong migrants. Chinese criminal gangs have become very active in drug-smuggling and people-smuggling, but they do so as parts of the larger growth in global criminal activity.

Terrorism

Terrorism is political action against a state and its citizens that pursues its goals through extreme violence, often on a spectacular or mass scale, and that is generally criminalized through legislation, proscription, and exclusion. It has become, since the 1960s, one of the most important targets for police and security service operations and it has entered the public consciousness as a major—and perhaps permanent—source of concern at work, in travel, and during leisure. X-ray and security checks at airports and other public places have become an accepted, if unwelcome, weapon in what many politicians describe as 'the war against terrorism'.

Violent political conflict has a history as long as the human species. Its organized form as the internal opposition of political groups to state authorities has a history almost as long. Eric Hobsbawm (1969) has termed this 'social banditry' when it takes the form of redistributive political action pursued through violent acts that are criminalized by the state. Social bandits engage in a range of criminal activities in support of their political aims, and their overall political strategy and tactics are labelled as criminal by the state they attack. In rural societies, social banditry is generated by a sense of grievance and wrongdoing and a desire to secure vengeance and justice. Examples of such social banditry include the idealistic robber of the Robin Hood myth, the guerrilla or resistance fighter, and the violent avengers who terrorize their opponents.

Pacification of their societies by industrializing states, especially those that established liberal and democratic structures, greatly reduced the level of social banditry and institutionalized the legitimate and non-violent opposition of political parties. Even in these societies, however, criminalized forms of political violence could still erupt. Many European governments of the nineteenth century were concerned about the activities of 'anarchists', who were widely seen as motivated by the French Revolution. Anarchists were thought to form secret societies and organizations through which they could plot acts of violence, and a number of bombings and assassinations did take place in this period.

The most protracted forms of political violence, however, have been linked with separatist and nationalist claims, as in the Irish Republican Army (IRA) in the United Kingdom from the late nineteenth century until the establishment of the Republic of Ireland in 1922. The IRA attacked political or military targets and saw itself as engaged in a war against an imposed state.

From the 1960s, these forms of political violence were renewed, but they also began to be transformed as dispossessed groups generated by international conflicts began to take their struggles to the metropolitan and colonial states they saw as responsible for their oppression. This was the beginning of the form of violent political conflict described as terrorism.

The violent political organizations of the late 1960s and 1970s—groups such as the IRA, the Red Army Faction, the Red Brigade, and ETA—were formed, like the IRA of fifty years earlier, as highly centralized and tightly coordinated organizations with a structure of command modelled on that of conventional armies. Indeed, many used militaristic terminology in their names and in their tactics. They emerged in the political upheavals of the 1960s and saw themselves pursuing radical, leftist policies through violent means because they were unable to pursue their goals through conventional political means. They often saw themselves as part of an international struggle, though their international links were limited and each group tended to operate on a national basis. Their targets were politicians and businessmen, embassies and banks, and national airlines.

The rise of Islamist terrorism

The first signs of a change in the nature of terrorism occurred in the wake of the Arab–Israeli War of 1967, which led to the dispossession of large numbers of Palestinians in the Israeli-occupied territories. The involvement of Western states in this conflict, where support generally went to Israel, led many Palestinians to see Israel and Western governments as legitimate targets for acts of violence. Many came to see their conflict in religious terms, drawing on Islam to construct an ideology of political opposition. Groups such as Al-Fatah and Hezbollah organized themselves to pursue the goal of Palestinian liberation and autonomy through all means necessary, and many of their supporters came to see this as a first step in a holy war (*jihad*) through which the boundaries of the Islamic world could be extended across the globe. This Islamist ideology—often misunderstood as 'Islamic fundamentalism' (see Box 7.11)—was strengthened by the Iranian revolution in which the regime of the Western-oriented Shah was replaced by a radical Islamic caliphate under the Ayatollah Khomeini. Iran became a major centre for fomenting and supporting Islamist terrorism, and hijack and kidnapping became the principal means through which struggles against particular states were globalized.

A continuing failure to resolve the Palestinian situation radicalized other states in the Middle East, and numerous state-sponsored terrorist organizations arose. A crucial step was taken, however, in the heart of Asia, where

Russian intervention in Afghanistan led to the formation of *mujahideen* guerrilla groups who went on to build training camps across the country and to build links with radicals and terrorist groups in Pakistan and the Middle East. A variety of groups began to take their struggles to an international level and to broaden their targets from the political and the military to civilians. Bombs were set off at Western embassies in Kenya and Tanzania and at US embassies in the Middle East; hotels, restaurants, and buses became targets in Israel; and the World Trade Center in New York was bombed in 1993. This shift also involved a change in tactics, as car bombs and suicide bombs became the main weapons of attack.

The most visible sign of this shift in targets was the destruction of the twin towers of the World Trade Center on 11 September 2001. In this attack, hijacked airliners were flown directly into the towers and, simultaneously into the Pentagon in Washington. This led directly to a US-led invasion of Afghanistan, which was seen as the coordinating and training centre of international terrorism. Osama bin-Laden, a Saudi Arabian millionaire, was identified as the leading figure in an organized terrorist group called Al-Qaeda, and the war in Afghanistan was supposed to destroy his power base. Continuing American involvement in Afghanistan fuelled Islamist radicalism and wider public opinion across the Middle East, and terror attacks continued. In the search for states supporting this spread of terrorism, the United States led an invasion of Iraq, incorrectly seen as the source of international terrorism. While this invasion successfully removed the oppressive regime of Saddam Hussein, it created yet a further pretext for Islamist violence. American and British soldiers became targets of attack by Islamist groups from Iraq and the surrounding countries, and opposition to Western governments reached a higher level than before. The direct consequences may have included further increases in political terror, most notably in night clubs in Indonesia in 2002, in the Madrid train bombs of 2004, the London transport bombings of 2005, the Glasgow airport attack in 2007, and the Pakistan hotel bombings of 2008.

This growth in Islamist terrorism is often interpreted on the model of the violent political conflict of the past. Thus, it is seen as the product of a centralized and coordinated organization, headed by Osama bin-Laden, that plans its numerous coordinated attacks in immense detail. Actions such as the events of 9/11 certainly require meticulous planning, but it would be wrong to see these and similar

Briefing: Islam and Islamist ideologies 7.11

It is important to recognize a distinction between Islamist ideologies and the beliefs of Islam. Islamist ideologies are those that may be based on particular interpretations of Islam but that ally this with ideas that are opposed to secularism and that support the establishment of political systems in which their interpretation of Islam is promoted against all other forms of belief. Many Muslims, whether liberal or more traditional in their beliefs, reject such views and advocate a tolerance towards other religions and systems of political belief. Many commentators incorrectly and insultingly describe some violent political groups as 'Islamic terrorists', when they should be referring to Islamist terrorism. Islamist ideology should not be seen simply as 'Islamic fundamentalism' and it should certainly not be equated with Islam *per se*.

➜ *Connections*

You will find a full listing of recent attacks on p. 632 in Chapter 16. Pages 631–3 of that chapter also give a fuller discussion of the political context of and political responses to international terrorism.

attacks as part of the master plan of an army-like organization. We have shown that organized crime borrows certain elements from conventional business practice but applies these in a far looser and decentralized way. Islamist terrorism, too, has learned much from conventional military and security practices, but these are employed in novel ways through decentralized networks in which chains of command are complex and fragmentary.

Al-Qaeda does not exist as a monolithic organizational entity. The word means 'base' or 'model', and it was formed to promote a model of how the Islamist cause could be promoted and to establish an intellectual base from which activists could draw inspiration (Jason Burke 2004). It was probably formed in 1988 in Pakistan as a way of helping to maintain the political unity of those who had fought against the Russians in Afghanistan. It had, however, a purely nominal existence until 1996, when bin-Laden and a number of other politico-religious factions began to build training camps in Afghanistan and it became an important coordinating element in a larger network of militant groups. Its influence within this network came from bin-Laden's ability to provide finance, resources, and a safe base for terrorist operations.

Actual operations are planned by the many local groups linked to this network and there is little or no overall coordination. The 9/11 bombings did involve a greater degree of planning and coordination than many other attacks before or since, and the bin-Laden group does seem to have retained overall control. The initial idea came from a group from Egypt, the United Arab Republic, and Lebanon living in Hamburg, and it was through Osama bin-Laden that a number of Saudi Arabian activists in Afghanistan were drawn in to support the operation without having any part in its planning. The finance for the operation—estimated at $500,000—came from bin-Laden and was laundered through the international banking system to make it untraceable. The American-led invasion of Afghanistan in 2001 disrupted this network and made it impossible for the country to be used as a safe base. Bin-laden set up a more mobile base in Pakistan and continued his attempts to inspire Islamist terrorism: he and his associates issued videos in support of terrorist attacks and encouraged others to follow suit. However, Al-Qaeda has even less of a directive role in this terrorism than before.

Islamist terrorism is now planned and executed by very small groups with multifarious, but loose, links to each other. Actual terrorist operations are generally planned by small groups or clusters of individuals, linked by ethnicity and family background and, perhaps, worshipping at the same mosque. The London underground attacks of 7 July 2005 were largely planned and carried out by a small group of British Asians from Leeds, while the failed attempts of later that month were undertaken by a small group of Somalis from south London. A willingness to participate in acts of terrorism is something that individuals drift into and to which they gradually become more committed as a result of their ideological radicalization through religious events and groupings allied to, but not parts of, particular mosques in their own country and in Pakistan. Loose and informal connections with people met informally, if at all, are the means through which they acquire the necessary knowledge and materials for their attacks. Those who become involved in terrorist activities know very few other participants, making it especially difficult for security services to build up intelligence through the usual mechanisms of tracing known contacts. Their acts are not an expression of widely held subcultural beliefs in their locality—indeed, public opinion in their communities is generally strongly opposed to such acts. Nevertheless, their radical views can often be interpreted by outsiders as mere religious fervour, and, embedded in their localities, they may be all but invisible to these outsiders.

 ## *Stop and reflect*

In this section, we have explored a number of issues relating to organized crime and violence and its increasingly transnational character. Review your knowledge by considering the following:

- Contemporary organized crime in the United States cannot simply be traced back to rural roots in the Sicilian mafia. It is a specific adaptation to contemporary economic and political conditions.

- Organized crime takes the form of loose networks, often with a family or neighbourhood base, but connected through formal mechanisms of communication and control.

- Patterns of organized crime in the United States, Russia, Japan, and Hong Kong all show a similarity and overlap with conventional business activity.

- Is organized crime a bigger social problem than informal street crime?

We have drawn on parallels between organized crime and international terrorism. Review your knowledge by considering the following:

- New forms of terrorism arose from the 1960s and have had their focus in Islamist ideologies produced in the Middle East.
- International terrorism has a loosely structured organization, with acts of terrorism largely initiated and planned by small, local groups rather than by a vast international conspiracy.
- People may drift into terrorism, their radical views sustained by their subculture, but terrorist acts are not expressions of subcultural values and are not supported by Islamic communities.
- Why has Islamist terrorism led to so much hostility towards Islamic communities?

Key concepts

- addiction 247
- career deviance 231
- craft crime 235
- crime 234
- deviance 227
- drift 231

- labelling theory 228
- moral career 231
- normalization 230
- own 232
- primary deviation 230
- project crime 235

- secondary deviation 230
- underworld 236
- white-collar crime 243
- wise 232

Workshop 7

Study 7 Bank robbers

Martin Gill (2000) has carried out one of the few ethnographic studies of commercial robbery—that is, robbery aimed at business and commercial premises and property. He interviewed a sample of 341 people imprisoned for robberies of commercial properties such as banks and building societies, or cash-in-transit vans, aiming to uncover the motives behind their robberies and to study the ways in which they identified targets and planned their crimes. Gill reports that most of the robbers had been convicted for the first time in their teens, generally for assaults, car crimes, or burglaries. Most were in their twenties before they first committed a robbery, but few regarded themselves as exclusively robbers. The overriding motive was, unsurprisingly, financial gain, but many robbers reported that their desire for money was associated with unemployment or a desire for excitement. The money gained from robberies was most typically spent on drugs, alcohol, and gambling, and on living the 'high life'. It was generally spent in a relatively short period rather than being invested to meet long-term living expenses.

Much of Gill's research concerns the organizational structure of robbery, and particularly the actual planning and carrying-out of robberies. The planning of a robbery varied considerably. In the case of banks and cash-in-transit, planning took more than a week, while building-society, post-office, and off-licence robberies were generally planned only over a day or two. This reflected robbers' perceptions of whether a particular target was a 'soft' or 'hard' one. Supermarkets and off-licences, but also building societies, were generally regarded as soft targets that required little or no planning. Robbers might, on the spur of the moment, drive into town and look for a likely place to rob with only a very minimal reconnaissance. Large-scale cash robberies directed at banks, on the other hand, required more meticulous preparation in advance and might involve periods of surveillance. It was not uncommon in such cases to rely on information received from friends or acquaintances, and this might some-times involve the cooperation of someone on the inside of the organization targeted. Hard targets also tended to involve more robbers: a bank or bank van might typically involve a team of three or more robbers. Physical security measures such as closed-circuit television cameras were rarely deterrents to rob-bery, as robbers simply hid their faces or wore disguises.

Gill draws on his results and a series of case studies to reflect on attempts to construct a typology of robbers. The clearest divi-sion that he found was that between the amateurs and the pro-fessionals, who could be distinguished by the amount of planning and organization that they did and by the sizes of their targets. There was, however, much overlap between these cate-gories. Gill sees far more uniformity among robbers of all types, with their willingness to engage in robberies depending on their rational calculation of the particular rewards and the costs

involved in the specific situations in which they find themselves: their assessment of the risk and the opportunities, the presence of cameras, screens, and other security measures, and so on.

➲ Gill stresses the rationality of robbers. Refer back to our discussion of rational action theory in Chapter 2, p. 52, and see how useful you think this approach might be in explaining Gill's findings.

❷ How valid are Gill's conclusions likely to be, considering that his sample consisted of those who had been caught and convicted for their robberies?

❷ Read the case studies presented by Gill (2000: ch. 4). What evidence do they provide for the various theories of crime that we have considered in this chapter? What evidence is there for labelling processes, differential association, and drift, for example?

Media watch 7   Phone theft

The problem of crime is often depicted as a problem of youth crime, so you will find it useful to consider some aspects of this. Look back at our discussion of mobile phone theft at the begin-ning of this chapter, p. 227.

The Chairman of the Youth Justice Board in Britain saw these trends in crime as showing the growing importance of gang crime committed by young people against other young people. He claims that there are 400 'problem estates' in Britain where gangs of up to sixty members operate. These gangs are said to recruit their members from those excluded from school. Gang activity on these estates, he said, encouraged a 'culture of bul-lying and intimidation' that undermined authority and order at school and on the streets. Gang members steal mobile phones, trainers, and designer clothing, they are involved in drug use, and they coerce girls into sex. This crime is missed in the British Crime Survey, the Chairman argued, because only those aged over 16 were interviewed.

Reporting on these views, the *Independent* newspaper identi-fied what it held to be the five types of tactic used by these juve-nile gangs:

● *the blitz*: a brief attack by a group of youngsters, generally on an older person;

● *the snatch*: a crime where one gang member targets the victim;

● *the confrontation*: a crime where the victim is surrounded by gang members, who threaten and intimidate until the targeted goods are surrendered;

● *the con*: a crime where one gang member distracts the victim and lures him, or her, to where the other gang members are waiting;

● *the trap*: a robbery that takes place when an outsider enters a gang's territory and is surrounded by its members.

Consult the official statistics on crime (see the Home Office website listed in the 'Online resources' section below) and see what information you can discover about the extent of this kind of juvenile crime. Do the statistics tell you anything about whether the perpetrators of the crime are acting as members of a gang? What are the problems of drawing any firm conclusions from these data?

The Youth Justice Board held that these kinds of crime tend to lead to custodial sentences, and it advocated a greater use of community service as a penalty. Do you think such a shift in sen-tencing would be successful in reducing the amount of crime and the likelihood of juvenile offenders drifting into long-term criminality?

Use the Index and the Contents page of this book to find the sections in Chapter 9, 'Education', and Chapter 13, 'Cities and communities', that might be relevant to explaining youth crime. Can you find any material that would help to assess the accuracy of Lord Warner's depiction of schools and communities?

Go to your library and find some books on juvenile crime and delinquency. The classic sources are Cohen (1955) and Yablonsky (1967).

Discussion points

Review the various 'Stop and reflect' points in this chapter. You may find it useful to consider these in relation to our discussion of socialization and identity in Chapter 4. The topics that we considered can usefully be revised in three groups: the most general issues raised about deviance; general issues related to crime and criminality; and issues related to organized crime and terrorism.

Deviance, reaction, and identity

In 'Understanding deviance and control' we set out a number of general ideas that were applied to deviance in later parts of the chapter:

- How important do you think it is to distinguish between 'difference' and 'deviance'?

- Make sure that you understand the meaning of primary deviation and secondary deviation, and that you understand the role of labelling and stigmatization in establishing role deviance.

- Try to think of examples of processes of 'drift' in and out of deviance.

Many writers and commentators on deviance still look to biology for the causes of crime. Look back at our discussion of biological and cultural determinism in Chapter 4, pp. 133–6, and then consider the following questions:

- Lombroso and other biological theorists used terms such as 'atavism', 'degenerate', 'lower races', and 'born criminal'. Can these be considered to have any scientific meaning, or are they mere value judgements?

- How much attention should sociologists give to recent developments in genetics that have claimed to identify the genes responsible for particular kinds of behaviour?

Crime and criminal careers

We began our discussion of crime with an account of the distinctive features of the criminal law, distinguishing it from civil law, constitutional law, and other specialist forms of law. We then looked at criminal behaviour as a specific form of deviance. A number of the issues that we looked at concern the formal and informal social organization of crime:

- Make sure that you understand the terms craft crime, project crime, underworld, and white-collar crime.

- How plausible is it to describe career crime as a job? Why are women less likely than men to engage in a career of theft?

- What problems do you think might be involved in calculating the economic significance of corporate crime?

- Compare the data in Figures 7.2 (p. 235) and 7.4 (p. 240). Why are the numbers in each category of offence so different in the two tables? Which type of crime reported to the police is most likely to result in a conviction or caution? And which is the least likely?

Drugs and pleasure

Our sections on drugs and sexuality looked at diverse ways in which people pursue pleasure, and we paid particular attention to the ways that their actions come to be seen as conformist or deviant:

- Why is there such great diversity in the social reaction to different drugs and other mood-changing substances?

- How would you define the following terms: occasional user, regular user, addiction, hedonism, retreatism?

- Make sure that you understand the main ideas of Becker and Young.

You should give some attention to the particular methodological problems involved in trying to find accurate information about these matters. You will find some useful background in Chapter 3:

- Using the data in Figure 7.5 (p. 251), draw a pie chart showing the users of different types of drug. Are the data in the figure likely to be reliable? Why is this?

- What are the main problems involved in obtaining accurate information about drug use?

Organized crime and terrorism

We discussed the relationship between formal and informal mechanisms of control in the organization of criminal and terrorist actions.

- Why does the conventional view of organized crime tend to see it as tightly structured and bureaucratic?

- To what extent do you think that ideas of anomie might be useful in explaining involvement in political terrorism?

- Consider some of the issues concerning ethnicity and religion discussed in Chapters 6 and 11. How important is the existence of religious subcultures in ethnic communities for the emergence and perpetuation of terrorism?

Explore further

Good overviews of the subjects in this chapter are:

Becker, H. S. (1963), *Outsiders: Studies in the Sociology of Deviance* (New York: Free Press). *This is a landmark study that still repays a close reading.*

Heidensohn, F. (1985), *Women and Crime* (London: Macmillan). *A very useful and comprehensive overview of the gendering of criminal activity.*

Croal, H. (1992), *White Collar Crime* (Buckingham: Open University Press). *An up-to-date account of the nature and significance of white-collar crime.*

Plummer, K. (1975), *Sexual Stigma: An Interactionist Account* (London: Routledge). *A classic study of homosexuality that makes powerful use of symbolic interactionist theory.*

Further and more detailed information can be found in:

Matza, D. (1964), *Delinquency and Drift* (New York: John Wiley & Sons). *An important work that emphasizes the fact that much criminal behaviour results from 'drift' and circumstances, rather than from commitment to a criminal career.*

Goffman, E. (1963), *Stigma* (Englewood Cliffs, NJ: Prentice-Hall). *Like all Goffman's work, this is very readable and has been massively influential. He sets out a general model of the stigmatization of deviance and difference.*

Dorn, N., Murji, K., and South, N. (1992), *Traffickers* (London: Routledge). *An important book by some of the leading figures in the study of the organized criminal drug trade.*

Coomber, R. (2006), *Pusher Myths: Re-Situating the Drug Dealer* (London: Free Association Books). *A comprehensive review of material on dealing and pushing drugs.*

Turk, Austin T. (2004), 'The Sociology of Terrorism', *Annual Review of Sociology*, 30: 271–86. *An overview of themes in the study of terrorism as a deviant act.*

Online resources

Visit the Online Resource Centre that accompanies this book to access more learning resources and other interesting material on crime and deviance at:
www.oxfordtextbooks.co.uk/orc/fulcher4e/

The site of the Institute of Criminology at Cambridge has many useful links:
www.crim.cam.ac.uk/library/links/criminology.html

A huge site that contains almost everything you could possibly want to know (and a lot that you don't want to know) about crime and criminology:
http://faculty.ncwc.edu/Mstevens/415/criminology.htm

The Criminology Information Service page at the University of Toronto has many links to 'grey' and alternative sources:
http://link.library.utoronto.ca/criminology/crimdoc/index.cfm

The official website on crime and law enforcement in Britain is that of the Home Office. This contains links to research reports and much statistical information:
www.homeoffice.gov.uk

International material can be found through the United Nations site on drugs and crime:
www.unodc.org

On drugs, the website of the Institute for the Study of Drug Dependency is the most comprehensive available:
www.drugscope.org.uk

The leading international investigator on terrorism is Paul Wilkinson and you will find useful information on the site of his research centre at St Andrew's University:
www.st-andrews.ac.uk/~wwwir/research/cstpv

You can find the official viewpoint on the website of MI5, the British security service, at:
www.mi5.gov.uk

The website of MI6, the British Secret Service, can be found at:
www.mi6.gov.uk/output/sis-home-welcome.html

Body, Health, and Medicine

Contents

Psychiatric careers

Andrew Solomon, a New Yorker, published his first novel in 1994, aged 30, but felt no enthusiasm about its critical success. He felt constantly tired, barely ate anything at all, and contact with other people just seemed too much of an effort. He feared going to a birthday party organized for him by his family, and on his only trip outside the house on the day of the party he lost control of his bowels.

Andrew consulted his doctor, who diagnosed him as suffering from depression, and he was prescribed a course of drugs to control his anxiety. While taking the medication he spent most of his time in bed, having to force himself to do such basic things as wash. He had to be fed, like a baby, by his father.

Over the next six months he slowly began to feel better, and he began to live a more normal life again. Though others saw him as having recovered, Andrew felt that it was simply the symptoms that had gone away and that the underlying depression remained. Feeling that death would end this, and that a serious and 'visible' illness would legitimate his death, he sought out homosexual encounters in public parks in the hope that he would get AIDS. He failed to contract the disease, but to his own surprise he felt relieved about this and began to feel that his recovery was now really under way and that he knew how he could control his own depression.

Deborah Tallis's depression led her to overdose on her medication, and she was taken into hospital. She was classified as a risk to herself and was 'sectioned' under the Mental Health Act. She stayed in hospital for eight months. When she was released she felt herself to be back in exactly the same situation, and after another six months she was back in hospital.

As her spells of hospitalization increased, she found it more and more difficult to cope alone in the outside world. She moved continually from the community to hospital and back again over a period of more than six years. When she is in hospital, she wants only to be outside again. When she is released, her difficulties in coping and getting welfare benefits make her long for the relative security of hospital.

Sources: Guardian, 5 February 1997; *Observer,* 6 May 2001.

What is depression, and why is it so difficult to treat? If it is an illness, why does it seem less responsive to treatment than other diseases? In this chapter we look at the ways in which both psychiatric and physical illnesses are subject to social construction. They are products of a long-term transformation in medical understanding that began in the eighteenth century, and have since then been subject to commercial and state regulation. Control over minds and bodies has become a major feature of state policies in relation to their populations, and contemporary medicine cannot be understood apart from its political and economic context. Deborah Tallis would be the first to recognize that her personal troubles are inextricably linked to the public issues of financing medical and welfare provision.

The section on 'Understanding bodies' looks at the ways in which individual bodies and populations have been controlled, using the theories of Foucault. Aspects of individual health and population demography are considered in 'Health, reproduction, and disability', where we explore the impact of industrial development on health. In the final section on 'Medicine, minds, and bodies' we look at the medical control and regulation of bodies, in life and in death, and at the shaping of mental problems by medical interventions. We consider, in particular, the gendering of medical interventions in relation to cultural conceptions of femininity and beauty.

Concepts and theories

Michel Foucault described in some detail the role of the state in controlling the bodies of its members. He related the development of the medical profession and modern forms of medical practice to the transformation of modern states and their growing capacity to exercise powers of surveillance over their populations.

Sex, bodies, and populations

Foucault saw the late eighteenth century as the point at which a **disciplinary society** began to be built. There was a growing concern to secure the human foundations of national wealth through the application of new forms of social power over human biology. Foucault refers to these forms of power as the demographic control (or *regulation*) of whole populations, and the anatomical control (or *discipline*) of individual human bodies.

Regulating populations

The idea of a national 'population' came to be used as an economic and political category, as the leading nation states strived to expand their national wealth and productive powers at the end of the eighteenth century. A population was seen as something more than an aggregate of individuals. It was seen as what Durkheim (1895) was to call a 'social fact', an entity with specific properties of its own. Nation states recognized that a nation's level of productivity, rate of employment, rate of growth, wealth, and so on depended, to a crucial degree, on the size and well-being of their population and the productive powers of its members. These population factors depended on the sexual behaviour of its members. As Foucault (1976: 25–6) put it:

> At the heart of this economic and political problem of population was sex: it was necessary to analyse the birth rate, the age of marriage, the legitimate and illegitimate births, the precocity and frequency of sexual relations, the ways of making them fertile or sterile, the effects of unmarried life or of the prohibitions, the impact of contraceptive practices.

States identified a whole new range of social facts to investigate: rates of birth and death, trends in life expectancy, rates of suicide, levels of health and disease, patterns of diet, and so on. The sexual conduct of the population became the object of analysis and a target for intervention by nation states, and there was a growing concern with the suppression of forms of sexuality not directly linked to procreation and, therefore, to the reproduction of the population. Observation of birth, death, and marriage rates in censuses and surveys, the compilation of official statistics by government agencies, the undertaking of public health and housing schemes, and control over migration were all developed as ways of regulating the 'social body'.

Foucault saw the introduction of demographic controls as creating a **biopolitics** of population. This involved new disciplines and forms of discourse to shape and give direction to the demographic controls. Statistics and later demography, for example, defined ways of mapping a population in numerical terms and measuring its key characteristics. These new forms of knowledge became central to state policy. Indeed, the word 'statistics' has its origins in the idea of

---

THEORY AND METHODS   8.1

Michel Foucault

Michel Foucault (1926–84) was born in Poitiers, France. The son of a doctor, he studied philosophy at the École Normale Supérieure in Paris. While there he joined the Communists, though he left the party in the early 1950s. Disillusioned by the failure of philosophy to provide him with answers to the great questions of human existence, he turned to the study of psychology and psychopathology. He spent the period from 1952 to 1955 carrying out research into psychiatric practices in mental hospitals and wrote a short book on mental illness.

During academic visits to Sweden and Poland he switched his attention to the history of philosophy and science, and particularly to the history of medical science. He soon completed his first major book in this area, *Madness and Civilization* (1961), and this was rapidly followed by *The Birth of the Clinic* (1963).

More general works in history and theory and a diverse array of specialized investigations led to his masterly *Discipline and Punish* (1975). By this time he had already begun the research for what he intended to be a six-volume history of sexuality, though only parts of this (1976, 1984a, 1984b) were to appear before his death.

collecting facts relevant to the state. In a related way, political economy provided ways of mapping the resources that were available to a population and the division of labour through which these resources were used. Similarly, sociology studied the properties of human populations as 'societies'.

Medical experts played a key part in the development of new forms of knowledge. A medical point of view was established, according to which populations are complex organic wholes—social bodies—that can have 'pathological' problems requiring effective treatment. The health of the social body was seen as dependent, in large part, on the health of the individual bodies of its members. Public-health measures—such as sanitation and housing improvements—were seen as ways of improving the general health of the population. Fear of the effects of such diseases as cholera and typhus were eventually met by the introduction of sewerage and freshwater schemes, urban paving and rebuilding, by regulations over the burial of dead bodies, and through the expansion of hospital medicine. Social problems were to be treated through an informed social policy aimed at restoring normal 'health', and public-health measures were linked to other techniques of regulation that massively expanded during the nineteenth century. The police and the prisons, the workhouses, and poor-law welfare administration all contributed to the regulation and control of human populations using the new ideas of social science.

Disciplining bodies

The second form of power, anatomical control, involved new disciplines of the body. Foucault described these as comprising the **anatomo-politics** of the body. This form of power rested on a view of the body as a mechanism with capabilities and skills that had to be optimized in order to increase its usefulness and to integrate it into efficient economic systems.

Until the eighteenth century, physical controls over the body were aimed at reaffirming the power of the state and deterring others. In many cases this involved public spectacles of torture and execution, such as hanging, burning, disfigurement, or dismemberment. Foucault (1975: 3) illustrated this with the public execution set out for anyone who attempted to murder the French king:

> The flesh will be torn from his breasts, arms, thighs and calves with red-hot pincers, his right hand, holding the knife with which he committed the said parricide, burnt with sulphur, and, on those places where the flesh will be torn away, poured molten lead, boiling oil, burning resin, wax and sulphur melted together and then his body drawn and quartered by four horses and his limbs and body consumed by fire.

Anatomical controls were not, however, purely physical in nature, and Foucault traces a shift in social control from attempts to shape the *flesh* of the body to attempts to shape its *mind*. From the late eighteenth century, new techniques of social control were developed that affected the body only as a way of influencing the mind. Surveillance and the shaping of motives, operating through consciousness and language, were seen as more effective methods of control than force and coercion. This kind of control involved harnessing and intensifying the energies of the human body through processes of treatment and training.

Disciplines of training into new habits of behaviour were the tasks of the prisons, clinics, schools, workshops, and barracks that brought people together for their various purposes. These organizations were established from the sixteenth century, but were massively expanded with the consolidation of the capitalist market in the nineteenth century. The emergence of scientific medicine was central

The structure of Pentonville prison epitomizes the disciplinary gaze.

© Getty Images/Ian Waldie

to the establishment of new disciplines of the body in these organizations. Medicine and reform—the clinic and the prison—were particularly closely associated, as many forms of criminal behaviour were seen as the results of treatable medical conditions. The growth of psychiatric medicine, in particular, involved a close association between the criminalization and the medicalization of behaviour (Scull 1979).

Criminals were controlled through private and enclosed disciplines aimed at their reform. Prison discipline has only incidentally been concerned with physical intervention on the body, as methods of punishment have principally been concerned with altering the mind in order to shape motivations and desires. Prison inmates were trained in new ways of behaviour so as to produce conforming, obedient individuals who could, in due course, be returned to a 'normal' and productive life. Moral training and industrial training in work habits were at the heart of this new discipline of the body.

> ⮕ *Connections*
>
> In Chapter 14, pp. 525–8, we discuss more fully the 'carceral' organizations in which this discipline takes place. You will find this a useful background for both the present discussion and our discussion of Goffman's work on the hospital treatment of mental patients later in this chapter.

Conceptions of health and illness in traditional societies made little distinction between disorders of the body and disorders of the mind. They saw illness in religious terms and linked 'sickness' with 'sin'. Physicians and surgeons did not exist in most societies, and there was little or no medical treatment. Where it did occur, it was barbaric and used unfounded techniques. Even this kind of intervention was largely confined to the aristocratic and professional strata. The illnesses and emotional problems of labourers and peasants were of little concern to anyone else. For the most part, those in rural villages remained dependent on herbal and folk remedies passed down by word of mouth from one generation to the next and sometimes meted out by the local wise man ('wizard') or wise woman.

The expansion of scientific medicine in the eighteenth and nineteenth centuries changed all this and introduced characteristically modern ways of handling physical and psychological disorders. A new bio-medical model of illness was established, and doctors—as the possessors of this knowledge—established themselves as the 'experts' in the treatment of bodily ills. Centralized hospital medicine allowed doctors to use their control over knowledge to build a power base. The shift from aristocratic **client control** over medicine to autonomous **professional control** by doctors themselves meant that doctors could define the nature of health and determine forms of treatment

(Jewson 1976; see also T. Johnson 1972; I. Waddington 1973). Forms of hospital medicine and general practice were slowly established, initially in the private clinics and the workhouses, and later in large public hospitals. This involved an increasingly complex division of labour among doctors, nurses, and other professionals, along with ancillary workers and administrators.

Central to the rise of scientific medicine was a new orientation towards the sick. The medical professions were organized around what Foucault called the **medical gaze**. This is a specific way of seeing and defining the sick that entailed specific forms of investigation, teaching, and clinical intervention. Through the medical gaze was built an image of the 'sick body' as something that could be technically manipulated. The sick were no longer seen as persons, but simply as 'pathological' or dysfunctional bodies. They were systems of organs, cells, and tissues that required treatment whenever they were subject to 'disease'. This new viewpoint culminated in the germ theory of disease, systematized during the 1870s and 1880s. As scientific technicians, doctors could adopt a detached, neutral, and disinterested orientation towards a particular 'case' and its 'symptoms'. Each case could, furthermore, be given a clinical description that could be bureaucratically organized and filed as a 'case record'.

In all countries, medical experts have become the core members of an administrative apparatus that comprises the various levels of staff that run the wards, consulting rooms, and dispensaries. Bureaucratically organized systems of staffing have expanded continuously since the nineteenth century, and include many different categories of 'specialist' doctor (physician, surgeon, psychiatrist, dentist, geriatrician, gynaecologist, paediatrician, and so on), nurses (midwives, psychiatric nurses, district nurses, health visitors), technicians (radiographers, audiologists, haematologists), social workers, and managers. Medicine has expanded into specialized organizations (asylums, sanatoriums, isolation hospitals) and into associated and subsidiary positions and organizations: Medical Officers of Health, general-practice surgeries, health centres, pharmacies, school and occupational nursing, family-planning clinics, and residential homes for the elderly. Administrative apparatuses vary considerably in their levels of organization into health regimes. Even where state centralization created such organizations as the National Health Service, the degree of coordination has generally been quite loose (Freidson 1970).

This looseness and lack of coherence in health regimes led Foucault to reject the concept of a health 'system'. The 'disciplinary society' is one in which organizations and agencies are interconnected in complex and extensive networks of power. However, they are rarely formed into tight and centralized systems. Foucault describes such a network as an 'archipelago'—literally, a group of islands—so as to emphasize that there is only a loose interconnection among the constituent organizations.

Controlling sexuality

Foucault saw the attempt to discipline sexuality as central to the new techniques of anatomical control. Sex came to be seen as a central and potentially dangerous force that had to be channelled in appropriate and productive directions. In all areas of social life there was an attempt to define and to consolidate images of normality: the good worker, the well-educated child, the law-observing citizen, and so on. The 'pathologies' of the feckless, unemployed poor, the ill-educated truants, and criminals had to be controlled so that they did not 'infect' the 'healthy' members of society. The norm of sexuality was defined in relation to an image of the heterosexual couple, the 'Malthusian couple' whose sexual activity is limited to the procreation of children and, thereby, to increasing the size of the population. On this basis, norms of sexual development were defined that described the behaviours that were felt to be appropriate.

Public attention was directed towards the maintenance and protection of the marital, heterosexual sexuality of the 'normal' family. There was a corresponding 'medicalization of the sexually peculiar' and a 'psychiatrization of perverse pleasure' (Foucault 1976: 44). 'Unusual' and 'unnatural' forms of sexuality were identified as 'lesions', 'dysfunctions', or 'symptoms' that reflected deep organic disturbances in the body. Those who were sexually different were fixed in the medical gaze and isolated as objects of investigation and treatment. They were seen as suffering from 'nervous disorders' and sexual 'perversions'. Medical power drew out, isolated, and solidified these sexual disorders and made them objects of public concern, transforming many types of sexual conduct into behaviours that could be pathologized or even criminalized.

Childhood masturbation, for example, became a major target of medical attention. Described as 'onanism' and as a wasteful and dangerous activity, it was seen as something for which parents, teachers, and others needed to be constantly observant. Similarly, the male medical establishment saw female sexuality as dangerous and in need of control. Many female disorders were seen as sexual in origin. 'Idle' or 'nervous' women, for example, were seen as suffering from 'hysteria'—literally, a disorder of the uterus. Such women were in need of medical treatment that could restore them to a healthy state and, therefore, to their domestic, child-bearing, and family roles.

A whole range of sexual practices came to be identified as distinct types of 'perversion'. Psychiatric opinion recognized not only the 'homosexual', but also the 'zoophile' and the 'zooerast', the 'auto-monosexualist', the 'mixoscopophile', the 'gynecomast', the 'presbyophile', and so on

(Foucault 1976: 43). Many of these categories had only a short medical life, before being superseded by newer ones. Today, for example, the 'homosexual', the 'sado-masochist', and various types of 'fetishist' form the core elements in the psychiatric imagery of contemporary sexuality.

Several perversions were also seen as carrying the threat of other forms of illness. Diseases linked to sex, such as the venereal diseases of syphilis and gonorrhoea, were seen as ever-present consequences of unnatural sexual pleasures, much as AIDS has been seen. Concern about the spread of these diseases in the nineteenth century led to great public concern over prostitution, which itself reflected male attitudes towards female sexuality.

Foucault has provided a very powerful account of the disciplines of the body and the regulation of populations in modern societies. His argument, however, tends to present a highly flexible picture of the body that recognizes few significant physical limits to the ways in which the human body can be shaped by social forces. The body is known only in and through discourse, and, as a result, Foucault tends to play down the importance of the physical, material aspects of bodies that exist independently of medical and other forms of discourse. Later in this chapter we will look at some of these material features of populations and bodies, before going on to consider the social construction of health and illness through medical discourse. First, however, we must give some further consideration to the idea of surveillance.

Surveillance of populations

Regulation and discipline depend on practices of **surveillance**. Those who are to be controlled through the new techniques of bio-politics and anatomo-politics must be observed and monitored by the various agencies whose job it is to supervise and superintend their behaviour. The power of surveillance has been central to the growth of nation states, which have developed complex apparatuses for collecting and processing information on those who live within their boundaries. In this section we will look at the establishment of censuses and surveys along with mechanisms for the analysis and reporting of official statistics.

The birth of the census

Central to systems of surveillance were new mechanisms for counting the population and keeping track of its growth. In Britain and in many other countries, the churches had been responsible for the regulation of births, marriages, and burials, together with occasional local censuses, since the sixteenth century. The new systems of the eighteenth and nineteenth centuries, however, established national systems backed by the full force of the law. In 1800 an Act of Parliament established a regular census, a full count of the whole English population. The first national census took place the following year, and, with the sole exception of 1941, a census has been taken every ten years since then. The cost of the Statistical Service, however, led the government to set up a review of the Census in 2002. The task of the review was to see whether the kind of information collected in the census could more cheaply be collected from computerized tax and benefit records, supplemented by a sample survey. The internal review proposed that the Census continue but that its results and procedures be more closely integrated with other official data sources.

In 1837 a national system of 'civil registration' was set up for England. Under this system, all births, marriages, and deaths had to be registered at local offices, which reported these to a General Register Office in London. Similar systems were set up for Scotland and Ireland a few years later (J. Scott 1990: ch. 4; see also Nissel 1987; Higgs 1996). This system of civil registration is still in operation and provides many of the basic demographic statistics published by the government.

Registration and statistical services had been established in virtually all the major European countries, in the United States, in Australia and New Zealand, and in Japan by the middle of the nineteenth century. Alongside the collection of data on their populations, states also began to compile statistics on crime, health, and a whole array of economic matters. Publication of statistics on court trials, for example, began in Britain in 1805. Prison statistics followed in 1836 and police statistics in 1857. By the time Durkheim carried out his investigations into suicide (Durkheim 1897), official statistics on this subject were available for a large number of countries.

Censuses in Britain have been overseen by local enumerators, who issue standard forms to each household in their area. These forms collate information on the names, ages, sexes, places of birth, and occupations of all members of the household, together with an indication of their marital status and their relationship to each other. To this core of information is added a varying set of questions concerning travel to work, education, housing conditions, car ownership, and ethnicity. The household forms, when completed, are used for the compilation of registers and, in recent years, computer records, and are stored by the Office for National Statistics (ONS), formerly the Office of Population, Censuses and Surveys (OPCS).

Civil registration records are also stored by the General Register Offices for England and Wales, Scotland, and Northern Ireland, and it is from these registers that birth, marriage, and death certificates are produced. The birth registers record the name, sex, place of birth, and date of birth of each child, together with the names of its parents, the occupation of its father, and the name and address of the person (usually a parent) registering the birth. A marriage register records the date of the marriage, the names, ages, and occupations of each partner, the names and occupations of their fathers (but not of their mothers), and whether the partners were bachelor, spinster, or widowed at the time of the marriage. The death registers are much shorter, giving simply the name, age, sex, and occupations of the deceased, the cause and place of death, and the name and address of the informant.

The original records and registers from the census and civil registration are stored under conditions of official secrecy, though the census records are opened for public examination after 100 years. Staff in the ONS, however, have full access to all the original records and use them to produce periodic statistical reports. Civil registration data are summarized quarterly in a publication called *Population Trends*, while census data are summarized in national and county reports and in the so-called small area statistics. Taken together, the census and civil registration data provide regular benchmark counts of the whole population and a record of trends between these benchmark years. In addition to aggregate totals, the statistical summaries give breakdowns and comparisons by age, sex, class (as computed from occupational data), and a whole variety of other factors.

The ONS brought together various government statistical agencies around the Government Social Survey (GSS), which was formed in the Ministry of Information in 1939 to monitor public morale during the Second World War. Drawing on the successes achieved by many private and academic surveys, the GSS used sampling methods obtain national data that could complement the comprehensive data from the census and civil regist. The GSS was able to produce detailed informati range of topics much more cheaply than could a census. Some of the early wartime surveys lo availability of steel for corset production and domestic brushes and brooms, though mo results came from surveys on food consu tudes towards sexual disease.

In the post-war period, a number surveys were established, including th Survey, the General Household S Force Survey (see Box 8.2, p. 272 from each of these annual sur results are combined with cens in such compilations as *Social* with health service and oth periodic reports on drink ease and illness, employ

The ONS oversees coordinates them

Government social surveys

In addition to occasional surveys and alongside the Census and civil registration, the ONS is responsible for three major social surveys that provide essential information for planners and academics.

The *Family Expenditure Survey* began in 1957 and carries out interviews with people in 11,000 households. These people keep detailed records of their expenditure over a period, and they provide details on their incomes. In addition to providing information on tax changes and on income distribution, typical patterns of expenditure can be identified. These data are used in the preparation of the Retail Price Index.

The *General Household Survey* began in 1970. It undertakes annual interviews with those aged over 16 in 12,500 households. Topics covered include household composition, housing, employment, education, health, and income.

Additional topics are added from year to year. It was reduced in scope in the 1980 cost-cutting review, and it was a suspended in 1997–8 and 1999–2000 in order to save money and carry out a review. It was reinstated in 2001 and continues in operation.

The *Labour Force Survey* began in 1973. It was carried out every two years until 1983, annually from 1984 to 1991, and is now a quarterly survey. It draws its information from a regular 'panel' of individuals in 60,000 households. Questions covered in the interviews cover employment, hours worked, vocational training, education, job-search methods, nationality, and ethnicity.

➲ You can find the official government statistics home page at **www.statistics.gov.uk**. From this page you can download many statistical tables and publications. Survey work can be found at **www.statistics.gov.uk/ssd**.

---

departments. Criminal statistics are collected in the Home Office, which publishes *Criminal Statistics* and various reports from the regular *British Crime Survey*; health statistics are collected by the Department of Health; employment and unemployment statistics as well as educational statistics are collected by the Department for Education and Skills, which publishes the *Employment Gazette*; and financial and trade statistics are collected in the Treasury. A cost-cutting review in 1980 made substantial cutbacks in the statistical service in order to reduce its public-service role and limit its work on social statistics, but there is still a massive output of statistical data. In 2000 'National Statistics' was formed as a central organizing agency for all government statistics.

Stop and reflect

n this section we have examined the growth of regulation and scipline in the control of populations and human bodies. We ed the ideas of Foucault to bring together a number of cerns.

e development of nation states and the idea of a national pulation was an important feature of the growth of veillance and control. Medicine and statistics were ral to this.

ine introduced new techniques of social control aimed shaping of the body and the influencing of the mind. dical gaze introduced conceptions of the sick body rofessional expertise.

ur discussion of sexuality in Chapter 5, pp. 179–83, der what this tells us about how control over ecame central to control over populations.

We also looked at the ways in which new techniques of measurement through censuses, surveys, and registration became central to social surveillance. This resulted in the collection and compilation of official statistics.

● Nation states have established regular population censuses and a number of regular surveys aimed at collecting data about their people.

● Criminal statistics, unemployment statistics, demographic statistics, and a variety of other statistics are shaped by the bureaucratic procedures through which they are produced. They reflect administrative concerns rather than sociological concepts.

● Can official statistics have any useful role in explorations of health and illness?

Health, reproduction, and disability

Foucault's work highlighted the importance of examining the ways that populations are regulated and individual bodies are disciplined. In this section we look at the material structure of populations—what Durkheim called 'social morphology'—and at the material health, disease, and diet of individual bodies. We will show that both social morphology and individual health have undergone a distinctive pattern of change since 1800.

Fertility and mortality

Total world population seems to have fluctuated at a level of about half a billion until the modern period, when it began to climb steadily. By 1950 it had risen to 2.5 billion, and in 2001 it stood at 6.1 billion. Europe's total population (see Figure 8.1) is about half as big again as the total population of the United States. This, in turn, is half as big again as the population of Japan. Europe, the Americas, and Africa are roughly equivalent to each other in terms of population size, but by far the most populous area of the world is Asia. Almost two-thirds of the world's population lives in Asia, and almost a quarter of the world's population lives in China. The significance of this is clear when population is compared with economic development, an issue that we discuss more fully in Chapter 16. Just 20 per cent of the world's population lives in the most developed areas: in North America, Europe, Australia, New Zealand, and Japan. The remaining 80 per cent of people live in the world's poorest countries, where population growth is also most rapid. The population of India, for example, has increased by over 20 per cent each decade, and its growth in population between 1991 and 2001 was greater than the total population of Brazil, the fifth most populous country in the world. In 2001 India became the second country in the world, after China, to achieve a population of more than one billion (see **www.censusindia.net**).

Britain is quite small and so has a very high population density. With a population of just over 59 million, it has about 1 per cent of the total world population. Within the European Union, it has about the same population as France and Italy, but significantly less than Germany (Coleman and Salt 1992; *Social Trends* 2005). The British population figure of 59 million is a substantial increase over the figure of 38 million recorded in 1901, and the population is estimated to rise to almost 64 million by the year 2021. Despite this substantial increase, the *rate* of growth in the twentieth century was much lower than it was in the nineteenth century. The first Census, in 1801, recorded a population of just over 10 million, a figure that

Figure 8.1   World population, 1800–2001

Region	Population (m.)		
	1800	1900	2001
Europe	203	408	726
North America	7	82	317
Latin America, Caribbean	24	74	527
Asia	635	947	3,721
Africa	107	133	813
Oceania	2	6	31
Total	978	1,650	6,134

Note: Figures do not total exactly because of rounding in the original source.
Sources: Social Trends (1996: table 1.21; 2002: table 1.17).

had doubled by 1851 and had almost doubled again by 1901. By contrast, the estimated population size for 2025 is less than double the 1901 figure. The fastest period of population growth in the twentieth century was during its first decade, and the growth rate has declined since then. Despite a small boom in the 1960s, this decline in the rate of growth was especially rapid in the last thirty years of the twentieth century and it is expected to continue. These trends are summarized in Figure 8.2, p. 274.

Marriage and fertility

The size of a population and its rate of growth or decline are largely determined by the balance between fertility (births) and mortality (deaths). Whenever the birth rate is higher than the death rate, there is an increase in the so-called natural growth rate of the population. This terminology is a little unhelpful, as it implies that changes in population that are due to other factors are somehow 'unnatural'. Nevertheless, it remains the case that the balance between births and deaths is fundamental to the development of any particular population.

The basic measure of the **fertility** of a population is its so-called crude birth rate. This is the annual number of live births per 1,000 population. This widely used figure gives a result very similar in form to a percentage figure, but it is calculated on a base of 1,000 rather than 100. The crude birth rate in England and Wales stood at 35.2 per 1,000 between 1860 and 1870. It declined very rapidly from the 1870s to the 1920s, reaching 27.2 in the period 1901–10. The drop in the rate across the British Isles was particularly sharp while men were away at the front during the First World War. The rate increased in the years immediately after the war, but the decline set in again fairly rapidly and continued through the 1930s.

Figure 8.2 UK population, 1851–2021 (000)

Year	England	Wales	Scotland	Northern Ireland	UK
1851	16,764	1,163	2,889	1,443	22,259
1901	30,515	2,013	4,472	1,237	38,237
1931	37,359	2,593	4,843	1,243	46,038
1961	43,561	2,635	5,184	1,427	52,807
1971	46,412	2,740	5,236	1,540	55,928
1981	46,821	2,813	5,180	1,538	56,352
1991	48,204	2,899	5,107	1,601	57,807
2001	49,450	2,910	5,064	1,689	59,113
2021 (projected)	53,954	3,106	4,963	1,811	63,835

Sources: Coleman and Salt (1992: table 3.1); Central Office of Information (1995: table 1); *Social Trends* (2002: table 1.1); *Population Trends* 121 (2005: table 1.2).

When is the right time to have a baby?
© Alice Chadwick

Despite the onset of the Second World War in 1939, the birth rate increased through most of the wartime years, and there was a substantial baby boom in the years 1945–8. From a low point in the middle of the 1950s, the birth rate increased through the 1960s. This was a period of relative prosperity and affluence, and there was a second baby boom between 1957 and 1966. Following this boom, the rate declined once more, and it has continued to decline. The decline since the 1960s has been especially rapid. The crude birth rate fell from a level of 18.8 in 1964 to one of 10.7 in 2009.

As its name implies, this 'crude rate' is a very rough-and-ready figure, which does not directly reflect changes in the age and sex composition of the population. What is called the 'general fertility rate' does a rather more precise job of measurement. This is the number of births per 1,000 women in the usual child-bearing age range of 15 to 44. Figures show that this rate fell from 94 to 55 between 1964 and 2001. The general fertility rate, however, is also a little misleading, as it obscures variations from one age group to another. Age-specific fertility rates show, for example, that there were 73.3 births per 1,000 women aged 20–24 in 2004, compared with 99.4 births per 1,000 women aged 30–34.

Changes in the age-specific rates—and, therefore, in the overall birth rate—are consequences of changes in the age of marriage and the age at which child-bearing begins. If people marry late, then there will be fewer years of marriage in which to have children. Similarly, if married women delay having their first child, they will also reduce the total number of years that are available for child-bearing. The age at marriage for women was between 25 and 26 throughout the period from 1900 to 1940. The age at marriage for men in the same period was between 27 and 28. After 1940, people began to marry much earlier, and the average marriage age had fallen to 22 for women and 24 for men by 1970. During the 1980s and 1990s, however, age at marriage began to increase once more. At the turn of the century it stood at about 24 for women and 26 for men.

There are great differences in the age of first marriage internationally. In most of Europe, figures range from 27 to 30, with slightly lower ages in the Baltic states and parts of Eastern Europe. Australia, Japan, and the United States show a similar pattern to Europe. In many parts of Africa and Asia, however, people tend to marry below the age of 25.

In Britain, late marriage is especially marked among professional and managerial workers. Late marriage, however, does not necessarily mean that people begin their families later. As we show in Chapter 12, the rate of marriage itself has fallen as more and more people choose to cohabit. Many 'late' marriages take place between people who have already been cohabiting for some time. Despite these trends, the so-called age of maternity—the age at which a woman has her first child—has increased. In 1951 the average age at maternity was 28.4 years. This fell to 27.3 in 1964, and 26.5 in 1977. During the 1980s and 1990s the age of maternity increased, and by 2005 it had risen to above 27.

Mortality

The basic measure of **mortality** is the crude death rate, the annual number of deaths per 1,000 population. Death rates were very high in Britain in the eighteenth century, but began to fall during the nineteenth century. By 1870 the rate stood at 23.0 per 1,000, and this had dropped to 13.5 by 1910. Death rates altered very little during the rest of the century, though high rates were recorded—for obvious reasons—in the wartime years. The death rate is between 10 and 11 persons per 1,000.

The aggregate figures, of course, mask significant differences among the age groups. There are fewer than one per 1,000 deaths among those aged between 1 and 15 years, while there are 44.7 per 1,000 among those aged 65–79 and 141.4 per 1,000 among those aged 80 or more. If crude death rates are compared across the country, the highest death rates—for obvious reasons—appear in those areas where there are relatively large numbers of retired persons. Many of these deaths are among people who have retired to the seaside. About a third of the population in East Sussex and the south of the Isle of Wight are over pension age, and these areas have the highest death rates in the country.

A more useful comparison of death rates uses the so-called standardized mortality rate, which takes account of the age structure of the population. A figure of 100 indicates that an area or group has exactly the death rate that would be expected among people of its age composition; a figure above 100 indicates higher-than-average death rates, and a figure below 100 indicates lower-than-average death rates. Using age-specific measures for Great Britain as a whole, death rates are lowest in East Anglia and the south-west, and they are highest in Scotland and the north of England.

Mortality rates reflect the increase in life expectancy that has taken place over the century. People are now living longer than ever before, and women live longer than men. Life expectancy for a male born in 2003 was about 76 years, compared with 80 for a female. The corresponding life expectancies for 1901 were 45 for men and 49 for women, an increase in average life span of 50 per cent. A hundred years earlier, in 1801, life expectancy was about 37 years (Coleman and Salt 1992: 38).

This does not mean, however, that large numbers of people died at age 37 in 1801 and at about 50 in 1901. Life expectancy at birth is very low when rates of infant mortality are high, but those who survive their childhood can expect to live rather longer than these minimal figures suggest. Although life expectancy at birth in 1901 was just under 50, those who actually managed to survive until age 45 could certainly have expected about another twenty-five years of life. Changes in life expectancy, then, reflect two quite separate changes: the rate of infant mortality and the rate of post-infant mortality. Globally, the average life expectancy is just under 67 years. In North America and Western Europe expectancy is generally above 77, but in sub-Saharan Africa life expectancy is generally below age 55.

One of the major changes in mortality during the twentieth century was the reduction in levels of infant mortality. This is officially measured by the number of deaths of infants aged under 1 year old per 1,000 live births. At the end of the nineteenth century, infant mortality accounted for one in five of all deaths. Most of these were due to diarrhoea, dysentery, and other forms of gastric infection. These were diseases of poverty, poor sanitation, and bad hygiene (Coleman and Salt 1992: 54). The rate of infant mortality fell constantly over the course of the twentieth century. It fell from 147 in 1901 to 70 in 1931, 32 in 1951, 23 in 1961, 10 in 1981, and 6.9 in 1994. The greatest improvements in infant health have been those that have increased survival chances during the critical first four weeks of life. This so-called neonatal mortality rate stood at 24.48 per 1,000 in 1951. By 2004, total infant mortality stood at 5.1 per 1,000.

Infant mortality is not constant across Britain, but varies quite considerably from one region to another. Rural areas of Oxfordshire, Cambridgeshire, and Warwickshire, like the affluent districts of London, Surrey, and Hampshire, have infant mortality rates of between five and six per 1,000. The poorer urban areas of Birmingham, Wolverhampton, and Bradford have rates that are more than double these levels. Rates of infant mortality also vary by ethnicity: rates for infants born to mothers from the Caribbean and Africa are one-and-a-half times those for mothers born in Britain. Rates for mothers born in Pakistan were double the British-born rate.

Age, sex, and ethnicity

Any population is diverse in terms of its sex and age structure. Very slightly more than a half of all births in Britain are male, and males outnumber females in the population throughout childhood and the early years of adulthood. Death rates for males, however, are higher than they are for females at all ages, and women tend to live longer than men. As a result, women outnumber men from about the age of 50. Among those who are 80 years old or more, there are twice as many women as men.

The age composition of a population can vary quite considerably from one period to another. From the middle of the nineteenth century until the 1920s, there were

relatively large numbers of infants and young children in Britain. About one-third of the population was aged 15 or less in 1901. At the same time, there were very small numbers of people aged over 70. As a result, the British population was, overall, quite young. A decline in the birth rate, however, has meant that the total number of children in the population has declined from its earlier level. About one-fifth of the population is now aged under 16, while one-sixth of the population is aged 65 or more. Baby booms in the 1940s and the 1960s (peaking in 1964) have produced bulges in the age distribution of the population in successive years as the members of these cohorts have aged. At the same time, there has been a growth in the number of elderly people. In 1993, 18.3 per cent of the population were of retirement age or above (60 for women, 65 for men), the corresponding figure having been 6.2 per cent in 1901 (see Pilcher 1995: figure 1.2). In 2000, 13 per cent of men and 18 per cent of women were aged 65 or over.

It is estimated that 23 per cent of the population will be aged 65 or over in 2031, and about a third of these people will be aged 80 or more. Those over 80 will be the survivors of the post-war baby boom, while those in their sixties will be the survivors of the 1960s baby boom. Looking at these trends in the numbers of the young and the old from a different angle, those of working age (16 to 65), whether actually working or not, made up about two-thirds of the population in 2001 and they will have fallen to below 60 per cent by 2025 (see Figure 8.3 and Box 8.3).

Britain is not unusual among advanced industrial societies in this respect, although its population is now somewhat older than the European average. The problems of an ageing population are especially marked in Japan. There are major differences, of course, from the non-industrial societies, which tend to have much younger populations.

Figure 8.3 Age and gender, United Kingdom, 1961–2001

Year	% of population			
	Under 16	16–39	40–64	65 or over
1961	25	33	32	12
1971	25	33	30	13
1981	22	35	28	15
1991	20	35	29	16
	Under 16	16–34	35–64	65 or over
2001				
Male	21	26	39	14
Female	19	25	39	18

Sources: *Social Trends* (2002: table 1.5; 2005: table 1.2). See also Pilcher (1995) and Vincent (1995).

Briefing: an ageing population   8.3

The problems of an ageing population are increasingly debated in newspapers and frequently make front-page news. Greater life expectancy has meant that a larger number of retired people must be supported by the younger working population. This puts great pressure on the pension system, as the contributions made by those in employment are used to pay pensions for those who have retired, leaving less money available for the pensions of younger workers when it comes to their turn to retire. Low stock-market values, on which many pensions depend, during the early years of the century have made this problem even worse. It is proposed that the age of retirement rise from its present level of 65 to 68 by the year 2050, as improved health has meant that people are now capable of working for longer. It has been estimated, however, that the increase in average life span may continue to grow, and the very elderly will make heavier demands on the health-care system and on the need for residential care.

Sources: Guardian, 10 May 2002, 25 July 2005; www.guardian.co.uk/money/2006/may/25/politics.business.

About one-third of the Chinese population is under 15 years old, and only 6 per cent are aged 65 or more. Where Britain is unusual among industrial societies is in the ethnic composition of its ageing population. Members of ethnic minorities (predominantly black and Asian) are significantly younger than the rest of the population. Almost one-third of the ethnic-minority population is under 16 and only less than one in ten is aged over 60. In thirty years' time, if present trends continue, the population of working age will be disproportionately black and Asian, while the retired population will be disproportionately white.

We showed earlier that the so-called natural growth of a population depends upon the balance between its birth rate and its death rate. A further variable that has an effect on population, which should by no means be regarded as 'unnatural', is migration. **Immigration** (the movement of people into a country) tends to increase the population, while **emigration** (the movement of people out of a country) tends to reduce it. The net effect of migration on a population is the balance between its levels of immigration and emigration from year to year. As we show in Chapter 6, pp. 209–10, migration into Britain had little impact on the overall size of the population until relatively recently.

Emigration more or less balanced immigration until the growth of immigration during the 1950s and 1960s. Migration has, however, altered the ethnic composition of the population. Just over 5 per cent of the population now assign themselves to a non-white ethnic category, about a half of them describing themselves as Asians and about a half as 'black' Africans or African Caribbean. The majority of these people, however, are not 'immigrants' but were born in Britain.

The demographic transition

Industrialized societies have been described as showing a particular pattern called the **demographic transition** (W. S. Thompson 1929; Kingsley Davis 1945). According to this point of view, population change shows a succession of three stages (see Figure 8.4, p. 279). Stage 1, which in Britain preceded the Industrial Revolution of the eighteenth century, is a period of high death rates combined with high birth rates. As a result, population growth is fairly slow. Industrialization initiates the transition to Stage 2, where death rates begin to fall as the improved food supply increases longevity and reduces infant mortality. Birth rates, however, remain high, and so population begins to increase rapidly. This period of rapid population growth ended in Britain at the close of the nineteenth century, when birth rates began to fall. Stage 3, then, is a period of low death rates combined with low birth rates, resulting in only slow population growth.

The late and more rapid industrialization of other European countries meant that they underwent the demographic transition somewhat later than Britain. It is now the common experience of all the industrialized societies. It has been suggested that the non-industrialized countries of the world today will eventually undergo a similar transition as they industralize. Many think that this will resolve the problem of overpopulation that the poorer countries currently face. However, these countries have been able to learn from the European experience. They have been able to adopt many measures to improve individual and public health, so lowering death rates, before improved industrial productivity can have any effect on their birth rates. As a result, Stage 2 of the demographic transition has shown a much more dramatic increase in population than occurred in Britain. This makes it much less likely that Stage 3 will be entered. Large families remain the norm, and there are often religious proscriptions against birth control. Some governments, such as the Communist regime in China, have tried to encourage family limitation, but with only limited success. While the death rate in China has fallen to 6 per 1,000, the birth rate stands at 17 per 1,000. In India, death rates of 12 per 1,000 are countered by birth rates of 33 per 1,000. The demographic transition *may* describe

The contemporary nuclear family.

© Alice Chadwick

the future of the newly industrializing countries, but it is by no means an inevitable transition for them. This becomes clear if the reasons for changes in birth and death rates in Britain are examined.

Birth rates in Britain have been shaped by both economic and cultural factors. The costs involved in having and bringing up children are considerable, and they include the costs of housing, education, and food. They also include the lost earnings of a parent who takes responsibility for childcare, or the costs of paying for a professional nanny or childcare. These costs lead people to have fewer children when times are bad and there is much unemployment or less full-time work. They also have fewer children if they seek to improve the standard of living of their existing family. In the former case, parents may simply *defer* births. In the latter case, however, they are more likely to *reduce* family size. The effects of these economic influences depend upon cultural factors. These include changing ideas about the appropriate or ideal number of children in a family, expectations concerning the age of marriage, attitudes towards contraception, and the normative expectations that are attached to female identity. If, for example, there is a weakening of the traditional ideal of female domesticity and an increase in opportunities for women to take on paid employment, there is likely to be a reduction in the number of children born. These issues over family limitation were first raised by Malthus (see Box 8.4).

Edwardian families were much larger than today's.

Figure 8.4 The demographic transition

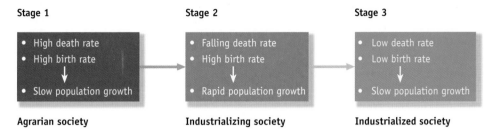

Stage 1	Stage 2	Stage 3
• High death rate • High birth rate ↓ • Slow population growth	• Falling death rate • High birth rate ↓ • Rapid population growth	• Low death rate • Low birth rate ↓ • Slow population growth
Agrarian society	Industrializing society	Industrialized society

---

THEORY AND METHODS   8.4

Malthus on population

Writing at the end of the eighteenth century, during Stage 2 of the demographic transition, Thomas Malthus (1798) tried to anticipate future population trends. He saw that the population of Britain was growing rapidly and he expected this to continue into the future. He calculated that population would increase at an 'exponential' rate, doubling every generation. The supply of food, on the other hand, could not expand so rapidly, as there were limits to the productivity of agriculture. As a result, population would outstrip food supply; Britain was heading for a famine that would reduce its population.

The only way to prevent this catastrophe, Malthus held, was for people to exercise 'moral restraint' by postponing marriage, remaining chaste before marriage, and having sex less often during marriage. This restraint would lower the birth rate. Malthus rejected the use of contraception on religious grounds, as being counter to God's law. While attitudes towards contraception have changed since Malthus's time, the Roman Catholic Church is still opposed to it.

In general, the long-term population trend in Britain has resulted from a desire for improved standards of living and an increase in the number of women who enter or remain in paid work. Both of these factors imply that women and men have made conscious and deliberate decisions to reduce the number of children they wish to have (J. Banks 1954). A crucial condition for this decision, however, has been the availability of effective forms of contraception. Methods of 'family planning' have become both more easily available and more acceptable over the course of the century, making it possible for people to translate their decisions about family size into practice. This was not possible, for most people, before the end of the nineteenth century. The desire to reduce family size was not, in any case, so strong until then. For much of the nineteenth century, children were seen as a source of income for a family—and this was true for even quite young children. Restrictions on child labour and the introduction of compulsory education in 1870 turned young children into more of a financial burden, altering the calculations that parents made about family size. The average number of children per family was seven in the 1860s, but this had fallen to four by 1900.

Although contraceptives were more easily available from the 1920s, they were not used by the mass of the population until the 1950s. It was in this period that family size reached its famous and much-parodied level of 2.4 children. The introduction of the contraceptive pill in the 1960s allowed far more effective planning of births and allowed the increasing numbers of women who took on paid employment to defer or end their child-bearing period.

Death rates since the middle of the nineteenth century have been influenced mainly by changes in medical treatment and public-health provision. In the nineteenth century and the first part of the twentieth century, public health was of the greatest significance in this respect. Improved sanitation, better living and working conditions, changes in diet and nutrition, and many effects of increasing disposable income all helped to reduce the *incidence* of disease by making people less susceptible. Medical treatment, on the other hand, has mainly had an effect since the early years of the twentieth century, when techniques of vaccination and immunization improved the survival chances of infants. We look further into this in the following section.

Health and disease

A major concern for people such as Malthus was that population growth would outstrip food production and that this would result in large-scale famine, disease, and death. The most pessimistic expectations have not materialized, but patterns of death and disease have changed quite markedly since the end of the nineteenth century.

The health transition

In parallel with the demographic transition, there has been a change in patterns of disease. This can be described as a **health transition**. This transition, shown in Figure 8.5, involves a change in the nature and scale of the principal diseases responsible for ill health and death as societies industrialize.

Stage 1 of the health transition is that of pre-modern, agrarian societies. The principal causes of illness and death are acute infectious diseases. These are spread from one person to another through direct contact, through polluted water, or through parasitic carriers such as fleas and mosquitoes. Diseases such as tuberculosis, malaria, and plague are endemic in these societies, along with cholera, typhus, leprosy, and sleeping sickness. Young children are particularly susceptible to measles, smallpox, and diphtheria. Whole populations are at risk from these diseases, and only the very wealthy have a degree of immunity. The incidence of these diseases is greatly affected by poor harvests and by warfare, which reduce or disrupt food supply and result in deteriorating living and working conditions. In these circumstances, epidemics are regular occurrences.

Stage 2 of the health transition, corresponding to the period of industralization, involves some improvement in the standard of living for many people, though the problem of urban poverty increases. Acute infectious diseases (particularly tuberculosis, cholera, and typhus) remain at a high level. They are, however, particularly concentrated among the new urban poor, whose living conditions make them the most vulnerable. Tuberculosis accounted for 13.2 per cent of all deaths in Britain in 1880; typhus, dysentery, and cholera accounted for 7.3 per cent; measles, scarlet fever, and whooping cough each accounted for just less than 1 per cent. Alongside these infectious diseases, respiratory diseases such as pneumonia accounted for 17.6 per cent of all deaths. Improved public health through sanitation, housing, and nutrition had some effect on the diseases of the poor, but it served mainly to confine the diseases to the poor districts and to insulate the majority of the population from their worst effects.

Stage 3 of the health transition involves an enhanced control over infectious diseases, which fall to low levels. It is not always realized how little direct effect medical treatment had until comparatively recently. The decline in tuberculosis, for example, began in about 1850, but the tubercle bacillus was not discovered until 1882, and drug treatment was not available until 1947. Nevertheless, vaccination and the use of antibiotics from the 1930s and 1940s did have a significant effect on health, particularly on that of children. This was possible once the underlying improvements in living conditions had been made (McKeown 1979). There has been a rapid growth in medical and surgical techniques since the 1940s. As a result of these medical advances, there have been the significant falls in infant mortality and the general increase in life expectancy already discussed.

In Stage 3, rates of the degenerative diseases, such as cancer, heart disease, and strokes, are high. They become the principal causes of chronic illness and death. These diseases result largely from bodily deterioration with age, or from environmental conditions (such as dietary changes and the use of alcohol and tobacco) that have their greatest effects as bodies age. People now live long enough to suffer from different kinds of disease. In the early twenty-first century respiratory diseases continue to account for about one in ten of all deaths in Britain, but tuberculosis accounts for only a fraction of 1 per cent. Circulatory diseases (those of the heart and blood vessels) account for 46 per cent of all deaths, compared with just 7 per cent in 1880. Another major cause of death is cancer, which accounts for 25 per cent of deaths (2.5 per cent in 1880). The incidence of lung cancer among men has declined since 1951, but among women both lung cancer and breast cancer have increased sharply since the 1960s.

Britain is now above the European Union average for both circulatory disease and cancer. The highest rates of death from cancer among European women are found in Denmark, Ireland, and Britain; the lowest rates are in Greece, Spain, and France. Among men, the highest rates of death from circulatory disease are found in Austria and Germany, and the lowest rates are those of France and Spain.

Changes in patterns of death in the twentieth century reflect, in part, a real increase in the level of such diseases

Figure 8.5 The health transition

Stage 1

- High rates of acute infectious disease
- Regular epidemics

Agrarian society

Stage 2

- Concentration of infectious diseases among urban poor
- Enhanced public health

Industrializing society

Stage 3

- Low rates of infectious disease
- High rates of chronic degenerative disease
- Enhanced medicine

Industrialized society

as cancer as a result of changes in living conditions. An increase in smoking in the first half of the century, for example, was responsible for the increase in the prevalence of both lung cancer and heart disease. However, these trends also reflect increased life expectancy. Putting matters crudely, a greater control over infectious diseases means that people are now living long enough to face the circulatory and cancer problems of old age that their parents and grandparents avoided because they died much younger. These diseases are, therefore, commonest among the oldest age groups. By contrast, over a half of deaths among men aged 15 to 39 result from injury or poison (associated with drugs or alcohol), and not from disease at all. Many of these injuries result from road-traffic accidents, which account for nearly 40 per cent of all accidental deaths.

Health problems are especially acute in the poorer countries, yet these are precisely the countries with the lowest spending on health care. At the beginning of the twenty-first century, Cameroon, Indonesia, Nigeria, Sri Lanka, and Sudan each spent less than 2 per cent of its GDP on health care. In Germany, 10 per cent of the national income is spent on health care, compared with 9.3 per cent in France and 6.8 per cent in Britain.

Health and well-being

Of course, not all people suffer from serious **illnesses**. A national survey in 1993 found that over three-quarters of British adults rated their own health as 'good' or 'very good'. Nevertheless, about 40 per cent reported that they had a long-standing illness or disability.

On average, people see their doctor about four times each year, and it is he or she who provides most medical treatment. More serious illnesses are often referred on for more specialist treatment at hospitals, though this may involve a long wait until a clinic appointment or hospital bed is available. Much effort has been put into reducing waiting time for hospital treatment, which has always been very long in Britain. The British health-care system is not typical. In the United States, for example, the bulk of the health system operates on a private basis rather than as a public service, and it is normal for paying patients to make direct approaches to specialist practitioners.

For all age groups—and among both men and women—problems of the musculoskeletal system (arthritis and rheumatism) were among the most common long-standing disorders. Among those aged 45–64, almost a quarter report these problems. For those aged 65 or over, the proportion rises, especially among women: almost two-thirds of women report such problems. Among older men, however, heart and circulatory problems outweighed arthritis and rheumatism. The most common heart and circulation problems faced by older people were high blood pressure and angina, though large numbers of people experienced diabetes or abnormal heart rhythms. Many older people, of course, experienced both musculoskeletal problems and circulatory difficulties, along with other long-term disorders.

Among common medical conditions that are chronic rather than physically dangerous are fatigue and sleep problems, irritability and worry, anxiety, depression, and 'stress'. People aged 35–54 are particularly likely to report stress or pressure in their life; men and those in non-manual jobs are more likely to report this than women and those in manual jobs. A growing amount of evidence, however, shows that medically diagnosed stress is more common among manual workers than non-manual workers. On the other hand, rates of depression are much higher among women than among men, and they are especially great among women in manual-working households.

Asthma has shown an increased incidence since the 1980s. This is an illness that is particularly likely to affect children and that has been linked to growing levels of air pollution. Many other childhood diseases, however, have shown a long-term decline. Measles and whooping cough, despite occasional epidemics, are at a lower level than they were even fifty years ago, and diseases such as diphtheria (which killed about 10,000 children each year in the second half of the nineteenth century) and polio are kept under control through immunization programmes.

The largest single cause of death globally is heart disease, accounting in 1999 for 13.7 per cent of all deaths. In second place was cerebrovascular disease (stroke), accounting for 9.5 per cent of deaths, and in third place was deaths from acute respiratory infections. HIV/AIDS was the fourth largest killer, accounting for 4.2 per cent of deaths worldwide (WHO 1999).

A major health issue of the 1980s was AIDS (acquired immune deficiency syndrome). This is sexually transmitted, but can also be contracted through infected blood. It could often prove fatal, until improved treatment allowed its effects to be kept under control. The number of new cases reported in the United Kingdom has increased considerably since the 1980s, though it has dropped slightly in recent years. Of these known cases, about 6 per cent resulted from infection as a result of the injection of drugs. About the same number were contracted through infected blood (generally from a transfusion), and 73 per cent were as a result of unprotected homosexual intercourse. In the late 1990s, however, the number of cases resulting from sex between men fell and was overtaken by the rapid rise in cases that were due to sex between men and women. To put these numbers in context, the incidence of many less serious sexually contracted diseases is much higher, and also increasing. The number of cases of gonorrhoea and syphilis had decreased substantially, but increased sharply in the second half of the 1990s. Chlamydia, another sexually transmitted disease, shows a rising trend.

Figure 8.6 Prevalence of HIV/AIDS, various countries, 2002

Country	% of total population
Japan	< 0.01
USA	0.61
Russia	0.90
UK	0.11
Australia	0.15
Thailand	1.80
Haiti	6.10
Malawi	15.96
South Africa	20.10
Zimbabwe	33.70

Source: Lichtenstein (2002: table 19.1).

Rates of HIV infection vary considerably across the world. Although it came to prominence in the United States and Europe, the prevalence there is among the lowest in the world. Rates are higher in the countries of the former USSR and in South East Asia, but they reach their highest levels in Africa. As shown in the 2002 data from which Figure 8.6 is drawn, in sixteen African countries more than 10 per cent of the population was infected with AIDS. In Zimbabwe, one-third of the population was estimated to be affected by the disease. The causes of infection vary. In the United States and Europe the disease was initially spread through unprotected gay male sex. In Eastern Europe infected intravenous drug use has been the main agent, though this has also been responsible for a significant minority of cases in the United States and some European countries. In Africa, on the other hand, AIDS has spread predominantly through heterosexual relations. Nelson Mandela spoke out about the experience of AIDS in his own family in order to increase awareness of the issue within Africa.

When account is taken of the burden of disease—the number of years that someone lives with a debilitating disease—psychological conditions appear as an important factor. Depression is the fifth most significant cause of disease burden. In Europe and the United States, it is estimated that depression is actually the second largest cause of death if account is taken of its impact on alcohol, tobacco, and drug use and of the health consequences of these. The European country with the highest life expectancy is Sweden, where average expectancy is almost two years longer than in Britain. France and Germany have higher rates of death from cancer (among men and women) than does Britain, though Britain has higher rates of death from heart disease.

Diet and fitness

The health and fitness of a population reflect a whole complex of environmental factors. Among the most critical have been patterns of eating and exercise. Under-nourishment was chronic throughout the eighteenth and nineteenth centuries, when large numbers of people died in the Irish famines. Lack of food left many people unhealthy and prone to infectious diseases. At the time of the Boer War (1899–1902), 38 per cent of potential army recruits were rejected as being undersized or unfit for military service.

The quality of the national diet has generally improved since the end of the nineteenth century. Levels of poverty have declined, though lack of food remains a problem for many people. Many of the poor are forced to eat cheap but unhealthy diets. Although the quantity of food eaten by the majority of the population has increased over the period, its nutritional quality has not always increased at the same pace. Compared with the typical nineteenth-century diet, there has been a reduction in fibre intake and an increase in fat, sugar, and salt intake, as well as a greater consumption of alcohol and tobacco.

 Global focus Pandemics   8.5

There has been growing concern over the global spread of disease as a 'pandemic', an epidemic of an infectious disease spreading rapidly and across large parts of the world. This hit newspaper headlines and caused mass panic when cases were reported of 'Avian flu' in 2004–5 and 'Swine flu' in 2008–9. A Swine flu pandemic was declared by the WHO in the summer of 2009 and was declared over in early 2010.

There have been very real problems of the global spread of disease: the most serious influenza epidemics were the Asian flu of 1957 and the Hong Kong flu of 1968. Deaths in recent outbreaks have been far fewer, causing some to see the concern over pandemics as a 'moral panic' that raises public concern above the level of the actual scale of the problem.

You might like to look at our discussion of moral panic on p. 235 and see if you think this does offer an explanation of the attention given to influenza outbreaks in the mass media.

There have been major changes in diet since the 1960s. Most significant has been a shift from red meats (beef and lamb) and dairy products to poultry and vegetables. The increased consumption of vegetables reflects a growing level of vegetarianism and concern for healthy eating, especially among the young (P. Atkinson 1983; Twigg 1983). There has also, however, been a decline in the consumption of fresh vegetables and an increase in the consumption of processed vegetables. This is associated with a growth in the consumption of 'convenience foods' of all kinds, including sweets and snacks. A national survey for the mid-1990s found that young people in the 16–24 age group were especially likely to eat confectionery and to do so on five or six days of each week. These trends are, perhaps, reinforced by the decline in the idea of the 'family meal' as the focus of family life. Households of all kinds rely more and more on convenience foods, rather than the traditional 'hot meal' with a 'pudding', and household members eat at different times of the day (Blaxter and Paterson 1982; Murcott 1982; Charles and Kerr 1988).

Smoking has declined considerably since the early 1970s. In 1972, 52 per cent of men and 41 per cent of women were smokers. By 1994 these figures had fallen to 28 per cent and 26 per cent, respectively. The fall levelled off for a while and there has recently been a further fall. The highest rates of smoking are found among those in the 20–24 age group, where almost a third are regular smokers. Trends in smoking have been influenced by bans on smoking in public places and places where food is served, which have been introduced in many countries. Similarly, the incidence of excessive drinking—consumption of alcohol above medically approved limits—is highest among both men and women in the 18–24 age group.

Disability and disadvantage

'Disability' might seem to be a straightforward idea. Many who regard themselves as fully fit in body and mind label themselves as 'able-bodied' and those who differ from them as 'disabled', as lacking in certain 'normal' physical abilities. Thus, the visually impaired, the deaf, wheelchair-users, and others may all be defined as having disabilities that prevent them from leading a normal life. They are regarded as incapacitated or handicapped, as unable to take on normal social responsibilities. This leads people to operate with an individualized model of disability, treating it as an individual 'problem', as a personal tragedy, with psychological or biological causes. Many disabled people, seen as unable to live like the rest of their society, are often seen as requiring incarceration in a 'home', segregated from the rest of society, where they could be looked after by professional carers (Goffman 1961b; P. Morris 1969).

This view has been questioned by those who advocate a social model of disability, first set out by pressure groups acting on behalf of the disabled. An influential statement was that of the Union of the Physically Impaired Against Segregation: 'In our view it is society which disables physically impaired people. Disability is something imposed on top of our impairments by the way we are unnecessarily isolated and excluded from full participation in society' (UPIAS 1976: 14). According to the social model of disability, disability has to be seen as a failure on the part of a society to provide appropriate services and facilities that meet the needs of those with particular impairments. Those with particular bodily impairments *become* disabled when the social conditions under which they live exclude them from participation in things that other members of their society take for granted.

Oliver (1983, 1996) has shown that the conventional view tends to medicalize a social condition and so to hand control of a serious problem to the medical profession.

Impairment and disability

The social model of disability rests on a distinction between impairment and disability. An **impairment** exists when someone has a defective bodily part (a limb or an organ), and it includes such things as blindness and visual impairment, deafness, vocal difficulties, paralysis, amputation, arthritis, epilepsy, and problems of brain disorder and function. Impairment can result from congenital and perinatal conditions, from disease and illness, and from injury. A **disability**, on the other hand, is a disadvantage that is caused for the physically impaired by particular forms of social organization. Examples of disability include the inability to negotiate stairs, use keyboards, use telephones, read documents, get dressed, communicate, or drive a car (see Albrecht *et al.* 2001).

Thus, impairment is not, in itself, a cause of disability. A disability exists when social conditions impose restrictions on impaired people. As such, it may result from prejudice or simply from the way that accepted institutions happen to operate. What might be called institutional discrimination, like institutional racism, may disable the impaired even where none of the participants intends to do so.

It has recently been argued that 'disablism'—prejudice and institutionalized discrimination against the impaired—should be seen in the same way as sexism and racism. Disablism is a form of oppression, social exclusion, and disadvantage exercised over the impaired by other members of their society (Barnes and Mercer 2003).

Typically, disability results from the stigmatization of impairments (Goffman 1963b). Stigmatization occurs when an impairment becomes a mark of social difference that is responded to in prejudiced and socially stereotyped ways. It is treated as something that undermines the identity of the impaired person as a 'normal' member of society.

A stigmatized impairment signifies a 'spoiled identity', something that is disfiguring physically or metaphorically. Goffman gives particular attention to the ways in which individuals seek to manage their spoiled identities. He looks, for example, at the ways in which they seek to avoid embarrassment and prejudice by 'passing' as normal, hiding their impairment. Davis (1961) has documented the mechanisms of 'deviance disavowal' through which impaired individuals may gradually encourage those with whom they interact to accept their impairment as unimportant or unnoticeable. In many situations, however, such disavowal is not possible, and people must handle the negative reactions to their spoiled identities. In striving for 'normality', impaired people adopt coping mechanisms that enable them to present and sustain an impression of a 'capable self', rather than the 'disabled self' that others might impute on the basis of their spoiled identity (Corbin and Strauss 1985).

It is certainly important to recognize that impairment is not the *cause* of disability. It is also important, however, to recognize that impairment is a bodily condition or circumstance that allows the disabling processes of a society to have their effects. Some advocates of the social model of disability have deliberately emphasized a strong formulation of the model, minimizing the reality of physical impairment, in order to further a political programme of eliminating the social conditions responsible for disability. In fact, the social model has to be combined with a proper awareness of impairment as a condition that makes disability possible and that must, therefore, be analysed in its own right. Carol Thomas (1999) has argued that disability and impairment must be recognized as separate and quite distinct conditions affecting social activity:

> Disability is about restrictions of activity which are socially caused. That is, disability is entirely socially caused. But some restrictions of activity are caused by illness and impairment. Thus, some aspects of illness and impairment are disabling. But disability has nothing to do with impairment.

Thomas 1999: 39

While the social conditions for disability must be removed, the potential for medical intervention on impairments should not be ignored. The provision of contact lenses or glasses for the short-sighted, for example, may be a far more effective solution to their impairment than treating it as a disability requiring a restructuring of the social conditions that necessitate good eyesight (the ways in which books and newspapers are produced, the rules governing car driving, and so on). Similarly, the provision of hearing aids may be a more appropriate solution for hearing impairment than attempts to redesign televisions and radios for use by the hearing impaired. Such medical intervention on impairment may not be possible or appropriate in all cases, but it is important to recognize the

> **⊃ Connections**
> Consult some published official statistics on disability. Do these statistics recognize the distinction between impairment and disability? How useful are they likely to be in devising policies for reducing levels of disability? In considering these questions, you may like to think about the kinds of questions that need to be asked in social surveys if they are to produce better information. For example, could questions on difficulties in holding or grasping objects be rephrased as questions about the design of objects?

interdependence of medical intervention and social change in reducing the potential for disability.

Learning spoiled identities

Some of these issues have been explored in relation to blindness and deafness. Robert Scott (1969) has looked at the ways in which the medical and care services available to blind people reinforce the kind of behaviour expected by the experts who provide the services. Those taken into 'special' schools and training organizations are rewarded when they conform to staff expectations—they are praised for their 'insight' into their own condition and they are punished when they deviate from them—and they are criticized for 'resisting' the views of staff. In these ways, their behaviour and their own sense of identity is shaped into a dependent role—the blind role—that is seen as a normal and natural consequence of the impairment.

In their study of deafness, Evans and Falk (1986) looked at the effects on deaf children of attending a residential school. They show how children who are born deaf are socialized into the expectations of the official culture of the school. In learning the sign language that allows them to communicate with staff and with each other, they also learn the attitudes and identity expected of them. They are schooled for the world of the deaf rather than being schooled for living in a hearing world. This is not a completely deterministic process. Some visually impaired people, Scott shows, resist these definitions, despite the punishing sanctions applied by the service providers. They may calculatedly and manipulatively adapt the blind role when it suits their purposes, maintaining an independent sense of identity, or they may actively oppose the institutionalization of the blind role.

In many cases, however, the social reaction to impairment and the construction of a disability role is based around a discourse of 'rehabilitation'. Wendy Seymour (1998) has shown how those with spinal-chord injuries are encouraged by health professionals to recognize and address the 'damage' to their bodies and to reassess the ways in which they might live in the future. This discourse revolves around an ideal of how the body should be and a model of the ways in which a disabled person can be brought back towards this ideal image. In some cases this may be allied with the medical interventions aimed at reconstructing the body and transforming it into a more 'normal' form. Such attempts have sometimes encountered resistance from the disabled themselves, especially where they have the support of groups of similar others. Some

deaf parents of deaf children, for example, oppose the use of cochlear implant operations, which restore an approximation to normal hearing in the completely deaf, on the grounds that such interventions deny the identity that a child already has within a deaf community with its own way of life and way of communicating.

 ## *Stop and reflect*

This section has presented a large number of statistics about population and health, and these cannot be summarized here. You will find it useful to glance back over the various tables and diagrams that we have given.

- Population change is the result of the balance between fertility, mortality, and migration.
- In modern societies, changes in population can be described in terms of a demographic transition.

The demographic transition is associated with a parallel health transition.

- Causes of illness and death have altered considerably with the development of industrial societies.
- Is it useful to see impairment as a condition distinct from disability, and to see the latter as the result of stigmatization and social exclusion?

Medicine, minds, and bodies

Illness is generally seen as having an objective, physical reality. It is a result of the influence of germs, viruses, and other specific biological agents. Our discussion in 'Health, reproduction, and disability' may have seemed to accept, rather uncritically, the idea that there can be an objective and straightforward definition of health. It should be clear from our discussion of Foucault, however, that this is not the case. It is now necessary to return to this theme and look more critically at the ideas of health and illness.

The conditions recognized as illnesses vary quite considerably from one society to another, as do the particular ways in which they are defined and treated. For the sociologist, health is whatever is regarded as the normal biological condition of an individual in a society that has institutionalized a medical gaze and conception of reality. Illness is any perceived departure from this condition that is subject to medical treatment (Freidson 1970).

People in different societies may be affected by a similar viral infection, but their conditions may be socially defined quite differently. In contemporary societies, such a person is likely to be seen as 'ill'. In many pre-modern societies, which lack a concept of 'virus' and have no institutionalized medicine, they may be seen as suffering from the effects of witchcraft or evil spirits. In the same way, it is only recently—and still only in part—that those who suffer from persistent fatigue and depression have been defined as suffering from chronic fatigue syndrome (sometimes

called ME or myalgic encephalomyelitis) rather than being seen as malingerers. The social construction of health and illness makes it impossible to set out any kind of general and absolute idea of what it is to be healthy. Conceptions of health are inextricably linked to ideas of personal identity and social acceptability.

Consider the case of dental health. It might be thought that this could be defined in terms of the presence or absence of tooth decay. Much dental treatment, however, is preventive and opens up many ambiguous areas of treatment. The removal of crowded teeth, the straightening of crooked teeth, and the whitening of yellowed teeth are treatments that owe as much to cosmetic considerations as they do to preventive dentistry. It is impossible to decide with any certainty which particular dental interventions are necessary for good health.

In the same way, it might be thought that those who are overweight are unhealthy. However, it is impossible to define what is meant by being overweight independently of social considerations. Conceptions of what it is to be overweight, as we show below, are impossible to disentangle from ideas of what it is to be slim and attractive. This kind of ambiguity has drawn doctors into medical treatments aimed at slimming and into various types of cosmetic surgery.

Sociologists do not, of course, deny that there is a biological basis to illness, nor do they fail to recognize physical suffering. This would be obviously absurd. Two fundamental points are being made in theories of the social construction of illness. First, even biological concepts of health are imprecise. The World Health Organization defines health in relation to 'well-being', for example, but the Royal College of General Practitioners sees it as 'adjustment' to circumstances. Medical definitions leave many areas of uncertainty that can shift as medical knowledge changes. This medical knowledge is itself the product of a complex social process of clinical and scientific investigation. Secondly, social contexts shape both the meanings that are given to biological conditions and people's reactions to them. While doctors need to employ biological conceptions of illness in order to diagnose and treat particular disorders, the sociologist is more interested in the social behaviour of those who are labelled as 'sick' and those who do this labelling. Medicine and sociology have complementary concerns. An understanding of health and illness requires both a biological knowledge of the causes of illness and a sociological understanding of how sick people behave and how others react to their sickness.

Medical control and the body

Foucault (1976) showed the way in which the medical gaze transformed the prevailing view of the human body and introduced new disciplines of anatomical control. Organized medicine has been expanding its power by extending its claims to competence to more and more areas of social life. Matters that used to be the responsibilities of priests, social workers, teachers, and others are now seen as 'medical' matters. Illich (1977) sees this **medicalization** as undermining the power of ordinary people to make their own decisions. The right to make decisions is handed over to the technical 'expert' (see also Zola 1975).

In this section we will look at the idea of the sick role, which has been widely used as a way of understanding how these disciplines of the body have been organized in contemporary societies. We will also look at some of the reproductive technologies through which the fertility and sexuality of women have been disciplined. Finally, we look at the discipline of the body in death.

The sick role

In his discussion of health and illness, Talcott Parsons (1951) described the emergence of what he called the **sick role**. This role is defined by normative expectations that people who are ill should behave in ways that minimize the disruptive effects that their illness can have on ordinary social life. Those who are ill may not be able to continue with their usual activities, or they may behave in unacceptable ways. In either case, there may be much disruption of normal, everyday life. Minor forms of illness and disability are often disregarded, but disorders that are long-lasting or debilitating are likely to cause particularly pressing problems for others as well as for the sufferer. Deviance that might result from such illnesses can be minimized and normalized if the ill person conforms to the expectations of the sick role. Through their knowledge of the sick role—a knowledge that is acquired during their socialization—people learn how to be ill in socially acceptable ways.

There are three principal elements in the normative expectations that define the sick role. A sick person:

- is exempted from any personal responsibility for her or his illness;
- has permission to withdraw from many normal family and work commitments;
- is obliged to seek medical help and to become a 'patient'.

In most Western societies, illness is not seen as something that sufferers bring upon themselves. It is something that is beyond their control. The physical or organic character of an illness is seen as having no direct connection with the previous behaviour of the sick person. This general principle is not, of course, completely clear-cut, and there are many areas of ambiguity. The health risks resulting from heavy smoking are now well known, and there has recently been some discussion about whether heavy smokers should be entitled to receive medical treatment for lung cancer. Even more controversially, public opinion on AIDS/HIV-infection has sometimes tended to see it as a 'self-inflicted' illness: as a consequence of deviant sexual behaviour and, therefore, as less deserving of treatment than other illnesses. These are, however, highly problematic and contentious areas (see Box 8.6). In most cases, exemption from responsibility is given to the sick person, who is then permitted to act in ways that would not normally be tolerated.

The recognition of 'sickness', then, is one way of normalizing deviant behaviour. When people are recognized as suffering from a sickness for which they have no responsibility, they are seen as having a legitimate right to abandon many of their normal day-to-day responsibilities. They may be entitled to take time off work without loss of pay, they can take to their bed and leave domestic chores to other household members, and they may even be able to disregard some of the normal niceties of polite behaviour. None of these dispensations would usually be allowed to people experiencing problems that were seen as their responsibility. The person who becomes incapable of work because of a drinking spree, for example, is not normally seen as having a legitimate right to take a day off. Those who find themselves in such a situation may often invent a 'bug' or a bout of 'flu' to legitimate their time off work. In doing so, they trade on the social acceptability of the sick role.

Briefing: self-inflicted illness and non-diseases   8.6

Should smokers receive NHS treatment for illness caused by their smoking? Some have argued that such illnesses are self-inflicted and, in a situation of limited resources, should not receive treatment at the public expense. This issue first hit the headlines in the early 1990s, when Harry Elphick, a heavy smoker aged 47, was refused hospital treatment at Wythenshawe Hospital in Manchester for his heart condition. Mr Elphick stopped smoking, but died a week before his next hospital appointment.

In early 2002 a woman aged 35 wrote to the *Guardian* to complain that her GP had refused her a repeat prescription for the contraceptive pill unless she stopped smoking. In this case, the refusal of the prescription was justified by doctors on the grounds that the combination of heavy smoking and oestrogen (the active ingredient in the pill) would increase the woman's risk of heart attack or stroke.

Alcohol, like tobacco, has been seen as a possible cause of self-inflicted harm and disease: through liver and heart damage, cancer, and the effects of drunken violence, alcohol is estimated to cost the NHS £3 billion a year. A report by Alcohol Concern suggested that heavy drinkers needed to be identified in order to reduce the burden on the health service. The Chairman of NICE (the National Institute for Health and Clinical Excellence) has said:

> Alcoholism rots the liver and if the patient is going to continue drinking, giving them a liver when there is already a shortage of organs is not a sensible use of resources. . . . We are not punishing alcoholics. It is just that it is pointless spending all that money and using a liver that could be used for someone else.

A recent survey on medicalization asked doctors to name the main things for which they were consulted that they thought should be regarded as 'non-diseases' that required no treatment. The top ten non-diseases named were:

1. Ageing
2. Work
3. Boredom
4. Bags under the eyes
5. Ignorance
6. Baldness
7. Freckles
8. Big ears
9. Grey or white hair
10. Ugliness

Sources: Independent, 28 January 1997; *Guardian*, 21 February 2002; 1 March 2002; 10 April 2002; *Daily Mail*, 28 November 2005.

❓ *Under what circumstances do you think that such patients should be refused medical treatment? What considerations are relevant to this decision?*

❓ *What does this debate tell us about the relative powers of doctors and patients in constructing the sick role?*

This permission to withdraw from normal commitments is not absolute, but is conditional on the person seeking medical help. The sick role is a temporary role, and the sick person must see her or his state of sickness as undesirable, as something to be escaped from as soon as possible. Those who 'wallow' in their illness and who show no sign of trying to recover will rapidly find that the permission to withdraw from normal interaction and the exemption from responsibility are taken away from them. They will be seen as 'malingerers'. The normal assumption is that real sufferers will visit a doctor's surgery or arrange a visit from a doctor to their home. It is normally doctors who confirm that a person is ill and so legitimate occupancy of the sick role. The sick person is permitted to continue in this role by those family members, friends, and work colleagues who accept the medical definition of the illness. Doctors authorize the sick person's withdrawal from normal life and make available their medical expertise to treat her or him as a patient.

Central to an understanding of the sick role, then, is the doctor–patient relationship. The relationship between the role of the doctor and the role of the patient is one of authority. There is a fundamental difference in power between the two, rooted in the claim that the doctor makes to scientific expertise (T. Johnson 1972). The patient must submit to the doctor's power, because continued occupancy of the sick role rests upon an acceptance of medical authority. People who deny the authority of a doctor must give up any claim to have a legitimate sickness. They may, indeed, be ill, but they cannot expect any allowance to be made for this by others because they have rejected the institutionalized requirement to seek and to accept medical help. (However, see the issues raised in Box 8.7, p. 288.)

This difference in power between doctor and patient is brought out in the use of the very word 'patient', a word that originally described someone who exercises 'patience' and is, therefore, 'passive'. This power difference is magnified

New technology Online diagnosis   8.7

To deal with a shortage of doctors, nurses, and health provision, many governments have introduced online and telephone diagnosis systems.

In Britain, logging on to **www.nhsdirect.nhs.uk/index.asp**, allows people to consult a database of symptoms to try to identify their medical problems and recommended action. Linked to the online service is a 24-hour telephone service on which patients can speak to a nurse, who will advise on symptoms and treatments. It is intended to integrate these services with the existing 'out-of-hours' call-out service provided by GPs.

Some private medicine providers also provide online diagnosis systems on a charging basis. For example, the Australian website **http://yourdiagnosis.com/start.htm** is run by Macquarie Health Corporation.

❓ What are the implications of such systems for the power of the medical professon? Do they reduce this power or increase it?

---

when there are also differences of class, gender, or ethnicity between doctors and their patients.

Reproductive bodies

Difference in power between doctors and their patients are especially marked in the medical care of pregnancy and childbirth. In these medical encounters, the doctors are overwhelmingly male and the patients are exclusively female. Their power relations are shaped by the wider context of gender differences and gender inequalities. Medical intervention in child-bearing is an intervention in the central defining characteristic of sex–gender roles in contemporary societies.

Over the last century-and-a-half there has been a major shift in the way child-bearing is controlled. Until well into the nineteenth century, childbirth took place within the private sphere of the home, perhaps with the help and support of female relatives and neighbours. The rise of modern medicine brought childbirth and the whole surrounding area of sexuality, pregnancy, and child health into the medical arena, under the control of doctors. Obstetricians, gynaecologists, and paediatricians, supported by midwives and other nurses, achieved a high level of control over these aspects of women's lives (Oakley 1984). By 1927, 15 per cent of all births took place in hospital, and by 1980 this figure had reached 98 per cent.

Pregnancy and childbirth are not, of course, illnesses. Their incorporation under the medical gaze, however, has eliminated or reduced many of the dangers to health that women and their babies previously faced. Death during childbirth, for example, was once far more common than it is today, and we have also shown how much neonatal and infant mortality have been reduced. A consequence of this involvement of medical experts has been that pregnant and would-be pregnant women have been required to adopt a variant of the sick role that legitimates the further medicalization of their lives. As a patient, they must accept the

authority of the doctor (H. Roberts 1985). They must subordinate their own knowledge of their body and their control over it to the expertise of the doctor. The obstetrician, for example, expects to have the same degree of control over a woman's reproduction as a neurosurgeon has over patients during brain surgery.

The medicalization of reproduction has involved an expanding complex of reproductive technologies, under the control of doctors. Many of these technologies have, of course, made childbirth safer, but they have also introduced new health risks. Changes in medical technology have led to a significant increase in the health risks that women face when undergoing treatment.

There are four principal technologies of reproduction (Stanworth 1987a: 10–11):

- contraception technologies;
- childbirth technologies;
- foetal technologies;
- conception technologies.

Contraception technologies are among the oldest available and include a whole array of techniques for preventing and terminating pregnancies. The legalization of abortion in Britain in 1968 reduced the very large number of deaths and injuries that resulted from illegal 'back-street' and self-induced abortions. The technology of termination, however, means that abortion of a foetus is now possible at a much later age. There have been renewed debates about the ethics of abortion and who has the right to decide whether an abortion should take place. Condoms and barrier methods of contraception have been used for a very long time, and about one-third of sexually active people use them—the rates are higher among those with more than one sexual partner (see Figure 8.7). One of the greatest revolutions in contraceptive technology, however, has been the introduction of the contraceptive pill. As a technology, working

Figure 8.7 Use of condoms in the previous four weeks, by number of new partners of the opposite sex, 2001

Great Britain	Percentages	
	Existing partner only	One or more new partners
Males		
Used on every occasion	20	46
Used on some occasions	9	17
Not used at all	70	38
Females		
Used on every occasion	17	37
Used on some occasions	8	16
Not used at all	76	48

Note: Numbers rounded up in original source.
Source: *Social Trends* (2004: table 7.23).

through the regulation of hormones in the woman's body, it is highly effective. It has, however, been linked with thrombosis and some forms of cancer.

Childbirth technologies include such procedures as the long-established Caesarean section and the somewhat newer induction of deliveries. Drug technologies for inducing births have allowed hospitals to schedule childbirth to correspond with staff shifts and rotas, reducing the number of overnight births, but induction is not without its dangers to women and their babies. Particularly important forms of childbirth technology have been those concerned with monitoring and treating the pain and distress of the mother and baby. Painkilling injections and foetal-monitoring equipment, for example, were introduced as ways of making childbirth more comfortable and of increasing the chances of the baby being born healthy.

Foetal technologies are those that monitor foetal development and eliminate birth defects. These include the use of ultrasound and X-ray to examine the foetus, amniocentesis to identify genetic problems, and, most controversially, genetic engineering. The results of monitoring programmes have been used to identify potential 'problems'—such as a foetus likely to develop into a baby with Down's syndrome—and to recommend terminations. The aspiration of many medical scientists involved in the area, however, is that it may be possible, instead, to intervene directly and alter the genetic material of the foetus.

Finally, *conception technologies* are concerned with the promotion of pregnancy and the treatment of infertility. Informal arrangements for the 'donation' of ova and sperm and for 'surrogate motherhood' have long existed, but the medical profession has increasingly become involved in formalizing and medicalizing these arrangements. The development of drug treatments for infertility and the use

of *in vitro* fertilization (so-called test-tube reproduction) have expanded the power that the medical profession has to decide who may have children and when they may have them. The most recent technology to be explored in this area is the genetic cloning of embryos. Experiments on animals led to the first successful cloning of a sheep, and there have been successful clonings of human embryos.

The development and expansion of new reproductive technologies must be seen in relation to the occupational strategies of medical experts. While technologies may remove some dangers, they create new risks, and their introduction and use have not been led by their health effects alone. Doctors involved in such high-profile work at the leading edge of research are able to enhance the status of their professional specialism and strengthen their arguments for higher levels of funding. The expansion of reproductive technologies is also driven by the interests of the big drug and medical supply companies, for whom reproduction has become big business.

In this context, women can become quite powerless. For this reason, feminists have seen it as critical to the whole debate over women's health and their control over their own bodies (Dworkin 1983). Reproductive technologies allow the medical profession to weaken—and perhaps to break—the link between sex and motherhood. A predominantly male medical profession usurps activities that were formerly a primary concern of women, making women's bodies into objects of the new technologies. Reproductive technologies are integral parts of the socially structured medical practices that centralize control over the regulation of populations and human reproduction.

Learning to die

It may be accepted that physical illness is socially constructed in various ways, but surely death is an undeniable biological fact? In one sense, of course, this is true, though there are numerous differences of medical opinion as to exactly when someone can be regarded as 'dead'. There are very real medical difficulties involved in determining the moment of death and in deciding whether those in a persistent vegetative state on a life-support machine are 'dead'. The problems in deciding the brain state of those in comas are notoriously difficult. A Belgian man thought to have been in a vegetative state from 1983 to 2006 was found to have a fully functioning brain and to have been consciously aware of his situation for the full twenty-three years. This has raised questions about the ability of doctors to detect brain states and, therefore, to decide on the moment of death. There has been much debate over the rights of relatives to switch off the life-support systems of patients who are in long-term comas. In a wider sense, however, death must also be seen as a socially constructed event defined by values and norms. While people do, of course, die—an undeniable physical event, however difficult it might be to identify in some cases—numerous and very different subjective meanings can be given to this event. For some, death is the end of existence, for others it is merely a point of transition to some higher, 'spiritual' life. For yet others it may mark the point at which the 'soul' is released for rebirth in another body. Physical death is the end stage of a social process of 'dying', and this can be understood in the same way as other forms of social behaviour.

Dying, then, must be understood as a social process. This was one of the central insights of Durkheim's study of suicide (1897). Durkheim showed that suicide could be understood only if it was recognized that rates of suicide varied considerably from one social group to another. Douglas (1967) extended this argument, showing the varying social meanings given to unexpected deaths by the perpetrator (for example, in a suicide note), by friends and relatives, doctors, the police, coroners, and others.

In their powerful study of death, Glaser and Strauss (1965) have shown that, except in cases of sudden accidents resulting in instantaneous death, a person's death is a process that takes time. Sometimes this is days, sometimes weeks, sometimes years. In many cases, dying is the final phase of a long occupancy of the sick role, and it involves the continued 'management' of the patient, which today generally takes place in a hospital. Relatives and medical staff have certain expectations about when and how a patient will die, and they construct a **death trajectory** that they expect the patient to follow. The trajectory becomes, in effect, a role expected of the dying person.

It is difficult for these role expectations to be imposed on a dying patient when the patient is unaware that he or she is dying, and Glaser and Strauss have shown the considerable variations in role behaviour that occur with varying degrees of awareness. Doctors and nurses make medical assessments of a patient's condition, which they record in case notes and that influence their behaviour towards the patient. Medical professionals must decide how much of this information is to be passed on to the patient and to his or her relatives. In some cases, patients and relatives may be made fully aware of the situation, while in others they may be kept in the dark.

The participants in a death, therefore, act on the basis of varying states of awareness. Where all participants share a common state of awareness, there may be a high degree of consensus over the death trajectory to be followed. When awareness varies, however, there will be much scope for conflict and misunderstanding and for deviance on the part of the dying patient. The person may, for example, be perceived as dying in unexpected or 'inappropriate' ways. Glaser and Strauss identify four different **awareness contexts** that surround dying in hospitals. These are:

- *closed awareness*: the patient is kept in ignorance of the condition and does not know that he or she is dying;

- *suspected awareness*: the patient suspects that he or she is dying;

- *mutual-pretence awareness*: both staff and patient know, but maintain the fiction that the patient does not know;

- *open awareness*: patient and staff are all fully aware.

In a closed-awareness context, the patient does not know his or her true condition, and the medical staff strive to ensure that this remains the case. They employ various tactics to prevent the patient from even suspecting the truth. Doctors will not tell patients they are dying, unless asked a direct question, and all staff may talk 'around the houses' in order to avoid making any direct statements that would give the game away. Staff and relatives engage in collusion and secrecy and try to construct plausible accounts of events and experiences that might otherwise lead the patient to question his or her chances of recovery. In these circumstances, it is difficult to make patients conform to expectations about how to die properly, as they do not know that they are dying.

Because of collusion and the potential for misunderstanding, closed awareness is difficult to sustain, and often slips into a situation of suspected awareness or open awareness. Where a patient discovers the truth, he or she may, nevertheless, pretend not to have done so, and the staff—if they are aware of this pretence—are also likely to try to maintain the fiction. This context of mutual pretence is also particularly difficult to sustain.

An open-awareness context is far easier for staff to manage. In this situation, expectations of proper behaviour can be explicitly imposed on patients. Their awareness means that they can be seen to have responsibility for their own actions as dying persons: not for the fact that they *are* dying, but for *how* they die. When people know that they are dying, they are expected to present a *dying self* to the world, and this self-presentation is expected to conform to particular standards that define a 'proper' death:

> The patient should maintain relative composure and cheerfulness. At the very least, he [*sic*] should face death with dignity. He should not cut himself off from the world, turning his back upon the living; instead he should continue to be a good family member, and be 'nice' to other patients. If he can, he should participate in the ward social life. He should co-operate with the staff members who care for him, and if possible he should avoid distressing or embarrassing them. A patient who does most of these things will be respected. He evinces what we shall term 'an acceptable style of dying'.

Glaser and Strauss 1965: 86; see also Glaser and Strauss 1968

Patients who do not die 'properly' are sanctioned to make them conform to the role expectations. They will be reprimanded, scolded, and ordered; they will be coaxed and coached in how to behave; and they may even be offered rewards for cooperation. Staff may be more likely to be friendly and helpful if the patient cooperates with ward routines, and the relatives of the patient are drawn into this process of social control.

Medicalization and the mind

We have looked at the sick role in relation to physical illnesses, but a whole array of other illnesses are seen as having mental rather than physical effects. Schizophrenia, depression, and other mental illnesses are often seen as having an organic basis and as being treatable through drug therapies. They are, however, generally seen as a different type of illness from the purely physical.

Mental disorders are seen in a rather more ambiguous light than are physical and physiological disorders. A lack of public understanding about mental disorders is associated with an unwillingness on the part of sufferers to recognize their own symptoms. There is, in a very real sense, public disagreement over whether mental illness is really an illness at all. Many think that those who feel depressed should 'pull themselves together', that psychological states are less 'real' than physical states, and that, in many respects, people are responsible for their own mental states.

If people are seen as having at least a degree of responsibility for their own illness, then the sick role cannot be played in the usual way. From this point of view, mental illness—unlike physical illness—comes to be seen as a type of deviant behaviour itself. Mentally ill people not only deviate from expectations about normal, everyday behaviour; they also deviate from the expectations surrounding the sick role. Many of the ambiguities and contradictions inherent in the treatment of the mentally ill and in the low prestige of psychiatric doctors can be explained by this ambivalence over the character of mental *illness* itself.

Becoming schizophrenic

Scheff (1966) set out a model of the forms of mental illness diagnosed by psychiatrists as forms of 'schizophrenia' or 'psychosis' (see also Coulter 1973). These diagnoses are usually employed where people experience serious delusions or hallucinations and come to be seen as a threat to themselves and to others. Scheff aimed to show that these forms of mental illness, which often involve long periods of hospitalization, can be understood as forms of deviant behaviour.

Schizophrenia is rooted in what Scheff calls **residual rule-breaking**. 'Residual rules' relate, not to specific kinds of interaction and relationship, but to the very nature of social interaction itself. These rules involve deeply embedded assumptions about the nature of ordinary, day-to-day encounters. They include the expectations that people engaged in a conversation should face one another, maintain a certain distance, take proper turns in the conversation, remain attentive to what is going on, and so on. Those who violate these expectations on a regular basis or in especially visible ways tend to be seen as particularly strange, bizarre, or frightening. They violate the very expectations without which 'normal' interaction is impossible. Their behaviour is seen as unreasonable (Busfield 1996).

Behaviour that may be seen as violating residual rules includes withdrawal, hallucination, muttering, unusual gesturing or posturing, and distraction. Many of these behaviours are acceptable in some contexts, but objectionable in others. Kneeling down, talking to someone unseen, and seeing visions might be regarded as perfectly acceptable behaviour in a Christian Church—they define a devout act of prayer—but they are not regarded as appropriate in a job interview. It is when such types of behaviour occur in inappropriate situations and in ways that threaten normal interaction that they are likely to be seen as deviant.

Nevertheless, residual rule-breaking is quite frequent in everyday encounters. We all, quite regularly, encounter those who seem to be distracted while we talk to them, or who continually interrupt and refuse to allow others to speak. In most cases, this behaviour goes unnoticed, is ignored, or is explained away—it is normalized in one way or another. People are seen as 'tired', 'busy', 'under the weather', or as in some other way experiencing difficulties that account for their behaviour in terms of 'normal' motivations. When residual rule-breaking is normalized, it has little continuing significance.

In some cases, however, the behaviour goes beyond the bounds of what is regarded as normal, exceeding the normal tolerance levels of friends, family, or work colleagues. It may, for example, be particularly visible, extreme, or long-lasting. In these circumstances, the behaviour is seen as being unreasonable, abnormal, and incomprehensible. It is seen, therefore, as needing to be acted upon. In contemporary societies, such behaviour is likely to be labelled as a symptom of 'mental disorder'. In other societies, argues Scheff, the same behaviour might be seen as symptomatic of 'spirit possession' or of 'witchcraft' (see Szasz 1970). The term 'mental disorder' is likely to be used today because our culture has become permeated by medical and psychiatric concepts—often only partially understood—that make the imagery of mental 'abnormality', 'madness', and 'insanity' familiar.

Stereotyped images of mental disorder are learned from early childhood and are reinforced in the mass media. These images are conjured up through the use of such terms as 'crazy', 'loony', 'mad', 'insane', or 'deranged'. In appropriate circumstances, these labels may be applied to others or even to ourselves. People grow up with a particular image of mental disorder and, therefore, of the ways in which they expect those who suffer from it to act. As a result, there is a specific version of the sick role, the **insanity role**.

Many forms of depression and anxiety may be normalized by families, or treated within the conventional framework of the sick role; those who seem to experience seriously disruptive mental problems are more likely to be treated in terms of the insanity role. As with the sick role proper, the medical profession is called in to accredit the insanity. The person's friends and family may, for example, call in the general practitioner, who may refer the case to a psychiatric specialist. In these ways, residual rule-breaking is medicalized, and the medical professionals initiate a process of treatment.

When people act in terms of the insanity role, incorporating it into their sense of identity, residual rule-breaking is transformed into the form of secondary deviation called 'mental illness':

> When the deviance of an individual becomes a public issue, the traditional stereotype of insanity becomes the guiding imagery for action, both for those reacting to the deviant and, at times, for the deviant himself [*sic*]. When societal agents and persons around the deviant react to him uniformly in terms of the traditional stereotypes of insanity, his amorphous and unstructured rule-breaking tends to crystallize in conformity to these expectations, thus becoming similar to the behaviour of other deviants classified as mentally ill, and stable over time. The process . . . is completed when the traditional imagery becomes a part of the deviant's orientation for guiding his own behavior.

Scheff 1966: 64

But why should anyone conform to such a role? Scheff argues that this is because residual rule-breakers are encouraged by others to accept the image of insanity as an 'explanation' for the problems that they have been experiencing. At the same time, they are refused the opportunity to act in more conventional ways: if mentally ill people deny their illness and do not accept the treatment, then this simply shows how ill they really are. They may, for example, find it difficult to enter or retain employment or to continue with normal domestic responsibilities. The people labelled are, furthermore, likely to be highly suggestible to the opinions of others. The hostility they may feel and the strength of the opinions held by professionals all leave them feeling highly vulnerable.

To see schizophrenia as a form of deviance is not to deny that many people do face serious mental problems and that they may need help in dealing with them. Nor is it to deny that there may be a biological basis to some forms of residual rule-breaking. The point that Scheff is making is that mental illness is always to be seen as a social fact as well as a physical fact. Psychiatric diagnoses—such as 'schizophrenia', 'phobia', and 'neurosis'—are made in social contexts

and are applied to people who have already been labelled as a problem by others. It is only those who have come to be seen as problematic by non-psychiatrists—by friends, relatives, or colleagues—who come to the attention of psychiatrists. For this reason, psychiatrists have most of their professional contact with those who have entered the stage of secondary deviation and are already playing the insanity role. In this context, psychiatric diagnoses cannot be seen as neutral acts independent of processes of social control.

The moral career of the mental patient

Goffman (1961*b*) also explored the life of seriously ill schizophrenics and psychotics, paying particular attention to their 'moral career'. This term refers to the changing sense of self that develops as they experience the particular contingencies and constraints that occur with their hospitalization.

Goffman saw the transition from primary deviation to secondary deviation for the mentally ill as involving a movement from the status of a *civil person* to that of a *patient*. Whereas the civil person is an individual with full civil rights as a member of society, the patient loses certain rights and powers. Hospitalized mental patients in Britain, for example, cannot vote in general elections, and hospital staff have the power to act on their behalf in many areas of life. As we show in Chapter 14, the admissions procedures adopted by mental hospitals emphasize the new status that the person has acquired. With the status of patient, the person fully enters the insanity role, and a career of mental illness becomes possible.

The patient stage of the insanity role is seen by Goffman as having three phases. First, there is the *home-patient phase* (Goffman calls this the pre-patient phase). This is when the person remains at home, but is under the supervision of a general practitioner. Second is the crucial *in-patient phase*, when the person has been hospitalized, voluntarily or forcibly, and begins a period under the close control of hospital staff. Third is the *ex-patient phase* that follows the patient's release. Ex-patients experience a continuing public reaction and may face many constraints on their opportunities. They are seen in terms of their status as a former mental patient and this may, for example, make it difficult for them to get a job. Many ex-patients relapse into illness, re-entering the hospital for further in-patient treatment. Goffman's argument is summarized in Figure 8.8.

Goffman's own work was concerned mainly with the in-patient phase. He saw the mental hospital as an arena in which staff and patients struggle with each other to define the reality of the patient experience. Patients will initially respond to hospitalization by denying that they are sick. They selectively draw on pre-hospital experiences that allow the presentation of a convincing and self-respecting account of the reasons for their new status: 'It's all a mistake', 'I was under a lot of pressure', 'I'm not like all the other

Figure 8.8 The career of the mentally ill

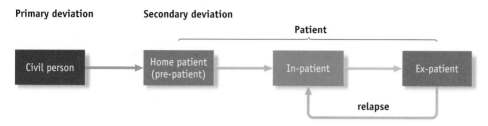

patients', and so on. These kinds of accounts are difficult to sustain in the long term, as they are incompatible with the medical definition of the situation that staff are constructing.

This medical definition is embodied in the case notes and underpins the treatment carried out. It is structured into the very power relations of the hospital. The staff construct an image of the patient as a sick person. He or she is seen as someone who has suffered some kind of collapse or breakdown on the outside and is currently unable to act in his or her own best interests. As the patient attempts to put a positive interpretation on his or her situation, so staff will make comments or highlight evidence that contradicts this. When patients attempt to show staff how 'normal' they are, this is simply taken as a sign of how ill they are: they are so ill that they cannot even recognize their own illness.

Striking evidence in support of Goffman's argument comes from a remarkable study carried out by Rosenham (1973). In this study, Rosenham and seven colleagues feigned psychiatric symptoms—they claimed that they heard voices—and they got themselves admitted to psychiatric hospitals in various parts of the United States. Following admission, they gave up the pretence of hearing voices and began to act in 'normal' ways once more. In all cases, it was some considerable time before staff accepted that they were 'well enough' to be discharged. One of the researchers remained in hospital for a month and a half before being released. On their release, being ex-patients, none of the researchers was defined as having been 'cured' or as having returned to mental health. All were diagnosed as being 'in remission', a diagnosis that meant that the doctors felt that their 'illness' could recur at any time.

Goffman's study focused on the activities undertaken by staff to manage the lives of their patients. The staff included not only the doctors and the nurses, but also cleaners, porters, administrators, athletics instructors, therapists, and many others. When in hospital, Goffman argued, patients must conform not only to the medical definition of their 'case', but also to the demands of the organizational routines on which staff work activities depend. Patients must, for example, fit into ward routines and staff shift patterns, they must receive their meals and post at times convenient for the catering, delivery, and cleaning staff, they must have

their visits properly regulated, and so on. The hospital—like any organization— is a *negotiated order*, a stable system of recurrent relationships and interactions that results from conflict, bargaining, and compromise among the various participants. Each participant has different kinds and amounts of power resources that they can bring to the situation (Strauss *et al.* 1963). The patient, of course, is the least powerful participant. He or she is enticed into accepting the staff definition of the situation by the rewards that can be offered for conformity.

A key to this system of rewards in the hospitals that were studied by Goffman was the ward system. The various wards were arranged in an informal hierarchy of conditions, facilities, and privileges, and patients could be moved from one ward to another in accordance with their perceived 'progress'. This progress, of course, was measured by the extent to which the patient had come to accept the staff definition of their situation as that of a person in need of treatment. Protestations of sanity and rejection of the hospital routines were regarded as signs of illness or of a lack of insight. Patients with such signs could be punished through being 'demoted' from a privileged ward to a less privileged one. A patient who accepted the medical staff's definition of the situation and cooperated with attendants and orderlies was seen as developing an insight into his or her illness. Such patients could be rewarded through 'promotion' up the ward system.

Deprived of the social supports that sustained their self-image in the outside world, patients are particularly vulnerable to these processes of control. They are, therefore, likely to show a gradual submission to staff views. In order to achieve a speedy release from hospital, 'the patient must "insightfully" come to take, or affect to take, the hospital's view of himself' (Goffman 1961b: 143). By accepting the staff definition of the situation, patients reconstruct their biographies as those of people who are 'ill', but are 'getting better'.

'Community' care

Both Scheff and Goffman looked mainly at the situation of schizophrenics and psychotics, and especially at those who receive hospital treatment. With the expansion of psychiatry, however, there has been a shift away from the nineteenth-century model of the asylum as the principal focus of psychiatric treatment. The total number of patients in mental hospitals in England and Wales increased continually over the twentieth century until its peak year of 1954. After this year, however, the number declined constantly, despite an increase in the total population over the same period. Thus, the rate per 10,000 people had declined to a level in 1980 that was close to its level of 100 years before. Today, approximately three-quarters of all psychiatric patients are treated on an out-patient basis. Data for the United States show a similar pattern, the peak year for hospitalization being 1955.

What was happening over this period was that more and more patients were being treated 'in the community', rather than as hospital in-patients. This is the process of decarceration that we discuss in Chapter 14, pp. 545–7. This change in treatment was associated with a shift in the psychiatric gaze. The expansion of psychiatry led its practitioners to give relatively less attention to the severe psychotics and schizophrenics and relatively more attention to the less severe 'depressive' disorders. Depressive states had long been recognized as illnesses by the psychiatric profession, but it was only during the twentieth century that more precise diagnostic criteria were established.

> ⊙ *Connections*
> Read our discussion of Goffman's concept of the total institution in Chapter 14, p. 524, and consider how useful you think it is in understanding mental hospitals. Look also, in the same chapter, at our discussion of decarceration on pp. 545–7.

At first, such patients were treated in hospital, but they rapidly became candidates for out-patient treatment.

It has been suggested that new drug therapies using tranquillizing drugs such as Largactil (chlorpromazine) were responsible for this change in treatment, but this has been overstated. These drugs undoubtedly had some effect in controlling symptoms and so allowing patients to be treated at home, but the shift away from treatment in a mental hospital began before tranquillizer treatment was at all widely available. Scull (1984) has convincingly argued that decarceration became a possibility only because of changes in the system of welfare provision. With the establishment of improved welfare systems from the 1930s, and especially since the Second World War, the cost of hospital treatment has been far greater than the cost of out-patient treatment for a person receiving welfare benefits. Given the choice, then, medical authorities have preferred to treat patients in the community rather than in the asylum.

By the 1960s a formal policy of 'community care' had been adopted. Long-term patients, thought not in need of active medical treatment, were processed through hostels, 'half-way houses', and training centres, while others remained at home. Instead of becoming or remaining in-patients, they have the status of home patient, and the task of care is placed upon their families and their neighbours. Many mental problems are now treated by general practitioners and a growing number of counsellors. This process was especially rapid in the 1980s, as Thatcherism promoted the commercialization of care by encouraging private hostels and residential care homes. It has been estimated that the total cost of community care for elderly

Care in the community?
© Alice Chadwick

people suffering from dementia, depression, or anxiety is more than £2 billion. These costs include not only medical treatment but also the cost of such things as home helps and meals on wheels.

The lack of proper funding for community-care programmes has meant that many schizophrenics and psychotics who are released from mental hospitals have had to live in rundown hostels or have become homeless. These are the very conditions that perpetuate their difficulties and that may allow them to drift into other forms of primary deviation. There have been a number of well-publicized cases of schizophrenics in community care who have become involved in dangerous actions or crimes of violence that would not have been possible if they had been hospitalized (see Box 8.8). It has been shown, however, that the number of murders committed by the mentally ill has fallen since 1957. In 1979, 121 murders were committed by those classified as mentally ill, but by 1995 this had fallen to 60. Critics of government policy suggest that the decrease in hospitalization cannot, therefore, be seen as having brought about a greater risk of such murders and violent attacks. Whether mental illness should be treated in hospital or in the community is not a matter that can be resolved by the murder statistics.

Depression, stress, and gender

The largest number of people suffering mental disorders and being treated 'in the community' are those suffering from depression. Like many psychiatric diagnoses, 'depression' is only loosely defined. It is seen as involving feelings of general helplessness, and is closely associated with 'anxiety' and 'stress', as well as with extreme lethargy, loss of appetite, and both suicide and attempted suicide. The disorder is highly gendered, and women form the core of those receiving treatment for depression.

Studies of depression (Busfield 1996: ch. 10) have come to focus on various distressing experiences that put people under 'stress' and so predispose them to feelings of depression and anxiety. Events associated with stress have been said to include job change, moving home, divorce, bereavement, loss of work, being the victim of crime, illness, heavy demands at work, and so on. Stress levels have been found to vary with subordination and oppression, as people in these situations are more likely to experience unemployment, ill health, family breakdown, violence, poor housing, and crime. Women and the poor, for example, have higher rates of diagnosed and self-reported depression than have men and the more affluent. It has been estimated that between 12 per cent and 17 per cent of women have suffered from clinical depression at some stage in their life, compared with only 6 per cent of men. Women are also far more likely to be taking or to have taken tranquillizers: 23 per cent of the population in 1984 had been prescribed tranquillizers at some stage in their

Briefing: schizophrenia and community care 8.8

There have been a number of notorious cases of schizophrenic patients released into the community and subsequently carrying out violent acts. Christopher Clunis, for example, stabbed a complete stranger in the street, killing him. Clunis's career as a mental patient had included treatment at ten different hospitals before the events of 1992. He had also stayed in a probation hostel, two prisons, a sheltered housing scheme, and five bed and breakfast hotels. He had been seen by five different Social Services departments. The family of the victim, Jonathan Zito, pressed for an official inquiry, which found that Clunis's records had not been properly kept, that there had been no proper plan for his care after his last release into the community, and that no one had overall responsibility for supervising his case.

In 2005, paranoid schizophrenic Anthony Joseph stabbed Richard Whelan on a north London bus after an argument about Joseph throwing chips at Whelan's girlfriend. Joseph had been released on bail in relation to other offences, despite there being an arrest warrant out for him, and he had been bailed to false addresses. An investigation in 2008 blamed problems with the Police National Computer for the breakdown in the bail system.

➲ *When you have read our discussion of the meaning of community in Chapter 13, you might like to return to these cases and think about the implications for the idea of care in the community.*

life, and women were twice as likely as men to have used them (Blackburn 1991: 103).

In practice, the idea of 'stress' is difficult to define with any precision. The question of what is and what is not stressful is very much a subjective matter, and it may be as much a *consequence* of depression and anxiety as it is a *cause*. The fact that women are far more likely to experience depression than men, for example, has been related to the way in which emotions are structured into gender identities. Conventional gender identities involve an expectation that women will express their emotions and take on the 'emotional work' of dealing with others, and this has become a central part of their responsibilities within families (Duncombe and Marsden 1993; see also Hochschild 1983). Men, on the other hand, are expected to 'hold things in'. When men do express their emotions, this is more likely to be outwardly, in the form of violence or in the use of alcohol. The inward direction of emotions by women has been seen as responsible for the self-blame and lower self-esteem that predisposes them to depressive

Figure 8.9   The structuring of depression

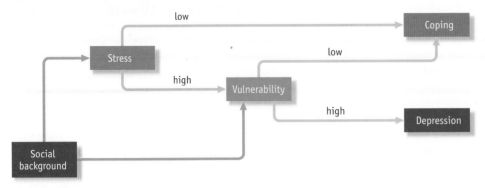

Source: Adapted from Brown and Harris (1978: 48).

responses to stress. It has been suggested, for example, that, because women tend to have more emotionally charged relationships with others to whom they are close, they are, themselves, more likely to be emotionally affected by the problems faced by others in their family and the circle of close friends.

These issues were explored by Brown and Harris (1978) in their investigation into the links between potentially stressful life events and depression in a large sample of women in south London. They show that women who become depressed are far more likely to have experienced serious and severe stressful events (life-threatening illness in the family, loss of job, and so on) over a long period than were those who did not become depressed. They argue, however, that the susceptibility of women to stressful events depends upon what they call 'vulnerability'. By this they mean the social supports that are available through social ties and social networks and that help, or hinder, people's ability to cope with stress. They identify four particular 'vulnerability factors' that predispose certain women to depression:

- the absence of an intimate relationship;
- the lack of employment outside the home;
- three or more children under 14 at home;
- the loss of their own mother before the age of 11.

Those women who have these experiences—especially the first one—are far more likely to experience depression if they are faced with stressful events. Women with an intimate partner, with few or no small children, without paid employment, and who have not lost their mothers appeared to find it easier to cope with stressful events and were less likely to fall into depression. The important point made by Brown and Harris is that these factors do not, in themselves, induce depression: they make people more or

less vulnerable to the stressful events that actually trigger depression (see Figure 8.9). Further stress after the onset of depression reinitiates the process and deepens depression.

The vulnerability factors are clearly linked to conventional gender roles and to ideas about the domesticity of women. Having small children at home and being responsible for them is a central feature of the *captive wife* described by Gavron (1968). It is the combination of this with involvement in paid work that has placed conflicting pressures on many employed women in contemporary Britain. Their two principal roles—employee and mother —involve contradictory expectations and may make it more difficult to cope with stress. Those factors that help women to combine the two roles may, thereby, reduce the impact of stressful events on them. The availability of effective childcare facilities, for example, helps those who have many small children.

Femininity, medicine, and beauty

As the boundaries of medicalization have expanded, there has been a counter-movement in which patients have been seen by governments as 'consumers' of health with the right to choose in medical matters in the same way as they choose the education of their children, the type of car they drive, and the kind of food they eat. The power of patients to choose is limited in many ways, just as their powers to choose in other areas of life are limited. However, the growing popularity of alternative medicines is a sign, perhaps, of the weakened authority of doctors. Patients are able to exercise considerable consumer power in areas such as cosmetic treatment, where medicine has stretched

Briefing: media representations 8.9

There has been much controversy over the media representations of women's bodies in advertising campaigns. It has often been claimed that only very thin models ever get depicted in newspaper and television advertising. The September 2009 issue of US magazine *Glamour* published a near-naked photograph of 'plus-sized' model Lizzie Miller as part of an article on body image. The editor claimed that this was 'the beginning of a revolution' in how women's bodies are depicted.

? *Does this publication mark a change in media representations of women? The photograph was on page 194 and was not in an advertisement—what is the significance of this? (The photograph of Lizzie Miller can be found at www.bbc.co.uk; search for 'The pic that caused a storm'.)*

beyond the more clear-cut boundaries defined by notions of 'disease' and 'illness' to engage with ideas of 'beauty'.

In this section, we look at two very different ways in which people 'choose' their own state of health—cosmetic surgery and eating disorders—seeing these in relation to contemporary images of femininity.

Images of femininity

Contemporary Western culture attaches a strong positive value to the idea of the slim, attractive woman, seen as both independent and self-assured. This cultural ideal contrasts sharply with the traditional image of female domesticity. The traditional image was vociferously challenged by the women's movement of the 1960s and 1970s in the wake of Friedan's critique (1962) of the 'feminine mystique'. This critique encouraged the view that caring for a family is a mundane and undemanding task and that women needed to develop their potentialities outside the home.

The new image of femininity closely combines conceptions of 'beauty' and 'attractiveness' with conceptions of 'health' and 'fitness' (Wolf 1991; Kathleen Davis 1995). A whole complex of industries and processes now surround this image. The cosmetics industry, the fashion industry,

Thinness as glamour: image and reality.

© Getty Images/Gustavo Caballero

© Getty Images: Zubin Shroff

pharmaceuticals companies, and other organizations concerned with dieting and 'healthy eating', as well as the medical profession itself, are all involved in perpetuating the new cultural ideal. These are, in turn, reinforced by advertising images of all kinds, and not only by advertising for 'beauty' products themselves. Consumer pressure groups and television programmes that publicize the health implications of food also tend to reinforce the image of the healthy and fit woman.

Cultural ideals can change rapidly, and the ideal female body of the 1950s and 1960s became the 'full figure' of the 1980s and after. It has been shown that, over the period from 1959 to 1979, the average size of women depicted in fashion and other magazines decreased substantially. At the same time, changes in diet have meant that average weight in the population as a whole has increased. While women are getting larger, models and media ideals have been getting thinner. Pressures to be slim have grown, and the size of the ideal body image has diminished (Mennell *et al.* 1992). The British Medical Association has estimated that a healthy woman has 22–26 per cent body fat, while models and actresses have an average of 10–15 per cent body fat. In mid-2000, the British government organized a seminar at which fashion editors and others discussed the idea that the mass media were promoting unrealistic body images, but the editors held that they were reflecting, not creating, the views of their readers.

> **⊙ Connections**
> You might find it useful to turn to Chapter 10 and look at our discussion of images of women in the media in 'Representation', pp. 367–9.

Through their socialization, women have come to internalize this conception of femininity and to accept it as an ideal. The strength of the image is such that the great majority of women learn to scrutinize and monitor their size, shape, and food intake. They compare themselves with the cultural ideal, and feel themselves to have some kind of spoiled identity (Goffman 1963*b*). They may feel they are overweight or fat, or they may feel they have some particular blemish that marks them out as different from other women: their nose is the wrong shape, their breasts are too small or too big, or they have too many wrinkles.

The tyranny of the cultural ideal means that it is almost impossible not to develop a negative self-image. In pursuit of the cultural ideal, women seek to control and to shape their bodies in the desired direction. Dieting—restricting the amount of food eaten—becomes, for many, a normal part of their life. Large numbers of women are drawn not only into diet, exercise, and jogging, but also into body-building, the use of slimming pills, and increasingly into

cosmetic surgery. Young girls are also exposed to these pressures and grow up feeling that it is unusual not to diet for weight loss. Their attitudes are affected by the views about health and fitness held by their own families and friends and by the classes on 'healthy eating' that now figure in the school curriculum.

Diet and eating habits have changed considerably over time. As a result of poor diets and overeating among the relatively affluent, many people have become medically overweight. Few people engage in any strenuous activity during an ordinary day. They drive to work, are mainly involved in sedentary, non-manual work, and take little or no exercise. Less than half the British population is at a weight that is medically recognized as appropriate for their height and body shape. Significant numbers of men and women are classified as 'obese' or dangerously overweight. This increase in the problem of being overweight is also apparent in the United States, where over 60 per cent of adults are estimated to be obese or overweight. As shown in Figure 8.10, the problem of being overweight is marked by a sharp social-class gradient. It also varies with age, being lowest among young people. Obesity has been linked with the incidence of heart disease and other serious medical disorders.

Among many young people—and especially among young women—there is also a serious problem of being medically 'underweight'. This problem affected between 5 and 7 per cent of those surveyed in 1993. In the 16–24 age group, 14 per cent of males and 18 per cent of females were underweight. This is caused principally by a deliberate restriction of food intake as part of a slimming diet. Lack of body weight is linked to menstrual and fertility problems in women, as well as to such conditions as osteoporosis (brittle bones).

We will look at two different responses to the desire to lose weight, both of which aim at empowerment and control. In the case of those women who choose to undergo

Figure 8.10 The overweight problem

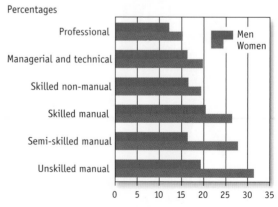

Source: *Social Trends* (2002: chart 7.20).

cosmetic surgery, we will show that control is sought through a faith in medical experts and the quick surgical fix. In the case of those women who experience eating disorders, we will show that control is sought through the adoption of a strict and disciplined way of life.

The surgical fix

Various forms of plastic surgery have been performed for many centuries in the past, but it was not until the Crimean War that these techniques became at all reliable. Surgical techniques were driven by the need to repair the war-ravaged bodies of male soldiers, and great advances were made in the two world wars. In the second half of the twentieth century plastic surgery for the aesthetic improvement of healthy bodies became a major area of medical specialization.

Plastic surgery is now the fastest-growing medical specialism, and cosmetic surgery accounts for about 40 per cent of all plastic surgery. About two million Americans received cosmetic surgery in 1988. An example of cosmetic surgery is discussed in Box 8.10. Ninety per cent were women undergoing face lifts, breast augmentations, liposuction (fat removal), and so on. This is, perhaps, the clearest expression of a consumerist 'choice' orientation in contemporary medicine. Having a new nose or new breasts is seen in almost the same way as having a new hairstyle: it

is something chosen by a woman in order to achieve a particular, desirable presentation of self.

Kathleen Davis (1995) has shown that cosmetic surgery is seen as an option by women who compare themselves with others and develop a fear and loathing of a particular aspect of their own body. This comes to be seen as a blemish that in some way discredits them as women. Their nose, their breasts, or their buttocks, for example, do not fit with the image of what they feel they 'really' look like. It does not match the rest of their body.

Davis argues that these women are not in search of absolute perfection or an exceptional beauty. They are, rather, responding to a perceived stigma. She notes, however, that the perceived stigma is rarely disfiguring, or even apparent, in any objective sense. The cultural pressures on women have led many to be hypersensitive towards their appearance. They are constantly concerned about anything that is 'not quite right'. They hope to rectify a specific blemish that, they feel, prevents them from appearing 'ordinary' and is responsible for their (actual or imagined) exclusion and derogation by others. They feel different and feel they are constantly noticed by others because of their assumed peculiarity. These women use the word 'ordinary' when they mean having an appearance that is within the normal aesthetic range for contemporary women. An ordinary woman is not noticed in her everyday encounters. Their perception of normality, however, is heavily influenced by the cultural ideal of femininity.

The first step towards cosmetic surgery, then, is a feeling of being blemished. The second step is deciding that cosmetic surgery is an appropriate solution. In a society where more areas of life have become medicalized, the surgical fix becomes a realistic possibility for ever-increasing numbers of people.

Those that take this decision, Davis argues, are involved in a renegotiation of their identity and sense of self. It is seen as a last-ditch attempt to rectify a situation perceived to be unbearable:

> **Cosmetic surgery is not about beauty, but about identity. For a woman who feels trapped in a body which does not fit her sense of who she is, cosmetic surgery is about exercising power under conditions which are not of one's own making. In a context of limited possibilities for action, cosmetic surgery can be a way for an individual woman to give shape to her life by reshaping her body.**

Kathleen Davis 1995: 163

Women come to believe that by controlling their bodies they are controlling their lives. Cosmetic surgery comes to be seen as a way of enhancing their power. Their identity is renegotiated, however, in relation to a prevailing image of femininity and a medicalized definition of reality. Their freely chosen option of the surgical fix is as much a sign of subordination as it is of empowerment. The dilemma of

Briefing: having a face lift   8.10

Cosmetic surgery can involve major surgical intervention, as this account shows:

> I saw a face lift performed—the surgeon's hand inside the woman's face, punching and tearing, her separated skin only anchored at the nose and mouth. . . . The laser has added a further dimension to face lifting. The woman's face is now cut, separated, trimmed and reattached, the skin then burnt with a laser to get rid of the fine lines around the mouth.

A survey in the United States found that in 2007 there were 11.7 million surgical and non-surgical procedures for plastic surgery; 91 per cent of these were performed on women. The number of surgical procedures had increased by 142 per cent since 1997. The five most popular surgical cosmetic procedures in 2007 were: liposuction (456,828 cases), breast augmentation (399,440), eyelid surgery (240,763), abdominoplasty (185,335), and breast reduction (153,087).

Sources: Joanna Briscoe, *Guardian*, 18 February 1997; **www.cosmeticplasticsurgerystatistics.com/statistics.html**

cosmetic surgery is that the desire for power and control is pursued by subordination not merely to a cultural ideal of femininity but also to the power of the medical profession.

Femininity, weight, and eating

There has been growing public concern and something of a moral panic over anorexia nervosa. Anorexia comprises a number of physical symptoms that revolve around an abnormally low body weight for the age, height, and sex of the sufferer and is brought about by a sustained and deliberate restriction of food intake. Although the condition first appeared as a medical diagnosis in the middle of the nineteenth century, it is only since the 1970s that it has become of epidemic proportions. Its actual incidence is difficult to gauge, but the rate increased substantially during the 1980s and has stabilized since the mid-1990s. It is thought to be a serious problem for one in every 200 or 250 women between the ages of 13 and 22. About double this number are thought to be significantly affected in some way by problems of anorexia. The number of deaths is small, but they may amount to over 10 per cent of those who receive long-term medical treatment as hospital inpatients. The condition is found mainly, but not exclusively, among young, white, and relatively affluent women, and it is the causes and consequences of anorexia in this group that have been so keenly discussed.

The loss of body weight in anorexia may vary from a condition of being mildly underweight to a state of extreme emaciation. Medical discussions have followed a physiological model in which the former leads inexorably to the latter. The medical view does, however, correctly identify a number of physiological changes that result from extreme weight loss and that characterize established sufferers. These physical effects include secondary amenorrhoea (cessation of menstruation as a result of hormonal changes), feelings of extreme coldness as a result of a lowered rate of metabolism and blood circulation, disturbed sleep, the growth of fine body hair, and a thickening of head hair. There are also likely to be stomach and intestinal upsets, such as constipation and abdominal pain. These are, however, much worse in the related problem of bulimia, where 'binge' eating is followed by induced vomiting or diarrhoea. Abstinence from food over a long period of time reduces body weight below the level at which normal physiological mechanisms can operate to regulate the state of the body, and total physical breakdown is, indeed, inevitable unless treatment is accepted (R. L. Palmer 1980).

In relatively affluent and comfortable families, there is often great pressure on children to succeed in their lives. In the case of young women, this is likely to involve an encouragement—experienced as pressure—to take up opportunities not available to earlier generations of women. This encouragement involves a rejection of, or at least an ambivalence towards, the traditional feminine role and an implicit endorsement of the new cultural ideal. This new ideal of independent and assertive femininity, however, is something that many young women find difficult to accept. They are anxious about their ability to meet these expectations, concerned about how they could ever compare with the ideal.

It is these anxious individuals, it seems, who are especially likely to be drawn into anorexic behaviour (Bruch 1973, 1979; Chernin 1985). Their anxiety makes them uncertain about their own goals, unable to decide what to do. They become confused about who they are and what they might be in the future. This uncertainty over their identity, and the associated feeling that they have no control over their own lives, leads them to focus their attention on more immediate goals set by parents and teachers. Educational success, for example, becomes an end in itself, and, striving to please, they tend to adopt a perfectionist attitude towards their school work. In doing so, they set unrealistic goals and so are constantly unable to meet their own rigorous standards. If they do meet these standards, they feel that they must, after all, have been too low. This is the classic example of the inferiority complex described by Adler (1928).

In their search for a solution to their problems of identity, these young women have not completely abandoned the cultural ideal of femininity. It is something that is still important to them, but about which they feel ambivalent and inadequate. Like others of their age, and like many of their mothers' generation, they are drawn to the ideal and to the practices of bodily control associated with it. Slimming and fitness training, for example, may be adopted as exploratory experiments of their ability to meet this ideal. Such experiments often begin around the time of puberty and are associated with the natural weight gain and changes in body shape that occur at this time. For those who misinterpret the nature of these changes, they can be seen as signs that they are getting 'fat'. It is in these circumstances that the drift into anorexia becomes a possibility.

Many young women begin to diet, perhaps by avoiding what they see as unhealthy or fatty foods. Many—perhaps most—are unsuccessful in losing weight and may drift in and out of dieting for the rest of their lives. Some of those who are successful, especially the anxious perfectionists, are likely to feel a degree of pleasure in having achieved their goal. They enjoy the feeling of accomplishment and control that it gives them. Achieving a weight loss provides a sense of purpose that seems to resolve some of the confusions that they feel about the direction that their lives should take. Dieting becomes one area of life where it seems possible to exercise total control (Bordo 1993: 148–50).

The anorexic solution

The person who drifts from experimental dieting into incipient anorexia is one who gets great satisfaction from finding, at last, something that she has chosen and that she is good at. Dieting seems to resolve her sense of identity even more than immersion in school work. It becomes something that is very difficult to give up. If it is the one area where she feels that she can 'succeed', then what does she have left if she gives it up? She becomes committed to the activity into which she has drifted, gaining satisfaction and even enjoyment from it. Continued weight loss, rather than a fixed target weight, becomes her goal. The original aspiration to achieve attractiveness and independence is partially displaced into a mastery of the body for its own sake. She begins to enter what we describe in Chapter 7 as secondary deviation. She begins a *career* of anorexia, which becomes a way of life that, paradoxically, becomes increasingly detached from the cultural ideal of femininity.

The anorexic way of life revolves around a commitment to *ascetic* practices and values that are deeply rooted in our culture and were first explored by Max Weber (1904–5; see also B. Turner 1996). Asceticism is the pursuit of a disciplined life of self-denial and abstention from material comforts and pleasures. The asceticism of the early Puritans, he argued, was the basis of their business success. In the favourable circumstances of seventeenth- and eighteenth-century England, it helped the expansion of the capitalist system. These values subsequently became much weakened, but they became the basis of a so-called work ethic that limited consumption and leisure by subordinating them to the expansion of production. As we suggest in the discussion of drug use in Chapter 7, the work ethic involves the idea that consumption and leisure can be enjoyed only *after* work commitments have been met in full. The right to enjoy one's leisure must be earned through hard work (J. Young 1971).

> ⊃ *Connections*
>
> We discuss Weber's argument in Chapter 11, pp. 397–8, and you might find it useful to review what we say there. You might also find it useful to look at our discussion of hedonism and the work ethic in Chapter 7, pp. 249–50. These issues are well covered in Lupton (1996).

The work ethic is linked to a specific structuring of sex–gender roles. Participation in the 'public' world of paid work and politics has been mainly an activity of men. Women have largely been confined to the 'private' domestic world of unpaid work. In the conventional family household, women have been responsible for intimate and emotional matters and the man has been the 'breadwinner'. It is precisely this feminine role that many young women today reject, reflecting a fundamental cultural shift involving a weakening of the work ethic and the possibility of a more open pursuit of pleasure.

For those who are ambivalent towards the contemporary images of femininity and who drift into anorexic practices, the adoption of a purer form of asceticism, closer to the Puritan original, is highly conducive. In this sense, the anorexic way of life is an ascetic way of life. Asceticism for the anorexic is a response to anxiety and inner loneliness, as much as it was for the Calvinist. In her case, however, the anxiety does not concern religious salvation but personal autonomy and independence.

Bordo (1993) sees these women in a state of implicit 'protest' against the culturally institutionalized images of femininity that, in crucial respects, they fear and seek to avoid. This is not, however, an absolute rejection, and their feelings are highly ambivalent. As young girls, they are socialized into an acceptance of these images, which become deeply embedded parts of their sense of self. Nevertheless, they find it impossible to embrace them wholeheartedly as examples to follow in their own lives. The anorexic, then, is in protest against these prevailing images of women—attracted by them, but fearing and rejecting aspects of them as well. This protest, however, is not a conscious and planned political protest, but a *bodily* protest. The anorexic engages in what calls a 'hunger strike' against contemporary femininities.

In the stage of secondary deviation marked by the adoption of an ascetic way of life, the central element in the young woman's identity is no longer an aspiration to a cultural ideal of femininity. Instead, it is the maintenance of an image of a person who is in control of her own life through her control over her body. The anorexic way of life establishes a regime in which size must be constantly reduced. The search for a slender, controlled body involves a constant watch for any increase in weight and for any unwanted bumps that must be eliminated. With continued weight loss to well below 'normal' levels, the sufferer becomes committed to being thin rather than to meeting the cultural ideal of femininity itself. Being thin—and so being 'straight' rather than 'curvy'—is *safe*, as it allows her to withdraw from the competitive pressure to be an attractive and independent woman. A return to normal weight is feared for the problems of identity that would return with it.

As the goal becomes that of attaining ever greater slenderness, any soft flesh comes to be seen as unsightly, as fat. Sensations of emptiness become a sign of health and achievement, while eating above the very restricted level that has been adopted leads to feelings of being 'bloated' and, therefore, 'fat'. Paradoxically, the slimmer a woman gets, the more obtrusive becomes any normal roundness in body shape, and the greater becomes the internal pressure towards continued size reduction. As the sufferer gets drawn further into these patterns of behaviour, so the inevitable physical hunger pains and other physical symptoms of starvation also come to be seen as things that must be suppressed or ignored and, therefore, controlled. This victory over pain may even be secretly enjoyed as yet another sign of control.

It has been suggested that a sufferer from anorexia experiences perceptual distortions as a direct result of her physical condition—she misdescribes her own body as fat rather than thin. This view, however, has been challenged. It may simply be that words are used to obscure her new, secret identity as someone who has escaped from contemporary femininity through the hunger strike. By describing herself as fat, the anorexic legitimates a continuation of the ascetic practices that she believes have helped her to escape from the tyranny of the cultural ideal.

As her physical condition worsens, however, a sufferer may begin to feel that there is something wrong with her. This is tempered by a continuing commitment to her lifestyle and new identity as someone who is in control. Wearing many layers of clothing will keep her warm, partly offsetting the physical coldness that she feels, but it may also help to hide the extent of her weight loss from friends and family. She continues to tell herself that she fears putting on weight because she would no longer be attractive or healthy, and she may put these arguments to others if challenged about her appearance or behaviour. These explanations, however, become less convincing.

From reading magazines, watching television, and talking to others, the anorexic adopts the idea of an 'eating disorder' to account for her behaviour. As she struggles to understand her own feelings, she may come to accept, in private, the idea that she is suffering from anorexia. Because anorexia has been socially defined as abnormal or unacceptable—by family, by friends, and in the media—this self-definition is likely to remain a private matter. Outwardly, the anorexic wishes to appear as normal, but privately she feels that only she may know the practices and routines through which this appearance is produced. The idea of anorexia is incorporated into her identity and given a positive interpretation, but it must remain secret, something that can be admitted only in private. By maintaining an outward front-region appearance of normality and conformity, she can feel that she is able to remain in control.

In the back region—in the privacy of her bedroom—the sufferer voraciously consumes books about anorexia and eating disorders, and she comes to redefine and to reconstruct her biography in the same terms that they use. There is, however, a curious ambivalence about the medical diagnosis. This is likely to be rejected at the same time as many of its features are accepted. There can be no easy acceptance of the idea of being ill when the sufferer feels that she is in control.

Successful reversal of the anorexic condition has been shown to depend on a self-recognition of it and an acceptance of the need to struggle against the illness. Such a decision is by no means easy, as a positive view of anorexia has become a central feature of the sufferer's identity. Any departure from the ascetic regime that she has been following for so long is likely to result in feelings of guilt, and guilt is likely to lead to re-adoption of the regime in an even more rigorous form. The ascetic shaping of the body and its physical consequences reinforce one another. Eventually the deteriorating physical condition of the sufferer may destroy the possibility of any proper control and autonomy. Lack of energy, depression, and sheer starvation make almost all physical and mental activity impossible. The search for control *over* the body can all too easily end in the control of the searcher *by* her own body.

 ## *Stop and reflect*

In this section we have looked at the medicalization of ever more areas of life. We looked not only at physical health and mental health, but also at the medicalization of reproduction and beauty.

- There is no necessary conflict between medical and sociological views of health and illness. Both are important, but they have differing purposes and concerns.

- Illness in contemporary society is organized in terms of a sick role that establishes norms of behaviour for the sufferer and for others. Death is also disciplined through definite role expectations.

- Depression has its origins in particular life conditions that are experienced most particularly by women.

- Why did Goffman say that hospital treatment of mental illness involves a definite 'moral career' for patients?

We argued that the medicalization of life raises important questions about the meaning of 'health'.

- Reproductive behaviour has increasingly come to be defined in medical terms. Sex and motherhood have both come under the medical gaze.

- Contemporary concerns about feminine beauty have had a major impact on women's lifestyles. They have been a major causal factor in the growth of cosmetic surgery and eating disorders.

- To what extent is the mass media responsible for the growth in eating disorders?

Key concepts

Workshop 8

Study 8 Enforcing normality

L. J. Davis (1995) has explored the cultural assumptions underpinning conceptions of deafness in Europe and the United States. Taking a historical approach, Davis shows that the idea of disability was something that became organized during the eighteenth and nineteenth centuries as part of a more general project to control the body. It emerged at a time when categories of crime, sexuality, gender, disease, and so on were all emerging in relation to transformations in the state and the economy. Those with problems of hearing came to be regarded as 'deaf' and, therefore, as subject to particular forms of regulation and control.

Western culture, Davis argues, is based around an assumption that it is normal for humans to speak and hear—just as it assumes that the norm of gender is seen as masculine, the norm of race is seen as white, and the norm of sexuality is seen as heterosexuality. Such an assumption, he claims, rests upon a particular view of the body and power. It is possible to imagine, he argues, that a developed sign or gesture language preceded oral language and so has an equal right to be considered as the norm. He makes what he admits is an extreme point in order to highlight the arbitrariness of the cultural assumption and the fact that its relevance for the future can be questioned.

'Normalcy' is socially constructed, and we cannot avoid living in a world of norms, constructed from averages and typical occurrences. The idea of the disabled body emerged in relation to a conception of the normal body. The focus of discussion, therefore, should be on the constructions or representations of disability rather than the disabled person as an object. It is the way in which normalcy is constructed that makes disability into a 'problem'. It was in the eighteenth century that deafness came to be a matter of central cultural concern. It became the visible subject of discourse among those professionals who felt that an inability to participate in the spoken culture of the Enlightenment reduced the level of a person's humanity. The deaf as a social category were brought into being by this discourse. Prior to that time the deaf were isolated within their own families and there was no public, enlightened discourse from which they were excluded. Writings about deafness began to appear at the same time as writings about language and communication: the Enlightenment view that language was central to humanity defined the 'problem' of deafness as a condition that was not truly human. It developed alongside the discourse of nationalism, as the shared language of a national population was seen as central to civilized human existence.

Davis raises the question of how the deaf can challenge their categorization. The disabled generally have received less political attention than many other minorities. Discussions of sexism, racism, and heterosexism, for example, are now commonplace, but the social model of disability has only slowly led to corresponding ideas of 'disablism'. Those with hearing problems are less visible as a minority even than many other disabled groups, and there has been little criticism of 'audism'. Concerns over the categorization of hearing problems as disabilities, Davis argues, has led many deaf people to define themselves as members of a 'linguistic minority'—and he suggests that a similar challenge to the general idea of disability might be posed by a term such as 'physical minority'.

❷ How useful is it to think of deafness as having been invented in the eighteenth century?

❷ Collect some advertisements for hearing aids from your local newspaper. What image of the deaf is conveyed in the advert?

❷ Consider the debate over the cochlea implant (discussed on p. 285 above). What are the main issues that deaf parents should consider when deciding whether to allow their deaf children to be surgically treated and given a form of hearing?

Media watch 8   Care in the community

The process of decarceration, with its shift to care in the community for the mentally ill, has resulted in the closure of large numbers of hospitals. For years, mental patients were treated in the large 'asylums', many of which had been built in Victorian times. One hundred Victorian hospitals have been closed during the course of this policy, with just twenty now surviving. Many of the patients now released had spent the bulk of their lives within the hospitals, and they have found it difficult to come to terms with the outside world.

Sixty-year old Annemarie Randall was an adopted child who was treated violently by her adoptive parents. She married at 16 and suffered violence from her husband. Two children died as newborn infants before a healthy son was born. When her son was 6 years old, Annemarie's husband insisted that his pregnant mistress move into the house, and Annemarie and her son moved out. Six years later her son, Robert, was killed in a road accident. Annemarie blamed herself for having bought his bicycle, and she began a period of self-abuse. She left her flat and wandered the streets; she stabbed herself with a bread knife eleven times, and she attacked herself with razor blades and broken glass. It was not long before she was picked up by the police and was sent to a mental hospital.

She spent four years in Oakwood Hospital, Maidstone; she was given insulin therapy and ECT (electro-convulsive therapy); she spent a great deal of time in a padded cell. She escaped from the hospital a number of times, but was always brought back. When she was released, she spent her time in hostels and bed-sits and, for a while, lived with an older woman whom she nursed

through the final stages of cancer. When her friend died, Annemarie once more fell into depression and was taken into Banstead Hospital, in Surrey. She spent ten years in Banstead until it closed, when she was transferred to a small hospital and then to a hostel. Although life had been comfortable in Banstead, Annemarie felt that she had not been given the opportunity to talk to therapists and had, instead, been given unhelpful drug treatments. She now lives alone, apart from her cat, suffering from chronic heart and blood problems that she believes will eventually result in a fatal stroke.

Source: *Observer*, 7 April 2002.

⮕ Consider our account of Goffman's model of the moral career of the mental patient and the argument of Brown and Harris about the social origins of depression.

❷ What elements in Annemarie's life story support the Brown and Harris argument?

❷ Which aspects of her story demonstrate the impact of organizational processes on her sense of self?

❷ Consult the article that we have cited: you can find it at www.guardianunlimited.co.uk. In the article you will find other accounts of patients' lives. Note down further evidence that helps you to explore the above questions. Do any of the accounts provide evidence on the effectiveness—or otherwise—of the policy of care in the community?

Discussion points

Review the various 'Stop and reflect' points in this chapter. You may find it useful to consider these in relation to our discussion of socialization, identity, and deviance in Chapters 4 and 7. We considered a number of substantive areas, as well as the methodological problems of using official statistics.

Medicine, health, and illness

In our discussion of medicine, we looked at both physical illness and mental illness. We showed that each must be seen as socially constructed:

- Make sure that you understand how the following terms can be used: medical gaze, medicalization, sick role, and moral career.

- Consider the implications of the increasing use of technology in relation to contraception and childbirth.

- Try to grasp the key ideas associated with: Foucault, Parsons, Scheff, and Goffman.

The social body

Foucault figures again in our review of the social body. You should spend a little time thinking about the links between his views on medicine and his arguments about population:

- How does Foucault distinguish between regulation and discipline?

- How would you define the terms anatomo-politics and bio-politics? How do these relate to his idea of surveillance?

Understanding fertility and mortality requires a little bit of statistical knowledge, and you should try to practise some of your skills and consolidate your knowledge of the statistical concepts used to study populations:

- What do you understand by the following demographic measures: crude birth rate, crude death rate, age-specific fertility, standardized mortality rate, life expectancy, neonatal mortality, ageing population? Do not worry about giving precise definitions, but just ensure that you understand the general idea.

- Using the figures in Figure 8.1 (p. 273), draw a pie chart to show the distribution of world population across the various regions. Using the data in Figure 8.2 (p. 274), calculate the periods in which the UK population increase has been most rapid. What conclusions would you draw from the figures in these graphs?

- How would you word a question on ethnic identity for use in a government social survey? How would you expect the conclusions reported on pp. 276–7 to be affected by a change in question wording?

Food, beauty, and lifestyle

Issues of beauty and eating have increasingly come to be seen in medical terms, and we discussed a number of matters that have arisen. Issues of health and lifestyle are now closely associated with each other.

- What is the significance of the idea of the family meal? What factors have contributed to its decline?

- Why do you think there has been a growth in smoking among young people?

- Why do you think that the cultural ideal of femininity is so important to most women?

- What do you understand by the following terms: cosmetic surgery, asceticism, hunger strike?

Explore further

Good general discussions of the issues covered in this chapter can be found in:

Foucault, M. (1963), *The Birth of the Clinic* (New York: Vintage Books, 1975). *Hard going, but it repays the effort.*

Coleman, D., and Salt, J. (1992), *The British Population: Patterns, Trends and Processes* (Oxford: Oxford University Press). *A large and comprehensive summary of population trends since the nineteenth century.*

Pilcher, J. L. (1995), *Age and Generation in Modern Britain* (Oxford: Oxford University Press). *A very useful and well-written overview of population issues related to age and ageing.*

Freidson, E. (1970), *The Profession of Medicine* (New York: Dodd Mead). *An important study of the medical profession and its power.*

Goffman, E. (1961), *Asylums: Essays on the Social Situation of Mental Patients and Other Inmates* (New York: Doubleday). *Once again, we recommend a book by Goffman. This one was said to have inspired the feature film 'One Flew Over the Cuckoo's Nest'.*

Lupton, D. (1996), *Food, the Body and the Self* (London: Sage). *A useful overview of the sociology of food that considers many of the issues discussed in this chapter.*

Busfield, N. J. (1996), *Men, Women and Madness: Understanding Gender and Mental Disorder* (London: Macmillan). *A good, recent account of the gendered character of mental illness.*

Stanworth, M. (1987) (ed.), *Gender, Motherhood and Medicine* (Cambridge: Polity Press). *Important for Stanworth's Introduction and for other contributions on the new reproductive technologies.*

Bordo, S. (1993), *Unbearable Weight: Feminism, Western Culture, and the Body* (Berkeley and Los Angeles: University of California Press). *A collection of Bordo's papers that examine anorexia from a feminist standpoint.*

Wolf, N. (1991), *The Beauty Myth: How Images of Beauty are Used against Women* (New York: Wm Morrow). *A good critique of the cultural ideal of beauty and how it constrains and coerces women.*

Busfield, J. (2000), *Health and Health Care in Modern Britain* (Oxford: Oxford University Press). *An excellent overview of the whole area that is comprehensive and authoritative.*

Interesting video resources on topics covered in this chapter include:

One Flew over the Cuckoo's Nest, a film that explores issues of mental illness and illustrates many aspects of Goffman's argument.

My Left Foot, a film that raises issues of disability in relation to those of class and ethnicity.

The Hand Maiden's Tale, a novel by Margaret Atwood and a film that explores a futuristic society in which women are enslaved for enforced reproduction.

Life is Sweet by Mike Leigh touches on the issues of anorexia.

Online resources

Visit the Online Resource Centre that accompanies this book to access more learning resources and other interesting material on the body, health, and medicine at:
www.oxfordtextbooks.co.uk/orc/fulcher4e/

Much useful information can be found through the World Health Organization at:
www.who.int/home-page

World Health Organization statistical information can be found at:
www.who.int/whosis

The United Nations Population Fund can be found at:
www.unfpa.org

The British government's Department of Health website is useful for official information and policies:
www.doh.gov.uk

The website of the British Sociological Association's Medical Sociology Study Group contains information on seminars and conferences and links to a variety of sources on the sociology of health:
www.britsoc.co.uk/medsoc/

The website of the Beat: The Eating Disorder Association is at:
www.b-eat.co.uk/Home

We have discussed Foucault a great deal in this chapter. Casey Alt has set up a video introduction to The Genealogy of Modern Medicine at:
http://caseyalt.com/foucaultmed.html

PART THREE

CULTURE, KNOWLEDGE, AND BELIEF

Education

Contents

09

More choice or less?

Choice of school is now an accepted parental right, but what happens if too many parents choose the best school in the area? If a popular state school has three applications for every place, only a third of the children who have applied will get the school their parents want. The school can select the child, rather than the family choosing the school.

In theory popular schools should expand and make more places available, but there is inevitably a considerable time lag if schools do this. Anyway, many popular schools would not want to, since their size is part of their character and they would risk losing their ethos and popularity if they became too big.

Parents can face very difficult choices, since they have to take into account not only the quality of schools but also the likelihood of getting into them. They can drop down the scale in order to be surer of getting a place at a reasonably good school, but then have to settle for 'second best'. They may look further afield but then face long and expensive journeys. They may decide to opt for private education, with all its costs, though their children will still have to pass through a selection process.

There are always some schools somewhere with places available. If schools have spare places because they are unpopular, this probably means, however, that they are remote or perform badly or have more than their fair share of problems. As the *Guardian* has put it, 'the end result is a combination of unacceptable and unobtainable schools'.

Sources: *Guardian Education,* 29 January 2002; *Independent,* 28 April 2005.

Parental choice has become one of the accepted principles of British education, but many parents are unable to exercise that right effectively, as our opening piece shows. Furthermore, information in league tables about examination success increases demand for the 'best' school. The right to choose and league tables are now established features of the British educational scene, but they are, in fact, recent innovations, and in this chapter we examine how and why they came into existence, and the problems they raise.

High demand for some schools makes them more selective. The issue of selection has dominated the educational debate since the 1960s because it conflicts with another principle, equality of opportunity. Later in the chapter we examine this question and the relationship of equality of opportunity to class, gender, and ethnicity. But we begin by considering the broader relationship between education and society, and then outline the development of education in Britain.

Concepts and theories

The key issues of the sociology of education focus on the relationship between education and society. Our starting point here is the significance of education in the socialization process, before moving on to inequality, and finally the relationship between capitalism and education.

Education and socialization

Education is central to the socialization process. As we show in Chapter 4, p. 114, *primary* socialization is carried

out within the family, but this takes the process only so far. Both Émile Durkheim (1925) and Talcott Parsons (1959) argued in their different ways that education plays a key role in *secondary* socialization by performing functions that the family cannot perform.

One way in which education does this is by providing the skills needed for the specialized occupations of industrial societies. As the division of labour became more specialized, it was no longer possible for skills to be handed down within the family. Children could acquire them only through formal education. How well schools perform this function has become a matter of growing concern in Britain, as occupational and technological changes have altered the skills required.

More fundamentally, education turns children into members of society by socializing them into the common values and norms of their society. Through education, children learn religious and moral beliefs. They also develop a sense of national identity, learning national languages and customs, the symbols of nationality, and the history of the nation.

Durkheim was particularly concerned with the moral aspects of this process. It was through school discipline that children learned to behave in a moral way. Punishment and the authority of the teacher played an important part in this, but he argued that it was not just a matter of forcing children to obey but also of getting them to appreciate the moral basis of society. They needed to understand the reasons for moral behaviour, so that they behaved morally because they wanted to do so. Social rules had to become internalized as part of the individual's personality, so that discipline became self-discipline.

Durkheim emphasized the moral aspect of education because he was concerned with the increasing individualism of nineteenth-century French society. For Durkheim, the key function of education was that it subordinated the individual to society and made people aware of their responsibilities to each other and to the wider collectivity. This view of education has more recently been expressed by Hargreaves (1982), who drew extensively on the work of Durkheim. He argued that British schools and teachers had become dominated by a culture of individualism. They were far too concerned with meeting the needs of the individual child and too little concerned with the school's functions for society. He called for schools to promote social solidarity by generating a sense of community among their pupils and linking this to the wider community and society as a whole.

Parsons too recognized the moral significance of education, but in the rather different social context of mid-twentieth-century America he placed more emphasis on the value of individual achievement. It was through education that children acquired this and learned how to achieve it. This value was central to the functioning of an industrial society, but families could not instil it, for they treated children in a *particular* way according to who they were, not according to how they achieved. In school, however, success depended upon achievement, and this was measured by the *universal* standards of examinations, which took no account of who you were and simply measured how well you performed.

Although they differed in their emphasis, both Durkheim and Parsons viewed education in terms of the *functions* that it performed for society. Education does do the kinds of things that Durkheim and Parsons saw it doing, but, as we show in Chapter 2, pp. 45–8, there are problems with **functionalism**.

First, functionalists argue from the needs of society as a whole. But can we speak of the needs of whole societies? Who defines these needs? Does education perform functions for society or does it rather serve the interests of those who rule it and control education?

Secondly, functionalists assume that the members of a society share common values. Many different cultures exist within most societies, however, and there can be conflicts between them, often grounded in religious differences (see Box 9.1, p. 312). Education may not so much create a sense of common membership of a society as perpetuate particular cultures within it and reinforce social divisions.

Education and inequality

The relationship between education and inequality has been one of the main concerns not only of the sociology of education but also of educational policy, which has gone through many processes of reform intended to produce greater equality.

Equality of opportunity?

As we have just shown, Parsons argued that education instilled the value of achievement, which was closely linked to another shared value, a belief in equality of opportunity. This was crucial to the allocation of human resources, for it enabled people with ability to find their way into the jobs that required those abilities. In industrial societies status was not determined by birth but by achievement.

It also performed another key function by getting those who did not succeed to accept failure. Industrial societies motivated people to achieve by providing them with superior rewards. This inevitably resulted in inequality, but those who did not succeed accepted this because they thought that everyone had had an equal chance to succeed. Thus, the stratification of society was legitimated by the belief that equality of opportunity existed.

Parsons considered education to be the main mechanism of equality of opportunity. In schools there was competition on equal terms, for examinations applied universal standards and examination performance determined educational success. Furthermore, it was clear to all that success was the reward for achievement. The problem with this approach is that it assumes that competition is on equal terms. Others have argued that this is not the case and we now need to consider their views.

> **⊃ Connections**
> We discuss equality of opportunity and the related concept of meritocracy in Chapter 18, pp. 697–9.

Controversy and debate Faith schools   9.1

The British government's September 2001 White Paper on education welcomed faith schools into the state-maintained sector, though they had in fact long existed there. In England in January 2001, 35 per cent of state primary schools and 17 per cent of secondary schools were already faith schools, mainly Church of England or Roman Catholic. Figure 9.1 shows the distribution by religion of state schools in England in 2007. In Scotland in 2007 there were 289 state-funded faith schools, but, apart from one Jewish school, all were Christian. In the independent sector in England in 2007, out of 2,300 schools around 900 were faith schools. Of these, 38 were Jewish, 115 were Muslim, and most of the rest were Christian.

Figure 9.1 State schools by religious character, England, 2007

	Primary	Secondary	All
Christian	6,221	573	6,794
Jewish	28	9	37
Muslim	4	3	7
Sikh	1	1	2
Other religions	1	1	2
No religious character	11,106	2,756	13,862
Total	17,361	3,343	20,704

Source: *Social Trends* (2008: 32).

The state pays the teachers in state faith schools and 85 per cent of the school's capital costs. Faith schools are allowed greater freedom than other state schools in appointing staff and selecting pupils. They are required to follow the national curriculum, though in 2010 the Labour government controversially amended its new curriculum for sex education to allow them to teach sex lessons in a way that reflected their religious character. They were still, however, required to follow the curriculum and cover such topics as abortion, contraception, and homosexuality.

Those in favour of faith schools claim they are popular, meet local needs, strengthen moral beliefs, and achieve high educational standards. Those against argue that they reinforce social divisions, generate conflict between communities, and prevent the social integration of minorities. Some have suggested that there should be *multi-faith* schools that would both meet the needs of the various local religious communities *and* make children aware of other faiths.

The possible indoctrination of children in creationist views of the origin of species has been another major issue. The three Emmanuel Foundation Schools sponsored by the Christian car dealer Sir Peter Vardy have attracted criticism from scientists for including creationist theories in lessons. Sir Peter defended this practice on the grounds that they presented both Darwin's evolutionary theory and creationism, leaving things 'up to the children' (BBC News Report 2006).

Sources: BBC News Reports, 11 April 2006, 27 November 2009; *Guardian*, 2 September 2008; *Social Trends* 2008; see also Gardner *et al.* (2004).

❷ What did Durkheim consider to be the key functions of education? Do religious schools perform these functions?

❷ As faith schools have long existed, why has this recently become such an issue?

❷ Do faith schools integrate or divide society?

❷ Should schools present both creationism and Darwinian evolution, leaving it 'up to the children' to choose between them?

Class, culture, and language

It has long been argued that class background shapes educational success through material advantages and disadvantages. The better-off can buy educational success, either by buying entry to better schools or by buying assistance with education, such as private coaching or extra books. It is not just money that counts, however, for it has been shown that such factors as health and quality of housing, which are related to class background, influence educational success (see Lee 1989).

Others have argued that it is not so much a matter of *material* as *cultural* advantages and disadvantages. One approach of this kind has been labelled **cultural-deprivation theory**. This held that working-class children have been disadvantaged by working-class values and beliefs. These placed a low value on education and focused on the immediate rewards of earning money rather than *deferring gratification* until qualifications had been obtained. This could, for example, result in a lack of parental interest in education, which Douglas (1964) found to be the single most important factor in explaining children's educational attainments. It could also result in children leaving school early in order to earn money. Similar arguments have been put forward to explain some ethnic minorities' lack of achievement in education.

Such approaches have been criticized for the negative views they present of particular class or ethnic-minority cultures. These views often seem to reflect prejudices rather than real knowledge of the culture concerned. It is also difficult to separate out cultural from situational factors.

Do faith schools 'light the way' in education?

© Hymers College, Hull

Leaving school early, for example, may mean not that education is undervalued but rather that a family desperately needs more earners. A lack of interest in education may reflect *material* rather than *cultural* deprivation.

Basil Bernstein developed an approach to class differences centred on differences in the use of language. In his early work (Bernstein1961), he distinguished between two speech patterns:

- **Restricted codes**. This refers to speech patterns where meanings are implicit. They are typical of situations where people have so much in common that they do not have to spell out what they mean. Few words are needed. Sentences tend to be short and have a simple grammatical structure. Much may be communicated by gesture or tone of voice rather than the words themselves. While this form of language works well in situations where people know each other, its capacity to communicate is limited because it is *context-bound* to a particular situation.

- **Elaborated codes**. This refers to speech patterns where meanings are made explicit. People spell out fully what they mean in longer and more complex sentences. While restricted codes are *particularistic*, elaborated codes are *universalistic*. They are 'context-independent' and enable those who do not share a particular social situation, or do not know each other, to communicate.

Educational success requires an ability to use elaborated codes. These are the language of instruction. Restricted codes are no use for essay-writing! Bernstein argued that while middle-class children can typically communicate in both restricted and elaborated codes, working-class children are accustomed to restricted codes only and therefore likely to be less successful in education. He did, however, recognize that schools can teach elaborated codes to those who have not acquired them beforehand.

These cultural differences were linked by Bernstein to differences in class situation. Middle-class people speak in elaborated codes because their non-manual

Figure 9.2 Language and class

Language and context	Restricted code	Elaborated code
Speech forms	Small vocabulary and short, simple sentences	Large vocabulary and longer, more complex sentences
Meaning	Implicit	Explicit
Communication context	Particularistic and context-bound	Universalistic and independent
Family structure	Positional	Person-centred
Class	Working	Middle

❓ Imagine that a parent is telling a child to switch off the television and go to bed. How would this be expressed in speech using restricted and elaborated codes?

Ball's argument is that middle-class families have far more social capital than working-class families. This is demonstrated through the competition for places in higher education and the planning of careers. The families of students from working-class backgrounds have little knowledge of higher education and the best routes into it. The families of middle-class students have that knowledge and the contacts that can help with choice of course and university, and make the right connections between higher education and professional careers.

Social capital could be especially important at times of crisis, if, for example, an exam has been failed or a student is on the edge of dropping out, and an appropriate intervention can help to restore the situation. This shows that social capital is not just something possessed but involves work, requiring the expenditure of time and effort, the investment of 'emotional capital' (Ball 2003a: 95).

Private education played an important role in the accumulation of social capital. As Ball (2003a: 86) puts it:

> In effect when parents invest in private education for their children they are buying into a broad and complex body of social capital that is made available to the children and in relation to which the young people develop their own investment skills.

This brings out the links between economic capital and social capital, for a family's finances determine whether it can buy social capital in this way.

The use of social capital within state education is closely linked to the development of educational policy. As we shall show in the section on 'A regulated marketplace' (see pp. 337–9), the post-1980s emphasis on choice of school and parental involvement in school management has played into the hands of those with social capital.

Education and capitalism

The functionalist approach to education assumed that education met the needs of society. Marxist writers have argued that we should not refer to the needs of society as a whole, for within societies there is a fundamental conflict of interest between capital and labour, which have different needs. Education does not meet the needs of society but serves the interests of the owners of capital.

The supply of labour

Samuel Bowles and Herbert Gintis (1976) carried out the classic study of the relationship between capitalism and education in the United States.

To Bowles and Gintis, education was the main means by which capital subordinated labour. Capitalism required obedient and disciplined workers prepared to carry out boringly repetitive work in a highly unequal society. Labour could not be subordinated by the use of force alone, because on its own this was self-defeating by generating resistance. Effective subordination depended on getting workers to accept the capitalist system through education. This not only led to the reproduction of class; it was also crucial to the **reproduction of labour**.

In explaining how education does this, Bowles and Gintis referred not to the *content* of education but to the *structure of social relationships* within it. Their key concept is the **correspondence principle** (Bowles and Gintis 1976: 131). Relationships of authority at school corresponded with those at work. Competition between students corresponded to the competition between workers that employers seek to encourage. Students were *externally* motivated by the award of grades, not the satisfactions of learning, just as workers were motivated by pay, not the satisfactions of work. Children were prepared for work because schools taught them how to behave like workers.

In focusing on these aspects of education, Bowles and Gintis drew attention to what Ivan Illich (1973) had called the **hidden curriculum** (see Box 9.4). While the formal curriculum provided children with skills, knowledge, and qualifications, the hidden curriculum more importantly taught them how to work and obey.

The correspondence principle also operated in another way by relating levels in education to occupational levels. The lower levels of education emphasized obedience to rules, as required in low-level occupations. Intermediate levels required students to work independently without continuous supervision, as did middle-ranking positions in organizations. In higher education students were expected to internalize the institution's norms, so that they were self-motivated and self-disciplined, just as those in senior posts were expected to be. If students were unable to make it to the next stage of education, they moved into the occupational level corresponding to the stage they had reached. Thus, while reproducing labour, education also reproduced the occupational divisions of the class structure.

While this approach started from a different theoretical perspective, it overlapped in many ways with the functionalist approach. The points made by Bowles and Gintis about the importance of school discipline and competitiveness to life in the wider society were similar to those made by Durkheim and Parsons. Although Bowles and Gintis saw education as serving the interests of capital rather than the needs of society, they too were examining the importance of education to the socialization process, the economy, and the maintenance of social order.

But does education actually function in this way to produce subservient students? Does it actually provide employers with the workers they need?

THEORY AND METHODS   9.4

Illich and the 'hidden curriculum'

Ivan Illich (1926–) was born in Vienna, studied theology and philosophy in Rome, obtained a Ph.D. in history at the University of Salzburg, and became for a time a Catholic priest. His career led him to Latin America, where he became a severe critic of economic development. He saw this as destroying the skills, knowledge, and self-sufficiency of pre-industrial societies and forcing people into a passive dependence on experts and organizations.

One of his most well-known books is *Deschooling Society* (1973), where he called for the abolition of schools. He argued that education has been confused with schooling and that most learning occurred outside schools, which do nothing for the poor and turn people into passive consumers.

Illich originated the widely used concept of the hidden curriculum. This strikingly expressed the idea that schools do not just teach the subjects of the formal curriculum. They also teach values, attitudes, and patterns of behaviour through the organization and social relationships of the school. This hidden curriculum maintains the existing social order and has a far greater influence on social life than the formal curriculum. While this is an important insight, the concept has been used in widely varying ways to refer to almost any aspect of education outside the formal curriculum. It is also a misleading term, because it does not refer to an identifiable curriculum but to the whole context of education in the school.

An oppositional culture

Bowles and Gintis treated the working class as culturally passive, absorbing and accepting the values of school and employer. They argued in a similar way to those who have claimed that there is a *dominant culture* imposed by the ruling class on the rest of the population. Another stream of research has, however, examined how *resistant subcultures* grow out of the experience of the working class.

> **⮑ Connections**
> We discuss the concepts of dominant culture and subculture in Chapter 10, pp. 355-6.

In *Learning to Labour* Paul Willis (1977) carried out a well-known study of the emergence of an **oppositional subculture** in a school. He argued that this subculture was hostile to authority, rejected the value of mental work, and celebrated physicality and violence. The authority of teachers was constantly challenged, but in subtle ways that undermined it while stopping short of open confrontation. This oppositional culture was generated by the school itself, though its content was provided by the wider culture of the working class.

His study was based mainly on the observation of twelve working-class 'lads', selected because they were members of a minority opposition group. They were not therefore representative of boys in the school or working-class boys in general. Indeed, Phillip Brown (1989) has argued that most working-class children adopt a strategy of limited compliance rather than opposition. They recognize the importance of qualifications and go along sufficiently with the school to 'achieve modest levels of attainment' that will improve their job prospects.

Willis's focus on working-class boys may now seem a little dated. Oppositional cultures are not just found among boys, and class is not the only basis of opposition. Carolyn Jackson (2006) explores the emergence of 'ladette' behaviour among schoolgirls and its consequences for achievement and order in the classroom (see Media watch 5 on p. 186 for a discussion of ladettes). She found that 'girls, just as much as boys, suggested that it is not seen to be cool for them to work hard in school' (Jackson 2006: 79). Arguably, with the decline of class organization and greater ethnic diversity, oppositional subcultures based on ethnicity have become more salient (O'Donnell and Sharpe 2004). Jeffrey Smith (2007) has, however, shown that traditional working-class identities rejecting schoolwork are alive and well in a school he studied on a housing estate (see Chapter 5, p. 179).

Whatever the extent and the basis of an oppositional subculture, the main point here is that it cannot be assumed that education socializes children into the work habits and obedience that capitalist production requires. Education does not automatically reproduce labour.

The workers the employer needs?

If education does not always produce subservient workers, perhaps in other respects it does not always produce the labour the capitalist economy needs. Britain's poor economic performance during the twentieth century has been ascribed to education's failure to produce the skills required by modern industry. This was to become a key issue in the 1970s, when declining competitiveness and rising unemployment led to much discussion of the reasons for British economic decline. Politicians, employers, and trade unionists called for the reform of education to make it more relevant to economic needs.

This was partly to do with changing economic requirements. The decline of traditional industries and occupational changes meant that there was less need for unskilled manual labour. As we show in Chapter 17, pp. 671–2, the changes associated with post-Fordism led to employers seeking adaptable, committed, and cooperative workers rather than simply obedient ones. The kinds of workers that Bowles and Gintis saw the education system producing no longer corresponded to the needs of the employer.

The approach taken by Bowles and Gintis rightly draws our attention to the importance of the relationship between education and capitalism. As we show in the section on 'Education and economy', pp. 334–7, an understanding of this is crucial to an understanding of recent changes in British education. It is also clear, however, that there is nothing automatic about the relationship. Education does not always meet the needs of the employer.

 ## *Stop and reflect*

In this section we first considered the part played by education in the process of socialization.

- Durkheim saw education as turning children into moral members of their society.
- Parsons paid more attention to the way in which it instilled values of individual achievement.
- Do faith schools exemplify their notions of the functions performed by education?

We then considered the relationship between education and inequality.

- Parsons considered that education was the main mechanism providing equality of opportunity.

- Others have argued that education reproduces the material and cultural advantages and disadvantages of social background.
- How do the concepts of 'cultural capital' and 'social capital' help us to understand the relationship between education and inequality?

Lastly, we examined the relationship between education and capitalism.

- In their different ways both functionalist and Marxist perspectives argue that education meets economic requirements.
- Does education provide the workers that employers need?

The development of education in Britain

As we showed in the 'Concepts and theories' section, key issues in the sociology of education have been whether education provides equality of opportunity and meets economic needs. Before examining these questions further, we must set them in context by outlining the development of educational institutions in Britain.

The nineteenth-century growth of education

At the beginning of the nineteenth century there was no national system of education. In England elementary education for the poor was provided by charity, church, and private schools. Secondary education was not widely available and was provided mainly by the so-called public schools, which catered not for the public in general but for fee-paying pupils, and a scattering of grammar schools in the towns. The only universities were Cambridge and Oxford, which were very exclusive institutions admitting only about 300 fee-paying students a year in the mid-eighteenth century (Royle 1987: 368). They were primarily concerned with educating the sons of the upper class to become Church of England clergy.

In eighteenth-century Scotland education was more developed at both ends of the spectrum. There was a system of publicly funded local schools provided by the Church, though this failed to keep up with the growth of urban populations. The local schoolmaster was expected to be a graduate able to teach up to university-entrance level. Five universities existed, and during the later eighteenth century they established a high academic reputation through such leading thinkers of the Scottish Enlightenment as David Hume and Adam Smith. Student numbers were higher and university education was far more accessible than in England and Wales. About a quarter of the students at Glasgow University at the end of the eighteenth century were of working-class origin (Royle 1987: 373).

Education of all kinds expanded in the nineteenth century. The 1870 Education Act in England and the 1872 Act in Scotland created national networks of schools administered by local boards (Royle 1987: 354). The public schools too grew, with the creation between 1837 and 1869 of thirty-one new boarding schools in England, which provided an elite classical education (Royle 1987: 360–1). The founding of the University of London in 1828 was a key step in the growth of higher education, and new colleges were eventually set up in the provinces and industrial cities.

The expansion of elementary education had more to do with religious, moral, and political than economic concerns. At this time, industry required practical workshop skills rather than technical knowledge or even literacy. Schools for the poor were seen as a means of establishing order and countering radicalism in the new industrial cities. There was also a popular demand for education, and radicals called for it to be taken out of religious hands and made available to all on a free and equal basis. Education became a battleground between conservatives and radicals, though both agreed that more education was needed.

The expansion of 'public-school' education for the middle and upper classes was linked to state and empire rather than commerce and industry. The bureaucratization of the nineteenth-century state (see Chapter 14, p. 525) meant that there was a growing emphasis on qualifications. The route to office in the growing imperial state was through success in examinations.

> Ambitious middle-class parents knew they would have to make the necessary sacrifices to buy a public-school education for their sons if they were to make their marks in the world. Purchase of office had been the eighteenth-century method; purchase of education replaced it in the nineteenth. (Royle 1987: 390)

The public schools, together with Cambridge and Oxford universities, produced a cohesive ruling class with bureaucratic skills, the shared culture of a classical education, and a gentlemanly set of norms and values centred on public service and sportsmanship.

Nineteenth-century education clearly reproduced the class structure. In England elementary education was considered the most that the working class required. Too much education was seen as threatening the social order. The public schools provided education for the upper class and those in the middle class who could afford them. Grammar schools were the main providers of education for the middle class. Some became increasingly exclusive, keeping the children of the local poor out because fee-paying parents did not want their children rubbing shoulders with those from a lower class. In Scottish education there was more of an ideal of classlessness, though in practice the town schools were dominated by the middle class and the poor were 'left to attend charity mission schools created especially for them in working-class districts' (Royle 1987: 358).

State schools for all

A national system of schooling was slowly constructed between 1870 and 1944. Free and compulsory elementary education was gradually built up after the 1870 (and 1872) Acts. Further Acts at the beginning of the twentieth century began to create a national system of secondary education, though it was not until the 1944 Act in England (in Scotland the 1945 Act) that free secondary education was made available to all.

The 1944 Act has been seen as a major social advance that transformed education. It created a *tripartite* structure of schools for children of different abilities. There were grammar schools and technical schools, and secondary-modern schools for the rest. In Scotland there were academic 'senior' schools and non-academic 'junior secondaries'. This was a selective system that distributed children into types of school on the basis of their performance in examinations at age 11. It was described as meritocratic, because it supposedly allocated children entirely on the basis of their ability or merit (for a discussion of meritocracy, see Chapter 18, p. 699). It exemplified the *correspondence principle* of Bowles and Gintis, for types of school corresponded to types of occupation.

If private education is included, there were, however, not three but five different levels in secondary education:

- public schools;
- direct-grant grammar schools (charging fees);
- grammar schools;
- technical schools;
- secondary-modern schools.

In many ways the post-1944 system perpetuated the existing structure of British education. The top two categories continued to provide a superior education for the small minority of families who could afford to pay for it. For most of the population, education meant either a grammar school or a secondary modern, the fourth category of technical schools never becoming widely available. The grammar schools became the elite institutions of the state sector, while the secondary moderns were essentially a continuation of elementary education for the working class.

The 1944 structure soon attracted criticism for maintaining class inequality and wasting talent. Most working-class children ended up in secondary moderns, and the

Briefing: development of a national school system in England   9.5

Elementary education

1833   The state began to provide some funding for religious schools.

1844   Factory Act required children in employment aged 8–13 to spend half the week in school.

1870   Education Act to provide cheap, publicly funded local schools.

1880   Attendance made compulsory up to the age of 10.

1891   Right to free elementary education established.

1893   School-leaving age raised to 11.

1899   Leaving age raised to 12.

Secondary education

1902   Education Act to create national secondary education: state grants for grammar schools in exchange for some 'free places' for children from elementary schools; new state-funded secondary schools created on grammar-school model.

1918   School-leaving age raised to 14.

1944   Education Act introduced tripartite system of grammar, technical, and secondary-modern schools. Free secondary education for all.

1947   School-leaving age raised to 15 (1972 to 16).

Early Leaving Report of 1954 showed that over half of those who did get into grammar schools dropped out or failed to get three GCE O level passes (GCE O level was the examination that preceded GCSE). It was rejected by the Labour Party, but there was also some middle-class dissatisfaction, for middle-class children who failed the 11+ examination also ended up in secondary moderns. From a national point of view, it was argued that an elitist system wasted talent and created social divisions. Comparisons were made with other economically more successful countries, like the United States, that did not have selective state education.

Comprehensive schools were put forward as the answer to these problems. The principle of comprehensive education was that all children within a particular area would go to the same secondary school, irrespective of ability or background. Education was gradually reorganized along comprehensive lines through local-authority action and the 1964 Labour government's education policy, except in Northern Ireland, where the grammar/secondary modern division persisted. Although comprehensive schools came to dominate elsewhere, the fact that selective schools (and private education) still existed and 'creamed off' many of the more able students meant that a fully comprehensive system had still not, however, been established. Furthermore, the selective principle still operated *within* most comprehensive schools through the streaming of children into different ability groups.

Higher education for some

The founding of the University of London in 1828 broke the Oxbridge monopoly of English higher education and established a major new institution that soon became the biggest in the country. It also helped to spread higher education, for the colleges emerging in the industrial cities taught external London degrees until they had acquired the expertise and status to award their own and become 'red-brick' universities. By the 1930s there were twenty-one universities in Britain, but higher education was still relatively undeveloped in Britain as a whole, as comparison with other industrial countries shows (see Figure 9.3). It is important, however, to take account of variations within Britain, for higher education was particularly undeveloped in England, while Scotland compared favourably with most other European countries.

It has, indeed, been argued, notably by Wiener (1980), that the character of British education largely accounts for Britain's failure to keep pace with other industrial countries and eventual economic decline in the 1960s

Figure 9.3 Higher education in industrial countries, 1934

Country	Number of inhabitants per university student
Great Britain	885
England	1,013
Scotland	473
Wales	741
Italy	808
Germany	604
Holland	579
Sweden	543
France	480
Switzerland	387
United States	125

Source: Simon (1991: 30).

and 1970s. An anti-industrial culture had developed in elite educational institutions during the nineteenth century.

British industrialists concerned with increasing international competition had played an important part in establishing the new colleges in industrial cities during the 1870s and 1880s. Civic leaders insisted, however, that they taught the liberal arts as well as applied studies, and they eventually became universities teaching a broad range of subjects. Any aspirational educational institution modelled itself on the public schools or on Cambridge and Oxford universities, where the arts were dominant. Where science was taught, it was pure rather than applied science. Comparisons with Germany showed that technology was much more highly valued there and the provision of education in technology and applied science much greater.

Mass higher education began with its expansion between the 1950s and the 1970s. This was driven by the increasing numbers of 18-year-olds with the qualifications for entry and a government commitment to provide higher education for all who could benefit from it. During 1957–72 full-time students in higher and further education rose from 148,000 to 470,000 (Simon 1991: 597). In the 1970s this growth slowed down and barely kept pace with the increasing number of 18-year-olds, until the current burst of expansion began in the late 1980s.

The 1960s growth of higher education had taken a binary form. The 1964 Labour government decided to halt the creation of new universities and build up a distinct sector from existing colleges and new polytechnics. The rationale for this binary system was that a new sector would boost the development of vocationally relevant institutions that would not be dominated by the elite universities. It inevitably created, however, a two-class system of higher education, with the polytechnics being seen by many as second-class rather than different institutions. The polytechnics themselves tried to become more like universities by awarding degrees and developing university-type courses. They were eventually allowed to take the title of university with the abolition of the binary system in 1991.

Comparative issues

We now briefly consider the distinctiveness of the British system by making some comparisons with other societies.

The 1944 Education Act had established a national system that was less centralized than the French system but much more centralized than the American. There was no centrally controlled national curriculum as in France.

There was, nonetheless, more of a national system in Britain than in the United States, where funding was decentralized and local communities had more control. In Britain state education was centrally funded and school organization was at least shaped by national education policies. The British system was, however, a mixed one that allowed the competing principles of the 'tripartite' structure and comprehensive schooling to coexist according to local decisions. In most European countries there was a uniform national structure.

Under the tripartite system established by the 1944 Act, selection and specialization took place at age 11. Internationally speaking this brought about a very early separation of the academic and non-academic routes. Even after comprehensive education had been introduced, the continued existence of many grammar schools and a large private secondary sector have perpetuated early selection and specialization. In many other countries separation into academic and vocational routes occurs only after age 15 or 16.

We showed above that the expansion of higher education was slow in Britain as a whole. Into the 1980s a far lower proportion of 18-year-olds entered higher education than in comparable countries (Halsey 1997: 642). Those who did had their fees paid by the state and, at that time, a generous system of maintenance grants. Graduates were a small and highly subsidized elite. British higher education was also elitist in another way, for the more vocational polytechnics were widely considered to be lower in status than universities. Although the polytechnic institutions of France, Germany, and Sweden were not strictly comparable, they were high-status institutions, often having higher status than universities.

It is, however, difficult to compare national educational systems, because there are so many sources of variation within them. This is particularly the case in Britain. It is, indeed, difficult to speak of a British system. There are important historical differences between England and other parts of Britain, especially Scotland, while in England itself different systems coexist. Furthermore, what applies to schools may not apply to higher education. Thus, private schooling is highly developed in Britain but higher education is dominated by public-sector institutions, while the opposite is the case in Japan.

Although institutional differences are undoubtedly important and certainly shape the way that education is delivered, they may, anyway, tell one little about how it is actually experienced. As Box 9.6 (p. 322) shows, an apparently model system of education looks very different when the daily realities of school life are brought to light. What is clear, however, is that British education has developed in a quite distinctive way and has emerged from a very particular history.

Global focus Education in Japan   9.6

Education in Japan developed rapidly towards the end of the nineteenth century. Indeed, by 1910 Japan, although much less developed economically, had overtaken Britain in participation rates. Enrolment ratios are the proportion of the relevant age group participating in formal education (see Figure 9.4).

This rapid development was driven partly by economic needs, as Japan embarked on industrialization and sought to replace imported foreign experts. The political functions of education were also of immense importance, since education was a means of indoctrinating the population with nationalism, loyalty to the emperor, and obedience to the government. The content of the curriculum, textbooks, and the recruitment of teachers was closely controlled by the state.

The Japanese system of education undoubtedly contributed to Japan's post-war economic miracle. It produced highly educated engineers and an obedient labour force. It was also highly meritocratic, because of the competitiveness of Japanese education, its unstreamed and comprehensive character, and the links between educational achievement and career success. Indeed, Dore (1987) considered Japan to be the most meritocratic society in the world.

Some saw this as a model system but more recently it has been much criticized. Such a highly competitive system had resulted in an 'examination hell', with lots of after-hours work in private crammers subjecting Japanese children to terrible pressure. This, combined with the overcontrolled and oppressive atmosphere of schools, has produced many pathologies—bullying, suicides, violence, and school refusal. There has, indeed, been a growing concern with the inability of Japan's conformist schools to produce the creative and innovatory people increasingly needed in a post-Fordist world. Reform attempts have been made but schools remain highly controlled and intensely competitive.

Sources: Dore (1976, 1987); Yoneyama (1999).

Figure 9.4 Occupational structure and educational participation in Japan and Britain, 1870 and 1910 (%)

| | Percentage of labour force in non-agricultural occupations | | Enrolment ratios (%) | | | | | |
| | | | Primary | | Secondary | | Tertiary | |
	Japan	Britain	Japan	Britain	Japan	Britain	Japan	Britain
1870	17	85	28	40	1	2	–	–
1910	41	92	98	100	12	4	2	2

Source: Dore (1976: 40).

Stop and reflect

In this section we have outlined the development of educational institutions in Britain.

- The nineteenth-century growth of elementary education was driven by religious, moral, and political, rather than economic, concerns.

- A national system of primary and secondary schooling was constructed between 1870 and 1944.

- Make sure that you know the main features of the 1944 Education Act.

- Why were comprehensive schools introduced and did they replace the 1944 structure?

- Can one meaningfully speak of a British system of education?

Inequality and education

In 'Education and inequality' we discussed different approaches towards the relationship between education and class inequality. In 'The development of education in Britain' we showed that attempts have been made to reform education in order to increase equality of opportunity. Whether these reforms did so has been the subject of considerable sociological research, which we now draw on in order to examine their impact on patterns of inequality. We start by considering class inequalities and then move on to gender, ethnicity, and disability.

Class

Nineteenth-century education clearly reproduced the class structure, but twentieth-century reforms, first the 1944 Education Act and then the introduction of comprehensive schools, were intended to provide equality of opportunity, irrespective of class background.

The tripartite system

The 1944 Act made free secondary education available to all, with access to grammar schools determined by performance at the 11+ examination alone. Did this create equality of opportunity?

In a classic study, Halsey *et al.* (1980) examined the impact of organizational changes in education on patterns of class inequality. They studied the educational careers of 8,529 men by examining four age 'cohorts' (an age cohort consists of all those born between two dates). Since two of their cohorts were educated before the 1944 Education Act came into operation and two afterwards, the researchers could make a 'before and after' comparison.

Under the tripartite system, entry to selective schools was crucial in determining educational success. Only those going into these schools could obtain academic qualifications and go on to university. Halsey *et al.* found that class continued to determine boys' chances of getting into these schools. Making grammar-school education free and selecting on the basis of the 11+ examination made no appreciable difference to class differentials. About one-fifth of the working-class children in their earliest (1913–22) cohort and their last (1943–52) cohort entered selective schools (Halsey *et al.* 1980: 63).

The 11+ examination was basically an intelligence test, which assumed that there was some general underlying ability called intelligence, which could be measured objectively. Any such ability is not, however, independent of class (or ethnicity). Tests of this sort have been shown to embody cultural and linguistic assumptions that are themselves linked to class and ethnic background (see Chapter 18, pp. 706–7). Performance at intelligence tests can, anyway, be improved through training, which families with superior resources can buy. As we showed earlier, Bourdieu argued that examinations are not objective because they are framed by the dominant culture. The greater success of those from higher classes in intelligence tests and examinations reflected both their material and cultural advantages.

Class differences then carried through to university entrance. The increasing availability of university places meant that the proportion of working-class children getting into university certainly increased but so did the proportion of those from higher classes. Indeed, while the proportion of working-class children at university tripled, the proportion of children from the higher classes nearly quadrupled (see Figure 9.5). Those in classes I and II clearly benefited far more than the other classes. Their entry to university increased by 19 per cent, as compared with a 6 per cent increase for the intermediate classes, and a mere 2 per cent for those at the bottom.

Comprehensive schools

Did comprehensive schools make any difference? It is difficult to explore this still-debated question because a fully comprehensive system was not created. As selective schools still existed and could 'cream off' the more academically successful children, comparisons between the tripartite system and comprehensive schools could not easily be made.

Anthony Heath (1989) argued that comprehensive reorganization made no real difference, but his conclusion was challenged by McPherson and Willms (1989), who examined later data from Scotland, where comprehensive reorganization had been more extensive. Their evidence showed that since comprehensive reorganization the gap between the examination performance of working-class and mid-

Figure 9.5 Attendance at university by birth cohort, 1913–1952 (%)

Father's social class	Birth cohort	
	1913–32	1943–52
I and II (service)	7.2	26.4
III, IV, and V (intermediate)	1.9	8.0
VI, VII, and VIII (working class)	0.9	3.1

Note: This study used the Goldthorpe class categories (see Chapter 19, p. 755).
Source: Adapted from Halsey *et al.* (1980: 188).

Education in Japan: meritocratic but conformist.
© Getty Images/Paul Chesley

dle-class children had narrowed slightly, as working-class children started to catch up. Differences remained great, however, and it is clear that the performance of children in comprehensive schools was still substantially related to their class background.

Stephen Ball's case study (1981) of 'Beachside' comprehensive school showed some of the reasons why. Like many comprehensives, Beachside was internally streamed into three ability bands. He found that banding reproduced the traditional academic/non-academic split in British education. Band one, the academic band, consisted mainly of middle-class children, bands two and three of working-class children. On entry children were allocated to bands on the basis of primary-school reports. There was some movement between bands in the first term but little after this point, certainly little movement into band one. Band differences in curriculum, syllabus, teaching methods, and relationships with teachers created two different kinds of education within the school.

The significance of primary-school reports for banding showed that selection originated largely at the previous stage of education. Success in primary education was, therefore, critical to future success in education. Douglas *et al.* (1968) demonstrated that the social-class composition of the primary school had a persistent influence on secondary-school performance. Children from predominantly working-class primary schools did less well in whichever type of school they went on to at age 11.

Beachside comprehensive did make a limited shift to mixed-ability classes, largely it seems because of persisting discipline problems in band-two classes, where an oppositional culture had established itself (see our discussion of this on p. 316). The mixing of children with different abilities was, however, limited. 'Sets' for children of different abilities emerged in some subjects, notably maths and languages, while mixed-ability classes came to an end after the third year.

Ball argued that mixed-ability classes did not, anyway, change teacher attitudes. Teachers still classified children in terms of their ability and treated them accordingly. He made the important point that the classroom mixing of children of different abilities did not mean that there was mixed-ability *teaching*. His research showed that the shift to mixed-ability classes enabled the more effective socialization of children into the school and better control of their behaviour. The social divisions found within banding were, nonetheless, broadly reproduced in mixed-ability classes.

Class background or school?

It would be easy to conclude from all this that class background is decisive in shaping educational success, that schools do not really matter. Indeed, Bernstein (1970) famously declared that 'education cannot compensate for society'. Was he right?

Halsey *et al.* (1980) certainly believed that the school mattered. Whether children went to public schools or grammar schools made little difference to their examination performance, but whether they went to selective schools (public and grammar) or secondary moderns was critical. Class had a major influence on the kind of school a boy ended up in, but its influence then diminished as the school took over. It has, indeed, been argued that grammar schools, with their strong academic culture, provide a better route upwards for those working-class children who do manage to get into them than comprehensive schools do.

Rutter *et al.* (1979) carried out a rather different study of twelve non-selective secondary schools in the London area. Although they found that the composition of a school's intake influenced both academic success and delinquency rates, differences in the schools as 'social institutions' were systematically related to their results. Mortimore (1997: 479) reviewed the literature on school

Does education enable upward mobility or reproduce inequality?
© Alice Chadwick

differences and concluded that they account for about 10 per cent of variations in examination performance.

Parental interest in school choice shows that parents are in little doubt about the school's significance. Phillip Brown (1995) argued that middle-class interest in school choice has increased as middle-class jobs have become more insecure. Organizational changes, intensifying international competition, and declining security of employment mean that the middle class can no longer rely on an easy passage for its children into stable bureaucratic and professional careers, while mass higher education has produced larger numbers of graduates seeking such careers. Middle-class parents have responded by using their material and cultural capital to maximize their children's educational advantages.

This has been translated into a pressure for greater choice in education. The more choice there is, the greater the opportunity for middle-class parents to use their advantages to get their children into higher-quality, higher-status institutions. We will return to this issue on pp. 337–8 and p. 340, where we examine the consequences of providing greater choice.

Higher education for more

Higher education expanded rapidly after the late 1980s, with the proportion of 18-year-olds entering it doubling from 15 per cent in 1988 to 30 per cent in 1994. How did this impact on class inequality?

This expansion certainly increased greatly the access of those at the bottom of the class structure to higher education. Thus, between the years 1991–2 and 1998–9 the participation of those with an unskilled manual background doubled, rising from 6 to 13 per cent. No other class category came close to doubling its participation rate, and this might suggest that expansion has disproportionately benefited those at the bottom (see Figure 9.6).

On closer examination, however, it becomes clear that it is actually those from the highest social classes who have increased their participation most. The most striking feature of Figure 9.6 is in fact the disproportionate increase in those coming from a professional background and the very high proportion of the children of professional parents who gain entrance to university. Later figures show that manual workers (the bottom three classes in Figure 9.6) increased their participation from 11 per cent in 1991–2 to 19 per cent in 2001–2, while non-manual workers (the top three classes) increased theirs far more, going from 35 per cent to 50 per cent (*Social Trends* 2004: 45).

Data from the HEFCE suggest that those at the bottom of the scale may have caught up a small amount since 2004–5 (see Figure 9.7). These data are not directly comparable with the data on students' class background, since they are based on the *area* students came from. Areas were classified into five groups, from the most advantaged to the most disadvantaged. Between 2004–5 and 2009–10, those from the most disadvantaged increased their participation by four percentage points, while those from the most advantaged increased theirs by only two percentage points. The gap between the two groups had narrowed slightly, but was, however, still slightly greater than in 1994–5. Furthermore, while in 2009–10 fewer than one in five from the most disadvantaged areas were making it into higher education, in the most advantaged areas more than one in two were getting there. This does not really change the picture of the better off benefiting most from the expansion of higher education.

A recent study of intergenerational social mobility rates in different countries concluded that rates in Britain were comparable to those in the United States and lower than in Canada and Scandinavia. Social mobility had in fact been falling in Britain, and this was at least partly explained by the close and increasing relationship between family income and educational achievement, particularly access to higher education. By enabling much greater access to higher education for the children of the better-off, the 1990s expansion of higher education had reduced, not increased, the social mobility between generations (Blanden *et al.* 2005).

Figure 9.6 Social class and participation in higher education, Great Britain, 1990s (%)

Social class	1991–2	1998–9	Change
Professional	55	72	+17
Intermediate	36	45	+9
Skilled non-manual	22	29	+7
Skilled manual	11	18	+7
Partly skilled	12	17	+5
Unskilled	6	13	+7
All	23	31	+8

Source: Glennerster (2001: table 11).

❷ Who has benefited most from the expansion of higher education?

Figure 9.7 Proportion of young people entering higher education from different social backgrounds, England, 1994/5–2009/10 (%)

	1994/5	2004/5	2009/10
Most advantaged areas	50	55	57
Most disadvantaged areas	13	15	19

Source: HEFCE (2010).

The Labour government made the relationship between education and social mobility a major issue in 2009. A committee chaired by Alan Milburn declared that the professions were a 'closed shop' that excluded the poor. Entry was still determined by family wealth and private education. It was estimated that only 29 per cent of students, and only 16 per cent of those at the top Russell group of universities, came from the bottom half of the socio-economic scale. The committee called on universities to take more account of applicants' backgrounds when offering places (*Guardian*, 21 July 2009).

Some universities already do this, a practice that has unsurprisingly caused a backlash from schools and parents who think their children have lost places to those with lower qualifications. Should a student from a professional background with an A and two Bs lose a place to a student from a working-class background with, say, two Bs and a C?

This is not just a matter of equalizing opportunities. It is claimed that research carried out by the University of Bristol shows that students from 'poor' schools outperform at university those with the same A-level grades from 'better' schools. If universities want to admit those students likely to perform best at university, they should consequently make offers to those from 'poor' schools that are one or two grades lower. So argues Steve Smith, President of Universities UK (*Sunday Times*, 28 March 2010).

As with greater school choice, middle-class families have undoubtedly been using the opportunities provided by the expansion of higher education to pass their advantages on to their children. Some universities have tried to counteract this through their admissions policies. Whether they should do this is a matter of considerable debate.

Gender

The literature on education and class has been mainly concerned with the persistence of inequalities in educational achievement. In examining gender inequalities we find not so much persistence as transformation. Historically, girls were excluded and sidelined, but in recent years they have overtaken boys.

The separation of girls

According to the nineteenth-century domestic division of labour, girls were destined for housework and child-rearing, and had little need for formal education beyond elementary level.

By 1880 elementary education was compulsory for all children up to the age of 10. The limited skills taught were differentiated by gender, girls learning domestic skills and boys craft skills and elementary arithmetic. Education was seen as less necessary for girls, and it was considered acceptable for them to stay at home helping their mothers and acquiring domestic skills (Abbott and Wallace 1990).

> ➔ *Connections*
>
> As the education of women has reflected persisting nineteenth-century ideas of their place in the world, you may find it helpful to refer to our discussion of this in Chapter 5, pp. 163–5.

Secondary schools for upper- and middle-class girls were gradually established during the second half of the century. One model for their education was provided by Cheltenham Ladies College, founded in 1854, which saw its function as providing an improved training for women's traditional roles. North London Collegiate, which opened as a day school for girls in 1850, had the very different mission of providing an academic education for girls. It was a model for the Girls' Public Day School Company, which was funding thirty-eight schools by 1901 (Royle 1987: 363). Secondary schools for girls were well established by the beginning of the twentieth century, but were far less numerous than those for boys.

Women were excluded from universities for most of the nineteenth century. It was in 1878 at the University of London that they were for the first time allowed to take degrees. Cambridge and Oxford were particularly slow to open their doors to women. Some separate colleges for girls were established around 1880, but women were not allowed to receive full degrees until 1920 in Oxford and 1948 in Cambridge. The numbers of women in higher education remained low for a long time. In 1961 only 13 per cent of students at Cambridge and Oxford were women (Royle 1987: 381).

Integration and discrimination

The 1944 Education Act made free secondary education available to all, but secondary education for girls did not mean that they pursued the same curriculum as boys. The role expectations of both staff and students steered girls and boys towards specialization in different subjects as they moved higher up the school and into higher education. Girls moved towards those that were extensions of the domestic role and boys towards technical and scientific ones. The introduction of a national curriculum in the 1980s counteracted this to some extent by establishing the same curriculum for boys and girls up to age 16.

Requiring girls and boys to take the same subjects did not, however, remove gender issues from the curriculum, as the debate over the gendering of science shows (Heaton and Lawson 1996). Feminists argued that science was taught in a 'masculine' way. Three responses to this problem emerged:

- *girl-friendly science*: making science more attractive to girls by introducing topics that interest them;

Is science a masculine activity?

© Hymers College, Hull

- *feminine science*: replacing competitive masculine behaviour in the laboratory with a more cooperative feminine approach;
- *feminist science*: challenging masculine ways of thinking by arguing that scientific method should give more weight to feminine intuition.

This debate exemplifies the conflict between the liberal and radical tendencies in feminism (see Chapter 5, p. 156, for a discussion of this). Liberal feminism seeks equal opportunities for women within the existing system, but radical feminism argues that this results in women thinking and acting like men. According to radical feminism, masculine ways of behaving and thinking should be challenged and replaced by feminine ones. If the 'feminist-science' approach is adopted, this can, however, lead to the response that scientific method, as it stands, is essential to science and, if it is treated as masculine in character, this means that girls cannot be as good at science as boys.

Research by Spender (1982) and Stanworth (1983) showed the importance of different gender-role expectations in the classroom. Boys got more attention and interest than girls. Boys tended to receive higher marks than girls for comparable work and were expected to perform better in examinations. This was due not just to teacher

expectations but to the children's expectations and behaviour. Boys, for example, demanded more attention.

This led some to conclude that girls would be better off in schools for girls only or girls' classes in mixed schools. The debate on this continues, with the Schools Minister arguing in late 2008 that separating the sexes for science teaching would get more girls taking science and engineering courses. But, according to Professor Alan Smithers, research does not provide any consistent evidence that girls perform better when taught on their own (*Independent*, 25 and 26 November 2008).

The educational superiority of girls

More recently girls have performed better than boys at A-level and have done so increasingly (see Figure 9.8). Their growing examination success has been reflected in their access to higher education, where they have steadily increased their participation and in 2000 considerably outnumber men (see Figure 9.9, p. 329). It was reported in 2009 that the higher-education participation rate for women was 49 per cent, as compared with 38 per cent for men. Furthermore, while 64 per cent of women obtained firsts or upper seconds, only 60 per cent of men did (*Higher Education Policy Institute*, 5 June 2009).

How is girls' greater success to be explained?

There is, first, the claim that attempts to counteract educational discrimination against girls have worked. These include such initiatives as GIST (Girls into Science and Technology) and the introduction of single-sex classes. More generally, there has been a greater awareness of, and sensitivity to, gender issues in schools.

Figure 9.8 Achievement of two or more GCE A levels or equivalent by gender, United Kingdom, 1990/1–2003/4

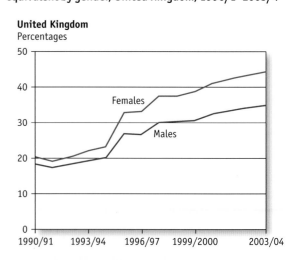

United Kingdom
Percentages

Source: Social Trends (2006: 42).

❷ Why do you think that girls have become increasingly successful in A level examinations?

Figure 9.9 Students in higher education* by type of course and gender, United Kingdom, 1970/1–2006/7 (000s)

	Undergraduate		Postgraduate		All higher education
	Full-time	Part-time	Full-time	Part-time	
Males					
1970/1	241	127	33	15	416
1980/1	277	176	41	32	526
1990/1	345	193	50	50	638
2000/1	511	228	82	118	940
2006/7	563	267	120	143	1,094
Females					
1970/1	173	19	10	3	205
1980/1	196	71	21	13	301
1990/1	319	148	34	36	537
2000/1	602	320	81	124	1,128
2006/7	706	451	125	181	1,463

*Includes both home and overseas students, and students at the Open University.

Source: *Social Trends* (2009: 34).

❷ Why do you think that there are more women than men in higher education?

There is, secondly, the argument that changes in assessment have resulted in better results for girls. They tend to perform better at coursework, while boys do better when assessment is by unseen examination. Growing use of coursework may have led to the greater success of girls. There are also signs that a shift from assessment by coursework back to assessment by unseen examination may have recently reversed this tendency at GCSE level (*Independent*, 27 August 2009). Whether this could account for the magnitude of the change in entry to higher education must, however, be doubtful.

There is, thirdly, the broader argument that changes in patterns of employment account for the superior performance of girls. The growing employment of women arguably raised girls' expectations and confidence (see Chapter 5, p. 174). The decline of traditional male jobs led to the disillusionment and disaffection of many boys, who no longer bother with education and take refuge in an oppositional culture, of the kind described by Willis (1977) (see p. 317). Weiner *et al.*(1997) have suggested that a growing insecurity of employment may have had similar effects on middle-class boys. These theories are linked to wider notions of a male identity crisis, which we discuss in Chapter 5, pp. 176–9.

Against this, Mac an Ghaill (1996) has pointed out that a wide range of male peer groups and masculinities, not just oppositional cultures of the kind described by Willis, can be found in schools. And for some working-class boys, new vocational routes opened up into areas such as business studies, technology, and computing.

There has certainly been a growing worry about boys' educational performance and calls for something to be done to help them catch up. In 2000 the government launched pilot schemes to provide separate classes for boys, in order to restore discipline and improve results. The worry about boys' examination performance has been accompanied by a concern with their much higher rate of exclusion for misbehaviour. In English schools the rate of exclusion for boys has in recent years been four times higher than the rate for girls (Department for Education and Skills 2006).

Arguably, however, too much attention has been paid to boys' problems and girls' less visible problems have been neglected. According to Osler *et al.* (2002) girls are more involved than boys in some of the less formal and less visible forms of exclusion, such as isolation within the school and self-exclusion through disengagement from work or withdrawal from school.

The educational success of girls should not, anyway, be taken to mean that older gender patterns have disappeared. Thus, gender still plays a part in subject choice, which steers boys and girls towards different careers. The introduction of a national curriculum reduced gender differences in subject choice before age 16, but by A level traditional gender differences had re-emerged and these continued into higher education. At the beginning of the twenty-first century this was still evident. In 2001 93 per cent of the students sitting the vocational A level in Health and Social Care were female, while in Computing 79 per cent of entrants were male (*Independent*, 16 September 2001).

Male domination of education has also persisted in other ways. As academics move up the career ladder in higher education men become more numerous, which also means that university procedures and decision-making bodies tend to be dominated by men (Hodges 2000). Senior positions in schools, governing bodies, local education authorities (LEAs), and the Department for Education and Skills have also been male-dominated (Weiner *et al.* 1997).

Ethnicity

Variations in educational achievement have been linked to ethnicity, though the relationship between ethnicity and achievement is particularly complex.

Ethnicity and achievement

A growing concern with ethnic variations in educational achievement led to the Rampton (1981) and Swann (1985) reports, which showed that there were important ethnic differences in attainment. A considerable literature then developed to explain the relationship between ethnicity and educational achievement. Some claimed that ethnic variations could be explained by differences in inherited intelligence (Herrnstein and Murray 1994). Alternatively, it was argued that cultural differences explained these variations. Thus, African Caribbean culture placed a low value on education, though some Asian cultures valued it highly. Others have suggested that growing up in a white-dominated society with few positive 'black' role models leads to low self-esteem, low aspirations, and educational underachievement among African Caribbean children.

> **⊃ Connections**
> We examine biological explanations of ethnic differences in Chapter 6, pp. 191–3, and biological explanations of differences in intelligence in Chapter 18, pp. 706–8.

There are many problems with the literature on the educational performance of ethnic minorities. First, there is the problem of categories. The collective term 'ethnic minorities' conceals great differences in ethnicity and educational achievement (see Figure 9.10). Some are performing at higher levels than the white majority, some at lower levels. Indeed, recent research has drawn attention to low levels of achievement amongst white children (Cassen and Kingdon 2007). The notion that it is ethnic minorities who underachieve is simply wrong.

Secondly, there are major gender variations within ethnic groups. Trevor Phillips, the chairman of the Commission for Racial Equality, has pointed this out. In 2004, 36 per cent of black Caribbean children achieved five or more GCSE grade A–C passes. This aggregate figure concealed the fact that 44 per cent of black Caribbean girls achieved these

Figure 9.10 Attainment of five or more GCSE grades A*–C in year 11, England and Wales, 1992–2006 (%)

Ethnic origin	1992	2006	Change
White	37	58	+21
Black	23	50	+27
Indian	38	72	+34
Pakistani	26	52	+26
Bangladeshi	14	57	+43
Other Asian	46	77	+31
Other ethnic groups	46 (1996)	56	+10

Source: *Social Trends* (2006: 41; 2009: 39)

❷ What does this table tell us about ethnic variations in educational achievement?

grades but only 27 per cent of boys. This led him to call for separate classes for black boys in order to improve their particular performance (*Independent*, 7 March 2005).

There is, thirdly, the difficulty of distinguishing between *ethnicity* and *class*. Particular ethnic groups, such as African Caribbeans, may perform badly because of their class rather than their ethnicity. In an important study of nineteen 'multi-racial' comprehensives in the early 1980s, Smith and Tomlinson (1989) found ethnic differences at age 16 in GCE/CSE grades (the examinations that preceded GCSE). Class was, however, far more strongly related to attainment than ethnicity. It was also quite possible that ethnic differences masked class differences. The relatively low grades achieved by African Caribbeans could well have resulted from their mainly working-class backgrounds.

A recent study has supported this. Cassen and Kingdon (2007) found that African Caribbean boys had a lower educational performance than white boys. But when ethnic groups at the same class level were compared, it was white boys that were performing worse. Thus, when boys on free school meals were compared, 62 per cent of whites fell into the bottom 10 per cent of performers, as compared with 43 per cent of African Caribbeans. White boys at the bottom at age 11 tended to stay there, as compared with other ethnic groups, who improved their position. This study also found that 14 per cent of the variation in achievement was related to school quality, indicating the importance of school character (see p. 325).

Similar problems arise with ethnic variations in achievement at universities. While 66 per cent of white students obtained a first or an upper second in 2007–8, only 47 per cent of Asian students did so, and only 38 per cent of black students. It has been suggested that these differences may, however, reflect ethnic differences in such factors as age distribution, the courses taken, and the part-time or full-time status of students, which are all related to levels of

Figure 9.11 Permanent exclusion rates in primary, secondary, and special schools, England, 2004–5

Ethnicity	Rates per 10,000 pupils
White British	13
White Irish	21
Mixed white and black Caribbean	41
Mixed white and black African	24
Mixed white and Asian	9
Other white	9
Black Caribbean	39
Black African	14
Other black	36
Indian	4
Pakistani	8
Bangladeshi	6
Other Asian	4
Chinese	2

Source: *Social Trends* (2007: 29).

❷ What is the significance of differences in these rates for patterns of educational achievement?

achievement. Floya Anthias argues that ethnic differences may again mask class differences, since ethnic minority students tend to come from lower class backgrounds and class is linked to performance in higher education (*Guardian*, 27 October 2009).

When examination performance at school is considered, it is important to take account of change and not to see a particular level of performance as a fixed feature of a particular group (see Figure 9.10). All groups have been improving their performance, while some non-white groups that were previously disadvantaged have been catching up, and others have leaped ahead. Account should also be taken of very pronounced ethnic variations in rates of exclusion (see Figure 9.11).

Racism in schools?

Ethnographic studies, such as Cecile Wright's (1988), have demonstrated the existence of racially discriminatory behaviour in schools. Observational and interview techniques have been used to investigate the interaction between different ethnic groups and teachers. They have shown teachers interpreting the behaviour of African Caribbean children as disruptive and then reacting in an inappropriately punitive way. This fits with the much higher rate of exclusion of black children from school because of 'bad' behaviour.

Rattansi (1988) referred to the *institutional racism* embedded in taken-for-granted features of school organization and curriculum (see Chapter 6, p. 195, for a discussion of this term). By this he meant that such matters as dress requirements or school-meals arrangements or aspects of the curriculum failed to take account of non-white cultures.

Mason (2000) recognized the existence of these practices but was concerned that the term 'racist' had become overused. He argued that many such practices should be viewed as *ethnocentric* rather than *racist*. They show an ignorance and disregard of other cultures that is typical of a widely found ethnocentrism, but they are in principle no different from practices that discriminate against the customs and cultures of, say, people from Ireland or Poland who live in Britain. Mason preferred to keep the term 'racism' for beliefs that involved the idea of biologically distinct races.

Ethnocentrism and racism do not themselves determine children's behaviour, for much depends on how children respond. Brah and Minhas (1988) described the emergence of an oppositional response by Asian schoolgirls. They were well aware of the operation of ethnocentric stereotypes and responded to the notion that Asians had language difficulties by pretending not to understand their teachers' instructions and speaking Urdu in class. Their resistance to the ethnocentric culture of the school took a collective form as they created mutual support groups. Fuller (1983) reported a rather different response by African Caribbean girls, who reacted to low teacher expectations by combining defiance with educational success. Well aware of the importance of educational qualifications, they showed they could achieve results as good as anyone else's.

Nor is it simply a matter of the interaction between teachers and pupils, for interactions between the pupils themselves have an important bearing on all this. In a study of excluded black students, Wright *et al.* (1998) showed how the stereotypes of male black youth held by white students, which combined 'fear' and 'awe', interacted with those of teachers to generate an oppositional black masculinity that reinforced the stereotype.

Policy responses to ethnocentrism and racism in schools may have gone some way to counter racism and ethnocentrism.

Multicultural education recognized cultural diversity and tried to treat cultures as different but equal. It involved changes to the curriculum that would better reflect cultural diversity by, for example, bringing black writers into the study of literature and recognizing religious diversity, but it has come under much criticism. It provoked a hostile reaction from those who believed it threatened British national identity or justified unacceptable cultural practices, such as the wearing of the *burqa* by Muslims. It was also criticized by black activists for colluding with *cultural racism* (see Chapter 6, p. 217) and trying to assimilate minorities into a racist society that it did not openly challenge.

The second more radical response was *anti-racist* education. This more directly challenged racism by insisting

How significant is ethnicity in educational achievement?
© Alice Chadwick

that it must be recognized and confronted. It sought to raise awareness of all aspects of racism and train teachers in anti-racist policies. Its broad definition of racism treated all forms of disadvantage or discrimination affecting ethnic minorities as racist, labelling as racist practices that Mason would consider ethnocentric. It certainly brought racism out into the open but has been criticized for intensifying and racializing conflicts between ethnic groups.

Disability

As the literature on class, gender, and ethnicity shows, aspirations are important to success in education. Do those with disability have the same aspirations as the non-disabled? Earlier studies had shown a big gap in aspirations, but Burchardt (2005) found that the aspirations of disabled people born in 1970 had more than caught up with those of the non-disabled. Survey data showed that 62 per cent of disabled young people wanted to stay on at school after 16, as compared with 60 per cent of the non-disabled. Indeed, the occupational aspirations of the disabled were higher, with 33 per cent of the disabled seeking employment in a profession, as compared with 24 per cent of the non-disabled.

Data on educational outcomes showed, however, that the ambitions of the disabled were in many ways frustrated. Only 62 per cent of the disabled stayed on in full-time education after age 16, as compared with 71 per cent of the non-disabled. By age 18/19, the qualifications achieved by the disabled were falling well below those obtained by the non-disabled. Some 48 per cent of the disabled achieved qualifications at NVQ level one or below, as compared with 28 per cent of the non-disabled. By age 26 the disabled were showing a lack of confidence and evidence of disheartenment that had not been apparent at age 16.

Burchardt's report (2005: 49) concludes that 'high aspirations with relatively low chances of fulfillment are arguably the worst possible combination', because of the disappointment and frustration that they generate. Government policies aimed at providing incentives to the disabled to seek work, as in the New Deal for Disabled People, miss the point, since there is no lack of motivation. It is the lack of opportunities in education (and employment) that need tackling, by, for example, providing more financial support.

Controversy and debate Education and disability: integration   9.7
or segregation?

Should those with a disability be educated in special schools that provide for their particular needs or should they be integrated into mainstream schooling?

Following the 1978 report by Baroness Warnock, the 1981 Education Act established a framework for educating children with 'special needs' in mainstream schools. The needs of such children would be assessed and their schools would be given additional support by local education authorities. This was a reaction against both the traditional 'dumping' of many such children in special schools and the absence of any special provision in mainstream schools for those with learning difficulties.

According to the Audit Commission, between 1981 and 1991 the number of special school places in England fell from around 130,000 to around 100,000, but, contrary to public perceptions, it has only slowly declined since. In 2001, 61 per cent of children with special needs in England were educated in mainstream schools but 34 per cent were still in special schools (most of the remainder were educated in independent schools).

This integration policy reflected broader changes in the way that the disabled were viewed. Traditionally, disability had been considered an individual medical problem that required treatment in a specialist institution. Increasingly, the problem was seen as lying with society, which discriminated against and excluded those with special needs, depriving them of their rights. Integration was part of a broader process of decarcerating people from institutions (see Chapter 14, pp. 545–7, for a discussion of this) and providing 'care in the community' (see Chapter 8, pp. 293–5).

Those critical of the integration policy argue that the specialized staff and facilities of special schools make them much better at meeting special needs, while support in mainstream schools is erratic, inadequate, and difficult to obtain from local-education authorities. They claim that the disabled suffer neglect and bullying in mainstream schools, which are anyway sometimes reluctant to admit them and often exclude them. Indeed, a report published in December 2009 claimed that children with special needs were eight times as likely as others to be excluded from school.

Those in support of integration argue that segregation is wrong and that the problems faced by mainstream schools would be solved if they were properly resourced. Those with 'special needs' can benefit greatly from contact with other children. It is also argued that some specialist schools are themselves inadequately staffed and resourced, and have changed little since the time when Baroness Warnock made her report.

Sources: Audit Commission (2002); *Guardian*, 10 June 2005; *Independent*, 16 December 2009; *Sunday Times*, 12 June 2005;

Stop and reflect

In this section we examined various patterns of inequality.

Class inequalities:

- In spite of their intentions, neither the 1944 Education Act nor comprehensive schools made much impact on class differences in educational achievement.
- Why do you think that class inequalities have been so persistent?

Gender inequalities:

- The gendering of occupational and educational expectations disadvantaged girls until recent times.
- Why have girls recently outperformed boys in many public examinations?

Ethnicity:

- Variations in educational achievement have been linked to ethnicity.
- Would it be true to say that ethnic minorities underachieve?
- Should class, gender, and ethnicity be treated as separate dimensions of inequality?

Disability:

- Disability is another source of inequality in educational achievement.
- This reflects lack of opportunity rather than any absence of aspiration.
- Should those with a disability be educated in special schools?

Education in transformation

In the 1980s a further transformation of British education began. There was a new emphasis on gearing education to the needs of the economy and developing its training function. Parental choice and greater competition between educational institutions exposed education to market forces. Local education authorities (LEAs) lost much of their control over education, while central state regulation greatly increased. The proportion of students staying on in education after the age of 16 rose sharply and higher education rapidly expanded.

This transformation was initiated by Conservative governments during the later 1980s and we first examine the various changes they introduced. We then consider whether Labour governments after 1997 reversed or continued these changes.

Education and economy

As we showed on p. 320, education has been held responsible by some for Britain's declining international competitiveness. Britain's economic problems in the 1970s, increasing international competition, and the consequences of globalization resulted in a growing concern with education's contribution to the economy.

Education and economic success

Bowles and Gintis (1976) (see p. 316) argued that the key function of education was the supply of labour to the capitalist economy. Economic changes have made this function even more important. In Britain, unskilled manual labour has declined and work requiring skills and qualifications has become more important. The spread of information technology into all areas of life means that new skills in processing and communicating information are needed. Knowledge and the capacity to use and communicate it have become vital to the economic success of countries and the earnings of individuals. Furthermore, in a world of growing economic integration, investment in education has become one of the main ways of increasing international competitiveness (see Box 9.8).

It is now widely agreed that education is important to economic success, but which aspects of it matter most to the economy? Does education need to train workers in technical skills? Or are employers looking less for specific skills, which may soon go out of date, and more for adaptable and flexible workers with transferable and interpersonal skills? How important are communication skills? Or is it basic standards of literacy and numeracy that especially need improvement?

While it is clearly possible for governments to try to improve all these aspects of education, given limited resources they imply conflicting priorities. Here it is interesting to see which skills are considered by those English employers experiencing skill gaps to be lacking in their employees (see Figure 9.12). Technical and practical skills come top of the list, but communication skills and

Global focus Education and globalization 9.8

Growing state intervention in education has been, partly at least, a response to globalization. Global economic integration, the mobility of capital, and neo-liberal policies have reduced the capacity of governments to protect industries against foreign competition or direct the development of national economies. One of the few ways in which international competitiveness can be increased is through investment in human capital by putting resources into education and training.

This argument particularly relates to the old industrial societies. Their traditional manufacturing industries cannot compete with developing countries where labour costs are far lower. This also applies to clerical work and data processing, which can now be done by overseas teleworkers. The industrial societies can compete only by upgrading their skills and capitalizing on their knowledge and expertise.

All this means that it is those who are highly educated who do well. According to Reich (1997), people who can do only routine production and service work will lose out, while it is the highly educated 'symbolic analysts'—scientists, consultants, engineers, and financial experts—whose skills and knowledge are in global demand. The implication is that inequality will be more related to level of education than ever before.

Data from the OECD suggest that the UK is falling behind here. In 2000 the UK was ranked fourth amongst OECD countries in the proportion of young people graduating from universities, but by 2008 had dropped to twelfth. The proportion had increased between these two years, but only from 37 to 39 per cent. Other countries had increased their proportion of graduates faster.

Sources: Brown and Lauder (1997); Reich (1997); *Guardian*, 10 September 2008.

---

transferable skills, such as teamworking, problem-solving, and management, are not far behind. If general and professional information technology skills are added together, information-technology skills rise up the list. Literacy and numeracy, however, are down towards the bottom. Foreign-language skills are right at the bottom, reflecting perhaps the status of English as a *lingua franca*.

Figure 9.12 Skills gaps experienced by English employers, 2007 (%).

England
Percentages

Note: This figure shows the skills found lacking by those English employers experiencing skills gaps.
Source: National Employers Skills Survey, as reported in *Social Trends* (2009: 37).

The new vocationalism

The concern to improve education's supply of labour to employers led in the 1980s to the **new vocationalism**. This aimed to make education more relevant both to the occupational requirements of the economy and to students' need for jobs. The established liberal and academic traditions of British education were challenged. The liberal approach to education aimed to develop an individual's full potential in all aspects of life and did not particularly concern itself with education for work. The academic tradition valued knowledge for its own sake and was not concerned with how it was used.

Knowledge was now considered less important than the capacity to learn, communicate, and work cooperatively with others. A more vocational, more motivating, more student-involving education was needed that would raise the numbers of 16–19-year-olds staying on in education. Widespread changes followed in both secondary and tertiary education:

- *Course construction*. The modularization of courses into shorter, more flexible units with specified objectives.

- *Skills*. A shift of focus from knowledge to work-related skills, such as skills in information technology, communication, problem-solving, and personal management.

- *Learning*. More emphasis on student-centred learning through project work rather than teaching factual information, on group cooperation rather than individualist competition.

- *Enterprise.* Development of entrepreneurial skills by encouraging students to take part in profit-making business activities.

- *Assessment.* Profiles, records of achievement, and transcripts to recognize what has been achieved and replace traditional grading systems, together with certification that a defined level of competence has been reached.

It was no good, however, developing work-relevant skills if they were not valued. This was a deep-rooted problem in Britain, where academic qualifications had always been more highly valued than vocational ones. The response to this problem was to build a new system of National Vocational Qualifications (NVQs), which tested competence in specific work situations. General NVQs (GNVQs) were developed to meet the requirements of groups of related occupations, such as health care, and provide a vocational route into further and higher education. Advanced GNVQs or 'vocational A levels' were created to give equality of status with A level and provide a route into higher education through vocational qualifications. Alan Smithers (1994) described all this as 'a quiet educational revolution'.

Can entrepreneurial skills be learned in schools and colleges?

© Hymers College, Hull

Figure 9.13 Academic education versus the new vocationalism

Academic education	New vocationalism
• Teaching	• Learning
• Knowledge	• Competence
• Subject-specific skills	• Transferable skills
• Individual achievement	• Teamwork

↪ Think about the course that you are taking.

❓ Does it reflect the new vocationalism?

The new vocationalism may have brought about a quiet revolution, but it upset some on both the right and the left of politics. It was resisted by supporters of the academic tradition, who thought that traditional, knowledge-based A levels were a 'gold standard' to be defended at all costs. It also conflicted with the **authoritarian populist** strand in Conservative policy, which rejected the views of experts and called for a return to the common sense and 'natural instincts' of the people (Dale 1989). Left-wing critics argued that it subordinated education to the requirements of work in a capitalist economy. Indeed, it seemed to

vindicate the Bowles and Gintis (1976) analysis of the relationship between education and capitalism. Was education only for work?

A regulated marketplace

The drive to make education more responsive to the needs of British society led also to an introduction of market principles intended to reduce state control, though they actually involved extensive state intervention and much greater state regulation. We will first consider changes in schools and colleges and then move on to higher education.

Market forces

The introduction of market principles in the 1980s reflected the Conservative government's **neo-liberal** belief that the British economy could be revitalized by allowing market forces to operate more freely. This involved two key interacting processes: greater competition between institutions and greater parental choice.

Before the 1980s reforms, entry to state schools was based on catchment areas. Children were allocated to schools by the Local Education Authority (LEA) according to the area they lived in. If parents did not like the local school, they either had to educate their children privately or move house into the catchment area of a 'good' school.

The 1980 and 1988 Education Acts gave parents the right to choose which school their children attended. In theory, popular schools could expand, while unpopular schools might be forced eventually to close. Schools were also allowed to specialize in areas like technology and modern languages. An internal market had been introduced, and schools now had to compete for pupils. Glossy school brochures multiplied.

Competition was encouraged in other ways by reducing LEA control over schools. The delegation of management and budget control to the schools themselves gave them greater freedom to compete, for they could decide how to use their resources most effectively. They could increase their resources by attracting more pupils, but in this new competitive climate they also began to raise more money from parents, sponsors, and commercial operations.

Similar changes occurred in further education, where colleges were removed from local-authority control and had their funding transferred to a national funding council appointed by the government. They were now controlled by new governing bodies on which local industry was heavily represented. Funding linked to student numbers forced the colleges into competition with each other and also with those schools providing post-16 education.

Another kind of competition was also introduced. Educational services had previously been provided by the LEAs. Schools could now choose whether to buy LEA services or go to private suppliers. The LEAs had to

Figure 9.14 Schools enter the marketplace

Before the 1980s	After the 1980s
• Catchment areas	• Open entry
• LEA allocation of places	• Parents' right to choose
• LEA coordination of provision	• Competition between schools
• LEA control	• Governor authority, delegation of management, opting out
• LEA services	• Private services

compete on the same basis as private companies to win contracts from schools. Education services, just like many other local-authority services, had been privatized (Blakemore and Griggs 2007: 138–45).

Choice, selection, and inequality

It was claimed that these changes in education increased parental choice, but they also increased the capacity of schools to select.

Choice results in a growing inequality between schools and therefore in the resources and facilities available to their pupils. As money follows pupils, resources flow to popular schools. If there is a high demand for places, popular schools can be more selective in deciding which child to accept. By selecting children with greater ability, they improve their results and become still more popular. At the other extreme, 'sink' schools emerge that face a downward spiral of pupils, resources, and results.

As both our opening piece and Media watch 9 at the end of this chapter suggest, the opportunity to choose schools has turned out to be illusory for many people. Popular schools simply cannot expand sufficiently to accommodate the demand for places in them. As these schools become more selective, the choice for many parents is reduced, and those who cannot get their children into their school of choice have to settle for less desirable schools.

The capacity to exercise choice effectively is inevitably related to social class. There are straightforward material factors, such as the availability of transport and the pressures of work, which limit the choices of those who are poor. Cultural and social capital (see pp. 314–16) also play their part, as knowledge of education and involvement in networks help some parents to get their children into better schools. The better the school is (in reputation at least), and the more competition there is for places, the more strongly these mechanisms operate.

In a study of school choice in Greater London, Ball *et al.* (1995) found two patterns of choice that corresponded to social class:

• *Working-class locals*. Their choice was governed by practical considerations and immediate concerns, such as transport arrangements.

- *Middle-class cosmopolitans.* They gave higher priority to school reputation and longer-term career concerns, and had more money for travel or private education.

A growing competition for jobs, together with the inflation of qualifications by mass higher education, led middle-class parents to use their full weight in the education market in order to give their children a competitive edge. To do this, they needed greater choice. Phillip Brown (1995) claimed that there has been a shift in the ideology of the middle class from meritocracy to parentocracy. He contrasted these two ideologies through two equations:

- **meritocracy**: ability + effort = merit;
- **parentocracy**: resources + preference = choice.

There is also an ethnic dimension to this whole issue of choice. Research has shown that parents from ethnic minorities are concerned to find a school 'with a critical mass of children from their own ethnic background'. There are also patterns of 'ethnic aversion', when schools are avoided because of their ethnic composition. This applies particularly to schools with a high proportion of refugee children. Those at the bottom of the ethnic hierarchy were least able to exercise choice effectively and ended up at locally labelled 'bad' schools. Patterns of ethnic disadvantage were reinforced by the machinery of choice (J. Williams 2005).

Thus, in these various ways, greater choice means more inequality. It increases inequality between schools. It creates a new line of division between those who get the school of their choice and those who do not. It reinforces existing inequalities, as those with superior material and cultural resources are better placed to pursue their preferences and obtain the kind of education they want for their children.

More state regulation

The government did not, however, simply leave education to the operation of market forces and the exercise of parental choice.

The 1988 Education Act introduced a national curriculum for children aged 5–16. This was a fundamental change in British education, which had never before experienced such a regulation and standardization of its content. As Chris Pole (2001: 4) has pointed out, this considerably changed the role of the teacher: 'By the end of the 1980s, central government was firmly inside the classroom, reducing the role of the teacher from that of professional who had previously made decisions about the curriculum to that of technician who merely delivered it.'

With the national curriculum went national testing. GCSE already provided a national test at age 16, but new tests were introduced at younger ages. National testing enabled the construction of league tables that allowed the comparison of schools' performances. A major problem with these tables was, however, that performance was largely determined by a school's intake. This created a powerful incentive for schools to be more selective and exclude children likely to perform badly.

It was not only the children who were tested, for a new system of school inspection run by the Office for Standards in Education (OFSTED) was introduced. This involved not only the inspection of the workings of a school but also meetings with parents at which teachers were not present. OFSTED reports were then made available to parents. This fitted well with the government's belief in parent power and parent choice.

The heavier state regulation of education was in constant tension with the emphasis on free competition elsewhere in government education policy. In their day-to-day running, schools had been given greater freedom from local-authority control, but they were now instead tightly controlled by the central state.

More higher education

Higher education was expanded massively from the late 1980s, though expansion was not matched by increased funding. The proportion of 18-year-olds in higher education doubled from 15 per cent in 1988 to 30 per cent in 1994, and continued rising. Funding per student declined, however, during the 1980s and the 1990s, dropping by almost half in real terms. Higher-education institutions responded by allowing the staff–student ratio to rise from 1 to 10 in 1985/6 to 1 to 21 by 2003/4 (Association of University Teachers 2005).

Universities have tried to find new sources of income. They have recruited more overseas students (who pay much higher fees), expanded their postgraduate courses (again seeking overseas students), and developed distance-learning programmes. The academic marketplace has gone global. They have also tried to raise more money from renting out accommodation, from conferences, and appeals to their *alumni*.

Pressure on students increased in various ways. The most obvious were the shift from grants to loans, and eventually the introduction of student fees. Students have increasingly earned their way through university by taking paid work in term-time as well as vacations. They have also come under other forms of pressure through library, equipment, and accommodation shortages, larger classes, and cramped conditions in university buildings.

Research too has been affected by a financial squeeze. This is the result not only of reduced state funding but also of greater competition for research money from the Higher Education Funding Council. This became more intense when the polytechnics became universities in 1992 and began to seek a share of the limited funds available. Researchers have been forced to seek funds increasingly from industry or government departments. This means that research has become more directed by the interests of outside organizations and more secretive, since they may not wish information to be disclosed to competitors or to the public.

Under these pressures, universities, like other organizations, have had to become more competitive and more flexible in their internal workings. More flexible courses have been created through modularization and credit-accumulation structures. Universities have also, like schools and many other employers, moved towards greater flexibility of employment (see Chapter 17, pp. 673–5). They have a *core* of full-time, permanent staff members, and a *periphery* of part-timers and short-term contract staff. This provides them with a 'numerical flexibility' that

enables them to respond to changes in their financial situation.

Universities, like schools, came under closer state scrutiny, as their teaching and research were audited and graded. As with schools, results have been published and league tables constructed. Funding became linked to research performance, while league table position affected student recruitment and through this the funding of teaching.

Thus, although greater competition and flexibility were introduced into higher education, there was also a tighter and more bureaucratic control by the state. Both teaching and research came under closer surveillance. The institutions of higher education had lost much of their earlier autonomy and now had to operate within a framework imposed by the state.

 New technology E-Universities?   9.9

Information and communication technology (ICT) is transforming education but can be used in many different ways. E-moderators (teachers and trainers who work with learners online) can adopt different roles. Gilly Salmon (2004: ch. 6) has sketched out four scenarios to help us think about the range of possibilities and the choices that we face. She takes us on a voyage to a new planetary system.

Planet Contenteous

On this planet 'content is king'. The latest technologies are used to make as much content as possible available to everyone. The traditional transmission model of teaching is dominant. Experts pass on their knowledge to students. Students are assessed frequently through automated testing of their ability to reproduce, comprehend, and critique the material they receive. Communication skills are at a premium, but communication is increasingly at a distance and there is little interpersonal contact between staff and students. The e-moderator combines the roles of e-librarian, e-lecturer, and e-mentor. The most successful can become media stars.

Planet Instantia

Here the key things are instantaneity and flexibility. E-learning takes place through integrated information technology devices that are available everywhere in the institution and are online all the time. Learners are concerned with whether their own particular and immediate needs are met. They ask: 'Is this learning just for me, just in time, just for now, and just enough?' Assessment is concentrated on performance in meeting work or professional needs and is integrated with learning activities. E-moderators facilitate 'autonomous learning' and focus on developing the skills this requires. They are professionals, loyal

to their organizations, and tend to have a 'human resources' background.

Planet Nomadic

This planet provides 'portable learning for mobile lifestyles'. Here wireless technology is the norm. Learning is independent of time and place. Assessment is largely through projects and outcomes, which students can choose, or at least negotiate. E-moderators are as mobile as their students. They may work for different organizations and move around the globe. They are also mobile intellectually and freely cross subject boundaries. They are enthusiasts who enjoy helping people to learn, get on well with students, and have themselves moved from e-learning to e-moderation, working when the spirit moves them.

Planet Cafelattia

Here ICT is used for the exchange of knowledge, for collaborative activities, and for community purposes. Technology does not replace social interaction but provides a means of achieving it. Academics do not have a monopoly of knowledge and there is an egalitarian spirit of sharing experiences of all kinds. There is a 'strong social context to learning' and learners 'express themselves freely'. Assessment is not performance-oriented but a means of enhancing the process of learning and takes a group or peer form. E-moderators can think globally *and* act locally. They have highly developed social skills and typically come from a background in community work or social movements.

Source: Salmon (2004: ch. 6; note that this is not in the 1st edn).

❓ Which of these planets is your institution on (or heading for)?

❓ Which would you like to inhabit?

Regulated choice under Labour

Education had been transformed by the neo-liberal policies of the Conservatives, but most of the changes they introduced were strongly opposed by the Labour Party. Would Labour government after 1997 roll back the Conservatives' reforms?

School diversity, selection, and regulation

Comprehensive schools have long been one of the battlefields of education policy. Historically, the Labour Party promoted a universal system of non-selective comprehensive schools, while the Conservatives supported diversity and selection. Things have, however, changed, and, in a famous outburst in February 2001, Alistair Campbell, the prime minister's press adviser, declared that 'the day of the bog-standard comprehensive is over', while New Labour enthusiastically pursued diversity and, in practice at least, accepted selection.

Labour endorsed the neo-liberal principle of providing choice in a competitive marketplace. There was to be no return to the 'old-labour' allocation of school places according to catchment area by the Local Education Authority. The problem with providing choice, however, was that this would almost inevitably conflict with equality of opportunity, which was a key principle of education policy. How could 'better-off' parents be prevented from using their various advantages to get their children into the 'best' schools?

This had always been a problem, even when catchment areas ruled, since the 'better-off' could buy their way into the catchment area of a favoured school. School diversity and the encouragement of choice made the problem worse. Faith schools, academies, and specialist schools were all allowed some degree of selection. More generally, any oversubscribed school—and the best schools were likely to be oversubscribed—had to select those they accepted on some basis. If schools were engaged in any kind of selection, this increased the opportunities of the 'better-off' to make their advantages count.

To counter this, the government issued detailed mandatory guidelines on school admissions. For example, oversubscribed schools could not interview children or their parents, or ask discriminatory questions on application forms. They were also not allowed to require parents to enter into agreements with the school—for example, to provide some form of financial assistance. One thorny problem was that catchment areas lived on in admissions criteria as 'priority areas'. Parents could still buy their way into a 'good' school by acquiring property in these areas. To prevent this occurring, schools were encouraged to allocate places by lottery.

Apart from all the problems of enforcing the 'admissions code' and preventing both schools and parents cheating, it cannot equalize the process through which parents *choose* schools. Simon Burgess *et al.* (2009) have shown that choice of primary school is strongly influenced by class background. Most parents (94 per cent) do get the school of their choice, but poor parents tend to pick schools near where they live, while middle-class parents are guided more by the school's academic performance, particularly in areas where there are lots of competing schools and there is plenty of choice. This is partly a matter of cost and ease of travel but also of class differences in cultural and social capital (see p. 337). All this has the effect of increasing the social segregation of schools by class.

Greater diversity has made English education in particular (for other parts of the UK see Box 9.12 on p. 342) more hierarchical than ever, with the addition of new layers below the elite public and grammar schools (164 grammar schools still existed in 2010). Specialist schools are one layer, which has been further differentiated with the creation of 'advanced specialist schools', charged with raising standards and training teachers. Another consists of city academies, which the government has been enthusiastically creating (see Box 9.10). Faith schools too have been encouraged (see Box 9.1 on p. 312). In 2006 trust schools with greater independence from local education authorities were added to this mix. A comprehensive *system*, albeit incomplete, has been replaced by a diversified hierarchy of schools, with ordinary comprehensives at the bottom.

The Labour government also went further along the path of 'parent power'. School diversification gave parents greater choice, in principle if not always in practice. Parents were given a greater role in the management of the independent trust schools created in early 2006. In February 2010 the then Prime Minister announced a plan to allow parents to trigger a ballot on a change of leadership at their children's school if they were dissatisfied with its results (*Independent*, 7 March 2010).

The process of privatizing education has continued. Labour allowed private companies to take over the management of failing schools and even some local education authorities. Many of the new schools set up by the government, such as specialist schools, city academies, and trust schools, were privately sponsored by business and religious interests. In 2009 private companies were given permission to set up schools for children excluded from state schools. School building has been financed by private finance initiatives, while services once provided by local education authorities have been increasingly provided by private agencies.

Privatization has not, however, meant any reduction in state regulation. In 1998 the government took new powers to take control of schools judged to be failing, while those that miss targets have been subject to a range of coercive

Controversy and debate Academies   9.10

City academies were launched in 2000 to replace failing secondary schools. It was claimed they would be innovative schools that would raise standards by bringing in business skills and enterprise. In 2008 the Labour government announced an increased target of 400 such schools. By May 2010, out of 3,100 secondary schools, 203 were academies.

As set up by Labour, academies were partially privatized state schools. They had to follow the national curriculum and were subject to OFSTED inspections, but sponsors had considerable discretion over the content of teaching, the employment and payment of teachers and managers, the appointment of governors, and the selection of pupils. Sponsoring organizations would provide 10 per cent of the founding costs, the rest of their funding and their running costs coming from the local authority, which would ultimately decide whether they should be set up. Thus, private sponsors could largely control schools that were still mainly state funded.

Much concern has been expressed about the character and motives of sponsors. As with faith schools (see p. 312), there were fears that religiously motivated founders would indoctrinate children. Labour policy did, indeed, shift from seeking individual entrepreneurs and philanthropists as sponsors towards a safer sponsorship by other schools, universities, and local authorities.

After the 2010 election, the new Conservative/Liberal Democrat coalition government immediately proposed an extension of the academy principle. Primary schools would be allowed to become academies. Academies were no longer to be seen as replacements for failing schools but as the normal form that schools would take. Indeed, schools with outstanding OFSTED reports would be 'fast-tracked' to academy status and were promptly invited to apply for it. The decision to create an academy would be removed from local authorities, as would their funding, which would come directly from the government.

Critics have been concerned that this would result in a two-tier system, with academies draining teachers and funds from other schools. Local links would go if the funding and control of education were further centralized in government hands. Class divisions could widen, with schools in middle-class areas rushing to enjoy the benefits of academy status.

Sources: Blakemore and Griggs (2007); *Guardian*, 7 June 2010; *Independent*, 15 October 2004, 17 October 2008; *Observer*, 6 June 2010.

❓ Does the development of academies demonstrate continuity or change in education policy?

Frontiers Educational choice Swedish style   9.11

The Conservative Party declared in 2009 that, if elected in 2010, it would allow new schools to be created on the Swedish model.

According to this model, parents are given a voucher, which they can use to buy education of their choice for their children. They can use the voucher at a state school or at one of the 900 or so 'free' schools, many of them profit-making, that have been set up in Sweden since this system was introduced in the 1990s. They can, indeed, use the voucher to set up their own school. Parents are not allowed, however, to buy entry to a chosen school and admission operates on a first-come, first-served basis until a school is full. 'Free' schools have control of their own budgets but have to teach the seventeen-subject curriculum laid down by the government.

The Conservative Shadow Schools Secretary announced in 2009 that he would like to see up to 3,000 such schools created. They would be outside local-authority control and supported by the central government to the tune of around £6,000 per pupil per year. It was initially stated that only charities and non-profit-making organizations would be allowed to create schools, but concern that too few bodies of this kind would come forward led to a reconsideration of this. Reportedly, 'dozens of parents' groups, prep schools and educational chains such as Montessori and Steiner have signed up to Tory plans to introduce a Swedish-inspired system of independent state schools' (*Sunday Times*, 18 October 2009).

Sources: *Daily Telegraph*, 26 July 2009; *Guardian*, 14 April 2008; *Independent*, 1 October 2008; *Sunday Times*, 18 October 2009.

interventions to bring them into line. The OFSTED school inspections regime has been intensified, with 'tougher' inspections leading to greater pressure on head teachers to improve results and more being sacked for failure to do so (*Independent*, 7 March 2010). In 2009 the government took new powers to control the content of qualifications, while the Secretary of State for Education was to have the right to decide which books children must study at GCSE or A-level. The 'admissions code' has imposed a very detailed regulation of school admissions procedure. There is not only a continuing preoccupation with standards but also a growing concern with behavioural problems, linked to wider public order and criminality issues (Blakemore and Griggs 2007: 145–53).

Students pay for HE expansion

Higher-education expansion continued under Labour and the participation rate of 18-year-olds had risen to 42 per cent by 2006–7 (and was higher in Scotland—see Box 9.12). This was, however, well short of Labour's target of 50 per cent. In spite of this expansion, the UK has fallen from fourth (2000) to twelfth (2008) in the OECD league table of graduation rates in thirty leading countries (*Independent*, 10 September 2008). In early 2010 the government announced an extra 20,000 places in science and related subjects, but, with cuts in the universities' teaching budget of around £215 million in 2010–11, further expansion seems unlikely, unless at the cost of teaching quality (*Guardian*, 2 February 2010).

Labour also continued to shift the funding of higher education from the taxpayer to students and their parents. It was, indeed, under Labour that the student payment of fees was introduced, with reductions and exemptions for low-earning families. The rationale for this shift was the higher earnings that graduates could command and the avoidance of increased taxation. Higher taxes would mean that lower-paid workers would be financing, through the taxes they paid, the education of people who could consequently earn considerably more than they did.

From 2006, universities (in England) were allowed to increase their fees up to £3,000 per year, this figure rising to £3,240 by 2010. Payment was made easier, since the fees could be financed by loans that are not repayable until a graduate is earning at least £15,000 per year. Universities

---

 Briefing: British education? 9.12

Although we often refer to British education, and the British government certainly has an education policy, devolution has allowed Scotland, Wales, and Northern Ireland to go their own various ways. Their divergence did not, however, start with devolution. Scotland in particular had long had its own institutions. Blakemore and Griggs (2007: 249) indeed suggest that 'much of the driving force behind support for the whole project of devolution was to preserve Scottish distinctiveness in education'. Northern Ireland had not gone through the comprehensive revolution and had kept selection at age 11. Wales was less different institutionally from England, but had preserved a cultural distinctiveness around the teaching of Welsh literature and language.

Scotland did not introduce the national curriculum brought in by the 1988 Education Act in England and Wales. Scotland has not followed other more recent English changes, such as SATS at ages 7, 11, and 14, specialist schools, and special literacy/numeracy strategies. Private companies have not been allowed to take over state schools. Performance-related pay for teachers was not brought in and there is no Scottish OFSTED. Scotland rejected up-front HE tuition fees and reintroduced means-tested grants for students. HE participation rates have been higher in Scotland, rising above 50 per cent in 2001/2, although then dropping back somewhat.

The Welsh National Assembly has less autonomy than the Scottish Parliament, but it too has refused to follow some English changes. Thus, Wales has not gone down the path of school diversification, has kept the private sector out of state schools, has no OFSTED, and has abandoned the literacy/numeracy strategies. Welsh schools do, however, follow the national curriculum. Although HE students have to pay up-front fees, means-tested maintenance grants were reintroduced in 2002.

While Northern Ireland has stood aside from school diversification, privatization, and OFSTED inspections, its starting point and issues have been rather different, because of its selective schools, and Catholic/Protestant divide. In higher education, it has not diverged from the English pattern.

Scotland and Wales especially have clearly resisted the Thatcherite and New Labour programme of moving education towards a regulated marketplace. The UK Labour government more recently showed signs of following some of their initiatives, by reintroducing means-tested maintenance grants and reducing the amount of testing in schools.

Source: Blakemore and Griggs (2007: 249–54).

charging increased fees were required to conclude an Access Agreement with the Director of the Office for Fair Access, known appropriately as OFFA, to show that they have safeguarded access for under-represented groups. In 2009 the universities floated a proposal to increase fees up to £5,000 per year, and there was talk of this figure rising to £7,000 (*Sunday Times*, 26 July 2009). The government's response was to defer a decision until the report of a review of higher education in the summer of 2010, safely after the general election.

University income depends on the success with which universities can attract students. One way of doing this is to undercut other institutions by charging lower fees, but this kind of competition has been inhibited by the fear of appearing to be a low-quality institution. Competition has instead taken place through the bursaries that universities offer students, the facilities they provide, and the effectiveness of branding and marketing. League table position has played an important role in marketing. Universities jostle for position in the student satisfaction survey and, it has been claimed, through degree-grade inflation.

There has been concern that the greater burden placed on students and their families might hold back the growth of higher education. UK applications for the year 2006/7, when top-up fees were introduced, did fall. Every year since, however, they have increased. Recession and higher unemployment no doubt had much to do with this. Applications for 2009 entry were up by 10 per cent on the previous year, and in January 2010 were up again by 22 per cent. Significantly, in January 2010 applications from the over-25s had gone up by 63 per cent, while those from 21–24-year-olds had risen by 45 per cent. There was also a 45-per-cent increase in people reapplying (*Guardian*, 9 February 2010). All this suggests that the constraints on further expansion are not fees but capacity and funding.

Continuity and change

While there are differences of emphasis and detail between Conservative and Labour education policies, the continuities are very striking. Diversity, privatization, competition, league tables, and choice have been as characteristic of Labour as of Conservative policy. Labour, like the Conservatives, both expanded higher education and transferred much of the cost of doing so from the state to students and their families. Both have combined the development of market mechanisms with increasing state regulation. Both have increased the pressure on children, students, teachers, schools, colleges, universities, and local education authorities to improve standards.

Blakemore and Griggs (2007: 153) conclude that Labour education policies should be described as 'right-wing' rather than 'left-wing', since they were closer to the Conservative policies of the 1980s than those of 'old labour'. This was perhaps most evident in Labour's abandonment of the 'old-labour' notion that state education should be based on non-selective comprehensive schools, and in the promotion of schools—academies, specialist schools, faith schools—that were inevitably selective.

This is not to say that there were no left-wing elements in Labour policy. After 2005 Labour considerably increased spending on state education. State childcare and nursery provision, which many regard as the most important means of improving educational opportunities for the poor, were significantly improved. Labour also tried to increase the access to higher education of those from poor backgrounds, particularly by putting pressure on elite universities to admit more students from state schools (Blakemore and Griggs 2007: 154).

Indeed, Labour governments placed great emphasis on increasing equality of opportunity. They here used the New Labour rhetoric of 'levelling up' and 'inclusion' (see Chapter 15, pp. 579–80). Greater equality of opportunity was to be achieved by forcing up the standards of institutions, bringing state schools up to the standards of the private sector, and raising the standards of poorly performing state schools to those of the best. New schools in the inner city would replace poorly performing ones. Pockets of illiteracy and innumeracy were to be eliminated by special policies that targeted them. The expansion of higher education would mean that more young people would be able to go to university.

The raising of standards and the widening of access may be highly desirable goals, but it is difficult to see that they will actually increase equality of opportunity, because so many other changes are operating against this:

- the increasing diversity and hierarchy of educational institutions;
- greater competition for resources and growing inequality *between* educational institutions;
- more selection placing hurdles in front of those with disadvantages;
- parental choice giving advantages to those with more knowledge and resources.

Opportunities have increased, but this does not mean that there is an increasing *equality* of opportunity. Some of those from disadvantaged backgrounds will benefit, since they can obtain educational qualifications that they would not otherwise have achieved. Those with knowledge and resources are, however, much better placed to exploit these opportunities. The possession of cultural and social capital has become more important than ever.

The overall similarity of Conservative and Labour policies points to two main conclusions. First, differences between Labour and Conservative policies have been far less than the differences between pre-1980 and post-1980 policies. As we argue in Chapter 15 (see pp. 581–2), this applies across the whole range of state policies. Secondly, education policy must be placed in the context of broader changes in economy and society. Neo-liberal beliefs in market forces, competition, and individual choice lie at the heart of the post-1980 transformation of education. The rise of neo-liberalism was itself a response to the crisis of profitability in the 1970s, increasing international competition, the growth of individualism, and a shift towards a more consumerist demand for greater choice in all spheres of life.

Stop and reflect

In this section we have examined the transformation of education since the 1980s. We first considered the changing relationship between state and economy in Britain.

- Governments have placed increasing emphasis on the economic functions of education.
- Consider the relationship between globalization and education policy.
- Do recent changes in education provide support for the approach taken by Bowles and Gintis?

We went on to examine the introduction of 'a regulated marketplace' in first schools and then higher education.

- Market principles were introduced by diminishing local-authority control, increasing competition, and providing more parental choice.

- Do these changes result in less or more state control?
- Consider the implications of these changes for patterns of inequality.

Lastly, we discussed the character of government education policy.

- The reforms of the 1980s were driven by 'neo-liberal' beliefs. Make sure that you understand the meaning of this term.
- Did the post-1997 Labour governments simply continue the policies introduced by the previous Conservative governments?
- Has the 'bog-standard' comprehensive had its day?

Key concepts

- authoritarian populism 336
- correspondence principle 316
- cultural capital 314
- cultural-deprivation theory 312
- education 310
- elaborated codes 313

- functionalism 311
- hidden curriculum 316
- meritocracy 338
- neo-liberalism 337
- new vocationalism 335
- oppositional subculture 317

- parentocracy 338
- reproduction of class 314
- reproduction of labour 316
- restricted codes 313
- social capital 315

Workshop 9

Study 9 The employability of graduates

The economy's need for more highly educated employees has become one of the truisms of education policy. Not only is it argued that a knowledge-based economy requires more and better graduates; it is also claimed that higher education is a passport to a good job and higher earnings. In *The Mismanagement of Talent*, Brown and Hesketh (2004) subjected these notions to a searching critique, supported by research into company selection practices and the experience of graduates.

They reject the idea that we now live in a knowledge-based economy. In the most advanced economy in the world, the US economy, only one-fifth of the current labour force could reasonably be described as 'knowledge workers'. In the United Kingdom the proportion of knowledge workers is probably higher and may be around one-third of the labour force, but most workers are still engaged in service or routine production work. They conclude that 'there is no prospect of the graduate labour market expanding in line with the increased supply of graduates' (Brown and Hesketh 2004: 63).

The result is inevitably an intense graduate competition for jobs. The employability of graduates is supposedly a matter of whether they have acquired the right skills and knowledge for the job, but so many applicants for any given job have these skills and knowledge that their possession does not make someone employable. Brown and Hesketh (2004: 7) argue that employability should be redefined to include what they call the realities of 'positional conflict'. Whether one secures employment depends on one's competitive position, and this is a matter of the 'personal capital' that has been accumulated.

Personal capital includes the 'hard currency' of qualifications, work experience, and other objective achievements but also the 'soft currency' of interpersonal skills, leadership qualities, appearance, and accent (Brown and Hesketh 2004: 35). Cultural and social capital (see pp. 314–16 of this chapter) are clearly of great importance here, as is the status of the educational institutions attended. In spite of their demands for better-qualified labour and their recruitment rhetoric, many companies still select on the basis of elitist criteria. The assumption is that 'the best students go to the best universities because they are the most difficult to get into' (Brown and Hesketh 2004: 219).

From their interviews with graduates, Brown and Hesketh constructed two ideal types: *players* and *purists*. Players saw the search for employment as a competitive game with rules that had to be learned and followed if one was to be successful. Purists saw this search as a technical and meritocratic process of matching abilities with job requirements in which those who were best for the job would win out. Players would present themselves in ways that enabled people to win the game, while purists would act as they really were. Players saw their work as a means of developing their career, while purists saw it as expressing their true selves. The players' approach to their career was to maximize their advancement by moving around between employers, while purists were more concerned with progression within an organization (Brown and Hesketh 2004: 125).

Interviewees did not fit these types exactly, but roughly one-third could be placed in each, with a third falling between them. Graduates falling into one type might anyway change their strategy as a result of their experience. One might expect that the players would tend to win out, but Brown and Hesketh warn that their success depends on properly understanding the rules of the game, learning to play it effectively, and convincing employers that they are genuine and not 'faking it'.

The intensification of graduate competition for jobs has broader implications for education. It creates great anxiety among the middle classes, which increases the competition for access to elite institutions at every level. One aspect of this is the ongoing debate over entry criteria to universities and the complaint that some universities, pushed by government policy, are now privileging those from state schools. Another is the greater importance attached to choice and the frantic parental manœuvring to get children into the 'best' schools.

⮞ The arguments around the growth of a knowledge-based economy are quite similar to the debate over 'post-industrial' society and you may find it helpful to read our discussion of this in Chapter 17, pp. 669–70.

❷ What aspects of the academic marketplace (see pp. 337–9) does this examination of employability highlight?

❷ Do you see yourself as a player or a purist?

Media watch 9 How do you choose a school?

Providing opportunities for parents to choose their children's schools has been a central plank of both Conservative and Labour education policies. Exercising the right to choose has, however, proved a complex business.

A new system of coordinated admissions was introduced on an experimental basis for London schools in 2004. Parents had been making multiple applications to schools in different areas and then sitting on the offers until they discovered whether their favourite school had offered a place. It was a perfectly rational thing to do, but it greatly delayed offers to other children, as the schools waited for responses to their first round of offers. This was clearly unfair to those waiting, in some cases till the beginning of the school year, to know where their child would go. The new coordinated scheme allowed parents to state a preference to their education authority for at least three schools, in rank order. A computer program would then offer a place at the highest-ranked school possible, taking account of the schools' vacancies and admissions criteria. Problem solved?

Not exactly . . . Schools want to give preference to those who have made them their first choice. Some Local Education Authorities therefore operate a first-preference system, which gives priority to those who have made a school their first choice. Surrey is one such authority. This led to a difficult situation for one family, whose predicament was described in a *Guardian* article. The family wanted to apply for a place at a prestigious grammar school, but this would mean facing the hurdle of an 11+ exam. Their second choice was a local comprehensive with a good reputation, but this was in high demand and their child might not get in if it was not their first choice. Their third choice was a much less desirable school. If they went for their first choice and their child failed the 11+, they could well end up with their third. So they felt forced to go for their second-choice school.

The first-preference system clearly made this situation particularly difficult, but there is a fundamental problem here that no system can avoid. If parents go for a first-choice school that is in high demand or is highly selective, they risk not getting a place and then having to settle for a much less desirable school than one they could otherwise have got. Choosing a school requires careful study not only of schools' qualities and achievements but also of their admissions criteria and a careful calculation of your child's chances. As Stephen Ball (2003*a*) has argued, the middle-class activation of social capital involves uncertainty and anxiety.

Source: Guardian Education, 26 October 2004.

❷ Parents are told they have choice, but who does the choosing?

❷ Which parents benefit most from parental choice?

Discussion points

Educational capital

Read the sections on 'Cultural capital' and 'Social Capital' in 'Education and inequality' and make sure that you understand their meaning.

- Why is the term 'capital' used in these concepts?
- What is the relationship between 'cultural' and 'social' capital?
- Consider whether the notion of subcultural capital is a useful extension of these ideas.

  Relate these concepts to school and university choice, as discussed in 'A regulated marketplace' and 'Regulated choice under Labour'.

- Can those with greater cultural and social capital be prevented from gaining advantages from it?

Graduate employability

Read the sections on 'Education and economic success' (p. 334), 'More higher education' (p. 338), and 'Students pay for HE expansion' (p. 342), and Media watch 9.

- Why do you think that higher education has expanded?
- What have been the consequences for the employability of graduates?
- Has higher education been over-expanded?
- What is meant by 'personal capital'? Consider its relationship to the concepts of 'cultural' and 'social' capital.
- How much personal capital do you have and how does this affect your employability?

Explore further

The following cover most of the issues dealt with in this chapter:

Apple, M., Ball, S., and Gandin, L. (2009) (eds), *The Routledge International Handbook of the Sociology of Education* (London: Routledge). *This wide-ranging reader is divided into sections on perspectives and theories, social processes and practices, and inequalities and resistances.*

Ball, S. (2004) (ed.), *The Routledge Falmer Reader in the Sociology of Education* (London: Routledge Falmer). *A personal collection of classic and contemporary texts.*

Halsey, A., Lauder, H., Brown, P., and Stuart Wells, A. (1997) (eds), *Education: Culture, Economy, and Society* (Oxford: Oxford University Press). *A comprehensive reader, which became a standard work.*

Particular topics can be followed up through:

Archer, L. (2003), *Race, Masculinity, and Schooling: Muslim Boys and Education* (Maidenhead: Open University Press). *A discussion of the complex interaction of gender and ethnicity through an analysis of the views of Muslim boys.*

Ball, S. (2003), *Class Strategies and the Education Market: The Middle Classes and Social Advantage* (London: Routledge Falmer). *A theoretically informed discussion of class strategies that draws on interviews with parents and children.*

Brown, P., and Hesketh, A. (with Williams, S.) (2004), *The Mismanagement of Talent: Employability and Jobs in the Knowledge Economy* (Oxford: Oxford University Press). *A powerful critique of the notion that mass higher education enhances employability.*

Chitty, C. (2009), *Education Policy in Britain* (2nd edn, Basingstoke: Palgrave Macmillan). *Very clear and up-to-date coverage of policy-making from 1944 to New Labour.*

Gardner, R., Cairns, J., and Lawton, D. (2004) (eds), *Faith Schools: Consensus or Conflict* (London: Routledge Falmer). *Provides different perspectives and lots of material from Britain and other countries on a hot topic.*

Illich, I. (1973), *Deschooling Society* (Harmondsworth: Penguin). *A classic critique of schooling that argues that education should not be confused with what goes on in schools.*

Jackson, C. (2006), *Lads and Ladettes in School* (Buckingham: Open University Press). *Explores how girls as well as boys adopt laddish ways of behaving in schools, linking up theories of masculinity and femininity to the sociology of education.*

Tomlinson, S. (2005), *Education in a Post-Welfare Society* (2nd edn, Buckingham: Open University Press). *A very useful account of recent educational policies and the way that they have combined centralization and competition.*

Online resources

Visit the Online Resource Centre that accompanies this book to access more learning resources and other interesting material on education at:
www.oxfordtextbooks.co.uk/orc/fulcher4e/

The Guardian Education website is a useful source of articles, special reports, and data on all aspects of education:
www.education.guardian.co.uk

The British Educational Research Association publishes the *British Educational Research Journal* (an online version is available to subscribing libraries) and organizes conferences:
www.bera.ac.uk

The website of the Department for Children, Schools, and Families provides information about government policy and funded research on education and training:
www.dcsf.gov.uk

The Sutton Trust funds research into the educational opportunities of under-privileged young people and produces important and influential reports that are available online:
www.suttontrust.com

Communication and the Media

Contents

10

Battle of the networks

Social networking sites (SNS) have been rising and falling. Friends Reunited, the one-time front-runner, was down to 1.8 million users in April 2009, after losing a quarter of them in a year. Bebo too lost a quarter of its UK users but still had 9.1 million. MySpace lost 18 per cent and was down to 6.9 million. Facebook's UK users were up 9 per cent at 29 million. Having just started up, Twitter increased its UK users forty-fold to 2.4 million.

These are free sites. Free availability has now become something of a norm. Within certain rules, users can freely generate their own profiles and attach their own photos, videos, and music. They build their own links and create their own networks. These sites appear to be a quite new phenomenon, entirely separate from the previously existing media.

But how separate and how different are they? To survive they have to make money, and the easiest way to do this is through advertising. What matters to advertisers is the number of views by users. The intense competition for users is driven by commercial pressures similar to those that operate in the world of newspapers, and commercial broadcasters.

Business models based on adverts are themselves, however, under threat, since the imposition or infiltration of ads runs against the ethos of SNS users. The effectiveness of ads is anyway doubtful, since users are more likely to rely on recommendations. Theirs is the world of TripAdvisor or comparison websites rather than pop-ups.

Arguably, the SNS can only survive by becoming part of larger media empires seeking to extend their reach. Friends Reunited was owned by ITV from 2005 to 2009, and then sold to the DC Thomson media group. Rupert Murdoch's News Corporation owns MySpace. AOL owns Bebo, and Google owns YouTube. In spite of its rapid rise to fame, it is not clear how Twitter can make money, and its financial future is uncertain. How long will it remain independent?

Source: Clark (2009).

The social networking sites and the media operate in the same commercial world but new technologies have certainly revolutionized communication. The Internet, mobile phones, and social networks can bypass 'the media' and challenge the state's control of communication. The techniques of the 'flash mob' (see Chapter 13, p. 479) can be used to assemble demonstrators. As the Iran election crisis of 2009 showed, photos and videos can be circulated and sent across frontiers to document state violence.

For most people, most of the time, the traditional media nonetheless remain the chief providers of news and entertainment. Indeed, much of the day-to-day content of the material downloaded to computer and mobile screens is sourced from them. Newspapers and broadcasters have websites that put their material on the Net, which is simultaneously a rival medium and a means of extending their reach. Political leaders may have blogged, tweeted, or joined Facebook, but they have not abandoned the television studios or cut their links to the editors of national newspapers.

We live in a media-saturated world. What influence do the media have on the way we feel, think, and act? A lot of research has gone into trying to answer this question, and we discuss in this chapter the issues that it raises. Who determines the content of the media and the messages they transmit? Is it the journalists, the editors, or the corporations? Or are they all simply trying to give us what we want in order to maximize audiences and sales?

It is, furthermore, not only the Net that is new. The traditional media themselves have been transformed. There is now a bewildering amount of choice, as terrestrial, satellite, and cable delivery systems provide us with hundreds of channels. But is this sense of choice illusory? Do we choose or are choices made for us? We consider whether governments manipulate the flow of information, and whether commercialization distorts media content.

Communications have also become global. Does this mean that national cultures are disappearing? Is the culture of the United States, the main exporter of films and television programmes, becoming *the* global culture? Or does the culture of the audience force producers to take account of the local? Later in the chapter we examine the globalization of the media and its impact on cultural diversity.

Concepts and theories

Before discussing these issues, we first need to be clear about the connections between communication, language, and the media. The term 'media' is widely used in a taken-for-granted way and it is important to be clear about what it means. We then go on to consider theories of the reationship between the media and society, and between media and culture. This leads us to examine the central issue raised by the study of the media, the way they influence people and the degree to which they do this.

Communication and language

Animals communicate, but only humans communicate through language. The distinctive feature of language is that words carry meanings, which we learn initially through socialization and education. Communication through language depends upon these meanings being shared.

We also communicate in many non-verbal ways, through, for example, body language, but the same processes of attaching and learning meaning apply. Thus, we learn that the 'thumbs-up' sign means that 'things are OK'. We communicate through images too. A holiday snap can communicate our well-being on holiday and inform people that we have been somewhere fashionable. The term 'image' has, indeed, been extended to mean not just a representation of something but also the impression of ourselves that we communicate to others. We create an image through the style we adopt. The clothes that we wear communicate a great deal about us (see Box 10.1). These non-verbal ways of communication carry learned and shared meanings and may also be considered languages.

Languages are much more than a means of communication, for they also express and shape the way that we see the

---

Frontiers Communication through dress 10.1

One way in which we communicate our identity is through dress, and the structuring of this communication tells us a lot about a society. In some communities there are rigid dress codes that allow no individuality and require complete conformity. Religious communities have operated codes of this kind, and examples such as the *burqa* or the 'habit' readily spring to mind.

Religious dress codes may appear totally resistant to change, but some religious communities have allowed greater choice of religious dress as they adapt to social change. Free choice of dress to express personal identity is indeed seen as a characteristic feature of the more complex world we now live in, though codes still operate. William Keenan (2004: 55) suggests that the result is a 'dual dress economy':

> To survive within and pass successfully through the differentiated and multiple cultural environments we inhabit today we need to

be able to adapt our dress code responses. The idea that we have at least two wardrobes, that we inhabit a dual dress economy, where a formal and a casual option is available to us, where classical and modern items mix and mingle as a matter of course within our dressways, could be said to be the characteristic message given out by the postmodern dress code system.

❷ What does what you are wearing today communicate about your identity and your community?

❷ What processes and influences shaped your choice of clothing?

❷ What does your choice of dress say about the kind of community/society you live in?

world and the way that we see ourselves. If you say that you are British, you are not just stating which country you live in. This presupposes a way of seeing the world that divides it up between nation states. It indicates that you see yourself as British, rather than, say, English or Scottish, and carries with it ideas of national character. The importance of language is not only that it allows us to communicate, but also that it gives us an identity. Without it we would not know who we are.

Communication occurs not only through face-to-face interaction but also through various forms of recorded and transmitted images and sounds. These means of communication are generally termed the **media** (note that this is the plural of medium), because they mediate between those who give information and those who receive it. We usually use the term to refer to television, newspapers, and radio, sometimes films, but there are many other means of communication, such as paintings, books, or graffiti, which all mediate between people providing and people receiving information. The Internet is a particularly interesting medium, because the user-generated content of Web 2.0, from Wikipedia to social networking sites, blurs the distinction between those providing information and those receiving it.

The media and society

The media are central to the way our society functions. Newspapers, radio, and television are the principal means through which people obtain information. Indeed, if the media do not cover an event or an issue, it is unlikely that anyone other than those immediately involved would know anything about it. The media not only inform us selectively about events; they shape them. Politicians or public relations agencies or advertisers construct 'media events' in ways that will maximize their coverage by the media and create images of a favourable kind.

The media play a key role in cultural, economic, and political activities. They largely create popular culture. They are crucial to the functioning of the economy because of their role in the marketing of goods and services. Politicians use them to manipulate voters, and elections may well be won or lost through them. Indeed, one of the

What does the wearing of the *burqa* communicate?
© Getty Images/Yoray Liberman

first things that the leaders of any revolution or military *coup* will do is to seize control of the radio and television studios.

The relationship between the media and society has been discussed from a number of perspectives and in this section we examine the main approaches that have emerged.

Manipulation and domination

The development of technology enabled the media to reach ever larger numbers of people, at first through newspapers but then more particularly through radio and television, which could broadcast messages to huge audiences simultaneously. The media became **mass media** in the sense that they could reach the broad masses of the population.

The notion of 'mass' is not, however, just a descriptive term but carries with it a particular perspective on the character of industrial society, which sees it not as divided by organized classes or communities but as a mass of individuals. Industrialization and urbanization had atomized society, which had become a mass of isolated individuals after traditional community and family structures disintegrated. Social isolation meant that people were particularly open to influence by the media (see Figure 10.1).

Nineteenth-century theorists, such as Pareto and Mosca (see Chapter 20, p. 791), had distinguished between the elite and the masses. During the 1930s and 1940s, the Frankfurt school (see p. 356), followed later by Kornhauser (1960), were much concerned with the dangers of political manipulation of the masses. Fascist leaders, such as Hitler and Mussolini, had been very skilful at using the media to mobilize and control people. As Strinati (1995: 5) has put it, mass-society theorists believed that 'mass media equalled mass propaganda equalled mass repression'.

> ### ⊃ *Connections*
> Louis Wirth's notion of an 'urban way of life', which we discuss in 'Urban society', Chapter 13, pp. 475–6, embodied ideas very similar to those of **mass-society** theory. He argued that the decline of community led to social disintegration and instability in the city.

They also believed that the rise of a 'culture industry' would result in the creation of a standardized and commercialized mass culture, a view of culture that we discuss further on pp. 355–6.

The **dominant-ideology** approach too saw the media as highly influential, though it held a very different view of the nature of society (see also our discussion of this in Chapter 20, p. 794). It rejected the idea that industrialization and urbanization produced a mass of isolated and disorganized individuals and drew from Marxist theory the notion of a society divided into classes. It argued that *subordinate* classes are dominated by the ideas and beliefs of a *ruling* class. In Marx's famous words (1845–6: 93): 'The ideas of the ruling class are, in every age, the ruling ideas: i.e. the class, which is the dominant *material* force in society, is at the same time its dominant *intellectual* force.' This approach to the media has been much influenced by the ideas of Antonio Gramsci, who was critical of the economic determinism of some Marxists and argued that they failed to recognize the role of ideas in class domination and class conflict. According to Gramsci, the ruling class maintained its authority not just by coercion but by establishing hegemony. By **hegemony** he meant the ideological domination of society by the ruling class, which persuaded other classes to accept its values and beliefs so that a general

Figure 10.1 Mass-society theory

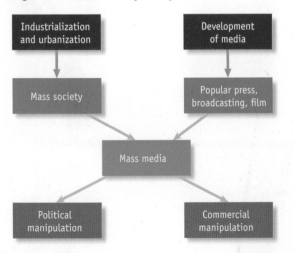

> ### THEORY AND METHODS   10.2
> ....
>
> ### *Antonio Gramsci*
>
> Antonio Gramsci (1891–1937) was born in Sardinia. He studied at the University of Turin but left to become a socialist journalist. He was closely associated with the factory-councils movement of the Turin workers, which sought to establish a system of direct industrial democracy. He was one of the founders of the Italian Communist Party in 1924 and was arrested because of his political activities in 1926. He died in prison in 1937. It was during his years in prison that he wrote his major work, *Prison Notebooks*. Unlike most Marxist theorists, he developed his ideas not in a university context but out of his practical experience of political work. His most well-known contribution to Marxist theory is the concept of hegemony. An introduction to his work can be found in Ransome (1992).

consensus emerged around them. According to Gramsci, the reason why socialist and communist movements had failed was that the ruling class had won the battle of ideas. A revolutionary movement could not succeed unless it first challenged the hegemony of the ruling class and wrested the control of ideas from it.

Miliband (1969) spelled out the ways in which the ruling class was able to control people's ideas through the media. These were largely in private ownership, which was concentrated in a few hands. The owners of the media were not only major capitalists in their own right but also closely connected with ruling circles. They used their control of the media to support right-wing parties by presenting ruling-class interpretations of events and preventing the discussion of alternative interpretations.

More generally, it has been argued that the media play a key part in getting people to accept inequality, for they gain most of their knowledge of the world from the media, which treat inequality as a normal, natural, and inevitable fact of life. The media also divert people's attention from the exploitation and inequality characteristic of capitalist society by glorifying and encouraging consumption (Murdock and Golding 1977).

But how dominant is the dominant ideology? There is a tension in this approach between the notion of a dominant ideology and the idea that subordinate classes have their own beliefs, which can contest dominant ideas (J. Clarke *et al.* 1976). Abercrombie *et al.* (1979) argued that the importance of such an ideology has been exaggerated, that capitalism is maintained primarily by what Marx called the 'dull compulsion of economic relations'. Workers accept capitalism because they have no real choice. They have to work in order to live, and it is the capitalist economy that provides them with employment. Their beliefs have little to do with it.

Is the idea of a dominant ideology anyway still relevant in the age of the Internet? This, especially in its Web 2.0 forms (see Box 10.3), has arguably democratized discourse by making it possible for ordinary people to escape media domination and make their own voices heard.

David Beer and Roger Burrows (2007: 3.7) query, however, the 'rhetoric of democratization'. Who actually participates in Web 2.0 activities? Which voices get heard 'above the din that is Web 2'? What new hierarchies and social divisions have emerged in this new world? What commercial interests are financing it and exploiting it? As we argued in our opening piece, Web 2, however different it may appear to be, operates in the same commercial world as the traditional media.

Consumption and production

Both mass-society and Marxist theory assumed that the content of the media is shaped by those who produce it. This ultimately means those who own and control the

---

 New technology Net and Web 10.3

The 'Net'

- The Internet is a network of interconnected computers.
- Its origins lay in a military network developed in the United States in the 1960s.
- After technical developments in the 1970s, the Internet was established in the 1980s to transmit information between American universities and laboratories.

The 'Web'

- The World Wide Web is a network of interlinked files accessed via the Net. The Hyper Text Transfer Protocol (http) comprises the rules that enable their transmission between computers.
- The World Wide Web was created by Tim Berners-Lee in 1990, while he was working at the Cern European Particle Physics laboratory in Geneva.
- The invention at the University of Illinois of an easy-to-use web browser called Mosaic, later to become Netscape Navigator, resulted in the rapid expansion of the Web after 1993.

'Web 2.0'

- The term Web 2 was invented in 2004 to describe a new version, which allows users to contribute and share content, instead of simply browsing existing sites.
- 'Wikis', such as Wikipedia, allow users to contribute and edit material on web pages, which provide a history of editing changes.
- 'Folksonomies', notably flickr and Youtube, create networks of web pages through tagging, so that searches can find pages labelled with a particular tag.
- Social Networking Sites—for example, MySpace and Facebook—enable users to create a profile of themselves with links to networks that can be used to arrange meetings and get-togethers (see pp. 499–500).

Sources: Berners-Lee (2000); Gauntlett (2000b); Beer and Burrows (2007).

means of production, though journalists and programme producers, do have a degree of autonomy. They are professionals with their own values and their own occupational associations. The media do depend on creative people with specialized occupational skills. An understanding of media content requires the study of those who actually produce it, as in Tunstall's classic study (1971) of journalists at work.

Tunstall recognized, however, that professionals work under constraints. They have to operate within the organizations that employ them. They are controlled by editors, who are ultimately controlled by owners. Their careers depend on the approval of others and they are in competition with colleagues. They are also dependent on those who provide them with information (Tunstall 1995). At most, they have a very limited autonomy.

An alternative approach argues that the content of the media is determined by consumers. Thus, the content of, say, newspapers, is shaped not by their owners but by the readers who buy them. Newspapers and broadcasters are ultimately concerned with circulation and audience figures. According to this approach, the market rules and the media will serve up whatever the consumer wants.

The problem here is to explain why the readers hold the views they do, since this approach takes these views as given. It also treats those who own and control the media as passive, when there is plenty of evidence that many of them hold strong opinions and see the media as vehicles for their interests and beliefs. It is, nonetheless, true that most media operations have to make profits and cannot afford to alienate readers or audiences. The market at least constrains the production of content.

Production and consumption certainly interacted in the mass media, but they were clearly separated processes. Internet consumers have become increasingly active in production. In the world of Web 2.0 (see Box 10.3 on p. 353), it is no longer easy to make the distinction between production and consumption. Users simultaneously produce and consume. They construct the product by providing information or videos or photos or links at the same time as they use the service.

As Beer and Burrows (2007: 3.2) have put it:

Perhaps the key-defining feature of Web 2.0 is that users are involved in processes of production and consumption as they generate and browse online content, as they tag and blog, post and share. Indeed, it is the mundane personal details posted on profiles, and the connections made with online 'friends', that become *the* commodities of Web 2.0. It is the profile, the informational archive of individuals' everyday lives, that draws people into the network and which encourages individuals to make 'friends'.

The content of Web 2 is at least provided by the users. In this respect it is radically different from the traditional media. In providing the content of Web 2, the users are, however, unwittingly carrying out unpaid casual labour for essentially money-making commercial operations. There is also the issue of who owns the information provided by users. Facebook users challenged Facebook on this when Facebook put into its 'terms and conditions' its right to make any use it chose of user information and to prevent users from deleting it.

A public sphere?

The autonomy not only of media professionals but also of a public sphere has been an important issue in the study of the media. The concept of a **public sphere** refers to a space where people can freely discuss matters of general importance to them as citizens. The eighteenth-century idea of human rights, especially the right to vote, and the rights to free speech and free assembly, was crucial in establishing this notion.

Jürgen Habermas developed an influential theory of the development and decline of the public sphere. He saw this as first emerging in eighteenth-century coffee houses, where people of all kinds could meet and freely discuss any matter in a non-commercial atmosphere, uncontrolled by church or state. He considered that the rise of commercialized and manipulative mass media led to the decline of the public sphere. This contrast was, however, overdrawn. The coffee houses were hardly accessible to the public as a whole, while the mass media do in various ways allow for the discussion of matters of public interest. In Britain, the BBC was established within a public-service framework, and public-service ideals remain influential in British broadcasting. Habermas's ideas have, nonetheless, struck a chord among those concerned with the decline of the public functions of the media (Boyd-Barrett 1995).

The relationship between the state and the public sphere has been a complex one. The public sphere needs protection from commercial pressures if it is to flourish, and such protection depends on state regulation. The state is in other ways, however, an enemy of the public sphere, for governments seek to control or manipulate the content of the media and turn them into an instrument of government. The public sphere needs protection from the state as well. The BBC has had an uneasy relationship with governments, and, as we shall show later, its ideal of public service has at times appeared to mean service to the state.

The public sphere has also been encroached upon by private matters. Media space and time have become increasingly taken up with material from private life, which pushes out the discussion of public affairs. While commercial pressures have largely driven this, politicians and other public figures have used the media to project their personalities and families. Media revelations can, however, do considerable damage to public figures, who have called for privacy legislation to regulate unwelcome media intrusions.

Social networking sites (SNS) fill the public sphere with private matters. Indeed, arguably the distinction between the public and the private has broken down in these sites, which distribute private information to all and sundry. The extensive flow of private material into SNS, particularly Facebook, has not been inhibited by the risk of dangerous revelations or malicious use of personal information (Beer and Burrows 2007: 3.4).

We return to these issues on pp. 361–3 and in the section on 'Decline of the public sphere?', pp. 378–82.

The media and culture

Culture has been central to the issues that we have been discussing. If the media shape the way that people think and live, they do it largely through their impact on popular culture. In this section we will examine what we mean by this term and the main approaches to it, but we first need to set it in the context of the development of different kinds of culture.

Folk, high, and popular culture

The distinction between **folk culture** and **high culture** originated with pre-industrial society, where there was a *high* culture of the aristocratic elite that was separate from the *folk* or *low* culture of the ordinary people. Folk culture consisted of local customs and beliefs that were handed down by word of mouth from one generation to the next. While high culture was associated with the arts, folk culture was associated with crafts.

With industrialization and urbanization, a new, increasingly commercialized culture emerged. It was a mixture of elements of the old folk culture and the new way of life in the industrial cities. It affected the content of the media, as they sought larger circulations and audiences, but it was in turn shaped by media influences. This new form of culture came to be called **popular culture**.

While the term 'popular culture' is widely used, it is not easy to specify what it means. Three different meanings are commonly found:

- *That which is not high culture.* This elitist way of defining popular culture assumes that we know what high culture is and implies that popular culture is inferior. Even within its own terms it is difficult to apply, for the boundaries between the two are hard to establish, and particular items of culture move across them. Thus, Shakespeare and Dickens originally provided popular entertainment but are now treated by many as high culture.

- *What most people like and do.* This raises the issue of how popular a cultural trait has to be in order to be classified as popular. Pop songs are commonly

regarded as part of popular culture, but the latest fashion in rock music may not actually be at all popular in this sense. The notion of a culture of the majority does not, anyway, fit easily with the diversity of culture, which varies, for example, by class and ethnicity.

- *Culture created by the people.* This gets round the problem of how popular something needs to be in order to be part of popular culture. Folk music, pigeon-fancying, train-spotting, and rugby league—the list is endless—can all be regarded as popular in this sense, even if they are all minority interests. But does pop music originate from the people or from recording studios funded by transnational corporations? The notion of 'the people' is, anyway, more than a little vague. Does it include the middle class?

The distinction between popular and high culture is rejected by post-modernists. They do not distinguish between different kinds of culture, but treat all its manifestations as equal, and combine them freely. Plentiful evidence of the mixing and interpenetration of cultural styles can certainly be found in contemporary culture, whether in architecture, cinema, or advertising. As Strinati (1995) points out, this does not mean, however, that these distinctions no longer have any meaning. Indeed, post-modernists' jokey references to high culture actually presume its existence, since they would otherwise be pointless. 'Rather than dismantling the hierarchy of aesthetic and cultural taste, post-modernism erects a new one, placing itself on top' (Strinati 1995: 242).

> **⊙ Connections**
>
> We are referring to post-modern culture here, but there is a broader post-modern perspective in contemporary thought and sociological theory, which is discussed in Chapter 2, pp. 61–3.

Mass culture, dominant culture, and subcultures

According to mass-society theory, which we examined above, popular culture is **mass culture**. The 'genuine' folk culture of the people was destroyed by a highly commercialized and standardized mass culture, which also undermined the standards of high culture.

Theodor Adorno and Max Horkheimer, prominent members of the Frankfurt school, used the term 'culture industry' to describe the production of mass culture (Adorno and Horkheimer 1986). Culture had become something that was made and sold, just like any other industrial product, in order to make a profit. It was, according to this view, forced on the masses by the culture industry and turned people into passive consumers of material that did not meet their 'real needs'. Hollywood,

THEORY AND METHODS   10.4
···

The Frankfurt school

The Frankfurt school is the name given to a group of left-wing thinkers associated with the Frankfurt Institute of Social Research. Founded in 1922, the institute moved to New York during the Nazi period, returned to Frankfurt in 1949, and was disbanded in 1969. Theodor Adorno (1903–69), Erich Fromm (1900–80), Max Horkheimer (1895–1973), and Herbert Marcuse (1898–1979) were prominent members of the school. Jürgen Habermas (1929–) has continued to develop their ideas.

The Frankfurt school found much of its inspiration in the work of the young Karl Marx on alienation (see Chapter 2, p. 29, for a discussion of this concept). It emphasized the way that the culture industry integrated workers into a capitalist society. The growth of mass consumption gave capitalist societies more stability, though there were still crisis tendencies in capitalism. Habermas (1973) has produced an influential theory of a sequence of crises that spread from the economic through the political to the cultural sphere.

which members of the Frankfurt school experienced during their Second World War exile in the United States, was a prime example of the culture industry.

Mass culture was also crucial to the maintenance of a capitalist society. Workers were willing to accept boredom and exploitation at work because they could escape during their leisure hours into the pleasures of popular culture, by watching films or listening to popular music. This overwhelmingly negative view of the commercialization of culture has, however, been rejected by the 'culture-industries' approach, which questioned its monolithic treatment of cultural production and viewed this as much more diverse and contested (Hesmondhalgh 2007: 17).

A debate between elitist and populist interpretations of popular culture has run through the literature. The elitist view valued the high culture of the arts and treated popular culture as commercial and trivial. Populist views, on the other hand, recognized the vitality and creativity of popular culture and argued that it expressed the experience of ordinary people. They saw popular culture as authentically rooted in subcultures related to ethnicity or class.

Subcultures are the cultures of particular groups within society. The term is generally used to refer to youth cultures or the cultures of subordinate classes. The concept of subculture implies the existence of a dominant culture, a notion similar to that of dominant ideology, which we discussed above.

Some Marxist writers have seen subcultures based in subordinate classes as resisting the **dominant culture** and, potentially at least, challenging the social order. Thus, the subcultures that emerged among the young in the working class and middle class in the 1960s were described as 'counter-cultures' (Clarke *et al.* 1976). The 1960s styles of the 'mods', 'teds', and 'skinheads' were interpreted as challenges to the dominant culture (Hebdige 1979). A slightly more recent example would be 'punk'. As we noted in our discussion of the dominant-ideology approach, there is a tension in this literature between the idea that a dominant culture is imposed by the ruling class and the possibility of subcultural resistance to it.

This discussion situates the analysis of culture within the framework of class relationships in a capitalist society and enables us to make important links between the structure of a society and its culture. It helps us to understand not only the content of culture but also how the existing structure of a society can be both maintained and periodically challenged through culture.

It also, however, neglects those aspects of culture linked to gender and ethnicity, and the complexity of the relationship between dominance and resistance in subcultures. 'Hip-hop' and 'Rap' provide an interesting example of subcultural resistance along the ethnicity dimension. It has been claimed that rap music is a 'cultural response to historic oppression and racism, a system for communication among black communities throughout the United States' (Wikipedia, entry on hip-hop, January 2010). But, in the hostile attitudes towards homosexuality expressed by many rap artists, it can arguably be seen as incorporating some aspects of the dominant culture. Or should this be interpreted as resisting tolerant strands in that same culture? The same applies to attitudes towards women. Like other forms of subcultural resistance, rap has also been deradicalized, commercialized, and exploited by business corporations in the music industry.

Cyberculture

The Internet and the World Wide Web have provided a new medium for culture, generally labelled **cyberculture**, because it exists in cyberspace, 'the conceptual space where computer networking hardware, network software and users converge' (Gauntlett 2000*b*: 220).

The Internet and the Web made possible a culture apparently free of many of the constraints that operated in other media. The Web was decentralized and outside the control of governments, elites, and business corporations. Information could be freely exchanged without anyone censoring or editing it. When on the Net, people were anonymous and could assume, and play with, any identity they chose. With others they could construct their own virtual communities, their own society, their own world. They were free of their relationships, their communities, even their bodies.

Sherry Turkle (1997) argues that they can become 'free of themselves'. They are no longer constrained by a 'unified self' and can be many different selves, exploring instead of suppressing those parts of their personality that do not fit their dominant identity. In a world of screens, this virtual world can become more real to people than the 'real world' and can shape their behaviour in the 'real world'. Aspects of identity developed in the virtual world can form the basis for relationships in the 'real world'.

> **➔ Connections**
> We discuss virtual communities in Chapter 13, pp. 499–500, and you might like to follow up these issues there.

Marginalized groups that have difficulty in asserting or even maintaining their particular cultures can communicate and rebuild their worlds through cyberculture. Dispersed minorities and deviant groups that find it hard to make their voices heard can establish a presence there, develop their specific culture, and create a virtual community.

With the growth of what Silver (2000) has labelled 'critical cyberculture studies', the celebration of cyberculture has, however, been moderated by a growing awareness of its limitations. Many familiar constraints are at work behind the scenes.

The inequalities found in society at large are present in the world of the Internet too. The rapid rise in the numbers of those using the Internet led people to view cyberculture as a new popular culture, but there is plentiful evidence of a 'digital divide' between 'haves' and 'have-nots'. The digital divide in the United States has been described as a 'racial ravine', while cyberspace has also been considered a predominantly male space, with a typically male 'frontier culture' (Silver 2000: 26–7). This divide has been magnified by the emergence of a 'technopower spiral', with the introduction of advanced tools intelligible only to a technically competent elite (Jordan 1999: 101).

Nor is cyberculture free of commercial and political pressures. Commercial pressures are blatantly present in the pop-up advertising that finances so much 'free' activity. Commercial interests also steer and manipulate users in covert ways (see p. 381 of this chapter and the discussion of Web surveillance in Chapter 14, p. 550–2). Governments can find ways of censoring Web content, as in the pressure exerted by the government of China on Microsoft and Google (see Box 10.20, p. 382).

This raises the broad question of quite how different cyberculture is from other cultural media. That it is different to some degree is undeniable. It does provide opportunities for individuals and groups to engage in cultural exploration in a *relatively* unconstrained way. Cyberculture is by no means immune, however, from the social processes of manipulation, domination, and commercialization that operate in society at large and shape culture in general.

Media influence and the audience

Much of this literature assumes that the media have considerable influence on what people think and do. How much influence they have has, however, been extensively debated and researched. In this section we first examine theories of the influence of the media and then go on to the main methods used in the study of their influence.

Models of media influence

Three main approaches to the influence of the media can be found:

- the media-effects model;
- the active-audience model;
- the media-themes model.

Also known as the 'hypodermic model', the *media-effects* approach assumes that audiences are passive and simply absorb injections of material from the media. It is characteristic of mass-society theory, some Marxist theories, and those who blame the media for the ills of society. Its view of the audience as passive has been challenged by the second model.

According to the *active-audience* model, audiences do not simply receive messages from the media. They select what they want to hear and interpret media messages according to their existing ideas and beliefs. To put it in a nutshell, they hear what they want to hear and see what they want to see. In which case, the media tend to reinforce rather than change people's views.

Research on audience response has shown that people do not just absorb representations. They often identify with film and television characters in unexpected ways. A study of responses to westerns showed that some Native Americans rejected them and criticized the portrayal of 'Indians', but others actually identified with the Indian-hating John Wayne because they appreciated the freedom of the cowboy way of life. Audience members can also identify with minor or deviant characters, or select aspects of a character, say beauty or strength, to identify with. They can interpret and reconstruct characters to suit their particular needs and fantasies (Eldridge *et al.* 1997).

While the active audience model's emphasis on selection and interpretation provided a healthy correction to the previous notion of influential and all-powerful media, it went in some ways to the opposite extreme by exaggerating the freedom and choice of the audience. The *media-themes* model pursues more of a middle path. This is the approach advocated by the Glasgow University Media Group (GUMG) and developed through its studies of television news. It recognizes that audiences are active but argues that the media do, nonetheless, influence them. In many ways it combines the insights of the other two approaches.

The GUMG found that the themes of media reporting corresponded closely with the ideas of audience groups. This was a matter not just of the main arguments in a programme but also of subtler themes in the language used and the images created. Indeed, members of the audience might reject opinions that did not fit their pre-existing beliefs but still pick up ideas and images that affect their view of the topic.

Media influence was then reinforced by social interaction. Thus, striking events or stories acquired 'social currency' and were passed around in conversation, which reinforced them in people's minds. The GUMG studies have shown how perceptions of key social issues, such as those surrounding AIDS, child abuse, food panics, mental illness, sexual violence, strikes, and the conflict in Northern Ireland, were influenced in this way by media coverage (Eldridge 1993a). (See also Media watch 10.)

The GUMG has brought the idea of media influence back in, but its model of it is much more complex than the media-effects one. It recognizes that audiences are selective and interpretative but argues that audience activity actually increases media influence by involving the audience's interest and emotions. An active response is far more likely to result in something being carried away from a programme, discussed with others, and incorporated into ways of thinking and acting.

Approaches to media research

Methods issues have been quite central to the debate over media influence, for different approaches have tended to use different methods. Here we will briefly consider the four main methods used:

- content analysis;
- textual analysis;
- audience research;
- production research.

Early approaches focused on *content analysis*. Typically this involved quantitative studies of how often a particular item was covered by the media. These could establish the extent of a topic's coverage, and certain basic aspects of it—whether it was covered, for example, in news reports, editorials, or commentaries. It could provide useful information on, say, how often strikes were reported in newspapers or on television.

There are two main problems with this approach. There is, first, the problem of meaning, for researchers are interested not just in how a topic is covered but in the slant of the coverage. It is not just a matter of how often a newspaper covers strikes but also of how it reports and interprets them. Does it adopt a managerial or a union perspective? A purely quantitative analysis of content cannot tell us this. There is, secondly, the problem of effect. Content analysis cannot tell us anything about how a given article or programme actually affects the audience.

The problem of meaning has been addressed by the more qualitative techniques of *textual analysis* (see also our discussion of discourse analysis in Chapter 6, p. 196). This approach drew on the techniques developed to analyse literary texts. It was also influenced by semiotics, the study of the meaning of signs, and is sometimes called the semiotic approach. It sought to penetrate behind words and images to uncover their meaning. The words or pictures used in reporting a strike could, for example, present a managerial account by emphasizing the stoppage of work and the loss of production. Alternatively, they could present a union perspective by focusing on workers' grievances. Through careful analysis of the text, its meaning could be revealed and its bias identified.

Important as this approach was because of its capacity to uncover deeper meanings, it lacked objectivity. The researcher had to make assumptions about the meaning of

---

THEORY AND METHODS   10.5

Audience understandings of AIDS

The GUMG study of media influence on the knowledge and understanding of AIDS showed the importance of both the words and the pictures used by the media, and the associations created by media coverage.

- *Words*. Content analysis showed that the media made frequent reference to 'mixing bodily fluids' and the 'exchange of bodily fluids'. Audience research found that these words had stuck in people's minds and led them to fear that kissing could cause AIDS through contact with saliva, even though scientists had rejected this idea.

- *Pictures*. Media coverage often showed AIDS sufferers looking thin, haggard, and depressed. This image too stuck in some people's minds and led them to think that this appearance would enable them to recognize people with the AIDS virus. This undermined the health-education message that people with this virus can look quite normal for many years before they develop AIDS symptoms.

- *Associations*. Much of the early media coverage associated AIDS with homosexuality. There was little reference to lesbians, but this association led people to think wrongly that lesbians were a high-risk group.

Source: Adapted from Kitzinger (1997: 6–11).

➲ Consider the news coverage of Africa or terrorism or Islam and see whether you can identify similar patterns of influence.

the text, which other researchers might interpret differently. Would ordinary readers or viewers interpret it in the same way? The focus on *text* is also not so appropriate to broadcast media, where communication is through *talk*, often characterized by interaction between broadcasters and interviewees or audiences. Here the techniques of conversation analysis can be applied (Hutchby 2006). There is also yet again the problem of effect. Textual analysis cannot, on its own, tell us anything about the impact of the text on the audience.

To find out about this, it was necessary to carry out *audience research*. A commonly used method for doing this was to show a programme to an audience and assess its effect by making before and after comparisons. While this approach could provide evidence of effect, it ran into other problems of its own:

- *The research situation*. The audience was put into a contrived situation. Would they react to the programme in the same way outside this laboratory situation?

- *Long-term effects*. Studies of this kind could not get at the long-term and cumulative effects of exposure to the media. Do people gradually build up a way of looking at things through repeated exposure to a particular perspective?

- *The social context of influence*. Such studies could not take account of the way that audience ideas changed after they had discussed a programme with others.

All research methods have advantages and disadvantages. Thus, in spite of its limitations, *content analysis* has

a vital contribution to make. It is a starting point that can identify issues for audience research by mapping media coverage of a topic. It can perform an auditing function by dealing with such questions as whether the media report on events in a balanced way, giving equal time or space, for example, to the views of different political parties. Barrie Gunter (2008: 9) calls it 'a cornerstone of our knowledge about the impact of the media'. John Robertson (2007) demonstrates its usefulness in his analysis of the content of television news.

Audience research, whatever its problems, is, however, the only way of addressing the question of media effects. It has also become more sophisticated in order to deal with the problems raised above. The GUMG, for example, has developed discussion-group techniques and script-writing exercises in order to probe into longer-term effects and examine the social context of media influence (Kitzinger 1997).

While research has focused mainly on the content of the media and its reception by audiences, these need to be set in the broader context of the wider society. Under what financial, political, and technical constraints is the content of the media produced? This leads back to the issues of ideological domination and cultural production, which we examined above (see pp. 352–6), and their relationship to state, economy, and class structure.

The link between the wider society and the content of the media is the process of production and this is where *production research* comes in (Cottle 2003). If the content of the media is to be explained, it is not enough to refer simply to the structure of the wider society or the dynamics of capitalist industrialism. What goes on in studios or

What techniques should be used to research talk shows?

© Getty Images/Dan Kitwood

editorial offices? How, for example, is the news constructed (see our discussion of this on p. 364 and in Media watch 10 at the end of this chapter)? Observational techniques can be used to examine the actual process of programme production, and conversation analysis can show how interviews, debates, and audience participation are structured by broadcasters. The study of content and audience needs to be complemented by production research.

 Stop and reflect

In this section we first examined different approaches to the study of the relationship between media and society.

- We discussed the concepts of 'mass media' and 'mass society', and the alternative 'dominant-ideology' approach.

- Do these approaches exaggerate the extent to which people are manipulated by the media?

- Make sure that you are familiar with Habermas's concept of the public sphere.

- What are the main threats to the functioning of such a sphere?

We then examined different types of culture.

- Make sure that you know the meaning of the following terms: high and folk culture; popular culture and mass culture; post-modern culture; dominant culture and subculture; cyberculture.

- Does cyberculture enable freedom of communication?

Finally, we identified models of media influence and examined methods of media research.

- We identified the 'media-effects', 'active-audience', and 'media-themes' models of media influence.

- We examined the 'content-analysis', 'textual-analysis', audience-research, and production research methods of media study.

- Which method would you use to investigate the media coverage of terrorism?

The rise of the mass media

Industrial societies not only produce and distribute goods and services; they also produce and distribute information and entertainment. Industrialization not only led to mass production; it also created mass media. In this part of the chapter we will examine the growth of these media and situate this within the development of a capitalist industrial society.

The print revolution

The earliest known book was printed in China in the year 868, and metal type was in use in Korea at the beginning of the fifteenth century, but it was in Germany around the year 1450 that a printing press using movable metal type was invented.

Capitalism turned printing from an invention into an industry. Right from the start, book printing and publishing were organized on capitalist lines. The biggest sixteenth-century printer, Plantin of Antwerp, had twenty-four printing presses and employed more than a hundred workers. Only a small fraction of the population was literate, but the production of books grew at an extraordinary speed. By 1500 some twenty million volumes had already been printed (Febvre and Martin 1976).

The immediate effect of printing was to increase the circulation of hand-written works that were already popular, while less popular works went out of circulation. Publishers were interested only in books that would sell fairly quickly in sufficient numbers to cover the costs of production and make a profit. Thus, while printing enormously increased access to books by making cheap, high-volume production possible, it also reduced choice.

The great cultural impact of printing was that it facilitated the growth of national languages. Most early books were printed in Latin, the language of educated people, but the market for Latin was limited, and in its pursuit of larger markets the book trade soon produced translations into the national languages emerging at this time. Printing indeed played a key role in standardizing and stabilizing these languages by fixing them in print, and producing dictionaries and grammar books. Latin soon became obsolete.

Newspapers

In Britain, newspapers first established themselves in the eighteenth century. They were initially concerned mainly with providing the middle class with business information, but a radical press grew up at the end of the century (E. P. Thompson 1963). The popular press first emerged in the 1820s with Sunday papers containing stories of murders and executions. In the second half of the nineteenth century, the *Daily Telegraph* pioneered the growth of a cheaper, more popular middle-class press. Finally, in the 1890s, the *Daily Mail*, followed by the *Daily Express* and the *Daily Mirror*, created a mass market for daily newspapers.

Newspapers had become a mass production industry by the end of the nineteenth century, and their financial basis changed as advertising became a greater source of earnings. Papers could now become cheaper than ever, but a large circulation to attract advertisers was also now more important than ever. Content was increasingly driven by commercial pressures.

In their pursuit of wider readership, newspapers changed in character. Headlines became bigger and there was more illustration. Coverage of political and economic matters declined, while sport, crime, sex, and human-interest stories increased. Between 1927 and 1937 the *Daily Mirror* halved the proportion of its news covering political, social, economic, and industrial issues (Curran and Seaton 1991: 67).

We discussed earlier the idea of a public sphere (see p. 353). The rise of mass-circulation newspapers extended this by making news and views available to larger numbers of people. These newspapers had, however, driven out of business the radical press, which had generated political debate by challenging the dominant ideology. Furthermore, the decline of serious content in the mass-circulation newspapers, as the popular press became more concerned with entertainment than information, hardly promoted public discussion.

The transformation of the press into a mass-production, mass-circulation industry led to the concentration of ownership. Production had become capital intensive and large amounts of money were needed to set up a newspaper, while costs were reduced if the machinery was used to produce more than one. Small-circulation papers could not compete with the new mass dailies. By 1910, 67 per cent of national daily circulation was in the hands of three owners and 69 per cent of national Sunday circulation in the hands of another three. By 1921 the Harmsworth brothers (see Box 10.6) owned papers with a circulation of over six million (Curran and Seaton 1991: 51–2).

The era of the press barons raised acutely the question of press influence and the power of its owners. They made no secret of their intentions to use their papers for political purposes. They certainly exercised a detailed control over editorial content. But did their views actually influence their readers? Curran and Seaton (1991: 61) have argued that it was not so much their direct as their indirect influence that mattered: 'Their main significance lay in the way in which their papers provided cumulative support for conservative values and reinforced opposition, particularly among the middle class, to progressive change.'

The barons' era has gone, but ownership is still concentrated, and the issues it raises have not gone away. We will return to them in 'Ownership and control'.

Cinema

The history of the press is long and readership built up steadily over a long period, but 'movies' burst upon the world at the end of the nineteenth century. They arrived in England in 1896 and by 1914 there were already 500 cinemas in London. As Corrigan (1983: 27) has put it, 'by 1914 going to the picture palace had become a normal activity'. The reproducibility of film meant that multiple copies could be made and films could be shown simultaneously to audiences across the world.

Going to the cinema could become a mass activity, however, only if ordinary people had the time and money for it. The reduction of working hours provided more leisure time, and in the 1920s and 1930s cinemas benefited from the enforced leisure resulting from higher unemployment. The introduction of unemployment benefit meant that the unemployed could afford cheap seats. Films appealed particularly, however, to the young and to women. John Eldridge *et al.* (1997) have suggested that film-going was the first permissible leisure activity outside the home for women.

📌 **Briefing: press barons**   10.6

In 1921 the following newspapers were owned by the Harmsworth brothers:

- **Lord Northcliffe (Alfred Harmsworth):** *The Times, Daily Mail, Weekly Dispatch, London Evening News;*
- **Lord Rothermere (Vere Harmsworth):** *Daily Mirror, Sunday Pictorial, Daily Record, Glasgow Evening News, Sunday Mail;*
- **Sir Lester Harmsworth:** a chain of local papers in the south-west of England.

Source: Curran and Seaton (1991: 50).

Briefing: the Hollywood star system   10.7

'Far more than the type of movie, stars were the commodities that most consistently drew audiences to the movies. A "star vehicle", a movie constructed around the appeal of one or more particular stars and sold on that basis, was bound to have a set of conventional ingredients. . . . An Elvis Presley movie, for instance, offered its star several opportunities to sing, a number of girls for him to choose his romantic partner from, and a plot in which he would be misunderstood by older characters. The repetition of these standard ingredients created an audience expectation of these elements. . . . The studio system was committed to the deliberate manufacture of stars as a mechanism for selling movie tickets, and as a result generated publicity around the stars' off-screen lives designed to complement and play upon their screen images.' (Maltby and Craven 1995: 89)

❓ *Is the Hollywood star system still operating? Can you think of any contemporary examples of it?*

Films are often seen as an art form, with inspirational directors drawing on the creative talents of writers, actors, and camera crew to craft unique products. Such films have been made, but most have been produced on an industrial basis. Picture houses in Britain were eventually showing two new programmes each week, each typically containing two feature films. To meet this demand, studios had to churn them out on a routine basis and to a tight schedule. Like any other form of mass production, they were large-scale operations with a high division of labour and a bureaucratic structure.

Production and distribution were integrated and concentrated in the hands of Hollywood companies. Control of distribution was crucial, for this guaranteed outlets for production and shut out the competition. Distribution networks were able to dominate the market because film copies were cheap to produce and could be rented to a large number of cinemas at the same time. The distributors built up cinema chains to give them direct control of outlets and kept their grip on audiences through the star system (see Box 10.7), for stars were the best guarantee of a large audience.

By 1914 Hollywood already had 60 per cent of the British market. In the 1920s it became completely dominant, producing 95 per cent of the films shown in Britain in 1925 (Corrigan 1983: 26). In the 1930s and 1940s Hollywood accounted for 60 per cent of world film production (Maltby and Craven 1995: 66).

As with the popular press, there has been a concentration of ownership and control in a small number of large corporations. With films, however, there is the additional twist that ownership and control have been internationally concentrated in the hands of American corporations. This raises the issue of the Americanization of popular culture, which we return to on pp. 383–5.

Radio and television

Radio and television are broadcasting media, which have quite different characteristics from cinema:

- *Domesticity*. They penetrate into the ordinary life of family and household.
- *Continuity*. They provide an endless daily programme rather than a one-off entertainment.
- *Immediacy*. They can go 'live' and communicate events to an unlimited audience as they happen.
- *Variable usage*. In the cinema people simply watch the screen, but television and radio can be combined with many other activities.

In Britain, radio provided the model for the early organization of television. In the 1920s radio was put under the control of a publicly owned monopoly, the British Broadcasting Corporation (BBC). Television then developed under the BBC's control during the 1930s. Broadcasting took this form in Britain as part of a general tendency towards the public ownership of important national services at this time.

BBC radio was established as a public service by Reith, the first Director-General of the BBC, on two basic principles:

- Universality through a national service, though with some regional programmes.
- Mixed programming to provide a mix of education, information, and entertainment, and cater for different tastes and interests.

As we argued above, the changing character of the press was making it less appropriate as a vehicle of the 'public sphere'. The control of British broadcasting by an independent public corporation meant that first radio and then television were able to take over this function to some degree, though the BBC had an uneasy relationship with the state. The government expected the BBC to be a cooperative instrument of the state and refused to allow the BBC to cover matters of political controversy or to make parliamentary broadcasts. Indeed, during the General

Strike of 1926 the BBC eventually found itself assisting the government to bring the strike to an end (Curran and Seaton 1991: 143).

British broadcasting was transformed in the 1950s by the breakthrough of television and the ending of the BBC's monopoly. The number of TV licence-holders rose from 344,000 in 1949/50 to 1,165,000 in 1959/60 (Curran and Seaton 1991: 196). In 1954 a law was passed to introduce commercial television or 'Independent Television' (ITV), as it was misleadingly but cleverly called, since it may have been *independent* of the BBC but it was *dependent* on a range of commercial interests. Pressure from the advertising and entertainment industries had combined with the Conservative Party's belief in market forces to end the BBC's monopoly.

The ending of the BBC's monopoly did not, however, destroy the public-service tradition. Indeed, it led in some ways to television becoming a more effective medium for the public sphere. Commercial television loosened up the relationship between politics and television, and allowed increasing discussion of controversial matters. Both radio and television were able to develop their political function of informing the public about political debates and presenting opposition as well as government views. The key issue now became 'balance', the fair provision of airtime to different political views.

There was some danger that commercialization and the competition for audiences would undermine public-service principles, but their effects were limited by state regulation. The Independent Broadcasting Authority (IBA) restricted the amount of advertising, required that non-fiction programmes occupy a specified proportion of airtime, and limited repeats and imports. The public-service tradition survived.

> ### Briefing: the concentration 10.8 of media ownership
>
> Concentration of ownership became a feature of all areas of the media, with a higher level of concentration in these industries than in industry generally. In Britain:
>
> - two companies dominated the production of gramophone records by the 1930s;
> - two companies dominated cinema by the 1940s;
> - five companies accounted for about 70 per cent of newspaper circulation in the 1950s;
> - commercial television in the 1960s was dominated by five network companies with monopoly positions in particular regions.
>
> *Source*: J. Scott (1990: 142).

The effects of commercial competition were also limited by monopolistic tendencies within the industry. There was little competition between ITV companies once they had won their franchises, for they operated as a national network based on regional monopolies. Competition was also limited by programming conventions. Thus, the BBC and ITV learned to schedule unpopular programmes at the same time, maximizing the audiences for, say, documentaries in the interests of both organizations. After an initial period of frantic rivalry, BBC and ITV had settled down to live quite comfortably with each other during the 1960s and the 1970s, though a period of more drastic change awaited them, as we show later in the 'The limits of choice'.

Stop and reflect

In this section we moved on to outline the rise of the mass media.

- We first examined the print revolution.
- We then explored the interrelationships between the growth of the mass media, the development of capitalism, and industrialization.
- We outlined the emergence of mass-circulation newspapers, cinema, and broadcasting.
- We argued that a growing concentration of ownership took place as the mass media developed.

We discussed the impact of the mass media on the public sphere.

- Return to the earlier discussion of the public sphere and make sure that you are clear about its meaning (see p. 353).
- Consider how mass-circulation newspapers affected the public sphere.
- We suggested that first radio and then television took over the function of providing a public sphere.
- Did commercialization weaken television's contribution to the public sphere?

The influence of the mass media

The growth of the mass media had created organizations with an enormous potential for influencing people. Industrial techniques gave newspapers and films a huge production capacity, while their distribution networks could reach large numbers of people at more or less the same time. The broadcast media could reach people instantly and give them the illusion of being present as events happened.

Concentration and monopolization gave great power to the small number of organizations that controlled each of the media. In some cases this put power in the hands of individual owners prepared to use it for political purposes.

But how much influence could those who owned and controlled the media actually exercise? As we showed in the first part of the chapter, there is no consensus on this, and different models of media influence have led people to very different conclusions. In this section, we examine media influence in a number of key areas—information, representation, and morality.

Information

Although the Web is growing in importance, the mass media are still the most important sources of information in our society. We rely on 'the news' to tell us about major events and report them in a truthful and accurate way. Journalists and editors assure us that their professional values require them to provide accurate and objective information, and a balanced and representative range of opinions. But do they provide this? Is it even possible for them to do so?

Constructing the news

The starting point of the sociological study of the news is its social construction. The facts never speak for themselves.

This is partly because of the news production process. Space and time are limited and editorial **gatekeepers** select what goes into newspapers and news programmes. The news also has to be trimmed and packaged to fit newspaper layout or the structure of a broadcast news programme. The shift towards rolling news on news channels, and instant 'breaking news', have impacted on the process of news production and affected news content (see Box 10.9).

News does not just arrive on the editor's desk. Information is gathered by journalists, who are organized into a reporting network by their newspaper or broadcaster, which directs and distributes them, steering them towards information of one kind rather than another. International reporting shows this particularly well. It is inevitably patchy and decisions to send journalists to one place rather than another can have an enormous bearing on international coverage. A searchlight can be trained on a country with a particular problem, say the destruction of rainforest in Brazil, by sending a camera team to cover it for television. Problems that are not highlighted in this way hardly exist on the world stage.

The journalists themselves are guided by 'news values', which shape what they find newsworthy. They often claim that these are objective and self-evident. Galtung and Ruge (1999) did find some evidence for this. The more recent, the closer, and the bigger an event, the more likely it was to be covered. They also found, however, that news of interest

---

New technology Rolling and breaking news   10.9

Technology has made it possible to provide direct and continuous news transmissions. Rolling news channels with 24-hour news coverage have multiplied, and regular programmes are interrupted by breaking news. The viewer gets a sense of being present, of participating as events unfold, with direct access to what is going on. Martin Bell (2003) points out that there is, however, 'a lack of authenticity' in much of the coverage:

> It consists of correspondents perched on the roofs of hotels and television stations, exchanging guesswork with other correspondents on other roofs, about the crisis of the moment.

Instant reporting often means the transmission of unchecked rumours rather than properly investigated news stories:

> In times of crisis, of war and terrorism, the rolling-news channels have special responsibilities as the primary source of news for millions of people. They are defined by F-words. They aim to be first and fastest with the news. Their nature, too often, is to be feverish, frenzied, frantic, frail, false, and fallible.

Source: Bell (2003).

→ Next time you watch a rolling-news channel, bear in mind Martin Bell's scepticism!

to the poor, ethnic minorities, and women was neglected. The selection of news reflected the male, white, middle-class character of the media elite (Galtung and Ruge 1981). John Robertson suggests that this process is not deliberate and results from a subconscious 'self-censorship'. Media professionals believe in a notion of 'newsworthiness', which 'may make the profoundly ideological choices made about news stories seem, both to the audience and the producers, to be quite "natural"' (J. Robertson 2007: 9).

Some aspects of the selective process are, nonetheless, quite deliberate. As Tunstall (1996) has put it, each newspaper looks for the 'good story for us', the story that fits the style of a paper and its political slant. Journalists are well aware of the need to find such stories and present them in the way required by their organization. They can be forced to conform, since editors, ultimately controlled by owners, can bring strong pressures to bear on them.

This was shown well by what happened to the *Sunday Times* after it had been bought in 1981 by Rupert Murdoch, who shifted its political stance to the right. A new editor was appointed and journalists were pressed to conform through the editorial hierarchy. Their articles were amended through editing. If they resisted, they could find that their pieces appeared less often, facing them with 'professional death'. It was also easier to conform than to struggle every day to maintain their views. Isobel Hilton has suggested that many ended up internalizing these controls and becoming their own censors (see Box 10.10). In the

end, the choice was to give in or to resign. Curran and Seaton (1991: 104) report that at least a hundred journalists left the *Sunday Times* between 1981 and 1986.

Much of the news is not, anyway, gathered by journalists so much as presented to them. News agencies are an important source of material, particularly from other countries. International agencies do try hard for purely commercial reasons to present information in as neutral a way as they can, since they have to sell it into countries with widely varying cultures and political regimes. Gurevitch (1996) points out that this does, however, make it easier for national editors then to manipulate the material for their own purposes. Furthermore, sources are not generally given for agency material, which frequently originates from the state. An apparently neutral agency source does not make the news objective.

It is also considerably easier for journalists to write stories on the basis of information they have been given than to seek out the information themselves. It is this that keeps the public-relations industry in business, providing material that presents its clients in a favourable light, and the capacity to employ public-relations companies clearly depends on resources. In practice, this means that business corporations and governments are able to dominate the flow of information to the media.

The Glasgow University Media Group has demonstrated how the news favours explanations that reflect the views of dominant groups in British society. Their content analysis of strike coverage makes this point particularly well, for it is characteristic of strikes that management and union provide opposite accounts of them. The television reporting of strikes did recognize that there were two views but generally privileged the managerial account (Philo 1990: 169–70). In later work on the television news reporting during 2000–2 of the Palestinian–Israeli conflict, the GUMG examined conflicting accounts of the events and found that the Israeli perspective dominated news coverage. Their analysis of news content and its impact on the audience can be found in Media watch 10 at the end of this chapter.

The study of news construction and the analysis of news content have demonstrated that the news is neither objective nor impartial. Broadly speaking, those with power and wealth are able to manage the flow of information and interpretation through the media. But it is important to recognize that they do not always succeed. Investigative reporting exists. Governments and business corporations are at times seriously embarrassed by the activities of journalists.

As Eldridge (1993*a*: 20) has put it, 'the media occupy space which is constantly being contested'. Subordinate groups organize and challenge the dominant ideology. Conflicts within the elite itself often provide journalists with leverage through the leak of information that governments would like to keep quiet. This is where the journalists'

Briefing: a journalist under pressure   10.10

Isobel Hilton, the Latin American correspondent of the *Sunday Times* in the early 1980s, describes the pressures she experienced after its takeover by Murdoch:

What would happen is that you would write a story and it would disappear. The copy would vanish around the building and people would write little things into it and take out other things. It would eventually appear in a very truncated form with the emphases changed. It had all been done at stages along the way. To try and make a fuss about this on a Saturday when everything was very busy was very difficult. . . . The sense of intimidation was so strong that people actually started censoring themselves because it is very unpleasant to get into this kind of argument all the time. It is not just a collection of incidents, it's a collection of incidents *and* the atmosphere, which is in the end so depressing. You stop functioning as a journalist. There are things that you just don't bother to pursue because you know you just won't get them into the paper.

Source: Curran and Seaton (1991: 104).

occupational values of independence, objectivity, impartiality, and balance come into play. Even if these values do not and cannot produce objective news, they can enable the voice of dissent to be heard.

Government information

The construction of the news provides many opportunities for governments to influence it. Bob Franklin (1994) provides an account of some of the main ways in which British governments can influence the media:

- *Censorship*. The media are not allowed by the Official Secrets Act to publish information on 'sensitive' military or security matters, or information obtained in confidence from foreign governments or international organizations. The broad wording of these restrictions leads editors to play safe, which considerably widens the effect of censorship.

- *Control of the BBC*. The BBC depends on the government for increases in the licence fee to cover rising costs. Governments have at times threatened to withhold increases. The government also appoints the BBC's Board of Governors.

- *Provision of information*. Briefings by the prime minister's press secretary through the lobby system are an important source of information for journalists. This system feeds government information from unattributed sources into the media. Information from state agencies is released (or suppressed) to suit their purposes.

- *Pressure on investigative journalists*. There are well-known examples of governmental attacks on specific programmes, such as the 1988 Thames Television documentary *Death on the Rock*, which investigated the shooting of three unarmed members of the IRA in Gibraltar. Thames Television's failure to obtain renewal of its franchise in 1991 has been attributed to its conflict with the government over this programme.

- *Relationships with newspapers*. Those favourable to the government can become a mouthpiece for its views.

In 2000 a Freedom of Information Act (FOI) was passed in the UK by a Labour government with a manifesto commitment to it. This Act introduced a 'public right to know' the information held by public bodies, but this was restricted in important ways. There is a ministerial veto, which was used to prevent disclosure of the minutes of the Cabinet meetings that discussed the legality of the 2003 Iraq war. There are also exemptions for some bodies, which can decide that the public interest in non-disclosure outweighs the public interest in information. It can also take a long time to obtain information. This Act has, nonetheless, caused the state serious discomfort (see Box 10.11).

Briefing: MPs' expenses　10.11

The Freedom of Information Act (FOI) came into operation in 2005. The parliament that had passed this Act did, however, make strenuous efforts to prevent disclosure of its members' expenses claims. These failed, for legal and political reasons, though some crucial details, notably the private addresses of MPs, were blacked out. This was supposedly because of the threat to their security, but it also hid their manipulation of second-home allowances and tax exemptions to benefit from property deals. Full information was then provided by the *Daily Telegraph*, which had obtained a disc containing the complete record of recent expense claims. This information has in the public's eyes discredited many MPs, led to resignations and de-selections, and proposals for far-reaching constitutional reforms. The Freedom of Information Act played a crucial role in this process, but so did an old-fashioned leak to a newspaper of information unobtainable under the Act.

While the Act can evidently be used to force public bodies to reveal things they would prefer to keep secret, state officials can find ways of avoiding disclosure. A contest over disclosure takes place, with both sides learning from previous experience and developing new tactics. One civil servant interviewed by the Constitution Unit at University College London declared as follows:

I am afraid I am very negative about the FOI. It is used a lot in my area by pressure groups who are opposed to what we are seeking to do. There are a lot of 'fishing trips', trying to get information which they can use in public, or even in the courts, to undermine our policy. And they will use any information received very selectively to support their own aims . . . So in the future, I'll be making sure that there is nothing for them to get at. Part of our problem is that we have had a lot of internal material and our record keeping has been good. But I've told my team to make sure in future we minimise what we write down and minimise what we keep. So we'll be getting rid of emails quickly and we won't worry if the record is incomplete, so long as it contains nothing we wouldn't want to see released. (Waller *et al.* 2008: 57)

Representation

The media can influence their audience not only through the information they provide but also through the way they represent people. In this section we consider the representation of class, gender, ethnicity, and disability.

Class

Representations of class have a long history. Dodd and Dodd (1992) argued that, in the late nineteenth century, middle-class commentators created an image of the British working class that shaped later representations of it. The working class was invariably situated in industrial communities of the north. It was contrasted with the middle class by making a set of oppositions that represented workers as physical and practical in character rather than intellectual; decent and simple rather than sophisticated; local rather than national.

This image of the working class persisted through the twentieth century and can be found in the writings of Orwell, Hoggart, and Sillitoe, and in films such as *Saturday Night and Sunday Morning* or *Letter to Brezhnev*. It can also be found in soap operas, as in *Coronation Street*'s close-knit community located in a northern city.

Continuities can be found with the 1980s soaps *EastEnders* and *Brookside*, but these also broke new ground. Although they too focused on local communities, they were concerned 'not so much with what holds a community together but with what threatens to splinter or disrupt it' (Geraghty 1992: 137). These soaps were aimed at a wider audience that included male and young viewers and tried therefore to break away from the *Coronation Street* model. There was more emphasis on social diversity, conflict, deviance, and crime. *EastEnders*, for example, was the first to recognize the multi-ethnic character of the British working class. As the Dodds have pointed out, the values of community were still there, however, for the community is defended against the criminal and racist forces threatening it from the outside.

Although the image of the working class was created by the middle class, it was adopted by intellectuals of working-class as well as middle-class origin. It was then adapted to the audience needs of television and became part of popular culture through the soap opera. The extent to which it has shaped conceptions of the working class is an open question, but the soap operas have certainly reached a mass audience. At a time when class communities were in decline (see Chapter 13, pp. 496–7), the only community in the lives of many working-class people was in the soap opera.

Gender

Feminists have often criticized the media for reinforcing traditional gender stereotypes. Tuchman (1981) claimed that women were portrayed mainly in terms of their sexual attractiveness and their performance of domestic roles. The exclusion, marginalization, and trivialization of women's activities resulted in what she called the 'symbolic annihilation of women' (Tuchman 1981: 183).

But have media representations of women changed? Television content in Britain and the United States has increasingly featured 'strong women' performing male occupational roles in, for example, the police, or the armed forces, or the professions more generally. Arguably, television has over-compensated for its past deficiencies and misleadingly gives women more power than they really have. Against this, there is in some programmes the continued representation of women as primarily concerned with romance, marriage, and domesticity (Bernstein 2002).

This somewhat contradictory picture is found also in soap operas, which as a 'feminine genre' have been the focus of much feminist interest. Research here has emphasized that the significance of soap operas is not just a matter of how they represent women but also of the pleasure that they give them. As Pilcher (1999: 114) has summarized it: 'soap operas are potentially both a ghetto, where femininity is valued but firmly based within the domestic and the personal, and a beneficial cultural space, where women audiences can actively enjoy the struggles of strong, independent, women characters'. It is also necessary to take account of social interaction within the audience, as argued by the GUMG (see p. 358). A study of the soap-opera audience has claimed that much of the pleasure that women take in soaps results from the opportunities they provide for discussion of the characters and events. This can build solidarity among women and resistance to patriarchy (M. Brown 1994).

The content of girls' and women's magazines has been another major focus of interest. McRobbie's well-known study of the teenage magazine *Jackie* started off a debate that raised important issues of method. McRobbie argued that stories, images, problem pages, and articles on fashion, beauty, and pop music combined to focus girls on personal and emotional matters, as though these were the only things that mattered. Relationships between boys and girls were treated solely in 'romantic' terms. As McRobbie put it, 'the girl is encouraged to load all her eggs in the basket of romance and hope it pays off' (McRobbie and McCabe 1981: 118).

This approach went well beyond content analysis by using techniques of textual analysis to discover hidden meanings, but inevitably had to make assumptions about the text's meaning. Martin Barker (1989) criticized McRobbie for treating the reader as a passive receiver of messages. Frazer (1987) studied reader responses to *Jackie* through discussions among girls and found they distanced themselves from the fictional characters, criticized the magazine, and were well aware of the process through which it had been produced.

> ⟳ **Connections**
>
> We discuss femininities and masculinities in Chapter 5, pp. 158–9, and recent changes in gender on pp. 169–79. Read these pages with this discussion of media representations.

Do girls' magazines shape the way they think?
© Getty Images/M Nader

In later work, McRobbie (1996) acknowledged these criticisms and adopted more of an 'active-audience' approach. She found that the content of such magazines as *Just Seventeen*, *More!*, and *19* was focused on sexuality rather than romance. They treated the reader as more 'knowing', and adopted an ironic, mocking attitude towards traditional femininities. The young women professionals who produced and edited them were highly educated and familiar with gender politics. These magazines promoted a bolder, more confident, more challenging identity for women, though in some respects they still reinforced established femininities through their predominantly heterosexual assumptions.

While the literature on gender has been dominated by feminist concerns, there has been a growing interest in media representations of men. Representations of sportsmen have embodied **hegemonic masculinity** (see Chapter 5, p. 159) in their emphasis on competitiveness, strength, and aggression. Alternative gay masculinities have been generally mocked and marginalized, though some soap operas have introduced 'gay' characters and taken them seriously (Bernstein 2002).

Men's magazines, as Edwards (1997) has argued, have been permeated by traditional images of masculinity. This applies particularly to those celebrating laddism, which have gloried in such images, though even here a certain irony has crept in. As Pilcher (1999: 128) has put it, they are 'sexist but in an ironic, self-conscious "should know better" way'.

There is an interplay here between representations of men and women. Changing representations of women have challenged the established model of femininity and, therefore, the hegemonic masculinity that depends on this. This challenge, together with the assertion of gay sub-cultures, resulted in some questioning of the hegemonic model but also provoked a masculinist response. The challenge should not, anyway, be exaggerated, for the hetero-sexuality at the heart of the established models seems as pervasive as ever, if not quite so compulsory.

Ethnicity

The media have reinforced racial as well as class and gender stereotypes. Solomos and Back (1996: 184) argue that media racism has two core features: the culture of black people is presented as alien to the British way of life, and their presence is seen as a threat to British culture.

> **⮑ Connections**
> It is important to bear in mind the cultural form taken by racism in Britain. As we show in Chapter 6, pp. 217–18, the discrediting of an openly biological racism led to its replacement by a 'new racism' emphasizing national cultural differences.

The press in particular has presented a negative image of black people, though the content of this image has shifted over time. Solomos and Back (1996: 83) have suggested that there have been three successive stereotypes:

- the 1960s 'welfare scrounger';
- the 1970s 'mugger';
- the 1980s 'rioter'.

The emphasis was always on the problems presented by black people rather than their contribution to British society, or the problems that British society created for them.

Thus, welfare scrounging was emphasized rather than the contribution of black immigrants to the staffing of the National Health Service. The black mugger was highlighted rather than the rising numbers of racist attacks on blacks by whites. Headlines such as 'Black War on the Police' presented the disorders in 1980s British cities as 'race riots', in which blacks attacked the police, rather than as the outcome of urban deprivation, exclusion, or changes in methods of policing (we discuss these disorders in Chapter 13, pp. 503–5).

Similar negative images can be found in television. Alvarado *et al.* (1987) identified four historical stereotypes of black people:

- the 'exotic', as in British media coverage of international tours by the Royal Family;
- the 'dangerous', as in the portrayal of Indians in westerns;
- the 'humorous', as in sit-coms like *Till Death Do Us Part*;
- the 'pitied', as in coverage of famines.

Such representations place blacks, and other minorities treated in a similar way, in a special 'different' category, whether to be feared, patronized, or ridiculed. Deliberately presenting positive images might seem one way of counter-acting negative ones but can also reinforce stereotypes. Thus, black success stories, such as very occasional Oscars for black film stars, not only show that some blacks can succeed but may also suggest that success is exceptional and that most fail. Furthermore, success or failure is seen in individual-ist terms and does not take account of the disadvantages and deprivations that make such stories exceptional.

Arguably, negative images are best countered by the representation of minorities as ordinary people. *Eastenders* was the British soap opera that led the way with the Karims of the 1980s, though the Ferreira family, introduced in 2003, was considered unrealistic by British Asians and axed in 2005. They tried again with the Masoods in 2007, claiming to provide stronger storylines for them and

Controversy and debate The 'Scottish Six' 10.12

There is a nationality as well as an ethnicity representation issue. There has long been a Scottish demand for a devolved six o'clock, sixty-minute BBC news programme *produced in Scotland*. Alex Salmond, the First Minister of Scotland, called for a 'Scottish Six' and set up a Scottish Broadcasting Commission in 2007 to examine Scottish broadcasting issues. The Commission reported in September 2008 that 'the UK's broadcasters were failing to properly serve their audiences in Scotland or to spend a fair share of their money on Scottish programmes' and made proposals, welcomed by Salmond, to

remedy this. It did not, however, recommend a 'Scottish Six'. Although digital technology makes the production of such a programme easier, the likelihood of its happening appears to be receding, partly, it seems, because of financial pressures on the BBC but also because the multiplication of TV channels fragments the potential audience.

Should the TV news be devolved?

Source: Guardian, 16 June 2008, 8 September 2008.

adventurously embarking one of the characters on a gay affair (*Guardian*, 22 June 2009).

This may not, however, be the best approach. A study of this issue by Trevor Phillips was commissioned by Channel 4, after Jade Goody and Danielle Lloyd had been accused of abusing the Bollywood star Shilpa Shetty during an episode of *Celebrity Big Brother*. Its report found that black and Asian viewers criticized soaps for tokenism and stereotyping, as in Asian shopkeeper characters. They praised those reality shows, such as the *X Factor* or *Strictly Come Dancing* or *The Apprentice*, which allowed individuals from the ethnic minorities to show their skills and talents (*Guardian*, 17 July 2008).

It is not just a matter of representations but also of the ethnic composition of media organizations themselves. Greg Dyke famously described the BBC as a 'hideously white' organization in 2001. About 8 per cent of its workforce came from ethnic minorities but only 2 per cent of its managers. In 2007 the *Guardian* claimed that, although the situation had changed 'on screen', senior media management was still overwhelmingly white. The *Guardian*'s 2006 Media 100 list had not contained a single black or Asian

Do adverts reinforce ethnic stereotypes?
© Alice Chadwick

face (*Guardian*, 2 April 2007). In the 2008 report cited above, Trevor Phillips concluded that television was still 'hideously white where it matters', in its senior positions (*Daily Telegraph*, 17 July 2008).

Disability

Media representations of disability reflect the broader cultural identification of the disabled as 'different'. This way of treating them has a long history, stretching back through medieval times to ancient Greece and Rome. Those with some perceived disability, such as 'dwarfs', were a source of entertainment in households and royal courts. They could be the target of abuse and humiliation, as their difference removed them from the constraints that normally regulated behaviour. 'Freak shows', where visitors would pay money to see people with some disability, real or fake, were at one time a common feature of travelling fairs and circuses.

The mass media continued this treatment of the disabled as different. This is reflected in both their absence and their presence. Research on television programmes has shown that the disabled rarely appear in normal roles. When they do appear, they are typically presented as 'dependent, unproductive and in need of care'. Storylines, and this applies to newspaper coverage as well, have taken a 'personal tragedy approach' that focuses on the suffering of the disabled, their medical treatment, or their achievements in spite of their disability (Barnes and Mercer 2003: 94).

In the *Cinema of Isolation*, Martin Norden (1994) identified three stages in the portrayal of the disabled in films. The first stage, between the 1890s and the 1930s, was an exploitative continuation of the 'freak-show' tradition. In the second stage, 1930s to 1970s, a more exploratory 'personal-tragedy' approach was taken. Disabled individuals struggled to overcome their difficulties. This was followed by a third and more positive stage in which disability was treated in a more 'incidental' way. While some normalization was taking place, examples of negative stereotyping in films continued to appear.

As pointed out above, one of the problems with research in this area is the lack of research into audiences. *Disabling Prejudice*, a report by Jane Sancho (2003), commissioned by UK broadcasting organizations, has, however, carried out important audience research. A postal survey of a representative panel, which therefore included disabled people, was carried out, with a response rate of 75 per cent. This research identified five different types of respondents, demonstrating the importance in media research of differentiating the audience (Sancho 2003: 7–8):

- *issue-driven* respondents (14 per cent of sample), who were disabled or associated with disabled people, and were 'vocal and active on behalf of disabled groups';
- *transformers*, who were younger people (9 per cent), some of whom were disabled, and were less critical but

looked for role models and wanted more opportunities for the disabled and 'a normalization of portrayals';

- *progressives* (36 per cent), who were mainly non-disabled, educated, and middle class, and considered that television had 'a role to educate and normalize';
- *followers* (26 per cent), who are described as 'mainstream', mainly non-disabled, with no interest in the disability issue, who saw television as entertainment, and were 'surprised by more hard-hitting portrayals';
- *traditionalists* (15 per cent), who were older viewers, some of whom were disabled, who had a stereotyped and prejudiced view of minority groups, saw television as entertainment, and were 'shocked by hard-hitting portrayals'.

One of the interesting findings of this research was that the audience seemed to have advanced further than the professionals who were also interviewed. Some 69 per cent of survey respondents said 'it would not bother them if a disabled person read the main evening news', and 63 per cent thought 'it would be good to see more disabled presenters on different programmes'. However, the professionals 'are inclined to believe that audiences are not ready to accept an increase in disability portrayals yet . . .' (Sancho 2003: 16).

Media organizations are under pressure to normalize the representation of the disabled. As with gender and ethnicity, greater organization, 'voice', and anti-discrimination legislation have made an impact. As Barnes and Mercer (2003: 132) have put it, 'disability politics has been caught up in the wider flow of identity politics and the celebration of difference'. Media research has been crucial here, for it is research that has brought to light the way that people are represented and has informed the campaigns of minority groups.

Moral issues

We focus here more specifically on the way that the media handle behaviour judged to be criminal or immoral. Some have held them responsible for criminal or immoral behaviour. Others have accused them of generating moral panics through the exaggerated and distorted reporting of events.

Sex and violence

The powerful visual impact of film meant that, almost as soon as films were introduced into Britain, concerns were raised about their dangers. They were seen as generating crime, promiscuous sexual behaviour, and violence. There was particular concern because of the large numbers of women and children who went to the cinema. Some claimed that children learned how to commit crime by seeing crimes on the screen. Others worried that screen stories of romantic love affairs would undermine marriage and threaten the family. The film industry decided to stave off state regulation by setting up its own British Board of Film Censors in 1912, and this still operates, though its standards and rules have changed (Eldridge *et al.* 1997).

Later developments in the media have intensified worries about their corrupting effects. Broadcasting media, especially television, penetrate into the home and are easily accessible to children. The content of videotapes, video-games, and the Internet has been not only easily accessible but also more difficult to regulate because of the way their material is distributed and disseminated.

Videotapes have attracted much blame. A well-known example of this was the James Bulger case in 1993, when the murder of a 2-year-old child by two 11-year-old children was blamed on horror videos. One particular video, *Child's Play 3*, was blamed, though there was no evidence that either of the children had seen it (Newburn and Hagell 1995).

There is a long history of research into whether the media are responsible for rising violence, but it is an exceptionally difficult issue to investigate. This is partly because of definitional and measurement problems:

- *The definition of violence.* It is hard to define this objectively. What some would consider a violent act, others would not. Is smacking a child a violent act?

Controversy and debate What is violence? 10.13

The following are all actions that might be considered in some way violent:

- a cruise missile attack;
- a fatal shooting;
- a 'beating-up';
- a boxing match;
- verbal abuse;

- an execution by lethal injection;
- an execution by beheading;
- corporal punishment.

❓ Which of these would you consider 'violent'?

❓ Can you rank them in terms of degree of violence?

❓ What do you think makes one act more violent than another?

- *The acceptability of violence.* Boxing is considered by some but not others to be a legitimate form of violence, as is the use of military force.

- *The measurement of violence.* It is difficult to assess the amount of violence involved in different kinds of violent act. This applies to both attempts to measure violent behaviour and attempts to assess the amount of violence in the media.

Studies of television and violence have commonly found evidence of a relationship but have had difficulty in isolating the effect of media violence from the wide range of other factors that may be said to cause violent behaviour. If violent children are found to be big watchers of violence, this may be because they are attracted to violent programmes. Experiments can be designed to investigate causality by exposing groups in laboratory situations to different amounts of violence and then measuring their aggressiveness. Such experiments have demonstrated a relationship between exposure and aggressiveness but are open to the criticism that the experimental situation is artificial and bears no relation to the social situations in

which people actually watch the screen. In Study 10 at the end of this chapter, we report an important attempt to get beyond these methodological problems.

Although many studies may be flawed and a causal link between television-watching and violence may not be proven, this does not mean that there is no relationship between the two. Crude notions that one causes the other may not stand up to examination, but the research by the GUMG (see p. 358) has shown that on a number of issues the media do influence the audience in subtle and long-term ways. The discussion of moral panics shows how complex this influence may be.

Moral panics

The literature on 'moral panics' provides another approach to these questions. The argument here is not that the media cause people to behave badly but rather that they report bad behaviour in an exaggerated and distorted way. This results in a societal reaction out of proportion to the initial problem, a reaction that can itself generate deviance.

The concept of the **moral panic** was first developed in Stan Cohen's study (1972) of the 'mods and rockers' of the 1960s. These were rival youth groups that engaged in some minor violence in Clacton during the Easter weekend of 1964. The newspapers reported widespread violence and large numbers of arrests with such headlines as 'Day of Terror by Scooter Groups' (*Daily Telegraph*) and 'Youngsters Beat Up Town—97 Leather Jacket Arrests' (*Daily Express*). These exaggerated reports awoke public fears and a hostile reaction to the youth groups, which were seen as a major threat to public order. Mod and rocker subcultures received publicity, which led more teenagers to adopt these styles, further increasing public fears. Mods and rockers became what Cohen called the 'folk devils' of their time.

Do the media generate moral panics?
© Alice Chadwick

THEORY AND METHODS   **10.14**

Moral panics

- Can you think of a recent moral panic?
- What form did the primary deviance take?
- What role did the media and the politicians play in its amplification?
- Were any folk devils created?
- Can you identify any secondary deviance that resulted from this process?
- Why do you think this moral panic occurred?

➲ You may find it helpful to read *Sociology Review* articles on this topic by Marsha Jones (2009) and Tammy Boyce (2009). See also our discussion of deviance in Chapter 7, pp. 229–31.

Cohen's analysis of this moral panic made an important contribution to the theory of deviance, which we outline in Chapter 7, pp. 228–31. Its two key notions were:

- *The labelling of behaviour.* What were little more than subcultural styles, the riding of scooters and the wearing of leather jackets, became defined as deviant behaviour.
- *Deviance amplification.* The social reaction to the *primary* deviance, the minor violence in Clacton, generated *secondary* deviance, the spread of deviant subcultures. This developed the distinction between *primary* and *secondary* deviation made by Becker

(1963) and Lemert (1967), though Cohen used the term 'deviance' rather than 'deviation'.

The concept of a moral panic was an important addition to the vocabulary of sociology. It identified mechanisms in the media representation of deviance and showed how the media could amplify it. The main problem that it faces is whether a moral panic actually affects people's attitudes and behaviour. A readership accustomed to exaggerated media stories may well view them with some scepticism. Newspapers may also pander to *existing* popular taste in constructing folk devils. The effects of media labelling and amplification may therefore be more limited than this concept suggests.

 Stop and reflect

In this section we considered the various ways in which the mass media have been said to influence people.

We first examined the media presentation of information.

- We showed how the social construction of news shapes the way that information is presented by the media.
- Do those with wealth and power control the news?

We then considered the media representation of class, gender, ethnicity, and disability.

- Do the media reflect or perpetuate stereotypes?

Lastly, we considered the influence of the media on moral issues.

- We examined the difficulty of establishing the influence of the media on violent behaviour.
- We explored the notion that the media generate 'moral panics'.
- Should the media be held in any way responsible for 'immoral' behaviour?

The limits of choice

We have examined the growth of the mass media and their influence on culture and society, but times have changed. The media have now lost much of their previous mass character with the shift to multiple outlets providing specialized programmes to particular, not mass, audiences.

The multiplication of the media has greatly increased consumer choice. Until quite recently there were only four television channels in Britain—BBC1, BBC2, ITV, and Channel 4. Hundreds of channels now compete for audiences. Similar changes have happened in other media, as cinemas went multiplex and a wide range of special-interest magazines appeared. The Internet has hugely expanded access to information. Globalization has increased the international availability of both information and entertainment.

But how much diversity is there, and how much real choice? These are the questions that we examine in this part of the chapter. We first examine diversity, before considering ownership and control, the fortunes of the public sphere, and the implications of globalization.

Diversity and choice

Greater choice has come about through a combination of technical, economic, political, and cultural changes, which we examine first. We then consider how real the greater diversity and choice have actually turned out to be.

Technology or politics?

Technological change has opened up new ways of delivering information to the household. Satellite and cable delivery systems, together with digital transmission, have made hundreds of television channels possible. Satellites make programmes available across national boundaries. The

Internet is an alternative delivery system that can provide almost limitless digital material. Telly-surfing and web-surfing have become part of everyday life and interchangeable, as the boundaries blur between TV, computer, and phone.

Choice of viewing has been enhanced by a shift of power from the programme scheduler to the viewer, from a 'push' to a 'pull' system. The breakthrough here was the video cassette recorder (VCR), which liberated the viewer from what was immediately available. Further technical advances have provided huge personal storage facilities and made searching much easier. The spread of subscriber and pay-per-view TV has enabled consumers to buy more precisely what they want.

Politics was also involved, however. In Britain, the 1980s Conservative governments held a neo-liberal ideology that advocated deregulation and competition (see the discussion of Thatcherism in Chapter 15, pp. 576–9). It was argued that greater competition would result in more choice for the consumer, though this was not its only motivation. It would also cut costs by forcing programme producers to be more efficient and could be used to weaken the unions, which were seen as having a stranglehold over BBC and ITV production.

THEORY AND METHODS   10.15

Measuring audiences

All TV channels need to find out how big an audience their programmes attract. The commercial channels set their rates to advertisers on the basis of audience size, while the BBC needs to show that its audiences are big enough to justify the licence fee. Data on audiences are also important to academic research.

Audiences are measured by research companies commissioned by the Broadcasters Audience Research Board (BARB). Audience data are provided by a panel of 5,100 volunteers, selected to represent the main characteristics of the British population. The volunteers are rewarded with gift vouchers. Viewers are required to register on a handset every time they enter a room containing a TV and to deregister when they leave it. Viewing data are continuously transmitted to the processing companies.

Source: http://www.barb.co.uk.

➲ What problems do you think there are in collecting and interpreting the data? Think about the selection process and viewing habits. Visit the BARB website for more information. You may find it helpful to refer to 'Selection and sampling' in Chapter 3 (see pp. 90–3), and the discussion of audiences on p. 357 of this chapter.

Competition certainly increased as cable and satellite delivery systems developed, but changes in the state regulation of ITV were also important. The 1990 Broadcasting Act forced the ITV companies into competitive tendering for franchises and required BBC and ITV to make more use of independent producers. The Independent Broadcasting Authority, which regulated the content of commercial television, was replaced by a 'lighter-touch' Independent Television Commission. As in other areas of life, the promotion of market forces required a combination of regulation and deregulation.

Behind these changes lay the growth of large media corporations, which we examine in 'Ownership and control' (see pp. 376–8). Hesmondhalgh (2007) argues that it is quite wrong to see these changes as simply a consequence of technological development. They were deliberately brought about by governments 'in order to support the interests of large, commercial, cultural industry companies' (Hesmondhalgh 2007: 115).

Post-Fordism and post-modernism

Product diversity in the economy as a whole has been increased by broader changes in production and consumption that have been labelled **post-Fordist** (see Chapter 17, pp. 671–3). The saturation of markets with mass-produced goods has resulted in the production of a more diverse range of products aimed at *niche* rather than *mass* markets. Advertising has similarly become more sophisticated and increasingly targets particular markets.

Post-Fordist changes have occurred in the media too. The creation of Channel 4 in 1982 has been seen in terms of a public-service concern to provide programmes for minorities, but it also made commercial sense, as these minorities were niche markets for advertisers. Entirely specialized television channels, providing sport or films, and specialized radio stations, such as Classic FM, have taken this process one stage further. There is also the proliferation of special-interest magazine titles. If you are selling pesticides to gardeners, the best way to reach them is to put adverts in a gardening magazine or attach them to a gardening programme on commercial radio or television.

Another important post-Fordist change has been the emergence of more flexible forms of organization that contract out functions to a network of smaller specialist firms (we discuss network organizations in Chapter 14, pp. 533–5). This has occurred in television with the introduction of the *publisher* model to replace the *producer* model. Both the BBC and the ITV companies were traditionally *producer-broadcasters*—that is, they largely made the programmes that they transmitted. Channel 4 was set up as a *publisher-broadcaster* to commission programmes made elsewhere, and the other channels too now do this extensively.

Greater diversity or more of the same?
© Alice Chadwick

The state played a part in this through the 1990 Broadcasting Act, which forced both BBC and ITV companies towards the publisher model by requiring them to take at least 25 per cent of their output from independent producers. Small and often short-lived independents have multiplied. This has diversified production and enlarged the range of products available. It has also greatly reduced security of employment and weakened the union organization of workers in the television industry.

The cultural changes associated with **post-modernism** (see p. 355) have contributed to diversity in other ways by

Figure 10.2 The sources of diversity

Technology	New delivery and storage systems
Politics	Deregulation and competition
Consumption	Niche marketing
Production	Post-Fordist product diversification
Organization	Publisher broadcasting
Culture	Post-modern pluralism

creating a non-hierarchical plurality of cultures. The distinction between *high* and *popular* culture has become ever more blurred, as the domination of an elite *high* culture has been increasingly challenged by *popular* forms of culture disseminated by the media. Culture has also become less hierarchical as diverse class, ethnic, and national subcultures have become increasingly valued in their own right.

It is, however, not only the coexistence of a plurality of cultures that is characteristic of post-modernism. It is also the way that they are mixed and combined. People move more freely across cultural boundaries, as they consume culture just like any other product. They adopt styles and follow fashions in dress or food, picking and mixing from the various cultural resources available to them. Styles from different places and times are combined, whether in architecture or popular music or television adverts. This can be done for effect, to surprise and attract attention by deliberately breaking cultural rules. As Strinati (1992) points out, there is often a subversive jokiness in the combination of apparently incompatible styles.

So, there are multiple sources of greater diversity, and choice has apparently greatly increased. Before celebrating this, however, we must also consider processes diminishing and limiting it.

Increasing or declining diversity?

These changes have undoubtedly put ITV and the BBC under greater pressure, and this pressure has reduced their programme diversity.

The multiplication of channels inevitably reduced the audiences for the main BBC and ITV channels. This was particularly serious for ITV, which had to compete with Channels 4 and 5 for advertising revenue and a host of other channels for audiences. If audiences fall, advertisers will not pay for advertising or will, at least, force down the rates they pay. The BBC also has to compete, as it can justify the licence fee only by having a large audience.

The growing competition for audiences has arguably reduced diversity. BBC1 and ITV have shown more frequent episodes of popular programmes, especially soap operas, and this has driven other programmes from peak viewing times. The main BBC and ITV channels are wary of taking risks, as they once did, with minority programmes at peak times. Nor can they force 'educational' programmes on a mass audience, as they also once could, by scheduling them at the same time, for there are plenty of other channels for watchers to migrate to. Educational, documentary, and minority programmes have been relegated to non-peak times or left to the niche channels, which have fewer resources for making them.

Thus, while a greater diversity of channels has provided more consumer choice, increased competition has also led

Briefing: how much choice do YOU have? 10.16

- Look at one of the weekly magazines listing television programmes.
- How many channels are listed?
- How many do you have access to?
- List the things that limit your choice of viewing.

to the pursuit of popularity by the main terrestrial channels and this has probably lessened programme diversity in the *mass* TV media.

Access

Diversity may make choice possible, but, as always, the exercise of choice depends on income, knowledge, time, and control.

Almost everyone in Britain has access to a television, but access to satellite, cable, and digital transmissions requires extra expenditure, and some events, particularly major sports, have become accessible only by this means. The exercise of choice is related to income, and those living in poverty will be increasingly excluded from full media participation. A section of the population may be deprived of what is increasingly regarded as a normal part of social life (see 'Poverty and deprivation', Chapter 18, pp. 725–6).

Knowledge, time, and control are closely related to the division of labour and distribution of power in the household. Gray (1992) studied household use of VCRs. She found that men had more knowledge of the technology and exercised more control over the choice of programmes. Housework, anyway, reduced the time, especially uninterrupted time, available to women for television-watching. Indeed, some of the women she interviewed saw television and VCR as a last-resort leisure activity, for household obligations made it difficult to escape work at home and they preferred to go out. Women apparently benefited less than men from the opportunities for increased choice.

Choice is not simply a matter of the availability of options and depends on access to the alternatives and the capacity to choose.

Ownership and control

Greater competition has also led to greater concentration, as control of the media fell into fewer hands. In this section we first consider changes in the pattern of ownership and then its significance for political choice.

Ownership

As we showed on pp. 361–2, ownership became more concentrated as the media developed. This process has continued and become more complex with the multiplication of media:

- concentration within media;
- multi-media ownership;
- transnational ownership.

Ownership has become concentrated within particular media. Murdoch's News Corporation's papers have at times accounted for one-third of the weekly sales of British national papers. With the creation of ITV plc, ITV has finally lost its original regional ownership structure, and has proposed a merger with Channels 4 and 5 to produce one single commercial broadcaster in England, though Scotland and Ulster still have their own companies. As in any other area of the economy, concentration is a way of increasing profits by eliminating competitors and creating economies of scale.

Even more striking has been the growth of *multi-media* empires. Conglomerates have emerged with wide-ranging interests spanning newspapers, book and magazine publishing, television companies, film studios, and radio stations. Ownership across the media facilitates the promotion of related products, such as books based on television series, transfers of content between, say, cinema and television, and the pooling of communications expertise. Rupert Murdoch's News Corporation, with its major interests in film and television, as well as newspapers, again provides a good example (see Box 10.17).

These empires have extended into the Internet. News Corporation bought MySpace in 2005. Time Warner merged with America Online (AOL) in 2000, though the two have recently split apart again. The BBC has created online services that are closely interconnected with its programmes. ITV bought Friends Reunited, but has recently sold it. It has, however, created ITV.com to compete with the BBC's online services.

A small number of large transnational corporations arguably dominate the world's media. The global extent of News Corporation's transnational activities can be seen from the Box 10.17 on 'Planet Murdoch'. According to Terry Flew (2007: 86), News Corporation is, however, the only one of the top four largest media corporations that should be considered really global in character (2007: 86). The other three, Time-Warner, Disney, and Viacom, should be seen as nationally based with some overseas operations rather than as truly global (see our discussion of this issue in Chapter 16, p. 625). We explore the significance of these corporations in the later section on 'Media globalization'.

Global focus 'Planet Murdoch': Rupert Murdoch's News Corporation in 2004   10.17

Area	Newspapers	Book and magazine publishing	Television, radio and film
Global		Harper Collins UK, US, and Australia Inc. (operations in 30 countries)	20th Century Fox
Asia and Middle East		Harper Collins (India)	Star TV (satellite covering China, India, Saudi Arabia, and 50 other countries) Phoenix satellite TV China Network Systems
Australia	*The Australian* and over 100 other titles	Various magazine titles	Fox Studios Foxtel
Europe (outside UK)			Sky Radio Sky Italia Balkan News Corporation
Latin America			Sky Latin America Direct TV Latin America
United Kingdom	*The Times, Sunday Times, News of the World, Sun*	*TES, TLS*	BSKYB (satellite)
United States	*New York Post, Weekly Standard*	*Gemstar TV Guide*	Fox Entertainment, 35 Fox TV stations Cable Network Programming Direct TV
Other	Interests in Fiji and Papua New Guinea		

Note that in 2005 News Corporation began to acquire Internet companies and has since bought MySpace.

Source: Shah (2004).

Newspaper politics

But how much does ownership matter? Here we focus on the consequences of the concentration of newspaper ownership for the political process. Do owners politically manipulate their readers or merely follow their views?

There is little doubt that British newspapers were moving to the political right during the period from the 1960s to the 1980s. The *Sun* in particular moved from supporting Labour to supporting the Conservatives in 1979. The Labour Party faced a largely hostile press in the 1980s, and by 1987 papers supporting the Conservative Party accounted for 72 per cent of national daily circulation (Curran and Seaton 1991: 124).

Their shift to the right can be explained in two different ways. First, there is the argument that it resulted from the interests of capital. As owners of capital, the owners of newspapers have a general interest in maintaining capitalism. More specifically, their profits are heavily influenced by labour costs, and they therefore have a direct interest in 'bashing the unions'. Tunstall (1996) suggests that their support for Thatcherism was linked to its attack on union power. The anti-union legislation passed by the Thatcher government certainly helped Rupert Murdoch to take on and defeat the print unions in the crucial battle over the movement of newspaper production to Wapping in 1986. This defeat destroyed their previously considerable control of newspaper production.

The alternative explanation refers to market pressures. In the end profits depend on selling newspapers, and no owner can run a paper at a loss for long. People are unlikely to buy papers on a regular basis if they express unpopular views. The electorate as a whole shifted to the right in the later 1970s, and arguably newspapers simply followed it in order to maintain their sales. There were good commercial reasons for the rightward shift of the press.

The significance of this shift is difficult to assess. The *Sun*'s support for the Conservatives has been considered a major factor in their election victories, but, as we showed earlier (see p. 361), it is very difficult to demonstrate media effects on behaviour. Through its support for Thatcherism, the press probably played some role in the Conservative victories of the 1980s and 1990s, but it is difficult to assess how important this was, since the Labour Party was weak during this period for other reasons.

This was not, however, the end of the story, for in March 1997 the *Sun* changed sides (as did some other right-wing newspapers). It supported Labour in the 1997, 2001, and 2005 general elections. It may be that the *Sun* simply recognized that Labour was going to win and wanted to be on the winning side so that it could influence the government. One may note that the 2003 Communications Act assisted Rupert Murdoch's activities by removing various rules designed to prevent media corporations becoming too big.

Murdoch's strong opposition to Britain joining the Euro might have been expected to prevent him supporting a pro-Euro Labour government. However, Murdoch reportedly told Tony Blair that the *Sun* would support Labour if it changed its policy and called a referendum on the Euro (given the unpopularity of the Euro, a referendum would probably block entry). Labour did, indeed, change its policy, and newspapers owned by Murdoch just happened to be the first to break this news (*Independent*, 20 April 2004).

It is clearly difficult to assess the significance of newspaper support for the outcome of elections but it is also clear that politicians take it very seriously. In deciding whom to support, newspaper-owners are influenced by their established ideological positions, which are related to their target readership. They also have clear interests as owners in securing governments with policies that favour their corporate interests. They have to bear in mind, however, the danger of losing influence if they back the wrong horse. In the 1980s there was no problem, as all these considerations pointed the same way—support for the Conservatives. Since the middle of the 1990s Murdoch in particular faced more difficult choices, but his interests kept the *Sun* supporting Labour, until September 2009, when it was announced that it would support the Conservative Party in the lead-up to the 2010 general election.

Decline of the public sphere?

We discussed earlier (on p. 354) the concept of a 'public sphere', and the impact of the rise of the mass media on it (see pp. 361–3). How has the public sphere fared in more recent times?

The commercialization of the media

We showed earlier (see p. 361) that commercial pressures have long been shaping the content of newspapers. This process continued after the Second World War and threatened the public sphere through the commercial manipulation of content, notably the displacement of information and debate by entertainment.

A widening gap emerged between the popular and the 'quality' press, where the coverage of public affairs was maintained. Curran and Seaton (1991) claimed that this gap had important political consequences, for working-class readers were denied serious coverage of public affairs.

Why did the Sun dump Labour in 2009?

© Alice Chadwick

This was not because there was no demand for this material. Market research showed that people wanted it, but their lack of purchasing power meant that advertisers were not interested in supporting newspapers that might meet this demand. 'An elite press thus came to dominate by default the field of serious journalism, thereby reinforcing elite domination of political life' (Curran and Seaton 1991: 118).

Both the ITV network and the BBC have come under increasing commercial pressure since the 1980s. ITV companies found that the arrival of Channel 5, followed by the multiplication of satellite and cable channels, intensified the competition for audiences and advertisers. The BBC's licence fee did not increase sufficiently to cover its rising costs, and it sought alternative sources of money, by, for example, creating magazines linked to programmes.

One of the effects of commercialization has been the steady breakdown of the barrier between programme content and advertising. Advertising agencies seek to break through this barrier because advertising that is *integrated* with content is more effective than advertising *segregated* in slots. Integration enables the use of what Vance Packard (1963) famously called 'hidden persuaders'. It also reaches a larger audience through repeats and international sales, and cannot be bypassed by the 'zapper' or recording technologies.

Graham Murdock (1992) has traced this process. In the early 1980s both BBC and ITV came to accept sponsorship. The televising of sport was a key battleground, for advertisers wanted to associate their products with healthy activities and reach large, often international, sport audiences. The BBC gave way on this, and by 1986 was showing some 350 hours of sport per year sponsored by tobacco companies, which were not allowed for health reasons to advertise their products in ITV slots. ITV sponsorship rules were relaxed by the 1990 Broadcasting Act, which allowed sponsorship of an increasing range of programmes, including weather forecasts but excluding news programmes.

Sponsorship is now an accepted and ever more widespread part of television. The Independent Television Commission banned the influence of programme content by sponsors, though Murdock (1992) has pointed out that sponsorship gives commercial interests the power to determine which programmes are made.

'Product placement' is a particularly insidious way in which commercial interests can influence the viewer. Although this has not up till now been allowed in British television, advertisers try to 'beat the system', and placement has occurred increasingly through films, which, sooner or later, get shown on television (see Box 10.18). The situation may well be changing in Britain. ITV has run into serious financial problems, because of increasing competition from other channels and the impact of recession, which has led to the government proposing abolition of the

Briefing: product placement 10.18

'It has been billed as the Bond that will break with tradition. In *Quantum of Solace* Daniel Craig will not ask for his martini, "shaken not stirred", and won't announce that he is "Bond, James Bond". But at least one 007 tradition is going strong: *Quantum of Solace* is expected to have more paid-for corporate product placements than other Bond movies before it . . .

The list of confirmed products to feature in the new film includes Heineken, Virgin Atlantic, Coca-Cola, Smirnoff . . . Ford, Omega, Sony, and Aston Martin. But perhaps the biggest sponsorship deal is a new one involving a British private jet company, Ocean Sky. It lent five of its jets . . . which were used to fly the cast and crew out to Panama for a week. . . . In return Ocean Sky will feature eight times in the film. The scenes will include interior and exterior shots of the planes and one will show a woman in full Ocean Sky uniform, made by the fashion designer Hugo Boss, behind an Ocean Sky-branded check-in desk.'

Source: Hughes (2008).

ban on product placement, though it would stay in place for the BBC and all children's programmes (*Independent*, 13 September 2009).

Commercialization also mixes information with entertainment to produce 'infotainment'. Hallin (1996) examined this process in American television. In the 1960s professional journalism became well established in the networks' news divisions, which were insulated from commercial pressures. Increasing competition in the 1980s led, however, to the spread of 'reality-based programming'. This mixed news and entertainment in magazine-style programmes that became the main output of the news divisions.

One consequence of this was a greater interest in the private lives of public figures. Presidential elections in the United States came to revolve largely around personalities rather than policies. Politicians were, of course, happy to exploit and manipulate this interest in private lives, but commercial pressures lay behind the shift of news content that brought this about. Hallin saw some virtues in a more popular and less elitist presentation of news, but he was concerned about the way in which 'the nation's political agenda' was being shaped by 'profit-seeking programmers and advertisers' (Hallin 1996: 259).

The state and the public sphere

The relationship between the state and the media is central to the maintenance of the public sphere.

The state has sought to maintain the public-service functions of the media. In Britain, the media regulator, the Office of Communications (OFCOM), has been charged by the Communications Act of 2003 with a duty to 'further the interests of citizens in relation to communications matters'. The state sets the framework for public-service broadcasting by regulating the programmes of public-service providers, which include not only the BBC channels but also ITV, Channel 4, and Channel 5. ITV has, for example, been required to provide arts, religious, children's, and regional programmes.

The continuing shift to digital broadcasting is expected, however, to undermine existing public-service provision by ITV, as unregulated channels take more viewers without having to carry the public-service burden. OFCOM remains committed to public-service broadcasting and has been pursuing two ways of solving the problem. One is simply to relax ITV's public-service obligations. The other is to find new funding for public-service programmes by 'top-slicing' the BBC's licence fee, a move rejected by the BBC. The BBC itself has problems justifying the licence fee, given the number of other channels that people may choose to watch, the availability of programmes online to non-licence payers, and its earnings from its own commercial operations. It is clearly difficult to reconcile the multi-channel world of choice with the maintenance of a strong public sphere.

The state also contributes to the public sphere by providing important information to the public. In 1980s Britain, the flow of information to the media about politics and policies grew enormously. Television gained access to parliament. New 'league-table' information, of great interest to the public, on the performance of hospitals, schools, and universities became available for the first time.

Since the 1980s, governments have also, however, engaged in increasing manipulation of the media. The 'packaging' of politicians and policies for the media developed rapidly at this time. The political parties increasingly employed media consultants, public-relations experts, and advertising agencies to promote their policies and personalities (B. Franklin 1994).

While all parties did this, the governing party had control of the apparatus and resources of the state. The Conservative governments of the 1980s made much greater use of the media than had occurred before. The prime minister's press secretary more actively managed and coordinated the flow of information to journalists. By 1989 the government had become Britain's biggest advertiser, as huge amounts of money were spent on promoting the government's privatization policies.

There were also growing government attempts to censor and regulate media information. The government attacked media coverage of the Falklands War and the conflict in Northern Ireland. New bodies were established to regulate

Figure 10.3 The state and the public sphere

The state's positive contribution	The state's negative contribution
• Public-service framework of TV	• Censorship
• Regulation of commercial interests	• Promotion of government policy
• Provision of information	• News management

broadcasting, the Broadcasting Complaints Commission of 1981 and the Broadcasting Standards Council of 1988. The 1990 Broadcasting Act required the practice of 'due impartiality' in matters of 'political or industrial controversy or relating to current public policy'. While this might appear unexceptional, it enables governments to attack media they judge to be giving too much publicity to opponents.

The post-1997 Labour governments further developed these techniques. The prime minister's press secretary tried to take control of the government's relationship with the press. Special political advisers, nick-named 'spin-doctors', were appointed to ministries to handle the presentation of policies, and, some have said, actually to shape those policies in ways that would gain good publicity. Although the Freedom of Information Act was passed in 2000, the state has tried hard to control the release of information (see p. 366).

Government news management has involved not just the dissemination of 'good news' but also the concealment of bad news. When the twin towers of the World Trade Center came down on 9/11, Jo Moore, a special adviser at the Department of Transport, notoriously e-mailed colleagues to tell them that it was 'a good day to bury bad news'.

The state's relationship to the public sphere is ambivalent. The control of the commercialization of broadcasting and the maintenance of public-service provision depend on state regulation. The state provides a great deal of important information to the public. The state is also, however, an instrument of governments seeking to manipulate and restrict the information made available. The state is both the main protector of the public sphere and the greatest threat to it.

The Internet and the public sphere

Commercialization and government manipulation may have threatened the public sphere, but has not the Internet created great new opportunities for developing it?

Although created for military purposes (see Box 10.3 on p. 353), the Internet was then developed as a means of exchanging knowledge for education and research. It was decentralized, committed to 'free speech', and open to all, qualities that made it a highly suitable vehicle for the public sphere. The invention and expansion of the World Wide Web opened up the Internet to the public at large.

The Web was designed to perform public-sphere functions. Tim Berners-Lee, more responsible than anyone else for creating it, was an idealist dedicated to the principles of communication, cooperation, and participation.

> When I proposed the Web in 1989, the driving force I had in mind was communication through shared knowledge, and the driving 'market' for it was collaboration among people at work and at home. By building a hypertext Web, a group of people of whatever size could easily express themselves, quickly acquire and convey knowledge, overcome misunderstandings and reduce duplication of effort. This would give people in a group a new power to build something together.

Berners-Lee 2000: 174

The creation of the Web was, however, followed by its commercialization. Rapidly growing Internet usage provided an opportunity to access an expanding and relatively affluent market. Companies could display their products through an 'electronic shopfront' (Goggin 2000: 105). Advertisers found a new medium for reaching consumers. Pornographers could transmit powerful erotic images directly to individuals. Banks could transact their business cheaply online. By the end of the 1990s, e-commerce had really taken off and has continued to grow.

Arguably, this commercialization has eaten into the public-service functions of the Web. It is not only that commercial activity has occupied growing amounts of Internet space. Technological advances have made it possible for commercial interests to accumulate information about individuals' interests and target them with tailored advertising. Consumers' profiles can be bought and sold. Portals can steer the browser towards the products that sponsor them or advertise through them. Google, which is by far and away the dominant search engine, stands accused of steering users towards its own comparison websites. Net-users are exposed to many kinds of *covert* commercial manipulation.

Goggin (2000) cautions us, however, against jumping to the conclusion that commerce has taken over the Web, which still facilitates plenty of cultural, educational, political, and individual activity:

> Some of the traditional public spaces have been reinvented and reconceived online, often deliberately so—whether libraries, community or selfhelp groups, public broadcasters, news, public service announcements or information services. An individual or group's ability to make a space for themselves on the Internet—public or private—is still arguably far greater than in other media.

Goggin 2000: 111

The public functions of the Internet can, therefore, coexist with its commercial functions, but it is not just a matter of their survival. Arguably, the vast expansion of the Web would not have occurred unless people could make money out of it. It was only by making the Internet user-friendly that the market for services and products could be maximized. Like commercial television, much 'free' Internet provision, such as search engines, is financed by advertising. Without commercialization, the Internet would have remained a high-minded but exclusive club for a highly educated elite. Indeed, the survival of Social Networking Sites is in some doubt, because of the hostility of their users to advertising (see p. 349).

Frontiers News on the Net   10.19

One area in which it is claimed the Internet contributes to the public sphere is through the diffusion and democratization of news. Established news providers, such as the newspapers or the BBC, can reach out faster and further by putting material online. Arguably, news has also been democratized, for it is no longer controlled by established commercial or political organizations but can come from anyone able to blog. 'News receivers' can become 'news producers'. The news provided by Web sources can escape the state regulation and manipulation that distort the news from newspapers and broadcasters.

There are also problems, however, with online news. The instant transmission of news may be the transmission of unchecked rumour (see Box 10.9 on p. 364). Untrained news producers on the Web may lack the standards of detachment and impartiality that, in principle at any rate, govern reports by established providers. The source may be obscure. Such news may be manipulated, even planted, by regimes. If people turn increasingly to the Web for news, they may use established providers less, and these may lose commercial viability. Newspapers may shut down, and the established public sphere may be diminished.

Sources: Gunter (2003); *Sunday Times*, 5 June 2005.

❓ When you want to find out 'the news' about something, where do you look?

❓ Do you think that Web sources are 'better' than established providers?

➲ As an exercise, compare news coverage of an event by an established provider and by Web sources.

In China the media have long been tightly controlled by the Communist Party. The Internet has provided a new means of criticizing the government and voicing dissent. Print journalists have taken to the Net to publish what the censors have blocked.

The government has responded by blocking websites, introducing filtering software, monitoring Internet cafés, and registering their users. According to Jonathan Watts of the *Guardian*: 'An Internet police force—reportedly numbering 30,000—trawls websites and chat rooms, erasing anti-Communist comments and posting pro-government messages.' Censorship has recently been extended to text messages on mobile phones.

The government has enlisted major Western IT corporations in its censorship and surveillance activities. The Chinese market is so big that these companies have been reluctant to risk exclusion from it. Yahoo helped the government identify a dissident, subsequently jailed for ten years, through his e-mail account. Microsoft has blocked Chinese searches on key words, such as 'democracy'. Cisco has provided surveillance software. Google agreed in 2006 that its Chinese branch would obey Chinese cen-

sorship laws, though in January 2010, after a 'cyber attack' seeking information about human rights activists, it reportedly decided to end this compliance and, if necessary, abandon the Chinese market.

It is technically possible for determined users to find ways round the Great Firewall and some have held that this dooms it to failure. James Fallows (2008) argues that the point is that most people will not bother.

> Chinese bloggers have learned that if they want to be read in China, they must operate within China, on the same side of the firewall as their potential audience.... And being inside China means operating under the sweeping rules that govern all forms of media here: guidance from the authorities; the threat of financial ruin or time in jail; unavoidable self-censorship as the cost of defiance sinks in.

Sources: Watts (2006); Fallows (2008).

❓ Can the Internet undermine authoritarian regimes?

Internet and mobile-phone technology make possible the bypassing of state media controls. They enable the cross-border organization of dispersed or fragmented opposition movements and the transmission of information about demonstrations and protests against repressive states. The use of Twitter by the anti-government protest movement after the 2009 election in Iran provides a case in point.

The state's capacity to intercept, monitor, and block transmission has been increasing (see Box 10.20). The public sphere of the Internet has become a battleground between the state and technically sophisticated users of Web 2.0. Furthermore, in some countries, the state penetration of SNS networks has made it easier for the authorities to obtain information about dissidents and counter their activities. States can also plant information to discredit their opponents or create stooge identities to muddy the waters (Morozov 2009). State regulation should not, however, just be seen as an interference with free public discourse. It provides the only means of policing 'abuse' of the Net by racist and hate groups, and paedophile networks.

There are also reasons for doubting whether the Internet can *replace* the media as the main vehicle of the public sphere:

- *Access.* The Net is still a long way from being as accessible as radio, television, or newspapers, which are the main source of information for most people.

- *Amateurism.* Much Net information is not produced according to the professional standards of journalism (see Box 10.19 on p. 381).

- *The interface with politics.* The connection between the Net and mainstream political discussion and communication is limited.

- *Depoliticization.* The opportunities provided by Web 2.0 for gossip, socializing, and the spreading of private material may distract attention from public matters.

There are, then, good grounds for the view that the Net can contribute importantly to the public sphere. Although commercialization has diverted its content away from the goals and values of those who created it, this has arguably made it much more accessible without destroying its public functions. Governments are, however, making greater attempts to monitor, regulate, and, indeed, use it for their own purposes. And, while the growth of SNS can be a vehicle for opposition groups, it can also lead to the intrusion of the private into the public sphere. The established media still have a crucial function to perform in the public sphere.

Media globalization

Global communication has potentially opened up a new world of choice by giving people access through cinema, radio and television, computer and phone to a wide variety of different cultural experiences. The key word here is *potentially*. Some claim that globalization has actually destroyed diversity by imposing on the world the culture of the advanced nations, above all that of the United States. The global diffusion of American culture has been seen as a **media imperialism** that promotes continued domination by American corporations, values, and policies. Note that the term 'cultural imperialism' is sometimes used instead.

Media imperialism

We examined earlier the growth of Hollywood film production (see p. 362). According to exponents of the media-imperialism approach, notably the political economist Herbert Schiller, the interrelated US entertainment, communications, and information industries became globally dominant. American values were spread worldwide through the popular culture disseminated by these industries. The media were a particularly effective instrument of economic and political influence because of their 'direct, though immeasurable impact on consciousness' (Schiller 1969: 115). A media imperialism had replaced the earlier military imperialism that had failed.

More recently, Robert McChesney has developed these ideas from a similar 'critical political economy' perspective. He argues that before the 1980s national media systems were able to coexist with imported media content, but during the 1980s and 1990s transnational, mainly US, media corporations expanded their activities into other countries. Ownership of the media became increasingly concentrated in the hands of a small number of giant multi-media corporations (see p. 376). This process went hand in hand with the spread of neo-liberalism, as processes of deregulation and privatization opened up countries to the operations of these corporations.

> In short order, the global media market has come to be dominated by nine transnational corporations: *General Electric* (owner of NBC), *Liberty Media, Disney, AOL-Time Warner, Sony, News Corporation, Viacom, Vivendi*, and *Bertelsmann*. . . . Between them, these nine companies own: the major US film studios; the US television networks; 80–85 per cent of the global music market; the majority of satellite broadcasting worldwide; all or a part of a majority of cable broadcasting systems; a significant percentage of book publishing and commercial magazine publishing . . . a significant portion of European terrestrial television; and on and on.
>
> *McChesney 2003: 29*

McChesney has moved away from the notion that this is simply a matter of American media imperialism. The USA is the largest source of these transnational media corporations but *Sony* (Japan), *News Corporation* (Australia), *Vivendi* (France), and *Bertelsmann* (Germany) have originated elsewhere. Whatever their base or origin, they advance 'corporate and commercial interests and values' (McChesney 2003: 35).They spread not American domination but that of a global corporate capitalism.

There is, nonetheless, evidence of increasing American domination of cinema and television in some regions. Between 1987 and 1996 Hollywood's share of the European film market rose from 56 per cent to 70 per cent. By 1996 Hollywood had 83 per cent of the Latin American market. Mexico had at one time produced a hundred films a year but by 1995 was making only forty and by 1998 less than ten (United Nations Development Programme 1999: 33). In the 1990s some 62 per cent of television-programming in Latin America came from the United States, 8 per cent from Asia and Europe, and only 30 per cent from within the region (United Nations Development Programme 1999: 34).

Cultural pluralism

The claim that the world is dominated by American or, more broadly, Western corporations is opposed by those who argue that the emergence of local production has led to a growing cultural pluralism. Annabelle Sreberny-Mohammadi (1996) listed a number of ways in which national cultures can resist media imperialism:

- *The domestication of output.* Home-produced programmes can oust imports because they are more attractive for linguistic and cultural reasons.

- *Reverse flows.* Ex-colonial countries can start to export their own programmes to the old imperial societies. Increasing international migration has paved the way for this. Bollywood films provide a good example.

- *Going global.* Local producers can themselves create transnational corporations. For example, ZEE TV, a Hindi-language Indian commercial station, took over TV Asia in Britain and has extended its operations to the USA.

- *Controls on distribution.* Television imports to terrestrial channels in Britain have been limited to a quota of some 14 per cent of programmes. It is more difficult to control satellite television, but some countries, such as Singapore, Malaysia, Saudi Arabia, and Iran, have banned the sale of satellite dishes.

American penetration of markets does vary considerably. It is high, as we saw above, in Latin America, though Brazil is an important independent centre of production there. It has been much lower in some Asian markets, especially India. Indeed, according to a UNESCO survey, Bollywood produced 1,091 feature-length films in 2006, and the USA only 485. There has been a remarkable growth of film production in Nigeria (known as Nollywood), which in 2006 made 872 films (UNESCO Institute for Statistics 2009). Production is one thing, distribution

Global focus 'Reality TV' goes global   10.21

The *Big Brother* format was created in 2000, and by early 2004 there were already twenty-four different versions across the world. The twenty-fifth was *Big Brother Middle East*, which was the first in a Muslim area. There was much local concern that unmarried men and women would be sharing the same house and might fall in love. Nonetheless, the programme went ahead but with separate living rooms and prayer rooms for men and women. Cameras in the bathroom, dance marathons, and the practice of chaining people together for long periods were all dropped!

In 2005 *The Apprentice* arrived in China. There it was called *Wise Man Takes All*. In the American and British versions contestants compete to secure employment with such well-known entrepreneurs as Donald Trump and Alan Sugar, who set them complex tasks, judge their performance ruthlessly, and fire those who do not perform. In the Chinese version the show has more of an educational character. Contestants have to submit business plans, to be judged by a panel of business-school professors, and the winner receives one million *yuan* to invest in his or her business. There is no humiliation of contestants and no one gets fired!

Sources: Independent, 28 February 2004, 18 August 2005.

❓ Does the international spread of 'reality TV' weaken or strengthen local cultures?

something else, and here the USA remains well ahead of the field, but it is still significant that production thrives outside Hollywood.

The notion of Americanization is also open to the criticism that it is based on the *media-effects* model of media influence, which we discussed on p. 357. It assumes that American programmes automatically inject American values. Studies of the impact of the American *Dallas* series, which was exported to more than ninety countries, showed that it is not as simple as that. *Dallas* apparently celebrated the values of American capitalism, but Ang (1985) demonstrated that Dutch viewers were perfectly capable of enjoying the story and its emotions while disapproving of its values and rejecting them.

Bollywood: a reverse flow?

© Getty Images/Arko Dattaut

Controversy and debate Al-Jazeera   10.22

CNN has been a powerful vehicle for the global diffusion of the American view of the world, but in the Middle East its domination of 24-hour news broadcasting has been challenged by the rise of Al-Jazeera, an Arabic satellite channel launched in Qatar in 1996 and modelled on CNN.

Al-Jazeera's news coverage has been heavily criticized by US leaders and officials. It has been accused of giving a voice to Al-Qaeda by broadcasting Osama bin-Laden's videotapes. It has been criticized for showing 'raw' the bloody consequences of warfare and insurgency in Iraq. It has been seen as a mouthpiece of the insurgents because of its 'slanted' reporting of the civilian deaths and destruction caused by military operations. Its offices in Kabul and Baghdad were bombed by American planes, and its operations in Iraq have been shut down.

Al-Jazeera is seen as an Arabic alternative to Western news channels, but its position is not as simple as this. It has

drawn Arabic criticism because it has given voice through interviews to Israeli and American politicians. It has also been seen as siding with Sunni Muslims against Shias. The rival Al-Arabiya news channel, set up by Saudi interests in Dubai in 2003, is popular in Iraq and Saudi Arabia.

What does the future hold for Al-Jazeera? It has global ambitions. It launched an English-language channel, presented by David Frost, in March 2006. A new competitor for its audience in the Middle East is, however, coming over the horizon. The BBC launched its own Arabic news channel, funded by the British Foreign Office, in 2008.

Sources: *Economist*, 24 February 2005 (Special Report: 'Arab Satellite Television'); Miles (2005); Gibson and Rattansi (2006).

❓ What does this account tell us about media globalization, American global domination, and cultural pluralism?

As we showed, audience identification with film characters is a complex process. The audience may simply reverse the apparent values of a Hollywood film by siding with the 'bad guys' rather than the 'good guys'. People respond to cultural imports within the context of their own situation and values.

Global corporations anyway recognize that they can market their products more effectively by adapting them to local needs. Indeed, the term 'glocalization' was invented to describe the Japanese marketing strategy of adapting global products to meet local requirements. It should not, therefore, be assumed that the global destroys the local, though this also means that an apparent local pluralism may hide a sophisticated corporate strategy. Local production may disguise corporate penetration of a local economy.

Dominant cultures

The debate over Americanization and cultural imperialism has mainly revolved around the relationships between societies but needs also to be placed in an internal context. We need to return here to our earlier discussion of 'mass culture' (see p. 355). The diffusion of cultural products from the dominant developed societies can be seen from the 'culture-industry' approach as maintaining capitalism by spreading capitalist values within a society and turning people into passive consumers.

Interpretations of Americanization here differ. Those holding *elitist* views of British culture (see p. 356) have

been hostile to Americanization. They have viewed it as a commercial intrusion responsible for the mass culture that threatened to swamp British cultural traditions. It has been interpreted very differently from a *populist* perspective. This view claimed that America was popular because American culture gave them what they actually wanted. America was a source of democratic and popular forms of culture that had been suppressed in a class-dominated Britain. Young members of the working class could draw on American culture to resist and challenge the dominant culture.

Similarly, the defence of 'the local' against Americanization may be a defence of the local regime. As Sreberny-Mohammadi (1996) has pointed out, local producers will generally be under the control of their nation state, which may well be trying to stamp out local resistance to its authority. The banning of satellite dishes may be little to do with preserving local culture and a lot to do with maintaining the existing social order. In highly patriarchal societies, male domination may be threatened by the import of programmes embodying a different conception of the role of women. Some aspects of Americanization or Westernization may well be liberating.

This clearly applies as well to attempts by state authorities to erect barriers to Internet and mobile-phone traffic, as in recent events in Iran and China. But this brings out another dimension to this problem. In these situations the Western media corporations may collude with local regimes to keep out Western ideas that threaten the regime's authority. In Iran, Nokia Siemens Networks supplied a monitoring centre, described as 'lawful intercept functionality', to *Irantelecom*, the state-owned telephone company. This enabled the regime to monitor the external links of the protest movement that emerged in the wake of the 2009 election, indeed resulting in the boycotting of Nokia phones by supporters of the movement (*Guardian*, 14 July 2009). In China, Western corporations have similarly colluded with the state (see Box 10.20 on p. 382).

Thus, the activities of Western media corporations must not only be placed in the context of conflicts *between* national cultures but also set in the conflicts of interest and authority relationships *within* societies. There is here a certain ambivalence in the role of these corporations. By transmitting Western ideas they may undermine authoritarian regimes, but they may then also collude with the regime to filter out threatening material, in order to maintain access to markets.

 Stop and reflect

In this section we examined the movement from a small number of mass-media outlets towards a world of more specialized multiple media.

- Technical change, neo-liberal politics, post-Fordist organization, post-modern culture, and globalization have created greater media diversity.

This diversity has in principle provided more choice, but in practice within limits.

- The exercise of choice depends on access, which requires resources, knowledge, time, and control.
- The concentration of ownership has increased not only within particular media but also across the media and internationally.
- What implications has this concentration had for political choice?

We also considered the impact of media changes on the public sphere.

- Revisit the discussion (on pp. 361–3) of the impact of the growth of the mass media on this sphere.
- The commercialization of newspapers and broadcasting have weakened its autonomy.
- The state is a guardian of this sphere but also a threat to it.
- Has the Internet revived it?

Technical change and neo-liberal capitalism have facilitated media globalization.

- This has potentially provided access to a far greater range of cultures and experiences.
- Has it led to Americanization?

 Key concepts

- cyberculture 356
- dominant culture 356
- dominant ideology 352
- folk culture 355
- gatekeepers 364
- hegemony 352
- hegemonic masculinity 368

- high culture 355
- mass culture 355
- mass media 352
- mass society 352
- media 351
- media imperialism 383
- moral panic 372

- popular culture 355
- post-Fordism 374
- post-modernism 375
- public sphere 354
- subcultures 356

Workshop 10

Study 10 Television and violence

The impact of television watching on violence has been a much-debated issue. As we argued on p. 371, it is one thing to show an association between watching violence on television and violent behaviour, but it is more difficult to show that the watching led to the violence, rather than the other way round. People with a violent disposition or in a situation that made them violent might simply be attracted to violent programmes.

The results of a sophisticated longitudinal study that tried to tackle this problem have been published by Johnson *et al.* (2002). This was a seventeen-year study, beginning in 1975, of 707 families with a child under 10 in the state of New York. Data on television viewing and aggressive or criminal behaviour were collected by interviews with the children and their mothers in the 1980s and 1990s. Information was also collected on other aspects of these families, such as intelligence, education, income, psychiatric disorders, and child neglect, and on neighbourhood characteristics, including levels of aggression and school violence.

The study found a significant association between the amount of television watched in the early teenage years (at an average age of 14) and aggressive acts reported later (at average ages of 16 and 22). Thus, it was reported that 25 per cent of those who had watched more than three hours of television per day in their early teenage years were involved later on in assaults or fights resulting in injury. This compared with 18 per cent of those who watched between one and three hours, and 6 per cent of those who watched less than one hour.

There was also an association between amount of television watched in early adulthood (at an average age of 22) and aggressive acts reported later (at an average age of 30), though this was not so strong.

There were important differences between boys and girls. The early teenage boys who watched a lot of television were far more likely to be involved in assaults or fights later on—some 42 per cent of those who had watched more than three hours a day, compared with 27.5 per cent of those watching one to three hours, and only 9 per cent of those watching less than an hour. The association was much less strong with girls at this age.

The picture changed dramatically later on. There was a much stronger association between television-watching and later aggression among young adult women than young adult men. While 17 per cent of the women who watched more than three hours of television engaged in aggressive acts later, only 4 per cent of those who watched between one and three hours did so (none of them watched less than an hour).

These associations suggest that large amounts of television-watching may lead to violence later, but what about other possible explanations? There was still a significant association between amount of watching and amount of later aggression after controlling other variables, such as poverty or bad parenting, which might account for both. What about the argument that those with aggressive tendencies were more likely to watch a lot of television in the first place? An association was found between amount of watching and later violence, whether or not there was a history of previous violence.

What conclusions can be drawn from this study? The authors state that their study could not, by its very nature, demonstrate a *causal* connection between amount of television-watching and later violence. Some environmental factor they had not taken into account could possibly explain the association. Only a controlled experiment could demonstrate causation, and a study of that kind would be unethical. The leader of the research team was, however, confident enough to state: 'Our findings suggest that, at least during early adolescence, responsible parents should avoid permitting their children to watch more than one hour of television a day' (*Independent*, 29 March 2002).

Note that this study did not show an association between *amount of violence* seen on television and later violence. The association was between *amount of watching* as such and later violence. The authors refer to other studies that show there are on average between three and five violent acts per hour of prime-time television and between twenty and twenty-five in an average hour of children's television.

Sources: Johnson *et al.* (2002); *Independent*, 29 March 2002.

❷ Can you think of any possible explanation of the association between amount of television watching and later violence other than the violent content of television programmes?

❷ Given this study's results, should children's television-viewing be restricted to one hour a day?

❷ Try making a content analysis of the violence portrayed in a drama or some other similar programme on television (record it first). List incidents of violence, their duration, their consequences, different types of violence, the relationship in which the violence occurs and its context. Before doing this you must think carefully about the meaning and types of violence, and construct lists and grids to help you record what you see (see p. 371 of this chapter and the discussion of domestic violence in Chapter 12, pp. 461–3). How far can a content analysis take one in investigating the significance of violence on television?

Media watch 10 News from Israel

In *Bad News from Israel* (2004), Greg Philo and Mike Berry from the Glasgow University Media Group examined the process of news production, the content of news broadcasts, and their impact on audiences. They interviewed journalists and other broadcasting professionals. They analysed TV news coverage of Israel from September 2000 to April 2002. They investigated audience responses through a questionnaire distributed to students in Britain, the United States, and Germany, and through the extensive use of focus groups, in which journalists and other broadcasting professionals participated.

This study is set in the context of the historical conflict between Israel and the Palestinians. Two key events are identified:

* the displacement of Palestinians from homes and land when Israel was created in 1948;
* the establishment of Israeli military control of the occupied territories after the 1967 war.

Recent events can be understood and explained only when placed in the context of these historic events. Very different accounts of these historic events have, however, been provided by the two sides, which makes the job of the journalist extremely difficult.

Content analysis showed that TV news-reporting was dominated by Israeli perspectives. The Palestinians were seen as the source of trouble and Israel as only responding or retaliating. There was more coverage of Israeli than Palestinian casualties, even though more Palestinians died, and a different language was used to describe Israeli and Palestinian casualties. Israeli deaths but not Palestinian ones were, for example, described as 'mass murder' (Philo and Berry 2004: 259). Israeli perspectives tended to dominate the headlines.

Philo and Berry comment on the lack of historical explanation in news reports. This could partly be due to the production process. News bulletins had to fit a time frame. A concern for audience ratings favoured images of violence, fighting, and destruction, rather than dry explanation. A focus on bombings rather than the situation that gave rise to them suited, however, the Israeli view of the conflict, while the 'war-on-terror' language of news reports demonstrated the dominance of an Israeli/American perspective. There are, of course, lobbies for both sides, but the dominance of this perspective reflected the greater power of the pro-Israel lobby in Britain and the United States, and the superior effectiveness of the Israeli public-relations machinery.

The content of the news is clearly important, but what *effect* does it have on the audience? This was partly assessed through questionnaire responses, but the focus groups were crucial, since they made it possible to explore the reasons given for answers and to discuss the issues raised. Focus-group members also participated in a news-writing exercise to see whether they reproduced the language and explanations found in news broadcasts.

Most participants in the audience study had little idea of the history, which 'made it very difficult for people to understand key elements of the conflict' (Philo and Berry 2004: 216). But there was plentiful evidence that the audience had absorbed many features of the news treatment of the conflict. It was, for example, often seen as initiated by the Palestinians with the Israelis then responding, while the news-writing exercise showed the audience reproducing the themes of TV news. Those who obtained information from other sources could, however, be critical of TV news coverage and present alternative views.

Discussion in the focus groups brought out a 'strong feeling ... that the news should explain origins and causes and that journalists should speak more directly to viewers about what was happening and why' (Philo and Berry 2004: 240). When people learned more about the history of the conflict through the focus-group discussions, their interest in the news increased, while 'incomprehension led to detachment and increased the sense of powerlessness some people felt when watching terrible events with which they could not engage or relate to' (Philo and Berry 2004: 257). This led Philo and Berry to argue that the existing structure and content of TV news programmes should be changed in order to provide better information for people.

❷ What do we learn from this study about the uses and limitations of content analysis?

❷ Why do Philo and Berry think there should be more explanation of origins and causes?

❷ How do you think journalists should deal with conflicting accounts of events?

❷ Should the structure and content of the main television news programmes be changed, and if so, how?

Discussion points

Television violence

Before discussing this issue, read the section on 'Moral issues' and Study 10.

- Why do some people think that violence on TV makes people more violent?
- Why do others think that TV violence has no such effect?

Consider what 'violence' means, and how violence should be defined.

- Can we really speak of violence in general?
- How can violence be differentiated? What kinds of violence are there?
- Is there good evidence that TV violence makes people more violent?
- Or is the concern with TV violence just a 'moral panic'?

Cultures

Before discussing this, read 'The media and culture', and the later sections on 'Media globalization'.

- Consider the terms 'high culture', 'folk culture', and 'popular culture'. How are they to be distinguished? Find examples of each.
- How would a post-modern approach view such distinctions?
- Do *you* think these distinctions are meaningful?

What is cyberculture?

- How free is it from the constraints operating in other media?
- Why is it thought that globalization is leading to Americanization?

- Does globalization mean that local cultures are disappearing?

What were the last three television programmes that you watched?

- Where was each produced?
- Did any of them show signs of American influence? Consider the type of programme, its format, and style.
- Did these programmes reflect your own national culture in any way?

The public sphere

Before discussing this, read 'A public sphere?' (p. 354), 'The rise of the mass media', and 'Decline of the public sphere?'. Make sure that you are clear about the meaning of the 'public sphere'.

- Which institutions and organizations of your society contribute to its public sphere?
- Why is it important that a society has a functioning public sphere?
- What reasons are there for thinking that the public sphere is in decline?
- Is there still a functioning public sphere in your society?
- Do you think that your society needs a larger or stronger public sphere?
- Has the Internet/Web revived the public sphere?
- Will the Internet/Web become the main medium of the public sphere?

Explore further

The following references cover most of the issues dealt with in this chapter:

Eldridge, J., Kitzinger, J., and Williams, K. (1997), *The Mass Media and Power in Modern Britain* (Oxford: Oxford University Press). *A discussion of the power of the media, examining their history, and reviewing different approaches to their influence.*

Lievrou, L., and Livingstone, S. (2006) (eds), *The Handbook of New Media: Updated Student Edition* (London: Sage). *A wide-ranging collection of pieces focusing on the uses and implications of new media technologies and networks.*

Newbold, C., Boyd-Barrett, O., and Van den Bulck, H. (2002) (eds), *The Media Book (London: Arnold). A clear and comprehensive introductory reader that works through all the key issues in media studies.*

Particular topics can be followed up through:

Abercrombie, N. (1996), *Television and Society* (Cambridge: Polity Press). *Although this is focused on television, it is a very clear and full analysis of all aspects of the sociology of the media.*

Bell, D., and Kennedy, B. (2000), *The Cybercultures Reader* (London: Routledge). *A very extensive collection of pieces out on the frontiers of the study of culture.*

Curran, J., and Seaton, J. (2002), *Power without Responsibility: The Press and Broadcasting in Britain* (6th edn, London: Routledge). *A theoretically informed account of the development of the press and broadcasting from the nineteenth century onwards.*

Flew, T. (2007), *Understanding Global Media* (Houndmills: Palgrave Macmillan). *A clear and systematic examination of theories of media globalization, covering approaches ranging from political economy to cultural studies.*

Gauntlett, D. (2008), *Media, Gender and Identity: An Introduction* (2nd edn, London: Routledge). *A lively and theoretically informed examination of gender issues, dealing with both femininity and masculinity.*

Gillespie, M., and Toynbee, J. (2006) (eds), *Analysing Media Texts* (Maidenhead: Open University Press). *A stimulating and accessible collection of pieces on the analysis of texts, with a DVD-ROM that provides activities related to each chapter.*

Hesmondhalgh, D. (2007), *Cultural Industries* (2nd edn, London: Sage). *A penetrating and very up-to-date analysis of cultural production and the way it has changed since the 1980s, setting it in its economic and technological context.*

Seabrook, J. (2004), *Consuming Cultures: Globalization and Local Lives* (Oxford: New Internationalist). *A highly readable discussion of the impact of globalization and Americanization on cultural diversity, with lots of examples.*

Strinati, D. (2000), *An Introduction to Studying Popular Culture* (London: Routledge). *A clear and comprehensive guide to the study of popular culture.*

Online resources

Visit the Online Resource Centre that accompanies this book to access more learning resources and other interesting material on communication and the media at:
www.oxfordtextbooks.co.uk/orc/fulcher4e/

The Resource Center for Cyberculture Studies is 'an online, not-for-profit organization whose purpose is to research, study, teach, support, and create diverse and dynamic elements of cyberculture':
http://rccs.usfca.edu

Transparency, a site created by American writer and media critic Ken Sanes, provides very clear and theoretically informed accounts and reviews of contemporary material on the media and popular culture. Both lecturers and students have apparently found his work very helpful:
www.transparencynow.com

Based in the United States, the Center for Media and Public Affairs is a 'nonpartisan research and educational organization', and conducts research into many different aspects of media content and influence:
www.cmpa.com/index.htm

The Campaign for Press Broadcasting Freedom campaigns for the reform of the British media and is linked to the unions and the labour movement:
http://keywords.dsvr.co.uk/freepress

Religion, Belief, and Meaning

Contents

11

Pagan beliefs

Cassandra Latham is a qualified nurse and counsellor. She is also a witch. She makes charms and spells for the residents of her village in Cornwall, and she makes them available to a larger audience through her website (www.villagewisewoman.co.uk). Maureen Brown is a psychotherapist, and she, too, is a witch. Maureen has been a member of a coven in Croydon for twenty-six years.

Witches are followers of the Wiccan religion. There are about 10,000 in Britain today, and most are affiliated to the Pagan Federation, which has 100,000 members. Its practitioners adopt magical means to cast spells, mix love potions, and engage in other rituals aimed at enhancing a person's powers and abilities. These aspects of Wicca are familiar from story-book images such as those in the Harry Potter books. Wiccans, however, base their magic and rituals on their belief in a so-called Mother Goddess, closely associated with the Horned God. They celebrate the winter and summer solstices, the autumn and spring equinoxes, and they hold festivals at Lammas (harvest time in August) and Halloween (October).

Cassandra Latham: Village Wisewoman.
© Simon Burt of Apex Agency

Paganism is little understood. It is often confused with Satanism or with the demons depicted in *Buffy the Vampire Slayer*. In fact, it is a very respectable religion. The Pagan Federation comprises druids, witches, shamans, wizards, and others who are united by their adherence to ancient Celtic, Germanic, and Norse beliefs. For a long time, those beliefs have been ignored and were actively suppressed in the witchcraft persecutions of the sixteenth and seventeenth centuries. The Witchcraft Act was not repealed until 1951, and Wicca, like other Pagan religions, has grown rapidly since then—and especially since the 1970s. Contemporary Wicca and Paganism have few direct links with past generations of believers and are, in many respects, recent creations: Wicca was effectively founded as an organized religion by Gerald Gardner in the early 1950s.

Sources: *Guardian,* 28 October 2000; *Sunday Times Magazine,* 23 December 2001.

For every person in Britain today who subscribes to Pagan beliefs, there are many more who subscribe to more conventional religious beliefs. For these people, religion is something for Sundays and holy days, and is practised largely in and through a church. Others adhere to highly emotional belief systems and may talk in tongues, engage in faith healing, or actively convert others on their doorsteps. In many societies of the past, levels of religious activity were much greater than for most people in Britain today. Many societies, however, have very high levels of religious activity. Religious participation is especially high in the United States. The strength of religious commitment is quite variable from one society to another.

In this chapter we will look at religions of all kinds and, in particular, at the historical trend in religion and belief in modern societies. In the section on 'Theories and concepts' we consider the nature of religion and the major sociological approaches to the subject. The second section on 'Religion in modern society' examines the decline in religious beliefs and practices and assesses whether modern societies have undergone a process of secularization. The final section, on 'The rise of new religions', looks at the significance of the many new religions that have experienced a growth in membership in recent decades.

Concepts and theories

A religion is a system of beliefs through which people organize and order their lives. This is often thought to involve a belief in a god or gods, but this is not the case with all religious beliefs. The central meaning of the word 'religion' is, in fact, simply the way in which shared beliefs establish regulations, rules, or bonds of obligation among the members of a community. In its broadest sense, then, religion involves devotion or attachment to a system of beliefs that defines the moral obligations and responsibilities people have towards one another. These beliefs define a code of behaviour that regulates personal and social life. It is notoriously difficult to produce any generally acceptable definition of religion. Wallis and Bruce, however, came up with a useful, if rather complex, definition. According to them, a religion comprises the,

... actions, beliefs and institutions predicated upon the assumption of the existence of either supernatural entities with powers of agency, or impersonal powers or processes possessed of moral purpose, which have the capacity to set the conditions of, or to intervene in, human affairs.

Wallis and Bruce 1992: 10–11

While this definition contains a number of quite complex ideas, it is a good starting point for our discussion, and you will find it useful to return to it from time to time.

The sacred and the secular

Religious beliefs and rites have generally been organized around objects and activities held to be sacred because they have superior power or dignity relative to the objects and activities of everyday life. Sacred things have 'a quality of mysterious and awesome power' (Berger 1967: 34; see also Durkheim 1912; Pickering 1984). They have a spiritual quality that leads them to be venerated as holy and to be set apart from everyday things. By contrast with natural objects, they are *supernatural*. These sacred objects are the basis of the moral standards by which the non-sacred, or *secular* world is judged. Religious activity involves special forms of communication and action—such as prayer and ritual—through which those in the secular world come into contact with the sacred world.

Religion forms what Berger (1967) calls a *sacred canopy*. This is an overarching framework of meanings that gives a larger, cosmological significance to the ordinary world of practical action and that legitimate particular social institutions. Everyday matters can be seen as significant if they have a place in a wider context of meanings. When covered by a sacred canopy, routine, day-to-day social reality comes to acquire a significance that goes beyond the immediate, practical interests and concerns of everyday life. Instead of appearing as arbitrary and precarious, it appears as part of some larger purpose. People conform to the expectations defined by this social reality because they feel a sense of duty or obligation to something beyond themselves. Sacred social institutions may compete for control over people's lives with institutions that are purely secular.

Religions differ from one another in terms of those things they regard as sacred or holy. Typically, the ultimate sacred object is some kind of higher power, such as a god, though this may often be seen in highly abstract terms. What are called theistic religions are those that involve devotion to a superhuman or controlling power seen as the source of all moral values and requiring an attitude of reverence or awe. Such a sacred power becomes the object of worship. The major monotheistic religions—Judaism, Christianity, and Islam—have all accorded this kind of devotion to a single, personified God. In Christian theology, for example, representations of God are at the heart of the spiritual significance given to sacred texts (especially the Bible), to sacred buildings (churches and chapels), and to sacred music and works of art.

Polytheistic religions, on the other hand, are organized around a large number of separate gods. The religions of ancient Greece and Rome, for example, were polytheistic. In fact, they invoked a similar set of gods. For the Greeks, Zeus ruled the spiritual world from Mount Olympus, along with Athena, Poseidon, Hermes, Artemis, and other gods. For the Romans, the counterpart gods were the spiritual ruler Jupiter, together with Minerva, Neptune, Mercury, and Diana. In both religions, the events of the natural and social worlds reflected the relations of cooperation and competition that existed among the various gods.

In practice, however, the distinction between monotheistic and polytheistic religions is difficult to draw with any precision. Early and medieval Christianity, for example, saw God—personified always in male terms—as standing at the head of a celestial hierarchy of other spiritual beings: seraphim, cherubim, thrones, dominations, virtues, powers, principalities, archangels, and angels. The various prophets and saints inspired by God also became objects of religious devotion, as did—above all—Mary, the mother of God. In this system of religious belief, then, monotheism was combined with the recognition of a vast number of lesser spiritual beings.

Not all religions are theistic. Buddhism, for example, has no conception of a personal god, although it does require that people regulate their lives by specific values and standards. It sees people as going through a series of reincarnations until they achieve an enlightened, sacred state that releases them from their earthly existence. They achieve 'nirvana'. The moral standards that Buddhists must follow, therefore, have an ultimate, supernatural significance, but are not derived from the demands of any supernatural being. Though recognizing no personified gods, Buddhists do revere those who have achieved perfect enlightenment. They are termed Buddhas and Bodhisattvas and are held up as exemplars for others to follow. The founder of the religion—often referred to simply as Buddha—was Sidartha Gautama, the most important of the Buddhist saints. Buddhism merges easily with other religions, and many of the gods of the traditional Brahman religion of India, from which Buddhism originated, were simply transformed into Buddhas. The number of holy entities recognized in some forms of Buddhism can, in fact, be very high.

Buddhism is a religion in which the ultimate state of existence (nirvana) is *transcendent*—that is to say, it goes beyond the everyday world and exists only on a purely spiritual plane. Similarly, the Christian heaven is an ultimate state that transcends the everyday world. In some non-theistic religions, however, the ultimate state of existence is *immanent* rather than transcendent. This means that it is rooted in the natural, practical world itself and is seen as an actual state of affairs that can or will result from practical actions. The secular world—as it is or as it might become—is itself given a sacred status.

Soviet Communism, for example, justified commitment to the existing political order in relation to the ideal Communist society that was being built. The state's role in building this ideal legitimated conformity to its demands. Despite the absence of gods and transcendent states of existence, Soviet Communism was a religion as we have defined it. Marxist-Leninist ideas were drawn upon to construct images of such sacred entities as the proletariat and the party, and these became objects of reverential attachment. Exemplary thinkers and practitioners of Marxism were accorded a holy status, and some became the objects of cult attachments. Marx, Engels, Lenin, and Stalin were all treated in this way. Lenin's body, for example, was preserved in a special mausoleum in Moscow and was the focus of many ceremonies of state. Party Congresses and other party meetings provided the ritualized contexts in which these ideas and values could be reaffirmed. Even after the collapse of the Communist regime, cult attachments persisted, and the new authorities did not rush to remove Lenin's body from public display.

Theories of religion

The pioneer sociologists of the nineteenth century recognized the central part that religion has played in human history. They were particularly concerned, however, with the implications of modern science for traditional forms of religion. Both Comte and Marx saw the specifically supernatural aspects of religious belief as being incompatible with an acceptance of modern scientific knowledge. Both of them held that traditional forms of religion would disappear as modern societies matured. Their claim concerned the secularization of modern society—the declining significance of religion in the day-to-day lives of people in the modern social world.

The founders of classical sociology—most particularly Durkheim and Weber—drew on these ideas and developed them into more sophisticated understandings of the social significance of religion and scientific knowledge. Durkheim, like Comte, saw modern society as evolving new forms of religion that were more compatible with scientific knowledge and with the structures of complex, advanced societies. Weber was more pessimistic. He anticipated the complete disappearance of all religion and held that individuals would be unable to make any sense of their lives. Weber undertook a range of comparative and historical studies of religion, looking particularly at the link between religion and the rise of capitalism. A useful overview of theories of religion can be found in Beckford (1989) and Aldridge (2000).

Comte and Marx: religion and science

Comte saw traditional religions as having either a theistic or a metaphysical character. They constructed sacred canopies around ideas of supernatural beings or abstract forces and powers. The Catholic Church in medieval Europe was typical of such a traditional religion (see Box 11.1). These kinds of religious ideas, Comte held, have been undermined by the growth of modern science. In the modern world, he argued, no theistic or metaphysical religion can stand up to the advance of scientific knowledge. He held, however, that modern societies did still require a system of beliefs that would function as religion had in the past to regulate social activities and produce social order. This new form of religion he found in science itself.

Positive, scientific thought, Comte held, would become the basis of a new kind of religion that could provide the cohesion and consensus necessary for social integration.

Briefing: Catholicism 11.1

Christians believe that Jesus was the Son of God, the Messiah prophesied in the Jewish religious texts. Christianity was adopted as the official religion of the Roman Empire in the fourth century AD. The Roman Church termed itself Catholic because it claimed to be a universally valid religion for all who lived within the Empire. The Roman Catholic Church has always had a centralized structure and is headed by the Pope, who has ultimate, infallible authority over its members. The authority of the Church is exercised through a hierarchy of cardinals, archbishops, bishops, and priests.

With the fall of the Roman Empire, the Roman Catholic Church was separated from the Eastern Orthodox Church, a federation of independent churches that rejected the authority of the Pope but retained the core beliefs and rituals of the Roman Church. The Orthodox Church remains strong in Greece, the Balkans, and Russia, while the Roman Catholic Church is strongest in Italy, Spain, and Latin America.

It could do this without resorting to theistic or metaphysical ideas. Only a scientifically based religion could provide sacred ideas and a moral code compatible with the modern scientific outlook. Central to all religious beliefs are ideas about the nature of social life itself, and Comte therefore held that the science of society—sociology—would be at the heart of this new religion. Comte set out to help build a positivist religion of humanity that could provide the necessary cement to hold modern societies together (B. Turner 1991: ch. 2).

> ### ⊃ Connections
> You might like to look back at our review of the development of sociological theory in Chapter 2. There you will find accounts of Comte and the various other theorists that we look at in this section. Comte's religion of humanity followed from his law of the three stages, which we discuss on p. 26.

A more radical view of religion was taken by Marx, though he too recognized the role it played in furthering social cohesion. Like Comte, Marx believed that theistic forms of religion would disappear as modern societies matured. He believed, however, that this would occur only when the capitalist features of these societies had been abolished and they had become socialist societies.

Marx saw theistic and metaphysical religions as expressions of the deepening alienation experienced in a modern capitalist society. Traditional religious thought is simply a distorted reflection of the real class relations that connect and divide people from one another. In a capitalist society, Marx held, class divisions take a particularly sharp form, but they are obscured by religious ideas of unity and common brotherhood. The cohesion and integration this produced simply served the interests of the dominant class and not the whole of society.

According to Marx, then, traditional religion has an *ideological* function and cannot be understood apart from underlying social divisions and conflicts. Although it appears to provide a sense of meaning for those who are subject to economic exploitation, this is an illusion. It merely obscures their subordination and oppression and makes it less likely they would challenge the existing social order. Religion deflects social conflict by encouraging people to accept their social position. It is, in Marx's words, both 'the sigh of the oppressed' and 'the opium of the people'. By providing illusions to live by, it effectively drugs people into the acceptance of social relations that exploit and alienate them. Religion will be swept completely away when capitalism is overthrown and when, in consequence, alienation and class divisions finally disappear from human history.

Durkheim: religion and individualism

Durkheim followed Comte in recognizing the part played by religious belief and ritual in social cohesion and social integration (Beckford 1989: 25–31). He also agreed with Comte that the theistic aspects of religion would disappear in modern society. Though he rejected Comte's religion of humanity, he did say that modern societies would come to be organized around a 'cult of man' or cult of individualism.

Durkheim approached religion from an analysis of its most primitive or elementary forms. These he found in the **totemism** of tribal societies. All forms of religion, he argued, had their origins in totemistic beliefs, though he believed that these survived only among native Australians and some North American tribes. These tribes, he argued, were divided into clans, which were the real bases of social solidarity. People felt strong sentiments of attachment to their clan, because it defined their relations to all other members of their tribe. Each clan identified itself with a particular animal or plant. This was its emblem or totem, and it symbolized the clan. Members of a clan might say, for example, that they are the fox clan, and that they are quite distinct from the beaver clan. These totems are, then, marks of social identity.

Because clan membership is fundamental to the whole way in which people live their lives, the totem has a sacred quality. It was in this imputation of sacredness to particular objects that Durkheim found the basis of all religion. In more advanced forms of totemism, sacredness is not so likely to be seen in natural objects such as animals, plants, winds, stars, rocks, rivers, and so on. Instead, social identity became focused around spiritual entities such as souls, demons, spirits, saints, or gods. A people might, for example, regard themselves as the 'chosen people' of a particular god. The further development of religion, as societies advance beyond the tribal stage, leads to the complete disappearance of its totemistic elements. The sacred objects of a society became more abstract.

Durkheim had a rather limited knowledge of the Australian tribes, and his views on totemism have been seriously questioned by later writers (Lévi-Strauss 1962). What has not been challenged, however, is his general view of the relationship between the sacred sphere and the religious attitude, on the one hand, and the structure of society, on the other.

Durkheim, like Marx, saw religion as having a social basis (see Box 11.2). The origin of the idea of the sacred was to be found in society itself. Religious forces and entities, he held, are mere representations of the moral forces and constraints experienced in social relations. In their social interaction, people build what Durkheim called **collective representations**, including shared images and ideas about the moral obligations they feel bind them together as members of their society. These representations are so fundamental to their social relations that they come to have a sacred character. They are, under some circumstances, personified as gods or other spiritual beings: the idea of god is an expression of society itself.

Ideas of divinity, then, are reflections of the ways in which people attempt to understand their social relations with one another. Religion is also central to the production of a sense of moral community. It is through religion that the symbols and ideas that sustain social life and that underpin the social order are sustained. Durkheim called these symbols and ideas, in French, the **conscience collective**. This is a difficult term to translate, and so is generally

---

THEORY AND METHODS 11.2

Religion and society

Religious force is only the sentiment inspired by the group in its members, but projected outside of the consciousnesses that experience them, and objectified. To be objectified, they are fixed upon some object which thus becomes sacred. (Durkheim 1912: 229)

Durkheim's statement is quite complex, and you will not fully understand it the first time that you read it. Read it through once or twice, picking out the key words and try to get the gist of what he is saying. The key words are 'sentiment', 'projected', and 'objectified'. Can you see how he applied these ideas to totemism?

left in the French. It refers to both the consciousness that is shared among the members of a society and the moral ideas that form their consciences. Because the *conscience collective* is so central to social life, Durkheim held, the disappearance of religion would mean the disappearance of social order itself. For this reason, he concluded that any society that is to persist must have some form of religion. This is why Durkheim is often said to have focused his attention on the functions of religion in creating social solidarity.

Although traditional forms of supernatural religion disappear as societies become more modern, other forms of religion take their place. This new form of religion, Durkheim argued, centres around the idea of the individual. Individualism is the system of ideas most compatible with the social division of labour and the market relations central to modern society. This is manifested in moral systems that emphasize human rights, freedom, and equality, and the encouragement of individual autonomy and choice in all things. Moral individualism, centring around a cult of the individual, is, according to Durkheim, the normal form taken by religion in modern society. This idea has been taken up in the discussions of Soviet Communism and 'civil religion' that we refer to on pp. 406–7 below.

> **⊃ Connections**
> Read our discussion of Durkheim's wider theoretical ideas in Chapter 2, pp. 32–7. We show there how he saw anomie and egoism as pathological expressions of the normal condition of moral individualism in modern societies. Can you see why religion was so important in Durkheim's theory of suicide?

Weber: religion and capitalism

Weber's particular concern in his sociology of religion was to look at the relationship between religious values and economic action. He carried out comparative studies of the religions of China, India, and ancient Israel, but his most important study was set out in a book on *The Protestant Ethic and the Spirit of Capitalism* (Max Weber 1904–5). The problem that he set himself to examine was why modern capitalism developed first in Western Europe, and he found the answer in its particular religious pattern.

Weber saw the central characteristic of modern capitalism as its spirit, its particular cultural attitude towards commercial activity. The **spirit of capitalism** is a system of beliefs that encourages the accumulation of income and assets through productive activity. This spirit encourages people to see excessive consumption as wasteful and, therefore, as something to be avoided. The profits of business have to be reinvested rather than consumed in luxurious and extravagant expenditure. This spirit emerged first

Briefing: Protestantism 11.3

This is a Christian religion that originated in Martin Luther's 'protestation' against the authority of the Roman Catholic Church in the sixteenth century. Luther emphasized the authority of the Bible, as the direct word of God. He rejected the Catholic view that priests were able to interpret God's wishes. Luther held that each individual must open his or her mind to God and must rely on conscience as the sole guide to conduct.

Contemporary Protestant churches include Lutheranism, Methodism, the Baptists, and Anglican churches such as the Church of England.

among those who became active capitalist entrepreneurs in the seventeenth and eighteenth centuries, and Weber wanted to uncover its origins. He concluded that these origins were to be found in certain characteristics of the Protestant religion (see Box 11.3).

Weber looked, in particular, at the forms of Protestantism that developed from the ideas of John Calvin. Calvinists believed that only a small minority—the elect—were destined by God for salvation and would join Him in heaven. The remainder were destined for eternal damnation. Nothing that people did during their lives could make any difference to their destiny, which reflected God's choice, and there was no way in which any individual believer could know whether he or she was destined for salvation or damnation. As a result, Calvinists experienced what Weber called 'inner loneliness': they felt completely on their own, having no one to whom they could turn for authoritative guidance on their eternal destiny.

This extreme anxiety about their fate caused great uncertainty about how to behave. Protestant ministers and teachers responded by stressing those aspects of Calvinism that might help resolve the anxieties of their parishioners. Calvin had said that success in a person's calling might be taken as a sign that he or she was destined for salvation. A calling or vocation was the particular way of life to which a person felt called by God. Calvin's followers concluded that God would hardly allow worldly success to those whom he had damned. The Puritan sects of the seventeenth century—especially the Quakers and the Baptists—developed an ethic that saw success in an occupation, business, or profession as giving people some indication of whether they were saved or damned. They began to encourage their members to be diligent and hard-working in their work and disciplined in all aspects of their lives. Those who worked hard found they were, indeed, likely to be successful, and this helped to lessen their sense of anxiety concerning their destiny (G. Marshall 1982).

Weber described this lifestyle as one of *asceticism*. The ascetic lifestyle involved hard work, discipline, the avoidance of waste, and the rigorous and systematic use of time. This rational and calculative attitude was applied in all aspects of life. In the Puritan world-view, eating and sexuality were seen as stimulating the bodily appetites and, therefore, as things to be controlled. Fasting, the avoidance of non-reproductive sex, and, outside marriage, a life of chastity and celibacy were all seen as means of self-control through which a mastery of the body could be attained (B. Turner 1996).

The pursuit of these values by seventeenth-century merchants in the Puritan sects led them to greater business success than their counterparts in other religions. Their ascetic way of life stressed the avoidance of excessive income and wasteful or luxurious consumption, and this led them to plough back their profits into their businesses and so to expand their scale of operations. Asceticism gave a new meaning to practical economic life. A distinctively modern view of commercial activity and an ethic of hard work were encouraged, and it was this new outlook and orientation that allowed capitalist business enterprises to expand on an unprecedented scale in the eighteenth and nineteenth centuries. The Protestant ethic, Weber argued, had given birth to the spirit of modern capitalism.

In the favourable conditions provided by the nation states of Western Europe in the seventeenth and eighteenth centuries, this spirit helped to produce the modern capitalist system of production. This system rapidly spread across Europe and into the wider world. In the longer term, however, the success of the capitalist system undermined sacred, religious meanings. In expanding capitalist societies, Weber argued, individuals are forced to work by economic necessity, and not by spiritual commitment to it as a calling. For most people there is simply no alternative to capitalist economic activity: if employers do not make a profit, then the pressures of competition will force them out of business; and if employees do not work hard, they will be sacked and replaced by those who will. The spirit of modern capitalism disappears, and modern life becomes increasingly empty and meaningless.

Weber's ideas on religious ethics and their influence on economic activity have been taken up in some contemporary discussions of the economic development of overseas Chinese communities in the Far East, where forms of religion now operate in much the way that the Protestant ethic operated in seventeenth-century Europe (Redding 1990).

Stop and reflect

In this section we have looked at the nature of religion and the principal sociological theories about the development of religion in modern societies.

- A religion is an overarching system of beliefs and practices that helps the members of a society or community to organize and order their lives.
- Central to religious thought is a distinction between the sacred and the secular.

We sketched the views of the main sociological theorists of religion. Their ideas are relevant to the many issues that we discuss in the rest of this chapter.

- Comte saw a conflict between religion and science, though he held that science could itself become the basis of a new religion and a new form of social cohesion.

- Marx related religion to class divisions and alienation. It is an important factor in the legitimation of social divisions.
- Durkheim saw modern societies as organized around a religion of moral individualism that corresponded to its social differentiation and division of labour.
- Weber gave an account of the rise of modern capitalism that saw the social ethic of the Protestant churches as a crucial factor in generating the attitudes and outlook of the capitalist entrepreneur.
- Is it necessary to choose between these differing views of religion?

Religion in modern society

Belief in God is often held to be less common in Europe and America today than was the case in the past. This loss of traditional religious belief is seen as an indication of the increasingly secular character of modern societies. Atheists have seen this trend favourably, seeing it as a liberation from superstitious and irrational beliefs. Those who remain committed to traditional religion, on the other hand, have seen it more negatively. For them, it undermines morality and destroys the possibility of a disciplined communal life. Most sociologists prefer not to take sides on these theological issues, seeing religious faith as a purely personal matter. They concern themselves only with the actual question of whether Comte was correct to see the growth of positive, rational knowledge as driving a process of secularization.

Secularization and modernity

The sociological concept of **secularization** involves two closely related ideas. First, it implies a *disengagement* of religion from public institutions. Religious beliefs and practices are detached from major social institutions and become purely private matters of individual belief and choice. Indeed, the word 'secularization' was originally used to denote the removal of a territory from the legal control of a church and was generalized from this to mean the declining public significance of religion. The idea of secularization, secondly, implies that there has been a *disenchantment* of social life. The disenchantment of the world is the process through which the ultimate spiritual meaning of practical life recedes as individuals lose their traditional religious beliefs. A society is disenchanted when sacred ideas are no longer of any relevance to people and practical matters are, in consequence, emptied of any ultimate spiritual significance. Disengagement involves a *privatization* of religious belief; disenchantment involves a *loss* of spiritual concerns.

The disengagement of religion

Disengagement is 'the process by which sectors of society and culture are removed from the domination of religious institutions and symbols' (Berger 1967: 113). This is apparent in the separation of church and state, the removal of education and welfare from control by religious bodies, and the withdrawal of churches from attempts to regulate economic behaviour and control matters of morality. In Europe, this disengagement was apparent in the transformation and weakening of the Roman Catholic Church.

Medieval Europe was marked by the cultural dominance of the Catholic Church, which was allied with the major states and was the main focus of unity across the continent. The Catholic Church established a virtually compulsory framework for religious observance. People were born into membership of the Church, just as they were born into membership of a particular state. There was no choice about either: place of birth fixed a person's subjection to church and state. The Church hierarchy was closely allied with the political hierarchies of the states of the Christian world, and the Pope was at least the equal of the European kings and princes.

Sociologists introduced the term **ecclesia** to describe the specific form taken by religion in this period. This type of religious organization is sometimes referred to simply as a 'church', but this word is now used so widely and in such a general sense that it has lost its original and more specific meaning. A church, in its broadest sense, is any form of association that is organized around the relations of its members to a sacred sphere of meaning and action. The word 'church' is even used to refer to the buildings in which religious activities take place.

An ecclesia is a specific kind of church, most clearly illustrated by medieval Roman Catholicism. It is a universal and inclusive religious organization that claims total spiritual authority over all those who live within a territory. It generally claims a degree of political authority too. The medieval Catholic Church claimed spiritual authority over virtually the whole of Europe. An ecclesia is organized around an orthodox doctrine. This is a systematically codified body of beliefs protected as the one true faith and given authoritative interpretation by the church's leaders. People are born into membership of an ecclesia and are socialized into its beliefs and practices. An orthodox doctrine may be the basis of a rigid social conformity: heretics (deviants from the religious orthodoxy) are not tolerated and may be relentlessly persecuted.

Redundant churches have been turned into trendy bars, restaurants, and retail outlets.

© Freud

The ecclesia can be distinguished from the **denomination**. A denomination is a church that is organized around *voluntary* rather than compulsory membership. It occurs where there is a separation between church and state. A denomination is a church that is disengaged from the many political and public functions undertaken by an ecclesia. A denomination does not claim a monopoly of religious truth and it accommodates itself to the legitimacy of secular states and to the beliefs of other denominations. This contrast between ecclesia and denomination is important when comparing different forms of religion (D. Martin 1962; see also Niebuhr 1929).

By the nineteenth century, neither Roman Catholicism nor Anglicanism could be regarded as ecclesia. They had come closer to being mere denominations. Anglicanism had, and still has, certain privileges and powers in relation to the state. It forms the established 'Church of England'. However, it is far weaker than it was in the past (B. R. Wilson 1966: 252). In virtually all the societies of Europe, religion became denominational, and states have gradually come to tolerate the existence of numerous separate denominations. At the same time, the various denominations are more tolerant of one another than any ecclesia would be towards unorthodox beliefs and practices. In Britain, for example, such churches as the Methodists and the Baptists emphasize voluntary commitment and accommodation to other religions.

Denominations often have a particular social-class or ethnic-group base, and religious struggles in a denominational society are often closely associated with the social struggles of these groups for power. For example, nonconformist (that is, non-Anglican) Protestantism was strongest in nineteenth-century England in the working-class communities of the industrial north. Methodist, Baptist, and Congregationalist chapels provided a focus for communal cohesion and bases for opposition to the Established Church. The conflict between 'chapel' and 'church' became an important thread in British politics, persisting well into the twentieth century. In big cities, where there were substantial numbers of Irish migrants, Catholicism played a similar part in building the solidarity of the Irish working-class communities. The differences between the ecclesia and denomination are shown in Box 11.4.

The disenchantment of the world

The second aspect of secularization is what Max Weber called the *disenchantment* or 'desacralization' of the world. By this he meant that modern societies experience a loss of the spiritual meaning that had been provided by traditional religious belief. While it is important not to overstate the depth and the consistency of religious belief in the past, Weber correctly identified a major difference between the medieval and the modern world-view.

THEORY AND METHODS   **11.4**

Ecclesia and denomination

The contrast between the ecclesia and the denomination—often referred to as a contrast between 'church' and denomination—is of great importance. According to Weber, an ecclesia is a form of administration that organizes religion into a structure of what he called 'hierocratic coercion'. It is characterized by:

- a claim to universal authority: control that is not restricted by kinship, ethnicity, or other particularistic claims;
- a systematic dogma and set of rites, generally recorded in texts that are objects of disciplined training;
- a professional priesthood, having specific duties and controlled through salaries and promotions;
- compulsory membership for all who live within the territory over which it claims authority.

A denomination, on the other hand, exercises fewer and more restricted controls over its members. Although it may have a professional priesthood, these do not have the powers held by priests in an ecclesia. Specifically, the denomination is characterized by:

- a tolerance towards other religions, which are recognized—in principle—as having an equally legitimate right to attract members and spread their views;
- a voluntary membership based on an act of choice made by a believer.

Examples of ecclesia are medieval Catholicism and Islam. Examples of denominations are the Methodist and Baptist churches in nineteenth- and twentieth-century Britain, and the many branches of Buddhism in Japan. Anglicanism is intermediate between the ecclesia and the denomination.

Most ordinary people in the medieval world did hold to a broadly Christian world-view. The details of Christian theology and its specific doctrines were often unfamiliar or poorly understood, but Christianity provided a taken-for-granted sacred canopy that helped to organize everyday lives. The spiritual content of this religion was reinforced by equally strong beliefs in a whole array of supernatural and magical powers. For most people, witches, spirits, and fairies were every bit as real as the angels and saints of orthodox Christianity. These heretical views were tolerated by the Catholic Church, so long as its own position was not threatened. More systematic and intellectually consistent Christian beliefs were held by the literate, though even here there was a willingness to believe in magical forces (K. Thomas 1971). Medieval people, then, lived in an enchanted world, a world in which the secular activities of everyday life were permeated by supernatural forces.

The Reformation of sixteenth-century Europe challenged the Catholic orthodoxy and popular beliefs. The new Protestant beliefs recognized far fewer spiritual beings and emphasized a much greater degree of doctrinal purity. In a wider context, this helped to produce the fundamental shift in intellectual outlook described as the Enlightenment. In one sphere of intellectual enquiry after another, knowledge was freed from religious constraints and opened up to rational criticism (Merton 1938a). As Comte had recognized, an increasingly scientific world-view gave greater priority to rational considerations over matters of faith. Protestantism and Enlightenment thought together destroyed the medieval world-view, encouraging a separation of religious from practical matters. Protestantism eliminated much of the spiritual content from religion, and scientific knowledge soon began to challenge all theistic religion. Traditional religious beliefs could no longer be taken for granted and became progressively more difficult to sustain.

Many people, then, experienced a loss of faith in traditional religious ideas. Miracles, mysticism, saints, and sacraments all played a much smaller part in everyday life when religion took a specifically rational form and placed less emphasis on the supernatural. As Berger (1967: 117) has written: 'The Protestant believer no longer lives in a world on-goingly penetrated by sacred beings and forces.' In the modern world, it is science and technology that are looked to for solutions to practical problems. While most people do not have the knowledge that would allow them to assess scientific ideas critically, their faith is now placed in the powers of the scientific expert rather than the world of spirits. They are also less likely to believe in the power and effectiveness of witches, demons, and fairies. Such ideas are confined to the world of fiction, fairy tales, and horror films. People find it more difficult to believe in things that run counter to scientific principles of explanation.

> **⮌ Connections**
>
> Does Weber's argument about disenchantment explain why the witchcraft beliefs of Cassandra and Maureen, whom we introduced at the beginning of this chapter, appear so strange to so many people? Later in this chapter (on pp. 417–18) we look at the growth of 'New Age' beliefs. You might like to come back to this discussion when you have read those pages and see whether you think that this new spirituality marks a move away from the disenchantment that Weber described.

With the growing rationalization of modern culture, the sense of spiritual meaning formerly provided by religion was lost. Weber took a particularly pessimistic view of this. He saw people living in a cold, soulless, and calculating world. They no longer had any sense of mystery about supernatural forces that could be understood only through magic or religion. They had lost sight of any values or goals except those that were tied to their immediate economic and political concerns. Modern society was becoming a vast and relentless machine, and individuals became mere 'cogs' in this machine. They played their parts out of necessity and not for any ultimate spiritual purpose.

In these circumstances, Weber held, it becomes more and more difficult to justify a commitment to any values and ideals (B. R. Wilson 1976; Wallis 1984). Individuals no longer feel they have any basis for choosing the values by which to live. They must make arbitrary choices among the competing values that face them, and they cannot rely on the guidance formerly provided by traditional religions. Such arbitrary choices provide them with no foundation for moral commitment to the rational and impersonal world in which they live. Practical matters lack any moral legitimacy.

Durkheim was less pessimistic than Weber. Like Comte, he accepted that there had been a decline in people's willingness to believe in spiritual beings and forces. He recognized, however, that a new form of religion—moral individualism—was developing, and that this could give a moral significance to social life. Moral individualism, as it developed, would help to offset the calculative and soulless aspects of modernity that Weber had identified. Only where moral individualism had not fully developed did modern life break down into anomie (see Box 11.5). For Durkheim, then, disenchantment could be seen as involving a decline in traditional religious beliefs, but not a decline in religion as such. Religion had been transformed, but not displaced. Religion in the modern world may be less spiritual and less theistic, but it could still sustain a sacred canopy.

THEORY AND METHODS   11.5

Anomie

Anomie is a term introduced by Durkheim to describe a failure of moral regulation. The word literally means 'without norms', and Durkheim used it to mean the absence of a normative framework or sacred canopy. Individual desires and interests for wealth and power are left uncontrolled.

Anomie is seen as a pathological condition that exists when the moral basis of modern society (moral individualism) has not properly developed. The full development of moral individualism produces the organic solidarity that Durkheim saw as the key to social cohesion in modern societies.

⮌ In Chapter 2, p. 36 and pp. 44–5, we look at how Durkheim and Merton defined anomie. We will use Merton's ideas later in this chapter.

Differentiation and religious pluralism

The Catholic Church in medieval society claimed a monopoly of moral authority. In a secular society, there are numerous denominations, and they must compete for believers. In this situation, religion becomes much more a matter of individual choice and preference (Berger 1961*a*, 1961*b*). The roots of this religious pluralism and the need for choice can be traced to certain central features of Protestant Christianity itself.

The Protestantism of Luther and Calvin, as we have shown, rejected the authority of priests and the church hierarchy. It emphasized the need for each individual to read the Bible and listen directly to the voice of God. Individuals had to use their powers of reason to arrive at their own decisions about what is right and what is wrong. The Protestant obligation to consider all matters rationally and critically encouraged, albeit unintentionally, the very existence of God to be questioned. By the nineteenth century, all the major elements of traditional Christian belief—the Trinity, miracles, and the Virgin birth—were legitimate subjects for rational debate. They were no longer simply matters of faith (B. R. Wilson 1966). Religious denominations felt an increasing need to ensure that their doctrines and teachings would appear plausible to rational believers. They could not rely on an uncritical acceptance of traditional authority.

These features of Protestantism have meant that none of its denominations has found it easy to maintain a plausible claim to a monopoly of truth. It has been said that 'Protestantism is essentially fissile': it tends always to split into competing schools of thought (Bruce 1985, 1986). Unlike Roman Catholicism, there is no unified and coherent system of Protestant doctrine and practice. Existing interpretations of the word of God are always open to challenge in the light of rational argument or personal inspiration, and so there is a strong tendency to schism and sectarianism. Protestant churches must compete to maintain the loyalty of those who have the obligation to make their own religious choices.

When religion is a matter of personal choice and private belief, societies face a problem of moral legitimacy. Traditional religion can no longer provide an authoritative guide for moral decision-making. There can be no intellectually convincing statement of what is right and what is wrong. Modern societies must live with the possibility of moral relativism. The moral individualism of modern society provides only a very weak basis for a shared commitment to any other ideals.

Contemporary societies are not, however, in a chronic state of anomie. In addition to the bonds of moral individualism, there do remain certain areas of *shared* belief. It is those who are most concerned with intellectual matters who are most likely to engage in rational criticism of accepted values. Most people, for most of the time, do not question the values into which they have been socialized. While these values are, in principle, subject to rational criticism, they are generally taken for granted in everyday situations. People are born into specific cultural and religious traditions, and these shape the way that they approach religious and moral questions. Religious commitment becomes weaker, but religious and moral beliefs tend to be relatively standardized throughout a society. As a result, competition between religions tends to be limited in scope. They can compete through the marginal differentiation of their ideas within a broadly shared religious framework.

Individual attachment to this framework is, however, weak and precarious. It is constantly subject to intellectual criticism, and there is always the danger that individual adherents will take these intellectual problems seriously. The inherited religious framework is in constant danger of erosion in the face of the secularizing tendencies built into modern society. Religious attachment must also compete with other calls upon people's time. When religion becomes a matter of individual preference, people see it as a leisure-time activity to be engaged in on a purely voluntary basis. It must, therefore, compete with the many other leisure-time activities that have become such important aspects of modern life. As B. R. Wilson (1976: 96) has argued, choice in religion becomes equivalent to the consumer choice between 'pushpin, poetry, or popcorn'.

Religion in Britain

Early Protestantism in Britain was divided into numerous churches organized as 'sects'. A **sect** is a schismatic group, a body of people whose views diverge from those of others within the *same* religion. Following the Reformation, the number of sects multiplied as they diverged from one another within the broadly Protestant framework. The sociological concept of the sect was used by Troeltsch (1912) in his study of how the early Baptists, Quakers, and Methodists split from the Anglican and other Protestant faiths in the seventeenth and eighteenth centuries. These sects were quite diverse. The followers of Devon-born Joanna Southcott believed that she had received messages from the Spirit of God warning of impending dangers and disasters. These prophecies were placed in a 'Great Box' to be opened only when humankind was ready to receive the true message. Her contemporary followers still await the opening of the box (www.panacea-society.org). George Fox's Society of friends—known as the 'Quakers'—believed in the power of quiet contemplation as a means to spiritual enlightenment. They believed in the importance of telling the truth at all times and refused to swear oaths, even in court.

Like the ecclesia, the sect claims to possess a monopoly of religious truth, but it is organized on a voluntary basis rather than through compulsory membership. Members are recruited through the conversion of non-members or through their personal decisions to join. People are born into an ecclesia, but they *choose* to join a sect. Sects establish sharp boundaries between members and non-members, and they expect a high level of involvement and commitment from their members. They stress the earnestness of individual faith, and there is a heightened sense of commitment and morality. They tend, therefore, to be highly emotional and to adopt an evangelistic stance towards non-members. A denomination is tolerant towards other religions, but a sect stresses its sole and exclusive claim to religious truth.

Sects also place a great emphasis on individual decision and choice. This has meant that there is a greater lay involvement in religion. There is far less differentiation between lay people and clergy than there is in either the ecclesia or the denomination, and so they have more fluid and democratic structures of leadership. Niebuhr (1929) showed that sects tended to evolve into denominations as they grew and matured. The early Protestant sects in Britain, for example, had gradually been transformed into denominations by the nineteenth century. The Protestant sects had rejected Episcopalianism—rule by bishops—and relied, instead, on quite informal and democratic structures of leadership. In their denominational forms, church government was formalized into congregational or presbyterian structures.

It was this transition from sect to denomination that allowed the secularizing potential of Protestantism to make itself felt in Britain. The emerging denominations relaxed their earlier claims to possess a monopoly of religious truth, and they accommodated to one another and to Anglicanism. This pattern of denominational pluralism—the competition of rival but mutually tolerant denominations—became the characteristic religious pattern in Britain and the United States. Sects such as the Jehovah's Witnesses and the Seventh Day Adventists have survived only through very active proselytization and conversion (see Box 11.6).

Church and nation

The high point of religious participation, for all denominations, was the second half of the nineteenth century, after which it declined quite considerably. Rates of church attendance and of membership fell rapidly, and only a quarter of adults in England were even nominal members of a religious group by the 1950s (B. R. Wilson 1966; Martin 1967). Between 10 per cent and 15 per cent of the population were regular Sunday churchgoers, compared with about 40 per cent a century earlier. This decline in membership and attendance was especially marked during the last decades of the nineteenth century. Decline began first among Anglicans, and it then set in among the nonconformist denominations.

Briefing: surviving sects   11.6

- *Jehovah's Witnesses* believe in the literal truth of the Bible. They hold that the world was actually created in seven days and that there will soon be an apocalyptic battle between God and Satan. The sect actively recruits new members through a door-to-door ministry.

- *Seventh Day Adventists* believe that Jesus Christ will soon return to earth and will rule for 1,000 years. Founded in the 1840s when William Miller prophesied the end of the world, the sect is active in missionary work and has Saturday as its holy day.

The decline in membership was greater in towns and cities than in rural districts, though the extent of the decline varied quite considerably from district to district within the major cities. Inner-city and working-class housing estates, for example, had very low rates of churchgoing, while middle-class suburbs showed significantly higher rates. The Catholic Church in Britain was more successful in retaining relatively high levels of church attendance, partly because of the large numbers of those who migrated to England from Ireland. For this reason, Catholics came to form a large proportion of the total churchgoing population.

While Protestantism in Britain took this highly pluralistic form, the Church of England remained the religion of the majority until well into the twentieth century (B. R. Wilson 1966: 119). The Church is the Established Church, having a constitutionally defined role in relation to the monarchy and the political system. The monarch is both Head of State and Head of the Church, appointing all bishops and archbishops and acting as 'Defender of the Faith'. The Church retained a strong association with the major social institutions of British society. As the Established Church, it was very much the church of the aristocracy, the old professions, and the middle classes.

Despite its official status, however, the Church of England is a denomination, not an ecclesia. It is a state church whose religious monopoly is limited by the existence of a substantial bloc of dissenting religion (Davie 1994). It has consistently sought to accommodate its practices to those of the leading Protestant denominations that have split from it over the years. Methodism, for example, has been particularly successful in attracting large numbers of working-class adherents, but the two churches have cooperated in a number of religious and secular activities.

A majority of people in England in mid-century (just under two-thirds) continued to describe themselves as 'Church of England' when asked. A nominal affiliation to the Church was seen as a part of what it was to be 'English'. It was an expression of English national identity and allegiance to English social institutions (B. R. Wilson 1966: 24). Other religions in Britain had much smaller numbers of adherents. About one in ten people was a Catholic, and there were similar numbers in the Church of Scotland. There were as many Jews as there were Catholics, and one in ten of the population was a member of smaller nonconformist denominations. In 1966 these smaller denominations included about 700,000 Methodists, 280,000 Baptists, 200,000 Congregationalists, and about 250,000 people in total spread among the Unitarians, Presbyterians, Quakers, and Salvation Army. Between 1 and 2 per cent of the population were affiliated to small sects, such as the Christian Scientists and the Jehovah's Witnesses. Religious pluralism was especially high in Wales, where there were many dissenting sects and denominations. As in England, however, religion was linked with national identity. The chapels were the carriers of a distinctively Welsh identity, nurturing generations of Liberal and Labour supporters and politicians.

Only a very few people were willing to describe themselves—at least in public—as non-religious. An opinion poll in the middle of the 1960s found just 6 per cent of the English population stating 'none' as their religion. Only 9 per cent claimed that they had no belief in a 'spirit, god or life-force'. Almost a half of the people (43 per cent) claimed that they said regular prayers, and the majority wished to retain religious instruction in schools (Forster 1972).

Britain was a nominally Christian nation, and for the majority it was an Anglican nation. Although the level of emotional commitment to religion was low, involvement in the major rituals of the Christian calendar persisted. Church services were important markers of various critical stages in the life course. Two-thirds of all children were baptized into the Church of England between 1885 and 1950, and a quarter of the population in the early 1960s had been confirmed into the Church. One-fifth of children attended Sunday school over the period from 1895 to 1940. In this period the marriage rate was high and marriage in church was very common. The proportion of church marriages declined from the high level of 70–80 per cent that it achieved between 1850 and 1880. Nevertheless, over a half of all marriages were still being solemnized in the Church of England until after the Second World War.

Religion in the United States

While England had a national church, and there were similar institutions in Scotland and Wales, this was not the case in the United States. While the US Constitution guaranteed religious freedom for all its citizens, it gave no privileged position to any denomination. Political differences in the United States did not, therefore, take a religious form—there were no nonconformist or dissenting churches that could link religious opposition to an established religion with political opposition to an established state (Tocqueville 1835–40). The numerous religions that migrant settlers brought from their home countries to the United States all found their place within a strong pluralistic structure. Some of the older Protestant sects did retain a sectarian form, though they have often found it difficult to survive. The Shakers, for example, have died out, while the Amish have been much reduced in numbers (see Box 11.7).

Despite their different histories, Britain and the United States have moved towards similar forms of denominational pluralism (B. R. Wilson 1966: ch. 6). Levels of church membership in the United States have been higher than in Britain, however, and church involvement has substantially increased since the turn of the century. Twenty per cent of the US population were church members in 1880, and by 1962 the figure had increased to 63 per cent. Membership of Protestant denominations, for example, increased from 27 per cent of the population in 1926 to 35 per cent in 1950. The number of Catholics increased from 16 per cent to 23 per cent over the same period. Until well into the post-war period, almost a half of all Americans attended church every week.

 Briefing: declining sects   11.7

- *Shakers* originated in the United States in the eighteenth century. They were celibate communities that lived apart from the rest of society and followed a simple life. They originally practised religious activities that involved shaking, trembling, or convulsions. There are no longer any Shaker communities, and they are now famous for their highly valued antique furniture, produced in their communities to simple, clean designs.

- *Amish* originated in a Swiss sect of Anabaptists in the seventeenth century. They maintain a strict Puritan lifestyle, living apart from the world in isolated communities. They are now found in Pennsylvania and the Midwest. Contemporary 'Old Order' Amish still dress in the same way as their founders and they make no use of modern technology such as cars and televisions (Sim 1994). The community received national media attention in 2006 when a school became the target of a gunman who killed five young girls.

The religious melting pot

These high levels of church attendance and membership do not mean that the United States is not a secular society. An important study by Herberg (1955) showed that mainstream religions in the United States were losing their specifically theological character and were coming to be more closely identified with a sense of national identity. Herberg traces this to the particular experience of migration in the United States.

The United States is a nation of migrants. Successive waves of migrants arrived with their specific ethnic identities and religious affiliations. There was never a single, dominant denomination, and nor was there a single, dominant ethnic group. While the great bulk of all nineteenth- and twentieth-century migrants were white, they were ethnically diverse: there were Germans, Poles, Irish, Dutch, Norwegians, Russians, and many others. This produced what has been called an ethnic 'melting pot' (Glazer and Moynihan 1963). While first-generation migrants retained strong emotional ties to their home countries, second- and third-generation migrants tried to forge stronger identities for themselves as Americans and identified themselves closely with the social institutions of American public life.

> **⮕ Connections**
>
> The idea of the melting pot has been central to many discussions of race and ethnic relations. We discuss this and the associated idea of assimilation in Chapter 6, pp. 197 and 207–8. You will find it useful to consider those discussions alongside our discussion of Herberg's argument.

Being religious and being American.
© Alice Chadwick

Central to the American way of life—or so it seemed to the newcomers—was regular churchgoing, and members of the ethnic minorities sought acceptance by mainstream American society through their own churchgoing. At church, they met those who had already successfully completed the process of migration and settlement, and they could get much needed practical help, including help with the language. Most importantly, they could acquire a sense of belonging in their new society. In their dealings with others, religious differences were minimized, as they built a shared sense of being religious and, therefore, of being 'American'.

Commitment to a church was a matter of practical commitment to the American way of life and American national identity. It was not a sign of high levels of religious faith or devotion. High levels of church membership and attendance went hand in hand with secularization. Religions in the United States were disengaged and American society was disenchanted. It was the particular situation of the United States as a nation of migrants that led to such high levels of church involvement in a secular society. Churchgoing was an expression of one's citizenship, of being a 'good American'. To be a good American did not, however, require adherence to any particular religion. Someone could be a good American by being a good Protestant, a good Catholic, or a good Jew.

The various denominations identified themselves with the American state and society and the American way of life. As a result, the moral teachings of the principal religions became more and more similar, and their theologies became looser and more liberal in character. Once religiosity is identified with national identity in this way, a withdrawal from or denial of religion comes to be seen as a withdrawal from or denial of the American way of life. People are locked in to high levels of church attendance and to the public statement of religious values. To do anything else would be 'un-American'. Churchgoing strengthens a sense of national community. It reinforces the symbolically bounded imagined community that unites all together in a common activity and with a common identity.

Civil religion

In both Britain and the United States there has been a close association between religion and national identity. In Britain, this was the nominal affiliation of a majority of the population to the Church of England. In the United States, it took the form of high levels of church attendance. This identification of religion and national community has led many sociologists to suggest that secular societies can be seen as organized around a characteristic pattern of **civil religion**.

In a civil religion, the secular world itself has a sacred character (Bellah 1967, 1970; Bocock 1974; see also Warner 1953). Secularized religions of this kind are a result of the partial, but not complete disenchantment of the modern world. Despite growing disenchantment, modern societies have been able to rely on a residue of traditional attachment to established social institutions. The traditional symbolism of national identity provides a common cultural framework for all members of society, cutting across differences between particular denominations. The nation itself can become an object of religious veneration, and distinctive civic rituals are focused on it. Presidential inaugurations, Thanksgiving, Independence Day, Veteran's Day, and other public occasions in the United States, for example, provide opportunities for the expression and reaffirmation of a sense of shared national identity and commitment.

Bellah, like Herberg, sees the United States as having been united by a religious belief in the sacred character of America and a consequent loyalty to the American nation. God is almost seen as an American. Where children's prayers end with 'God bless Mummy and Daddy', political speeches end with 'God bless America'. Saintly figures from American history have been central to the maintenance of American values. The story of Abraham Lincoln's rise 'from the log cabin to the White House', for example, is central to the mythology of America as an open, classless society and to the maintenance of the 'American Dream'.

Involvement in civic rituals is a way in which existing religious organizations can maintain a role for themselves in a secular society. In Britain, for example, the Church of England remains the nationally Established Church. It is closely involved in major parliamentary occasions and in the celebration and commemoration of national values and events. The Royal Family has for long been associated with the civic rituals of the major national occasions, and many specific rituals surround the Royal Family itself: the Coronation, the Queen's Birthday, the Christmas speech, the Trooping of the Colour, the State Opening of Parliament, Remembrance Day, and so on. The link between the nation, the monarch, and the church has been central to the legitimation of the state.

This view of religion and ritual in British society was first explored in an influential article on the Coronation of Queen Elizabeth II in 1953 (Shils and Young 1953). The Coronation was seen as one of a number of occasions—others might be royal weddings—in which a sense of national community could be affirmed and the basic moral values of the society reinforced. The Coronation of 1953 was the first major televised spectacular in which a large mass audience could simultaneously participate in the same civic ritual. Twenty million viewers watched seven hours of live coverage of the Coronation. Even in 1981, 39 million people watched the televised wedding of the Prince of Wales, and there was a doubling in sales of video recorders.

> **⊃ Connections**
>
> You will find it useful to look at what we say about national identity in Chapter 16, pp. 598–600. Pay particular attention to the idea of nationalism as allegiance to an imagined community.
>
> The situation that we are describing is that which existed in its strongest form until the 1960s. How far do you think it still applies to Britain? How have the personal problems of the Royal Family affected the Church of England and its role in civil religion? What does public reaction to the deaths of Diana, Princess of Wales, and the Queen Mother tell us about religious beliefs and attitudes towards the monarchy? Were these reflected in celebrations of the marriage of Prince Charles to Camilla Parker-Bowles?
>
> The religious aspects of views on Princess Diana are discussed in Bramley (2002).

The idea of civil religion offers, perhaps, the best framework for understanding the religious character of Soviet Communism that we mentioned earlier. The Marxist–Leninist creed identified the revolutionary role of the proletariat with the Soviet state and its leaders, and many public ceremonials and rituals reinforced its moral values and legitimated its power (C. Lane 1981). Public occasions were marked by the parading of portraits of Communist leaders as national symbols from the Communist past. On the anniversary of the Communist Revolution, the major national event of the year, lengthy military and industrial parades marched past the political leaders in their enclosure above Lenin's mausoleum. The Red Flag, the Red Army, and Red Square were the symbols of Soviet identity.

It is important not to overemphasize the consensual character of civil religions (K. Thompson 1992). For many people, involvement in public ceremonies and rituals reflects a pragmatic acceptance of them rather than any kind of normative commitment. In a disenchanted society, people may not be individually and genuinely committed, in terms of their personal and private beliefs, to the moral authority of political leaders and national symbols. They

Presidential inaugurations: a ceremony of the civil religion?

© Roberto Schmidt/AFP/ Getty Images

may, nevertheless, conform to the rituals and observances as public acts, and as part of the routine of their daily lives. This conformity may reflect the power of taken-for-granted attitudes, or the wish not to deviate from what is taken to be public opinion. It may result from calculations of personal advantage, or it may be enforced by coercive political authorities (Abercrombie *et al.* 1979).

> ⮕ *Connections*
>
> We look at the political structure of the Soviet Union in greater detail in 'Totalitarianism and command societies', in Chapter 20, pp. 802–5. You may like to return to our discussion of civil religion when you read that chapter. What evidence is there from television and newspapers of a civil religion in the new post-Communist Russia?

Stop and reflect

In this section we have looked at patterns of secularization in modern society. We began by looking at the concept of secularization itself.

- Secularization can be seen in terms of the two processes of disengagement and disenchantment.

- In Europe, secularization involved a transition from the Catholic ecclesia to a situation of denominational pluralism. Many denominations evolved from earlier sects.

- In modern societies, religious belief has become more of a private matter, and religious activities have to compete with the other activities among which individuals must choose to allocate their time.

- If beliefs have become simply a matter of choice and lifestyle, can they still be regarded as 'religious'?

We then turned to reviewing religious practices and beliefs in Britain and the United States from the middle of the nineteenth century to the 1960s.

- There was a decline in religious participation in Britain, but a majority of the population continued to see themselves as nominal members of the Church of England.

- There was an increase in religious participation in the United States, where a nation of migrants saw church membership as a symbol of American national identity.

- Civil religion is a secularized form of religion that identifies religion with national identity and state ceremonial. Is it compatible with the existence of privatized religions of choice?

The rise of new religions

In the previous section we traced patterns of religious belief and practice up to the 1960s. As in so many other areas, the 1960s were a turning point for religion. Old and established forms of religion have declined since then, and those that have prospered have done so by adapting their beliefs and practices to the new times. Moreover, civil religion has weakened, and now exists in only a very feeble form. The residue of traditional social attachment on which it could trade in the past has continued to decline in the face of growing disenchantment. Traditional authority in the state and other social institutions is increasingly difficult to sustain, and, with the decay of tradition, so civil religion is weakened. At the same time, however, new religious sects and cults have multiplied. While the scale of religious involvement remains quite low, new forms of religion have become an important element in the lives of many people.

Belonging and believing

The post-war period in Britain has seen a continued decline in church membership and attendance. Although church involvement in the United States remains higher than in Britain, membership is no longer growing and attendance seems to be falling. There has been a considerable weakening of religious belonging. People are now less likely to belong to organized religions or to be actively involved in

their rituals and practices. There has not, however, been a comparable decline in religious belief. The majority of people continue to subscribe to broadly religious beliefs, though their adherence is very loose. Their beliefs are not tied to particular doctrines or practices and they are a matter of only very low-key adherence.

For many people, then, religious belief is a real, but rather unimportant part of their lives that has no particular significance for their moral or political attitudes. For a minority, however, the common religion does not suffice. These are the people who are attracted into active and reinvigorated Protestant sects or into new, non-Christian forms of cult religion. In this section we will look at trends in religious behaviour and the nature of the common religion, and we will then turn to a discussion of the variety of new religions.

From civil religion to common religion

The proportion of the British population who belonged to a Christian church had fallen to around 12 per cent by the end of the twentieth century. This is less than half the level it was at the end of the nineteenth century. About two-thirds of church members were Protestants and one-third were Catholics. Just under 6 per cent of the British adult population in 2007 attended a church service on a regular weekly basis. Only 15 per cent of the population attended church at least once each month. The rate of decline in church attendance is greatest among Roman Catholics.

Church membership and attendance are highest among older women and among non-manual workers than they are, in general, among men and manual workers. Among those who see themselves as 'frequent' or 'regular' church attenders, two-thirds are women. Among Protestants, members of the Anglican denominations (the Church of England, the Church in Wales, the Episcopal Church in Scotland, and the Church of Ireland) were in a minority. The great majority of active Protestants are members of Presbyterian, Methodist, or Baptist denominations (Davie 1990). Church membership remains particularly high in Northern Ireland, among both Catholics and Protestants. About a quarter of Catholics in England are first-generation migrants from Northern Ireland or the Republic.

Britain has one of the lowest levels of church membership in Europe. Although comparative figures are notoriously difficult to compile, it seems that about 15 per cent of the adult British population are members of one church or another, compared with just over 20 per cent in France and Denmark, and about 30 per cent in Finland and Norway. Overt religious activity is still very high in the United States. Over two-thirds of the population of the United States claim to be church members, and just over a half of the population still attends a church at least once each month.

Figures 11.1 and 11.2 show some recent trends in church membership and church allegiance in Britain. A comparison of the two tables brings out clearly the discrepancy between the numbers claiming a nominal adherence to a religion and the numbers who are actively involved as members of one or another church. About 37 million people in 2000 claimed to have some kind of religious allegiance, over a half of them claiming to be Anglican. Very few of these nominal Anglicans were active members or attended church regularly. It would seem that only about one in twenty of those who claim to be Anglicans are actually members of the Church. This discrepancy was less marked for other denominations. In most cases, about a half or more of their adherents were active members.

Figure 11.1 Active membership in Christian churches, United Kingdom, 1975–2000

Church	1975	1985	1995	2000
Anglican	2,297,571	2,016,593	1,785,033	1,653,980
Roman Catholic	2,518,955	2,204,165	1,914,396	1,768,036
Presbyterian	1,641,520	1,384,997	1,088,098	988,812
Other Protestants	1,345,273	1,318,644	1,299,916	1,277,927
Orthodox	196,850	223,686	196,995	234,690
Total	8,000,169	7,148,085	6,284,438	5,923,445

Sources: Davie (1994: 46, table 4.1); *Religious Trends* (2001: table 2.22).

Figure 11.2 Expressed church allegiance, United Kingdom, 1975–2000

Church	Allegiance (m.)			
	1975	1985	1995	2000
Anglican	28.2	27.1	26.1	25.6
Roman Catholic	5.6	5.6	5.7	5.8
Presbyterian	2.9	2.7	2.6	2.6
Other Protestants	3.1	3.3	3.2	3.2
Orthodox	0.4	0.4	0.5	0.5
Total	40.2	39.1	38.1	37.7
Hindus	0.3	0.4	0.4	0.5
Jews	0.4	0.3	0.3	0.3
Muslims	0.4	0.9	1.2	1.4
Sikhs	0.2	0.3	0.6	0.6
Others	0.8	1.3	1.6	1.7
Total	2.1	3.2	4.1	4.5
Totals	42.3	42.3	42.2	42.2

Source: Religious Trends (2001: tables 2.3.1 and 10.7.2).

❷ How do you think a question on religious allegiance might have been worded for these surveys?

❷ Is it useful to study religious beliefs using survey methods?

The Anglican and Catholic churches both lost large numbers of members between 1975 and 2000. The Protestant sects and denominations have held up slightly better than the Anglicans. Nevertheless, the Baptists, the Methodists, and the Presbyterians each lost about a quarter of their members between 1970 and 2000. Among Christian churches, only the Orthodox Church has shown an increase in numbers, largely as a result of migration over the period.

About two-thirds of children born between 1885 and 1950 were baptized into the Church of England, but the figure had fallen to a half by 1960. By 2000 the figure had dropped to only just over a quarter. There were 122,000 infant baptisms and 36,300 confirmations in 2000. Less than one in ten children was then attending Sunday school, compared with one in five during the period 1895 to 1940. There was also a decline in church marriages, as couples became more likely to have a civil ceremony. One-third of English marriages were civil marriages in the period from 1952 to 1962, compared with one-quarter in 1929 and just one in eight in 1879 (B. R. Wilson 1966: ch. 1). By 2000, however, well over a half of all marriages took place in a register office or in 'approved premises', such as hotels and public halls. Marriage itself had become less popular (see Chapter 12, pp. 448–51).

These falls in membership and attendance have been associated with organizational changes in the churches. The number of Church of England ministers declined from over 20,000 in 1900 to 10,750 in 2000, and the number of Methodist ministers declined from 3,800 to 2,456 over the

Global focus World religions　　　　　　　　11.8

Figure 11.3 shows the growth in various religions across the world since 1900. Which religions have shown the greatest rate of growth over this period? Which have been the slowest to grow?

You can calculate growth rates by subtracting the 1900 figure from the 2000 figure and dividing this amount by the 1900 figure. Christianity, for example, has grown by (1999.6–558.1)/558.1, or by 2.58 times. Note that you cannot calculate this accurately for Baha'is, who were so small in numbers in 1900 that there were not enough of them to be recorded in this table. (The technical reason for this calculation problem is that it would involve you dividing by zero—and anything divided by zero is infinity.)

Now calculate similar growth rates for the increase between 1970 and 2000.

Can you come up with any explanation for the rates of change that you have found? Total world population increased from 1,620 million in 1900 to 3,696 million in 1970 and 6,055 million in 2000—what does this tell you about the overall trend in religious attachment? Can you find any evidence for secularization in this table?

Comparative measures of church attendance are very unreliable, but some broad patterns are clear. Rates of church attendance are especially low across northern Europe, Russia, China, and Central and East Asia. Moderately high rates are found through the Americas, and the highest rates of all occur in Nigeria, the Philippines, Ireland, and South Africa. Data were not collected for many Muslim countries in Africa and the Middle East, where attendance at religious services might be expected to be very high.

Figure 11.3　World religions, 1900–2000

Religion	Allegiance (m.)				
	1900	1970	1980	1990	2000
Christian	558.1	1,236.4	1,482.6	1,747.5	1,999.6
Muslim	199.9	553.5	759.0	962.4	1,188.2
Hindu	203.0	462.6	578.7	686.0	811.3
Chinese folk religion	380.0	231.9	288.4	347.7	384.8
Buddhists	127.1	233.4	275.7	323.1	360.0
Animists	117.7	160.3	180.9	200.0	228.4
Sikhs	3.0	10.6	14.2	19.3	23.3
Jains	1.3	2.6	3.2	3.9	4.2
Jews	12.3	14.8	14.0	13.2	14.4
Baha'is	0	2.7	3.8	5.7	7.1
Other religions	14.0	93.8	105.4	116.7	130.0
Non-religious	3.2	697.5	774.2	853.8	918.2

Source: Religious Trends (2001: table 1.2.2).

same period. The number of Catholic priests in England and Wales, by contrast, increased for a while as the number of migrants from Eire and Northern Ireland also increased. It has now fallen back in line with declining membership. In Scotland, the number of ministers in Presbyterian denominations had fallen from 3,600 to less than 1,500 by the mid-1990s (Bruce 1995: 32–3), and to less than 1,100 by 2010. An important trend, however, has been an increase in the number of women clergy. About 17.5 per cent of Anglican ministers and 19 per cent of Methodist ministers in 2006 were female.

These trends show a decline in religious *belonging*, as measured by conventional churchgoing and church involvement (see Box 11.8). They do not, however, give any direct evidence of a decline in religious *believing* (Davie 1994). In fact, religious belief appears to remain quite strong. A survey carried out in the 1980s found that 76 per cent of people in Great Britain believed in God, 50 per cent engaged in regular prayer, and only 4 per cent described themselves as atheists. In 1990, 71 per cent claimed to believe in God, 53 per cent prayed or meditated, and 44 per cent said that they drew personal strength from their religious beliefs. Fifty-three per cent of people believed in 'Heaven', and 25 per cent believed in 'the Devil' and in 'Hell' (Davie 1994: 79, see also Jowell *et al.* 1991). In a survey in 1995, only 11 per cent said that they definitely did not believe in God, while 21 per cent had no doubts at all about the existence of God (see Figure 11.4). During 1996, the then leaders of all three major political parties claimed that they prayed regularly to God. By

Figure 11.4　Belief in God, Great Britain, 1995

	(%)
Do not believe in God	11
Do not know if God exists and cannot find evidence for God's existence	15
Believe in a higher power of some kind	12
Believe sometimes	12
Doubt, but believe	23
God exists, with no doubts	21
Can't choose/not answered	7
	100

Source: Social Trends (1997: table 13.23).

1999, only 32.5 per cent of the population claimed to believe in God (Voas and Bruce 2004).

In the United States, religious belief seems to be somewhat higher. A massive 95 per cent of the population claim to believe in God. In many cases, Americans subscribe to creationist ideas that run counter to the conclusions of contemporary science. In the early 1980s, a survey reported that 44 per cent of Americans believed that God had created human beings within the last 10,000 years.

Though most people in Britain and the United States describe their religious beliefs as 'Christian', they are not those of conventional Christianity. For many people, Christian and non-Christian ideas have been fused into loose and amorphous systems of personal belief. They claim no specific biblical or priestly authority for these beliefs, regarding them as things that they simply accept or have worked out for themselves. Forty-two per cent of those who believed in God saw this god as 'some sort of spiritual or vital force' rather than as the personal God of traditional Christianity (Bruce 1995: 50).

Beliefs in a god are directly and closely linked with 'superstitious' beliefs and practices and with beliefs in astrology, psychic phenomena, ghosts, and paranormal experiences. Just under a quarter of the British population in 1991 believed that good-luck charms were effective, just over a quarter believed in the accuracy of horoscopes, and 40 per cent believed in the powers of fortune tellers (Jowell *et al.* 1991). For many people, these beliefs were held alongside beliefs in alternative medicine, the power of crystals, and reflexology.

This was true also of those who identified themselves as Catholics, a significant number of whom held unorthodox beliefs or rejected certain aspects of traditional Catholicism. These 'heterodox Catholics' formed a majority among Catholic non-attenders at church. They were younger than the average English Catholic—two-thirds of them were under age 35—and they were more likely to be second or later generation than recent migrants. A survey of their attitudes concluded that they might never have been anything more than nominal Catholics (Hornsby-Smith *et al.* 1982; see also Hornsby-Smith 1987, 1991).

Organized religion, both conventional denominational religion and state-oriented civil religion, is no longer a major factor in the lives of most people. Those religious beliefs that they do retain are loose and free-floating and are not organized into any formal participation in churches or rituals. Mainstream religious belief in Britain is no longer tied to conventional Christianity or to regular church attendance.

What Davie (1994) has termed the common religion is a non-sectarian and eclectic form of religious belief. People 'continue to believe in God, but . . . are reluctant to express this belief in either churchgoing or church membership' (Davie 1990). Their conception of God, furthermore, bears

Briefing: mainstream religion 11.9

We have argued that mainstream religion is no longer tied to conventional Christian church beliefs, though people may generally describe themselves as 'Christian'. It is impossible to summarize mainstream religious beliefs and attach a conventional label to them. Even many of those who attend Church of England services cannot be easily described as 'Protestant' or 'Anglican' in their beliefs. The beliefs that comprise the 'common religion' are diverse and quite variable.

❓ *You might like to talk to friends and family about their beliefs to see if they are similar to those described here. Is it possible to depict mainstream religious beliefs in a simple creed that summarizes the key features in the way that we have done for smaller religious groups?*

little relationship to the scriptural God of the Christian tradition. The common religion is a private system of belief that draws on a pool of shared ideas that derive from both Christian and non-Christian sources (see Box 11.9).

What is striking, however, is that the common religion has no significant moral implications for how people should live in society. There is some sign of a growing sense of the environmental implications of these religious beliefs—of the need to protect the earth and its natural resources—but there is no equivalent sense of any need to build or to defend particular kinds of social order. The common religion does not provide the moral bonds and regulations that were central to traditional religion. In a secular society, the uncommitted mainstream religion of the vast majority of the population is a sprawling and amorphous array of beliefs that form a framework of taken-for-granted ideas that, for most people, are an integral, if rather marginal, aspect of their day-to-day lives. This raises the question of whether such collective beliefs can still be said to constitute 'religious' beliefs in the fullest sense of the term.

> ➔ *Connections*
> The idea of the common religion raises questions about the definition of religion. What do you think about this? Look back at the definition given on p. 393 at the beginning of this chapter.

Varieties of new religion

The common religion is a widely shared framework of ideas, but for many people it is not enough. Nor does the more general framework of moral individualism meet their need for truly spiritual values. Some of these seekers after the sacred have turned to more fundamental forms of traditional Christianity, but others have found a greater appeal in new religions. The number of these new religions, both Christian and non-Christian, has increased since the Second World War, in both Britain and the United States. This growth has been especially rapid since the 1960s. These new religions are often described as cults, though this term has been given a wide variety of meanings.

In the original definition given by Troeltsch (1912), the **cult** was contrasted with the sect. Troeltsch defined the cult as a loosely organized grouping without sharp boundaries and with no exclusive system of beliefs. Cult beliefs are not rigid and exclusive; they are open and flexible. They comprise a set of common themes and ideas, and individual members can contribute their personal views to the pool of ideas. A cult is very open to new recruits, it is tolerant towards other beliefs, and it makes no demand that its members should completely abandon their other beliefs. Many people today, for example, adhere to cult beliefs in UFOs and alien abductions. These beliefs are remarkably diverse, and those who adhere to such beliefs are united by little more than their common concern and interest. There is no central organization or rigidly codified and enforced set of beliefs.

Cults are often short-lived. They depend upon the personal leadership of a founder or key member, and they dissolve when this leader dies. An example of a long-lasting cult is spiritualism, which has drawn its adherents from the membership of many churches, as well as from those who are members of none (Nelson 1969). Troeltsch argued that, if a cult can establish a more secure base of recruitment, it can establish a more permanent organization. Such a cult may even develop into an ecclesia, as happened when early cult Christianity was taken up by the Roman emperor and became the Roman Catholic Church. On the other hand, however, cults may remain apart from political and economic power and evolve into sects.

The word 'cult' has also been used in popular discussions, but here it tends to be a derogatory term. For many people, then, a cult is a contemporary religious organization, often a tight and exclusive sect, whose aims and methods they reject. Cults are accused of brainwashing or kidnapping those who join them, and they are often accused of financial, sexual, or political deviance. Because the original sociological meaning of cult has been obscured by its contemporary popular use as a label for religious deviance, many sociologists now prefer to use the more neutral term 'new religious movement'. This term, too, can be a little misleading, as all religions were, at some stage, new, and many of the growing religions of the 1960s have long-established roots.

The established Christian and non-Christian denominations and sects—Methodists, Baptists, the Reformed Church (Presbyterian and Congregationalist), Anglicans, Catholics, Jews, Spiritualists, Mormons, Jehovah's Witnesses, and the Salvation Army—have, in general, continued to decline in numbers or have, at best, maintained their membership through active proselytizing. The big growth in numbers of members and believers has largely occurred among those sects that have returned to or have emphasized the fundamental beliefs of their faith and those religions that have based themselves on radically new sets of ideas that are often non-theistic in character.

In the rest of this chapter, we will look at the four main forms of religion in which there has been a growth of activity. They are:

- inspirational Protestantism;
- world-rejecting religions;
- world-affirming religions;
- religions of ethnic protest.

Inspirational Protestantism comprises a number of fundamentalist, reformed, and evangelical sects and denominations that have split from the established denominations or that have been set up in direct opposition to them. Examples are the Pentecostalist churches and the Southern Baptist Convention. World-rejecting religions are a variety of generally non-Christian sects and cults that reject established religion and many aspects of modern society. They adopt a 'utopian' or millennial point of view. Examples are the Unification Church and Krishna Consciousness. World-affirming religions, on the other hand, include a variety of sects and cults that embrace the values of modern society. They aim to provide their members with better

---

THEORY AND METHODS   11.10

Sect and cult

We have identified four concepts that form a typology of religious organizations. These are ecclesia, denomination, sect, and cult. You should review the definitions of ecclesia and denomination on p. 399.

A sect is characterized by:

- a claim to a monopoly of religious truth;
- voluntary, not compulsory membership;
- a high level of emotional commitment;
- non-hierarchical forms of leadership.

In so far as the concept of a cult can still be used in its original sociological sense, it refers to religious groups that are characterized by:

- great openness to all who wish to join;
- loosely defined beliefs and concerns;
- non-institutionalized forms of leadership.

means to achieve them. Examples are Scientology and Transcendental Meditation. Finally, religions of ethnic protest are religions of migrants and ethnic minorities who have been excluded from full participation in the mainstream of modern society. The religion becomes a means of protest and opposition to their exclusion and oppression. Examples are Rastafarianism and some contemporary forms of Islam.

Inspirational Protestantism

Those who are attracted to inspirational Protestantism do so in reaction to the increasingly liberal religious attitudes of the mainstream Protestant denominations. As we have shown, Protestant beliefs have encouraged and reinforced the tendency to secularization, and this has meant that the beliefs of the Protestant denominations themselves have been marked by a disenchantment. To those who look for traditional religious beliefs, the Protestant denominations have little to offer. Moving in an increasingly liberal direc-

Presbyterianism in Northern Ireland is a basis of ethnic loyalism.

© Neil Jarman

tion, the Protestant denominations have estranged many of their own adherents.

These people decry the loss of distinctively religious content in the teachings of the churches. They resent the abandonment of what they still regard as religious certainties, especially when it is bishops and other senior leaders of the churches who seem to be denying the central tenets of their belief. When, in the early 1990s, the Bishop of Durham gave a rational, liberal interpretation of the Virgin birth, many of the most active members of the Church felt that he was no longer speaking as a truly Christian clergyman.

Those who retain traditional Christian beliefs lose confidence in a church that they see as moving rapidly away from them in an increasingly secular direction. They reject attempts to be relevant to contemporary concerns and to update the liturgy and rituals. They disapprove of the translation of the Bible into contemporary English. The involvement of the churches in social work and political controversies is seen as a departure from their primary purpose of preaching the gospels. The Protestant denominations have lost members, at least in part, because their liberal beliefs are out of line with the more conservative religious beliefs and attitudes of many of their members. These disaffected Protestants are attracted to the more fundamentalist Protestant sects that have managed to increase their memberships in recent years. These sects have prospered by retaining traditional beliefs in an increasingly secular age. As Bruce (1983: 466) has argued: 'The group of Protestants who do most to preserve their faith from the ravages of the secular world have survived the last quarter century in better shape than have those who argued for compromise with the modern world.'

Most of the Presbyterian denominations in both Scotland and Northern Ireland, for example, have experienced declining membership over the course of the century. The more conservative Free Presbyterian Churches, however, have experienced huge increases in membership since the middle of the 1950s. Ian Paisley's Free Presbyterians have built up a massive 10,000 membership in Northern Ireland since its formation in 1951, its role as the defender of the 'loyalist' ethnicity of Ulster Protestants having helped to strengthen its appeal (Bruce 1983).

The Protestant sects that have attracted this growth in membership have been the inspirational sects, and we now need to look a little closer at the nature of inspirational Protestantism and those who support it.

Fundamentalism and Pentecostalism

Two principal forms of inspirational Protestantism can be identified in Britain and the United States. These are fundamentalism and Pentecostalism. Fundamentalists adopt a particularly conservative attitude towards their religion. They subscribe to the Protestant reliance on the Bible as the direct word of God and, therefore, as the fundamental source of all knowledge, and they hold its meaning to be self-evident to all who read it. The Bible requires no interpretation by priests or others: it is not allegorical or mythical, it is literally true. God's will and the truth of human creation are claimed to be discoverable by a simple and direct reading of the Bible.

Things are not, of course, this simple, as no text can be understood in a strictly literal sense, without interpretation. The meaning of the Bible, or, indeed, of any other text, is far from straightforward. This is clear from the number of divergent forms of biblical fundamentalism. There are, for example, differences between reformed and evangelical Protestantism. Calvinist or Reformed Protestants believe in a doctrine of predestination according to which only a small group of the elect are destined for salvation. Evangelical forms of fundamentalism, on the other hand, encourage people to choose God and, through being 'born again', to *achieve* salvation.

In reality, then, fundamentalism must rely on the authoritative interpretations given to the Bible by preachers and teachers who have played a leading role in the social organization and development of particular sects. Fundamentalists are inspired by the direct word of God, as recorded in the Bible, but they must rely on charismatic, inspiring preachers to guide their reading. Fundamentalist readings of the Bible are attractive to those who, by prior belief or social background, are predisposed towards conservative responses to its message.

Pentecostal Christians also subscribe to the literal truth of the Bible, but they combine this with an overriding emphasis on personal religious experiences, such as spiritual possession, speaking with tongues, healing, and the working of miracles (Bruce 1985). In this kind of religion, the word of God in the Bible is supplemented by the direct voice of God. Pentecostalists believe that they can learn God's wishes for them through opening their hearts and minds to His spirit. They believe that they can learn from direct spiritual inspiration and from observing the religious experiences and inspiration of others in their church. Pentecostalism is discussed in Box 11.11.

Large numbers of Pentecostalists in Britain are African Caribbean. First-generation migrants arrived in Britain in the 1950s with more conservative religious attitudes than most of the white population. They were particularly attracted by Pentecostalism. It has been estimated that just under one in five African Caribbeans attends church regularly, about four-fifths of these attending Pentecostal churches. Pryce (1986) has shown the high level of support for Pentecostalism in a particular area of Bristol. African Caribbeans in Bristol reported that they were oppressed as both black and working class. Their religion helped them to minimize the significance of this oppression while they awaited salvation in the next world. Black Pentecostalism,

Briefing: Pentecostalism   11.11

According to the Bible, the Holy Spirit descended on the disciples on the fiftieth day (Greek *pente koste*) after the Passover festival. The Holy Spirit gave the disciples gifts of prophecy, healing, and speaking in foreign tongues. In the contemporary Christian calendar, this is celebrated at Whitsun.

Pentecostal churches believe that these gifts are still available to true believers, and their services are designed to create the conditions for this. Services involve loud and joyful singing and prayer, and members of the congregation may exhibit signs of the Spirit's 'gifts'. The Pentecostal movement began in the United States around 1900 and soon spread to Britain. The principal Pentecostal church in the United States is the Assemblies of God. In Britain, most Pentecostalists are members of the Elim Pentecostal Church or the Apostolic Church. There are also many independent black Pentecostalist churches.

then, is a form of *cultural defence* (Bruce 1995: 78) for African Caribbean ethnicity.

The new Christian right

The social and political influence of fundamentalism grew particularly rapidly in the United States during the 1960s and 1970s. Underlying this growth was a view that a weakening of the civil religion and an associated spiritual decline in American society into permissiveness and moral relativism needed to be reversed through a reassertion of traditional Christian values. Moral individualism, also, was felt to be unsatisfying in itself, because it lacked the enchantment and spirituality of traditional religion. Specific targets were the liberal intellectuals seen as responsible for this spiritual decline.

This demand for moral revival emerged in what Bruce has called conservative social milieux or subcultures. These are loose networks of individuals and organizations united by shared beliefs and values but not formed into any single organization or political movement (Bruce 1984: chs. 3 and 7). These milieux are particularly strong in the southern states, but they extend nation-wide. Those who live in the conservative milieu build supporting institutions that strengthen them and extend their influence. Separate and distinct schools and colleges, for example, have allowed conservative Protestants to socialize their children away from the permissiveness and liberalism of mainstream schools. Similarly, the publication of fundamentalist books, films, and music helps to enlarge the subculture of fundamentalism. Most recently, these cultural efforts have been solidified through radio and television evangelism. There are now a number of satellite and cable television channels dedicated to evangelistic Protestantism and its charismatic leaders.

Evangelical crusades have been important in attracting new recruits to particular churches, and in preventing the sons and daughters of subcultural adherents from falling away from their faith. Conservative Protestant movements have, however, recruited mainly from the children of people already predisposed towards traditional, conservative forms of religion through allegiance to one or another of the conservative Protestant churches. The crusades have been occasions for reviving and revivifying the religious beliefs of those already predisposed towards conversion.

When existing religious world-views lose their plausibility, many young people in the conservative milieux find the message of the fundamentalist churches attractive. This cultural affinity builds on the close personal links they and their families have to the churches and other institutions of the subculture of fundamentalism. Personal social relations are also able to reinforce their commitment once their religious choice has been made. More than a half of all converts to the conservative Protestant churches are recruited between the ages of 12 and 20, and they have generally been introduced to the church through a parental Christian influence (Bruce 1984: 56–7). For these reasons, fundamentalist churches have made few converts from outside the milieux, and the evangelical crusades have not resulted in the mass conversion of the uncommitted:

> The people who go forward are almost all the sons and daughters of believers. What they signify with such a move is not that they have found a new and previously alien belief system convincing but rather that they have come to make a positive commitment to a set of beliefs with which they are already familiar.

Bruce 1984: 102

It was from these conservative cultural milieux that the so-called new right emerged in the 1970s. Media evangelists were key figures in mobilizing cultural support for the Moral Majority, which was formed in 1979 as an organizational focus for the new Christian right. Conservative Protestants formed the leading members of the new right in the political sphere, though it also built its support through alliances with right-wing thinkers in the Catholic, Jewish, Mormon, and other churches. This movement built a large bloc of support that helped to secure the election of Ronald Reagan in his first term as president.

> **⤷ Connections**
> If you want to know more about the growth and influence of the new right in the United States and Britain, turn to Chapter 15, pp. 576–80.

The processes that helped the formation of the new Christian right in the United States were much weaker in Britain. The conservative Protestant churches have, however, been the least likely to embrace the move to toleration and secularism in politics. Bruce has shown that smaller religious organizations in Scotland and Northern Ireland, especially those with a predominantly working-class membership and a strong regional identity, have maintained a sectarian stance towards other churches and have opposed moves that would undermine their own particular identity (Bruce 1986). In Northern Ireland, conservative Protestantism has developed into a strong social force with an anti-Catholic character, and these fundamentalist churches have been particularly important social bases of support for the Orange Order, a Masonic body that pursues charitable and, above all, political goals. Orangeism in Northern Ireland, drawing widely in its recruitment from among the Protestant population, has been especially strongly shaped by the views of those associated with the conservative Protestant sects.

World-rejecting and world-affirming religions

Conventional forms of Christianity can no longer meet the religious needs that many people feel. They seek forms of religion that seem to be more in accord with contemporary life. The work of Merton, whose ideas on anomie we looked at in Chapter 2, pp. 44–5, can illuminate this. Merton looked at the strains and tensions that can occur in cultural systems and at the varying responses that individuals may make to these. The growth of affluence and consumerism in the 1950s and 1960s generated two characteristic responses to the mainstream religious culture on the part of those who felt unable to achieve their goals through the conventional means available to them:

- *Retreatism*: this involves a rejection of the goals and means of the conventional society and a withdrawal from it;
- *Innovation*: this involves seeking out alternative ways of achieving the conventional goals.

Wallis (1984: 4–6, 9) argued that each of these responses was associated with the growth of a particular kind of religion. Corresponding to the retreatist response are the **world-rejecting religions** that denigrate the central values and assumptions of the modern world. Examples of such religions are The International Society for Krishna Consciousness (ISKCON) and the Unification Church (see Box 11.12, p. 416). ISKCON—popularly known as Hare Krishna—is based around a form of Hinduism that requires an ascetic and communal way of life from its followers. Corresponding to the innovative response are the **world-affirming religions** such as Transcendental

Briefing: Moonies   11.12

A characteristic world-rejecting religion is the Unification Church, popularly known as the 'Moonies' after its founder, the Reverend Moon. Drawing on both Christian and Buddhist sources, the religion rejects the materialism of the contemporary world and advocates a disciplined, ascetic lifestyle. It requires that its members should give their income and assets over to the use of the church. Moonies see their task as bringing about a physical kingdom of God on earth that actualizes the spiritual kingdom that had been established by Jesus. The Reverend Moon is believed to be the new Messiah who leads adherents towards this goal. A good study is E. Barker (1984).

Meditation (TM) and Scientology. These religions embrace many of the central cultural goals and values of contemporary societies but claim to offer new means to achieve them. TM, founded by the Maharishi Mahesh Yogi, stresses the personal and practical benefits of regular meditation, while Scientology uses methods closer to psychotherapy (see Box 11.13).

Many of these religions take a cult form. They engage in worldly activities and allow people to drift in and out of participation as they sample the beliefs on offer. TM, for example, is associated with a political party (the Natural Law Party) that fights general elections on policies that advocate the benefits of TM and 'yogic flying' for solutions to individual and social problems. Even such groups as the Unification Church and Scientology, which are relatively closed to outsiders, do not typically hold on to their members for long periods.

Utopian religion and world rejection

World-rejecting, utopian religions grew rapidly in the 1960s, when many young people were attracted by retreatist responses. In the early 1960s this had been expressed in the hippie, drug-user subculture of American and European youth, which, as Jock Young (1971) showed, rejected the work ethic and the impersonality and bureaucracy of modern society. In place of these values, hippies emphasized spontaneity and hedonism. The subculture proved especially attractive to white, middle-class, college drop-outs. It was the perceived failure of hippie utopianism to achieve its aims that produced many recruits for new religions that offered more radical solutions. Those who identified with the values of the hippie culture, even if they had not directly experienced it, sought new ways of meeting its values of community and fellowship.

These religions see present-day problems as symptoms of a departure from an authentic and more natural way of life, and their appeal derives not so much from the specific content of their beliefs as from the communal lifestyles with which the groups have been identified. Familiarity with the beliefs generally came *after* young people had joined the groups. Potential members have been attracted by the communal group solidarity that the religions espouse, and it is this—rather than brainwashing—that has tied people to them. These religious communities appeared to offer an escape from the impersonality of modern society and a solution to the perceived loss of community in the wider society.

> ⮔ *Connections*
> You might like to read the discussion of Jock Young's work in Chapter 7, pp. 249–50. This will give you an overview of the hippie subculture.

These religions tend to have a clear and specific conception of a god or gods, regarded as the source of moral norms and obligations. They have a sense of their religious mission that is sometimes allied with a search for political influence and social change. Some, however, are millenarian. That is to say, they anticipate the destruction or collapse of the world, followed by their own salvation. The Children of God, for example, await the return of Jesus to save the world. Yet other groups anticipate the arrival of extra-terrestrial life forms (Festinger *et al.* 1956). What such groups tend to hold in common is a view that;

> . . . the prevailing social order . . . [has] departed substantially from God's prescriptions and plan. Mankind [*sic.*] has lost touch with God and spiritual things, and, in the pursuit of purely material interests, has succeeded in creating a polluted environment; a vice-ridden society in which individuals treat each other purely as means rather than ends; a world filled with conflict, greed, insincerity and despair. The world-rejecting movement condemns urban industrial society and its values, particularly that of individual success as measured by wealth or consumption patterns. It rejects the materialism of the advanced industrial world, calling for a return to a more rural way of life, and a reorientation of secular life.

Wallis 1984: 10

The utopian religions tend to organize themselves as total institutions, and there is a great emphasis on their separate, enclosed, and disciplined communal life. This often involves engaging in economic and fund-raising activities that help to provide for the group's own subsistence. Those religions that have been particularly successful in this and have become very wealthy have often attracted criticism, especially when the wealth seems to provide extravagant lifestyles for their leadership.

Social control within the group operates mainly through persuasion that draws on people's commitment to the

Briefing: Scientology 11.13

A characteristic world-affirming religion is Scientology. Founded by the science-fiction writer L. Ron Hubbard, Scientology draws on psychotherapy to provide practices and techniques that alter the consciousness of its members and enable them to act in more positive and effective ways to achieve their worldly goals: a better job, a higher income, or greater happiness in what they are doing. It claims to give its members spiritual powers, such as the ability to see, hear, and manipulate people and objects at great distances, purely by mental forces. The religion works through training and therapy sessions in closed communities, but it has many similarities to a conventional business operation: recruits pay fees for their training and counselling, and many full-time workers are employed to manage the church. An inquiry in the 1990s alleged widespread financial fraud on the part of the church. Prominent adherents today include the Hollywood actor Tom Cruise. A good description of Scientology can be found in Wallis (1976). Scientology recruits through high street stalls offering 'Free Stress Tests'.

recruit those who are searching for a more direct experience of the sacred than established religions can provide. The religions provide a feeling of certainty in a relativistic culture, and Wallis suggested that world accommodation is the end-stage for all world-rejecting sects and cults.

Therapeutic religions and world affirmation

The second response that we identified to the mainstream religious culture is the innovative response of the world-affirming religions. These religions have a worldly character. That is to say, they embrace the goals and values of modern society. They combine their religious orientation with an acceptance of magical and manipulative techniques that allow their members to achieve conventional goals through unconventional means.

Many of these religions adopt a psychotherapeutic stance towards the solution of their members' problems, and they 'straddle a vague boundary between religion and psychology' (Wallis 1984: 35). They generally lack any developed theology or ritual, and their conception of God, if any, is that of a diffuse, universal force that manifests itself in individuals. They are oriented towards the perfectibility of the individual through specific therapeutic practices, and they work towards promoting individual achievement within the existing society. They might claim, for example, that they can unlock a person's potential by providing him or her with the appropriate discipline or training. These advantages are held to be open to anybody who joins the group and learns its techniques.

These religions have deeper roots and a more long-lasting base of recruitment than do the world-rejecting religions. They expanded considerably during the 1950s and 1960s, and they recruited from among relatively affluent people in their twenties and thirties who were seeking ways of helping themselves towards greater individual achievement, happiness, and success in a consumer society (B. R. Wilson 1966: 216).

While Scientology has tended to adopt a sectarian form of organization, the so-called New Age movement is a much looser world-affirming cult. It combines elements of Eastern religions with mythology and Jung's psychoanalysis to form a complex and diverse system of beliefs that embraces crystal healing, the use of essential oils, astrology, acupuncture, herbalism, dowsing, UFOs, Paganism, certain aspects of witchcraft, and various other strands. New Age ideas became especially popular in the 1980s, and have had an impact on mainstream culture beyond their own adherents. Those who see themselves as part of the New Age movement promote their preferred therapies and ideas through advertising, setting up shops, and publishing books. These promotional activities bring non-believers into contact with the movement, and they have been behind the massive popularity of such techniques as aromatherapy. This technique, which involves the use of

group and their love for its leaders, its ideals, and their fellow members. In these circumstances, individual identity is subordinated to collective identity. Although the exercise of coercion over members is not usual, it does occur, and a degree of coercive control may be accepted by members as necessary to maintain the group in a hostile environment. In some extreme cases, suicide may be accepted as a necessary way to affirm the group's identity and beliefs when under threat from the outside. This is known to have been the case with the mass suicides of members of the Heaven's Gate group in San Diego in 1997, and it is thought to have played a major part in the destruction of the Branch Davidian group in Waco, Texas, in 1993. Durkheim (1897) called this fatalistic suicide.

The end of the long period of sustained affluence in the mid-1970s was marked by static or declining membership for the world-rejecting religions. In response, some of them became more world-accommodating in character and have since recruited older people. The term **world-accommodating religions** describes those religions that adopt an attitude of mild disapproval or of acceptance of the world as it is, rather than an attitude of complete rejection. In such groups, religious beliefs often come to be seen as separate from the principal activities of everyday life (Wallis 1984). As religions become world accommodating, they tend to attack established religious organizations rather more than they do the secular world, and they

World-rejecting and world-affirming religions

	World-rejecting	World-affirming
Conception of good	Personal entity distinct from humanity	Element of every human life
Present world	Debased: its values all contrary to the ideal; in need of total transformation	Much to offer if one has the means to secure the good things available
Commitment required	Complete, including separation from family and career; movement is a 'total institution'	Partial, a largely leisure-time pursuit while one continues one's activity in the world
Economic base	Wealth and labour of converts, supplemented by street solicitation of donations	Fees for goods and services marketed by the movement
Sexual morality	Ascetic (i.e., tightly regulating sexual activity) or antinomian (permitting promiscuous sexual relationships)	Largely indifferent to sexual conduct
Conversion	Rapid, abrupt after contact, attitude of 'surrender' required from outset	Typically a sequence of stages of progressive personal transformation
Leader	God's emissary or representative	Technical innovator
Social organization	Communal	Corporate
Examples	Unification Church, ISKCON, Children of God, People's Temple, Manson's Family	Transcendental Meditation, Human Potential Movement, Est (Erhard Seminars Training), Silva Mind Control, Scientology

Source: Wallis (1984).

essential oils, appeals to those, for example, who are also attracted to the forms of alternative medicine and personal strategies of well-being that challenge the authority of medical experts.

Despite the growth in their numbers, the world-rejecting and world-accepting religions together comprise only a very small proportion of the population. The membership of any one group is tiny. There have, for example, never been more than 1,000 'Moonies' in Britain. There are less than 500 members of ISKCON, and only a few hundred members of TM (E. Barker 1989).

Religions of ethnic protest

Religious beliefs have long played a central part in defining and developing ethnic identities. In many religions, a particular ethnic community is seen as being in some way special to the gods. Jewish holy texts, for example, define the Jews as the chosen people of God, and the indigenous religious beliefs of Japan trace the origins of the Japanese to *Ama-terasu*, the sun goddess. As A. Smith (1991: 7) has

shown, for most of human history, religion and ethnic identity have been very closely entwined, each people having its own gods and sacred texts, and its distinctive religious practices, priests, and places.

Migration into Britain and the births of second- and later-generation members of migrant families have altered the religious mix. Migrants from the Caribbean, as we have shown, brought conservative Protestant religions with them, but migrants from elsewhere have brought about an expansion of non-Christian religions. Those from India, Pakistan, Bangladesh, and East Africa have swelled the numbers of Hindus, Muslims, Sikhs, Jews, and others. This religious diversity is increased by the divisions within each religion. About one in ten British Muslims is Shi'a, while most of the rest are Sunnis. The Sunnis, however, are divided into Barelwi, Deoband, and Tablghi Jamaat branches. Similarly, Hindus are divided into loose traditions, as well as being divided by caste (Bruce 1995: 79 ff.).

In the early twenty-first century there are more than one million Muslims in Britain, just under a half a million Hindus, and the same number of Sikhs. Membership of these religions has tripled since 1970. The state has long financed denominational schools—through the system of voluntary aid—for Anglicans, Catholics, Methodists, and Jews, and there is a growing demand for similar support for Muslims.

Growth in the numbers of those affiliated to ethnic-minority religions is not, however, what is meant by the term 'religions of ethnic protest'. A multi-ethnic, multi-religion society is an essential condition for the emergence of religions of ethnic protests, but it is not the same thing. Religions of ethnic protest are those that have grown within particular ethnic-minority communities and are used by their members to voice their protest at their exclusion, on the grounds of their ethnicity, from full participation in their society.

> **➲ Connections**
>
> You will probably find it useful to remind yourself about what we say on ethnicity and ethnic identity and on migration in Chapter 6, pp. 194–5 and 215–17. You will also find useful our discussion of ethnicity and national identity in Chapter 16, pp. 598–600.

Rastafarianism and the Nation of Islam

The two most characteristic religions of ethnic protest in contemporary Britain are Rastafarianism and the Nation of Islam.

The deeply felt experience of deprivation and exclusion found in the poor, inner-city districts of Britain, where many African Caribbean people are forced to live, contrasts sharply with the optimistic expectations of the migrants who arrived in Britain during the 1950s and 1960s. Many of the first generation, as we have shown, have given voice to their situation through inspirational Protestantism. Those of the second and third generations—like their young white counterparts—have sought answers in newer and more radical forms of religion. Among these people, Rastafarianism has had a particularly strong appeal, as its social ethic seems to talk directly to their experiences (see Box 11.15).

Membership grew particularly during the 1970s with the success of the singer Bob Marley and the popularization of reggae. Its musical style, along with its style of dress and the use of cannabis (ganja), have sprung from and contributed to the wider growth of a consciousness of black identity (Alexander 1996). Its lifestyle and ethic of social nonconformity were attractive to many inner-city African Caribbeans. Many of these adherents were attracted by its musical and fashion styles, and they did not necessarily make any serious commitment to its religious beliefs and practices. The committed Rastafarian refuses to become involved in crime and deviance for its own sake, stressing the need to build a sense of black dignity (Pryce 1986).

Drawing on a shared memory of the African diaspora, this black consciousness forms part of what Gilroy (1993)

Briefing: Rastafarianism   11.15

Rastafarianism originated in Jamaica. Marcus Garvey had claimed that Africans were the 'lost tribe' of biblical Israel, and that this tribe had been further dispersed across the world by the enslavement of Africans and their transportation to the West Indies and the Americas. Africans, African Americans, and African Caribbeans were, therefore, seen as a chosen people of God. Their oppression and exploitation could be ended only by a return to Africa and the establishment there of societies free of colonial and post-colonial domination. Seeing the former Emperor of Ethiopia Haile Selassie (otherwise known as Ras Tafari) as a Messiah, Garvey advocated and encouraged such a return. There are estimated to be about 70,000 believers world-wide, but the religion is not united under a single leadership.

has called the 'Black Atlantic', a cultural framework that links Africa, Britain, the Caribbean, and the Americas. This consciousness, however, is not without its divisions. In 1996, Rastafarians attended a service for the dead Crown Prince of Ethiopia at an Ethiopian Orthodox church in London. The Rastafarians saw the Prince as the son of a God (Haile Selassie), a direct descendant of King Solomon and the Queen of Sheba. He was also heir to the throne of their spiritual homeland. The Ethiopian Orthodox Church, part of the Eastern Orthodox Church, refused to be publicly linked with these claims, and many Ethiopians resented the presence of the Rastafarians in their church.

The Nation of Islam was central to the civil-rights movement in the United States. One of its principal aims is the promotion of black consciousness, and it was a major force behind campaigns stressing 'Black Power' and 'Black is Beautiful'. Those who were excluded from the ethnic melting pot also felt excluded from any sense of American identity and participation in the civil religion. Total membership in the United States is estimated at about 100,000. Membership in Britain, where they began recruiting in 1986, is relatively small, and is thought to be about 2,500. In the United States, it takes a high-profile stance in African American politics. Its leader, Louis Farrakhan, has been at the centre of attempts to build cross-faith solidarity among African Americans (Lincoln 1973).

The British Nation of Islam (see Box 11.16, p. 420), which is more closed and secretive in its organization than the American one, is in some rivalry with the Rastafarians for recruits. It has been suggested that those African Caribbeans who identify with Africa are attracted to the Rastafarians, while those who identify with black Americans are attracted to the Nation of Islam. In many

Briefing: Nation of Islam 11.16

The Nation of Islam, also known as the Black Muslims, was founded in the United States by Fard Mohammad and his deputy Elijah Muhammad in the 1930s. They promoted the adoption of Islam by African Americans as a return to the pre-slavery religion of their ancestors. Those who join the Nation of Islam adopt new Muslim names, and many of the men wear smart suits and a bow tie as a mark of their membership. For many years the chief spokesman for the group was Malcolm X, but he was expelled in the 1960s. The beliefs of the group are far from pure Islam, and there is much reliance on the Christian New Testament. Some activists hold that the founders of the Nation of Islam are orbiting the earth in a spaceship.

The current leader of the Nation of Islam, Louis Farrakhan, was excluded from Britain between 1986 and 2001 because of claims that his views would encourage racial hatred. These claims were based on Farrakhan's views on Jews and white people. He has said that Judaism is a 'gutter religion' and that Jews are 'selfish, self-centred, vindictive, and unforgiving'. White people have been described as 'our mortal enemy', and Farrakhan has denounced sexual relations between blacks and whites. Slavery, he argues, was a Jewish conspiracy against Africans, and African Americans should be given eight or ten states to form a black USA.

You might like to look at our summary of black nationalism in Chapter 6, Box 6.9, p. 215.

The globalization of economic, political, and cultural relations has posed a threat to many local, indigenous communities that had not previously been drawn directly into the modern world. As we show in Chapter 16, pp. 614–17, these communities have not been isolated from the expanding world-system—far from it—but they have not until now been so directly penetrated by forces that come from outside their own immediate world. In many parts of Africa, the Middle East, and the Far East, for example, strongly anti-modern and, therefore, anti-Western sentiments have been aroused. Similarly, migrants from these areas to Western and Central Europe have generally experienced an exclusion from mainstream society that reinforces their sense of difference from white Westerners. The post-colonial experience—in the metropolitan centres and in the local communities—provides fertile ground for an emphasis on 'traditionalism' and traditional religion.

Fundamentalism occurs in areas that have been relatively secure from outside influence and have suddenly experienced major disruptions to their way of life. In those parts of the world that have a Christian tradition, as we have shown, Christian fundamentalism has attracted large numbers of adherents, while Muslim areas—which make up a significant proportion of all areas that are greatly affected by the forces of globalization—have shown a growth in radical forms of Islam often misleadingly called Islamic fundamentalism.

This radical Islam stresses that traditional religious truths, far from being undermined by modern society, have an ever-greater relevance to its problems. Essential religious truths are reaffirmed in a context where the

respects, the Nation of Islam adopts conservative attitudes, stressing traditional morality and the value of the family. To this moral conservatism, however, it adds a radical political programme of black consciousness-raising and black segregation.

Islam in a global context

Islam is the second largest religion in the world today and a major force in many societies of the world (see Box 11.17). It has been estimated that almost a quarter of the population of the world is nominally Muslim. Its growth over the centuries has been linked with huge advances in knowledge and scholarship—indeed, one of the earliest sociological writers, Ibn Khaldun, wrote from an explicitly Muslim standpoint in the fourteenth century. Today Islam has become an important element in the everyday lives of millions of people across the world. In many places, however, particularly radical forms of Islam have grown in recent years.

Briefing: Islam 11.17

Islam is a monotheistic religion that shares much of the Old Testament tradition with Jews and Christians. Its main beliefs, however, are contained in the Qu'ran, which contains the teachings of the sixth- to seventh-century prophet Muhammad. The Qu'ran is seen as the revealed will of God (Allah). It has no priestly hierarchy or authoritative interpretation of its orthodoxy, and no distinction is made between the spheres of religion and politics. Sunni Muslims are the more orthodox, while Shi'as have added to the original teachings of Muhammad. The largest areas of settlement are in the Middle East, the Indian subcontinent, South East Asia, Turkey, and West Africa. The largest single community is found in Indonesia. In Western Europe, the largest numbers of Muslims are in France, mainly migrants from north and west Africa, with smaller groups in Britain and Germany.

Friday prayers in a Muslim Mosque
© Getty Images/Paul Chesley

form of 'Islamism', a radical reading of holy texts that allies their principal tenets with social exclusion and nationalism. This need to rework and recreate tradition is made all the more necessary by the fact that migration and the globalization of cultures make each local group more aware of the diversity that exists within Islam. No set of beliefs can any more be simply taken for granted. They have to be taken back to their basic principles.

A key characteristic in radical Islam has been its development in reaction to a specifically *Western* form of modernization. This form of Islam achieved its earliest success in Iran in 1979, where it produced a revolutionary overthrow of the pro-Western regime of the Shah and established a Shi'ite Islamic Republic. Powerful and important radical Islamist movements played a major role in Lebanon, in Egypt, in Syria, and in Afghanistan, and Islamist regimes have been established in Algeria and Sudan. Moderate—generally Sunni—forms of Islam are the official creeds of many Arab states. The growth of Islamist regimes has been greatest wherever globalization results in the oppression or exclusion of those from a particular ethnic group—in many cases, therefore, radical Islam strengthens a sense of national identity.

The image of 'Islamic fundamentalism' in the West focuses on its links with the political violence, kidnapping, and hijacks undertaken by terrorist groups such as Hezbollah and Al-Qaeda, though these are minority activities. More typically, Islamists argue their position in peaceful, though forcible, discussion. Nevertheless, political regimes based on Islamist principles have tended to take a very restricted view of personal and political rights, such as those of women.

There is some evidence of a growth of radical Islamist views among some young second-generation Muslim migrants in Britain. While many have abandoned their religion altogether, the experience of unemployment, poor housing, and racial discrimination leads others to be receptive to radical solutions. Just as disadvantaged African Caribbean youths have embraced Rastafarianism rather than the Pentecostalism of their parents, so many young Muslims find Islamist ideas appealing.

globalizing forces of modernity have disrupted highly valued traditional ways of life. The reassertion of traditional ideas and values, however, is not a simple restatement of an unchanging tradition. It is, rather, a creative reinterpretation of that tradition through a selective drawing on inherited social meanings in the light of their present circumstances. It is a reworking of the shared values and beliefs of a Muslim community aimed at uncovering their central principles in the face of modernizing forces seen as imposing a 'Western' or 'American' way of life. It takes the

 Stop and reflect

In this section we have looked at the emergence of a number of new forms of religious belief and practice and at how there has also been a growth of traditional beliefs.

- There has been a continuing decline in both church attendance and church membership. At the same time, the civil religion has weakened, in both Britain and the United States.

- There is strong evidence for the existence of a loose and unorthodox common religion that has little similarity with traditional Christianity.

- Where do the various beliefs that comprise the common religion come from?

We looked at how the growth of liberal Protestantism has encouraged many believers to seek out more inspirational forms of Christianity.

- Conservative Protestantism takes two main forms: fundamentalism and Pentecostalism. These forms of conservative Protestantism have been closely associated with the new right and the moral majority.

The new religions that have grown in numbers have tended to be non-Christian sects and cults.

- World-rejecting religions are utopian or millennial and reject many aspects of contemporary social life. World-affirming religions are therapeutic and tend to embrace the values of modern society.

- Why are so many people worried about the rise of religious cults?

We finally looked at the relationship between religion and ethnicity. We showed how Britain had become a multi-ethnic, multi-religious society, and we examined global changes in religion.

- There has been growing support for religions of ethnic protest.
- Islam is one of the fastest-growing religions in the world.
- Why is there such a strong link between religion and ethnicity?

Key concepts

- civil religion 406
- collective representations 396
- conscience collective 396
- cult 412
- denomination 400

- ecclesia 399
- sect 402
- secularization 399
- spirit of capitalism 397
- totemism 396

- world-accommodating religion 417
- world-affirming religion 415
- world-rejecting religion 415

Workshop 11

Study 11 The New Age

We have pointed to New Age beliefs as a contemporary form of world-affirming religion, and we have noted that certain New Age beliefs even form a part of the 'common religion' espoused by many people in Britain. Paul Heelas (1996) has traced the growth and development of New Age ideas, showing how they originated in the late nineteenth century but flowered in the 1960s and 1970s during the so-called 'Age of Aquarius'. The phrase 'New Age' was introduced in the last third of the nineteenth century when the ideas of Swedenborg and others were taken up in such belief systems as Theosophy and Jungian psychotherapy.

Behind the borrowings from Buddhism, Hinduism, Christianity, Paganism, and spiritual therapies, the core element in New Age belief systems is what Heelas calls 'self-spirituality'. The

individual self is seen as a sacred object. The task of the believer is to make contact with the spirituality that lies within the individual person. People must distance themselves from the contamination and pollution of the profane world in order to discover the sacred inner world. This is expressed in practices of healing and therapy in all areas of human life, the aim of which is 'enlightenment'.

Heelas argues that the New Age reintroduces pre-modern ideas of mysticism, shamanism, and magic as a response to the cultural uncertainties of contemporary life. New Age beliefs help to resolve the anxieties and uncertainties that face the contemporary self. Paradoxically, however, New Age beliefs appeal because many of them are in tune with modernist ideas: they promise the rational promotion of people's interests and desires.

- Review our discussion of the reflexive project of the self in Chapter 4, p. 149. Return to this discussion of the New Age when you have familiarized yourself with the key arguments of Giddens on this.

- Visit your local bookshop and examine the books in the 'Mind, body, and spirit' section. (Most shops have a section with this title or something similar.) What specific issues and topics are covered in these books, and which of them would you characterize as New Age? Are these books sold alongside other New Age materials (such as music cassettes or tarot cards)? Are there any other shops in your local high street that sell New Age materials (jewellery, ornaments, incense, aromatic oils, and so on)? Try to compile a list of the particular techniques and themes stressed in the New Age.

- How many people in your class or lecture group subscribe to any New Age beliefs, and how many engage in, or have some interest in, New Age practices such as aromatherapy? Do they typically regard their beliefs as 'religious', and do they see any incompatibility with other religious ideas? What does this tell you about a common religion?

- What differences—apart from the obvious differences of intellectual content—do you find between the New Age and a religion such as Islam? What are their respective views of the self and their views of morality? Does the New Age specify a particular moral way of life to which individuals should conform? Find out about the beliefs of Baha'i: to what extent can this be seen as a New Age Islam?

In addition to Heelas (1996), you will find useful background information in Roszak (1971), Reich (1971), Ferguson (1982), and Merchant (1992). These cover the background and influence of New Age ideas in a number of contexts.

 Media watch 11 Moral panic over Islam

A growing moral panic over the role of religious teaching in mosques was brought to a head in the public and press reaction to the London bombings in the summer of 2005, the bombing conspiracies uncovered in the summer of 2006, and the car bomb at Glasgow airport in 2007. Great concern was expressed about the role of 'radical clerics' in encouraging and supporting violent political opposition and acts of terrorism.

Abu Hamza Al-Masri came to Britain from Egypt in 1979 and was regularly portrayed in the press as a leading spokesperson and supporter of Al-Qaeda from his base in the Finsbury Park Mosque in London. He came to particular prominence in 2002, when he addressed a meeting of Al-Muhajiroun, whose members openly support Al-Qaeda, and when he spoke in support of Osama bin-Laden. He was banned from preaching at his mosque, and the government launched plans to deport him. Subsequent to this he was arrested and in 2006 was jailed for seven years. The United States launched extradition proceedings in connection with terrorist charges.

Omar Bakhri Mohammed lived in Britain for twenty years but was banned from returning after a visit he made to Lebanon. It was allegations that he supported the London bombers that led to his exclusion.

Columnist Melanie Phillips had earlier commented that 'Muslim clerics in Britain were appalled at militant figures from "Mujahidin-type organisations" who run what are advertised as prayer groups from private homes but which are in reality recruiting missions' (**www.melaniephillips.com**). The blame, she argued, lay with the failure of Muslim communities to regulate their own affairs.

This is part of a wider concern about the conservatism of many Islamic clerics. Much press comment has centred on the recruitment of clerics from Middle Eastern countries and from poor, rural backgrounds, rather than training imams in Britain. It is claimed that such clerics are out of touch with the views of most British Muslims and that more 'modern' attitudes should be promoted in the mosques. Such issues have sparked a wider debate over education in separate faith schools and the extent to which religious attitudes and practices should be expressed in public life. In many schools, wearing of the *hijab* by girls has been banned as incompatible with a standard school uniform. This is not unique to Britain. In France, a new law prohibited the wearing of any religious symbols or emblems at school, and this was widely seen as a law aimed specifically at Muslims.

Collect copies of daily newspapers for a week and mark all the stories that refer to religion, distinguishing those that relate to Islam and those that relate to other religions. Then consider the following questions:

- What differences can you see in the type of language used to describe followers of each religion and their activities?

- Is religion linked to other social phenomena in the articles (for example, to health or crime)? Can you see any differences in the claims made about Muslims and non-Muslims?

- If you have examples of different kinds of newspapers, can you identify any differences in their treatment of Muslims?

Sources: The Times, 20 October 2004; *Guardian*, 19 October 2004; **www.bbc. co.uk/bbcfour/documentaries/profile/abu-hamza.shtml; http://news. bbc.co.uk/1/hi/world/europe/3619988.stm.**

Discussion points

Theories of religion

Make sure that you are familiar with the main ideas on religion of Marx, Durkheim, and Weber. Try to make sure that you understand the idea of the sacred and the secular and the importance of the distinction.

- Can Weber's ideas on the influence of the Protestant ethic on the spirit of capitalism help us to understand the contemporary relations between religion and economic activity?

Secularization and mainstream religion

The idea of secularization has dominated discussions of religion in the modern world. We drew on the work of Weber to explore some of its implications. We started off by seeing secularization as involving the two processes of disengagement and disenchantment:

- Try to draw up a classification of forms of religious organization in which you distinguish between ecclesia, denomination, sect, and cult. Give examples of each type. Which description is most appropriate for each of the following contemporary religions: Krishna Consciousness, Jehovah's Witnesses, Children of God, Pagans, Hinduism, Shinto, Unification Church, Scientology, Rastafarianism, Nation of Islam? If you are not familiar with the beliefs and organizations of these religions, use your library resources to find out more about them.

- We have presented some evidence to show that women are more likely to be active churchgoers than are men. In view of this, why do you think that there was such opposition to the ordination of women in the Church of England?

- Why does Steve Bruce claim that 'Protestantism is essentially fissile'? What are the implications of this?

- Figures 11.1 (p. 395) and 11.2 (p. 396) give some evidence on church membership and church attendance in Britain. How do you think that these data might have been collected? What other kinds of data would be useful to assess the extent of secularization?

New religions and growing religions

We examined a number of new and growing forms of religion, some of which are renewed and more strident expressions of traditional religious beliefs:

- How useful is the distinction between world-rejecting religion and world-affirming religion?

- Is conservative, inspirational Protestantism characteristic of particular regions or classes?

- How would you go about collecting evidence on the extent and significance of New Age beliefs in Britain today?

- How useful is it to see the spread of Islam as a religion of ethnic protest and a response to globalization?

- What are the implications of the banning of religious dress in French schools? Is this government action directed specifically at Muslim pupils?

The study of religious belief raises some of the most fundamental questions about the nature of knowledge and the role of science. You might like to consider some of these issues. (We do not expect you to come up with the answers!)

- What is religion? Do you think that the definition given by Bruce and Wallis (p. 393 above) is useful?

- Are the claims of religion and science compatible with one another? Is it possible to be both a rational scientist (for example, a sociologist) and a religious believer?

Explore further

Extremely good general accounts of religion can be found in:

Bruce, S. (1995), *Religion in Modern Britain* (Oxford: Oxford University Press). *A brief and very readable account of contemporary trends in British religion.*

Bruce, S. (2003), *Politics and Religion* (Cambridge: Polity Press). An interesting and thoughtful discussion of the worldly impact of religion.

Ling, T. (1968), *A History of Religion, East and West* (Houndmills: Macmillan). *A very useful comparative study of the origins and development of the major religions.*

Turner, B. (1991), *Religion and Social Theory* (2nd edn, London: Routledge). *A useful overview of theories that discusses many of the key issues.*

Wallis, R. (1984), *Elementary Forms of the New Religious Life* (London: Routledge and Kegan Paul). *A classic account of the variety of new religions. You should follow this with a reading of Wallis (1976) and E. Barker (1984).*

Wilson, B. R. (1976), *Contemporary Transformations of Religion* (Oxford: Oxford University Press). *One of the key sources by the principal writer on contemporary forms of secularization.*

More detail can be found in the following. You should *try* reading the books by Durkheim and Weber, but be warned that they are rather difficult.

Barker, E. (1984), *The Making of a Moonie* (Oxford: Basil Blackwell). *A study of the Unification Church.*

Durkheim, E. (1912), *The Elementary Forms of the Religious Life* (London: George Allen & Unwin, 1915, but also in various other editions). *Sets out Durkheim's argument about totemism and the origins of religion.*

Festinger, L., Riecken, H. W., and Schachter, S. (1956), When *Prophecy Fails* (New York: Harper & Row). *A wonderful case study of a millenarian, flying-saucer cult. The methodological appendix is particularly good for highlighting the practical and ethical problems of participant observation. The research was* fictionalized in Alison Lurie's novel Imaginary Friends (New York: Coward, McCann, 1967).

Herberg, W. (1955), *Protestant, Catholic, Jew* (New York: Doubleday). *A classic study of mainstream American religions in relation to ethnicity.*

Wallis, R. (1976), *The Road to Total Freedom* (London: Heinemann). *A study of Scientology.*

Weber, Max (1904–5), *The Protestant Ethic and the Spirit of Capitalism* (London: George Allen & Unwin, 1930, but also in various other editions). *Sets out Weber's account of the part played by religion in the rise of modern capitalism.*

Witness (1985). *Fictionalised film account of an Amish community in Pennsylvania, starring Harrison Ford.*

 ## Online resources

Visit the Online Resource Centre that accompanies this book to access more learning resources and other interesting material on religion, belief, and meaning at:
www.oxfordtextbooks.co.uk/orc/fulcher4e/

A useful general source is the Virtual Religion Index at Rutgers University:
http://virtualreligion.net/vri

Trends in organized Christian religions are covered by the Church of England at:
www.cofe.anglican.org

and by the World Council of Churches at:
www.oikoumene.org

A more independent source of factual information on a variety of religions can be found at:
www.adherents.com

For new religious movements you should consult the Inform website:
www.inform.ac/index.html

Links to information about many different religious organizations can be found at:
www.academicinfo.net/religindex.html

For conferences and seminars on the sociology of religion, consult the website of the British Sociological Association's Sociology of Religion Study Group at:
www.socrel.org.uk/index.html

PART FOUR

SOCIAL ORGANIZATION
AND CONTROL

Family and Life Course

Contents

12

How many households are normal?

Most people's idea of a normal household is a married couple with children. Does this any longer correspond with the reality of people's lives? In 2008 only 21 per cent of British households consisted of a couple with dependent children, compared with 35 per cent in 1971. In 2008 considerably more households, 30 per cent, actually consisted of individuals living entirely on their own (*Social Trends* 2009: 15). Marriage used to be considered the cornerstone of family life, but by 2000 over two-thirds of respondents from the *British Social Attitudes* survey thought that 'it is all right for a couple to live together without intending to get married' (Park *et al.* 2001: 32).

One might conclude from this that family life is in decline, and some have indeed reached this conclusion and argued that this decline is responsible for many of the ills of today's society. There is, however, an alternative view that family life in particular and households in general have simply become more varied. Family life should not be measured against some impossible ideal that is no longer appropriate. Indeed, some have argued that the traditional family was constrictive and damaging to all concerned.

What we mean by 'the family' has been the subject of much debate, and in this chapter we begin with this question. Family life involves relationships between people at different stages of their lives, and we go on to examine ways of thinking about the 'life course'. In the next section, we discuss the historical development of the family and the division of the life course into distinct stages. In the last section, we examine a range of contemporary family issues, from divorce and parenting to ethnic diversity, from the domestic division of labour to domestic violence and sexual abuse.

Concepts and theories

Before examining the development of the family and changes in the life course, we must first be clear about the concepts used in this area and the different approaches to the study of the family.

What is the family?

This might seem a question that does not have to be asked. Surely everyone knows what a family is. When we refer to 'our family', or indeed someone else's, there is usually little doubt about what we mean by this.

A little reflection shows, however, that it is actually far from clear what 'our family' means. It may refer to those with whom we share a household. It may mean a wider group that includes our parents and/or our children, whether or not they live with us. Divorce(s) and remarriage(s) may make this an extensive and complex group with uncertain boundaries. It may mean a much wider group of relatives with whom we have occasional contact by phone or at family meetings. It may mean a group of blood relatives, extending perhaps to cousins, grandparents, uncles, and aunts, which includes people with whom we have no contact at all.

Families and family practices

Different views of the form the family *ought* to take have coloured notions of what the family *is*. Conceptions of the family are indeed highly politicized, and it is difficult to arrive at a neutral or objective description of it.

Traditionalists see the family as centred on marriage and a domestic division of labour between a breadwinning husband and a housewife responsible for childcare and housework. A definition of the family in these terms excludes single-parent families, and unmarried couples, heterosexual or homosexual, even though they may consider themselves to be families and act together in family ways. This definition also builds the domestic division of labour into the family, instead of treating it as just one way in which families can organize their work lives.

Controversy and debate   What is the family?   12.1

'The family is a social group characterized by common residence, economic co-operation and reproduction. It includes adults of both sexes, at least two of whom maintain a socially approved sexual relationship, and one or more children, own or adopted, of the sexually cohabiting adults.' (Murdock 1949: 1)

❓ This is a well-known and much-quoted definition of the family. What problems do you think that it faces in the light of the discussion in the text?

❓ Have a look at other definitions in dictionaries and sociological works (use indexes to locate definitions). How well do they cope with these problems?

❓ Do you think that the definition that we offer in the text is a satisfactory one?

To avoid these problems, Diana Gittins (1993) argued that, instead of referring to 'the family', we should refer to 'families'. By doing this we could recognize the various forms taken by the family and avoid privileging any one of them. This practice has now been widely adopted in sociology, but it does not really solve the problem, for families must logically have something in common that leads us to call them families. There would still seem to be the problem of what we mean by the term 'family'.

There is also the issue of how a family should be distinguished from other similar social units. Sue Heath has carried out research into relationships between young adults in shared households. The sharing of housing has become increasingly common as young adults delay forming couples until they are well into their twenties or thirties. These shared households can be seen as 'families of choice'. As Sue Heath (2004: 10) has put it:

> In the broader context of risk-laden transitions to adulthood, many of the sharers we met appeared to be looking to their peers to provide the sense of communality, support and intimacy that they might hitherto have drawn from 'settled' family commitments, commitments which they were deferring, whether by choice or constraint.

A friendship unit of this kind would not in the past have been considered a family, but, if it performs the functions of a family, should we not consider it to be one?

A more radical approach is to reject the whole idea of defining the family as a social unit. David Morgan (1996, 1999) has argued that, instead of concerning ourselves with what the family is, we should focus on 'family practices', on what families do and what *they* consider to be family activities (see Box 12.2 on p. 432). This is in many ways a refreshing and liberating approach. It suggests that, instead of engaging in rather sterile discussions about the boundaries and membership of family units, we should

concentrate on exploring what goes on in family life and how people view it.

The problem of what we mean by the family does not really go away, however. The notion of 'family practices' begs the question of how we distinguish these practices from non-family ones. Furthermore, the notion of a family unit is still important to people, and the question of whether particular units should be viewed as families or not does matter to them. It matters, for example, whether gay couples or single parents with children see themselves as families and are treated as families. So, while recognizing the difficult issues raised by the question 'What is the family?', it is necessary to arrive at a working definition.

In moving towards a sociological definition, we should consider that families have two main things in common:

- *The closeness of family relationships.* Relationships are closer within a family than with people outside it. There is a boundary around a family, a sense of family identity that separates it off from other people.

- *A sense of obligation and responsibility.* Family responsibilities are not fixed and are continually negotiated by family members, but there is, nonetheless, something distinctive about them that makes family commitments different from, say, those to friends.

The **family** may then be defined as a small group of closely related people who share a distinct sense of identity and a responsibility for each other that outweighs their commitments to others. This group is commonly, but not necessarily, based on marriage, and on biological descent or adoption. Indeed, there is much to suggest that these criteria are becoming less important in the way that people think about the family unit. We have therefore put forward

Frontiers Family practices   12.2

According to David Morgan (1999: 16): '"Family" represents a constructed quality of human interaction or an active process rather than a thing-like object of detached social investigation.' He prefers to use the term 'family practices'. Instead of worrying about the composition of the family, we should study what families do and what people themselves consider to be family activities. He claims that much of the literature is too concerned with the family as an institution, while a focus on family practices makes it possible to give more attention to the everyday activities of family life, the ordinary ways in which families eat together, enjoy leisure activities, and care for each other, which are not trivial things but things that really matter to families. Family activities should also not be sealed off from other areas of life in a kind of 'family box', for family practices interpenetrate with, say, work practices or leisure practices. Family practices are not something that is fixed, but constantly change as people construct and reconstruct family life.

So how does Morgan define family practices? In his words:

'family practices' are those practices described as being in some measure about 'family' by one or more of the

following: individual actors; social and cultural institutions; the observer. . . . They are also practices which matter to the persons concerned and which are seen in some way as being 'special' or 'different'. To 'mean' something to somebody is not simply to be able to identify, but also to invest that object of identification with a degree of emotional significance. It should be stressed that this emotional/evaluative aspect need not be positive; in family matters, as many have noted, we are dealing with love and hate, attraction and repulsion, approval and disapproval. (Morgan 1999: 19)

➲ List up to five activities that you have engaged in during the past week that you consider to be family practices.

❓ Compare your list with those compiled by others. Is there any agreement between you?

❓ What are the differences and what do they suggest about views of the family?

❓ Do you agree that we should stop worrying about what the family is and get on with studying family practices?

a deliberately broad definition that includes established notions of the family but takes account of social change by avoiding the exclusion of people who live together in a family way but do not fit the traditional conception of the family.

Families, households, and kinship

Sociologists distinguish between families and households. A **household** consists of a person or group of people living in a particular residential unit. But is a common residence enough to make people a household? The Family Resources Survey of the Office of National Statistics defines a household as 'one person or a group of people who have the accommodation as their only or main residence and (for a group) either share at least one meal a day or share the living accommodation' (Annual Technical Report 2001/2: 58). This definition may seem rather convoluted, but such a survey, and this one collects important and widely used data, requires a clear and precise definition. The point to note here is that this definition goes further than common residence, since it assumes that the members of a household must in some meaningful way share its facilities. A household is, in other words, more than a collection of people who happen to live in the same place.

Family and household may well not overlap. The members of a family may live in different households. When

children leave home and set up their own households, this does not mean that they leave their family. Furthermore, the members of a household may well not be bound together by family ties. Indeed, some groups opposed to the idea that people should live in families have created households based on the idea of community rather than family.

Sociologists also distinguish between family and kinship. **Kinship** refers to a network of relatives (kin) who are connected by common descent or by marriage. Common descent means that all can trace their ancestry back to the same person, real or, as is often the case, mythical. Kinship therefore extends well beyond the smallish group that we usually take the term 'family' to mean, though there is also an intermediate term, the 'extended family', which we discuss below.

Kinship structures have been central features of small-scale societies, such as hunting and gathering bands or tribes, and social anthropologists have discovered many different principles of kinship in them. They have, for example, distinguished between *matrilineal* structures that trace descent from a female ancestor, and *patrilineal* structures that trace descent from a male. These differences have been very important in societies that have not developed state structures of coordination, because such societies have been largely organized around kinship patterns.

While most contemporary societies are not primarily structured in this way, kinship networks are certainly found within them and perform important functions for their members.

Nuclear and extended families

The most common forms of the family distinguished in the literature are nuclear and extended families. The **nuclear family** is usually defined as a two-generation unit consisting of parents and unmarried children. A distinction is generally made here between the 'family of origin' and the 'family of destination'. People will commonly be members of at least two nuclear families, the family of *origin* into which they were born and the family of *destination*, which they created themselves. Divorce and remarriage may mean that they create a series of such families.

The **extended family** includes other family members. It extends *vertically* to include at least three generations—that is, at least grandparents and grandchildren. It extends *horizontally* to include 'in-laws', cousins, aunts, and uncles,

A nuclear family.
© Alice Chadwick

though how far it extends will vary and depends upon perceptions of the composition and boundaries of the family. It is important to recognize that terms such as 'aunt' are not universal. The language of kinship and the kinds of relationship that exist between family members vary greatly between societies. In some societies, for example, aunts on the mother's side are distinguished from aunts on the father's side, and there is no common word for aunt.

There has been much debate over the relationship between these two forms of the family. Talcott Parsons (1949) argued that industrialization resulted in a shift from the extended family characteristic of traditional societies to the nuclear family typical of industrial societies (see our discussion of his theory on p. 434). Against this view, Peter Laslett and Richard Wall (1972) claimed that in Britain the nuclear family has always been the dominant form. Also against this view but in a different way, the well-known studies by Michael Young and Peter Willmott (1957) and by Michael Anderson (1971) found that the extended family still performed important functions in industrial societies. We examine this question in the next section (see pp. 442–3).

The nuclear family is usually defined in residential terms, as parents and children living together on their own, but in many ways its key feature is less a matter of 'who lives with whom' than of the family's relationship to other people. The nuclear family is a relatively isolated and inward-looking unit that is centred on domestic life and held together by close emotional relationships. It is this rather than whether or not a grandparent lives in the household that really marks out the nuclear family. Edward Shorter has nicely expressed this view of the nuclear family (see Box 12.3).

THEORY AND METHODS   12.3

The nuclear family

'The nuclear family is a state of mind rather than a particular kind of structure or set of household arrangements. It has little to do with whether the generations live together or whether Aunt Mary stays in the spare bedroom. Nor can it be understood with kinship diagrams and figures on family size. What really distinguishes the nuclear family—mother, father, and children—from other patterns of family life in Western society is a special sense of solidarity that separates the domestic unit from the surrounding community. Its members feel that they have much more in common with one another than they do with anyone else on the outside—that they enjoy a privileged emotional climate they must protect from outside intrusion, through privacy and isolation.' (Shorter 1976: 205)

Perspectives on the family

Here we work through the main perspectives on the development of the modern family and link them to contemporary debates.

Functionalist

Parsons (in Parsons and Bales 1956) took a functionalist approach to the development of the family, starting from the assumption that social institutions developed to meet the basic needs of society. There were two such needs that the family, and only the family, met: the needs for primary socialization and personality stabilization. Primary socialization was the process through which children acquired the basic values of society from their family during their early years. Family life also stabilized the adult personality by providing emotional support through marriage and enabling adults to satisfy childish impulses that could not be indulged in public, by, for example, playing games with their children.

This theory of the development of the family was set in a more general theory of social change. Parsons argued that the pre-industrial extended family was a multifunctional unit that met most of people's daily needs. Modernization involved institutional differentiation, with distinct and specialized institutions emerging to meet particular needs. The family lost many of its functions to other institutions, as production moved from the household to the workplace, and education and health care were provided by specialist occupations and organizations. The family itself became more specialized around its core functions of socialization and personality stabilization.

> ↻ *Connections*
>
> We deal with primary and secondary socialization in Chapter 4, pp. 113–14, and you will find it helpful to refer to this chapter for a more detailed discussion of these concepts. We discuss the functionalist approach in Chapter 2, pp. 45–7, and the theory of social change put forward by Parsons, also in Chapter 2, on p. 47.

Parsons claimed that the nuclear form of the family was particularly well suited to an industrial economy. Roles were specialized, with one adult earning money through paid work and the other bringing up the children. The small nuclear family without obligations to an extended family and with only one 'breadwinner' could be geographically mobile, which was important in a dynamic industrial society with a mobile workforce. This close fit between the nuclear family and the requirements of the economy integrated the institutions of industrial society.

The nuclear family also fitted an industrial society because it kept separate the worlds of work and family.

Industrial societies were based on values of *achievement* and *universalism*, which meant that people were rewarded according to their achievements and judged according to universal standards of qualification and competence. The family, however, operated on the basis of the opposite values of *ascription* and *particularism*. Thus, status was ascribed and depended on who one was—husband, wife, child, or grandparent, and so on—rather than on what one did. Parents would do their best to advance their children, whatever their children's abilities might be. If family units and work units overlapped, there would be endless tension and conflict between the incompatible value systems of work and family relationships. With the nuclear family the two worlds were kept separate and linked only by the male breadwinner.

This approach has been much criticized. It appeared to justify a gendered division of labour between male breadwinner and female housewife by arguing that this alone met the requirements of an industrial economy. It emphasized the fit between the nuclear family and industrial society, and did not take account of the tensions between the two. It said nothing about observable variations in the structure and composition of families in industrial societies. It also treated the family as a harmonious institution and did not deal with its internal conflicts and their consequences.

Marxist

A different theory of the development of the modern family was put forward by a 1970s group of Marxist writers, who explained its development in terms of the needs of a capitalist economy.

Their central argument was that the capitalist system exploits the free domestic labour of the housewife through the **domestic division of labour**. A key point here is that housework and child-rearing should not be considered family activities *outside* the operation of the capitalist economy but rather an *essential* part of it. The male breadwinner can work long hours for the employer only because the domestic work of looking after the household and bringing up children is done by the housewife. The family also reproduces labour by beginning the process of producing submissive workers, which is then continued by education (see Chapter 9, p. 316). Although domestic labour is therefore essential to the capitalist economy, employers pay only for the work of the male breadwinner and get the housewife's contribution free. If the housewife was paid for her labour, the wage costs of the capitalist employer would increase considerably.

It has also been argued that the family provides an outlet for the tensions and frustrations generated by the alienating work of a capitalist economy. Workers are under constant pressure from the employer to work harder and faster, often carrying out boring and repetitive work in very poor conditions, over which they have little control. Family life provides a temporary escape and a means of relieving the tensions generated by work, which may well be at the expense of wife and children, particularly if these tensions are expressed in a violent way. The bullied worker may restore his self-esteem by bullying his family. The build-up of an explosive discontent at work is avoided through the safety valve provided by the family and the 'emotional labour' of the wife.

Many housewives do, however, work in paid employment and have always done so. As the main role of the woman in the nuclear family was to be a housewife and the male breadwinner earned a 'family wage' to support the whole household, employers could pay women low wages. They could also treat women as a 'reserve army' that could be drawn into work when there was a labour shortage and returned to the home when demand was slack. Thus, the nuclear family also provided employers with a useful additional supply of cheap labour.

In spite of its evident differences from the functionalist approach, this analysis shared with it the assumption that a particular form of the family fits the requirements of the economy. It treated the nuclear family with a gendered division of labour as the standard form of the family, much as Parsons did, and similarly said little about variations in the structure and character of the family. It was an approach that was taken up by some Marxist feminists, such as Veronica Beechey (1987), who saw the dynamics of capitalism as central to the subordination of women.

> **Connections**
> We discuss the employment of women in paid work, and the concept of a 'reserve army', in Chapter 17, p. 665.

Feminist

An alternative feminist approach focused in a similar way on the domestic division of labour but rejected the idea that it can be explained by capitalism. This approach argued that the domestic division of labour preceded the rise of capitalism and resulted from an age-old domination of women by men. For these 'radical feminists', as they were called, it was not capitalism that was the problem, but **patriarchy**. By patriarchy they meant a universal structure of male authority that is found in all societies but expressed in many different institutional ways. It is the power that men have over women, not the dynamics of capitalism, that explains the domestic division of labour.

> **Connections**
> We discuss feminism, the concept of patriarchy, and the problems it raises in Chapter 5, pp. 156–7.

Thus, Delphy (1977) saw the exploitation of women's labour as rooted in 'the domestic mode of production' in the household, not in the capitalist mode of production. Men held a superior position within the domestic mode of production and exploited the labour of women through marriage. The family was an institution for the exploitation of women by men.

Walby (1986) too rejected the idea that the development of capitalism accounted for the emergence of a domestic division of labour, though she argued that there are other patriarchal structures besides the family. It was not so much that men kept women subordinated in the home as that men excluded them from the paid employment that would enable them to be independent. The capitalist employer actually wanted to employ women as a cheaper source of labour, and it was the patriarchal structures of the state and the trade unions that excluded women from work. Thus, Walby argued that women's domestic labour was a *result* of the exclusion of women from paid work rather than a *cause* of it.

The feminist perspective moves away from the functionalist notion of the family as a harmonious institution adapted to the needs of industrial society and also avoids the economic determinism of the Marxist approach. There are, however, problems with explanations that rely on patriarchy alone. If patriarchy is a universal feature of human societies, it cannot explain variations or changes in the relationships between men and women. We will return to this question in our section on 'The development of family life'.

Contemporary debate

These perspectives have been associated with very different evaluations of the contemporary family. Those who believe in 'family values' have a view of the family close to the functionalist perspective. They see the correct performance of the socialization function as critical to the maintenance of the social order and believe that only the traditional family can perform this function. They are much concerned with what they consider to be the decline of this family.

Their idea of the family is based on marriage, a gendered division of labour within the household, and sex only within marriage. They call for divorce to be made more difficult and do not consider that cohabitation is an acceptable alternative to marriage. Wives should focus their lives on the upbringing of children and the maintenance of the household. There is a general hostility here towards sex education, homosexuality, and abortion.

Single-parent families headed by lone mothers have come under attack from this perspective. These are not considered to be 'proper' families. The absence of a father figure is said to weaken the control of children and deprive boys of a male role model. Fatherless families have been blamed for rising crime, educational failure, lack of interest in work, and dependence on state welfare. According to

Charles Murray (1990), fatherless families are responsible for the emergence of an underclass (see our later discussion of 'Parenting').

Against this view, it is argued that single-parent families should not be held responsible for these problems. The difficulties of these families are seen not so much as the result of their one-parent character as of their poverty and their children's consequent lack of opportunity. The focus on the decline of the family as the source of social problems diverts attention from their broader economic and political origins. This approach is critical not of the family but of the existing social order, and is typical of a Marxist perspective.

> ⮑ *Connections*
> The theoretical assumptions behind these positions on the single-parent family are further discussed in Media watch 2 on p. 66.

In *The Antisocial Family*, Michele Barrett and Mary McIntosh (1991) combined a Marxist with a feminist approach. They argued that the family is the central mechanism through which inequality is passed from one generation to the next through the inheritance of wealth. They also emphasized the 'dark side' of family life. The family is not, as it is often seen, a refuge from the pressures of the world but a prison, which isolates women, leaves them vulnerable to domestic violence, and generates mental illness. The family oppresses women sexually and financially, through marriage and the domestic division of labour.

The problem is not only what the family does to people but also that it is a 'privileged institution', which devalues life outside it. As they put it, 'the family ideal makes everything else seem pale and unsatisfactory' (Barrett and McIntosh 1991: 77). Non-familial institutions, such as old people's homes, nurseries, or children's homes, may well provide better care or a more stimulating environment than the family, but they are always viewed in negative terms because of the dominance of the family ideal. Furthermore, people become so wrapped up in family life that they do not have time and energy for other relationships and activities. The family is presented here as an exclusive and suffocating institution, which 'sucks the juice out of everything around it, leaving other institutions stunted and distorted' (Barrett and McIntosh 1991: 78). To Barrett and McIntosh, the problem is not that the family is in decline but that it is too strong.

These consequences of family life are certainly recognizable, and, as we shall see in the section on 'Domestic violence and abuse', there is plentiful evidence for the 'dark side' of family life. This critique of the family also usefully counteracts the dominant and idealizing view of family life presented by those who believe in 'family values'. This negative view makes it difficult, however, to understand the continued strength of family relationships, which people actively maintain, presumably because they find them rewarding and satisfying, if not essential to their wellbeing.

Those who fear the decline of the family and those who would welcome it both have to contend with the plentiful research on family life which shows that families are flexible and adaptive structures (see, e.g. Charles *et al.* 2008*a* and 2008*b*). They are a resource on which people draw for support as they face the problems of everyday life but they are not just a means to an end, for family relationships are valued in their own right and family practices are an important source of meaning in people's lives. Negative and positive evaluations of the family by commentators and critics should not be confused with the sociological analysis of what people do in their family lives.

The life course

Families involve relationships between people of different ages who are at different stages of life. People also themselves move through these stages as they pass through the 'life course'. These generational relationships and stages are important aspects of family life, which have been receiving increasing attention from sociologists (Pilcher 1995; Hunt 2005).

Age and generation

People of different ages are often described as belonging to different generations. Two different usages of the term **generation** should, however, be distinguished.

- *Those born during a particular period.* Examples of this usage are the 'sixties generation' or the 'pre-war generation' or 'my generation'.
- *Kinship groups defined by parent–child relationships.* Children and their cousins; their parents, aunts, and uncles; their grandparents, great-aunts, and great-uncles; and so on: each of these constitutes a generation.

Pilcher (1995) has argued that this double usage creates confusion. She suggests that it is best to use the term **cohort** for all those born in a particular year or group of years and reserve generation for kinship groups. The term 'intergenerational relationships' would then refer to, say, relationships between parents and children or grandparents and grandchildren, rather than to the relationship between 'pre-war' and 'post-war' generations.

Intergenerational relationships are certainly central to the functioning of a family. The process of socialization operates through them, as adults pass on their knowledge, experience, and values to the young. This process can also operate in the other direction, as when the young pass on their knowledge of, say, information technology or the Internet to the old.

Intergenerational processes are also crucial to caring, and this demonstrates the importance of taking account of changes in the relationships between generations as families adapt to the social changes occurring around them. One consequence of the rise of the two-earner family, in which both parents take paid employment, is that a greater burden of childcare falls on grandparents.

While intergenerational relationships enable the family to function, they are also a source of tension and conflict. Growing longevity, the smaller size of families, and changes in social policy have made the old a greater financial and care burden on the young. This can lead to 'elder abuse'. It can also result in a broader conflict between those at work and those in old age, between those paying taxes and those receiving state benefits and care.

These relationships must be put in the context of the changing generational composition of families and households. Increasing longevity means that there are growing numbers of multi-generation families that include not only grandparents but great-grandparents. As the family has become generationally stretched, intergenerational relationships have become more complex and more salient.

Stages in life?

As we grow older, we pass through various stages in life. Childhood, youth, adulthood, middle age, and old age are terms commonly used to describe these stages.

The term 'life cycle' has often been used to describe this process. This term has biological origins and implies that a process of biological ageing shapes the stages of life. It contains the idea that there is a fixed sequence of stages that everyone passes through as they age. The traditional British notion that there are clearly bounded stages, such as adulthood beginning at the age of 21 or retirement starting at the age of 65, reflects a life-cycle way of thinking.

The idea of a life cycle cannot, however, easily accommodate two features of the stages:

- differences in stages between societies;
- changes in stages.

In many pre-industrial societies there has not been a youth stage but rather a direct transition from childhood to adulthood (Hunt 2005). There has also been considerable change in both the number and timing of stages in Britain. For example, the notion of a 'new middle age' of active but non-work life between adulthood and 'old age' has recently emerged and 'old age' has been shifted to a later time of life (Pilcher 1995).

In sociology, the more flexible term **life course** has now superseded life cycle. This accommodates better the *social construction* of life's stages and gets away from the idea that these are biologically determined or fixed. Furthermore, as Pilcher (1995) has pointed out, life course also carries with it a sense of the cumulative character of a person's movement through life. The way that a person starts the course and moves through it will shape the way that he or she finishes it.

If stages are so variable and changeable, do they have any real basis in social reality? Post-modern theorists have argued that it no longer makes much sense to see the life course in terms of stages. The boundaries between stages have become blurred and are no longer fixed at particular

---

Frontiers Disability and the life course   12.4

Mark Priestley has developed a life-course approach to the study of disability. He claims:

> This perspective is important, because it highlights how disabling societies and practices affect people of different generations in different ways (e.g. children, young people, adults or older people). It also allows us to consider some important disability issues at the very beginning and end of the life course (i.e. at birth and death). This in turn enables us to see more clearly how societies organize generational boundaries and life course transitions in a collective way, and how this shapes our understanding of disability in the social world. (Priestley 2003: 1)

An example of this approach is his examination of the distinctive way in which the young disabled are regarded.

The treatment of disabled adults as impaired, incompetent, and passive has been challenged effectively by disability activists, but this has not happened with disabled children, who are still treated in this way. They are still viewed as a distinct category, as a social problem, rather than as individuals with their own personalities, needs, and wishes. As they become older, they are denied the transition from youth to adulthood. For the disabled 'true adult status is neither envisaged nor attained' (Priestley 2003: 113). The disabled young are therefore locked into a kind of 'enduring adolescence' and also find themselves excluded from a youth culture centred on images of bodily perfection.

Does the notion of the stages of life still have any meaning?

© Getty Images/Philip Lee Harveyends

ages. Instead of living in a way appropriate to their stage in life, people choose lifestyles regardless of their age. Indeed, they go to great lengths to counteract or conceal their biological age through exercise regimes or cosmetic surgery. In an age of individualization, consumerism, and choice, life is no longer divided into stages (Hunt 2005).

The idea of stages in life is still, nonetheless, embedded in ordinary discourse, in the language that people use to describe themselves and each other. They still commonly call themselves 'young' or 'middle-aged' or 'old'. They mark transitions from one stage to another with twenty-first birthday or retirement parties. It therefore still makes sociological sense to conceive of stages in the life course, so long as this notion is used flexibly and takes account of changing conceptions of these stages. Indeed, charting changes in the way that people divide up the course of their lives is one means by which sociologists can study processes of social change.

Stop and reflect

We began this part of the chapter by considering what is meant by the family.

- In everyday usage the family is given many different meanings, and notions of the family have been highly politicized.

- Instead of seeking to define the family, should we simply refer to 'families' and 'family practices'?

We went on to outline different perspectives on the family.

- Make sure that you are clear about the functionalist, Marxist, and feminist approaches.

- How would these differ in their interpretation of the rise of single-parent families?

Lastly, we examined the concepts used to explore the life course.

- Why is the term 'life course' preferable to 'life cycle'?

- Is the notion of 'stages' in life still useful?

The development of family life

Many aspects of contemporary family life are 'taken for granted' or treated as 'natural' characteristics of the family. The existence of strong emotional bonds between family members is considered a natural feature of family relationships. The life course is seen as passing through certain natural stages. There is, however, nothing natural about family life, which is socially constructed. In this section we examine the processes of social change that have produced the contemporary family and life course.

The rise of the nuclear family

As we argued earlier (see p. 433), the nuclear family is usually defined as a residential unit consisting of parents and unmarried children, but what really matters is not so much its composition as its relationship to the wider society. The nuclear family is a relatively isolated and inward-looking unit centred on domestic life and characterized by intense emotional relationships.

The emergence of the nuclear family

According to the classic model of the development of the family, as presented by Talcott Parsons (1949), the extended family unit of pre-industrial society gave way to the nuclear family of industrial societies. In pre-industrial societies production depended on the amount of family labour available to work the land. Large families were economically advantageous, and the extended family was the most appropriate unit. In industrial societies, the household became increasingly separated from production and the nuclear family with one breadwinner became the dominant form. This view needs considerable qualification in the light of later historical research.

The nuclear family was, in fact, emerging long before industrialization. According to Lawrence Stone (1977), in the upper and middle classes the isolation of the nuclear family from the extended family began as early as the sixteenth century. Before this time there was no boundary between the two. Relationships between husbands and wives, parents and children, were no closer than their relationships with other relatives or neighbours. From this time on, the family became increasingly focused on the upbringing of children and the emotional needs of their parents. By the eighteenth century the nuclear family had become 'walled off' both from the community and the wider network of relatives.

In line with this view, Leonora Davidoff (1990) has argued that family life in the upper class became more private and more domestic during the eighteenth century. There was less involvement in public activities and a greater interest in the pleasures of home and family. In the upper-class country house, activities became less centred on the semi-public great hall and more on the small private rooms of the family. One important architectural change was the building of corridors, which allowed people to go from one room to another without disturbing each other. Servants were increasingly segregated in their own quarters.

Catherine Hall (1982a) has shown how a similar domesticity was emerging in the middle class. During the eighteenth century the better-off shopkeepers became dissatisfied with living over the shop and wanted their home to be separate from their workplace. Their wives 'were furnishing their living apartments elegantly, putting their servants into livery, and refusing to be seen in the shop themselves, as it was not considered to be ladylike' (C. Hall 1982a: 4).

In the family life of the lower classes, the great change in the eighteenth century was the break-up of the household as the unit of production. Previously, all members of the family had been expected to engage in productive activities—working on the land, keeping animals, producing craft goods, collecting wood, or foraging for food. Young people often became servants or apprentices in the larger households, where they were treated as members of the family. Indeed, the family at this time was taken to mean all members of the household. Servants and apprentices had the same status and were treated in much the same way as members of the biological family (Davidoff 1990).

The pre-industrial development of wage labour broke up the household as a unit of production. With the growth of capitalism in eighteenth-century Britain, production was carried out increasingly not by members of the family but by workers paid a wage for their labour. The family was becoming a unit of *consumption* rather than *production*. Its members no longer worked together but rather used the wages they had earned elsewhere to buy the goods they consumed as a family.

The family also became a more exclusive unit held together by kinship alone. Its members were linked now only by marriage and birth (or adoption). Apprentices and servants were no longer treated as family members. Apprentices now learned their trade in the workplace, while domestic servants increasingly became wage-workers. The family had become both biologically and emotionally a tighter 'nuclear' unit.

Husbands and wives

According to the sentiments school of sociologists and historians (see Box 12.5), family members have not always been bound together by strong emotional relationships. There was no affection in the relationships of the early family. It was only with the emergence of the nuclear family that family life developed an emotional quality.

Stone (1977) called this process the 'growth of affective individualism' (affective simply means emotional). People began to treat each other as unique individuals with personal and emotional needs. Family relationships took on a new quality as its members became concerned with their feelings for each other. The main function of the nuclear family increasingly became the satisfaction of emotional needs.

He argued that these changes could be seen in marriage. In the sixteenth century, marriage in the upper ranks of society joined together two kinship groups, for economic or political purposes. Mate selection was controlled by parents and the wider family. By the end of the eighteenth century emotional concerns had become much more important. Economic considerations and parental influence still mattered, especially when large fortunes or estates

were at stake, but love and companionship were also seen as essential. Rejection of a chosen partner on the grounds of incompatibility was allowed, and choice based on mutual attraction was becoming more common. It was also recognized that loveless marriages would inevitably lead to extramarital affairs.

One sign of these changes was the proliferation of match-making occasions for upper-class families. Balls, card parties, and other social events in the 'assembly rooms' that were being built in eighteenth-century towns enabled young members of the elite to meet potential marriage partners and exercise some choice over whom they married. London and Bath became the centres of the national marriage market established at this time.

Lower down the social order, in the middle class and among skilled workers, economic considerations remained more central to mate selection, because capital was scarce and the financial aspects of marriage were that much more crucial. Among the propertyless poor there was less at stake. Premarital sex was common and partners were freely chosen, and discarded, or abandoned. Desertion and bigamy were, according to Stone (1977), common, while 'wife sales' by 'mutual consent' provided an unofficial means of divorce (see Box 12.6).

Briefing: eighteenth-century wife sales 12.6

'As described in 1727, the husband "puts a halter about her neck and thereby leads her to the next market-place, and there puts her up to auction to be sold to the best bidder, as if she were a brood mare or a milch-cow. A purchaser is generally provided beforehand on these occasions." This procedure was based closely on the sale of cattle. It often took place in a cattle market and was accompanied by the use of a symbolic halter, by which the wife was led to market by the seller, and led away again by the buyer. . . . In the popular mind, this elaborate ritual freed the husband of all future responsibility for his wife, and allowed both parties to marry again. Very often, perhaps normally, the bargain was pre-arranged with the full consent of the wife, both purchaser and price being agreed upon beforehand.' (Stone 1977: 40)

❓ *What does the symbolism of this ritual tell us about the relationship between husband and wife?*

As marriage became more emotional, it also became less stable. The nuclear family was held together less by wider kin relationships and depended more on internal bonds. Women found themselves torn between the competing demands of children and husbands as family relationships became emotionally more intense. The eighteenth-century changes in marriage created 'very severe stresses' for the institution (Stone 1977: 404) and these have arguably been with it ever since.

Parents and children

The sentiments historians argued that the relationship between parents and children also became more emotional. It was the pioneering work of Ariès (1962) on the history of childhood that started the discussion of this aspect of the family.

Aries claimed that childhood did not exist in medieval times. Once children no longer required constant care, they were treated like adults. This was shown by the way that they were dressed. Until the seventeenth century there were no special clothes for children, who were dressed like small adults. Children did not lead separate lives and generally mixed with adults. They were expected to earn their keep, and to fight in war, as soon as they were physically able to do so.

Relationships between parents and children were at this stage unemotional. Adults took no pleasure in their relationships with children and were indifferent to their emotional needs. They left children alone for long periods,

put them out to wet-nurses, and showed little concern when they died, which they often did, for infant mortality was very high. Indeed, this meant that it was best not to invest too much emotion in them. The lack of parental feeling for children was shown by the harsh punishments that were used to discipline them.

According to Aries, it was in the seventeenth century that attitudes began to change, at first in the aristocracy and among educated people. Parents began to take pleasure from watching and playing with children, and began to treat them as different from adults. Clothes, games, toys, and stories specifically created for children made their first appearance. Also, a sense of special parental responsibility for the welfare and success of children began to emerge. Child-rearing now became a central function of the family in a way that it had not been before.

The idea that parents had previously lacked emotional feelings for their children has, however, been challenged by Linda Pollock (1983). She used diary and autobiographical material to show that sixteenth-century parents grieved for their children when they died and treated them less harshly than the sentiments historians suggested. Hugh Cunningham (1995) has reviewed the literature on this issue and concluded that there were, nonetheless, significant changes in attitudes towards children, particularly in the eighteenth century. A greater concern for their welfare and a greater sense of parental responsibility emerged in the middle class and spread downwards to the working class after industrialization.

Patriarchy and the domestic division of labour

The development of the nuclear family involved changes not only in the emotional quality of relationships but also in power relationships. The nuclear family was a patriarchal family in which men dominated.

> ➲ *Connections*
> We discuss the concept of patriarchy in Chapter 5, pp. 156–8.

The domestic division of labour was central to the patriarchal nuclear family of the nineteenth century. Men went out to work and controlled the family income, while women were confined within the home, doing the housework and bringing up children. As we showed earlier (p. 434), Marxist writers have argued that it was industrial capitalism that brought about this domestic division of labour. There is also, however, evidence of a pre-industrial division of labour between men and women. Harriet Bradley (1989) has reviewed the literature on this question.

Women were engaged in a wider range of productive tasks in pre-industrial Europe but tended to carry out those that were of lower status and linked to the home. Segalen's study (1983) of French peasant households showed that women worked in the house, the barn, the farmyard, and the garden more often than out in the fields. Middleton (1979) held that women in medieval Britain carried out many different agricultural tasks, but it was the men who did the high-status work of ploughing. In the towns, women were engaged in a variety of occupations, but the main crafts were male-dominated and women took part in craftwork in a less specialized and more intermittent way, generally through family connections.

Although a gendered division of labour existed, there was much variation and flexibility. In some places women were very active in trade and shopkeeping, which could give them independence and lead to their playing important public roles. Widows and unmarried women could indeed be heads of households in the same way as men. Bradley (1989) has stressed that the gendering of the pre-industrial division of labour was quite flexible. She suggested that the greater uncertainties of life in pre-industrial societies made it necessary for the various members of a household to cooperate in a flexible way.

With industrialization there was a much sharper separation of production from consumption. This resulted in a more systematic separation of the male and female spheres (see Chapter 5, pp. 163–5). In the middle class there was a clear separation of the male sphere of paid work and, more generally, public life from the female domestic sphere. Women were excluded from public activities and more than ever confined within the home. This separation was less marked in the working class, where many women went out to work, but this paid work was seen as secondary to their domestic role and subordinate to it.

It was also in the nineteenth century that an ideology of the domestic division of labour became established. The belief that women's primary responsibilities and duties lay in the home acquired a new moral force. Men and women were seen as having different identities, which were grounded in what were presumed to be their very different natures.

It is, then, clear that the gendered division of labour characteristic of the 'classic' nuclear family did not originate with industrialization. It existed in pre-industrial times but with a lot of local variation and flexibility according to household circumstances. With industrialization came a greater standardization of male and female roles and an ideological rationale for them that became deeply embedded in people's beliefs about the differences between the work of men and women.

The persistence of the extended family

Domesticity did not, however, mean that the nuclear family cut itself off from contact with relatives. According to Davidoff (1990), the nineteenth-century middle-class family was typically large, with families interlinked by marriage into an extensive network. People kept in touch with their relatives through letter-writing, visiting, and the exchange of gifts. The domestic focus of the middle-class household clearly did not prevent important relationships with a wide circle of relatives. Technological change later made this easier, with the telephone providing a new means of keeping in contact.

In the working class, the modern pattern of the nuclear family, focused on home life and separated from the workplace, had become generally established in the nineteenth-century industrial city, but this did not mean that the working-class family was completely isolated. Michael Anderson (1971) argued that in 'critical life situations' there was a continued dependence on the extended family. These situations occurred through illness, death, unemployment, difficulties in finding work or accommodation, and the problems of old age. In such circumstances it was only the family that people could fall back on and the extended family remained a crucial means of support.

In their well-known study of Bethnal Green, Michael Young and Peter Willmott (1957) found that the extended family was still alive and well in a stable working-class community in the 1950s. They particularly emphasized the importance of the mother–daughter relationship. Even when daughters had married and set up their own households, mothers and daughters relied upon each other for help and advice, and had frequent contact. In their sample, a fifth of those married couples with parents who were still alive had them living in the same street. This was not just a feature of family life there, for similar relationships could be found in other places, such as Liverpool, Wolverhampton, and Swansea (Willmott 1988).

Communities of this kind did then change, as the extensive rehousing of inner-city communities dispersed their members during the 1960s. Willmott and Young (1960) showed that the rehousing of Bethnal Green families to an estate in Greenleigh broke up extended family relationships and led people to lead a more isolated life focused on the nuclear family household. Women now depended much less on their mothers and more on their husbands. Changing leisure patterns, the rise of home ownership, and increasing domestic consumption resulted in a growing focus on the private life of the family. Furthermore, Geoff Dench, Kate Gavron, and Michael Young (2006) argue that the role of older women changed as the welfare state and professional social workers took increasing responsibility for welfare:

What seems to have happened is that the welfare state has appropriated the role which older women used to play. The growth of a national family—the nanny state in some accounts—has created an additional system of public care and support which now goes beyond helping ordinary families and is instead taking power and meaning away from them.

Dench et al. 2006: 118

Some studies have, nonetheless, shown that contacts with the extended family still survive (Willmott 1986; O'Brien and Jones 1996). Nickie Charles, Charlotte Davies, and Chris Harris (2008*a* and 2008*b*) found considerable continuity when they replicated in 2002 a study of family life carried out in 1960s Swansea. Three-generation extended family *households* had largely disappeared, but there was still a lot of contact between generations, particularly in the working class and amongst ethnic minorities. There was less contact in the later study between mothers and partnered daughters. The proportion having daily contact had fallen from 54 per cent in 1960 to 41 per cent in 2002. But this was still the main relationship between extended family members and 'still crucial for the functioning of kin groups' (Charles *et al.* 2008*b*: 4).

Arguably the extended family is once again becoming more central to people's lives. As life expectancy has increased, the number of old people has risen, and they have required more care, but state care for the old has declined with the closing of local-authority homes and geriatric wards. Similarly, with the closure of mental hospitals, care of the mentally ill has shifted back into the community via community care, but inadequate resources mean that in practice a growing burden has fallen onto families (see Chapter 8, pp. 293–5, for a discussion of community care). This is not only a matter of the greater dependence of the old on the family but also of the greater

Figure 12.1 Main stages in the development of the nuclear family

1 Pre-industrial emergence of domesticity.
2 Pre-industrial break-up of the household as a unit of production.
3 Increasing focus of the family on emotional life.
4 Separation of home from work by capitalist production and industrialization.
5 Separation of male from female sphere, standardizing of a domestic division of labour, and growth of a domestic ideology during the nineteenth century.
6 Further isolation of the nuclear family through the break-up of communities and the privatizing of leisure and consumption during the later twentieth century.

dependence of the family on the old. Increasing numbers of working women, especially the working mothers of small children, have made extended family assistance with childcare, particularly through grandparents, more important.

There is then plentiful evidence that the extended family has remained important to people in industrial societies. Extended kin are still a source of help and support, and this function may well have recently increased in importance. This does not contradict the idea that the nuclear family has become increasingly isolated. The separation of production from the household, the rise of domesticity, the spread of home ownership, the decline of local communities, and a growing focus on private life have gradually isolated the nuclear family. It does, however, show that the notion of a transition from the extended to the nuclear family is over-simple.

Frontiers Children in their own right   12.7

James, Jenks, and Prout (1998) have argued that the study of children has been dominated too long by the notion that childhood is a stage of socialization through which people pass on their way to be adults. They called for a new sociology of childhood that would focus on the child 'as being' rather than 'as becoming'. They identify four discourses of childhood, which could provide the basis for a new approach to the study of children:

1. *The social structural child*. Children should not be treated as marginal but 'as a constant and recognizable component of all social structures' (James *et al.* 1998: 210). As a category of people, children should have the same conceptual status as a social class.

2. *The minority group child*. Children are 'structurally differentiated within societies' (James *et al.* 1998: 211). Within all societies children are a minority within society, which,

like other minorities, is exploited and discriminated against.

3. *The socially constructed child*. 'There is no essential child' (James *et al.* 1998: 212). Childhood is constructed through social practices and perceptions, and is culturally and historically variable.

4. *The tribal child*. Children inhabit their own cultural world with a 'self-maintaining system of signs, symbols and rituals that prescribes the whole way of life of children within a particular sociohistorical setting' (James *et al.* 1998: 215).

❓ In the light of this approach, should we give up the idea of childhood as a stage of life?

Changes in life's stages

As the family developed, the life course changed. Stages in the life course that are now commonly taken for granted actually emerged historically at different times. In this section we examine the social construction of the stages of life.

Childhood and youth

As we showed earlier, attitudes towards children were changing, in the upper levels of society at least, by the seventeenth century, but childhood as a distinct stage did not become clearly established until the nineteenth century. Two key changes during this century were the restriction of child labour by the Factory Acts and the development of compulsory education, which was gradually lengthened, reaching age 16 in 1972. These changes created a space for childhood between infancy and adulthood, and kept children longer in the parental home (see Box 12.7 on p. 443).

Recent changes have to some extent undermined the distinctiveness of childhood. Television's penetration into the household has given children virtually unrestricted access to the adult world. Children became consumers, becoming indeed fully-fledged consumers of adult products, rather than of special products designed for children. Children have also been increasingly treated as individuals in their own right. Thus, the Children's Act of 1989 made changes in their legal status, treating them less as minors without rights and more as individuals, with the right to have their wishes and feelings taken into account—for example, by the courts or those running children's homes (Lavalette 1996; Winter and Connolly 1996).

There has, however, been a reaction against these changes that has re-emphasized the distinctive status of children. On the one hand, there has been a growing concern to protect them from drugs, violence, sexual abuse, exploitative child labour, and 'adult' television. On the other hand, politicians have sought to reassert parental authority over children and establish parental responsibility for their behaviour. Boyden (1997) has argued that these twin concerns with the protection and control of children have informed the globalization of a concept of childhood that is not in the interests of children (see Box 12.8).

Between childhood and adulthood comes youth, though it is a less clearly defined stage in the life course. Pilcher (1995) suggests that it is best treated as a stage of

---

Global focus The globalization of childhood   12.8

There has been much media concern with the global plight of children. As Boyden (1997: 191) has put it: 'international media coverage of the young paints an especially stark picture, of innocent and vulnerable child victims of adult violence and maltreatment; of "stolen" childhoods in refugee camps and war zones.'

In response, international agencies have been created with a mission to protect children from the adult world and provide them with a safe and happy childhood. The work of these agencies has led to the globalization of a particular notion of childhood based on a concern for the rights of children. Behind this concern for children's rights, however, lies the export of a particular conception of childhood. This is 'culturally and historically bound to the social preoccupations and priorities of the capitalist countries of Europe and the United States' (Boyden 1997: 192). These involved not only welfare concerns but also adult fears of children becoming undisciplined and getting out of control. Such a conception of childhood is two-edged, treating street children as 'both the most deprived and the most depraved members of society' (Boyden 1997: 196).

Boyden (1997: 207) is concerned that this conception can 'have the effect of penalizing, or even criminalizing the childhoods of the poor'. Governments treat street children as vagrants or delinquents, but, if their families are to survive, children must earn money by selling goods and providing services on the streets. These customary family practices become the target of inappropriate state intervention by governments that are anyway primarily concerned with maintaining order and protecting the interests of the rich rather than promoting the welfare of the poor.

Forcing children into school may actually be of little benefit to them, as the kind of work available when they leave does not require formal skills, and education may merely subject them to indoctrination by the state. They can more appropriately prepare for adult life by acquiring work experience and survival skills on the streets.

Boyden, then, is sceptical of the benefits to children and their families of the globalization of a concept of childhood that may appear grounded in a concern for universal rights but is in fact culturally specific and may not be appropriate to the cultures, customs, and circumstances of most poor countries.

➲ Look up newspaper reports of the treatment of children in poor countries.

❓ Are there situations where governments should intervene to protect or educate children?

❓ Should governments in poor countries leave children alone?

transition between the two, which involves two particular transitions:

- from compulsory, full-time education to employment;
- from family of *origin* to family of *destination*.

Modern conceptions of youth as a distinct stage date in Britain from the early 1900s, when special prisons, courts, employment, and welfare agencies for young people were established. Special organizations and institutions were required to deal with teenagers who were no longer really children but not yet recognized as adults.

It was not until the 1950s and 1960s, however, that distinctive youth cultures emerged. During these years of growing affluence, teenagers found jobs quickly and could earn large amounts of money. Their spending power and minimal financial obligations to the household made them important consumers. Products were created that marked youth out as having a distinctive style of clothing and leisure. Their earnings, greater independence, and lifestyle brought them into a conflict with 'the older generation' that sharpened awareness of age differences.

This greater independence was not, however, to last. A much higher proportion of young people now stay in some form of education or training to the age of 21. The ending of maintenance grants and the introduction of student fees have led to more dependence on the family during higher education. Rising debt and house prices have resulted in many staying with their family of origin into their twenties and thirties.

Adulthood, post-adolescence, and middle age

Adulthood became a more distinct stage, as its boundaries with childhood and old age grew sharper. It came to be seen as a time between education and old age, during which people made a productive contribution to society. Its boundary with old age became sharper with the notion of retirement from work and the creation of the old-age pension in 1908. Recently, however, both the early and the late boundaries of adulthood have come into question.

The early boundary has been challenged by those who argue for the existence of a new stage, variously labelled 'late adolescence', 'young adulthood', or 'post-adolescence'. We will call it **post-adolescence**. This is a period in the life of those in their twenties and thirties when they are relatively independent of their families of origin but have not acquired the responsibilities associated with adulthood, in particular those connected with marriage and parenthood. The mobile phone and Web 2.0 (see Chapter 10, p. 353) are an important means of creating and maintaining patterns of sociality during this period.

Some have evaluated post-adolescence negatively as a period of inability, or selfish refusal, to take on the responsibilities of adulthood. Heath and Cleaver (2003) suggest that it should be seen more positively as a time when people work out for themselves how to 'do' adulthood. They are experimenting with relationships and choosing how to live, though not freely, because they have to operate within the constraints of the housing and labour markets. Indeed, class position plays a key part in enabling or preventing this experimentation. Post-adolescence marks not just a new stage on the way to adulthood but also a rethinking of the criteria of adulthood, a social reconstruction of what adulthood means.

At the later end of adulthood, a 'new middle age', covering the later years of working life and extending into what used to be considered 'old age', has emerged. This time of life has been reconstructed as an active phase with its own distinctive features, as changes in employment, welfare, and health have enabled a period of active non-work. Earlier retirement has released some people from the constraints of paid work, while state-subsidized occupational pension schemes have provided them with the means to maintain a reasonable standard of living. The growing purchasing power of the over fifties has led to the creation of magazines, holidays, insurance schemes, retirement homes, and residential communities designed specifically for them. The University of the Third Age was set up to provide an educational forum for the exchange of accumulated knowledge and expertise.

Pilcher (1995) has pointed out that the capacity to enjoy a leisurely and affluent 'third age' is not, however, equally available to all. Lower-paid jobs and intermittent work histories, because of child-rearing, mean that women may have to resume or continue paid work into 'old age', while there is no retirement from housework. Redundancy may bring employment to an end before sufficient pension contributions have been accumulated to provide for a comfortable retirement (and the closing of many final-salary schemes will anyway make this retirement less comfortable). Those in lower-paid work without occupational pensions have to rely on state pensions, whose value relative to earnings has been declining since 1982, when they were linked to changes in prices rather than earnings. Some ethnic minorities are disproportionately represented in this group. The world of the third age may largely be inhabited by white, middle-class, males.

Old age

In contrast with the active, up-beat presentation of the *third age*, images of the *fourth age* tend to be negative, treating old age as a period of dependence, disability, and decline. It is important to understand that these images are not simply descriptions of the characteristics of old people. Like the other stages of life, old age is socially constructed, not biologically fixed.

Controversy and debate   Ages and stages?   12.9

There are four ages of life:

- The *first age* is the period of childhood, characterized by socialization and dependent status.
- The *second age* is the period of full-time employment, family-building, and adult responsibility.
- The *third age* covers the years 50–74 and is the 'new middle age' of active independent life, post-work and post-parenting.

- The *fourth age* is old age proper, characterized by increasing dependence on others.

Source: Pilcher (1995: 89).

❓ How well does the notion of four stages describe the life course?

❓ How would post-modern theorists view this notion of stages (see p. 437)?

There are two main ways in which people become classified as old. The *first* is based on chronological divisions. Old age is often taken to mean the age at which people become entitled to the state pension, which in the past meant that men became old at 65 and women at 60, though in future both will receive the pension at 65. Problems in funding pensions for a longer period, as people live longer, may well lead to this age rising towards 70. The *second* is the way that they look. Grey hair and wrinkles are, for example, commonly taken to indicate that people are old.

Once people are classified as old, they get treated as dependent, and as physically and mentally incapacitated, irrespective of their characteristics as individuals. This stereotyping of old age has led to those who would conventionally be considered old rejecting the term as inappropriate for them. People who *look* old frequently state that they do not *feel* old. There is, as Pilcher (1995) points out, a tension between external appearance and sense of identity.

The stereotyping of old age has been associated with patterns of prejudice and discrimination labelled 'ageism', in the same way as patterns of racial and sexual prejudice and discrimination are called 'racism' and 'sexism'. In the case of older women, ageism tends to be combined with sexism, for women are judged more in terms of personal appearance. Old women have also been particularly caricatured in folk tales and children's stories.

The stages of life are, therefore, anything but fixed. The boundaries between one stage and another have often shifted, and new stages have been created as views of the life course have altered. Arguably, the social constraints of a person's stage of life have been loosened as stereotypes have been challenged and people have exercised a more individual choice of lifestyle. A post-modern rejection of the idea of stages (see p. 437) probably goes too far, however, for the notion of stages of life still provides a framework within which people can locate and identify themselves and a means of ordering and managing their lives.

Generations and families

The age composition and generational shape of families has been changing. There are growing numbers of multi-generation family units that include grandparents and great-grandparents. Two long-term demographic changes operating since the nineteenth century were the main causes of this:

- greater longevity resulting in the older generations living longer;
- the earlier age of child-bearing reducing the age gap between generations (though in recent years the age of child-bearing has increased).

Four- and five-generation families have become more common. Thus, about half of all people over the age of 65 are now great-grandparents.

Multi-generation families have combined with a lower birth rate to restructure the family. While the number of generations in a family increases, a lower birth rate means that people have fewer siblings within their generation. The structuring of kinship networks is increasingly by relationships *between* generations rather than relationships *within* them. Families have been extended *vertically* rather than *horizontally* (see Figure 12.2).

These changes have also brought about a shift in the age distribution of the population. Greater longevity and a falling birth rate mean that the care of the old has become a greater burden on the young. The contrast in the age distributions of the population in 1821 and 2004 demonstrates this very clearly (see Figure 12.3). Furthermore, the smaller size of the lower age groups in 2004 indicates that there will in future be even fewer people of working age to support the growing numbers of old people.

The growth of this burden is not just, however, the result of demographic changes in age distribution, since social-policy changes have shifted more of the care of the old onto the family. The state funding of residential care has declined, which has increased the financial and social

Figure 12.2 Horizontal and vertical families

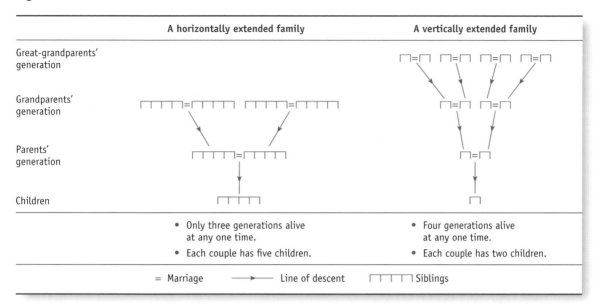

	A horizontally extended family	A vertically extended family
Great-grandparents' generation		
Grandparents' generation		
Parents' generation		
Children		
	• Only three generations alive at any one time.	• Four generations alive at any one time.
	• Each couple has five children.	• Each couple has two children.

= Marriage   ⟶ Line of descent   ⌷⌷⌷⌷ Siblings

Figure 12.3 Population by sex and age, Great Britain, 1821 and 2004 (m.)

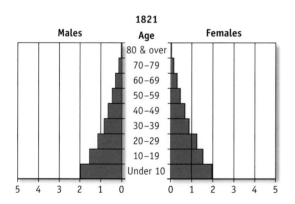

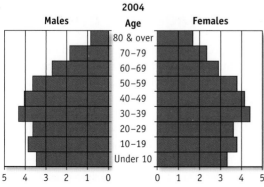

Source: Social Trends (2006: 11).

Grandparents can assist with childcare.
© Alice Chadwick

burden on the family. Furthermore, as Janet Finch (1989) pointed out, the care burden on the family has increased as the capacity of the young to look after the old has diminished. Families have become smaller and there are fewer children to share the responsibility for care of the old. Care of the old also tends to fall on daughters rather than sons, and the increasing employment of women means that daughters have less time available.

There is some danger, as we noted above, of treating the old merely as a burden. They can clearly make a very positive contribution to family life. Grandparents can, in particular, assist with childcare as mothers increasingly go out to work. The old do, nonetheless, require more care as they get older, and more of this care seems to be descending on the family at a time when it is less able to provide it. There is the potential

here for a growing conflict between generations. In this context, the problem of 'elder abuse', which was 'discovered' in the United States during the 1980s (Gelles and Cornell 1987), may become a more serious issue in the future.

Thus, changes in the life course have had important consequences for family structure, family relationships, and family life. As we have shown, the family gradually became more focused on the nuclear, domestic unit, but extended family relationships remained important. These extended family relationships have, however, themselves changed as families have become vertically rather than horizontally extended. Changes in social policy have then led to these vertical relationships placing a greater burden of care on the nuclear family at a time when it is strained by other processes of social change.

Stop and reflect

In this part of the chapter we first examined the historical development of the family as a distinct domestic unit.

- Make sure that you know the meaning of the terms 'nuclear family' and 'extended family'.
- What was distinctive about the 'sentiments approach' to the development of the family?
- With industrialization the family became a unit of consumption rather than production.
- Did this result in a transition from the extended to the nuclear family?

We went on to consider changes in the life course, the stages of life, and the relationships between generations.

- Should childhood still be considered a distinct stage?
- What is meant by 'post-adolescence' and 'a new middle age'?
- Intergenerational relationships have changed with the shift from a horizontally to a vertically extended family.
- What have been the consequences of this shift for family life?

Family life in transformation

By the middle of the twentieth century the nuclear family had become established as the main form of the family in Western industrial societies. This was a unit centred on marriage and children, focused on domestic life, and based on a gendered division of labour. This form of the family had become ideologically dominant and was enthroned as 'the family'.

Since the 1960s this model has been undermined by changes in sexual life, marriage, and employment. It has been challenged by a growing awareness of the dark side of family life. Greater ethnic diversity has led to more variation in family relationships.

These changes have led to a debate over the decline of 'the family'. Those who believe in 'family values' have defended the nuclear family model. Those critical of it have called for a greater acceptance of new forms of the family.

This debate has coloured the discussion of all the issues that we cover in this section.

Sex, marriage, and divorce

Marriage was a cornerstone of the established form of the nuclear family. Do the 'sexual revolution', declining rates of marriage, and a rising divorce rate mean that marriage is in decline?

A sexual revolution?

The 1960s has been generally considered a period of sexual liberation. This was particularly the case for women, who could at last start to free themselves from the risk of unwanted pregnancies through the contraceptive pill.

A redefinition of female sexuality took place as sex became seen as a source of pleasure, rather than a means of producing children. The sexual behaviour of women has arguably become more like that of men (see Chapter 5, pp. 179–80).

Jeffrey Weeks (1989) has set this sexual revolution in the context of post-war changes in capitalism and their impact on the working class in particular. Drawing on the ideas of the Frankfurt school (see Chapter 10, p. 356), he argued that post-war mass consumption commercialized all aspects of life and ended the social isolation of the working class. There was a shift from the traditional virtues of self-denial and careful saving to compulsive spending. Weeks associated this with a new pleasure-seeking attitude towards life, which spilled over into sexual behaviour and was manipulated through the more explicit use of sexual imagery in advertising.

The relationship between sex and marriage has been changing in some respects. According to the British Social Attitudes Survey, the proportion of respondents thinking that there was nothing wrong with premarital sex rose from 42 per cent in 1984 to 70 per cent in 2006 (Duncan and Phillips 2008: 4). The proportion thinking that extra-marital sex is wrong has, however, remained high at over 80 per cent (Hunt 2009: 28)

Marriage has itself changed. A growing importance has been attached to the sexual aspects of the marital relationship, and a satisfying sex life became one of the expectations of marriage (Richards and Elliott 1991). This continued the process of changing marriage from a primarily economic to a primarily emotional relationship.

> **➲ Connections**
>
> You may find it helpful to place this account of changes in the relationship between sex and marriage in the context of our discussion of changes in sexual behaviour in Chapter 5, pp. 179–81.

Marriage and cohabitation

The permissiveness of the 1960s was seen as a threat to the institution of marriage. Would people bother in future to get married? Would they instead simply live with whoever they chose for however long they chose?

Statistically, marriage appears to be in decline. The number of marriages per year has gone down steadily since the 1970s (see Figure 12.4). The number of marriages is not, however, a good guide to the popularity of marriage, as it in part reflects the size of the population and its age distribution. Rates provide a better guide. The proportion of adult men who were married dropped from 71 per cent in 1971 to 53 per cent in 2000, the proportion of adult

Did 'the pill' lead to a sexual revolution?

© Alice Chadwick

Figure 12.4 Marriages, divorces, and remarriages, United Kingdom, 1955–2005 (000)

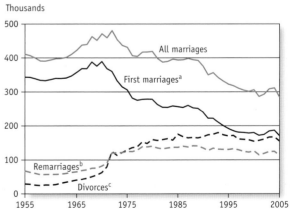

Thousands

[a]For both partners.
[b]For one or both partners.
[c]Includes annulments. Data for 1955–1970 for Great Britain only.

Source: *Social Trends* (2008: 20).

❷ Is marriage in decline?

women from 65 per cent to 52 per cent (*Social Trends* 2002: 42). More people are living on their own or cohabiting.

One of the most striking changes is the increasing number of people who live on their own. The number of households containing only one person rose from 11 per cent in 1961 to 30 per cent in 2008 (see Figure 12.5). This partly reflects an increase in the number of women outliving their partners, but, more recently, it results from the rising number of people under state pension age, particularly men, living on their own (*Social Trends* 2009: 15, 17).

Cohabitation, which refers to an unmarried couple who live together, has also sharply increased. In the UK as a whole in 1986, 11 per cent of non-married men aged between 16 and 59 were in cohabiting relationships, but in 2006 24 per cent were. The corresponding figures for women were 13 per cent in 1986 and 25 per cent in 2004 (*Social Trends* 2009: 21). Northern Ireland has, however, lagged behind, and only 15 per cent of men and women were cohabiting in 2006 (*Social Trends* 2008: 19).

Cohabitation relationships need to be differentiated and fall into three different categories:

- long-term relationships similar to marriage, which are often called consensual unions;
- short-term relationships with little commitment;
- pre-marriage relationships, a group that to some degree overlaps with the other two, for relationships can clearly change.

Cohabitation as an alternative to marriage became particularly established in Scandinavia, especially in Sweden. It is much more common there than in other European countries and has become institutionalized as a stable relationship very similar to marriage. The proportion of Swedish women who marry has consequently long been much lower than in other countries. In 1988 the proportion of women married by the age of 50 was only 55 per cent, as compared with 78 per cent in England and Wales (F. R. Elliot 1996: 15).

Cohabitation in Britain has commonly taken the form of a pre-marriage relationship. Thus, data from 1998 show that 76 per cent of cohabiting men and 71 per cent of cohabiting women expected to marry. Looking at this the other way round, about three-fifths of those who had got married in their thirties had cohabited before marriage (*Social Trends* 2002: 42). The rising rate of cohabitation did not then mean that cohabitation was replacing marriage, for cohabitation more often than not led to marriage.

It is important when considering these figures to set marriage within the life course of a person. The declining proportion of the population in marriages in part reflects a later date of marriage. The average age of first marriage increased considerably between 1971 and 2006, for men from 25 to 32, for women from 23 to 30 (*Social Trends* 2006: 25, 2009: 19). Marriage may be delayed for various reasons, such as the lengthening of education or the pursuit of a career, but this does not mean that people are less likely to become married *during* their life.

There is, nonetheless, evidence that cohabitation may increasingly be becoming seen as an alternative to marriage. Significantly, cohabitation became a longer-term relationship in the 1990s, the average length of cohabitation

Figure 12.5 Households by type of household and family, Great Britain, 1961–2008 (%)

Type of household/family	1961	1971	1981	1991	2001	2008
One person	11	18	22	27	29	30
Two or more unrelated adults	5	4	5	3	3	3
One-family households						
Couple						
No children	26	27	26	28	29	29
1–2 dependent children	30	26	25	20	19	18
3 or more dependent children	8	9	6	5	4	3
Non-dependent children only	10	8	8	8	6	6
Lone parent						
Dependent children	2	3	5	6	6	7
Non-dependent children only	4	4	4	4	3	3
Multi-family households	3	1	1	1	1	1
All households (= 100%) (m.)	16.3	18.6	20.2	22.4	23.8	25.0

Source: *Social Trends* (2009: 15).

❓ What have been the main changes in households and families since 1961, as shown by this table?

Controversy and debate   Gay marriage?   12.10

Gay couples have long sought the right to marry. Although gay couples had acquired registration rights in Scandinavia in 1996, it was in the Netherlands that same-sex marriages were first allowed, and two took place in Amsterdam City Hall on 1 April 2001.

Same-sex marriages are not allowed in Britain, but in 2004 the government passed a Civil Partnership Act to give to same-sex partners legal rights equivalent to those of married couples in such matters as property, inheritance, pensions, and benefits. Partners can now register at a Registry Office and sign an official document on its steps. The first civil partnership ceremonies took place in December 2005, and by the end of that month almost 2,000 couples had registered. In 2006 nearly 19,000 registered and in 2007 around 8,700 (*Social Trends* 2009: 21). The only way of ending a civil partnership is through a divorce.

❓ What does this tell us about the institution of marriage?

Celebrating a gay marriage.

© Getty Images/Martin Sanmiguel

jumping from twenty-three months in 1989 to thirty-three months in 1995 (Hunt 2009). According to *Social Trends* (2004: 33), 88 per cent of those aged 18–24 considered that 'it is all right for a couple to live together without intending to get married'. There were also signs that the government was in 2009 moving towards greater rights for cohabitees, who currently do not have the same legal protection as divorcees if they split up.

These moves have been opposed by defenders of the institution of marriage, and the Conservative Party has declared that, if it wins the 2010 general election, it will provide tax incentives to encourage couples to marry. Iain Duncan Smith, the MP who chairs the Conservatives' Centre for Social Research think-tank, has declared: 'Marriage is good for society, good for children, good for binding together communities. All of that says we should value marriage and try to stabilize it' (*Sunday Times*, 18 October 2009).

The greater acceptability of premarital sex, a higher rate of cohabitation, and more people living on their own, all indicate that marriage is considered less necessary than it once was. It remains, however, a generally accepted ideal. According to the British Social Attitudes Survey, in 2006 54 per cent of adults aged 18 and over agreed that, 'even though it might not work out for some people, marriage is still the best kind of relationship' (Duncan and Phillips 2008: 8). Its future was one of the key issues at the 2010 election and will no doubt continue to be the focus of intense political debate.

Divorce and remarriage

While many people are still keen to get married, the divorce rate has risen. Does this mean that marriage is in decline? The number of divorces in the UK certainly rose steadily after the 1960s (see Figure 12.4 on p. 449). There are, however, two reasons for qualifying such a conclusion. First, the divorce rate reflects not only the state of marital relationships but also the ease of separation. Secondly, there is also the high rate of remarriage.

An unhappy marriage leads to divorce only if the couple are able to end it. The 1969 Divorce Reform Act made divorce far easier and was followed by a big rise in divorce. In 1984 it became possible to divorce after one rather than three years of marriage. There were growing fears that the institution of marriage was being undermined, and the 1996 Family Law Act faced both ways, introducing 'no-fault' divorces but slowing down the process by requiring people to wait for nine months (fifteen if children were involved) and to undergo a conciliation procedure. Reacting to the fears that divorce was becoming too easy, the post-1997 Labour government threw out this law. Nonetheless, the spread of 'collaborative divorce' from the United States to the UK has further eased the divorce process by making it cheaper and less adversarial.

Permissive changes in the law have been crucial, but ease of separation depends not only on the law. It also depends on the practicalities of life after divorce. The growing employment of women in paid work, and the greater availability of state benefits, have made it easier for wives to leave marriages.

As the divorce rate went up at the end of the 1960s, so did the number of remarriages (see Figure 12.4 on p. 449). People have increasingly passed through more than one marriage. The term **serial monogamy**—that is, a sequence of marriages—is used to describe this process. The fact that so many divorced people remarry suggests that divorce indicates a dissatisfaction with a particular partner rather than a rejection of the institution of marriage.

Marriage in decline?

In assessing whether marriage has declined, much depends on the view taken of it. If marriage is taken to mean a life-long relationship, which provides the only proper framework for a sexual relationship, then sexual permissiveness, increasing cohabitation, and a rising divorce rate undoubtedly mean that it has declined. This is the view of marriage put forward by those who believe in 'family values', and they are in no doubt about its decline.

If the essence of marriage is taken to be a mutually satisfying relationship, it has arguably been strengthened rather than weakened by cohabitation and divorce. Neither has stopped people marrying, while both can be seen as improving the quality of marital relationships. Cohabitation enables a more informed selection of partners and a preparation for marriage, while the greater ease of divorce makes 'empty-shell' marriages less likely.

Parenting

The model of family relationships held by those who believe in 'family values' sees marriage as essential to parenting. According to this view, the only right way to bring up children is within the marriage that has produced them.

Marriage has, however, become increasingly dissociated from parenthood. This has occurred in three main ways:

- a rising number of childless couples;
- the increasing birth of children outside marriage;
- a rising rate of separation and divorce.

We will not concern ourselves here with childless couples but concentrate on the consequences of this dissociation for the parenting aspects of family life.

Cohabitation and parenting

The proportion of children born outside marriage in the United Kingdom has risen steadily, from about 10 per cent in the 1970s to 43 per cent in 2005, a relatively high figure internationally (see Figure 12.7). Most of the children born outside marriage in Britain are, however, born to a cohabiting couple. Cohabitation relationships may be less stable than marriages, but they do mean that two parents are present, and they may well lead to marriage. The joint, as opposed to sole, registration of births can be taken as an indicator of a stable cohabitation relationship. In England and Wales in 1975 less than half the children born out of marriage were jointly registered, but in 2006 about four-fifths were (*Social Trends* 2008: 24).

Furthermore, data from the British Social Attitudes Survey have shown that people are becoming more willing to accept cohabitation as a basis for parenthood. When respondents were asked in 2000 whether 'people who want children ought to get married', only 54 per cent thought so, as compared with 70 per cent in 1989, a considerable change in eleven years (Park *et al.* 2001: 37). In 2006, only 29 per cent of respondents thought that married couples made better parents than unmarried ones (*Social Trends* 2009: 21).

The political debate over the future of marriage is centred on its implications for parenting. To the Conservative Party, marriage provides the stability and commitment that good parenting requires and is therefore crucial to the upbringing of children. The Labour Party leadership agrees that a strong and committed relationship between the parents provides the best basis for parenting but does not believe that marriage alone can provide such a relationship. Both sides claim their position is supported by research, but it is very difficult to isolate the effect of marriage on parenting, since those who marry are probably those with the strongest relationships, anyway, and tend also to be better off financially (*Guardian*, 5 January 2010). The debate goes on, but people at large have clearly become more accepting of cohabitation as a basis for successful parenting.

Single-parent families

The proportion of families with dependent children headed by single parents has at least tripled since the beginning of the 1970s (see Figure 12.6). There are two main and roughly equal routes to single-parenthood: the birth of children outside marriage, and divorce. Another important, but less common, route is widowhood.

Figure 12.6 Percentage of children living in different family types, Great Britain, 1972–2007 (%)

Family type	1972	1981	1992	2007
Couple families				
1 child	16	18	17	18
2 children	35	41	38	36
3 or more	41	29	28	22
Lone-mother families				
1 child	2	3	5	7
2 children	2	4	6	8
3 or more	2	3	5	6
Lone-father families	1	2	2	2
All dependent children	100	100	100	100

Source: *Social Trends* (2008: 19).

❷ What changes in children's experience of family life does this table suggest have taken place since the 1970s?

❷ What issues are raised by the category 'couple families'?

❷ Does this table provide evidence for change or stability in family life?

Figure 12.7 Births outside marriage, European Union, 2005 (%)

Estonia	59
Sweden	55
Bulgaria	49
France	47
Slovenia	47
Denmark	46
Latvia	45
United Kingdom	43
Finland	40
Austria	37
Hungary	35
Netherlands	35
Czech Republic	32
Ireland	32
Portugal	31
Germany	29
Romania	29
Lithuania	28
Luxembourg	27
Spain	27
Slovakia	26
Malta	20
Poland	18
Italy	15
Greece	5
Cyprus	4

Source: *Social Trends* (2008: 25).

❷ Why do you think there are such wide variations in the rate of births outside marriage?

Single-parent families have been the focus of much debate. To right-wing commentators they are a defective form of the family that cannot function properly and causes social problems. They are seen as resulting from a lack of moral responsibility that is often blamed on the permissiveness of the sexual revolution. Those on the left attribute these families' problems to poverty and see them as needing support.

This debate has particularly centred on whether single-parent families are a source of social problems. They are mainly headed by women (see Figure 12.6 on p. 453), and it has been argued that the absence of a father results in inadequate socialization, since boys without an appropriate male role model fail to learn the correct patterns of male behaviour.

> ⟴ *Connections*
>
> Charles Murray (1990) has argued that single-parent families are largely responsible for the creation of an underclass. We discuss his theory of the underclass in Chapter 18, pp. 706–7. You may also find it interesting to compare this theory of paternal deprivation with the theory of maternal deprivation discussed in Chapter 4, pp. 130–1.

But is it the absence of a father that leads to problem behaviour? Rodger (1996) reviewed many alternative explanations. The key factor may be not whether fathers are *present* but whether they are actively *involved* in upbringing,

and this applies to two-parent families as well. Children in single-parent families may anyway be disturbed not by the absence of a father but by the conflict and disruption caused by separation and divorce. Single-parent families experience greater deprivation, and it may be the household's poverty rather than the absence of a male role model that is crucial. Rodger reported that research on delinquency in children has, anyway, linked it not to 'broken' but to 'bad' homes, to the way children are treated, supervised, and disciplined rather than the composition of the household.

One major concern of governments has been the cost to the state of supporting one-parent families. This led to the creation of the Child Support Agency (CSA) in 1993 to make absent parents support their children financially. The CSA's administration ran into huge and persistent problems, which eventually led to its abolition in 2006 and replacement by the Child Maintenance and Enforcement Agency with greater enforcement powers. The problem of the costs of one-parent families has also been addressed in another way, by getting single parents back to work and off income support through Labour's Welfare to Work programme, which has provided more state-funded childcare and put pressure on the mothers of school-age children to seek work.

Parenting after divorce

Divorce ends a marriage but it does not end a couple's relationship, at least where children are involved, for the divorced partners have to continue working out their

What proportion of single-parent families are headed by lone fathers?

© Lucy Dawkins

relationship as parents. Remarriage may then lead to complex parenting relationships.

Bren Neale and Carol Smart (1997) have explored the issue of parenting after divorce in the context of the shift, brought about by the 1989 Children's Act, from **custodial parenthood** to **joint parenting**. Under the earlier system of custodial parenthood, one parent, usually the mother, ended up with responsibility for care. Joint parenting required parents to share responsibility and cooperate in the continued care of their children. Disputes between parents are settled by a process of mediation rather than by decisions in the courts.

A growing concern with the problem of absent fathers motivated this change. According to Burghes (1994), 40 per cent of absent fathers had lost all contact with their children within two years, which was a problem not only for the children but also for the father. In recent years there has been a strong movement to reassert fathers' rights after divorce.

This issue has been linked to broader changes in family relationships by Beck and Beck-Gernsheim (1995). They held that the growing employment of women combined with their continued responsibility for childcare to generate growing marital conflict. Both parents then sought greater emotional satisfaction in their relationship with their children. The emotional intensity of the family increased, and, when divorce led to children staying with the mother, fathers felt all the more deprived.

They argued that the idea that wives now 'have everything', both a career and the children, has caused resentment in some fathers. Previously, fathers had been willing to allow 'non-working' mothers to have the children, as they would otherwise 'have nothing'. The growing insecurity of male employment added to this sense of injustice, as men found themselves ending up with neither jobs nor children. This led to the claim that 'true equality' should mean that, just as women are entitled to a career, men are entitled to the emotional satisfactions of parenthood. Gatrell's research (2008: 4) on couples suggests that 'many fathers play a greater role in their children's lives than would have been the case in the past'. It was therefore an assertion of fathers' rights, in combination with a social-policy concern with absent fathers, that promoted a model of joint parenting after divorce.

Joint parenting may have been an advance, but it was not sufficient to meet fathers' concerns and pacify the fathers' movement. It was claimed that men were still often excluded from contact with their children, that the courts were biased against men when arriving at access and residence decisions. It was also claimed that mothers benefited far more than fathers from state benefits after divorce. The Fathers 4 Justice organization called for children to be shared 'fifty–fifty' between parents, who should be given equal contact with children, and should share parental state benefits.

After divorce who should get the child?

© Alice Chadwick

In response to a highly publicized campaign, the government promised in 2005 to improve child contact arrangements. The courts would be given more power to deal with parents who flouted access orders—in other words, to force mothers withholding access to fathers to obey the law. There would also be new funding for child contact centres. The call for equally shared contact, for 'shared parenting', was, however, rejected as not being in the interests of children.

Reconstituted families

Post-divorce parenting has been made more complex by the reconstitution of families after remarriage. These new families have been traditionally called stepfamilies, but in sociology are termed **reconstituted** (or hybrid) **families**. This situation is by no means new, for the death of one parent led frequently to the reconstitution of families in earlier times. The contemporary reconstituted family is, however, new in two key respects.

First, the commonness of a divorce background means that reconstituted families are different in composition. Traditional stepfamilies generally took the form of the replacement of a dead or disappeared parent, but the contemporary reconstituted family often involves the bringing-together into one unit of children from different families after divorce or separation. In 2004–5, 10 per cent of families in Great Britain with dependent children contained one or more stepchildren, 81 per cent of whom were from the woman's previous family (*Social Trends* 2006: 28).

Secondly, the traditional stepfamily was an attempt to recreate a nuclear family that had lost a key member through death or separation. Stepfamilies sought to present themselves as no different from any other ordinary family. Increasingly, when marriages split up today, ex-partners are still around, maintaining some contact with their children, and taking part in their parenting. The reconstituted family cannot so easily present itself as a traditional nuclear family unit (Crow 2002).

Reconstituted families are generally regarded as experiencing additional tensions and problems. The marital relationship itself is likely to be less stable, as the divorce rate for second marriages is higher than for first marriages. Children have to establish new relationships with step-parents and possibly step-siblings. They experience conflicts of loyalty between their parents and between parents and step-parents. Parents have to juggle feelings and responsibilities between biological children and stepchildren. Ex-partners generally have access rights, and the conflicts of the previous family may well re-emerge and cast a shadow over the new one. The process of working out all these relationships is a long and complex one (Robinson and Smith 1993).

This somewhat gloomy view of the reconstituted family has, however, been challenged. It has been argued that it compares stepfamilies with an idealized and unrealistic image of the nuclear family. It also neglects the advantages of the new kind of extended family created through remarriage(s) (see Figure 12.8). In such a family a child can draw on the support and resources of a greater array of relatives. Family life can be flexible and adaptable, with few fixed boundaries and an opportunity for considerable choice of relationships within the family network.

One response to these changes in parenting has been to defend, and to try to revive, the traditional family, as the only context in which proper parenting can take place. The alternative is to accept the growing diversity of family life, and recognize that there are positive aspects to other forms of the family.

Frontiers A new form of the extended family   12.11

Figure 12.8 Jennie's extended family

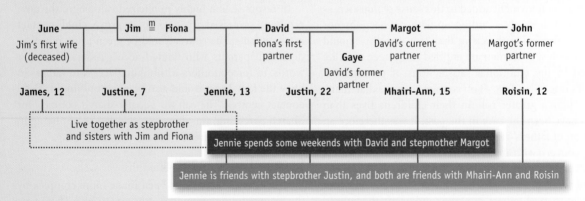

'Alongside the nuclear family of parents and their children, a new social organism is developing: the extended network of stepparents, stepchildren, cousins, aunts, uncles and grandparents. It is a grouping that is simply reflecting demographics, expanding and adapting to increased rates of divorce and remarriage. . . .

Take Jennie, 13, whose mother Fiona, 38 . . . separated from her partner David six years ago to marry Jim, 45. She now enjoys strong relationships with both sets of parents and their respective partners as well as various step- and half-relations across the country. For Jennie there have been many positive aspects to this complex merger of relatives and strangers.

"I like having this sort of family," says Jennie. "My mum seems much happier and so does my dad. I also feel I've got more people to support and care for me—I've always got lots of different relatives to visit and things to do".' (Cook 1996)

Ethnicity and family diversity

Increasing ethnic diversity is another source of family diversity. It is, however, important to bear in mind the diversity *within* as well as *between* ethnic groups, and to take account of change. Static stereotypes that exaggerate the differences between groups and ignore the diversity and change within them must be avoided.

African Caribbean families

The literature on family patterns in the Caribbean suggests that the lower-class Caribbean family is particularly centred on the role of women. Marriage is weakly institutionalized, men 'wander', and women commonly head households. Relationships between mothers and children are much stronger than those between fathers and children. Family life is held together by a network of women. Children are cared for through this network, and women other than the biological mother often take on a mothering role (Elliot 1996; Berthoud 2000).

This pattern is certainly evident among those of African Caribbean descent in Britain today. The rate of marriage is low, and lone-parent families are common (see Figure 12.9, p. 458). It should not, however, be thought that this is simply a matter of the persistence of an African Caribbean culture, for this pattern is stronger among those born in Britain than it was among the first generation of migrants. Some have explained it in terms of increased black male unemployment or the assertion of black cultural identity in response to patterns of racist exclusion.

Faith Robertson Elliot (1996) has linked the African Caribbean family form to the high involvement of women in economic activity, their distinctive attitudes to work, and independence from men. African Caribbean women have been more economically active than women from any other ethnic group. They see paid work as a basis for financial independence and are more likely to control the use of their earnings than Asian or white women. This high involvement in economic activity is, however, made possible only by the sharing of the mothering role with other women.

Asian families

Families from rural areas in South Asia typically take an extended form. They include three generations in the household, and are organized through a network of males. They are also strongly bound together by beliefs in brotherhood and family loyalty. Marriages are arranged and seen as a contract between two families. This type of family structure contrasts strongly with both the contemporary nuclear family in Britain and the mother-centred African Caribbean family.

Migration to Britain severely disrupted extended families of this kind, and many women especially found themselves socially isolated at home and unsupported by kin. A period of dislocation was followed by the rebuilding of extended family structures. The family network was an important resource for the individual, as well as a source of identity, a means of maintaining cultural distinctiveness, and a defence against local hostility.

F. R. Elliot (1996: 42) argued that South Asian communities have adapted to the British environment but according to 'their own cultural logic'. Sikh households have become more focused on couples, and women have renegotiated traditional authority patterns through the greater independence paid work has given them. They were able to do this because Sikh religious traditions emphasized equality and allowed Sikh women a degree of independence (Bhachu 1988).

In contrast, women from Pakistani and Bangladeshi cultures have been limited to homework or work in family businesses by the Islamic prohibition of contact with unrelated men. This can lead to the exploitation of women as cheap labour and their confinement within the home. They have, nonetheless, been becoming more assertive and influential within the family, and have also developed some independence through their own neighbourhood networks (Werbner 1988).

Marriage rates are very high (see Figure 12.9) and divorce rates very low within the minorities of South Asian origin. Divorce is permitted under certain circumstances but strongly discouraged. This lower rate of divorce can be linked to the greater strength of communal and kinship bonds, the patriarchal control of women by men,

Controversy and debate Black fathers   12.12

Black fathers have come under attack for not exercising their family responsibilities and failing to act as good role models for their children. David Cameron, leader of the Conservative Party at the time, followed Barack Obama in taking this line. In June 2008, Obama told a predominantly African American audience in Chicago that too many black

fathers are 'missing from too many lives and too many homes'. Obama was in turn criticized for disseminating white views of black men, disregarding the poverty in which many black families lived, and failing to acknowledge the responsibility of government for their situation (*Guardian*, 9 and 16 July 2008).

Figure 12.9 Families with dependent children, by ethnicity and family type, United Kingdom, 2001 (%)

	Bangladeshi	Black (African)	Black (Caribbean)	Chinese	Indian	Pakistani	White
Married couple	79	44	32	79	85	78	63
Cohabiting couple	3	8	12	3	2	3	12
Lone parent	18	47	57	18	13	19	25
	100	100	100	100	100	100	100

Source: *Social Trends* (2006: 25).

❷ What evidence can you find in this table to support the points made in the text about ethnic differences in family life?

and the lower involvement of women in paid employment. There is evidence that the family life of young Asian couples has become more focused on the marital relationship and less involved with wider kin networks but that they still have a strong sense of obligation to the extended family (Elliot 1996).

Some commentators have pictured young Asians as caught between cultures and in conflict with their parents, particularly over arranged marriages. Ethnographic studies have, however, suggested that they have often been able to make compromises between cultures or find ways of combining them. Thus, some have accepted the institution of the arranged marriage but become more involved in the arrangement process and have been allowed to defer marriage until completing higher education. Conflict does clearly occur, however, and some young Asians have rejected their parents' plans, chosen their own partners, or engaged in secret relationships (Elliot 1996; Berthoud 2000). The helpline of the Derby-based Honour Network, which began work in 2006, reported that it was receiving on average sixty-two calls for help every week from children afraid of being forced into marriage or suffering violence, possibly 'honour killings', if they refused (*Independent*, 26 September 2008).

There are accounts of British girls in families of Pakistani or Bangladeshi background being sent, often unknowingly, to marry men in these countries, though this problem is not confined to girls. Foreign and Commonwealth officials have reported that the injured party is male in at least 15 per cent of the cases they investigate. These officials reported in 2004 that since 2000 nearly a thousand cases of this practice had been investigated by British government officials, but these are, of course, only the ones that came to their attention. The police and social services have tried to mediate between families and daughters, but this can lead to girls finding themselves defenceless back in the families that have been pressurizing them (*Independent*, 25 March 2005).

Thus both the African Caribbean and the various Asian patterns of family life originated in agrarian societies but first persisted and then developed in their own ways within British society. As both are quite different from the standard nuclear family, their adaptation to life in an industrial society challenges Parsons's notion that the nuclear family is the form appropriate to it (see p. 434). They similarly show that family forms are culturally diverse and that the standard nuclear family is not really standard at all but just one cultural form that the family has taken.

Work and money

The traditional family has also been challenged by changes in work patterns, and we now move on to consider their impact on gender-roles within the family. We begin by discussing whether the growing employment of women has led to changes in the domestic division of labour, and then consider whether it has affected the management of money in the household.

> ➔ *Connections*
>
> The discussion of the domestic division of labour should be placed in the context of changing employment patterns, which we examine in Chapter 5, pp. 169–70, and Chapter 17, pp. 681–4.

A changing domestic division of labour?

Changes in employment have challenged the rationale for a domestic division of labour, not only because of the growing employment of women in paid work, but also because of the declining employment of men. Does this mean that the domestic division of labour is coming to an end?

The domestic division of labour established in nineteenth-century Britain was between the male *breadwinner* and the *housewife*, though this was not an absolute division. First, men did do some household tasks, though these were gendered. Some, such as gardening and house repairs, were defined as men's work, while others, such as routine cleaning and childcare, were defined as women's work. Secondly, many women did paid work, though this was regarded as secondary to their domestic work. Women in this situation have been said to carry a **double burden** or work a 'double shift', because they were still expected to carry out their domestic work.

A 1990 study by Warde and Hetherington (1993) of households in the Manchester area showed that the domestic division of labour still operated. Housework was overwhelmingly done by women rather than men. There was also a clear division of household tasks between men and women. Women did the more routine cleaning, cooking, and childcare tasks. Men mainly did jobs such as home repairs, home improvement, car maintenance, and also various intermittent tasks such as brewing alcohol, cooking barbecues, and collecting takeaways. Weeding the garden appeared to be the only ungendered task.

This suggested that little had changed, but, according to Jonathan Gershuny (1992), important changes have taken place. Gershuny used detailed diaries to measure the time spent by men and women on all their various daily activities, including housework and paid work. He found that, even though the distribution of housework was still far from equal, the proportion of housework done by men had been increasing. The *total* work done by men and women had become almost equal. If their total work was almost equal, it could not be argued that women carried an extra, 'double' burden.

Gershuny suggested that a process of lagged adaptation was taking place. There was inevitably a lag between women taking on paid work and households adapting to change, but they did eventually adapt. His data showed that, the longer a woman had been in paid employment, the more equal had become the sharing of the total household workload. There was also a generational dimension to change, for children socialized in a changing household may be expected to acquire different conceptions of gender-roles, which they then practise later on in their own households.

Sullivan (2000) has used national time-budget data to compare couples in 1975, 1987, and 1997. She found that women's share of domestic work had dropped overall by nearly a fifth between 1975 and 1997 (see Figure 12.10, p. 460). A decline had occurred across all her employment categories, and in both working-class and middle-class households, suggesting that this was a very general social change. In all categories, women, nonetheless, still did more domestic work than men in 1997. Her data also showed that the *more* that women were employed, the *lower* was their share of the domestic work, and that the *less* that men were employed, the *more* they did at home.

Sullivan analysed these data to discover how many 'egalitarian' households there were. She found that, when both partners were working full-time, the woman was doing *less than half* the domestic work in only 15 per cent of the couples in 1975, in 20 per cent of them in 1987, but in 32 per cent of them in 1997. Thus, by 1997, in a third of these couples the husband was doing more than the wife, though

Does a continued domestic division of labour mean that patriarchy continues?
© Alice Chadwick

in two-thirds the wife was still doing more than the husband. Sullivan (2000: 450) argued that her data indicated 'a general trend towards a more egalitarian domestic division of labour'.

Sullivan also put together the time spent in paid work and in domestic work to arrive at the total work contribution. She found that women's share of the total work-time was about 50 per cent in each of her three years, which broadly supports Gershuny's argument against the double burden, as it suggests that the total workload was equitably distributed. However, she also found that women doing more than five hours of paid work a week, particularly those in full-time work, did do more than half of the total work. This provides some support for the notion of the 'double burden', though Sullivan notes that these women were working only between 3 and 5 per cent longer than men, rather less than the amount suggested by other studies.

From this we may conclude that:

- the proportion of domestic work done by women has generally declined;

- women still do more housework than men;

Figure 12.10 Women's share of domestic work by employment status of partners, Great Britain, 1975, 1987, 1997

Employment status	1975	1987	1997
Both partners full-time	68	62	60
Husband full-time, wife part-time	80	70	69
Husband full-time, wife not employed	82	73	73
Other[a]	61	55	59
All	77	67	63

[a] This category consisted largely of couples with husbands either not employed or working part-time.

Source: Adapted from O. Sullivan (2000: 443, table 1).

- the amount of housework done by women is related to their employment status, and that of their husbands;
- the proportion of 'egalitarian' households has increased;
- there is, nonetheless, still some evidence to support the existence of a double burden.

Crompton, Brockmann, and Lyonette (2005) have carried out a comparative study of the domestic division of labour and attitudes towards it. They demonstrate significant and persisting international differences in the domestic division of labour between Britain, the Czech Republic, and Norway. Norway, with its Social Democratic welfare state, is the least traditional. The Czech Republic, which has been moving away from state socialism, is the most.

By comparing data from national surveys in 1994 and 2002, this study examines the relationship between attitudes and social change. Crompton *et al.* found that in all three countries *attitudes* towards domestic work, especially those of women, had become less traditional. The *actual* domestic division of labour had, however, changed much less, indeed reverting towards a more traditional division in Britain (see Figure 12.11).

They argue that Gershuny's process of lagged adaptation has 'stalled', a result, they suggest, of an intensification of work pressures. As international competition increases and companies demand greater commitment from their employees, men in demanding careers are forced to devote more time and energy to their paid work. This stalling, at a time when women's attitudes were changing, is linked to greater 'home life stress' among British and Norwegian women in households with a traditional division of labour.

There are a number of hidden issues in this whole discussion that need to be brought out. First, there is the problem of how housework is defined. Does this, for example, include gardening or car maintenance? Different conclusions will be reached according to the range of tasks included in a study.

Figure 12.11 Households with traditional and non-traditional division of domestic labour (%)

	Britain		Czech Republic		Norway	
	1994	2002	1994	2002	1994	2002
Traditional	46	49	63	58	40	39
Non-traditional	54	51	37	42	60	61
	100	100	100	100	100	100

Source: Crompton *et al.* (2005: 217).

Secondly, a focus on the amount of work done does not take account of its meaning. When men increase their share of housework, do they take on the boring routine jobs? Or do they focus on intrinsically more interesting tasks, such as gardening, which could reasonably be considered leisure rather than work (see our discussion of these issues in Chapter 17, p. 653)?

Thirdly, the listing of tasks takes no account of the hidden 'emotion work' that women do. Duncombe and Marsden (1995) carried out a study of forty couples who had been married for at least fifteen years. They found what they called a general 'gender asymmetry' in emotional behaviour. Men were reluctant to express emotions, and the emotional labour of the household had to be done disproportionately by the women. It has been argued (see p. 434) that it is through the emotion work of the wife that the male breadwinner copes with the tensions generated by work in a capitalist economy. It has also been suggested that this additional emotion work means that women carry not a *double* but a *triple* burden.

Fourthly, married couples are not the only couples. As about a third of couples are in cohabitation relationships, and these will inevitably be, on average, younger couples, it would be interesting to know how the domestic division of labour operates here. There are also same-sex couples. Gillian Dunne (1999: 68) studied lesbian couples and found that 'the allocation of household tasks bore no relationship to the gender-segregated patterns that characterize dominant trends for heterosexual couples'. In a review of the literature, Silverstein and Auerbach (2005: 42) concluded that 'just as gay dads are changing the gender ideology of families by "de-gendering" parenting, transsexual parents are reconstructing family roles in an even more dramatic way'.

Money management

The management of money is a key issue in most households. Studies of the distribution of tasks commonly find that this is one that is either shared or mainly done by women. Does this mean that women control household finances?

Routine *management* of money matters does not necessarily mean *control* of money. It may, for example, mean sorting out how the 'housekeeping' money is spent, but not deciding how much is allocated to it. Furthermore, as Crompton (1997: 92) points out, when income is low, sorting out the household budget may be 'more a chore than a source of power'. The statement that both partners are involved may also be quite misleading, for Pahl (1989) found that, when both were said to control finances, it was in practice the husband who made the major decisions.

Pahl (1993) identified four main ways of organizing household money in a randomly selected sample of 102 couples, who all had at least one child under the age of 16. The couples were sorted into the following groups according to whether they pooled their income in a joint bank account and according to the wife's response to the question 'Who really controls the money that comes into the house?'

- *Husband-controlled pooling* (39 couples). A joint account but the husband paid bills and checked the bank statement. This was typical of higher-income groups where the wife was not in paid employment. If the wife had a job, it was one of lower status than her husband's or part-time.

- *Wife-controlled pooling* (27 couples). This was particularly common among middle-income groups, where both partners were in full-time paid work. The higher the wife's earnings and educational level, as compared with the husband's, the greater the wife's financial control.

- *Husband control* (22 couples). This occurred typically on the traditional model of a housekeeping allowance. The husband had his own bank account and gave his wife an allowance. The man was the sole or main earner.

- *Wife control* (14 couples). This was most commonly found in low-income families, where both partners were unemployed and household income came mainly from social-security payments.

Thus, women had most control where there was least to control. There was otherwise a clear relationship between the paid employment of women and the influence they had over household finances. A later study by Vogler and Pahl (1993) showed that the traditional practice of husbands giving wives a housekeeping allowance was in decline. This was probably related to increasing male unemployment. The relationship between employment and control over money shows how important employment is to power in the household.

Domestic violence and abuse

The established form of the nuclear family has also come into question because of an increasing awareness of the family's 'dark side'. The family home is not only a place of comfort and affection but also a place where violence and sexual abuse occur.

Both family violence and sexual abuse have increasingly become major issues. There are three possible explanations and each may partly account for this.

- *Changes in behaviour*. This is the explanation that first springs to mind, but it is by no means the only one.

- *The redefinition of behaviour*. Behaviour once considered acceptable or only a minor form of deviance has been redefined as unacceptable or serious, as in the beating of children or 'date rape'.

- *Increasing awareness*. Unacceptable behaviour that was previously concealed has come to light, a rediscovery of the family's 'dark side'.

Child abuse and child protection

The problem of separating out changes in behaviour from changes in attitudes and reporting applies to both the physical and the sexual abuse of children. There is little agreement about what constitutes 'abuse'. Conceptions of this vary and change (see Corby 2000 for a discussion of these issues).

Violence against children is certainly nothing new, but it is only since the 1960s that it has been treated as physical abuse. Corporal punishment and firm discipline within the family had long been considered essential to the maintenance of social order. In the 1960s, however, the 'battered-baby syndrome' was discovered, and in 1973 the death of Maria Colwell at the hands of her stepfather led to a public inquiry that established child abuse as a 'problem'. The work of professionals in medicine and childcare was clearly important in bringing child abuse to light, but Hendrick (1994) has argued that it became a major issue because ideological conflict was increasing at that time. The Colwell case was used by the New Right to highlight the dangers of permissiveness and moral decline.

The *reported* abuse of children increased rapidly in Britain during the 1980s. The number of children on child protection registers in England and Wales increased from a rate of 1 per thousand children in 1984 to 4 per thousand in 1991. It then dropped back to 3 per thousand in 1999, largely, it seems, because of changes in registration procedure and the faster removal of cases from the register. Significantly, new registrations continued to rise during the 1990s (Corby 2000: 88–9). Clearly, with rates of this kind, changes in reporting and definition can have a big impact.

The discovery of the physical abuse of children was followed shortly by the discovery of sexual abuse. In the United States there was an increase of 71 per cent in reported cases during the three years 1976–9, an increase so great over such a short period that it could only be due to changes in reporting or definition (Russell 1986: 75). There is, however, some American evidence of a long-term increase in the sexual abuse of children (see Box 12.13).

Varying definitions of sexual abuse certainly have an enormous effect on reported rates. F. R. Elliot (1996: 156) points out that different definitions have resulted in estimates of its prevalence in Britain ranging from 3 to 46 per cent of children. A key issue here is whether non-contact offences, such as exposure or obscene telephone calls, are included.

In Britain there was an upsurge of concern with the sexual abuse of children within the family during the 1980s. This was clearly connected with the high publicity given to a series of cases in Cleveland. In 1987, 545 accusations of child sexual abuse were referred to Cleveland Council, and action was taken in 265 cases to protect the children involved. Social workers advised by doctors using new (and controversial) techniques of diagnosis removed a large number of children from families suspected of child abuse (see Box 12.14).

There was a very public conflict in Cleveland between the police, on the one hand, and social workers and doctors, on the other. The police rejected the medical evidence of sexual abuse and refused to act on it. Media coverage largely took the side of the police, and social workers found themselves heavily criticized by the media and politicians. They were, in fact, under attack from two different quarters, for failing to protect children and for overzealously removing them from their families. There was simply no agreement between the various professions involved about how much abuse had actually been occurring.

There has subsequently been a shift towards a more legalistic and formal system of child protection. Rodger (1996) has claimed that social work became more

---

THEORY AND METHODS   **12.13**

Child sexual abuse in the United States

Diana Russell (1986) carried out a study of sexual assaults through a survey of 930 women in San Francisco in 1978. Women of all ages (aged 18 or above) were interviewed, and rates of abuse could therefore be established for women born from the early years of the century up to the early 1960s. Russell concluded that rates of both incestuous and non-familial child sexual abuse had increased fourfold between 1909 and 1973. Instances of incestuous abuse amounted to 16 per cent of the total reported child abuse. There were, however, problems with the representativeness of these findings, as 36 per cent of those approached refused to participate. There is also the problem of recall varying with age.

How did Russell explain increasing child sexual abuse? She argued that it was due to changes in sexual behaviour and gender relationships. She pointed to the greater availability of child pornography and the permissiveness generated by the sexual revolution of the 1960s. She also suggested that a reaction against women's demands for sexual equality might be involved. Women's challenge to male power deflected men towards children as sexual objects, for children were dependent on adults and less able to resist their demands. This is consistent with the generally accepted explanation of child sexual abuse as being due to the availability and vulnerability of children rather than their sexual attractiveness.

---

bureaucratic and defensively concerned with rules and procedures in order to avoid criticism. It has also focused increasingly on the investigation and surveillance of families rather than on family support. There has, indeed, been a tendency for the state to intervene increasingly in family

---

Controversy and debate Should abused children be taken   **12.14**
away from their families?

The problems experienced with institutional care, its poor outcomes, and the dangers of abuse within it led to a policy of keeping abused children, if at all possible, with their family of origin and supporting that family. The highly publicized deaths of some children left with their families, especially the death in 2008 of Baby P, whose family had been regularly monitored by social workers but who, in spite of many danger signs, was left with it, led to calls for a reversal of this policy.

Fostering out such children at least results in the placing of an endangered child with another family, but it is, however, difficult to find a sufficient number of good foster parents. Some children have been bounced around between as many as forty or fifty different foster parents.

In 2009 there were calls for a re-evaluation of publicly provided care. Should more children be removed to publicly provided care in children's homes? According to Andrew Flanagan, the new head of the NSPCC:

There is a long-standing view that publicly provided care is not as good as care in the home. There is a presupposition that leaving a child in the home must be better. We need to open up that debate. Why is care not a good option? If it isn't, that is the thing that needs to be addressed. (*The Times*, 6 April 2009).

Source: Gentleman (2009).

matters, to concern itself with the health and behaviour of children, and the adequacy of parenting.

There is no real way of knowing whether child abuse has increased or whether there is simply greater awareness of it. It is clear from all this that the greater publicity given to child abuse and policy towards it have little to do with child abuse itself and much to do with changes in professional practices, ideology, and politics. We do, however, now have much better information on the amount of violence and abuse of British children, from a recent NSPCC survey, which is reported in Study 12 at the end of this chapter.

Marital violence and coercion

Attitudes towards violence between husband and wife have also changed markedly in Britain since the 1960s. Feminism has here played a crucial part in exposing the hidden violence within marriage and rejecting the idea that it is simply part of normal married life. The creation of women's refuges was an important practical consequence of the new attitude towards domestic violence.

Changes were made in British law during the later 1970s to provide greater protection for women. Housing rules were changed so that women leaving home because of male violence were no longer regarded as making themselves homeless and therefore losing the right to council housing. New laws gave women greater legal protection against violent husbands through injunctions that could be issued quickly by magistrates and followed by imprisonment if breached.

Action through the courts has, however, proved difficult, because of women's dependence on their men, fear of the consequences of taking them to court, and an unwillingness to testify against them. Courts have also had a reputation for treating men leniently and not imprisoning them for acts of domestic violence. To address this situation, the Home Office awarded funding in 2000 for twenty-seven projects designed to reduce domestic violence. Special Domestic Violence Courts have been established, and domestic violence awareness training has been introduced for magistrates, prosecutors, and lawyers (*Independent*, 8 June 2005).

The focus on husbands' violence against wives has been challenged. A national survey carried out in the United States in 1985 by Straus and Gelles (1986) showed that women were, in the domestic situation, at least as violent as men. The most common situation involved violence by both, but, after this, violence by women against men was more common than violence by men against women. Even in the severe-violence category, wives were violent more often than husbands (see Figure 12.12, p. 464).

A recent survey in Britain apparently demonstrated that domestic violence is overwhelmingly the violence of men. A survey of all police forces in the United Kingdom found

Briefing: marital rape 12.15

Marital rape is a key issue in the study of changing attitudes to domestic violence. Until recently it was not treated in most countries as a crime. The law assumed that men were entitled to sexual intercourse whenever they wished it, while married women were required by their marriage vows to obey men. In the United States the law on this point was not changed in most states until 1990. In Britain, it was not until 1991 that a House of Lords ruling established that rape could occur within marriage.

Diana Russell carried out a pioneering study of marital rape, using material from the same 1978 survey used for her study of child sexual abuse (see Box 12.13). Definitions of rape vary from the narrow legal definition of forced intercourse to the much broader notion of forced sexual activity of any kind. Russell adopted an intermediate definition that included forced oral and anal sex and forced digital penetration as well as intercourse. She found that 14 per cent of the married women in her sample reported they had experienced rape or attempted rape by a husband or ex-husband (Russell 1990: 57, 67).

Marital rape, as defined in this way, has been regarded as but one form of sexual coercion. Some feminists have argued that there is a continuum from entirely mutual sexual acts to rape, which then becomes a somewhat arbitrary line drawn across the continuum at a certain point. Indeed, Russell (1990: 74) argued that 'much conventional sexual behaviour is close to rape'. Twenty-six per cent of Russell's sample reported some kind of 'unwanted sexual experience' with their husbands, and interviewers then had to probe further to establish whether this experience fell into the study's definition of rape.

that on one day in September 2000 there were 1,300 reports of domestic violence. Of these, 81 per cent involved a male attacking a female. Only 8 per cent were attacks by females on males. Attacks by females on females accounted for 4 per cent and males on males 7 per cent (*Independent*, 26 October 2000).

There are also data from the 2001 British Crime Survey. Here, 6 per cent of women and 4.5 per cent of men reported that they had been subject to non-sexual domestic violence (abuse, threat, or force), during the past year. The figures for severe domestic force alone were 1.6 per cent of women and 1.2 per cent of men (Walby and Allen 2004: 14). These figures do indicate that men are more violent than women, but to nothing like the extent suggested by the 2000 survey of British police forces.

Figure 12.12 Marital violence in the United States, 1985 (per 1,000 couples)

	Husband and wife	Wife-to-husband	Husband-to-wife
Overall violence	158	121	113
Severe violence	58	44	30

Notes: Acts of severe violence were: kicked, bit, hit with fist; hit, tried to hit with something; beat up; threatened with gun or knife; used gun or knife. Overall violence included minor acts: threw something; pushed/grabbed/shoved; slapped or spanked.

Source: Straus and Gelles (1986: 470).

How are these very different conclusions to be reconciled? One explanation lies in the method of investigation used. Archer has reviewed eighty-two different studies of 'inter-partner aggression' in Western societies. He found that studies based on *reports* showed that women were more often the victims but *social surveys* showed that men were more often the victims. Surveys also showed that this was not because women were in some way acting in 'self-defence', as has often been argued, since women were at least as likely as men to initiate the violence. The discrepancy is explained by women being much more likely than men to report violence to the police.

The kind of information collected about the violence is also crucial. James Nazroo (1999) studied ninety-six couples in Britain. He too found that there were significantly more attacks by women on men than by men on women, but, when he looked at how dangerous the acts were, he found a very different situation. Men were far more likely to engage in dangerous violence with an intention to harm, while women were more likely to be seriously injured. Violence by men was also more likely to be continuous and repeated, and there were higher levels of anxiety about violence among women.

Nazroo's study was not based on a nationally representative sample, but his in-depth approach enabled him to probe into the character, meaning, and consequences of violence. His findings also point towards an explanation of the higher rate of reporting by women, and are consistent with the well-known fact that far more women than men are murdered.

Research has, then, revealed that there is much hidden violence towards women in Britain but also a hidden violence towards men that has attracted far less attention. This does not, however, detract from the view that the violence towards women is more serious, as its consequences are more serious.

This area is a difficult one to investigate, but there is no doubt that research has revealed a 'dark side' of family life. The inward focus of the nuclear family and its characteristic isolation of family life from wider kin and community networks have hidden violence and abuse from public view. Furthermore, the growing emotionality of family relationships, as the nuclear family developed, may well have created an emotional intensity that finds expression in greater violence and abuse. Those who believe in 'family values' face the problem that the very form of the family that they defend may also be the one most likely to generate behaviour that violates other widely held norms and values.

Global focus Domestic violence across the globe   12.16

The UN Population Fund's 2000 report stated that 'violence against women is a pervasive yet under-recognized human rights violation' that takes many forms: the infanticide of unwanted female children; suicides following domestic violence; rapes, sexual violence, and prostitution; genital mutilation; so-called 'honour' killings.

In many countries domestic violence towards women was considered legitimate, and often by the women themselves. Thus, a survey in Ghana found that 43 per cent of men and nearly half of women considered that wife-beating was justified if a woman used a family planning method without her husband's consent. In Egypt many women in rural areas thought that beatings were justified if women refused to have sex with their partners. Honour killings were reported to be on the increase and most commonly occurred in Muslim communities and societies.

The Population Fund's latest studies of this issue, *Programming to Address Violence against Women: 8 Case Studies Volume 2* (2009), can be found at www.unfpa.org/public/publications.

Source: United Nations Population Fund (2000).

Stop and reflect

This part of the chapter has examined the recent transformation of family life.

We began by considering changes in marriage.

- The rate of marriage has been falling as people increasingly live on their own or cohabit, while the divorce rate has risen.
- Does this mean that marriage is in decline?

We considered changes in parenting.

- Parenting has become increasingly separated from marriage.
- What have been the consequences of this for family life?

  We went on to examine ethnicity and family diversity.

- Increasing international migration has added to the growing diversity of family life.

- What are the implications of ethnic diversity for the functionalist theory of the family?

We also considered the domestic division of labour, and the management of the household.

- Do women in paid work still carry a 'double burden'?

Lastly, we discussed the 'dark side' of family life.

- Why has there been a growing concern with child abuse and domestic violence?
- Do studies of domestic violence show that women are as violent as men?

Key concepts

- cohabitation 450
- cohort 436
- custodial parenthood 455
- domestic division of labour 434
- double burden 458
- extended family 433

- family 431
- generation 436
- household 432
- joint parenting 455
- kinship 432
- life course 437

- nuclear family 433
- patriarchy 435
- post-adolescence 445
- reconstituted families 455
- serial monogamy 452

Workshop 12

Study 12 The extent of child abuse

Reliable information about the amount of violence and abuse experienced by children is very hard to come by. Most information is from official sources and is based on cases reported to the authorities. As families are secretive about such sensitive matters—child abuse can lead to criminal prosecutions, social-worker interventions, and the removal of children—data from such reports are bound to underestimate the size of the problem. There are also well-known problems with official statistics (see Chapter 3, pp. 99–101, where we discuss these issues).

We now have much better information about the situation in Britain from a national study carried out by the NSPCC and reported in *Child Maltreatment in the United Kingdom*

(Cawson *et al.* 2000). This was based on a national probability sample of households and achieved a response rate of 69 per cent. The sample consisted of 1,235 men and 1,634 women aged between 18 and 24. This age group was interviewed because of the difficulties involved in interviewing children themselves, but it did mean that there would be problems of recall, particularly with incidents in early childhood. The restriction of the study to people living in households, the response rate, and recall problems meant that the amount of abuse would be under- rather than overestimated.

It was found that a total of 24 per cent had experienced physical abuse of some kind from parents or carers. This figure was broken down into the following categories:

	%
Serious physical abuse	7
Intermediate physical abuse	14
Cause for concern	3
Total	24

Definitions are here crucial. *Serious physical abuse* was defined as the use of violence that either caused injury, or carried a high risk of doing so if it continued, and regular violent treatment. Such actions as choking, scalding, hitting with fists or objects, and violent shaking came into this category. *Intermediate physical abuse* either involved occasional violence that did not cause injury or regular physical treatment resulting in 'pain, soreness or marks lasting at least a day'. Regular smacking or slapping, if it left marks or caused pain, would be intermediate abuse. The *cause for concern* category referred to less serious physical maltreatment that occurred regularly and indicated 'problems in parenting or the quality of care which could escalate or lead to continued distress' (Cawson *et al.* 2000: 34–5). The category a respondent fell into was determined, not by self-assessment, but by the researchers' evaluation of the information provided by the respondent.

There are clearly many problems with these categories. They combine both the severity of the action and its frequency. The movement of the boundaries between them through small changes in definition would produce a different picture. It was considered important, however, to carry out some form of grading, since a global figure, covering everything from really serious injury to regular smacking, would not be very meaningful on its own. The global 24 per cent figure did, nonetheless, indicate that almost a quarter of the child population at least sometimes experienced treatment in their families that 'breached the standards shown by previous research to be accepted by over 90 per cent of the population' (Cawson *et al.* 2000: 37).

There were many other interesting findings on physical abuse. The person responsible was most often the mother (49 per cent of cases) rather than the father (41 per cent), though this is no doubt largely explained by mothers' greater involvement in childcare. Physical abuse appeared to be related to class, with 12 per cent of social grade DE respondents coming into the serious abuse category, as compared with 7 per cent of

C1s, 5 per cent of C2s, and 4 per cent of ABs. Girls (8 per cent) were more likely than boys (6 per cent) to have suffered serious abuse.

This study not only dealt with physical abuse but also covered emotional and psychological maltreatment. The problems of studying this are clearly even greater than those of studying physical abuse, where more objective indicators, such as physical damage, can be used. The approach taken was to identify from the literature the following seven dimensions:

- psychological control and domination, including attempts to control the child's thinking and isolation of the child;
- psycho/physical control and domination—that is, physical acts that control by causing distress rather than pain or injury;
- humiliation/degradation, including verbal and non-verbal attacks on sense of worth or self-esteem;
- withdrawal of affection and care, including exclusion from the family or from benefits received by other children;
- antipathy by showing marked dislike by word or deed;
- terrorizing by threatening the child, or someone or something loved by the child, or making the child do something frightening;
- proxy attacks on someone or something loved by the child or valued by the child.

A score was produced for each respondent. The maximum possible score was 14, but 7 was taken as a cut-off point indicating serious emotional maltreatment. Six per cent of respondents had scores of 7 or above. The most common maltreatment was terrorizing, which was experienced by a third of children, while a quarter had experienced extreme psychological domination, and almost a fifth had suffered from psycho/physical domination and humiliation.

Data were also collected on sexual abuse. This was defined as any of the following:

- acts involving a parent or carer;
- behaviour against the respondent's wishes;
- consensual sex with someone other than a parent who was five or more years older when the child was aged 12 or under.

Some 16 per cent of respondents reported acts of sexual abuse, though only 1 per cent reported abuse by a parent or carer, and 3 per cent abuse by another relative. Girls were more likely than boys to have suffered sexual abuse by a *parent* or *carer*, but there certainly were reports from boys, though numbers were too small for any generalizations to be made. It was, however, nearly always a male parent who was responsible. Class differences in abuse rates were minimal. Definitions are crucial, and if 16, the legal age of consent, rather than the age of 12, had been put into the definition, much more sexual abuse would have been reported.

This is just a brief summary of a major study and does not do justice to the amount of data it provides, the complexity of the issues, and the methodological discussion. It also reports on other aspects of maltreatment, such as neglect, and contains useful reviews of the literature and a bibliography. Further reports based on this survey are available from the NSPCC.

Source: Cawson *et al.* (2000).

❷ What problems are involved in seeking to establish the extent of child abuse?

❷ How can each of the problems that you have identified be expected to affect the results?

❷ Should child abuse be considered a normal feature of family life?

 ## Media watch 12 The family in 2020

There has been much concern in the media and amongst politicians about the consequences of the changes in the family that we have examined in this chapter. The bad behaviour of children is seen as a growing problem, which is commonly attributed to poor parenting, which is in turn blamed on the decline of marriage. The *Daily Telegraph* recently opened a front-page piece headlined 'Death of the Traditional Family' by pointing out that, according to the latest statistics, 'women are more likely to give birth before they turn 25 than get married'.

In an earlier article for the *Guardian*, Madeleine Bunting reflected on these changes and projected them forward to the year 2020. She saw cohabitation, divorce, births outside marriage, and single parenthood continuing to increase. She concluded that 'the brittle nature of the core relationship between the parents' will be accepted as a 'general rule of family life' in 2020.

She did argue, however, that parental relationships are becoming stronger and more important. She claimed that 'the major characteristic' of the twenty-first-century family is the charging of the parental relationship 'with a much greater intensity, commitment and pleasure'. Parenting is not just a matter of bringing up children but a process to be enjoyed in its own right for its own sake, and by fathers as well as mothers.

More generally, she argued that a growing family diversity did not mean that the family is breaking down but rather that it is undergoing a process of 'reinvention'. People value family life as much as ever, but the traditional family unit has been taken apart and the bits reassembled as people have 'adapted family structures in line with their aspirations to autonomy, self-definition and emotional integrity'.

Bunting suggested that, with more people living on their own, family relationships will for many not be as important in their lives as friendship. There will be a greater reliance on friends for help with the crises of life. This will leave some, particularly the old, in a vulnerable position, with loneliness and depression becoming more common. Women used to be responsible for care in the family, but 'the transfer of their labour from the family to the paid economy has opened up a care deficit'. This is made worse by the lengthening hours of work.

Does new technology offer a solution? According to Bunting, the new communications technologies of the Internet, e-mail, and mobile telephones can help family members stay in contact but cannot solve the problem of care. Care requires carers, and it is not clear where they will come from in 2020. Either carers will have to be paid more, or the gap will have to be filled by migrant labour.

Sources: Bunting (2004); Wallop (2009*b*).

❷ What is meant by the 'brittle nature of the core relationship', the 'greater intensity' of parenting, and the 'reinvention' of the family?

❷ Are families becoming a matter of choice rather than biology?

❷ Is friendship replacing family?

❷ Do you think that the family will be a weaker institution in 2020?

⮕ Revisit our discussion of what the term 'family' means on pp. 430–2, and consider the usefulness of our definition.

Discussion points

Domestic violence

Before discussing this, read the section on 'Domestic violence and abuse' and Study 12.

- Should domestic violence refer to acts of physical violence only?
- Should acts of domestic violence be graded according to severity?
- Can domestic violence be defined objectively or is it a matter of how actions are viewed by those involved?
- Should the smacking of children by parents be considered domestic violence?
- Has domestic violence become treated as a problem because violence has increased?
- Are males as much a victim of domestic violence as females?
- Does the nuclear family generate domestic violence?
- Is domestic violence a universal feature of human society?

Is the family in decline?

Before discussing this read 'Families and family practices' (p. 430), 'Contemporary debate' (p. 435), 'Family life in transformation', and Media watch 12.

- It is important to be clear about what you mean by 'the family'. What problems are there in defining it?
- Should we not worry about definitions and simply study 'family practices'?
- How important is marriage to the family?
- Does increasing cohabitation mean that the family is in decline?
- Does a higher divorce rate mean that the family has declined?
- What is the significance of the introduction of civil partnerships for the institution of marriage?
- Consider the increasing diversity of family life. What forms has this growing diversity taken?
- Does this diversity indicate the decline of the family or its vitality?
- Are the bonds of friendship replacing those of the family among young adults?

Explore further

The following provide general discussions of the nature of the family and family life:

Allan, G. (1999) (ed.), *The Sociology of the Family* (Oxford: Blackwell). *A standard and comprehensive reader on the family, with important and interesting contributions on key contemporary issues.*

Allan, G., and Crow, G. (2001), *Families, Households, and Society* (Basingstoke: Palgrave). *Provides useful and up-to-date coverage of the issues of diversity and change in the family, focusing particularly on the family and the life course.*

Brynin, M. and Ermisch. J. (2009) (eds), *Changing Relationships* (London: Routledge). *Uses the latest data to examine changing relationships within the family and between friends, and their contribution to social welfare.*

Gittins, D. (1993), *The Family in Question: Changing Households and Familiar Ideologies* (2nd edn, London: Macmillan). *A critical examination of the gulf between the ideology of 'family values' and the realities of family life, which challenges the whole idea of 'the family' and argues that only 'families' exist.*

Hunt, S. A. (2009) (ed.), *Family Trends: British Families since the 1950s* (London: Family and Parenting Institute). *Up-to-date*

information on family trends and policy relevant discussions of contemporary issues.

Roopnarine, J. L., and Gielen, U. P. (2005), *Families in Global Perspective (London: Pearson). A useful discussion of contemporary issues in Part One, followed by a wide-ranging examination of the family in different parts of the world.*

For further reading on specific topics, see the following:

Barrett, M., and McIntosh, M. (1991), *The Anti-Social Family* (2nd edn, London: Verso). *A classic critique of the family.*

Berthoud, R., and Gershuny, J. (2000), *Seven Years in the Lives of British Families* (Bristol: Policy Press). *This is an invaluable source of information on social change in the family, based on annual interviews with 10,000 adults.*

Chapman, T. (2004), *Gender and Domestic Life: Changing Practices in Families and Households* (Basingstoke: Palgrave Macmillan). *Moves beyond 'the family' to consider domestic practices in a range of households, including single-person, gay and lesbian, and communal households.*

Charles, N., Davies, C., and Harris, C. (2008*a*), *Families in Transition: Social Change, Family Formation, and Kin Relationships* (Bristol: Policy Press). *Gets at continuity and change by replicating a 1960s study of Swansea and very usefully examines theoretical issues raised by recent studies of the family.*

Cunningham, H. (2006), *The Invention of Childhood* (London: BBC Books). *Provides a useful and readable account of the development of childhood and changes in its social construction.*

Dench, G., Gavron, K., and Young, M. (2006), *The New East End: Kinship, Race, and Conflict* (London: Profile Books). *Updates the classic Bethnal Green study of the family and raises fundamental issues concerning the interrelationships between change in the family, the welfare state, ethnicity, and politics.*

Edwards, R. (2008) (ed.), *Researching Families and Communities: Social and Generational Change* (London: Routledge). *Brings together classic and recent studies, focusing on a range of important contemporary issues.*

Ferguson, H. (2004), *Protecting Children in Time: Child Abuse, Child Protection, and the Consequences of Modernism* (Basingstoke: Palgrave Macmillan). *A sophisticated examination of the development of child protection policy and practice that draws on the 'risk-society' ideas of Giddens and Beck.*

Heath, S., and Cleaver, E. (2003), *Young, Free and Single?: Twenty-Somethings and Household Change* (Basingstoke: Palgrave Macmillan). *Brings the life-course literature up to date and relates it to contemporary debates by very clearly reviewing the literature on 'post-adolescence' and presenting the results of a survey of young adults.*

Hockey, J., and James, A. (2003), *Social Identities across the Life Course* (Basingstoke: Palgrave Macmillan). *A re-conceptualization of the life course, which examines the interaction between structure and agency, assesses the post-modern perspective, and emphasizes the embodiment of identity.*

James, A., Jenks, C., and Prout, A. (1998), *Theorizing Childhood* (Cambridge: Polity Press). *This book brings together the new ideas on the sociology of childhood that were developed in a number of important projects and publications during the 1990s.*

Pilcher, J. L. (1995), *Age and Generation in Modern Britain* (Oxford: Oxford University Press). *A clear and thorough account of changes in the life course, examining all its stages and discussing the relationships between generations.*

Silva, E., and Smart, C. (1999) (eds), *The New Family?* (London: Sage). *This collection pushed out the frontiers on the family with contributions that challenge established views of it both within society and within sociology.*

 ## Online resources

Visit the Online Resource Centre that accompanies this book to access more learning resources and other interesting material on family and the life course at:
www.oxfordtextbooks.co.uk/orc/fulcher4e/

The Institute of Economic Research at the University of Essex carries out research into families and households and is particularly well known for its longitudinal and life-course studies. Electronic versions of publications and papers are available at:
www.iser.essex.ac.uk

Information about the University of Leeds Centre for Research on Family, Kinship, and Childhood and its research activities can be found at:
www.leeds.ac.uk/family

The Centre for Research on Families and Relationships (CRFR) is a collaborative venture between Glasgow Caledonian University, and the Universities of Aberdeen, Edinburgh, and Glasgow. Information about its research and publications is available from:
www.crfr.ac.uk

The UN Population Fund has an online exhibition that reports on projects addressing violence against women in a number of countries:
www.unfpa.org/endingviolence/home.html

The Family and Parenting Institute has recently stirred up the debate on the future of the family by arguing that the nuclear family is dead:
www.familyandparenting.org

Cities and Communities

Contents

Dubai: a global consumer city

In Dubai a global city of consumption has emerged from the desert. Dubai has some oil but lacks the reserves of neighbouring states. Investment has gone instead into hotels, shopping malls, apartment blocks, theme parks, artificial islands, and tourist attractions.

Located midway between Europe and the Far East, Dubai is at the heart of a global communications network. The Dubai-based Emirates airline ordered forty-two Boeing 777s, the biggest order that Boeing has ever received. Dubai Ports has acquired port facilities all over the world, in 2006 buying P & O, the British shipping and ports company, and awakening fears in the United States that an Arab corporation would gain control of American ports.

Huge construction projects have drawn in migrant labour. A labour force of some 250,000 workers has come mainly from India and Pakistan. They have been described as slave labour. They cannot easily leave, since on arrival they are required to hand their passports to their employer. They are closely controlled and crammed into shared accommodation in camps. There were reports in 2005 and 2006 of strikes, demonstrations, and riots by construction workers complaining about low pay and exploitation, but they were forced back to work. According to Adam Nicolson (2006), it would cost one of these workers the equivalent of six months' wages to buy one night's stay in one of the luxury hotels.

Dubai now faces difficult times. The global recession of 2008–9 has hit hard an economy focused heavily on tourist consumption. With its desert location, high temperatures, and heavy consumption, Dubai requires huge amounts of water and is entirely dependent on expensive desalination. Its residents have one of the highest carbon footprints in the world, but Dubai has invested heavily in the construction of artificial islands vulnerable to rising sea levels.

'Dubai is not just a city living beyond its financial means; it is living beyond its ecological means' (Hari 2009).

Sources: Nicolson (2009); Hari (2009).

As the example of Dubai shows, cities are dynamic places. Capitalism drives this urban dynamism, as the ceaseless search for profit transforms the urban landscape and urban society by revolutionizing production and consumption. Cities are also the control centres of the global capitalist economy, the location of transnational corporation head-quarters and the financial markets that move capital around the world. We begin this chapter by examining the changing relationship between cities and capitalism.

What, however, is it that makes the city distinctive? How is urban society different from rural society? Can one speak, as the sociologist Louis Wirth (1938) argued, of an 'urban way of life'? Have the differences between life in the city and life in rural areas now largely disappeared as both are shaped by the dynamics of consumer capitalism?

According to some urban sociologists, social isolation and the absence of community are the distinctive features of urban society. Others have, however, claimed that strong communities *can* form in the city. The strength of community has been one of the main issues of urban sociology, and we take this up at various places in this chapter.

Social change in the city has taken new directions in recent years. As cities grew, they developed a centralized structure and acquired a local state that provided urban management and public services for their residents. More recently, major economic activities have been decentralized to the city's periphery, while the local state and public services have been subject to privatization. After examining centralization and the growth of urban management, we consider decentralization and the decline of city management.

Changes in the city are most obvious in its buildings, in the new clubs and bars of the inner city, or the retail and leisure complexes along the motorways that ring it. These changes in buildings are closely connected with changing relationships between people. In this chapter we examine the changing relationships in the city between classes, sexes, and ethnic groups. We discuss increasing inequality and rising violence. In the changes of the city we can see the changes that have been taking place in society as a whole.

Concepts and theories

Here we begin by discussing the relationship between the development of the city and the rise of capitalism. We go on to consider theories of the differences between urban and rural life, which leads us to the study of community, and the debates around this.

Capitalism and the city

The development of capitalism has been the driving force behind the growth of the city, while the city has played a key part in the rise of capitalism. If we are to understand the dynamism of the city and the character of urban society, we must first examine the relationship between capitalism and the city.

This relationship was central to Max Weber's work on the city. To Weber (1923), the *medieval city* was 'a fusion of fortress and market'. It was there that the markets central to the rise of capitalist economies were first established, in the context of emerging legal and political institutions that protected property, established the rights of citizens, and gave merchants and craftsmen the stability and security they needed to engage in their economic activities. The independence of the city was crucial too, for this allowed capitalism and citizenship to emerge within a feudal society hostile to both. This is where the fortress came in, for political independence depended on military security.

A network of independent cities provided a framework for the early development of international capitalist trading in Europe, but these early cities did not maintain their leading economic and political role. Although the medieval city created favourable economic and political conditions for the growth of capitalist *trading*, these later inhibited the capitalist transformation of *production*. The guild regulations of the cities protected traditional crafts, and

Figure 13.1 Capitalism and the city

Type of city	Relationship between capitalism and the city
The medieval city	• Cities as early centres of capitalist trading
	• Citizenship and self-government
	• Military and political independence
	• European economy controlled by a network of trading cities
The industrial city	• New centres of industrial production outside the medieval city
	• Growth of industrial cities shaped by capitalism
	• City incorporated by nation state
	• Growth of collective consumption
The consumer city	• Cities reshaped by investment in means of consumption
	• Cultural restructuring
	• Marketing of city image
	• Increasing employment in production of services and images
The global city	• Cities as control centres of emerging global economy
	• Empires administered by imperial cities
	• In the post-colonial world, global cities are headquarters of transnational corporations and manage the global flow of money
	• New network of cities outside national control

new forms of production could be more easily established outside the city walls. Cities also lost their independence as they fell under the control of the developing political and administrative structures of the nation state. These changes were symbolized by the dismantling of medieval city walls, which marked the city's subordination to the modern state and its incorporation within a national economy.

> ⊃ **Connections**
>
> You may find it helpful here to refer to Chapter 16, p. 606, where we examine the rise of the nation state, and Chapter 17, pp. 648–9, where we discuss capitalism and industrialism.

Capitalist production led to industrialization and the growth of a new kind of city, the *industrial city*, in the nineteenth century. It was this that resulted in the urbanization of society, in the emergence of the first societies that were predominantly urban in character. Industries employed large numbers of people and became the centres of new concentrations of population far greater in size than the older cities dating from medieval times.

The industrial city was quite different from the medieval city. The medieval city was shaped by the contours of the land, for its streets and walls followed the land's shape. In a capitalist society urban land was not just ground that was suitable to be built on but had a market value. Land was bought and sold. As Lewis Mumford (1961) emphasized, the spatial patterns of the capitalist city were not *dictated* by the shape of the land but were *created* by a market in land. And re-created, for cities have been involved in a constant process of restructuring as developments in production, communication, and consumption have changed property values and altered land use.

Industrial capitalism shaped the city not only through these economic transformations of its physical structure but also through the changing relationship between capital and labour. This aspect of the city was explored by Manuel Castells, who argued that capitalism could function only if the employer was provided with an educated, healthy, and housed labour force that was able to work (Castells 1977). Employers, if they were to make profits, could not bear the costs of providing these services themselves. The costs were, therefore, increasingly borne by the state through what Castells called **collective consumption**. By this he meant that the education, health, and housing consumed by labour were not obtained from the market on an individual basis but were collectively provided by the state, largely through local authorities in cities. Labour movements played an important part in forcing the state to provide these services.

As services were expensive to provide, the rising costs of collective consumption led eventually to urban crisis and political conflict. In the 1970s, cities cut back on services and came into conflict with political movements struggling to maintain them. Castells believed that collective consumption was essential to the maintenance of capitalism, and saw no way out of this crisis, but in the 1980s public services were privatized and consumption was individualized, a process that we examine in 'City management in decline'.

Out of this process emerged the *consumer city*. Central areas of the city had always been devoted to consumption

Consumer city
© Lucy Dawkins

Shanghai: a global city
© istockphoto.com/Nikada

but towards the end of the twentieth century cities were reshaped as capital flowed into the construction of shopping malls, peripheral stores and leisure facilities, and new pubs and clubs in city centres. Cities began to market themselves as centres of consumption, attracting consumers and tourists from whole regions, indeed from other countries, as travel became easier and cheaper. The image of the city became all-important, and cities engaged in 'cultural restructuring' (see p. 506) to maximize their attractiveness (Miles and Miles 2004).

This did not mean that urban production had become a thing of the past. The production of goods was in decline but the production of services was growing and providing increased employment. Furthermore, as the cultural aspects of city life became more important, the production of culture increased. A decline in the production of goods should not be confused with a decline of production in general, for the services and images consumed in the city all have to be produced. Consumer cities are still full of employees engaged in production, in producing services and images (and goods too). The expanding areas of production are, however, more directly and immediately

related to consumption, and the shape of the city is determined increasingly by the requirements of consumption.

One group of cities, *global* or *world cities*, has come to play an increasingly important role in directing the development of the world economy. In their first guise, the global cities were imperial cities that administered colonial empires. Now they are financial centres that manage the flow of money and investment around the world. The headquarters of transnational corporations (TNCs) are located in them. They form a new urban network that directs economic forces that have an enormous impact on national economies but are largely outside the control of the nation state. Indeed, Saskia Sassen (2001) has argued that global cities have become in many ways detached from national economies. We examine the rise of global cities on p. 492.

The independence of the *medieval city* enabled the emergence of an early form of capitalism within it, but cities lost their independence with the rise of the nation state, while capitalist production initially developed outside them. New industrial cities eventually grew up that were shaped by industrial capitalism, class conflict, and state intervention. The growth of individualized consumption then reshaped cities into centres of consumption. With the rise of a network of global cities, the city has regained some of the directive autonomy that it had in much earlier times.

Urban society

The new cities of the nineteenth and twentieth centuries presented a sharp contrast to the predominantly rural societies in which they emerged. How different was the social life of the city from the social life of rural areas? And is it still different?

The urban way of life

Louis Wirth (1938) has made the most well-known attempt to identify the differences between urban and rural life. He saw the defining characteristics of the **city** as:

- the large size of its population;
- its high population density;
- its social diversity.

These resulted in a quite distinctive **urban way of life**, though Wirth was careful to emphasize that the city's influence on surrounding areas meant that this way of life was found to some degree outside the city. The large and dense population of cities resulted in a high division of labour. People performed specialized roles, and this meant that social relationships were segmental and secondary.

Relationships were **segmental** because people did not know each other as rounded individuals and saw only the segment or section of personality related to a person's role as, say, shop assistant or employer. This contrasted with rural society, where people knew about many different aspects of each others' lives and had all-round relationships that were not limited to particular roles.

The term 'secondary' referred to a distinction made by Charles Cooley (1909), another member of the Chicago school of sociology, between *primary* and *secondary* groups. **Primary groups** involved face-to-face interaction, of the kind found in the family or among friends. **Secondary groups** were much larger associations in which relationships were distant and impersonal, as in organizations, such as factories, unions, or political parties, where their members did not know each other as individuals.

According to Wirth, urban society was weakly integrated. City-dwellers had frequent but brief and superficial encounters rather than enduring relationships. Their involvement in the organizations that dominated city life was limited to the task or activity concerned. Thus, although people were crammed together, they felt isolated and 'on their own', a feature of city life also emphasized by Georg Simmel (see Box 13.2, p. 476). This weak integration meant that city life was unstable and social order liable to

> ## THEORY AND METHODS 13.1
>
> ### Louis Wirth
>
> Louis Wirth (1897–1952) was born in Germany but pursued his career in the United States. He received his doctorate at the University of Chicago and spent almost the whole of his career there. He was a member of the Chicago school of sociology, which established 'urban sociology' as a specialized field in its own right. He believed that the urbanization of society had done more to shape its character than either industrialization or capitalism. His short 1938 essay on 'Urbanism as a Way of Life' is generally considered to be the most influential piece in urban sociology. He was not only an academic, for he also acted as a consultant to numerous housing, anti-poverty, and planning agencies.

break down. People living in cities were more likely than those living in rural areas to suffer mental breakdowns, commit suicide, or become victims of crime. Weak integration and instability also meant that city-dwellers were easily manipulated by politicians and the media.

Urban diversity

Gans (1968) argued that Wirth focused too much on the inner city and ignored the majority of the urban population, who lived in quite stable communities that protected them from the worst consequences of urban living. He also argued that there was not just one way of life in the city. Five different ones could be distinguished.

- *Cosmopolites*. Students, artists, writers, musicians, entertainers, and other intellectuals and professionals, who chose to live in the city for cultural and educational reasons. Insulated from city life by their subcultures, they had no wish to be integrated and were detached from the neighbourhood they lived in.

- *The unmarried and childless*. The geographically mobile, who lived in areas of high population turnover and were not interested in local services because of their stage in life. They too had little interest in the neighbourhood in which they lived, did not seek local ties, and did not suffer from social isolation.

- *Ethnic villagers*. Groups with a common ethnic background. Heavily reliant on kinship and the primary group, they were little involved with secondary associations and lived outside the formal controls of society in highly integrated communities that identified strongly with their neighbourhood.

- *The deprived*. The poor, the emotionally disturbed and handicapped, single-parent families, and people experiencing racial discrimination. Forced to live in

'The Mental Life of the City'

In a famous essay with this title, Georg Simmel explored the individualism of city life and its consequences.

Simmel argued that in cities endless variety and constant change result in a continuous stimulation of the senses that leads to an 'intensification of emotional life'. People protect themselves against an intolerable level of excitement by becoming detached, reserved, indifferent, and *blasé*. Although they are physically very close in 'the metropolitan crush of persons', they are distanced from each other emotionally. They can experience a more intense loneliness in the city than anywhere else.

In the city individualism becomes extreme. The only way to stand out from the mass of people and establish a distinct identity is to be different, and a person's distinctiveness has to be highly visible if it is to register with people in a world of brief and fleeting contacts. As Simmel put it:

> This leads ultimately to the strangest eccentricities, to specifically metropolitan extravagances of self-distanciation, of caprice, of fastidiousness, the meaning of which is no longer to be found in the content of such activity itself but rather in its form of 'being different'—of making oneself noticeable. (Simmel 1903, in Levine 1971: 336)

➲ Next time that you are in the centre of a city, look around and see whether you can identify in people's appearance and behaviour 'the mental life of the metropolis'.

'Making oneself noticeable' in the city?
© iStockphoto.com/TerjeBorud

deprived areas with the cheapest housing, they did suffer from social isolation.

- *The trapped*. Old people on small pensions, or the downwardly mobile, who had been left behind when others moved out to the suburbs and had to continue to live in an area after its character had changed. They had lost their social ties, and they too suffered from social isolation.

Of these five ways of life, only two, the *deprived* and the *trapped*, experienced the social isolation that Wirth saw as typical of urban life. Gans argued that ways of life depended not so much on people's urban or rural location as on their class situation and stage in life. He concluded that there was no such thing as 'an urban way of life' and also nothing distinctive about suburban life either (Gans 1995). The age of an area and the cost of its housing had a greater bearing on the characteristics of the people who lived in it than its location.

Giddens (1981) too has rejected Wirth's idea that there is a distinctive urban way of life. He argued that there were in the past sharp differences between urban and rural society, but modern capitalism has eliminated them by transforming both. What really matters is that in both labour is sold to an employer in return for a wage. Similar goods are then bought with these wages, and the result is a similar lifestyle. It is wage labour, not where they live, that shapes most people's lives.

In a short essay Wirth had provided a coherent, wide-ranging, and forceful analysis of urban life that has been highly influential but also much criticized. Although he mentioned some of the positive sides of city life, notably the greater choice, freedom, and tolerance it provides, the image he presented of it was, on the whole, negative and emphasized its loneliness, insecurity, and superficiality. There was an anti-city bias in Wirth's approach that reflected a widely found nostalgia in industrial societies for the life of the rural village.

Community

Louis Wirth believed that city life was incompatible with community. A contrast has, indeed, been commonly drawn between the integrated communities of rural society and the isolation of the individual in the city. It has also been argued, however, that this contrast is misleading, that city life is perfectly compatible with community, while plenty of conflict can be found in supposedly integrated rural communities.

Urbanism and community

Wirth followed in the steps of the nineteenth-century theorists who contrasted traditional communities with the urban industrial society they saw emerging around them. The best-known exponent of this view is Ferdinand Tonnies, who distinguished between community (*Gemeinschaft*) and association (*Gesellschaft*).

According to Tonnies (1887), in *communities* there were strong and emotional bonds of unity based on kinship and sustained by close, personal relationships within a small population. In contrast, *associations* were characterized by rational and impersonal relationships between isolated individuals. These relationships were typical of business enterprises and large populations, such as those of the industrial city or the nation state. While custom ruled in communities, relationships were regulated by contract and law in these larger groups and organizations. In communities there was a strong emotional attachment to the place where people lived, but this was absent in the city. The distinction made by Tonnies between community and association corresponded closely to Wirth's distinction between primary groups and secondary associations.

But is urban society so hostile to community life? Gans demonstrated that communities of what he called 'ethnic villagers' could be found in American cities. Young and Willmott (1957) showed that a strong working-class community still existed in Bethnal Green in 1950s London (we discuss the working-class community on p. 486).

Indeed, it can be argued that urban life actually enables the formation of communities through a process of gravitation. Fischer (1975: 1326) has claimed that cities allow thinly spread minorities, such as artists or students, to gravitate together and produce a 'critical mass' that enables them to establish 'thriving social worlds'. This kind of argument can also be applied to ethnic or religious minorities, who in cities can form communities that would be impossible to create in rural areas or small towns, where their members would be individually isolated and excluded.

Mike Savage and Alan Warde (2002) have, nonetheless, argued that the presence of communities in cities has been overstated. They suggest that those studying communities have found evidence of social integration partly because

Figure 13.2 Rural integration and urban isolation

	Rural integration	Urban isolation
Ferdinand Tonnies	**Community**	**Association**
	• Emotion	• Reason
	• Unity	• Individuality
	• Custom	• Contract and law
	• Loyalty to place	• Non-attachment to place
Louis Wirth	**Ruralism**	**Urbanism**
	• Primary group	• Secondary association
	• 'All-round' personality	• Segmental roles
	• Personal relationships	• Impersonal relationships
	• Integration	• Isolation and disorder

Figure 13.3 Changing views of the relationship between cities and communities

Communities and cities incompatible	**Wirth, Tonnies**
Communities do exist in cities	**Gans, Young, and Willmott**
Cities facilitate formation of communities	**Fischer**
Social isolation is nonetheless a feature of city life	**Savage and Warde**

they were looking for it. They neglected isolated people, who are inevitably less visible and more difficult to contact. Furthermore, people move through many different situations in their daily lives and can sometimes behave as members of a community but at other times experience social isolation. People's involvement in a city community does not mean that they live their whole lives within it.

What is community?

This term has been given many different meanings and used in countless different ways, often loosely to refer to any group assumed to share a common way of life, as in references to the diplomatic community or the black community, or simply to those who live in the same place, the local community. These everyday usages should be distinguished from the use of the term in sociology, where it indicates that a group has certain sociological characteristics.

While sociological definitions themselves vary in their emphasis, they do share certain common features. A **community** may be said to have the following characteristics:

- *Common situation*. Those living in a community will share some common feature that binds them together.

This may be their place of residence, but may also be their class, their ethnicity, their religion, or some other feature. A distinction is commonly made between *residential* and *non-residential* communities.

- *Common activities*. Communities involve all-round relationships between people. They are all-round in the sense that they are not limited to work, or politics, or sport, or any other single activity, but extend into most areas of life.

- *Collective action*. People have some sense of a common interest, and may well organize collective action in pursuit of this common interest. Thus, those living in a particular place may organize action to prevent a road being built through it or to raise money for a community centre.

- *Shared identity*. There is a sense of belonging to a distinct group that has an identity. With this identity goes a certain emotional charge, a feeling of belonging to a larger unit and some loyalty to it.

Definitions are important not only for what they contain but also for what they leave out. In the above definition, we deliberately make no reference to *integration* or *place*, which are commonly seen as characteristics of community. This is because there has been much argument over their links with community and we will now examine the issues they raise.

The classic discussions of community assumed that communities were unified or integrated. This was particularly considered to be the case with rural communities. Those who have studied rural society have often found high levels of conflict, however. Frankenberg (1966) found plenty of conflict in the Welsh village that he studied in the 1950s. One example of this was the conflict within the village football committee over whether outside players, who would increase the team's strength but diminish its local character, should be selected. The conflict in the committee was apparently settled by resignations but then spread into the wider community, as those who had left sabotaged the committee's actions. Eventually the conflict became so intense and widespread that village football collapsed and village interest switched to other activities. These went through the same cycle of intensifying conflict followed by collapse. There was no apparent end to these sequences, though some of the people involved were driven out of the village or left.

Thus, features of the community that are commonly thought to produce integration actually generated a conflict that weakened it. The emotionality of community life, its frequent face-to-face contacts, and the multiple connections between those involved made conflict more intense and harder to resolve through avoidance or compromise. In the end village unity could be maintained only by 'adopting an enemy, real or imagined, outside' (Frankenberg 1966: 273).

It is also commonly assumed that communities are identified with places. The classic community studies certainly demonstrated the importance to many communities of a sense of place, and recent studies have confirmed this (Charles and Davies 2005). There are also non-residential communities whose members do not live in the same place.

The significance of spatial location has been particularly questioned by those who have studied social networks. Ease of travel in the city enables the creation of network communities spanning large areas, and community relationships can be liberated from the constraints of place. They do not even require face-to-face contact. The invention of the telephone enabled the creation of voice-to-voice networks, but the ultimate liberated community is provided by the spatially unlimited *virtual communities* of the Web, which we discuss on pp. 499–500.

Furthermore, William Flanagan (1993) has emphasized that people who live in an area with a residential community may not be a part of that community. Their particular social network may connect them more strongly with people in other parts of the city, or nation, or world. The cosmopolites identified by Gans provide a good example of this. Global communications and extensive international migration, which mean that local people may hardly figure in some social networks, have made this more true than ever before.

THEORY AND METHODS   13.3

Your place

Flanagan (1993) has pointed out that 'each of us lives in our own city'. Each person has a personal map of the city, where the areas that he or she knows and uses are highlighted. Two people who say that they live in the same city may have very different personal maps and, therefore, live in two quite different cities. As Flanagan (1993: 39–40) also points out, the fact that we each have a personal map also means that much of the physical city will be unknown to us and be a 'world of strangers'.

- Photocopy a local map and distribute it to several different people. Ask them to mark with a highlighter pen the places they have visited during the past week and the routes they have taken.

- Compare the maps. From what you know of the people concerned, how would you explain the differences between their personal maps?

- You could develop this into a small project by administering a short questionnaire to find out their occupational status, family situation, leisure patterns, and so on.

There are strong arguments for moving away from the old *container* idea of community to a *network* conception of it. The container idea saw communities as consisting of all those who lived within certain geographical boundaries. They were seen as *members* of that community, who belonged to it. People's social relationships are not actually, however, contained in this way and extend across such boundaries. Some living in a particular place may have minimal connections with locals and may well be in networks that span the globe (Crow and Allan 1994).

If we adopt a network conception of community, these problems can be overcome. A network conception allows for greater openness, for individuals' varying connectedness with a particular community, and for a person to be a member of multiple communities. It also makes room for the approach to community developed by Gerard Delanty (2003). He advances the view that people actively construct communities through communication with others as they search for meaning and a sense of belonging in a meaningless and fragmented world.

A network conception of community is still perfectly compatible with the idea of a local community. A local community can be said to exist when many local networks overlap to produce a high local density of social relationships. The important idea of the 'local community' can be retained, but there is no assumption that all those living in the place are involved in the community network.

Socioscapes

The rather different concepts of 'socioscape' and 'sociosphere' have been put forward by Albrow *et al.* (1997) as a way of describing local relationships in the contemporary city. A study of the London area of Tooting showed that many living there were in networks created by global migration. They were part of an 'imagined community' based on a global network that was non-spatial in character. Furthermore, different networks coexisted within the same area without coming into much real contact with each other. There was no local community as such.

Albrow uses the term **sociosphere** to refer to the separate worlds of those living in such an area, worlds that may be based on very different structures, from the relics of traditional communities to global networks. Some people may have an almost entirely local life, while others may be what Gans called cosmopolites (see p. 475). But, however global their networks are, all do, nonetheless, have a local existence, where 'their sociosphere touches the earth', for everyone lives somewhere. The lack of local contact between those who live in a place means, however, that there is no local culture of the kind described by the classic studies of local communities. People use the locality in many different ways, according to their needs, but pay little attention to each other. 'They live stratified existences, just as airliners operate in different air spaces according to the length of their journeys and cross each other's path at different heights in co-ordinated but unconcerned ways' (Albrow 1997: 53).

The sociospheres intersect in a **socioscape**, a concept derived from Appadurai's term (1990) 'ethnoscape'. An ethnoscape is a space that people *pass through* rather than *live in*, much as tourists pass through a landscape rather than settling in it, experiencing it from the perspective of their own worlds. People similarly pass through a socioscape, carrying with them their own very different worlds. Since they live in the area, they do also, however, interact on a regular basis, for they have established routines and ways of getting on with each other that enable them to coexist, though their interactions do not produce anything as substantial or as stable as a local culture or community. The term 'socioscape' refers to these regular but superficial interactions.

These are interesting concepts, which try to get to grips in an innovative way with the interaction between the global and the local in particular places. The researchers

---

New technology Flash mobbing
13.4

'They appear in public places as if by chance, perform random acts of communal silliness, then disappear'. Flash mobbing is one of the stranger features of contemporary urban life. It occurs when people suddenly assemble in a public place to carry out briefly some unexpected activity together and then disperse.

The first British occurrence was in August 2003 when around 200 people gathered at 6.30 in a sofa store in London's Tottenham Court Road and used their mobiles to make calls praising the sofas on offer. This was the 'London Mob No. 1: Sofa So Good'!

Another example has been 'rick mobbing' or 'rick rolling', when hundreds of people turn up at a railway station in the rush hour and sing 'Never Gonna Give You Up' before leaving.

New technology makes these events possible. They are organized through e-mail, social networking sites, and mobile phones. But why do people carry out such apparently bizarre acts? What is it about city life that motivates them to behave in this way? Is it a reaction against the individualism and anonymity of city life? Does Georg Simmel provide the answer (see Box 13.2 on p. 476)?

Source: North (2008).

deviant groups. This area was seen as particularly exemplifying the disintegrated character of urban life, as described by Louis Wirth (see p. 475).

Processes of area specialization, and changes in the use and social composition of areas, have undoubtedly been important aspects of the development of urban society. The biological assumptions of urban ecology have, however, been strongly criticized as inappropriate to the analysis of social behaviour. In nature, if one species is better adapted to a particular environment, it will force out other, less well-adapted, species. But in a city many other processes are going on. There may be successful local resistance to invasion, for people can organize to keep out the invaders. Furthermore, local politicians and planners may well intervene and control changes in the occupation and use of areas, as we will now show.

Ethnic competition

John Rex and Robert Moore (1967), in their well-known study of race relations in Birmingham, found the ideas of the Chicago school useful, especially the notion of competition for areas and the concept of a zone of transition. Their analysis also demonstrated, however, the importance of external intervention, for the control of areas was not simply a matter of competition between groups and depended on the allocation of housing.

They examined the role of urban **gatekeepers**, such as landlords, building-society managers, and Housing Department officials, in the distribution of accommodation. These were quite literally gatekeepers, as they controlled access to housing, though the term has also been used more generally to refer to those who control access to any resource. The local authority's procedures for allocating council housing were particularly critical in determining which groups occupied which housing in which areas.

Eligibility for council housing depended first on being a resident for five years and then on the number of points accumulated, which took account of such matters as existing housing conditions, health, and war service. Rex and Moore pointed out that these criteria inevitably disadvantaged the ethnic minorities, who were forced into lodging houses by the five years' residence rule. Furthermore, when they had met this requirement and accumulated enough points to make them eligible for council housing, they generally found that they were allocated poor-quality housing in slum areas. Rex and Moore noted that the criteria used by the Housing Visitor, who allocated council housing, were not made public, and there was plenty of scope here for discrimination on racial grounds.

This study demonstrates well the limitations of an ecological model in understanding ethnic competition for areas. Such competition has certainly occurred but within a framework of local authority regulation and a structure of ethnic relationships. The criteria used by local authorities have, however, changed since then and allocation on the basis of need has generated much resentment in some areas when locals on waiting lists have found themselves overtaken by immigrants judged to be in greater need (Gavron 2006).

Class segregation

The growth of the city led to class as well as ethnic segregation. Distinct working-class communities became established in the inner areas of cities, while the middle class moved to the suburbs.

As we showed in our earlier discussion of community, nineteenth-century theorists and their twentieth-century followers thought that urbanization resulted in the decline of community because city life was incompatible with it. This was far from the case. When urban society had settled down after the turbulence of industrialization and the population movements of urbanization, relatively stable communities could emerge.

Many features of working-class life encouraged the growth of strong communities. The workers in one area would often be employed largely in one particular trade, such as mining or dock work, and sometimes largely by a single local employer. Conflict with this employer and the growth of trade unions could generate local solidarity, while the deprivations and insecurities of life in early industrial cities made people reliant on local structures of support. Opportunities for social or geographical mobility were limited and most people lived most of their lives within a restricted area. Common situation, collective organization, mutual dependence, and social segregation produced the conditions in which strong communities could become established.

Once they were established, the strength of their networks, organizations, and identities enabled communities to perpetuate themselves and resist external changes. In the most famous study of a working-class community in Britain, that of Bethnal Green in 1950s London by Michael Young and Peter Willmott (1957), the authors expected to find that post-war social changes were leading to the breakdown of community, but instead discovered that it was alive and well.

The middle class became concentrated in the suburbs. The building of most suburbs was financed by the sale of houses to owner-occupiers, and middle-class people were more able to afford homeownership and the cost of travelling in and out. Suburban living also enabled the middle class to separate itself off socially by spatially distancing itself from the working class.

As Savage and Warde (2002) have argued, suburbanization reinforced social inequality. By excluding those with lower incomes from new residential areas, it consolidated a distinctive middle-class culture and strengthened middle-class solidarity. The process of suburbanization itself contributed to class formation.

Gendered urban space

The growth of the city was also associated with gender segregation, which was linked to the separation of home life from work life in the nineteenth-century city (see Chapter 5, pp. 163–4).

The public life of the city became dominated by men, who could travel freely through it, and there has been much discussion in the feminist literature of the 'male gaze' of the wandering man or *flâneur* (the French term often used), which expressed male domination and treated women as sexual objects. The presence of women in public places was associated with prostitution, as in the term 'street-walker'. The male domination of public space was particularly apparent in the predominantly male character of sporting events and sports places. As Doreen Massey (1994) has observed, this started early in life (see Box 13.5).

Elizabeth Wilson (1995) has cautioned us, however, against taking this view of the male domination of the city too far, for the city is also a place of opportunity for women. Employment in the city made it possible for women to escape from unpaid labour in the household, while shopping became one of the few legitimate public activities for women.

One consequence of the growth of female white-collar work in the city and the rise of the department store was the appearance in late-nineteenth-century cities of a range of eating places specifically designed for women. So, women too could wander in the city, albeit within certain limits, and men could not in the end keep them out of public life.

Suburbanization hardened the separation of gender roles in the household. The male breadwinner commuted into the city, while the housewife remained at home with little else to do but engage in housework and child-rearing. As compared with the inner city, there was little local employment for women. Furthermore, transport was designed to meet the needs of the male commuter, and the poor provision of local public transport within the suburb confined the housewife even more to the home. Distance from other members of the family intensified the housewife's social isolation and substituted telephone for face-to-face contact.

Thus, suburbanization not only segregated classes; it also segregated men and women, reinforcing gender, as well as class, inequalities.

Managed cities

During the nineteenth century, institutions were established to manage the sprawling concentrations of population brought about by urbanization. To understand the rise of the 'managed city', we must place it in the context of the growth of capitalism, class relationships, state intervention, and collective consumption, which we outlined and discussed earlier in this chapter (see pp. 472–4).

In Britain a local state was constructed by the national state in the nineteenth century. Parliament passed laws that enabled the development of local democratic institutions and empowered local government to create a wide range of authorities and services. This provided an opportunity for the labour movement to gain a foothold by first establishing its political presence on local councils and local school boards. What has been called 'municipal socialism' led to councils taking water and gas supply into public ownership, and developing modern transport systems. The management of the city later extended to planning the use of land.

We examine elsewhere the issues of order (Chapter 14, pp. 526–8), health (Chapter 8, pp. 280–1), and education (Chapter 9, pp. 318–19). We concentrate here on the public provision of housing and the development of planning.

Housing classes

Perhaps the best example of collective consumption in the city is the public provision of housing.

The rapid growth of the industrial city in the nineteenth century soon produced severe problems of overcrowding

---

⬤ Briefing: the male domination of public space 13.5

'I can remember very clearly a sight which often used to strike me when I was nine or ten years old. I lived then on the outskirts of Manchester, and "Going into Town" was a relatively big occasion; it took over half an hour and we went on the top deck of a bus. On the way into town we would cross the wide shallow valley of the River Mersey, and my memory is of dank, muddy fields spreading away into a cold, misty distance. And all of it—all of these acres of Manchester—was divided up into football pitches and rugby pitches. And on Saturdays, which was when we went into Town, the whole vast area would be covered with hundreds of little people, all running around after balls, as far as the eye could see. . . . I remember all this very sharply. And I remember, too, it striking me very clearly—even then as a puzzled, slightly thoughtful little girl—that all this huge stretch of the Mersey flood plain had been entirely given over to boys.' (Massey 1994: 185)

❓ *Does this male domination of open space still occur? Observe your local park at the weekend and see who makes most use of its space and sporting facilities.*

in poor-quality housing. There were calls for slum clearance and house-building programmes. The 1890 Housing Act enabled both processes to start, but for a long time progress was slow, and it was not until the 1960s that they came to a climax. In London, one in ten houses was demolished between 1967 and 1971. At its high point in 1979 the public sector accounted for what must now seem a quite astonishing one-third of British households.

Up to this time, the social significance of the ownership and control of housing had been rather neglected in sociology, but Rex and Moore (1967) tried to remedy this through their concept of **housing classes** (see Box 13.6). This started a debate over whether the housing situation should be treated as a separate dimension of stratification.

In their study of Birmingham (see p. 486), Rex and Moore argued that lack of housing was a more serious problem in people's lives than lack of employment. They claimed that ownership of domestic property was as important in determining class situation as the ownership of industrial property, though there were also important differences within the categories of owners and non-owners. They concluded that 'there is a class struggle over houses and this class struggle is the central process of the city as a social unit' (Rex and Moore 1967: 273).

The whole idea of *separate* housing classes has, however, been found wanting, as position on the housing market is so closely related to other aspects of stratification. If housing situation is largely determined by income, there is little to be gained by creating a separate housing dimension of stratification, though it must be said in defence of Rex and Moore that they did show that access to housing was not *only* a matter of income. They showed how the local state

played an important part in distributing 'life chances' and reinforcing patterns of inequality (see the discussion of gatekeepers on p. 486).

Planning

Nineteenth-century British cities grew, but twentieth-century cities were increasingly planned, and the planning process has shaped the environment in which we now live.

Planning was strongly influenced by notions of the ideal city. Two influential conceptions were Howard's *garden city* (see Figure 13.9) and Le Corbusier's *radiant city* (see Figure 13.10). Howard's garden city sought to combine the advantages of urban and rural life. Le Corbusier presented the radiant city as a 'vertical garden city' that would preserve open space for grass and trees and prevent urban sprawl but in a more realistic way compatible with large concentrations of population. The radiant city was, nonetheless, radically different from the garden city in its size, architecture, and transport arrangements.

Jane Jacobs (1961: 16–23) has argued that both these conceptions were, in spite of their differences, fundamentally anti-urban in spirit, as they devalued street life, imposed

Figure 13.9 Ebenezer Howard's garden city

Published at the end of the nineteenth century, this vision of the city envisaged a group of six garden cities, each the size of a small town, surrounded by green belts, and linked to a larger central city, the whole complex comprising a 'Social City'. Each garden city would be self-sufficient, with its own industries, residential areas, and cultural, recreational, and service facilities. The residential areas would be divided into neighbourhoods, to facilitate the growth of communities. There would be an emphasis on public transport, and cycling would be encouraged. Housing would be small scale and traditional. Howard believed in the collective ownership of land and the development of public welfare services at local level.

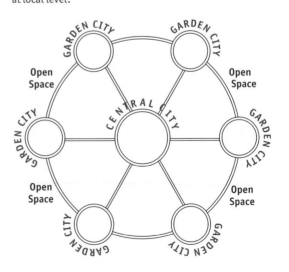

Source: Adapted from Howard (1898).

Figure 13.10 Le Corbusier's radiant city

This 1920s vision of the city saw it as 'towers in a park'. Population density would be far higher than in the garden city or, indeed, existing cities, but the construction of tower blocks sixty storeys high would leave most of the land free of building and available as green spaces for sport and leisure. There would be a great central open space for restaurants, cafés, and various public buildings. The techniques of mass production would be used to standardize building and cut its costs. This city was designed for the car, with arterial roads, one-way systems, and underground routes for heavy vehicles and deliveries. Although Le Corbusier too believed in the public ownership of land, there was less concern for community in his vision of the city, which sought to maximize the freedom of the individual by, for example, facilitating travel by car.

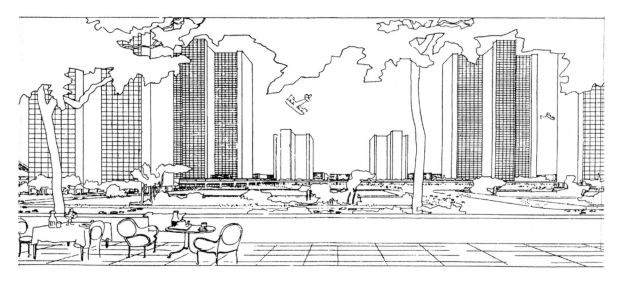

'*Note*: The centre of the city seen from one of the terraced cafés surrounding the Great Central Station square. The station can be seen between the two sky-scrapers on the left, only slightly raised above ground level. Leaving the station, the "speedway" continues to the right in the direction of the Park. We are in the very centre of the city, the point of greatest density of population and traffic; there is any amount of room for both. The terraces containing the cafés are much frequented and serve as boulevards. Theatres, public halls, etc., are scattered in the open spaces between the sky-scrapers and are surrounded by trees.'

Source: Le Corbusier (1947: 258–9).

conformity, forced activities into zones, and left no space for the spontaneity, diversity, innovation, and dynamism, which she saw as the essence of urban life. Their elitist blueprints catered for the interests of planners, architects, and engineers but did not allow for popular involvement and did not give people any say in the construction of the environment in which they would have to live, travel, and work.

More down-to-earth concerns with the growing size of cities, overcrowded housing, and uncontrolled building motivated politicians' interventions. Legislation, especially the 1947 Town and Country Planning Act, established a

Figure 13.11 Garden city versus radiant city

Garden city	Radiant city
• Small population	• High population density
• Decentralized	• Centralized
• Green belts	• Green spaces
• Neighbourhood housing	• Tower blocks
• Public transport and cycling	• Cars and trucks
• Collectivist	• Individualist

framework for planning. Implementation involved local councils, their planning committees, and the officials who influenced and implemented local planning decisions.

What has been the impact of planning on the development of towns and cities? The construction of self-sufficient 'new towns' (see Figure 13.12) and the preservation of green belts around cities showed the influence of Howard's ideas. These fitted well with the anti-urban sentiments of the British elite, which has always valued country rather than city life. The protection of the countryside and agricultural land was one of the main themes of British planning. In spite of these views, population growth after the Second World War and a rising demand for homes in suburban and rural areas created pressures that could not be resisted and led to development in rural areas (Murdoch and Marsden 1994).

Le Corbusier's conception of the city became influential in the 1950s. The high-density and industrial building techniques that he advocated provided cheap solutions to the problems of overcrowded cities and badly built slums. His ideas were seized upon by city councils, architects, engineers, and builders. His legacy is visible in the tower blocks, system building, and urban motorways of British cities.

Figure 13.12 New towns, Great Britain

Source: Lawless and Brown (1986: 134).

In the 1960s there was some shift of emphasis from transformation to conservation. The 1967 Civic Amenities Act gave local authorities greater power to protect listed buildings and trees. Particular areas of historic or architectural interest could be designated Conservation Areas, though development in them was allowed, if it could be presented as consistent with the area's character. In general, employment, transport, and housing were higher priorities than conservation and the reshaping of the urban environment continued apace.

Planning is a bureaucratic process carried out by experts, but group interests are heavily involved and exert pressure on the planners. Incoming middle-class residents seek to conserve rural areas, but farmers often want to sell their land to developers, and local workers are primarily interested in new economic activities that will give employment. Conservation Areas in cities have been used by the urban middle class to protect the quality of its environment and increase the value of its property, bringing them into conflict with developers alive to every opportunity to build more houses in sought-after locations. So-called slums in working-class areas have, however, been cleared without much concern for conservation and little reference to the people whose homes were demolished.

Those who are most organized and have most resources are most able to represent themselves effectively, pay for professional assistance, and influence planning procedures. This not only means that the middle class is likely to be more effective than the working class in protecting its interests; it also means that the interests of capital tend to prevail over those of conservation groups seeking to halt development. Planning is not a neutral bureaucratic process, for decisions are shaped by class interests and class power.

 Stop and reflect

In this section we outlined the process of urbanization and linked it to other processes of change.

- In Britain, industrialization led to urbanization, but this was also the result of the development of a global trading economy and the growth of empire.

We then considered the structure of the centralized city that resulted from nineteenth-century urbanization.

- Cities developed zones that were differentiated by function, class, and ethnicity.

- Key functions were located in the centre and communications radiated from it.

- What contribution did the ecological approach make to the study of the city and what were its limitations?

We went on to examine the emergence of managed cities.

- In the nineteenth century a local state was constructed and collective consumption began to develop.

- Key features of the managed city were public services and housing, and planning.

- How useful is the concept of 'housing classes'?

- What ideas and interests shape the planning process?

The contemporary city

Here we explore recent changes in the city that have reversed many of the tendencies examined above. Decentralization has spread the city out and blurred its boundaries with the countryside. Inner cities have been 'hollowed out' and become problem areas. Long-established communities have been broken up. Local government has lost power and resources, and social order has been threatened by violence.

Cities have not just experienced decline, however. There have also been processes of gentrification and regeneration. Cultural restructuring and investment in new economic activities have given cities a new lease of life. New kinds of community have emerged. Although global economic changes inflicted considerable damage on industrial cities, global cities have benefited from them. Out of all these changes has emerged a new kind of city—the post-modern city—and we conclude the chapter with a discussion of this.

Deurbanization or deruralization?

After a long period of urbanization, the halting of city growth and the actual decline of some city populations suggested that some degree of deurbanization was happening. It can also be argued, however, that the influence of the city has actually penetrated further into rural areas. Has deurbanization or deruralization been taking place?

Urbanization had been going on for so long that it seemed an unstoppable process, but in the 1950s it began to slow down and eventually reverse in both Britain and the United States. Large cities lost population to towns and rural areas—a process called deurbanization (sometimes counter-urbanization). This resulted from two important processes:

- the decline of urban employment;
- the decline of urban residence.

Between 1951 and 1981 some two million manufacturing jobs were lost in the larger cities of Britain. Between 1961 and 1978 Greater London lost 47 per cent of such jobs, though increasing service employment partly

> **Connections**
> It is important to emphasize that the decline of city populations occurred in only a limited number of rich countries. In most countries of the world urbanization has continued, and the world as a whole is becoming more urban (see Chapter 16, pp. 621–3).

compensated, and the decline in total employment was only 17 per cent. The decline of urban employment was due partly to a general collapse of manufacturing, as competition from low-cost countries increased. There was also a shift of employment towards the outskirts of cities, smaller towns, and rural areas, where land was cheaper and communications were easier (Lawless and Brown 1986; D. King 1987).

Those who worked in cities have increasingly lived outside them. Road- and house-building, together with the spread of car and home ownership, made it easier for people to live outside cities and commute. Motorways and rail electrification brought a huge area of the country, including the Midlands, East Anglia, and even parts of Wales and Yorkshire, into commuting range of London. Information technology enabled some to telework and made it possible to pursue city careers a long way from cities.

London has, nonetheless, recently started growing again. In the 1990s its population began to rise rapidly, from 6.8 million in the 1980s to 7.5 million in 2001, with predictions of over eight million by 2016. London is exceptional, however, because of its global functions as a centre of financial services and its attractiveness to immigrants at a time of increasing global migration (see Media watch 13 at the end of this chapter). The other fortunes of global cities have been different from those of cities in general (see Box 13.7, p. 492).

Does the movement of jobs and homes out of the city anyway indicate a process of *deurbanization* or *deruralization*? If people with an urban culture and urban living patterns are dispersed into rural areas, closely linked by commuting and shopping patterns to cities, do not these areas become urbanized? Furthermore, declining employment in an ever-more capital-intensive agriculture has led rural inhabitants to seek urban employment, while the new stores and services around the edge of cities are accessible from rural as well as urban areas. Rural areas are also increasingly devoted to the provision of leisure pursuits for city-dwellers. Are the golf courses, theme parks, and garden centres in country areas in any sense rural?

The term 'deurbanization' certainly draws our attention to important changes in the distribution and location of population and employment, but it must be put in the context of a broader urbanization of rural areas that makes it ever more difficult to argue that social life in rural areas is still distinctive. As we saw earlier, some sociologists have been sceptical of the notion that urban and rural societies are any longer different from each other (see p. 476). They were different during the period of city growth, but the processes we have just been examining suggest that this difference may be disappearing.

Figure 13.13
The centralized city

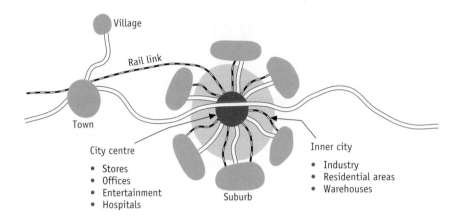

City centre
- Stores
- Offices
- Entertainment
- Hospitals

Inner city
- Industry
- Residential areas
- Warehouses

The decentralized city

We now turn to examine the emergence of a new type of city, the decentralized city, with multiple centres and activities dispersed to the city's periphery.

Decentralization and dedifferentiation

Decentralization is associated with a process of dedifferentiation, reversing the differentiation that we discussed earlier (see p. 484). The various parts of a city have become less specialized in their activities and land use. Retail stores, for example, are spread through the city and are no longer concentrated in a shopping district. While at one time there were distinct inner-industrial areas, small industrial estates are now dotted around the city.

New urban development is particularly focused on the periphery of the city as new stores, warehouses, leisure facilities, hotels, schools, and hospitals are built there. The term 'edge city' has come into use to describe the new shape of cities. People increasingly travel out of the city for shopping or leisure, and many now work on the city's edge. With this growth of the periphery, cities have spread out and incorporated outlying towns and villages into an urban network.

These changes are linked to changes in communications. The centralized city typically had radiating railway lines, which brought people in and out of the centre. The decentralized city has a network of motorways that link its multiple centres and give access to the periphery. The prime location for many commercial organizations is now the motorway junction. Graham and Marvin (2001) argue that the growth of networks connecting together the most valued parts of cities but bypassing places and people of low value is leading to the fragmentation of cities and 'splintering urbanism'.

The best and probably only example of a totally decentralized city is Los Angeles, which has no discernible

Figure 13.14
The decentralized city

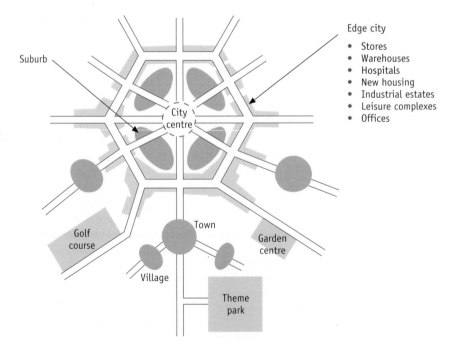

Edge city
- Stores
- Warehouses
- Hospitals
- New housing
- Industrial estates
- Leisure complexes
- Offices

Globalization has led to the emergence of a new kind of **global city** that is centrally involved in the growing economic integration of the world. The rise of the global city and the shifting of capital out of the old industrial cities were part of the same process.

In her study of *The Global City* Sassen (2001) argued that the *dispersal* of production from the old industrial societies to other parts of the world made greater coordination necessary and resulted in the *concentration* of control in a small number of global cities. These are the 'command' cities, where transnational corporations (TNCs) and financial institutions have their headquarters.

Sassen concentrated her attention on London, New York, and Tokyo and argued that, although they have very different histories, cultures, and national traditions, these three cities have become increasingly alike because of their similar global functions. These three cities are linked together in a global financial network that has produced 'one transterritorial marketplace' (Sassen 2001: 327). Their geographical positioning means that, as one closes down at the end of the day, another opens for trading.

Sassen also argued that the global role of these cities has partially *unhooked* them from their societies. They have followed patterns of economic growth different from those of the national economy. At a time when the industrial cities in Britain, America, and Japan were in decline, their global cities were booming.

These cities produce the services and financial innovations required by TNCs and the international financial industry. They are, therefore, centres of managerial, legal, insurance, marketing, communications, public-relations, design, and accountancy occupations. They are also centres of innovation, where the latest technologies are applied to the development of these services.

While these global functions have revived the fortunes of the cities concerned and provided them with new sources of employment, not all those who live in them have benefited. As we show on p. 494, London contains areas that have experienced severe deprivation, as growing global economic integration led to the decline of traditional industries.

A growing inequality has resulted from the occupational changes generated by London's global financial functions. While higher-paid managerial and professional occupations have expanded, so have the low-paid occupations of the clerical workers, cleaners, and security staff employed in the office blocks. Other low-paid occupations, such as restaurant workers, bar staff, and shop assistants, have expanded to meet the consumption needs of the higher paid. Sassen suggested that this gap between the higher and lower paid has been widened by the global city's orientation to world markets and diminished sensitivity to local poverty, local problems, and local politics.

The notion that global cities are new is in some ways misleading. As we showed earlier (pp. 483–4), London and other comparable cities have long performed global functions. But they did so within the framework of the imperial state, and there is certainly something new in the emergence of a network of global cities that are partially unhooked from national economies. This network has opened a new chapter in the evolving relationship between capitalism and the city (see p. 473).

centre. Most cities still have a clear centre and a communications system focused on it. One of the great problems of the contemporary city is how to reconcile the centralized structure inherited from the past with the decentralizing tendencies of the present, and produce a working city out of them.

Concentrated deprivation

Decentralization 'hollowed out' the city, as the loss of economic activity, employment, and population from inner areas drained their resources and concentrated deprivation in them. Changes in the character of the local state, such as privatization and a tighter central control of local government funds, made the problems of the inner city worse.

The problems of the inner city have been described in Paul Harrison's study (1985) of Hackney, one of London's inner-city boroughs. Jobs in manufacturing dropped by 40 per cent between 1973 and 1981. Furthermore, the

Figure 13.15 The experience of deprivation, London, 1985–6 (%)

Form of deprivation	Percentage experiencing deprivation as a major problem in	
	Most deprived areas	Least deprived areas
Health of someone in the family	33.8	29.1
Vandalism and theft	30.3	14.5
Poor public transport	20.4	11.2
Unemployment	20.1	6.7
Street/estate violence	17.7	4.6
Poor housing	16.4	1.3
Being alone and isolated	12.1	6.9
Poor local schools	8.2	3.0
Conflict at home	7.1	4.5
Racial harassment	7.0	1.4

Source: Adapted from Townsend (1991: table 5.6).

industries that were left—for example, in clothing and footwear—were labour intensive and highly vulnerable to competition from poor countries with cheaper labour. Then, in the early 1980s, employment by Hackney Council, the largest employer in the borough, was hit by various government policies aimed at reducing local authority expenditure (P. Harrison 1985: 49–51).

Poverty and ill health were linked and concentrated in the inner city. The concentration of deprivation in the inner city was demonstrated by the 1985–6 study of London by Peter Townsend and his colleagues (Townsend 1991). Of the ten most deprived areas that they studied, only two were in outer London. Townsend and his colleagues also showed a clear relationship between deprivation and death rates. The death rate for those under the age of 65 was almost twice as high in the most deprived areas as in the least deprived. Townsend reported that other studies of Manchester, Birmingham, and Liverpool showed similar links between inner-city deprivation, ill health, and premature death.

It is not only in the inner city that such deprivation is found. Meegan (1989) described the intense deprivation experienced by those living on estates in Kirby and Speke on the edge of Liverpool. The fortunes of this area changed drastically when the transnational corporations that had invested there during the 1950s and 1960s either closed their plants or reduced their labour forces.

A recent Fabian Society report has described Britain's council estates as 'social concentration camps' (Gregory 2009). The practice of concentrating the provision of public housing in estates isolated from the wider community has intensified deprivation in these estates, setting up cumulative mechanisms as various forms of deprivation reinforce each other.

> By the age of 30, public housing tenants born in 1970 are twice as likely as the population as a whole to suffer from mental health problems, eleven times more likely to be not in employment, education or training, and nine times more likely to live in a workless household.
>
> *Gregory 2009.*

These problems show that the distribution of deprivation reflects not only changes in the city and economic shifts in employment but also the operation of housing policy. Furthermore, an unintended consequence of policies aimed at alleviating deprivation by providing public housing has actually been to make deprivation worse.

Gentrification

Inner-city decline has resulted in deprivation for some but opened up opportunities for others. In some parts of inner cities, property developers and middle-class owner-occupiers have moved in to 'upgrade' areas, a process known as gentrification. Instead of moving out to the suburb, some middle-class people, typically young singles and childless couples, settle in the inner city (Butler 1996). Changes in class composition have led to the appearance

Gentrification.
© Lucy Dawkins

of boutiques, galleries, delicatessens, restaurants, and similar enterprises that have also helped to revitalize inner-city areas.

Following Warde (1991), gentrification can be defined as involving four processes:

- the displacement of one group of residents by another of higher social status;
- the transformation of the built environment, as housing is renovated and new shops and services arrive;
- the emergence of a new urban lifestyle with a distinctive pattern of consumption;
- rising property values.

Why does gentrification occur? The decline of the inner city itself provides an opportunity, as lower property prices attract both developers and owner-occupiers. The disappearance of factories, warehouses, and docks have made cheap ex-industrial buildings and sites available for 'loft-living' conversions and developments.

Savage and Warde (2002) linked gentrification to changes in household formation, composition, and employment. Rising population after the post-war baby boom led in the 1960s to a greater demand for housing, which could not be satisfied by suburban house-building. Gentrified areas provided housing particularly suitable for the smaller households that have become steadily more common. The growing employment of women in salaried occupations was also a factor, for living in the city suited dual-career couples by giving easier access to work and to cheap domestic labour from those living in the deprived areas.

Cultural reasons for preferring to live in the inner city have played a significant part in the process. These may involve access to the cultural facilities of big cities or a rejection of suburban values and lifestyles. Some people are attracted into the city by the opportunity to pursue deviant lifestyles in a more anonymous, more tolerant urban society.

Suburbanization, as we showed earlier, segregated classes residentially, while gentrification is a movement of middle-class groups back into predominantly working-class areas. Has it reversed class segregation? Tim Butler (1996: 104) has argued that in gentrified areas of Hackney 'there is little evidence that spatial togetherness leads to any lessening of social distance'. Furthermore, while gentrification upgrades areas, it pushes house prices out of working-class reach, reduces the rented accommodation available to those who cannot afford to buy houses, and generally displaces the lower paid. There is little to suggest that gentrification has diminished class differences or class segregation.

Degendering urban space?

We argued earlier that the spatial differentiation of the centralized city further separated the spheres of home and work. Suburban life distanced housewives from the public life of the city centre and left women isolated in the home, often without transport. Have recent decentralizing and dedifferentiating tendencies reversed this process?

Decentralization means that the local availability of services has increased in most suburban areas, as have employment opportunities, and suburban isolation has therefore diminished. The new superstores and leisure services on the edge of cities offer part-time work consistent with the domestic role. Public transport to the city edge may be poor, however, so access to many of these decentralized activities may still be dependent on car ownership

---

 Frontiers Gentrification, Sex Work, and the City 13.8

In the modern industrial city, sex work was segregated into 'red-light districts', typically located in zones of transition (see p. 485). In San Francisco, around the year 1917, the expansion of the central business district and 'crack-downs' on prostitution moved the red-light area from the Barbary Coast to the Tenderloin, where it remained until the 1990s, when the city authorities decided to remove prostitutes from the streets.

Bernstein (2007: 33–4) argues that this resulted largely from the gentrification of the Tenderloin.

As in other U.S. and West European cities, rigorous, combative policing became a 'front-line strategy' for purging sex workers

and other perceived members of the 'deprived underclass' from newly desirable downtown real estate . . . The transformation that was underway in San Francisco thus did not solely concern the fate of a few hundred street prostitutes and their customers but was about a wide-sweeping reallocation of urban space, in which the inner city found itself being reclaimed by the white middle classes, while those at the social margins were pushed to the city's literal periphery.

Sex work did not disappear but took new dispersed forms, operating from private houses, hotels, and entertainment venues, using the phone and the Internet.

Source: Bernstein (2007).

and availability, which is itself gendered, as men tend to control car use.

Gentrification too has arguably contributed to the degendering of the domestic division of labour. One of the attractions of inner-city living is that it provides easier movement between workplace and home for dual-career households trying to juggle with the competing demands of work and family.

The situation in declining areas of the inner city is quite different. Single parents with small children, who, after the collapse of many city communities, may well lack local support networks, can be confined to the home by the demands of childcare. Their incomes are not high enough to buy it, and state nursery provision in Britain has been minimal, even if recently improving. This has forced many women to take up low-paid homework and work for long hours within the home.

New housing estates with leisure facilities often limited to male-dominated clubs and pubs may leave women with little alternative, apart from bingo, to private leisure in front of the television. Bingo is a predominantly female activity, which, Dixey (1988: 126) has argued, 'plays a vital role in providing a semi-public space which is local and handy, and, as an extension of the community, brings feelings of rootedness and "at-homeness"'.

According to a study of Manchester and Sheffield by Ian Taylor, Karen Evans, and Penny Fraser (1996), men still

dominate urban space. Their street survey found that men consistently outnumbered women in public spaces at all times of day and night, particularly at night. They came across only 31 women for every 100 men in the streets during the early evening hours (Evans 1997).

Valentine (1992) has suggested that a vicious circle comes into operation. The male dominance of public space in cities leads to women avoiding some areas by day and all areas by night, which increases male dominance, which intensifies women's fears (see Box 13.9). The responses of both the police and the media to incidents of violence against women reinforce their fears by suggesting that by putting themselves at risk in dangerous places they are partially to blame for the violence against them.

Even though some of the social changes that gendered urban space have been reversed, there is in the end little to suggest that recent changes in the city have done much to degender the use of space within it.

Changing communities

In this section we examine the implications of recent changes for community life in both urban and rural areas. We also consider the emergence of a new kind of community, the 'virtual community'.

Declining working-class communities

Working-class communities may still have been flourishing in the 1950s (see p. 480), but this situation was about to change. Slum clearance and relocation shattered the residential base of many of these communities during the 1950s and 1960s.

In their classic study, Peter Willmott and Michael Young (1960) followed what happened to forty-seven young married couples who moved from Bethnal Green in London to Greenleigh, a council housing estate twenty miles away. The move to Greenleigh immediately broke up the extended kinship network that had been a prominent feature of Bethnal Green, while fewer public meeting places, such as pubs and shops, meant less opportunity for social interaction. Greenleigh also brought together people from many different places who were strangers to each other. People lived a much more private existence focused on the household and the nuclear family.

Where communities survived these changes, they were weakened by the more general growth of privatism that we examine in Chapter 19, p. 375. These focused people's energies increasingly on home and household. When Bethnal Green was restudied in the early 1980s, it had become much more home-centred (see Box 13.10).

The changes in the inner city that we have been examining above further weakened those working-class communities that were still there. The decline of urban

---

● Briefing: a landscape of fear?   13.9

A study of Manchester and Sheffield showed that women's use of the city was shaped by safety concerns and a 'landscape of fear', which identified areas to be avoided. These varied according to the time of day, and shopping areas that attracted women in day-time became a 'dead space' that was avoided or passed through hastily at night. For an analysis of night-time life in the city, see Study 13 at the end of this chapter.

Source: Taylor *et al.* (1996).

➔ *Try comparing male and female responses to these questions.*

❷ *Have you ever felt frightened in a public place? If so, when did this last happen? At what time of day did it happen? Where did it happen?*

❷ *What frightened you about the situation that you were in? Is there any part of the city you live in (or a city that you visit) that you would avoid visiting? During the day-time? At night?*

❷ *In what ways do you think that the city could be made safer?*

Briefing: Bethnal Green revisited   13.10

'One striking difference was how home-centred most Bethnal Green families had now become. In the 1950s, this had been a feature of the Woodford families. Mothers with a three-month old child are, of course, likely to spend more time in the home than outside it. But it was noticeable how many husbands in Bethnal Green today were almost as much around, when they could be, as Woodford husbands. DIY, even in rented property, and television—not to mention the baby—were clearly strong competitors of the pub and the football ground. . . .

But whatever the draw towards the home, or occupation within it, the corollary in Bethnal Green to this new home-centredness was the emptiness of the streets and corridors and staircases in the housing estates. Markets still flourished. Children sometimes played outside. Small groups of adults occasionally congregated. But no longer could it be said that people in Bethnal Green were (in Young and Willmott's words) "vigorously at home in the streets . . ."' (Holme 1985: 45).

Who looks after people when communities collapse?

© Alice Chadwick

manufacturing damaged their economic base. Those left in inner-city areas were disproportionately the old, the unemployed, one-parent families, the homeless, and the chronically ill. Socially isolated, they looked to support from the welfare state rather than from relatives or community, though arguably the expansion of the welfare state has itself impacted on community provision. Thus, Geoff Dench *et al.* (2006: 118) argue that the welfare state, with its 'army of social workers', has taken away the authority of the older women who used to hold the community together through family networks.

It would be easy to conclude that working-class communities are in terminal decline. In a recent study of communities in Wales, Charles and Davies (2005: 687) conclude, nonetheless, that, 'despite the laments of older respondents, communities rooted in close-knit networks of kin and friends are still very much in evidence in Swansea, especially in working-class neighbourhoods and amongst the minority ethnic population'.

Rural communities

Decentralization also impacted on rural communities. The spread of urban commuters into rural areas meant that the dividing line between urban and rural came to run *through* villages rather than *between* them and the city. As commuters leading essentially urban lives became an increasing proportion of village inhabitants, the village community could be weakened and divided. Ray Pahl (1965: 18)

commented on this long ago: 'The middle-class people come into rural areas in search of a meaningful community and by their presence help to destroy whatever community was there.'

In his study of class relations in East Anglia, Howard Newby (1977) interpreted this situation rather differently. He argued that a common opposition to newcomers had strengthened the sense of community between agricultural workers and farmers. In the nineteenth century the landowners had tried with little success to create a spirit of community between themselves and labourers. They failed because the class structure and the conflicting interests of landowners and labourers generated an oppositional culture among the latter. This culture was, however, weakened by the decline in the number of agricultural workers. The invasion of outsiders from the city then strengthened the bonds between farmers and their workers by generating a shared hostility to the newcomers.

Thus, according to Pahl, the incomers destroyed the community, while, according to Newby, they stimulated the emergence of a community. These apparently conflicting interpretations are, however, perfectly compatible, for Pahl and Newby were referring to different kinds of community. Pahl was concerned with the decline of the residential community, as village unity and identity became weaker, while Newby drew attention to the strengthening of a countryside community, in the face of an invasion from the outside. As one kind of community declined, another was formed.

Ethnicity and community

Ethnicity as well as class has provided a basis for city communities. As we showed in the first part of the chapter, Gans argued that *ethnic villages* had a distinctive way of life based on strongly integrated communities (see p. 475). Immigrant communities are nothing new in Britain, but increased immigration in the 1950s and 1960s led to their proliferation in British cities.

Various aspects of the situation of ethnic minorities facilitate community formation. They tend to be spatially concentrated, while ethnicity itself provides a strong basis for community because of the distinctive linguistic, cultural, and religious traditions that can bind members of an ethnic minority together (see Media watch 13 at the end of this chapter for a discussion of ethnic concentration). This is reinforced by the ethnic conflicts and racism that commonly accompany ethnic diversity. Indeed, racism is, as Jewson (1990: 171) has put it, 'a particularly intrusive, explicit, involuntary, and powerful determinant of collective identity'. Ethnic communities are not just the product of shared customs and beliefs. They are also the result of common experiences of exclusion and discrimination, and the creation of organizations for mutual support and protection.

While attention has been focused on the ethnic communities of black and Asian minorities, whites too have ethnic identities. Jeffers *et al.* (1996) examined the emergence of what they call 'defended communities' among whites in the East End of London and on the Beaumont Leys estate in Leicester. These communities *saw* themselves as threatened by blacks and Asians, though this did not mean that any actual threat existed. The scarcity of housing and jobs in these areas easily generated fears and conflicts. As we showed on p. 485, ethnic competition for housing has been a long-standing feature of city life.

The formation of ethnic communities can result in people leading parallel lives without much contact with each other, and this in turn can create conflict situations leading to riots (see p. 503). In the wake of the riots in British cities in 2001, it was proposed that there should be a national programme to promote community cohesion, in the sense of cohesion *between* communities. An Institute of Community Cohesion has been set up at the University of Coventry. A central principle of community cohesion is not only that there is 'a common vision and a sense of belonging' but also that 'the diversity of people's different backgrounds and circumstances is appreciated and positively valued' (Cantle 2007: 17).

Jeffers *et al.* (1996) have examined the success of seven community initiatives to overcome ethnic and racial divisions in Bristol, Leicester, and Tower Hamlets in London. They concluded that one important factor in their success was whether the various ethnic groups were interdependent. When they were interdependent because they shared a common interest, maybe in a sporting activity or in improving a housing estate, an appropriately organized initiative could reduce ethnic and racial conflict.

The form taken by state initiatives could have a considerable bearing on these relationships. Government funding strategies that encouraged competition for public resources often generated ethnic conflict, as ethnically based groups competed for funds and claimed they had 'special needs'. On the Bancroft estate in Tower Hamlets, both blacks and whites were, however, dependent on a multi-ethnic Tenant Management Committee for access to modernization funds, and racial conflicts on the estate declined. Ethnic interdependence can be promoted if government interventions are designed appropriately.

Jeffers *et al.* (1996) point out that much also depended on how such initiatives were carried out. They needed to strike a difficult balance between working against racism in public and allowing people to maintain their private attitudes and feelings, even if these were racist in character. It was important that cultural differences were not ignored or suppressed but instead recognized and accommodated. The Coventry Institute of Community Cohesion has explicitly recognized the importance and value of difference.

Ethnicity has then provided a basis for community in contemporary Britain, but ethnic communities were not only generated by the distinctive customs and cultures of groups. They also arose because of patterns of exclusion, racial discrimination, and the competition of groups for resources. Attempts have been made to reduce ethnic conflicts by constructing multi-ethnic community organizations that seek to establish a broader community cohesion.

Gay villages

The hollowing-out of the city (see p. 493) has provided the space for another kind of community to emerge, one based on sexual orientation. Taylor *et al.* (1996) have examined the growth of a gay village in the centre of Manchester.

They advance an argument similar to Fischer's 'gravitation' theory by suggesting that the sheer size of the city's population meant that it contained a sufficient number of gay people to sustain an openly identifiable gay area (Taylor *et al.* 1996: 182). Also, the existence of various ethnic communities in Manchester, including a Chinatown and distinct Indian and Jewish areas, facilitated the tolerance of a gay village as just one more minority culture. As Zukin (1995) has pointed out (see Box 13.11), even though it is not based on ethnicity, a gay community has many features in common with an ethnic minority and may present itself as ethnically distinct.

The emergence of gay communities must be set in the context of changing attitudes towards sexual orientation (see Chapter 5, p. 181). The partial decriminalizing of gay sexuality by the Sexual Offences Act of 1967, the rapid spread of openly gay pubs and clubs in the 1970s, and the emergence of a distinctive gay lifestyle prepared the way for the establishment of gay villages. But these were not simply the result of a growing tolerance that enabled gays to associate openly in public.

Indeed, Taylor *et al.* (1996) suggested that it was the 1980s resurgence of political and media hostility to gays, partly occasioned by the association of AIDS with gay sexual activity, that precipitated the withdrawal of gays into their own space. Gay communities are the result of 'gay-bashing' as well as gay association. Thus, while gay villages clearly require a degree of tolerance, they also stem from a more general intolerance, which leads gays to travel considerable distances to find an area where they can be open, relaxed, and at home with others of the same sexuality.

The creation of a gay village in Manchester was also linked to gentrification, as it upgraded a derelict area of inner-city warehouses. There was investment in shops and places of entertainment, and the renovation of buildings and streets, which involved both commercial interests and local-authority regeneration programmes. The so-called 'pink pound', the exceptional spending power of gay consumers, with their lower family and household commitments, attracted the interest of entrepreneurs, both gay and straight. To a local authority, a gay village could be a means of reviving a flagging local economy, revitalizing a derelict area of the city, and attracting tourists.

Virtual communities

In our earlier discussion of community (see pp. 477–9), we examined the network conception of community and argued that this was superior to the older container notion. **Virtual communities** provide the purest example of a network community.

Older communications technologies allowed the *extension* of communities, but it is the Net that has enabled the creation of the virtual community. National postal systems and telephone networks made it possible to extend existing communities without everyday face-to-face contact but did not provide an independent basis for community in the way that the Net does. The bulletin boards, chat rooms, multi-user domains, and social networks of the Net make it possible for whole groups of people to interact electronically.

The idea of virtual communities has been promoted by enthusiasts such as Howard Rheingold (www.rheingold.com), who have engaged actively in building such communities. A by now classic example of them is 'The Well', which describes itself as 'a cluster of electronic villages on the Internet, inhabited by people from all over the world' (www.well.com/aboutwell.html). Such communities can be constructed by any group of like-minded people. As Rheingold (2000: 173) has put it:

> The great value of virtual community remains in its self-organizational aspects. Any group of Alzheimer's caregivers, breast cancer patients, parents of learning disabled children, scholars, horse-breeders—any affinity group—can start an e-mail discussion group, a chat-room, or a Web-forum.

But are these really communities? Sceptics argue that so-called virtual communities are little more than a means of exchanging information. If relationships are formed, they are brief and not sustained. They are also partial, concerned only with some shared interest, and do not involve

 Controversy and debate Gay communities and city interests: the Gay Games in New York   13.11

'The games are more than an athletic competition for a special group. They are supposed to exemplify the solidarity and pride of homosexuals, burnished by political organizations and ravaged by AIDS. In the publicity surrounding the games, as well as in the athletic and cultural program, homosexuality is represented as if it were an ethnicity with its own traditions and roots. It is also represented as a lifestyle, with its own entertainment forms and consumption choices. Lifestyle is

inescapably linked to marketing, as it is often pointed out that most individual homosexuals in the United States have higher incomes than most households. Thus the Gay Games have drawn the support of large corporate sponsors (manufacturers of consumer goods), feature T-shirts and other commercial memorabilia, and are praised for bringing tourist dollars to the city.' (Zukin 1995: 264)

New technology   LunarStorm: a Swedish Web community?   13.12

Advances in mobile phone technology have made possible the creation of extensive 'mobile virtual communities'. One such Web community, called 'LunarStorm', has been created in Sweden. It has claimed a membership of over a million, with nearly half of all Swedish teenagers between the ages of 12 and 17 visiting it each month. It has, however, suffered considerable loss of traffic to rival networks, such as Facebook and MySpace.

It is a commercial operation, run by the LunarWorks company, which provides a LunarMarket and operates LunarMobil phones with a special direct text link to LunarStorm. When people join LunarStorm, they accept the right of LunarWorks to send them product information and commercial offers. LunarWorks collects useful intelligence about which products or services are likely to appeal to particular members through the information provided about their usage of its services through 'cookies'. Members also have to accept the company's right to sell any data it collects on its membership, though not the personal details of particular members.

Source: www.lunarstorm.se.

❓ Do you think that such an organization can be meaningfully considered a 'community'?

---

the whole person. Some consider that electronic contact cannot be sufficient for the creation of a community, for a 'real' community must have face-to-face interaction (Wellman and Gulia 1999).

Furthermore, some of these communities are, more or less disguised, commercial operations (see Box 13.12). They provide yet another means of targeting people with advertisements and selling them goods and services. Some are, indeed, sponsored by mobile phone companies, for the growing linkages between the Net and mobile phones mean that these companies have an evident interest in stimulating electronic interactions that provide them with revenue.

There is also the argument that virtual communities operate at the expense of real communities. Participation in a virtual community and long hours on the Net isolate people from their local community, arguably providing a pale substitute for real community relationships.

In defence of virtual communities, it is claimed that they are far more than a means of communication. Many of them do provide emotional support for their members. Some become highly organized, with rules to regulate interactions, sanctions against those who break them, and governing institutions. Some generate face-to-face interaction, when community members arrange real meetings and conferences. Some result in common action, when they bring people together in a common cause that leads to fund-raising or political action.

The dangers of commercialization can be exaggerated. Rheingold (2000) thinks that opportunities for commercial exploitation are limited and that commercial operations will succeed only if they allow genuine communities to emerge, a process that requires considerable time and skill: 'If you squeeze your community to make a profit at the same time as you are trying to coax it into taking its first breath, you will simply kill your enterprise' (Rheingold 2000: 173).

Wellman and Gulia (1999: 185) have reviewed the literature and conclude that there *are* meaningful virtual communities that maintain 'strong, supportive community ties' and 'may be increasing the number and diversity of weak ties'. Weak ties should not be neglected because they may be a bridge to stronger relationships and anyway have considerable social significance in their own right.

They make the important point that virtual communities should not be contrasted with some mythical rural community that no longer exists in an individualized and privatized world. Social relationships 'online' are much like 'offline' ones, which too are 'intermittent, specialized, and varying in strength'. Weak electronic ties are, anyway, better than no ties at all and can perform important functions by extending networks into new areas.

In deciding whether virtual communities are real communities, conception of community is clearly crucial. If face-to-face interaction or location in the same place is made a defining characteristic of a community, they are not communities. They do not fit the traditional 'container' model of a community, but they are perfectly compatible with the network conception of community, which we argued for above (see p. 479).

Community diversity

So many different kinds of community exist that one cannot sensibly speak of a general decline of community. Communities based on class have been generally in decline but not communities based on ethnicity. Residential communities have been weakened by privatism, as people's lives have become focused on the home, but virtual communities are anchored in the mobile computer.

The changes that weaken one kind of community may well enable another to establish itself. Thus, the movement of commuters into villages weakened local residential communities but stimulated the emergence of a defensive countryside community. The emptying-out of inner-city working-class communities may lead to the creation of new communities, such as gay villages or middle-class communities generated by gentrification.

One kind of community may, indeed, be in conflict with another. Thus virtual communities may arise at the expense of residential communities, and ethnic communities may become stronger at the expense of multi-racial communities. Communities can, however, coexist and it should not be assumed that a person can be part of only one community at any one time.

What does seem clear is that people do experience a need for the practical and emotional benefits of community, and commonly seek to identify themselves with a community of some kind. It is important to understand that communities do not just emerge in the right conditions but are actively constructed by people. If the social basis for one kind of community breaks down, they are likely actively to seek to create a community of another kind. This is where the Net comes in, for it provides new opportunities for them to do this.

City management in decline

We showed in 'Managed cities' how urbanization led to the growth of a local state to establish order, manage the city, and provide collective consumption. In recent years the privatization of local services has reversed these processes, while urban disorder has re-emerged.

Privatization

In Britain the local state came under attack from a Conservative government seeking to reduce local-government powers and spending after its victory in the 1979 election. Local government lost much of its autonomy as a result, and its finances became regulated by the central state. The Conservatives initiated an extensive programme of **privatization** based on the principle of individuals choosing services from providers competing in a marketplace.

As we showed earlier (p. 472), Castells (1977) believed that collective consumption was necessary to the maintenance of capitalism, since it provided the capitalist employer with a supply of healthy, educated, and housed workers. Saunders (1986: 316) took a different view. Collective consumption was not a requirement of capitalism but rather a 'holding operation' that covered people's basic consumption needs until they were able to take responsibility for meeting these needs themselves. In future most people would satisfy their consumption requirements through private purchases, leaving a minority that was unable to do so dependent on what was left of the welfare state. Privatization was not something forced on people by the government, for it met a real desire by consumers for greater control over their lives. Saunders (rightly) did not expect some future Labour government to reverse it.

> **⦿ Connections**
> These changes in the local state need to be placed in the context of changes in the state as a whole. We discuss these in Chapter 15, pp. 576–8.

Some of the main forms taken by privatization in the city were:

- compulsory competitive tendering;
- delegation of education budgets;
- deregulation of bus services;
- sale of council houses;
- privatizing of public space.

Compulsory competitive tendering required local authorities to allow private companies to compete for contracts to provide services and give contracts to the cheapest provider. Local authority services were, in effect, privatized, since they had to behave like private companies in order to compete with them. Refuse collection, road maintenance, street cleaning, and school meals provision were privatized in this way.

This was linked to the *delegation of education budgets* to schools. The funds for local education authority services were largely transferred to schools, which could then buy in services from a provider of their choice.

The *deregulation of bus services* took away their monopoly of routes from municipal bus companies, which now had to compete with (sometimes transnational) private companies. As we show elsewhere, privatization is closely linked to globalization (see Chapter 14, pp. 542–3).

The *sale of council houses* too was driven by government policy, which forced local authorities to allow their tenants to buy their houses. Between 1981 and 1989 1.5 million council houses were sold. New council-house building fell and rent subsidies to council-house tenants were reduced.

Although the sharp decline of council housing in the 1980s was the result of government policy, there had been a steady increase in owner-occupation during the twentieth century (see Figure 13.16, p. 502). Saunders (1990) has pointed out that house ownership is particularly high in Britain and societies originally settled by the British—Australia, Canada, New Zealand, and the United States—in contrast with the countries of continental Europe. He argued that it is related to a strong culture of individualism going back to medieval British society.

Saunders saw private ownership as meeting real needs, giving people greater control over their lives, security and identity. In enabling greater homeownership the

A transnational company operates a local bus service. Find out how many countries this bus company operates in.

© Lucy Dawkins

Conservatives certainly generated considerable popular support, particularly in the working class, which helped them to stay in government until 1997. It did have disadvantages. For some people, it turned into a personal disaster, when they lost their jobs, found themselves unable to service their loans, and lost their homes. It also led to a shortage of social housing, exacerbating tensions between local whites and incoming migrants in areas like East London and providing an opportunity for the British National Party to exploit local white discontent (Gavron 2006).

Another less obvious form taken by privatization was the *privatizing of public space*, which had been one of the central features of urban life (Bianchini and Schwengel 1991). Examples of it are:

- *Shopping malls.* The essentially public shopping street has been replaced by privately owned or privately managed shopping malls. Access to these is controlled by private security companies, who can exclude buskers and expel 'undesirables'.

- *Privately controlled streets.* Homeowners' Associations and Business Improvement Districts in the United States have acquired the authority to carry out surveillance and control the streets.

- *Fortified estates.* Walled estates with controlled entry, surveillance by camera, and patrol by private security companies have been built, not only in American but also in British cities.

- *Privately managed parks.* The transfer of park management to private companies is commonly found in American cities (Zukin 1995).

The privatizing of public space reflects not only the spread of private ownership but also a growing concern with public order. The exclusion of 'undesirables' is in part a response to rising crime, the growth of begging and busking, squatting in shop doorways, and 'sleeping rough' in the parks. These are in turn at least partly a consequence of unemployment, homelessness, and the closing of mental hospitals.

It is also linked to the privatizing of law enforcement. The financial crises of the state, local and central, have led to the transfer of security and policing to the private sector, which

Figure 13.16 Housing tenure changes, Great Britain, 1914–2007 (%)

Year	Types of tenure		
	Owner-occupiers	Council tenants/ social sector	Other rented
1914	10	0	90
1945	26	12	62
1961	43	27	31
1971	53	31	16
1981	54	34	12
1991	67	24	10
2001	70	21	9
2007	69	18	12

Sources: Jewson (1989: 130); *Living in Britain* (1996: 229); *Social Trends* (2002: 167; 2009: 142).

Is it important to keep
public spaces in cities?
© Alice Chadwick

Figure 13.17 Major riots since the 1980s

1980	April	Bristol (St Paul's)
1981	April	London (Brixton)
	July	London (Brixton)
	July	London (Southall)
	July	Liverpool (Toxteth)
	July	London (Brixton)
1985	Sept.	Birmingham (Handsworth)
	Sept.	London (Brixton)
	Oct.	London (Broadwater Farm)
1991	Aug.	Cardiff (Ely)
	Sept.	Oxford (Blackbird Leys)
	Sept.	Tyneside (Meadowell)
1992	May	Coventry (Wood End)
	July	Bristol (Hartcliffe)
1995	June	Bradford (Manningham)
	July	Leeds (Hyde Park)
	July	Luton (Marsh Farm)
	Dec.	London (Brixton)
2001	April	Bradford (Lidget Green)
	May	Oldham
	June	Burnley
2005	Sept.	Belfast
	Oct.	Birmingham (Lozells)
2009	Sept.	Birmingham (city centre)

pays lower wages and provides a cheaper service. This process has gone furthest in the United States, but it has been happening in Britain too (see Chapter 15, p. 585).

Riots

Riots were a common feature of the pre-industrial and early industrial city, but during the nineteenth century conflict became increasingly organized, managed, and contained. The main form it took was class conflict, and this was organized in the industrial sphere by unions or in the political sphere by political parties. Violent riots still occurred from time to time, but were exceptional events. In the 1980s, however, rioting re-emerged. Beatrix Campbell (1993: p. xi) went so far as to claim that 'riot became routine' in the 1980s and 1990s.

The one thing that most riots have had in common is their occurrence in working-class areas with high levels of unemployment and deprivation, whether areas of the inner city, such as Brixton, or outer estates, such as Meadowell, or deindustrialized mill towns, such as Oldham. High local unemployment is one of the most important conditions leading to rioting, and there are fears that rising unemployment in the wake of the economic crisis of 2007–8 will trigger new riots, but it can only provide a partial explanation. Riots have not occurred in all areas of high unemployment and were not a feature of the 1930s, when unemployment and deprivation were very much higher.

Ethnicity has been a major factor in many riots. Jewson (1990) suggested that a common feature of the 1980s riots was the involvement of ethnic minorities experiencing racial discrimination and exclusion from full participation in British society. He argued that in Britain political organization has been on class lines, and there was no tradition of organized ethnic politics. Ethnic minorities had not been politically incorporated as they had in the United States, where they were represented in city governments. This situation has clearly now changed in cities like Leicester.

The ethnicity dimension is linked to another feature of some riots in British cities—conflicts with the police. In some communities a counter-culture associated with drug-dealing and petty crime brought people into conflict with the police. Police stop-and-search tactics that discriminated against blacks resulted in a deterioration of relationships between the police and black communities during the 1980s and early 1990s. Although this issue still festers, the police have scaled down this practice and tried to deal with accusations of 'institutional racism' (for a discussion of this concept see Chapter 6, p. 221).

Ethnicity was not a major factor in generating the outer estate riots of the early 1990s, though other forms of exclusion were involved. According to Campbell (1993: 303), 'these estates had been living with permanent high unemployment and decline, while they were encircled by evidence of prosperity and renewal'. An extreme example of this was the proximity of the Scotswood Estate to the Gateshead Metro centre (see Box 13.18 on p. 510). Conflicts with the police were again also a feature, for the estates had become centres of burglary, car theft, ram-raiding, and joy-riding.

In the 2001 riots, ethnicity was again a central feature. In Oldham, where the most serious disorder took place, rioting occurred against a background of deteriorating relationships between whites and Asians, mainly with a Bangladeshi or Pakistani background, in a town with high unemployment and poor housing. There were white suspicions that scarce local resources were being channelled towards the Asian community, who in turn considered that they were being discriminated against. There were Asian fears of racist attacks and claims that the police were racist and not providing protection, though Asian self-defence actions and counter-violence led to white accusations of attacks by Asians. Both Asians and whites claimed that they were being excluded from 'no-go' areas. Both the British National Party (BNP) and Islamic militants were said to have exploited local fears and discontents (*Independent*, 17 and 28 May 2001).

The background to the 2001 riots was investigated by the Community Cohesion Review Team, set up by the government and chaired by Ted Cantle. This also considered ethnic relations in other cities, such as Leicester and Nottingham, where there had not been riots. It argued that an ethnic polarization, which generated mutual fear and

 Briefing: ethnic polarization   13.13

'Whilst the physical segregation of housing estates and inner-city areas came as no surprise, the team was particularly struck by the depth of polarization of our towns and cities. The extent to which these physical divisions were compounded by so many other aspects of our daily lives was very evident. Separate educational arrangements, community and voluntary bodies, employment, places of worship, language, social and cultural networks, mean that many communities operate on the basis of a series of parallel lives. These lives often do not seem to touch at any point, let alone overlap and promote any meaningful interchanges.

A Muslim of Pakistani origin summed this up: "When I leave this meeting with you I will go home and not see another white face until I come back here next week."

Similarly, a young man from a white council estate said: "I never met anyone on this estate who wasn't like us from around here."

There is little wonder that the ignorance about each others' communities can easily grow into fear; especially where this is exploited by extremist groups determined to undermine community harmony and foster divisions.'

Source: Home Office (2001).

➔ *For a discussion of ethnic concentration, see Media watch 13 at the end of this chapter.*

❓ *Under what conditions does the formation of communities lead to a polarization of this kind?*

❓ *How can polarization be broken down?*

suspicion, lay behind the riots (see Box 13.13). Some of its main recommendations were:

- the need for a clearer concept of the rights and responsibilities of citizenship, which should be embodied in a statement of allegiance;

- the development of 'a new compact or understanding between all sections of the community', which should include an expectation of competence in the English language, a recognition of women's rights, a commitment to the 'full representation of all minority groups', and 'respect for both religious differences and secular views';

- a 'community cohesion strategy' for each area, which should include 'a new and vigorous approach to recruitment and career progression, in all key agencies, such as the police, local authorities, health authorities and regeneration agencies';

- a 'programme of cross-cultural contact' in schools and moves to desegregate education by getting all schools to offer 25 per cent of places to 'other cultures or ethnicities within their local area', and establishing ethnically mixed catchment areas for new estates;

- a change in regeneration strategies to avoid funding area projects linked to the interests of distinct ethnic communities but also action to 'bust myths' about the way that resources were distributed;

- more action by the police to ban 'inflammatory marches' but also a recognition by minorities that they have tolerated 'certain types of criminality'.

Polarization is not just a consequence of ethnic differences. Indeed, perhaps the most extreme example of urban polarization in the United Kingdom has resulted from the religious divisions of Northern Ireland in general and Belfast in particular. The residential segregation of Catholics and Protestants has increased during recent decades. In Belfast it has become almost total in public housing and working-class areas. Where Catholic and Protestant areas are not kept apart by roads or commercial properties, they are separated by the high walls of the 'peace lines' (*Independent*, 6 April 2004).

In this context it is not surprising that riots returned to the Northern Ireland scene in September 2005. There were violent disorders in seven locations within Belfast and five locations outside. The riots were apparently initiated by Protestants, and the event that triggered them was the rerouting of a traditional Protestant march away from a Catholic area. The rioting was fuelled by Protestant discontent with government housing policy, which, it was claimed, favoured Catholics, and also conflicts between the police and Protestant paramilitaries.

There were deeper, long-term causes of Protestant anger. There was said to be a Protestant sense of abandonment by the British government as it searched for an accommodation with Sinn Fein and the republican movement. Further in the background lay the decline of traditional Protestant working-class communities. These had suffered from the consequences of deindustrialization and were losing out demographically to Catholics. They were also experiencing a crisis of identity in the face of a new confidence among Irish Catholics (*Guardian*, 12 and 13 September 2005; Howe 2005).

In 2009 sectarianism spilled over into racist attacks on East Europeans in Belfast. In April groups of Hungarians, Lithuanians, Slovakians, and Poles, who had been living close to a Protestant working-class area, were forced out. They were followed in June by Romanian families, most of whom then decided to leave Northern Ireland. Sectarian and racist violence were interrelated. In the words of one observer, sectarianism had created a subculture where 'anyone slightly different becomes a target for intimidation' (*Guardian*, 17 June 2009).

Riots are very complex social events, and in understanding and explaining them it is important to separate out:

- the underlying social conditions;
- the dynamics of conflict generation;
- the triggering incident;
- later responses to the situation;
- the explanations of those involved.

The *underlying social conditions* can be linked to the changes in the city that we have examined earlier—the decline of the inner city, concentrated deprivation in the inner city and outer estates, and ethnic segregation.

The *dynamics of conflict generation* involve the vicious circles that easily develop around policing, criminality, and resources. Conflicts over these issues intensify discontent and create a combustible situation. Politicization through the involvement of external political agents, such as the British National Party, can play an important part in this.

Some *incident*, very often of a quite minor kind, can ignite a riot, but the way the riot unfolds depends on *responses* to the situation by groups, organizations, and state agencies. It might take on a quite new character in its later stages.

After the riot those involved provide their own *explanations*, which derive from their particular experiences and beliefs, and their concern to justify their actions. Rioters focus attention on the injustice or unfairness of the incident that precipitated the riot and accuse the police of worsening the situation by overreacting to legitimate protests. The 'authorities' deny that legitimate grievances have played any part in generating a riot and accuse extremists or looters of engineering it for their own purposes. Alternatively, the media are blamed for publicizing previous riots and triggering off 'copycat' incidents.

There is no single or simple reason why such a complex event as a riot occurs. It passes through many stages in its development and at each one new factors can influence its course. It involves complex interactions between many different groups of people with varying perceptions of what is going on. The explanation of a riot must take account of the whole process and not fasten on one particular stage or one particular group's view of it.

Urban regeneration

We have given much attention to changes that are symptoms of urban decline—the problems of the inner city, the decline of the local state, and the return of the riot. Cities have also, however, become centres of regeneration, and we move on here to the role of culture and sport, and the part played by the state, in urban revival.

> **⊃ Connections**
>
> We have already touched on urban regeneration in our discussion of gentrification (see pp. 494–5), which can revive particular areas. In Study 13, at the end of this chapter, we examine the part played by the night-time economy of clubs and pubs in reviving the urban economy.

Cultural restructuring

Culture has been making a growing contribution to the city economy. Zukin (1995: 2) has argued that 'cultural consumption' has become a central activity of the contemporary city:

> With the disappearance of local manufacturing industries and periodic crises in government and finance, culture is more and more the business of cities—the basis of their tourist attractions and their unique competitive edge. The growth of cultural consumption (of art, food, fashion, music, tourism) and the industries that cater to it fuel the city's symbolic economy.

By the 'symbolic economy', Zukin means the production and distribution of images rather than goods. Tourism, for example, sells sights, captured as images by the camera, rather than objects. Employment has steadily increased in a range of occupations concerned with the symbolic economy. Advertising, public relations, the media, designers, and software companies in various ways all make and sell images. Goods are, of course, still produced, but their design has become an ever larger component of their value.

The image of the city itself has become a means of 'place marketing'. Culture, tourism, and investment are here closely tied together. Cultural attractions enable image-makers to sell cities to tourists, who bring money into the city, make it more widely known, and attract corporate investment. This process is linked to the growth of global tourism (see Chapter 16, pp. 625–7) and is yet another aspect of the increasing integration of cities in the global economy.

Higher education is tied into this cultural complex, for universities are major employers and became an increasing source of local consumer demand as governments increased the proportion of 18-year-olds in higher education. The image of the city is important in attracting student consumers as well as tourists.

Cultural restructuring is one of the chief ways of regenerating cities in economic decline (see Box 13.14). The revival of Glasgow as 'European City of Culture' in 1990 has provided the best-known example in Britain, but the

> **📌 Briefing: the cultural restructuring of Lancaster**　　13.14
>
> 'As industry has departed from the city centre Lancaster has been reconstructed as a modern consumption centre preserving the shells of past rounds of economic growth to house new functions—the old customs house as a maritime museum, the warehouses of the riverfront as gentrified homes, canal-side mill buildings as new pubs. One of the main thrusts of all of this is to construct "Lancaster" as an object of the tourist gaze. It has many of the ingredients of a modern tourist mecca: a castle (which in 1991 will become entirely usable for tourist purposes); a river and a gentrified river front; the folly on the hill (Ashton Memorial) just restored at a cost of some £1.5 million; four museums, three of which have been recently completed; well-conserved old, interesting streets with 270 listed buildings; cultural events including the Lancaster Literature festival, and so on.' (Bagguley *et al.* 1990: 161)
>
> ❓ *Can you think of any examples of cultural restructuring in the area where you live?*

process has been going on in towns and cities up and down the country, and across Europe. In Spain, the Guggenheim made Bilbao a tourist destination and demonstrated that architecturally exciting art galleries could lead a city renaissance.

As employment in manufacturing has collapsed, the heritage industry has turned industrial landcapes into tourist attractions. The conversion of ex-industrial buildings into museums, galleries, and restaurants combines nostalgia for the past with the attraction of the new, as in the conversion of Southbank power station into Tate Modern. Cultural restructuring not only provides local employment and brings in tourists but also makes places more attractive to live and work in, and therefore attracts other symbolic economy businesses that can locate themselves where their employees want to be.

Sport cities

The attraction of major sporting events can similarly promote a city's image, bring in visitors and investment, and improve facilities. Urry (2002) pointed out that such events can enable a city to reinvent itself by creating a new identity unrelated to the city's past or location. The intense global competition to host major sporting events, especially the Olympic Games and the football World Cup, shows the importance that cities attach to them.

Will the London Olympics in 2012, as claimed, bring economic benefits, regenerate East London, improve London transport, and provide important new sporting facilities? The experience of other Olympic cities tells an interesting story.

Barcelona 1992

This has been considered a model of regeneration. Barcelona's beach area was brought back to life through the construction of the Olympic village, and a new port was built. The city's image was transformed, and it subsequently became a major tourist centre. It is also claimed that the Games inspired later Spanish sporting achievements.

Atlanta 1996

Commercial sponsorship enabled the Games to break even. The Olympic Park is said to have regenerated the area, while the stadium became the home of the Atlanta Braves baseball team. Other sporting facilities and the Olympic village were taken over by a local university.

Sydney 2000

This has been considered the most successful recent Olympic Games, but the cost to public finances was A\$1.5bn, and there were no obvious economic benefits. The Olympic Park has been labelled a 'white elephant' that diverted money from other public facilities, such as hospitals and schools.

Athens 2004

This left huge debts, amounting to 50,000 Euros per Greek household, and four years afterwards twenty-one out of the twenty-two venues lay abandoned, though transport infrastructure had been improved.

Beijing 2008

The consequences of the Beijing Olympics are not perhaps of great relevance to London, given the rather different character of the Chinese state, but the preparations for them reportedly resulted in 1.25 million people losing their homes.

Sources: on Beijing, UN Centre on Housing Rights and Evictions (2008); on Sydney, Hodgkinson (2007); Osborne (2008).

Taylor *et al.* (1996) have discussed the part played by sport in the regeneration of Manchester and Sheffield. Manchester's (unsuccessful) bids for the Olympic Games were an important part of that city's regeneration strategy, and the bidding process alone attracted funds and improved facilities. Sheffield's success in attracting the World Student Games in 1992 was more of a mixed blessing, generating jobs and sports facilities but also imposing a financial burden that led to cuts in local authority services and jobs.

Manchester's successful bid for the 2002 Commonwealth Games was similarly double-edged. It was claimed that this would regenerate the eastern side of Manchester, attract tourists and capital, generate jobs, and enhance Manchester's image world-wide. Expenditure on the Games did, however, lead to the shutting-down of fourteen Housing Department offices, redundancies among council employees, and the closure of two swimming pools and a boxing club (*Guardian*, 25 July 2001).

Sport stadia play a crucial part in the competition to host major sporting events. The Commonwealth stadium and national velodrome were built in east Manchester to provide the main venue for the Commonwealth Games. The Millennium Stadium has brought major events to Cardiff. The building of new stadia can, however, lead to the closure of old ones, and this can have a devastating effect on the local businesses that have grown up around them and the community that depends upon them.

The attraction of major sporting events, and, indeed, cultural restructuring, require local actions. They need investment by local entrepreneurs but also the active involvement of local authorities in promotion, coordination, reconstruction of the urban landscape, and the provision of facilities. The (somewhat mixed) story of sport cities shows that the economic fortunes of cities depend not only on movements of capital outside their control but also on local initiative, for this can be critical in shaping where the capital flows.

The state's role

The central state became involved with the Conservative government's attempts at urban regeneration during the 1980s. Regeneration was to be brought about by private capital, and the state's role was initially merely to relax planning regulations and provide tax incentives through Enterprise Zones.

A more interventionist approach followed with the creation of twelve Urban Development Corporations, notably the London Docklands Development Corporation (LDDC), which bypassed local authorities. These corporations could compulsorily purchase large areas, invest in infrastructure, and ignore normal planning restrictions.

The LDDC certainly attracted international capital to build the office blocks, most famously at Canary Wharf, that now dominate the east London skyline, but did not provide much employment for local people accustomed to dock-work and other kinds of manual labour. While there was a huge expansion of private housing in the area, the prices were out of the reach of most locals, while funding cuts halted council-house building (Coupland 1992).

The City Challenge programme of 1993 initiated a period of greater local involvement. It brought in local authorities as major partners, and took more account of local needs and local people (Pratt and Fearnley 1996). This programme also went beyond the built environment to target particular areas' housing, education, and crime problems.

The Labour government's 2000 Urban White Paper basically continued this programme. It put forward a coordinated approach to regeneration that would deal with the multiple problems of particular areas. It also focused increasingly on the 'community', through New Deals for Communities and Neighbourhood Renewal Units.

The modernist idea of constructing a whole city, whether in the total vision of the 'ideal city', which we examined earlier (see pp. 488–90), or the 'new town' (see p. 489), appeared long gone in Britain, until the government came up with its eco-town proposals in 2007. These were, however, envisaged as much smaller units of between 5,000 and 20,000 inhabitants, and only four of the many proposals have got to the planning stage, which they may or may not survive. The focus of urban regeneration has been rather more on the local community and the neighbourhood. This has been described as a process of 'post-modern' regeneration that creates 'islands of renewal' in a piecemeal and fragmentary way (Wilkinson 1992).

The post-modern city

The idea that cities have recently entered a new stage in their development has led to the notion of the **post-modern city**, which is similar to the concepts of post-Fordism and post-modern organization and related to the changes they describe. Here, we use this concept to draw together the various changes examined in the section on the 'contemporary city' and link them to changes in city culture and city life.

Like the post-modern organization, the post-modern city is decentralized. The shifting of production and services to the periphery has hollowed out the city and decentralized its activities to the city's edge, where large units readily accessible by car and truck have been constructed on greenfield sites. In the past people typically used public transport to head into the centre for shopping and services, but they now drive in their cars to facilities on the periphery.

> **⊃ Connections**
>
> See Chapter 17, pp. 671–3. for our examination of post-Fordism and Chapter 14, p. 536, for the post-modern organization. Post-modernism is discussed in Chapter 2, pp. 61–3, and post-modern culture in Chapter 10, p. 355.

The post-modern world is particularly focused on consumption and culture, and this is reflected in urban life. The economy of the post-modern city is based less on the production of goods and more on the consumption of goods and services. Cities that were once known as centres of production, as cotton or hosiery or pottery or steel 'towns', are now known for their shopping centres. City politicians have recognized these changes and tried to revive their economies through cultural restructuring and the improvement of the city's image to draw in tourists, investors, and consumers in general.

Style and appearance rule in the architecture of the *post-modern* city. In the *modern* city, function shaped appearance. Products and buildings were mass-produced in standard forms, to provide efficiently functioning structures that were universally applicable and almost indistinguishable. One tower block functioned and looked like another. Post-modern architecture has reacted by playfully creating façades that have nothing to do with the function of the building, often borrowing and combining styles from the past.

This emphasis on style and surface appearance took on an all-embracing form through the simulation of complete worlds. In the *modern* city people went to the cinema to transport themselves into another world, for this was the only way that most people could 'escape reality'. The film industry went on, however, to create complete entertainment cities in the various versions of Disneyland, where we can visit, and for a time stay in, another world and accompany its characters. The experience of other places is simulated in a safe and sanitized environment. In the *post-modern* city people can escape reality by entering other worlds.

Figure 13.18 Modern and post-modern cities

The modern city	The post-modern city
• Centralized	• Decentralized
• Production	• Consumption
• Manufacturing	• Symbolic economy
• Function	• Style
• Faceless architecture	• Façades
• Reality	• Simulation
• Collective consumption	• Private consumption
• Public life	• Private life
• Integration	• Fragmentation

Las Vegas: the ultimate post-modern city?
© Getty Images/Robert Glusic

A process of what Bryman (1999) has called Disneyization has spread Disney principles into many areas of consumption. Theming, the contriving of an experience of another world, is found not only in Disneyland and theme parks but in themed hotels, themed restaurants, and themed shopping centres (see Box 13.17, p. 510). Theming has found its most famous expression in Las Vegas, where visitors to its hotel-casinos can sample simulations of Venice, Rome, ancient Egypt, and so on. The Disney company has constructed on theme park principles a whole new town in Florida, called Celebration, to recreate the feeling of a traditional American small town.

Theming is linked to placelessness, which is one of the most remarked-upon features of the contemporary city. The location of a particular city and its history become irrelevant as theming creates a fictitious place that isolates the themed area from its geographical and historical context. The standardized superstores, shopping malls, hotel chains, and burger bars that are such a feature of the contemporary city have no sense of place about them. The

domination of the high street by brand-name chains selling identical products has resulted in the 'cloning' of urban centres and loss of the distinctiveness of place. Perhaps the ultimate example of the placeless urban experience is the cruise ship (see Box 13.16, p. 510), a floating city that is not only wholly contrived but always moving between places and insulated from them.

The isolation of the individual from place is reinforced by the increasingly private character of life in the postmodern city. The privatizing changes that we have examined in this chapter, the privatizing of consumption and entertainment, the spread of homeownership, the privatizing of public space, focus people more on their domestic and private lives. As public and communal life have declined, people are less inclined to go out into their city and experience what is left of its particular qualities as a place. The particularity of the place where they live loses importance in their lives.

In the post-modern city, urban society has fragmented. The city has been fragmented by decentralization and the

Briefing: the cruising city   13.16

Steven and Malcolm Miles argue that in the cruise ship 'consumer capitalism' has created a 'placeless city':

> in its determination to find new markets through the commodification of city life, consumer capitalism has reached the stage where it can now actively transcend place in the form of a mobile city, a city without place, but *with* consumption. (Miles and Miles 2004: 134)

The cruise ship provides round-the-clock consumption for its passengers. Services are available throughout the day. Food and entertainment are continuously provided. A wide variety of shops, personal services, and leisure activities make available anything a person might wish to buy 'under one roof'. This is a captive market, since opportunities to purchase goods and services elsewhere are extremely limited.

Indeed, although cruises are sold on the basis of visits to romantic tourist destinations, it is the cruise ship itself that is for many people the main attraction. Contact with local destination cultures is carefully controlled. The local culture that is made available is inevitably commercialized, sanitized, and non-authentic. The consumption of local products is also minimal, since cruise ships are fully stocked with consumables before they leave their home port. Passengers hardly experience the places they visit.

The society of the cruise ship, like urban society, is stratified and segregated. There is the division between passengers and crew, but the passengers themselves are divided into classes, while the crew are stratified into occupational hierarchies. The crew are ethnically diverse but also ethnically stratified, as different ethnicities occupy different occupational positions. Segregation excludes from specific areas of the ship members of different passenger classes and categories of crew.

The placeless city has, however, gone beyond cruising with the construction of mobile residential ships. The first such ship, *The World*, has 110 private apartments and claims that it enables people to travel the world without leaving home. The projected *Freedom Ship* describes itself as a 'floating city' with 18,000 living units, 3,000 commercial units, 2,400 time-shares, and 10,000 hotel rooms. It claims that it will have a 'world-class' medical facility, a school system, and an international trade centre. The *Oasis of the Seas* cruise ship, launched in 2009, also calls itself a floating city and is organized by 'neighbourhood' rather than by deck.

Sources: Miles and Miles (2004); www.aboardtheworld.com; www.freedomship.com; www.oasisoftheseas.com;

❓ *What do you think is meant by 'the commodification of city life'? (Visiting the glossary and the index will help you with this.)*

➲ *Assess the claim that 'cruise ships are the cities of the future' (Miles and Miles 2004: 140).*

 ## Briefing: a themed shopping centre   13.17

'Looking across the river from Scotswood, the residents see another miracle of the Enterprise Zone, the £200 million Gateshead Metro Centre, Europe's biggest retail park, which was built on 115 acres of derelict land, and was fuelled by tax allowances and an exemption from rates until 1991. It provided a crèche for customers, but not for its projected four thousand workers. Looking like an eyeless fortress, topped with stiff plastic flags around its periphery, the Metro Centre is a cornucopia of pastiche—customers walk around two million square feet of retail space down colour-coded routes, along 42nd Avenue, or around the Grecian Terrace, or through the Victorian Arcade lit darkly with a night sky all day long. People go for the day to the Metro Centre; they have been seen with flasks and sandwiches as if they were on holiday. The Metro Centre is a shopping resort.' (B. Campbell 1993: 305)

❓ *In what ways can such a shopping centre be considered post-modern?*

dispersal of population. The public life that once brought people at least superficially together has declined and public space is increasingly seen as dangerous and best avoided. Cities have also become more divided by inequality. The well-off have withdrawn behind their fortifications, while the poor have been isolated in inner-city areas of deprivation and outer-city estates. Ethnic diversity has produced some strong communities but also juxtaposed and polarized cultures that do not communicate much with each other.

It would be wrong, however, to suggest that the city has changed completely. Decentralization does not mean that city centres no longer exist, and central shopping areas have fought back against the peripheral stores, often by creating a kind of 'inner periphery' of enclosed shopping malls or retail parks. There are still rush hours, as those living in the suburbs travel into work in the centre, while city centres have acquired new life from the clubs and pubs that pull in people from suburban areas at night (see Study 13 at the end of this chapter).

The post-modern city is superimposed on the modern city, which still surrounds us and still structures our lives. While being aware of continuities, we do need to find ways of grasping change, and the notion of the post-modern city helps us to do this. It highlights the reversal of many previous tendencies and connects together into a coherent pattern many of the features of the contemporary city.

Stop and reflect

In our section on 'The contemporary city' we began by discussing the relationship between recent changes in capitalism and changes in the city.

- In rich countries both deurbanization and deruralization have occurred.
- Global cities have grown in size and become detached from their surrounding areas.
- How has globalization affected urban society?

We then examined the emergence of a new kind of decentralized city.

- Decentralization led to the 'hollowing-out' of cities.
- Deprivation was concentrated in both the inner city and outer estates.
- More recently a reverse process of gentrification has occurred in central areas.
- Has urban space been degendered?

We went on to examine the effects of social change on a range of communities.

- Revisit pp. 477–8 and make sure that you are clear about the meaning of 'community'.

- Although some communities have been weakened, others have become stronger, and some new forms of community have emerged.
- How would you explain the emergence of gay villages?
- Are virtual communities real communities?

We moved on to consider the decline of city management and processes of urban regeneration.

- Privatization has resulted in the decline of 'collective consumption'.
- Urban riots 'returned' in the 1980s.
- Cities have also, however, been regenerated through 'cultural restructuring', investment in sport stadia, and government initiatives.

Lastly, we examined the broad notion of the 'post-modern' consumer city.

- Make sure you understand the meaning of 'theming' and 'placelessness'.
- How have they affected the city's appearance and the experience of city life?
- Can a cruise ship be described as a 'floating city'?
- Has the 'post-modern' city replaced the 'modern city'?

Key concepts

- city 475
- collective consumption 473
- communitarianism 481
- community 477
- gatekeepers 486
- global city 492

- housing classes 488
- post-modern city 508
- primary groups 475
- privatization 501
- secondary groups 475
- segmental relationships 475

- socioscapes 479
- sociospheres 479
- urban ecology 485
- urbanization 482
- urban way of life 475
- virtual communities 499

Workshop 13

Study 13 Cities in the night

At night British city centres are taken over by young drinkers frequenting a mass of late-night bars and clubs. In a lively and intriguing article, 'Receiving Shadows', Dick Hobbs *et al.* (2000) explored the causes and consequences of the rise of a night-time economy that has become a central feature of the 'post-industrial' British city.

This new economy has emerged against the background of industrial cities in decline. As we showed on pp. 493–4, the movement of production to lower-cost locations elsewhere has emptied industrial cities of much of the manufacturing that was once at the heart of the urban economy. The vacuum left by local deindustrialization has been filled by services, as cities have reinvented themselves as centres of leisure and consumption. The night-time economy of bars and clubs has also provided flexible employment for the young, who can combine night-time work with day-time jobs or studies.

The growth of this economy has not, however, simply been an economic process. Hobbs *et al.* (2000) argue that it is also closely connected with a 'new urban governance'. Local government went into partnership with private capital in a 'municipal capitalism' that contrasts with the 'municipal socialism' of old (see p. 487). City councils engaged in an intense competition to regenerate their cities by attracting scarce capital to them. Instead of limiting and regulating city-centre bars, they encouraged them, by relaxing licensing and planning rules in order to attract breweries, pub chains, and leisure companies to invest.

The rapid growth of licensed premises has brought about an intense and homogenizing competition between the various bars and clubs for the young drinkers' market. Old-style pubs, with a diverse, local clientele, give way to 'fun pubs'. Stone floors are replaced by wooden dance floors, entertainment is introduced, and 'a cross-section of quality bitters is replaced by a narrow selection of strong lagers' (Hobbs *et al.* 2000: 709). In the city centre investigated by Hobbs *et al.*, only four of the fifteen traditional pubs there ten years previously had survived.

Areas that are shopping and business districts in the daytime take on a different character during night-time. The line between day and night is a division between work and leisure, safety and danger. Night-time gives 'a release from the rigours and restraints of the daylight hours' but also 'inspires fear and apprehension'. It is a time of 'liminality', by which is meant enjoy-ment of a separate area of life outside its normal boundaries. People can escape the routines of ordinary existence and abandon normal restraints in the experimental pursuit of excitement and illicit pleasures (Hobbs *et al.* 2000: 710–11).

Pubs and clubs exploit this desire for liminality and seek to give people the feeling that they are in a distinctive community of free and equal people, in order to attach their customers to a particular venue. Hobbs *et al.* consider this an illusion. There is no real community or freedom or equality, but rather commercial manipulation and control by business interests, maintained by a subculture of criminality and violence.

They examine this subculture in another article, based in part on a covert ethnographic study carried out by a member of the research team working as a bouncer (Winlow *et al.* 2001). A 'door culture' had emerged among the bouncers 'as a strategy of economic and personal survival, control and domination within a hostile and chaotic working milieu' (Hobbs *et al.* 2002: 355). Verbal skills, local knowledge, and physical presence were important attributes of bouncers, but it was their fighting skills that were crucial. Bouncers often had a criminal record, and there was plenty of scope for criminal abuse of their power.

> As informed by our interviewees, this scope for abuse ranges from the potential for an 'over-the-top' heavy handed response to problem punters, to the opportunist theft from a marooned handbag, to the planned conspiracy to supply, wholesale, a venue's drug of choice. (Hobbs *et al.* 2002: 360)

The maintenance of order in the city at night-time had largely fallen into the hands of bouncers. Manchester city centre attracted about 75,000 people on Friday and Saturday evenings and they were controlled by almost 1,000 bouncers, as compared with some thirty police officers charged with public-order duty. The maintenance of order in the night-time world of the city had effectively been privatized and placed in the hands of people with criminal connections and often a criminal record. The state had apparently abandoned its historic monopoly of the right to use physical force (see our discussion of this in Chapter 15, p. 559).

Registration schemes for bouncers operated by local authorities are supposed to provide a degree of official control and exclude those with a criminal record, but Hobbs *et al.* (2002) do not consider that they are effective or could ever be, even if their role were strengthened by legislation and the proposed creation of a Security Industry Authority. They conclude that 'local police divisions with their wealth of local knowledge and experience are likely to remain better situated to manage and enforce regulation at both a formal and informal level' (Hobbs *et al.* 2002: 363).

Sources: Hobbs *et al.* (2000, 2002); Winlow *et al.* (2001).

❓ What does this study tell us about the relationship between capitalism and the city?

⮕ Go into your local city and try systematically comparing a traditional pub and a cheap alcohol bar under the following headings: the environment; the venue; processes of commercial operation; mechanisms of social control; staff appearance and behaviour; staff interactions with customers; customer appearance and behaviour.

 Media watch 13 Cosmopolitan London

In September 2005 a speech by Trevor Phillips, Chairman of the Commission for Racial Equality, was given much media attention. Phillips argued that a process of ghettoization was taking place in British cities. Multiculturalism has, in Phillips's view, failed, and the populations of British cities are becoming segregated into ethnic communities that do not intermix.

He claimed that research showed that the residential concentration of people of Pakistani origin in Leicester and Bradford is increasing: 'The number of people of Pakistani heritage in what are technically called "ghetto" communities trebled during 1991–2001; 13% in Leicester live in such communities (the figure was 10.8% in 1991); 13.3% in Bradford (it was 4.3% in 1991).' He concluded that 'the fragmentation of our society by race and ethnicity is a catastrophe for all of us' (T. Phillips 2005).

Leo Benedictus (2005) carried out for the *Guardian* an analysis of the residential distribution of different ethnic groups in London, using data from the 2001 Census. He found that around a third of the population of London had been born outside Britain, and many more of its residents were descendants of immigrants who identified with minority ethnic groups. He claimed, however, that 'there are no true ghettoes in the city', since ethnic minorities only rarely amounted to more than 50 per cent of the population of a ward.

The Bangladeshis had become the most concentrated ethnic group. In 1991 there were about 37,000 of them in Tower Hamlets, but there were 67,000 by 2001. Over a third of Tower Hamlets residents considered themselves to be Bangladeshis, and in one ward they amounted to nearly 60 per cent of the population. Pakistanis were much less concentrated and were less than 20 per cent of the population in all wards in their areas.

Indians were mainly concentrated in a large area of west London, where in some wards they were over 50 per cent of the population. What appeared to be a solid Indian area was, however, divided by religion, with a Hindu part to the north and a Sikh part to the west, though in some wards they overlapped. The notion of a solidly Indian area here was misleading, because it concealed two different communities.

Afro-Caribbeans were concentrated in three distinct blocks, in the east, south, and west, where there were large and overlapping black African and black Caribbean populations. The notion of three 'black' areas may again, however, be at least partly misleading, as may be the term 'Afro-Caribbean': 'The two halves of the black community often live close together, sharing shops, schools and history, and yet they have acquired a reputation for not getting along—nowhere more famously than in Peckham . . .' (Benedictus 2005).

The Chinese population was much more dispersed than any of these groups and was nowhere more than 6 per cent of the population of a ward. This was said to be because they prefer to set up their restaurants at a distance from each other!

The white British were concentrated in a ring of outer boroughs, where in a large number of wards they amounted to over 75 per cent of the population, and in one east London ward over 90 per cent.

This is just a brief outline of the distribution of some of the larger ethnic groups, and it is important to bear in mind the sheer ethnic diversity of London. Benedictus (2005) claimed that London is probably the most ethnically diverse city in the world. 'Altogether, more than three hundred languages are spoken by the people of London, and the city has at least fifty non-indigenous communities with populations of ten thousand or more.'

Sources: Benedictus (2005; a *Guardian* special report, with maps, is obtainable from its website); T. Phillips (2005).

⮕ See what you can find out about the original meaning of the term 'ghetto' and the history of its use.

❓ Do you think that 'ghetto' is an appropriate term for the ethnic-minority residential patterns found in Britain?

❓ Under what conditions do ethnic groups become residentially segregated?

Discussion points

Community

Before discussing this, read the sections on 'Urban society', 'Community', 'Changing communities', and Media watch 13.

- What are the key features of a community?
- How important is identification with a place?
- What are the differences between 'container' and 'network' conceptions of community?
- Is city life compatible with community life?
- Should 'gay villages' be considered communities?
- Do communities integrate people?
- Are virtual communities 'real' communities?
- Visit a virtual community on the Web and see what features of 'community' it has.
- Do virtual communities increase or decrease a person's participation in community life?
- Do you think that you are a member of a community?

- Why do you think it is a community?
- What effect does it have on your social relationships?

The post-modern city

Before discussing this read 'Capitalism and the city', 'Cultural restructuring' (p. 506), and 'The post-modern city'.

- What is distinctive about the city that you know best?
- Has it undergone a process of cultural restructuring?
- What image do you think the city has?
- Has there been a shift from manufacturing to services?
- Has there been a shift from production to consumption?
- Is this city losing its distinctiveness?
- List any ways in which it is becoming 'placeless'.
- Do you think that the identity of the city matters any longer to the people who live there?
- How post-modern do you think this city is?

Explore further

Clear and comprehensive coverage of the main issues and the literature on cities and communities can be found in the following texts:

Byrne, D. (2001), *Understanding the Urban* (Houndmills: Palgrave).

Crow, G., and Allan, G. (1994), *Community Life: An Introduction to Local Social Relations* (Hemel Hempstead: Harvester Wheatsheaf). *This is an extremely useful introduction to community, which brings the concept up to date by developing a network perspective.*

Savage, M., Warde, A., and Ward, K. (2003), *Urban Sociology, Capitalism and Modernity* (2nd edn, London: Palgrave Macmillan).

Wide-ranging collections of articles and extracts can be found in these readers:

Kasinitz, P. (1995) (ed.), *Metropolis: Centre and Symbol of Our Times* (London: Macmillan).

Legates, R. T., and Stout, F. (2007) (eds), *The City Reader* (4th edn., London: Routledge).

Westwood, S., and Williams, J. (1997) (eds), *Imagining Cities: Scripts, Signs, and Meanings* (London: Routledge).

For further reading on particular topics:

Delanty, G. (2009), *Community* (2nd edn, London: Routledge). *Ranges across multiculturalism, globalization, postmodernism, and the virtual world in order to reconceptualize this concept in a way appropriate to the contemporary world.*

Dench, G., Gavron, K., and Young, M. (2006), *The New East End: Kinship, Race, and Conflict* (London: Profile). *Following up on the work of Young and Willmott, this examines the impact of immigration and the welfare state on East London communities and ethnicities.*

Eade, J. (1997) (ed.), *Living the Global City: Globalization as Local Process* (London: Routledge). *An innovatory and influential collection of pieces on the relationship between global and local changes in London.*

Jarvis, H., Cloke, J., and Kantor, P. (2009), *Cities and Gender* (Routledge). *A wide-ranging study of this issue, covering European, American, and third world cities.*

Miles, S., and Miles, M. (2004), *Consuming Cities* (Basingstoke: Palgrave Macmillan). *A lively, wide-ranging, and sophisticated examination of the relationship between consumption and urban life, illustrated with detailed examples from around the world.*

Minton, A. (2009), *Ground Control: Fear and Happiness in the Twenty-First Century City* (London: Penguin). *A critique of the impact of urban planning policies, the privatization of public space, and urban regeneration, which proposes an alternative, continental approach that celebrates shared space.*

Sassen, S. (2001), *The Global City: New York, London, Tokyo* (2nd edn, Princeton: Princeton University Press). *Second edition of a classic study that argues that these three cities form a transterritorial marketplace, detached from their national economies.*

Smith, M., and Kollock, P. (1999) (eds), *Communities in Cyberspace* (London: Routledge). *This interesting collection goes beyond the hype to examine the realities of communities formed on the Internet.*

Taylor, I., Evans, K., and Fraser, P. (1996), *A Tale of Two Cities: Global Change, Local Feeling, and Everyday Life in the North of England. A Study in Manchester and Sheffield* (London: Routledge). *A plentiful and fascinating source of material on recent changes in these two cities and how they have affected many different aspects of the lives of those who live in them.*

Thorns, D. (2002), *The Transformation of Cities: Urban Theory and Urban Life* (Basingstoke: Palgrave Macmillan). *This thoughtful and wide-ranging book moves from the industrial city to the 'sustainable' city via topics such as the global city, consumption in the city, and urban social inequality.*

Zukin, S. (1995), *The Culture of Cities* (Oxford: Blackwell). *Highly readable analysis of cities as centres of cultural consumption and production, which examines the Disneyfication of the city.*

 ## Online resources

Visit the Online Resource Centre that accompanies this book to access more learning resources and other interesting material on cities and communities at:
www.oxfordtextbooks.co.uk/orc/fulcher4e/

For information about virtual communities on the Internet, visit the website of Howard Rheingold, one of the pioneers of their development, but bear in mind that he is promoting the idea:
www.rheingold.com

The *Guardian* special report on the ethnic diversity of London (see Media watch 13) can be found through the *Guardian* website:
www.guardian.co.uk

'Britain's Estates are Social Concentration Camps', a summary of the 2009 Fabian Society report 'In the Mix', can be found in the *Independent*:
www.independent.co.uk

Organization, Management, and Control

Contents

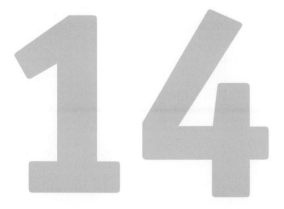

Organizing the McDonald's way: the McDonald's operations manual

'It told operators exactly how to draw milk shakes, grill hamburgers, and fry potatoes. It specified precise cooking times for all products and temperature settings for all equipment. It fixed standard portions on every food item, down to the quarter ounce of onions placed on each hamburger patty and the thirty-two slices per pound of cheese. It specified that French fries be cut at nine thirty-seconds of an inch thick. And it defined quality controls that were unique to food service, including the disposal of meat and potato products that were held more than ten minutes in a serving bin.

Grill men were instructed to put hamburgers down on the grill moving from left to right, creating six rows of six patties each. And because the first two rows were farthest from the heating element, they were instructed (and still are) to flip the third row first, then the fourth, fifth, and sixth before flipping the first two.'

Source: Love (1986: 141–2, quoted in Ritzer 1996: 32).

We spend much of our daily lives working for organizations or trying to obtain goods or services from them. Schools, hospitals, companies, trade unions, churches, government departments, armies, prisons, and theatres are all organizations. We tend to think of them as very different in character because they carry out such different tasks, but they do all have certain basic features in common.

Most of the organizations that we come across are bureaucracies, and we have mixed feelings about them. Bureaucratic organizations do meet important needs by providing us with, for example, employment, health care, and education. They also often seem impersonal, obstructive, and unconcerned with our particular requirements. In this chapter we discuss the way that bureaucracies work but also consider whether there are alternative, less bureaucratic and more effective ways of organizing activities.

An orderly society depends on discipline. Hospital patients are required to accept treatment, soldiers to obey orders, employees to do their work, and students to write essays. But why do people act in the way required by organizations? How do organizations know that they are behaving correctly? We examine the basis of discipline, methods of control, and the surveillance techniques used to monitor people's behaviour.

Organizations require management. Those who run them have to ensure they achieve their goals. What is the best way to do this? One way is to divide work up into simple tasks, give workers detailed instructions, and see that they carry them out, as in a McDonald's restaurant. Is it, however, better for managers to leave it to the workers to decide how best to carry out tasks and concentrate themselves on motivating workers to do their best? How then can people best be motivated? We examine these issues too in this chapter.

We also consider who actually controls an organization. In most organizations there are many experts, but do they control what goes on? In a business organization, are the managers in control or those who own it? Many industries and services have been privatized, but what difference does private or public ownership make? We consider too the global corporation and the degree of control it exercises over operations in different countries.

You will find that we discuss many different organizations, from departments of government and business corporations to mental hospitals and prisons. As you read the chapter, try and apply what you learn to any organizations that you have experience of.

Concepts and theories

We begin by considering briefly what we mean by organizations, before discussing Max Weber's analysis of bureaucracy, which has been central to the sociological study of organizations. One of the defining features of bureaucracy is discipline, and we go on to examine Foucault's influential analysis of this. We also consider his concept of carceral organization and Goffman's similar notion of the total institution.

Organizations

The term **organization** is used in a very general way in sociology. Do not worry too much about the definition of this term, but it is worth sketching out briefly what sociologists have in mind when they use it. An organization is basically a structure for carrying out a particular social activity on a regular basis and will generally have the following features:

- a specific goal;
- a defined membership;
- rules of behaviour;
- authority relationships.

Continuity is a key characteristic of an organization. It has an existence independent of the particular individuals who make it up at any one time. There may be frequent changes of personnel, as people enter and leave or move between different positions, but the organization goes on.

The range of social units that come into the category of organizations is not well defined. It is clear that business corporations, trade unions, hospitals, schools, churches, and armies are all organizations, for they all have the features listed above. It is equally clear that some social groupings, such as a community or a class, are not, for they do not have specific goals or rules of behaviour, though they may provide the social basis for organizations that do.

The term 'organization' is also used to refer to the *process* through which a group becomes organized. Social-class organization provides a good example of this. A social class consists of those who share a common economic situation (see our discussion of class in Chapter 19, pp. 746–7) and is not itself an organization, but it can become organized through the creation of class organizations, such as trade unions or political parties.

There is some ambiguity in the use of the terms 'organization' and 'institution'. Strictly speaking, organizations are not institutions. **Institutions** are established practices that regulate the various activities that make up social life.

A wedding or a funeral is, for example, an institution but not an organization. These practices, however, became increasingly organized as society developed, and the term 'institution' is often used to refer to the organizations that now carry them out. Thus, churches, schools, hospitals, and prisons are often described as institutions, though they should really be called organizations. Goffman, whose work we shall discuss shortly, used the term 'total institution' to refer to mental hospitals and other organizations of this kind.

Bureaucracy

Bureaucracy is only one type of organization but one that has become increasingly widespread. Most of the organizations that we come into contact with are bureaucratic, though not all. Small businesses, for example, are not usually run on bureaucratic lines. In this section we consider the meaning of bureaucracy and the issues raised by bureaucratic organization.

Weber's ideal type

Weber's *ideal type* of **bureaucracy** has been the starting point of the sociological study of organizations. The term 'ideal type' can be a little confusing, and it is important to be clear about its meaning, which we discuss in Chapter 2, p. 38. Weber's ideal type was a statement not of what bureaucracies *ought* to be like but rather of the *key features* of bureaucratic organization.

According to Weber (1914), bureaucracies have the following characteristics:

- *Specialist expertise.* Bureaucracies contrast with earlier forms of organization where there was no systematic specialization of tasks. Expertise depends on education and training, and bureaucracies require qualifications for entry. As Weber (1920: 225) put it: 'bureaucratic administration means fundamentally the exercise of control on the basis of knowledge.'

- *Hierarchy.* There is a hierarchy of officials, with those in higher positions having authority over those lower down. The duties of the different positions are laid down in writing, and behaviour is closely supervised.

- *Impersonal rules.* Particular cases are dealt with by reference to general rules. Bureaucrats are expected to apply rules impersonally and take no account of the particular character of the person with whom they are dealing. This applies whether they are dealing with each other or with the outside world.

- *Discipline.* Bureaucrats are required to obey the rules and carry out their duties in a disciplined way. The bureaucrat is expected to be self-disciplined, but, if the rules are broken, the official concerned is punished.

- *Salaries.* Bureaucrats are paid salaries. This means that they do not have to earn their living as they perform their duties. Their private interests and their public duties are clearly separated.

- *Careers.* Bureaucrats have full-time and permanent posts. Their security of employment enables them to act impartially without fear or favour. They are promoted on the basis of merit and seniority.

The interrelationships between these elements are central to the ideal type. Thus, career officials can operate impersonally because of the independence and security provided by their salaries and their permanent posts. Similarly, disciplined behaviour is bound up with hierarchy and the application of impersonal rules in a non-emotional way.

Since Weber's time there have been numerous studies of bureaucracy that have criticized or revised the ideal type. Martin Albrow (1970) argued that much of the criticism of Weber was ill-founded, because it misunderstood or oversimplified what he wrote. The critics of Weber have been concerned with the *efficiency* of bureaucracy, while Weber was primarily interested in its *rationality*. Weber's writings on bureaucracy should certainly be placed in the context of his general interest in broader processes of rationalization (see Chapter 2, p. 39). He did, nonetheless, make many statements that indicated his belief in the technical efficiency of bureaucracy:

> The decisive reason for the advance of bureaucratic organization has always been its purely *technical* superiority over any other form of organization. The fully developed bureaucratic mechanism compares with other organizations exactly as does the machine with the non-mechanical modes of production. Precision, speed, unambiguity, knowledge of the files, continuity, discretion, unity, strict subordination, reduction of friction and of material and personal costs—these are raised to the optimum point in the strictly bureaucratic administration . . .

Max Weber 1914: 973

The functions of rules

Much of the literature on bureaucracy has focused on the operation of rules. One question it raises is whether obedience to the rules results in effective organization. It also raises more fundamental issues to do with their use and interpretation by different groups.

Robert Merton (1940) examined the *dysfunctions* of rules. He argued that obedience to the rules could prevent

an organization achieving its goals, instead of enabling it to function efficiently. Obedience is considered so crucial that officials are trained to obey rules to the letter, and this can lead to decisions inappropriate to a particular situation. The application of rules can become 'an end in itself' rather than a means of achieving the organization's goals. Merton called this a **displacement of goals**, for the bureaucrat's goal became the correct application of the rules rather than the achievement of the organization's goals. Bureaucrats therefore acquired what Merton called a *trained incapacity* to work effectively.

In his study of an American factory, Alvin Gouldner (1954a) argued that the operation of bureaucratic rules should be understood not in terms of the needs of the organization as a *whole* but rather in terms of the interests of *various groups* within it. Thus, while some rules might be imposed on workers by managers, others were forced on management by workers, while still others emerged in a more 'democratic' way through consultation and discussion. Gouldner identified three patterns of bureaucracy (see Figure 14.1, p. 520):

- *Mock bureaucracy.* This referred to rules, such as no-smoking rules, that were not enforced by management, except when the insurance inspector visited. This non-enforcement helped to create solidarity between managers and workers against the interfering outside world.

- *Representative bureaucracy.* This referred to rules implemented with the consent of workers. Thus, workers accepted the need for safety rules. He called this kind of bureaucracy representative, because the workers themselves were involved, in part through union safety committees, in developing and implementing these rules.

- *Punishment-centred bureaucracy*. This referred to rules that one side tried to impose on the other against resistance. Management tried to enforce a non-absenteeism rule on the workers. The workers tried to force management to fill vacancies according to the procedure laid down by a collective agreement, which required any new job to be offered to existing workers and restricted the managers' freedom of action.

Gouldner emphasized that in other situations a particular rule might fall into another pattern. On an oil rig, the evident dangers of smoking might mean that a non-smoking rule would become an example of representative rather than mock bureaucracy. Arguably, the diminishing cultural acceptance of smoking has anyway shifted non-smoking rules into this pattern. The fundamental point is that rules do not exist in some vacuum but have to be interpreted and enforced before they become a social reality. The interests of groups and the relationships between them are crucial in shaping the way that this happens.

This important study also documented a process of bureaucratization and observed its consequences. Gouldner showed how the *succession problem* created by the arrival of a new boss led to a greater reliance on rules. The new boss lacked his predecessor's informal contacts. He was also under instructions to increase production by tightening up on worker behaviour, thereby violating what Gouldner called the *indulgency pattern* established by his predecessor. As he tried to enforce the rules, he met worker resistance, lost the workers' cooperation, and fell back even more on the formal structure of supervision and control. The workers then retaliated by 'working to rule' and insisting that management obeyed the rules laid down in the collective agreement. A vicious circle of conflict developed and led to the unofficial strike that Gouldner (1954b) analysed in a follow-up study.

In another well-known study, Anselm Strauss *et al.* (1963) examined the use and interpretation of rules in a mental hospital. Hardly anyone knew all the rules, which were frequently ignored or forgotten, and then reinvented when a particular crisis showed they were needed. The rules were only actually used in conflicts between groups, as when nurses invoked 'the rules of the hospital' to fend off the demands some doctors made on them. Rules also always required interpretation before they could be implemented. Did they apply to *this* person, in *this* situation and, if so, to *what* degree and for *how* long?

The various occupational groups in the hospital—psychiatrists, psychologists, nurses, students, occupational therapists, social workers—not only had different interests but had been trained in different ways and held varying and strongly held professional ideologies. Whether a rule should be implemented and how this should be done were always matters for negotiation. Strauss *et al.* saw the hospital as based on what they called a **negotiated order**.

In a similar way to Gouldner, Strauss *et al.* drew attention to the realities of rule use. Rules should not be seen as fixed and objective structures that somehow exist in their own right and regulate people's behaviour. They are always subject to interpretation and implementation. It is important, however, to be aware of differences between organizations in the way that rules are applied. Hospitals are different from factories. The negotiated order of the hospital reflected a distinctive occupational structure, where staff had a degree of autonomy because of their professional or semi-professional status. This autonomy gave them a greater capacity to negotiate than ordinary employees usually have.

For and against bureaucracy

It is wrong to think that Weber was an uncritical advocate of bureaucracy. He was certainly impressed by its efficiency but he was also very concerned about its implications for both creativity and democracy.

He was particularly interested in the character of the bureaucratic state and the relationship between bureaucrats and politicians. Bureaucrats should in principle be the servants of government, but they tended to become a force in their own right. Although they were supposed to be detached and objective, they had their own interests, while their expertise and authority made it difficult for politicians to resist them.

Weber was very aware of the dangers of bureaucratic domination under socialist regimes. He was sceptical of the socialist belief that the abolition of the private

Figure 14.1 Gouldner's patterns of industrial bureaucracy

Pattern of bureaucracy	Example of rule	Who enforces the rule?	Management–worker relationship
Mock	No smoking	Outsiders	Solidarity
Representative	Safety	Management *and* workers	Agreement
Punishment-centred	Non-absenteeism	Management	Conflict
	Vacancy-filling	Workers	Conflict

ownership of industry and the introduction of a planned economy would lead to a more equal and more productive society. He thought that the bureaucrats in charge of planning would become a secretive, selfish, and all-powerful elite. The result would be repression and inefficiency. A capitalist society based on market principles was more flexible and more responsive to people's needs.

While the development of state socialist societies has borne out Weber's fears, capitalist societies too became increasingly managed and controlled by bureaucratic organizations. This occurred particularly through the nationalization of major industries and services, the growth of state welfare, and the state management and state planning of the economy. Then, in the 1970s and the 1980s, the economic crisis of the old industrial societies revived a belief in market forces and led to an attempt to shift from bureaucratic control to market regulation, in part through privatization (see p. 542).

Debureaucratizing tendencies have occurred within business corporations as well. Debureaucratization can be seen both in the search for new organizational forms (see pp. 533–5) and in changing management techniques (see pp. 539–42). These changes too became particularly evident recently, as technological change, growing international competition, and globalization increased the pressure on business organizations to be flexible and responsive.

There has also been a re-evaluation of the importance of emotion in organizations. Weber (1914: 975) had stressed the rational and non-emotional character of bureaucracy: 'The more perfectly bureaucracy develops, the more it is "dehumanized", the more completely it succeeds in eliminating from official business love, hatred, and all purely personal, irrational and emotional elements which escape calculation.' The rediscovery of the emotional aspects of organizations began with the emphasis placed by the human-relations school of management on the emotional needs of the worker and the significance for productivity of relationships with supervisors and other workers (see pp. 539–40). From a different perspective, the Weberian model of bureaucracy has been criticized by feminists for its typically male concerns with hierarchy, formality, and impersonality rather than the female qualities of caring and sharing (see pp. 536–8).

In spite of its negative image, bureaucracy continues, however, to perform key functions in today's society. 'Bureaucracy' is all too often used merely as a term of abuse. When people are asked to fill in forms, or find themselves regulated by apparently unnecessary rules, or wait endlessly for their case to be dealt with, or feel that they are being treated in too impersonal a way, they accuse organizations of 'bureaucracy'. This fails to take account of the vital role it plays in many areas of life. Health and safety rules protect us against accident and disease. The protection of the environment requires the bureaucratic implementation of legislation. Impersonal treatment guards against favouritism and corruption.

Bureaucracies, at least in principle, treat people impartially and equally. They may work slowly but they usually also work thoroughly. When bureaucracy protects us, treats us fairly, and operates efficiently, we never sing its praises. It is important to take a balanced view of its positive and negative aspects.

Discipline, carceral organizations, and total institutions

Discipline is not only a key feature of bureaucratic organization. According to Michel Foucault (1975), it is a central feature of society as a whole, for we live in a 'disciplinary society'. In this section we discuss Foucault's analysis of discipline and examine the organizations that most embody it.

Discipline

Foucault's disciplinary society is based on techniques of control first developed in the seventeenth and eighteenth centuries to produce what he called 'docile bodies'. These techniques attained their most developed form in the nineteenth-century prison, which became a model not only for other organizations but also for techniques of surveillance and control that have spread throughout society.

According to Foucault, discipline involved:

- control of the body;
- surveillance;
- punishment.

Discipline required a detailed *control of physical activities* through the systematic subdivision of space, time, and bodily activity. Thus, criminals were spatially confined in prisons divided into blocks or wings, which were in turn subdivided into cells. Time was divided up by the timetable, which broke it down into short periods, and provided a means of organizing activity, and eliminating idleness. Bodily activity was split up through drills and exercises. The loading and firing of a gun, for example, was carried out through a specified sequence of movements. Once activity had been divided up, it could be reassembled in a coordinated and directed manner.

Discipline was dependent on *surveillance*, the continuous observation of those subject to discipline by those enforcing it. Foucault stressed the importance of visibility.

People were under the gaze of those who controlled them, though the controllers remained invisible. The military camp, for example, was laid out in lines of tents with prescribed spaces between them, specified routes, and carefully positioned entrances and exits, so that all movement could be observed. This principle was eventually extended to many other areas of life. 'For a long time this model of the camp or at least its underlying principle was found in urban development, in the construction of working-class housing estates, hospitals, asylums, prisons, schools . . .' (Foucault 1975: 171–2).

Discipline involved new methods of *punishment* centred on the prison. In pre-industrial times, offences, even relatively minor ones, were punished by public execution of the offender. This might involve torture and bodily mutilation, particularly when the offence challenged the authority of the ruler. Rulers were concerned primarily with the public demonstration of their authority, by displaying their power over subjects' bodies. Laws were implemented and offenders punished in an erratic and arbitrary way. In the late eighteenth century a much more systematic approach to law enforcement and the punishment of criminals emerged. Punishment was increasingly by imprisonment, with its duration related to the seriousness of the crime. Punishment was now concerned not with demonstrating royal power but with maintaining order.

Carceral organization

According to Foucault, these disciplinary techniques were most developed in the nineteenth-century prison. The growth of systematic punishment through imprisonment initiated a process of **incarceration**, which basically means shutting people away from society. The regime of the nineteenth-century prison was different from that of earlier prisons because it cut off prisoners' contact with the outside world. The new prison also controlled prisoners by isolating them from each other, and keeping them under constant surveillance. Foucault used the term **carceral organization** to refer to organizations that controlled people in these ways. We examine nineteenth-century incarceration and the new prison in 'Disciplined organizations'.

The process of incarceration extended beyond the prison, however. This was partly because the prison became the model for other carceral organizations, such as hospitals and factories, which similarly isolated and watched people. It was also because the techniques of control

Guy Fawkes and his co-conspirators in the Gunpowder Plot of 1605 are publicly hanged, drawn and quartered. Why were they punished in this way? Why are people not punished in this way nowadays?

© Getty Images/Hulton archive

Frontiers Aesthetic organizations 14.2

The classic studies of how organizations control their members have focused on the use of incentives and punishments to secure obedience to the rules. Control operates through the conscious minds and rational actions of the organization's members. They might not always obey, but disobedience too was treated as a conscious and rational process, as in Gouldner's 'patterns of bureaucracy' (see pp. 519–20).

There has been a growing interest in the control of people through their bodies rather than their minds. This can be seen in Foucault's emphasis on the discipline of bodies. It can also be found in recent interest in the aesthetic character of organizations. By this is meant aspects of their physical environment, such as office décor, furniture, and building design, which impact on the senses. The physical environment

is used to make employees feel in certain ways about each other and about the organization. It is not the symbolism of the physical environment that counts here, for this operates through the mind, but the feelings created through the senses.

The concept of aesthetic labour, which we discuss in Chapter 17, p. 660, conveys the similar idea that the bodily characteristics of the worker have in many occupations become an essential part of work and a condition of employment.

An exploration of these issues can be found in Gagliardi (1996). For an analysis of the aesthetic character of organizations and a case study of a hotel chain, see Witz et al. (2002). Felstead, Jewson, and Walters (2005) discuss the aesthetic aspects of the 'collective office'—see Chapter 17, p. 675.

---

developed within prisons have been generalized *throughout* society. Thus, according to Foucault, people at large have been increasingly controlled by dividing them up into isolated compartments and keeping them under surveillance. The same principles governed the construction of the housing estate as the prison. The working class was controlled by isolating workers on estates, where they were under police surveillance. This generalization of techniques of control led him to use the terms 'carceral city' and 'carceral society'.

Giddens criticized Foucault for over-extending the idea of carceral organization. Giddens held that factories are not carceral organizations. Some factories may well have adopted disciplinary and surveillance techniques similar to those used in prisons, but workers remain 'free wage labour', able to leave if they wish. Workers have not been isolated from the rest of society and, unlike prison inmates, can organize themselves in unions to resist the power of the employer (Giddens 1981: 172). While Foucault's notion of the generalizing of control techniques is interesting and insightful, Giddens clearly has a point.

The process of incarceration was reversed in the 1960s, temporarily at least, by **decarceration**. In both Britain and the United States there was a shift from locking up 'the mad and the bad' to dealing with them through community programmes. Andrew Scull (1984) has argued that this was a response to the financial crisis generated by welfare capitalism. Arguably, however, this was not so much decarceration as an extension of carceration into the wider

society, by spreading surveillance into the community through, for example, electronic tagging.

This reversal was temporary, anyway, and a process of recarceration began in the 1980s as the rate of imprisonment began to increase rapidly in the United States and other advanced societies. Loic Wacquant (2009) argues powerfully that recarceration is essentially a political process bound up with the growth of the neo-liberal state. Neo-liberalism sought to revive market forces by demolishing worker organization, individualizing labour, and shifting from welfare to workfare. As the economic and welfare responsibility of the 'social state' was rolled back, the penal state grew. This was to discipline an insecure and fragmented labour force, 'warehouse' those who were disruptive or 'superfluous', and strengthen the authority of the state within the more restricted area of life in which the neo-liberal state operated.

> If the same people who champion a minimal state in order to 'free' the 'creative forces' of the market and submit the dispossessed to the sting of competition do not hesitate to erect a maximal state to ensure everyday 'security', it is because the poverty of the social state against the backdrop of deregulation elicits and necessitates the grandeur of the penal state.

Wacquant 2009: 19

Scull and Wacquant are in their different ways linking recent changes in punishment and imprisonment to the changes in the state and economy, to crises of capitalism.

We return to these issues in the later section on 'Dec-arceration and recarceration'.

> ⊃ *Connections*
> Interesting and important interconnections between the penal and other aspects of the development of the state are raised here. We discuss neo-liberalism in Chapter 15, pp. 564–5, and workfare in the same chapter on pp. 564–5.

Total institutions

Although some organizations, particularly those that employ people, may make heavy demands on our time and energy, most leave us with a separate private life. This does not happen in those labelled **total institutions** by Erving Goffman in his book *Asylums* (1961*b*). His study of these institutions was based on his observations of life in a mental hospital, but he was struck by the similarities between mental hospitals and other organizations, such as prisons, boarding schools, monasteries, merchant ships, and military barracks, that apparently performed very different functions.

> ⊃ *Connections*
> Goffman was particularly interested in people's daily rituals and face-to-face interactions, with the construction, maintenance, and change of their sense of identity, and with the way that they present themselves to others and are seen by others. We outline his views on these issues in Chapter 4, pp. 124–5, and you may find it helpful to place the discussion of total institutions in the context of his broader approach.

Total institutions had in common the following features, though not all would be found in every institution:

- *The disappearance of private life*. All daily activities were carried out within the same organization. Any sense of a separate work or private life disappeared.

- *Life in common*. Each daily activity was carried out at the same time by all the inmates together. Eating, for example, became a communal activity. People were moved around in batches that were treated alike.

- *Planned and supervised activities*. Activities were timetabled and controlled in accordance with an overall plan for the organization.

- *Inmate/staff division*. There was a sharp division between staff with access to the outside world and inmates separated from it. There was little contact or communication between the two groups, which held stereotyped images of each other.

- *The mortification of the self*. Inmates experienced the 'death' of their previous identity. They lost their roles in the wider world, at work or in the family, roles that were central to their sense of identity and self-esteem.

Goffman particularly emphasized the way that people were systematically stripped of their previous identity. When they entered a total institution, they were required to change their clothing, while personal objects important to their sense of self were removed. Routine humiliations forced them to act in ways that contradicted their previous identity. This stripping of identity involved the penetration of the private space that protected their identity from the surrounding world. Goffman called this process a 'contamination' of the self:

> The model for interpersonal contamination in our society is presumably rape; although sexual molestation certainly occurs in total institutions, there are many other less dramatic examples. Upon admission, one's on-person possessions are pawed and fingered by an official as he itemizes and prepares them for storage. The inmate himself may be frisked and searched to the extent—often reported in the literature—of a rectal examination. Later in his stay he may be required to undergo searchings of his person and of his sleeping quarters, either routinely or when trouble arises. In all these cases it is the searcher as well as the search that penetrates the private reserve of the individual and violates the territories of his self.
>
> *Goffman 1961: 35–6*

Goffman was particularly interested in the changes brought about by total institutions in the inmates' sense of self, and their responses and adaptations to the situation they found themselves in. He described these organizations as 'forcing houses for changing persons' (Goffman 1961*b*: 22).

Goffman's concept of the total institution is similar to Foucault's notion of the carceral organization, though Foucault was more interested in the techniques of control developed in these organizations than in changes of the self. Although Goffman recognized that some of the features of the total institution could be found in other organizations, he treated total institutions as a distinct class of organizations, while Foucault argued that the control techniques of the carceral organization were extended throughout society.

Stop and reflect

We began this section by discussing the concept of organization before examining Weber's ideal type of bureaucracy and the issues that it raises.

- Make sure you understand the distinctive character of bureaucratic organizations.
- Later studies of bureaucracy argued that many of its features could be dysfunctional for the achievement of an organization's goals.
- Make sure that you understand the following terms: the dysfunctions of bureaucratic rules; the displacement of goals; and trained incapacity.
- Other studies have argued that there are different types of bureaucratic organization, as in Gouldner's typology of mock, representative, and punishment-centred bureaucracy.
- Consider what is meant by a 'negotiated order'. Do all organizations have this?

- Why do you think that bureaucracy has acquired a negative image? Has this view of it been taken too far?

We then considered discipline, carceral organizations, and total institutions.

- Make sure that you understand the following terms: carceral organization and total institution.
- According to Foucault, discipline involved control of the body, surveillance, and punishment.
- Are there good reasons for thinking that we live in a 'carceral society'?
- Goffman claimed that many organizations are 'total institutions'.
- A key feature of these organizations was the 'mortification of the self'. What is meant by this?
- Can you identify the features of a total institution in any organization that you have been in?

The administrative and managerial revolutions

We tend to see the nineteenth-century transformation of society as driven by industrialization, but it was also transformed by technologies of social control. There was an administrative as well as an industrial revolution. In this section we first examine the emergence of the disciplined organizations that were at the heart of the administrative revolution. We then consider the growth of management, the changing relationship between managers and owners, and the rise of public ownership.

Disciplined organizations

Discipline was the key feature of the new organizations, which developed ways of much more closely controlling people, whether in the army, or the factory, or the prison. These organizations emerged through a process of bureaucratization.

Bureaucratization

Bureaucracies of a kind had long existed, and we will briefly consider these earlier forms of bureaucracy in order to highlight the distinctiveness of the new bureaucracies of the nineteenth century.

Weber (1914) recognized that earlier forms of bureaucracy had been created by the empires of ancient Egypt, Rome, and China to administer the huge territories they conquered. The officials in these early bureaucracies were, however, usually paid in kind, taking a share of the produce from the land they governed. They were often simply allowed to extract as much from it as they could. They then became preoccupied with the exploitation of the people they governed, failed to carry out their official duties, and were largely outside the ruler's control. This was not a disciplined bureaucracy in the modern sense of the term.

The creation of salaried bureaucrats was crucial to the rise of modern bureaucracies. Payment by salary, as Weber recognized, meant that bureaucrats could be full-time officials devoted wholly to their duties and under the control of their superiors. Salaries could be paid, however, only if rulers had funds at their disposal, which they could acquire only if there was a money economy for the state to tax. The growth in Europe of a highly commercialized capitalist economy was therefore an essential condition for the emergence of the modern career bureaucrat.

Bureaucratization resulted from rulers' attempts to gain greater control over their territories. The appointment of salaried officials enabled rulers to escape an administrative dependence on the loyalty of uncontrollable feudal lords, a dependence which had been the central problem faced by the medieval monarch. There was also a parallel process of military bureaucratization, as rulers developed disciplined and professional military forces that were loyal to the state (Dandeker 1990).

> **⮑ Connections**
>
> Later on bureaucratization was linked to other aspects of the development of the state, which we examine in Chapter 15. See especially, pp. 559–60, and the discussion of the relationship between state welfare and bureaucratization on pp. 567–8.

While the foundations of modern bureaucracy had been laid by these earlier changes, it was during the nineteenth century that there was a general bureaucratization of society. According to Weber (1914), modern societies developed bureaucratic organization partly because of the problems of administering large, heavily populated territories, but the pre-industrial empires too had faced difficulties of this sort. What distinguished modern societies was the multiplicity of administrative tasks found within them and the importance of expertise in carrying these out. All this resulted from what Weber called 'the increasing complexity of civilization', which was due to the greater wealth, increasing social problems, and growing size of organizations in industrial societies.

The bureaucracies that emerged in the nineteenth century were highly rational organizations. They operated on the basis of the expertise of their officials and the knowledge stored in their files, rather than on traditional customs and beliefs. They functioned in a disciplined and unemotional manner, and their activities were calculated, systematic, and predictable. As we showed in our earlier discussion of his work, Weber considered that the sheer technical superiority of bureaucracy over other forms of organization meant that it would triumph in all fields of human activity, in the business corporation, the church, and the university, as well as the state.

Incarceration

The prison was as typical an organization of the nineteenth century as the factory. Incarceration in a prison eventually became the normal method of punishment for almost all offences, and the prison a characteristic organization of modern society.

The prison embodied all the new techniques for instilling discipline that Foucault identified. Local jails had certainly existed earlier, but prisoners had not been incarcerated. They had not been shut off from contact with the outside world, or confined in cells, or subjected to silence rules, as they were in the new prison or penitentiary, as it was called to emphasize its punitive and disciplined character (see Box 14.3 on p. 527). Techniques of surveillance and control were steadily tightened and culminated in the 1842 opening of Pentonville, a new model prison, in London. Prisons had become carceral organizations.

The ultimate example of discipline and surveillance the *panopticon*, the name given to Jeremy Bentham's nineteenth-century design for a prison. This was a circular building with the cells on the periphery and guards in a central tower. The cells extended the full width of the building and had a window on each side, so that prisoners could be observed from the tower and were silhouetted by the light coming from the outer window. Venetian blinds in the tower windows would make the guards invisible to the prisoners, who would not know whether they were under observation at any particular moment.

Cellular subdivision, the total visibility of those under control, and the invisibility of those in control, were all exemplified by this design. It also minimized costs by enabling the supervision of a large number of prisoners by a small number of guards. No prison was ever built exactly according to Bentham's design, but its basic principles of surveillance and control have been commonly applied in prison construction.

The growth of imprisonment was linked to the development of industrial capitalism. A more systematic means of punishment was needed because of the disorder that accompanied industrialization. Craftworkers reacted against changes that threatened their livelihoods, through, for example, the Luddite machine-breaking movement. Workers challenged the authority of the employer by organizing themselves in unions and taking strike action. Economic fluctuations produced unemployment, and some of those without any means of subsistence resorted to crime. There was a general problem of disorder in the new industrial cities, where masses of people were concentrated outside the traditional rural structures for maintaining order.

Crime also increased because there were new laws to protect the private property crucial to the functioning of a capitalist society. Industrial capitalism involved the widespread trading and movement of goods, which created new opportunities for crime and meant that property required greater protection (Ignatieff 1978).

Prisons were a means of isolating and managing those who threatened social order, as was the asylum for the mentally ill, which was also established at this time. In pre-industrial society, deviants could be absorbed and managed locally within the community. This was not possible in the new industrial cities, so they were separated and controlled in carceral organizations.

The state was closely involved in the process of incarceration. Governments passed the laws that defined

Why are so many prisons in nineteenth-century buildings?
© Alice Chadwick

 Briefing: from jail to penitentiary 14.3

The eighteenth-century jail

'It was common for wives to appear daily at the gates bearing meals for their jailed husbands. They were given the run of prison yards from dawn until locking up, and a judiciously placed bribe would make it possible to remain inside at night. The sexual commerce between the inside and the outside was vigorous. As far back as the seventeenth century, one prisoner had observed that whores flocked to prison like "crowes to carrion". . . . Walls often no more than eight feet high could not stop passers-by from tossing food, notes, and letters over the other side, or stop prisoners from conversing with people in the street, or on occasion splashing them with dirty water.' (Ignatieff 1978: 34–5)

The nineteenth-century penitentiary

'At Gloucester an eighteen-foot wall was constructed around the institution. Outsiders required written permission from the magistrates to get inside. For next of kin, visits were allowed only once every six months. No food, bedding, books, or furniture were allowed in from the outside. The penitentiary enforced a new conception of the social distance between the "criminal" and the "law-abiding". Walled away inside Gloucester, "deviants" lost that precarious membership in the community implied by the free access once allowed between the old jail and the street.' (Ignatieff 1978: 101–2)

❓ *In what ways did the new penitentiary embody the techniques of discipline identified by Foucault?*

behaviour as criminal, increased the powers of local magistrates, and created new police forces to catch the new criminals (Ignatieff 1978). The state also funded, directed, and inspected both prisons and asylums.

Conceptions of deviance were changing. Criminals had previously been considered innately wicked, and the mad were treated as uncontrollable animals. In the nineteenth century it was increasingly believed that both the bad and the mad could be reformed through the application of scientific expertise. Prisons and asylums were places where deviants could be cured as well as disciplined and isolated.

It was indeed at this time that the medical model of madness emerged. Asylums became seen as mental hospitals where the mentally ill could be treated by psychiatry, which was at this time establishing itself as a branch of medicine.

Factory discipline

The maintenance of discipline was also of great importance to the new industrialists. Discipline was crucial to profitable production. Punctuality and uninterrupted work during fixed working hours were essential, for the division of labour made one worker's labour dependent on that of others, while expensive machinery had to operate continuously if owners were to maximize the return on their capital.

Sidney Pollard (1965) argued that the employment of children presented the early British industrialists with a particular problem of discipline. In the early nineteenth-century cotton industry, some 40 per cent of employees were under the age of 18. Child labour was nothing new, but when production was in small workshops or households children were controlled by parents or guardians. According to Pollard (1965: 217), 'the new mass employment removed the incentive of learning a craft, alienated the children by its monotony, and did this just at the moment when it undermined the authority of the family, and of the father in particular' (see Figure 14.2).

In early nineteenth-century Britain employers relied overwhelmingly on dismissal or the threat of dismissal to maintain discipline. This was a method that could work only when alternative sources of labour were freely available, which at this time was generally the case, for there was considerable labour migration, and unemployment was often high. The use of fines or deductions from pay to maintain discipline was also widespread. Corporal punishment too was widely used, particularly where children were employed.

Techniques of labour management developed slowly, for the early entrepreneurs were preoccupied with such matters as machinery, transport, and finance. Specialized managers to take over responsibility for these various matters, and indeed for the management of labour, did not yet exist. Some of the more advanced employers, such as Robert Owen, did invent more subtle methods of control, but these were quite exceptional (see Box 14.4). In the harsh conditions of the Industrial Revolution, the means used to maintain discipline were overwhelmingly negative and relied, as Pollard (1965: 243) has put it, on 'compulsion, force and fear'.

The factory was not a prison, but it was certainly a place of punishment, and the prison was there in the background

Briefing: silent monitors   14.4

In the early industrial factory new techniques were invented to monitor work performance. Best known of all were the 'silent monitors' of Robert Owen. He awarded marks for the past day's work to each superintendent, and each of them, in turn, judged all his workers; the mark was then translated into the colours black–blue–yellow–white, in ascending order of merit, painted on the four sides of a piece of wood mounted over the machine and turned outward according to the worker's performance. These daily marks were entered in a book as a permanent record, periodically inspected by Robert Owen himself.

Source: Pollard (1965: 225).

to back up the authority of the factory-owner. Behind the employer stood the magistrate and laws that made worker organization illegal and breach of the contract of employment a crime. Industrialists (and farmers) could use the courts to discipline their workers. Thus, the prison and the courts played an important part in maintaining discipline in the factory.

Management and ownership

It was the growth of larger and more complex businesses that led to the emergence of specialized and professional management. In this section we examine first the development of 'scientific' management. We go on to consider the increasing power of managers and changes in their relationship with owners. Lastly, we consider the growth of public ownership and its implications for management.

Figure 14.2 Controlling child labour

Different means used by firms to discipline children in British industry, 1833

Negative means	No.	Positive means	No.
• Dismissal	353	• Kindness	2
• Threat of dismissal	48	• Promotion or higher wages	9
• Fines, deductions	101	• Reward or bonus	23
• Corporal punishment	55		
• Complaints to parents	13		
• Confined to mill	2		
• Degrading dress, badge	3		
Total	575	*Total*	34

Source: Factory Commission Survey of 1833 (Pollard 1965: 222).

Scientific management

As we showed above, the techniques used to manage labour in the early factories relied on punishment. Later in the nineteenth century, there was more use of incentive schemes intended to increase productivity by paying workers according to how much they produced. This approach was most systematically developed by the school of thought known as **scientific management**, which emerged in the United States in the 1880s.

The most famous exponent of scientific management was the engineer Frederick Taylor, who published his *Principles of Scientific Management* in 1911 (scientific management is sometimes referred to as Taylorism). Its key ideas were as follows:

- *The subdivision of labour.* Work is broken down into the smallest possible tasks requiring a minimum of skill. Workers can then be trained easily to carry out a particular task in the shortest possible time.

- *Measurement and specification of work tasks.* 'Time-and-motion' study shows scientifically the best way of performing a task, the exact movements required, and the time that they should take (see Figure 14.3).

- *Selection and training.* Workers are selected according to their ability to carry out a particular task and then trained in the best way to carry it out.

- *Motivation and reward.* Workers are solely motivated by the wages they earn. They should be paid not by the hour but according to the amount they produce.

Figure 14.3 Scientific management in action. How long does it take to open a drawer?

An American corporation's unit time values for clerical tasks

Actions	Minutes
Opening and closing	
File drawer, open and close, no selection	0.04
Folder, open or close flaps	0.04
Desk drawer, open side drawer of standard desk	0.014
Open centre drawer	0.026
Close side drawer	0.015
Close centre drawer	0.027
Chair activity	
Get up from chair	0.033
Sit down in chair	0.033
Turn in swivel chair	0.009
Move in chair to adjoining desk or file (4ft. max.)	0.050

Source: Braverman (1974: 321), quoting a 1960 guide to office clerical time standards.

The price per item produced should be determined by the time taken to carry out the movements involved.

- *Individualism.* Workers are motivated by individual self-interest. Social contact distracts them and should be kept to a minimum. Unions are unnecessary, as rates of pay can be determined scientifically, and there is therefore no basis for a conflict of interest between workers and managers.

- *Management.* Management is completely separated from labour. Production is planned by management, which gives workers detailed instructions to follow obediently and exactly.

This method appeared to be scientific because it was based on experiments, and involved the careful measurement of behaviour by work-study engineers trained in its techniques. It was certainly an engineering approach to the management of labour, for it treated workers as machines without feelings or culture, and there was no recognition that work was a meaningful activity. This meant, however, that it was not really scientific at all, for it was not based on a genuinely scientific knowledge of people. Its claim to be scientific was, nonetheless, an important means of legitimating it in an age when science was identified with progress. Weber (1914) considered it to be the ultimate example of rational factory organization but also of the dehumanizing consequences of rationalization.

Scientific management was essentially a means for exploiting labour more effectively. Its emergence in the United States towards the end of the nineteenth century is usually explained by declining industrial profits at this time and the rise of labour movements (Clegg and Dunkerley 1980). Declining profits stimulated employers to develop positive ways of increasing productivity through incentives, rather than simply relying on punishment or the threat of dismissal. Scientific management was also a means of responding to the growing power of unions by taking a tighter managerial control over labour. It particularly attacked the power of the craft unions of skilled workers, since it deskilled labour by subdividing it into the simplest possible tasks.

While it developed new techniques of management, it also embodied the features of industrial capitalism identified by Marx and the technology of organizational control analysed by Foucault. The division of labour, its individualization, and the reliance on monetary incentives were considered by Marx to be typical of capitalist production. The subdivision of tasks, the training of the body in specified movements, and the individualist isolation of the worker exemplify Foucault's analysis of new disciplinary techniques. Scientific management also involved the close surveillance of labour by management, for it required the constant monitoring of a worker's movements and performance.

➲ Connections

See 'Capitalism', in Chapter 17, p. 648, for an outline of Marx's analysis of the capitalist mode of production. In Chapter 17, p. 657, we discuss the implications of scientific management and deskilling for the meaning of work.

Managerial capitalism

The growing size and complexity of organizations made management more important, and this led to the rise of managers as a distinct and powerful group. Some have argued that they took control of industry away from the owners of capital, though others have rejected this view and claim that control actually passed at this time into the hands of finance capitalists.

Ownership and control were originally fused in the person of the industrial entrepreneur, who combined the work of financier, works manager, engineer, and accountant. The problems of coordinating an increasingly specialized division of labour, rapid technical development, and the growing size of companies made it impossible to carry on in this way. Owners kept overall control, but the detailed control of company activities was delegated to a managerial bureaucracy. Increasingly, specialist managers developed a degree of professional autonomy. Thus, personnel management and marketing, for example, eventually became distinct fields in their own right, with their own career structures, qualifications, and professional institutes.

Ownership too changed. In the first half of the nineteenth century ownership was *personal*. Factories were owned by an individual, a family, or a small number of partners. Mid-century legislation then made possible *impersonal* ownership through joint-stock companies. These were owned by shareholders, who could be any members of the general public who had invested in the company through the Stock Exchange. The new companies were controlled by directors, elected by and responsible to the shareholders. These companies allowed businesses to draw on a much wider pool of capital to finance investment. Apparently rather technical changes in company law were immensely important, for they made possible the growth of the giant corporations that dominate the world economy today.

There have been widely differing interpretations of these changes. There were those, such as Berle and Means (1932) and Alfred Chandler (1962), who argued that ownership and control had actually become separated. They claimed that share ownership had become so fragmented among a mass of small shareholders that owners no longer had any control over corporations. Control had passed into the hands of managers, and a **managerial revolution** had taken place. Some indeed argued that the exploitative capitalist had been replaced by the 'socially responsible' manager, who was concerned not so much with profitability as with keeping the company going by balancing the competing claims of all those who had a stake in it, from shareholders to trade unions. A post-capitalist social order had emerged.

Marxists, such as Hilferding (1910) and Aaronovitch (1961), claimed that ownership was more important than ever. The spread of share ownership reduced the power of *individual* owners, but enabled financial organizations with large shareholdings to become the *effective* owners. Effective owners were those who were able to use their ownership of shares to exert influence over the company, even though they did not own a majority of its shares. Economic power was concentrated, as a small number of large banks became the effective owners and gained control of the large corporations that monopolized production. The age of industrial capital had been followed by the age of **finance capital**.

These writers too argued that ownership was separated from production, since finance capital was interested only in profit and not concerned with the management of production, so long as this was profitable. It was not, however, the managers but the finance capitalists, those who controlled the big banks and other financial organizations, who had ultimate power. They could hire and fire managers at will. Indeed, their concern with profit alone made them more ruthless than traditional industrial entrepreneurs, who had been deeply involved in the day-to-day running of their businesses.

John Scott (1997) has examined this debate in the light of the accumulated research and concluded that owners still exercise control. By owners he means, however, not small individual shareholders, for he agrees that they are powerless, but those in effective possession, who are typically a loose grouping of major shareholders. Scott has called these groupings 'constellations of interests'. They are dominated by financial institutions, such as insurance companies, banks, and pension funds, but often include other non-financial companies as well and also some executives and wealthy families with large shareholdings. They are linked together by interlocking directorates. These involve the directors of one company having seats on the boards of others (see Figure 14.4).

The opposed theories of managerial revolution and finance capital have each recognized important aspects of social change, but neither can be accepted in its entirety. Managers do, indeed, have day-to-day power and much autonomy in their decision-making, but they are constrained by the interests and pressures of the leading shareholders. These shareholders are in most cases not a tightly integrated group but a looser constellation of interests. The insights of the two theories need to be combined if we are properly to understand how business is controlled.

Figure 14.4 Ownership and control

The network of control

In contemporary Britain, just under a half of the top 250 enterprises are controlled through constellations of interests. Their controlling constellations overlap a good deal and form a large intercorporate network of controllers, linked through cross-shareholdings and interlocking directorships. Less than a hundred enterprises are at the heart of this network (J. Scott 1997).

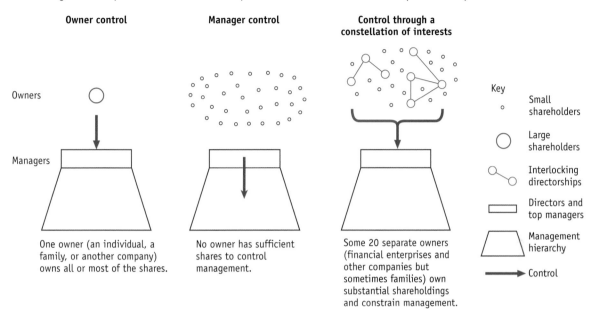

Public ownership

In some societies the state began to take over the ownership of certain industries and services. This led to another aspect of the managerial transformation of capitalism, the growing state management of production.

Public ownership was seen by socialists as an essential step in the transition from a capitalist to a socialist or communist society. Marx and his followers considered that the private ownership of the means of production was the main feature of capitalism. Some Marxist writers believed that the growing concentration of private ownership under finance capitalism made it easier, however, for the state to take control of industry, for it would only have to take over the small number of companies already in effective control of the economy.

Public ownership did develop in Britain but for rather different reasons. It began during the later nineteenth century with moves by city councils to control the supply of water, gas, and electricity, and improve methods of urban transport. The first major expansion of state control was driven by the imperatives of war. During the First World War the government took control of coal-mining, the railways, shipping, and the munitions industry. All this was dismantled at the war's end, but there was some movement towards greater state control and public ownership during the inter-war years. This was motivated by nationalist rather than class concerns, by the problem of

reorganizing Britain's more archaic industries, particularly coal-mining, and by the belief that new services, such as broadcasting and civil aviation, should be kept under state control.

The main extension of public ownership was carried out by the Labour governments of 1945–52 (see Figure 14.6 on p. 532). This was certainly in part motivated by the labour movement's belief that key areas of the economy should be brought under public control, but it mainly resulted from continued nationalist concerns with the backward, inefficient, and fragmented character of key industries and services. Public ownership was seen as a means of overcoming backwardness, of reorganizing these industries and services into more effective and modern units. Significantly, this extension of public ownership was described as the nationalization, not the socialization, of ownership.

What difference did nationalization make? Those who had hoped for a socialist transformation of the economy

Figure 14.5 Interpreting changes in ownership

Issues	Managerial theorists	Marxists
Ownership	Dispersed	Concentrated
Controllers	Managers	Banks/financial corporations
Social order	Post-capitalist	Finance capitalism

Figure 14.6 The growth of public ownership, United Kingdom, 1850–1950

Years	Main extensions of public ownership
1850s–70s	Municipal ownership of water, gas, and trams
1892–1912	Nationalization of telephone companies
1914–18	State takes temporary control of transport, coal-mining, and munitions
1920	Law passed to combine 120 railway companies into 4 regional groups
1926	British Broadcasting Corporation created
1926	Central Electricity Board created to buy and distribute electricity
1933	London Passenger Transport Board created to control buses, trams, and underground lines
1938	Coal Act takes coal reserves into state ownership
1940	British Overseas Airways Corporation created
1946	Bank of England nationalized
1946	Coal, cable and wireless, and civil aviation nationalized
1947	Road and rail transport nationalized
1947	Electricity generation nationalized
1948	British Gas created
1948	National Health Service created
1949	Steel industry nationalized

were soon disappointed. Since each industry was run by its own relatively independent board, nationalization did not result in the increased planning of economic development. Although some token worker–director schemes were introduced, workers and their unions found that they had no greater influence over management than before nationalization. The nationalized industries anyway had to operate within the framework of a capitalist economy and were soon themselves required to make a normal commercial profit on their operations.

This is not to say that nationalization achieved nothing. It was, however, more a vehicle for the state reorganization and coordination of *particular* industries and services than a means of controlling the economy or changing the capitalist relations of production. It led to greater state control but not to workers' control.

In state socialist societies, public ownership and state planning did become the norm. The ruling party directed economic development and planned production. Although factories were supposedly controlled by workers' councils, these actually became a means through which the ruling party controlled and disciplined labour, except in Yugoslavia. There, after a degree of independence from the Soviet bloc had been achieved in the later 1940s, workers' councils did acquire some real autonomy. There were no independent trade unions in state socialist countries, including Yugoslavia.

Broadly speaking, in state socialist countries the state was in control and Weber's bureaucratic nightmare had been realized. As we pointed out in our discussion of Weber's view of bureaucracy, he was deeply concerned that bureaucratization would weaken democracy and result in a loss of freedom and creativity. He considered that this was particularly likely to happen under socialism, for the power of the bureaucrat would no longer be balanced and limited by the power of the owner of private capital.

 Stop and reflect

This section has been concerned with the administrative and managerial revolutions that began in the nineteenth century. We began by examining the emergence of disciplined organizations.

- We argued that the prison should be considered as typical an organization of the nineteenth century as the factory.
- What was new about the nineteenth-century penitentiary?
- Discipline also had to be maintained in the factory.
- Why was discipline so important there?
- How was the factory related to the prison?

We went on to consider the development of management and the changing relationships between managers and owners.

- Make sure that you understand the following terms: scientific management; managerial revolution; and finance capital.
- What was scientific about scientific management?
- Ownership and management became increasingly distinct.
- Did this mean that owners lost control?
- From the 1850s to the 1950s public ownership increased in Britain.
- Did the extension of public ownership change capitalism?

Towards new structures of control

The techniques of control developed during the nineteenth and early twentieth centuries enabled a massive expansion in both the productive capacity of industrial capitalism and the apparatus of the modern state. These techniques have, however, been challenged in recent times. New methods of control began to emerge that reacted against bureaucratic structures. We examine these in this section and consider whether they have transformed organizations or merely further developed the framework established by the administrative revolution.

Debureaucratization?

Although Weber was highly critical of bureaucracy, he thought that its technical superiority would make it the dominant form of organization in modern societies. As we showed on p. 519, the efficiency of the bureaucratic model has, however, been questioned, and we consider here alternative forms of organization. We also discuss the feminist argument that bureaucracy is patriarchal in character and organizations should be feminized.

Organic organization

Rigidity was one of the main features of bureaucracy revealed by case studies of organizations. More flexible organizations, claimed to be more appropriate to situations of rapid technical change or market uncertainty, have been developed.

In their classic study of the Scottish electronics industry, Burns and Stalker (1961) examined the emergence of a more flexible form of organization, which they called *organic* and contrasted with *mechanistic* organization, which they also found within this industry.

The *mechanistic* type had a clearly specified division of labour, coordinated by a hierarchy of managers. Everyone knew exactly what their job required and what their responsibilities were. Decisions were taken at the top, where knowledge of business matters was concentrated. Orders came from the top down, and subordinates were expected to obey instructions. This structure led to conflicts between *line* and *staff* managers, an example of the conflict between hierarchy (line) and expertise (staff) commonly found in bureaucratic organizations. As Gouldner (1954a) pointed out, there is a tension in the Weberian model of bureaucracy between authority based on expertise and authority based on hierarchical position.

The *organic* type was much more flexible. Jobs changed as the company's projects changed and relationships evolved within the organization. Roles were not clearly defined, and there was little sense of particular responsibilities.

Figure 14.7 Mechanistic and organic organizations

Mechanistic	Organic
• Rigid division of labour	• Flexible tasks
• Hierarchy	• Network
• Authority based on position	• Authority based on expertise
• Obedience to authority	• Collective problem-solving
• Instructions	• Advice and consultation
• Defined duties/ responsibilities	• General commitment to goals
• Vertical communications	• Lateral
Stability	*Change*

Source: Adapted from Burns and Stalker (1961: 119–22).

Positions were still stratified by seniority, but authority was exercised by those with most expertise, wherever they were located, and through a network rather than a hierarchy. Communication was lateral rather than vertical. The ethos of the organization was not obedience to authority but collective problem-solving. Commitment was not to the duties of the job but to the goals of the company and wider values of technical progress.

The *mechanistic* organization was clearly the more bureaucratic of the two. Its machine-like character made it inflexible, and it responded poorly to the demands of change in an industry with a high rate of technical innovation. Burns and Stalker concluded that the more flexible *organic* form was much more appropriate to such an environment. They did not, however, argue that it was generally superior to the mechanistic form or that bureaucratic organization was outmoded, for they recognized that the *mechanistic* form was more appropriate to situations of stable production.

Network organization

A more radical and more recent departure from the classic bureaucratic organization is the network organization, which is a much more open structure based on *information technology*. Computer networks can link not only those inside a company but those outside, so that a factory, its component suppliers, and retailers are all interlinked. Instead of operating through the detailed regulation of its members' behaviour, the network organization plugs them in on a contractual basis when it requires their work. It operates on the basis of market rather than bureaucratic coordination.

Thus, the organization can subcontract work through the network to self-employed teleworkers or specialist outside organizations that provide services when required.

Are network organizations non-bureaucratic?

© Alice Chadwick

Instead of directly employing designers or marketing specialists, it can simply call them in through the network when it needs them. At the other end of its activities, instead of selling its products, it can produce according to the orders coming through the network from retailers or franchised outlets. Rapid communication and a highly flexible structure make a network organization highly appropriate to post-Fordist production, which we discuss in Chapter 17, pp. 671–2.

It is hard to establish the boundaries of a network organization or to distinguish between its internal and external activites, as in the Benetton case discussed by Stewart Clegg (1990). If it is defined by its own employees, Benetton consists of certain design and production facilities in north Italy. But are not Benetton's thousands of retail outlets, franchised operations not staffed by Benetton employees but selling only Benetton products, part of its organization? What about the hundreds of small firms and the homeworkers who make the products or carry out certain stages in their production, such as finishing off clothing?

The subcontracting of components production or the use of homeworkers to finish goods is nothing new, but what distinguished Benetton was that the bulk of its production was carried out in this way. Clegg (1990: 121) suggested that it should be thought of 'less as an organization *per se* and rather more as an organized network of market relations premised on complex forms of contracting made possible by advances in microelectronics technology'.

Virtual organization

The ultimate network organization is the virtual organization that exists only in an electronic form, and this is promoted by some as the future form that organizations will take. It is important, however, to distinguish between organizations that make an extensive use of electronic communications and virtual organizations. Most organizations of any size will communicate electronically, and this may well enable them to develop more of a network structure, but it does not make them virtual organizations that operate almost entirely on an electronic basis.

Virtual organization is particularly appropriate for organizations whose activity mainly involves information and communication, and this would include some financial organizations. Not all such organizations can, however, take such a form. Call centres, which carry out such functions, are far from virtual in character and have many of the characteristics of much older workplaces (see Chapter 17, p. 670). Apparently electronic organizations, such as Amazon, have offices, warehouses, and distribution systems that are hardly virtual (see Chapter 17, p. 648).

Virtual organization may also be appropriate for short-lived operations, which assemble people electronically for a particular purpose and are disbanded once a project is completed. Social movements, such as the anti-globalization movement (see Chapter 16, p. 634), may be largely virtual organizations that bring people together for particular demonstrations, though these are anything but virtual.

The advocates of virtual organization have argued that it has a special character that distinguishes it from all previous forms of organization. It is claimed that it is by its very nature decentralized and unhierarchical. This claim may well, however, reflect ideal conceptions of what the world of the Internet should be like rather than being a description of how such organizations actually operate. Even virtual communities have rules and some form of government by those who formulate the rules and enforce them.

> **➜ Connections**
> We have a section on virtual communities in Chapter 13, pp. 499–500, and you may find it interesting to compare them with virtual organizations.

It is important to stress that information networks of all kinds actually facilitate central control. They do certainly enable the flow of information across the organization, so that communications can be lateral and less dependent on central coordination or a managerial hierarchy. They also enable the decentralization of management. They do, however, provide those who control an organization with access to very detailed information about the behaviour and performance of its members. Electronic communication, particularly when combined with the huge potential for surveillance that this provides (see our discussion of this on pp. 550–1), can be a highly effective vehicle of central control.

Cultural alternatives

Much of the early literature on organizations assumed that their principles were universal, but later studies have argued that there are important international variations in their character.

The economic success of East Asian countries led to a growing interest in their organizational patterns and the possibility of learning from their experience. We will consider here Stewart Clegg's account (1990) of the Japanese and Chinese patterns of organization.

Japanese industrial organization typically involves less specialized and more flexible occupations than a Western industrial organization. Workers are not seen as having particular skills but are expected to carry out any task required by management. They are moved through the various operations in a factory and acquire a knowledge of the connections between its various parts, which improves communication and develops lateral networks. Research and development are less separated from production, for personnel will have had experience of each other's work. Management is similarly unspecialized, and there is a regular rotation of managers through different functions.

> **➔ Connections**
>
> To understand the wider context in which this kind of organization has developed, refer to the discussion of Japanese industrial relations in Chapter 17, p. 679.

Chinese business organization in Taiwan is radically different from both the modern Western and Japanese models. Taiwan businesses are organized on a family basis. The head of the family that owns the business controls it, and the key tasks of managerial surveillance and control are kept, so far as possible, inside the family. Authority is related to age. Relationships are personal, familial, and based on trust—quite opposite in character to the impersonal and formalized relationships of bureaucratic organizations.

As Clegg points out, the key point is that, while small family businesses everywhere will tend to have these features, in Taiwan they are found in large organizations as well. Indeed, the need to provide an inheritance for sons, who will receive equal shares of the father's estate, has driven the expansion of Taiwan family businesses. When profits lead to the accumulation of capital, new businesses are founded, which are run by members of the family, usually by sons, who inherit them on their father's death.

These examples show that unbureaucratic forms of organization can work well in the contemporary world. They also show that there is no such thing as a single East Asian model. Japanese and Taiwanese businesses are organized on very different principles but both have been highly successful. The success of these models suggests that the structures promoting organizational effectiveness are culturally specific. What works in one society with one set of beliefs and practices will not necessarily work in another.

Clegg warns, however, against jumping from a universalism that ignores culture to a cultural determinism that explains everything by it. Both Japan and Taiwan are predominantly Confucianist in culture, but they have developed very different organizational patterns. Clegg proposes an *embedded* view of organization. This accepts that organizations are based in a particular societal context but includes in this not only the culture but also the institutions, laws, and policies of the society. It also recognizes that their character is not *determined* by their context, for they are actively *constructed* out of the 'materials available' (Clegg 1990: 7).

THEORY AND METHODS   **14.5**

Modern and post-modern organizations

Modern (Fordist)	Post-modern (post-Fordist)
● Differentiated	● Dedifferentiated
● Specialized roles	● Unspecialized
● Centralized	● Decentralized
● Hierarchy	● Network
● Mass production	● Flexible production

Stewart Clegg (1990) argued that the changes that we have been discussing in this section have created **post-modern organizations.** He identified *modern* organization with the Weberian model of bureaucracy and *post-modern* organization with various alternative organizational structures. Organic organizations, the East Asian models, and network organizations are all examples of post-modern organization, and Clegg is at pains to emphasize that there is no single post-modern form. Modern and post-modern organizations broadly correspond with the distinction between Fordist and post-Fordist production (see Chapter 17, pp. 671–3).

Feminizing the organization

Another line of criticism has come from those who argue that Weber's emphasis on the formality and impersonality of bureaucracy conceals its gendered character.

Bureaucracy and patriarchy have arguably been historically interrelated and mutually reinforcing. Nineteenth-century bureaucratization took place in a highly patriarchal society and produced male-dominated organizations. During the twentieth century these organizations increasingly employed women, but in junior clerical positions, where they were excluded from promotion.

Banking provided a good example of this. Up until the 1960s sex discrimination in banking was quite explicit, with separate salary scales for men and women, and the requirement that on marriage women had to resign from their jobs, though they were usually then reappointed to non-career grades. It was not until the 1980s that this situation really changed, after the recruitment practices of Barclays Bank had been referred to the Equal Opportunities Commission (Crompton 1997).

Patriarchy operated not only through the exclusion of women from bureaucratic careers, but also through the dependence of the male career on gendered domestic roles. This applied both inside and outside the office. Inside the office, secretaries became 'office wives', who carried out personal caring functions and provided emotional support for the boss. Outside the office, the successful male career

Can organizations be feminized?

© Alice Chadwick

 Briefing: solicitors and secretaries 14.6

'The most claustrophobic example of control through sexuality (no-one had yet labelled it "harassment") concerns a legal practice which was, for a country town, quite large. The atmosphere was one of compulsory jocularity: solicitors and secretaries gaily exchanged insults and sexual banter with each other all day, and there was a great deal of friendly fondling and patting of bottoms. They also intermarried and had a shared social life of parties and barbeques. Ex-secretaries with their babies were regular visitors, and often came back to work on a part-time or temporary basis. Beneath the enforced egalitarianism and informality there was a rigidly enforced sexual division of labour. The partners could not imagine taking on a woman lawyer or the possibility that any of the "girls" might have the capacity to do "law". . . . The women were clear that their role was to service men and were willing to put up with what was constant sexual innuendo. The overall feel of the place was not dissimilar to a brothel. While the secretaries made continuous use of mockery and parody, it seemed only to reaffirm them in "traditional" boss–secretary relationships.' (Pringle 1989: 93–4).

❓ *Have you come across examples of sexual behaviour or the use of sexual language in organizations that you have worked for?*

❓ *What effect has this had on work relationships?*

depended on the housewife, whose servicing and emotional labour enabled the husband to give time and energy to his organization. The bureaucrat's self-disciplined devotion to duty, which was central to Weber's ideal type, depended on the domestic division of labour.

If gender is important to office relationships, what about sexuality? The classic literature on organizations has focused on their rational and non-emotional character, leaving sexuality out. Rosemary Pringle has argued, however, that sexuality pervades the life of the office 'in dress and self-presentation, in jokes and gossip, looks and flirtations, secret affairs and dalliances, in fantasy, and in the range of coercive behaviours that we now call sexual harassment' (Pringle 1989: 90).

Some have treated this as inappropriate behaviour that spills into the work setting but is nothing to do with work. Thus, Rosabeth Moss Kanter (1977) recognized the existence of sexual behaviour in the office but treated it as a hangover from pre-bureaucratic relationships that should be eliminated. This approach maintained the Weberian view of bureaucracy as an impersonal structure in which emotional and sexual relationships should play no part.

Others have argued that it is an integral part of authority relationships. According to this view, sexual harassment at work is not just an overflow of non-work behaviour into the work situation; it is one of the means by which male superiors establish their power over female inferiors. It is also used to justify the exclusion of women from occupations that involve 'serious' work by treating them as irrational reservoirs of sexuality and emotionality (see Box 14.6).

Treating sexual behaviour at work as sexual harassment presents other problems, however. Pringle accepted that sexual behaviour is a means by which women are subordinated but also pointed out that it can make women 'the pathetic victims of sexual harassment'. Account must also be taken of 'the power and the pleasure' that women can get from sexual interaction at work (Pringle 1989: 101–2).

Feminist responses to the patriarchal character of traditional bureaucracies have varied. Some have argued that they should be forced to open their senior positions to women, but, although the opening-up of careers to women may reduce discrimination, it does not necessarily make organizations less patriarchal in character. Women may have to act like men in order to reach and hold senior positions. Crompton and Le Feuvre (1992: 116) reported that many of the women managers they studied 'had felt constrained to behave as "surrogate men"—even to the extent of remaining childless'.

Women in senior posts can, nonetheless, make a difference. Watson (1992) claimed that 'femocrats' in the relatively open Australian state bureaucracy have been able to make some important changes in policies, laws, services, and the bureaucracy itself that are favourable to women.

A more radical approach has argued that organizations cannot be feminized by women in senior positions because bureaucracies are inherently masculine in character. Their emphasis on hierarchy, formality, and impersonality is typically male. Women should instead seek to create a different kind of organization that embodies the female qualities of 'caring and sharing'.

There are two strands to this argument:

- a belief that activities can and should be organized in a more democratic, more participatory, and cooperative way;
- the notion that women are more able than men to create this kind of organization, as the organizations created by the women's movement are said to have shown.

As Witz and Savage (1992: 20) have pointed out, the problem with this approach is that it assumes 'gender differentiated modes of social action'. It presupposes that women are socialized into more participatory, cooperative, caring, and sharing patterns of behaviour. This kind of socialization is itself, however, a consequence of patriarchy, since it is male domination that pushes women into caring roles in the household. The notion of the feminine organization is, in other words, itself bound up with patriarchal assumptions.

Witz and Savage suggest that we should recognize that organizations require both 'male' and 'female' activities, and that both men and women can carry out both sets of activities, instead of attaching different principles of organization to gender. What matters is the relationship between these activities, and the way they are divided and distributed between men and women. Witz and Savage argue that work activities should be degendered. As they nicely put it: 'men can no longer go on simply organizing the world; they have to take responsibility for tidying it up too' (Witz and Savage 1992: 26).

Continued bureaucracy

Bureaucracy has been challenged and bureaucratization to some degree reversed. Has a process of **debureaucratization** taken place?

A growing awareness of the disadvantages of bureaucracy and of the existence of alternatives that seem to work better has led to the construction of less bureaucratic forms of organization. The growth of organizational studies has contributed to this process by stimulating reflection on organizational character and structure, drawing attention to structures embodying different principles and values, and designing more appropriate organizations for specific purposes. Organizations have also had to adapt to changes in their environment, to advances in information technology, changing markets, and feminist challenges.

These changes have occurred only in some organizations, however. George Ritzer has argued that the broad tendency of organizational development is towards greater rationalization and bureaucratization, which he calls the McDonaldization of society (but see Box 14.7). He claims that the principles of the fast-food restaurant exemplify the rationalizing tendencies identified by Max Weber as characteristic of modern society. McDonald's offers efficiency, calculability, and predictability. It also tightly regulates its employees (see the opening extract of this chapter), and even controls the behaviour of its customers, by, for example, providing uncomfortable seats that 'lead diners to do what management wishes them to do—eat quickly and leave' (Ritzer 1996: 11).

There has, furthermore, been no debureaucratization of society as a whole. Bureaucratic organization remains the principle way of organizing large-scale activities, and information technology has simply improved their coordination and increased central control of them. Although the bureaucratic model has been challenged in some businesses, where greater flexibility and higher commitment have become crucial to competitiveness, in others bureaucratic organization is still considered the best way of coordinating the routine production of standard goods and services. Bureaucratic organization also remains central to activities concerned with health, safety, equal opportunities, and protection of the environment, where objectivity, consistency, and impersonality are essential.

As we show in Chapter 15, p. 583, although deregulatory government policies may have diminished state regulation in some important areas of activity, the overall level of regulation has increased—and regulation almost always means bureaucratic organization. The term 'debureaucratization' is a useful means of drawing attention to important changes in some organizations, but these must be placed in the context of continued bureaucratization elsewhere.

Figure 14.8 Three ways of feminizing organizations

- *Femocracy:* increasing women's access to senior positions.
- *Feminine organizations:* creating alternative feminine organizations.
- *Degendering activities:* redistributing activities equally between men and women.

Marek Korczynski (2001) argues that Ritzer's concept of McDonaldization fails to grasp the full character of service bureaucratization. The Weberian rationalization of production certainly operates in service organizations, but these are distinctive in the *simultaneity* of production and consumption, which operate according to different principles. The discipline of production conflicts with the customer's pleasure in consumption, and at least some service organizations have to satisfy customers in an immediate way. The requirements of a customer orientation contradict those of rational organization and set up tensions within the organization.

Korczynski discusses this issue after studying five call centres in different countries. Employees were expected to empathize with customers and seek to meet their needs. Indeed, they were selected partly on their capacity to do this and trained to do it. Managers tried also, however, to minimize costs and to control employee behaviour by standardizing responses and limiting the length of calls. A rationalized emotional labour was required from employees, and this set up tensions within them, particularly when they had taken on this work out of a desire 'to help

people'. Torn between the 'pleasures and pains' of call-centre work, they found it both satisfying and highly stressing.

Korczynski points out that this may not apply to all call centres, as some may operate on a more professional basis, while others may be concerned solely with sales. He also argues, however, that

> there are many other forms of front-line work that can be illuminated through the lens of the customer-oriented bureaucracy. The work of the nurse, the care assistant, the retail worker, the bank teller, the restaurant worker, the hotel worker, the bar-worker can all be analysed usefully against the ideal type of the customer-oriented bureaucracy. (Korczynski 2001: 98)

Note that we also discuss call centres in Chapter 17, pp. 660–1.

❓ Have you ever worked in a customer-oriented bureaucracy? Did you experience such tensions and contradictions? If so, what form did they take and how did you deal with them? If not, why do you think that there were no contradictions or tensions between customer service and rational organization?

The transformation of management

The organizational changes examined above were paralleled by changes in management techniques. Management thinking shifted from an emphasis on formal to informal structures, from authoritarian to integrative styles of control, from specialization to general commitment. In this section we consider this shift by examining the human-relations approach and human resource management. We then consider the impact of privatization and globalization on management.

Human relations

The **human-relations school** of management grew out of, but also reacted against, the scientific-management approach that we examined on p. 529. The human-relations approach emerged from interpretations of the experiments conducted during 1924–32 at the Hawthorne factory of the Western Electric Company in the United States. These experiments are important not only because of their significance for the development of management thought but also because of their methodological implications.

The first experiments were in the scientific-management tradition. They examined the effects of changes in lighting on worker productivity. The experimenters found, to their surprise, that almost any changes they made, whether, for example, they increased or decreased the amount of light, resulted in higher productivity. They also found that productivity rose in the control group as well as the experimental group. They concluded that the conduct of the experiment had itself raised productivity. The interest shown by the investigators in the workers had changed their attitudes to their work, and this had more effect on their behaviour than the experimental changes. They had discovered what has been labelled the 'Hawthorne effect'—that is, the effect of a study on the behaviour of those being studied.

This discovery led to many further experiments that showed productivity was not a matter of individual responses to incentives, as assumed by scientific management. Production was regulated by the group, which established output norms and put pressure on those who over- or under-produced to conform to them (see Box 14.8 on p. 540).

The behaviour of work groups was in turn seen as largely the result of supervisory style. The restriction of output was interpreted as a defensive response by workers fearing managerial interference in their work lives. Supervisors

Briefing: the work-group rules!   14.8

The rules established by one group observed during the Hawthorne experiments.

- 'You should not turn out too much work. If you do, you are a "rate-buster".
- You should not turn out too little work. If you do, you are a "chiseller".
- You should not tell a supervisor anything . . . to the detriment of an associate. If you do, you are a "squealer".
- You should not attempt to maintain social distance or act officious. If you are an inspector, for example, you should not act like one.' (Roethlisberger and Dickson 1939: 522)

Figure 14.9 Human relations versus scientific management

Aspects of management	Scientific management	Human relations
Motivation of worker	Money	Social needs
Unit of analysis	Individual	Work group
Organizational structure	Formal	Informal
Work tasks	Subdivided	Rotated, enlarged, enriched
Management style	Coercive	Integrative
Interpretation of worker behaviour	Rational, calculative	Irrational, emotional

who allayed workers' anxieties, and encouraged their participation in decision-making, obtained higher levels of production.

The human-relations approach is generally considered an advance on scientific management. It recognized the importance of group influences on the individual, and took account of the informal as well as the formal structure of the workplace. It established the significance of workers' emotional needs and argued for an essentially integrative style of management to meet these needs. It led to schemes that sought to make work more meaningful by rotating tasks between workers, and by enlarging and enriching jobs to include more varied work. It also promoted the rise of personnel managers as human-relations specialists. In general, it treated workers as human beings rather than machines—hence the term *human relations*.

It was claimed that the Hawthorne experiments provided a scientific basis for the human-relations approach, but the results of the experiments have been interpreted in other ways (Carey 1967). Rose (1975) argued that the restriction of output was not necessarily a response to supervisory practices, for, at a time of high unemployment, it was quite rational to restrict output in order to make a job last as long as possible. He claimed that the conclusions drawn by the human-relations approach reflected a particular interpretation of the experiments' results.

The human-relations approach derived not only from the results of the experiment but also from a particular social theory. One of the leading exponents of the approach, Elton Mayo, who directed some of the experiments, believed that the integration of workers in a work community could counteract societal tendencies towards excessive individualism. Influenced by Émile Durkheim's ideas, he believed that the problem of *anomie* could best be solved by developing integrated industrial communities (for Durkheim's theory of anomie, see Chapter 2, pp. 35–6).

The human-relations approach has been criticized for its managerial assumptions, its focus on the work situation alone, and its neglect of technology (see Chapter 17, pp. 657–8 for a discussion of the significance of technology). Its understanding of worker behaviour was, nonetheless, an advance on scientific management. It was also based on a substantial body of research, which greatly increased our knowledge of social behaviour at work.

Human resource management

Human resource management (HRM) is the name given to a new emphasis in management thought since the 1980s on the central importance of a company's labour force in creating competitiveness. Like the human-relations approach, HRM seeks to integrate workers into the company, but it has gone considerably further in its aims and techniques. According to HRM, personnel issues are too important to be left to personnel managers. They must become a central concern of *all* managers, especially top management, for a company's human resources are its most important resources. It is also more ambitious than the human-relations approach in its mission to change the whole culture and organization of the workplace.

Exponents of HRM argue that *cultural* change is crucial to competitiveness, because it is employee attitudes and beliefs that really matter. Management should not seek a bureaucratic obedience to company rules but rather the total commitment of employees to the company. Mission statements, cultural change programmes, staff development, and appraisal are typical techniques for developing this commitment. The selection of employees is also crucial, to make sure that company recruits are capable of commitment.

Cultural change requires *organizational* change. Organizations should be decentralized to shift responsibility downwards in order to empower the workforce. Instead of allocating workers to specified tasks, managers should create flexible teams that can take responsibility for carrying out whatever work is required to meet the objectives of the company. Workers should be involved in the process of quality improvement.

This highly integrative approach to the management of labour leaves little room for an independent trade unionism. Unions are, after all, based on the assumption that there is a conflict of interest between employers and employees, while HRM emphasizes the cultural unity of a company as it engages in an intensely competitive struggle with its rivals. HRM is, therefore, wary of collective bargaining and seeks to individualize the relationship between employee and company, through individual contracts, appraisal, and performance-related pay.

HRM requires cultural and organizational changes in management as well as labour. Managers must alter their own customary ways of thinking, if they are to bring about cultural change and introduce the new programmes to achieve it. Intermediate layers of management should be stripped out, partly because they are no longer necessary if responsibility is devolved, and partly because HRM calls for a closer and more direct relationship between management and labour.

> **⮕ Connections**
> HRM and the Japanese-style integration of employees into the company are closely linked to 'the "new" industrial relations', which we discuss in Chapter 17, p. 679.

These ideas have been linked to Japanese-style management practices. Japanese companies began to out-compete many Western companies in the 1960s, and one reason for their success appeared to be their much higher levels of employee commitment. Core Japanese workers have been expected to stay with their company throughout their careers and subordinate themselves totally to it. They have had to take part in quality-circle meetings and suggest ways of improving production. They have had to work long hours and sacrifice weekends and holidays to the requirements of their company. They have been expected to spend much of what leisure time is left at company social events or engaging in bonding activities with colleagues after work. It is no accident that the Japanese have a word—*karoshi*—for death through overwork (see Box 14.10 on p. 542).

Some have taken a sceptical view of HRM and treated it as little more than managerial rhetoric. Karen Legge (1995) found little to distinguish it from the standard prescriptions of personnel management, and argued that

THEORY AND METHODS 14.9

Critical management studies

Critical management studies (CMS) emerged in business schools in the 1980s and has established itself as a distinctive perspective in the study of management. It brings together many different critiques, from Marxist, Foucauldian, and feminist approaches, of the managerial ideologies dominant in the 1980s. Grey and Wilmott (2005) have identified three common threads in CMS:

- de-naturalization;
- anti-performativity;
- reflexivity.

De-naturalization rejects any notion that management structures and practices are natural. Hierarchy or competition, for example, are often treated as self-evident features of management. CMS rejects the idea that any aspect of management should be taken for granted in this way.

Anti-performativity opposes the idea that management should be evaluated solely in terms of its success in attaining the goals of the organization. Ethical and political criteria matter.

Reflexivity refers to the importance of reflecting upon the assumptions that inform business-school teaching and research. These must always be subject to questioning and challenge.

CMS has attracted a following among academics in business schools but faces the problem that business schools earn their money by training managers who come from, or seek careers in, organizations that operate on the basis of the assumptions it is criticizing. The ultimate test of CMS is whether it can move beyond academic critique to impact upon the practices of management in business organizations.

practice anyway fell far short of its exponents' claims. She saw HRM as a management fad generated by those, such as business gurus, management consultants, business schools, and publishers, who make money by riding new bandwagons (see Box 14.9). Managers used HRM qualifications to advance their careers, while personnel managers became HRM missionaries at a time when the decline of labour organization had diminished their role as managers of industrial relations.

Storey (1995a) argued, however, that HRM is distinctive and that management has really been changing. He presented survey evidence that showed the growing use of HRM techniques, though he found that few companies had adopted the full HRM package. HRM is also interrelated with other changes, such as post-Fordist methods of production, which we examine in Chapter 17, pp. 671–3.

Briefing: work in a Japanese car factory   **14.10**

'In recent years demand for the company's product has been brisk and two hours of overtime are routinely required. . . . With overtime the working day from start to finish is typically 11 hours long. . . . Even though their day is long, workers can expect little free time for rest and relaxation in the course of the working day. The scheduled meal breaks are often taken up with company business, such as Quality Circle meetings. When the norm is 32 suggestions per worker per year, membership of an 8 or 10 person Quality Circle imposes real obligations. Workers are formally entitled to 2 days off each week but, in recent years, they have been obliged to work 6 days so that the company can extract more output from existing capacity. Their one day off may not be completely free because loyal workers are expected to join in company sports and social events. Finally, the day off may be taken mid-week at the convenience of the company and the inconvenience of the worker's family. In the summer of 1987 Nippon Car chose to work Saturdays and Sundays because the local electricity utility charged a lower tariff at weekends.' (K. Williams *et al.* 1994: 61)

Similar pressures for more competitive, more flexible, more customer-oriented organizations lie behind all these innovations, and they have been influenced by a growing interest in the merits of non-Western alternatives.

New management styles and new methods of control have certainly developed in some companies, but this does not mean that older techniques of management have been superseded. HRM techniques may not be appropriate in businesses where production is labour intensive, work tasks are routine, and profits depend on producing large quantities of goods at the lowest possible cost. In such circumstances, the most effective management of human resources may be simply to use financial incentives or coercion to get employees to work as hard as possible. In some companies the most effective management of human resources may not require HRM techniques at all!

Privatization

The literature on organizational and management change makes little reference to ownership, but in a capitalist society the control of an organization lies ultimately in the hands of its owners. We showed earlier that there had been a considerable extension of public ownership in Britain since the mid-nineteenth century. Since the 1980s this has been substantially reversed by privatization. Private capital has been drawn into public services in many different ways, but here we will focus on public utilities sold to the private sector.

> **⟳ Connections**
> We examine privatization in Chapter 15, pp. 577–8 and 581–2, and its consequences for industrial relations in Chapter 17, p. 678.

We argued earlier that nationalization made little difference to the capitalist character of British society. The nationalized industries had to operate within a capitalist society and therefore operated on capitalist principles. This implies that it mattered little whether businesses were privately or publicly owned, but the privatizing Conservative governments of the 1980s and 1990s clearly did believe that ownership was important. They associated public ownership with sluggish, bureaucratic, inefficient, and unresponsive organizations and claimed that privatization would make them dynamic, efficient, and responsive to consumers. We cannot here make a general assessment of the effects of privatization, but what consequences did it have for organization and management?

Kate Mulholland (1998) examined the impact of privatization on managerial careers. She found that it led to changes in career paths and in the relationship between the employing organization and the manager. Previously this relationship had been one of trust and commitment, with the manager giving loyal service in return for a salary and a secure career. After privatization, employment depended on performance. The bureaucratic career was replaced by a 'portfolio career', where individuals took responsibility for their own futures, moving between organizations, and capitalizing on their employability. A division opened up between 'public-sector survivors', who tried to hang on to their jobs, and 'movers and shakers', who were constantly on the lookout for better opportunities elsewhere.

The privatization of the utilities had enabled the most senior managers to operate more freely, for they became relatively independent of both owner and market control. Ownership was now dispersed among many small and passive shareholders, while the monopolistic position of the utilities left them relatively free from market regulation. This freedom enabled them to diversify company operations into other activities both at home and abroad. They sharply increased their salaries, while also benefiting from share ownership and share options. They abandoned the industrial-relations and career conventions of the public sector.

The senior managers were not wholly free of external constraints, however, for they were subject to new bureaucratic controls. They were supervised by new regulatory authorities, such as the Office of Water Regulation (OFWAT). Their prices, standards of service, investment programmes, and impact on the environment were all

Controversy and debate Gas and electricity prices 14.11

One of the benefits of privatization was said to be lower prices owing to competition between the suppliers. The new regulatory agencies were charged with ensuring that a proper competition took place and fair prices were charged. OFGEM (the Office of the Gas and Electricity Markets) decided in 2002 that it did not need to regulate prices any longer, since there was enough competition in the marketplace. According to Martin Hickman (2009), there is, however, no effective competition.

> The Big Six energy suppliers don't need to collude to fix prices—they simply watch what their rivals are charging and tweak tariffs accordingly. They leave millions of people on expensive tariffs, leaving the juiciest rates for price-sensitive internet surfers. They have little to fear from the regulator OFGEM. They have run rings around it, even managing to keep their outrageous right to inform customers of price increases two months later. With the regulator in their pocket and a weak government, they have almost complete control of the market.

One consequence of privatization is that the bulk of the British energy supply industry is owned by foreign companies. Of the Big Six only British Gas (which the Russian company Gazprom has shown interest in buying) and SSE are British owned. E.ON and Npower are German-owned, EDF is French, and Scottish Power is owned by a Spanish company. This has led to suspicions that British customers are disadvantaged, as foreign-owned companies favour their domestic consumers.

Sources: Hickman (2009); Wallop (2009*a*).

---

subject to regulation. These authorities were controlled by bureaucrats with a high degree of autonomy, but the effectiveness of regulation has been a matter of considerable debate (see Box 14.11).

Thus, privatization involved both debureaucratization and bureaucratization. A limited debureaucratization took place internally and through some shift from state control to market control. New external bureaucratic controls were, however, created to regulate with debatable effectiveness the behaviour of the privatized utilities.

Globalization

While privatization reversed earlier nationalizing tendencies, one process that has not gone into reverse has been the rise of transnational corporations (TNCs), not only in manufacturing but also in services (see Box 14.12, p. 444). Their growth has created some corporations whose operations are so extensive that they are considered to be global in character (see Chapter 16, p. 625, for a discussion of this). Here we will consider the organizational and management issues raised by globalization, but it is first worth pointing out the relationship between globalization and the process of privatization we have just considered.

Globalization interacted with privatization in various ways. State ownership tended to keep the operations of companies within national boundaries, while privatization released them from this restriction. Privatization also allowed foreign companies to buy into previously nationalized activities and build up transnational operations (see Box 14.11). Globalization has in turn promoted privatization, since with the increased mobility of capital has gone the diffusion of neo-liberal ideologies that call for

privatization (see Chapter 16, p. 616). Bodies like the World Bank have put pressure on governments to privatize, as a condition of receiving loans.

Concentration and globalization have led to decentralizing changes in organizational structure. According to the traditional *functional* model, a corporation was divided into specialized departments, such as personnel, research and development, and marketing, that were coordinated by a centralized management structure. As corporations became transnational and grew larger, they shifted to *divisional* structures with *product* or *area* divisions, each having a complete range of specialized departments within it. Sometimes product and area structures were combined in *matrix* structures that tried to get the best of both worlds (Child 1984). Coordination was carried out at the divisional level, and management was largely decentralized to this level, though financial control and strategic direction remained centralized in the corporate headquarters, which was always firmly located in a particular country.

Since the 1980s, American and British companies have become increasingly decentralized along *project* lines (Scase 2002). Cumbersome bureaucratic structures coordinating many different operations were broken down into more flexible units able to carry out particular projects. These were leaner operations, where occupational boundaries were broken down, high levels of commitment and cooperation were required from employees, and performance could be closely monitored. This could deliver impressive results, but Richard Scase (2002) has commented that it was geared to short-term performance and liable to burn out those involved. This essentially American model has been widely diffused, but adoption has been far from

Global focus Global Tesco   14.12

Tesco's increasing dominance of the UK retail sector has attracted growing comment. In 2010 Tesco had around a 30 per cent share of the UK grocery market, roughly twice as much as its nearest competitor. In 'Tesco towns', notably Inverness, Swansea, Salisbury, Perth, and Cambridge, it has around half the market. This is not only because of its superstores but also because of its local convenience stores. A campaign to prevent it further dominating local markets failed when Tesco appealed successfully against the Competition Commission's April 2008 ruling that local planners could stop new stores opening where one company was becoming too dominant.

In 2009 Tesco had 2,362 stores in the UK, but it is not just a UK operation. It had declared in 2000 that 'food retailers will have to go global to succeed', and it expanded into other European countries, into Asia, and into America. In Europe in 2009 it had 127 stores in the Czech Republic, 164 in Hungary, 117 in Ireland, 125 in Poland, and 74 in Slovakia. In Asia it had 71 stores in China, 137 in Japan, 30 in Malaysia, 280 in South Korea, 614 in Thailand, and 100 in Turkey. It had 125 stores in the USA. Indian regulations prevent foreign-owned stores selling directly to consumers,

but in 2008 Tesco began investing in three wholesale 'hubs' in India to supply retailers, hotels, and restaurants, and signed a deal to supply the TATA conglomerate's Trent retail arm.

Tesco also has a global reach through its sourcing of products. It has been criticized by ActionAid for using its huge purchasing power to force down the prices it pays for South African fruit and therefore the wages of South African farmworkers.

> Tesco is the UK's biggest buyer of South African fruit. Despite the company's commitment to corporate social responsibility and the Ethical Trading Initiative (on minimum labour standards)— and the existence of good national laws to protect farm labourers—ActionAid found unacceptable conditions among the temporary labourers interviewed on Tesco accredited farms. (ActionAid 2005)

The mainly women farmworkers were paid below the minimum wage, exposed to pesticide spraying, and excluded from benefits provided by labour legislation.

Sources: ActionAid (2005); *Guardian*, 13 August 2008; *Independent*, 5 March 2009; Tesco plc 2009.

---

universal, and companies in continental Europe have continued to operate on more bureaucratic lines.

Some aspects of this leaner model originated in Japan. As we showed in 'Cultural alternatives' (on p. 535), there has been much interest in the less bureaucratic organizational structures found in East Asia, while HRM has tried to apply Japanese-style techniques for generating employee commitment and loyalty. A debate has developed between those who believe that Japanization has been taking place and those who argue that Japanese organizational forms are dependent on the Japanese context and cannot travel.

> **Ͽ Connections**
> We discuss globalization and the rise of transnational corporations in Chapter 16, pp. 623–4. In Chapter 17, p. 679, we discuss whether Japanese industrial relations practices have been transplanted into Britain.

Japanese companies themselves provide an interesting test case, given the number of foreign plants that these companies have set up since the 1970s. There is much anecdotal evidence of the diffusion to the 'transplants' of typical Japanese practices, such as quality circles, exhaustive selection procedures, and various kinds of

management–worker mixing. Case studies suggest, however, that there are barriers to the full implementation of Japanese management techniques outside Japan. One such study has concluded that overseas Japanese companies find it 'difficult or impossible to Japanize because they cannot recreate Japanese levels of workforce consent and commitment' (K. Williams *et al.* 1994: 87).

But do Japanese companies even try to Japanize their foreign operations? A study of the HRM practices of Japanese companies in Australia has suggested that a distinction be made between the *core* and *periphery* of Japanese companies (Dedoussis and Littler 1994). Even in Japan itself, the distinctive features of Japanese management, such as lifetime employment, do not operate within the periphery, which consists of small subcontractors that supply the core company (see Chapter 17, p. 679). Dedoussis and Littler argue that overseas plants are part of this periphery, particularly when they are 'screwdriver' operations assembling Japanese components abroad in order to penetrate local markets. There is no need to introduce there the expensive personnel practices used to create and maintain worker loyalty in core plants at home.

Global corporations do put pressure on countries to standardize the economic and financial environment within which they operate. Governments deregulate and

Japanization? Workers at the Japanese-owned Auto Parts Alliance factory in Guangdong, China.
© Getty Images/Peter Parks

privatize in order to attract investment, and this results in the partial dismantling of distinctive national structures, often within special zones (see Chapter 16, p. 624). Globalization has not, however, standardized corporate structures and cultures. Both the American and the Japanese model have had limited applicability outside their country of origin.

Decarceration and recarceration

We showed on pp. 526–7 that incarceration in prisons and hospitals was a characteristic feature of the new industrial society emerging during the nineteenth century. In the 1950s and 1960s a process of **decarceration** got under way as community alternatives to imprisonment and

hospitalization were developed. But there was then a reaction against this and a process of recarceration began. In this section we examine these processes but also consider the privatizing of prisons, for the rising prison population has been increasingly accommodated in privately managed prisons. Lastly, we consider surveillance, for arguably recarceration has extended to the whole of society as surveillance has spread and intensified.

Decarceration

In the 1960s there was a growing criticism of the incarceration of people in prisons and mental hospitals. Goffman's analysis (1961*b*) of the dehumanizing effects of 'total institutions' on their inmates became one of the fashionable texts of the time (see p. 524). It was argued that such organizations did not help either to cure or to rehabilitate those shut up inside them and, indeed, often made them worse by 'institutionalizing' them. The symptoms displayed by patients in mental hospitals were attributed to the organization itself or the adoption of an inmate role, with patients losing their ability to cope with the outside world. It was claimed that prisons actually increased criminality, because inmates were brutalized by their prison experiences and learned new criminal skills while they were inside.

The alternatives put forward involved various forms of *community care* for the mentally ill and *community corrections* for criminals. Community care was made easier by the availability of new drugs that made it possible to treat mental patients without taking them into hospitals. There were 130 large mental hospitals in England Wales in 1975 but by 2005 only 14 much smaller ones were left. Crimes were punished increasingly by fines rather than imprisonment, and new forms of punishment were created, such as community service, suspended sentences, or residence in supervised hostels (see Figure 14.12, p. 548).

According to Andrew Scull (1984), the emergence of superior community-based alternatives did not, however, explain decarceration. He claimed there was no evidence to support the idea that treatment in the community was more effective than hospital care. Furthermore, those who believed in community care had no idea what it really meant.

> What has the new approach meant in practice? For thousands of the old, already suffering in varying degrees from mental confusion and deterioration, it has meant premature death. For others, it has meant that they have been left to rot and decay, physically and otherwise, in broken down welfare hostels or what are termed . . . 'personal-care' nursing homes. For thousands of younger psychotics discharged into the streets, it has meant a nightmare existence in the blighted centres of our cities, amidst neighbourhoods crowded with prostitutes, ex-felons, addicts, alcoholics, and the other human rejects now repressively tolerated by our society.

Scull 1984: 2

Scull also argued that 'community corrections' were an inadequate way of controlling and rehabilitating criminals and delinquents. Those charged with supervising them were overloaded with cases, and supervision became a token process involving no more than short weekly interviews. Criminals drifted into decaying inner-city areas, where they were largely left alone by the police. As both the mentally ill and the criminals congregated in these areas, there was the danger of a violent backlash against them from the local inhabitants.

Scull saw decarceration as a response to the crisis of welfare capitalism. The expense of the welfare state had generated a financial crisis. It was cheaper to deal with deviants through community programmes and welfare payments than to lock them up in heavily staffed and expensive organizations. This was not just a matter of their running costs, but also the need to rebuild them, as most dated from the nineteenth century and urgently needed replacement.

⊙ Connections

You may find it helpful to look up our discussion of changes in welfare in other chapters. See Chapter 8, pp. 293–5, and Chapter 15, pp. 579–80.

Controversy and debate Electronic tagging   14.13

Electronic tagging, otherwise known as the 'home detention scheme' (HDS), was introduced in the 1990s and has now become an established part of the British courts' repertoire of punishments. It involves the wearing of a device that enables the private security companies operating the scheme, under contract from the Home Office, to know whether the wearer is within a particular area, normally their home, during a specified time period.

Electronic tagging was seen initially as a means of preventing reoffending. It would permit the early release of offenders from prison, so that they could maintain or re-establish their family and community lives, and possibly return to work, while continuing their punishment. It has been claimed that it helps an offender to resist peer pressure to re-engage in criminal activity after release. Increasingly, however, it has been seen as a means of relieving the problems caused by the overcrowding of prisons.

Mike Nellis has claimed that, instead of being an extra means of supervising offenders, it is becoming the dominant means, displacing the traditional functions of the probation service. This marks 'an emerging shift in the community field from a humanistic to a surveillant paradigm' (Nellis 2003: 63). Powerful commercial interests are involved, for tagging is carried out by private companies using the products of companies selling ever more advanced surveillance machinery.

Sources: Independent, 22 March 2002; Guardian, 14 October 2005; Nellis (2003).

❓ Why do you think that electronic tagging was introduced?

❓ Do you think its use should be extended?

❓ Is the growth of electronic tagging evidence of decarceration?

Scull's theory of the decarceration of the mentally ill has been criticized for its economic determinism. The critique of the 'total institution' together with a movement in psychiatry away from a *medical* towards a *behavioural* model of psychological problems was at least partly responsible for the shift from hospital to community-based treatments (Nettleton 1995: 246). Scull was, nonetheless, right to draw attention to financial pressures, and Baggott (1994: 200) has concluded that in Britain it was the 'economic argument which has been the driving force behind the development of community care policies'.

There has been a more fundamental critique of the whole notion of decarceration. Stanley Cohen (1985) argued that community punishments do not decarcerate but extend surveillance and control into the society at large. Instead of surveillance and control being concentrated in specific institutions, they now operate in the outside society through probation, community service, and electronic tagging (we discuss surveillance in a separate section below). This leads us back to Foucault's argument that the disciplinary and surveillance techniques of the carceral *organizations* of the nineteenth century were but the first step towards a disciplinary or carceral *society* (see p. 523).

Recarceration

Mental illness in the United Kingdom is, in principle, now handled by community care, with only the most serious cases leading to hospitalization. Highly publicized cases of murder by the mentally ill, growing concerns with public safety, and attempts to get the homeless off the streets have, however, contributed to what two community psychiatrists have called a process of 'reinstitutionalization'. Turner and Liebe (2002: 253) contend that: 'Whether you call something a continuing care unit, a 24-hour nursing staffed hospital or a medium secure rehabilitation unit does not really matter, since essentially you are reproducing the asylum.'

So far as punishment is concerned, there has been a rise in imprisonment going back to the 1970s. According to Loic Wacquant (2009) recarceration was bound up with the growth of the neo-liberal state (see p. 523).

This was most evident in the United States, where incarceration returned to favour as a way of solving the problem of rising crime by taking criminals off the streets. This was particularly the case with drug offenders, with those in prison for possession now accounting for over 50 per cent of all federal prisoners and 20 per cent of those in state prisons (Holleman *et al.* 2009). Prison terms became longer, most notoriously with the 'three-strikes' laws introduced in most states during the 1990s. This meant that in some states conviction for three crimes of any kind resulted in mandatory life imprisonment.

The prison population in the USA increased at a staggering speed, roughly doubling in every decade, rising from 316,000 in 1980 to 740,000 in 1990, to 1,428,000 in 2000, and to 2,290,000 in 2009 (*Guardian*, 15 February 2000; Walmsley 2009: 1). The USA has much the highest rate of imprisonment in the world (see Figure 14.10), and well over a quarter of the world's prisoners are held in US prisons (Walmsley 2009: 1).

In Britain, the rate of increase was much slower, though rising sharply since the early 1990s (see Figures 14.10 and 14.11, p. 548). The rates for England and Wales, and Scotland, are very similar and the highest in Western Europe, but the rate for Northern Ireland is substantially lower. There has been a particularly sharp rise in the number of children aged between 10 and 14 given custody sentences in Britain, a fivefold increase in ten years. According to a Barnardo's report, 'we are almost alone in western society

Figure 14.10 Rates of imprisonment in selected countries

Country	Prison population per 100,000 inhabitants	Date
United States	756	2007
Russian Federation	629	2008
South Africa	335	2008
Estonia	322	2007
Chile	305	2008
Poland	237	2007
Iran	222	2007
Brazil	183	2008
Spain	160	2008
England and Wales	153	2008
Scotland	152	2008
Saudi Arabia	132	2002
Kenya	130	2006
Australia	129	2008
China	119	2005
France	96	2008
Italy	92	2008
Germany	89	2008
Northern Ireland	88	2008
Ireland	76	2007
Sweden	74	2007
Denmark	63	2008
Japan	63	2006
India	33	2006

Source: Walmsley (2009).

➲ Note that definitional and recording practices do vary between countries.

❓ What factors do you think affect the rate of imprisonment in a country?

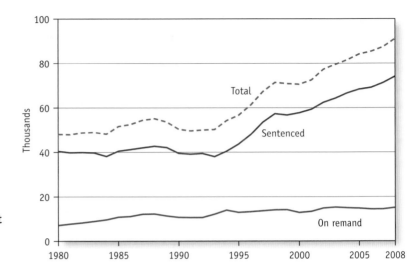

Figure 14.11 Prison population, Great Britain, 1980–2008 (000)

Source: Social Trends (2009: 138).

in routinely incarcerating large numbers of children aged between 10 and 14 who commit crime' (*Guardian*, 22 September 2008).

A rising prison population has led to the building of new prisons, but prison-building has not been able to keep pace. There have been recurrent overcrowding crises, with rising numbers of prisoners per cell and a growing pressure on educational and exercise facilities. With cuts in expenditure leading to lower staffing levels and reducing prisoners' out-of-cell time, rehabilitation work with offenders has suffered. One expedient adopted to deal with the crisis was the purchase of a prison ship from the United States, which was moored in Portland Harbour between 1997 and 2006. Another has been early release and the greater use of imprisonment at home through electronic tagging.

It should be emphasized, however, that in Britain there has been what Cavadino and Dignan (2002) have called a 'twin-track' strategy, making greater use not only of imprisonment but also of non-custodial punishments. With lesser offences, attempts have been made to keep the prison population and costs down by non-custodial punishments, and shorter sentences (see Figure 14.12).

It should also be emphasized that punishments are not only inflicted by the courts. There are 'non-court disposals', such as cautions, fixed penalty fines, and penalty notices for disorder, which are administered by the police and the Crown Prosecution Service (CPS). In 2007 over half the offences 'brought to justice' were dealt with outside the courts. There are also many new kinds of non-criminal order, such as Anti Social Behaviour Orders (see Chapter 15, p. 585) and parenting orders. Increased use of these various measures has been seen as a way of avoiding court proceedings, debureaucratizing and speeding up the process of

dealing with offences, and reducing costs. It means, however, that the police, the CPS, and other agencies have taken over judicial functions previously carried out by the courts. Concerns have been raised about inconsistencies and

Figure 14.12 Changing patterns of punishment, England and Wales, 1938–2007 (%)

Sentencing of adult offenders	Percentage of offenders			
	1938	1975	1994	2007
Imprisonment	33	13	18	24
Probation	15	7	12	–
Community service	–	1	11	–
Combination order[a]	n.a.	n.a.	2	–
Community sentence[b]	–	–	–	34
Fines	27	55	35	16
Suspended sentence	–	11	1	9
Discharge	23	12	18	14
Other	1	1	2	4
	100.0	100.0	100	100
Total no. of offenders	38,896	209,709	215,500	312,300

[a]After the 1991 Criminal Justice Act probation could be combined with other penalties.
[b]Community sentence now includes probation, community service, and other community punishments.
Sources: Cavadino and Dignan (1997: 207, table 8.1); *Social Trends* (2009: 135).

❷ What are the main changes that have taken place in methods of punishment?

❷ Do these figures suggest that there has been a process of decarceration?

The prison ship in Portland harbour. Was this the way to solve the overcrowding of British prisons?
© Getty Images/David Goddard

failures to deal properly with serious offences (*Independent*, 6 August 2009).

Thus, although incarceration has increased, there is evidence to support the idea of decarceration as well, though, as suggested by Stanley Cohen above, decarceration has arguably resulted in the extension of carceral controls into the wider society, through community penalties, non-criminal orders, and electronic tagging. A parallel can here be drawn between the notions of debureaucratization and decarceration. Both these concepts usefully draw our attention to important changes in techniques of control, which have partially reversed previous tendencies. But, just as debureaucratization has occurred in some organizations within an increasingly bureaucratic society, a limited decarceration has taken place within an increasingly carceral society.

Private prisons

As prison populations rose, prisons were privatized. In this section we consider the consequences of this process, drawing on a study by Adrian James *et al.* (1997).

It was in the United States, with its rapidly rising prison population, that in the 1970s the private prison was first revived. Privatization was supposedly justified by cost savings, but the small savings private prisons produced were achieved almost entirely by breaking the prison guard unions and reducing wages (Holleman *et al.* 2009). Prisoner labour has become a resource, and in many states can now be contracted out to private employers. Hanna Holleman *et al.* (2009: 21) claim that 'the prison-industrial complex has become a major industry, with the standard *accoutrements* of conventions, trade fairs, and Wall Street analysts devoted to it'.

The American example was then followed by Australia, various European countries, including Britain, and more recently New Zealand. The international scope of privatization has, indeed, resulted in leading American companies, such as the Corrections Corporation of America, becoming transnational corporations involved in prison management in Australia and Europe, another example of the interaction between privatization and globalization.

In Britain, privatization began in 1992 with the handing-over of the management of the Wolds Prison in Yorkshire to Group 4. Two other prisons have had their management privatized, while eight have been constructed and managed by private companies. There were many reasons for privatization:

- the belief that the private sector would manage prisons more efficiently and more economically than the state;
- the hope that private prisons would be innovative, improving the conditions for prisoners, and reducing disorder;
- the weakening of union power, for the powerful Prison Officers' Association was seen as an obstacle to reform in state-managed prisons.

At Wolds, Group 4's contract required it to achieve higher standards—for example, in prisoner education—than were required elsewhere in the prison service, but gave Group 4 a relatively free hand in how it achieved them. In order to make a fresh start, Wolds employed staff without previous experience of working in prisons. Unlike other British prisons, it was to have remand prisoners only, which meant that it was dealing with non-convicted prisoners who were legally 'innocent until proved guilty'.

The regime established at Wolds set out to minimize the carceral aspects of imprisonment. Its management declared that, since the prisoners were on remand only, they should have as much freedom as possible within an environment that was as normal as possible, and should make productive use of their time. Thus, they were allowed out of their cells for fifteen hours a day and were to receive six hours of education and gym each week. Maintenance of contact with their lives outside the prison was a high priority and they were encouraged to have substantial daily visits and given access to card-phones.

The American practice of 'direct supervision' was introduced. This involved prison officers having closer contact with prisoners and treating them more positively. The idea was that greater officer involvement would make destructive prisoner behaviour less likely and enable the construction of cheaper prisons that did not have to withstand violent assault. In Wolds, direct supervision occurred through Unit Supervisors, who took charge of living units of fifty prisoners and had a general responsibility for meeting prisoners' needs. It was believed that this would lead to closer relationships between staff and prisoners.

The realities of prison life turned out to be somewhat different. Problems in controlling prisoners led to restrictions on their movements, while 'trouble-makers' had to be segregated under a tougher regime. Supervisors complained of isolation, and more staff had to be appointed to the units. Many services, such as education and library services, were contracted out to external providers, which had difficulty supplying them to the required level, because competition for contracts had forced them to cut costs.

In assessing the Wolds experiment, James *et al.* (1997) concluded that it was, nonetheless, innovatory and successful. The majority of the prisoners they interviewed thought that relationships with staff were better than elsewhere, while the staff too thought relationships were good. They noted that there was also some evidence that the relative freedom of movement in Wolds had led to more bullying and drug use. It was the staffing problems of the Wolds that gave James *et al.* most cause for concern, and they argued that in private prisons inexperienced staff face greater stress and insecurity.

In 2009 the eleven private prisons in England and Wales accommodated 11 per cent of the prison population, with the government committed to building another five to cope with rising numbers. This was the most privatized system in Europe, and considerably higher than the 7 per cent in private prisons in the USA, though lower than the 17 per cent in Australia. Private prisons had a somewhat mixed reputation, with evidence that some in Britain were performing considerably worse than those in the public sector. Their reputation was worse in the USA, where in 2009 two Pennsylvania judges were convicted of accepting bribes from private prison companies for jailing youngsters. When private prisons are paid according to the number of prisoners they house, this creates an incentive to imprison more! (*Independent*, 29 June 2009; *Sunday Times*, 8 March 2009).

Organizational surveillance

Surveillance was one of the key features of Foucault's disciplinary society (see p. 521). Those who control organizations have always wanted to watch those they control, and it is becoming increasingly easy to do this. Felstead, Jewson, and Walters (2005) argue that the construction and organization of the 'collective office' has increased the visibility of those working there (see Box 14.14). Technology has now made it far easier to watch workers at a distance through web-cams and CCTV, with the added bonus that they do not know when they are being observed.

Technology has also, however, made it less necessary to have people actually in view, for their location and activity can be tracked electronically. Thus electronic tagging

Frontiers From panopticon to polyopticon   14.14

Felstead, Jewson, and Walters (2005) argue that in some work-places there is a shift from panopticon to polyopticon surveillance. The panopticon (see p. 526 of this chapter) enables those in authority to view subordinates from a central location. The polyopticon provides 'all-round, 360–degree, observation by both senior and junior co-workers at all times' (Felstead *et al.* 2005: 84). In the polyopticon everyone is watching everyone else.

Felstead *et al.* observed this kind of surveillance in a 'collec-tive office', where employees had no fixed work stations and were

frequently moving around a workplace with glass walls and uninterrupted lines of sight. Senior staff as well as junior staff were highly visible, and their behaviour too was open to view and subject to gossip and comment. In the polyopticon control was not just vested in those with authority, for all employees were potentially agents of control.

➲ For an account of the social dynamics of the 'collective office', see Chapter 17, pp. 675–6.

means that convicts can be imprisoned in their own homes outside the view of guards or warders. Tagging has also been introduced by employers to track the movements of security, warehouse, and delivery workers. In call centres it is not necessary to watch operators to see whether they are answering calls correctly and efficiently, as call durations are monitored electronically and conversations are recorded. In retail operations, sales volume tracking ena-bles managers to check not only what is being sold but who is doing the selling. Surveillance of this kind is much tighter than it ever was in the traditional workplace, where work-ers could devise ways of avoiding the supervisor's eye or pretend to be working when they were not.

As communication becomes increasingly electronic, surveillance becomes easier and tighter. Cheap surveil-lance software allows managers to monitor communica-tions, while some systems even enable them to detect and track union activities. Written communications can be destroyed, but electronic messages leave traces that cannot be removed by those who have sent them. It was never easy, if not impossible, to monitor private face-to-face conversa-tions, but such conversations, and movement around the workplace to conduct them, are disappearing as electronic communication becomes the norm (Lyon 2001).

David Lyon (2001) has pointed out that an individual-izing of surveillance parallels the individualizing of work. Payment is increasingly linked to the individual worker's performance. A worker's location, performance, and other activities can now all be monitored electronically on an individual basis.

A surveillance society?

Surveillance does not just occur *within* organizations. Through electronic linkages one organization's data can easily become another's. As Lyon (2001: 37) has put it, the surveillance containers that once 'were pretty well sealed' are now 'leaky'. This applies particularly to information collected by state agencies, which can be passed from one to another.

Private information is becoming increasingly available to outside interests. Tesco is reportedly constructing a pro-file not only of its own customers but of every consumer in the country, with information not only on what they buy, and where and when they buy it, but on their lifestyle, their travel habits, and even such matters as how charitable they are and how eco-friendly. This commercially valuable information is sold by Dunnhumby, the Tesco subsidiary that collects the data, to other retail organizations as well (*Guardian*, 20 September 2005).

According to Lyon (2001: 17), 'the fiction that the inside of a home is a haven from outside demands and pressures is subverted by the ways in which electronic devices take data into and out of the house, sometimes without our knowledge'. The cookies and other spyware planted on computers, when websites are accessed, transmit informa-tion about their users to commercial and criminal organi-zations. The state too is seeking to collect data on Internet use (see Media watch 14 at the end of this chapter).

Body surveillance techniques that record physical and biological data about individuals are being rapidly devel-oped. People can be identified by palm prints, iris, or retina patterns, and DNA, which can now be analysed from the traces left by breathing on, say, buildings, cars, or furniture. CCTV can be programmed to identify and track individu-als from stored profiles of their facial features or to home in on those engaging in specified movements defined as suspicious. Information about health or drug-taking hab-its can also be obtained in unexpected ways. Workers at a British Toyota plant were surprised to find that their urine was being routinely and automatically analysed when they went to the washroom (Lyon 2001: 9).

Surveillance not only penetrates into people's private lives and bodies; it also extends globally. Airlines routinely collect and exchange data about passengers' travelling hab-its and medical conditions. Police surveillance has been globalized, not only to trace individual criminals and pass data on them between countries but also to identify and track the international movement of targeted groups, such

**Watch where you go
in London!**

© Lucy Dawkins

as minorities. The computerized Echelon system intercepts virtually all electronic communications across the world, to pick out and store messages including names or other words listed in 'dictionaries' compiled by intelligence agencies (Lyon 2001).

It is the increasingly routine character of surveillance that makes the notion of a 'surveillance society' particularly appropriate (Ball and Webster 2003). There is, of course, a deliberate targeting of those considered to be a particular threat, but huge amounts of data are routinely collected about ordinary people as they go about their daily activities. Using the telephone, surfing the Web, going through a supermarket checkout, just walking or driving along a road covered by CCTV can all result in the collection of information somewhere about one's behaviour, movement, and lifestyle (see Media watch 14). This routine information can

inform marketing. It can become a commodity to be bought and sold. It can be trawled by state agencies searching for criminals, or terrorists, or simply opponents.

Lyon (2001) insists that an information society is inevitably a surveillance society. But although it is the development of information and communication technology that makes greater surveillance possible, technological determinism is, he argues, wrong. These technologies are invented and applied because those with power seek to maintain and extend their control through surveillance. They are also driven forward by a capitalist society, where the relentless competition between business organizations gives them strong incentives to increase surveillance, to find ways of extracting more work from their employees and obtain more information about the consumers who buy their products.

 Stop and reflect

In this section we explored the emergence of new techniques and structures of control that partially reversed the processes of bureaucratization and incarceration. We began by considering debureaucratization.

- Make sure that you understand the following terms: mechanistic and organic organization; network organization and virtual organization; McDonaldization and customer-oriented bureaucracy.

- There are important international differences in the character of organizations and in some East Asian societies less bureaucratic forms of organization have been effective.

- What have been the organizational consequences of the increasing employment of women?

- Do you think that society *is* becoming less bureaucratic? Do you think that it *should* become less bureaucratic?

We went on to examine the changes that had occurred in management.

- Make sure you understand the terms: scientific management; the Hawthorne effect; the human-relations approach; human resource management.
- Is HRM anything more than the latest version of the human-relations approach?
- The privatization of the British utilities resulted in important, and partially debureaucratizing, changes in organizational character and managerial careers.
- Globalization has exerted debureaucratizing pressures on company organization, but distinctive national organizational structures have persisted.

Lastly, we explored processes of decarceration, recarceration, and increasing surveillance.

- Make sure that you are familiar with Scull's theory of decarceration.
- In what ways have decarceration and recarceration occurred?
- Do you think that you live in a 'carceral society'?
- Why have prisons been privatized and what have been the consequences of this?
- What is meant by the notion that the 'panopticon' has been replaced by the 'polyopticon'?
- It has been claimed that an 'information society' is necessarily a 'surveillance society'. Why should this be the case?

Key concepts

Workshop 14

Study 14 CCTV surveillance at work

There is much awareness of the growing use of CCTV to watch the streets, but rather less of the growing surveillance of the workplace, though that is where most of the money invested in CCTV is spent. McCahill and Norris (1999) carried out a study of twenty-four retail and manufacturing businesses in a northern town in England.

CCTV was partly used to protect businesses against external threats to their profitability. On the manufacturing sites, it was used to maintain perimeter security; in the stores, to deter shoplifting and card frauds. The visibility of cameras was an important means of deterrence, and some were placed to record till transactions in order to deter card fraudsters. The cameras were used not only to observe theft in progress but also to identify potential shoplifters from a 'rogue's gallery' and alert security staff. CCTV recordings could be used to train staff to identify known shoplifters and spot suspicious activities.

There were also internal threats from the employees themselves. CCTV monitored staff handling of cash, where camera visibility was again an important deterrent, but also to observe cleaning staff and loading bays. If employees were suspected, they were often targeted by a covert camera. Monitoring of cash handling was also carried out via EPOS (Electronic Point of Sale) systems, which enabled managers to obtain a printout for each till of expected and actual takings. At the manufacturing sites CCTV was used to prevent staff pilfering.

Managers found that CCTV could help monitor and improve staff performance. Store managers could observe customer service and procedures at fitting rooms, which were also crucial to the prevention of shoplifting. Staff were subject to a quite penetrating surveillance of their body language when dealing with customers. Staff movement and activity were also checked, to make sure they were actively engaged in serving customers and not just standing around or chatting among themselves. At manufacturing sites, CCTV enabled managers to check that workers complied with health and safety regulations, and handled goods and machinery correctly. Carelessness that caused damage could be recorded and the recordings used to discipline those involved. The amount of time spent on work breaks could be checked.

Surveillance could be subverted, however. One CCTV operator turned a 'blind eye' and did not report workers engaged in pilfering, because he identified with them rather than management and, indeed, took part in the pilfering himself. Operators subverted the system in other ways, by neglecting their screens or watching what people got up to 'for fun'. Some security managers responded by installing their own covert systems to make themselves independent of CCTV operators.

McCahill and Norris argue that, in evaluating CCTV surveillance, account must be taken of its unintended consequences. Fiddling and pilfering are accepted practices, particularly in poorly paid work, and their suppression may lead to higher wage demands, industrial conflict, or loss of staff. Managements may, in fact, prefer workers to take part of their earnings in this way, since this reduces wage costs and losses may be covered by insurance.

Surveillance may also destroy trust, since it implies a managerial distrust of employees. Workers may take the attitude that, as they are not trusted, they may as well behave in an untrustworthy way, if they can get away with it. Workers may only comply, and work properly, when they know they are in view. To understand surveillance and its consequences, it must be placed in the context of the overall relationship between employers and employees, between managers and workers.

This study showed that surveillance for one purpose, say reducing theft, may become surveillance for another, say monitoring worker performance. It showed that surveillance itself does not result in discipline and control, for these depend on human actions. Indeed, the commonly found notion that surveillance is purely a matter of installing the appropriate technology is quite wrong, for its effectiveness depends on operators, who have their own interests and inclinations. Surveillance technology has potentially increased managerial control over workers, but whether this does actually increase depends both on managerial actions and on worker responses. Lastly, tighter surveillance may appear to be obviously in the managerial interest, but its costs and the damage it does to relationships may outweigh its benefits.

❷ Look up the discussion of bureaucratic rules on pp. 519–20. What are the implications of greater surveillance for 'mock bureaucracy' and 'indulgency patterns'?

❷ Look up the discussion of Foucault's concept of a 'disciplinary society' on pp. 521–2. What does the above study tell us about the relationship between discipline and surveillance?

❷ Think of somewhere where you have done paid work. What managerial surveillance practices were you aware of? Think of electronic ones but also of other ways in which your work was observed and checked. Were you able to escape surveillance? Did an 'indulgency pattern' operate?

 Media watch 14 State surveillance

Britain is at the forefront of the development of techniques of state surveillance and this has generated much media attention and debate.

DNA profiling was a British invention, and the UK has by far and away the largest DNA database in the world. DNA is taken from all those arrested, even if they are entirely innocent and not charged with any crime, let alone convicted. In 2009 DNA from around 10 per cent of the UK population was stored on the police database. This figure rises to 30 per cent for black people, and the DNA of one million children is stored.

In England and Wales, profiles have in the past been stored for life, though, following a European Court for Human Rights ruling, the DNA of innocent people will in future be retained for only six years, except in the case of terror suspects, whose DNA will be kept for life. The DNA of youths convicted of a serious or second crime, and the DNA of adults convicted of any crime, would still be held for life. In Scotland, the situation is different, and profiles of those arrested for serious crimes have been kept for a maximum of five years, while in minor cases they are destroyed at the end of an inquiry.

The argument for storing as many DNA profiles as possible is that they greatly aid the catching of criminals, though others claim that the effectiveness of DNA profiling has been greatly exaggerated. Against this it is argued that the retention of the

DNA of innocent people is an invasion of their privacy, treats them quite unwarrantably as potential suspects, and risks criminalizing them.

Another police surveillance scheme monitors the movements and activities of 'domestic extremists'. Originally coined to describe animal-rights activists, this term was expanded to 'include all forms of domestic extremism, criminality and public disorder associated with cause-led groups'. Anyone engaging in a demonstration or public protest could find themselves included.

The National Public Order Intelligence Unit (NPOIU) has a database of named 'extremists'. The NPOIU works with the National Extremism Tactical Coordination Unit, which assists companies, universities, and other public bodies targeted by protesters, and the National Domestic Extremism Team of detectives who investigate protesters. Their vehicles are tracked by number-plate recognition cameras. Forward Intelligence Teams and Evidence Gatherers supply the NPOIU database with photos and videos of people attending meetings. Spotter cards with photos are then compiled to help identify protesters. The legality of a database holding such information on individuals engaged in non-criminal activities and peaceful protests has been challenged.

There has been much media concern with the government's proposed creation of a so-called big-brother scheme to collect information about every phone call made, the address of every e-mail and text message sent, and details of every Internet site visited. The initial idea of creating a central database was abandoned, but a proposed second version would require communications companies to store all this information and make it available to the police and security services. It has been suggested that such a scheme could include social networking sites, such as MySpace, Bebo, and Facebook. The content of messages would not be recorded, but a huge amount of information would, nonetheless, be collected about people's contacts and networks.

Opposition to this scheme, together with doubts about its practicality, resulted in the government shelving it in November 2009. Some such scheme might, however, be revived in the future, while the proposal itself indicates the surveillance ambitions of state agencies and the lengths to which they might go.

Sources: On DNA profiling, *Independent*, 12 November 2009; on the surveillance of domestic extremists, *Guardian*, 26 and 27 October 2009; on the 'big-brother' database, *Independent*, 10 November 2009.

❷ Do the benefits of increasing state surveillance outweigh its dangers?

 Discussion points

For and against bureaucracy

Before discussing this, read 'Bureaucracy' and 'Debureaucratization?'.

- Why did Weber think that bureaucracies were highly rational organizations?

- What did he think were the negative consequences of bureaucracy?

- What dysfunctions of bureaucratic organization were demonstrated by later studies?

- Why have bureaucracies been considered patriarchal organizations?

- Should organizations be feminized?

- What alternatives are there to the bureaucratic organization of work?

- Can these be developed in any work situation?

- Is debureaucratization possible?

- Is debureaucratization desirable?

Decarceration

- Before discussing this, read 'Discipline, carceral organizations, and total institutions', 'Decarceration and recarceration', and Media watch 14.

- What did Foucault mean by 'carceral organization'?

- What did Goffman mean by the 'contamination of the self' in total institutions?

- Why was incarceration such a feature of nineteenth-century British society?

- Why was there a process of decarceration during the second half of the twentieth century?

- Is it better to care for the mentally ill in the community?

- Is it better to punish offenders with community sentences?

- Is electronic tagging a good alternative to imprisonment?

- Does greater surveillance mean that we live in a 'carceral society'?

- Is greater surveillance of any benefit to ordinary people?

Explore further

Further reading on bureaucracy, organization, and management can be found in the following:

Clegg, S. R. (1990), *Modern Organizations: Organization Studies in the Postmodern World* (London: Sage). *A classic journey from the Weberian model to East Asian and post-modern organizations.*

Clegg, S. R., and Hardy, C. (1999), *Studying Organization: Theory and Method* (London: Sage). *A wide-ranging reader that seeks to convey the diversity of the field of organization studies.*

Grey, C., and Wilmott, H. (2005), *Critical Management Studies: A Reader* (Oxford: Oxford University Press). *A wide range of readings critical of management orthodoxy, and including both classic and contemporary critiques.*

Ritzer, G. (2007), *The McDonaldization of Society: An Investigation into the Changing Character of Social Life* (5th edn.; Thousand Oaks, CA: Pine Forge Press). *A wide-ranging and highly readable application of the Weberian approach to contemporary life, which argues that it is becoming ever more rationalized and bureaucratic.*

Scase, R. (2002), *Living in the Corporate Zoo* (Oxford: Capstone). *A lively and perceptive analysis of current corporate practices that discusses their implications for organization, management, careers, education, and life in general.*

Storey, J. (1995) (ed.), *Human Resource Management* (London: Routledge). *A collection of readings on HRM, which includes supporters and critics.*

Styhre, A. (2007), *The Innovative Bureaucracy: Bureaucracy in an Age of Fluidity* (London: Routledge). *A study of two major companies that challenges the view that bureaucracies are inefficient.*

Further reading on punishment, imprisonment, incarceration, and decarceration can be found in the following:

Cavadino, M., and Dignan, J. (2007), *The Penal System: An Introduction* (4th edn., London: Sage). *A systematic analysis of punishment and imprisonment, which deals with privatization and discusses Scull's approach.*

Goffman, E. (1961), *Asylums: Essays on the Social Situation of Mental Patients and Other Inmates* (New York: Doubleday). *A classic set of essays on life in a mental hospital.*

Scull, A. (1984), *Decarceration: Community Treatment and the Deviant: A Radical View* (2nd edn., Cambridge: Polity Press). *Forcefully advances a theory of decarceration and includes an appendix which updates the original study and responds to critics.*

For further reading on particular topics, see the following:

Ball, K., and Webster, F. (2003) (eds.), *The Intensification of Surveillance: Crime, Terrorism and Warfare in the Information Age* (London: Pluto Press). *An up-to-date and wide-ranging collection.*

Elger, T., and Smith, C. (1994) (eds.), *Global Japanization: The Transnational Transformation of the Labour Process* (London: Routledge). *Examines the degree of Japanization in many different countries.*

Lyon, D. (2001), *Surveillance Society: Monitoring Everyday Life* (Buckingham: Open University Press). *A powerful statement of the proposition that we live in a surveillance society.*

Scott, J. (1997), *Corporate Business and Capitalist Classes* (Oxford: Oxford University Press). *An examination of the growth, power, and influence of big business.*

Online resources

Visit the Online Resource Centre that accompanies this book to access more learning resources and other interesting material on organization, management, and control at: www.oxfordtextbooks.co.uk/orc/fulcher4e/

The HRM Guide Network provides a series of linked websites with articles, features, and links on Human Resource Management: www.hrmguide.co.uk

The International Centre for Prison Studies at Kings College London annually produces the *World Prison Population* List: www.kcl.ac.uk/schools/law/research/icps

The State, Social Policy, and Welfare

Contents

Choosing health care

'For the first time patients in the NHS will have a choice over when they are treated and where they are treated. The reforms we are making will mark an irreversible shift from the 1940s "take it or leave it" top down service. Hospitals will no longer choose patients. Patients will choose hospitals.

By 2005 all patients and their GPs will be able to book appointments at both a time and a place that is convenient to the patient. This might include NHS hospitals locally or elsewhere, diagnostic and treatment centres, private hospitals or even hospitals overseas. They will be able to compare different waiting times in different hospitals. By then the latest IT systems will allow GPs and patients to see which hospitals have capacity available to treat more patients quickly and book on line.'

Source: Department of Health (2002).

In this document the UK government committed itself to an 'irreversible shift' in the way health care is provided. This is but one example of the fundamental changes that have recently taken place in state policy. Does it mean that the founding principles of the welfare state have now been left behind? Is welfare becoming a matter of consumer choice rather than public need? Did the Labour governments that ruled Britain between 1997 and 2010 abandon the welfare state that the Labour Party did so much to create and defend after the Second World War?

Before dealing with these questions, we need to outline the earlier development of the state. We take for granted a framework of services provided by the state, but, if we go back to the early nineteenth century, none of these existed. There were no state schools, there was no state medical care, and there were no state pensions. If you fell on hard times, there was precious little help from the state. Why did the state become so involved in our welfare? How was the welfare state created and what were its key principles?

We have already made many references to 'the state'. This may seem a remote and vague abstraction, but the state's influence is actually present in everything that we do. It regulates the contents and packaging of the food we eat, the television programmes we watch, the construction of the house we live in, what is taught in school, the way we drive down the road, and the environment in which we work, study, or play. Indeed, the state is involved in so many activities that it is difficult to pin down what we mean by it, and that is the first problem we shall address in this chapter.

Concepts and theories

What do we mean by 'the **state**'? We begin by discussing this vexed question and different perspectives on its development, before moving on to the issues raised by state welfare.

What is the state?

People commonly think of the government as being 'in charge of the country'. The government is, however, but a small part of what we call 'the state'. The government would be powerless without civil servants, tax collectors, diplomats, and the police, to name only the more obvious employees of the state. When sociologists refer to 'the state', they mean both the government and the complex of organizations that enable governments to govern.

It is fairly easy to say what the government is. We know that in Britain a group of about twenty Cabinet ministers is collectively responsible for taking key decisions on our behalf. It is much more difficult to define what we mean by the state, because it is such a complex and extensive structure.

The best way to approach this question is to identify the functions that states perform. The **state** can then be said to consist of the institutions and organizations that perform these functions. Most sociologists would agree that the state is involved with the following things:

- the maintenance of order;
- policy-making and implementation;
- taxation;
- political representation;
- the management of external relationships.

The *maintenance of order* involves most obviously legal and penal systems, and a police force, with the military to back it up when necessary. It also depends on a horde of inspectors, regulators, and other officials, such as air-traffic controllers, traffic wardens, auditors, health-and-safety officials, and school inspectors.

Policy-making and implementation extend into all areas of society. Most of the work of government departments is concerned with policy, but this is also a key function of local government, for local authorities are charged with carrying out many important policies.

Taxation provides the resources that enable the state to exist. Taxation is also one of the main ways through which governments implement their policies. Thus, it is partly through its taxation policies that a government controls the economy, and regulates the distribution of income and wealth.

Political representation occurs through parliamentary bodies and political parties. Governments may largely ignore the views of elected representatives and treat parliaments as a rubber stamp for government decisions. All contemporary state structures have such bodies, however, if only to legitimate their actions by presenting them as 'the will of the people'.

The management of external relationships has always been a key function of the state. It was initially mainly concerned with territorial boundaries, which were the subject of diplomacy and war, but it has increasingly become concerned with economic and environmental issues, which are regulated by international institutions, such as those of the European Union and the United Nations, which we discuss in Chapter 16, pp. 637–9.

While sociologists broadly agree that the state does these things, they hold differing views on the question of whom the state does these things for. Thus a *functionalist* approach to the maintenance of order would treat this as an activity performed by the state to meet one of the basic needs of society. A *Weberian* approach would see the maintenance of order in terms of the control of society by its rulers. A *Marxist* approach would argue that the maintenance of order is a means by which one class uses the state apparatus to dominate and exploit another. In societies split by ethnic or religious divisions, the maintenance of order can similarly be seen as one way in which other dominant groups control subordinate ones.

The development of the state

In this section we first draw on the work of Max Weber to consider his account of the development of the state. We go on to discuss the notion of democracy and democratization. We then draw on the Marxist approach to set the development of the state in the context of class relationships.

Authority and control

In his account, Weber was primarily interested in the process through which rulers acquired control of their territories. Control of physical force was crucial to this, though Weber emphasized that the state did not rule through force alone but also by establishing its authority. In 'Politics as a vocation', he declared that the state's defining feature was that it 'successfully claims the monopoly of the legitimate use of physical force within a territory' (Weber 1919: 78). There are three key notions here that are central to the understanding of the state's development:

- monopoly of the use of force;
- legitimacy;
- territory.

States seek to gain a *monopoly of the use of force* because otherwise they cannot command the allegiance and obedience of their citizens. The efforts made by rulers to establish such a monopoly led to the early development of the state in Europe. In the feudal societies of medieval Europe the use of military force was decentralized in the hands of local lords. Rulers had no direct control over their subjects and rather little control over the local lords themselves. These were obliged by their feudal oaths to provide military service to the ruler, but rulers frequently had great difficulty in getting them to do this and often faced revolts. The beginnings of the modern state can be seen in the ruler's subordination of the feudal lords. The destruction of their castles and the creation of military forces paid to serve the ruler were crucial steps in this process.

A monopoly of the use of force was not, however, sufficient on its own, for control of the population depended on the *authority* of the ruler, which itself required **legitimacy**. People obey rulers not simply because they are forced to do so but because they recognize the authority of those they obey. They accept this authority when they consider it legitimate. This notion of legitimacy becomes clearer when one considers the three types of authority identified by Weber:

- traditional authority, when particular individuals or groups have held a customary authority since ancient times;
- charismatic authority, which is held by particular individuals through personal qualities of leadership;

- rational–legal authority, which is held by politicians and officials whose actions are legitimate because of the positions they occupy and who exercise powers laid down by law.

Weber had created what he called 'ideal types' (on these see Chapter 2, p. 38), in order to explore the logic of these different types of authority. The types certainly correspond to distinct and identifiable patterns of political leadership, but it should be emphasized that they are often found in combination. For example, political leaders whose authority is rational–legal, because it is based on their position as prime minister or president, may well also develop a charismatic relationship with their followers.

Weber argued that there was a tendency for traditional and charismatic authority to give way to rational–legal authority as societies developed, though charismatic leaders could still emerge at any time. This movement towards rational–legal authority took place through bureaucratization, which provided rulers with a corps of professional administrators, who had specified official duties and were under the ruler's direct control. Whether these administrators have remained under the ruler's control is another matter, for they have often taken over, or tried to take over, the running of the state. In democratic states, there is always a tension between the top state officials and the elected political leaders, a tension that Weber explored at length in his work.

The state's authority is exercised within a *territory*. The emergence of a consolidated national territory under a unified national administration was a central feature of the construction of nation states. This territorial aspect of the state leads us to the issue of how it has managed its external relationships, which have greatly influenced its internal development.

The development of the state apparatus has indeed been largely driven by international conflict. It was war, above all, that led to the centralization of the state in order to mobilize and control the population. The demands of war lay behind the development of taxation, which was the main function of the administrative apparatus of the early state. Michael Mann (1986: 485) has shown that in Britain from the twelfth to the nineteenth centuries between 70 and 90 per cent of state expenditure was on the military.

Democratization

As states developed, democratization took place. Indeed, most rulers nowadays seek to legitimate their authority by claiming they have been democratically elected. We first need to consider what democracy means and the issues that it raises.

Democracy means rule by the people. It comes from the ancient Greek words *demos*, the people, and *cratia*, rule. It contrasts with *aristocracy*, rule by an elite defined by birth, and *monocracy* (more commonly called monarchy), rule by a single individual.

> **⊃ Connections**
>
> We have examined important aspects of the development of states in other chapters. The bureaucratization of the state is covered in Chapter 14, p. 525, the development of the nation state in Chapter 16, pp. 606–7. Authority is discussed in Chapter 19, p. 749.

But how is 'the people' defined? In the so-called democracies of ancient Greece, women and slaves had no political rights, for they were not considered citizens. The definition of citizenship is crucial to democracy. Simply living in a country does not make one a citizen, for citizenship is conferred only on those considered full members of a society (see Chapter 18, pp. 697–8, for a discussion of citizenship). A large part of the population may in this way be excluded from political participation.

There is then the issue of how 'the people' can rule. A distinction is made here between *direct* and *representative* democracy. *Direct* democracy means that citizens collectively take political decisions. While this may be possible in very small societies, in social units of any size it is impossible. The referendum may allow all citizens to vote on a particular issue but can only be used to decide a limited range of matters where there is a fairly clear and simple choice. Generally, democracy has taken a *representative* form, where government is carried out by representatives of the people, who are chosen through elections.

For elections to be meaningful, there must be a free choice for the electorate. If only one party is allowed to put up candidates or there are restrictions on political activity, there is only the semblance of democracy. Single-party states are not usually considered to be democracies, though they may well claim that the existence of elections and parliamentary bodies makes them democratic. Representative democracy requires a multi-party system, free competition between parties, and free political activity. This kind of political system is often labelled 'liberal democracy', because it is based on liberal ideas of the freedom (liberty) of the individual. The rule of law and the existence of an independent judiciary are also crucial, to protect the rights and freedoms of the individual against the state, and prevent governments, once they have been elected, from encroaching on them.

There must also be voter participation in elections. Concerns with turnout are not, however, simply a matter of democratic principle, for the main political parties tend to lose out when turnout falls and fear that single-issue or politically 'extreme' parties, with highly committed supporters, will benefit from this. Recent declines in the turnout at British elections have led to a discussion of ways to increase it by greater use of the postal vote or e-mail voting. Some have proposed making the vote compulsory, as in Australia, with fines for non-voters.

By **democratization** is usually meant two main processes, the emergence of representative assemblies with

Frontiers Internet democracy   15.1

Can the Internet solve the problems faced by democracy? It has been claimed that it provides a 'technology of democracy' by making information freely available, facilitating communication, and enabling organization by opposition or campaign groups. It has also been argued that it can counteract declining popular participation and involvement in the political process.

The Internet particularly provides a vehicle for campaigning groups. It is a useful additional tool for established organizations, such as the environmental movement, and has become an absolutely crucial means of contact for loosely organized campaigning organizations, such as the anti-capitalist, anti-globalization movement and also for local campaigns, such as anti-road protests. It plays a key part in the organization and functioning of dispersed groups, such as exiled opposition or diasporic movements. It must be added that it also facilitates the organization of 'hate' groups that are far from democratic in spirit.

With the election of President Obama in 2008, the Internet was plugged into mainstream politics. Large numbers of small donations via the Internet helped the Obama campaign to raise huge funds. Social networking sites like Facebook and YouTube were used to create many thousands of local organizing groups. Indeed, some have claimed that 'the Internet elected Obama'. Obama's success has, however, stimulated the Republican Party to develop its own networks, using Twitter in particular to organize anti-Obama demonstrations.

Sources: The Tech Herald, 8 November 2008; Pilkington (2009).

? Has access to the Internet increased your political activity?

---

political power and the extension of the right to vote to all adults. Parliamentary assemblies existed in medieval times, but it was only after a series of revolutions, in seventeenth-century Britain and eighteenth-century America and France, that such bodies began to acquire real power. The extension of the vote took much longer. In most countries only men with a certain amount of wealth or income were initially allowed to vote, while colonial peoples were largely excluded until after the Second World War.

As we argued above, the existence of parliaments and elections is not enough to make a society democratic, for democracy also requires party competition and free political activity. These were not found in the totalitarian regimes of Germany, Italy, and Spain, or the state socialist countries of the Soviet bloc, which we discuss in Chapter 20, pp. 802–5. With the defeat of fascism in the 1940s and the col-lapse of state socialism at the end of the 1980s, the 'liberal democracies' were apparently victorious, and this led Francis Fukuyama (1989) to proclaim 'the end of history' in a much-publicized essay. What he meant by this rather misleading phrase was that the historical struggle between different political systems had come to an end. Liberal democracy had won.

This notion of the victory of 'liberal democracy' hardly conveys, however, the reality of contemporary world politics. The collapse of the Soviet Union was not the same as the triumph of democracy, which still had to be fought for in the successor states, as the 'orange revolution' in the Ukraine showed. Many countries are ruled by nominally democratic but repressive regimes with little regard for the liberties essential to a functioning democracy (see Box 15.2).

Global focus Democracy in China?   15.2

Will China's transition to capitalism be accompanied by democratization?

As we note in Chapter 16, p. 616, China's movement towards capitalism has been controlled by the state. The Chinese Communist Party has held on to power and suppressed any movement that challenged it. In 1989 the huge demonstration for democratic reform in Beijing's Tiananmen Square was crushed by the military at the cost of an estimated 400 to 800 lives. The regime suppresses dissent, imprisons without trial, executes more than any other country, controls the media, and censors Internet traffic. There is little sign here of democracy.

Doug Guthrie (2009) is well aware of all this but argues that democracy is gradually emerging. The 1989 movement was crushed, but its very existence showed that change was under way. Communist Party control has diminished as market reforms give more autonomy to companies and managers. Information is flowing more freely through Chinese society. Institutions are changing, with the increasing autonomy of the National People's Congress, a growing emphasis on the rule of law, and local experiments with greater democratic participation. He concludes that democratic reform is 'an inevitability' (Guthrie 2009: 278).

Class and state

A very different perspective on democracy has emerged from the Marxist analysis of the relationship between capitalism and the state. This places the state in the context of class relationships and treats it as an instrument of class domination. The institutions of representative democracy are seen here as a means through which the capitalist bourgeoisie could pursue its interests.

The domination of the state by capital was challenged by the growth of labour movements. Marx believed that class conflict would lead to the emergence of a revolutionary labour movement (see Chapter 20, pp. 788–9), but most European labour movements pursued an alternative, non-revolutionary strategy of gaining control of the state by parliamentary means. Before they could do this, they had to force through a democratization that would enable workers to use their weight of numbers to elect pro-labour governments. The power of the state could then be used to reform society and create a fairer and more equal distribution of resources. In this way a non-revolutionary transition could be made from a capitalist to a socialist society.

Labour governments were certainly elected, notably in Britain and Scandinavia, but did this mean that the state became an instrument of the working class? A transition to socialism was never really on the agenda. In spite of their rhetoric, Labour governments accepted that the economy should be run on capitalist lines. They did introduce welfare reforms, but, as we shall see in 'Welfare capitalism', it was arguably the middle class that benefited most from these.

Why did Labour governments not introduce more radical reforms? In a classic study of Labour government in Britain, Ralph Miliband (1969) argued that the economic power of capital inevitably limited any government's freedom of political action. The resources of private capital, which were so much greater than those of labour movements, enabled it to bring pressure to bear on governments, parliaments, and the civil service. Miliband also emphasized the ideological **hegemony** of the ruling class (see Chapter 20, pp. 790–1, for a discussion of this concept). Radical alternatives were developed only weakly, because the mass media and education were dominated by conservative views.

History has not ended: the 'orange revolution' in Ukraine 2005.

© Getty Images/Sergei Supinsky

Labour governments are now arguably more than ever constrained by the economic power of capital. As we show in Chapter 16, p. 624, increasing global economic integration means that capital can be shifted more easily than ever from one country to another. If governments pursue policies that threaten the interests of capital, it is liable to be moved elsewhere, with serious consequences for the national economy, and this enables large companies to blackmail governments into pursuing the policies that favour them.

If we are to understand the development of the state, we must certainly place this in the context of class relationships and the relationship between capitalism and the state, but there is a danger of then treating the state as no more than the instrument of a class. There is also the problem of economic determinism, of explaining the development of the state solely in terms of changes in the economy.

These problems have been recognized by Marxists themselves, and Nicos Poulantzas criticized Miliband for his 'instrumentalist' view of the state. Poulantzas (1975) argued that the state could act in the interest of capital *as a whole* only if it had a degree of independence from it, what he called a **relative autonomy**. This enabled the state to arbitrate between the conflicting interests of different sections of capital and take a long-term rather than a short-term view of the interests of capital. There was still, however, an underlying economic determinism in his approach, as he still saw the state's actions in terms of the interests of capital.

Theda Skocpol (1985) held that the state had much more autonomy than this. She returned to the Weberian tradition to emphasize the territorial character of the state, which involved it in interstate relationships. States face outwards as well as inwards, and their international involvements have given rulers some independence from the economic power of capital. Thus, as we shall show in 'The state takes responsibility' (p. 568), the imperatives of the First World War allowed the British state to take control of the economy and, at least to some extent, override the interests of private capital.

Governments do have some freedom, though the term 'autonomy' is rather misleading, since it suggests that the state can somehow be an independent force. It is better to see governments as having a limited freedom of action that has to be exercised within the various constraints, both internal and external, acting upon the state. They are also constrained by the consequences of democratization, for, in the liberal democracies at least, rulers can rule only if they succeed in persuading the electorate to give them the power and authority to do so.

State welfare

States have since earliest times been involved in the maintenance of order, the raising of taxes, and conflicts over territory. It is only since the nineteenth century that they have become drawn into the provision of welfare. Since then the questions of how much welfare they should provide, who should get it, and what means they should use in providing it have become ever more important issues.

While most countries have developed some form of *state welfare*, not all of these have developed a *welfare state*. The term **welfare state** is used by some to refer broadly to all states that provide welfare, but others use it to refer only to states that have at least attempted to provide welfare on a 'universal' basis for the whole population. We use it in the latter sense.

Theories of state welfare

The functionalist approach to the development of state welfare, as taken by Wilensky (1975), explains it in terms of the 'new needs' generated by industrialization, which destroyed self-sufficiency. People moved from the land to the city, where they became dependent on employment in paid work. Industrial economies were prone to sudden slumps, when people were thrown out of work and lost the capacity to support themselves. Furthermore, traditional means of community support were largely absent in the new industrial cities. Urbanization created new concentrations of population, where there were severe problems of health and housing. The state stepped in to deal with the problems created by industrialization.

There can be little doubt that the development of state welfare was in some sense a response to the problems generated by industrialization, but the difficulty with this approach is that it assumes that the 'new needs' would be met. It does not deal with the contested political process through which the welfare state was established. Nor can it explain international differences in social policy.

These issues have been addressed by those who link the development of the welfare state to class conflict. According to this approach, the welfare state developed because of the growth of a labour movement. The starting point here is not so much the needs of an industrial society as the class conflict generated by capitalism. Thus, Esping-Andersen and Korpi (1984) have argued that state welfare was most developed in countries such as Sweden, where the working class was well organized and gained political power through a strong labour movement.

According to Esping-Andersen (1990), decommodification is central to the development of the welfare state by labour movements. In order to understand this term, we must first consider **commodification**, which refers to the process through which capitalism turned all aspects of life, including health care and education, into 'things' (or commodities) that were bought and sold. Access to them then depended on people's capacity to buy them, which was in turn related to their 'market situation'—that is, their earning power or wealth. **Decommodification** was the opposite process, through which people became independent of the market by means of the state provision of welfare as a matter of right.

Decommodification led to what Habermas (1981*a*) has called **juridification**. By this he meant that welfare was provided through legal (or juridical) and administrative procedures. Rights to welfare were specified by laws, which were administered by state agencies. Although welfare had become a matter of legal entitlement, the application of laws to particular cases always required interpretation by administrators. This frequently led to disputes between agencies and clients, and reference to the courts for the resolution of conflicts. State provision generated its own problems.

According to Esping-Andersen, decommodification was crucial to the collective solidarity and therefore to the strength of labour movements. If welfare was provided by the state on a universal basis, this would prevent divisive conflicts between the higher paid, who had to pay for state welfare through taxes, and the lower paid, who received it. Greater worker unity would then strengthen the collective power of workers. This was one reason why labour movements have tried to use their political power to create welfare states.

This general emphasis on the role of labour movements in the development of state welfare has in turn been criticized on the grounds that it was often initially created not by Labour or Social Democratic governments but by Liberal or even Conservative ones, which was the case in Britain (Pierson 1998). It can, nonetheless, still be argued that the pressure of a labour movement generally lay in the background, leading other parties to introduce state welfare to prevent the growth of a revolutionary movement or stop a labour party gaining power.

The development of state welfare must also be set in the context of bureaucratization and interstate relationships. State welfare was in part a product of the administrative revolution, which we examine in Chapter 14, pp. 525–6. International considerations played their part, for the military and economic effectiveness of the nation state depended on its having educated and healthy soldiers and workers. The provision of state welfare on a national basis was also a means of unifying society at a time of war. As we shall see on pp. 568–9, war and the development of state welfare have at times been closely associated with each other.

Market versus state

A central issue in the contemporary discussion of welfare is the relationship between the market and state provision of welfare. Two main types of social policy have emerged:

- the market model;
- the welfare-state model.

The *market model* is based on the principle of selective state benefits for the poor. Benefits are means-tested—that is, they are given only to those whose means (income and wealth) fall below a certain level. Everyone else is expected to buy welfare from the market by, for example, subscribing to private health insurance. Apart from the state provision of a safety net for the poor, welfare is the responsibility of the individual not the state. This approach is often called 'liberal', because its supporters believe in the freedom (liberty) and responsibility of the individual.

The *welfare-state* model is based on the idea that state welfare should be not selective but universal, in two senses. It should provide benefits for all, irrespective of income. It should also provide a comprehensive range of benefits, including pensions, health care, education, and employment. By providing equal and comprehensive access to welfare, the welfare state seeks to reduce the inequality generated by market forces. It also does this by funding state welfare through 'progressive' taxation, which requires those with higher incomes to pay more tax (as opposed to 'regressive' taxation, such as sales taxes, which bear most heavily on the poor). One of its central principles is that employment should not be left to market forces. The state should manage the economy in order to maintain full employment.

The relationship between these welfare principles has been the main issue in the development of state welfare. Those who support a 'market model' argue that limited state resources should be targeted on those with most need. Dependence on the state should be discouraged, and people should take responsibility for their own welfare. In a society dependent on a market economy, state intervention and taxation should be kept to a minimum. This approach is usually linked to a belief in the virtues of capitalism and the importance of maintaining the free market central to the workings of a capitalist economy.

Those who advocate the welfare state argue that benefits should be universal because this commits the whole society to the welfare state and prevents a backlash against high taxation from those who rely on private schemes. Universal welfare also establishes high standards of state welfare, as it has to meet the needs of the middle as well as the working class. Universal benefits avoid the problem of the 'poverty trap', which occurs in means-tested systems when claimants' incomes increase and they lose benefits, leaving them no better off and with no incentive to seek work and support themselves. In its hostility to the market principle, this approach has been particularly supported by socialists seeking to restrict the scope of the market or engineer a socialist transformation.

Until the 1970s it seemed as though there was a general tendency for the social policies of industrial societies to move towards welfare-state principles. In the 1970s, however, the market model was revived by **neo-liberalism** (which simply means 'new liberalism'). Neo-liberals sought to restore the individual's freedom and choice, which they thought had been taken away by the growth of state welfare. They called for the targeting of state welfare on those who were most in need. The rest of the population should be encouraged to enter private insurance schemes. This would not only keep state expenditure down; it would also prevent people from becoming dependent on the state, and enable market forces to work. We discuss neo-liberalism further in the later section on 'Thatcherism and the transformation of the state'.

Neo-liberalism is often associated with the idea that the state should be 'rolled back', to allow market forces to operate and provide individuals with greater choice. Neo-liberal policies have indeed rolled back the *welfare* state, but this has not meant that the state as a whole has taken a back seat. Andrew Gamble (1994) has argued that neo-liberalism, like liberalism itself, actually requires a strong state to protect the rights and freedom of the individual and create the conditions in which markets can flourish. As we shall see in 'A weaker or stronger state?', the neo-liberal policies of the Thatcher governments in 1980s Britain actually led to greater state regulation.

From welfare to workfare

The notion of workfare has been another departure from the classic welfare-state model. Jessop (2002) goes so far as to argue that there has been a shift from a welfare to a workfare state. The idea of 'workfare' first emerged in the United States, and influenced Conservative policy in Britain, but was then taken up enthusiastically by the 1997 Labour government in its 'welfare to work' programme.

Exponents of **workfare** argue that social policy should be designed to get those who have become dependent on state welfare back into work. Thus, it is claimed that unemployment can be reduced by improving the work skills and general readiness for work of the unemployed. Social policy becomes a means not of insulating people from the market by decommodifying welfare (see our discussion of decommodification on p. 564) but of increasing their market effectiveness.

Improving work skills through better education and training also improves the quality of the labour force and increases national competitiveness. The development of

workfare is part of the process of constructing what Evans and Cerny (2003: 24) have called the 'competition state'. This is 'the successor to the welfare state', which reshapes welfare to fit a globalizing world.

Workfare is related to a movement away from the idea that people are simply entitled to welfare. This has been expressed in two main ways:

- A process of what Peter Dwyer (2004) has called 'creeping conditionality' has weakened welfare rights by making the provision of welfare increasingly dependent on the fulfilment of certain conditions. State benefits for the unemployed, lone parents, and the disabled have become conditional on attendance at interviews designed to get them back into work. Thus, 'unemployment benefit' has been replaced by the 'job-seeker's allowance'.

- There has been a growing emphasis on the responsibilities of the citizen. People should take responsibility for their own welfare instead of depending on the state to provide it (J. Lewis 2003). Thus, instead of relying on the state to provide them with pensions, people should save for the future, and the state should give them incentives to do this.

These conceptions of welfare have both been rejected by Anthony Giddens. In *Beyond Left and Right* (1994), he argued that both the market and the welfare-state approaches to the provision of welfare were out of date. He called for a 'third way' programme of 'positive welfare' that would address what he saw as the real welfare problems of the contemporary world. The notion of a 'third way' became one of the slogans of the 1997 Labour government, and Giddens further developed his ideas on welfare in *The Third Way* (1998). We discuss the 'third way' in more detail, and whether Labour policy may be described in these terms, later in this chapter on pp. 579–80.

> **⮎ Connections**
> Different concepts of welfare provision are linked to corresponding notions of citizenship. The market model is linked to *liberal* ideologies that emphasize the importance of political democracy and see citizenship in terms of civil and political rights. The *welfare-state* model is based on a social-democratic concept of citizenship that sees it as also involving social rights to employment, education, health, and welfare. This principle of citizenship has been undermined by the 'creeping conditionality' that makes welfare payments dependent on the meeting of certain conditions by claimants. See our discussion of citizenship in Chapter 18, pp. 697–8.

> **⮎ Connections**
> Social policy links here to education policy, which has come to be seen as one of the main ways in which governments can increase national competitiveness in a globalizing world. See Chapter 9, pp. 334–5.

Stop and reflect

In this section we began by considering what is meant by 'the state' and then examined different approaches to its development.

- We argued that the uncertain boundary of the state made it best to define it in terms of its functions.
- Make sure that you are familiar with the main features of the Weberian and Marxist perspectives on the state.
- We examined the process of democratization but treated with scepticism Fukuyama's notion that the triumph of liberal democracy had resulted in the end of history.

We went on to examine different approaches to state welfare.

- Make sure that you understand the meaning of the following terms: commodification and decommodification; the market and welfare-state models; means-testing; progressive and regressive taxation; workfare.
- Was the development of the welfare state a process of decommodification?
- The welfare-state model of the provision of welfare developed to replace the market provision of welfare but has been challenged by a revived market model.
- New Labour (and Anthony Giddens) have claimed that there is a 'third way' that transcends these two models.

The development of the state in Britain

In this section we examine the development of the state in Britain from the early nineteenth century through to the 1970s, setting it in the context of the theoretical issues that we have just discussed.

Liberal capitalism

Our starting point is the period of liberal capitalism during the first half of the nineteenth century. Industrialization was taking place, but there was minimal state interference with the activities of the early industrialists—hence the term liberal capitalism. Indeed, state regulation initially declined, though in the 1830s new forms of bureaucratic regulation began to appear.

Deregulation

The politically dominant ideas were those of the eighteenth-century economist and philosopher Adam Smith, who believed in a society of freely competing individuals. Smith argued that competition in a free market would be to the benefit of all. It would not only reduce prices but also increase wages, for employers seeking to expand production would compete for labour and wages would rise. The capitalist employer's search for profits would also make sure that industry produced only goods for which there was a demand. If this was insufficient, prices and profits would fall, and industrialists would switch their investment into producing the things that people really did want to buy.

Although Smith believed that the state should allow market forces to operate freely, he did recognize that it had

some important duties to perform. These involved not only defence and the administration of justice, but also other tasks important to the community that could not be carried out by profit-seeking entrepreneurs. This aspect of his ideas is often forgotten by his modern-day followers.

During the first half of the nineteenth century, important aspects of economic activity were deregulated. In 1815

Briefing: free trade   15.3

The apparently obscure repeal of the Corn Laws in 1846 was one of the most important events of nineteenth-century history and typical of the era of liberal capitalism. The Corn Law of 1815 had been introduced to protect the interests of British farmers and landowners by keeping out cheap foreign corn. Its repeal in 1846 marked the victory of the industrial over the agricultural interest. Cheap food imports meant that industrialists could pay lower wages to their workers. It was argued that this would make British industry more competitive and enable it to expand production. British agriculture would be forced to become more efficient and diversify its products. There was more to it than this, however. If other countries were able to export food to Britain, they would be able to buy industrial goods from Britain. This repeal was a key step in the development of an international division of labour, which we discuss in Chapter 16, p. 608.

the regulation of wage rates and food prices was ended, though the freeing of international trade took longer. The key step in this was the ending of import duties on corn in 1846 (see Box 15.3), which was followed by a general removal of import duties in the 1850s and 1860s.

These were the actions of a capitalist state. Deregulation was in the interests of industrialists, who wanted to be free to develop their activities without state interference. They wanted wage rates to be set by the labour market, not by the state. They also wanted free trade, in part to assist exports but also because imports of cheap food would allow them to pay lower wages. Whether liberal capitalism was in the interests of workers, as Adam Smith believed, was another matter. Skilled workers in high demand could certainly use their market power to push up their wages, but workers with weak bargaining power could be freely exploited. Agricultural labourers found that their bargaining position was greatly weakened by the import of food produced by cheap agricultural labour abroad.

Allowing market forces to operate freely did not, however, mean that the state was weak. Indeed, the very reverse was the case, for market forces could operate freely only within an orderly society. The maintenance of order required a strengthening of the state at a time when capitalist industrialism was generating disorder. Strikes, rioting, machine-breaking, and crimes against property were threatening both production and social order, while trade unions and radical political movements emerged to challenge the capitalist employer and the state. In response, there was a general tightening-up of law and order, which

we outline in Chapter 14, pp. 520–7. The military quelled riots and demonstrations, and the law was used to suppress trade-union activity.

Limited state intervention

There was a growing awareness of social problems as Britain became an industrial society, population increased, and new industrial cities rapidly grew. Unemployment became a recognized problem, for industrial workers were entirely dependent on paid work, though the economists of the time saw unemployment as the inevitable result of the operation of market forces and believed that there was nothing that could be done about it. Indeed, they believed that the labour market central to a capitalist economy would work only if there was a steady supply of labour seeking employment.

Employers needed workers to labour for long hours in the unpleasant work conditions of the early factories. The poor had to be forced to work, and in 1834 the Poor Law Amendment Act introduced a new system of relief to do just that. Only those who entered a 'workhouse' would be given support. Conditions there would be made worse than those experienced by the poorest paid worker, so that only the absolutely desperate would enter. Families were broken up, men and women segregated. This law unsurprisingly generated enormous hostility among the poor. It illustrates well the attitude of the state to poverty during the period of liberal capitalism.

People who fell on hard times were otherwise dependent on the local community, charity, self-help schemes

Women having their dinner at a workhouse in London, around 1900.

© Getty Images/General Photographic Agency

> ➲ *Connections*
> We refer in this section to aspects of welfare discussed in other chapters. In Chapter 17, pp. 664–5, we examine the problem of unemployment. In Chapter 18, pp. 704–6, we discuss the distinction between the 'deserving' and 'undeserving' poor.

through 'friendly societies', and pawn shops. In 1830 in London alone there were an estimated 500–600 unlicensed pawnbrokers, in addition to some 342 licensed ones (Royle 1987: 186).

In some areas of welfare the state did begin to intervene, for there was a growing concern with work conditions in the factories, with the length of work hours, but also with issues of morality, health, education, and family relationships, which were all affected by unregulated labour in mines and factories. From 1833 a series of Factory Acts began to restrict the hours of work, though many employers resisted or circumvented them, and implementation was very slow. The 1833 Act also required employers to provide two hours of education per day for child workers. In 1844 another Act prohibited women and children working in the mines.

The other main area of state intervention was in public health. The 1848 Public Health Act required the establishment of local boards of health and the appointment of medical officers in places with higher than average death rates. The state did not become involved in health care as such, though in the 1840s workhouses began to provide some very basic medical care for the poor.

Although the state's actual involvement in welfare was limited by the liberal principles dominant at the time, there was a new bureaucratic approach to social problems. This involved state investigation, the collection of information, legislation, regulation, and inspection. Inspectors' reports then fed back into the process. There were still many barriers to effective regulation, but a bureaucratic state-welfare machinery was coming into being.

Origins of state welfare

New attitudes towards poverty and new policies towards welfare gradually emerged during the later years of the nineteenth century. The work of Booth (1901–2) and Rowntree (1901) created more awareness of poverty and understanding of its causes (see Chapter 18, pp. 713–16). In Britain it was during the years before the First World War that the breakthrough to the state provision of welfare was made, though in Germany the development of state welfare had started much earlier (see Box 15.4).

The state takes responsibility

During the ten years or so before the First World War of 1914–18 the British state began to take responsibility for the unemployed, the sick, the old, and the young. The initial focus was on improving the welfare of children through state-funded school meals, a school medical service, and the 1908 Children's Act, which made parental neglect of children's health an offence and the community responsible for the care of neglected children. In 1908 state pensions were brought in for the over-seventies. In 1911 the National Insurance Act established unemployment benefit, sick pay, maternity and disability benefits, and free medical treatment from general practitioners.

The state welfare introduced by these measures was, however, limited in important ways. It was limited by the insurance principle, for both unemployment benefit and health benefits depended on weekly national-insurance contributions paid by those in employment. As Derek Fraser (1984: 166) has put it, 'the state was compelling its citizens to provide insurance for themselves rather than providing simple state medicine and sickness benefits'. Only those who had paid contributions were entitled to benefits, and non-working wives, who had not contributed, were excluded. The health care provided by the 1911 Act was limited to general-practice medicine, and a national hospital system had to await the creation of the National Health Service in 1947.

Global focus State welfare in Germany   15.4

State welfare developed much earlier in Germany than in Britain, even though industrialization occurred there much later. In Germany legislation providing social-insurance schemes for accidents, sickness and disability, and old age was passed in the 1880s, a good twenty years earlier than in Britain. This legislation was initiated by Bismarck in an attempt to detach the German working class from the Social Democratic Party, which it failed to do. The background to this early welfare legislation was the early extension of the vote, which was given to all adult males in 1871, and the early growth of a socialist political movement, both occurring much earlier than in Britain. This shows the significance of democratization and class organization in the development of state welfare.

Some have argued that this burst of legislation marked the beginning of the welfare state, but the dominance of the insurance principle meant that it was a long way from the welfare-state idea that all citizens are entitled to welfare by right. Nonetheless, its importance can hardly be exaggerated, for the state had taken a substantial responsibility for people's welfare in quite a new way.

Democratization and the labour movement

To understand these reforms we must take into account the changing character of class relations, going back to the mid-nineteenth century. At this time, the strategy of the British ruling class shifted from *repressing* discontent to *containing* it by incorporating the growing labour movement. By **incorporation** is meant the process of including working-class organizations in institutions of bargaining and political representation.

Incorporation involved democratization. The vote was gradually extended to all adult males by the Reform Acts of 1867, 1884, and 1918, which led to a growing competition for the working-class vote between the two main political parties of the time, the Conservative and Liberal parties. It also led gradually to the independent political organization of the working class, and in 1906 the unions finally created the Labour Party to represent them in parliament.

It was not the Labour Party that was responsible for the welfare legislation of the years before the First World War. This was introduced by the Liberal government of 1906–14. It was, however, the growth of the labour movement and the development of socialist ideas that had put pressure on the political elite to head off the threat of more radical changes. The Liberal Party, which relied on the support of organized labour, felt particularly threatened by the emergence of the Labour Party. It was, therefore, ultimately the class conflict and class organization generated by a capitalist industrial society that resulted in the development of state welfare.

The First World War

The development of state welfare must also be placed in the context of interstate conflict. The growing international rivalry that led towards the First World War made its own contribution to the development of state welfare. Many British politicians were keenly aware of the superior development of state welfare in Germany (see Box 15.4). The significance for national military strength of a healthy population and an integrated society was well recognized.

The First World War itself then gave an additional momentum to the development of the state. Often described as the first 'total war', it made huge demands on the populations and resources of all the participating countries. In Britain, the state intervened massively to organize production and control society. Some of its main interventions were:

- conscription to the armed forces in 1916;
- the creation of the Ministries of Food, Health (1919), Labour, Munitions, and Shipping;
- state control of wages and prices, food and raw materials, housing and rents;
- state control of industrial production and transport;
- state arbitration of industrial conflict;
- a sixfold increase in state expenditure.

The war had a lasting effect on the development of the state and its relationship with British society (see Runciman 1993). Higher state expenditure and taxation never fell back to their pre-war levels. The wartime experience of state control provided a model for its later extension, preparing the way for a more state-managed form of capitalism. The state's involvement in industrial relations stimulated both unions and employers to strengthen their organization at a national level and establish relationships with the state. The 1918 extension of the vote to women (over the age of 30) followed their heavy involvement in the war effort.

Welfare capitalism

It was during the Second World War and the years immediately after it that the *welfare state* proper was established. Here we examine its creation and set it in the context of corporatism, for welfare depended upon the state management of the economy by corporatist means. We also consider the implications of the welfare state for social inequalities by discussing its patriarchal character and its redistributive consequences.

The Second World War and the post-war settlement

The Second World War had a far greater impact on the development of state welfare than the First World War had done. It was during the Second World War that Keynesian policies to manage the economy gained official acceptance. The Beveridge proposals (see Box 15.5, on p. 570) for a new system of social insurance emerged during the war years. The 1944 Education Act, which we discuss in Chapter 9, p. 319, at last established secondary education for all.

Why did the Second World War have such an impact? Welfare ideas and policies had developed considerably since the First World War, while the Keynesian idea of the state management of the economy had emerged in the inter-war period. The labour movement had grown in strength and the Labour Party participated in the wartime coalition government. The war itself had a more general

Briefing: Beveridge and the welfare state   15.5

William Beveridge (1879–1963) has been seen as the architect of the welfare state. He was Director of the London School of Economics during the years 1919–37. In 1941 he was appointed chairman of a committee of civil servants charged with inquiring into the whole field of social insurance. The Beveridge Report of 1942 emerged from the work of this committee. In 1944 he became a Liberal MP for a year and then a Liberal peer.

The Beveridge Report made wide-ranging proposals for reform. It called for a war on the 'five giant evils' of 'Want, Disease, Ignorance, Squalor, and Idleness'. Beveridge was torn, however, between his universalist desire to 'cover everything and everyone' and his belief in contributory insurance through employment, which meant that benefits would be related to years of employment. The report immediately became a bestseller and generated a popular impetus for welfare reform.

Glennerster (2000).

and more immediate impact on the British people through the extensive bombing of British cities, which destroyed or damaged about a quarter of the British housing stock. The government recognized that the construction of a welfare state was the price that had to be paid for the wartime mobilization and sacrifices of the British people.

The outcome was what is generally called the 'post-war settlement'. This was a settlement in two rather different senses. First, it settled the broad framework of social policy until the 1980s. Secondly, it was a compromise between capital and labour. The labour movement accepted capitalism, while business accepted the welfare state and greater state intervention in the economy. The settlement was broadly accepted by all the main political parties.

The welfare state and corporatism

A Labour government was elected in 1945, and by 1948 the Keynesian welfare state had been established. It was based on three key principles:

- full employment;
- universal welfare;
- free health care and education for all.

Full employment was considered essential to welfare and would be maintained by the Keynesian management of the economy. *Universal welfare* was provided by the National Insurance Act of 1946, which introduced a basic minimum level of welfare for all. *Free health care* was provided by the National Health Service (NHS) in 1948, and *free secondary*

education had already been provided by the 1944 Education Act.

While these measures transformed state welfare, they did not provide equal welfare for all. There was, certainly, an extensive *decommodification* of welfare, as education and health care were now freely available to all, but the persistence of private medicine and private education meant that superior education and health care could still be bought. There was a complete range of benefits for the whole population 'from the cradle to the grave', but this was less than universal. While there was a basic minimum for all, the actual level of benefits depended on the contributions made during employment. The insurance principle, which related benefits to contributions, still remained (Glennerster 2000).

Welfare depended not only on specific social policies but also on the effective management of the economy to provide jobs, give people a good standard of living, and fund state expenditure on welfare. It was thought that effective management of the economy depended on the participation of unions and employers in making and implementing policy. From the 1950s to the 1970s, Conservative and Labour governments tried to involve both of them in economic management through various corporatist arrangements.

Corporatism involved the state developing a cooperative relationship with the organizations (or corporations) of major interest groups, such as unions and employers' organizations. It recognized their power and tried to bring them into the state apparatus by appointing their representatives to policy-making bodies. In exchange for being given some influence over policy, they were expected to become agents of the state and implement government policies on, for example, prices and incomes. One of the remarkable features of this period was the attempt by government after government, both Conservative and Labour, to control price and wage increases (Fulcher 1991).

As we showed earlier, the British ruling class had shifted from a strategy of repressing the unions to one of incorporating them during the second half of the nineteenth century. The corporatism of the 1960s and 1970s was the final stage of this process.

An egalitarian welfare state?

It was widely believed that the British welfare state would lead to greater equality. It was, however, based on inequality between men and women, and less redistributive than expected.

It assumed a gendered division of labour between men in paid employment and women at home carrying out unpaid domestic and childcaring tasks. Men in paid work would support women doing domestic work, and married women, therefore, received a lower rate of benefit until the 1975 National Insurance Act. The insurance principle also

What was the connection between the Second World War and the welfare state?
© Getty Images/John Turner

meant that they received lower benefits because they had made fewer contributions, owing to years off work rearing children. As Pateman (1989) argued, men were treated by the British welfare state as full citizens but women as wives and mothers.

The welfare state depended on women carrying out much of the work of caring for children, the sick, and the old on an unpaid basis. In other words, it was based on the provision of welfare by the state *and* by women. This was not just a matter of unpaid work but also of the absence of state childcare facilities, which led to British state childcare provision being the lowest in Europe (Phillips and Moss

1988). The assumption was that mothers looked after pre-school children. If they chose to work, they had to make their own childcare arrangements without assistance from the state.

Secondly, the welfare state was expected to be redistributive. It would provide universal benefits and equality of access to education and health, but the poor would benefit the most, since progressive taxation would place more of the burden of paying for it on those with higher incomes. Increased spending on social security and social services should redistribute resources from those with higher to those with lower incomes.

In important ways the welfare state soon departed, however, from the principles of universalism and free and equal access through:

- means-testing;
- charges;
- income-related benefits.

The *means-testing* of state benefits had become quite widespread by the 1970s. While this was an apparently reasonable way of containing costs, it created a complex poverty trap and moved away from welfare-state universalism.

Health care soon became less free as *charges* were introduced for prescriptions and for some services, such as dentistry. These charges inevitably took a higher proportion of income from those with lower pay.

The principle of *relating benefits*, such as unemployment benefit and pensions, *to income* was introduced in the 1960s. This meant that a lower income resulted in lower benefits.

These were all processes of recommodification, for they made welfare more dependent on market situation (Glennerster 2000).

Redistribution through taxation and state spending has diminished. So far as taxation is concerned, the growth of indirect taxation has placed a greater burden on those with lower incomes. An increasing proportion of the money raised by tax has come from indirect taxes on products widely used by the poor, such as beer, cigarettes, and petrol. There is also a general sales tax—VAT. If you are too poor to pay income tax, you still pay tax on most things that you buy and at the same rate as the rich.

So far as spending is concerned, Julian Le Grand (1982) showed that public expenditure has mainly benefited the better-off, and this has been confirmed by later studies reviewed by Colin Hay (1996). The better-off made more use of the NHS, because of their greater knowledge of what they could get from it, and their social and cultural connections with those who provide care. Their children stayed in education longer and gained higher qualifications, which improved their career prospects and earnings potential. There were similar patterns in housing expenditure and transport subsidies. Le Grand (1982: 3) concluded that 'almost all public expenditure on the social services in Britain benefits the better off to a greater extent than the poor'. Note that this conclusion was reached on the basis of

> **⟲ Connections**
>
> We discuss the meaning of commodification and decommodification, and the opposed principles of means-testing and universalism, on pp. 563–4,. The issue of equality of access to education is taken up in Chapter 9, pp. 325–5.

1970s data, before the changes in social policy introduced during the period of Conservative government after 1979.

Arthur Gould (1993) developed this argument further. He pointed out that the middle class benefited not only because of its capacity to exploit state welfare but also because of the jobs it provided for the middle class. The welfare state has generated large numbers of salaried white-collar, professional, and semi-professional occupations in health, welfare services, and education.

Three worlds of welfare

In this section we set the British experience in an international context by considering different systems of state welfare and their consequences. Esping-Andersen (1990) has provided a framework for doing this, and we will first outline his 'three worlds of welfare' before examining their consequences for employment and social stratification.

As we showed earlier, Esping-Andersen's central concept was the decommodification of welfare, which essentially means making people's welfare independent of the market. He carried out an international comparative study of the extent of decommodification in 1980. This study measured the degree of decommodification in pension provision, and sickness and unemployment benefits. These measures were then combined into an index to capture the extent to which the 'average worker' had become independent of the market.

When countries were ranked according to their position on this index, he found that they clustered in three groups. He also examined the history of their social policies and found that these corresponded with his three clusters. This led him to identify three types of state welfare (see Figure 15.1). Not all countries fitted his clusters neatly. Britain, for example, showed a relatively low level of decommodification, but its social policy combined liberal and social-democratic principles. Esping-Andersen pointed out that particular societies always combined different principles of social policy to some degree and therefore never fitted his types of state welfare exactly.

Two of his types correspond broadly with the two models of social policy we examined in 'Market versus state', p. 564. The *liberal* type corresponded to the *market* model, providing state welfare for the poor only and expecting everyone else to take responsibility for their own welfare and buy it on the market. The *social-democratic* type was essentially based on the *welfare-state* model of providing universal state welfare.

The third *conservative* type sought to protect traditional structures against both the individualism of the market and the egalitarian tendencies of socialism. The state provided more welfare than in the liberal model but channelled it largely through workers' entitlements to benefits

Figure 15.1 Esping-Andersen's three types of welfare

Type of welfare	Degree of decommodification	Principles of social policy	Countries
Liberal	Low	Individualistic self-reliance	Australia
			Canada
			United States
Conservative	Medium	Loyalty to state and preservation of existing social order	France
			Germany
			Italy
Social democratic	High	Equality and social solidarity	Denmark
			Netherlands
			Norway
			Sweden

and pensions. The assumption was that the male worker would provide for his family through a 'family wage' and through the benefits and pensions paid to him. Traditional gender roles were maintained, and the family was expected to play a central part in welfare. State benefits could be quite generous but were related to occupation. The links between occupation and welfare meant that welfare depended on the labour-market situation and was only partially decommodified.

Esping-Andersen was interested not just in the development of state welfare as such but also in its important, and often overlooked, consequences for employment and social stratification (see Box 15.2 on p. 574). Welfare work was a crucial source of 'post-industrial' employment, particularly for women, at a time when manufacturing jobs were shrinking. Depending on the type of social policy, employment in welfare services could lead to 'good' or 'bad' jobs. The outcome was very different patterns of social stratification. He examined Sweden, the United States, and Germany as examples of each 'world of welfare'.

In Sweden the development of a universalist welfare state led to the creation of many public-sector jobs in health, education, and social services. These enabled Sweden to maintain full employment even though manufacturing industry was contracting, while a strong labour movement kept up the wages of service workers and prevented the emergence of bad jobs. A non-patriarchal welfare state enabled women to pursue full-time and relatively uninterrupted careers in service jobs. The principle of providing welfare for all also resulted in a high degree of social solidarity stretching across the working class and the middle class. The gender segregation of occupations was, however, high in Sweden, where managerial, professional, and technical occupations were dominated by men and caring occupations by women.

In the United States, too, health, education, and social services provided increasing employment, but the reliance on market provision expanded private-sector services, subsidized in various ways by the state. Private-sector expansion and a weak labour movement resulted in a dual labour market with a widening gap between good and bad jobs. The good jobs were in well-paid managerial and professional occupations with plentiful 'fringe benefits' providing welfare. The bad jobs involved routine and menial work in low-paid services, where pay was low and workers received hardly any additional benefits. The result was increasing inequality and social division. The good jobs were monopolized by white males and the bad ones were carried out largely by women, and by black and Hispanic workers, though Affirmative Action and Equal Opportunities programmes have opened up routes for these groups into better jobs.

In Germany there had been less service expansion, and employment was still largely dependent on a highly productive manufacturing industry, though this provided diminishing employment. Declining employment was managed through early retirement, but unemployment too was high. Lack of service jobs and the preservation of the traditional family resulted in fewer women entering the labour market than in Sweden and the United States. The result was a large number of economically inactive people, consisting of housewives, the unemployed, and pensioners, supported by a relatively small and highly taxed labour force in manufacturing industry. The main line of social tension was between insiders jealously guarding their jobs and unemployed outsiders.

Where does Britain come in? In 1980 Britain was probably closest to the Swedish case, but it then moved away from it towards the American. The British welfare state had some universal features, but low-paid and insecure private-sector jobs in areas such as cleaning and care were expanding on American lines. Britain was moving from a social democratic welfare state towards the liberal/market model.

Figure 15.2 Welfare worlds, employment, and social divisions

Country	World of welfare	Development of post-industrial employment	Social divisions
United States	Liberal	'Dual' expansion of 'good' and 'bad' private-sector jobs and low unemployment	Concentration of women, blacks, and Hispanics in 'bad' jobs but 'equal-opportunities' programmes
Germany	Conservative	Low expansion of service jobs and high unemployment	Tax-paying 'insiders' with jobs/unemployed 'outsiders'
Sweden	Social democratic	Expansion of 'good' public-sector jobs and low unemployment	Private-sector male workers/public-sector female workers

This is one of the problems with Esping-Andersen's typology, for there has been a general tendency, eventually even in Sweden, for all countries to move towards the liberal/market model. More generally, it is argued that he made the character of paid employment too central to his typology at a time when, in developed countries, it was occupying a diminishing part of people's lives (Pierson 1998). Feminists have argued that he dealt only with women's paid work and ignored their unpaid and uncommodified domestic labour (Crompton 1997).

Nonetheless, in evaluating Esping-Andersen's work it is important to recognize its originality and the comprehensiveness of its framework. It brought statistical and historical analysis together in a fruitful and broadly convincing way. It provided a framework for the comparative study of state welfare. It also broadened the study of social policy by examining its consequences for employment, occupational structure, stratification, and social conflict. We will return to his typology when we place later changes in comparative perspective.

 ## *Stop and reflect*

In this section we first considered the state's role during the period of liberal capitalism.

- Important areas of economic activity were deregulated.
- What was the significance of the 1834 Poor Law Amendment Act?
- Did state intervention decline during this period?

We went on to examine the growth of state welfare.

- The origins of the British welfare state were in the years before the First World War.
- The principles of the welfare state were established during/after the Second World War.
- The welfare state was linked to the management of the economy through corporatist structures involving both unions and employers.

- The egalitarian goals of the welfare state were compromised by the continued importance of market power in access to welfare, the state's patriarchal character, and the lack of redistribution.
- Was the growth of state welfare driven by class conflict or international conflict?

We set the development of the British welfare state in a comparative perspective.

- Make sure that you are familiar with Esping-Andersen's typology of state welfare and the consequences of the different types for employment and social divisions.
- How does Britain fit into his typology?

Crisis and transformation

We now move on to the transformation of the British state during the 1980s. This transformation was central to the development of all aspects of government policy since, and that includes the policies of the post-1997 Labour governments.

The crisis of the 1970s

The transformation of the state was rooted in the crisis of British society in the 1970s. In order to understand contemporary policies and issues we must go back to this crisis and examine why it occurred.

The decline of profitability was at the heart of the 1970s crisis. The profitability of British industry declined during the 1960s and 1970s to the point at which much of it was hardly making a profit at all. This is shown by the net profit rate, which measures the return on capital after allowing for the cost of replacing worn-out or out-of-date equipment. The net profit rate of British manufacturing as a whole fell from 17.5 per cent in 1960 to a low of 1.7 per cent in 1981. The crisis was particularly severe in Britain, but it occurred in other countries too (see Figure 15.3).

Profit is the driving force in a capitalist economy. If profitability falls, then industry collapses, companies go bankrupt, and workers lose their jobs. Without the expectation of profit, there will be no investment and no creation of new jobs. Governments face growing financial problems, as higher unemployment leads to higher welfare expenditure at a time when their income from taxation falls. They are likely to face a growing discontent and increasing disorder. So the crisis spreads rapidly from the economy to the state.

Figure 15.3 Net profit rate of manufacturing industry, selected countries, 1960 and 1981 (%)

Country	1960	1981
Canada	17	14
France	18	1
Germany	29	8
Japan	44	13
United Kingdom	18	2
United States	22	10

Note: Figures to nearest 1%.
Source: Armstrong *et al.* (1984: 464).

Contradictions and competition

The internal causes of crisis lay in the problems created by the system of welfare capitalism established by the postwar settlement. These problems became particularly severe, however, because of increasing international economic competition, which particularly threatened the economies of the old industrial societies.

As we showed on p. 570, the establishment of a welfare state in 1940s Britain has been interpreted as a settlement between capital and labour. Although this settlement apparently solved the problem of class conflict, welfare capitalism then generated 'vicious circles', which led to greater conflict in the 1960s and the crisis of the 1970s. These vicious circles have been seen by Marxist writers as resulting from the contradictions of welfare capitalism (Gough 1979). By this they mean that essential elements of welfare capitalism were in fundamental conflict with each other.

One of these vicious circles centred on state spending. The welfare state led to growing expenditure on health, education, pensions, and social services generally (see Figure 15.4, p. 576). This led to what has been called the **fiscal crisis** of capitalism (Gough 1979: 125). The higher taxation of both companies and workers, who demanded higher pay in compensation, diminished the profitability of industry. As the economy got into a worse state, it became more difficult for the government to raise the taxes it needed.

This vicious circle interacted with another one, centred on the maintenance of full employment. This was one of the key principles of the welfare state, but it increased the bargaining power of workers, who could take strike action in pursuit of higher wages with little fear of losing their jobs (see Chapter 17, p. 576), and resist attempts by employers to change work practices in order to increase productivity. Thus, the full employment of the 1960s and 1970s had consequences that weakened the competitiveness of British industry.

These economic problems were particularly serious because increasing international competition led to a general crisis of profitability, as Figure 15.3 shows. Even Japan suffered, though not as severely as the old industrial countries. Britain's crisis was one of the worst, because of economic weaknesses dating back to the nineteenth century. Three main problems are commonly identified:

- an archaic industrial structure, resulting from early industrialization;
- the domination of financial and trading interests, established in the nineteenth century;
- the absence of an effective state industrial policy.

Figure 15.4 Welfare spending, Great Britain, 1900–2001

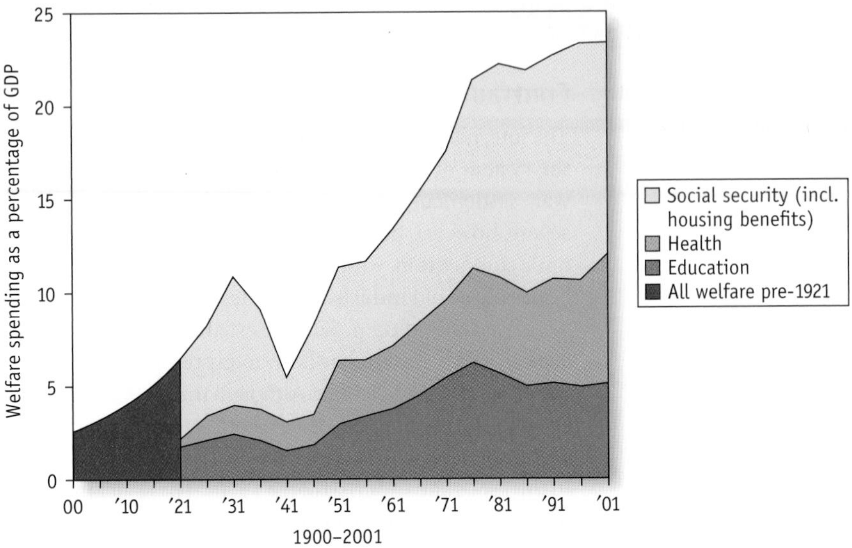

Source: Glennerster (2001: 228).

Thus, the problems generated by the contradictions of welfare capitalism were worsened by an increasing international competition, which Britain was poorly equipped to meet because of the legacy of its nineteenth-century industrialization.

From economic to political crisis

Crises can, however, be managed. They lead to breakdown and transformation only if crisis management fails. As we showed on p. 570, the governments of the 1960s and 1970s responded to Britain's growing economic problems by seeking to construct a system of corporatist cooperation between the state, the unions, and the employers. Although numerous attempts were made to achieve this, they all failed and corporatism eventually collapsed in the later 1970s.

Why did corporatism fail? It failed largely because it required the unions to control their members, but this conflicted with their basic goals, for they had been created to represent their members' interests. It failed also because of the organizational structure of both unions and employers' associations. In Britain these bodies were weakly centralized and had little control over their members. They were reluctant to act as agencies of the state and could not deliver on the agreements that governments forced them into. In other countries, such as Sweden, where more centralized organizations had emerged, corporatism was more successful (Fulcher 1991).

While the corporatist experiments of the 1960s and 1970s may now seem rather remote, their failure and the way they failed shaped the transformation of the British state in the 1980s.

By the late 1970s the post-war settlement was becoming strained. First, the institutions of the welfare state were

coming under growing criticism, because it was becoming more apparent that the welfare state was falling short of its egalitarian goals, and because they were seen as unresponsive to consumers and providing insufficient choice. Secondly, UK governments had been unable to handle the growing economic crisis and the state's role in managing the economy was increasingly questioned.

British politics polarized as alternatives emerged on the left and the right. They agreed that there was a crisis, and their diagnoses were remarkably similar. It was a crisis of profitability, and the welfare capitalism established in the 1940s had failed. Their ways out of the crisis were, however, very different.

According to the left, capitalism was collapsing, and a transition should be made to a socialist society. The left-wing alternative was not, however, viable in a capitalist society. Sweden was the capitalist society that came closest to a socialist transition, but this was never a realistic prospect even there (see Fulcher 1991a: 303–6).

To the right, capitalism was collapsing and needed reinvigoration. The right was politically resurgent in many countries in the 1970s. In Britain, the right-wing alternative won at the polls, and after the 1979 election eighteen years of Conservative government began.

Thatcherism and the transformation of the state

Thatcherism emerged victorious out of the polarizing of British politics in the 1970s. It was more than a new set of policies, for it sought to bring about long-term changes in the basic assumptions of British politics. It rejected the values of compromise, consensus, welfare, and equality, putting in their place enterprise, market discipline, consumer choice, and freedom. In this section we will first examine the beliefs and principles of Thatcherism before considering the changes made to the structure of the British state.

Thatcherism

The roots of Thatcherism can be found in the thinking of the New Right, which became dominant in the Conservative Party during the 1970s. This combined two rather different strands of thought, *neo-liberalism* and *neo-conservatism* (Hay 1996). The prefix 'neo' indicates that both were new versions of old ideas, and there was at the time much talk of a return to Victorian values.

Neo-liberalism was a restatement of beliefs in individual freedom and market forces, beliefs that had been dominant during the period of liberal capitalism in the early nineteenth century (see p. 561). Britain's economic problems were seen as the result of the growing power of the unions, increasing state intervention, and the growth of the welfare state. These all interfered with the operation of market forces and took freedom, choice, and responsibility away from the individual. Neo-liberals advocated the curbing of union power, an ending of dependence on the welfare state, and the restoration of the rights and responsibilities of the individual.

Neo-conservatism was a reassertion of the traditional values of the Conservative Party. It involved strengthening morality, reviving the traditional family, and restoring 'law and order'. The problems of Britain were seen as moral rather than economic. This strand was also strongly nationalist and concerned both to defend British sovereignty against federal tendencies in Europe and to protect British identity by controlling immigration. Stuart Hall and Martin Jacques (1983) used the concept of **authoritarian populism** to describe this aspect of Thatcherism. They argued that Thatcherism generated support for extending the *authority* of the state by appealing to *popular* anxieties about union militancy, permissiveness, crime, and immigration.

These two strands of Thatcherism were in some conflict with each other. The neo-liberal belief in freedom, choice, and market forces conflicted with the neo-conservative emphasis on order, morality, and tradition. Market forces are no respecters of tradition and ignore moral concerns. Neo-liberalism and neo-conservatism could unite, however, in their joint hostility to welfare dependence on the 'nanny state' and to the power of trade unions. They could also unite in the defence of property, for the protection of property rights was central to both.

Hay (1996) argued that the authoritarian populism of the *neo-conservative* strand was crucial in generating political support for Thatcherism. It was, however, the *neo-liberal* strand that mainly informed the policies that transformed the state.

Marketization

The central objective of the Conservative transformation of the state was **marketization**. This basically meant expanding the role of market forces in British society. It is very important to grasp that, although this involved a withdrawal of the state from some of its activities, it also led to the extension of state control as well. We examine this issue later on p. 583.

There was a shift from the corporatist management of the economy to a reliance on market mechanisms. The corporatist structures that involved unions and employers in policy-making were dismantled. The government neither consulted with union and employer organizations nor used them to implement its policies. Although it continued to control the wages and salaries of public-sector employees, it did not try to control wage levels in the economy as a whole through incomes policies but left the market to set them.

The market sphere was more generally expanded through **privatization**, which transferred production, services, and property from the public to the private sector. Some of the main ways in which this occurred were as follows:

- Publicly owned companies were sold to the private sector. British Airways and British Telecom were examples of this kind of privatization.

- Local and central state services were increasingly carried out by private companies under contract. Examples of this were the school-meals service or refuse collection or privately operated prisons.

- Public property was sold, as when councils were forced to sell council housing to tenants wishing to buy their houses.

- Privatization occurred in a rather different way by encouraging or forcing people to pay for services they had previously relied on the state to provide. Thus, people began increasingly to pay privately for health, education, and the care of the old.

When services could not be privatized, 'internal markets' were introduced. This meant that services remained in public ownership but those who provided the service were required to behave *as though* they were operating in the private sector. Thus, schools and colleges were forced to compete with each other, as were hospitals. Hospital trusts were created 'on the model of commercial companies, run by chief executives with boards of directors consisting chiefly of businessmen' (A. M. Pollock 2005: 45). A fundamental change made to the NHS was to separate *purchasers* from *providers*, opening the way to the state payment of private companies to provide treatment and care. The boundary between public and private health was blurred by the provision of private care by hospital trusts and the use of public funds to buy care from private hospitals.

The reduction of state expenditure and taxation was one of the most important goals of neo-liberalism. This was certainly attempted, but the Conservatives were unable to bring about an overall reduction, largely because higher unemployment resulted in higher social-security spending. The overall level of taxation was not brought down, but income-tax rates were reduced by shifting the burden of taxes from income tax to indirect taxes on goods and services.

The 1980s changes in the state were quite fundamental and reversed many long-term processes of change. They reversed the corporatist tendency, dating back to the First World War, to involve the unions and the employers in the management of the economy. They reversed the nationalization of important industries and services, which also went back to the First World War. They reversed the growth of local-authority services, which dated back well into the nineteenth century. Furthermore, the clear distinction that had been established between the public and the private spheres began to break down as public activities were privatized.

Away from the welfare state

The Conservative governments of the 1980s were hostile to the universalism of the welfare state. They argued that people should not be dependent on the state and should take individual responsibility for their own welfare through insurance and savings schemes provided by the private sector. State welfare should be targeted on those unable to provide for themselves. Conservative policy was also driven by the need to save money on public spending.

Some of the main changes in welfare policies during the Thatcher years were as follows:

- *Priority to control of inflation.* Employment was central to most people's welfare, and the maintenance of full employment was one of the principles of the welfare state. This principle had already been abandoned in 1976 by a Labour government, but the first Thatcher government made it clear that the main aim of government economic policy was to control inflation.
- *Delinking of pensions to earnings.* After 1982 pensions were increased in line with price increases, not increases in average earnings. This cut the cost of the basic pension by a third during the next ten years (Glennerster 1995: 182). Retirement would now result in an ever greater drop in living standards for those dependent on the state pension alone.

- *Reductions in unemployment benefit.* As we show in Chapter 3, pp. 101–2, entitlement to unemployment benefit was restricted and benefits were cut. This was the beginning of the move from welfare to workfare.
- *Increased means-testing.* The shift from universal benefits to means-tested ones did not start with Thatcherism, but it certainly continued. Child benefit remained universal, but its level was frozen, so inflation reduced its value and cost.
- *From grants to loans.* The freezing of maintenance grants for students forced them to rely increasingly on loans, preparing the way for abolishing the student grant.
- *Less state support for the old.* State support for the residential care of the old was sharply cut by means-testing it and making local authorities responsible for it.
- *Parental responsibility for children.* The Child Support Act of 1991 created the Child Support Agency, designed to transfer the financial support of single-parent families from the state to the absent parent (see Chapter 12, p. 454).

There was, broadly speaking, a shift towards **welfare pluralism**, the provision of welfare by a number of agencies rather than just the state—yet another example of reversal, for the state had gradually displaced other welfare agencies to become the dominant provider of care in the 1940s. Welfare pluralism was the result not just of privatization, important as this was, but also of a greater reliance on voluntary organizations, charities, the family, commercial sponsors, and the funding of projects through the new state lottery.

State welfare in decline?

State welfare had moved away from the central principles of the welfare state. We identified these earlier as full employment, universal welfare, and free and equal health and education. Full-employment policies had been abandoned. Welfare had become increasingly selective and benefits had been cut in various ways. Free health and education were still available, but people found themselves under a growing pressure to buy them.

In Esping-Andersen's terms, a process of *recommodification* had taken place. Welfare was once again becoming a commodity provided by the market, with access more dependent on market situation. The level of employment depended less on government policy and more on the competitiveness of British businesses in international markets and the attraction of foreign investment. State benefits had been restricted, reduced, and means-tested. The quality of health care and education depended increasingly on purchasing power and the operation of market mechanisms.

This does not, however, mean that state spending on welfare declined. Indeed, the proportion of national income spent on state welfare continued to rise (see Figure 15.4 on p. 576). The major components in this rise were spending on health and social-security benefits. More and more people became dependent on state benefits, largely because of higher unemployment, the rise in non-working single parents, and higher rents, which led to the increased payment of housing benefit.

Nor did a movement away from *welfare-state* principles necessarily mean that *state welfare* was in decline. It is important to keep in mind the distinction between the welfare state and state welfare, and the existence of different models of state welfare, which we discussed above on p. 563. Whether a movement from the welfare state to the market model means that there has been a decline in state welfare depends on one's views on the merits of these two models. It is also important to recall that there had been a sense in the 1970s that the welfare state was not providing good enough services. In Glennerster's words (1995: 192):

> What Mrs. Thatcher saw, with her populist insight, was that there was a growing dissatisfaction with state services that gave little choice to their users, in which the professional view was dominant and the parent or patient in the waiting-room seemed to count for little. In a growingly sophisticated consumer society this compared poorly with the market sector.

The 1980s *can* be seen not as a period of decline in state welfare but rather as one of reform, which addressed long-standing problems in the welfare state and injected a healthy dose of market discipline.

New Labour

The transformation of the state in the 1980s was carried out by Conservative governments, but between 1997 and 2010 Labour was again in power. The election of 1997 appeared to be a political watershed, as Labour had won its largest ever majority and then went on to win two more general elections in 2001 and 2005.

In this section we consider how much impact the return of Labour government made on the British state and its social policies. After considering New Labour's 'Third Way', we focus on the key areas of state welfare and the relationship between the public and private sectors. We then examine the accommodation of diversity through devolution and the emergence of *sharia* law.

A 'third way'?

'New Labour' claimed that it was pursuing a distinctive **third way** between the 'old left' and the 'new right'. After a series of general-election defeats, the Labour Party needed to distance itself from 'old labour' but still present itself as different from the Conservatives.

This notion should also be put in the context of broader social changes, notably the growth of individualism and globalization. The policies of 'old labour' were based on collectivism and the state direction of the economy. With the decline of trade-union membership, the growth of consumerism, and the greater emphasis on individual freedom and choice, basing a party on collectivism was no longer a viable strategy. Governments could also not realistically pursue economic policies that ignored the global mobility of capital (see Box 15.6 on p. 581). A 'third way' was needed that would recognize the existence of individualism and globalization but also take account of their costs and limits.

As a political position, the 'third way' was most clearly advanced by Tony Blair (1998) in a Fabian Society pamphlet. A longer and more academic reflection on 'third-way' politics was produced by Anthony Giddens (1998) in *The Third Way*, though many of the ideas that informed this book had already been developed in *Beyond Left and Right* (1994). Here we outline some of the main points made in *The Third Way*.

- Social problems cannot be solved by leaving things either to the market (the 'new right') or to the state ('old labour'). Politics should be based on an 'active' civil society, where community organizations and voluntary agencies play a key part. Citizenship is about the obligations as well as the rights of citizenship.

- The state requires further democratization to counteract distrust in politicians and the formal political process. A decentralizing devolution of power will strengthen not weaken the state by giving it greater legitimacy and reconnecting government and citizens.

- A new mixed economy should be created. The public sector should draw on the dynamism of the private sector through joint projects, while keeping the public interest paramount. Business should be involved in partnerships with government and community.

- Equality remains a key issue but 'the cultivation of human potential should as far as possible replace "after the event" redistribution' (Giddens 1998: 101). 'The new politics defines equality as *inclusion* and inequality as *exclusion* . . .' (Giddens 1998: 102; emphasis in original).

- An outmoded welfare state should be replaced by 'positive welfare'. Instead of reliance on the bureaucratic state, there should be greater self-reliance. The state should provide the conditions in which people can take charge of their own welfare.

- A new role is required for the nation state. Globalization is not destroying the nation state, which is the main defence against political fragmentation, but to be effective this must become more *cosmopolitan* and accommodate ethnic and cultural diversity. It should also become part of a global system of governance that can alone manage economic and environmental problems that are global in character.

Much of the policy and rhetoric of recent Labour governments are informed by ideas of this kind. There are important departures from 'old labour' thinking, notably the emphasis on the responsibilities rather than the rights of citizens, and the redefinition of equality in terms of inclusion rather than redistribution. Whether this was a 'third way' or an adoption of the neo-liberal principles of Thatcherism is a moot point.

Welfare and workfare

What actually happened to state welfare when Labour returned to power in 1997? Did it reverse Conservative policies, continue them, or pursue a 'third way'?

Labour did not entirely abandon redistribution. An 'old labour'-style minimum wage was introduced, though the main thrust of policy was on reducing poverty, especially child and pensioner poverty. Labour set itself the goal of abolishing child poverty, and it was claimed in 2006 that a quarter of children in poverty had already been lifted out of it through tax credits and benefits. Pensioner poverty too was reduced through tax credits. According to Polly Toynbee (2006), 'Labour has redistributed more to the poor than any government since the war.'

The focus was, however, on poverty rather than on inequality, and the gap between rich and poor, which had been widening during the years of Conservative rule, continued to increase after Labour came to power. In a later piece, Polly Toynbee (2009) declared that, 'on Labour's watch, class has become more rigid, destiny for most babies is decided at birth, and the incomes of rich and poor families have drawn further apart'. Indeed, it was claimed that 'Britain under Gordon Brown is a more unequal country than at any time since modern records began in the early 1960s' (Elliott and Curtis 2009). Elliott and Curtis also report that, according to the Institute of Fiscal Studies, poverty too increased during 2007–8. This was against a background of growing economic recession and harder times, which may be expected further to worsen the position of those at the bottom.

Welfare policy was also a matter of helping people to help themselves. The phrase 'a hand up, not a hand out' was one of the government's slogans. This could be seen in Labour's policy towards the unemployed. While in opposition, Labour politicians had criticized the Conservatives' abolition of an unconditional unemployment benefit, but when in government Labour continued down the same track. Its 'Welfare to Work' programme required unemployed people receiving state benefits to accept a subsidized job, carry out voluntary work, or take up full-time education or training. As Gordon Brown put it when delivering his first budget in 1997: 'when the long-term unemployed sign on for benefit they will now sign up for work or training'.

Indeed, 'routes into work' became absolutely central to Labour's social policy, not just towards the unemployed, but to anyone on benefit. A tougher stance towards those living 'on welfare' was signalled by moves to get lone parents off benefits and back to work. In 2008 the government brought out a Green Paper on welfare reform that proposed the abolition of incapacity benefit and income support, and various measures to get people off benefits and into work of some kind, backed by the threat of cutting their benefits if they did not comply. Drug addicts, for example, would be forced to tackle their habits or risk losing benefits. These proposals were supported by the leadership of the Conservative Party, who claimed that these had been their ideas all along. There is much evidence here of a shift from a welfare to a workfare state.

Did Labour governments significantly reduce pensioner poverty?

© Alice Chadwick

> **Connections**
> We are not dealing with education policy here, because this was covered in Chapter 9, pp. 340–4. Education policy is an important part of social policy, however, and in considering the issues we discuss here you should refer to Chapter 9.

As we have shown, the rhetoric of the 'third way' equated social inequality with social exclusion. Labour set up a cross-departmental Social Exclusion Unit, with eighteen Policy Action Teams, immediately after the 1997 election. 'Welfare to Work' and the ending of child poverty were presented as policies to end exclusion. Another means of ending it was by improving access to education, through programmes like Sure Start.

Levitas (2005) argues that New Labour here gradually shifted away from its earlier redistributionist discourse. Exclusion was detached from inequality. The very use of the term 'exclusion' diverts attention from inequality by drawing the main line of division in society between the included and the excluded rather than, say, the rich and the poor. As Susanne MacGregor (2003: 72) has put it:

The attention given to social exclusion in Britain at the turn of the 21st century has been primarily about redrawing the boundaries between acceptable and unacceptable behaviour. But this effort has focused almost entirely on distinguishing the genuinely unemployed from those who are not, the genuine asylum-seeker from the economic migrant, the disreputable from the respectable poor. This concentrates on bad behaviours among the poor, ignoring the drug taking, infidelities, frauds and deceptions and other human frailties found among the rich, the better off and the not-quite-poor.

Many of the ideas expressed in the 'third way' can be traced in Labour's policies. Whether they are sufficiently distinctive to merit a 'third way' label is more debatable. The movement away from redistribution, the shift from welfare to workfare, the emphasis on the individual's responsibility for welfare show broad continuities with the Thatcherite transformation of the 1980s. This does not mean that Labour government made no difference. A Conservative government would not have introduced a minimum wage, or targeted poverty in the way that Labour did. From a longer-term perspective, however, the division between different eras in social policy lies in 1979 rather than in 1997.

Continued privatization and marketization

In proposing that the private sector be given a greater role in public services and emphasizing the importance of choice, the 'third way' advocated marketization and privatization.

 Global focus Globalization and international convergence? 15.6

Changes in state welfare in Britain need to be set in a global perspective. Has Britain been merely conforming to global tendencies moving all countries away from the welfare-state model of state welfare?

It has been argued that countries can no longer afford the cost of a welfare state in a world of increasing international competition and global economic integration. There are three main steps in the argument:

- First, international competition has put pressure on the old industrial societies, which had higher costs and found themselves out-competed by the new industrializers, to reduce the costs of state welfare.

- Secondly, a growing global economic integration has made it easier for capital to move around the world. Any country whose government adopts welfare policies judged to diminish its competitiveness or likely to increase inflation will find money leaving its shores for lower-cost and safer places.

- Thirdly, the economically more successful countries, such as Japan and the other Asian tigers, have not developed welfare states on the European model. Lower rates of taxation have made them more competitive. Furthermore, in Japan the development of company welfare schemes enabled companies to integrate and control workers. Their competitive success can be partly explained by the high commitment and high productivity of workers integrated in this way (see Chapter 17, p. 679).

Will Esping-Andersen's three worlds of welfare (see pp. 672–4 of this chapter) therefore become one? Nick Ellison and Chris Pierson (2003: 2–5) argue that countries in his 'conservative' and 'social-democratic' categories have moved in a neo-liberal direction, but there is not a general convergence towards one model. National governments have a 'bounded autonomy'. They adapt national welfare systems but view the pressures of globalization through the 'lens of the domestic policy agenda' and preserve national distinctiveness. Governments' political concerns to maintain their electoral popularity and pressures from organized interest groups set limits to change. There still are many different worlds of welfare.

There are many different ways in which privatization has occurred. There is first the transfer of ownership from the public to the private sector. This kind of privatization was carried out massively by the post-1979 Conservative governments and opposed by Labour at the time. By 1997 Labour had, however, itself embraced privatization, notably in the modernization of the London Underground and its plans to privatize at least part of Royal Mail (Heffernan 2000). Moreover, it did not reverse the Conservative privatizations, with the exception of Railtrack, which was only a very limited reversal, since the train operating and leasing companies were left in private ownership.

Another form taken by privatization is to draw private capital into the financing of public services and public enterprises, without transferring ownership. The Conservatives began using private capital to finance unprivatized parts of the public sector through the Private Finance Initiative, and Labour continued this through its Public Private Partnerships. Private capital, for example, was used extensively and expensively to finance almost all hospital and school-building. Private capital was also drawn into public service delivery. Failing schools and failing education authorities were turned over to private management (see Chapter 9, p. 340). Under Labour's Welfare Reform package, private companies were to be paid to get those on benefits back into work.

In opposition, Labour had opposed attempts by the Conservatives to revitalize health care through market mechanisms. Once in government, Labour abolished the internal market, but, nonetheless, made extensive and increasing use of market mechanisms. Great emphasis was placed on the provision of choice to patients and the principle that funding should follow them. Private clinics and hospitals were widely used to supplement NHS provision. If all this indicates considerable continuity with Conservative policies, it should be recognized that Labour hugely increased spending on the NHS (see Study 15 at the end of this chapter for further discussion of Labour's health policies).

Why was there so much privatization under Labour? It was partly driven by the problem of how to increase investment in the public sector without increasing public-sector borrowing or raising taxes, which partly motivated privatization under the Conservatives. More fundamentally, there was the same conviction that private management can succeed where the public sector has failed, that private management possesses superior skills. As with the Conservatives, the provision of greater choice to the consumer was an important consideration, most notably in Labour's plan for the NHS (see Study 15). Labour privatization ultimately reflected the capitalist character of the British state and the growth of a consumer capitalism characterized by an ideology of individual choice.

Did Labour pursue a 'third way' here? The involvement of the private sector in the provision of public-sector

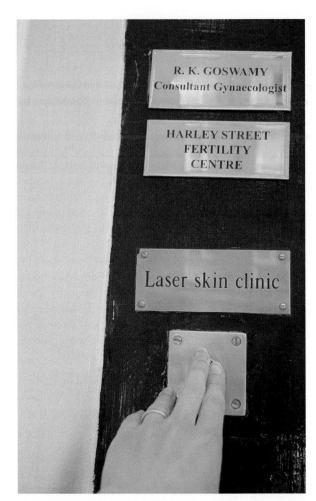

Is greater use of private clinics the best way to increase NHS capacity?
© Alice Chadwick

services was certainly one element in Giddens's 'third-way' prescription. New Labour, however, hardly steered a middle path between the 'new right' and the 'old left', and may be judged much closer to the former here. Indeed, Labour went much further in bringing private capital and consumer choice into public-service provision than the Conservatives ever did. Here New Labour accepted and further developed the transformation of the state initiated by the Conservatives in the 1980s. Arguably, while party differences clearly remained, a broad new consensus around the neo-liberal policies of the 1980s had arrived.

A weaker or stronger state?

The transformation of the state revived market forces and extensively privatized public ownership and public services. It was often claimed that this would lead to the 'rolling-back' of the state. In this section we consider whether the state has actually been rolled back, and whether it has become weaker or stronger.

Increased regulation

Deregulation was one of the watchwords of the 1980s, but attempts to revive market forces actually led in various ways to greater regulation.

This is not to say that there were no processes of deregulation. There were certainly clear examples of this. The deregulation of local bus services allowed private companies to enter the field of public transport and led, at least initially, to intense competition to provide it. The deregulation of financial services permitted building societies to become banks and freed up the movement of capital between countries. The deregulation of opening hours allowed the 24/7 opening of stores and pubs.

Deregulation did not automatically mean, however, that competition would increase, at least not in the long term. One of the consequences of allowing competition to take place is that the strongest companies rapidly come to dominate the market. Although capitalism is generally characterized as a system of free enterprise, it also manifests strong monopolistic tendencies. When the British water, gas, and electricity industries were privatized, there was the evident danger that new private monopolies would emerge to replace the public ones that had previously provided these services. A whole range of new bureaucratic bodies, such as OFWAT, OFTEL, and OFGAS, were created to maintain competition and protect the consumer through regulation. The maintenance of competition actually requires strong regulation by the state, not its withdrawal.

The abandonment of state incomes policies, which we described on p. 577, did not mean that the state simply withdrew from the labour market. It combined deregulation with regulation in its policies towards labour. The unions, by their very nature, obstructed the free operation of the labour market. The whole point of union organization is, indeed, to mobilize the collective power of labour, in order to protect individual workers against exploitation by the employer, who has far greater market power. The Conservative governments' drive to free up the labour market resulted in a whole series of laws being passed during the 1980s and the early 1990s to restrict the activities of the unions, laws that were left largely intact by New Labour. The unions became more regulated than they had ever

been before, and their opposition to regulation was ruthlessly suppressed.

Another example of the combination of deregulation and regulation can be found in the changes to the licensing laws. The laws that regulate the sale and consumption of alcohol have been gradually relaxed since the later 1990s, in part as a means of regenerating city centres hollowed out by the shift of economic activity to the city periphery (see Chapter 13, pp. 512–13). In 2005 changes in the law finally allowed 24-hour drinking in those premises licensed to provide this. This reform was, however, coupled with increased regulation. The police and local councils were given new powers to 'crack down' on disorderly behaviour and disorderly premises, while tougher penalties were introduced for shops caught selling alcohol to minors.

The maintenance of law and order

There has also been a greater emphasis since the 1980s on law and order. In part this resulted from the Conservatives' 'law and order' electoral strategy, dating from the 1970s. It was also connected with the policy changes of Thatcherism, which generated greater disorder.

The policies of the 1980s contributed to growing disorder in three main ways:

- unemployment and crime;
- urban deprivation and riots;
- industrial-relations policy and strikes.

Crime rates rose (continuing their 1970s rise). Recorded offences increased by 56 per cent between 1979 and 1990. While this was probably partly due to changes in recording and reporting, an increase of this magnitude suggests that crime itself had increased. Loveday (1996: 84–8) summarized plentiful evidence of an association between high rates of local unemployment and crime. The Conservatives' adoption of a tough anti-inflationary policy in the 1980s clearly contributed to higher unemployment, and government policy can therefore be held partly responsible for increases in crime.

Riots resulted partly from increased urban deprivation. Higher levels of unemployment and associated deprivation were linked to the rioting that became a regular feature of city life (see Chapter 13, pp. 503–5). Feelings of deprivation became particularly acute as the individualist consumerism promoted by the neo-liberal ideology of Thatcherism took hold.

Strikes became more violent. Government industrial-relation policies led to new confrontations in the 1980s, and industrial disorder reached new heights in the violent battles of the 1984–5 miners' strike. The use of police against strikers was a feature of the government's handling of this and other 1980s strikes (see Chapter 17, pp. 677–8).

⊃ Connections

We examine many of these changes in other chapters: the regulation of trade-union activity is discussed in Chapter 17, pp. 676–8; the introduction of market forces and greater state regulation are discussed in relation to education in Chapter 9, pp. 337–8.

Why has there been a greater emphasis on law and order since the 1980s?

© Alice Chadwick

There was also a discernible shift in social policy from the principle of removing the causes of disorder through state welfare to the containment and suppression of disorder through the police and the courts. The Conservatives rejected the idea that disorder resulted from social conditions and saw it in terms of the moral responsibility of individuals for their actions. This was the other side of the individualism of the 1980s. If individuals failed to act responsibly, they had to be punished and forced to obey the law.

The state was strengthened through various changes in policing. Control of the police was centralized and largely taken out of the hands of locally controlled police authorities. The police were given new equipment and trained in

What is anti-social behaviour?

© Alice Chadwick

new tactics for dealing with public-order situations, a process that has been described as *para-militarization*. As P. A. J. Waddington (1996: 124) put it: 'No longer are officers deployed as a collection of individuals acting more or less at their own discretion; police now act as squads under superior command and control.' Kettling is a recent example of this.

The powers of the police were extended. In 1984 they acquired the power to hold for questioning for seven days those suspected of terrorism. In 1986 they were given greater powers to ban and control demonstrations and marches. The 1994 Criminal Justice Act changed the 'right to silence' by allowing the silence of defendants when questioned by the police to be used against them in court. It also increased police powers in dealing with such groups as football hooligans, travellers, squatters, hunt saboteurs, and road protesters. Changes in policing were backed up by changes in the penal and judicial process, with punishments for serious offences being made more severe (see Chapter 14, pp. 547–9).

These authoritarian tendencies continued under New Labour, notably with the introduction of Anti-Social Behaviour Orders (ASBOs), Family Intervention Projects (FIPs), and further anti-terror legislation. The police, local authorities, and social landlords were all able to initiate proceedings leading to an ASBO, which typically restricted the movement of offenders. FIPs were created to tackle 'neighbours from hell', anti-social families considered a threat to their community. Anti-terrorism laws enabled the Home Secretary to impose highly restrictive control orders on those suspected of terrorism and to lengthen detention before trial. This legislation was also arguably misused in police stop-and-search operations and control of demonstrations, and in local councils' surveillance activities (*Guardian*, 22 January 2009). New Labour's style of government can also be seen in its education policy, in its tough school inspection regime and severe penalties, such as the closure of failing schools and the suspension of failing education authorities (see Chapter 9, pp. 340–2).

There were evident continuities with Conservative policies. The *authoritarian populism* considered a feature of 1980s Conservatism (see p. 577) turned out to be a feature of New Labour as well.

Privatizing law and order

While the state's apparatus for maintaining law and order was being strengthened, it was also being privatized, though this resulted from long-term privatizing tendencies as well as new policies. Privatization has taken three main forms:

- the growth of private security;
- the privatizing of law and order functions;
- active citizenship.

Private security companies probably employed more people by the 1990s than the public police force. This was a long-term process going back to the 1920s, which was linked to changes in industry and retailing, such as the growth of large commercial sites (Johnston 1992). The widespread introduction of bouncers to police entry to clubs and, in effect, to control the surrounding area has led to the claim that the maintenance of order in cities at night has been privatized (see Study 13 on p. 512). Gated communities staffed by guards provide another example, and there has also been the appearance in some local areas of street patrols by private security companies, funded by local residents.

There has been an extensive *privatizing of law-and-order functions*. Prisoner escort duties, to and from courts and prisons, have been privatized. Prison-building has been privately financed and the management of some prisons has been privatized (see Chapter 14, pp. 549–50). Electronic tagging is operated by private companies (see Chapter 14, p. 546). 'Non-essential' police functions have been transferred to private companies.

Active citizenship involves private citizens in police functions. There are various state-sanctioned schemes, such as Neighbourhood Watch. Television programmes such as *Crimewatch* and hotlines providing information to the police are other examples. Active citizenship may also take non-legitimate forms, such as vigilante activity.

These privatizing processes raise the possibility of police functions becoming fragmented between various competing organizations. In this vein, Les Johnston (1996: 63) listed seven alternative providers of policing in British cities, ranging from public organizations to private security companies, and vigilantes.

Privatization extends to the conduct of military and security operations overseas, notably in Iraq after the 2003 invasion. By spring 2004 there were some 20,000 employees of 60 different private security organizations operating in Iraq. Many of these companies were transnational and recruited retired military or police personnel from a wide variety of countries. As always, privatization and globalization were closely linked processes. According to Deborah Avant (2005: 3): 'A burgeoning transnational market for force now exists alongside the system of states and state forces.'

These various processes of privatization may be seen as reversing the nineteenth-century development of a public police force. They raise the issue of whether the modern state is losing the 'monopoly of the legitimate use of force', which, as we showed earlier (see p. 559), was considered by Max Weber to be its key feature. At the very least, the privatization of the maintenance of order blurs the distinction between public and private services in the performance of a key function of the state.

Accommodating diversity

In this section we shift to another issue. The 'third way' had called for devolution and a new form of the nation state that would accommodate ethnic and cultural diversity (see p. 579). Here we examine two ways in which this has been happening—the devolution of government and the introduction of sharia law.

Devolved government

The **devolution** of government to Wales and Scotland in 1997 and 1998 seemed to be quite a sudden change in the character of the United Kingdom. Movements to provide greater autonomy for Wales and Scotland had, however, long existed, and there had been an earlier attempt to bring devolution about in 1979. It was arguably not so much the 1990s devolution of government as its previous absence, with the very special exception of Northern Ireland (see Box 15.7), that marked out the British state. Russell Deacon (2002: 15) points out that 'Britain had become the only large state in Europe that still had its legislative and executive power concentrated in just one parliament'.

Long-term processes combined with political changes to bring devolution about. There had always been tension between the component nations of the UK, because its unification had subordinated the Celtic nations to the English and generated nationalist movements for independence, particularly in Ireland (see Box 15.7). One of the cementing forces of the Union had been a collective participation in imperial expansion, but by the 1960s the Empire was collapsing. Industrial links, together with an accompanying class organization and class conflict, kept nationalism quiet in Scotland and Wales, but by the 1980s their industries were collapsing and class organization was weakening, while in Scotland North Sea oil suggested a possible basis for economic independence. Meanwhile the growth of the EU had opened up the possibility of 'independence within Europe'.

The determined opposition of the Thatcher governments to devolution blocked the process for a time, but also gave it new life by bringing Labour and the Scottish nationalists into their early 1990s alliance. It is then not really surprising that under the 1997 Labour government devolution rapidly occurred.

Devolved government has not, however, been a systematic or clear-cut affair. Varying institutions were created that sufficiently met the demands of the nationalist movements to head off, at least for the time being, a fragmentation of the British state. Devolution has gone furthest in Scotland, with the creation of a Scottish executive and a parliament with some policy-making and limited tax-raising powers. There was less support for it in Wales, which has an advisory assembly rather than a parliament,

Waving the saltire: why
© Getty Images/Jeff J. Mitchell

with less scope for policy-making. Northern Ireland is for historical reasons a more complex case, as discussed in Box 15.7. Although a sense of English national identity has been growing, no English parliament has been created and attempts to construct regional assemblies in England have so far been rejected. Defence and taxation remain in the hands of the UK government, parliament, and civil service, which anyway continue to control most areas of policy. Sovereignty still inheres in the UK parliament.

Where devolution has made a difference is in education and social policy. Broadly speaking, the devolved administrations have reverted to less market-driven policies, reacting against the neo-liberalism of Thatcherite Conservatism and New Labour. Thus, Scotland and Wales led the way in reintroducing maintenance grants for students. In Scottish and Welsh education there has been less diversification of schools, less selection, and less privatization. In Scotland free personal care was introduced for older people, and in Wales a standard contribution by the state, while in England personal care is means-tested. The Scottish National Party (SNP) government has been phasing out prescription charges and abolishing hospital parking fees. Scottish policy has been described as more collectivist and welfarist, and Welsh policy as more universalist and egalitarian, than the consumerist and marketing policies of the UK government (Birrell 2007).

Briefing: Ireland: the first devolution 15.7

Until 1922 the whole of Ireland was part of the United Kingdom. Home rule for Ireland was already on the British political agenda by the 1880s, but it was only after a war of independence that the Irish Free State was created in 1922. At the same time Ireland was partitioned, with the six Protestant-dominated counties of the north separating themselves from the Catholic Free State and remaining part of the UK.

The creation of a Northern Ireland government, with its own parliament at Stormont, was the first devolution in the United Kingdom. As Russell Deacon (2006: 90) points out, this was in spite of the fact that there was little desire for devolution there: 'Elsewhere in Britain devolution was sought or granted as a product of nationalism but in Northern Ireland the population either wished to be united with another country (Ireland) or was fervently unionist and wished to be governed from Westminster.' Although the UK government remained sovereign and kept control of taxation, the armed forces, and foreign relations, Stormont had extensive powers over other areas and was given a free hand by Westminster.

Devolution came, however, to an abrupt end with a resumption of direct rule from Westminster in 1972. The background to this was growing violence, as the Protestant-dominated Stormont government came into increasing conflict with a civil-rights movement seeking to end discrimination against Catholics. The movement had its roots in the growth of a Catholic middle class no longer willing to accept Protestant oppression. As conflict intensified, a new Provisional wing of the Irish Republican Army (IRA) emerged, claiming that, since

the armed forces had not protected Catholics, it would do so. Northern Ireland then became locked in armed conflict as both sides sought a military solution and engaged in ethnic cleansing.

After repeated attempts to find a political solution had apparently succeeded in the Good Friday Agreement of 1998, devolved government returned in November 1999, but for only seventy-two days. Attempts to restore it failed, and between 2002 and 2007 it was suspended. Conflicts grounded in religious differences made it extremely difficult to create a functioning government including both sides. Deacon (2006: 203) comments that Northern Ireland had the 'strongest religious sectarian political parties in Europe', that at a time when religious political divisions were diminishing elsewhere they were increasing there. Paramilitary violence actually increased for a time after the 1998 Good Friday Agreement (Deacon 2006: 205). In 2007 a devolved government, with a Unionist (Protestant) first minister and a *Sinn Fein* (Catholic) deputy, and containing representatives of all four political parties, at last resumed.

This recent absence of a stable devolved government makes it difficult to assess the consequences of devolution for social policy. It has, however, been argued that, as in the other devolved administrations, there has been a reaction against the policies of Thatcherism and an attempt to 'put the clock back' (Blakemore and Griggs 2007: 256).

➲ *We refer to religion in Northern Ireland in Chapter 11, pp. 409–15, and to riots there in Chapter 13, p. 505.*

So does all this mean that the UK is breaking up? Tom Nairn forecast the break-up of Britain in his well-known book of 1977, and still maintained in *After Britain* that 'a dissolution of the old multinational state is indeed under way, and there is now almost no one who believes otherwise' (Nairn 2000: 4). It is clearly Scotland that now leads the way in this. In the 2007 election the Scottish National Party became (by one vote) the largest party in the Scottish parliament and formed a minority government committed to a 2010 referendum on independence. Scottish national identity is certainly strong, with survey data showing that nearly two-thirds of Scottish residents see themselves as Scottish rather than British (Bechofer and McCrone 2008: 96).

Whether this would translate into a vote for independence is, however, doubtful, since only 49 per cent of those

describing themselves as 'Scottish, not British', which means those most likely to vote for independence, were actually in favour of it (Bechofer and McCrone 2008: 99). The 2010 change of government and the heavy public expenditure cuts that followed could well, however, give new momentum to the SNP's drive for independence.

Sharia law

While devolution sought to accommodate the long-standing national diversity within the UK, the issue of *sharia* law arose from immigration and increasing ethnic diversity. Although this might seem to be a matter for Muslims, since they are the ones who practise *sharia*, British Jews too have been allowed to operate their own courts. The principle at issue is whether ethnic or religious minorities should be allowed to have their own courts or whether there should be 'one law for all'.

Sharia law is derived from verses in the Qu'ran, interpreted in the light of the *hadith*, the collected sayings and doings of the Prophet Muhammad. Four main law schools, providing different interpretations, have combined with local traditions and customs to produce considerable variation in the principles and application of *sharia* law. The impact of the West resulted in the introduction in most Islamic countries of secular Western legal codes alongside *sharia* but also generated a reaction against them in many Islamic countries, notably in Iran, Malaysia, Nigeria, Somalia, Sudan, and Afghanistan under the Taliban. Within Islam there has been a Salafist movement seeking to return to the original teachings of the Qu'ran and the *hadith*, as expounded during the *Salaf*, the first three generations of the Muslim faith. Some countries, notably Saudi Arabia and the Gulf states, had never really moved away from *sharia* in the first place.

In the UK, *sharia* courts operate under the 1996 Arbitration Act, which allows people to resolve disputes by going to an impartial tribunal. Provided that both parties to a dispute agree to do this, the tribunal's decisions have the force of law. This Act was intended to be a means by which people could settle disputes cheaply and quickly through arbitration and avoid having to go through the civil courts. It provided an opening, however, for the advocates of *sharia* to give the force of law to the judgments of *sharia* courts. Jewish *Beth Din* courts too operate on this basis, and in principle any ethnic or religious group could set up its own tribunals under the 1996 Act. Although *sharia* law covers all aspects of life, most of the cases going before *sharia* courts in the UK are concerned with marital or family matters, though business disputes are also often settled in this way.

According to the 2009 report on *sharia* law by the Civitas think tank, there were at least eighty-five *sharia* courts operating in the UK, far more than most people knew about. There were the well-known courts in London, Bradford, Coventry, and Manchester but also others operated by Muslim councils and 'dozens of informal tribunals run out of mosques or online' (Maceoin 2009: 69).

To some Muslims, subordination to *sharia* law is a matter of religious belief. It is important to emphasize *some*, since a 2007 survey found that 59 per cent of Muslims living in the UK rejected the idea of living under *sharia* law, with 28 per cent preferring it. On specific questions, there was more support for the pronouncements of *sharia* law. Thus, 51 per cent thought that 'a Muslim woman may not marry a non-Muslim' and 61 per cent agreed with the statement that 'homosexuality is wrong and should be illegal' (Mirza *et al.* 2007: 5, 47). Significantly, support for *sharia* varied with age, the young supporting it more than the old. Some prominent non-Muslim figures, such as the Archbishop of Canterbury, have supported it, the Archbishop on the basis that the acceptance of *sharia* would promote social cohesion, 'because some Muslims did not relate to the British legal system' (*Guardian*, 8 February 2008).

Critics have pointed out that *sharia* pronouncements in the UK often conflict with UK law and human rights, and the Civitas report provides many examples of *fatwas* (*sharia* legal judgments) that illegally discriminate against women, non-Muslims, and homosexuals. The position of women has attracted particular attention. They have an inferior status in *sharia* courts, while *sharia* rulings on marriage, divorce, financial rights, the care of children, and inheritance discriminate against them in various ways. In 2008 the Muslim Institute proposed a new marriage contract that would improve the position of women under *sharia* law, and received support from important UK Islamic organizations, but met strong opposition from conservative clerics (Maceoin 2009).

The Civitas report points out that women face particular problems with divorce. Men can easily divorce their wives, but women cannot so easily divorce husbands. This makes it very difficult for women to escape abusive and violent husbands. In the eyes of the community, Islamic marriages and the *sharia* rules governing them take priority over civil marriages. Women cannot easily avail themselves of British or European laws that protect their rights, if they are under family and community pressure to seek remedies through *sharia* courts. Furthermore, the 1996 Act's requirement that participation be voluntary, that both parties must agree to the resolution of a dispute by an arbitration tribunal, carries little weight if there is communal or family coercion forcing compliance (Maceoin 2009).

Advocates of *sharia* law challenge the notion that all citizens should be governed by the same law. Does this mean that increasing international migration and ethnic diversity will result in diverse legal systems within diverse societies? There are many ethnic minorities that do not demand their own laws. Furthermore, as we showed above, differing opinions on *sharia* clearly exist amongst Muslims. The Canadian experience is here instructive. In the Canadian province of Ontario, an Islamic Institute of Civil Justice was founded in 2003 to provide *sharia* arbitration under a 1991 Arbitration Act. After a 'furious debate led by Muslim women who argued that they had gone to Canada to get away from *sharia* law', the Arbitration Act was amended to ensure 'one law for all' (Green 2009: 8).

A new economic crisis

We have argued that the economic crisis of the 1970s lay behind the transformation of the state since the 1980s. In 2007 a new economic crisis began to unroll, a crisis that has been widely considered the worst since the depression of the 1930s. In this section we first examine the nature and causes of this crisis, before moving on to the state's response to it. Is another transformation of the state beginning in the wake of this crisis?

The crisis

The immediate origins of the crisis that began in 2007 lay in a house market bubble, especially in the United Kingdom and the United States. Prices seemed to rise endlessly, making houses an apparently safe investment, both for those buying and for those lending to them. Banks and building societies competed aggressively to lend, with commission payments and bonuses spurring their sales staff on. They were eager to lend not just because of the interest they could earn but, more importantly, because a new market had developed for the loans themselves. The loans could be 'securitized', packaged up and sold on to other financial institutions looking for apparently safe and profitable ways to invest their money.

House prices could not go on rising for ever, and it was hardly surprising that the house market bubble eventually burst. Few, however, expected that this would lead to a full-blown and global crisis of capitalism. Why did this happen?

Many so-called sub-prime borrowers had been persuaded to take loans they could not afford and defaulted on them. When house prices began to fall, the financial institutions that had made the loans or bought them as investments faced problems in getting their money back. But what really turned this situation into a crisis was the heavy indebtedness of these institutions. They had themselves borrowed vast amounts of money, often from abroad, to make the loans or buy the loan packages. Major US investment banks had borrowed as much as thirty times their capital.

The banks had made good profits from this 'leverage', and their share prices had risen, but they did not realize how dangerous their situation was. They thought they were safe, because they had used sophisticated new financial techniques supposed to eliminate risk, but these were poorly understood and promised more than they could deliver. Apparently rock-solid US financial institutions—the New York investment banks Bear Stearns, Merrill Lynch, and Lehmann Brothers, the mortgage finance corporations Fanny Mae and Freddie Mac, and the global insurance giant AIG—had hugely overextended themselves and faced bankruptcy.

The crisis then spread rapidly and globally. One big name after another was rescued by governments, but, when Lehmann Brothers was allowed to go bankrupt in 2008, there was a global financial panic. Was any bank safe? Banks became reluctant to lend. Interest rates rose. Capital was hoarded.

This was no longer just a crisis for the banks. It spread through the whole economy because the hoarding of capital froze the financial system. Normal economic activity is lubricated by the movement of money between those with money to lend and those needing finance, but with the 'credit crunch' this ground to a halt. Ordinary companies needing to finance their daily activities and ordinary people wanting to buy homes found that loans had suddenly become very hard to obtain. Governments tried desperately to get interest rates down and banks lending again.

This financial freeze set off cumulative deflationary mechanisms. Bankruptcies, rising unemployment, and falling wages, sales, and prices interacted to depress economic activity. Fearful of the future, people started to save more and spend less. Deflationary spirals of this kind are hard to reverse, as the well-known Japanese case has shown. When the Japanese economic bubble burst at the end of the 1980s, the economy entered a downward deflationary spiral from which it still has not really recovered (Fulcher 2004: 122). In 2008, global economic interconnectedness meant that it was not one country that was spiralling down but most of the global economy.

Behind these crisis mechanisms lay more fundamental changes in the character of capitalism. First, neo-liberal capitalism had deregulated financial activities. This had allowed banks and building societies to engage in speculative activities that they had not previously been allowed to do. In the neo-liberal spirit of allowing markets to operate freely, regulatory institutions operated 'light-touch' policies. Secondly, it was easy to borrow money. It was cheap for consumers, companies, and banks to borrow, because of low interest rates and the flow of money into the old industrial societies from the exporting countries of the Far East (see Box 15.8, p. 590). Thirdly, financial globalization meant that money could move rapidly around the world, facilitating its flow into banks eager to borrow in order to finance speculative ventures, but also making it easy for capital to leave in a crisis.

A debt bubble had been growing since the 1980s. More and more consumption, more and more economic activity, were financed through debt. By the time the crisis hit, total US debt had risen to well over three times its national income. Heavy debts place individuals and companies in a vulnerable situation, since changing circumstances may mean they cannot service, let alone repay, the money borrowed, and then face bankruptcy. The bursting of the housing bubble was just such a circumstance. Collapsing banks, company bankruptcies, and rising unemployment then only made the situation worse. Governmental injections of money and the lowering of interest rates prevented a complete collapse, but debt levels remain dangerously high.

Without a debt-financed consumption there would arguably have been an earlier crisis of overproduction. The intense competition characteristic of capitalism, the

Global focus China and the crisis   15.8

China has been central to the global crisis that began in 2007. One important reason for the crisis was the flow of money from countries with a surplus, notably China, into the West. In China growing exports had generated a large surplus, which was invested in the United States. It was the flow of money from China that kept interest rates low and allowed the huge growth of debt that lay behind the financial crisis. This flow also financed consumption of China's exported goods.

Economic growth in China has provided one way out of the recession. China too suffered from the global recession, but its economy continued to grow at around 8 per cent. Some have argued that it is China (and India, with 2009 growth of around 6 per cent) that can pull the world out of recession. Much depends on whether domestic consumption can be increased in China, to decrease its dependence on exports and bring in imports from countries in recession.

This crisis may well accelerate the forecast shift of global economic power from the USA to China, as its growth outpaces that of the USA. The global role of the dollar as a reserve currency may well be gradually replaced by the Chinese *renminbi*. One straw in the wind is the report that Arab oil states plan to replace the use of the dollar for oil trading with a basket of other currencies that would include the *renminbi*.

Sources: Fisk (2009); O'Grady (2009).

---

technological advances driven by competition, and the spread of capitalist production to new countries all combined to push production to new heights. The only way that consumption could absorb the flood of products was through increasing personal debt. Furthermore, increasing debt had arguably only delayed a crisis of overproduction and, by allowing production to expand even further, actually made the eventual crisis worse. It is the overproduction tendency of capitalism, which Karl Marx long ago drew attention to, that is the most fundamental problem of all (Fulcher 2004: 106–7).

The state's response

As major financial institutions and manufacturing companies faced bankruptcy, governments intervened to force them into mergers with stronger rivals, provide them with financial support, or take them over. Although Lehman Brothers was allowed to fail, with apparently disastrous consequences, others were considered 'too big to fail' in both the USA and the UK.

The Royal Bank of Scotland (RBS), the UK's biggest bank, came within days of bankruptcy in October 2008 and was forced to accept an injection of capital that gave the state 60 per cent ownership of it, this figure rising to 84 per cent in February 2009 after more capital was needed (*Sunday Times Business*, 4 October 2009).

This might lead one to think that the neo-liberal era of Thatcherism and New Labour has come to an end. Indeed, some thought that 'old labour' nationalization policies were back, while others actually called for a nationalization of all the banks, which had through their reckless and self-interested practices brought the economic crisis about. There was not, however, any ideological shift in the UK Labour government's posture. Its gradual and reluctant

bank takeovers were driven by the perceived need to keep the financial system working rather than any belief in the virtues of public ownership. The intention was to return RBS and other banks in which the state had a substantial stake to the private sector as soon as possible.

There was also widespread government intervention to support economic activity and maintain employment. This can reasonably be described as a return from the neo-liberal reliance on market mechanisms to a Keynesian management of the economy (see p. 569). Instead of 'balancing the books', governments have been running deficits. The car industry, with its massive overproduction crisis, received financial support. Industrial policies to subsidize the 'green' industries of the future appeared on the scene. Quantitative easing increased the supply of money. These attempts to reduce the depth and length of the recession have been internationally coordinated through the G20 and the EU. So, does all this indicate that a global rejection of neo-liberalism is under way?

Again, this reversion to pre-Thatcherite economic interventions seems likely to be short-lived. The problem with the deficit financing of economic intervention is that it requires heavy borrowing. Such borrowing is expensive and becomes a burden on future governments, which have to pay interest and eventually repay the loan. Furthermore, if extensive borrowing makes it look as though countries are in economic trouble, higher interest payments are required and loans may be refused. There are heavy pressures on governments to reduce their deficit as soon as possible.

In the UK in 2009 and early 2010, the Labour government and the Conservative opposition were in conflict over the handling of this. Labour argued that the deficit should not be reduced too sharply or too quickly while the economy was struggling to escape from recession, while the Conservatives insisted that there should be immediate and drastic action to reduce it. After the 2010 general election, the Conservative/Liberal Democrat coalition government moved quickly to cut public expenditure and raise taxes. There is the risk that these actions may push the UK economy back into recession. With governments elsewhere behaving similarly, there may well be a return to the global recession from which governments had thought they were escaping.

Another apparent reversion from neo-liberalism is the call for greater regulation of the banks to prevent the excesses of the recent past. There is a broad international consensus that banking practices, salaries, and bonuses now require tighter regulation, though governments disagree on the specifics and are wary of damaging their financial industries. While regulation is stridently opposed by the exponents of free-market capitalism, it is, nonetheless, wrong to see it as inimical to the period of neo-liberal capitalism that began in the 1980s. As we argued above (see p. 583), policies of deregulation were matched by the creation of numerous regulatory bodies to supervise the workings of markets. More effective regulation of the banks, if it does occur, will at best enable financial markets to work better and prevent banks engaging in risky practices that endanger the current system. This would not be a reversion to the policies of an earlier age but rather a consolidation of neo-liberal capitalism.

As the crisis unrolled and its magnitude became apparent, the writings of Karl Marx were often recalled (Boyes 2008; King 2009). Could capitalism be entering some final crisis? The scale of the crisis was such that it was quite plausible to think so at the time. Governments intervened, however, to prevent a catastrophic collapse, in a way unimaginable to Marx, though they may well be storing up trouble for the future. They may be sowing the seeds of another crisis by allowing the biggest corporations to believe that, whatever they do, however risky their activities, they will not be allowed to fail (Ferguson 2009). Thus, some have argued that in bailing out the banks governments have interfered dangerously with the normal workings of capitalism. Indeed, Marx himself had argued that crisis bankruptcies were beneficial to capitalism since they got rid of unprofitable businesses and enabled profitable ones to expand and take their place.

It is important to add that, while Marx believed that crises would get bigger and more threatening to the system, he did not argue that a crisis would on its own bring about the end of capitalism. This would happen only if it was overthrown by revolutionary action. There has certainly been popular indignation. The high pay and bonuses of the bankers held responsible for the crisis aroused anger, as those with much lower incomes felt the pain of unemployment, reduced earnings, and the repossession of their homes. Popular discontent may well lead to disorder, as it did in the 1980s, but there is no sign that a revolutionary overthrow of the capitalist social order is imminent. Anticapitalist movements exist but only on the margins of political activity. Recent elections and opinion polls do not suggest that the crisis has resulted in a movement of opinion towards the Left.

This is a very big change from the situation, say, a century ago when there were powerful social movements that could envisage a non-capitalist world and were working to produce one. Furthermore, the collapse of the Soviet Union at the end of the 1980s rather decisively demonstrated the non-viability of an alternative system. A state-protected capitalism seems here to stay.

 # Stop and reflect

In this section we began by linking the crisis of the 1970s to the transformation of the British state.

- Corporatist attempts to manage the 1970s crisis failed, and politics became polarized.
- Margaret Thatcher's Conservative Party won the 1979 election and initiated the 1980s transformation of the state.

We went on to analyse the Thatcherite transformation.

- Make sure you understand the meaning of neo-liberalism, neo-conservatism, authoritarian populism, and marketization.
- What were the main features of the state's transformation?

- How did state welfare change and do you think that it declined?

We then considered Labour government after 1997.

- Did Labour pursue a 'third way'?
- Was 1997 or 1979 the year of political transformation?

We discussed whether the state had been weakened or strengthened by these changes.

- Privatization and deregulation had diminished the public sector.
- In what ways was regulation increased?

continued

- Neo-liberals had called for the state to be 'rolled back'. Do you think it was?

We went on to consider the state's accommodation of greater diversity.

- Is devolution likely to lead to the break-up of the UK?
- Should different ethnic groups be allowed to have different laws?

Lastly, we examined the economic crisis that began in 2007 and the state's response to it.

- Why did the bursting of the housing bubble lead to a general economic crisis?
- Is another transformation of the state's relationship with capitalism taking place?

Key concepts

- authoritarian populism 577
- commodification 563
- corporatism 570
- decommodification 560
- democracy 560
- democratization 560
- devolution 586
- fiscal crisis 575

- hegemony 562
- incorporation 569
- juridification 564
- legitimacy 559
- marketization 577
- neo-conservatism 577
- neo-liberalism 564
- privatization 577

- relative autonomy 563
- state 558
- third way 579
- welfare pluralism 578
- welfare state 563
- workfare 565

Workshop 15

Study 15 A privatized NHS?

In April 2000 the Labour government unveiled its plan for transforming the NHS through a massive increase in its resources. There were to be over 100 new hospitals by 2010 and 7,500 new consultants, while waiting times for hospital treatment would be reduced from an average of seven months to a maximum of three. By 2005 patients would be able to choose which hospitals to be treated in (see our chapter opener on p. 558). League tables and the publication of death rates would inform choice.

Transforming the NHS was not just about increased resources, however. It was also about a radical marketization of health-care provision. Hospitals would compete, money would follow patients, and 'payment by results' would be introduced. The 2004 NHS Improvement Plan revealed that the government 'intended to introduce for-profit clinical providers on a large, potentially unlimited scale, and make NHS hospitals and other organizations

compete with them in a full health-care market, no longer supervised by or answerable to parliament' (Pollock 2005: 237).

Private providers were invited to set up Independent Treatment Centres to carry out routine operations, which would be paid for at higher rates than NHS providers. Reportedly, a quarter of the contracts for the new polyclinics, intended to be the place where most routine health-care needs are met, have been awarded to private companies (*Independent*, 20 January 2009). Privatization provided 'entry points' for private, often transnational companies, seeking access to state-funded health care (Pollock 2005: 68, 128).

Another step has been taken towards turning hospitals into private corporations with the award of 'foundation status' to hospitals performing well. These can then raise private capital, pay their staff at higher rates, and contract out health care freely to private companies. According to Allyson Pollock (2005: 130), they 'will be freed from NHS oversight via the strategic health authorities and be subject only to an independent regulator, who will be primarily concerned with their financial viability'.

Improved performance was not left solely to the operation of market forces, for there was also more central regulation. The National Institute for Clinical Excellence (NICE) was created to ensure that the most cost-effective treatments were used. National Service Frameworks lay down standards of treatment. A 'health super-regulator', called the Commission for Healthcare Audit and Inspection, was established to monitor performance and scrutinize complaints. Another body, the Commission for Social Care Inspection, regulates nursing and the care of old people. This auditing apparatus has monitored the NHS's success in achieving the literally hundreds of targets laid down by the NHS plan.

These processes of change have not, however, been applied uniformly through the UK. Devolution has made a difference, at least in Scotland. Blakemore and Griggs (2007: 256) point out that in Scotland 'the NHS is beginning to seem to be distinctively different . . . because the Scottish system is not being reorganized at the same pace or on the same scale a it is in England and Wales'. In Scotland health care has remained more integrated and under central control.

❷ Which of Esping-Andersen's three worlds of welfare does the UK government's policy on health come closest to?

❷ Do you think the Labour government's health policy indicates a commitment to the principles of the welfare state or an abandonment of them?

❷ Has the 2010 Conservative / Liberal Democrat government continued the privatization process?

Media watch 15 For and against NHS marketization

After publishing its NHS plan the Labour government pressed ahead with the marketization of the NHS (see Study 15). According to Polly Toynbee of the *Guardian*, 'manic marketization is driving the NHS into cut-throat chaos'. She accepted there were good reasons for using the private sector to cut waiting lists and she was not against patient choice, but she feared that the government's increasing emphasis on competition would 'cause nuclear melt-down in the NHS'.

Toynbee raised many questions. What would be the effect of competition on cooperation? How could organizations both cooperate and compete? What would happen to units driven into financial failure by competition? Would they actually be closed down? As she put it, 'just watch how many services will need rapid rescue when wards or clinics prove indispensable (or local protest threatens marginal seats)'.

Marketization has increasingly turned the NHS into a purchaser rather than a provider of services. Toynbee thought that turning primary care trusts into purchasers would destroy the local relationships that had built up between doctors and health visitors, school nurses, community nurses, and midwives, as these became 'self-employed entrepreneurs' or were bought up by organizations that sell their services to the trusts.

She worried about the consequences of introducing 'payment by results', particularly if this spread to emergency and chronic care. Paying for 'cold surgery' was one thing, but how could the medical care of the old, with their complex medical problems, be paid for in this way? She feared that payment by results could lead to 'expensive overtreatment', as hospitals earned extra money through unnecessary procedures or medication. Payment by results 'will create a tidal pull for extra patients to fill hospital beds—and coffers'.

Julian Le Grand, one of the architects of government health policy, responded a few days later. He argued that the NHS had

failed to live up to its principles. There had been long waiting lists, unhappy patients with no choice of care, unless paid for privately, and no incentives to reward providers of good care or force bad providers to improve. Increased funding alone would not remedy its deficiencies.

Targets had helped but they were 'too blunt an instrument' and required a constant monitoring of performance. Giving patients choice was a step forward but could not on its own provide sufficient incentives. That is why it was necessary to introduce payment by results as well, 'where money follows choice'. Le Grand claimed that the 'overtreatment' danger should be avoided by making general practitioners the purchasers, for 'experience has shown GPs to be good gatekeepers, effectively managing referrals to hospitals and drug costs'.

Alternative providers were needed to make choice work. The government was therefore introducing new providers—foundation trusts, social enterprises, and independent centres for diagnosis and treatment.

Toynbee described the outcome of successive NHS reforms as 'a cat's cradle of contradictory policies' leading to chaos, but Le Grand saw health policy as having 'an underlying logic and consistency' that would produce 'a service that is responsive, fair, efficient, free, and robust enough to last'.

Sources: Toynbee (2005); Le Grand (2005).

When considering these questions, use material from Study 15 as well:

❷ Do you think that the Labour government's health policy led to a 'cut-throat chaos' or had 'logic and consistency'?

❷ What do you think are the advantages and disadvantages of: greater choice; payment by results; increased competition?

Discussion points

Thatcherism and New Labour

Before discussing this, read the sections on 'Thatcherism and the transformation of the state', 'New Labour', and 'A weaker or stronger state'.

- What is meant by the 'third way'?
- What continuities can you find between the policies of Thatcherism and New Labour?
- What differences can you find?
- Do you think that the post-1997 Labour governments continued Thatcherism, reversed it, or pursued a 'third way'?
- Did the British state enter a new era in the 1980s?

- How would you explain the transformation of the British state?

Worlds of welfare

Before discussing this, read the section on 'Three worlds of welfare', and Box 15.1 on p. 573. Try surfing the Net to find out about the debate over health care in the United States.

- What did Esping-Andersen mean by the 'three worlds of welfare'?
- Which world does Britain fit in?
- Is the United States moving from one world to another?
- Are the three worlds becoming one world?

Explore further

The following examine aspects of the development of the state and its recent transformation:

Avant, D. (2005), *The Market for Force: the Consequences of Privatizing Security* (Cambridge: Cambridge University Press). *This book starts from Weber's famous words on the state's monopoly of the use of force to examine its privatization in Iraq and many other parts of the world.*

Gamble, A. (1994), *The Free Economy and the Strong State: The Politics of Thatcherism* (2nd edn, London: Macmillan). *An influential examination of the crisis of the 1970s, the rise of Thatcherism, and the transformation of the state during the 1980s.*

Hay, C. (1996), *Re-Stating Social and Political Change* (Buckingham: Open University Press). *A sophisticated review of the literature on the state and an account of its development from the 1940s to the present, with a lot of helpful tables and diagrams.*

Held, D. (2006), *Models of Democracy* (3rd edn, Cambridge: Polity Press). *An authoritative examination of the various forms that the democratic state can take.*

Miliband, R. (1969), *The State in Capitalist Society* (London: Weidenfeld & Nicolson). *A classic study of the relationship between capitalism and the state, which deals not only with government but also with the civil service, the military, the judiciary, the mass media, and education.*

Wainwright, H. (2003), *Reclaim the State: Experiments in Popular Democracy* (London: Verso). *A discussion of alternatives to the neo-liberal state, drawing on examples of experimentation in various countries.*

Clear and full accounts of the development of state welfare in Britain are provided in:

Fraser, D. (2009), *The Evolution of the British Welfare State* (4th edn, London: Macmillan).

Glennerster, H. (2006), *British Social Policy since 1945* (3rd edn, Oxford: Blackwell).

Hill, M., and Irving, Z. (2003), *Understanding Social Policy* (8th edn, Oxford: Blackwell).

Lowe, R. (2004), *The Welfare State in Britain since 1945* (3rd edn, London: Macmillan).

Contemporary social policy and welfare issues are also examined in:

Blakemore, K., and Griggs, E. (2007), *Social Policy: An Introduction* (3rd edn, Maidenhead: Open University Press). *A comprehensive examination of social policy that also covers education policy and criminal justice issues.*

Ellison, N., and Pierson, C. (2003) (eds), *Developments in British Social Policy 2* (Basingstoke: Palgrave Macmillan). *All aspects of Labour's social policy are covered here.*

Levitas, R. (2005), *The Inclusive Society: Social Exclusion and New Labour* (2nd edn, Basingstoke: Palgrave Macmillan). *This is a penetrating analysis of Labour's policies on social exclusion and their relationship to inequality.*

Pollock, A. M. (2005), *NHS plc: The Privatization of our Health Care* (London: Verso). *A powerful and authoritative account of the privatization of health, from Thatcherism to New Labour.*

Online resources

Visit the Online Resource Centre that accompanies this book to access more learning resources and other interesting material on the state, social policy, and welfare at:
www.oxfordtextbooks.co.uk/orc/fulcher4e/

A debate on the 'third way' hosted by the Nexus think tank, with contributions from sociologists and social policy experts, can be found at:
www.netnexus.org/library/papers/3way.html

A site maintained by the *Guardian* newspaper, providing access to news on welfare issues and public services can be found at:
www.guardian.co.uk/society

The Centre for the Analysis of Social Exclusion at the London School of Economics can be found at:
http://sticerd.lse.ac.uk/case

develop together in their own way and avoid the evils of both capitalism and socialism. There was a third route to modernity.

These distinctions now appear more than a little dated. Any idea of the ex-colonial countries pursuing a common path disappeared quickly, as the cold war between the United States and the Soviet Union forced them into one camp or the other. The Second World then collapsed with the break-up of the Soviet bloc. It is, anyway, difficult to see the countries of the Third World as any longer sharing common features. While the Asian 'tigers' rival the old industrial societies, some African countries seem stuck in an almost permanent condition of deprivation and poverty.

Globalization makes the notion of distinct worlds ever more out of date, though this idea was always somewhat misleading. There have long been close 'one-world' relationships between the so-called First, Second, and Third World countries. Indeed, as we will show on pp. 607–8, a capitalist *world economy* has long existed. It has never made much sense to conceive of three different worlds within it.

Globalization

Our sense that the world is increasingly becoming one place is most commonly expressed by the term 'globalization'. After discussing the meaning of this term, we will return to the issue of the nation state and the impact of globalization upon it.

What is globalization?

This word is often used as a short-hand term for growing economic integration, but, although there is an important economic dimension to globalization, it embraces all aspects of our lives, and all institutional areas of society. Processes of cultural and political as well as economic globalization are at work. Religion and the media, crime and sport, work and leisure have all been globalized. To make sense of globalization we have to provide a definition that can apply to all these different areas and activities.

Globalization refers to a complex of interrelated processes, which have in common the idea that relationships and organizations have increasingly spread across the world, bringing about a growing awareness of the world as a whole. Its key components are:

- the destruction of distance;
- the stretching of relationships beyond national boundaries;
- a growing awareness of the world as a whole;

- an increasing interdependence between different parts of the world.

Globalization *destroys distance* through communications technologies that bring places closer together, as in such terms as the 'shrinking' or 'compression' of the globe (see Figure 16.2). Faster travel does this, but it is most strikingly exemplified by the telecommunications technologies that allow the instant communication of information between distant places. As Anthony Giddens has put it, this is 'action at a distance'. Globalization is 'the intensification of world-wide social relations which link distant localities in such a way that local happenings are shaped by events occurring many miles away' (Giddens 1990: 64).

A key aspect of this 'action at a distance' is the development of relationships and organizations that *cross national borders* and *extend beyond the nation state*. Held *et al.* (1999: 15) consider that 'globalization implies first and foremost a stretching of social and economic activities across frontiers . . .'. Transnational organizations provide the clearest example of this stretching process, and Sklair (1991: 6) has argued for a 'conception of the global system based on transnational practices'.

Figure 16.2 A shrinking world

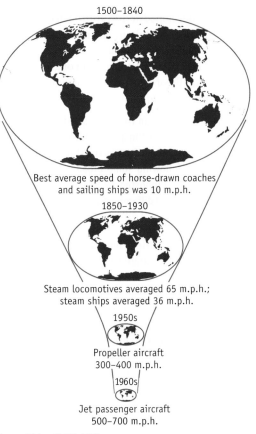

1500–1840

Best average speed of horse-drawn coaches and sailing ships was 10 m.p.h.

1850–1930

Steam locomotives averaged 65 m.p.h.; steam ships averaged 36 m.p.h.

1950s

Propeller aircraft 300–400 m.p.h.

1960s

Jet passenger aircraft 500–700 m.p.h.

Source: Dicken (1992: 104).

Globalization is not just to do with communication and organization. It also involves the growth of an *awareness or consciousness* of the 'world as a whole' or the 'world as a single place'. Thus, Robertson (1992: 8) has argued that globalization means 'the intensification of consciousness of the world as a whole'. People now see themselves less as members of this community or that country and more as members of humanity, of a single threatened species. Notions such as 'one earth', the 'new world order', or the 'global economy' are examples of this consciousness. Indeed, Giddens (1999: p. i) considers that the growing use of the word 'globalization' is itself an indicator of it. Another term used by Martin Albrow (1996) and Robertson (1992) to convey the notion of this new global awareness is 'globality'.

This growing awareness is linked to the increasing *interdependence* of widely separated areas of the world. This interdependence is another key feature of globalization. It is particularly evident in economic matters. Vegetables from Kenya, or wine from New Zealand, or cameras from Japan are produced for global markets. Producers in one country are dependent on retailers and consumers in another, and vice versa. An economic crisis in one part of the world can be swiftly transmitted to another. Environmental concerns have intensified the awareness of interdependence, for global warming ignores state boundaries.

Global organization

The notion of global organization is central to the discussion of globalization but requires further analysis. It is important to distinguish between transnational and international organizations, since they have very different implications for the nation state:

- International organizations, such as the United Nations (UN), are controlled by the representatives of nation states and operate through national structures.
- Transnational organizations, such as transnational corporations (TNCs), operate across national boundaries and have some autonomy from the nation state.

There are problems with equating global organization with *transnational* as opposed to *international* organization, in the way that Sklair, for example, does (see previous section). Many TNCs actually operate in only a small number of countries and are hardly global in character (see p. 625). On the other hand, an international body, such as the UN, is about as globally extensive as one can get. It makes little sense to treat all TNCs as global organizations but then exclude the UN. Globalization should, therefore, be taken to refer to the growth of both international and transnational relationships and organizations.

As Held *et al.* (1999) have emphasized, a distinction also needs to be made between regional and global organizations. By 'regional' organization is meant here the organization of distinct regions of the world, such as Europe or Africa. Both regional and global organizations extend beyond the nation state, but they are very different in character. As groupings of nation states that have a common interest, regional organizations such as the European Union (see pp. 637–9) act in some ways like self-interested superstates. A global organization, such as the UN, which represents all nation states and tries to reach compromises and agreements between them, is quite different in character.

Global organizations not only extend across the world; they also penetrate into local society, both shaping what happens locally and adapting to it. The term **glocalization** has been employed to refer to the interpenetration of the global and the local. It was first used by Japanese business corporations to describe the adaptation of their managerial practices to local cultures and conditions. It was then

Global food: who is more dependent, those who produce the food or those who sell it?

© Alice Chadwick

THEORY AND METHODS   16.3

Place polygamy and the globalization of biography

In *What is Globalization?* (2000a) Ulrich Beck argues that globalization not only reaches down into local society; it penetrates into our personal lives. Globalization means that we live simultaneously in many different social worlds. He gives the example of a German lady who travels between homes and social networks in Bavaria and Kenya, belonging to neither place and to both. He calls this 'place polygamy':

> Transnational place polygamy, marriage to several places at once, belonging in different worlds: this is the gateway to globality in one's own life; it leads to the globalization of biography.

> By this he means not only that we may have homes, friends, and families in different countries but that this brings many different worlds into our lives. Furthermore, the simultaneous presence of different worlds means that the conflicts between them are reproduced inside each one of us.

> Globalization of biography means that the world's oppositions occur not only out there but in the centre of people's lives, in multicultural marriages and families, at work, in circles of friends, at school, in the cinema, at the supermarket cheese counter, in listening to music, eating the evening meal, making love, and so on.

Source: Beck (2000a: 73).

❓ We outline some of Beck's other ideas on the consequences of globalization (for work, employment, and leisure) in Chapter 17, p. 674.

taken up by Roland Robertson (1992) and has since become widely used by, for example, Ulrich Beck (2000a). Beck has gone further and emphasized the ways in which the global penetrates into people's lives, so that the conflicts between different worlds are reproduced within individuals (see Box 16.3). We should not then treat global relationships and processes as though they exist solely at some high level above national societies, for the global impacts on the local and, indeed, the personal, while local responses affect global structures.

Globalization and the nation state

The relationship between globalization and the nation state has been the subject of a long and continuing debate.

In one of the classic discussions of globalization, Anthony Giddens (1990) treated the development of the nation state as interconnected with globalization. The nation state existed from its very beginnings in a system of nation states, which was initially European but then expanded to become global. Some have seen this system as weakening the sovereignty of the state, but Giddens insisted that sovereignty has always been dependent upon the system. It has been through the international system that states have recognized each other's sovereignty and sorted out their boundary disputes. Loss of sovereignty to a supranational UN has been exaggerated, for the UN has actually presided over the establishment of many new nation states during the post-colonial era. The very existence of the nation state was therefore bound up with the growth of a global system of states.

A chorus of recent writers has, nonetheless, declared that globalization is now resulting in the decline of the nation state. Manuel Castells refers to its 'demise' (1996: ii. 275), and argues that 'globalization, in its different dimensions, undermines the autonomy and decision-making power of the nation state' (1996: ii, 261). Zygmunt Bauman (1998: 57) refers to its 'withering away' . . . According to Martin Albrow (1996: 64), 'the nation state loses control of the forces it previously contained' (we outline some theories of this kind in Chapter 2, p. 63).

The specific arguments made by these various authors are as follows:

- The growth of international law and organization leads to a loss of national sovereignty.
- Global economic integration undermines national control of the economy, constrains the actions of national governments, and weakens the state.
- National governments are challenged 'from below' by transnational social and religious movements.
- The growth of global communication makes it more difficult for states to police their borders.
- National unity is fragmented by a growing ethnic and religious diversity that stimulates communal demands for autonomy from the state.

Does all this mean that the nation state is on the way out? Albrow (1996) claimed that national societies are being superseded by a global society. Others have suggested that weaker versions of the old nation state will survive. Thus, Bauman (1998) argued that global capitalism promotes the proliferation of weak states able to maintain order but not strong enough to control the movement of capital between countries and its activities within them.

It is often claimed that nation states can no longer control their borders. Ohmae argued in *The Borderless World* (1990) that the global flow of information is 'eating away' the boundaries between states. The broader term 'deterritorialization' has been used to describe the decline of social organizations based on *bounded* units, from the nation state to the local community. Instead of being members of distinct units, people are linked by networks that spread across all boundaries.

> **⊃ Connections**
> You may find it interesting to follow up this issue in our
> discussion of container and network conceptions of
> community in Chapter 13, pp. 478–9.

Bauman has, however, made the important point that the significance of borders depends on social position. He has sharply contrasted the situation of the rich and poor:

> For the inhabitants of the first world—the increasingly cosmopolitan, extraterrestrial world of global business-men, global culture managers or global academics—state borders are levelled down, as they are dismantled for the world's commodities, capital and finances. For the inhab-itants of the second world, the walls built of immigration controls, of residence laws and of 'clean streets' and 'zero tolerance' policies, grow taller; the moats separating them from the sites of their desire . . . grow deeper, while all bridges, at the first attempt to cross them, prove to be drawbridges.

Bauman 1998: 89

Paul Hirst and Grahame Thompson (1996) have firmly rejected the idea that the nation state is in decline. They have criticized the belief that transnational corporations are, somehow, free-floating organizations detached from nation states. TNCs still have national headquarters and national cultures. They still depend on the nation state's institutions and support for their activities. Hirst and Thompson also argued, like Giddens, that international political organiza-tions do not take authority away from nation states, for these are represented in such bodies and participate in their deci-sion-making, while these bodies inevitably depend on nation states to implement their policies. They concluded that government has certainly become a multi-layered mat-ter, but the nation state remains essential to it.

Thus, the impact of globalization on the nation state raises a range of important questions, which are linked to

the most pressing issues of the world today. We will come across them at many points in this chapter.

The timing of globalization

Globalization is commonly treated as a recent process. The world does seem to have 'shrunk' since the 1960s, with the much greater speed of travel and communication resulting from key developments at that time, such as the introduc-tion of wide-bodied passenger jets and geostationary satel-lites. People, goods, information, images, and money began to move around the world much more freely. Globalization might then appear to be a recent phenomenon and some sociologists have treated it in this way. Albrow (1996) argued that globalization occurred during the transition from the modern to the global age, a transition that he dated very precisely to the years 1945–89.

Robertson (1992) considered, on the contrary, that glo-balization began in the fifteenth century with the European voyages of discovery and the beginnings of the European colonization of the world. Similarly, Immanuel Wallerstein (1974), whose ideas we will examine in the next section, argued that a capitalist world economy was already coming into existence at that time. Certainly, by the time of the nineteenth century there were major communications advances—steam travel, the telegraph, and the telephone —which 'shrank' the world (see Figure 16.2, p. 602). We take the view that globalization should be treated as a long-term process that stretches back to the fifteenth century.

Hirst and Thompson (1996) have challenged what one might call the 'onwards and upwards' notion of globaliza-tion. They claimed that the world economy was more inte-grated by trade and finance during the period before the First World War than it is today, though they did recognize that some globalizing processes, such as the growth of TNCs, have recently accelerated. The global movement of people through international migration, which we examine on pp. 608–11 and pp. 625–9, certainly slowed down after the First World War, before accelerating again after the Second. It should not be assumed that globalization is a continuous and ever-increasing process of world integration.

 Stop and reflect

We began this chapter by considering the nation state, and its relationship to the nation and to nationalism. Reflect on your own nationality.

- What nation state are you a citizen of?
- List the main rights and obligations that citizenship of your nation state involves.

- What do you consider your nation to be?
- What are its distinguishing features?
- Does your nation correspond with your nation state?
- How important is nationality to your sense of identity?

We then considered issues raised by the development of post-colonial nation states.

- Modernization and dependency theory provided contrasting approaches to development.
- While evidence from different countries can be found to support each of these approaches, both gave insufficient attention to local diversity and initiative.
- Does the action approach provide a better way of addressing development issues?

We then went on to globalization.

- Although this is often taken to refer to the growing economic integration of the world, it embraces all aspects of people's lives.
- Make sure that you are clear about its key components (see p. 602).
- What is meant by the notion of a 'shrinking' world?
- Consider Beck's concept of 'place polygamy' and its consequences. Think about what you have done in the past week. Can you find examples of the 'world's oppositions' in your daily life?

Empires in a global economy

In this part of the chapter we examine the early stages of globalization, from the rise of nation states and empires, through the growth of a world economy, to world wars.

From nation state to empire

The origins of European nation states can be traced far back in history. Anthony Smith (1994) argued that the ethnic elements of nationality already existed in medieval times. The peoples of Europe had a sense of their distinctiveness because of differences of language and culture, and the historical myths that traced their origins back to distant ancestors.

Linguistic diversity had always existed in Europe, but distinct national languages had to be created. In medieval Europe educated people communicated with each other through the international language of Latin. The creation of national languages involved the displacement of Latin, the consolidation of local dialects into a standard and stable language, and the elimination of rival languages. The fifteenth-century invention of the printing press and the growth of the printing trade played a crucial part in this process (see Chapter 10, p. 360).

At this time Europe was divided between dynastic states, of the kind that we describe on p. 548. In the sixteenth and seventeenth centuries the monarchs ruling these states consolidated their territories and began to build new administrative structures that gave them more control over their populations and resources. They constructed

royal administrations to collect taxes and maintain order within distinct national territories with defined borders. Nation states were now emerging.

Interstate conflict played an important part in the process by driving rulers to find new ways of raising armies and financing wars. The nation state, international warfare, and international relations emerged together. Giddens (1985) argued that the growth of nation states can be understood only if they are seen as parts of an international system.

In the British case, it was, according to Linda Colley (1992), the long eighteenth-century conflict between Britain and France, lasting until Napoleon's defeat in 1815, that forged the British nation. This conflict made three crucial contributions:

- *national administration*: the construction of an effective system of national taxation and the building of a 'massive military machine';
- *national identity*: the creation of a British identity, with religion playing an important part in this, for war with Catholic France unified the Protestant peoples of Great Britain and Northern Ireland;
- *empire*: the unifying of the various British sub-nationalities through their combined involvement in building, administering, and exploiting the Empire.

Then, in the nineteenth century, a unified national administrative structure was constructed through the administrative revolution, which we examine in Chapter 14, p. 525. The railways, improved postal services, and the telegraph created national communications networks.

Within this framework other changes integrated and strengthened the nation. The nineteenth-century democratization of government involved the British people, and those of other European states, in national politics. State education, state employment, and national military service generated loyalty to the state. Governments standardized national languages, built national monuments, revived

---

⮕ Connections

Other closely related aspects of the development of states are discussed elsewhere. The bureaucratization of the state is discussed in Chapter 14, p. 525, and the development of the ruler's authority in Chapter 15, pp. 559–60.

ancient myths of national origin, and generally glorified the nation (Hobsbawm 1977). Industrialization and urbanization broke down local ties and brought people into larger groupings where they could identify with the 'imagined community' of the nation.

The rise of the nation state and the construction of overseas empires were closely interconnected. Territorial conflicts in Europe extended to territorial conflicts elsewhere in the world, while overseas rivalries contributed to nation-building in Europe. The construction of these empires must, however, also be set in the growth of a global economy.

The emergence of a global economy

The beginnings of a global economy can be found in the late-fifteenth-century expansion of Europe through voyages of exploration that led to trading relationships with other continents and the emergence of a 'capitalist world economy'.

A capitalist world economy

The concept of a 'capitalist world economy' comes from Immanuel Wallerstein's work (1974) on world systems. A **world system** is, in his terms, a unit within which there is a complete division of labour that extends across various ethnic and cultural groups. World systems can take the form of world empires or world economies. **World empires**, such as ancient Rome or imperial China, had a single political centre and were integrated by a bureaucratic administration. **World economies** had multiple political centres and were integrated economically rather than politically.

Wallerstein argued that a capitalist world economy first established itself in Europe and then gradually extended to include the whole world. After the collapse of the Roman world empire, no other imperial power had been able to take control of Europe, which fragmented into competing states. Although Europe was politically divided, it became economically integrated by the capitalist merchants in the trading cities of north-west Europe, who created a network of economic relationships that eventually extended across the whole world. A capitalist world economy had come into existence.

The central feature of this world economy was the relationship between its *core* and its *periphery*. It was initially dominated by a group of *core* countries in north-west Europe—Britain, France, and the Netherlands—but this later included Germany and the United States. These were the economically most advanced areas, where the manufacturing of goods was already well established, and were later to be at the centre of the Industrial Revolution.

The *periphery* supplied raw materials to the core and imported manufactured goods from it. Initially it consisted of East European countries, but in the late fifteenth century began to expand to include Africa, Asia, and America. Military domination by the strong states of the core countries kept state structures weak in the periphery. The construction of overseas empires played an important part in this, though the core also dominated the periphery by financial means.

The importance of Wallerstein's approach is that he established that:

* we should not examine national economies in isolation but always consider their place in the whole system of economic relationships;

* from its very beginnings the development of capitalism brought about a growing economic integration of the world;

* the end of empire did not end the core's domination of the periphery. Thus, when Latin American countries

---

Controversy and debate   Re-orienting world thinking   16.4

In the 1970s Andre Gundar Frank (see p. 600) found Wallerstein's ideas congenial and began working with him. Frank saw the lack of development in Latin American countries as resulting from their position in the capitalist world economy. By the end of the 1980s, Frank and Wallerstein were, however, moving apart, and in his 1998 book *ReORIENT: Global Economy in the Asian Age*, Frank accused Wallerstein, and indeed Marx, Durkheim, Weber, and many others, of giving a Eurocentric version of world history.

In *ReORIENT*, Frank claimed that Asia was economically ahead of Europe until the nineteenth century. Europe's early

economic development resulted from the earlier growth of Asian economies. It was only in the nineteenth century that the West overtook Asia. The later rise of Asian economies in the second half of the twentieth century, and their future dominance of the world economy, should not be seen as something new but rather as a return to their earlier world dominance.

In his 2009 book, *When China Rules the World*, Martin Jacques pursues a similar theme and claims that a resurgent China is becoming the dominant world power.

became independent from Spain and Portugal, their domination by core countries continued, for Britain and the United States still controlled their economies.

Industrialization and the international division of labour

While a world economy was *created* in the sixteenth century, it was industrialization that really *integrated* it by generating a much closer interdependence between the core and the periphery. This interdependence resulted from the international division of labour established in the nineteenth century. The industrial societies specialized in producing manufactured goods and the rest of the world in raw materials and food (usually called primary products, to contrast them with the secondary, processed goods made in the industrial countries). This global division of labour was said to be in the common interest, as each country could concentrate on what it was best at doing.

Interdependence meant, however, that some were more dependent than others, and the result was increasing international inequality. The primary producers found that most of the benefits of the international division of labour seemed to go to the industrial countries. It was the growing awareness of this that led to the *dependency* theory of the relationship between the industrial and primary producer countries (see p. 600).

There were many reasons for the growth of international inequality between the industrial societies and the primary producers:

- *Profits on capital.* The industrial countries were the source of the capital that financed tea estates in India or rubber plantations in Malaya, and took the profits from primary production.

- *Control of prices.* These were controlled by trading corporations and markets located in the industrial countries. The prices of industrial goods were kept high, while raw material prices tended to fall.

- *Product dependence.* The economies of the industrial countries were highly diversified, but the economies of the primary producers were often dependent on one product, such as coffee in Brazil or bananas in the Caribbean. A fall in the price of these products had a catastrophic effect on these countries.

- *Imperialism.* Through their empires the industrial countries were in political, administrative, and military control of many primary producers, and could make sure that colonial economies were subordinated to imperial interests.

Nineteenth-century empire-building was linked to industrialization. The spread of industrial methods of production from Britain to other countries led to an increasing international competition for markets and raw materials.

The best way to protect markets and raw-material supplies was to erect an imperial fence around them. Economic concerns were not, however, the only motivation behind imperial expansion. Having an empire was regarded as one of the defining characteristics of a 'great power', and late-comers to the competition, such as Germany and Italy, scrambled for areas with little obvious economic value.

A divided world

Different parts of the world had become increasingly integrated through both the administrative structures of empires and the capitalist world economy. Globalization was well under way. The world was also, however, becoming more divided.

Ethnic and racial divisions

The growth of a world capitalist economy generated a series of migrations that created ethnically more diverse societies. At a time when people were learning to identify themselves as nations, they also began to think of themselves as belonging to distinct races.

It is estimated that between 1500 and 1800 some six million Africans were transported by the slave trade to the colonies of America and the Caribbean (Emmer 1993: 67). This was not the only trade in African slaves, for they were also traded to the Islamic countries of North Africa and the Middle East.

The defining characteristic of **slavery** is that it treats people as property. Slaves are the possessions of slave-owners, who can buy and sell them at will (see Box 16.5).

The labour provided by slaves was crucial to the emerging capitalist world economy. They were used to work the gold and silver mines of South America, to produce sugar in Brazil and the Caribbean, to grow tobacco and cotton in North America. Native populations had often been exterminated by a combination of colonial conquest and colonist-spread disease, or else were hard to subdue into a reliable labour force. Slaves transplanted from their societies of origin and forced into submission were a cheap and controllable source of labour.

This trade in people was also central to the capitalist world economy in another way, for it formed one side of the Atlantic trade triangle of the eighteenth century. Goods shipped from Britain and France were used to buy slaves on the West African coast, who were transported across the Atlantic and sold to plantation-owners. The ships could then return to Europe with a cargo of colonial products, typically sugar or tobacco or cotton. From Europe they shipped industrial products back to Africa for sale there (see Figure 16.3).

While most people have heard of the slave trade, there was a far greater transportation of indentured labour after

Briefing: the slave-ship *Zong* jettisons its cargo 16.5

The *Zong* was a Liverpool slave-ship that sailed in 1781 from West Africa to Jamaica with a cargo of slaves. On the initiative of its captain, and with the crew's compliance, 131 sick slaves were thrown overboard as it approached its destination, in order to save drinking water and to make a claim on the ship's insurers. When this became known, Granville Sharp, a leading campaigner against the slave trade, tried to bring a prosecution against the crew for murder.

Two cases came to court in 1783, when the shipowner's insurance claim was contested by the underwriters. The Solicitor-General represented the slave-owners and declared in court that a prosecution for murder 'would be madness: the blacks were property'. The judge agreed and stated that 'the case of the slaves was the same as if horses had been thrown overboard'.

The only response of the British state to this and similar cases seems to have been the Act of 1790, which ruled out insurance claims 'on account of the mortality of slaves by natural death or ill treatment, or against loss by throwing overboard of slaves on any account whatsoever'.

Source: Walvin (1993: 18–21).

the nineteenth century abolition of slavery (in the West, for it still exists in some parts of the world—see the Wikipedia entry on 'slavery in modern Africa'). Unlike slavery, indentured labour involved the payment of wages, but in other respects it was little different, since workers were subject to enslaving contracts. Some thirty million indentured workers were transported from India to other British colonies, to work, for example, on sugar plantations in the Caribbean or to build railways in East Africa (Massey and Jess 1995: 12).

There was also an extensive migration of settlers from Europe to the 'new world', particularly during the

Figure 16.3 The transatlantic slave-trade triangle

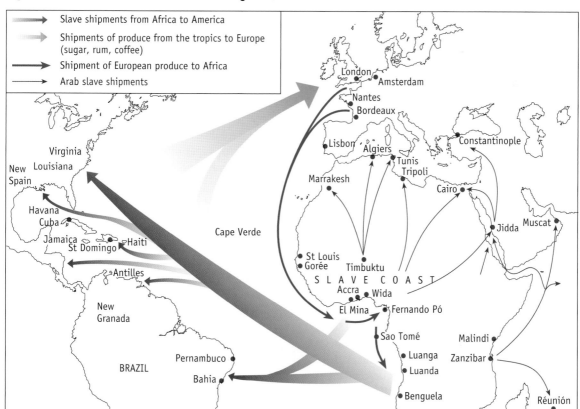

Source: Potts (1990: 42).

Figure 16.4   International migrations, 1820–1910

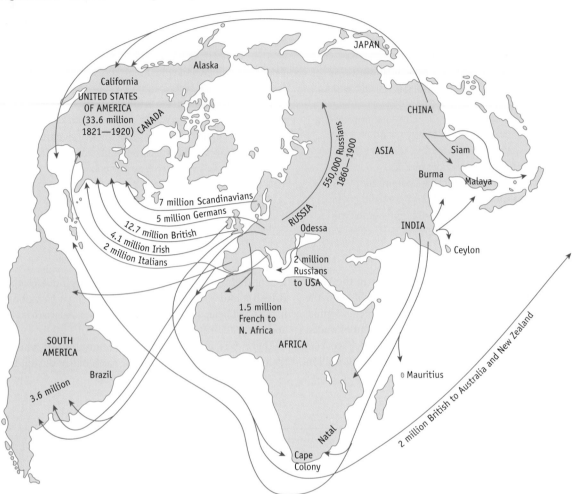

Source: The Times Atlas of World History (1978: 209).

nineteenth century (see Figure 16.4). Between 1815 and 1914 some sixty million people left Europe for America, Africa, and Australasia combined (Hirst and Thompson 1996: 23). Between 1860 and 1920 around thirty million emigrated from Europe to the United States alone (Castles and Miller 2003: 51). Some migrants were motivated by dreams of making their fortunes in the colonies or on the American frontier, but, for many, emigration was the only means of escaping from poverty or even death, from famine in Ireland or anti-Semitic pogrom in Eastern Europe.

These international migrations created ethnically diverse societies stratified by ethnicity. In the United States, white Anglo-Saxon Protestants (WASPs) were dominant, other groups of European origin, such as Italians, Irish, and Poles, came below them, and the black descendants of African slaves were at the bottom. In many British colonial territories, Asians occupied an intermediate position between the British settlers and native populations. These

hierarchies resulted from differences in power and wealth, but notions of superiority and inferiority were quickly attached to ethnicity. Stereotyping resulted in crude characterizations used to justify inequality. The ethnic stratification of these colonial societies was seen as reflecting in-born racial characteristics rather than resulting from power and wealth.

Race was identified with skin colour. Europeans justified their rule over Africa and Asia by claiming the superiority of the white race over the black, brown, and yellow peoples of the world. This belief in racial superiority helped to bridge class divisions in Europe. Subordinated workers

> **⊖ Connections**
> We discuss race and ethnicity in Chapter 6, pp. 195–6, and stratification in Chapter 19, pp. 745–6. You may find it helpful to refer to these discussions while reading this section.

could now see themselves as members of a superior white race that ruled the world.

Imperial divisions

By the end of the nineteenth century, almost the whole world was divided up between the rival empires of the European states, the United States, and latterly Japan. Where they did not formally incorporate territories, they established competing spheres of influence, as in China.

Expansion overseas not only gave these countries new territory; it also consolidated them as nation states. The economic benefits of imperialism produced employment and higher wages, while the discontented or adventurous could emigrate to the colonies. Empire also provided a sense of national superiority that strengthened popular identification with the nation. Hobsbawm (1987) noted

that the politicians of the time were well aware of the 'social benefits' of imperialism.

Unlike Wallerstein's world empires (see p. 607), these overseas empires were not complete world systems but parts of a *system of nation states*. The empires of Rome and China had been for a time contemporary civilizations, but they were isolated from each other and each had arguably established a 'world of its own'. The overseas empires of the nineteenth century had not established such complete worlds and were in constant competition, at times engaging in wars with each other.

Industrial production, railway systems, and bureaucratic administrations provided nation states with a new capacity for war. It was now possible to organize and mobilize whole populations and whole economies for 'total war'. A popular nationalism motivated and legitimated this mobilization, way beyond the expectations of

Figure 16.5 Africa under European rule, 1913

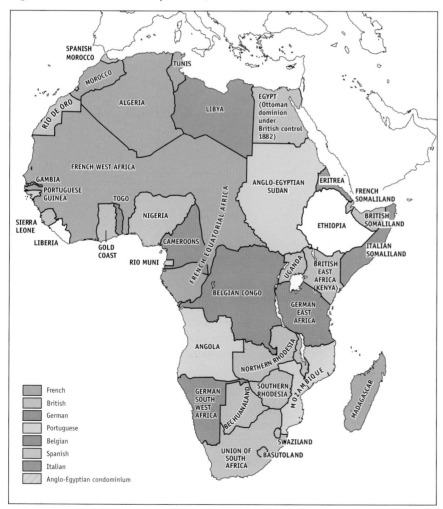

Note: With the exception of Ethiopia and Liberia, the whole of Africa was divided up between the European empires by 1913.
Source: *The Times Atlas of World History* (1978: 240).

governments. At the beginning of the First World War governments were surprised by the enthusiasm with which people plunged into a conflict that was to kill at least twenty million of them (Hobsbawm 1987).

Conflict between nation states had gone global. Periodic warfare between rival overseas empires had begun as soon as they acquired colonies, but the nineteenth-century division of the world brought about a more intense economic, political, and military competition between them. It also led to the construction of complex alliances stretching across the world, as in Britain's 1902–21 alliance with Japan to contain the expansion of Russia.

The First World War was still essentially a European war that drew in allies and colonies, but the Second World War between 1939 and 1945 was truly global in its scope. This time German expansion in Europe was linked to Japanese expansion in Asia. The European and Pacific 'theatres' were connected by global alliances, which joined the United States to the Soviet Union, Britain, France, and China, and joined Japan to Germany and Italy.

Ideological divisions

The cold war was a world war of a different kind. It was a war between rival socio-economic systems led by the Soviet Union and the United States. It started as the Second World War ended and lasted until the Soviet Union began to collapse at the end of the 1980s. The world was more divided into two blocs than ever before. Countries that tried to remain neutral found themselves under heavy pressure to join one side or the other. Many were split by political struggles or civil wars between forces sponsored by the two sides.

The cold war in some ways marked the end of the imperial stage of globalization. The European colonial empires collapsed, partly because both the United States and the Soviet Union supported independence movements. There was also an ideological dimension to the conflict between 'capitalism' and 'socialism' that was absent from the earlier conflicts between the colonial empires.

There were, nonetheless, continuities with the imperial past. The United States continued to regard Latin America, the Caribbean, and the Pacific as its sphere of influence and took military action against Soviet attempts to penetrate them. Much of the Soviet Union was not ethnically Russian and consisted of countries conquered by the pre-revolutionary Russian Empire, while its 'allies' were controlled by military occupation. The Soviet Union was the last European empire.

The conflicts between nation states had led to the construction of empires that both integrated and divided the world. They integrated the world by bringing almost all peoples into a small number of political and military structures that stretched across the continents. They divided the world through the racial divisions they generated and the rivalries that led to world wars. The world was both more integrated *and* more divided than ever before.

Stop and reflect

In this section we first considered the development of nation states, the growth of a capitalist world economy, and the construction of overseas empires.

- Make sure that you are clear about the meaning of 'nation state', 'world empire', and 'capitalist world economy'.
- The ethnic components of nationality have long existed, but it was in the nineteenth century that the modern nation state was constructed.
- A capitalist world economy originated in the fifteenth century, and after industrialization an international division of labour was established.

- Most of the world was divided up between overseas empires. Should they be considered 'world empires'?

We have also been examining the early stages of globalization.

- Return to our definition of globalization on p. 602 and consider in what ways globalization occurred during the centuries covered by this section.
- It is often said that globalization integrates the world. In what ways did the world become more integrated and in what ways more divided during these centuries?

Development and globalization in post-colonial times

In this section we consider the problems of development faced by post-colonial nation states, and discuss the issues raised by population growth and urbanization. We move on to globalization, examining global movements of capital and people, and global challenges to the nation state. Lastly, we discuss whether we can be said to live in 'one world', taking up the issues of global warming and world government.

New nation states

We begin by outlining the foundation of most of the world's nation states during the post-colonial era and considering their problems of development.

From empires to state nations

The overseas empires, which had appeared so permanent at the end of the nineteenth century, were self-destructive. The European states could not administer their huge colonial territories without involving and educating local people to do most of the work for them. Education brought local people into contact with the political movements and democratic institutions of the home countries. Nationalist movements calling for the same institutions to be established in the colonial territories inevitably emerged. The Second World War then weakened the empires' control over their colonial territories.

The cold-war period then brought the age of empire to an end. The United States and the Soviet Union dominated world politics, and both opposed the overseas empires of the European powers. As we noted above, the Soviet Union had itself acquired something of an empire, but it was unable to sustain the military expenditure required by the cold war and its collapse brought the last of the European empires to an end.

As the empires collapsed, new nation states were created. Between its foundation in 1945 and the end of the century the membership of the United Nations tripled from 50 to over 150. The new nation states faced difficult political problems. They rarely corresponded to a people with a clear national identity. Their boundaries were determined by the way the empires had divided territory between them. They often included ethnically diverse peoples, with different languages, religions, and cultures. They had, therefore, to construct new nations within their state boundaries and for this reason have been called *state nations* rather than *nation states*.

The new state apparatus would often be dominated by one ethnic group at the expense of others, and subordinate ethnicities frequently found this situation intolerable. Military *coups* and civil wars became a feature of the newly independent states.

Aid or trade?

The new states faced the question of how they could catch up with the developed industrial societies. Would the rich countries of the West, which had exploited them for so long and continued to dominate their economies, assist them? According to modernization theory, which we examined earlier (see p. 600), economic growth should spread from rich to poor countries. Economic aid would help this process along.

More economic aid has often been seen as the solution to the continuing problems faced by the new states. The G8 summit in 2005 and the accompanying Live-8 Concert focused on the provision of more aid to solve the problems of Africa. Arguably, the problem with economic aid is not, however, whether there is enough of it as whether it can actually do much to help poor countries.

The economic benefits of aid are problematic. When it takes the form of a loan, debt repayments can become a huge burden. Debt cancellation has indeed become one of the main objectives of those seeking to help poor countries. Economic aid has often been misdirected into large and highly visible prestige projects, typically dams (see Box 16.6, p. 614), or siphoned off by corrupt elites. Even if it is directed into projects likely to benefit the masses, a country's infrastructure and institutions may not be up to the task.

Aid-giving countries also generally attach 'strings'. Aid may be given on condition that it is spent on projects that benefit exporting companies in the donor country. It has often been steered politically to countries adopting the 'right' political and ideological stance. Loans have been made conditional on governments pursuing neo-liberal policies that may not be appropriate to their circumstances (see p. 616).

In *Dead Aid* (2009), Dambisa Moyo has called for aid to be stopped within the next five years. She claims that 'aid has been, and continues to be, an unmitigated political, economic, and humanitarian disaster for most parts of the developing world' (Moyo 2009: p. xix). She believes that aid creates a self-perpetuating dependence on donors that prevents Africans from acting independently for themselves. This prevents economic growth. She prefers the

Briefing: the biggest dam ever   16.6

The Three Gorges dam in China, completed in 2009, will create a reservoir stretching some 400 miles up the Yangtse. It has cost £15 billion, of which roughly a third has been paid for by the World Bank.

The dam will enable better control of the Yangtse, which periodically floods huge areas. It will also provide cheap hydroelectric power to meet rising industrial and consumer demand in a huge and rapidly developing country. It will displace an estimated 1.9 million people, who will be moved into 114 resettlement townships.

Environmental groups in China and abroad have been very concerned about its multiple impacts on the environment. Large quantities of silt are expected to accumulate above the dam, and there is the danger that, as happened with the Aswan dam in Egypt, this will be prevented from reaching the agricultural lands beyond in both China and other South East Asian countries, which have historically been refertilized by periodic floods. It is also feared that the reservoir will accumulate pollution from the cities up river, which contain a population of thirty-one million, and the areas flooded, which will include '1,300 local mines, 300,000 square metres of latrines, and 2.8 million tons of rubbish, as well as graveyards, abattoirs, medical centres and other potential hazards'.

Source: Gittings (2002).

kind of relationship recently developed by China with some African countries, where, she claims, 'Africans are treated as equals', to their relationships with the West (Moyo 2009: 110).

Trade is more important than aid. Many poor countries are heavily dependent on the export of one product and the price of, say, bananas, or tea, or coffee is far more important to them than the amount of aid they receive. They also find that, although they have often been forced to open their borders, the European Union, the United States, and Japan maintain their barriers to the import of agricultural goods, while subsidizing their own exports. Aid and debt relief are generally easier options for rich countries' politicians than the lifting of trade barriers, which may damage powerful economic interests. Indeed, as Moyo argues, dramatic declarations of increased aid can be used to divert attention from a failure to address the trade barrier issue.

Aid can help countries stricken by disasters, though Naomi Klein (2007) has argued that the 'collective shock' following disasters has provided the United States with an opportunity to introduce neo-liberal policies benefiting American corporations. Specific aid projects may well be beneficial in the long term. It is, however, doubtful whether aid in general leads to much economic development. Other aspects of the economic relationships between rich and poor countries are much more important.

Development strategies

If development depends largely on the efforts of the poor countries themselves, what strategy should they pursue?

Industrialization is arguably the best way to achieve economic growth. As we showed earlier, the international division of labour made non-industrial societies dependent on industrial ones. This suggested that the new states needed to industrialize if they were to achieve economic independence and raise standards of living.

But how is industrialization to be achieved? The strategy advocated in the 1950s and 1960s was *import substitution*, which involved the state setting up industries and protecting them against cheap imports by erecting tariff barriers. This policy could rapidly establish new industries, but these could then devour state resources, and become out of date and inefficient in the absence of competition.

The emphasis shifted in the 1970s to the state promotion of *export* industry, for Japan had taken this approach and very successfully penetrated the markets of the West. A group of other countries, notably South Korea, Taiwan, Singapore, Brazil, and Mexico, which were labelled the newly industrializing countries (NICs), followed Japan along this path.

Ashton and Sung (1997) have argued that state education policy, rather than state direction of the economy, was the key to the rise of the East Asian tiger economies. In the case of Singapore, development resulted not from centrally directing investment but from providing conditions that attracted to Singapore companies that would produce high-value goods and services. These companies were provided with the skilled labour they needed by state policies designed to upgrade labour force skills.

Since the 1980s, economic globalization has shifted policy from the state direction of development to the provision of conditions that will attract foreign capital. This is partly a matter of the easier movement of capital but also to do with the greater speed and volume of the movement of goods, information, and people. The goods and services that result from investment can be more easily exported to rich countries.

The availability of cheap labour in poor countries is important in attracting capital, but it is clearly not as simple as this. According to Ashton and Sung, it is suitably educated labour that is crucial. In India, the availability of

The 'Make Poverty History' demo at the 2005 G8 summit: can more aid do this?

© Getty Images/Nicolas Asfouri

English-speaking labour has facilitated the outsourcing of call-centre jobs from Britain, while Bangalore became a major centre of software production because it had a labour force that was both English-speaking and highly educated.

The degree of state regulation, the extent of trade unionism, and the level of taxation are also important. The growth of TNCs has led many countries to create Export Processing Zones, where foreign companies can operate freely with minimal constraints of regulation and taxation, and where unions may well be banned (see p. 624).

Since the 1980s the free movement of capital has been promoted by the American-dominated World Bank and International Monetary Fund (IMF). These important organizations have advocated free market policies, making them a condition of aid. They called for fiscal austerity to reduce both wasteful government spending and loose monetary policies that would cause inflation. They pushed for privatization to get rid of inefficient public enterprises, introduce market discipline, and reduce government expenditure. Trade barriers should be lifted in order to increase trade. These policies reflected the 1980s dominance of neo-liberalism in the United States.

Such policies have, however, attracted much criticism. Water privatization was advocated as a means of solving water shortages by bringing in investment, but it has been heavily criticized for giving Western companies highly profitable monopolies at the expense of the poor, who find they have to pay high prices for previously free water. Joseph Stiglitz (2002), a senior figure at the World Bank between 1997 and 2000, argued that, although free-market policies could bring benefits in some circumstances, their indiscriminate and over-hasty imposition could be disastrous. Valuable state projects could be destroyed. Mass unemployment could result. Assets could be plundered.

The contrast between the Russian and Chinese experiences is instructive here. After the collapse of state socialism, Russia followed IMF advice, and the resultant 'shock therapy' led to mass poverty, while China's gradual and controlled transition 'entailed the largest reduction in poverty in history in such a short time span' (Stiglitz 2002: 181–2). China did not engage in mass privatization but allowed capitalism to emerge within the existing social order. Foreign capital was attracted by China's huge market and reserves of cheap labour, but within an institutional framework controlled by the state.

The focus in this section has been on industrial development, but other areas of the economy should not be neglected. The growth of tourism has become very important to the economic development of some societies (see pp. 625–7). Furthermore, the economies of most of the new states are mainly agricultural, and it makes little sense to ignore agricultural development.

In agriculture, two different strategies can be found. One is to invest capital in large, modern units with economies of scale and the latest technology, able to produce for export markets. The technological advances of the 'green revolution', which invented new, more productive crop varieties, required this kind of unit. Countries such as Colombia, Mexico, and the Philippines went down this route. It could work well but only within fertile areas, leaving most of rural society with its productive potential untapped. Success tended to be short-term, for these crops needed an ever greater use of expensive and environmentally damaging fertilizers and pesticides.

Some countries have tried to increase agricultural production within small-scale traditional units, sometimes combining this with land reform to break up large estates and return the land to those who worked it. Taiwan is a good example of this strategy. Cooperatives and community development projects have been set up in many countries to help traditional farmers raise production by pooling resources, acquiring modern technology, and improving organization. Results have, however, often been disappointing, largely it seems because inappropriate structures imposed by bureaucrats have alienated local people (Hulme and Turner 1990).

A more flexible approach, of the kind advocated by the 'action perspective' (see p. 601), would give locals more

New technology Mobiles in Africa   16.7

Fixed telephone lines are scarce in Africa, but mobile ownership has been increasing rapidly, and by the end of 2007 there were 280 million mobile subscribers, a penetration rate of 30 per cent. In Kenya the number of mobiles rose from 1 million to 5 million in five years, while the number of landlines has stayed at 300,000, most of which are in government offices.

On a continent where communications are poor, mobiles can transform daily life. Before mobiles, information about crop prices could be obtained only by making often long journeys to markets. Now they can be obtained instantly and without travelling. Middlemen can be bypassed by producers and consumers. For many people, mobiles make it at last possible to obtain financial services, carry out cashless transactions, and access the Internet.

Sources: P. Mason (2007); D. Smith (2009).

Controversy and debate Poverty in Africa   16.8

Sub-Saharan Africa has not only failed to develop; it has gone backwards since the 1970s, with GNP per capita actually lower in 2002 than in 1975. Average life expectancy has been falling since 1990 and in 2003 was only 46 years, as compared with 63 years in South Asia and 69 in East Asia (Commission for Africa 2005: 102–5).

What are the causes of this situation? The Commission for Africa set up in 2004 by Tony Blair highlighted 'poor governance' as the main obstacle to development. Governments were often undemocratic, corrupt, and incompetent. Wars and other civil conflicts created and perpetuated poverty. These political problems, together with transport difficulties, deterred investment. Manufacturing had developed late, and Africa was still heavily dependent on the export of primary products, but agriculture had been held back by lack of investment, transport problems, and trade barriers. Poor health and weaknesses in education contributed to stagnation. Debt was a huge burden. Governments spent more on debt servicing than health.

The Commission concluded that 'internal factors have been the primary culprit for Africa's economic stagnation or decline' (Commission for Africa 2005: 113) but recognized that Africa's relationship with the developed world was also important. Poor governance was partly a legacy of the colonial period, while external business interests were complicit in corruption, but 'governance is in large measure made at home' (Commission for Africa 2005: 106).

What should be done? The most important task was to improve governance, since 'without progress in governance, all other reforms will have limited impact'. Developed countries could help with this but it is 'first and foremost the responsibility of African governments and people' (Commission for Africa 2005: 14). Conflict should be tackled by building up the capacity of African states to prevent and manage it. More resources should be provided for health and education. Africa needed to produce more marketable goods, though rich countries' barriers to trade had to be removed.

How should these changes be resourced? Donor countries should immediately provide an extra $25 billion in aid per year, and a further $25 billion a year by 2015, and there should be 100 per cent debt cancellation.

How did developed countries respond? The G8 leaders promised an extra $50 billion in aid at their meeting in Edinburgh in July 2005. The debts of eighteen countries, which had met certain conditions, such as trade liberalization and privatization, would be cancelled. Critics argued that these conditions would harm the countries concerned and far more countries needed to have their debts cancelled. On trade barriers there were fine words but no specific measures. The European Union has, however, promised reforms that would reduce barriers to the import of sugar.

Source: Commission for Africa (2005).

❷ Should the main responsibility for African poverty be placed on African countries?

❷ Will increased aid solve the problem of African poverty?

❷ Can one generalize about Africa?

---

involvement and more choice. The spread of mobile phones (see Box 16.7) and village banks (see p. 601) can here greatly help the growth of local enterprise.

The search for an appropriate strategy is a difficult one. Particular strategies and specific models have been strongly advocated by their supporters, but these generally fail to take account of the varying circumstances, institutions, and cultures of poor countries. What works in Singapore will probably not work in Somalia. Top-down strategic thinking also often fails to take account of local diversity, or involve local people. Strategies are anyway constrained by external forces, as the imposition of policy conditions by the World Bank and the IMF shows. If governments have little freedom of manœuvre, no choice of strategy is possible.

International inequality

How successful have developing states been in closing the gap with developed countries? Figure 16.6 on p. 618 shows a strikingly divergent picture. In 1960 most developing regions had an average per capita income about one-tenth that of the rich countries (the OECD). The East Asian and Pacific region have reduced this gap and in 1998 had almost one-fifth the income of the rich countries. The relative gap between the rich countries, on the one hand, and 'sub-Saharan Africa' and the 'least developed countries', on the other, widened considerably, however, as their income sank to about one-eighteenth that of the OECD. Given this divergence, it makes little sense, as we argued above (see p. 601), to refer to developing countries as the Third World.

Figure 16.7 (p. 618) shows a similar picture emerging from changes in the broader Human Development Index, which combines data on life expectancy, education, and income. The rich countries have, on the whole, maintained their relative advantages, though East Asia and the Pacific have closed the gap to some degree, while sub-Saharan Africa has fallen further behind.

Figure 16.6 A comparison of the incomes of developing regions and high-income OECD countries, 1960–98

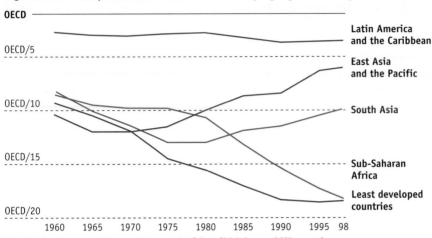

Note: Regional average GDP per capita as a ratio of that of high-income OECD countries.

Source: United Nations Development Programme (Human Development Report) (2001: 16).

This divergence suggests that there is some truth in both the modernization and dependency perspectives discussed earlier on pp. 600–1. Development has diffused to some societies, though this has not been the automatic process envisaged by modernization theorists and has largely resulted from the strategies pursued successfully by some states. In others development has been weak, and they have remained highly dependent on the rich countries, reliant on primary product exports and, indeed, on aid. An adequate theory of development would have to incorporate something from both perspectives and take account of both the diverse experiences of poor countries and the importance of local initiatives.

An over-populated world?

As they struggled to develop, poor countries found themselves faced with a rapid growth of population, much of which collected in large cities. In this section we examine

Figure 16.7 Global inequalities in human development, Human Development Index, 1975–2002

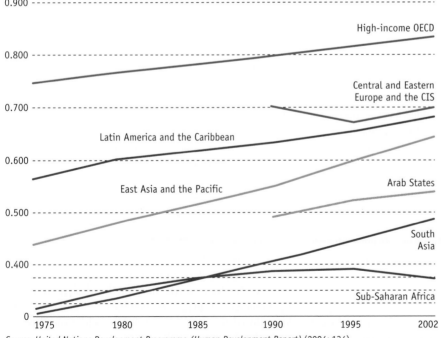

Source: United Nations Development Programme (Human Development Report) (2004: 134).

population growth and then consider whether over-urbanization is taking place.

Over-population?

Population increase is mainly a result of there being more births than deaths, though migration may have some impact on population size when the population is small. The post-1945 population increase in poor countries was quite simply the result of rapidly falling death rates as the technology of disease control spread from the industrial countries. Malaria, for example, could be wiped out by spraying wetlands with DDT.

Death rates had fallen in the industrial countries too, but this had happened gradually over the previous century and was cancelled out by falling birth rates. Industrial countries had passed through a **demographic transition**, moving from one relatively stable state to another as they shifted from high birth and death rates to low birth and death rates (see Figure 16.8). In poor countries death rates fell very rapidly after the Second World War but birth rates remained very high.

It is easy to see why death rates could decline so rapidly in poor countries, but why did birth rates stay so high?

In the industrial societies birth rates had declined because people had less need for large families and wanted smaller ones. With education becoming a longer and more compulsory process, children became less a source of additional income and more a cost. Family income would be maximized by women going out to work rather than having children. Also, pensions, state health care, and residential homes for the elderly meant that there was less need for children to provide support in old age.

In poor countries most of this did not apply. Much of the population was still engaged in agriculture, and more children meant more farmhands. Child labour was and still is common not only in agriculture but also in workshops and factories, while in the cities children make good beggars, thieves, and scavengers. A larger family means a larger income, and, in societies where there is little state provision for the sick or old, more support in illness or old age.

By the 1960s there was a growing concern with a *population explosion*. Although having more children might be a rational strategy for the individual household, an increasing population had serious consequences for countries trying to develop. It led to higher unemployment and increased welfare expenditure, pressure on the land, and over-urbanization. It resulted in growing poverty, which could lead to disorder. There was also much concern with the impact of rising populations on the environment.

If population increase was a serious problem, what was to be done about it? The first approach was to spread birth-control techniques through family-planning clinics and free contraception. Another was to bribe or coerce people to limit their families.

In China, a coercive one-child-per-family policy was adopted. In terms of results, this was highly successful, and a birth rate of thirty-seven births per 1,000 people in 1952 was reduced to eighteen per 1,000 by 1979 (Hulme and Turner 1990: 125). This policy had, however, consequences widely considered unacceptable. The preference for boys led to the selective abortion and infanticide of girls, and their abandonment in orphanages, where some were left unfed to die. The policy has been officially relaxed to allow those born since it was introduced to have two children, and those in rural areas whose first child is a daughter to have another child. Reportedly, there is still plenty of enforcement, with those already having one child being subjected to regular pregnancy tests and facing pressure to be sterilized, under threat of financial penalties and loss of jobs (*Sunday Times*, 15 February 2009).

Fears of an uncontrolled population explosion have diminished somewhat. The United Nations has recently revised downwards its estimates of future population growth. According to its medium scenario, it expects world

Figure 16.8 The demographic transition

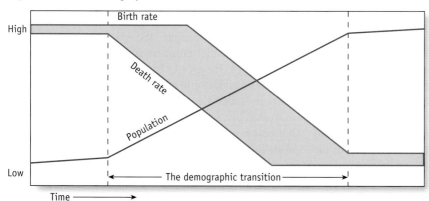

➲ See also our other discussion of the demographic transition in Chapter 8, pp. 277–9.

A Cambodian girl goes through garbage looking for things to sell.
© Getty Images/Paula Bronstein

population to rise from 6.1 billion in 2000 to around 9 billion in 2050 but then to stabilize at this level (United Nations 2004*a*: 2).

There is strong evidence of falling fertility, which in many countries has dropped below the level at which the population is replaced. The replacement fertility rate is 2.1 children per woman in countries where mortality is low. In the 1970s fertility in only twelve 'developed countries' was below replacement level, but by the 1990s forty-one had dropped below this level. More surprisingly, while in the 1970s only one 'developing country' was below replacement level, by the 1990s nineteen were. In these countries, average fertility levels had dropped from over 5.9 children per woman in the 1970s to about 3.9 children per woman

in the 1990s (United Nations 2003*b*: p. xviii). Many poor countries are now going through the demographic transition, with later marriage, the spread of contraceptive techniques, smaller numbers of children, and increasing divorce rates. The greater education of girls is considered to be a critical factor in reducing birth rates.

There is also the impact on population of increased mortality, because of the return of apparently conquered but now resurgent diseases, such as malaria and tuberculosis, and the spread of AIDS (see pp. 629–31). It is estimated that in 2025 the population of the thirty-eight most AIDS-affected countries in Africa will be at least 156 million lower than it would otherwise have been (United Nations 2003*a*: 28).

Figure 16.9 Fertility rates in selected countries, 2000–2010 (projected)

Country	2000–5	2005–10
Niger	7.45	7.19
Sierra Leone	6.50	6.47
Zambia	5.65	5.18
Iraq	4.86	4.26
Ghana	4.39	3.84
Saudi Arabia	3.81	3.35
Philippines	3.54	3.23
Bangladesh	3.22	2.83
India	3.11	2.81
Ecuador	2.82	2.58
Mexico	2.40	2.21
Turkey	2.23	2.14
		2.1 replacement rate
United States	2.04	2.05
Iran	2.12	2.04
Brazil	2.25	1.90
France	1.88	1.89
Sri Lanka	2.02	1.88
Thailand	1.85	1.85
United Kingdom	1.70	1.82
Sweden	1.67	1.82
Australia	1.76	1.79
China	1.70	1.73
Italy	1.29	1.38
Germany	1.35	1.36
Russia	1.30	1.34
Japan	1.29	1.27
World	**2.65**	**2.55**

Source: United Nations Department of Economic and Social Affairs (2006: table A.15)

❓ What patterns do you see emerging from this list and how would you explain them?

➲ Consider the implications of fertility rates for age distribution, labour force, and welfare.

➲ What do you think are the implications of this list for patterns of migration?

Population growth *may* then be less of a problem than it was thought to be. There are, however, many variables operating here, and the UN's various growth scenarios in *World Population Prospects* predict a range of outcomes for total world population in 2050, from eight billion to twelve billion (United Nations Department of Economic and Social Affairs (2006: p. ix) and a wider spread for dates further into the future. Even if the medium scenario is correct, its prediction of nine billion in 2050 would still mean that the world's population had increased more than threefold in 100 years, putting pressure on resources and speeding up global warming.

Over-urbanization?

As with population growth, urbanization in poor countries is often considered out of control. League tables do certainly show that the cities of Asia, Africa, and Latin America are overtaking in size those of Europe and North America (see Figure 16.10).

The notion of over-urbanization is based partly on the idea that urbanization in the poor countries of Africa, Asia, and Latin America has been much faster than in the developed countries at a comparable stage in their development. The rate of urbanization in nineteenth-century Britain did not get much above 1 per cent a year, while annual rates in poor countries reached between 3 and 6 per cent during the period 1950–90.

Cities in poor countries have been called *parasitic* rather than *generative*. They are said to drain resources from rural areas and contribute nothing to them, instead of creating economic growth, as cities are supposed to do. Urban elites have been criticized for leading unproductive lives, focused on the consumption of imported goods, and assisting foreign capital in the exploitation of their societies.

It is also argued that cities cannot cope with their increasing populations. Employment opportunities have not kept pace, and large numbers of people have been forced into the informal economy, which includes such activities as begging, scavenging, and prostitution, in order to survive.

Figure 16.10 The world's largest five cities, 1950–2015

1950		1990		2015 (projected)	
City	Population (m.)	City	Population (m.)	City	Population (m.)
1 New York	12.3	1 Tokyo	25	1 Tokyo	36.2
2 London	8.7	2 New York	16.1	2 Mumbai	22.6
3 Tokyo	6.9	3 Mexico City	15.1	3 Delhi	20.9
4 Paris	5.4	4 São Paulo	14.8	4 Mexico City	20.6
5 Moscow	5.4	5 Shanghai	13.5	5 São Paulo	20.0

Sources: United Nations Population Fund (1996: 32–3); United Nations (2004b: 9).

Figure 16.11 Have poor countries become over-urbanized?

Aspects of urbanization	Yes	No
Rate of urbanization	Higher than in rich countries	Comparable rates at a similar stage
Size of cities	Larger than in rich countries	Differences in boundary definitions
Contribution to economy	Parasitic	Generative
Living conditions	Cities unable to provide decent living conditions	Living conditions better than rural areas

Many have to live in shanty towns without decent housing or sanitation. Unmanageable concentrations of population have built up that cannot be provided with proper services and are a source of crime and disorder.

However, comparisons between the cities of rich and poor countries may well exaggerate the differences between them. Many cities in poor countries have grown larger by extending their boundaries, while some cities in the old industrial countries have retained old boundaries that no longer reflect their true size. Thus, London has kept administrative boundaries that give no real idea of its spread. Greater London in 1991 had a population of 6.4 million, which made it the twenty-third largest city in the world, but a definition in terms of its metropolitan region would have given it a population of 12.5 million, making it the world's sixth largest (United Nations Centre for Human Settlements 1996: 17).

While the world as a whole is certainly becoming increasingly urban, poor countries are not predicted to have significantly higher urban populations than rich ones. In 2030 the population of Africa is predicted to be 53 per cent urban, of Asia 54 per cent, and of Latin America 85 per cent. These are certainly high figures but in 2030 the population of Europe is predicted to be 80 per cent urban and of North America 87 per cent (United Nations 2004b: 6).

Over-urbanization? A shanty town in Ho Chi Minh City, Vietnam.

© Getty Images/Paul Chesley

The concept of 'over-urbanization' may also present too negative an image of city life in poor countries. There may not be enough employment in the formal economy to absorb migrants, but they are drawn to cities because these offer better prospects than the areas they come from. Conditions may be bad in the cities but worse elsewhere. The condemnation of apparently squalid shanty towns also neglects the success of community-based, self-help initiatives in improving them and obtaining transport, water supplies, and electricity.

Flanagan (1993) has suggested that the differences between the cities of rich and poor countries have been exaggerated. Many cities in rich countries are afflicted by serious poverty and unemployment. Furthermore, in an increasingly globalized world, all cities face problems generated by the dynamics of the international economy. He concluded that the study of the 'Third World city' has been a separate field for too long and needed to be integrated with the study of cities in the developed world.

Global movements of capital

Global economic integration is nothing new, see pp. 607–8, but in recent years the transformation of communications has speeded it up. After outlining this, we examine the growth of transnational corporations, the new international division of labour, and the notion of 'global capitalism'.

Transformed communications

Steam power transformed the speed of travel in the nineteenth century, air travel in the twentieth (see Figure 16.2 on p. 602). But too much emphasis can be placed on speed. The cheapness of transport, which is closely associated with volume, is fundamental to global integration. It was the wide-bodied passenger jets introduced in the 1960s that made cheap mass travel possible. The container revolution of the 1970s cheapened the sea transport of goods and enabled a huge growth in trade.

It is not only travel that matters but also the communication of information. In the nineteenth century the telegraph and the telephone 'destroyed distance' by separating communication from travel. The launching of geostationary satellites in the 1960s and 1970s further transformed communication. Satellites made global communication cheap and enabled the transmission of huge quantities of information and money, which now circulates mainly in an electronic form. Digital transmission greatly increased the amount of information that could be sent.

Since the 1990s, the spread of the World Wide Web on the Internet has brought about another communications revolution, though different parts of the world are plugged unequally into the global information network. Although

Figure 16.12 World Internet usage, 2008

World regions	Usage growth 2000–8 (%)	Users as % of population
Africa	1,100	6
Asia	474	17
Europe	274	49
Middle East	1,286	23
North America	132	74
Latin America/Caribbean	861	30
Oceania/Australia	173	60
World as a whole	*342*	*24*

Source: Internet World Stats (2009).

Internet use is increasing fast in the less developed regions of the world, it is still at a much lower level there (see Figure 16.12). There is also a divide within countries, with Internet use concentrated among those who are educated, young, male, and live in cities.

Transnational corporations

Faster communication facilitated transnational economic organization through the **transnational corporation** (TNC). The key feature of the TNC is that it does not just *trade* across borders. International trading is as old as national frontiers. TNCs actually *produce* goods and services in more than one country. They first emerged in the nineteenth century, but it was the new economic conditions stemming from the collapse of empire and increasing international competition in the 1960s and 1970s that made them a dominant force in the world economy.

Increasing international competition and declining profits drove companies in the old industrial countries to set up operations in countries where labour costs were lower. Another strategy, typical of the vehicle industry, was to buy up or merge with competing companies in other countries. Transnational organization was also stimulated by the erection of tariff barriers to protect domestic producers, since one way of getting round this was to produce goods and services inside other countries. That is one of the main reasons why Japanese companies built factories in Europe.

Global corporations have also come to dominate agriculture. According to an ActionAid report, two companies, Chiquita and Dole, control half the world's trade in bananas. Dupont and Monsanto dominate two-thirds of the world seed market for maize. Three companies control 85 per cent of world tea production (ActionAid 2004). Vandana Shiva (2000) has argued that agriculture is increasingly dominated by 'life-science' corporations, which cut across agribusiness, biotechnology, and the chemical and pharmaceutical industries.

TNCs provide services as well as goods, and there are global hotel chains, global advertising agencies, and global car rental companies. There are also global superstores like the US-based Wal-Mart, which has operations in Argentina, Brazil, Canada, Central America, Chile, China, India, Japan, Mexico, and the United Kingdom, where it owns Asda. Another example is Tesco (see Chapter 14, p. 644).

While access to cheap labour and control of markets largely motivated the growth of TNCs, the growth of tourism played its part, and changes in culture and way of life were also very important. The global expansion of McDonald's provided burgers for American travellers, whether business executives or tourists, but more importantly provided a standard and fashionable fast food for local people. The popularity of McDonald's was largely a result of the globalization of the media, which has spread American culture and the consumption of American products worldwide.

> ➲ **Connections**
>
> The globalization of the media is an important aspect of globalization. We discuss the growth of global media corporations in Chapter 10, pp. 376–7, and the issue of Americanization on pp. 383–5.

TNCs are a threat to the authority of the nation state, since they challenge its control over the economy. By shifting investment from one country to another, they can move capital and employment between countries, and, as this chapter's opening piece shows, TNCs can find ingenious ways of avoiding taxation. If they do not like a government, they can move their operations elsewhere or, at least, threaten to do so, putting pressure on states to act in ways that will maximize their profits.

A new international division of labour?

One of the main consequences of the growth of TNCs was the emergence of what Frobel *et al.* (1980) called a new international division of labour (see Figure 16.13). According to the old international division of labour, the industrial societies specialized in exporting manufactured goods, while Africa, Asia, and Latin America provided primary products (see p. 608). According to the new one, the industrial societies export capital and expertise, while the poor countries provide cheap labour.

One feature of this new international division of labour has been the creation of Export Processing Zones or Free Trade Zones, such as the *maquiladoras* of Mexico, which export a huge range of goods and services to the United States. To attract capital, the Mexican government has cut taxes and allowed unregulated production. Attempts by the low-paid workers to form independent trade unions have been obstructed and crushed by the employers and the state.

Figure 16.13 Changes in the international division of labour (IDOL)

Groups of societies	Old IDOL	New IDOL
Industrial societies	Manufactured goods	Capital and expertise
Rest of the world	Primary products	Cheap labour

The exploitation of cheap labour in poor countries has resulted in the increasing employment of women and children. TNCs prefer young women workers, for they can be paid less and are considered easier to control than male workers, and easier to dispose of by returning to the household if the employer needs to shed labour. Child labour has similar advantages and is widely exploited in many poor countries.

There can be no doubt that capital has moved into poor countries to exploit cheap labour, but the concept of a new international division of labour is in some respects misleading.

First, this new division of labour has not replaced the old one. Although the old industrial societies lost some manufacturing to the newly industrializing countries (NICs), they still have important exporting industries, such as, for example, the arms industry. Furthermore, poor countries are still heavily involved in producing food and raw materials for the rich ones. The old international division of labour lives on.

Secondly, much of the cheap labour carried out in poor countries involves little investment, if done in small workshops or even at home. This applies particularly to international telework, when companies based in rich countries have their calls answered, their software written, or their data processed by cheap labour in poor countries. There may be little transfer of capital to the poor country where the goods or services are produced.

Thirdly, rich countries attract capital from poorer countries. Thus, in the mid-1990s South Korean capital was drawn into Britain, particularly to Wales, where the closure of steelworks and coal mines had depressed wage levels. Chinese companies have been investing in European car companies, buying parts of MG Rover in 2005, after this had gone bankrupt, and Volvo in 2010.

Fourthly, most of the money moving between countries is not productively invested. There is a huge circulation of speculative money that moves between currencies, commodities, and shares, to make profits from differences in rates between countries and movements in financial markets elsewhere. This 'casino capitalism' stands outside the international division of labour.

The concept of a new international division of labour gives an over-simple picture of the movement of capital and the complex international relationships between capital and labour. It is, however, quite correct in drawing attention to the way in which cheap labour in poor countries has been drawn increasingly into the production of manufactured goods and services for rich ones.

Global capitalism?

As we showed earlier (see pp. 607–8), a capitalist world economy was emerging as early as the late fifteenth century, and this took on a more integrated character with the creation of an international division of labour that spanned the world in the nineteenth century. The notion of a 'global capitalism' went beyond this, however, for, with the late-twentieth-century growth of transnational corporations and the increased circulation of capital around the world, capitalism now seemed to be organized at a new level that transcended the nation state. Furthermore, alternative systems were eliminated with the collapse of state socialism. Russia, together with its satellite states, and China went capitalist.

But how global is this global capitalism? The notion that it is global can give the impression that the circulation of money is evenly spread across the world. This is far from the case. Most transnational investment has been between rich countries. Europe, Japan, and the United States have directed most of their investment at each other. China, South East Asia, and Latin America have recently been attracting more, but little has flowed into Africa (Held and McGrew 2007: 91–2).

Has the nation state really been transcended?

Hirst and Thompson (1996) have claimed that very few TNCs are really transnational, as their main operations are always located in a particular country. Even if they produce in many countries, they must have a national base where their headquarters and other central functions are located. They rely on national educational and financial institutions, and benefit from mutually supportive relationships with the government. TNCs are not at all averse to using the diplomatic and military power of their home country to advance their operations elsewhere. If they are still dependent on nation states, this means that national governments can exert some influence over them.

Dicken (2007) similarly argues that *transnational* corporations are at the same time *national* corporations. He is also sceptical of the commonly used term 'global corporation'. Some TNCs, such as Coca-Cola, or Hilton, or McDonalds, do have operations in most countries of the world, but most TNCs do not really have a global character and operate in a small number of countries.

Economic nationalism is far from dead and has indeed shown signs of increasing in recent years, leading some to claim that 'globalization is dead'. The failure in 2006 of the World Trade Organization's attempts through the Doha round of negotiations to further remove national barriers to trade led to such claims (Jacques 2006). Then, as the global financial crisis spread in 2008, governments became increasingly concerned with protecting their own financial institutions and maintaining investment and employment within their own borders.

'Globalization is dead' makes a dramatic title but, however, clearly overstates what has been happening. To start with, important as the economic aspects of globalization are, this is a much broader process that reaches into all aspects of people's lives. If one just considers its economic aspects, powerful transnational corporations still exist and large amounts of money still flow around the world. The countries of the East still use their cheap labour to supply goods and services to the West. Capitalism is still globally organized.

The key point is that global capitalism has not superseded the nation state but has a much more complex relationship with it, challenging its control of the economy and evading its taxes, but still dependent upon it. One consequence of the global financial crisis is that huge corporations, not only banks but manufacturing companies such as General Motors and Chrysler, found that they could not survive without the assistance of the state and therefore had to accept a degree of supervision by it.

There is also a further important point to be made here. It is not only that national organization persists but also that the power of the nation state varies and changes, and impacts upon the process of globalization. The global dominance of the United States lies behind this process, which has been a vehicle for expansive US corporations (Held and McGrew 2007: 110). Martin Jacques (2009) argues that China is in the process of taking over this leadership role and its growing penetration of African countries is already attracting attention. While we recognize the importance of globalizing changes, the dynamics of global capitalism cannot be understood unless the power of nation states is taken into account.

> **⊃ Connections**
>
> The crisis of capitalism that began in 2007 is examined in more detail in Chapter 15, pp. 588–9.

Global movements of people

The literature on global economic integration has focused on the movement of capital, rather than the movement of people. One of the main features of globalization is, however, the greater movement of people across national borders. Here we examine two very different examples of this, global tourism and migratory labour.

Global tourism

International tourism has become one of the main activities in the global economy. Its growth has been phenomenal,

Briefing: sex tourism   16.9

Sex tourism is one form of global tourism that has grown rapidly. It is another example of the exploitation of the cheap, unregulated labour in poor countries by people from rich ones. Tourists can engage in immoral or illegal activities more cheaply, more easily, and more safely than they can in their own countries. Prostitution in sex tourist destinations is largely organized by local entrepreneurs, though expatriates from the countries that supply the tourists can become involved. Major corporations based in the West also make profits from sex tourism. O'Connell Davidson (1998: 86) has argued that 'the airlines which transport prostitute users half way around the globe and the hotels (many of which are owned by international conglomerates) in which they stay, as well as the travel agents which arrange their flights and accommodation, are probably the prime beneficiaries of sex tourism'.

on television, travel books, and global online information. Global tourism results from globalization but also promotes it.

As with the circulation of money, the circulation of tourists is mainly between the rich countries of the world, between the United States, Europe, and Japan. The United States and European countries are the main earners from tourism and dominate the top ten positions in the earnings league table, though China comes fourth and Turkey ninth (World Tourism Organization 2009). Tourism has, nonetheless, become very important to the economies of poor countries and is the main 'export' in many of them.

Tourism can be seen as the spearhead of global capitalism. It can penetrate rapidly into areas of the world that have little capacity to produce goods or other services for the world market. Indeed, the most traditional societies attract tourists because of their traditionality. Their religious festivals, cultural objects, and way of life can suddenly acquire a monetary value. Tourism also creates paid labour in bar and hotel work, and prostitution. It generates a greater demand for food production and transport, and may well provide the basis for the local manufacturing of souvenirs. The earnings from tourism will increase the circulation of money and the import of goods, and establish new consumption patterns.

The question of who gains from tourism has been much discussed. Poor countries apparently gain a new economic activity that generates employment, encourages local businesses, and earns foreign currency. But how much of the benefit stays in the country concerned? Global tourism is organized by TNCs, which return most of the profits on tourism to rich countries (see Box 16.9). Price competition

from 25 million international tourist arrivals in 1950 to 924 million in 2008 (World Tourism Organization 2009).

Global tourism is clearly a consequence of faster and cheaper international travel, but it has also generated this itself, by increasing the demand for travel and opening up routes to new destinations, which have often acquired airports in order to receive tourists. Similarly, greater global awareness through media coverage has stimulated tourist interest in new holiday destinations, but tourist travel has also generated a demand for travel programmes

Thai bar girls: global tourism can increase local employment but at what cost?
© AFP/Getty

between companies drives down the wages paid to locals, who may be required to risk life and limb in dangerous but unregulated work (see Box 16.10). Agriculture may well suffer from a shortage of labour as people take up new jobs, while tourism may be seasonal and not support people through the year. Land and property prices may be pushed out of the reach of local people.

This leads to the wider issues of the cultural and environmental impact of tourism. Tourists often pursue the 'authentic', but cultures may lose their authenticity when commercialized, though commercialization may at least keep them alive in some form. Hotel-building and the sheer weight of tourist numbers may damage the natural environment, though tourists may also provide an incentive to preserve vanishing species and maintain natural environments. Much depends on the kind of tourism involved. The rise of 'alternative tourism' and 'eco-tourism' suggests that a tourism more compatible with the preservation of culture and environment has become commercially viable.

Whether tourism benefits poor countries is a complex matter, which ultimately depends on value judgements, on the relative value attached to employment, the environment, culture, and so on. What can be said is that surveys have indicated that ordinary people in poor societies take a positive view of tourism and say they want more of it (D. Harrison 1994).

Migration

As we showed earlier (see pp. 608–10), there was an extensive international migration during the nineteenth century. There was a new wave after 1945, as the growing economies of North America, north-west Europe, and Australia sucked in labour from the peripheral countries of Europe and from the colonial/ex-colonial territories of Africa and Asia.

Stephen Castles and Mark Miller (2003: 7–9) have identified five main tendencies in recent patterns of migration:

- *globalization*, as more countries experience it at the same time;
- *acceleration*, as international movements of people increase;
- *differentiation*, as different types of migration develop;
- *feminization*, as the labour migration of women workers increases;
- *politicization*, as politics is increasingly affected by migration.

The increasing migration of women has been the focus of much interest (see Study 16 at the end of this chapter). In rich countries the demand for female labour has been rising. Service occupations that typically employ women have expanded, as has paid domestic work. In the Arabian Gulf States, the growing employment of women in professional and managerial occupations led to the recruitment of Asian maids to do the housework, and this has happened in Hong Kong and London too. Female migrants have been drawn into prostitution and sex tourism, while there has also been a growing trade in 'mail-order' brides. Asia was their main source initially, but more recently they have come from Eastern Europe, after the collapse of the state socialist economies led to unemployment and poverty there.

 Frontiers trekkers and porters   16.10

'Nepal's spectacular beauty draws 40,000 Britons a year, most of whom are unaware of the ugly underbelly of the trekking business.

A hundred thousand men are estimated to be carrying the industry on their backs. It is a measure of how little importance is attached to their welfare that there is no register of how many are working in areas known to be dangerous. They come, they go. Some never return. There was talk last year of a dozen bodies or more appearing after a sudden thaw at the Gokyo Pass in the Everest region: twenty porters are said to have died in the Makalu-Barun National Park in the past few years.

They die perhaps partly because of the convenient myth that they are supermen. Physically small, the prowess they display in lifting and carrying seemingly impossible loads never fails to impress the pampered Western tourist. . . .

Most porters risk life and limb for the equivalent of the price of a pint of a beer. When they pocket as little as £2 or £3 a day, buying their own weatherproof gear is simply not an option. . . .

Proper shelter, decent medical care in the event of an illness and, above all, adequate protective gear to face the extreme conditions—these are the sort of expenses trekking agencies could work into their overheads—but Deepak Thapa (a Nepalese journalist) is pessimistic about the chances of agencies putting their own house in order. He sees no political will to improve. Any change, he says, will be in response to foreign consumer pressure, when trekkers themselves insist on ethical treatment of porters before making a booking.'

Source: Guha (2000).

Illegal immigration has grown, as national barriers have risen but the pressure to migrate has increased. Entry barriers rose in Europe and the United States as the economic transformations of the 1970s and 1980s led to industries collapsing, unemployment increasing, and popular demands for restrictions on immigration. Rising populations, the failure of economic growth, famine, and war increasingly drove people in poor countries to seek entry to rich ones. The response to a growing illegal immigration was a further tightening of entry controls in rich countries. Airlines, employers, educational institutions, and social-security offices all became agents of control in the UK. Highly organized people-trafficking then developed, as migrants tried to find ways around these controls.

Some employers have had an interest in employing illegal entrants, and economies can become highly dependent upon them. In the United States, the 1986 Immigration Act introduced fines and imprisonment for employers hiring illegal migrants, but huge protests from agricultural and industrial interests followed, particularly in California and New Mexico, where there was also a widespread employment of illegal migrants in housework and gardening. Concessions were made and enforcement was ineffective. It was illegality that made Mexican and Central American labour so cheap, for illegals were extremely vulnerable and willing to work for very low wages, while their employers avoided having to make social-security payments (N. Harris 1995).

While it is mainly the poor who want to migrate, in the hope of a better life elsewhere, it is easy to buy your way into countries if you have wealth or, increasingly, skills. Thus, the United States Immigration Act of 1991 allowed the entry of up to 10,000 migrants willing to invest $1 million and create ten jobs within six months. Australia and Canada have operated similar schemes with lower requirements. Indeed, Harris argued that there is an international competition to attract wealthy immigrants, with one country trying to outbid another. This supports Bauman's contention that the significance of borders depends on whether you are rich or poor (see p. 605).

As host countries put up the barriers to migrants, the number of refugees and asylum-seekers increased. This was partly because, by claiming asylum, migrants could circumvent immigration controls, but also because famine, wars, and oppression have forced so many more to leave their countries. The United Nations High Commission for Refugees (UNHCR) reports that the global number of 'persons of concern', which includes internally displaced people as well as refugees, rose from fifteen million in 1990 to forty-three million at the end of 2009 (UNHCR 2010).

It is often thought in Britain that these refugees arrive overwhelmingly on its shores. At the end of 2009 the UK came tenth in the UNHCR table of countries with refugees. With an estimated 270,000, it had less than half the number

Why did asylum-seekers become such a big issue in Britain?

© Alice Chadwick

of Germany (594,000), and far fewer than Pakistan (1.7 million), Iran (1.1 million), and Syria (1.1 million). In the European Union, which was the main destination of asylum-seekers, France was the main receiver of applications in 2009, with 42,000 claims for asylum, while the UK came second with 30,000 (UNHCR 2010).

Politicization

Castles and Miller (2003) listed politicization as one of the main tendencies in recent patterns of migration. This is yet another area where globalizing changes interact with the nation state.

Immigration policy in Britain has been torn between contrasting views of immigrants as a threat and a resource. Three main issues are raised:

- identity;
- economy;
- population.

Immigrants are viewed as a threat to traditional national identity. 'Traditional' identities are themselves, however, the product of past waves of immigration. Castles and Miller (2003: 289) suggest that ideas of national identity have to come to terms with greater diversity, because 'monocultural and assimilationist models of national identity may no longer be adequate for the new situation'. Migrants develop multiple identities, and arguably such identities are an inevitable product of the multi-layered world and multi-ethnic societies that globalization is producing.

Migrants are seen as benefiting the economy, because they provide cheap labour and skills in scarce domestic supply. Without them, important parts of the economy would grind to a halt. In Britain, agriculture, construction, care and cleaning services, education, hotels and restaurants, medicine, and transport have all become dependent on immigrant labour, which, one may note, the countries of origin may themselves need (see Box 16.11). Migrants can, however, be considered a threat by those with whom they compete for jobs, housing, and local resources. Rising unemployment in 2008–9 made this a bigger issue in Britain and led to demonstrations by workers who considered they had been elbowed out of jobs by foreigners.

The impact of migration on population size has also become an issue. The UK population has entered a period of growth, and is projected to rise from sixty-one million in 2007 to seventy-one million in 2031. Since the 1990s, migration has become a more important factor in accounting for population increase, which has led to headlines about 'a small overcrowded island' and calls for a halt to immigration. Over half the projected increase between 2007 and 2031 is expected to be 'natural', because of a higher birth rate and a lower death rate, as people live longer, though part of the higher birth rate is itself due to immigration, as the birth rate of immigrants is higher (*Social Trends* 2009: 6). The birth rate has, one may note, been below the replacement rate since 1973 and still was during the years 2005–10 (see p. 621), and there is also the growing burden of an ageing population. This suggests that some immigration and a larger population are necessary to maintain the size of the *economically active* population.

Government policy has to steer a path between various conflicting imperatives. Broadly speaking, the UK government tries to allow entry to those needed by the economy, while restricting their right to stay. It has tried to clamp down on illegal entry and to return to their countries of origin those with no right to stay. The proximity of general elections results in periodic lurches towards 'tougher' policies seen as popular with the electorate.

The UK government's hands are, anyway, considerably tied. EU membership and the recent enlargement of the EU to include many poor countries in Eastern Europe mean that it cannot refuse entry to those who want to come in from this area. The 1951 UN Convention on Refugees requires it to allow in those who are genuinely fleeing persecution. Furthermore, the European Convention on Human Rights prevents it from sending people back to countries where they may be 'exposed to torture, or inhuman or degrading treatment or punishment'.

National governments' attempts to control immigration are constrained both by global changes increasing migrant flows and by international restrictions on the state's freedom of action. But this is not simply a 'decline of the nation state' issue, for governments are themselves caught between conflicting imperatives, between needing and fearing immigrants.

Global challenges

In the previous two sections we considered the issues raised by the global movements of capital and labour. Here we examine three particular global challenges—global disease, global terror, and global social movements.

Global disease

HIV/AIDS probably originated in Africa around 1900. It is thought to have travelled from Africa to Haiti and then to

---

 Controversy and debate Should Britain import nurses? 16.11

UK health care has become heavily dependent on nurses (and doctors) from overseas, but every nurse who comes to Britain is one less in his or her country of origin. In order to stop the drain of nurses from countries that cannot afford to lose them, an NHS code of practice bans the recruitment of nurses and doctors from poor countries. Over 3,000 nurses from countries on this list were, however, registered in Britain during 2004–5. Of the 200 nurses trained in Swaziland during 2004–5, 150

came to Britain, at a time when the nurse shortage there was becoming acute because of the AIDS epidemic, which was also killing many nurses (300 during 2003–4). These nurses were recruited in Britain by private agencies and private-sector nursing homes, often working there for a short time but then entering the NHS.

Source: Guardian, 20 December 2005.

the United States, arriving there around 1970 but not being diagnosed as a specific disease until the early 1980s. By the end of 1986 it had been reported to the World Health Organization (WHO) as present in eighty-five countries. By 1990 the WHO estimated that there were approaching a million cases of AIDS worldwide and between eight million and ten million cases of HIV infection (the precursor of AIDS). There were an estimated 5.5 million cases of HIV in Africa, 1 million in both North and South America, 500,000 in both Asia and Europe, and 30,000 in Oceania (www.avert.org). The rapid and global spread of HIV/AIDS in the 1980s resulted from its high infectivity but was clearly linked to the growth of global travel.

By 2007 the number of people living with HIV worldwide had tripled to an estimated thirty-three million. In that year the number of deaths due to AIDS was estimated at 2.1 million in the world as a whole. Two main patterns of infection were found. In many sub-Saharan African countries there was a generalized epidemic, and AIDS was the main cause of death. Elsewhere, there was an epidemic mainly among those at greatest risk. According to the 2007 Epidemic Update (UNAIDS 2008), these were:

- men having sex with men;
- injecting drug users;
- sex workers and their partners.

Why has HIV/AIDS hit sub-Saharan Africa so hard? Barnett and Whiteside (2006: 144) argue that 'HIV/AIDS epidemics are related to income inequality and absence of social cohesion. Dislocation, inequality, civil unrest, population mobility, radical changes in community beliefs and standards have been constant motifs in the story of HIV and AIDS in Africa.' They consider that Africa has suffered more from these problems than any other region of the world. This is partly a consequence of its history, stretching back through colonial times to the slave trade, but also of economic crisis during the last thirty years, compounded by bad government and the consequences of the structural adjustment forced on countries by the World Bank (see p. 616).

Sub-Saharan Africa is one of the poorest areas of the world, and poverty interacts with HIV/AIDS in vicious circles. Poverty is associated with poor health, which increases vulnerability to HIV/AIDS, and makes it more difficult to obtain treatment. Illness and death then make it harder for families to earn a living. Poverty increases the risk of HIV/AIDS, and HIV/AIDS increases poverty.

Gender inequality is an important factor. In Sub-Saharan Africa women are disproportionately infected with HIV/AIDS, especially in the Central African Republic, South Africa, Swaziland, and Uganda. The UNAIDS report argues that it is not only that women's access to condoms and information about health is restricted, it is also that 'gender norms that prescribe an unequal and more passive role for women in sexual decision-making undermine women's autonomy, expose many to sexual coercion, and prevent them from insisting on abstinence or condom use by their male partners' (UNAIDS 2008: 67).

Traditional expectations of male behaviour, such as having multiple sexual partners, make the situation worse by leading males to behave in ways that spread infection. The report calls for greater investment in girls' education,

Figure 16.14 Global rates of HIV infection, 2007

Adult prevalence (%)
- 15.0% – 28.0%
- 5.0% – <15.0%
- 1.0% – <5.0%
- 0.5% – <1.0%
- 0.1% – <0.5%
- <0.1%
- No data available

Source: UNAIDS (2008: 5).

programmes directed at men and boys to change gender norms, and reforms to provide women with greater independence and more legal rights (UNAIDS 2008: 64).

Barnett and Whiteside (2006) argue that HIV/AIDS may force people to think about health in new ways. In the past, the response to infectious disease has been to contain and isolate it, on the model of the leper colony, but this cannot work in a global society where there is so much communication, interaction, and change. Health has been seen as a characteristic of individual bodies rather than a 'public good' linked to overall well-being. Thus, dealing with HIV/AIDS is a matter not just of condoms and retrovirals, but of tackling poverty and inequality. Furthermore, HIV/AIDS is not just a disease that impacts on the individuals who catch it but one that has consequences for whole communities and societies.

They claim that HIV/AIDS is the first global epidemic that has joined together people across the world in 'a common consciousness about its threats and implications' (Barnett and Whiteside 2006: 4). They argue that this is not a problem that the nation state can easily deal with. At the international level, a dedicated UN agency, UNAIDS, has in a flexible and effective way coordinated the work of various UN HIV/AIDS organizations. Subsequently, UNAIDS attracted much criticism, however, because it gave in to the George Bush administration's attack on its policies of decriminalizing sex work and employing drug-users in outreach work. More recently it seems to have revived these policies and recovered its mission (Dube and Csete 2008).

Global terror

On 11 September 2001 two airliners under the control of Al-Qaeda hijackers slammed into the World Trade Center in New York and demolished its twin towers. Another airliner crashed into the Pentagon and a fourth failed to reach its target and came down after passengers attacked the hijackers. Nearly 3,000 people were killed. This was neither the beginning nor the end of Al-Qaeda terrorism (see Figure 16.15, p. 632), but it was its most dramatic manifestation so far.

Before '9/11' a number of analysts had already been arguing that a 'new terrorism' had come into existence (G. Martin 2004). Its main features were

- organizational decentralization;
- operational asymmetry;
- religious centrality;
- weapons of mass destruction.

Through *organizational decentralization* terrorist organizations became a network of relatively independent cells. There could still be an important degree of central coordination—at the time of 9/11, Al-Qaeda had a clear base with training camps in Afghanistan. Cells could, however,

operate independently in different countries and sometimes with only a loose connection with Al-Qaeda.

In a world where one country, the United States, was unassailably dominant, there was an *operational asymmetry* between the USA (and its allies) and its opponents. Its opponents have had to engage in unconventional and unexpected attacks that bypassed national defences. This was a big change from the cold war, where the relationship between the orthodox military machines of the United States and the USSR dominated international conflict.

There was a *religious centrality* to contemporary terrorism, as compared to the left-wing ideologies or ethno-nationalism of the terrorism of the recent past. This did not mean that religion was the source of terrorism but rather that terrorists drew on it to justify their actions. They saw terrorism as a weapon in the absolute struggle between good and evil. This led to the commission of violent acts, regardless of the consequences to the actor and the victims.

There was a willingness to use *weapons of mass destruction*. Fuel-laden airliners, as in 9/11, could become such weapons. There were and are fears that biological, chemical, or radiological weapons could be used.

This new terrorism can reasonably be described as global. At the time of 9/11, Al-Qaeda's main base and training camps were in Afghanistan, but the attacks were planned by a cell in Germany and financed from Dubai. Immediately afterwards, suspected members of Al-Qaeda were arrested in Belgium, Britain, France, Germany, and Spain. The Al-Qaeda network has extended through the Middle East into Europe, Africa, and Asia. As the chronology of attacks (see Figure 16.15, p. 632) shows, the targets of Al-Qaeda have been worldwide.

Terrorists also use the global communications network to publicize their attacks. The crashing of the planes into the World Trade Center and the Pentagon was a global terrorist drama. It was an attack on well-known symbols of American capitalism and military domination in a media-saturated world, with instant transmission to all points of the globe. The audience was global, and people everywhere were able through live television to feel they were watching the event. Osama bin-Laden's tapes and videos of terrorist acts have similarly been diffused rapidly across the world by the Internet and the media.

The events of 9/11 have stimulated state counter-measures. These have used the apparatus of the nation state to engage in a 'war on terror'. This took a conventional form with the invasion and occupation of Afghanistan to destroy Al-Qaeda bases. The global character of the terror network has been combated through the tighter regulation and closer surveillance of the movement of people, money, and messages. Nation states across the world have flexed their muscles by introducing anti-terrorist laws that increase their powers, often at the cost of established civil rights.

Figure 16.15 A chronology of global 'Islamist' terror

Year	Country	Target	Method
1992	Yemen	International hotels	Car bomb
1993	United States	World Trade Center, New York	Car bomb
1993	India	Mumbai	Bomb
1994	Japan	Philippine Airlines 434	Bomb
1995	Saudi Arabia	US base at Riyadh	Bomb
1996	Saudi Arabia	US base on Gulf coast	Lorry bomb
1998	Kenya/Tanzania	US embassies	Lorry bombs
1999	Russia	Apartment blocks	Bomb
2000	Aden	US warship	Exploding dinghy
2001	United States	World Trade Center and Pentagon	Aircraft hijack
2002	Tunisia	Djerba synagogue	Lorry bomb
2002	Pakistan	Karachi bus carrying naval personnel	Suicide bomber
2002	Russia	Moscow theatre	Hostage taking and bomb
2002	Indonesia	Bali bars	Car bombs
2002	Kenya	Mombasa hotel used by Israeli tourists	Suicide bombers
2003	Saudi Arabia	Western compounds in Riyadh	Suicide bombers
2003	Morocco	US and Jewish targets in Casablanca	Suicide bombers
2003	India	Mumbai	Bomb
2003	Turkey	Istanbul synagogues	Suicide bombers
2003	Turkey	British embassy and HSBC bank, Istanbul	Suicide bombers
2004	Russia	Moscow Metro Station	Suicide bomb
2004	Egypt	Sanai tourist locations	Bombs
2004	Spain	Commuter trains in Madrid	Bombs
2004	Russia	Beslan school	Hostage taking and bombs
2005	United Kingdom	London underground trains and bus	Suicide bombers
2005	Egypt	Sharm al-Sheikh hotels	Suicide bombers
2005	India	Delhi	Bombs
2005	Jordan	American hotels in Amman	Bombs
2006	Iraq	Police academy in Baghdad	Suicide bombers
2006	India	Mumbai trains	Bombs
2006	Iraq	Sadr City	Car bombs and mortars
2007	India	Sunijhanta Express	Bombs
2007	Algeria	Government buildings in Algiers	Suicide bombers
2007	Kurdistan	Yazidi communities	Bombs
2007	Iraq	Markets in Baghdad	Bombs
2008	Iraq	Markets in Baghdad	Suicide bombers
2008	Algeria	Police academy	Suicide bomb
2008	Yemen	US embassy	Car bomb, rocket
2008	India	International hotels, Mumbai	Active shooter and bombs
2008	Pakistan	Danish embassy	Car bomb
2009	Indonesia	Jakarta hotels	Bombs
2009	United States	Northwest Airlines 253, Detroit	Bomb
2010	Russia	Moscow Metro	Bombs

⮑ Note that this is a list of only some major attacks. Whether they should be described as 'Islamic' is a contentious matter. The terrorists see themselves as engaged in an Islamic *jihad*, but other Muslims have rejected the idea that such actions are in any **way** Islamic or anything to do with *jihad*. We, for this reason, use the term 'Islamist' (see Chapter 11, p. 421). The degree of Al-Qaeda involvement is uncertain, since attacks are often carried out by relatively autonomous groups only loosely associated with it.

Such counter-measures can be counter-productive by increasing support for terrorism.

A big problem for the nation state has been the changing character of Al-Qaeda. Audrey Kurth Cronin (2006: 32) has made this point forcefully by declaring that 'the Al Qaeda of September 2001 no longer exists'. It changed its way of operating in response to the state's counter-measures. Awareness of electronic surveillance resulted in greater use of messengers. The destruction of Al-Qaeda bases in Afghanistan led to its organizational dispersal into other countries. Instruction in the techniques of terrorism was carried out via the Internet rather than in training camps. Websites and chat rooms provided advice and helped to bond members together. 'In a sense, members of the movement no longer need to join an organization at all, for the individual can participate with the stroke of a few keys' (Cronin 2006: 39).

Cronin (2006: 41) has been critical of 'war-on-terror' strategies that treat Al-Qaeda as a unified and centralized organization, when it has become a 'virtual organization', a loose coalition of independent terrorist groups linked by a mission. She argued that, instead of seeking to defeat Al-Qaeda militarily, the West should focus on counter-measures in the media and cyberspace. It should exploit the internal differences within a diverse movement. It should undermine Al-Qaeda's support by capitalizing on its many mistakes, especially its alienation of potential supporters by its bloody attacks on innocent people, many of them Muslim.

As Jason Burke (2005) has put it, with reference to the July 2005 bombings on the London underground:

> . . . we need to face up to the simple truth that bin-Laden, al-Zawahiri *et al.* do not need to organize attacks directly. They merely need to wait for the message they have spread around the world to inspire others. Al-Qaida is now an idea, not an organization.

Global social movements

Global communication has assisted the growth of transnational movements. The 'new social movements' of feminism, the peace movement, and, above all, environmentalism, have become globally organized.

The new social movements challenged the authority of the nation state by appealing to universal values and human rights. They have used information and communications technology to create networks that extend across national boundaries and enable them to spread their messages and mobilize international opinion against the regimes, policies, and actions of particular states. They have attached themselves through non-governmental organizations (NGOs) to the United Nations and promoted their causes through its programmes and conferences. They have used the global media to generate publicity by staging spectacular dramas, such as Greenpeace's interception of ships at sea.

These movements both reflected and created a new awareness of the responsibility of individuals for the fate of the world. They showed the sense of insecurity and risk, and distrust of experts, which Ulrich Beck (1992) and Anthony Giddens (1990) have examined in their analysis of 'risk society' (see Chapter 4, pp. 143–5). This changed way of viewing the problems of the world has resulted in political actions of a more individualized kind, such as:

- direct action against the destruction of the environment or harm to animals;
- consumer boycotts of environmentally harmful products or goods manufactured by child labour or exported by politically unacceptable regimes;
- personal activities such as recycling or the purchase of forest to prevent its destruction.

'Green consumerism' has stimulated travel companies to switch to eco-tourism (see p. 627) and stores to stock 'green products'. Moves of this sort have, however, been viewed with some scepticism, for they can just mean relabelling existing products in order to cash in on the 'green market'. Yearley (1991) suggested that companies make such changes to their products where they can do this easily and cheaply, to create a 'green' image. Campaigners can, nonetheless, then draw attention to practices that do not fit the image and press a company to justify itself. He concluded that 'on balance, green consumerism is likely to benefit the environment' (Yearley 1991: 100).

The growth and impact of the environmental movement has been quite dramatic. As environmental problems were almost by definition global in their scope, the environmental movement became globally organized. Through effective organization and lobbying, environmental NGOs acquired official recognition as legitimate participants in international policy-making, already outnumbering national representatives by around seven to one at the 1992 Earth Summit (Yearley 1996). The movement has achieved some spectacular successes against particular governments, most notably when France called off its nuclear testing programme, after environmentalist attempts to halt the 1995 Pacific tests.

The strength of global movements can, however, also be their weakness. Their global network does put them beyond the reach of individual nation states and enables them to mobilize international opinion against a

> **Connections**
>
> Our main discussion of social movements is in Chapter 20, pp. 815–19, and you may find it helpful to look this up as you read this section.

government. They can, therefore, be very effective in stopping particular government actions, but to have a long-term impact on policy they need to penetrate the structures of the decision-making and resource-controlling state. They are much less effective at this. Green political parties have remained peripheral, and this applies also to their international role. The movement may be highly vocal, but at international meetings it can be shut out of the negotiations by national representatives.

During the 1990s, sections of the environmentalist movement joined up with the descendants of older movements in anti-globalization and anti-capitalist demonstrations. These brought together environmentalists, socialists, anarchists, and other campaigning groups in a common opposition to the policies of the World Trade Organization (WTO), the World Bank, and other such organizations. There is not really an anti-globalization movement as such but rather a network of radical groups united only by their hostility to global capitalism.

At the 'Battle for Seattle' in November 1999, when radicals demonstrated at a meeting of the World Trade Organization, the Internet played a key role in mobilizing so many different groups in the same place at the same time. Another such demonstration took place at the G8 meeting in Edinburgh in June 2005. The authorities have, however, learned from experience. They have developed techniques for sealing off demonstrations with security forces, while the targeted organizations have moved to more secure and more remote venues for meetings.

According to Held and McGrew (2007: 149), a 'global redistributive politics is in the making.' Nation states are no longer the main agents of this. It operates through movements, such as the Trade Justice Movement (www.tjm.org.uk), and NGOs. Held and McGrew (2007: 150) claim that when these organizations 'can exploit international public opinion, divisions within the G8, and between the G8 leaders and their publics, significant advances can be made in promoting a progressive political agenda'. An example of this would be the impact of the 'Make Poverty History' campaign on the 2005 Edinburgh G8 meeting.

Can these movements change the world? Held and McGrew (2007: 150) argue that their internal divisions, the constraints of global markets, and US global dominance 'limit the prospects for fundamental or structural change'. A global crisis, originating from the contradictions of global capitalism, might, however, create the conditions in

Drama at a demo at the G8 Summit in Edinburgh 2005: what impact have such demonstrations had?
© Getty Images/Carl de Souza

which such change could occur. A global crisis did begin to unroll in 2007 (see Chapter 17, pp. 588–9). It is too early to know what consequences it will have, but so far it appears that international efforts have been directed at restoring the functioning of global capitalism rather than reforming it, let alone transforming it.

One world?

The global social movements discussed above have helped to bring about a growing awareness of the world as a whole, but has this been matched by global political organization?

Saving the earth

Environmental issues are generally considered a key area for global political organization. Nuclear radiation and pollution do not recognize national boundaries. Deforestation in one country affects the climate of another. Rivers cross borders. The consequences of climate change due to global warming impact on all countries. Ulrich Beck (2000*a*) has argued that the environmental issue can be the basis of a new and vigorous global politics.

There has been an active and global environmentalist movement, but has political organization developed far enough to regulate the environmental relationships between nation states? The United Nations has taken on the function of coordinating national responses to environmental issues. Its 1972 Stockholm Conference on the Human Environment was followed by the founding of its Environment Programme. 'Earth Summits' took place at Rio de Janeiro in 1992 and at Johannesburg in 2002.

At these summits, environmental politics demonstrated not so much a common interest in 'saving the earth' as conflicts of interest between countries. Poor countries accused rich countries, the world's main polluters and consumers of raw materials, of trying to solve the problems they had created by restricting development elsewhere. The poor referred pointedly to the 'pollution of poverty'. China and India have continued to build heavily polluting coal-fired power stations to meet their growing energy needs.

This conflict led to the compromise notion of **sustainable development**, which has come into widespread use as a way of reconciling environmental and developmental concerns. A good definition of it is the Brundtland Commission's: 'development which meets the needs of the present without compromising the ability of future generations to meet their own needs' (Adams 1995: 355).

The British government established an advisory Sustainable Development Commission in 2000. In 2005 a Sustainable Development Strategy, *Securing the Future*, was produced. The Department for International Development has a Sustainable Development Minister, regional divisions covering the world, and a cluster of working groups. Sustainable development is an easy goal to commit to but difficult to implement in a demonstrable way. It can easily become part of the rhetoric of good intentions.

A growing concern with global warming has switched international attention away from development issues. A broad agreement on the need for a binding treaty to

Demonstrators at the 2009 Copenhagen Climate conference: what did the conference demonstrate?

© Jens Noergaard Larsen/ AFP/Getty Images

contain global warming by limiting carbon dioxide emissions was reached in Kyoto in 1997. A further conference was held in Bonn in 2001, to try to resolve the problems left over from Kyoto. At Bonn, 186 countries signed up to implement the Kyoto treaty and accepted mandatory targets for the reduction of carbon emissions.

Conflicts between heavy polluters and light polluters were partly resolved through 'carbon sinks' and 'carbon trading'. Polluters could offset pollution by claiming carbon credits from carbon sinks created by planting forests or from agricultural practices that absorb carbon. Carbon credits could also be traded, so heavy polluters could buy credits from elsewhere and those countries reducing emissions could benefit financially. Clever and typically capitalist financial solutions had been found to overcome some of the international conflicts on this issue, though it soon became clear that these expedients would have no serious impact on global warming.

Kyoto was, anyhow, limited in its coverage. While ratification by a sufficient number of countries eventually activated the treaty, important countries remained outside. The United States and Australia, the world's largest per capita polluters, refused to ratify it, while rising polluters, the rapidly industrializing countries of China and India, were not included.

Acceptance of the growing seriousness of the problem led these countries to enter the process of negotiating a successor treaty at Copenhagen in December 2009. Important international meetings prepared the way. Large numbers of officials, advisers, diplomats, campaigners, and media people, not to mention political leaders, including President Barack Obama from the United States and Premier Wen Jiabao from China, assembled at Copenhagen (*Independent*, 9 January 2009). But no successor treaty emerged.

Old conflicts between rich and poor countries resurfaced. The rich countries were not willing to make the large cuts in emissions demanded of them by the poor countries. The rich have argued that carbon emissions are increasing most quickly in countries such as China and India, which are therefore the ones that must exercise most restraint. The poor countries were not prepared to sacrifice their carbon-generating development goals when the rich ones, which are the highest carbon emitters and mainly responsible for global warming and also most able to reduce emissions because of their more advanced technologies, have been trying to delay effective cuts into the distant future.

China's emissions are certainly rising fast, and China has indeed overtaken the United States as the world's largest emitter. This does not, however, put China in the same league as the USA and other developed countries when per capita emissions are compared (see Figure 16.16). China's per capita emissions were 4.6 tonnes in 2006, well below Australia's 19 or the USA's 19.7 or the United Arab Emirates 32.85 or even the United Kingdom's 9.2 (United Nations Statistics Division 2009).

After the failure of Copenhagen, what are the options?

- A further attempt at negotiating a treaty.
- National emissions reduction policies.
- Actions by companies and individuals to reduce their carbon footprints.
- Climate engineering projects.
- Adaptation rather than prevention.

Which is the best way to 'save the earth'?

Figure 16.16 CO_2 emissions per capita, 2006

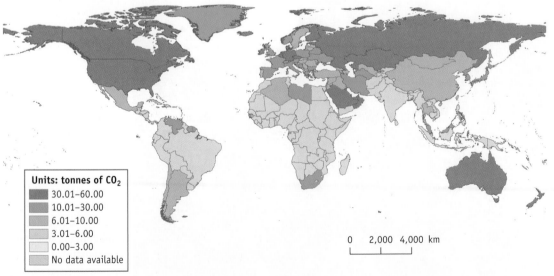

Units: tonnes of CO_2
- 30.01–60.00
- 10.01–30.00
- 6.01–10.00
- 3.01–6.00
- 0.00–3.00
- No data available

0   2,000 4,000 km

Source: United Nations Statistics Division (2009).

World government?

As the 'one-earth' story shows, one consequence of globalization has been the emergence of global institutions that seek to manage international conflicts, regulate international behaviour, and deal with world problems.

Central to this process has been the development of the United Nations. Founded in 1945, it was initially a forum for the discussion of international issues and the settlement of international disputes after the Second World War. Its charter recognized human rights that were universal and therefore applied to all countries. The UN was seen by some as an embryonic 'world government' that would eventually supersede the nation state.

It was also, however, built upon nation states. While many of its activities have a transnational character, it is essentially an international organization dependent on the nation states that are its members. When the UN sends a military force into a country, this is composed of units from national armies, which remain largely under the control of their respective nation states. The UN is entirely dependent for its resources on contributions from these states, which they are often slow to provide and may withhold. Furthermore, the UN's charter recognized not only universal rights but also the sovereignty of the nation state.

The UN's activities were constrained during the cold war by superpower polarization. The conflict between the United States and the Soviet Union dominated world politics. After the Soviet Union's collapse at the end of the 1980s, it was declared that there would be a 'New World Order', in which the UN would assume a much more important role. The UN intervened in Iraq, Bosnia, and Somalia, and there was increasing reference to 'human rights' as a justification for intervention. As we have just shown, there was also more intervention in matters of development and environment. Interventionism was stimulated by the increasing numbers of NGOs attached to the UN, which could act more flexibly and independently than the organization itself (Kegley and Wittkopf 1999).

What has been called a 'transnational civil society' was forming. This consisted of NGOs, transnational movements such as the Global Justice Movement, and organizations such as Greenpeace. World government was not just a matter of the activities of international agencies set up by nation states but also involved the representatives of this transnational civil society (Held and McGrew 2007).

However, a 'new world disorder' rather than a 'new world order' emerged. The collapse of the Soviet Union created many new nation states, some of which were weak and divided, out of its territory. The number of nation states in the world multiplied, and they sought the recognition, legitimacy, and protection provided by membership of the United Nations, but also fragmented it. It has also been argued that the end of the cold war resulted in the re-emergence of old conflicts between civilizations (see Box 16.12, p. 638).

In reality, the post-Soviet world was dominated by the United States rather than the United Nations. UN interventions have been dependent on the agreement and resources of the USA. This has been particularly evident since 9/11 and the declaration of a 'war on terror'. The UN has condemned terrorism, passed resolutions against it, and adopted anti-terrorist conventions and treaties, but it was the United States (and its allies) that took action. International action meant in practice that action was determined and carried out by the most powerful nation states, as in the 2003 invasion of Iraq.

This world may now be passing. Martin Jacques (2009) claims that a 'shift in global hegemony' from the United States to China is taking place. This began around the turn of the century, but 2008 was a critical year. The global financial crisis weakened the United States, while China began to play a more active global role. Thus, China proposed that a new global currency be created to replace the dollar and began to internationalize the role of its own currency. The current global dominance of the United States, especially in military matters, may continue for some time, but Jacques clearly has a point.

Instead of a world government appearing, a system of world governance has emerged, which the most powerful nation states dominate. The term 'world governance' indicates that global regulation involves a complex institutional process that brings in many different actors at different levels rather than simply actions by some kind of government. While the UN is a central institution in this, there is an array of global institutions, such as the World Bank or the World Trade Organization, carrying out different regulatory and mediatory functions. Around these institutions a transnational civil society has developed that links them to broader social movements. Nation states are no longer as autonomous as they were, but they remain the main actors within this structure and the critical units in the implementation of international policies and interventions.

European Union

Between the global and national levels of organization lies the regional level, where, in the case of the European Union (EU), political integration has gone much further than at global level. Regional organizations may be regarded as stepping-stones to global organization or as obstacles to it.

States have certainly lost some of their law-making and judicial powers to European bodies. EU legislation is initiated by the European Commission, while in some matters European law and courts take precedence over national legal systems. Closer economic union through the Euro constrains the economic policies of national governments by, for example, removing their power to

Frontiers Civilizations in conflict   16.12

In a much-quoted article, Samuel Huntington (1993) argued that after the end of the cold war world politics would be dominated by conflicts between civilizations. His main arguments were:

1 The ideological divisions of the cold war have given way to an older and more fundamental division of the world between civilizations.

2 Civilizations are basic cultural entities defined by differences of language, history, religion, customs, and identity. Huntington lists seven/eight main civilizations—Western, Confucian, Japanese, Islamic, Hindu, Slavic-Orthodox, Latin American, and possibly African.

3 Globalization intensifies conflicts between civilizations because it increases interaction between peoples from different civilizations, making them more aware of these differences and of what members of each have in common.

4 Economic and social change results in the decline of local and national identities, leading people to identify increasingly with their religions, which are central to differences between civilizations.

5 Conflicts of culture are less easily resolved by compromise than political and economic conflicts, and polarize people into 'us and them' distinctions.

6 Conflicts of civilization can occur both between communities and between states, taking the form of both ethnic cleansing and war between states.

7 One particular 'fault line' of conflict, that between the Western and Islamic worlds, has existed for 1,300 years, has recently intensified, and is seen by both sides as a conflict of civilizations.

This approach seems to resonate with recent world events but is open to considerable criticism:

1 Huntington's civilizations are units very different in character, including a nation state (Japan), religions (Islam), regions (Latin America), and a vague grouping of countries (the West).

2 Civilizations are not distinct units and borrow extensively from each other, as when medieval Christian Europe acquired cientific knowledge from the Islamic world.

3 Identities are complex, and there are many bases of identity other than civilization, such as class, gender, nationality, community, and ethnicity, which become salient in different situations.

4 Increased interaction between people of different cultures may lead to conflict but may also lead to multicultural tolerance and hybridization (we discuss hybridization in Chapter 6, pp. 220–1).

5 There are great variations and divisions within the civilizationsi dentified by Huntington, such as the division between Shi'a and Sunni branches of Islam.

6 The expansion of the European Union could bring countries from Huntington's different civilizations within one political organization.

7 Civilizations should not be seen as entities but as ideological constructs used by political and religious leaders to manipulate people and to justify their policies and actions.

⮕ Taking account of these criticisms, consider whether Islamist terrorism (see section on 'Global terror', p. 631) can be explained as a conflict of civilizations.

---

set interest rates. Some policies, as in agriculture and fishing, have long been determined within European institutions.

European unification has also diminished national control of frontiers. Control over borders has traditionally been important to nation states, for their territorial integrity and policy implementation depended on having frontiers. One of the features of European integration has been the weakening of border controls within the EU, and, over much of its area, their virtual disappearance. A key issue here is the extent to which the control of immigration operates at national level or becomes an EU responsibility.

European integration has threatened the integrity of nation states in another way, as sub-nationalisms can bypass national capitals by making their own links with Brussels. Loss of sovereignty downwards through devolution (see Chapter 15, pp. 586–7) combines with loss of

sovereignty upwards to European institutions to diminish the nation state.

Nation states have not, however, been superseded by the EU, because they are centrally involved in the making of European law. National leaders negotiate and decide policy through the Council of Ministers, the most powerful body in the European Union. Furthermore, the Presidency and other positions in the European Commission rotate between countries. Even if each state has lost some autonomy, it has also gained some new influence over other states.

While the European Commission supervises and monitors the application of European laws and treaties, they are implemented by national administrations. There is not as yet a European police force or a European army, though both are admittedly on the EU agenda. The institutions of the European Union can act only through the apparatuses of the nation states that make it up, which leads to a highly variable implementation of laws and treaties.

Figure 16.17 Is the nation state in decline?

Areas of change	Arguments for decline	Arguments against
Advances in communications	Loss of control over borders	Increased state surveillance
Transnational organization	Rise of the TNC	TNC dependence on state
Global social movements	State policies challenged	Movements ignored and resisted by state
Terrorism	Vulnerability to the 'new terrorism'	Development of counter-terrorist state
International government	Authority lost to international bodies	State involvement in international regulation
Identity	Revival of sub-nationalisms and ethnic diversity	Creation of new nation states

> ⊃ *Connections*
> This section raises a number of issues related to the definition and development of the state, which we discuss in Chapter 15, pp. 558–60.

The EU has experienced a massive enlargement that increased its size from fifteen countries in 1995 to twenty-seven in 2007, and other countries, such as Turkey, are waiting in the wings. Turkey, with its secular state tradition but predominantly Muslim population, is a particularly interesting case, given Huntington's thesis of conflicts between civilizations (see Box 16.12).

Enlargement raises acutely the question of how individual nation states relate to the EU. Federalists argue that the EU will only be able to function if there is further centralization to combat national fragmentation. Nationalists argue that greater national diversity within the EU must be recognized and more must be left to the nation state to decide. The rejection by some countries of the proposed European constitution suggests that there are limits to the process of centralization.

A global society?

Some have argued that globalization is leading to a global society. Anthony Giddens (1999) suggested that we already live in one. While there is no denying that a process of globalization has been taking place and that this has generated a global level of organization and a new global consciousness, this section has shown that the nation state has not been superseded. We can no longer say simply that we live in national societies but it makes no sense to conclude that we now live *instead* in a global one. We must make room too for the existence of distinct regional groupings, such as the EU, which lie between the national and the global. The persistence of subnational communities and the creation of new ones, which we examine in Chapter 13 (see pp. 496–501), should also be put into the picture.

As the range of social relationships expands and new larger-scale units emerge, lower-level ones do not disappear but persist in a changed form and interact with higher level ones. Society is neither national nor global but multi-level in character, with communal, national, regional, and global levels of organization.

 Stop and reflect

We began this part of the chapter by examining the collapse of global empires and the creation of most of the world's nation states. We then examined the problems of development they faced and the strategies they adopted.

- Will more aid enable them to catch up?
- Increasing population has been seen as one of the main problems faced by poor countries. Has it been exaggerated?
- Cities in poor countries have grown rapidly. Are they over-urbanized?
- What do you think is the main problem faced by poor countries in achieving improved standards of living?

We moved on to consider global movements of capital and labour.

- Communications technology has enabled the greater and faster movement of both capital and labour.
- So-called transnational corporations have grown, but are they truly transnational?
- Globalization has resulted in greater movements of people, through both tourism and labour migration.
- In what sense is global tourism the 'spearhead of global capitalism'?

(continued)

- Is increased migration a threat to the nation state or a resource?

We have in various places examined topics that involve the impact of globalization on the nation state.

- Go back to the earlier section on 'Globalization and the nation state' on p. 604 and make sure that you understand the positions outlined there.
- Why have sub-Saharan countries experienced such high rates of HIV/AIDS infection?

- What is meant by the 'new terrorism' and how can states best combat it?
- How meaningful is the notion that we live on 'one earth'?
- Should the United Nations be considered a 'world government'?
- Do you think we now live in a global society?

Key concepts

- action approach 601
- demographic transition 619
- dependency theory 600
- development 600
- globalization 602
- glocalization 603
- modernization theory 600

- nation 598
- nationalism 599
- nation state 598
- slavery 608
- sustainable development 635
- Third World 601
- transnational corporation 623

- underdevelopment 600
- world economy 607
- world empire 607
- world system 607

Workshop 16

Study 16 Global women

Care, housework, and sex work for people in rich countries are increasingly done by women from poor countries. *Global Woman* (2003), edited by Barbara Ehrenreich and Arlie Russell Hochschild, explores the issues that this raises in a wide-ranging collection of pieces.

In rich countries, women's employment in paid work has grown enormously, and this has diminished their capacity to carry out unpaid domestic and caring work in the household. This gap has been filled through the employment of other women, whether as au pairs, maids, or nannies. A globalization of women's work has occurred in two ways, for women in professional and managerial work have found themselves increasingly required to travel around the world, while the cheapest source of

domestic labour has been migratory labour from poor countries. Poverty is not the sole reason, however, for women seeking employment in rich countries, since many migrants come from better-off backgrounds and are seeking to escape the confinements of home life in their own countries.

Ehrenreich and Hochschild point out that all this is not simply a result of women's employment. In many rich countries, it is the state's failure to provide adequate child care to support women drawn into the labour force that has forced households to buy the services of other women. Furthermore, in rich countries men, many of whom have lost employment, have not been willing to fill the gap. As Ehrenreich and Hochschild (2003: 9) have put it: 'So, strictly speaking, the presence of immigrant nannies does not enable affluent women to enter the workforce; it enables affluent *men* to continue avoiding the second shift.'

Men are also responsible for the importation of women to do sex work and as sexual partners. This can reflect Western male conceptions of oriental women as exotic or as still having those traditional feminine virtues that are disappearing in the West. Many sex workers do not migrate voluntarily but are coerced by men and trafficked into prostitution.

Ehrenreich and Hochschild claim that the migration of women throws new light on the globalization process. Although poor countries have generally been treated as dependent on rich countries, these have now become dependent on poor country services. In their words:

> The First World takes on a role like that of the old-fashioned male in the family—pampered, entitled, unable to cook, clean, or find his socks. Poor countries take on a role like that of the traditional woman within the family—patient, nurturing and self-denying. A division of labour critiqued when it was 'local' has now, metaphorically speaking, gone global. (Ehrenreich and Hochschild 2003: 11–12)

This is not only a transfer of labour from poor to rich countries but, as Hochschild (2003: 26) suggests, a transfer of 'emotional resources'. Migrant nannies substitute the children of their employers for their own, providing love for the former at the cost of depriving the latter.

In 'Maid to Order', Ehrenreich examines the increasingly commercialized 'cleaning-service chains' that employ migrant women and have turned the household into a capitalist workplace. She calls for this hidden work, and the relationships of exploitation involved in it, to be made visible.

> The feminists of my generation tried to bring some of it into the light of day, but, like busy professional women fleeing the house in the morning, they left the project unfinished, the debate broken off in mid-sentence, the noble intentions unfulfilled. Sooner or later, someone else will have to finish the job. (Ehrenreich and Hochschild 2003: 103)

➔ See Chapter 12, pp. 458–60, for a discussion of the domestic division of labour, and Chapter 17, pp. 681–4, for the growing employment of women.

➔ Consider the implications of Study 16 for dependency theory (see p. 600) and the international division of labour (see p. 608).

❓ Does the globalization of women's work weaken or strengthen patriarchy?

Media watch 16 Galapagos tourism

We showed in this chapter that one aspect of globalization is the growth of global tourism. This has contributed importantly to the economic development of poor countries but at the same time can distort their economies and damage the environment. 'Eco-tourism' and 'sustainable tourism' seek to reconcile the conflicting imperatives of economic growth and conservation.

The Galapagos islands are off the Pacific coast of Ecuador and contain many intriguing plant, animal, and bird species found nowhere else on earth. Charles Darwin visited the islands in 1835, and his observations of different finch species helped to develop his theory of evolution. These special features of the islands have made them a major tourist destination.

Ecuador has allowed tourist numbers to rise. In 1987 it limited their annual entry to 25,000 in order to protect the environment, but some 160,000 tourists now enter annually. Each pays an entry fee of $100 and in other ways boosts the national economy. Increased tourism has put pressure on the environment through incursions into protected areas, the consumption of local products, the introduction of alien species, the generation of waste and pollution, the growth of local souvenir industries, and the rising population providing goods and services for tourists.

Human habitation is restricted to 3 per cent of the land area, and 90 per cent of it has National Park status. There is also a marine reserve where fishing is restricted. The population has, nonetheless, increased from around 6,000 in 1990 to around 30,000 in 2010. People are employed not only in tourism but also in the fishing industry, supplying, for example, shark fins to East Asia. Conflicts have emerged between tourism's interest in conservation and the fishing industry's calls for greater access to marine stocks. Some alternative employment has been created in conservation work.

In 2008 the Ecuador government came under pressure from international bodies to protect the Galapagos from further damage. It has rejected calls to limit the number of tourists, because of their contribution to the economy, but has recently started expelling an estimated 6,000 illegal migrants drawn in by employment in the tourist industry.

Source: Gumbel (2005); Carroll (2008).

❓ Does tourism preserve or destroy the environment?

❓ Is the economic development of poor countries compatible with protection of the environment?

Discussion points

Global warming

- Read 'Saving the earth' on pp. 635–6.
- Why did the December 2009 Copenhagen conference on climate change fail to produce a treaty?
- Was China or the United States the main obstacle? (Look up the newspaper coverage online.)
- Do you think that it is possible to arrive at an effective international treaty?
- Are national emissions limitation programmes now the best way forward?
- What problems do national policies face?
- Should attention and resources now be devoted to adaptation rather than prevention?

Migration and the nation

- Read 'Migration' (pp. 627–8). What is distinctive about recent patterns of migration?
- Why has illegal migration increased?
- Read Study 16. Why do women migrate from poor countries to rich ones?
- Migrants have been considered both a threat and a resource. List ways in which they might be considered either.
- What are the implications of migration for countries of origin?
- Should migration into Britain be reduced, increased, or held stable?

Explore further

The following provide general accounts of globalization:

Bauman, Z. (1998), *Globalization: The Human Consequences* (Cambridge: Polity Press). *A compact, strongly written and perceptive discussion of the relationship between the globalization of the elite and the localization of the poor.*

Cohen, R., and Kennedy, P. (2000), *Global Sociology* (London: Macmillan). *A clear, interesting, comprehensive, and user-friendly survey of all aspects of globalization, containing lots of examples and dealing with a wide range of issues.*

Held, D., and McGrew, A. (2007), *Globalization/Anti-Globalization: Beyond the Great Divide* (2nd edn, Cambridge: Polity Press). *A thorough, clear, and up-to-date examination of the concept of globalization and the debates around it.*

Held, D., McGrew, A., Goldblatt, D., and Perraton, J. (1999), *Global Transformations: Politics, Economics, and Culture* (Cambridge: Polity Press). *An extremely detailed, comprehensive, and authoritative account of all aspects of globalization.*

Steger, M. (2003), *Globalization: A Very Short Introduction* (Oxford: Oxford University Press). *The best introduction to this concept.*

For particular aspects of globalization see:

Castles, S., and Miller, M. J. (2009), *The Age of Migration: International Population Movements in the Modern World* (4th edn, Basingstoke: Palgrave Macmillan). *The standard work on migration, but also relevant to most of the issues discussed in this chapter.*

Dicken, P. (2007), *Global Shift: The Internationalization of Economic Activity* (5th edn, London: Sage). *A mine of information on TNCs and the economic aspects of globalization.*

Elliott, L. (2004), *The Global Politics of the Environment* (2nd edn, Basingstoke: Palgrave Macmillan). *Clear and full information on the development of international politics on this issue.*

Meetham, K. (2001), *Tourism and Global Society* (Basingstoke: Palgrave). *A useful examination of an often taken-for-granted aspect of a globally integrated world.*

On development issues see:

Long, N. (2001), *Development Sociology: Actor Perspectives* (London: Routledge). *Breaks away from the established approaches to development by presenting an alternative action approach.*

Townsend, P., and Gordon, D. (2002), *World Poverty: New Policies to Defeat an Old Enemy* (Bristol: Policy Press). *Contains contributions that analyse inequality and poverty in both rich and poor countries.*

United Nations Development Programme (2009), *Human Development Report: Overcoming Barriers: Human Mobility and Development* (**http://hdr.undp.org/en**). *Latest in this important series, focusing on migration.*

This book provides a stimulating and thought-provoking challenge to classic accounts of global economic development:

Frank, A. G. (1998), *ReORIENT: Global Economy in the Asian Age* (Berkeley and Los Angeles: University of California Press). *A critique of orthodox accounts of the growth of the capitalist world economy, arguing that Asia's significance in this has been ignored.*

Online resources

Visit the Online Resource Centre that accompanies this book to access more learning resources and other interesting material on globalization at:
www.oxfordtextbooks.co.uk/orc/fulcher4e/

The 1999 BBC Reith lectures given by Anthony Giddens on globalization can be found at:
http://news.bbc.co.uk/hi/english/static/events/reith_99

Belinda Weaver's site at the University of Queensland library provides links to a huge range of materials on all aspects of globalization and the debates around it:
www.journoz.com/global

For documents, reports, statistics and discussion of world poverty visit:
http://zunia.org

For information on the global environmentalist movement and the latest Earth Summit, visit Greenpeace International at:
www.greenpeace.org/homepage/international

The United Nations homepage is at:
www.un.org/en/index.shtml

PART FIVE

PRODUCTION, INEQUALITIES, AND SOCIAL DIVISIONS

Work, Employment, and Leisure

Contents

Amazon.com

Amazon.com provides the world's largest flow of online goods, with worldwide sales of around $19 billion in 2008. It started in 1994 as an online book shop based in a Seattle garage. It has now diversified into a huge range of products, supplied from its 'fulfilment centres' (warehouses) spread across North America, Europe, and Asia.

Amazon exemplifies the new world of e-commerce, but behind the scenes labour is exploited in an old-fashioned way. Employees at its Bedfordshire warehouse have reportedly not been allowed sick leave, even with a doctor's note, and were penalized if they took a day off. After a five-day week, they were required to do a compulsory overnight shift from Saturday through to Sunday. Those packing Xbox games consoles were expected to do 140 an hour. Those picking items off shelves were said to walk up to 14 miles a day.

Workers have approached the Graphical, Paper, and Media Union (now part of Unite) with grievances about work intensity, excessive working hours, and poor wages, together with blocked promotion. The union's attempt to secure recognition was, however, successfully obstructed by the company.

Sources: *Gall (2004); Newall and Foggo (2008); 'Amazon.com', Wikipedia.*

Work is constantly changing as technology develops, but, as our opening piece shows, capitalism continues to shape relationships between employers and workers. We begin this chapter by examining the character of the industrial capitalism that has shaped the world we live in.

While capitalism continues on its way, do we now live in a largely post-industrial world? Employment has certainly shifted from industrial production into services, though arguably services themselves are becoming increasingly organized on industrial lines. In this chapter we consider many different kinds of work, from work in factories to work in offices and call centres, and also work in the home.

Home and work are often treated as quite different parts of our lives, but home too is a workplace. We discuss unpaid domestic labour, the mechanization of housework, and the rise of DIY. We also examine paid work in the home for outside employers. Homework of this kind has actually been growing in importance with the spread of telework.

The home has also become the main focus of leisure. Work and leisure might seem totally different activities, but they are in fact bound together. One could not exist without the other. We also examine in this chapter the changing relationship between work and leisure, focusing on changes in sport.

Concepts and theories

Our experience of work, employment, and leisure has been shaped by two powerful forces that have transformed the world—capitalism and industrialism. We begin by discussing their meaning and the relationship between them. We then move on to consider the emergence of a distinct world of work and the relationship between home and workplace, work and non-work.

Industrial capitalism

Capitalism and industrialism have been closely linked, for industrial capitalism has transformed the world. They must,

however, be distinguished, for they refer to different aspects of economic organization (see Figure 17.1 on p. 650).

Capitalism

The basic feature of **capitalism** is the financing of economic activity by the investment of capital to make a profit. Capital simply means accumulated money that is available for investment. Money can be invested in this way in any economic activity, in trade, production, services, or agriculture. Capitalism did indeed first develop in trading activities during medieval times, and it was not until much later that capitalist production became established. It was, however, capitalist production that transformed society (see Box 17.1) and it is on capitalist production that we shall focus.

It was Karl Marx (1858) who first systematically analysed capitalist production. He argued that its central feature was the private ownership of the means of production. The **means of production** were the workplace, tools, and raw materials that made the production of goods possible. It was the capitalist who provided the money to set up a workplace, equip it with machinery, and buy the necessary raw materials. These means of production were therefore the private property of the capitalist and were not owned by the producers, the workers who actually made the goods.

Production was carried out by wage labour. Capitalists employed workers to produce goods in exchange for a wage. Instead of being able to consume or sell what they had made, workers received a wage in return for their labour. The producers had lost control of the product of their labour, which was owned by the employer. They worked not in order to produce something they could use or sell but to earn wages. They had become, as Marx put it, 'wage slaves'.

Market relationships came to dominate capitalist societies. In order to make a profit, the capitalist had to sell products in the market. Equally, producers could not consume what they had produced or produce what they consumed. Instead, they had to use their wages to buy in the market everything they needed or wanted. The link between production and consumption had been broken and was now mediated by market relationships.

> **⊃ Connections**
>
> Marx argued that capitalism experienced periodic crises of overproduction. We examine the latest of these crises, the one that began in 2007, in Chapter 15, pp. 588–9.

Marx emphasized that under capitalism those who produced lost control not only of the *product* of their labour but also the *process* of production. The capitalist employer determined what machinery should be used, how the work should be divided between employees, the hours of work, and the speed of work. This loss of control over product and process resulted in the *alienation* of the worker, a concept that we discuss on p. 651.

The interests of the owners of capital and labour were, according to Marx, in conflict. The capitalist's concern to maximize profits by squeezing as much work as possible out of labour, while paying it as little as possible, meant that the interests of the owners of capital and their workers were inevitably opposed. Marx argued that this conflict divided society into two classes, the capitalist bourgeoisie and the working class (see Chapter 19, p. 747, for a discussion of his theory of class conflict). Increasing conflict

---

THEORY AND METHODS   **17.1**

Marx and Engels on capitalism

Although Marx's name is associated with attempts to overthrow capitalism and replace it with communism, he was greatly impressed by capitalism's enormous productive potential. In the *Communist Manifesto*, Marx and Engels (1948: 85) wrote:

> . . . the bourgeoisie, during its rule of scarce one hundred years, has created more massive and more colossal productive forces than have all preceding generations together. Subjection of nature's forces to man, machinery, application of chemistry to industry and agriculture, steam-navigation, railways, electric telegraphs, clearing of whole continents for cultivation, canalization of rivers, whole populations conjured out of the ground—what earlier century had even a presentiment that such productive forces slumbered in the lap of social labour?

between these classes would lead eventually to a revolutionary transformation of society that would bring capitalism to an end.

Industrialism

Capitalist production existed before the Industrial Revolution. In sixteenth- and seventeenth-century Europe production in households and workshops was increasingly financed and controlled by the owners of capital. These then began to bring their workers together in larger units called factories and in the eighteenth century developed the techniques of industrial production in order to make higher profits on their capital.

Industrialism refers to the new method of organizing production that became fully established in the nineteenth century. While the development of *power-driven machinery* was central to industrialization, its defining feature was the way that production was organized. It was *concentrated* in large workplaces (factories), where work was *divided into specialized tasks* and *coordinated by managers*.

Production was transformed through the introduction of *power-driven machinery*, initially driven by water but then by the steam engine. The nineteenth-century introduction of steam power led to the rapid spread of industrialism, for steam engines could be set up anywhere, while travel was transformed by the steam-driven locomotive and the steamship. Hand tools had been controlled by the worker, but in a real sense the worker was now controlled by the power-driven machine, for this determined the speed of work and shaped the work environment.

Industrialization *concentrated* production in large workplaces. Workers could be controlled better if they were brought together under one roof, while the harnessing of water and steam power made it necessary to concentrate

Figure 17.1 Capitalism and industrialism

Capitalism	Industrialism
• Profit drives economic activity	• Power-driven machinery
• Private ownership of means of production	• Concentration of production
• Employment of wage labour	• Systematic division of labour
• Control of process of production by employer	• Coordination of production by specialized management
• Conflict of interest between capital and labour	• Organization of workers in unions

production in factories with power-driven machinery. The factory changed the social character of work, bringing large numbers of workers together and enabling them to organize themselves in unions.

The development of technology and the concentration of production led to the *division of labour* into specialized tasks. This did not begin with industrialization, but factory production resulted in a much more systematic division of work into specialized tasks than had existed before. This made workers highly interdependent, for the work of each depended on the work of all.

A whole new range of functions and occupations emerged to enable the *management and control* of the workplace. The concentration of labour, new technology, and the specialization of tasks in the industrial factory generated new problems of coordination, expertise, and control. Employers could neither ignore these problems nor handle them on their own and began to employ increasingly professional and specialized managers.

Capitalism and industrialism have been closely related, because it was the capitalist's pursuit of more profitable ways of organizing production that drove industrialization forwards. We do, therefore, frequently refer to *industrial capitalism*, but it is important to distinguish between capitalism and industrialism. As we have shown, capitalist production existed before production was organized on industrial lines. Furthermore, capitalist industrialism has not been its only form, and a non-capitalist system of production was created in state socialist countries, notably the Soviet Union, its satellite countries in Eastern Europe, in China, and in Cuba. State socialism was, however, in the end unable to establish itself as a viable alternative and collapsed at the end of the 1980s (see Chapter 20, pp. 804–5).

The world of work

Capitalist production and industrialization separated production from the household. Previously, most production had been carried out in the household, in a workshop attached to it, or on a family farm. Under industrial capitalism the workplace became a world of its own—the world of the factory, the office, the laboratory, the factory farm. Indeed, people now spoke of the world of work as though it were a quite separate part of life.

Employment relations

A distinct set of relationships emerged between employers and workers. These consisted of the organization and management of work, which we examine in Chapter 14, and industrial relations, which we consider here.

The term *industrial relations* refers to the bargaining relationships that developed between employers and workers, not only in factories but in all other kinds of workplace. These relationships became a distinct area of organizational and institutional development.

Organization started when workers began to form unions because they were individually weak. They were dependent on employment for a living, but, unless they had skills in short supply, the employer could easily dismiss and replace them. Worker organization then stimulated

A union meeting: why do workers need unions?
© Alice Chadwick

counter-organization by employers, who created employers' associations.

Organization led to the gradual **institutionalization of industrial conflict**. By this is meant its increasing organization and regulation. Unions and employers made collective agreements to regulate the relationship between them. These specified wage rates and conditions of employment, and procedures for dealing with disputes and negotiating agreements. Governments often became involved by creating institutions of mediation or arbitration, to avoid as much as possible the disruption and disorder resulting from open conflict.

Conflict did not, however, come to an end with institutionalization but took place within the framework of the negotiation procedures set up to regulate it. Open conflict anyway still occurred when negotiations broke down. Institutionalization also itself generated conflicts between the leaders of organizations and their members. One consequence of this was the rise of unofficial strikes, when workers took action locally in defiance of their leaders.

We examine these issues in 'Industrial conflict' on pp. 654–6.

The meaning of work

With the creation of separate workplaces, the experience of work became a distinct part of daily life. This experience was shaped by the work situation, the technology, management practices, and work environment.

According to Karl Marx (1844), work had been and should be a creative means of self-expression, but the emergence of capitalism turned it into a non-creative activity. Traditional craftsmen had worked at their own pace in their own workshops with their own tools, creating whole and unique products, which also belonged to them. The pace of factory work was, however, set by a machine in an environment controlled by the employer. Work was fragmented by the division of labour, and workers had no sense of making a complete object. They produced standard and characterless goods owned by the employer. Instead of work being a means of self-expression, it had become merely a means of earning a living.

This loss of the creative aspects of work was characterized by Marx as a process of **alienation**:

- As the worker had lost control of the product, it had become an alien object. The worker had no feelings for it, no attachment to it, or pride in it.

- With loss of control over the product went loss of control over the production process, which dominated the worker as an alien and oppressive force.

- Workers also became alienated from each other, as they competed for employment in a labour market.

- Since it was creativity through work that was the distinctive feature of human beings, the loss of creativity was dehumanizing and alienated 'man' from his true self.

Émile Durkheim (1893) challenged this view and argued that the growing division of labour should not have such degrading consequences, because it created a new interdependence between workers. This would give them a sense of participation in a common enterprise that would make work more, rather than less, meaningful. Instead of producing alienation and conflict, the division of labour would lead to cooperation and harmony. Durkheim used the analogy of the human body, where organs were specialized but worked harmoniously together to produce what he called an **organic solidarity**.

Durkheim's views were not, however, that different from Marx's, for Durkheim did recognize that the division of labour would have these integrative consequences *only if* people were able to carry out freely chosen tasks appropriate to their abilities. The difference between them was that Marx believed this was impossible in a capitalist society, while Durkheim thought it would normally be the case. When it was not, perhaps because social change had been too rapid, society was in an abnormal state of *anomie* (see Chapter 2, p. 35).

Marx and Durkheim were concerned with the general impact of industrial capitalism on work, but many different work situations have emerged within industrial societies, and we examine these on pp. 656–63.

Outside the world of work

Industrialization not only created a new world of work; it also changed people's ways of thinking about their work and non-work activities.

Work at home

We discussed the experience of work as though work always means paid work outside the home. Commonly used terms such as 'going to work', 'hours of work', or 'workplace' define work in this way. Where, however, does this notion of work leave housework or homework?

One of the problems here is that the definitions of the various kinds of work that go on in the household are far from clear. It is important first of all to distinguish two key terms:

- **Domestic labour.** This refers to all work that maintains the household. It includes both housework and domestic production, as well as other tasks that we discuss below.

- **Homework.** This is paid work carried out at home for an outside employer.

Domestic labour takes up a large part of daily life. Although not traditionally counted as economic activity, it undoubtedly makes an enormous contribution to the economy. People can do paid work only if they are fed, clothed, housed, and kept both mentally and physically well, but most of this work is provided by unpaid domestic labour. A recent attempt to measure its contribution concluded that in the United Kingdom it was equivalent to 77 per cent of Gross Domestic Product (see **www.statistics. gov.uk/hhsa**).

Domestic labour itself consists of many different kinds of work. The routine cleaning and maintenance tasks of *housework* are different from *domestic production*, such as baking cakes, making clothes, or growing vegetables. Other tasks, such as roof repair or decoration, are concerned with *domestic capital*, for they maintain or increase the value of property. There are also *management tasks* that deal with family finances, the distribution of work between its members, and the supervision of their work. *Emotional labour* is yet another kind of domestic work, concerned with the household's emotional needs, which

are in part generated by the stress of paid work (see Chapter 12, pp. 434–5).

Domestic labour can also be carried out in various ways:

- the unpaid labour of the household members;
- waged domestic labour, when maids, gardeners, or au pairs are paid to carry it out;
- informal cooperation, an important and often omitted source of labour, ranging from mutual baby-sitting arrangements to local systems for exchanging tokens representing amounts of labour.

Domestic labour is not the only kind of work carried out at home. There is also homework. Since industrialization, most people have earned their living in a separate workplace but some continued to carry out paid work for an employer at home. Recent developments in communications and information technology have given homework, particularly in the form of telework, a new boost.

The home is then a workplace, within which many different kinds of work go on. The 'sociology of work' should concern itself not just with paid work outside the home but with all work going on in the society. Glucksmann (1995) developed the concept of the *total social organization of labour* (TSOL) to convey this idea. The TSOL refers to 'the manner by which all the labour in a society is divided up between and allocated to different structures, institutions, and activities' (Glucksmann 1995: 67). This concept makes central to the study of work the relationships between the different forms that it takes.

Employment and unemployment

With industrialization, work became identified with employment. Those who made their living by providing goods and services without working for an employer were now the exception rather than the rule, and were called *self-employed*. If people lost their jobs or were unable to find paid work, they fell into the new category of the *unemployed*. If they were unemployed, they were 'out of work', even though they might be working hard to grow their own food or make their own clothes.

The definition of unemployment presents many problems. They are not simply all those not in employment, for those who are ill, retired, or in full-time education are not considered unemployed. To be unemployed, people must at least be *available* for paid work, and availability is not easy to define. Some may be available for work but not actually seeking it, because, for example, they have developed an alternative lifestyle. Should they be considered unemployed?

Definitions are important, for the official definition of unemployment determines the size of the figure for the

Is this domestic labour?

© Alice Chadwick

Figure 17.2 Who are the unemployed?

Which of the following would you consider to be unemployed?
• Those receiving Jobseeker's Allowance?
• People who are 'out of work'?
• People who are 'out of work' but seeking it?
• Part-time workers unable to find full-time work?
• Retired people who still want to work?
• Students unable to find vacation work?
• People between jobs?
• Househusbands and housewives?

unemployed, which is a politically sensitive issue. As we show in Chapter 3, p. 102, there have been many recent changes in the official definition of unemployment, which have mostly had the effect of reducing it!

Work and leisure

In daily life we usually distinguish between work and leisure. This distinction makes a sharp division between work and non-work activities, and commonly treats them as opposite in character. Work is generally seen as routine and unsatisfying, while leisure provides freedom, choice, self-expression, and creativity.

Should, however, such a sharp distinction be made? Stanley Parker (1976) showed how in some situations work is not sharply distinguished from leisure. He identified three different work–leisure patterns and linked them to differences between occupations:

- *The segmentalist pattern*. This broadly matched the conventional work–leisure distinction. It was found among routine clerical or unskilled manual workers, particularly those, such as fishermen or miners, working in harsh or dangerous conditions. Their work was a means to earn a living that provided few opportunities for work satisfaction and gave them little control over what they did. Leisure was an escape from alienating work. (See 'The working-class world', Chapter 19, pp. 762–4).

- *The extension pattern*. This did not fit the conventional distinction, for work interests spilled over into non-work time. It was characteristic of business people, professionals, and skilled workers, whose work was involving and satisfying. Work was not a negative experience and leisure not an escape from it.

- *The neutrality pattern*. An intermediate pattern, with no sharp opposition between work and leisure but also no extension of work into leisure time. It was typical of semi-skilled manual and clerical workers.

The extension pattern suggests that too sharp and general a contrast should not be drawn between work as a negative experience and leisure as a positive one. Work can be a positive experience, while the growth of leisure industries, and the manipulation of the consumer by the mass media and advertising, imply that leisure is not simply a time of choice, freedom, and creativity. There are pressures to consume as well as to work. Furthermore, the pressure to consume may lead to passive forms of leisure, such as television-watching. Indeed, some work activities may well be more creative and self-expressive than many leisure activities.

Arguably, the work–leisure distinction reflects a particularly male way of looking at the world. It does not take account of the housework that has been the main daily activity of many women, for housework by wives is neither paid work nor leisure. Furthermore, when women are employed in paid work, they generally have to carry out housework at other times. Thus, non-work time can become leisure only if the housework is done by someone else. The work–leisure distinction has applied, therefore, most clearly to the lives of married men in full-time employment with full-time housewives.

There are then problems with the distinction between work and leisure, but, as we shall show in 'The creation of leisure', pp. 665–7, industrial capitalism did, nonetheless, lead to a significant separation of work and leisure activities.

 Stop and reflect

We first explored the significance of capitalism and industrialism.

- Make sure that you understand the meaning of these two key terms.
- What is the relationship between them?

We went on to discuss the emergence of a separate world of work in the workplace.

- Make sure that you understand the approaches of Marx and Durkheim to the experience of work.
- How do they differ and do they have anything in common?

We then moved outside the 'world of work' to examine the relationship between workplace and home, between work and non-work.

- We distinguished between 'domestic labour', work concerned with the maintenance of the household, and 'homework', which is work carried out at home for an outside employer.

- We argued that people can be 'out-of work' for many reasons, but it is only when they are available for work that they are unemployed. Do you agree?

- Daily activities are commonly seen as divided between work and leisure. What problems are there with this distinction?

The impact of industrial capitalism

In this section we examine the main features of the new world of work created by industrial capitalism. This concentrated labour in the workplace and generated industrial conflict. It made the experience of paid work a central feature of people's lives and separated work from non-work in their minds.

Industrial conflict

In industrial capitalism there was, as we argued above, a conflict of interest between the owners of capital and their employees. Industrialization concentrated workers together in large units and made it easier for them to organize themselves in unions and stand up to the capitalist employer.

Workers organized themselves in different ways, however, and pursued different strategies, as did employers. Before considering industrial conflict, we need to consider the process of organization on both sides of industry.

Organization and strategy

The first strong unions in Britain were the *craft* unions that established themselves in the middle of the nineteenth century. They organized workers within a particular craft or occupation, such as printing, and their main strategy was to keep wages high by controlling the supply of labour. They controlled entry to the craft and restricted jobs to their members. They were in conflict as much with other crafts and less skilled workers as with employers. Employers tried to counter their strategy by using less skilled labour, a process known as **deskilling**, either breaking work down into simpler tasks or introducing machinery that could be

operated by less skilled workers (we discuss deskilling on p. 657).

A similarly exclusive strategy has been operated by professions, whose associations have acted much like craft unions. They too established their bargaining power by restricting entry, and controlling the training and certification of members. Thus, during the nineteenth century the British medical profession established control of entry through the registration of medical practitioners and the control of medical education. As with the craft unions, this involved the exclusion of women from membership (Witz 1992).

The second form of organization was the *industrial* or *general* union created by less skilled workers unable to control entry. These unions relied more on collective bargaining and the strike weapon. They were inclusive, seeking to organize as many workers as possible, regardless of their skill. Their open and inclusive character led them to adopt socialist ideologies based on the principle of class organization. This approach resulted also in the building of national federations that could mobilize the strength of the whole working class.

Employers responded by constructing counter-organizations. Faced by unions that stretched across a whole industry, they created matching employers' associations. They could respond to strikes by locking out all union members, seeking to exhaust the unions' funds by forcing them to support large numbers of out-of-work members.

The third main form of worker organization was the *labour* or *social democratic* party, which sought to advance the collective interests of labour through political rather than industrial action. In a democratic political system, such a party could bring to bear the numerical advantages

Figure 17.3 Labour organization, strategy, and employer response

Labour organization	Membership	Strategy	Employer response
Craft union	Skilled workers	Control of entry	Deskilling
Industrial union	All workers in an industry	Collective bargaining	Employer associations
Labour party	All workers	Use of political power	Influence on parties and state

of the working class, for workers' votes far outweighed those of the employers. The employers' response was to support and fund political parties themselves, and use their economic power to exert pressure on any labour government.

→ *Connections*
We discuss labour movements and the development of the British Labour Party in Chapter 20, pp. 794–5. In Chapter 15, pp. 562–3, we discuss the relationship between labour movements and the state.

Strikes

The term 'industrial conflict' is often taken to mean strike action, but this is quite wrong. When considering industrial conflict it is important to make a number of basic distinctions:

- between *institutionalized* and *open* conflict;
- between *different forms* of open conflict;

- between *collective* and *individual* expressions of conflict.

We discussed the *institutionalization* of industrial conflict on p. 651. As we argued there, institutionalization did not mean that conflict ceased, even if there was no open conflict.

Open conflict commonly takes the form of strike action, but in some situations it may be more effective to use other weapons. Workers can bring considerable pressure to bear on employers by refusing to work overtime or 'going slow', without breaking agreements or contracts, and continuing to draw their pay. Open conflict may also take the form of an employer-initiated lockout.

If workers are unorganized or unable to act collectively, discontent may take the form of *individual* actions, such as going sick or simply staying away from work. The term 'absenteeism' is used for this kind of individual refusal to work. The line between individual and collective action may, however, become blurred, for unions may advise their members to go sick or coordinate absenteeism.

Figure 17.4 UK strikes, 1895–2004 (five-year annual averages)

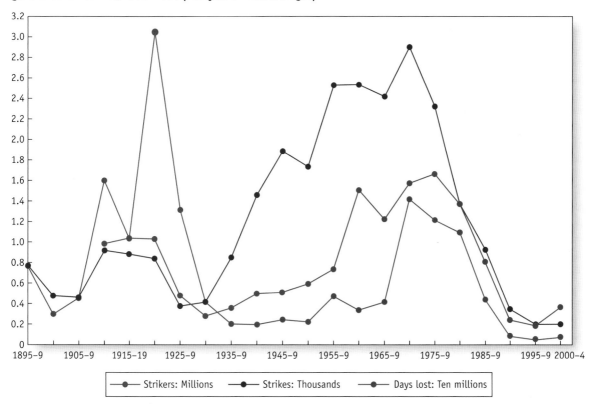

Sources: Grint (1999: 163); Office for National Statistics (2006).

❓ Why did the number of strikes between the 1930s and the 1970s increase so much more than the number of strikers and worker days lost?

❓ Why have strikes declined since the 1970s?

While industrial conflict must not be confused with strikes, they have been the most disruptive weapon used by workers and have been extensively studied. The most common method used has been to analyse trends and variations in the amount of strike action, though there have also been some important case studies of particular strikes (Gouldner 1954*b*; Lane and Roberts 1971; Friedman and Meredeen 1980). British strike data are available from the Office of National Statistics. The Workplace Employment Relations Survey is an important source of data on both strike and non-strike action (Kersley *et al.* 2005).

As we show in Chapter 3, pp. 99–100, there are many problems with official statistics and this is certainly the case with those on British industrial disputes. First, strike records depend on employer reports and the preparedness of employers to treat a work stoppage as a strike. Secondly, very small disputes that involve fewer than ten workers or last less than one day are excluded (unless they result in the loss of more than 100 worker days).

Strikes are mainly measured by *worker days lost* and *strike frequency*. *Strike frequency* figures are unreliable because most strikes are short. The shorter the strike, the less likely it is to be reported or included by the official definition. Problems with frequency data particularly affect international comparisons, for reporting and definitional practices vary considerably between countries. Strike frequency data are, nonetheless, important, because they indicate workers' readiness to take strike action. The *worker days lost* figure is more reliable, since it is mainly determined by large or long strikes that are certain to find their way into the statistics.

Figure 17.4 on p. 655 shows the long-term trend of strikes in Britain. The days-lost peak in the 1920s reflects the General Strike of 1926, and other large strikes around that time. In a well-known study, Ross and Hartman (1960) argued that there had been a general decline of the strike in all the main industrial societies as industrial conflict became institutionalized, but, as Figure 17.4 shows, strike measures rose to new heights in the 1950s, 1960s, and 1970s.

Relatively full employment at this time and growing union membership undoubtedly played a part in generating strikes, but it was argued that the archaic organizational and institutional structures inherited from the past were also responsible (Fulcher 1991). Major attempts were made in the 1960s and early 1970s to reform British industrial relations. These failed, and brought the governments concerned into disastrous conflicts with the unions, but had very important consequences by preparing the way for the legislative onslaught on them in the 1980s. We examine this in 'Industrial conflict' on pp. 676–8.

The experience of work

We now turn to consider the experience of work. We discuss, first, the effects of different technologies on manual work and then examine factors outside the work situation. We go on to clerical, service, and sex work.

Technology and the meaning of work

The classic work on this is Robert Blauner's *Alienation and Freedom* (1964). He developed and applied the concepts of Marx and Durkheim, which we discussed earlier on p. 651.

Blauner considered that technology was central to the way work was organized and experienced. It developed through four stages:

- craft production;
- machine-based factory production;
- assembly plants;
- automation.

Although these were historical stages in the development of technology, each of them still existed. He took printing as his example of craft production, textiles for the machine-based factory, the car industry for the assembly plant, and chemicals for automation. These examples were appropriate at the time of his study in the 1950s, but major changes in technology have happened since. In the car industry, for example, many operations are now carried out by computer-controlled machinery. All the technologies examined by Blauner do, nonetheless, still exist.

In order to study the effect of different technologies on the experience of work, Blauner had to operationalize the concepts of Marx and Durkheim so that he could measure the degree of alienation workers experienced (see Figure 17.5). His first step was to sort out the different ways in which the work situation could affect the worker. From the writings of Marx and Durkheim he extracted four dimensions of alienation:

- powerlessness;
- meaninglessness;
- isolation;
- self-estrangement.

Self-estrangement largely resulted from the effects of the other three dimensions on the experience of work. It referred to workers' inability to express themselves through their work or to involve themselves in it. It is similar to Marx's idea that workers are alienated from their true selves.

Indicators had to be found for each dimension. Blauner established, for example, the following indicators for powerlessness:

- non-ownership of the means of production and the product of labour;
- inability to influence general managerial policies;
- lack of control over the conditions of employment;
- lack of control over the immediate work process.

So far as non-ownership was concerned, he agreed with Marx that this characterized all workers under capitalism. But whereas this was for Marx the essential point, Blauner was primarily interested in how the degree of alienation varied within capitalism. His other indicators of powerlessness varied from industry to industry, producing different degrees of alienation.

He applied his dimensions to each of his four industries, using data from an attitude survey in the United States and case-study material. He found that printing retained much of the character of a pre-industrial craft and showed low levels of alienation (see Figure 17.5). Alienation increased with industrialization, reaching its maximum level with car assembly plants, returning with automation to a level characteristic of pre-industrial work. Although he accepted that under capitalism all workers experienced some alienation, he claimed that much of it could be removed by more advanced technologies that made work satisfying and meaningful again.

Harry Braverman (1974) challenged the idea that automation has reversed the tendency towards increasing alienation. He argued that technological development had deskilled workers by separating mental from manual work. Mechanization turned work into a series of simple, repetitive tasks that required little training or mental effort. Mental work was concentrated in management, in the occupations that planned, organized, and controlled the work process. The advantages of deskilling were that it made labour cheaper and increased employer control of the work process. According to Braverman, automation was but the latest stage in this process.

He was very sceptical of Blauner's argument that workers in the chemical industry had meaningful work. The monitoring of chemical processes was a routine matter that required little skill. The only knowledge it needed was the capacity to read a dial. A case study by Theo Nichols and Huw Beynon (1977) supported this view and argued that control work could be lonely and meaningless. Furthermore, however automated an industry was, it also employed many workers carrying out traditional kinds of manual work.

A more general issue is raised by both Blauner and Braverman. What is the significance of technology for the experience of work? Workers' power must partly relate to the strength of union organization and does not just vary with technology. Furthermore, styles of management can change work satisfaction through, for example, job rotation, job enlargement, and job enrichment.

Figure 17.5 Operationalizing the concept of alienation

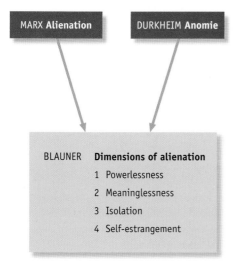

Indicators of powerlessness	Printing	Textiles	Cars	Chemicals
1 Separation from ownership	✓	✓	✓	✓
2 Inability to influence management	✗	✓	✓	✗
3 Lack of control over conditions of employment	✗	✓	✓	✗
4 Lack of control over work process	✗	✓	✓	✗

BLAUNER **Dimensions of alienation**
1 Powerlessness
2 Meaninglessness
3 Isolation
4 Self-estrangement

➲ Try applying Blauner's dimensions to any work situation that you have experienced.

➲ In Chapter 3, p. 94, we discuss whether Blauner accurately operationalizes Marx's ideas. Look at what we say there and see what you think.

> **➜ Connections**
> We discuss different approaches to management in Chapter 14, pp. 528–9 and 539–42.

From technology to orientation

The main challenge to the technological approach came from the *Affluent Worker* study by John Goldthorpe *et al.* (1968*a*) of Luton workers in the 1960s. This argued that the attitudes people bring to work shape their experience of it. The study covered all three of the technologies examined by Blauner.

The study did find that technology affected *work satisfaction*, but also that there was remarkably little variation in workers' *attitudes* to their work. These were instrumental, for they saw work as a means to earn the money they needed, rather than a means of self-expression. What mattered in their lives was not their work experience or work relationships but their private life at home, their possessions, and their families. As their work situations were so different, these attitudes could not have been generated by their work and must have been brought into the workplace.

The *Affluent Worker* study introduced the important concept of **orientation to work** to describe the attitudes that workers brought into work. Orientations were shaped by prior socialization, social background, earlier experiences of life, and media influences. Orientation to work then mediated between the characteristics of the workplace, such as its size and technology, and workers' experience of it. The Luton workers typically held an *instrumental* orientation to work, but Goldthorpe *et al.* also identified

Is this worker in control?
© Alice Chadwick

 Briefing: catering work   **17.2**

Gabriel (1988) examined the experience of work in catering. One of the workplaces that he studied was the catering department of a community centre in a northern British city. He found that catering had been deskilled through mechanization and industrialization, and the application of the techniques of scientific management, often known as Taylorism (see Chapter 14, p. 529):

> The cook-freeze kitchen was a faithful adoption of Taylorist principles in mass catering, splitting up cooking from planning, breaking up work-tasks into simple and tightly controlled routines, and reducing the skill, initiative and thinking required of the cooks to a virtual minimum. . . . All freedom and creativity, the hallmarks of craft cooking, are eliminated through rules aimed at preventing the cooks from 'messing about with the recipes'. Monotony and lack of variety prevailed, each day being the same as the next. (Gabriel 1988: 87–8)

He also found, however, that women made their work more meaningful by taking responsibility for meeting production targets, and controlling the pace and distribution of work. Their shared interests and common home backgrounds also made work bearable by generating a feeling of togetherness that 'provided consolation for jobs devoid of interest'. They, nonetheless, felt trapped in their jobs and unable to seek more interesting work, because the department's work hours and holiday periods were compatible with their domestic and childcare obligations.

❓ *Think about any paid work that you have recently done. How meaningful was it? What aspects of the work situation made it more or less meaningful? Could you make it more meaningful yourself? Did the meaning of your work matter to you?*

Figure 17.6 Orientations to work

Orientation	Meaning of work	Involvement in organization	Involvement in work	Relationship between work and non-work life
Instrumental	Work as source of income	Calculative only	Work not a central life interest	Sharp separation
Bureaucratic	Service to organization in exchange for career	Moral obligation to organization	Career a central life interest	Social aspirations and status related to career
Solidaristic	Work as a group activity	Identification with enterprise or work group	Work a central life interest	Strong occupational community

Source: Adapted from Goldthorpe *et al.* (1968*a*: 38–41).

bureaucratic and *solidaristic* orientations (see Figure 17.6). The solidaristic one was typical of the more traditional worker community, the bureaucratic one of white-collar workers.

This study did not claim that Luton workers were typical of workers in general. The high wages of this area had attracted mobile workers from all over the country and selected out those who were highly instrumental. The authors of the study were well aware of the distinctive character of the Luton labour force and, indeed, studied it for this very reason.

White-collar work

White-collar work has often been treated as quite different from manual work. In the classic British study of white-collar workers David Lockwood (1958) argued that white-collar workers had a more personal relationship with their superiors, while their work was non-repetitive and required some skill, responsibility, and judgement. As we showed above, Goldthorpe *et al.* (1968*a*) considered that a distinct bureaucratic orientation to work was associated with white-collar work.

> ⟴ *Connections*
> Braverman and other Marxist writers have argued that a process of proletarianization turned white-collar workers into members of the working class. We discuss changes in the class situation of white-collar workers in Chapter 19, pp. 766–8.

According to Braverman, however, the same deskilling processes operated in white-collar as in manual work and its distinctiveness has entirely disappeared. Bureaucratization created standard procedures that took much of the discretion and personal contact out of clerical work. Career opportunities declined as the number of routine jobs grew. Mechanization and the application of the principles of scientific management subdivided tasks and deskilled, just as they had done with manual work. The call centre standardization of employees' responses to enquiries is a recent example (Korczynski 2001).

Rosemary Crompton and Gareth Jones (1984) examined the effects of automation on a largely female white-collar workforce in three workplaces—local-authority departments, an insurance company, and a bank. The result was a greater fragmentation of work into specialized, low-skill, routine tasks. Instead of giving clerks more control over their work, automation actually shifted control into the hands of senior administrators. It had in this case increased powerlessness and alienation. Greater contact with the public did, however, make work more satisfying and more meaningful for the bank clerks.

They also examined the significance of the career, which was central to the notion of a bureaucratic orientation to work. Here they made two main points:

- White-collar occupations have become increasingly stratified by a promotion barrier. Only a small number of positions involving skill and responsibility had good promotion prospects and were filled by entrants with high qualifications.

- It was mainly men who got promoted. The lower grades were largely filled by women, whose promotion prospects suffered because of lower educational qualifications and career breaks to have children.

White-collar work lost therefore much of its distinctiveness, as it was subjected to the same processes of change as manual work. The distinction between manual and white-collar work has also diminished because all kinds of work increasingly involve information technology. Computer-controlled production and electronic communication mean manual workers have to learn the technical skills associated with non-manual work.

Customer service work

Employment in industrial societies has shifted from manufacturing to service occupations. 'Service work' includes both white-collar work that involves little or no contact with customers, and customer service work where interaction with customers is central. Customer service work has become steadily more important, with:

- the growth of occupations, from airline cabin crew, to hairdressers, and nurses, that involve such interactions;
- the increased emphasis on marketing products by providing a good service to customers.

Customer service work typically involves **emotional labour**, which we discuss in Chapter 4, pp. 141–3. Some work involves caring functions that draw upon the emotion of the employee and are a necessary part of the work, as in nursing. Customer service workers are also required to manage their own emotions in order to conform to the image promoted by their employer, as shown by Hochschild's study of airline cabin crews (see our discussion of this in Chapter 4). Bolton (2001) has argued that changes in health-service management mean that nurses too have experienced a growing pressure to present a 'smiley face' when they have to deal with difficult patients. Emotional labour can involve 'multiple identities' and an 'emotional juggling' that is itself a special skill.

Emotional labour commonly requires **aesthetic labour**. Employees are expected to 'look good' and 'sound right'. The key feature of aesthetic labour is the embodiment of certain capacities and attitudes. Employers select workers according to their bodily appearance and then modify this in order to conform with a company's image and style. While this has, arguably, always been a feature of occupations that involve contact with customers, Nickson *et al.* (2001: 178) show that commercial pressures are driving

more organizations to demand 'aesthetic skills and competences'. Increasing competition forces commercial organizations not only to improve their service but also to present a more attractive image.

Emotional labour can give work meaning. It can make work satisfying, if the worker draws satisfaction from contact with customers. Emotional labour also requires the development of special skills and may be more meaningful for this reason too.

Emotional labour takes many different forms (see Box 17.3). If it becomes too demanding, it can intrude into areas of workers' lives that they consider private and 'off limits'. If heavily scripted and controlled by an employer—and call centres are notorious for this—customer service work can easily become routinized and emptied of meaning. Workers can feel their emotions and bodies are no longer their own.

One way of dealing with this situation and protecting themselves is for workers to put on a mask. The 'smiley face' may be no more than that. Customers and/or employers may then, however, detect a lack of sincerity. If customers report that they do not feel genuinely cared for and threaten to remove their custom, an employer's business may suffer. The employer may respond by seeking to recruit more malleable employees, or by retraining and remotivating workers to express more emotion.

Emotional labour, like any kind of labour, can become a battlefield, but the battle may take very different, indeed opposite, forms. Conflict may arise because an employer tries to restrict the emotional involvement of workers, in order to speed up the process of dealing with customers. Conflict may also occur because an employer tries to

Customer service work involves emotional and aesthetic labour.
© Photo courtesy of ATOC

Frontiers Types of emotional labour 17.3

Sharon Bolton and Carol Boyd argue that a more differentiated approach to emotional labour is now required. They criticize Hochschild's emphasis on the control of employees' emotions by employing organizations. They claim that emotional labour is much less under the control of management than physical labour is.

> Cabin crew do not have to 'love' the product, the passengers or the airline. They do not have to feel estranged from the emotional labour process. Unlike the factory worker they own the means of production and, therefore, the capacity to present a 'sincere' or 'cynical' performance lies within the emotional labourer. (Bolton and Boyd 2003: 293–4)

They present a typology of four kinds of emotion management:

- *Pecuniary* management displays a purely instrumental and generally superficial display of emotion to keep the customer happy for commercial reasons, according to company norms.
- *Prescriptive* management conforms to professional and organizational safety and service standards, which may

supersede company concerns with customer service, as when abusive or irate passengers have to be controlled.

- *Presentational* management refers to emotional exchanges with colleagues, as when cabin crew have a laugh with each other in 'unmanaged spaces' and engage in a workplace humour that reinforces comradeship and relieves boredom.
- *Philanthropic* management refers to 'the freedom to give that little bit extra', when a genuine concern for the well-being of passengers or colleagues leads cabin crew to go beyond what is required by pecuniary or prescriptive rules.

Emotional labour is not just at the service of the employer but also meets the social and personal needs of the worker. Cabin crew 'juggle' with different kinds of emotional labour and have to reconcile their conflicting requirements.

➲ Bolton and Boyd studied cabin crew. Can this typology be applied to other kinds of customer service work?

---

intensify the emotional involvement of workers, in order to increase customer satisfaction. These various tensions are discussed in Korczynski's analysis of 'customer-oriented bureaucracy in call centres' (see Box 14.7, on p. 539).

Sex work

Sex work is a kind of customer service work that raises in an acute form the emotional issues discussed above. This work involves an emotional and sexual activity normally restricted to the sphere of private life. Sex workers not only transgress deeply internalized boundaries but are also stigmatized for doing so. How do they cope with this situation?

Sophie Day (2007) studied the experiences and ideologies of London sex workers attending a clinic. They insisted that sex work was no different from any other; it was 'simply work'. This applied to any kind of sex work.

> I find the vehemence of the stance I have described, where one and all are 'simply working', even more striking when the job is recognized to enjoin all manner of variations in the sale of sex—as a form of labour, glamour, domesticity, intimacy and therapy.

Day 2007: 52

Work was sharply separated from private and home lives, where their emotions and relationships belonged. The separate existence of a private life was a means of countering popular and legal perceptions of them as

prostitutes selling themselves in public, and it enabled sex workers to maintain their self-esteem. Some women adopted a middle-class persona when carrying out escort work that required it, and saw this as mental rather than physical work but work, nonetheless, from which they still had to distance themselves.

Day points out that in making this separation sex workers were subscribing to the general belief in a capitalist society that the self is divided between the public sphere of work and the private sphere of home. In their case, sexual behaviour normally considered to be a purely private matter took place in both spheres but with different meanings. The same can, however, be argued for other services provided (mainly) by women, such as childminding or cleaning, which are both paid work in the public sphere and part of private life. Sex workers certainly had to work at maintaining the public/private distinction and 'many were preoccupied with shoring up the flimsy divisions between the two domains' (Day 2007: 42).

This applied to their bodies as well. They saw themselves as having a private and a public body. Clients were given access to the public parts of their body only and the private body, where contact involved intimacy and pleasure, was generally reserved for their private relationships. If they did become sexually aroused at work, this embarrassed them. Where they drew the dividing line varied, but the division was always there and they worked hard to maintain it: 'most women had techniques—including a range of physical barriers, performative skills and calculations—that made it possible to live and separate "two bodies"' (Day 2007: 43).

Elizabeth Bernstein's study (2007) of COYOTE sex workers in San Francisco presents a rather different picture. COYOTE is a national sex workers' rights organization that was founded in San Francisco. Bernstein argues that sex work *can* involve an emotional labour that makes it more meaningful to both client and worker, notably in the provision of 'bounded authenticity' by middle-class sex workers operating in private locations (see Chapter 5, p. 180, for her concept of bounded authenticity).

> In my own research, evidence of middle-class sex workers' efforts to manufacture authenticity resided in their descriptions of trying to simulate—or even produce—genuine desire, pleasure, and erotic interest for their clients. Whereas in some cases this involved mere 'surface acting' . . . it could also involve the physical and emotional labour of manufacturing authentic (if fleeting) libidinal and emotional ties with clients, endowing them with a sense of desirability, esteem, or even love.
>
> *Bernstein 2007: 103*

The way that many sex workers of this kind described their experiences showed that there was 'genuine feeling' on their part. This was also shown by their blogs, where they expressed themselves and discussed their experiences (*Belle de Jour*'s blog provides a UK example of this). Unlike the sex workers studied by Day, they did not distance themselves from their work, which was integrated with their private lives and general lifestyle. A central theme of Bernstein's study (2007: 69) is the 'privatization of public women'. The COYOTE sex workers openly challenged the 'symbolic dualisms' of 'private and public, home and work, "good girls" and " bad girls" . . . sexuality and market' (Bernstein 2007: 111). They did not divide their bodies into public and private parts but rather sought to integrate bodily pleasure with their work.

Bernstein does not argue that her account applies to all sex workers. She contrasts the provision of 'bounded authenticity' by middle-class sex workers with the 'quick, impersonal sexual release' provided by the 'street-level sex trade'. It is not clear, however, that the differences between Day's and Bernstein's accounts relate simply to class background. Day reports that around half of those in her study came from middle-class backgrounds, and she did not find a clear relationship between class and attitudes to sex. Indeed, the sex workers she studied seemed rather detached from their class background and acted out the kind of class character required by their clients. There were clearly other differences between the studies, since Day drew much of her material from a project linked to a London clinic, while the COYOTE members studied by Bernstein in San Francisco were a distinctively activist vanguard in sex work matters.

Job satisfaction

The classic studies of the experience of work had examined its variations between industries. Michael Rose (2003) has, however, argued that differences in satisfaction are more closely related to occupational differences between jobs than work differences between industries.

Rose analysed data from the British Household Panel Survey in 1999. He found that the material advantages of the

Figure 17.7 A job satisfaction league table

Occupation	Number of cases	Overall job satisfaction score*
Top ten (of 88)		
Miscellaneous childcare	64	75
Caretakers	24	71
Hairdressers, barbers	27	70
Educational assistants	49	69
Farm workers	22	68
Gardeners and ground staff	23	65
Managers in building and contracting	23	65
Care assistants and attendants	138	64
Secretaries, PAs, typists	118	64
Nursery nurses	42	64
Bottom ten (of 88)		
Laboratory technicians	36	36
Metal working production and maintenance fitters	103	36
Assemblers/line workers (electrical/electronic)	56	34
Primary and nursery education teachers	98	34
Assemblers/line workers (vehicles/metal)	21	33
Plastics process operatives, moulders and extruders	28	32
Postal workers, mail sorters	56	32
Sewing machinists, menders, darners, embroiderers	32	32
Waiters and waitresses	33	24
Bus and coach drivers	31	23
All employees		**50**

*The score is the percentage scoring above the median for the whole sample.
Source: Rose (2003).

❷ Can you identify any common features in the top ten occupations and in the bottom ten?

job, including not only pay but hours of work, security of employment, and promotion opportunities, appeared more important to respondents than the work itself. *Extrinsic* factors to do with the contract of employment outweighed *intrinsic* ones to do with the work. The level of work-related stress seemed, nonetheless, crucial in shaping job satisfaction in some occupations, particularly among nurses, primary school teachers, solicitors, journalists, youth workers, production control clerks, and marketing managers. Degree of workplace influence was also important.

The ranking of levels of satisfaction in eighty-eight occupations produced interesting results (see Figure 17.7). Some professional and technical occupations, such as primary school teachers, management consultants, and laboratory technicians had low scores. Some manual workers, such as caretakers, farm workers, and gardeners, had high scores, though others, especially assembly-line workers, had low ones. Occupations involving personal and caring services scored highly, with hairdressers and barbers, care assistants and attendants, nursery nurses, secretaries and PAs, cleaners and domestics all towards the top end. Educational assistants came fourth from the top, but primary school teachers came close to the bottom! Waiters and bus drivers were right at the bottom, with very low scores.

This analysis of job satisfaction both consolidates and extends earlier findings. The importance given to extrinsic, contract of employment issues fits the instrumental orientation identified by the *Affluent Worker* study. The growth of consumerism and individualism, together with the rewards and pressures of neo-liberal capitalism (see Chapter 15, p. 577), have no doubt strengthened this orientation to work. Blauner's classic study of alienation is also supported, however, by the low position of assembly-line and other routine manual work, and the importance of influence in the workplace. But it is not just the alienating conditions of work that lead to low job satisfaction, for work-related stress, long hours, and insecurity at work also come out as key factors. It is also striking that so many personal service occupations, involving close contact with customers and employers, showed high levels of satisfaction, even though the extrinsic rewards of these jobs are often low.

Outside the workplace

We now turn away from the workplace to consider other consequences of the growth of industrial capitalism, its impact on work at home, and the creation of unemployment.

Continued work at home

Although production had largely moved from a domestic setting to outside workplaces, many different kinds of work still went on in the home.

Work in the home was in fact closely related to work in the workplace, which arguably could not go on without it. Thus, paid work depended on the unpaid work of women in the home to 'reproduce labour' (see Chapter 12, pp. 434–5). Labour was reproduced not only by producing and bringing up the next generation of workers but also by attending to the domestic needs of paid workers, whose time and energy could then be devoted to their paid work. When women themselves were employed in the factories, and many were employed in the textiles industry, this paid work was considered secondary to their main role as housewives, and they were expected to do the housework as well.

Women also carried out unpaid production at home. The household's clothing was not just provided through the purchase of factory-made clothes. Some were still made at home. Indeed, home production was greatly facilitated by one of the new industrial products, the sewing machine, which also made it easier to carry out paid work at home.

Employers could economize on workplace costs and wages by giving work that did not require factory machinery to women at home, who were in a weak bargaining position, because of their isolation and domestic responsibilities. A lot of homework was carried out in textiles, where spinning, weaving, and dyeing were factory processes but 'finishing-off' was done by homeworkers.

Most women who took paid work were not, however, employed in the textiles industry but in domestic labour in middle-class households. Women's employment in domestic service was certainly not new, but the character of this employment had changed significantly. Servants were now increasingly treated as wage labour, rather than members of the family. The development of industrial capitalism led not only to wage labour in factories but also to wage labour in the home.

This diminished in the twentieth century with the growth of clerical work and mass production. Servants became too expensive, as the growing employment of women in offices and factories pushed up women's wages. The gap they left was filled in three different ways:

- mass-produced labour-saving machinery reduced the time taken to do some household tasks;
- domestic production declined and finished products, particularly food products such as bread, were increasingly bought;
- middle-class wives did more housework.

In the 1970s, Oakley carried out a ground-breaking study of housework. She examined it in the same way as industrial sociologists like Blauner had studied factory work and found that it was similarly characterized by monotony, task fragmentation, time pressure, and social

Figure 17.8 Housework and industrial work

Workers	Percentage experiencing		
	Monotony	Fragmentation	Speed
Housewives	75	90	50
Factory workers	41	70	31
Assembly-line workers	67	86	36

Source: Oakley (1974: 87).

isolation. When she compared her findings with work-satisfaction data from the *Affluent Worker* study, she found that housework was more alienating than assembly-line work, the most alienating form of industrial work (Oakley 1974) (see Figure 17.8).

Oakley found no relationship in housework between technology and work satisfaction, but, as she pointed out, the relationship between machine and worker is different in housework. In industrial work the machine controls the speed of work, but the housewife controls the pace and rhythm of housework. The pressures of housework are different, for they come from the standards and routines that govern its performance. Dusting can, for example, be done daily or much less often. While mechanization could in principle save time, it could also lead to the more frequent repetition of tasks.

Oakley argued that in the absence of a wage the housewife had to find other rewards of a psychological kind. It was in meeting standards that housewives obtained what satisfaction they could from housework. Standards became powerful constraints that acted as external forces. They originated largely from socialization, which transmitted norms from one generation to the next.

Oakley had demonstrated that housework, like industrial work, could be analysed in terms of the satisfaction or dissatisfaction that it gave, but also that it was different in character. As with industrial work, the routines of housework were imposed, but not in the same way. Because they were psychological, the pressures generated by standards were actually greater than the external pressures of paid work. Paid workers could also leave the workplace and, at least temporarily, escape from its pressures. The housewife could not do this so easily.

The creation of unemployment

The distinction between employment and unemployment goes back to the emergence of capitalist production. If their paid work ceased, workers were now unemployed. A new category of people, the unemployed, had come into existence.

People could find themselves out of work in pre-industrial societies, but their pattern of work was irregular and included many different economic activities (see Box 17.4). With industrialization a sharper contrast between being in work and out of work emerged. Industrialists required their employees to work continuously for long hours, and work in manufacturing could no longer be combined with other kinds of work. When, however, production became unprofitable, factories closed. Unemployment then had a devastating effect on workers and their families, who had become entirely dependent on paid work for their livelihood.

Industrial capitalism by its very nature has provided insecure employment. The economic cycle has generated periods of intense work during booms, followed by recessions when demand collapses, production diminishes, and people are thrown out of work. Intense competition too can lead to the sudden closure of companies driven out of business. The high rate of technical change can result in the replacement of workers by machines and whole occupations can become obsolete.

Unemployment has had serious consequences for the individual and the society. For most of the population of working age, employment in paid work is the main source of income, but the impact of unemployment is not just financial. It reduces the variety of life, removes the satisfactions of work, makes the day structureless, diminishes social contacts, and damages identity and self-esteem (Warr 1983).

The experience of unemployment has been viewed as going through a number of stages. Four have been commonly identified:

* *shock*: on learning the news;
* *optimism*: an initially optimistic search for work;

Briefing: work in pre-industrial times   17.4

'A labouring family around 1700 normally got its support, not from just one or two sources, but from a variety of activities. . . . Even in places where few commons existed, many people had small cottage gardens where they could grow potatoes, cabbages, peas and beans; cottagers very commonly kept a pig or two, which could be fattened on almost anything; some had chickens or geese, a few kept bees . . . Some of this produce they sold in the market, much of it they consumed directly. For most of them farm labour was an important source of income; and increasingly country people were taking up ancillary employments—spinning, weaving, knitting, glove-making, metalworking, and the like—to supplement the livelihood they gained from agricultural wages, a smallholding, or common rights.' (Malcolmson 1988: 58)

- *distress and pessimism*: a growing concern about the future and a lowering of expectations when the search fails;
- *resignation and adjustment*: acceptance of the situation.

Unemployment is not, however, experienced in the same way by all. Ashton (1986) argued that its meaning varies. Those in middle-class occupations are more likely to be financially cushioned through savings but may suffer a more serious psychological loss, because their work allows self-expression and is important to their identity. Skilled workers may well experience unemployment in a similar way and have some cushioning through redundancy payments. Unskilled or semi-skilled workers are in a different situation. They are less likely to receive redundancy payments and are more affected by loss of income but suffer less from a loss of identity, as they express themselves less through their work.

The effects of unemployment also depend upon its duration. The longer people have been unemployed, the more difficult it becomes to re-enter employment, partly because motivation diminishes, partly because technologies and occupations change, so that previous experience becomes out of date. Long-term unemployment leads to poverty and dependence on the state. A vicious circle can develop that makes unemployment self-perpetuating.

THEORY AND METHODS   **17.5**
....

The reserve army of labour

The concept of the **reserve army of labour** was important to Marx's theory of capitalism. He argued that labour was increasingly replaced by machinery as capitalism developed. This process created a reserve army of the unemployed, which made workers available for the further expansion of production. The reserve army also kept wage levels down, forcing workers to accept a more intense exploitation of their labour, by increasing the competition for jobs.

Veronica Beechey (1987) argued that married women are part of the reserve. They can be drawn into production when there is a labour shortage and returned to the household when no longer required. This happened in Britain during the First and Second World Wars but also in the 1960s. The growth of part-time work later enabled women to combine employment with their domestic role.

Beechey emphasized that it is the 'sexual division of labour' and traditional assumptions about the role of women that make them part of the reserve army. Women's wage rates are lower than those of men, because their domestic role is primary. The availability of female labour therefore depresses wage levels.

Unemployment has wider consequences for society as a whole. There is plentiful evidence that it leads to higher levels of physical and mental illness, divorce, crime, and violence (Ashton 1986; Gallie and Marsh 1994). State benefits paid to the unemployed may seem inadequate to those receiving them but are a major item of state expenditure, while unemployment also reduces the state's tax revenue. Unemployment reduces spending power and the demand for goods and services, thereby throwing other people out of work and threatening to cause a cumulative decline of economic activity.

It must also be recognized that unemployment has some positive consequences for employers and for the state. A certain level of unemployment is arguably beneficial, because it damps down inflation, forces people to work harder to keep their jobs, and increases international competitiveness. Unemployment also provides a *reserve army* of people available for work (see Box 17.5), which helps to keep down wage levels, undermine collective bargaining, and reduce union militancy. Governments giving a higher priority to these matters may decide, as in early 1980s Britain, to allow unemployment to rise.

Leisure

Leisure as a category of daily activities came into existence with industrialization. In this section we examine its growth and, more specifically, the development of modern sport.

The creation of leisure

Recreational activities, such as sport or play, or painting or conversation, which are regarded nowadays as leisure pursuits, have existed since the earliest known human societies.

The *idea* of leisure as something distinct and separate from work resulted, however, from the impact of industrial capitalism on daily life. 'Leisure' is not a descriptive term for these activities but a way of thinking about them.

In pre-industrial times, the days of the landed gentry were largely occupied with such activities as field sports, gambling, social events, reading, eating, and drinking, which were not seen as leisure pursuits but as normal pastimes. Work was considered inappropriate to their class and socially demeaning. Their wealth enabled them to employ others to manage their estates and run their households. Their lifestyle demonstrated their wealth and signified their high social status to others.

Ordinary people necessarily spent most of their time in productive activities, as they tried to make a living. There were seasonal festivals, such as Christmas and Easter, and saints' days with fairs and sporting events, but there was no clear distinction between work and leisure time in daily life, for work hours were irregular and often seasonal. At harvest-time, for example, work would be day-long, while during slack periods of the year there might be no work available. The pre-industrial craftsman determined his own pace of work and could combine it with other non-work activities. Craftwork, anyway, had a creative quality and work was not a meaningless activity that had to be balanced by 'recreation' outside work hours.

With industrialization came a very different attitude towards work. Capitalist entrepreneurs put most of their time and energy into *generating* rather than *spending* wealth, while their employees were required to work regularly and continuously in a disciplined manner.

This focus on work might seem opposed to the whole notion of leisure, but it had the effect of creating leisure

as a distinct part of people's lives. As the regulated, supervised, and continuous work typical of the factory did not permit the mixing of work with non-work activities, work and leisure became separated. Employers concluded it was better to channel leisure into clearly organized holiday periods when their factories shut down than have production interrupted and disorganized by workers taking time off when they chose. Then, as workers became organized, their unions pressed for shorter working days and a fixed number of working hours per week.

The state too played an important part in the development of leisure by creating a legal framework for it. Health and welfare concerns, the pressure from religious movements to protect Sundays, and demands from the labour movement for shorter hours, all put pressure on governments to pass laws restricting work time. The

Southsea beach, 1895: why did seaside holidays become so popular in the nineteenth century?
© Getty Images/F J Mortimer

Factory Acts of the 1840s and 1850s restricted the hours of work of women and children. Sunday Observance Laws were enforced and extended to prohibit most commercial activity on Sundays. In 1871 four bank holidays were created. Later, in 1938, the Holidays with Pay Act was passed and paid holidays gradually became a normal feature of work-life.

The creation of 'free' leisure time for workers did not mean that they could be left to enjoy their leisure as they pleased. As early nineteenth-century factory-owners tried to control the work behaviour of their employees, a campaign began to regulate and 'improve' their non-work lives as well. This was not just due to the employer's need for disciplined labour, important though this was, for there was also the problem of maintaining order in the cities. The urban poor, who worked and lived in appalling conditions, engaged in disorderly, sometimes violent, political and recreational activities.

Leisure activities became increasingly regulated and organized. Traditional popular pastimes, such as drinking, bull-baiting, cock-fighting, and dog-fighting, could be tolerated and contained within the relatively stable framework of rural communities but endangered social order in the cities. By 1835 a law had been passed to prohibit sports involving cruelty to animals. From 1830 to 1914 a series of laws increasingly restricted the opening hours of public houses.

New leisure activities were developed, particularly by the growing middle class and the 'respectable' working class, who established their social status through pursuits different from both the landed gentry's traditional pastimes and the entertainments of the poor. They sought 'improving' recreations compatible with their religious values, and the growth of a civic, municipal culture in the new cities led to the emergence of publicly funded colleges, libraries, museums, and art galleries to improve the mind.

In a capitalist society the growth of leisure provided new opportunities for profit-making and led to the rise of leisure industries, such as tourism. The spread of railways enabled cheap and fast travel to seaside resorts. Organized tourism dates from 1841, when Thomas Cook of Leicester arranged a railway trip to a temperance meeting at Loughborough for some 400 people. Cook went on to organize international holidays, pioneer the conducted tour and the guidebook, arrange travel and hotel bookings, and ultimately create the package holiday. As Lash and Urry (1994: 262) have put it: 'Cook's . . . transformed travel from something that was individually arranged and full of risks and uncertainty into one of the most organized and rationalized of human activities based on considerable professional expertise.'

During the twentieth century new industries emerged to provide the *mass-consumer* products, such as cars, televisions, and washing machines, used during non-work time by most people. *Mass production* required a steady demand for products, and this stimulated the rise of yet another industry, advertising. Leisure time, leisure activities, and the marketing needs of both consumer goods and leisure industries in turn provided the conditions in which the modern *mass media* could emerge (see Chapter 10, pp. 361–2).

The significance of leisure had changed since the early years of industry. The first industrialists tried to make their employees work long hours, to keep costs low and to maximize profits. By the twentieth century the economy increasingly revolved around the consumption of goods and services during leisure time. Production had now become dependent in a quite new way on the earnings, non-work activities, and spending patterns of the population as a whole. Mass consumption also made it possible for governments to manage the economy in Keynesian fashion by controlling purchasing power through taxation or control of credit. Leisure, consumption, production, and economic management had become intertwined by the 1950s.

The organization of sport

As an organized industrial society with distinct leisure activities was established during the nineteenth century, sport began to develop its modern organization. Eric Dunning and Kenneth Sheard (2005: 30) argue that 'modern sports' emerged from 'folk-games' at this time.

Age-old folk-games had a local and traditional character, with local contests. There were no written rules, no specification of terrain or duration or number of participants. Player roles were not specialized, and there was no clear distinction between participants and spectators. One folk-game was not clearly differentiated from another. The players themselves controlled the game as it went on. High levels of physical violence were tolerated,

Figure 17.9 From folk-games to modern sports

Folk-games	Modern sports
Unwritten local rules	Written (inter)national rules
No specified terrain	A fixed 'pitch'
Unspecified duration	Fixed duration
Unspecialized roles	Specialized roles
Spectators can participate	Separated spectators
Undifferentiated games	Differentiated sports
Players control	Officials control
Violence accepted	Intolerance of violence
Physical prowess valued	Skill valued

and there was indeed an emphasis on physical prowess rather than skill.

Modern sports were formally organized with written rules standardized nationally, eventually internationally, to regulate competitions. Games took place on a fixed 'pitch' over a fixed period of time, with specified numbers of players. These performed specialized roles and were clearly separated from spectators. Sports became differentiated from each other. Games were controlled by officials appointed by national bodies. Gratuitous violence was not tolerated, and self-restraint was expected. Skill, rather than physical force, was emphasized.

Dunning and Sheard (2005) examined the transition from folk-games to modern sports in football. Between about 1750 and 1840, the folk version of football was taken up and adapted by boys' public schools. Rules were elaborated and eventually written down, while players were required to exercise more self-restraint. From about 1850 to 1900, this regulated form of football spread out from the public schools into society at large.

Although the process of increasing regulation first occurred in the public schools, and universities, it should also be seen in the context of maintaining order in the nineteenth century industrial city (see p. 667). Local sporting activities were increasingly organized within the framework of the club, with its members, officials, rules, and committees. This applied not only to football but to popular sports such as cricket, bowling, cycling, and swimming, and to tennis, golf, and croquet, which became socially exclusive middle-class sports.

As rules became more specific, different codes of conduct emerged within the public schools, which led to the differentiation of football's association and rugby branches. A central issue here was the degree of physical violence permitted, particularly in the acceptability of the rugby practice of 'hacking'. According to Dunning and Sheard (2005: 88), rugby 'adhered to a traditional concept of "manliness" which stressed courage and physical strength'. Association football 'advocated "manliness" of a more restrained and "civilized" kind'. The establishment of national associations—the Football Association (1863) and the Rugby Football Union (1871)—hardened this division to create separate sports.

Just as leisure in general became commercialized, so did sport (see Box 17.6). The emergence of the weekend stimulated this commercialization, particularly through the Saturday afternoon football match. Spectators began to pay, and players began to be paid. For some, sport had become work. Football became a capitalist enterprise towards the end of the nineteenth century, with local businessmen investing in clubs, and clubs becoming limited companies. The popularity of football and horse-racing provided the basis for a gambling industry. By the 1930s sixteen times as many people gambled through the football pools on the results of matches as actually went to watch them (Royle 1987: 269).

Commercialization was resisted by football's rugby branch, at the cost of losing the Northern Union clubs, who created the Rugby League in 1894. The bone of contention here was a movement towards the payment of players. The working-class players in the northern cities needed compensation for lost wages if they were to have time for the training and travel that competition made necessary. The Rugby Football Union (RFU) authorities refused to accept this step towards professionalism. The refusal stemmed from their social background, from the strongly held belief in the virtues of amateurism in the public schools and amongst the middle classes. As Holt (1989: 350) has put it, 'amateurism was both a code of ethics and a system of status'. Amateurism was also closely linked to imperialism, for 'the amateur ideal prospered in its purest form in the Empire' (Holt 1989: 351).

Strong as the rearguard action against commercialization and professionalism was, they could not in the end be resisted. The rugby establishment fought longest but eventually capitulated in the 1990s. The increasing intensity of national and international competition pressed clubs into finding more ways of making payments to players, and a transfer market grew. Management and administration became more professional. The sport became increasingly global and less regulated by the RFU. Rugby union became an 'open game', and players even began to transfer between its union and league variants (Dunning and Sheard 2005: 257–9).

Briefing: the commericalization of football   17.6

Key steps in commercialization took place in the nineteenth century:

- **Charging for entry to matches**
- **Wages for players**
- **Transfer fees**
- **Investment of capital by local businessmen**
- **Formation of a union by players**
- **Emergence of professional management**
- **Clubs becoming limited companies**
- **Formation of Football League (1888)**

Can you add steps that have happened since?

Stop and reflect

In exploring the impact of industrial capitalism, we first examined industrial relations and industrial conflict.

- Why did workers become collectively organized?
- How did employers counter worker organization?
- Consider the various forms taken by industrial conflict. List the ways in which conflict has been expressed in any work organization you have been in.

We went on to the experience of work and the ways in which this has varied.

- Make sure you understand the following terms: alienation, self-estrangement; deskilling; orientation to work; emotional and aesthetic labour.
- Blauner argued that degree of alienation was linked to the type of technology.
- The *Affluent Worker* study showed that attitudes to work reflected broader orientations to work.
- Customer service work involves emotional labour, which can provide work satisfaction, though tight supervision may empty it of meaning.

- How distinctive is sex work from other forms of labour?
- According to Rose, work satisfaction is more closely related to the job than the industry.
- What kind of paid work have you found most satisfying? Does your experience of work exemplify any of the above studies?

We then examined the changing relationship between 'work' and non-work, going on to leisure and sport.

- Industrialization concentrated production outside the household.
- Did it remove work from the home?
- In what sense did it create unemployment?
- Why did leisure emerge in the nineteenth century?
- Leisure itself became a source of work, as it became commercialized and industrialized.
- Sport became organized and regulated as a separate activity, and then commercialized.

The transformation of work, employment, and leisure

During the period of economic expansion from the Second World War to the 1970s, industrial capitalism continued to develop along the lines established before the war. Mass production and mass consumption flourished, while the high demand for labour resulted in full employment. The British labour movement continued to grow, and the unions saw off various attempts to reform them.

All this was changing by the 1980s. International competition had intensified with the rise of new industrial societies. The old industries of Europe and America struggled and contracted. Unemployment rose sharply, and new forms of insecure, part-time, and temporary employment emerged. The labour movement declined and unions came under increasing state regulation.

As jobs in manufacturing disappeared, service occupations grew. Men lost jobs, while the employment of women increased. Innovations in information and communications technology impacted on both production and consumption. Economic, political, and technological changes combined to transform work, employment, and leisure.

Post-industrialism, post-Fordism, and flexibility

How should the transformation of work and employment be described? We begin by discussing whether societies are now post-industrial. We go on to the notion of post-Fordism, and examine the 'flexible firm' and the 'flexible office'.

Post-industrialism

Daniel Bell (1973) popularized the notion of a **post-industrial society**. His starting point was the shift of economic activity from the production of *goods* to the provision of *services*. Manual work was in decline, and machine operators were being replaced by robots, while non-manual service occupations were expanding.

Financial occupations, teachers, advertisers, market researchers, scientists, and social workers all worked with different kinds of information. According to Bell, economies were now driven not by the search for more efficient ways of producing goods but by the generation of knowledge and the processing of information. Post-industrial society was an **information society**.

Employment has certainly been shifting from manufacturing into services, as Figure 17.10 shows. Some traditional industries, such as shipbuilding, have been almost wiped out. Since the miners' strike of 1984–5 the number of coal miners has fallen from 170,000 in 170 mines to a mere 4,000 in eight mines in 2005 (*Guardian*, 4 March 2005). Employment in services has soared, especially in financial and business services, but also in other areas: distribution; travel and tourism; communications and the media; leisure activities; personal services such as hairdressing, catering, and cleaning; education and health; care and welfare.

The term 'deindustrialization' has been much used, particularly when shipyards, or mines, or steel mills, or factories close, and many have closed since the 1970s. New industries, in electronics or biotechnology, have emerged, often in new science parks near universities, but there is no disputing the declining weight of manufacturing in the UK economy.

Does this mean that we are at least moving towards a post-industrial society? Although there is now less production of goods in the old industrial societies, it must be kept in mind that manufactured goods are still distributed and consumed within them. The production of goods has not ceased but has moved elsewhere, as other societies, notably China and India, industrialize. If we look at this from a global perspective, we do not live in a post-industrial world.

It should not anyway be assumed that service work is non-industrial. Industry should not be confused with manufacturing. As we showed on p. 649, the term 'industry' refers to the way in which production is organized, but industrial principles of organization can apply to the production of *services* as well as of *goods*. The characteristic features of industrialism are found in service organizations too. Catering, for example, provides a service, but, according to Gabriel (1988), has become industrialized (see Box 17.2 on p. 658). It can similarly be claimed that health care has undergone industrialization (see Box 17.7).

The growth of call centres provides another interesting case. This is undoubtedly service work, but it shows many of the features of industrial organization. Machinery, in the form of the phone or the monitor screen, determines the pace of work. A function that used to be dispersed through many local offices is concentrated in large workplaces. Call-answering has become a specialized work activity. The workplace is closely supervised by managers. Indeed, work conditions have been reportedly so poor that call centres have been described as the modern equivalent of the 'dark satanic mills' of the nineteenth-century textile industry (*Management Issues*, 8 January 2004).

The idea of post-industrial society draws attention to important and undeniable changes in economy and occupational structure. The term 'post-industrial' is, however, misleading, for industrial organization remains the dominant form of work organization, while industrialization is an ongoing process. The world is becoming more industrial not less.

Figure 17.10 Employee jobs by sex and industry, United Kingdom, 1978–2008

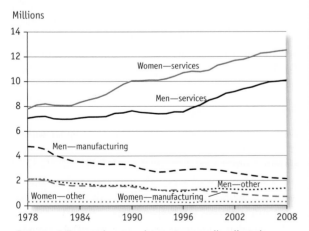

Millions

Data are at June each year and are not seasonally adjusted.

Source: Social Trends (2009: 53).

 Briefing: the industrialization of health care   17.7

The defining features of industrialism (see p. 649) can be found within health care.

- *Mechanization*: the use of ever more sophisticated machinery to investigate and treat illness and injury.

- *Concentration*: the emergence of large regional hospitals and the closure of small local ones.

- *Specialization*: the specialization of hospitals, as centres for the treatment of particular conditions, such as spinal injury; the specialization of medical, surgical, and nursing occupations, with, for example, physicians, surgeons, and nurses specializing in cancer care.

- *Management*: the creation of a distinct stratum of professional managers who distribute resources and develop policy.

Post-Fordism

Post-Fordism is a similar but more specific term used to describe changes in production and consumption. But, first of all, what was Fordism?

Fordism refers to the system of mass production created by Henry Ford in the car factories he set up in the United States during the early twentieth century. This became the model for the low-cost production of standardized goods for a mass market. Mass production and mass consumption were interdependent and linked by the advertising provided by the mass media.

> ⊃ *Connections*
>
> Changes in production and consumption were closely linked with changes in the media, which are discussed in Chapter 10, p. 374.

Fordist production exemplified the deskilling of work that Braverman considered characteristic of capitalist production, while, in Blauner's terms, its assembly-line

Is mass production a thing of the past?
© Alice Chadwick

technology maximized alienation. Work was fragmented into small tasks which could be carried out repeatedly by low-skilled labour with very little training. There was a clear division between a mass of semi-skilled workers and a small number of skilled workers carrying out key tasks. Production was controlled by a centralized management, sharply separated from labour. Trade unionism was strong and there was much open industrial conflict.

The very success of Fordism meant, however, that markets quickly became saturated. One refrigerator was enough for most households! Market saturation, together with increasing competition, resulted in a growing emphasis on quality, product diversity, and innovation. Long production runs were replaced by frequent changes of product and small batch production, to meet particular market opportunities and respond to changes of style. The Ford company had been famous for its standard model T Ford, obtainable in any colour, 'so long as it was black'! Car plants now provide a wide range of models, each with many variations in style and engine power, and any number of optional extras.

The decline of mass production was interwoven with the decline of mass consumption. With the decline of class and community as sources of identity and the growth of individualism, personal identity was increasingly attached to consumer goods. Identity was no longer a matter of the work people did or the place they came from but of what they wore, what they drove, where they took their holidays. Function became a less important product feature and the image projected more important. The shift from an emphasis on use or function to image can be seen particularly in advertising, which has both reflected and promoted this change.

The growing significance of image resulted in the **stylization** and **aestheticization** of consumption. Images were given meaning by styles. The concept of 'lifestyle' emerged as an organizing principle. The purchase of a group of products and experiences sharing a style enabled a consumer to establish an identity. The creation of styles by, for example, magazines has become crucial to marketing and a business in its own right. The importance of image led to the aestheticization of products, as culture became more influential in design, packaging, and advertising. Once a product's meaning rather than its function became crucial, culture came into its own, for meanings are essentially a cultural matter (Lury 1996).

The diversification of products, frequent changes of style, and a more aesthetic approach to design made the techniques of mass production less appropriate. Production was reorganized to meet the requirements of quality, diversity, innovation, and change. This involved the interrelated changes in work organization, personnel policies, and industrial relations described as **post-Fordism** (see Figure 17.12, p. 673).

The key features of the post-Fordist organization were a focus on skill, flexibility, and commitment. Workers

Why have image and style become so important?

© Lucy Dawkins

were expected to be adaptable and multi-skilled, which made trade unions organized on occupational lines less appropriate. Flexible production and quality products implied a highly motivated and highly trained labour force, a more decentralized management, and a more cooperative, less conflictual style of industrial relations. The techniques of human resource management (see Chapter 14, pp. 540–1) were designed to mobilize higher commitment and employee integration.

The concept of post-Fordism has generated considerable debate. Its advocates challenged the notion that capitalism continually deskilled and degraded labour and claimed that work would become multi-skilled and more varied. Paul Thompson (1993) argued, however, that requiring workers to do a wider range of tasks does not upgrade their work or increase its skill content. It would be more accurate to describe this as multi-tasking than multi-skilling. Wood (1989) has similarly claimed that many post-Fordist changes are merely minor modifications to basically Fordist methods. He prefers the term neo-Fordism—that is, a new form of Fordism—to post-Fordism.

Figure 17.11 From Fordism to post-Fordism at Ford

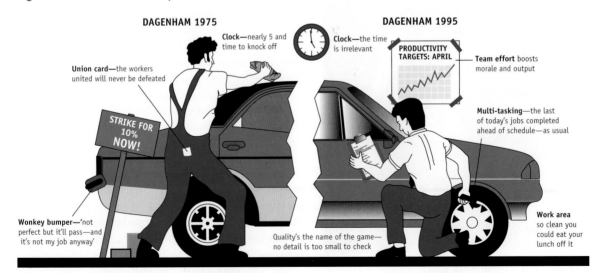

Source: Independent, 20 April 1995.

Figure 17.12 Fordism and post-Fordism

Aspects of production	Fordism	Post-Fordism
Product	Standard	Diverse
Priority	Cheapness	Quality
Market	Mass	Segmented/niche
Work tasks	Fragmented and repetitive	Multiple and varied
Skills	Mainly semi-skilled work	Multi-skilled worker
Labour force	Occupationally divided	Integrated and flexible
Management	Centralized	Decentralized
Industrial relations	Conflictual	Cooperative
Trade unionism	Multiple and independent	Single and integrated

taking place in catering, as described by Gabriel (1988), fit a Fordist rather than a post-Fordist model (see Box 17.2 on p. 658).

It is also important to emphasize that post-Fordist production remains capitalist in character. Employers still seek to maximize their profits and minimize their labour costs. Managers still control the production process. If anything, more is demanded from labour than before, for workers are required to produce higher-quality work, carry out a greater range of tasks, adapt to frequent changes of product, and work as long as it takes to complete the job.

The flexible firm

The flexible use of labour was central to the post-Fordist organization of production. John Atkinson (1984) constructed an influential and widely discussed model of the **flexible firm** (see Figure 17.13).

It must also be said that post-Fordist changes in some businesses do not mean the end of Fordism everywhere. There is still a market for many cheap, simple, functional goods that can best be produced by mass-production techniques. Fordism is arguably on the increase. The changes

Connections

The flexible use of labour is closely linked to new organizational forms, which we discuss in Chapter 14, pp. 533–6.

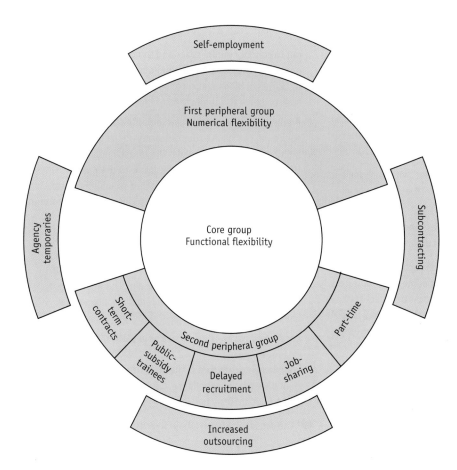

Figure 17.13 The flexible firm

Source: J. Atkinson (1984: 29).

Atkinson identified three different kinds of flexibility:

- *functional* flexibility, requiring workers to carry out any task;
- *numerical* flexibility, varying the size of the labour force;
- *financial* flexibility, such as performance-related pay.

This model drew attention particularly to numerical flexibility. The uncertainties generated by greater competition and faster change led employers to seek ways of adjusting the size of the labour force to their actual need for staff. One way of doing this is to employ more part-time workers, as when stores employ extra checkout staff during peak shopping times. Another way is to offer short-term contracts, perhaps for a particular production run or, in universities, the duration of a project. An extreme example is the zero-hours contract, which requires employees to be available but pays them only when the employer calls them in.

The flexible firm created a new division within labour, between *core* and *periphery* (see Figure 17.13, p. 673). The *core* consisted of permanent, full-time employees with security of employment, promotion prospects, and company benefits. In exchange, they were expected to be loyal and flexible workers. Employees in the *periphery* had a looser, less secure relationship to the organization. Atkinson divides it into two groups. The first consists of full-time workers with jobs rather than careers, the second of temporary or part-time workers. Further flexibility is provided by an outer ring of agency workers brought in under contract.

This division between core and periphery has impacted on the stratification of society and the organization of workers by dividing the working class (Coates 1989). In their study of low-paid employment in London, Yara Evans *et al.* (2005) found that the largely migrant cleaners, carers, and chambermaids working in transport, local authorities, major corporations, and top hotels were employed mainly through subcontractors and received lower pay and worse conditions than 'in-house' employees. Ulrich Beck (2000*b*) saw greater flexibility and insecurity of employment as combining with globalization to divide societies into four different groups (see the Box 17.8).

Critics have argued that there is nothing really new about the flexible firm. The practices of employing part-timers or

---

Global focus Globalization and Brazilianization   17.8

In *The Brave New World of Work* (2000*b*), Ulrich Beck lays out what he sees as the likely consequences of globalization for work, employment, and leisure. He describes this as Brazilianization rather than Americanization, for the future of Western societies can be seen in Brazil rather than the United States. Brazilianization produces 'a political economy of insecurity', with two key features:

- the growth of informal and temporary jobs, with 'inferior' productivity, working conditions, contractual terms, social security, and legal protection;
- deregulated labour relations that bypass and weaken collective bargaining and the power of unions.

He argues that Europe has been stable since the Second World War partly because of opportunities for people to be upwardly mobile and partly because of their willingness to accept factory work and discipline in exchange for 'greater income, social security and leisure time', which he calls a 'Fordist consensus' (Beck 2000*b*: 104–6). This stability is being undermined by a Brazilianization, which will fragment society into four groups:

'1 *The 'Columbus' class of the global age*. These are the winners from globalization, the owners of globally active capital and their top managerial executors. The income of this minority has been rising exponentially. . . . Like Columbus, they set out to conquer global space and subject it to their economic goals. . . . They have the technological and material resources of globalization at their command—but they pay a high price for this in the form of time poverty. . . .

2 *Precarious employees at the top of the skills ladder*. These earn a lot, but have to be constantly on the ball to avoid being pushed aside by rivals. They are temporary workers, the spurious self-employed, people with their own business, and so on, in high-paid positions that assume similarly high educational qualifications. . . . Leisure time is a foreign word. . . .

3 *The working poor*. The jobs of 'low-skilled' and 'unskilled' workers are directly threatened by globalization, for they can be replaced either by automation or by the supply of labour from other countries. In the end, this group can keep its head above water only by entering into several employment situations at once. . . .

4 *Localized poverty*. The localized poor of the global age are no longer needed. . . . Their position may be thought of as complementary to that of the globalized rich. The localized poor have time in abundance, but they are chained to space. (Beck 2000*b*: 106–7);'

❓ Can you identify such groups in British society today?

contracting out work are long established. Capitalist employers have always tried to cut employment costs at the expense of workers' security. They are simply finding new, or rediscovering old, ways of doing this (Pollert 1991).

The term 'flexibility' anyway gives too positive an image of change. Greater numerical flexibility can also be described as *casualization*. The labour movement has long struggled to improve the security of employment by getting rid of casual work, only to find it re-emerging under the banner of flexibility. Pollert (1988) has, indeed, claimed that the flexible firm is essentially a political notion put about by government and employers to spread and justify changes that reduced the employment security of workers.

Greater flexibility can also have negative as well as positive consequences for the employer, costing more than it saves. Temporary employees may be poorly motivated and unreliable. Subcontracted work may not be carried out to the correct standards. Product quality may suffer and safety may be compromised. Indeed, the fatal rail crash at Potters Bar in 2002 has been attributed to poor maintenance of the track by subcontractors using inexperienced casual labour.

Like post-Fordism, the concept of the flexible firm usefully highlights changes in employer practices. These concepts are simplified models of reality that help us to grasp processes of change by drawing contrasts and suggesting interrelationships between processes. The critics of these concepts do, however, rightly point out the dangers of exaggerating change and emphasizing its positive rather than negative consequences.

The flexible office

Another instance of greater flexibility is the more flexible use of space in what Felstead, Jewson, and Walters (2005) have called the *collective*, as opposed to the *personal*, office. In the collective office there are no longer fixed and personal places of work. People 'hot-desk' and 'touch down', moving around through relatively open spaces to use the available work stations. Felstead *et al.* emphasize that this new working environment should not be confused with the open-plan office, which retains individual and personal workplaces.

This spatial flexibility enables a company to cut considerably its office costs, for it no longer has to pay for the construction and upkeep of offices unoccupied by employees working elsewhere, travelling, or away ill. There is, however, much more to the flexibility of the collective office than this.

In the *personal office*, the bureaucratic principles of hierarchy and specialization resulted in highly specified positions in the organization. As Felstead *et al.* (2005: 65) put it, 'workstations and workplaces were demarcated as rigidly as occupational roles'. The spatial flexibility of the *collective office* matches the organizational flexibility of the post-bureaucratic company, where the emphasis is on teamwork, flexible job descriptions, and, indeed, the collective achievement of the company's goals rather than the individual performance of specified tasks.

> **⊃ Connections**
>
> The collective office reflects the new styles of management associated with post-bureaucratic organization and you may find it helpful to look up our discussion of this in Chapter 14, pp. 540–1.

The collective office has a very different culture of interaction. Informality, chance encounters, and social gatherings are characteristic features of the work experience. Information is collected not through communication channels but through the 'osmosis' of 'unobtrusive overhearing, eavesdropping and observing co-workers' as people move about and temporarily occupy work stations near each other (Felstead *et al.* 2005: 86). The separation of work and non-work breaks down as people interact informally at work and take work home.

This does not mean, however, that work is not controlled by the employer. Although not regulated by detailed rules, it is controlled by performance measures and appraisal. As with homework (see Study 17 at the end of this chapter), the burden of day-to-day management is placed on employees, who have to manage their own daily activities. Furthermore, informal social interaction is a means of instilling motivation and commitment to the organization, of binding the worker emotionally to the corporate mission. In this context, engaging in casual interpersonal interaction is not a permitted indulgence but a required behaviour.

Nor should it be assumed that employees simply conform. Felstead *et al.* describe the practice of 'stalling'. In the collective office employees are not supposed to take possession of particular spaces or work stations by, for example, leaving a jacket there. Employees do, however, seek to mark out their own territory. They may want to have a base or to work near a particular person or to make sure they have access to a particular facility. They may, therefore, lay claim to a work station by leaving personal items there. These practices will not seem unusual to anyone who has been in a university library! Management can respond with 'stall-busting' sweeps to clear away anything personal left at a work station or by instructing personnel to move around.

The collective office results from various contemporary processes of change. Advances in electronic communication and information technology allow people to work from multiple locations, not only in the office but while travelling or at home. Just as importantly, contemporary management philosophies and strategies emphasize flexibility, teamwork, and integration. Felstead *et al.* (2005: 9) emphasize that technology is not the 'prime mover', for

Office work can now be carried out anywhere.
© Alan Felstead

their research indicates that 'the crucial driver is cost saving'. The collective office does this by intensifying work and economizing on space. The competitive and profit-maximizing dynamics of capitalism lie behind the development of the collective office.

Changes in design have played a part in this. The architecture of the work space enables high visibility, and encourages movement and interaction. Felstead *et al.* do, indeed, devote considerable space to the aesthetics of control and point out that management was heavily involved in the design process.

Will all offices become collective offices? It must be kept in mind that the studies carried out by Felstead *et al.* (2005: 11) were of organizations selected because they had 'radically redesigned their office spaces' or 'supplied working facilities to staff on the move'. They were not representative of offices in general. It seems unlikely that offices concerned with routine tasks will go far down this track. Many, if not most, white-collar workers may well continue to experience the bureaucratic work environments that we described earlier (see p. 659).

Changes in industrial relations

The changes described above were linked to changes in industrial relations and labour organization.

Industrial conflict and the state

The 1979 Conservative government broke sharply with the previous relationship between the state and the unions. During the corporatist period of the 1960s and 1970s governments had tried to bring the unions into the state management of the economy (see Chapter 15, p. 570). In the 1980s, the Conservatives removed union representatives from state organizations and committees. The government sought to regenerate the economy by reviving market forces and, as it saw it, restoring the freedom of the individual. This brought it into conflict with the most basic principle of trade unionism, the subordination of individual to collective interests in order to protect the individual from the market.

Laws passed at roughly two-yearly intervals through the 1980s and into the 1990s regulated the unions' organization and behaviour. We cannot examine these laws in detail, but it is important to understand the main changes that they made.

- *Secondary action made illegal.* Industrial action in support of workers employed elsewhere became illegal. This attacked a key principle of labour movements: that workers in conflict with an employer can obtain support from other workers (see Box 17.9).

- *Restrictions on picketing.* Picketing refers to the practice of placing strikers at a workplace entrance to discourage or prevent workers entering. It had been used to great effect in the miners' strikes of the 1970s, when 'flying pickets' shut down power stations and prevented the distribution of coal. The 1980s laws restricted picketing to a worker's own place of work and the number of pickets to six.

- *Balloting*. Industrial action became subject to membership ballots, which meant that the unions had to follow complex and detailed procedures. Failure to ballot correctly made a strike illegal. The appointment of union officials and union financial support of political parties also became subject to membership ballots.

- *Banning of political strikes*. Strikes for political purposes or against legislation or privatization were made illegal.

These changes may seem reasonable restrictions on union behaviour. They can be justified on the grounds that they protect the individual, prevent unions from abusing their power, and require them to act democratically. They must also be placed in the context of class conflict, for they weakened the power of workers and strengthened the employer. They fundamentally changed the legal status of unions by reversing the 1906 Trade Disputes Act, which had given them immunity from the law in order to prevent employers using the courts against them.

Passing laws was one thing, enforcing them was another. The Conservatives' 1971 law to reform industrial relations failed because they could not implement it against union opposition. In the 1980s they acted more carefully and more effectively. They avoided the imprisonment of union members who disobeyed the law and instead introduced financial penalties. If a union broke the law, it was fined. If it refused to pay the fine, its assets were seized by the courts. Some unions did travel down this path and soon found themselves unable to function and forced to submit.

Enforcement also depended on police action. The government's struggle with the unions came to a climax with the 1984–5 miners' strike. Miners were arrested and prosecuted for public-order offences. There were battles between police and miners at mines and power stations,

---

Controversy and debate Industrial conflict at Gate Gourmet 17.9

Gate Gourmet is the world's second largest airline catering company and provides catering services to many major airlines, including British Airways (BA). It was constructed from a merger of several companies, including BA's catering company. By selling this off, BA could contract out catering and cut its costs. Gate Gourmet's headquarters are in Zurich, but it has 160 flight kitchens in 34 different countries. It is owned by the Texas Pacific Group, an American private equity investment company.

In August 2005 Gate Gourmet became involved in a long and far-reaching dispute with its British employees. The conflict began when workers walked out several times over Gate Gourmet's plans to change 'outdated' working practices. The company claimed that they had engaged in unofficial strike action and sacked 670 workers. The workers' union, the Transport and General Workers' Union (now merged into Unite), accused the company of deliberately provoking a strike. Unofficial action followed among baggage handlers at Heathrow, and BA had to cancel for a time all flights from Heathrow. This was secondary action prohibited by the 1980s industrial relations legislation, and BA later took action against the union officials involved.

The Gate Gourmet labour force consisted largely of women from ethnic minorities. According to Oxfam, they worked 'long hours for low wages, with little or no job security, sick pay or other employment rights'. Gate Gourmet nonetheless claimed that it was facing bankruptcy unless it could cut costs further. Both the company and the union accused BA of 'making unreasonable demands which have forced managers to squeeze more out of their already overworked staff' (*Independent*, 17 August 2005).

The conflict was eventually resolved by a September deal between the union and Gate Gourmet. Most of the sacked workers would be taken back by the company, but 144 were made compulsorily redundant, others taking voluntary redundancy. Those who returned had to accept new working practices. By December 2005 only 13 of the 100 workers who had reapplied for their jobs were back in employment. Gate Gourmet used the dispute to negotiate a better contract with BA.

This dispute set off a debate about workers' rights and industrial-relations law at the Trades Union Congress (TUC) conference in September 2005. TUC leaders called for a new 'trade union freedom' law to allow secondary action of the kind carried out by the BA baggage handlers. However, Alan Johnson, the Trade and Industry Secretary, spoke at the conference and condemned what he saw as a 'return to the 1970s', claiming that the government had provided workers with 'clear and effective social protection' through the minimum wage, improved maternity benefits, and unfair dismissal legislation (*Guardian*, 26 September 2005).

❷ What aspects of the contemporary employment and industrial-relations scene does this account demonstrate?

❷ Should there be a new trade union freedom law?

and police road-blocks intercepted and turned back miners moving across country on picket-duty (Percy-Smith and Hillyard 1985).

The Conservatives' reforms made it much more difficult for unions to strike. During the 1980s and early 1990s strike rates declined, while during the 1990s workers themselves increasingly resorted to the law. This indicated a shift from collective action to a more individualistic exercise of legal rights. In the twenty-first century there has been a pattern of large but short strikes, which have raised the number of strikers again (see Figure 17.4 on p. 655). Worker days lost and strike frequency have, however, stayed low, certainly in comparison with the period from the 1950s to the 1970s.

The economic crisis starting in 2007 might have been expected to increase conflict, as wage rates, hours of work, and working practices came under pressure from employers trying to cut costs. There have been some notable industrial battles, such as the Royal Mail conflict in the autumn of 2009 and the BA strike in March 2010, but worker days lost per year dropped from a recent peak of 1.04 million in 2007 to 759,000 in 2008 and 456,000 in 2009. Workers seem to have broadly accepted loss of earnings through wage freezes and reductions, and shorter hours, in order to hang on to their jobs. By endangering jobs, recessions actually weaken the bargaining power of unions and reduce strike rates. In spite of some high-profile disputes, this recession seems to be no exception.

The decline of trade unions

The decline in the strike rate reflected a more general tendency for collective organization and collective action to decline. The main changes identified by national industrial-relations surveys were the decline of union recognition and collective bargaining. The proportion of workplaces recognizing unions fell from 64 per cent in 1980 to 30 per cent in 2004. The proportion of employees covered by collective bargaining fell from 70 per cent in 1984 to 35 per cent in 2004 (Millward *et al.* 2000: 96, 197; Kersley *et al.* 2005: 12, 20).

The fall of union membership has been quite dramatic. The number of union members in employment in the UK fell from 11.7 million in 1980 to 6.6 million in 2000, then remaining around that level (Visser 2006: 43). This fall reversed a long period of union growth and has taken union membership back to its late 1930s level.

The absolute number of members is not, however, the best measure of union membership, because it does not take account of the size of the labour force—that is, the number of potential members. The extent of membership is best measured by **union density**, which is the proportion of employees who are union members (a measure that is also useful for comparing the rates of different groups of workers). In 1980 union density in Great Britain was 51 per cent, but by 2007 it had fallen to 28 per cent (*Social Trends* 2009: 60; Visser 2006: 45).

Why did this decline occur? Have employers become hostile to unions or have unions lost worker support? There were certainly cases when employers derecognized unions, but there is no real evidence of employers in general becoming anti-union. According to Millward *et al.* (2000), declining recognition was largely a result of the opening of new workplaces where unions were not recognized. This in turn 'can be put down to reduced enthusiasm for union representation by employees and a general withdrawal of the earlier presumption by large employers that joint regulation was the norm' (Milward *et al.* 2000: 232).

One possible explanation is the changing occupational, and industrial structure of the British economy. Union density varies greatly between occupations and industries, and employment has shifted from highly to weakly unionized ones. Many highly unionized workplaces in heavy industry and manufacturing were closed down during the recession of the early 1980s. Some services where employment has been increasing, such as the hotel and restaurant trade, and wholesale and retail distribution, have a very low union density (Sneade 2001). Part-time work and employment in smaller workplaces, both of which are associated with low union densities, have grown.

The decline of union density has been too widespread, however, to be explained solely by changes of this kind. Indeed, those categories of workers with the highest rates of union membership have shown the greatest decline (see Figure 17.14, p. 680), resulting in the union density of many groups converging towards a lowish rate of around 30 per cent. As the decline in union density has been so general and an anti-union government was in power between 1979 and 1997, it is plausible to argue that this contributed significantly to membership decline, but there is no easy way of assessing how important this was.

One particular way in which government policy may well have contributed to the decline of union membership is through privatization. The aspect of work most strongly related to union density is whether employment is in the private or the public sector. In the UK in 2007 the union density of public-sector employees was 59 per cent, as compared with 16 per cent in the private-sector (*Social Trends* 2009: 60).

Did the 1997 election of a Labour government make any difference? There was some change in the climate of industrial relations. The Employment Relations Act of 1999 granted unions a right to recognition, if a majority of employees voted for it, and generally improved workers' rights. The bulk of the anti-union legislation passed by Conservative governments has, however, remained in place. The process of privatization continued (see Chapter 15, p. 581) and, indeed, brought the government into conflict with unions. The decline of union membership slowed

Global focus The Japanese model   17.10

Japan's economic success and the high productivity of Japanese companies led to much overseas interest in the Japanese model of industrial relations (Dore 1973). In Japan, workers have been expected to be flexible, committed, and loyal members of the company, willing to subordinate themselves totally to its requirements. Worker integration and identification with the company were fostered in the following main ways:

- *Lifetime employment*. Workers normally stayed with one company throughout their working lives.
- *Company welfare*. The company provided welfare for employees, through, for example, company housing.
- *Management–worker integration*. Workers were integrated through the adoption of a common uniform, and social mixing during work-breaks and company-organized leisure activities.
- *Enterprise unions*. Unions were organized on company lines, so that there is a Nissan union, a Sony union, and so on.

One must, however, be careful not to treat this pattern as though it is found throughout Japan. It has been typical of large companies only and applied just to their full-time and male workers. Female employees had part-time status only (Broadbent 2003). Lifetime employment was possible only because fluctuations in demand were absorbed by an extensive small company sector with no security of employment, and by the part-time and temporary labour force.

Japanese industrial relations must also be put in the context of employer domination and the form taken by the Japanese state. Enterprise unionism was imposed on workers by their employers and reflected the historic weakness of the Japanese labour movement. Furthermore, although company welfare schemes are often attributed to traditions of employer paternalism, workers have been dependent on employers for welfare because state welfare has been less developed in Japan.

The Japanese model's integration of workers into the company fitted well the post-Fordist emphasis on integration and flexibility. In Britain some companies have applied a *Japanese-style* pattern of industrial relations. This involved single union deals, binding arbitration agreements, consultation and participation schemes, and single status for manual and non-manual employees. Lifetime employment, company welfare, and enterprise unionism were not compatible with British institutions. The adoption of even this watered-down version has not been widespread (Millward 1994: 123). In Japan itself the model has been weakened, as recent economic problems forced the large Japanese companies to shed labour and employ more part-time and temporary workers.

❷ Japanese industrial-relations practices are closely linked to Japanese organizational structures and management, which we discuss in Chapter 14, pp. 541–2 and 544.

Global focus Global unions?   17.11

Strong national labour movements developed in many countries, but globalization means they need to organize globally. The growth of TNCs and the greater mobility of capital have combined with neo-liberal government policies (see Chapter 15, p. 577) to undermine the power of *nationally* organized labour movements. Production can be moved to countries where the labour movement is weak. To counteract this, unions need to extend their organization across national borders.

Dan Gallin (2002: 237–43) identifies three key forms of international labour organization:

- *The International Confederation of Free Trade Unions* (ICFTU). The most extensive global labour organization, this is essentially a confederation of national union centres. It is handicapped by its national member units, which are 'accustomed to think and act within the confines of the nation state'.

- *The European Trade Union Confederation*. This has a similar problem and is limited by its dependence on the European Commission for funding. It is a regional rather than a global organization, and its Europeanism conflicts with the ICFTU's internationalism.

- *International Trade Secretariats* (ITS). These are international federations of unions operating in particular industries. They are more able to confront transnational corporations, can negotiate Global Framework Agreements with them, and on occasions act effectively against them. In 2007 the ICEM federation of chemical, energy, and mining unions had 467 affiliated unions with 20 million members in 132 countries (www.global-unions.org).

❷ Will unions ever be able to match the power of the TNC?

Figure 17.14 Changes in union density, 1989–2000 (%)

Variations in density	1989	2000	1989–2000
Men	44	30	−14
Women	33	29	−4
Full-time work	44	32	−12
Part-time work	22	21	−1
Manual work	44	29	−15
Non-manual work	35	30	−5
Production	45	29	−16
Services	37	30	−7
Workplaces with 25+ workers	49	36	−13
Workplaces with less than 25 workers	20	16	−4

Sources: Cully and Woodland (1997: 233); Sneade (2001: 437–40).

❓ Why do small workplaces and part-time workers have lower union densities?

❓ Why did women workers have a lower union density than men in 1989?

❓ Why are the densities of men and women now virtually the same?

but did not stop. In 1997 union density in the UK was 31 per cent; in 2007 it was 28 per cent (Visser 2006: 45; *Social Trends* 2009: 60). Labour government did not reverse union decline.

The decline of the UK unions must be placed in its global as well as its national context. Globalization (see Box 17.11 on p. 679) has undermined the bargaining position of nationally organized unions. This cannot, however, on its own explain union decline in the UK. Although union density has fallen below 30 per cent in the UK, in Sweden it has remained around 80 per cent, while in France it has fallen even further to around 10 per cent (Jensen 2004). Given such large international variations, the particular national trajectory of unions requires explanation. In the case of the UK, the government's 1980s onslaught on the unions would seem central to such an explanation.

> **⤷ Connections**
> Globalization has also affected the strength of organized labour in another way, through the increased movement of cheap, migratory labour from poor countries to rich ones. See the discussion of this in Media watch 17 at the end of this chapter.

Unions should not, however, be treated as passive organizations. How have they responded to decline? One response has been to merge. This can maintain, indeed greatly increase, the strength of individual unions, but does nothing for the size or strength of the whole movement. Another has been to increase membership by

making unions more attractive to underrepresented ethnic groups, young workers, and women.

The TUC launched a new organization campaign at its 1997 congress. Unions secured 2,872 new recognition agreements, covering 846,000 workers, between 1995 and 2004, particularly after the 1999 Employment Relations Act (Gall 2006: 15). Nonetheless, union density has continued to decline, and this has clearly disappointed the unions. It is, however, important to emphasize that they remain major organizations with a large membership. In 2007–8 the total membership of UK unions was over 7.6 million.

Changes in employment

There have also been big changes in employment patterns. Here we consider patterns of unemployment, the spread of part-time work, and the growing employment of women.

Higher unemployment

In the 1980s there was a huge rise in British unemployment, but by the beginning of the twenty-first century it had apparently fallen back to 1970s levels. Job losses in traditional industries and a general shedding of labour in manufacturing, as UK companies struggled to compete with competitors elsewhere, had been more than balanced by the growth of employment in the services sector. In the United Kingdom between 1978 and 2000, jobs in manufacturing dropped by 39 per cent, from 7 million to 4.2 million, while service jobs increased by 36 per cent, from 15.6 to 21.2 million (*Social Trends* 2001: 80).

The employment situation was more complex than this, however. Although it seemed as though unemployment was no longer such a serious problem, a large pool of hidden unemployment remained. Christina Beatty *et al.* (2007: 22) argued that in January 2007 there were 1.7 million 'hidden jobless', in addition to the 940,000 claiming unemployment benefit. The hidden figure included 650,000 who were unemployed but not claiming benefit, but the hidden jobless were mainly people on *incapacity* benefit. One million out of the 2.7 million on this benefit could have been expected to be in work.

In the UK as a whole, the unemployment rate for January 2007 rose from 2.6 per cent, according to the claimant count, to 7.2 per cent, when hidden unemployment was added. Significantly, much bigger regional variations showed up when this was added. In the south-east of Britain, the unemployment rate rose from 1.6 per cent to only 4.6. In Scotland, it rose from 2.8 per cent to 8.4; in Wales from 2.5 per cent to 8.9; in the north-east from 3.5 per cent to 9.6 (Beatty *et al.* 2007: 25). Incapacity benefit rates were much higher in the old industrial areas, especially the coalfields, of the north and west.

The high level of incapacity benefit is now seen as a serious problem, both for those who have become dependent on it and for the state that pays for it. The government announced in 2008 a target of reducing incapacity claimants by one million in ten years.

The above figures pre-dated the sharp rise in unemployment resulting from the growing economic crisis that started in the autumn of 2007 (see Chapter 15, pp. 589–91). Those claiming unemployment benefit in the UK rose from 0.9 million in January 2007 to 1.6 million in January 2010. We know, however, that many unemployed people do not claim benefit, because they are not entitled to it or choose not to claim. According to the more comprehensive Labour Force Survey figure (see Chapter 3, p. 102), the number of UK unemployed rose from 1.6 million in January 2007 to 2.5 million at the end of 2009. Unemployment would have risen faster but for workers and companies opting to preserve jobs by shifting from full-time to part-time work and preferring wage cuts to redundancy (*Guardian*, 12 November 2009).

Unemployment has been spreading across the economy. Financial services and construction were hit when the financial crisis struck and the housing market ground to a halt. As a more general crisis unfolded, unemployment spread, particularly into the retail sector, where the closure of Woolworths in early 2009 resulted in 27,000 losing their jobs. According to the TUC, it is the lower-paid retail, goods handling and storage workers, and general office assistants, who have suffered most (*TUC Newsroom*, 7 September 2009). When the inevitable public expenditure cuts begin to bite, it will be those in public-sector services who will feel the pain.

There is particular concern with the impact of unemployment on the young, partly because of their high rate of unemployment, partly because of fears that they will become a lost, workless generation. Around half of those losing jobs between June 2008 and June 2009 were between the ages of 16 and 24, and youth unemployment had risen close to a million (*Guardian*, 12 August 2009). In April 2009 the Chancellor of the Exchequer announced a £2.7 billion pound package of job creation and new education places to prevent a generation of young people from being 'abandoned to a future on the scrapheap' (*Guardian*, 23 April 2009). Whether such measures will achieve much in the face of future cuts in public expenditure, and in the higher education teaching budget, remains to be seen.

The growth of part-time employment

One of the most striking features of the changing pattern of employment in the United Kingdom is the growth of part-time work, usually defined as less than thirty hours per week. In 1951 only 4 per cent of workers were employed part-time, but by 2004 21 per cent were. There are many different forms of part-time work. There are job-share arrangements and term-time working. Some employees work annualized hours, a specified number of hours per year, which vary according to time of year.

Most part-time jobs, 81 per cent of them in 2004, are done by women, though the number of men in part-time work has also been rising (*Social Trends* 2005: 47). Significantly, the reasons given by men and women for taking part-time work are very different. Most women do not want full-time work, while most men do.

It has often been claimed that women have had to take it because of their domestic responsibilities, but Hakim (1995, 1996) has put forward a *rational-choice explanation*. She argues that part-time work is not forced on women but freely chosen. According to Hakim, there are two kinds of women, *career-centred* and *home-centred*. Home-centred women work part-time because they prefer to do so. Hakim believes that this preference should be considered a quite rational decision by women, who are perfectly able to make up their own minds about what they want to do and are not forced into part-time work against their will.

Hakim's view has, however, been strongly criticized by Ginn *et al.* (1996) and Crompton and Harris (1998). They argue that Hakim fails to explain why some women are home-centred and others not. She takes insufficient account of the childcare difficulties faced by women seeking to combine their work and domestic roles, and ignores the socializing processes that shape women's roles and expectations. This is not to say that women have no choice, but rather that their choices are shaped and constrained by the society within which they live.

Part-time work is clearly linked to childcare responsibilities. As the age of their youngest dependent child rises, women shift from part-time to full-time work, and those with no dependent children are the ones most likely to be in full-time work (see Figure 17.15, p. 682).

Part-time work must be set in its economic context. As we showed above (see pp. 673–5) the employment of part-time workers was a means by which employers pursued greater numerical flexibility. A growing demand for part-time workers is also related to the shift of employment into services, where the demand for labour fluctuates, with, for example, periods of peak demand in stores or restaurants. Part-time workers have also been cheaper to employ, because employers could avoid many of the obligations and costs laid on them by employment legislation by employing workers for less than sixteen hours a week.

The growing employment of women

In discussing part-time work we have already been dealing with one of the main ways in which women's employment has increased. Here we explore more generally the reasons for their growing employment.

Figure 17.15 Economic activity status of married and cohabiting women: by age of youngest dependent child, United Kingdom, 2004 (%)

Activity status	Age of youngest dependent child				No dependent children	All women aged 16–59
	0–4	5–10	11–15	16–18		
Working full-time	20	27	38	43	52	40
Working part-time	38	50	43	37	26	34
Unemployed	2	2	2	2	2	2
Economically inactive	39	21	18	18	20	24
All women (=100%) (m.)	2.2	1.7	1.2	0.4	5.3	10.8

Notes: Data for women aged 16–59. ILO definition of unemployment is used.

Source: *Social Trends* (2005: 47).

❓ Does this table show that women's childcare responsibilities determine their involvement in the labour market?

In the United Kingdom the involvement of women in paid work has risen steadily in the second half of the twentieth century. In 1951 43 per cent of women aged 15–59 were economically active, but by 2008 this figure had risen to 75 per cent. During the same period the proportion of men aged 15–64 who were economically active declined from 96 per cent to 84 per cent (Hakim 1993: 99; *Social Trends* 2009: 47). The gap between men and women in rates of employment has been steadily closing, though one must bear in mind the lower hours worked by women, because a higher proportion of them are employed part-time.

Women's availability for paid work has increased in various ways. A declining birth rate has reduced the time required for childcare. The mechanization of housework

has reduced the time needed to carry it out. There is also some evidence that men are taking an increasing share of housework, though this is still mainly done by women (see Chapter 12, p. 459).

> ➲ **Connections**
>
> The employment of women in paid work and the domestic division of labour are closely linked. We discuss the domestic division of labour in Chapter 12, pp. 458–60.

Greater availability for paid work does not itself explain the growing employment of women, however. Men may do more housework *because* women are going out to paid

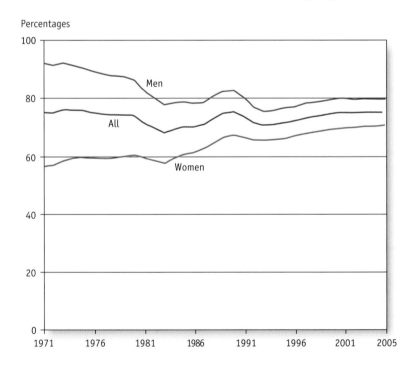

Figure 17.16 Employment rates by sex, United Kingdom, 1971–2005 (%)

Source: *Social Trends* (2006: 52).

Why are there more women lawyers?

© Alice Chadwick

work. The birth rate may have gone down *because* women are giving a higher priority to paid work. The higher household incomes that are *due to* the money earned by women make possible the purchase of domestic machinery. It is far from clear what is cause and what is consequence, and it appears likely that there are complex processes of interaction at work here.

One reason for women taking paid work is the growing financial pressure on households. The costs of increasing homeownership, consumerism, and rising levels of debt have led to increasing financial demands on households. Furthermore, the male contribution has been falling, as more men become economically inactive. Higher divorce rates have forced more women on to the labour market in order to support themselves, while the number of lone-parent families headed by women has increased. Labour's 'welfare into work' programme has also put pressure on lone mothers to find employment (see Chapter 15, p. 580).

The growing employment of women must also be placed in the context of changes in the demand for labour. Employment is gendered (see Figure 17.17). Women's occupations, such as those involving administrative and secretarial work, sales, and personal services, have been expanding, while male jobs, such as those in manufacturing and mining, have been in decline. As we showed above, the part-time work that disproportionately employs women has been growing. Employers also seek to recruit women for customer-service work involving 'emotional labour', because of the widespread belief that women have special emotional skills.

The traditional gendering of occupations has, however, been breaking down, and this too partly explains the

growing employment of women. There has been a dramatic increase in the entry of women to managerial and professional careers. The proportion of solicitors who were women rose from less than 1 per cent in 1946 to 31 per cent in 1994 (J. Elliot 1997: 12). The proportion of women who were administrative and executive local-government officers rose from 20 per cent in 1971 to 51 per cent in 1990 (Crompton 1997: 46). The proportion of women in all grades of hospital medicine rose from 23 per cent in 1983 to 35 per cent in 2003, in general practice from 19 per cent in 1983 to 38 per cent in 2003 (Allen 2005). Women still face the problem of getting through the 'glass ceiling' into the senior and better-paid posts, but there has clearly been an opening-up of these occupations that has greatly increased women's opportunities.

Equal-opportunities legislation and the efforts of the feminist movement have contributed to the opening-up process, but the increasing education of women has here been crucial (see Chapter 9, pp. 328–9, and Chapter 5, pp. 169–70). Women's growing educational success has interacted with higher occupational aspirations to enable women to compete with men and challenge the male domination of graduate and professional jobs.

The explanation of the growing employment of women in paid work is not a simple matter. Mothers forced to take poorly paid work in factories and supermarkets are in a very different situation from highly educated, single women pushing their way into male-dominated professions. Changes in the household and the economy interact in complex ways. Account must also be taken of changes in education and the challenging of patriarchy through the organization and political action of women.

Changes in household work

The changes in patterns of employment that we have been examining have been connected with many changes in the household and family. Here we examine changes in the relationship between the household and employment, and the growth of an informal economy.

Homework and telework

In recent years homework, defined as paid work for an outside employer, which includes both manual work and telework, has been growing. Between 1981 and 2002, the number of homeworkers working mainly in the home roughly doubled, from 346,000 to 673,000. If one considers those working mainly elsewhere but at least one day at home, there were 1,066,000 in 1997, rising to 1,242,000 in 2002 (Felstead *et al.* 2005: 55).

Employers' increasing use of homeworkers can be seen as another example of greater flexibility of employment, since they can be paid not by the hour but by the number

Figure 17.17 Employees by gender and occupation, United Kingdom, 2008 (%)

Occupation	Males	Females
Managers and senior officials	19	11
Professional occupations	14	12
Associate professional and technical	13	16
Administrative and secretarial	5	20
Skilled trades	19	2
Personal service	2	15
Sales and customer service	5	11
Process, plant, and machine operatives	12	2
Elementary occupations	12	11
All occupations	*100*	*100*

Source: *Social Trends* (2008: 51).

of garments they sew or the number of phone calls they answer. Homeworkers are, anyway, cheap to employ, partly because employers can avoid overheads but also because many homeworkers will work for very low wages. They have always been vulnerable to exploitation, because they are isolated, unorganized, and often unable to compete for jobs on the open labour market, owing, for example, to childcare responsibilities or disability.

Homeworking is sometimes presented as a choice made by those who prefer to work at home. This may be the case for some, but Phizacklea and Wolkowitz (1995) argued that many who work at home have no real choice, because of both internal and external constraints. By internal constraints they meant the socialized expectation that any paid work done by women should take account of the demands of childcare and housework. External constraints included high local unemployment, and the operation of the state benefit system and immigration law, which pushed both wives of unemployed men drawing benefit and illegal immigrants out of employment. They also included a lack of transport, qualifications, or affordable childcare.

Telework has been increasing particularly rapidly. A teleworker is basically a homeworker who uses information technology. According to the Labour Force Survey, the number of teleworkers in the United Kingdom increased from 0.92 million in 1997 to 2.4 million—8 per cent of the labour force—in 2005. This figure includes, however, the self-employed as well as employees (*Social Trends* 2006: 58).

Telework has a quite different image from the 'sweated labour' traditionally associated with homework, though whether this is justified is another matter. Telework is often taken to refer to consultants, designers, and writers working creatively in rural settings far removed from the city office, but also includes those carrying out routine secretarial, clerical, or sales work from ordinary homes in the suburbs.

Telework has much the same advantages and disadvantages as any other kind of homework. Although it allows some the freedom to work when they choose where they choose, it may lead to frequent domestic interruptions, and also isolates people from colleagues and the life of the workplace. It can also mean for others that home provides no escape from work, that the employer or customer can always reach them by phone or e-mail, interrupt their activities, and demand immediate attention. It is both the most flexible and the most intrusive form of homework (see Study 17 at the end of this chapter).

Telework has, however, brought about one major change in homework, which historically was locally based, with networks of homeworkers linked to nearby factories. Information technology has given homework a global reach, for satellite links can be used to employ teleworkers in cheap-labour countries to carry out telephone-answering,

data-processing, or software production (see Chapter 16, p. 624).

Waged domestic labour

As we showed on p. 663, waged domestic labour was the main source of paid work for women in the nineteenth century. It declined as labour costs increased, but since the 1980s it has expanded again, along with small businesses organizing and providing it.

The re-emergence of waged domestic labour is related to the employment of women, in two different ways (Gregson and Lowe 1994):

- as a response to the growing employment of middle-class women;

- as a source of employment for working-class women when other working-class occupations have been shrinking.

The revival of waged domestic labour has complex implications for social inequalities. To the extent that it facilitates women's careers and reduces women's unpaid housework, it promotes equality between men and women. It does so, however, at the expense of greater class inequality.

There has been a reconstruction of what Gregson and Lowe (1994: 234) call 'a class-mediated hierarchy of domestic tasks'. The more pleasurable housework and child-rearing activities are carried out on a shared basis by the middle-class couple, while the routine cleaning tasks are left to waged working-class labour. Thus, waged domestic labour results in the growing employment of women in lower-paid, unorganized, and unregulated work. It often provides work for migrant labour but at the cost of exploitative conditions of employment that are often made worse by the illegal status of many migrants.

The informal economy

With the growth of industrial capitalism, both goods and services were increasingly obtained from the market. The formal economy of transactions involving money became dominant, and, as we argued earlier (see p. 652), the formal economy was increasingly treated as though it were the only economy. In recent years there has, however, been a growing interest in the informal economy of the non-market provision of goods and services.

Many activities that were previously part of the formal economy have shifted into the informal economy through **self-provisioning**. Instead of paying workers to repair houses, shop assistants to serve them, or agricultural workers to harvest crops, people use DIY, self-service, and 'pick your own'. Greater self-provisioning can be linked to declining hours of paid work, higher unemployment, the development of domestic machinery, and the growth of a DIY industry.

The informal economy consists not only of unpaid labour within the household but also non-market exchanges within local networks and the acquisition of goods through 'foraging'. An example of non-market exchanges would be mutual baby/pet/granny-sitting arrangements within a group of households or barter exchanges 'in kind' of, say, garden produce. Such activities have sometimes been partially formalized through local systems for the exchange of tokens representing amounts of labour. Foraging activities range from traditional hunting and gathering activities, such as fishing, through refuse gleaning to shoplifting and other forms of pilfering and theft (Mars 1982).

Raymond Pahl has referred to a 'shift out of employment into work', which he linked to the decline of employment in the formal economy and the growth of 'patterns of getting by' that combined whatever paid work a household could get with greater activity in the informal economy (Pahl 1984: 179, 190). Increased taxation and regulation also played their part by driving activities out of the formal into the informal economy.

Somewhere between the formal and informal economies lies a grey area of cash transactions that are untaxed, often illegal, and certainly outside the laws that regulate formal economic activity. This includes a wide range of activities, from household repairs to car-boot sales, from prostitution to the sale of illegal drugs. Some of the gangmaster practices examined in Media watch 17, at the end of this chapter, come into this area.

This rise of the informal economy reversed the previous tendency to commercialize all goods and services, and revived the pre-industrial pattern of combining household production with foraging and paid work (see Box 17.4 on p. 664). As we showed above, there are also, however, opposite tendencies, such as the growth of waged domestic labour in the household. In a society where inequality is increasing, a widening gap has emerged between two-career households at the top, which can afford to buy time by paying for domestic labour, and unemployed ones at the bottom, which can afford plenty of time for informal activities but little else.

While the informal economy is an alternative source of goods and services, it is important to realize that it is dependent on the formal economy. Gangmasters supply labour to the formal economy. Self-provisioning depends on the mass production, marketing, and distribution of a whole new range of DIY products for home, car, and garden. Furthermore, while households with low incomes may turn towards self-provisioning to acquire the goods and services they want, they need sufficient income to buy the means of self-provisioning. Pahl (1984) found that employment was, for this reason, crucial to effective self-provisioning.

Between the formal and informal economies?
© Alice Chadwick

Changes in leisure

We argued earlier that industrialization had not only transformed work but had also created leisure (see pp. 665–7). In this section we examine the growing importance of leisure and the increasing consumption of sport, before discussing changes in the distinction between work and leisure.

A leisure society?

As industrial societies developed, increasing productivity and growing automation promised a world where machines rather than people would do the work. The daily hours of paid work declined and 'work-free' weekends and holidays became established, as we showed on p. 666. Working lives also became compressed between a lengthening education at one end and earlier retirement at the other.

Dumazedier (1967) suggested that a 'leisure society' had emerged. Leisure activities had steadily become a more important part of people's lives. Work was increasingly a means to the enjoyment of leisure. The commercialization of leisure activities, the growth of leisure industries, and the marketing of their products through the mass media made leisure pursuits the main focus of people's lives. There has been no let up in these tendencies, and, as we argued earlier (see p. 671), patterns of consumption rather than work have become the main source of identity for most people.

Leisure became privatized as leisure activities occurred increasingly at home. The *Affluent Worker* study (see p. 658) showed that the mobile and well-paid workers it studied in 1960s Luton had developed a privatized style of life. The spread of home and car ownership, and the ever greater development of the domestic machinery of leisure, continued this process. There have recently been some counter-tendencies, such as, for example, a sustained rise in visits to the cinema, but the time spent on activities outside the home is far outweighed by the time spent watching domestic screens of one kind or another.

Rapidly rising use of the Net reinforces privatism. In 2009 76 per cent of adults reported that they had used the Internet recently, as compared with 40 per cent in 2000 (Office for National Statistics 2009). People are increasingly connecting with the outside world from within their households rather than venturing out into public spaces or engaging in face-to-face contact with others. This applies to a wide range of leisure activities, to shopping, entertainment, socializing through SNS, and dating.

The privatizing of leisure has been reinforced by globalization. Satellite communications have connected homes to global entertainment and information networks. Global media corporations produce global products, whether sports events, soap operas, nature and arts programmes, or news coverage, for domestic consumption.

While mass consumption established new leisure habits, the post-Fordist shift to greater diversity and customization has enabled the tailoring of leisure activities to a person's own requirements. The multiplication and diversification of television channels, radio stations, and weekly magazines aimed at specific market niches rather than mass markets provide opportunities for this (see Chapter 10, pp. 373–4).

Lash and Urry (1994) have argued that the decline of the package holiday is another example, for this exemplified Fordist patterns of consumption. It involved:

- a complete package that combined holiday destination, travel, accommodation, catering, and entertainment;
- a standard product, with limited variation in accommodation or resort;
- advertising through the mass media and sale through travel agent chains;
- high volume to keep prices low.

Holiday destinations have now spread globally, while packages have become more varied, and a range of new holiday and travel experiences, often designed for minorities, as with 'green tourism', have emerged. The Thomas Cook company, whose founder created the package holiday, has reorganized itself into a global operation that specializes in providing holiday *information*, so that customers can construct their own packages instead of buying one out of the brochure.

> **⊃ Connections**
> Cruising has become a popular alternative to the package holiday. See Box 13.16 on p. 510 in Chapter 13.

Lash and Urry also suggested that travel could be replaced by what they call the 'post-tourist' experience of other places through 'travel by television' (see Box 17.12).

Google Earth has taken this process one stage further. Virtual travel is now a reality. It is now possible not only to zoom in on a place but also to stroll along a street, as Google makes available street-level images. Google sightseeing can now take you to see the Eifel Tower, the Imperial Palace of Japan, or Grand Canyon.

Viewing traditional sights through real or virtual travel may, however, no longer be sufficient to satisfy the post-tourist. According to Urry (2002), a key feature of tourism is the contrast between ordinary life and the extraordinary experience. Increasing familiarity through television with what were once remote sights makes ordinary what was once extraordinary, so people seek 'new out-of-the-ordinary experiences'. Urry gives as examples: the Leprosy museum in Bergen, the Japanese Death Railway in Burma, the Gestapo headquarters in Berlin, "boring tours" in Sydney, and space tourism (Urry 2002: 92).

The consumption of sport

Since sport was commercialized in the nineteenth century (see p. 668), its economic significance has continued to

---

THEORY AND METHODS   17.12

Post-tourism

'The post-tourist does not need to leave his or her house in order to see many of the typical objects of the tourist gaze. With TV and VCR most such objects can be gazed upon, compared, contextualized, and gazed upon again. The typical tourist experience is anyway to see *named* scenes through a *frame*, but this can now be experienced in one's living room at the flick of a switch, and it can be repeated again and again. It can be suggested that there is little difference between seeing a particular view through the viewfinder of one's camera and through the television set. The latter of course causes far less environmental damage. Tourism through virtual reality may be the twenty-first century solution.' (Lash and Urry 1994: 275)

grow. People spend money on spectating, viewing, sports clothing and equipment, sport books and magazines, subscriptions to gyms, and gambling—to name only the most obvious items of expenditure. They also spend on travel to sports events, on eating and drinking at them, and on accommodation. An estimated £16 billion was spent on sport in the UK in 2002 (Horne 2006: 26).

> **◑ Connections**
> Cities compete for the right to host major international sporting events because of the economic benefits they may bring to their economies. See Chapter 13, pp. 506–7.

Central to the recent process of commercialization has been the mediatization of sport. It was transformed by television between 1965 and 1985. Technical improvements in TV—in picture quality, the slow motion action replay, and satellite transmission across the globe—paved the way. Money flowed into sport through sponsorship, advertising, merchandizing, and exclusive broadcasting deals for major competitions. A key role in this was played by entrepreneurs, such as Jack Kramer, Mark McCormack, and Rupert Murdoch, who mediated between the sports organizations, the performers, the media, and advertising. Murdoch's Sky television deals transformed British football. Amateurism's remaining defences against the intrusion of professional sport finally collapsed (Horne *et al.* 1999: 266–8).

A feature of this transformation was the rise of the sport star. With the growth of the mass media, successful individuals became national figures, but with television they could be turned into global sport stars. This is not simply a matter of televised sporting success. Corporations use stars to endorse and promote their products, and pay them handsomely. Agents manage the image critical to their value, and move quickly to repair the damage if this is threatened by the star's behaviour or adverse publicity. The sport star, the club or team, the agent, the media, and the corporate sponsor create 'circuits of promotion' that benefit all concerned. Barry Smart (2005) considers that there are three outstanding commercial sporting figures—Michael Jordan, Tiger Woods, and David Beckham. Revelations about the private life of Tiger Woods in 2009–10 have required considerable image repair.

Lifestyle sports

Important as this highly mediatized world of sport is, it would be wrong to see the significance of contemporary sport solely in this way. People not only watch sport; they also engage in sporting activities themselves. Here the rise of 'lifestyle sports' is an important feature of changing leisure patterns. This term refers to such recently popularized sporting activities as skate-boarding, surfing, hanggliding, and scuba-diving, but also to new versions of older

What is a lifestyle sport?
© Bruno De Hogures/Getty Images

ones, such as rock-climbing (see Wheaton 2004). Many of its features would seem to apply to cycling or exercise activities in gyms and health centres. Rapid technical innovation and diversification are features of all these sports.

The key characteristics of 'lifestyle sports' are that they are individualistic, sometimes risky, and identity-forming. They are an individualist alternative to traditional competitive team and club sports, though they do develop their own subcultures and patterns of sociability. The key thing is the experience for the individual rather than the spectacle for the watcher. They can often involve a substantial element of risk. Catherine Palmer (2004: 67) suggests that the companies selling adventure sports will often hide this, presenting them as sports where nothing can really go wrong but where 'close calls and near misses' are part of the experience. Lifestyle sports create and recreate identity through the projection of an image and the adoption of a particular set of attitudes, an argot, and specialized dress and equipment. For a more detailed list of characteristics, see Wheaton (2004: 11–12).

Changing attitudes towards the body have contributed to the growth of lifestyle sports and in turn have been reinforced by them. Richard Holt and Tony Mason (2000: 170) suggest that amongst the growing numbers of women in sedentary office jobs there was a 'redefining of sport away from the competitive to the cosmetic' in the 1990s. Fitness, health, and body shape became important components of image and identity. The body has become a project rather than an object, and is seen as malleable and perfectible. Health is considered a responsibility of the individual, who can choose to adopt a more or less healthy lifestyle. People come under pressure to lose weight and to avoid obesity and the diseases associated with it (Horne 2006: 128–32).

Many of these developments in sport show the features of post-Fordism that we have found in leisure more generally. The greater diversity of lifestyle sporting activities, their customization for the individual, and their role in the formation of identity are typical of post-Fordist consumption patterns. Furthermore, the importance of style and image in these activities exemplifies post-Fordist stylization and aestheticization (see p. 671). Sport activities and goods have become a major focus of the mediatized consumption characteristic of contemporary capitalism.

The end of leisure?

As the range of sporting (and non-sporting) leisure activities has increased, the actual time available to enjoy them may well, however, have diminished. The historic decline in the hours of work did not necessarily mean that leisure time increased. More unpaid work in the household can hardly be treated as more leisure. Self-provisioning (see p. 685) has invaded leisure time. Rising longevity and the decline of public-sector residential care mean that many households have to spend more time looking after the old, the ill, and the disabled. Genuine leisure time is squeezed.

The separation of work and leisure into distinct time compartments has also become less sharp. There are now few blocks of time when most people are at leisure. This is partly because employment in leisure services has increased, so more people have to work during leisure periods. It is also because of the lifting of restrictions on trading and opening hours. Twenty-four-hour and Sunday shopping mean that many have to do their paid work during what had once been considered leisure time. Globalization destroys time differences in living patterns, for distinctions between different parts of the day cease to exist in a global society. 'Twenty-four/seven' sums up the new world of round-the-clock activity.

Industrialization had created leisure as a distinct part of life by separating work and leisure activities in people's lives. With commercialization and the growth of leisure industries, organized leisure activities became an ever more important part of the economy. In recent years leisure time has, however, been invaded by other household activities, while one person's leisure time has increasingly become another person's work time. Leisure activities have become privatized and individualized. Leisure has ended in the sense that the broad division of life into periods of collective work and leisure now seems specific to a time that has passed.

Stop and reflect

We first considered post-industrial and post-Fordist changes in production and consumption.

- Make sure that you understand the concepts of post-industrialism and post-Fordism.
- Consider whether you live in an industrial or a post-industrial society.
- What does it mean to say that post-Fordist consumption has been 'stylized' and 'aestheticized'?
- Beck claims that globalization is resulting in Brazilianization. Is Britain being Brazilianized?

We then examined the transformation of industrial relations since the 1970s.

- Although Japanese companies have invested heavily in Britain, there is little evidence of the Japanization of industrial relations.
- Governments used legislation to curb the power of the British unions during the 1980s and 1990s.
- Is this why union membership has declined in Britain?

We went on to consider patterns of employment.

- Declining employment in manufacturing has been counter-balanced by growing employment in services.
- Much unemployment has been hidden by shifting those out of work on to invalidity benefit.
- Non-standard forms of employment, particularly part-time work, have greatly increased.
- Why has the employment of women grown so much?

We then looked at the changing relationships between home and work.

- Telework enables more people to work at home, but at the cost of intruding into home life.
- What have been the consequences of the growth of waged domestic labour for patterns of inequality?
- What is meant by self-provisioning and what is its significance for work and leisure?

(continued)

We moved on to consider changes in leisure.

- Leisure activities have assumed greater importance in people's lives and leisure industries have provided increasing employment.

- Mediatization has been central to the continued commercialization of sport.

- New individualized lifestyle sports that contribute to identity formation have emerged.

- Do we live in a leisure society or has leisure come to an end?

Key concepts

- aestheticization 671
- aesthetic labour 660
- alienation 651
- capitalism 648
- deskilling 654
- domestic labour 651
- emotional labour 660
- flexible firm 673

- homework 651
- industrialism 649
- information society 670
- institutionalization of industrial conflict 651
- means of production 649
- organic solidarity 651
- orientation to work 658

- post-Fordism 671
- post-industrial society 669
- reserve army of labour 665
- self-provisioning 685
- stylization 671
- union density 678

Workshop 17

Study 17 Working at home

In their book *In Work, at Home* (2000), Alan Felstead and Nick Jewson investigate the relationship between the work and domestic lives of homeworkers who carry out paid work at home for an outside employer (see pp. 663 and 684 of this chapter).

For anyone doing research into homeworking, actually locating homeworkers is a difficult problem, which Felstead and Jewson solved by conducting a doorstep survey in nine different areas. In each, their researchers called on every other household, knocking on 15,623 doors in all. In-depth interviews with 338 respondents followed, enabling the researchers to 'listen to the voices of homeworkers' (2000: 9).

Felstead and Jewson map out the 'grim realities' of homework—its low pay, poor conditions of work, and health hazards—but what makes their approach distinctive is their analysis of 'technologies of the self'. These are 'ways in which people, more or less consciously and reflexively, mobilize and organize their attitudes, practices, and feelings in the course of their everyday lives' (2000: 116). Felstead and Jewson do not treat

homeworkers as passive victims of exploitation but see them as actively engaged in managing both their relationship with the employer and their domestic relationships. Homeworkers, more than other workers, have to develop techniques of *self-management*, and in doing so they move most of the burden of labour management from the employer to themselves.

One of the advantages of homework is said to be ending the separation between home and work life, but this means that the boundary between the two now runs *through* the household. Felstead and Jewson identify four techniques for managing this boundary:

- marking;
- switching;
- defending;
- intruding.

Marking establishes time and space boundaries between work and non-work lives. Homeworking mothers have to 'juggle' the demands of work and children. Spatial boundaries are needed to stop work stuff intruding into non-work areas, by, for example, confining work to a particular room.

Switching refers to techniques for moving between bounded activities. These involve the self-discipline required to 'switch on' work, but also to 'switch off' and resist workaholic tendencies. Homeworkers can create timetables by using media schedules, and limit their work by specifying the amount to be done in one day.

Boundaries are easily crossed—hence the *defending* of work time and space. Women especially have to develop defences, because of the pressures and expectations of housewife and childcare roles, by teaching children not to interrupt or finding ways of diverting them.

The *intruding* of work into non-work time and space nonetheless occurs, because of the unpredictability of workloads and employer demands. Techniques of negotiation and compromise are then needed to maintain domestic relationships.

Another set of techniques come into play to deal with the outside world. These are the management of:

- isolation;
- encroachments;
- work variability;
- homeworker invisibility.

Isolation can make it difficult for homeworkers to keep themselves going, in the absence of support from colleagues and contact with others. Some cope with this by maintaining contact by phone or e-mail, others by building in periods of the day when they leave the home.

Encroachments occur when employers, clients, or suppliers intrude on domestic time or space. Intrusion can be minimized by carefully scheduling visits or even creating special entrances for business callers.

Work variability can be a major problem, because work typically comes in unpredictable bursts of activity. Work flow can be regulated by negotiating with work suppliers. Another solution is simply to 'go with the flow' and organize life around alternating periods of intense and slack work. When work is intense, other members of the household may be drafted in.

The *invisibility* problem arises because neither colleagues in a regular workplace, nor people in general, may be aware that work is taking place or recognize how much work is going on. This may result in a homeworker losing status or credibility. Some deal with this by concealing the fact that they work at home.

In demonstrating the range of self-management techniques that homeworkers have to acquire, Felstead and Jewson dispel the idea that homework is an easy option. What comes through repeatedly from their interviews is the amount of self-discipline required. As one male respondent put it:

> The requirement is to be self-motivated and . . . it's the horror story sometimes. It's so difficult to explain to anybody who doesn't have the opportunity to work from home. A lot of people say it's a good idea. The way I feel at the moment, with the pressures that I have with the family, I wish I could go to the factory every day . . . I've really got to work a lot harder and discipline myself to accommodate the family and the business. (Felstead and Jewson 2000: 142)

Felstead and Jewson go on to explore ways in which the worlds of home and work are combined. They suggest that four types of *household understanding* can be distinguished. These are shaped primarily by power relations within the household and the degree to which household responsibilities are shared. Here, there is only space to deal with two of them.

In the *sole-responsibility* model, one person, generally the woman, takes complete charge of a highly gendered household organization. Where the woman is also the homeworker, this typically leads to an 'integration' of work and housewife tasks, with a lot of switching between them. In order to manage the large burden of work this imposes, the homeworker may maintain an 'open' boundary with the outside world, drawing on a network of support from friends and relatives. Where the man is the homeworker, a 'segregation' of work typically takes place, and he may be relegated to a shed, outhouse, or garage, where visitors are not allowed and the boundary with the outside world is 'closed'.

In the opposite *shared-responsibility* household, the division of labour is ungendered, work tasks are negotiated, and internal boundaries are few and flexible. Clear job demarcations are less important than the emotional quality of relationships, as people work together according to 'principles of consensus, equality, and mutual understanding' (2000: 158). Any failure to work in this spirit may, however, lead to an emotional exclusion from the household. In these households there is a joint 'integration' rather than a 'segregation' of work and domestic life, but barriers are likely to go up against the outside world. Its members provide mutual support and defend their emotional castle against intrusions from outside.

 While academic work at home is not strictly 'homework' as defined here, many of the homeworkers' 'technologies of the self' are also required in higher education. Think about your own experience and identify any techniques that you use.

Media watch 17 Gangmasters

Migrant workers now come into Britain from all over the world. Felicity Lawrence carried out an investigation for the *Guardian* into their conditions of work and the practices of gangmasters.

She uncovered a world of ruthless exploitation. Migrant workers are generally paid well below the minimum wage. They then have rent for overcrowded and squalid accommodation deducted from their wages. They may have to pay back large sums for visas and work permits, and travel arrangements. Tax and national insurance contributions may be deducted from their wages but never reach the authorities. If they object to loss of pay, they face threats and violence. Those working illegally are in a particularly vulnerable position.

Gangmasters are nothing new and have long supplied casual labour to agriculture. When farmers required seasonal labour, gangmasters traditionally provided it. The *Guardian* claims that a 'gangmaster culture' is now, however, spreading across Britain to provide labour for a wide range of businesses. One company the *Guardian* came across, the Monarch Catering Agency, provided labour not only for agriculture but for catering, office cleaning, hotels, food packing and processing, and motorway service stations.

This spread of gangmaster practices is partly the result of increased labour migration. Globalization has led to the greater flow of labour between countries. Migrants no longer come from particular areas, such as the Caribbean or the Indian subcontinent, but from a huge range of countries. Gangmasters mediate between migrant workers and potential employers, often travelling out to recruit them. The workers can then become totally dependent on gangmasters for jobs, documents, accommodation, and transport to work.

The spread of gangmaster practices also results from the increased importance of labour flexibility (see pp. 673–4). Labour supplied by gangmasters is attractive to employers not only because it is cheap but also because it can be turned on and off, as demand changes.

Intensified competition drives the spread of these practices. Thus, price competition between the big store chains results in lower payments for food products, which in turn force down labour costs. Only the immigrant labour supplied by the gangmasters will work for such low wages. International competition, as products are trucked or flown across borders, adds to the downward pressure on wages. The dynamics of global capitalism lead not only to the growth of transnational corporations but also to the spread of gangmaster operations.

The exploitation, illegal labour, and tax avoidance discovered by the *Guardian* investigation should not, of course, occur in a country with a minimum wage, laws regulating conditions of work, and law-abiding companies with personnel departments, codes of practice, and auditing procedures. The problem is the long chain from the retail companies through the producers to the labour supply agencies and the gangmasters. The formal structures operating at the top shade into informal, personal and temporary relationships at the bottom. When the authorities seek to enforce the law, they find it difficult to locate and identify those responsible for illegal activities. Gangmasters disappear and then pop up somewhere else under a different name.

In 2004 twenty-three Chinese cockle-pickers working for gangmasters in Morecambe Bay were caught by the tide and died. The government responded with the 2004 Gangmaster Licensing Act, providing protection for workers in agriculture, horticulture, shellfish gathering, and related industries. In its 2009 report, Oxfam found that, although the Act had provided considerable protection, there was still much exploitation, with unlicensed gangmasters still operating and workers afraid to report abuses. The main problem, however, was the extension of gangmaster operations into areas unregulated by the Act, notably construction, care homes, cleaning, hotels and hospitality, where 'severe exploitation' could be found.

Sources: Lawrence (2005); Oxfam (2009).

⮊ See if you can find media coverage of the deaths of the twenty-three cockle-pickers in Morecambe Bay on 5 February 2004. How does this disaster exemplify the analysis above?

⮊ See if you can find recent media coverage of gangmaster operations outside the industries covered by the 1994 Act.

Discussion points

Capitalism and conflict

Before discussing this issue, read the sections on 'Industrial capitalism', 'Industrial conflict', 'Changes in industrial relations', and Media watch 17.

- Why is there a conflict between capital and labour?
- What are the main forms taken by this conflict?
- What strategies are pursued by capital and labour?
- When and why did strikes decline?
- How did the state curb the unions during the 1980s and 1990s?
- Why has union membership declined in Britain?
- Is this decline irreversible?
- In what ways has globalization weakened the power of labour?
- Can globalization explain the decline of the British unions?
- What is the significance of labour migration for the relationship between capital and labour?
- Can the conflict between capital and labour ever be overcome?

The employment of women

Before discussing this issue, read the sections on 'The growth of part-time employment', and 'The growing employment of women' (p. 681).

- Were women excluded from employment in paid work in the nineteenth century?
- In which occupations have women become increasingly employed?
- Does the growing employment of women show that occupations are no longer gendered?
- Why do you think women seek paid work?
- Can women be divided into the 'home centred' and the 'career centred'?
- Have changes in the domestic division of labour made possible the growing employment of women?
- Why has there been a growing demand for women's labour?
- Is the increasing employment of women the result of changes in what women want?

Explore further

The following references provide general discussions of the sociology of work and leisure:

Critcher, C., Bramham, P., and Tomlinson, A. (1995), *The Sociology of Leisure* (London: Chapman and Hall). *A wide-ranging collection of pieces on leisure and its relationship to work.*

Grint, K. (2000) (ed.), *Work and Society: A Reader* (Cambridge: Polity Press). *This useful collection focuses on some newer themes in the study of work, such as conceptions of time, child labour, and globalization, but also deals with such familiar topics as gender and ethnicity.*

Grint, K. (2005), *The Sociology of Work: An Introduction* (3rd edn, Cambridge: Polity Press). *Covers the standard topics of the sociology of work and links them well to the main theoretical traditions of sociology but also deals with housework, gender, and ethnicity, as well as globalization.*

Horne, J. (2006), *Sport in Consumer Culture* (Houndmills: Palgrave Macmillan). *This lively examination of a wide range of sporting activities plugs the sociology of sport into debates about culture and consumption and theories of consumer capitalism.*

Noon, M., and Blyton, P. (2007), *The Realities of Work* (3rd edn, London: Macmillan Business). *A refreshing look at work from an employee perspective, covering the significance of time for the experience of work, emotional labour, survival strategies in the workplace, and informal work.*

Particular aspects of the sociology of work and leisure are examined in the following:

Anderson, B. (2000), *Doing the Dirty Work: The Global Politics of Domestic Labour* (London: Zed Books). *A wide-ranging study of paid domestic work, based on research in five European cities in different countries.*

Bolton, S. (2005), *Emotion Management in the Workplace* (Basingstoke: Palgrave Macmillan). *A critical analysis of the development of the important topic of emotional labour, by the leading British researcher in this field.*

Bryman, A. (2004), *The Disneyization of Society* (London: Sage). *Examines the way that Disneyization has spread into all areas of leisure and changed the experience of work.*

Crompton, R. (1997), *Women and Work in Modern Britain* (Oxford: Oxford University Press). *A clearly and strongly argued analysis of women's work that examines the growing employment of women, setting this in the context of change in both the family and the economy, and examining international differences.*

Felstead, A., Jewson, N., and Walters, S. (2005), *Changing Places of Work* (Basingstoke: Palgrave Macmillan). *Theoretically aware and research-based, this book is full of insight into the control and experience of work in the multiple locations (office, home, and travel) characterizing it today.*

Franklin, A. (2003), *Tourism: An Introduction* (London: Sage). *Treats tourism as a central, not peripheral, part of contemporary social life.*

Fulcher, J. (2004), *Capitalism: A Very Short Introduction* (Oxford: Oxford University Press). *The title says it all. The latest reprint has a new preface examining the crisis of capitalism that began in 2007.*

Gall, G. (2009) (ed.), *Union Revitalisation in Advanced Economies* (Houndmills: Palgrave Macmillan). *An up-to-date assessment of the union response to decline in Britain, Canada, New Zealand, and the USA.*

Maguire, J. (2002) (ed.), *Theory, Sport, and Society* (Amsterdam: JAI Press). *A collection of classic and contemporary pieces on the sociology of sport.*

Smart, B. (2005), *The Sport Star: Modern Sport and the Cultural Economy of Sporting Celebrity* (London: Stage). *A theoretically informed discussion of stars, including David Beckham, but covering a wide range of issues in the sociology of sport and the development of modern sport in Britain and America.*

Sturdy, A., Grugulis, I., and Willmott, H. (2001) (eds), *Customer Service: Empowerment and Entrapment* (Basingstoke: Palgrave). *A reader with many interesting pieces on the character of service work, including emotional and aesthetic labour.*

Online resources

Visit the Online Resource Centre that accompanies this book to access more learning resources and other interesting material on work, employment, and leisure at:
www.oxfordtextbooks.co.uk/orc/fulcher4e/

Visit the Trades Union Congress website for information on unions, membership, policies, conferences, etc. at:
www.tuc.org.uk

The Centre for Labour Market Studies at the University of Leicester carries out research into many different aspects of work, employment, and human resources, and provides electronic versions of working papers and research reports:
www.clms.le.ac.uk

Information about the projects being carried out by the Economic and Social Research Council *Future of Work* programme can be found at:
www.leeds.ac.uk/esrcfutureofwork

For information about global trade unions and their campaigns visit:
www.global-unions.org

Inequality, Poverty, and Wealth

Contents

Social exclusion

Mary is a single mother living in South London. Her only income comes from welfare benefits: she receives child benefit and income support. This gives her nowhere near enough to meet the basic needs of herself and her children. She would spend what she had on the immediate costs of basic food, but ran up bills for electricity and other household costs. The crisis came when one of her children needed new shoes.

A neighbour suggested a solution. The neighbour knew how to arrange a loan for her from Provident Financial. A £200 loan would pay off all Mary's bills and let her buy the shoes, and Mary would simply have to pay it off week-by-week through her neighbour. Unfortunately, Mary could not meet these repayments, and the size of her debt grew. She took out a further loan of £500 to clear the debts, but she could not meet these new repayments and took out a further loan for £1,000. Mary was unable to pay her debts, which now amounted to £1,700.

The reason for Mary's difficulties was that Provident Financial is one of a number of loan companies that specializes in dealing with those who are too poor to get regular credit. It covers the inevitable bad debts by charging a high rate of interest. An overdraft or bank loan typically costs between 15 per cent and 25 per cent in interest. Mary was paying various rates between 170 and 330 per cent (*Guardian*, 10 April 2002).

Mary is typical of many of those living in poverty, who must rely on loan sharks, pawnbrokers, and provident finance companies for excessively expensive credit. Their limited resources give them few opportunities for taking up the 'cheap' and easy loan offers that come pouring through the letterboxes of more affluent households every day.

The circumstances of the borrowers contrast sharply with those of the lenders. In July 2005, Mark Johnson was imprisoned for making illegal loans. This was the first case brought under a new attempt to crack down on loan sharks. Johnson had made numerous small loans that were repayable within weeks and with penalties for any missed payments. He took the benefits booklets of those who missed their payments. Real rates of interest charged by Johnson often reached levels of 8,000 per cent. A newspaper report showed that:

> Johnson's loan shark racket earned him a luxurious lifestyle. Despite claiming to be on benefits, he spent between £30,000 and £40,000 on a high-performance BMW 330 convertible and a Porsche Cayenne. He also attempted to buy a half-million-pound house with a mortgage application that the court was told was 'worthy of a Booker nomination' and stated his annual income as £132,000. (*Guardian*, 27 July 2005)

How extensive is poverty today? This is a remarkably difficult question to answer, as it is extremely difficult to measure poverty, and judgements about poverty reflect complex moral and political considerations. Some have even questioned whether the word 'poverty' is still appropriate: if standards of living are so much better today than they were in the past, perhaps it no longer makes sense to define anyone as 'poor'.

The question of poverty cannot be considered separately from the question of inequality. It is structures of social inequality that generate both poverty and wealth. One of

Mary's fellow citizens, the author J. K. Rowling, is reported to earn over £3 million per week. The average weekly pay rate in Britain is currently around £489.

In this chapter we look at evidence on the distribution of income and assets and on the patterns of deprivation and privilege that result. We will try to answer the big question with which we began: how much poverty is there today? These are highly contested political issues, and we look at the various explanations and justifications that have been given for social inequality.

Concepts and theories

Social inequalities are structures of advantaged and disadvantaged **life chances**. These are the opportunities that a person has to acquire income, education, housing, health, and other valued resources. There is much disagreement about which, if any, inequalities are natural. Natural inequalities are social inequalities that result, ultimately, from innate or genetic differences and have to be seen as necessary and inevitable features of any human society. All other inequalities are purely conventional and so are subject to social reform and social change.

There are many biological differences in human populations. These range from such minor details as hair and skin colour, through differences in height, weight, and physique, to differences of sex. More contentiously, some have seen intelligence as, to a greater or lesser degree, innate. These differences are difficult to associate directly with social inequalities: in Chapters 5 and 6 we look at the difficulty of defining sexual and racial inequalities with any precision. Some biological differences are, of course, directly linked to human abilities. The ability to run fast, for example, is determined by physique, and the ability to undertake mathematical tasks may reflect innate intelligence. These abilities may, in turn, determine the chances of attaining the kinds of resources that generate social inequalities. For example, being able to run fast may enable a person to be successful in competitive sports, while an ability to do maths may lead to success in the competition for highly paid jobs.

This does not mean that natural differences are simply translated into social inequalities. Social factors shape natural differences in all sorts of ways. A person's physique and running skills, for example, can be transformed through regimes of training, while mathematical skills develop only if innate intellectual capacities are cultivated through appropriate socialization and education. There are also other determinants of success and failure. Success in competitive sports, for example, can depend on whether a person is selected for a particular team and whether the team's organizers are able to resource and plan its activities. Similarly, success in the competition for jobs may depend on such things as the connections and contacts that can be mobilized, the existence of prejudice, discrimination, and other forms of bias in recruitment, and so on. The successful conversion of any natural ability into a social advantage depends upon socially structured opportunities and circumstances.

For these reasons, it is difficult—if not impossible—to separate out 'natural' from 'artificial' aspects of social inequalities. For example, there has been much discussion about whether it is possible to distinguish genetic from environmental effects on measured intelligence. In the section on 'Equality and inequality' we will look at the importance of these issues in arguments about the relationship between intelligence, inequality, and social justice.

Equality and inequality

Sociological and moral ideas are sometimes difficult to separate in discussions of equality and inequality. Although sociological arguments should never be pre-empted by value judgements and political opinions, it is important to be aware of the ethical and political implications of sociological ideas and research.

Citizenship and equality

Equality has attracted many different political interpretations. Critics of equality—most notably those of the New Right—have argued that inequality is inevitable and, therefore, morally acceptable. They have often added, however, that structures of inequality are acceptable only if they are 'open'. This openness requires that there be equality of opportunity. The meaning of equality, then, is highly contested, and it is important to be clear about which of the many possible ideas of equality is under consideration.

The work of T. H. Marshall (1949) helps to clarify these issues. He showed how the development of welfare policies has been shaped by ideas concerning the rights and obligations of **citizenship**. A citizen is a full member of his or her society. Full members have rights and obligations, institutionalized in state policies and the practices of state agencies, that are denied to others who live in the same society. For example, adults in contemporary Britain have rights and obligations that are not allowed to children, and these rights and obligations are only gradually extended to people as they age. No one age is critical in acquiring citizenship rights in Britain today, though most major rights are acquired by the age of 21. These age-related rights are shown in Box 18.1.

Until quite recently, citizenship rights were restricted to certain sections of the adult population. For example, those who held no substantial property—the great majority of the population—were denied voting rights in British elections until well into the nineteenth century. African Americans were completely denied all basic rights under the system of slavery and gained equal rights with white Americans only in the 1960s. British legislation on sex and ethnicity rights are shown in Box 18.4, p. 703. Marshall's argument is that state policy only gradually extends

citizenship rights to all adults and others have pointed out that this often occurs only as a result of pressure exercised by social movements.

Marshall shows that in Britain civil and political rights were slowly extended from the mainly male property-owners to all men and to women, regardless of property. It was not until 1928, however, that all women received full voting rights in elections. Social rights to full participation in the cultural and communal life—rights to education, health, and welfare—were established towards the end of the nineteenth century. Marshall saw these social rights as having been fully established with the major policy reforms of the 1940s.

The extension of citizenship rights reflects changing views about the respects in which the members of a society should be treated as equal to one another. A central theme in many discussions of equality is that, in addition to equal rights, all citizens should enjoy broadly similar life chances (B. Turner 1996, and see our discussion of Giddens's idea of the 'third way' in Chapter 15, pp. 565, 579–82). There are, of course, many different views as to *how similar* and in *what respects* life chances should be equalized. It is possible to recognize three different conceptions of equality:

- equality of opportunity;
- equality of outset;
- equality of outcome.

Those who promote **equality of opportunity** hold that access to all social positions should be governed by universalistic criteria: positions should be open to all on the basis of merit and not because of birth or social background. This involves a move from *ascription* to *achievement* criteria in recruitment to social positions and implies that education should be the central mechanism of occupational recruitment and mobility. In this way, occupational achievement can reflect innate and cultivated talents (intelligence and skills). This close association between individual merit and social achievement has been called **meritocracy**.

Proponents of **equality of outset** hold that equality of opportunity makes sense only if people start out from similar positions. Using the model of a competitive race for social advantage, advocates of equality of outset hold that a fair and equal competition requires that all participants begin from the same starting line. If some enjoy advantages at the start, then the outcome of the race will not result only from differences in merit. Equality of outset has often been seen as a necessary condition for equality of opportunity to be truly effective.

Advocacy of **equality of outcome** is the most radical position, holding that all should enjoy the same standard of living and life chances: the rewards received by the successful should be no greater than those that go to the

---

Briefing: a selection of age-related citizenship rights, England and Wales   18.1

Age	Rights
0	Have a bank account, borrow money, be named on parent's passport
5	Start full-time education, drink alcohol in private, see U or PG film unaccompanied
7	Open a National Savings account
10	Be convicted of a criminal offence, be fingerprinted, photographed, and searched in custody
12	Buy a pet animal
13	Be employed part-time, with restrictions
14	Enter a pub, own a rifle, shotgun, or airgun
15	See a 15 certificate film
16	Get married with consent, drive a moped, consent to sex (females), get a passport with parental consent, drink alcohol with a restaurant meal, leave school, get a National Insurance number, join a trade union, buy cigarettes, buy fireworks, work full-time, join armed forces (males), change name by deed poll, pay NHS charges (if not in education), consent to medical treatment
17	Drive a motor vehicle, emigrate, join armed forces (females), no longer subject to care order
18	Vote in elections, get a passport, sue or be sued, serve on a jury, qualify for basic rate income support, marry, make a will, consent to homosexual act (males)
21	Stand for election, hold a licence to sell alcohol
25	Qualify for higher-rate income support
65	Qualify for state pension

➔ *Some rights and obligations, and the ages at which they apply, differ in Scotland and Northern Ireland.*

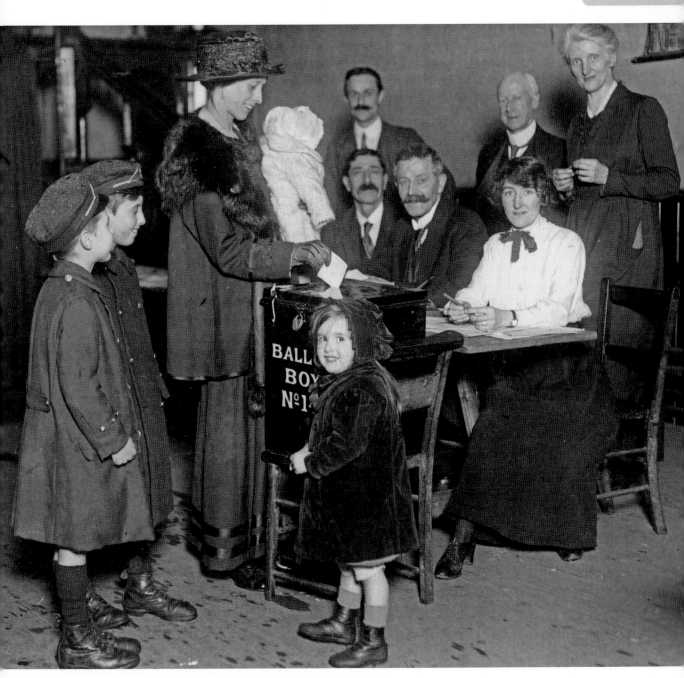

Votes for women (or most of them): the 1918 election.
© Getty Images/A. R. Coster

runners-up and the losers. Some see complete equality of outcome as an absolute goal in its own right. Others believe that it is a necessary condition for equality of outset, as winners of one race will otherwise have advantages at the start of the next. Views differ on whether this equality should be absolute and complete, or whether a limited degree of inequality can be allowed in order to motivate people towards achievement and success.

Structured inequality

All these views of equality see it as involving universalistic standards of judgement. **Universalism** means treating all people in the same way, without consideration for their particular characteristics. It rejects all arbitrary limitations on opportunities to participate fully in public life. In a universalistic system, all are free to achieve social goals through their own individual efforts. A **particularistic** system, on the other hand, restricts opportunities to certain social groups or categories: men, whites, Protestants, kin, and so on. The extension of citizenship rights in contemporary societies has involved a principle that economic resources be distributed on a purely universalistic basis.

Universalism operates most effectively through either a market mechanism or a bureaucratic mechanism. In a market system, individuals are rewarded according to the supply and demand for their skills or abilities. No account is taken of their particular circumstances or characteristics. The wages paid to engineers, for example, should depend on their technical knowledge and not on their gender or ethnicity. In a bureaucratic system, on the other hand, payments to individuals are based on political considerations that, again, should not vary with an individual's background. Someone who receives a welfare benefit would receive it because he or she has a specific need: the Jobseeker's Allowance, for example, is paid to all those who are unemployed and who meet certain universal criteria of eligibility, not only to those from particular ethnic groups.

> ### ⊃ Connections
>
> The distinction between market and bureaucratic systems for the provision of welfare is sometimes described as one between commodified and juridified provision. These terms are defined and applied in Chapter 20, p. 812, and Chapter 15, pp. 563–4.

Actual markets and bureaucracies do not work in quite this way. Even where universalistic standards are formally acknowledged, women and members of ethnic minorities, for example, have often been excluded or disadvantaged on grounds that have nothing to do with their abilities or needs. Purely universalistic principles, then, can be undermined by the informal and unofficial use of particularistic principles. Employers may, for example, discriminate against women, even when they are fully qualified for a job.

Social inequalities, then, are structured by a combination of formal and informal processes. The formal mechanisms of the job market and the welfare bureaucracy have been expected to operate according to universalistic standards, but this has been undermined by unofficial forms of bias and discrimination. Indeed, official policies themselves have sometimes been built around particularism and discrimination. The most important bases on which universalistic principles have been undermined is through ethnicity and gender. This was the argument of Martineau (1837) that was reiterated by Myrdal (1944).

We showed in Chapter 6 that racist discourse produces racial disadvantage. Skin colour and other visible markers of ethnic difference can be used to justify exclusion of some

from rights and advantages enjoyed by others. Terms such as black and white, for example, are widely used in Britain, the United States, and elsewhere as signs of racial difference. Although the concept of race has no biological foundation, it is used by many to disparage or disadvantage members of other ethnic groups. Through prejudiced attitudes and stereotyped identities, one ethnic group can assert its superiority over another. Racial disadvantage may also result from institutional racism.

Similar distinctions can be made concerning sex–gender differences. A sexist discourse is a system of ideas in which sex–gender categories play a central part and that disadvantages women in relation to men, or, far less often, men in relation to women. It is the use of particular language or categories, rather than people's intentions, that is so important in producing discrimination and disadvantage. To object to racist and sexist language is not to be 'politically correct'; it is to recognize the impact that language can have on people's life chances.

Sexism is a complex of structures and processes of discrimination and inequality built around a sexist discourse, and can be distinguished from the broader idea of institutionalized gender disadvantage. The latter occurs when, for example, women with young children are unable to take certain jobs because of a lack of childcare facilities. They would experience sexism if they were denied job opportunities simply because they were women.

A number of Acts have been passed to limit racism and sexism. These have generally been introduced only after long political struggles by excluded groups. Some

> ### Briefing: sexism in employment   18.2
>
> Discrimination against women in employment is nothing new. In the past it was often overt and accepted as legitimate. Women were formally excluded from many areas of employment, as this article from the 1920s shows:
>
> > The employment of married women in schools and in certain other capacities was discussed by the London County Council yesterday. The matter arose upon a joint report of the General Purposes Committee making recommendations that, with certain exceptions, married women should not be employed in the schools. Sir John Gilbert said that . . . the Council had a more than sufficient supply of well-qualified women and there was no evidence that the work of the Council had suffered through the non-employment of married women.
>
> *Source: Manchester Guardian, 17 February 1926.*
>
> ❓ *Would you expect to find similar public statements being made today?*

legislation, however, restricts citizenship rights and may itself be an expression of racist or sexist ideas. Immigration into Britain, for example, has been regulated through a series of Acts that have defined nationality in restrictive ways that will limit the numbers of immigrants from particular countries (Layton-Henry 1984). Discussion of the rights that ought to be enjoyed by asylum-seekers and of legislation aimed at controlling international terrorism has often invoked racist ideas. Legislation embodying racist ideas is likely to conflict with Acts aimed at regulating discrimination.

Poverty and citizenship

The distribution of economic resources invariably creates a structure of social inequality with extremes of poverty and wealth. Various attempts have been made to draw a poverty line—and more recently a wealth line—to highlight the points at which these extreme conditions occur. Poverty has often been defined in relation to the basic subsistence requirements, seeing the poor as those unable to meet basic human needs for food and housing. These attempts have not been successful. Poverty and wealth must be seen in relation to what is the normal standard of living in a particular society, rather than in relation to an arbitrary subsistence requirement. For this reason, poverty and wealth are related to the criteria defining citizenship.

Drawing a poverty line

The idea that poverty is a matter of subsistence rests on the view that human beings have basic physiological requirements for food, clothing, and shelter that can be established with scientific certainty and that can be used to draw a poverty line to distinguish the poor from the rest of society. People live in poverty if their income is too low for them to afford what is required for their physical survival.

Rowntree (1901), for example, used medical studies of nutrition to identify the calorie intakes required for individuals of different ages and sexes. What he called the standard diet consists of the cheapest and most basic foods that can supply these needs. Rowntree estimated the cost of this food and added an estimate of the amount he thought was needed for basic clothing, fuel, and housing. Rowntree's standard diet was based closely on the diet of the inmates of the York workhouse. It was, therefore, tied closely to official estimates of the minimum standard of living thought appropriate for people at the time.

Rowntree recognized that the amount of food and the type of housing needed, and therefore the monetary value given to a poverty line, depend upon the size and composition of a household. A couple need more money than a single person, and those with children need more than the childless. Rowntree calculated, for example, that a family with two adults and three children needed, in 1899, a weekly income of 21s. 8d. (about £1.08 in decimal currency). Rowntree used this household as an example and assigned households of varying sizes to positions above or below the line according to whether their actual income was equivalent to that needed by the example household.

This seems to provide an obvious and plausible definition of poverty. It is attractive to policy-makers because it seems to offer the possibility of a clear and attainable poverty policy. The aim of a poverty programme can be to ensure that the whole of the population has sufficient income to meet all its physiological subsistence needs, and governments and others can monitor progress towards this goal. Rowntree was, in fact, very influential among those responsible for official policy on poverty in Britain. Similar approaches were taken in the United States and many other countries.

Some commentators have gone even further and have held that people can be said to be living in poverty only if they are so lacking in resources that they are close to starvation. This leads them to claim that the absence of starvation conditions in contemporary Europe and America means that the struggle against poverty has been won in these countries. It is, of course, very important to distinguish between starvation and other kinds of human hardship. It is also true that the incidence of starvation is much lower in Britain today than it was in the nineteenth century. Similarly, it is very much lower than it is in many Third World countries today. However, poverty is still real, even when it does not lead to starvation or near-starvation.

Harsh as it was, Rowntree's subsistence standard was not a starvation standard. To his basic physiological subsistence measure, he added estimates for the kind of housing and clothing that he and others of his time felt it was appropriate for people to have. There was, then, a cultural element in his definition of poverty. Even the standard diet was based on customary ideas about appropriate kinds of food: it is, after all, possible to meet a specific calorie intake with caviar and smoked salmon or with bread and potatoes. Rowntree's conclusions about what should be included in the basic budget of a household reflected his culture-bound judgements and not simply the requirements of nutrition (see Box 18.3, p. 702).

Recognizing this point led Townsend (1974) to argue that poverty can be defined only in relative and never in absolute terms. A subsistence standard might appear to be absolute and physiologically determined, but this is not the case. It always involves historically and culturally relative standards. Researchers and policy-makers, therefore, must use a concept of **relative poverty**. People live in poverty if their way of life is deprived relative to that customary in their society. Customary standards change over time, and so the poverty line also alters. What might have been a

Briefing: the standard diet   18.3

Rowntree (1901: 99–102) gives long and complex day-to-day tabulations of the food needed for men, women, and children. To illustrate his method, the list below shows the diet that he specified for one particular day (Monday) for a man, a woman, and a child aged 3–8.

	Breakfast	Dinner	Supper	Calories
Man	bread 8 oz	boiled bacon 3 oz	bread 8 oz	3,560
	margarine ½ oz	pease pudding 12 oz	margarine ½ oz	
	tea 1 pt		cocoa 1 pt	
Woman	bread 4 oz	potatoes with milk 20 oz	bread 6 oz	2,987
	porridge 1 pt	bread 2 oz	vegetable broth 1 pt	
		cheese 1½ oz	cheese 2 oz	
Child	bread 2 oz	potatoes with milk 12 oz	bread 5 oz	1,824
	new milk ½ pt	bread 2 oz	new milk ½ pt	
	porridge ½ pt	cheese ½ oz		
	sugar ½ oz			

Note: 1 oz = 28.3 g.

minimum acceptable diet in Victorian Britain is not acceptable to people today. Townsend concluded that poverty must always be measured in relation to whatever standards of acceptability and unacceptability actually prevail in a society. To be deprived in a particular society—to live in poverty—is to be excluded from the kind and level of living that is regarded by its members as normal.

This view of poverty rests on a particular understanding of citizenship. To be a citizen, a full member of a society, is to be able to meet the expectations attached to parenthood, work, politics, neighbourliness, and friendship. Central to citizenship in modern societies are its social rights: rights to health, education, and welfare, and to the basic income that allows people to meet the normal obligations and standard of living expected of them. Social expectations of what is to count as a normal or acceptable way of life are institutionalized and become the basis for perceptions of deprivation. Legal definitions of important citizenship rights are shown in Boxes 18.1 (p. 698) and 18.4.

With the establishment of an idea of citizenship, demands for improved welfare facilities and for redistributive taxes can be made on the grounds that the existing distribution of resources does not allow everybody to participate fully as citizens of their society. Those who lack the necessary resources are denied the opportunity to exercise their citizenship rights in full. People live in poverty, then, if their lack of material resources deprives them of the opportunities that are normally open to citizens. They can neither meet their obligations, nor exercise their rights as citizens. The poverty line is a line in the distribution of resources that divides the deprived from the rest of the population.

Wealth and the wealthy

Wealth can also be defined in relative terms. The poor are excluded from full public participation, but the wealthy have resources that allow them to enjoy benefits and advantages not available to others in their society. The poor are deprived or excluded from public life; the wealthy, or the rich, are privileged because they can deny their special advantages to the general public (J. Scott 1994).

The standpoint from which both poverty and wealth are judged is the accepted view of what is normal for citizens in a particular society. The wealthy are able to enjoy life chances and lifestyles that are superior to those recognized as normal. They are able to enjoy what are culturally regarded as privileges, luxuries, or advantages. Poverty and wealth, then, are conditions that differ, in opposite directions, from the normal lifestyle of the citizen.

The poverty line is a point towards the bottom of the distribution of resources at which deprivation begins.

Briefing: Acts against discrimination   18.4

The main Acts that have regulated nationality and discrimination on the grounds of gender and ethnicity are listed below, though sections in many other Acts are also relevant.

British Nationality Act 1948	Distinguished 'UK and Colonies' citizens from 'Commonwealth' citizens
Commonwealth Immigrants Act 1962	Limited rights of immigration for Commonwealth citizens to those with employment vouchers
Commonwealth Immigrants Act 1968	Limited rights of immigration for UK and Colonies citizens to those with British parent or grandparent or from countries made independent before 1948
Immigration Act 1971	Required Commonwealth citizens who did not have a British parent or grandparent to be treated in the same way as any other foreigner
British Nationality Act 1981	Distinguished British citizens from two categories of overseas and dependent territories citizens, only British citizens having full rights of abode
Race Relations Act 1965	Made illegal discrimination on the basis of 'race, colour, or ethnic or national origin' in public places
Race Relations Act 1968	Made racial discrimination illegal in employment, housing, and other areas
Race Relations Act 1976	Set up Community Relations Commission and allowed cases to be taken to industrial tribunals
Race Relations (Amendment) Act 2000	Extended coverage of 1976 Act to public authorities such as the police
Representation of the People Act 1928	Gave full voting rights to all women over 21
Equal Pay Act 1970	Required equal pay for men and women doing work that was the same or similar
Sex Discrimination Act 1975	Made illegal sexual discrimination in employment, education, and other areas
Disability Discrimination Act 1995	Prohibited discrimination against disabled people in employment, education, retailing, access to transport and premises, education
Sex Discrimination (Gender Reassignment) Regulations 1999	Extended Sex Discrimination Act to transsexuals
Special Educational Needs and Disability Act 2001	Made discrimination illegal in education on the grounds of mental health or disability
Sex Discrimination (Election Candidates) Act 2002	Amended Sex Discrimination Act to allow positive measures by political parties to increase the numbers of women elected
Employment Equality (Sexual Orientation) Regulations 2003	Made illegal discrimination in employment or training on the grounds of sexual orientation. Related regulations prohibited discrimination on the grounds of religious belief

❷ *Look at the various laws concerning immigration and nationality. Do they have equal consequences for blacks and whites? You can find useful background to this question in Solomos (1993) and D. Mason (2000).*

Briefing: the changing value of money 18.5

It is very difficult to compare incomes over time, because of the changing value of money. As prices rise, a given *money wage* loses its purchasing power. As a very rough guide, £1 in the early 1900s bought about fifty times as much as £1 in the 2000s. To overcome this problem, money wages are often converted to *real wages* that reflect their purchasing power. Wages for 1906 and 2006, for example, can be compared 'at 2006 prices'.

In 1900, unskilled manual workers were paid an average of £1.05 per week, while skilled manual workers received £2 per week. In 2009, average weekly earnings were £489.

A good website for making price comparisons over time and in different countries can be found at: **www.ex.ac.uk/~RDavies/arian/current/howmuch.html**

THEORY AND METHODS 18.6

Relative and absolute poverty

An absolute view of poverty tries to measure it in terms of a fixed and unchanging baseline. Poverty is seen as defined by physiological subsistence or fixed human needs. A relative view of poverty measures it in terms of changing social standards of need. Poverty is defined relative to the level of comfort enjoyed by the majority of people in a society and that is socially recognized as normal or desirable for all.

poverty and wealth can then be counted and their lifestyles uncovered.

Inequality, intelligence, and genetics

Many of those who live in long-term poverty are members of ethnic minorities or are living in lone-parent, female-headed households. Politicians on the right, and some on the left, have often used the term 'underclass' as a way of denying that these poor people suffer from racism, sexism, or other forms of institutionalized disadvantage. Their argument is that the poor are poor because of natural, innate inequalities that divide people. The poor have certain innate biological characteristics that predispose them towards poverty. This is one of the most contentious issues in recent discussions of social policy.

The undeserving poor and the underclass

These ideas have a long history. In the eighteenth century, Malthus (whose views we look at in Chapter 8, pp. 278–9) saw poverty as related to population growth. He argued that restricting the welfare level—then already very low—would be an incentive to work and to limit families to a size that could be supported from wages. When this so-called moral restraint is absent, Malthus held, poverty tends to increase. There is a 'redundant population' of vicious, indolent, ignorant, and dependent individuals, who deserve nothing better than to perish in the struggle for subsistence. These were the 'undeserving poor', who were believed to refuse work, even when it was available.

Commentators and social investigators attempted to distinguish the undeserving poor from others who happened to live in poverty. In a remarkable account of life in the slum districts of London between the 1840s and the 1860s, Henry Mayhew showed that employment opportunities were unequally distributed. Many people could obtain only irregular or casual work that did not pay them

The wealth line, on the other hand, is a point towards the top of the distribution at which privilege begins. The wealth line divides the rich from everybody else. This line is more difficult to draw, and it has been far less well researched than the poverty line. It is, nevertheless, just as real. The poverty line and the wealth line are important lines of social division, and they may often become significant lines of social fracture. Poverty and wealth are polar positions in the distribution of resources, and one cannot be understood without the other. The causes of poverty cannot be separated from the causes of wealth, and policies aimed at reducing poverty will have repercussions for the existence of wealth.

Poverty and wealth, understood as economic conditions that are *relative* to social standards of citizenship, are integral features of any system of inequality. They could disappear only if there was a very flat and egalitarian distribution of resources, or if there was no consensus over minimum or maximum citizen entitlements. A society that accepted the legitimacy of whatever inequalities were generated by the free and unfettered operation of the market mechanism would have its extremes of income and assets, but it would have no poverty or wealth. This is why many neo-liberal governments in the 1980s and 1990s began to deny that poverty existed and, in many cases, abandoned the collection and publication of official statistics on poverty. However, this view did not go unchallenged, as many in the wider society still believed that there ought to be both a floor and a ceiling to the distribution of resources and life chances.

A task for sociology is to chart the extent of inequality that exists in a particular society and to identify the levels at which deprivation and privilege begin. The numbers in

Two faces of housing.
© Lucy Dawkins

enough to escape a life of poverty. These people were *forced* into degrading conditions by their circumstances. Nevertheless, there were others who *chose* a life of degradation by avoiding any form of steady work and who maintain themselves through street trading, begging, and criminal activities. Mayhew's work saw the distinction between the deserving and the undeserving poor as one between 'those who cannot work' and 'those who will not work'. He thought this moral distinction had a biological basis. The undeserving poor were, almost literally, a 'race' apart, people whose biological traits predisposed them towards a culture of poverty organized around habits of vice, ignorance, and barbarism.

This outlook dominated Victorian thought. The poor were seen as deserving public or charitable support only if they were willing to embrace the norms and values of respectable society and help themselves to escape from their poverty. These 'respectable poor' were deserving of help because their poverty was a temporary condition that could and should be alleviated. On the other hand, those who rejected respectability and pursued a life of

degradation and crime were seen as 'undeserving'. They were described as the 'dangerous classes' because of the threat that they were thought to pose to social order. (For a general review of this idea, see Stedman Jones 1971, and L. Morris 1994: ch. 1.)

Marx took a much more critical view of Victorian capitalism, but he also made a similar distinction. According to Marx, movement in and out of poverty depended, among other things, on the incidence of unemployment. Those who are put out of work in times of economic stagnation, he argued, become a reserve army of labour that can be called back into work when the economy is growing. Marx saw a segment of the long-term unemployed as a 'stagnant' group that could hope only for casual, irregular, and low-paid work. Their circumstances brought them closer and closer to the vagrants and criminals that Marx called the lumpenproletariat. Marx's contrast between this stagnant proletariat—forced into pauperism—and the 'depraved' lumpenproletariat—who chose it—repeated the conventional distinction between the deserving and the undeserving poor.

The growth of poverty in recent years has led to a revival of the notion of the undeserving poor in the form of the **underclass**. While this term has been used in a tentative and careful way in social research, many political commentators associated with the New Right have given it a moral dimension. In their hands, it has become a pejorative label with which to blame the victims of poverty for their own deprivation. They argue that there is a genetically inferior underclass of welfare recipients whose poverty is a consequence of their lack of intelligence and their cultural outlook rather than of any structurally determined differences in opportunity and advantage.

Those who have tried to use the word in a neutral, analytical sense have often found that their research has been distorted by political commentators. This is, of course, the fate of much sociological research, but it has been a particular problem in poverty research. In this and in the following chapter we will set out some criticisms of the idea of an underclass. We will show that, even when it is stripped of its moral dimension and used as a purely analytical concept, it misrepresents the realities of contemporary economic divisions.

The immediate source for much recent discussion of the underclass is work undertaken in the United States. Charles Murray's *Losing Ground* (1984), attempts to identify those of the poor who deserved support through the public welfare system and those who did not. Drawing on sociological research by Frazier (1932) and Moynihan (1965) on life in African American districts, Murray documents the poverty and 'social pathology' of the inner-city ghettos. The residents of these areas, he says, live in a culture of poverty (see Lewis 1961, 1966) that encourages fatalism and an acceptance of their situation as in the nature of things. Their concern is for the present and for immediate gratification. There is no interest in planning for the future. The inhabitants of these areas, Murray argues, show high levels of indolence, illegitimacy, drunkenness, and criminality. He places particular emphasis on the effects of being brought up in lone-parent, female-headed households. In these households, he claims, discipline is poor and boys have no appropriate male role models to show them the virtues of the work ethic and the morality of responsible parenthood.

The existence of large numbers of lone-parent households, Murray argues, is a result of the high level of welfare benefits. Dependence on these benefits, he argues, prevents people from taking responsibility for their own lives. When welfare levels are high, unmarried women are encouraged to have children that they could not otherwise support. Murray advocated a reduction in benefits, believing that this would encourage more self-reliance. Faced with reduced benefits, many more young women would remain childless and would go out to work, or they would marry a man who would support their children.

THEORY AND METHODS   **18.7**

Averages

There are a number of ways of measuring the 'average' figure in a distribution. The most common is what is technically called the *mean*. This comes the closest to what is meant by the word 'average' in everyday life—for example, in the points average of a football team. The mean for a set of figures is calculated by adding them all up and then dividing by the total number of cases. So, the mean income for a group of people is the total of all their incomes, divided by the number of people.

Other measures of average are the median and the mode. The *median* is the middle value in a distribution, the point at which it divides evenly in half. There are as many people above the median as there are below it. When a distribution, such as that of income, is skewed towards the top, the mean income will be higher than the median income. The *mode* is less widely used, but is the most frequently occurring value in a distribution. The mode is the 'typical' or most 'popular' value.

Murray and a number of others have tried to link the intelligence of those in the underclass with their 'race' (Jensen 1969; Herrnstein and Murray 1994; for critical commentaries, see Flynn 1980 and S. Fraser 1995). They have claimed that the disadvantaged position of African Americans can be explained by their lower intelligence than white Americans. Herrnstein and Murray, for example, have estimated that the median intelligence of black Americans is much lower than that of white Americans. This is a highly contentious claim, and all its various elements have been questioned.

Intelligence: heredity versus environment

Many aspects of Murray's argument have their roots in nineteenth-century discussions of 'eugenics'. A growing acceptance of Darwin's ideas on 'natural selection' after the 1860s led many to argue that there should be a scientific selection of those with the most desirable physical and moral qualities. Eugenists believed that human populations could be bred for appropriate characteristics, much as horses, domestic animals, and farm animals are bred for their speed, strength, or food value. They suggested that social arrangements should discourage the undeserving, unintelligent poor from breeding, while still encouraging the middle classes and other respectable members of society to increase their numbers. Poverty could be eliminated by selective breeding.

Some eugenists combined an emphasis on biological factors with a belief in the reality of race differences. Many of the poor were Irish or Jewish migrants, and eugenicists blamed their poverty on their assumed racial characteristics. A policy of eugenics can lead, all too easily, to a policy for the elimination of particular racial groups aimed at improving the genetic stock of the population.

A looser form of eugenics lay behind the development of attempts to measure intelligence and to associate it with social inequalities (Galton 1869). According to this point of view, the role of environmental factors had to be recognized alongside the part played by 'heredity'. This work led to the construction of IQ (intelligence quotient) tests to measure intelligence. The statistician Spearman (1904) introduced the concept of 'g' (general intelligence) to describe the general cognitive ability that lay behind specific linguistic, mathematical, spatial, and musical abilities and forms of intelligence. IQ tests promised the possibility that the relationship between material inequalities and social inequalities could be studied with mathematical precision.

THEORY AND METHODS   **18.8**

IQ

IQ is measured through tests of logic and mathematics. Tests are devised so that the mean score will be 100. Particular scores are represented as ratios of this average: an IQ of 110 is 10 per cent above average, while an IQ of 85 is 15 per cent below average. The tests are also devised so as to produce a 'normal distribution' of results. This is a statistical distribution of the frequency of scores that, when drawn as a graph, is described as a 'bell curve'. In the normal distribution, most people cluster around the mean and relatively few have very high or very low scores. The normal distribution has particular mathematical properties that make it useful for statistical purposes.

Attempts by Burt (1946) to use the idea of IQ in educational research have been seriously questioned after it was found that he had fraudulently manipulated some of his results (see Hearnshaw 1979; but see also Joynson 1989; Fletcher 1991; and Mackintosh 1995). A useful overview is in Gould (1981).

Figure 18.1 A bell curve

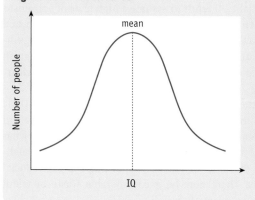

Arguments that link inherited intelligence to social disadvantage rest on the assumption that measures of social advantage and disadvantage correlate highly with measures of general intelligence, which can be accurately measured by IQ tests. If differential advantage is determined by differences in general intelligence, intelligence can be seen as genetically determined and so fixed from birth. Education and other environmental factors have little or no effect on the level of intelligence.

The concept of general intelligence has been heavily criticized, and there is no agreement that there is any such common factor behind particular abilities. Mathematical and verbal intelligence, for example, are not perfectly associated with one another. It may be more useful to regard intelligence as a set of intellectual capacities rather than a single one. Even if it is accepted that general intelligence exists, there is the problem of how it is to be measured. Many social scientists have questioned the value of the IQ score as a measure of intelligence. Tests have been shown to be culturally biased towards Western (American and European) culture and, within this, towards white, middle-class men. The cultural differences that shape the ability to perform in the tests do not necessarily reflect differences in intelligence. More fundamentally, perhaps, are doubts about whether performance in pencil-and-paper tests can be a proper measure of a person's ability to perform in 'real' situations. Indeed, there are wider doubts about whether performance in A level, degree, or other examinations is an adequate measure of the understanding of a subject or the ability to apply it in real-life situations.

Intelligence is a complex process that brings together numerous aspects of brain function, and doubts have been raised about its genetic basis. It is inherited not as a fixed quantity but as a capacity to learn the kinds of skills and understandings that make up a particular ability. The realization of this capacity depends on the stimulation received in the first few years of life and, to a much lesser extent, in later life. It has been found that pre-school, primary socialization is critical in raising or lowering measured intelligence. Formal education can have a continuing, if smaller, effect, and educational action programmes can significantly raise the IQ of children who enter them with relatively low IQ. Cross-cultural studies have shown that the relatively high IQ of East Asians, as compared with North Americans, is due to the length and type of schooling, the extent of parental support, and the cultural support for disciplined work.

⊃ Connections

Look back at our discussion of educational achievement in Chapter 9, pp. 330–3, for more information on the effects of schooling on different ethnic groups.

As we show in Chapter 6, most reputable scientists long ago rejected the concept of race. It is hardly surprising to find, then, that differences in intelligence between ethnic groups do not directly reflect genetic differences. The attributes that have been treated as racial characteristics show much greater variation *within* categories than they do *between* them. While the measured IQs of blacks and whites show a difference in median scores, many blacks have higher IQs than the average white, and many whites have a lower IQ than the average black. This is one reason why the evidence garnered by Herrnstein and Murray shows such a low level of association between IQ and social disadvantage. If intelligence is not genetically determined, but is partly influenced by environmental factors, then the impact of purely *inherited* intelligence on social disadvantage must be very slight.

The ability to perform well or badly in an IQ test is, to a very great extent, a consequence of the whole way of life of a group. It reflects education and social class, as well as ethnicity. The fact that those labelled black may score lower in intelligence tests has nothing to do with their skin colour.

Openness and meritocracy

The eugenic theories that we looked at in the last few pages have tried to relate social inequalities directly to natural inequalities. Genetic differences among individuals are seen as determining their intelligence and talents, and these, in turn, are seen as the basis of social inequalities. Those who are successful and those who fail have the positions they deserve on the basis of their naturally given abilities. Even if the genetic basis of this argument is rejected, however, there still remains the question of the relationship between social inequalities and the actual distribution of abilities. These abilities may be the product of environmental, rather than hereditary factors, but is it the case that structures of social inequality directly reflect their distribution? If they do, then the structure of inequality can be seen as a meritocracy. These issues have been examined in the debate around the so-called functionalist theory of inequality.

The functionalist theory of inequality

The functionalist theory of inequality (Davis and Moore 1945) is a much misunderstood theory, not least because of some of the rather simplistic statements made by its own supporters. Nevertheless, it does offer a useful, if partial approach to openness and inequality.

The theory assumes that the various social positions in a society require different skills and abilities for their performance. It is important that people with skills (or with the ability to acquire them) are encouraged, trained, and recruited to the appropriate social positions. This is especially important for those social positions that are critical for the survival or maintenance of the society. The theory concludes that societies will tend to develop a system of values that recognizes the differing functional importance of social positions. Attaching high rewards to important positions makes it possible to ensure that people with the required skills and abilities will, in fact, be motivated to take them on and to perform them effectively. The theory suggests, for example, that an industrial capitalist society that fails to recognize the functional importance of engineers and entrepreneurs for the continued production of goods that can be sold at a profit is likely to decline relative to its competitors, even if this decline takes some time (M. J. Weiner 1981; but see Rubinstein 1993).

> **⊃ Connections**
>
> This theory of inequality adopts the general functionalist approach that we discuss in Chapter 2, pp. 45–7. If you are uncertain about this theory, you might like to look at that discussion now.

The theory rests upon a model of supply and demand. It holds that, if the skills and abilities required for a social position are not especially unusual, and so are in easy and plentiful supply, there is no need for any great reward to be attached to them. This is the case, no matter how important a position may be: an important job that is easy to do is likely to recruit sufficient people so long as its wages are not too low in relation to alternative and similar occupations. If, on the other hand, the requisite skills and abilities are difficult to acquire, or are possessed by only a few people, they are likely to be in short supply. In these circumstances, high rewards will have to be attached to the position or not enough people will be recruited. This model is set out in the diagram shown in Figure 18.2; see also Box 18.9.

There are many problems with the functionalist theory of inequality. It tends to assume a high level of consensus in societies, and it assumes that people are motivated purely by rational economic considerations. Most significantly, it is not at all clear that it is possible to distinguish important from unimportant occupations in any clear-cut way.

The theory's main limitation is that it applies in whole only to those societies where social mobility is easy and typical among its various social positions. The theory has no place for ascriptive social factors and material inequalities (of outset or of outcome) that might prevent social mobility. There may be a considerable waste of talent

A parable of functional importance

The rulers of the planet of Golgafrincham decided to rid themselves of those in useless occupations: personnel officers, public-relations executives, hairdressers, and telephone sanitizers. These people—all rather dim—were told that the planet was doomed and that it was to be evacuated for another, safer planet. The telephone sanitizers and others were to be sent off into outer space as an advance party. One of them said:

> ... the idea was that into the first ship, the 'A' ship, would go all the brilliant leaders, the scientists, the great artists, you know, all the achievers; and then into the third, or 'C' ship, would go all the people who did the actual work, who made things and did things; and then into the 'B' ship—that's us—would go everyone else ... And we were sent off first.

A chronicler continues the story:

> It was ... an eccentric poet who invented the spurious tales of impending doom which enabled the people of Golgafrincham to rid themselves of an entire useless third of their population. The other two-thirds stayed firmly at home and lived full, rich and happy lives until they were all suddenly wiped out by a virulent disease contracted from a dirty telephone.

Source: Adapted from Douglas Adams (1980).

❷ What does this fictional account tell us about the difficulty of measuring functional importance?

❷ Is it feasible to try to assess the functional importance of different jobs today? How would you go about this?

whenever these occur on any scale, as talented individuals are prevented from rising into the positions where they could best exercise their talents. There may also be a dangerous incapacity at the top, as incompetents would face no pressure towards downward mobility.

In spite of this limitation, the functionalist theory of inequality does provide a useful, if partial, explanation of the mechanisms that are responsible for social inequality in actual societies, and of some of the ways in which particular structures of inequality may change over time.

Figure 18.2 The functionalist theory of reward and recruitment

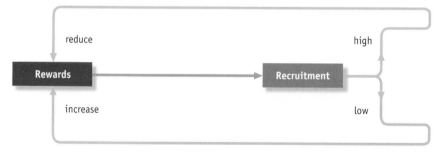

⚠ *Stop and reflect*

In this section we have looked at the relationship between equality, natural differences, and the openness of social structures.

- Social inequalities cannot be reduced to natural, biological differences. They are the outcome of complex social processes.

- Do you agree that the ideas of the underclass and the undeserving poor tend to confuse moral judgements with factual judgements?

We also looked at how ideas of equality and inequality must be seen in relation to the idea of citizenship, and we looked at some of the ways in which sexism and racism affect social inequality.

- Conceptions of citizenship rights and obligations set the basis for understanding poverty, wealth, and equality. Poverty must be distinguished from starvation and must be seen as a socially relative condition.

- Racism and sexism are major causes of systematic social disadvantage. For this reason, the association between intelligence and social inequality is far more complex than is often assumed.

- How plausible is it to claim that poverty is a historically and culturally relative condition? Does this view undermine the reality and objectivity of poor living conditions?

Inequalities in modern societies are organized around property and occupations. We looked at a set of issues related to the merit, skills, and functional importance of occupations.

- The functionalist theory of inequality offers a useful, but partial explanation of social inequality in terms of supply, demand, and cultural values.

- The functional importance of an occupation is difficult to measure. Judgements of functional importance can often involve value judgements.

- Does the attempt to talk about 'functional importance' involve the making of value judgements about particular occupations?

Equality, merit, and welfare

An open society can be an unequal society, and an unequal society can have extremes of poverty and wealth. Sociological research explores the extent of inequality, both of outset and of outcome, as well as its openness. This involves assessing the level of poverty and wealth and of changes over time. In this section we look at how these matters have been handled and at the conclusions that have been drawn from empirical research.

The drive towards equality

Central to the structure of inequality in modern societies is the distribution of economic resources among individuals and households. The economic resources of a household determine opportunities to purchase consumer goods, to obtain housing and use transport facilities, to provide for the future welfare of its members (for example, through saving for a pension or taking out an insurance policy), and to purchase such things as private health treatment and private schooling. The distribution of economic resources, then, underlies the whole range of household life chances.

Income and assets

Economic resources take the form of income and assets. **Income** is a flow of resources that a person or household receives during a particular period. It is the number of

Income and assets of the wealthy depend upon the operations of international money markets.

© Getty Images/Pierre Barbier

pounds, dollars, or euros that they receive each week, month, or year. Income comprises wages or salaries from employment, interest on savings and other personal investments, and profits from business or trading. It can also include income in kind, such as the provision of a company car, cheap housing, health insurance, and so on. Incomes of all types are usually subject to taxation, whether as direct taxes such as income tax, or indirect taxes such as council tax and sales tax or VAT. Rates of tax can vary with the type of income and the personal circumstances of the recipient. It is usual to distinguish between measures of income distribution before tax and after tax in order to recognize the redistributive effects of the tax system.

Assets, on the other hand, comprise the total stock of economic resources that a person or household has accumulated. These may be physical assets such as land or houses, or financial assets such as bank deposits, shares, or ISAs. Assets often generate income. A bank deposit, for example, earns interest. Similarly, an income may help to accumulate assets, as when part of an income is invested rather than spent. Assets are often referred to as 'wealth' by economists, but our earlier definition of wealth and the wealthy uses the word in a sense that is closer to its everyday meaning. To avoid any confusion, then, we will use only the word assets to refer to a person's stock of economic resources.

Much information on the distribution of economic resources comes from official statistics, and we show in Chapter 3, pp. 99–103, how difficult it is to rely on these for precise information. Nevertheless, there are comprehensive and long-standing series of statistics on these matters, and many statisticians and economists have gone to great lengths to clarify them and to make them more useful for social researchers (see especially A. B. Atkinson 1983). As a result, it is possible to arrive at a clear picture of overall trends in the distribution of economic resources.

The pattern of distribution

Britain and many other societies have been highly unequal over the whole of the first half of the twentieth century. This is clear from a series of studies in which the distribution of total income or assets is divided up according to the percentage held by particular 'slices' or statistical categories in the population. It is possible to look at the percentage of income or assets held by, say, the top 10 per cent of the population over a long period of time.

The particular slices identified in distributions of income and assets—the top 1 per cent, top 5 per cent, and so on—are not, of course, real social groups (see Box 18.10, p. 712). They are simply categories identified for statistical purposes. For this reason, it must not be assumed that, say, the top 1 per cent of income recipients are precisely the same people as the top 1 per cent of asset-holders. The statistical evidence does, nevertheless, allow us to draw some conclusions about the overall shape and extent of social inequality.

The top 1 per cent in Britain—a useful approximation to the wealthy—held 69 per cent of all personal assets in 1911. Their share declined to just over a half in 1938, and during the 1940s and 1950s it slipped below this level to 44 per cent in 1956 (see Figure 18.3). The relative share of the richest section of the population, then, fell by almost one-third over this period of half a century. The share of the top 5 per cent declined from over 80 per cent to 71 per cent over the same period, a much more limited rate of decline (A. B. Atkinson 1983: 168; Rubinstein 1986: 95). Looking at these figures from a different angle, it can be seen that, in 1956, 95 per cent of the population held only just over a quarter of all personal assets.

Figure 18.3 Distribution of personal assets, Britain, 1911–1971

	Percentage share of assets								
	England and Wales				Great Britain				
	1911	1923	1930	1938	1950	1955	1961	1966	1971
top 1%	69	61	58	55	47	44	37	31	29
top 5%	87	82	79	77	74	71	61	56	53
top 10%	92	89	87	85	—	—	72	70	68

Sources: Revell (1965); Hills (1995: table 14).

➲ You will be looking at a number of similar tables later in this chapter, so make sure that you understand this one now. Plot the data on to a graph that shows trends over time. You should show the dates along the horizontal (bottom) axis and the percentage of assets held along the vertical (side) axis. Draw a separate line on the graph for each of the three categories listed.

❓ What other kinds of graph or chart might be used to illustrate these figures?

THEORY AND METHODS   18.10

Slicing the distribution

In a study of the distribution of economic resources, individuals and households are arranged in a hierarchy according to the size of their income or the value of their assets. This hierarchy can, then, be sliced in various ways to identify the top 1 per cent, top 5 per cent, bottom 10 per cent, and so on. It is then possible to report the percentage of total income or assets that is held by those in each of these slices.

In an egalitarian society, any 1 per cent of the population would hold close to 1 per cent of assets, and any 10 per cent of the population would receive about 10 per cent of all income. Reporting the income and assets of various slices, then, is a way of showing how much a particular society departs from this egalitarian situation.

Each 1 per cent slice of the hierarchy is technically termed a percentile, each 10 per cent slice is a decile, and each 20 per cent slice is a quintile. Thus, there are 100 percentiles, 10 deciles, or 5 quintiles in any distribution. The median value is that which corresponds to the fiftieth percentile, or third quintile.

Income has always been more equally distributed than assets. Nevertheless, the earliest systematic study of income distribution showed that the top 3 per cent of the population received just over a third of all income in 1903 (Chiozza-Money 1905: 28, 42). If income had been equally distributed, each person would have received about £40 a year. In fact, those in the top 3 per cent slice of the population had incomes that were above £700 a year, while the very richest manufacturers and owners of large businesses each received more than £2,000 a year. At this time, average workers' wages were between £1 and £2 per week. Just a few years later, in 1910, it was found that 327 people received incomes over £45,000 a year—more than 800 times the wage of an unskilled labourer.

There seems to have been some slight redistribution of income away from those at the very top during the 1920s, and by 1938 the top 1 per cent of the population was receiving 16.6 per cent of before-tax income. Its share continued to decline until well into the post-war period, falling to 11.2 per cent in 1949, 8.2 per cent in 1964, and 6.2 per cent in 1974 (Rubinstein 1986: 80).

Both income and assets moved towards greater equality over the first sixty or so years of the twentieth century, although assets were more unequally distributed than income. A combination of economic change and social policy reduced the great inequalities that had been generated in the Victorian period, and those at the top saw a continuous, if limited erosion of their relative position. Much of this redistribution at the top, however, consisted of a redistribution of assets within large extended families. The families that had made massive fortunes from land, finance, and manufacturing in the nineteenth century were entering their third or fourth generation by the middle of the twentieth century, and their assets were being spread among ever larger numbers of heirs. At the same time, many wealthy families sought to avoid estate duty (inheritance tax) by transferring assets to children before the death of the head of the family. Nevertheless, the continuity of great wealth is striking. Over the nineteenth century and into the first half of the twentieth century, sixty-seven families each had three or more of their members leaving at least £0.5 million on their deaths (Rubinstein 1981).

Economic inequalities shape the other advantages and disadvantages that people experience. In Chapter 8, pp. 276–7, we show the ways in which a number of measures of health and mortality have varied over time and from one group to another. The evidence that we present in that chapter shows how health and mortality are related to gender and ethnic differences. Figure 18.4 shows how mortality rates vary from one occupational group to another. In this table, numbers

Figure 18.4 Inequalities of death (males), Great Britain, 1910–1953

Occupational group	1910–12	1930–2	1949–53
Professional and managerial	88	90	86
Technical	94	94	92
Skilled manual and non-manual	96	97	101
Partly skilled	93	102	104
Unskilled	142	111	118

Note: 100 indicates average mortality rate for population as a whole.

Sources: Black *et al.* (1980: table 7); Stacey (1987: table 8).

❓ For many people in the past, some partial relief from poverty was possible only in the workhouse or in a hostel. How does the position of the homeless differ today?

above 100 indicate that a group has an above-average rate of mortality, while numbers below 100 represent below-average mortality. The highest-paid occupations, the professional and managerial ones, have mortality rates that have been below average for the whole of the first half of the twentieth century. Mortality rates for unskilled workers—the lowest-paid group in the population—improved substantially between 1910 and 1953, but they were still significantly above average. In each year, there is a very clear gradient in mortality rates from the highest paid to the lowest paid.

> **➲ Connections**
>
> If you are unclear about the meaning of the standardized mortality rate, read our discussion of this in Chapter 8, p. 275. You will need to understand this if you are to make the best use of the evidence presented in this chapter.

Mapping poverty

The Victorian upper and middle classes were haunted by the prospect of a growth in urban poverty, especially in London's East End. Journalists, novelists, reformers, and the early social researchers were explorers in what came to be called 'Darkest England'. Best known among these writings are the novels of Charles Dickens, but systematic social investigations were also undertaken. In the 1840s, Friedrich Engels, Marx's collaborator, produced a report on the condition of the poor in Salford and Manchester, and in the 1860s, Mayhew (1861*a*) and Hollingshead (1861) produced sensational reports on conditions in London. Mayhew's surveys contain lively and vivid descriptions of the lives of the poor, and they remain among the major social documents of the nineteenth century. It was in the later work of Charles Booth and Seebohm Rowntree,

---

THEORY AND METHODS 18.11

Charles Booth

Charles Booth (1840–1916) was a wealthy Liverpool shipowner and merchant. He felt a responsibility to improve the conditions in which ordinary people lived, but was convinced that radical claims about the extent of poverty in London were overstated. He decided to undertake an investigation that would produce accurate figures on its true extent. Booth was surprised to discover that there were even more people living in poverty than the radicals had claimed. His work helped to shape the introduction of old-age pensions in 1908.

The work that Booth carried out was pioneering empirical sociology, although he was untrained in sociological theory or research methods. He originally intended to compile a full census of all residents of the East End, but he soon realized that this was an impossible task to undertake through house-to-house methods. Alternative methods were required. Booth gathered his information indirectly from School Board visitors and others who had a detailed knowledge of local residents. In this way, he was eventually able to extend his research to the whole of London, producing detailed street-by-street accounts of poverty in a massive work of seventeen volumes (Booth 1901–2). He compiled his results into a large-scale map of London, colouring each street: black or blue for poverty, red for comfort, and yellow for wealth.

Figure 18.5 The Booth class scheme

Category		Percentage in London (1889)	
H	Upper middle class (and above)	5.9	
G	Lower middle class	11.9	
F	Higher class labour	} 51.5	Working class
E	Regular standard earnings		
D	Small irregular earnings	} 22.3	Poor
C	Intermittent earnings		
B	Casual earnings	7.5 }	
A	Lowest class of occasional and semi-criminals	0.9 }	Very poor

Source: J. Scott (1994: table 2.1).

Figure 18.6 Distribution of poverty in London, 1886–1889

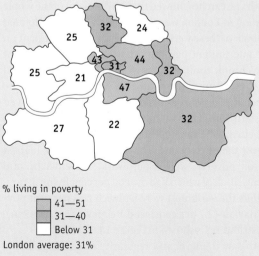

% living in poverty
- ▨ 41—51
- ▨ 31—40
- ☐ Below 31

London average: 31%

Source: J. Scott (1994: 25, figure 2.2), compiled from the various Booth reports.

however, that the parameters of poverty were uncovered with statistical precision.

Deprivation in darkest England

Booth began his work in 1886 with a study of social conditions in East London and some related analyses of Central London and Battersea. From this base, he broadened his enquiries into a comprehensive survey of the whole of London. His first priority was to devise a set of categories into which he could organize his materials. He defined eight categories of people according to the level and type of earnings available to their members (see Box 18.11, p. 713). He called these categories social classes, a claim that we look at in Chapter 19. Booth's main purpose was to use his categories to show the distribution of the population according to their various levels of living.

Booth saw poverty in relative terms. It was, he said, an inability to maintain 'the usual standard of life in this country' (Booth 1901–2: i. 33). He calculated that a family of five would require at least 21s. per week in order to achieve this standard of living (see also Pember-Reeves 1913). Those living in the 'ordinary poverty' of categories C and D, with incomes between 18s. and 21s. (90p to £1.05p) had insufficient means and could barely scrape by. Those who depended upon intermittent, irregular earnings lived a particularly precarious existence, as they faced the ever-present possibility of falling into deeper poverty. 'Chronic want', the lot of the very poor in categories A and B, occurred whenever income fell below 18s. The very poor relied, at best, on casual earnings from temporary and seasonal work or from small-time street trading. The 'loafers' of category A, forming what many now describe as an underclass, were the poorest of all. They had little in the way of legitimate income from employment, they drifted in and out of crime, and they were beset by vices of all kinds.

Booth's researches showed that 30.7 per cent of the whole population of London were living in poverty as he defined it. The bulk of these were the ordinary poor, dependent on low or intermittent pay, but a hard core of 8.4 per cent lived in chronic want. Poverty was heavily concentrated in the East End and a vast swathe of South London, where approaching 50 per cent lived in poverty. However, even the western boroughs had substantial amounts. Kensington and Chelsea, for example, had 21 per cent of residents living below the poverty line. The localities with the highest levels of poverty were Southwark, Greenwich, and Clerkenwell, all of which had over 60 per cent living in poverty, while the wealthiest were Dulwich (1.3 per cent poverty), Mayfair (2.7 per cent), and Belgravia (5.0 per cent). This distribution is shown in Figure 18.6, p. 713.

Booth saw the level and regularity of earnings as the heart of the problem of poverty. Among the ordinary poor (categories C and D), 43 per cent had only casual or irregular pay and a further 25 per cent were on regular but low

pay. Most of the very poor (categories A and B) suffered from similar problems, but Booth saw those he termed the 'loafers' as *choosing* to avoid employment. They were, he held, responsible in part for the depths of their own poverty. Even among the ordinary poor, Booth identified 13 per cent whose suffering he thought was made worse by their wasteful spending on alcohol of money that should have been spent on food. Others on similar incomes managed just about to scrape along because of the thrifty housekeeping of a 'good wife' (Booth 1901–2: i. 50). A substantial number of those living in ordinary poverty were in such dire straits because of the size of their families. Their incomes were insufficient to support the large numbers of children they had. In other cases, he claimed, poverty was due to serious illnesses that prevented people from working.

Booth wanted to find out more about the employment conditions responsible for low pay and irregular earnings, so he carried out an investigation into the London labour market. Of particular interest are his studies of those trades that employed women in large numbers. There were, for example, nearly 400,000 domestic servants in London, and 85 per cent of them were women. Many female servants were recruited as young girls directly from the workhouses, where they had been given a basic domestic training. At 13 years old, their pay averaged the equivalent of £5.30 a year, rising to £17.70 a year for those over 30. Many women had casual or irregular employment as homeworkers, employed to finish textile goods or assemble matchboxes. Such 'sweated' conditions, Booth held, were typical of all the East End trades. Both men and women had to work long hours in unsanitary conditions for low and irregular pay. In the docks, for example, casual labourers received between 60p and 75p per week, and they often had to go for weeks without any work at all.

> **⊃ Connections**
> You will find a discussion of contemporary forms of homeworking in Chapter 17, pp. 684–5.

Poverty and the welfare state

Shortly after Booth's research, Rowntree began an investigation of poverty in his home city of York. Rowntree wanted to see whether the amount of poverty found in London was typical of the rest of the country. His major survey was carried out in 1899, but he updated this in 1936 and 1950. He used similar research methods to Booth, but he also carried out a house-to-house survey (see Box 18.12).

We have already looked at the rather restrictive, absolute view of poverty that Rowntree adopted. Nevertheless, his poverty line, set at £1.08 per week, was actually a little

THEORY AND METHODS   18.12
···

Seebohm Rowntree

Benjamin Seebohm Rowntree (1871–1954) was the son of Joseph Rowntree, the founder of the large cocoa and chocolate business. The family were prominent Quakers and philanthropists. Seebohm worked in the family firm as labour director. He introduced a pension scheme, a works council, and arrangements for profit-sharing. He was Chairman of the company from 1925 to 1941. Rowntree was given responsibility for the welfare policy of munitions workers during the First World War and was centrally involved in the planning of post-war housing policy. His researches (Rowntree 1901, 1941; Rowntree and Lavers 1951) provide a long-term overview that stresses, in particular, the impact of age and the life cycle on poverty.

higher than that drawn by Booth. Using this poverty line, Rowntree concluded that 9.91 per cent of the population of York was living in what he called primary poverty. They simply had insufficient income for their own survival. A further 17.89 per cent had incomes that were above the poverty line, but were unable to budget properly and so experienced the 'obvious want and squalor' of what he called secondary poverty (Rowntree 1901: 115). Those in secondary poverty, he held, could escape this through better budgeting. In all, 27.8 per cent of York's population were living below the subsistence standard, a figure that was not much less than that found by Booth in London.

Rowntree saw low pay as the immediate cause of primary poverty in more than a half of all cases. He concluded

that the wages then paid to unskilled labourers were insufficient to maintain a normal family. He held, however, that the life cycle also had a major impact on poverty. The same family could pass from poverty to a degree of comfort as its members moved from child-rearing to maturity, but the husband and wife might move back into poverty in their old age (see Figure 18.7).

Studies by later researchers suggested that the level of poverty fell during the first three decades of the twentieth century. Rowntree decided to test this claim in a new study for 1936. He updated his primary poverty line to £1.53 per week for a family of five, and he found that just 3.9 per cent of the York population were then living in poverty. The amount of primary poverty, then, had fallen by two-thirds, and this finding was in line with the claim that income had become more equally distributed in the first part of the century.

This new study, however, also used a relative concept of poverty. This measure recognized that an absolute measure of subsistence income had to be combined with an allowance for insurance, newspapers, holidays, and various other things that could be regarded as necessities for most people. This new relative poverty line was set at £2.18 per week in 1936, and on this basis Rowntree found that 17.7 per cent of the York population were living in poverty (see Figure 18.8, p. 716).

Rowntree recognized, however, that he had still produced only a minimum estimate of the number of people who might actually experience poverty at some stage in their life. Some of those who had been poor in the past might be living in relative comfort at the time of his survey, because of the particular stage in their family life cycle. Similarly, many of those who were comfortable at the time of the survey might

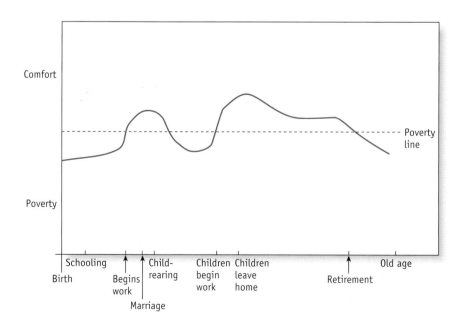

Figure 18.7 Poverty and the life cycle

Figure 18.8 Poverty in York, 1936 and 1950

1936		1950		
Class or weekly pay (£)	**% of population**	**Class or weekly pay (£)**	**% of population**	
Middle class (and above)	35.0	Middle class (and above)	not recorded	
3.18 or more	20.5	7.30 or more	34.98	Relative poverty line
2.68–3.17	8.0	6.15–7.29	11.90	
2.18–2.67	10.8	5.00–6.14	11.48	
1.68–2.67	9.6	3.85–4.99	1.43	
Less than 1.68	8.1	Less than 3.85	0.23	

Note: Pay levels identified by Rowntree have been converted to decimal currency.
Source: J. Scott (1995: table 2.16).

❓ The percentage figures do not add up to 100 per cent because Rowntree excluded servants and those living in public institutions, such as workhouses and hospitals. Do you think that the amount of measured poverty would increase or decrease if they had been included? What further evidence would you need to answer this question?

be expected to fall into poverty at some time in the future. Rowntree concluded that the numbers of these people needed to be estimated. He suggested that over a half of all manual workers would experience poverty at some stage in their life, even though a much smaller number would actually be living in poverty at any one time.

The principal causes of poverty, Rowntree argued, were old age (responsible for 14.6 per cent of all poverty), unemployment (28.6 per cent), and low pay (32.8 per cent). He therefore concluded that improvements in pension provision, an increase in the level of employment, and an increase in average pay would eventually lead to the disappearance of poverty.

In common with many of his contemporaries, Rowntree thought that by 1950 these very changes had come about. Unemployment was much lower than it had been in the 1930s and the country was coming out of a period of post-war austerity and entering a new era of affluence. Most importantly, the Beveridge proposals for establishing a welfare state had been implemented. Rowntree's own work from the 1930s had been taken up by William Beveridge (later Lord Beveridge) as the basis of his proposals on the level of welfare benefits. The key change, Rowntree felt, was improved old-age pensions. Rowntree set out to examine the consequences of these changes in a third, and final, survey of York (Rowntree and Lavers 1951). Setting his relative poverty line at £5.00 per week, he found that just 1.66 per cent of the population were poor, far fewer than there had been in the 1930s. The welfare state had, it seemed, confirmed a move towards equality.

Mobility and universalism

The distribution of income and assets—and, therefore, the levels of poverty and wealth—are largely determined by the ownership of property and earnings from employment. For all but the very rich it is occupational earnings that determine life chances. It is for this reason that an investigation into the occupational structure can tell us so much about a society. The openness of a structure of social inequality can be measured by the amount of **occupational mobility**, the amount of movement from one occupation to another.

An **open structure of inequality** is one in which people have the opportunity to rise from lowly paid occupations to those that give them superior income, assets, and prestige. Conversely, a **closed structure of inequality** is one in which people's chances in life are fixed at birth and they cannot rise, or fall, through their own efforts or achievements. An open structure, according to the functionalist theory of inequality, is one in which the ambitious and the talented are able to rise, and in which those without merit will fall. Britain may be an unequal society, but is it, nevertheless, a meritocracy?

> ➲ *Connections*
> We look in more detail at occupational mobility in Chapter 19, pp. 749–50, where we consider the question of when social *inequalities* are formed into patterns of *social stratification.*

Social mobility in Britain

The earliest and most important study of this question in Britain was that of David Glass and a team of colleagues at the London School of Economics in 1949. Glass allocated occupations to seven categories, each of which was homogeneous in terms of income, working conditions, and prestige. He was then able to compare the occupations of parents and children and to look at the occupational mobility of people over their working life. The research showed that positions in life were not completely fixed at birth. There was a degree of fluidity or movement from one type of occupation to another.

Glass found that there was rather more upward than downward mobility, but even this was very limited in scope. Most occupational mobility was short range: it was movement within a particular occupational category or between categories that were close in the occupational structure. People were unlikely to move into occupations that were very different from those of their parents or from those in which they had started their own working lives.

Glass concluded that the existence of only a limited amount of occupational mobility showed that Britain was far from being a truly open society. Openness was assessed against the yardstick of **perfect mobility**. This is the amount of mobility that we would expect to find if ability is randomly distributed and there are no barriers to the mobility of the able. In fact, there was nothing like perfect mobility in Britain. There was a kind of inertia that produced a pattern of *occupational closure*: people were more likely to remain where they were born than they were to rise or to fall.

Occupational closure was especially marked at the top and bottom of the occupational structure. The top category in Glass's schema contained the professional, administrative, and managerial occupations with superior life chances to all other occupations. If there was perfect mobility and openness, then everyone would have an equal chance of attaining one of these jobs. On this basis, only 3 per cent of the children of people already in these occupations would be expected to enter the same kinds of job. In fact, 40 per cent of them followed in their fathers' footsteps. Those who went into lower-level occupations than their fathers only rarely had to enter manual work. Their chances of remaining in some kind of relatively privileged non-manual work were very high.

THEORY AND METHODS   18.13

Measuring social mobility

David Glass's study (1954) of mobility in England, Wales, and Scotland used a sample of 10,000 adult men and women who were aged over 14 in 1949. His interviewers collected biographical details on each individual, especially on their education, qualifications, and work history. They also collected information on fathers' (but not mothers') occupations.

The occupational categories that were used in the Glass study are those of the Hall–Jones Classification. These are often seen as social-class categories, and we discuss these more fully in Chapter 19, pp. 752–7. You may like to keep that discussion in mind.

The two central concepts used in mobility studies are *intergenerational* mobility and *intra-generational* mobility. Intergenerational mobility is movement between generations and is measured by comparing a person's occupational level with that of his or her parents. In practice, most mobility studies have looked only at the father's occupation, a highly contentious approach. Intra-generational mobility

is movement within a single generation and is measured by comparing a person's current occupational level with that of his or her own first job.

Peter Blau and Otis Dudley Duncan studied occupational achievement using a sample of more than 20,000 men aged between 20 and 64 (Blau and Duncan 1967). Data were collected in 1962, using interviews and questionnaires. The fieldwork was undertaken in association with the US Bureau of Census. The occupations of their respondents were initially allocated to seventeen occupational categories (salaried professionals, managers, clerical, manufacturing, labourers, and so on) that were similar in terms of their life chances and social experiences. These seventeen categories were ranked according to the income and education of their incumbents. By comparing respondents' occupations with those of their fathers, Blau and Duncan were able to study intergenerational mobility.

The principal method used by Blau and Duncan was the construction of path diagrams as causal models of mobility.

The first steps in constructing a causal model are to guess at the most likely causal relations and to draw a flow chart of these influences. The next step is to calculate the actual strength of the various relations. Correlations among the variables are calculated, and regression coefficients are used as path coefficients to indicate the strength of a particular causal influence. You do not need to understand the mathematics of this, so long as the general principles are clear.

Correlation is a measure of how closely associated two variables are. If one changes in line with another, they are said to be correlated. The measure of how closely associated they are is called the correlation coefficient, but you do not need to know how to calculate this. Perfect correlation (one variable changing in direct proportion to another) has a coefficient of 1, while complete randomness has a coefficient of 0. The closer the value is to 1, the greater is the association between the two variables. If two factors vary in opposite directions (one going up while the other goes down), the coefficient has a negative value.

Occupational achievement

The argument that modern societies are open with no sharp boundaries between one level of living and another has been extensively explored in American sociology. It is useful to look at those studies for what they tell us about the United States and because the methods used have been taken up by British sociologists. The most important study in this area is that of Blau and Duncan (1967).

The amount of occupational mobility was measured in the same way as by Glass. They used an *index of association* that compared the actual mobility rates between two categories with those that would be expected solely on the basis of chance. In a completely open society —one with perfect mobility—this index would be 1.0. In fact, Blau and Duncan found that there was a high degree of self-recruitment, or closure, in the United States. The index of association was as high as 11.7 in the case of self-employed professionals. Despite the existence of a high level of self-recruitment throughout the occupational structure, there was also a great deal of upward mobility. There was a small amount of downward mobility, but only rarely did this involve mobility between non-manual and manual jobs or between manufacturing and agricultural work.

The high level of upward mobility was seen as a consequence of a massive growth in the numbers of non-manual and service-sector jobs, together with a corresponding decline in the number of manual and agricultural jobs. There was a surplus of non-manual jobs and a surplus of manual workers' children ready to fill them. Most of this movement was short-range mobility. There was little of the kind of long-range mobility that would indicate a truly open structure of inequality.

This was confirmed in some comparative work by Lipset and Bendix (1959), who undertook a secondary analysis of research into occupational mobility. Using a rather crude distinction between manual and non-manual occupations, they found similarities in all advanced industrial societies. Adding together the total amount of upward and downward mobility, they found the highest levels of overall vertical movement in Germany (31 per cent) and the United States (30 per cent). Levels in Britain and Sweden stood at 29 per cent, while France and Japan had levels of 27 per cent.

These similarities in levels of mobility were seen by Lipset and Bendix as reflecting certain common patterns in the development of industrial societies. It was only the less-advanced societies of Italy and Finland that had lower rates of mobility. The expansion of non-manual occupations as industry advanced, they argued, meant a growing demand for highly qualified workers. The children of those who were already in such jobs were too few to fill all the vacancies, even if none of them was downwardly mobile.

As a result, opportunities for upward mobility were created simply because of the changing occupational division of labour. Education became especially important for occupational recruitment, and those who acquired educational credentials through school, college, and university were able to move into managerial, technical, and professional occupations in large numbers.

Blau and Duncan looked at how occupational achievement, the occupational level to which people can rise or fall, was related to social origins. They asked how people's social background shaped their occupational destinations and, in particular, what part was played by education in linking origins and destinations. To explore these issues, they abandoned their initial seventeen occupational categories and used a quantitative measure of occupational prestige to place the occupations in a hierarchy. They held that the prestige of an occupation was closely associated with its income, and they went on to construct causal path diagrams of the factors involved.

Figure 18.9 shows the causal model for occupational achievement in the United States. The higher path coefficients are treated as the more important causal links. However, assessing causation is not straightforward, as correlation is not the same thing as causation. Correlation means only that there is a mathematical association between two measures, and this can be used as evidence for a causal relationship only if we have good reason to think that all the important variables have been included in the model. Blau and Duncan believed that they had measured everything that was important, and they drew conclusions about their relative importance.

It can be seen from Figure 18.9 that the greatest influence on both initial and current occupation was a man's level of education, which was itself influenced by his father's education and occupation. The direct effect of father's occupation, independently of educational factors, was very small. People's social origins determine their occupational achievements largely through the influence that they exert on their education.

> ➲ *Connections*
> You might like to review our discussion of educational selection in Chapter 9, pp. 311–16, and see what further light it throws on these claims.

The biggest causal influences in the diagram, however, are the so-called *residuals*, the unknown or unmeasured factors that are left over when all the known factors are measured. While the path linking education and occupation had a coefficient of 0.394, the unknown influences on occupation had a combined effect of 0.753. Blau and Duncan argued that this did not undermine their model, as they claimed to have uncovered the single most

Figure 18.9 Occupational achievement in the United States, 1967

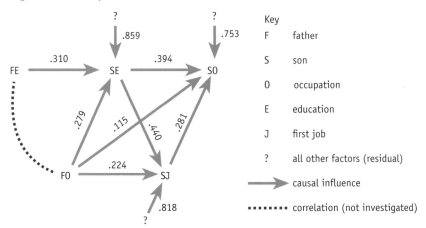

Key
F   father
S   son
0   occupation
E   education
J   first job
?   all other factors (residual)
⟶   causal influence
•••••••   correlation (not investigated)

Source: Blau and Duncan (1967: 170).

❓ It is often said that 'correlation does not mean causation'. How would you apply this judgement to these results? What unmeasured causal factors might be important in explaining these data?

important set of factors determining occupational achievement. Jencks (1972), however, has suggested that the massive size of the residuals indicates that factors such as 'luck' (for example, being in the right place at the right time to get a job) are far more important than any of the structural factors measured by Blau and Duncan.

Blau and Duncan gave particular attention to the effects of ethnicity on occupational achievement. The economic disadvantages that were experienced by African Americans, they argued, were due to their educational disadvantages. Because they had less chance of an education at high school, college, or university, African Americans were disadvantaged in the competition for jobs. These disadvantages reflected the existence of prejudice and racism. Even well-educated African Americans faced worse opportunities than did whites with a similar level of education. Because of the poorer educational facilities and economic opportunities that existed in the southern states, those living there were especially disadvantaged by comparison with those living in the north. Blau and Duncan (1967: 238) argue: 'It is the cumulative effect of the handicaps Negroes encounter at every stage in their lives that produces the serious inequalities of opportunities which they suffer.'

Occupational achievement in the United States, they conclude, was largely regulated by the universalistic values that were displacing more particularistic standards and ascribed characteristics. The effects of universalism, however, were partially counteracted by the persistence of racism and of disadvantages linked to ethnicity.

By contrast, the descendants of recent white migrants to the United States (Germans, Italians, Poles, and others)

had patterns of occupational achievement that were similar to those of the long-established white migrants. It took two or more generations for these patterns to appear, because of the strong influence that was exerted by parental background, but Blau and Duncan present much evidence to support the idea that, so far as white ethnic minorities are concerned, there was an ethnic melting pot that unified the life chances of indigenous and migrant groups.

Blau and Duncan saw the drive to universalism as persisting. Education has become ever more central to occupational achievement, they argued, because it measures ability and accredits academic success in the abilities that are required by the industrial system. This growing universalism is also apparent in the materialistic character of people's orientations. Material success, in the form of the pursuit of income and consumer goods, becomes the yardstick of occupational success. People are motivated by the material rewards that are attached to occupations. Like many observers, however, Blau and Duncan were pessimistic about the long-term impact of universalism on the ethnic disadvantages of African Americans.

> **➔ Connections**
>
> Blau and Duncan's emphasis on universalism and material success shows their acceptance of the functionalist theory of inequality. You might also notice the way in which their view connects with Merton's theory of anomie (discussed in Chapter 2, p. 45) and Parsons's theory of stratification (discussed in Chapter 19, pp. 747–9).

Stop and reflect

In this section we have examined trends in social inequality and openness from the late nineteenth century until the 1950s. We have shown that:

- Britain has had a high degree of economic inequality over the whole of this century, though the level of concentration in both income and assets declined over the period considered.

- The extent of poverty in London and in York at the turn of the century was extremely high. Booth estimated that about one in three of the London population lived in poverty. Rowntree suggested that this had fallen substantially by the 1950s.

We went on to show the connections between economic inequality and other aspects of life chances, and we put our figures in a comparative context.

- Inequalities in income and assets are associated with a whole range of other advantages and disadvantages in life chances. These include those of health, housing, and mortality.

- Evidence from studies of occupational mobility suggests that rates of mobility in Britain were similar to those in other industrial societies.

Inequality and social exclusion

The view that poverty had been eliminated in the advanced societies of the West persisted for some time after the Second World War. Gradually, however, academic commentators came to realize that the hopes that lay behind the establishment of welfare states had proved over-optimistic. Poverty was rediscovered and was seen as responsible for the exclusion of many citizens from vast areas of social life. Social policy through the 1960s and 1970s was concerned with alleviating poverty and social exclusion, eliminating the conditions that produce it, and promoting greater equality and social inclusion. From the late 1970s, however, governments aimed to reduce the level of spending on welfare provision and to promote greater enterprise and effort. As a result, inequality increased. By the 1980s, nevertheless, neo-liberal politicians were justifying welfare cuts on the grounds that there was no longer any poverty. If the welfare state had failed to eliminate poverty, it appeared to many on the political right that the 'enterprise economy' had done so.

The denial of poverty rested on an absolute concept of poverty. It was argued that living standards were far higher than they had been during the early years of the twentieth century: those who have not only food and shoes, but also cars, televisions, and washing machines, it was held, cannot be seen as poor in any meaningful sense of the word.

Much of this discussion about poverty and inequality has revolved around official figures derived from the public-assistance programmes of the welfare states. For example, although there has never been an official poverty line in Britain, the basic social-assistance level has been widely used for this purpose. Social assistance—in Britain, at various times called National Assistance, Supplementary Benefit, and Income Support—defines minimum incomes for households of different sizes, and welfare benefits are available, under certain conditions, to those whose incomes fall below these levels.

The social-assistance level is the official view of what ought to be the minimum standard of living for a full member of society, a citizen. This level of living has been institutionalized through legislation and administrative regulations. The level at which it is set varies with the financial constraints that a government currently faces, and it is also shaped by prevailing political prejudices and ideologies. Nevertheless, it does provide a benchmark level for estimating the officially recognized level at which poverty or deprivation occurs. Direct research on public perceptions of poverty have produced figures that are broadly comparable with those that have been arrived at by using the social-assistance level (Mack and Lansley 1985). The social-assistance level, then, is the closest thing that there is to an official poverty line.

Although British governments were denying the reality of poverty, the drive towards greater European integration during the 1970s and 1980s was associated with a series of Community-wide and Union-wide poverty and aid programmes. In these an alternative poverty line has been used. The European poverty programme measures the percentage of individuals and families whose *disposable income*—the amount that they actually have to spend after direct taxes—is 50 per cent or less of the national average (mean) income. This definition has effectively become the official poverty line for the European Union. It has been seen as the level at which people's resources 'exclude them from a minimum acceptable way of life in the Member State in which they live' (Article 1.2, 85/8/EEC).

This is, it must be noted, a relative definition of poverty. The line is drawn at a level of income that is likely to prevent people from participating fully in the societies of which they are citizens. It defines the acceptable social minimum in precise statistical terms. It is a matter not of particular administrative criteria (as with the social-assistance level) but of the way in which a social consensus is actually institutionalized in the structure of income distribution. Poverty is defined relative to the particular pattern of income distribution maintained by custom, by official policies, and by the economic processes of a society.

There are, then, two official poverty lines: the social-assistance line, which came increasingly under attack by Conservative and New Right critics in the 1980s and 1990s, and the European Union poverty line. Academic research on poverty has employed both of these poverty lines, recognizing that neither of them can give a perfect measure of the extent of relative poverty. This research into poverty has been combined with considerable research into the income and asset distributions within which poverty and wealth are generated.

Increasing inequality

Both of the official definitions of poverty are relative concepts. Poverty is not a matter of absolute physiological subsistence, but of conditions of living that are deprived relative to the range of acceptable conditions in a society. It is possible to assess poverty only in the context of a wider understanding of the extent of economic inequality and the differences in life chances with which these are associated.

Income and earnings

Income distribution altered only slightly between the Second World War and the middle of the 1960s. Between 1963 and 1977, however, there was a move towards much greater equality. This equalization was a result of government policy that built upon a period of affluence and economic growth. From 1978 to the end of the 1980s, however, policy was reversed and economic conditions worsened. Unemployment increased as recessions became more persistent, and there was a rapid increase in the level of inequality. This growth in inequality levelled off during the 1990s and stabilized by the turn of the century, by which time much of the post-war equalization had been reversed.

The top 20 per cent of the population's share of income before tax rose from 44 per cent in 1972 to 50 per cent in 1988 (*Social Trends* 1992). The share of the top 10 per cent increased from 21 per cent to 24 per cent over the same period, and the share of the top 1 per cent also increased. At the other end of the scale, the bottom 10 per cent received 4 per cent of all income in 1979, and their share had fallen to 2 per cent by 1991. Taxation had some effect on this (see Figure 18.10, p. 722). The share in after-tax income of the top 20 per cent had increased to 42 per cent by 2000, while that of the poorest 20 per cent had fallen to 7.6 per cent. Income inequality has increased slightly since 2000.

It is extremely difficult to compare statistics for one country with those for another. The share of total income going to the top 1 per cent of the population in 1970 seems to have been lower in Britain than it was in any other European country. In Belgium, Germany, and France, almost one-third of total income went to the top 10 per cent, while in Britain the figure was a quarter. On the other hand, the share of the bottom 20 per cent (just over 6 per cent) was broadly similar in Britain, Belgium, and Germany. Only France and Italy had a greater imbalance, probably reflecting the large agricultural population in these two countries.

Outside Europe, Britain and Australia were comparable in terms of economic inequality, but Japan and the United States were both considerably more unequal during the 1970s. By the middle of the 1980s, the growth of inequality in Britain had been more rapid and more marked than in any other country except New Zealand. Income inequality in Britain was greater than it was in Germany, the Netherlands, Sweden, and Canada, but it was lower than in France, Italy, New Zealand, and the United States (Hills 1995: 64; see also J. Scott 1994: ch. 5). Income distribution in Britain and the United States, however, is very similar. In 1992 the top 20 per cent of the population in the United States received 47 per cent of all income, while the bottom 20 per cent received just 4 per cent.

A major contributor to this growth in income inequality during the 1980s was a growth in unemployment that made more people dependent on low welfare benefits. The number of households in which neither partner was in employment grew particularly rapidly. At the same time, benefit levels were being reduced as governments tried to reduce levels of state expenditure. Relative to average earnings, both the state retirement pension and unemployment benefit have fallen in Britain. In 1970 Unemployment Benefit (now termed the Jobseeker's Allowance) was just over 40 per cent of average income, but in 1992 it was less than 30 per cent of average income.

There has also been an increase in the inequality of incomes attached to particular jobs. The distribution of income among manual workers, for example, remained virtually unchanged for almost 100 years from 1886 to 1976. Incomes of all manual workers tended to rise together by very much the same amount. From the late 1970s this was no longer the case. Long-established relativities were destroyed by an increasing demand for qualified and

The plight of the homeless offers a daily reminder of growing inequalities in society.

© Alice Chadwick

incomes and other high incomes as a result of the deregulation of the financial markets and the creation of a tax climate that encouraged a so-called enterprise culture. A quarter of all Chairmen and Chief Executives of large companies in 1986 had received salary rises of 23 per cent, and one in ten of them had been given a rise of 42 per cent in the year.

By 2008 average gross weekly earnings (before tax) stood at £562 for a man and £436 for a woman. The typical family of two parents and their dependent children had gross earnings of around £700 per week, but lone parents with dependent children average less than half this amount. These lone parents are heavily dependent on welfare benefits. Among retired households, there was a growing division between those who derived their incomes mainly or exclusively from the state retirement pension and those who were in private pension schemes. In 1979, 44 per cent of pensioners had occupational pensions, and the number had risen to well over a half by 2002. The average income of these private pensioners was far higher than the average income of those who depended on the state pension alone, despite pressure on pension schemes during times of recession.

These inequalities become clearer if they are seen in relation to particular occupations. Figure 18.12 presents some pay comparisons. A financial manager in 2003 earned more than six times as much as a waiter or waitress, whose pay amounted to £194 per week. Other high-paid groups included doctors and lawyers, while those in the higher profession, such as accountants and teachers, earned about half the pay of a top manager. The lowest-paid groups, after waiting staff, were cleaners, bar staff, and care assistants.

These comparisons, of course, give only an estimate of the differences. The actual differences are often much greater. A cleaner's wage shows little variation with age and experience, but solicitors and doctors are generally on progressive salary scales that allow many of them to earn far more than the incomes shown here. This is particularly true of many management careers. Pay for graduate entrants to a managerial career is broadly similar to that of

experienced workers, and by a decline in unionization and other mechanisms of wage regulation (see Chapter 17, pp. 678–80). Competitive, deregulated labour markets increased differentials among workers, and in very much the direction predicted by the functionalist theory of inequality.

Another factor responsible for increasing inequality during the 1980s was the huge growth in investment

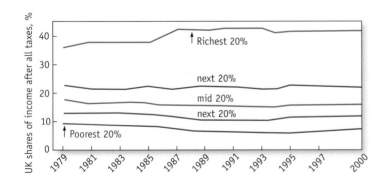

Figure 18.10 Income distribution, United Kingdom, 1979–2000

Source: Guardian, 7 April 1997, drawing on data from *Economic Trends*; *Social Trends* (2002: chart 5.11).

a nurse who is well established in a career, but the pay of top directors and executives goes well beyond the conventional scales. The highest-paid directors in large British companies receive, on average, at least ten times as much in income as a typical doctor, or forty times the income of a cleaner. The very highest-paid directors receive almost 150 times as much as the people who clean their offices. The highest-paid manager in Britain in 2007 was Sir Martin Sorrel, who received an annual salary of £23,372,504.

At the end of the 1990s, nearly one in twelve workers was earning less than £3 an hour. A national minimum wage was introduced in 1998, leading to the establishment of a minimum wage of £4.20 per hour by 2002. This had risen to £5.80 by 2009. This gives a maximum of £217.50 for a typical working week, though many low-paid workers are in part-time jobs that give them total incomes of less than £50 per week. Most part-time workers are women, which goes much of the way towards explaining the lower earnings of women as compared with men. However, women in full-time work typically earn significantly less than men in full-time work. These differences are reflected in the households of married or cohabiting partners: in more than a half of couples, the man earns at least £100 per week more than his female partner.

Incomes show great variation by industry and region. Earnings are highest in banking, finance, and insurance, and in the privatized energy and water industries. They are lowest in agriculture and fishing, in retail and wholesale distribution, and in hotels and restaurants. Wages and salaries are highest in London and the south-east. In the north of England, districts such as Cheshire, Redcar, and Cleveland are high-income areas, while Aberdeen is the only Scottish city in this category. The lowest incomes are found in parts of Wales, the Scottish border counties, and the Highlands.

Gross earnings tell only a part of the story, as taxation has a considerable effect on final income. The proportion of income paid in direct tax varies with the level of income, and there are, of course, variations from one society to another. Britain's tax rates are currently low by international standards. While an average of 16.3 per cent of income in Britain in 1994 was taken in direct taxes and National Insurance contributions, the tax burden in Germany was much higher at 21.4 per cent. Canada, France, Italy, and the United States all had higher levels of taxation than Britain, and only Japan had a lower rate (13 per cent). The effect of taxation in Britain is such that those on very low incomes pay little or no income tax,

Briefing: the top celebrity incomes   18.14

Many substantial incomes are earned in the entertainment industry by pop stars, film stars, and sports people. *Forbes* magazine has compiled a list that combines earnings with sales impact to produce a measure of overall 'celebrity' value.

Figure 18.11 Celebrity incomes, United States, 2009

The top 10 celebrities	Annual income ($m.)
1. Oprah Winfrey	275
2. George Lucas	170
3. Steven Spielberg	150
4. Madonna	110
5. Tiger Woods	110
6. Jerry Bruckheimer	110
7. Beyonce Knowles	87
8. Jerry Seinfeld	85
9. Phil McGraw	80
10. Simon Cowell	75

Source: Forbes (2009a).

➜ *Calculate how much bigger these incomes are than average earnings shown in Figure 18.12. What do the results tell you about the idea of functional importance? What criteria do you think govern the size of an income?*

➜ *Put your own income into the following website and see how you compare on a global scale:* **www.globalrichlist.com.**

Figure 18.12 Who earns what, Britain, 2009

Occupation	Median annual gross pay (£)
Managers	35,750
Professionals	34,049
Associate professionals and technical	26,797
Skilled trades	23,140
Personal service	12,482
Sales and customer service	9,618
Process, plant, and machine operatives	21,048
Elemantary occupations	12,630
All employees	21,320

Source: Office for National Statistics (2009).

those with slightly higher incomes pay about 10 per cent in tax, those with average earnings pay about a quarter of their income in tax, while higher earners may pay over one-third of this in income tax (*Social Trends* 1997: table 5.12).

Disposable income in Britain has actually increased overall in real terms since 1971. This increase has been greater for higher earners than for lower earners, leading to a growing gap between top and bottom. The disposable income of those at the bottom of the distribution has risen only slightly since the 1970s. Disposable income for those in the top 10 per cent, however, has increased substantially over the same period.

Direct taxation is *progressive* in its effect—the tax rate rising with income—but indirect taxes, such as VAT and customs duty, are *regressive*. The proportion of income paid in indirect taxes is greater in low-income households than it is in high-income households. A government that shifts the balance of taxation from income tax to a tax on food or fuel will have a redistributive effect in favour of highly paid households.

Asset distribution

So far, we have considered only income distribution. The ownership of assets is more concentrated than the distribution of income. Assets, it will be recalled, are the total stock of economic resources that a person or household has accumulated. Inequality in the distribution of personal assets narrowed continually from the 1920s to the 1970s, but it has not changed very much since then. The share of the top 1 per cent of the British population in personal assets declined from 47 per cent in 1950 to 17 per cent in 1993, most of this decline occurring during the 1950s and

1960s (see Figures 18.3 (p. 711) and 18.13). Figure 18.13 shows that the share of the bottom 50 per cent of the population in total personal assets barely altered between 1976 and 1991, but it has since increased slightly. This increasing concentration has been most marked at the very top, and the figures show a growth in polarization between top and bottom over the course of the 1990s. This trend is even more marked when the value of housing is excluded. The bottom 50 per cent now has just 3 per cent of non-housing wealth.

The top 1 per cent of asset-holders in the United States held 20.7 per cent of all assets in 1972, compared with 29 per cent in Britain (Rubinstein 1986: 147). In 1986, 160 American families had assets in excess of $200 million. These included such families as the Du Ponts, Fords, Gettys, and Rockefellers. The bases of these huge fortunes were financial, industrial, and commercial businesses, which have remained important sources of wealth throughout the century. In France, the top 5 per cent of households in 1992 held 40 per cent of all personal assets, while the bottom 25 per cent had just 1 per cent. The assets of a person in the top 10 per cent of the population were five times the average for the French population as a whole, and almost 800 times the average for those in the poorest 10 per cent. In 2009 the richest person in the world was Bill Gates, the founder and head of Microsoft, with $40 billion. He is followed by insurance specialist Warren Buffett with $37 billion. The richest person in Britain was Lakshmi Mittal with $19.3 billion. In second place was the Duke of Westminster with £11 billion.

Personal assets include houses, cars, and household goods, but the bulk of personal assets are held in monetary form. These include bank or building-society current

Global focus Inequality across the globe   18.15

The richest 1 per cent in the world (about 50 million people) have as much income as the poorest 57 per cent (about 2.7 billion people). This inequality reflects a global distribution of poverty: 80 per cent of the world's population have incomes below the US and European poverty lines. Two-thirds of the world's population is worse off than the poorest 10 per cent of Americans. This poverty is concentrated in Africa, India, and Bangladesh. While average age at death is 75 or older in North America, Australia, and Western Europe, it falls to 60 or so across continental Europe and Asia, and below 60 in Latin America, North Africa, and the Middle East. In many West and Central African countries, infant mortality is so high that the median age at death is less than 10 years. Gross national income per head is $34,100 in the United States and $24,430 in Britain, compared with $3,020 in South Africa and $260 in Nigeria. Countries such

as Russia and China show a growing polarization of wealth and poverty as a result of the growth of private enterprise and market production.

These inequalities are now central to the international disputes that have occurred at the meetings of the World Trade Organization. The world's largest trading blocs (the European Union, the United States, Japan, and Canada) have been forced to take account of the views of the poorer nations over customs tariffs on the agricultural and textile goods exported by these countries. However, continuing inequality has fuelled the anti-globalization protests that have erupted at meetings of the World Trade Organization and elsewhere.

Sources: Guardian, 2 October 2001; *Economic Journal*, 2002; *Guardian*, 26 June 2002; WHO (2005: annex table 1)

Figure 18.13 Distribution of personal assets, United Kingdom, 1976–2002

	Percentage share of assets					
	1976	1986	1991	1996	1999	2002
Top 1%	21	18	17	20	23	23
Top 5%	38	36	35	40	43	43
Top 10%	50	50	47	52	54	56
Top 25%	71	73	71	74	74	74
Top 50%	92	90	92	93	94	94
Bottom 50%	8	10	8	7	6	6

Source: Social Trends (2002: table 5.24; 2005: table 5.25).

❷ Extend the graph that you drew for Figure 18.3 and add the data in this table. Add lines for the extra slices shown. Do these extra data throw any new light on the trends that you have observed?

❷ Why not try drawing some pie charts for these data? Figure 18.14 shows a pie chart of the 2002 data.

accounts, unit trusts, Independent Savings Accounts (ISAs), and company shares. Just under a half of all adults in Britain have a bank or building-society savings account, but very few people hold any other kind of financial asset. For many people, however, their bank account is simply a temporary store for their income before the bulk of it is paid out again on household running costs. In some cases they may have negative monetary assets, as goods bought on credit or mortgage are debts rather than actual assets.

The great bulk of financial assets are held by a small number of the very wealthiest households. The top 5 per cent of asset-holders in 1961 held 96 per cent of all personally owned company shares. The number of shareholders has increased since then, and in 1995 about 17

per cent of the population were shareholders. About three-quarters of these shareholders owned shares in fewer than four companies. These were generally enterprises that had been privatized or converted from building societies into companies. For comparison, about 19 per cent of families in the United States own shares, with the top 1 per cent holding a half of all privately owned shares. These same wealthy families also hold almost one-seventh of all cash and bank deposits and one-seventh of all land and housing.

Deprivation and exclusion

Recognition that poverty had not declined so much as Rowntree expected, despite the expansion of welfare provision, was largely because of the work of Peter Townsend. A number of early papers and a major study of the elderly (Townsend 1963) were followed by a large national survey that set the scene for all later debates. Townsend's survey documented the scale of poverty in the 1960s, and he followed this with a survey of London that showed how the poor had fared during the 1970s and 1980s. In the United States a more impressionistic study by Michael Harrington (1962) discovered the 'other America' of the rural and urban poor. This growing poverty has increasingly been seen as a problem of social exclusion. Instead of being incorporated into the mainstream of the citizenry, increasing numbers suffer deprivations that exclude them from full participation in social life. Governments have, however, tended to focus on the social exclusion itself rather than addressing the underlying economic conditions that produce it.

Poverty in the United Kingdom

Townsend undertook an investigation of the extent and distribution of poverty in Britain in the 1960s, following

Figure 18.14 The national cake, 2002

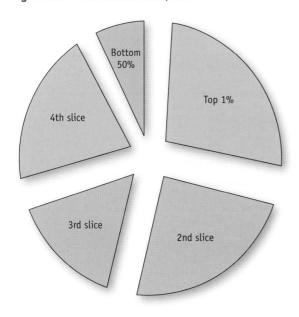

in the tradition of Booth and Rowntree. A study of poverty in London in the 1980s was designed to allow direct comparisons to be made with Booth's work of 100 years before.

Using the official poverty standard, based on social-assistance levels, Townsend showed that 7.3 per cent of British households were below the poverty line in 1968. A further 23.3 per cent were living on the margins of poverty with incomes only just above the income-support level and were in constant danger of falling below it. The corresponding figures for London in 1986 were 13.3 per cent in poverty and a further 13.3 per cent living on the margins (see Figure 18.15). The top 1 per cent of wealthy households in Townsend's survey had incomes 1,000 or more times larger than those living in poverty. If those below the poverty line and those on the margins are added together, these findings of 30.6 per cent of households nationally and 26.6 per cent of households in London living in poverty compare strikingly with Booth's discovery of 30.7 per cent of London households living in poverty (see Figure 18.5, p. 713).

Townsend saw poverty as a condition of relative deprivation, which he measured using indicators such as going without a week's holiday in the previous year, going without a cooked meal in the last fortnight, not having exclusive use of a toilet, sink, bath, or cooker, and so on. Most households experienced one or two of these deprivations, but 28 per cent of men and 30 per cent of women experienced true *multiple deprivation* (see also Coates and Silburn 1970). A family of four with an annual income of £2,500 or more in 1976 might experience two types of deprivation, but a similar family with an annual income of just £600 was likely to suffer from five or more deprivations.

THEORY AND METHODS   18.16

Poverty in the United Kingdom

Townsend's national survey (1979) involved interviews in 2,052 households drawn from a sample of 2,495, a completion rate of 82 per cent. These households contained 6,098 individuals, and the aim was to interview 'the housewife and all wage-earners' in each household. The interview schedule contained 175 questions on such topics as housing and living conditions, employment, income and savings, health, and disability. The main survey was carried out in 1968–9.

A number of related investigations were undertaken in various localities, but the main follow-up study was a survey of London carried out in 1985–6. A sample of 2,700 adults was used, and more detailed investigations were made in Hackney and Bromley (Townsend *et al.* 1987).

The official poverty line for a couple with two young children in 1968 was about £10.40 a week, excluding housing costs. In 1986 it was £70.15. A survey for 1996, when the official poverty line stood at £119, found that a majority of people in a national sample thought that a weekly income of £276, after tax, was necessary for such a family to avoid poverty.

The official poverty line now follows European Community definitions and defines a household as being in poverty if its income is 60 per cent or less than median household income. In 2007, the official poverty line for a couple without children was £199 after housing costs.

Figure 18.16 Poverty in the United Kingdom, new definition, 1994–2002

Percentage of individuals in households with less than 60% median income

1995	1997	1999	2002
24	25	24	22

Source: Sutherland *et al.* (2003: table 1).

Figure 18.15 Poverty in the United Kingdom and London, old definition, 1968–1989

	Percentage of households			
	UK 1968	UK 1979	UK 1989	London 1986
In poverty	7.3	12.0	20.0	13.3
On the margins	23.3	10.0	9.0	13.3
Total	30.6	22.0	29.0	26.6

Sources: Townsend (1979: table 7.2), Townsend *et al.* (1987: table 5.2), Oppenheim (1993: fig. 1).

One of the most important aspects of multiple deprivation was the condition of a person's housing. Of those actually living in poverty, 86 per cent experienced one or more serious housing problems from a list of major structural defects such as damp, leaking roof, and so on. Twenty-six per cent had three or more housing defects (Townsend 1979: table 13.11). Almost three-quarters of those on the margins of poverty had homes with one or more structural defects.

The poor were sharply divided from the larger category of manual workers. Townsend showed, for example, that among semi-skilled and unskilled manual worker families:

- 23 per cent lacked exclusive use of an indoor toilet, and 22 per cent did not have exclusive use of a bath or shower;
- 31 per cent lived in houses with serious structural defects;
- 54 per cent had only one room heated in winter;
- 91 per cent were without a telephone, and 35 per cent were without a vacuum cleaner.

These people, he argued, were living a precarious existence, and it needed only a relatively small change in their circumstances to tip them into the multiple deprivation of true poverty. Low pay or loss of earnings through unemployment could trigger the slide into poverty. Unemployment was, perhaps, the most significant factor. Two-fifths of unskilled and a quarter of semi-skilled males had had ten or more weeks of unemployment in the year of Townsend's survey, and a further 17 per cent had had at least one week of unemployment (Townsend 1979: table 17.4). Unskilled and semi-skilled workers who moved in and out of employment, who took on low-paid, seasonal, or casual work, or who, in general, had a precarious and marginal position in the labour market, faced the greatest risk of poverty. Forced into a dependence on welfare benefits, they often found it impossible to get by, especially when they had large families. They moved in and out of the margins of poverty, and periodically they fell into actual poverty.

The highest levels of poverty found by Townsend, both nationally and in London, were among single-person households (predominantly the elderly) and households with large numbers of children. Women are more often found in poverty than are men. This *feminization of poverty* is a result of the concentration of women in low-paid jobs and their disproportionate dependence on welfare benefits. Poverty was especially marked among men and women aged over 65. Over a half of all people of pensionable age were living in poverty or on the margins of poverty. The life-cycle effect on poverty that Rowntree had highlighted in his research was confirmed by Townsend, and this goes some way to explaining why there was a considerable turnover among those living in poverty.

The London survey found that the labour market operated in such a way as to concentrate poverty in certain areas. While the overall unemployment rate in London in 1986 was 11.9 per cent, it was more than twice this level in Hackney and Tower Hamlets. Townsend noted an increasing polarization between 'poor' boroughs such as Hackney, Tower Hamlets, Islington, Lambeth, and Newham, and affluent boroughs such as Harrow, Sutton, Bexley, Bromley, and Havering (see Figure 18.17, p. 728). He also found there to be a *racialization of poverty*, as members of ethnic minorities became concentrated in the occupations and boroughs that were especially likely to experience high levels of poverty. Young African Caribbean and Asian men, for example, had rates of unemployment that were almost three times the London average. Later research has shown that unemployment among young Asians in parts of Bradford in 1996 stood at 45 per cent, three times the national average level.

Growing poverty

Townsend's research showed the persistence of poverty into the post-war period. Although it did seem to decline somewhat during the 1960s and 1970s, it increased again during the 1980s (see Figure 18.15). This was a period of rapidly growing inequality, and poverty also deepened. The incidence of poverty was especially great among women and members of ethnic minorities.

The number of people in Britain whose final income after tax was less than a half of average income—the official European Union poverty level—was about 10 per cent of the population through the 1960s. The proportion fell below this level in the mid-1970s, but since 1978 it has increased. Although it fell back slightly after 1992, it rose to just under 20 per cent (Barclay 1995: 17) and had only fallen slightly by 2000, when 17.7 per cent of households (about 12 million people) were living in poverty.

> ### ⮑ *Connections*
> Remember our discussion of averages (Box 18.7 on p. 706)? The poverty line defined by 50 per cent or less of average income is based on a calculation of mean income. Calculations of the mean are affected by extremely high values—in this case the relatively small number of extremely large incomes. For this reason, many calculations of household poverty use median income instead. As we have shown above, the official European Union poverty line is calculated as households with 60 per cent or less of median income.

Those in the bottom 20 per cent of the income distribution—the bottom quintile of the income distribution—include large numbers of pensioner households and lone parents with dependent children. The most recent figures

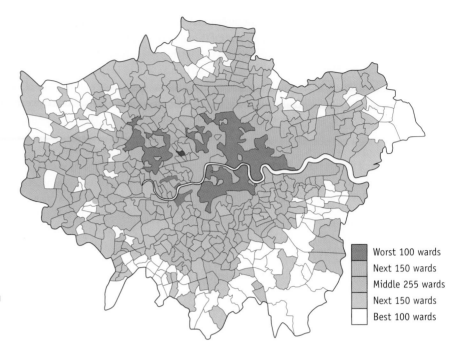

Figure 18.17 The distribution
of poverty in London 1986

Source: Townsend *et al.* (1987: 43).

Worst 100 wards
Next 150 wards
Middle 255 wards
Next 150 wards
Best 100 wards

available, those for 2002, show that one-third of the poor are in low-paid employment, a quarter are unemployed, and a quarter are retired. In a growing number of two-adult and family households, neither partner is able to find regular employment, and the whole household is plunged into poverty. This has created particular problems of child poverty. Thirty-two per cent of children live in poverty, the highest rate of any country in the European Union. About 200,000 people have no permanent home and live in 'bed and breakfast' accommodation, and 75,000 of these are officially classified as homeless. Nevertheless, the number of homeless rough-sleepers has fallen.

Black and Asian households are also overrepresented among the poor. Around two-thirds of Pakistani and Bangladeshi families are in the bottom one-fifth of the income distribution. Black and Asian households suffer from extremely high levels of unemployment, and Asian women in particular are disproportionately involved in low-paid home-working. Differences in unemployment worsened during the 1980s, with ethnic minorities being desperately hit by job losses. African Caribbean, Pakistani, and Bangladeshi males are more than twice as likely to be unemployed than are white males, and Bangladeshi females have an unemployment rate that is four or five times the rate for white females. Black and Asian people are twice as likely to be unemployed as white people.

These facts are results of a racialized employment structure. Just under 19 per cent of white males in 1982 were employed in professional and managerial work, but this was the case for only 5 per cent of African Caribbeans and 13 per cent of Asians. Conversely, while 16 per cent of white males were employed in semi-skilled and unskilled

manual work, this was the case for more than a third of African Caribbean and Asian men. As one of the most important studies in this area found, male ethnic-minority workers earn between 10 per cent and 15 per cent less than white male workers (C. Brown 1984).

Black women are doubly disadvantaged in the labour market. As black people and as women, they experience both racism and sexism. The employment rate for white women in 1995 was 68 per cent, but rates for Asian women ranged from 13 per cent for Bangladeshis to 17 per cent for Pakistanis. 'Sweated' textile trades of the kind studied by Booth are now important sources of low-paid work for many Asian and black women who work from home or in small workshops. It has been estimated that in the 1980s the pay of such women averaged 90p an hour, though some were earning as little as 10p an hour (Mitter 1986).

Using the official European poverty line, comparative research has shown that the countries with the lowest levels of poverty in Europe in 1985 were Belgium, the Netherlands, and Germany, each with about 7.8 per cent of their households living in poverty. The European average was 13.9 per cent of households, and the level in Britain was just below this. France, with 17.5 per cent of households in poverty, was just above the European average. The highest concentrations of poverty were found in Portugal, Greece, Ireland, and Spain, which all had massive problems of rural poverty. Research in Europe has highlighted the growth of poverty among ethnic minorities, women, and young people across the whole Union. Migrant workers from Turkey and North Africa, for example, have been especially heavily hit by unemployment and recession in France, Germany, and the Netherlands (Room 1990).

Poverty in the United States, as measured by an official subsistence measure, stood at 12–14 per cent throughout the 1970s and 1980s. On the basis of the official European poverty measure, however, the level of poverty in the United States would be 17 per cent, about the same as in France. About a third of those in poverty were rural or urban African Americans, and 2.4 million people were living in the inner-city ghettos of Chicago, New York, and other big cities, where poverty rates exceeded 40 per cent. Two-thirds of these ghetto residents were African Americans, and a quarter were Mexicans or Puerto Ricans (W. J. Wilson 1987). Levels of unemployment among African Americans were more than twice those of whites during the 1980s, and wages for those in employment were about three-quarters of white male wages.

It was findings such as these on the United States that led to the debate over the so-called underclass of urban poor. We have already discussed some aspects of this idea and the political definitions of them as the undeserving poor. Central to this debate has been the idea of a culture of poverty and an associated *cycle of deprivation*. According to this view, poor children are born into a culture that socializes them into inappropriate work habits and prevents them from overcoming their poverty. As they grow up in poverty, their own children are born in poverty, and so the cycle continues.

> **⬧ Connections**
> You should already be thinking about our earlier remarks on the underclass. If you were not, you should quickly review what we said in 'The undeserving poor and the underclass', pp. 704–6.

The evidence that we have reviewed shows that extremes of poverty still persist and that this is particularly concentrated in areas with large numbers of ethnic-minority and lone-parent households. The evidence provides little support for the idea that people are trapped in an underclass by a cycle of deprivation. Those living in poverty are not sharply divided from other manual workers, and households continually fall in and out of poverty.

Work undertaken by the British Household Panel Study showed that only one in six of those with incomes less than half the average in 1991 were still living in poverty by 1997. This was mainly because those who had been unemployed had found employment, though a person's position was also improved whenever other members of the same household (for example, a husband or wife) increased their earnings. Most of those who had moved out of poverty had moved into its margins, and not all would eventually escape the risk of falling back into poverty in the future. This is confirmed by the fact that others had fallen from the margins into true poverty. Families falling into poverty were the victims of redundancy, divorce, or the death of a partner, all of which seriously reduced family incomes. Almost a third of the whole population had some experience of poverty in the four-year period of the study. Those who were most trapped in long-term poverty—lasting four years or more—were pensioners and lone parents (S. Jenkins 1996; Berthoud and Gershuny 2000).

Poverty is not the condition of a distinct underclass; it is endemic to the lives of unskilled manual workers and their families, and it is an ever-present possibility for many other manual workers. A full exploration of this issue, however, depends upon a proper understanding of what it is to be a class, and we will return to the question of the underclass once more in the following chapter.

Disadvantaged life chances

Inequalities in economic resources are significant because of the differences in life chances that they produce. In this section we explore the deprivations in health and housing associated with economic inequalities, and we show how they are structured by gender and by ethnicity.

> **⬧ Connections**
> We look at overall trends in health, fertility, and mortality in Chapter 8, pp. 276–9 and 281–2. You might want to look at this as background for our discussion of inequalities in this section.

The normal length of a healthy pregnancy is somewhere between 38 and 41 weeks, but the actual length of pregnancy varies with the class of the mother. Pregnancies run to normal term in about 80 per cent of women from professional backgrounds, but this is the case for only 70 per cent of women from a manual-worker background. Children born into manual-worker families are far more likely than those born into professional families to have been either over-term or premature. These inequalities continue after birth, as the length of pregnancy, along with the mother's own health, affect birth weight and a child's later health. Birth weight is significantly lower in manual-worker families than among the professions (I. Reid 1977: tables 4.1 and 4.2). Figure 18.18 (p. 730) shows that rates of infant mortality are also higher among those born into manual-working households. Rates of infant mortality declined for all occupational categories over the course of the twentieth century, but they are still almost twice as high among unskilled manual households as they are among professionals and managers. Among those children who survive the first year of life, health chances in later life also vary by class background.

These and other health inequalities persist in later life. Rates of death, general health problems, and specific

Briefing: occupations and social class 18.17

Many discussions of inequality use occupational categories that are treated as social classes. This raises many important questions that we pursue in Chapter 17. For the present discussion we treat these purely as convenient occupational categories.

The first classification used in Figure 18.18 is the Registrar General's Classification, which has the following categories:

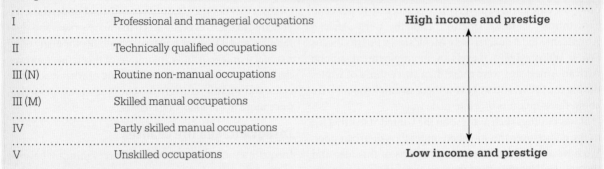

I	Professional and managerial occupations	**High income and prestige**
II	Technically qualified occupations	
III (N)	Routine non-manual occupations	
III (M)	Skilled manual occupations	
IV	Partly skilled manual occupations	
V	Unskilled occupations	**Low income and prestige**

The Registrar General's Classification is discussed more fully in Chapter 19, p. 753. The second classification is based on the new ONS classification, also discussed in Chapter 19. After reading Chapter 19, you may wish to return to this section to see what the use of the concept of social class adds to the conclusions that we draw.

problems such as total tooth loss are lower among professional and managerial workers than they are among manual workers (I. Reid 1977: tables 4.11 and 4.13). A number of other health chances show an occupational gradient with a strong association between health and economic resources.

Unskilled workers are two and a half times more likely to report that their own health is merely fair or poor than are professional and managerial workers. Research into causes of death has found that rates of tuberculosis and bronchitis show the same occupational gradient, and it is only slightly less marked for heart disease. Many of these inequalities are associated with differences in smoking behaviour, which, for both men and women, follow the

same occupational gradient (Black *et al.* 1980: table 34). Crude death rates, for both men and women, follow the same pattern. These occupational differences intersect with gender differences: standardized male mortality rates are twice the female rates in every occupational category.

Health inequalities also reflect ethnic differences. Figure 18.19 shows that the poorest rates of subjective experiences of health are found among Pakistanis and Bangladeshis. Figure 18.20 (p. 732) shows similar variations in rates of long-term illness or disability. Ethnic differences extend also to deaths. Still births in the United Kingdom are lowest for British-born mothers and highest for mothers born in Pakistan or Bangladesh. British-born mothers show the same relatively low risk of having their children die in the

Figure 18.18 Infant mortality, United Kingdom, 1921–2003

Occupational category	Deaths under 1 year per 1,000 live births				Deaths per 1,000 live births for children born within marriage			
	1921	1950	1970	1989		2003		
I	38	17	12	6.0		Neonatal	Post-neonatal	Infant
II	55	22	14	6.1	Managerial and professional	0.03	0.05	0.08
III (N)	76	28	16	7.0	Intermediate	0.07	0.09	0.16
III (M)				7.5	Routine and manual	0.04	0.19	0.23
IV	89	33	20	10.4				
V	97	40	31	11.0	All	0.05	0.13	0.18

Sources: Black *et al.* (1980: table 17), *OPCS Monitor* (1992), and *Health Statistics Quarterly*, 23 (Autumn 2004), table 8.

first year of life, while Pakistan-born and Caribbean-born women have much higher rates. A contrast between mothers born in Britain and those born in the Caribbean or the Indian subcontinent is also found in statistics on low birth weight and on such childhood diseases as rickets (deficiency of vitamin D). Among adults aged 20 or more, those born outside the United Kingdom showed higher than average rates for a number of death-inducing illnesses and accidents. Only in the case of bronchitis were rates consistently lower for the non-UK born.

Some of these differences can be explained by differences in lifestyle (for example, differences in diet and in the use of cooking fats), but far more significant is the over-concentration among ethnic minorities of low pay, unemployment, and poor housing. These conditions are known to increase the chances of health problems among all groups. People are made ill not by their ethnicity but by their poverty.

Housing conditions are central to multiple deprivation. The poor are more likely to live in poor-quality housing, and bad housing is a major cause of health problems. Very few of those in professional and managerial occupations live in overcrowded homes (the official criterion is more than 1.5 people to each room), but this is not unusual for unskilled workers. Townsend's research showed that overcrowded housing is often in a poor state of repair. Problems of cold and damp housing are especially significant for childhood and adult health.

Inequalities in housing were a massive problem for overseas migrants to Britain in the 1950s and 1960s. New migrants did not qualify for public housing and frequently lived in shared and poor-quality accommodation: in 1961 about a half of African Caribbean households were overcrowded, and even in 1974 almost two-fifths of ethnic-minority households lacked sole use of a bath, hot water, and indoor toilet. Migrants and their families were largely confined to run-down inner-city housing. By the 1980s, rates of overcrowding were far lower, although major inequalities persisted.

According to the 1991 Census, an average of just 2.2 per cent of the whole population was living in overcrowded conditions, but the rate was 47.1 per cent among those identifying themselves as Bangladeshi, and 29.7 per cent among Pakistanis. Rates among black Britons were lower, though there were sharp differences between Caribbean and African identifiers. Those identifying themselves as Black African had 15.1 per cent overcrowding, and they were less likely than the average household to live in self-contained accommodation. They also showed higher rates for the lack of basic bath and toilet facilities. (See also Ratcliffe 1981 and Karn *et al.* 1985.)

The Labour government, first elected in 1997, did not explicitly deny the existence of poverty as its Conservative predecessors had done. The existence of significant deprivation in income, assets, and living conditions was recognized, but this deprivation was seen not as a result of inequality but as reflecting *social exclusion*. On this view, exclusion of the poor from normal social contacts is what explains their poverty. For New Labour, a successful policy on poverty had to attack the social exclusion that produces it: the poor must

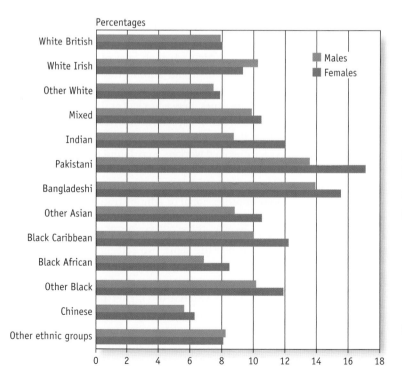

Figure 18.19 Health and ethnicity, England and Wales, 2001

Source: Office for National Statistics (2010).

⊃ This table shows age-standardized 'not good' health rates by ethnic group and sex. Age-standardized rates are rates of illness that have been standardized across the various ethnic groups by taking account of the varying age structures of each group.

⊃ Look at our discussion of ethnic identity in Chapter 6, pp. 194–5, for some help in interpreting these ethnic differences.

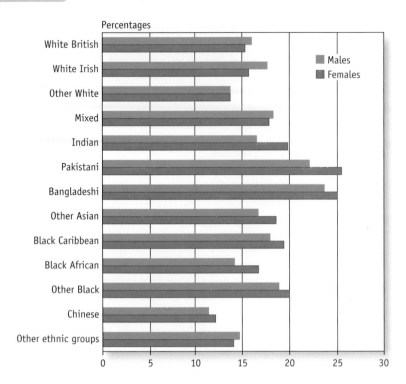

Figure 18.20 Long-term illness, disability, and ethnicity, England and Wales, 2001

Source: Office for National Statistics (2010).

be helped to build new networks of contacts through which they can build up job and housing opportunities, acquire information about education and health treatment, and so on. New Labour policy, then, reverses the causal relationship uncovered by sociological research: where research shows that a lack of economic resources is the cause of social deprivations and weakened social participation, New Labour sees the weakened social participation as the cause of deprivation and material poverty. The policy conclusion drawn is that there is no need to engage in any significant economic redistribution. Rather, it is necessary to encourage the deprived to improve the networking skills that will enable them to participate fully as citizens of their society.

Continuing closure

The Glass study of occupational mobility showed that Britain was far from being an open society in the first half of the twentieth century. The situation seems to have changed little since then. A series of projects directed by John Goldthorpe have demonstrated this well and have put the British situation in its international context.

Occupational mobility and stability

Goldthorpe's Oxford Mobility Study threw considerable doubt on the idea that Britain is a society of openness, meritocracy, and equality of opportunity. The study showed that barriers to social mobility remained sharp and that openness had barely altered since the 1940s.

Figure 18.21 shows Goldthorpe's findings on **outflow mobility** in England and Wales. Outflow mobility measures the proportion of individuals who have moved out of the social position in which they began their lives. Low levels of outflow mobility are signs of self-recruitment. The Oxford study found the highest levels of self-recruitment among higher professionals and less-skilled workers; clerical and supervisory workers show much lower levels of self-recruitment. Much of the mobility that does occur is simply short-range movement into neighbouring categories. There are particularly high rates of mobility between the two professional and administrative categories and between the routine occupations and the professional and administrative ones. Between a half and two-thirds of professionals and administrators are in the same kind of occupations as their fathers, and almost the same proportion of sons of less-skilled workers were found in manual work.

There has been very little long-range mobility, which Goldthorpe defines as movement from less-skilled manual jobs to professional or administrative ones. Eight per cent of sons of men in category II were downwardly mobile to unskilled work, and just under 8 per cent were upwardly mobile between the same two categories. Nevertheless, large numbers of manual workers did move up the occupational hierarchy: 18.4 per cent of the sons of skilled manual workers entered the higher professions, as did 15.4 per cent of the sons of supervisors. This reflects the opening-up of opportunities that occurred with the expansion of professional and administrative work in the post-war period, and the contraction of manual work over

Figure 18.21 Outflow mobility, England and Wales, 1972

Fathers' social class   Sons' social class

Fathers' social class	I	II	III	IV	V	VI	VII	Total
I Higher professional and administrative	48.4	18.9	9.3	8.2	4.5	4.5	6.2	100
II Lower professional and administrative	31.9	22.6	10.7	8.0	9.2	9.6	8.0	100
III Routine non-manual	19.2	15.7	10.8	8.6	13.0	15.0	17.8	100
IV Small employers, proprietors, and self-employed	12.8	11.1	7.8	24.9	8.7	14.7	19.9	100
V Lower technical and manual supervisory workers	15.4	13.2	9.4	8.0	16.6	20.1	17.2	100
VI Skilled manual workers	18.4	8.9	8.4	7.1	12.2	29.6	25.4	100
VII Semi-skilled and unskilled manual workers	6.9	7.8	7.9	6.8	12.5	23.5	34.8	100

LONG RANGE · Downward mobility · Upward mobility

Source: Heath (1981: table 2.1).

❓ In a table showing outflow mobility, as above, the percentages are calculated across the rows. A table of inflow mobility looks very similar, but the percentages are calculated down the columns. Why is this? Would it make any sense to add up totals for the columns above?

➲ Whenever you look at a table, make sure that you read the percentages in the correct direction.

the course of the whole century. For example, upward mobility had increased for people born after 1928 and who entered their working careers in the 1950s and 1960s. Those born since the 1930s were the first to go through the reformed secondary schools of the 1940s and their improved educational prospects coincided with an expansion of occupational opportunities.

Manual occupations are far more homogeneous than non-manual occupations. This is particularly clear from data on **inflow mobility**, which measures the proportion of individuals within an occupational category who have come from specific other categories. It is a measure of similarity in social background. Nearly three-quarters of manual workers are second-generation manual workers, many being third or later generation. On the other hand, only just over a third of professional and administrative workers are the sons of men in the same kind of work. As Blau and Duncan (1967) discovered for the United States, the professional and administrative categories expanded so rapidly that they had to recruit from outside their own boundaries and so are today very diverse in their social background. The contraction of manual work, on the other hand, means that it has been unnecessary to recruit large numbers from outside.

Figure 18.22 (p. 734) shows data on social mobility over time using a three-class model. About a third of all men were upwardly mobile between 1972 and 1997, while only one-sixth were downwardly mobile. There was some evidence, however, that the increase in upward mobility had fallen somewhat during the years 1992–7. Manual workers were coming to form a smaller proportion of the population, while the managerial and professional workers were becoming more numerous. The highest social class, nevertheless, remained highly self-recruiting, with little tendency for any sons of men in this class to be downwardly mobile.

Figure 18.23 (p. 734) presents the Oxford results in the same form as Blau and Duncan's data for the United States

THEORY AND METHODS   **18.18**

The Oxford Mobility Study

The study was carried out by John H. Goldthorpe and others, at Nuffield College, Oxford, in 1972. They used a sample of 10,000 adult males (aged 20–64) in England and Wales. A follow-up study in 1974 collected data on attitudes. The original intention was to compare the 1972 results with those from the Glass study (1954), but detailed comparisons proved impossible as the original Glass data no longer existed. Goldthorpe analysed the 1972 data in terms of seven occupational categories (see p. 755), which differ from those used by Glass. Like the Glass categories, however, these were intended to form a social-class classification, and we discuss this aspect of the work in Chapter 19, pp. 754–5. For some purposes, Goldthorpe followed Blau and Duncan (1967), and assigned occupations to individual scores on a 124-point-scale that reflects their income and prestige.

The main publications are *Social Mobility and Class Structure* (Goldthorpe 1980) and *Origins and Destinations* (Halsey *et al.* 1980), both of which are summarized in Heath (1981). A companion study for Scotland was undertaken by Payne (1987*a*), though this followed a different theoretical line.

Figure 18.22 Trends in social mobility, Great Britain, 1972–1997

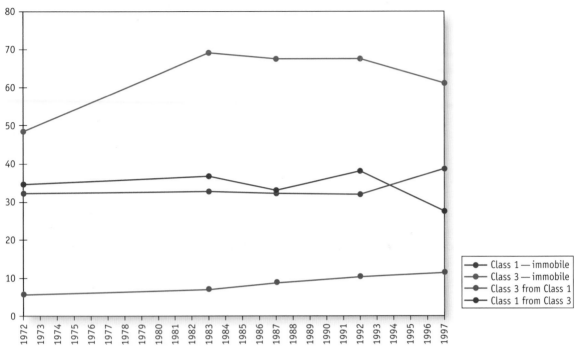

Source: Payne and Roberts (2002: figure 1, using data from the British Election Study).

(see Figure 18.9, p. 719). This shows that virtually all the relationships are weaker than they are in the United States, though the general model is confirmed. The residuals are, once more, very high. As has been indicated before, however, low residuals would suggest a society in which there is no freedom of action and everything is preordained by the facts of birth.

Although the Oxford study collected information only on men, Heath's summary (1981) used data from the General Household Survey to try to rectify this problem. Comparing women's occupations in 1975 with that of their fathers (still not their mothers), Heath found that the concentration of women's employment in routine white-collar

work and in semi- and unskilled work means that there are very high levels of downward mobility for those born into professional or administrative families. As we show in Chapter 19, p. 757, however, there is much evidence to suggest that women's occupations are badly handled in these occupational classifications. Nevertheless, the rates of downward mobility for women do seem to be significantly higher than those for men. An assessment of these gender inequalities, however, depends upon an understanding of patterns of marriage and household formation and the structuring of gender-roles within families.

Most discussions of openness have used measures of absolute mobility, as have our discussions in this chapter

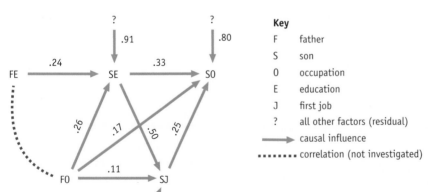

Key

F	father
S	son
O	occupation
E	education
J	first job
?	all other factors (residual)
→	causal influence
·······►	correlation (not investigated)

Figure 18.23   Occupational attainment, England and Wales, 1972

Source: adapted from Heath (1981: diagram 5.2).

➲ You can find a full list of the Goldthorpe categories in Figure 19.4 (p. 755).

so far. Goldthorpe, however, attaches particular significance to the measurement of relative mobility. **Absolute mobility** is a measure of the proportion of individuals who have been socially mobile, whether upwards or downwards. **Relative mobility** refers to the mobility chances of one group compared with another. The expansion of professional and administrative occupations may have increased the opportunities for all to rise up the occupational structure, but there may still be continuing differences in the chances of those from one category relative to another.

Calculations of relative mobility are very complex, and they need not detain us here. Goldthorpe shows, however, that the chances of the son of a manual worker rising into a professional or administrative occupation are a half of the chances of the son of a non-manual worker rising to a similar level, and a quarter of the chances of the son of a professional or administrative worker following directly in his father's footsteps. Looking at trends over time, Goldthorpe concluded that absolute rates had changed because of occupational change, while relative mobility rates were largely unaltered. The apparent openness of British society is an illusion that results from the focus on absolute mobility.

International comparisons

Goldthorpe and his co-workers have extended their work to the international level and produced an important comparative study of social mobility (Erikson and Goldthorpe 1993). The research compared the British situation with that in various European and non-European countries. This investigation involved the use of data from twelve national studies undertaken between 1970 and 1978, the original England and Wales data from the Oxford Mobility Study forming a part of this. As with the original Oxford study, a major limitation of the research is that it concerns only men aged 30 or over. Women and their experiences of social mobility are not considered.

The international study did not simply reanalyse existing data from the various countries. This would have meant replacing a variety of schemes with a crude division between manual and non-manual workers, as Lipset and Bendix (1959) had done. Instead, Erikson and Goldthorpe undertook a systematic recoding and re-examination of the original data from the projects, using a new set of occupational categories. The categories used in the Oxford study were slightly modified to take account of the different occupational structures in the various countries. Separate categories for farmers and for agricultural workers were added, small employers were separated from routine non-manual workers, and various other changes were made.

Erikson and Goldthorpe had hoped to uncover patterns of international variation in occupational mobility, but they found little sign of significant variations. There is what they call a standard pattern of mobility around which actual rates vary.

Typically in the advanced societies, about one-third of sons enter the same kinds of occupation as their fathers. Between a half and three-quarters have experienced some degree of social mobility, and there has been little change in this over time. Men born in the 1930s and the 1940s showed much greater cross-national similarity in their occupational mobility experiences than there was for those born a generation earlier. Rates of mobility are slightly below the norm in Ireland and in Poland, and above it in Hungary, but these three countries were beginning to converge towards the standard pattern. Overall, there is a tendency for mobility to increase at an early stage of industrialization, but thereafter there is no particular trend of increase or decrease in mobility. Erikson and Goldthorpe summarize the cross-national pattern of mobility as one of 'trendless fluctuation': mobility rates go up and down, almost at random, with no structural variations between societies over time.

This is rather a surprising conclusion. It might have been expected, for example, that there would be significant and systematic differences between Western and Eastern Europe, between areas with different national cultures, and between economies with different industrial structures. All these expectations were disproved, so far as absolute mobility patterns were concerned. All the major countries were remarkably similar, and there were no particular trends over time. The results of the research lead Goldthorpe and his colleagues to support the hypothesis first set out by Featherman, Jones, and Hauser (1975) that there is a broad *similarity* in mobility patterns in industrial societies: the similarities in mobility patterns outweigh any minor national differences (see also Lipset and Bendix 1959 for the earlier period).

To explore this idea further, they construct what they call a *core model*, to which the patterns of social mobility in England and France corresponded most closely. In this core model, the salaried managers and professionals are at the top of the hierarchy of occupational desirability and advantage. They have the greatest resources and the greatest barriers to entry from outside. Non-skilled jobs are at the opposite pole of the hierarchy and are the easiest to enter for those who are unable to maintain or to improve their social position. There is, for all occupational categories, a strong tendency towards the inheritance of occupational position.

The sectoral division between agriculture, on the one hand, and industry and services, on the other, forms a major barrier to mobility, as this economic boundary also tends to coincide with cultural and geographical differences. Mobility is fairly high between small business and the professional and administrative category, and between

Figure 18.24 Upward social mobility in seven countries

	Germany	France	Italy	Great Britain	Sweden	Poland	Hungary
Men							
1970s	31.7	25.9	—	32.8	35.1	22.1	26.9
1980s	33.6	29.1	29.0	33.1	35.3	24.8	34.7
1990s	33.3	29.9	35.9	31.7	36.6	26.3	35.9
Women							
1970s	25.8	27.8	—	27.5	23.9	19.5	23.2
1980s	29.6	32.9	38.5	29.0	27.5	31.7	38.8
1990s	32.2	33.2	36.7	30.6	33.5	34.1	42.0

Source: Breen (2004: 48, 66, tables 3.6 and 3.17).

skilled and non-skilled manual work. Variations from this core model were relatively minor and were due largely to particular historical circumstances and political policies. The broad picture, however, was one of similarity. Inheritance of occupational position was strongest in Ireland and weakest in Sweden, and Sweden appeared, overall, as the most open society. This was not simply a European pattern. Evidence from the United States, Australia, and Japan showed no great departure from the core model.

More recent information comes from later studies summarized in Figure 18.24, which shows the upward social mobility of both men and women in a number of countries. There is a broad similarity across all societies, though there are also quite significant differences. Between a quarter and a third of all men were upwardly mobile. The levels of upward mobility were broadly similar in Britain, Germany, and Sweden. France and Italy, on the other hand, showed lower rates of mobility. All societies, however, showed a slight tendency for rates of mobility to increase over time. The overall 'fluidity' or openness of the class structure (taking account of both upward and downward mobility) was lowest in Britain and Germany and highest in Italy, Sweden, and Hungary. The pattern was less clear for women. Women's rates of upward mobility are generally in the same range as for men, though they are closer to the bottom end of the range. In a number of countries, however, women's upward mobility rates have been increasing and are above those for men. Rates of downward mobility for women are generally much higher than they are for men.

 Stop and reflect

In this section we have looked at the rediscovery of poverty in the 1960s and the growing social divisions that have emerged during the 1970s and 1980s.

- Inequality of assets has stabilized and inequality of income has increased since the 1970s. This reflects changing economic conditions and shifts in government policy.

- Investigations into poverty show that, depending on how it is measured, the amount of poverty in Britain remains very great. On the official European poverty standard, just under 20 per cent of the British population are living in poverty. Britain today is a more unequal society than Germany and Sweden, but less unequal than France and the United States.

- What do you think are the major difficulties involved in making international comparisons of social inequality?

- Disadvantaged life chances are a feature of poverty. These have increasingly been feminized and racialized.

To develop your understanding of the impact of racism and sexism on social inequality, you may find it useful to look back at our discussions of sex–gender and ethnicity in Chapters 5 and 6. The final point that we made in this section concerned trends in openness over time.

- Openness has barely altered since the 1940s, despite the apparent increase in social mobility. Patterns of mobility are broadly similar in all the advanced societies.

- Why do people believe that British society is more open than sociological research shows it to be?

Key concepts

- absolute mobility 735
- assets 711
- citizenship 697
- closed (structure of inequality) 716
- equality 697
- equality of opportunity 698
- equality of outcome 698
- equality of outset 698

- income 710
- inflow mobility 733
- life chances 697
- meritocracy 698
- occupational mobility 716
- open (structure of inequality) 716
- outflow mobility 732
- particularism 699

- perfect mobility 717
- relative mobility 735
- relative poverty 701
- sexism 700
- underclass 706
- universalism 699
- wealth 702

Workshop 18

Study 18 Child poverty and social policy

Central to debates on inequality has been the question of child poverty. Lucinda Platt (2005a) has traced the relationship between sociological research and the policy agenda in Britain. She shows that the building of the welfare state in the middle of the twentieth century was the culmination of a long and pro-tracted struggle in which social research played a key role. This involved establishing definitions of poverty and also of child-hood. It was only when these definitions had been established that proper measures of child poverty could be made and could begin to influence the formation of government policy.

The impact of research on policy was immense, but not always in obvious and direct ways. Platt shows that research was far more likely to have an impact on policy if it could appeal to conserva-tive instincts and to philanthropic and religious bodies concerned with moral improvement. A mere identification of the facts about a particular issue was not sufficient. Thus, Platt points to the major impact of Rowntree's studies of poverty in York, showing that its influence on policy did not involve any direct translation of his ideas into specific policies. Rowntree's measures of pov-erty, produced in 1900, centred on the identification of a mini-mum necessary wage, but it was not until 1999 that minimum wage legislation was actually introduced. Similarly, Eleanor Rathbone undertook important work on family allowances in the first decades of the twentieth century, and she became a Member of Parliament and a government minister, yet family allowances were not actually introduced until 1945.

Particularly striking is Platt's argument that an improvement in provision for children depended upon the position of women. Both women and children were seen as dependants, and policy changes could be made on this basis. There was little support for the idea of paying a family allowance directly to mothers. Instead, policy debate focused much more on the idea of paying the man a 'family wage'. Gender issues were also inextricably linked with those of class, and policy debates were often con-cerned with the perceived failings of working-class mothers.

The development of pressure groups such as the Child Poverty Action Group from the 1960s is seen as having been very impor-tant in setting a research agenda, but Platt holds that the impact of current and future research will be limited by the same kinds of constraints that have operated in the past. Radical activism on the basis of sociological research findings is unlikely to be successful unless it can come to terms with the entrenched ideologies and practices through which policy is shaped.

⊃ Go to the website of the Child Poverty Action Group (www.cpag.org.uk) and find its manifesto for policy change. Identify its ten steps to a society free of child poverty.

❷ What kinds of social research are relevant to each of these steps?

⊃ Identify the main obstacles to change in each area.

Media watch 18 Wealthy families

At various points in this chapter we have mentioned particularly wealthy individuals. Figure 18.25 (p. 738) lists the 2009 compilation of wealthy individuals and families (not totally comparable with other sources used in this chapter). The full list covers the 2,000 wealthiest people in Britain, but we have extracted the 'top 20' from this list—there are actually twenty-three individuals and families because some are ranked equal.

The names in the list are quite diverse, and many will be unfamiliar to you. A number of those listed are members of old aristocratic families whose wealth still comes from land: the Duke of Westminster and the Earl Cadogan. Many others are from commercial and financial families, and only a small number have an industrial background.

Industrial interests in the top 20 of wealth include Lakshmi Mittal, owner of a steel-making empire and a pay TV company

called 'Bollywood for You', and Hans Rausing, the inventor of the TetraPack system for milk and juice cartons who is now involved with a company developing new plastic packaging materials. At number nine on the list is Rausing's niece Kirsten, who spends most of her inherited fortune on horse-racing. Other industrial and retailing interests include Sir Philip Green's British Home Stores, Sir Ken Morrison's Asda, and the Hinduja brothers. Financiers and property-owners on the list include the Reuben brothers, the energy-industry dealer Joe Lewis, the Fleming investment dynasty (James Bond author Ian Fleming was a family member), and the Oppenheimer diamond dynasty. Roman Abramovitch made a fortune in the Russian oil industry and is now the owner of Chelsea Football Club. Many names on the list will be unfamiliar to most people, though their products may be more familiar: Charlene de Carvalho is the daughter of a member

Figure 18.25 Britain's wealthiest people, 2009

Rank	Name	Worth	Source of wealth
1	Lakshmi Mittal and family	£10,800m.	Steel
2	Roman Abramovich	£7,000m.	Oil, industry
3	The Duke of Westminster	£6,500m.	Property
4	Ernesto and Kirsty Bertarelli	£5,000m.	Pharmaceuticals
5	Hans Rausing and family	£4,000m.	Packaging
6	Sir Philip and Lady Green	£3,830m.	Retailing
7	Charlene and Michel de Carvalho	£2,960m.	Inheritance, brewing, banking
8	Sammy and Eyal Ofer	£2,677m.	Shipping, property
9=	David and Simon Reuben	£2,500m.	Property
9=	Joe Lewis	£2,500m.	Foreign exchange, investment
9=	John Fredriksen	£2,500m.	Shipping
9=	Kirsten and Jorn Rausing	£2,500m.	Inheritance, investment
13	Sean Quinn and family	£2,295m.	Property, insurance
14	Earl Cadogan and family	£2,000m.	Property
15	Alan Parker	£1,800m.	Duty-free shopping
16	Sir Ken Morrison and family	£1,610m.	Supermarkets
17	Roddie Fleming and family	£1,550m.	Finance
18=	Alisher Usmanov	£1,500m.	Steel, mines
18=	Eddie and Sol Zakay	£1,500m.	Property
18=	Mahdi al-Tajir	£1,500m.	Metals, oil, water
18=	Mark Pears and family	£1,500m.	Property
18=	Nicky Oppenheimer	£1,500m.	Diamonds, mining
18=	Poju Zabludowicz	£1,500m.	Property, hotels

Source: The Rich List, in *Sunday Times*, 7 December 2009.

of a brewing family that goes under the better-known name of Heineken.

❷ Consult the reference book *Who's Who* and examine the entries for people listed in the table. Compile information on their education, family background, and other personal characteristics. Can you construct a portrait or profile of the very wealthy? You might like to look at Mills's attempt to do this for the United States in his *Power Elite* (Mills 1956).

❷ Some of those listed are individuals, while others are families. Do you think that the individual or the family is the appropriate unit of wealth holding? Should the listing have been consistent one way or the other?

❷ Find out the current level of the national minimum wage. How long would it take someone on the national minimum to accumulate enough wealth to enter this top 20? The person ranked at number 1,771 in the full list (TV celebrity Anne Robinson—by no means the weakest link on the list) had assets of £30 million. How long would it take to reach this level?

❷ What annual income would be needed to allow someone (after allowing for ordinary household expenses) to accumulate £30 million in, say, ten years? What does this tell you about the relationship between earned income and inherited assets?

Discussion points

Look back over the summary points in this chapter. You will find it useful to revise our arguments in relation to the conceptual issues involved in studying inequality, the problem of measuring poverty, and the question of occupational mobility and openness.

Equality, inequality, and citizenship

- What are the three conceptions of equality that were identified? How would advocates of each view regard (*a*) sexism and (*b*) racism?

- What does it mean to claim that poverty is 'relative' not 'absolute'?

- What do you understand by the term 'underclass'? Is it a useful sociological concept? How does it relate to the idea of a culture of poverty?

- What criticisms would you make of the functionalist theory of inequality?

- What implications can be drawn from measured differences in intelligence between social groups?

Measuring poverty and inequality

It is not easy to measure poverty, and definitions are often contested by politicians who wish to obscure its extent. We have, however, introduced a number of ideas that will help you to understand poverty and wealth:

- What do you understand by the following terms: life chances, real wages, secondary poverty?

- Booth's language for describing the categories of the population carries obvious moral judgements. Does the use of such words as 'loafers' and 'vicious' undermine his factual conclusions?

- Make sure that you understand the general ideas behind the terms: percentile, mean, and median. If you are still not happy reading tables and graphs, try the exercises suggested under Figures 18.3 (p. 711) and 18.13 (p. 725).

Openness and mobility

You will find that a good grasp of occupational mobility helps you to approach questions of inequality and opportunity. We look at some other aspects of occupational mobility in Chapter 19.

- How would you distinguish between intergenerational mobility and intra-generational mobility?

- What do you understand by the terms absolute mobility and relative mobility.

The study of occupational mobility has become a very complex area in sociology, and we have only touched upon some of the many issues here. You need to know only some very basic ideas.

- Make sure that you understand the general ideas behind the concepts of correlation and the path diagram. Do not worry if you do not understand this in detail. Try to concentrate on grasping the general principles. If you ever need to calculate correlations, you can always get someone else to do the maths for you!

Explore further

Good general coverage of the topics in this chapter can be found in:

Fraser, S. (1995) (ed.), *The Bell Curve Wars* (New York: Basic Books). *This collection of papers gives a good critical review of the arguments of Herrnstein and Murray.*

Hills, J. (1995), *Joseph Rowntree Inquiry into Income and Wealth*, ii (York: Joseph Rowntree Foundation). *One of the most up-to-date and thorough investigations into inequality and deprivation. Very useful tables and charts.*

Mack, J., and Lansley, S. (1985), *Poor Britain* (London: George Allen & Unwin). *A report on a survey into poverty undertaken for a television series on Breadline Britain. Now a little old, but raises a lot of important issues.*

Scott, J. P. (1994), *Poverty and Wealth: Citizenship, Deprivation and Privilege* (Harlow: Longman). *A comprehensive overview of the distribution of poverty and wealth. Concentrates on Britain, but puts this in an international context. Covers many of the issues raised in this chapter.*

Heath, A. (1981), *Social Mobility* (Glasgow: Fontana). *A useful compendium of the results of various studies of occupational mobility, presented in a digestible form. Should soon appear in a new, updated edition.*

Look at the brief discussion of Booth and Rowntree in Scott (2006*a*) and of Townsend and Wilson in Scott (2006*b*).

For more detailed considerations of specific issues, you might like to look at:

Black, D., *et al.* (1980), 'The Black Report', in P. Townsend and N. Davidson (eds), *Inequalities in Health* (Harmondsworth: Penguin, 1992). *A landmark study that the Conservative government tried to suppress. One of the first things that the 1997 Labour government did was to ask Sir Douglas Black to produce a new review of evidence on health inequalities.*

Erikson, R., and Goldthorpe, J. (1993), *The Constant Flux* (Oxford: Clarendon Press). *Puts the British results of Goldthorpe (1980) in an international context.*

Goldthorpe, J. H. (1980), *Social Mobility and Class Structure* (Oxford: Clarendon Press). *The basic report of the Oxford Mobility Study. Complex in places, but essential reading.*

Townsend, P. (1979), *Poverty in the United Kingdom* (Harmondsworth: Penguin). *Townsend's magnum opus. A massive report of more than 1,000 pages. A landmark study.*

Wilson, W. J. (1987), *The Truly Disadvantaged* (Chicago: University of Chicago Press). *Influential and contentious. Wilson's radical view of the underclass was soon overtaken by Murray's (1984) conservative view. Worth reading for the data and ideas about the ghetto poor, but be wary about taking on the terminology of 'underclass'.*

Also of interest here is:

Angela's Ashes. An autobiographical film on poverty in Dublin during the 1920s and 1930s.

Online resources

Visit the Online Resource Centre that accompanies this book to access more learning resources and other interesting material on inequality, poverty, and wealth at:
www.oxfordtextbooks.co.uk/orc/fulcher4e/

The Joseph Rowntree Foundation provides reports on its monitoring of poverty at:
www.poverty.org.uk

Broader material on low pay can be found through:
www.lowpay.gov.uk

Much material is produced by the Child Poverty Action Group:
www.cpag.org.uk/

General material on household income and expenditure, among other things, can be found through the Institute of Social and Economic Research at the University of Essex:
www.iser.ac.uk

See the Global Atlas of Inequality at:
http://ucatlas.ucsc.edu/home.html

Further aspects of global inequalities can be traced through the website of the World Trade Organization at:
www.wto.org

Stratification, Class, and Status

Contents

19

Knowing your place

> The rich man in his castle.
> The poor man at his gate.
> God made them high and lowly
> And ordered their estate.

('All Things Bright and Beautiful', Mrs C. F. Alexander, 1848)

The eighth Earl of Cadogan (Charles Gerald John Cadogan, Baron Cadogan, Baron Oakley, Viscount Chelsea) has one of the largest personal fortunes in the world. He owns major parts of London—he owns much of Chelsea and parts of Knightsbridge, and Cadogan Square is named after an ancestor—and he is a keen defender of the working classes.

The owners of a derelict site, just off the King's Road in Chelsea, wanted to develop it by building luxury homes. When the sixth Earl had sold the land in 1924, he had added a clause to the contract stating that the land should, for ever more, be used for the benefit of the working classes. The eighth Earl argued that the proposed luxury homes would be well beyond the means of the working classes and so would contradict his grandfather's wishes. On these grounds, he said, they should not be allowed. The developers of the land argued in the ensuing court case that the term 'working class' is outmoded and can no longer be given any meaningful definition. There were no longer people who could be described as working class—everyone who works is working class—and so a restrictive clause in the contract should no longer be upheld. The Earl held that, if he won his case, he would have proved the existence of the working classes as a distinctive part of British society. In fact, the case was lost on a technicality, though the judge did agree that the term 'working class' referred to those who would find it difficult buying or renting property and so still had a valid legal meaning.

Many houses are built on land that is subject to a 'working-classes' clause, aimed at cheap housing for the less well off, and many landlords have tried to break them. The Duke of Westminster—an even bigger London landowner than Earl Cadogan—successfully opposed the attempt by Westminster City Council in 1990 to sell off housing that had been built as dwellings for the working classes. The judge in that case decided that, even if the working class of the past no longer existed, most people would recognize the term and would be able to apply it with reasonable precision.

In the media debate around Cadogan's case, many complex issues were raised. The property developers had argued that old social hierarchies had crumbled and status distinctions were defunct. A leader in the *Guardian* argued that, even if there was some doubt about the precise meaning of the term, it was clear that thousands of low-paid workers in London could not afford decent housing. It supported Earl Cadogan as a champion of the poor. Mary Riddell in the *Observer* held a different view, arguing that the Earl's support for the working class was a reflection of self-interest rather than altruism. The aristocracy, she argued, needs the working class because 'Who else will buff its boots, pluck its grouse and dust its Vermeers?'

Sources: Independent, 11 April 2002; *Guardian,* 12 April 2002; *Observer,* 14 April 2002.

'Class' clearly remains a sensitive issue. For many people, Mrs Alexander's popular hymn defines the class relations of English society. In such views, class is a matter of hierarchy and knowing your place; it is something that ties people together into a cohesive social world. According to this view, a person's class is all a matter of breeding, of social background, and is reflected in social attitudes and lifestyle, in accent, and in style of dress. These social differences have often been seen as the source of snobbery and prejudice, leading many to conclude that Britain is a peculiarly class-ridden society.

Hunting and the traditional upper-class way of life: a thing of the past?

© Getty Images/John Dolan

Other aspects of a modern, urban, and industrial society point in a different direction. While trains and planes still divide passengers into first and second class, this is now done on the basis of their ability to pay, and second class is generally described as 'standard class' or 'tourist class'. More significantly, class has, for a long time, been seen by many people to be a matter of economic division and power. Class differences in attitude are rooted in the ownership and non-ownership of property, and these economic and social differences are perpetuated and multiplied over the generations.

How, then, should we see class? Is it a matter of hierarchy, cohesion, and deference? Or is it, rather, a matter of ownership, division, and disadvantage? Is Britain actually any more bound by class than other societies? And have there been any significant changes in class relations in recent years? We will consider these issues by looking at the idea of social stratification and its relationship to social inequality. We distinguish between class and status, and we show how Marx and Parsons studied these varying patterns of social stratification. In the section on 'The making of a class society' we look at the development of upper, middle, and working classes and the establishment of class societies. In the section on 'Transforming class society' we look at the contemporary disruption of class relations that has led some people to suggest that the advanced societies are no longer class societies and might even be post-industrial or post-modern societies.

Concepts and theories

Social stratification is not the same thing as social inequality. The inequalities described in Chapter 18 are central to any understanding of social stratification, but social stratification itself is something more than simply differences in life chances. **Social stratification** exists only when social inequalities involve the arrangement of individuals into *strata* or classes that lie one above another in a hierarchy of advantaged and disadvantaged life chances. When this happens, a society is said to be stratified.

The idea of stratification comes from geology, the science that studies the ways in which rocks of various kinds are formed into the levels or strata that make up the earth's crust and its surface layers of deposits. The concept of *social* stratification borrows these ideas to describe the levels or layers of a social hierarchy of advantage and disadvantage. An upper class, for example, lies on top of a middle class that, in turn, lies on top of a lower class. What is borrowed from geology, of course, is simply the general metaphor and image of stratification. Social strata are not lifeless objects, like rocks, but are actual social groups that are conscious of themselves and can act together. Like rock strata, however, social strata usually have a history of division and fragmentation. They are also likely to have undergone structural changes, and they may come into contact with newer strata that have risen from below.

Some of these ideas are illustrated in Figure 19.1. The first diagram shows the simplest image of three social strata arranged in a hierarchy of relative advantage and

Figure 19.1 Images of social stratification

➲ We introduce these images here simply to sensitize you to the idea of thinking in terms of social stratification. Do not try to work out the details now. Just try to keep them in mind as you read through the rest of our discussion.

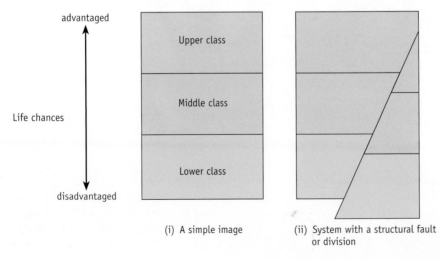

disadvantage. Many official and academic models of social stratification in contemporary society have taken just this form. In these classifications, however, it has been usual to recognize five, six, or seven social strata, not just three. However many strata are recognized, the simple image of stratification remains the same.

The second diagram in Figure 19.1 suggests how the idea of stratification can be extended to describe more complex structures with cross-cutting social divisions. Some commentators have described ethnically divided societies in these terms. They see two ethnic groups, a majority and a minority, divided from one another by a difference in colour or some other ethnic difference. Each ethnic group is internally stratified. Relations between whites and African Americans in the United States, for example, have been seen in this way (Warner 1936; Myrdal 1944).

A social stratum, then, is not merely a collection of individuals defined by their life chances in purely statistical terms. The members of a stratum are tied together through social relations and interactions that forge them into a real and cohesive social group. These social ties are those of occupational mobility, marriage, kinship, and informal association that close off one stratum and divide it from another. People who are unequal are members of different strata if there are social boundaries across which they rarely move: if, for example, they do not usually marry or interact with each other. Social strata are bounded social groups that are reproduced over time and across the generations. Social strata may, therefore, develop their own distinctive attitudes and values and may come into conflict with one another. A system of social stratification must be seen as a dynamic system that is shaped by shifting relations of antagonism or cooperation among the social strata.

Stratification and power

The advantages and disadvantages possessed by members of social strata constitute their power. This power derives from the various resources available to them. Property that generates a substantial investment income and that can, in turn, be used to buy education, housing, or health care gives power. It is for this reason that Weber claimed that social stratification was to be seen as a principal aspect of the distribution of power in society.

Marxists have seen property and other economic resources as the bases of social power, though this is only a part of the story. Alternatives to the Marxist view have proposed the importance of sex and race. Each of these has a part to play in a comprehensive account of stratification, but none can be taken as providing a complete theory of stratification. Indeed, it is doubtful if any such universal, single-factor theory could ever be workable.

Sex, race, and stratification

Many feminist writers have seen social strata as rooted in relations of sexual power based on biological differences of sex. Shulamith Firestone (1971) held that all societies are divided into opposed 'sex classes' that are the basis of gender inequalities. She claimed that 'all men' oppress 'all women', and that the struggle between men and women is the driving force in human history. Arguments such as this were central to the women's liberation movement as it developed in America and Europe from the 1960s.

Theories of racial stratification have generally been associated with more repressive political positions. The argument that social strata are rooted in inherited biological differences of race was particularly influential in the nineteenth century. Writers such as Ludwig Gumplowicz (1885) saw the conquest and domination of one ethnic group by another as the fundamental mechanism of social development. Gumplowicz believed that the conflict of races would lead to the survival of the fittest.

This racial interpretation of social stratification was taken up by more extremist political writers, and it was often allied with the eugenic arguments that we discuss in Chapter 6, pp. 191–3, and Chapter 18, pp. 706–8. The most extreme formulations were those of Gobineau (1853–5) and Chamberlain (1899), who advocated the repression of 'inferior' races and provided the basis for the later racialist programme of Adolf Hitler (1925) who attempted the extermination of races judged inferior.

Theories of sexual and racial stratification have undoubtedly recognized some of the key elements needed in any account of social stratification. Ethnic and gender divisions are, in different ways, central aspects of social inequality, and they play an important part in many systems of social stratification. They are not, however, forms of stratification themselves.

> **⊃ Connections**
> You might find it useful to review what we say about gender in Chapter 5, pp. 154–9, and about race and ethnicity in Chapter 6, pp. 196–204. We show how these are involved in patterns of social inequality in Chapter 18, pp. 699–701.

While ethnic divisions are fundamental in many systems of social stratification, this is not the case for *all* systems of stratification. Ethnic identities are cultural expressions of a sense of difference rooted in history, origins, language, religion, or some other ascribed group characteristics. These identities are relevant to social stratification when they rest on assumptions about the superiority or inferiority of particular ethnic groups. They play a part only if combined with economic or political resources that are not themselves simply a result of

Asian women are often confined to textile work.

© Getty Images/Robert Nickelsberg

ethnic differences. An emphasis on ethnic stratification becomes especially misleading, of course, if ethnic differences are assumed to involve real biological differences of race. As we show in Chapter 6, pp. 192–4, there is no scientifically justifiable concept of biological race. For this reason, there can be no valid theory of racial stratification.

Theories of sexual stratification must also be rejected if they attempt to reduce all social divisions and struggles to biological differences of sex. The fundamental problem with these theories is that, while they have recognized a significant aspect of *social inequalities*, they have not—and cannot—account for the long-term *stratification* of a society. Social strata reproduce themselves over time, ultimately through the sexual reproduction of their members. Separate social groupings of men and women cannot do this.

Sex and ethnicity affect relations of stratification in many very important ways—as we will show—and they have, of course, a major significance in areas of social life other than social stratification. Social inequalities are both gendered and racialized, and no theory of stratification can afford to ignore this. Ethnic and gender issues also have a fundamental importance as sources of social division and social inequality that goes well beyond their role in social stratification. They must be studied as important factors in their own right. An understanding of social stratification, however, requires a different starting point, one that incorporates aspects of ethnicity and gender but combines them in a larger picture. This has been provided for us by Weber.

Class and status

Weber saw social stratification as a central feature of social life, and his theoretical discussions have been enormously influential. The distinctions he made between class, status, and party have become commonplace in sociology, as has his related definition of authority. Here we use Weber's ideas to provide a comprehensive framework for understanding social stratification. (See J. Scott 1996 for a fuller discussion.)

Weber identified three distinct aspects or dimensions of the distribution of power: the economic, the communal, and the authoritarian. Each has a separate effect on the production of advantaged and disadvantaged life chances. He holds that:

- *economic* power is the basis of class relations;
- *communal* power is the basis of status relations;
- *authoritarian* power is the basis of authority relations.

We will look at each of these, concentrating on class and status, and we will show how other writers have helped to develop these issues.

Class and economic power

Class relations have an economic basis because they result from the distribution of property and other resources in the capital, product, and labour markets. Possession and non-possession of economic resources give people their power to acquire income and assets in markets. What Weber called **class situation** is a person's position in the capital, product, and labour markets as determined by the kinds of resources available to them. People occupy a similar class situation whenever they have similar abilities to secure advantages and disadvantages for themselves through their marketable resources.

The owners of company shares, for example, can earn an investment income and may be able to sell them for a profit on the stock market. Similarly, someone with educational credentials and technical expertise may command a higher income in the labour market than someone without this skill. A carpenter and an electrician both have skills that allow them to earn higher wages in the labour market than an unskilled labourer.

Economic power, Weber said, is a causal component in the determination of a person's life chances. This means that the inequalities in life chances examined in Chapter 18 are determined, to a greater or lesser extent, by differences in property and market position. Class situation not only determines a person's life chances; it also determines interests in protecting and enhancing these life chances. Weber held that people are likely to act, individually or collectively, in pursuit of their class interests.

Marx had earlier set out a similar view of the economic basis of class relations but went beyond Weber's understanding of class divisions (see Box 19.1). Central to Marx's theory was the claim that all societies, except for the most primitive tribal ones, are class societies and so 'The history of all hitherto existing society is the history of class struggles' (Marx and Engels 1848: 79). Marx saw ownership and non-ownership of property in the means of production—factories, machines, land, and other economic resources—as the key factor in the social divisions that give rise to class relations. These class relations may be masked or obscured by religious, ethnic, or other cultural differences, but they are always there as the fundamental determinants of people's actions.

The class that owns the means of production in a society, Marx argued, has the greatest amount of power and is able to oppress and to exploit the class of non-owners. In a capitalist society this creates a fundamental opposition between a 'bourgeoisie' or **capitalist class** and a 'proletariat' or **working class**. Capitalists include a whole range of property-owners directly concerned with the acquisition and use of capital in commerce, finance, and manufacturing. Proletarians, on the other hand, have no capital and must rely on the sale of their labour power for a wage. Only by securing employment from a capitalist can a proletarian obtain the money required to meet his or her needs.

Marx used the word 'capital' to refer to any physical or financial asset used in the economic sphere and that is a source of value. The personal assets of an individual or family, then, are not 'capital', in the strict sense, if they are simply consumed or enjoyed. A house, for example, becomes a form of capital only if its owners let it out for

---

Marx on class

Although the idea of class was central to virtually everything that he wrote, Marx never set out a systematic statement of his views. His followers have had to reconstruct a theory of class from his many writings, leaving much scope for rival views of 'what Marx really meant'. Nevertheless, his core ideas are clear enough. The main sources from which his views on class can be derived are the *Communist Manifesto* (Marx and Engels 1848) and the various volumes of *Capital* (see especially Marx 1864–5). Much of his work, including the *Communist Manifesto*, was written jointly with his collaborator, Friedrich Engels, but it is usual to refer to the principal ideas as being those of Marx alone. Marx's arguments were developed by many later Marxist writers. Of particular importance in relation to the study of class in British society are Miliband (1969) and Westergaard and Resler (1975).

---

rent or intend to sell it at a profit. The most important forms of capital are the assets used in production and finance. Capitalists are people who derive all or most of their income from their capital and who are involved in controlling the use of this capital.

Marx used the term 'exploitation' to describe the class relation that exists between capitalists and their employees. The workers' wages are only a small part of the total value of the commodities they produce during the working week, and by controlling this extra value—Marx called it surplus value—the capitalist benefits at the expense of the worker. Surplus value is the source of the profit that funds investment in machinery and allows a business enterprise to grow, and it is also the source of the personal income of the capitalist. The exploitation of labour, then, is the basis for both the accumulation of capital and the accumulation of wealth.

The class situations of capitalists and proletarians, therefore, are quite distinct. One is based on the ownership and control of capital, and the other is based on the exercise of labour power as an employee. Capitalist class situations comprise industrial entrepreneurs, bankers, and landowners, as well as investors who live on income from company shares. Proletarian class situations are those of skilled work, manual labour, office work, and so on. However, Marx's account of class cannot be accepted as it stands. Class relations are more complex than Marx's two-class model implies. Nevertheless, it is an extremely useful starting point.

Status and communal power

Weber's work developed in reaction to Marx. One of his main concerns was to show that it is impossible to explain everything in terms of economic factors alone, and he recognized the importance of non-economic factors in social stratification. Class situation is only *one* causal component in life chances. The other causal components are to be found in the non-economic factors of status and authority relations.

Status relations and status divisions emerge from the distribution of prestige or social honour within a community. In its most general sense, a person's status is his or her standing or reputation in the eyes of others. People rate each other as superior or inferior in relation to the values they hold in common with other members of their society or with a group within it. Those whose actions conform to these values receive approval and a great deal of prestige: they have a high status in their community. Those who deviate from these values or who conform to less central values are given a lower status and may be rejected as outsiders.

> ⟲ *Connections*
>
> You might recognize here some similarities between our discussion of communal approval and our discussion of deviance in Chapter 7. Try thinking about the idea of deviance as a social status.
>
> You might also like to look at the way in which community is defined in Chapter 13, pp. 477–9.

In small-scale societies, and in many face-to-face situations, status differences are based on detailed personal knowledge. People know one another as individuals through frequent interaction in many different situations, and they can easily make an overall judgement of reputation or social standing. Weber was more concerned with status in complex societies, where this kind of detailed knowledge is not usually available. In these societies, a person's status depends on the appraisal of a person's overall **style of life**.

A style of life is the way that people carry out the tasks associated with their most important social positions and the customs and practices they follow as members of particular social groups. Occupations, gender-roles, and ethnic-group membership may all be associated with particular and distinct styles of life, and it is these that are important in determining people's social standing. A feminine style of life, for example, may be valued less highly than a masculine one, and the way of life followed by Asians may be devalued by many whites. In these circumstances, women and Asians will be given a lower status than men and members of the ethnic majority.

One of the most important writers on this idea of status is Parsons (1940, 1953, 1970), who argued that people's social status is determined by the social positions that are most important in defining their membership of their society. Some societies define membership by birth or lineage, and a person's status reflects his or her kinship, gender,

and age roles. This is the case, Parsons argues, in many tribal societies. In these societies, older males generally have a high status as the elders of the society and are seen as superior in social standing to younger men and to all women. Young women may have an especially low status until they are married to a suitable man. A young woman's marriage chances may depend on whether she was born into a leading family or into one of the lesser families.

In modern societies, however, membership is no longer directly determined by birth in this way. Membership depends far more upon a person's public roles, and status depends on those particular roles to which people are able to achieve entry. The most important public roles for defining membership are work roles, which are organized into occupations. In modern societies, then, status is largely determined by occupation.

Occupations differ in terms of the skills, income, and authority that they involve, and Parsons argued that they are ranked and evaluated according to how these relate to communal values. Doctors, teachers, carpenters, bishops, and housewives all differ from one another in these respects. The result of this evaluation of occupations is a scale of occupational prestige. At the bottom of the scale are manual occupations, ranked by the level of their skill. Routine non-manual occupations come in the middle of the scale, and professional and managerial occupations are at the top.

People are often judged on the basis of vague and stereotyped knowledge of their occupations and other social positions. Their houses, their cars, their clothing, and their accents, for example, may be taken as indicators or symbols of their social status. As highly valued occupations are assumed to receive a high income, a rough scale of income is often used as an alternative way of deciding a person's status. In contemporary societies, then, income and consumption become symbols of status, and people may become motivated simply to achieve a high income rather than to enter a specific occupation.

> ⟲ *Connections*
>
> Compare this argument about occupational prestige with our discussion of the functionalist theory of inequality in Chapter 18, pp. 708–9. You may find it useful to go over that argument before continuing with this section.

Parsons is often criticized for exaggerating the amount of consensus in contemporary societies. It is certainly true that he stressed the part played by common values. He did recognize, however, that subcultures and subordinate value systems were also important. Modern societies are pluralistic in their values, and there may be competing criteria of social status.

Professional and administrative workers, for example, may follow the dominant cultural values and place their own occupations at the top of a scale of prestige, and are likely to place manual occupations at the bottom of the scale. Manual workers, on the other hand, might agree with the high valuation of professional occupations, but they may place skilled manual occupations above routine forms of administrative and clerical work. Similarly, the dominant values may stress occupational achievement, while other value systems place greater importance on ascriptive factors such as ethnicity or gender. Sometimes these different criteria of status may come into conflict with one another. It is possible, for example, for a person to have a high status as a doctor, but a low status as black or as a woman. Such people may experience status ambiguity or status inconsistency: the way that they are seen by others will depend upon *who* those others are.

According to Weber, **status situation**, like class situation, is a major causal component in life chances. Class situations are the economic relations through which control over marketable resources is organized for the attainment of income, assets, and other life chances. Status situations are the communal relations through which the prestige accorded to a particular lifestyle becomes the basis of life chances.

Because status has this effect on life chances, Weber paid particular attention to the distinct interests that people have in the preservation or enhancement of their prestige. He argued that people are motivated by their status interests as much as they are by class interests. Indeed, status interests may often be more important to people. Ethnic minority manual workers, for example, may unite with others from the same ethnic minority in a struggle for equal opportunities and rights, rather than uniting with other manual workers to raise the pay for their particular occupation.

Inequalities in life chances, then, must be seen as reflecting the effects of *both* class and status situations. A person's occupation, for example, is a position in the labour market that also has a place on a scale of prestige (Parkin 1971). Occupational prestige and position in the labour market work together to determine the life chances that people derive from their employment.

Ascribed status may also combine with the market situation to shape life chances. Women and members of ethnic minorities may be prevented by discrimination from taking those jobs in the labour market for which they are properly qualified. When they are in employment they may be given lower wages for doing the same or similar work to men or members of the ethnic majority. This intrusion of status into employment prospects shows how class relations are gendered or racialized. Where age is an important consideration, class relations may also be *aged*, and the life chances of the elderly, for example, may reflect their status as much as their class situation. The task of sociological analysis is to weigh the relative importance of class and status relations in different societies and at different times.

Authority and authoritarian power

Weber's third dimension of power was authoritarian power. His views on this were set out in his analysis of authority and bureaucracy, and you may like to look at our discussion of these matters in Chapter 14, pp. 518–20. Authority relations result from the distribution of authority and administrative power in organizations such as modern states and large business enterprises. In all organizations, there are those who command, those with delegated powers, and those who are simply on the receiving end of commands. A person's position within a structure of authority can be called a **command situation**. Command situations create interests in the maintenance or enhancement of powers of command and they can be considered alongside class situations and status situations as the third causal component in shaping life chances. This aspect of power is considered more fully in Chapter 20.

Boundaries and social closure

The investigation of class, status, and authority situations is only the beginning of an exploration into social stratification. It helps to explain patterns of social inequality, but it does not show how social boundaries come to be built and social strata formed. Social stratification exists when relatively closed social groups, differentiated from one another by their unequal life chances, reproduce themselves over time.

Social strata are demographically bounded social groups. They result from the social relations that tie together those in particular class, status, and command situations. Through social mobility, marriage and kinship, and free-time interaction, certain social positions become linked together and are separated from others. A social stratum is a cluster of social positions among which individuals can circulate and associate freely through their own mobility and that of their children, through marital and kinship connections, and through close and intimate interactions.

In contemporary societies, these relations have most frequently been studied in relation to occupations. Occupational roles are specific combinations of class, status, and command situations—each occupation, for example, involves particular marketable skills or resources, is given a particular level of occupational prestige, and involves a specific amount of authority over others. By looking at movement and interaction among occupations, it is possible to map the boundaries of social strata.

If it is regularly the case that, say, those who begin their working lives in lower-level supervisory work end up in junior management positions, then it is sensible to view these two occupational categories as parts of the same social stratum. This view would be strengthened by any evidence that the sons of lower-level supervisors enter work as junior managers, or that the daughters of junior managers regularly marry or form domestic partnerships with the sons of lower-level supervisors. In these circumstances, career mobility, generational mobility, and marriage relations reinforce one another to create regular and established patterns of connection within a single stratum. Similarly, if those who enter work as carpenters do not typically end their careers as doctors, if the daughters of carpenters rarely become doctors, and if the sons of carpenters rarely marry doctors' daughters, then these two occupations fall into different social strata.

Particularly important in the formation of stratum boundaries are the patterns of household formation that we discuss in Chapter 12, pp. 430–3. It is through marriage or cohabitation that households are formed, and it is within households that educational and occupational opportunities are shaped. This is why occupational mobility is generally measured in relation to household membership: for example, by measuring a man's mobility in relation to the occupation of his father (see Box 19.2). Households are also central to the organization of much free-time interaction, and an investigation of stratum boundaries must look at this. It is important to know, for example, whether lawyers interact with civil servants, other than in professional consultations: do they meet in each other's homes for drinks, entertain one another for meals, or attend the same clubs with their husbands and wives? If they do, then this is further evidence for considering them to be part of the same social stratum.

THEORY AND METHODS   19.2

Occupational mobility

It is important to be clear about two quite distinct ways in which occupational mobility is of interest to sociologists. In Chapter 18 we look at how rates of mobility can be used to measure the overall openness of a structure of inequality and the relative chances of changing occupational levels enjoyed by those in different occupations. In this chapter, on the other hand, we look at how patterns of occupational mobility are involved in the formation of social strata by defining boundaries of 'closure' around particular occupations. The study of openness cannot, of course, be completely separated from the study of closure, but it is important to keep these different concerns in mind. When you have read what we say about occupational mobility in this chapter, you might like to look at Chapter 18, pp. 716–19 and 732–6, and review our argument there.

Occupations, then, fall into the same social stratum if there is frequent mobility or interaction between them. Occupations form a stratum if they are connected through chains of frequent and relatively easy connection. Occupations in different social strata, on the other hand, are connected only through very infrequent movement and interaction. Boundaries between social strata, such as those shown in Figure 19.1, p. 744, can be identified wherever there is a natural break in the distribution of mobility and interaction, as this is where rates are significantly lower than elsewhere. If individuals are allocated to the various class, status, and command situations that make up the social positions of a society, an investigation of mobility and interaction will show how these positions are clustered together into various social strata.

Marx held that those in capitalist class situations form a social stratum because they circulate freely from involvement with one form of capital to involvement with another, they intermarry with one another, and their children inherit their capital and the advantaged life chances that it generates. In the same way, those in proletarian class situations come to form a separate social stratum: they move from one type of work to another, and from work to unemployment, they marry other workers, and their children have no choice but to enter employment as soon as they are able.

⦿ *Connections*

You may find these definitions very abstract, but do not worry. You will find that things fall into place as you follow through the rest of the chapter, and as we look at actual examples. For the moment, just try to understand the broad principles involved. You may find it useful to come back to this section after you have read the rest of the chapter. But first, we need some more definitions!

Consciousness and action

People have some awareness of the conditions under which they live. Where people share certain life experiences, they are likely to develop a shared awareness of the life conditions they have in common. The members of a social stratum, then, are likely to have some common awareness of the property or market conditions that they share, the authority relations that they are involved in, their social standing in the eyes of others, and their life chances in relation to others. They may, perhaps, have an image of the boundaries of their stratum and of how it relates to the other strata of their society. These images of society are important as cognitive maps that guide them in their relations with others. In modern societies they typically take the form of class consciousness (see Box 19.3).

THEORY AND METHODS   19.3

Class consciousness

Class consciousness is the shared consciousness of the members of a social class. It develops wherever the class situations of the members of a social stratum are the most important determinants of their life chances and of their shared experiences. Where status situations have an important effect on people's consciousness, it may be more appropriate to talk about status consciousness than class consciousness. The difference between social classes and other kinds of social strata are looked at in the next section.

In the past, these images of society have developed mainly through the direct, face-to-face interactions of stratum members and from the direct personal knowledge they have about those in other social strata. Through working together, living in the same neighbourhood, and being involved in the same leisure activities, people have forged a common outlook on life that has shaped their sense of community and solidarity. Where social strata are tightly closed, this solidarity has been particularly strong. Today, however, people's attitudes and opinions are shaped also by the media of mass communications. As we will show, the influence of the media and a decline in face-to-face sources of information and opinion have been the major factors responsible for reducing the strength of class consciousness and class identity in contemporary societies.

Where this common consciousness is especially well developed, it may take a political form. The members of the stratum may have a clear understanding of what they take their shared interests to be and of the kind of political programme that is likely to further these interests. In their individual actions (for example, as voters) and in their collective action (as, say, members of trade unions or social movements) they will strive to defend and promote their interests against those of other strata. This may lead them to advocate changes they think will be of particular benefit to them or that accord with their political goals.

Weber stressed the part that organized groups such as trade unions, political parties, interest groups, and social movements can play in focusing the consciousness of a stratum and in making people aware of the larger, nationwide and global interests they share with others. These bodies and associations were all described as parties by Weber. A **party**, in this sense, is any group united around a particular cause or interest and that claims to represent particular strata or social categories in the political sphere. The Labour Party and the Conservative Party, the GMB and Unison, and Friends of the Earth are all parties in Weber's sense.

The claims of parties cannot, of course, be taken at face value. Parties may claim to speak on behalf of people who actually ignore them or reject their views. Communist political parties in Europe, for example, have often claimed to represent the whole of the working class. While many of their members have been manual workers, no Communist Party in Western Europe has ever had the active support of a majority of its working class.

At the same time, the members of a social stratum can misunderstand their own situation and so act in inappropriate ways. Manual workers who are in similarly subordinate and exploited economic situations, for example, may fail to see that they have common economic interests and may also deny the relevance of these class relations to their lives. These views may be genuinely and authentically held, and they should not be rejected as mere 'false consciousness'. Sociological analysis must, nevertheless, pay particular attention to any apparent discrepancy between people's consciousness and their actual circumstances.

Systems of stratification

Life chances are shaped, then, by three aspects of power: *class situations* that result from differences of power in the economic sphere of property and the market; *status situations* that derive from differences of power in the communal sphere of prestige; and *command situations* that derive from differences of power in the sphere of authority. These operate alongside one another, but their relative importance can vary quite a lot from one society to another.

In some societies, class situations are the most important determinants of life chances, while in others the most important determinant is a command situation. It is not possible to say that any one of the three is more fundamental than the others in all circumstances. This was the point of Weber's criticism of Marx's economic determinism. The relative importance of the three components can be discovered only through empirical investigation. Any investigation of social stratification must identify the various class, status, and command situations that exist in a society and assess their relative influences on life chances and the ways in which they reinforce or counteract one another.

Weber used the term **social class** to describe those social strata that are formed when class situations are the most important factor. Social classes are clusters of households whose members owe their life chances principally to their specific property ownership and market positions. A society in which all or most social strata are social classes, in this sense, can be called a **class society**. An example of a class society would be a modern capitalist society in which it might be possible to identify, for example, a working class, a middle class, and an upper class.

The term **social estate**, on the other hand, refers to those social strata that exist when status relations are the most important factor. Social estates are clusters of households whose members owe their life chances principally to their specific social standing as superior or inferior to others. An example of a social estate would be the priesthood in a traditional society based on religion. A society in which all or most of the social strata are social estates, Weber said, can be called a **status society**. Weber said far less about **command societies**, where the life chances of members of social strata are determined by their command situations. An example of such a society would be the Soviet Union, where the whole society was dominated by a ruling elite whose members occupied the top positions of authority in the state. This aspect of social stratification is considered more fully in Chapter 20.

These definitions are what Weber called 'ideal types'. They do not exist in reality in their pure form, but only ever in combination. In a status society, for example, economic power always plays an important part, and class societies will also be shaped by the distribution of prestige. The task of the sociologist is to investigate the relative importance of each factor in the particular society with which he or she is concerned.

↪ Connections

We discuss Weber's methodology in Chapter 2. Look at p. 38 to see how he defined the ideal type. Can you see what it means to talk about the concept of a class society as an ideal type?

An example of a status society is the classical Indian **caste** system in which five strata were defined by the Hindu religion (Quigley 1993). Status divisions defined groups by their 'purity' or 'pollution' in terms of the values of the dominant social strata into four *varna* or pure castes.

The *Brahmins*, *Kshatriya*, and *Vaishya*—priests, landowners, and traders—were the 'twice born', who were believed to have been through several human reincarnations. The *Shudra*—labourers—had not been reincarnated. The lowest stratum were the menial workers who were regarded as untouchable or, literally, as outcastes (originally *Panchamas* and now *Dalit*). Contact with them was regarded as a source of pollution for the twice born and was possible only under closely regulated and ritually sanctioned conditions. Neither mobility nor interaction was possible across the caste lines, and each stratum was very tightly closed.

An example of a status society in which class and authority relations also played an important part is the slave and post-slavery society of North America that existed from the sixteenth to the nineteenth century. Stratification in the southern states during the era of segregation has been discussed as a further example of a caste system, drawing on parallels with the situation in traditional India. Weber suggested that all systems of stratification by ethnic identity tended to take a caste form. According to Warner (1936), African Americans in the Deep South were virtually an 'untouchable' caste, and the whole stratification system looked something like the second diagram in Figure 19.1 (p. 744). We discuss slavery at some length in Chapter 6.

↪ Connections

At this point, you might like to look in more detail at the argument of Warner. You will find a discussion of this in 'Theories of race and citizenship', Chapter 6, pp. 197–8.

It has also been suggested that the apartheid ('apartness' or separateness) system of ethnic relations that existed in South Africa from 1948 to 1991 can also be seen as a caste system of stratification, and that the post-apartheid state has had to grapple with the inheritance of this institutionalized racism. The American and South African situations show that caste, as a system of stratification by status, depends as much on force and law as it does on cultural values.

Britain, the United States, and most European societies can best be described as class societies. Ethnic segregation in the southern states of the United States was based on sharp status divisions, and ethnic divisions play an important part in the stratification of the northern states and in Britain. Nevertheless, the most important lines of social stratification have been those that result from relations of economic power. The principal social strata are social classes. Ethnic and other status divisions play their part alongside and within class relations.

We will look at these class relations in the rest of this chapter, and we will try to show how class and status operate together to produce contemporary patterns of stratification.

Classification by social class

While researchers have differed in exactly what they mean by class, there has been a common recognition of the need for a concept of class that grasps economically generated differences in opportunities and ways of living. Empirical research has, therefore, had to make class into a measurable variable.

The most widely used indicator of class has been occupation. This has been seen as a useful indicator of the differences in working and living conditions associated with the inequalities and differences in lifestyle that sociologists have referred to as class differences. Questions on occupation have been a standard feature of most social surveys, and occupations have been grouped into categories with similar economic circumstances and lifestyles. These occupational categories are taken as empirical measures of class differences. An individual person can be allocated to a social class so long as his or her occupation is known.

A number of different class schemes have been proposed, each giving a slightly different picture of the class structure. Most of these schemes claim a high degree of reliability in the allocation of individuals to classes. The question of validity is more complex. An indicator of class is valid if it corresponds to the concept of class. However, it is unclear whether any of the available class schemes give a completely valid definition of class (Nichols 1996). This is not to say that we must reject them all. It is, however, important to be aware of their limitations. In this section we will look at the main social-class classifications that have been used in Britain.

The official view of class

The classification of social classes used in many official statistics is the Registrar General's Classification. This was developed as a way of classifying data from the population censuses. Drawing on pioneering work by Charles Booth (1886), government statisticians in the office of the Registrar General devised a classification of the population into five principal 'social grades' or 'social classes' (Szreter 1984). This has generally been regarded as being the nearest that there is to an official listing of social classes for Britain as a whole. Because it has been so widely used in government statistics, it has also been used in a wide range of commercial and academic social surveys.

> **⊃ Connections**
> You might like to refer to our discussion of the rise of the census and the registration of population in 'Surveillance of populations', Chapter 8, pp. 270–2. That discussion looks at the major government surveys and series of official statistics.

The Registrar General's view was that social classes describe economic divisions of industry and employment. They are clusters of family households with similar residential and working conditions and that enjoy a similar social standing, culture, and lifestyle. The Registrar General's Classification was not, then, supposed to be a simple income or asset classification. It was intended to be a more general classification of social advantage and disadvantage.

A related scheme was introduced in 1951. David Glass, who was carrying out his important study of occupational mobility (Glass 1954), helped the Registrar General to establish an industrial classification of occupations that divided them into seventeen so-called socio-economic groups (SEGs). These have been used in a number of publications, including those from the General Household Survey. The seventeen SEGs can be reduced to a shorter set of six occupational categories that are sometimes referred to as 'economic classes'. The SEGs and economic classes are widely used in government statistics, but they have not been used in many non-official surveys. You will find that some government statistics use these economic classes, while others use the 'social classes' of the Registrar General's Classification.

The Registrar General's Classification revolves around three basic social classes—the upper and middle classes, skilled workers, and unskilled labourers—to which are added two 'intermediate' categories to cover those who do not fit neatly into the three principal social classes. The resulting five social classes are numbered in Roman figures from I to V. They have also been given an official label and description that make it possible to use them simply by classifying individuals and family heads according to the description. However, this is not a very reliable or precise method. The correct procedure, used in all official studies, is to allocate individuals to a detailed occupational category, of which there are currently over 500 listed in the official *Classification of Occupations*. The correct social class for each occupational category is shown in the same publication.

Since 1971 the Registrar General's Classification has incorporated a distinction between manual and non-manual forms of skilled work, a distinction that had already been used in some unofficial versions of the schema. As a result, the latest version has six social classes, which are shown in Figure 19.2. The incorporation of this manual/non-manual

Figure 19.2 The Registrar General's Classification

Social class	Official description	Example
I	Professional, etc., occupations	Exclusively non-manual: accountant, doctor, lawyer, university teacher
II	Intermediate occupations	Predominantly non-manual: aircraft pilot, farmer, nurse, police officer, school teacher
III (N)	Skilled non-manual occupations	Exclusively non-manual: clerk, shop assistant, secretary, waiter
III (M)	Skilled manual occupations	Exclusively manual: bus driver, carpenter, cook, miner, electrician
IV	Partly skilled occupations	Predominantly manual: farm worker, bus conductor, bar worker, postman, telephone operator
V	Unskilled occupations	Exclusively manual: labourer, office cleaner, kitchen hand, window cleaner

Class and economic divisions: manual workers.

© Alice Chadwick

division makes it relatively easy to collapse the whole scheme into a rough and ready distinction between manual (III (M), IV, V) and non-manual (I, II, III (N)) social classes. These have often been referred to loosely as the working class and the middle class.

Claiming that Britain had become a 'classless' society, the Conservative government in 1987 argued that it was time to abandon the practice of presenting official data in outmoded class terms. It suggested that there was no longer any need for an official classification of social classes. Although the Registrar General's Classification continued in use, it was put under review, and in 1994 a full academic review of the classification was set up. The initial report of the review group recommended that an official social-class classification should be retained and that it should combine the Registrar General's Classification with the SEGs. The aim of this change was to focus the whole classification more explicitly around employment differences. A team of sociologists and economists led by David Lockwood and David Rose (see Rose and O'Reilly 1998) produced a completely new classification, which has been adapted for official use. To understand this classification, it is necessary to know something about the other academic schemes on which it drew.

Non-official social-class schemes

The first unofficial social class scheme to achieve any widespread popularity among researchers in Britain was that of John Hall and David Caradog Jones in the 1930s and 1940s. This was used in the famous study of social mobility by Glass (1954). This so-called Hall–Jones Classification is slightly more complex than the Registrar General's Classification, and contains seven social classes, usually numbered in Arabic from 1 to 7 (see Figure 19.3).

The Hall–Jones Classification, like the Registrar General's Classification, has been widely used in social research, and a number of well-known studies have used it, or modified versions of it, to present their findings. The first attempt to rethink completely the approach taken to social class was that of John Goldthorpe and his colleagues when planning the Oxford Mobility Study (Goldthorpe 1980). In order to make comparisons possible with the Glass study of social mobility, Goldthorpe devised a broader classification. He began from a detailed list of occupational categories, taken from official sources, and organized these into seven social classes numbered in Roman numerals from I to VII. For some purposes he

Figure 19.3 The Hall–Jones Classification

Social class	Description
1	Professional and high administrative
2	Managerial and executive
3	Inspectional, supervisory, and other non-manual, higher grade
4	Inspectional, supervisory, and other non-manual, lower grade
5	Skilled manual and routine grades of non-manual
6	Semi-skilled manual
7	Unskilled manual

Figure 19.4 The Goldthorpe Classification

Social class	Description	
I	Higher professional and administrative; large managers and proprietors	Service class
II	Lower professional and administrative; small managers and proprietors	
III	Routine non-manual	Intermediate class
IV	Small employers, proprietors and self-employed	
V	Lower technical and manual supervisory workers	Working class
VI	Skilled manual workers	
VII	Semi- and unskilled manual workers	

Note: An 'elite' of property-holders is sometimes added as an additional social class at the top of the scheme.

added an extra social class of property-holders that he calls the 'elite'. The number of property-holders appearing in any sample survey, however, is so small that Goldthorpe relegates this social class to a footnote. It is not used as a category in the Oxford Mobility Study.

These social classes, Goldthorpe claims, are differentiated by their resources and their opportunities. Although the social classes do not form a strict hierarchy, he does recognize that social classes I and II (together forming a service class) enjoy superior conditions to classes V, VI, and VII (together forming a working class). Social classes III and IV are often referred to as 'intermediate' classes, though Goldthorpe does not see them in the middle of a neat social hierarchy. The seven social classes are generally listed in the order shown in Figure 19.4. The Goldthorpe Classification has been used in a large number of empirical studies.

The classifications that we have looked at have been devised for use in studies of British society, and they cannot necessarily be used in studies of other societies or in comparative research. It cannot be assumed that the number of social classes and the boundaries between them will be the same in, say, the United States or Japan as they are in Britain.

Goldthorpe has gone some way towards recognizing this problem, and he has tried to modify his classification for use in comparative research. The main changes that he made involved attempts to take account of the fact that agricultural work was more significant in many societies than it was in Britain. He divided a number of his social classes to handle the farmers and farm workers of France, Italy, and other societies with large agrarian sectors (Erikson and Goldthorpe 1993). So far, however,

these changes have been rather arbitrary and ad hoc, and the classification has only a limited value in comparative work.

A further social-class classification must be mentioned. Although it has not been very widely used in sociological research, the classification produced by the Institute of Practitioners in Advertising for a consortium of market-research organizations is often used in commercial and mass-media reports. This consists of six social classes that are labelled from A to E—you will often hear journalists talking about politicians seeking to attract the 'C1 voters'. This is not a rigorously worked-out social-class classification, and only five of the categories are positively defined. For the sake of completion, however, we show this in Figure 19.6 (p. 756).

A new official scheme

The government review of social classifications led to the production of a new scheme, replacing the Registrar General's Classification, that drew on everything that had been learned in the construction of the Goldthorpe Classification. David Lockwood and David Rose headed a team of investigators (Rose and O'Reilly 1998) who constructed and tested a scheme that was intended to be useful for both academic and official purposes. This new classification (termed the NS.SEC) includes as many as fourteen classes, but it can be converted into nine-, eight-, five-, and three-class versions, depending on the particular purpose of the research. This scheme is used in the compilation of official statistics and in academic social research. Its main categories are shown in Figure 19.5. In Figure 19.6, we summarize the various social-class classifications. Although we have tried to indicate the broad equivalencies that exist among the various classifications, these are only very approximate and there are no direct translations from one to another.

Figure 19.5 The NS.SEC Classification (Nine-Class Version)

Social class	Description
1	Higher managerial and professional occupations
2	Lower managerial and professional occupations
3	Intermediate occupations
4	Self-employed and own account
5	Lower supervisory and technical occupations
6	Semi-routine occupations
7	Routine occupations
8	Never worked and long-term unemployed
9	Not classified

Evaluating the class schemes

These social-class classifications have been used in a number of classic studies (see Box 19.4) and provide useful ways of organizing sociological data, so long as their limitations are understood. Many of these are limitations that are common to them all. The most important are:

- they depend on detailed occupational information, which may not be available;
- they have difficulties with those who have no current employment;
- they have not properly handled the class assignment of women.
- they have not taken account of property divisions.

In order to use any of these classifications, it is necessary to have detailed information about the work and employment relations of the people being studied. An occupational title alone is not enough, as occupations can be carried out under a wide range of work and employment conditions. An electrician, for example, could be in employment or self-employed. An engineer may be a professionally qualified chartered engineer who works as a self-employed consultant, a technically qualified manager in a large or small firm, or a skilled mechanic working in a car-repair workshop. The occupational listing that is used for both the Registrar General's Classification and the Goldthorpe Classification can be used only if the researcher has quite a substantial amount of information about the nature of the work that people do (Marsh 1986). This became even more important in 1980, when the official listing of occupational categories was directly linked to a more detailed listing produced by the then Department of Employment.

When detailed information is not available, it is not possible to classify people with complete reliability. Many researchers simply turn to the basic listings of social classes, as shown in Figures 19.2–19.5 and allocate people to whichever class seems appropriate. An electrician, for example, might simply be classified as an employed skilled worker (social class III (M), HJ 5, Goldthorpe VI, or NS.SEC 5, depending on the scheme used). Many uses of the classifications, then, are less precise and less accurate than might be thought. This does not necessarily make the results invalid, but it does show the need to treat them with great care.

Particularly difficult problems arise when people who are not employed have to be allocated to a social class. If occupation is the basis for allocation to a class, then how is it possible to decide the class situations of students, the unemployed, the retired, and women working at home? The unemployed and the retired have often been classified on the basis of their last major occupation. This can often

be appropriate, unless someone has been unemployed for a very long time. This is possible, however, only so long as a survey has included a question about it. If 'unemployed' or 'retired' is written down and no further questions are asked, it is impossible to assign the person to a social class.

The young unemployed cannot be handled so easily, as they have often had no previous employment. If they have been students, they can, like current students, be classified according to the occupation for which they trained. This, however, is not straightforward, as some of those who train for particular occupations may never enter them. Equally, not all courses of education lead to a specific occupation: training as a doctor may do so, but training as a sociologist or a historian is less likely to.

None of the classifications has treated women properly. Men and unmarried women have usually been allocated to occupational positions on the basis of their own employment, but married women—even if they are in employment—have generally been allocated to the occupational categories of their husbands. Married women working at home as full-time houseworkers have, then, been treated as mere dependants of their husbands or male partners. This has often been criticized on the grounds that it is unfair to classify women by their husbands' occupations. The real problem, however, is a theoretical and empirical one.

Classifying women on the basis of their male partners' occupations can be justified when they are full-time domestic houseworkers who are not in employment and have been out of the labour market for some time. In these circumstances, research has shown that their own previous occupations may be poor indicators of their current resources and opportunities (Goldthorpe 1983). For these women, it has been suggested, partners' occupations, where these are full-time, are far more appropriate as indicators of the actual opportunities and constraints that they face. Where a married woman has a current, full-time employment, this may be a more useful indicator than the employment of her partner.

There are, however, problems in using many of the existing social-class classifications for women in employment. These classifications were devised when the bulk of employees were male, and so they are geared towards men's work. As we show elsewhere in the book, there is a high degree of *occupational segregation* by gender (see Chapter 17, pp. 681–4). That is to say, women tend to find employment in occupations regarded as 'women's work' or that men tend not to enter. Employed women are concentrated in the lower professions, and in clerical, sales, and personal service work. Women working part-time are concentrated in shop work, cleaning, and catering. Women are therefore concentrated in certain specific occupations, and the existing occupational classifications give far less attention to those occupations. Almost a quarter of all employed women in 1971 were officially classified into just one of the 223 occupational categories then used for census data: that for clerks and cashiers. Over a half of employed women were assigned to just five of these categories.

Clerical and cashier work is not all of a type. It is carried out under a vast range of employment and working conditions and includes receptionists, proof readers, library assistants, stock-control clerks, postal clerks, meter readers, and so on (Arber *et al.* 1986). Existing classifications give far less attention to variations in women's work than they do to variations in men's work, though the new Office for National Statistics (ONS) scheme has tried to rectify this and to cover areas of women's employment more adequately.

All the classifications that we have looked at have used occupation as an indicator of class. If you have read our discussion of Marx in Chapter 2 and earlier in this chapter, you will know that he placed particular emphasis on property ownership as the basis of class division. This is not well handled by a focus on occupations. Goldthorpe did not properly separate out large property-owners from small ones, and the Hall–Jones Classification included property-holders and employers in all of the top four social classes. The Registrar General's Classification has even more problems. As Nichols (1996: 71) remarks, in the 1951 Census 'the "capitalist", the "business speculator", the "fund holder" and the "landowner" were lumped together into the same residual category as the "expert (undefined)" and the "lunatic (trade not specified)"' . In 1961, 'capitalist' was dropped as a census category altogether. The neglect of property ownership has been a major problem for all attempts to assess social class distribution.

 ## *Stop and reflect*

In this section we have reviewed the main concepts used in the study of social stratification. We set out a number of important theoretical points derived from the work of Weber:

- Social stratification must be distinguished from social inequality. It involves the formation of strata that are differentiated by their life chances. The boundaries of social strata are defined by relations of mobility and interaction.

- It is important to distinguish between class, status, and authority. Class involves economic power, status involves communal power, and authority involves authoritarian power.

- Collective action by the members of a stratum involves the formation of parties.

- How did we argue that gender and ethnicity can be related to patterns of social stratification?

We showed that Weber's ideas provide a basis for understanding the relationship between stratification, gender, and ethnicity. We also argued that some writers have more to say on class, while others concentrate on status.

- Marx is the principal theorist of stratification by class.
- Parsons is the principal theorist of stratification by status.
- Why do you think that it is important to distinguish class from status?

We stressed the ways in which these concepts could be used in comparative studies. We highlighted:

- Slavery as a system of social status rooted in force and coercion.
- Caste as a particular form of ethnic stratification.

We looked, finally, at the methodological issues involved in using class concepts:

- A number of social-class schemes have been used in sociological research. These include the Registrar General, the Hall–Jones, and the Goldthorpe classifications.
- Proper use of the classifications depends on the researcher having detailed occupational information. All the available schemes find it difficult to handle those who are not currently in employment.
- A major limitation of existing class schemes has been the inadequate way that they have dealt with the class position of women.
- Do you agree that the new ONS scheme deals properly with the class assignment of women?

The making of a class society

During the nineteenth century Britain truly became a class society. From the last third of the century until well into the first half of the twentieth this took the classic form of a division into a working class, a middle class, and an upper class. This is shown in the model in Figure 19.7, which represents the stratification system as a triangle in order to show the relative sizes of the social classes. A small upper class stands above a larger middle class and an even larger working class.

The class structure was not, of course, quite so neatly and rigidly divided into three social classes as this model suggests. The boundaries between classes were far from sharp, and each class was internally divided into subclasses or sections. It is for this reason that the social-class classifications that we looked at in the previous section have

divided the three basic classes into five or more social classes. Despite these qualifications, the image of British society as divided into three principal social classes gives an accurate view of the main lines of division that existed in the first half of the twentieth century. It also accords with the imagery and language employed by people themselves.

Figure 19.8 uses census data and the official socio-economic groups (SEGs) to show the distribution of men and women into various social classes. These official categories do not correspond exactly to the actual lines of social division, but they do give a general impression of the changing shape of the class structure and the composition of the various social classes.

The working class, broadly defined, amounted to over 80 per cent of the population in 1911. In 1951 it still included almost three-quarters of the population. Over this whole period, the number of semi-skilled workers in the working class was greater than the number of skilled workers, and the number of unskilled workers was much smaller. The middle classes increased from just over 12 per cent to about a quarter of the population in the same period. This was mainly a result of an increase in the number of clerical workers, though the number of professional and managerial workers also increased sharply. As we will show, the middle classes also included a number of small property-owners, who were counted along with all other property-owners in SEG 2A. This makes it difficult to estimate the number of large-scale capitalist property-owners and landowners who occupy positions at the top of the stratification system. At the beginning of the twentieth century, this stratum was popularly known as the 'upper ten thousand', and it certainly amounted to much less than 1 per cent of the whole population.

Figure 19.7 The British class structure, simplified model

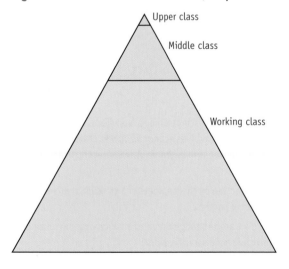

Figure 19.8 Stratification in England and Wales, (1911–1951)

Socio-economic group		Percentage of population				Social class
		1911	1921	1931	1951	
2A	Employers and property-owners	6.71	6.82	6.70	4.97	Some upper class, some middle class
1A/1B	Professionals	4.05	4.53	4.60	6.63	
2B	Managerial and administrative	3.43	3.64	3.66	5.53	Middle class
3	Clerical	4.84	6.72	6.97	10.68	
4	Foremen, etc.	1.29	1.44	1.54	2.62	
5	Skilled manual	30.56	28.83	26.72	24.95	Working class
6	Semi-skilled manual	39.48	33.85	35.00	32.60	
7	Unskilled manual	9.63	14.17	14.81	12.03	
		100	100	100	100	

Source: Adapted from Routh (1987: table 3.1).

❓ Which particular sections of the population showed the biggest growth during the first half of the twentieth century? Which has shown the biggest fall? You might like to draw a pie chart to illustrate the social class structure of the population in 1951.

Capitalism and class society

The most influential attempt to understand the origins and development of class structure in capitalist societies has been that derived from the work of Marx. According to Marx, the division between the dominant capitalist class and the subordinate working class would become ever sharper, while the middle classes would gradually disappear. Later Marxists recognized the growth in the number of clerical, managerial, and professional employees and tried to reconcile this growth of the middle class with Marx's own arguments.

Class polarization

Marx held that the growth of capitalism is marked by a drive towards economic concentration and monopoly. Driven by the need to expand the scale of production, capitalists issue company shares on the Stock Exchange and so allow other capitalists to invest in their businesses. As a result, the owners and controllers of capital become more closely tied together in a structure of concentrated business power. This becomes even more marked when banks and other financial enterprises become closely and directly involved in the financing of production. Small groups of *finance capitalists*, operating in both banking and industry, coordinate business activities at the national level and, increasingly, at the global level. This concentration of capital squeezes out small-scale capitalists and property-owners, leaving fewer—but wealthier—capitalists in existence.

These capitalists, Marx said, develop a class consciousness of their shared interests as employers and property-owners.

Through their intersecting investments in business, they develop a strong awareness of their dependence on property and of the economic gulf that separates them from their employees. This also leads them to recognize the need to ensure that the state maintains a framework of property and employment law to support their position and that it pursues policies in the interests of business. Marx saw this occurring when capitalists controlled the state, becoming what he called a *ruling class*.

The growth of wealth at one end of the stratification system, Marx argued, was matched by the growth of poverty at the other end. The opposition between capitalist and proletarian, he believed, would become ever starker as the capitalists became richer and the proletarians became poorer. This is the inevitable result of the way that a capitalist economy works through competition and the boom–slump cycle. Competition among workers keeps wages down, as there are invariably more workers than there are jobs. At the same time, there is a long-term tendency for the wage level to fall. Wages may rise in times of economic boom and prosperity, because of a temporary increase in the demand for labour, but the periods of slump and recession that follow will push them back down again. These recessions, Marx suggested, would become deeper and deeper as capitalism developed. The constant downward pressure on wages would lead to a growth in the amount of relative poverty. Although the pay and conditions of workers might improve over time, they always improve more slowly than those of the capitalists. The gap between rich and poor gets bigger as capitalism develops.

Marx saw economic deterioration as having implications for the class consciousness of workers. Their consciousness is rooted in the need to sell their labour power on the market. They have no control over it: they come to be seen as commodities and as mere appendages to the machines on which they work. Through their common experience of exploitation and alienation—a condition shared by all workers—workers begin to develop their class consciousness. They may initially unite around the common interests of their particular trade or occupation and form a trade union to promote their interests. As their economic position worsens, so their class consciousness is likely to deepen. This is especially likely where they work in large factories that bring together many different kinds of workers, and where they live close to each other in the same parts of the industrial towns and cities. In these circumstances, Marx said, they develop a broader awareness of their shared class interests. Occupational consciousness and solidarity gives way to true class consciousness and solidarity.

> ⤵ *Connections*
> You might find it useful to read our discussion of various aspects of Marx's wider views on capitalism. His views on work and the alienation of labour are covered in Chapter 17, pp. 649, 656–7. Also in that chapter, pp. 648–9, and in Chapter 14, pp. 528–32, you will find a discussion of ownership and of business organization. It might also be useful to review our definitions of absolute and relative poverty in Chapter 18, pp. 701–2.

For Marx, capitalist societies would show an ever greater **polarization** between wealth and poverty, and the two main classes would become more sharply divided in their class consciousness. He sometimes suggested that each recession would run deeper than the one before, and so wages would be constantly driven down in real terms until they reached a bare subsistence level. This is the *pauperization* of workers.

The growing scale of poverty—whether relative or absolute—was linked by Marx to an expectation that the development of capitalism would be marked by ever-deepening recessions. There is some evidence to support this view as a description of what happened in the first half of the nineteenth century, but matters have become more complicated since then. Capitalist production has, indeed, followed a pattern that shows successive periods of boom and slump, of expansion and recession, and recessions have often been both deep and long. However, there does not seem to be any long-term tendency for recessions to get deeper with every downturn in the economy. It is undoubtedly the case that periodic recessions have produced high levels of relative poverty, but the level of poverty has not shown a long-term increase, and there has been no straightforward increase in class consciousness with increases in poverty.

Intermediate class situations

Marx believed that the polarization of the class structure between capitalist and proletariat would be sharpened through the disappearance of all intermediate classes. In the early stages of capitalism a number of other classes existed between the capitalists and the proletariat. These included the peasants and small-scale property-owners, shopkeepers, and other relatively advantaged groups that together formed the 'middle classes'. Marx believed that those who occupied these class situations would lose their advantages because their property would be destroyed by the expansion and concentration of capitalist production. Intermediate class situations would show a **proletarianization** as their occupants were forced to become wage labourers. Using the simple model that we presented in Figure 19.7 (p. 758), Marx's model of class polarization can be summarized as shown in Figure 19.9.

The evidence does not seem to support Marx on this. As he himself began to realize towards the end of his life, there has been a massive growth in the numbers of those in the intermediate class situations that cannot be regarded as either capitalist or proletarian in the strict sense. The huge armies of managers and professionals who hold positions of authority in large state bureaucracies and big business enterprises may be propertyless, but they enjoy vastly superior life chances to manual workers and they have close working relationships with capitalist employers. The rise of this so-called new middle class runs counter to Marx's view of class polarization.

A number of Marxist writers developed new theoretical ideas to take account of this. They saw capitalism entering a new stage in which large bureaucratic organizations would play a greater part. As business enterprises became more bureaucratic, so the numbers of managers, clerks, foremen, and others involved in the supervision and control of manual workers would increase. The old propertied middle class might disappear, but a new propertyless middle class was expanding. This class was distinct from both the capitalists and the proletarians: its members lacked property and had to find employment through the labour market, but their jobs involved them in the exercise of authority

Figure 19.9 Class polarization

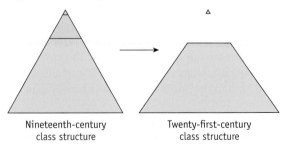

Nineteenth-century   Twenty-first-century
class structure   class structure

over others and they enjoyed relatively advantaged life chances. The continuing expansion of this kind of work has led to successively more sophisticated attempts to understand the class situations involved (Wright 1985, 1997).

The issues raised in the debate over the claims made by Marxism can be examined in relation to the three social classes that we identified earlier. These are the working class, the middle class, and the upper class.

The working class

The economic basis for a working class is the employee relationship of wage labour (technically termed their **market situation**) and the organizational setting of large-scale production (their **work situation**). Employees involved in the direct production processes of large organizations are typically, though slightly misleadingly, described as manual workers. They are involved in a complex division of labour in which each type of work is coordinated with that of others with a variety of skills and abilities. What unites them as proletarian workers is the similarity in market and work situations: they are employees and are subject to the authority of employers or managers. They are, however, differentiated by the levels and types of skills possessed. Skilled or 'time-served' workers who have served an apprenticeship that trains them for a particular job and whose skills are important marketable assets are distinct from semi-skilled workers with on-the-job training in skills that are less easily transferable from one employer to another. Unskilled workers involved in heavy labouring work and in routine manual tasks are distinct again. Skill differences comprise the market capacities that underlie varying opportunities to obtain higher wages and better conditions of work. These skill differences are the basis of the internal divisions of the working class that most social-class classifications have tried to capture.

The making of the working class

The typical work organization for manual workers is a factory, but they also work in coal mines, shipyards, steel plants, and other settings where large numbers of workers are brought together under common management for the purposes of large-scale production. These working conditions have been the basis for the development of a distinctive working-class outlook and consciousness of class. Those employed in small-scale units of production, on the other hand, have been somewhat separate from the mainstream of proletarian manual workers. They have distinct work situations. Workers in small factories or workshops, farm workers, and those in domestic service, for example, all have conditions of work that involve them in a far less extensive division of labour and in closer and more personal supervision by their employers.

They have less direct contact with other manual workers and they are less likely to develop a common consciousness and sense of solidarity.

For manual workers in large-scale production to form the core of a working class, there must be a high degree of mobility and interaction among them. It must be possible for workers to move from, say, unskilled to semi-skilled work, for the children of these workers to enter apprenticeships, and for skilled workers to fall into unskilled or semi-skilled jobs if work technology changes. This mobility among the different skill levels ties people into a distinct social class. This will be reinforced whenever the similarities in their conditions of work, the interests that they have in relation to their employing organizations, and the proximity into which they come lead them to think, feel, and act in similar ways. In these circumstances, they will interact frequently with one another outside the workplace. This is exactly what happened to manual workers from the second half of the nineteenth century.

In the early years of the nineteenth century, manual workers were still, for the most part, employed in relatively small organizations, and they were divided by trade and geography (E. P. Thompson 1963). Although there were great similarities in their market situations, their work situations and their subjective experiences differed markedly. It was only as the scale of production was increased and the disciplinary practices of the factory were extended that they were forged together into something closer to what Marx called a class for itself, a class capable of acting consciously in its own interests (Foster 1974; see also R. J. Morris 1979; A. J. Reid 1992).

> **⊃ Connections**
> These ideas on discipline are taken further in our discussion of Foucault in Chapter 8, pp. 267–70. We look in more detail at what Foucault says about large-scale organizations in Chapter 14, pp. 521–4.

As the century proceeded, their work situations became more homogeneous, their life chances became less diverse, they were more likely to experience the common threat of periodic unemployment, and the level of mobility among the different kinds of manual work increased (Savage and Miles 1994). Few manual workers, and few of their children, moved into non-manual jobs, but there were relatively high rates of mobility between unskilled, semi-skilled, and skilled work. This was the case for both women and men.

Marriage relations were similar. There were relatively few marriages across the manual/non-manual line, but marriages between the skilled and the unskilled were common. The wives of male skilled workers could withdraw from the labour market and concentrate on domestic work and family obligations. This was widely regarded as a sign of the 'respectability' of the skilled worker and his family. These women could, however, re-enter the labour market if their husbands' work became insecure. Where both partners were employed in unskilled work, often casual or irregular, the income of the household depended on them both remaining in employment.

Intermarriage among manual-worker households in particular localities created large and extended kinship networks that reinforced the bonds that already existed among neighbours and leisure-time associates. These dense networks of social relations were the basis for a strong sense of local class solidarity. As the industrial cities and suburbs grew in size (see Chapter 13, pp. 486–7), new migrants were drawn into these proletarian communities. The fusion of kinship and friendship around a particular locality and place of work was the basis on which a distinctive working-class culture and way of life could be built.

A number of organizations and institutions helped to forge the unity and cohesiveness of this social class. Public houses and working men's clubs, music halls, local dance halls and cinemas, and other places of leisure became important centres of shared relaxation and entertainment. Cooperative and Friendly Societies organized around mutual self-help and solidarity helped to counter some of the economic insecurities faced by manual workers and gave them a sense of common purpose. Trade unions and the Labour Party were other sources of informal solidarity and cohesion and helped to build a shared sense of political commitment and of the need for political action in defence of working-class interests.

Industrial and political associations took class action to the national level. Trade unions dealt with employing organizations that were nationally organized, and the Labour Party, after its formation in 1906, represented working-class interests in the national parliament. The strength of the Labour Party in national elections grew continually until the early 1950s, and it was especially rapid after 1918. Through the trade unions and the Labour Party, manual workers developed a broadened sense of *national* solidarity, though this was always much weaker than their local communal solidarity. For most people, the nation—and, therefore, the national working class—were abstractions with much less solidity and reality than the more local solidarities of the neighbourhood and the workplace.

The final element in the making of a working class was the explicit adoption of the language of class and the willingness of manual workers to describe themselves as 'working class'. The term was taken up with pride as a marker of social identity. It became a taken-for-granted way of defining position in society. It described 'us' (manual workers), and distinguished 'us' from 'them' (the middle classes and the bosses). Manual workers were conscious of themselves as a social class with distinct interests and concerns. They were a 'class for itself', a social class charac-terized by the solidarity of its members and by exclusion from any solidarity with those in other social classes.

The working-class world

One of the best pictures of working-class life is found in a study carried out by Dennis and his colleagues (1956) in the West Yorkshire coal-mining town of Featherstone, referred to as 'Ashton' in the book. Located just south of Leeds, close to Pontefract and Castleford, Featherstone was simply a small rural village until the first coal mine opened in 1868. A second mine was opened in 1877, and a number of additional shafts were sunk over the following thirty years. The population grew from about 600 to almost 14,000 by the time the survey was undertaken in the early 1950s.

Most families in Featherstone depended upon mining for their livelihood. Although one of the mines had shut down in 1935, most of its employees had been able to move to others in the area. Two-thirds of all men worked in coal mining, most of them in Featherstone itself, but some were employed in a clothing factory and on the railway. Relatively few women were in paid employment, and most married women worked as housewives. However, some young and unmarried women were employed in domestic service, shop work, dress-making, teaching, or nursing. Featherstone families were tenants in housing built by the local authority or by the mining companies. By the time of the survey, the mining industry had been nationalized, and the cottages along with the mines had become the property of the National Coal Board.

Featherstone was a town of long rows of terraced houses and a few old 'back-to-backs', surrounded by the waste heaps produced by the mining industry. Despite its bleak and sombre physical appearance, it was a community with a real sense of solidarity rooted in the work relations that the majority of the people shared and in their shared memories of the impact that the mines had had on the town and its people. Memories of the general strike of 1926, the depression of the 1930s, and the closure of one of the mines in 1935 were central to their responses to contemporary events and problems.

Coal production was complex and hazardous. It involved the cooperation of workers with many different kinds of skills. The largest group of workers was the colliers who actually worked at the coalface and cut the coal with mechanical drills and who could earn between £9 and £14 a week, depending on the number of hours of overtime that they worked. The wages of all workers were far from secure, and insecurity of wages was a major reason for a strong commitment to trade unionism. The miners felt that they were very weak as individuals and that it was only through collective action that they could hope to redress the imbalance of power between themselves and their employer.

The making of a class society 763

Featherstone households, like other working-class family households, were organized around a strict domestic division of labour and a separation of men's activities from those of women, as we describe in Chapter 12, pp. 440–3. Both men and women supported this view of the family and gender-roles, women seeing it as their job to look after their husbands properly (see also E. Roberts 1984). Male manual work was such a central part of family life that gender divisions were secondary in importance to a sense of class identity. For both men and women, class was a taken-for-granted aspect of their life and was underpinned by the ideas of the male breadwinner and the female housewife. In the face of the stark and obvious divisions of class that separated them from other members of their society, there was little scope for any sense of an autonomous and shared gender identity that cut across class lines.

The class consciousness of the miners was concretely rooted in their shared ideas of work and masculinity—their pride in being 'real men who work hard for their living' (Dennis *et al.* 1956: 33; see also Zweig 1948). Real work was manual work, and so non-manual workers—clerks and managers—could never be seen as working class. The division between 'us' and 'them' was rooted in a strong sense of the solidarity of working men and their role in providing for their families through physically hard and demanding work.

Leisure as well as work was a means through which solidarity was developed, and men who worked together also wanted to enjoy their leisure together (see Box 19.5, p. 764).

Some leisure activities were directly linked to the workplace through the Miners' Welfare Institute, which provided a billiards room, a regular Saturday night dance, and meeting space for various clubs and associations. Most leisure activities, however, were organized separately from the workplace in the town's six working men's clubs, where men met to drink and gamble and to play cards, dominoes, and darts. The town's seven pubs played a similar role in the life of the men.

Individuals, couples, and families regularly watched westerns, adventures, and comedies at the local cinema in nearby Pontefract, and this was the main leisure activity in which men and women participated together on a more or less equal basis. Some families were involved in religious activities, though involvement with church or chapel was far less than it had been in the past. The colliery brass band played at fêtes, parades, and concerts in the town and represented it in competitions with other bands. A main form of leisure activity was watching the local rugby football team. Following football did not mean simply—or even mainly—being interested in the technical side of the game. More important was its part in expressing local solidarity through an assertion of Featherstone's superiority over other towns.

Featherstone was marked by a very strong sense of localism. This was very common in working-class communities. More than 90 per cent of the residents of Bethnal Green in 1934 had been born in East London, and even in the 1950s over a half of local residents had actually been

A Working Men's Club in Durham in the 1950s.

© Getty Images/Alex Dellow

born in the borough (Young and Willmott 1957). More than a quarter of working-class families in a national survey in 1951 had relatives living within a five-minute walk of their own home. In these circumstances, as we show in Chapter 13, p. 486, extensive kinship networks tied people together and created a strong sense of community. The centrality of women in the maintenance of their family households meant that wider kinship links were also maintained through the women. 'Mum' played a key role, and visiting mum was important in sustaining bonds of social solidarity. Around these networks of kinship were circles of friendship that made themselves felt in communal support and in leisure-time activities.

These features of life in Featherstone were typical of working-class communities across the country until the 1950s. They have been documented in numerous other studies, such as those in nearby Leeds (Hoggart 1957) and Huddersfield (Jackson and Marsden 1962; Jackson 1968), in Salford (R. Roberts 1973), and in many other places (McKibbin 1990).

> **⮎ Connections**
> Look at Chapter 12, pp. 442–3, for a discussion of some further material on working-class kinship in East London and elsewhere.

Britain was the earliest nation to industrialize and to develop a strong working class, but it was not unique. In Germany, workers in coal, iron, and steel—most markedly in the Ruhr—were forged into a strong and nationally organized working class by the end of the nineteenth century. Germany was one of the first countries in which a strong Communist Party developed on the basis of a clear working-class consciousness. The worker's movement in Germany was important in the development of Marx's ideas on class, and the German Socialist and Communist parties were central forces in European politics. Similar developments occurred in France, where workers in the engineering industries of Alsace were active participants in socialist politics. Industrial developments in the United States led to the emergence of strong working-class communities in steel towns such as Pittsburgh and more diverse industrial cities such as Chicago. In the United States, however, migration had produced ethnically diverse working-class cities, and class solidarity was cross-cut by ethnic differences. Strong ethnic identities precluded the formation of a strong class identity. Relatively high rates of mobility meant that class consciousness and the language of class were much weaker in the United States than in most of Europe, and the American labour movement was correspondingly weaker and less socialistic in character (Sombart 1906; Archer 2008).

Middle classes

Those described as the middle classes were those employed in professional, managerial, administrative, and various technical occupations in business and public-sector organizations. This included such occupations as personnel managers, doctors, civil servants, lawyers, and teachers. In the past, of course, many of these people would have been self-employed, and many doctors and lawyers today are partners in practices rather than employees. However, the growth of large-scale organizations from the middle of the nineteenth century reduced the numbers of the self-employed and created many new categories of employees.

Figure 19.10 shows this growth in professional and office work around the turn of the twentieth century. The old professions (the clergy, lawyers, doctors, and teachers) showed relatively modest increases between 1880 and 1911, and the rate of growth was below that of manual workers in the same period. On the other hand, the number of civil-service and local-government clerks was almost three times as high in 1911 as it had been in 1880, the numbers of authors and journalists doubled, and the number of scientists was five times as high. By 1911 male clerks in all industries accounted for 5.7 per cent of all male employees.

Marxist writers have been partly correct to treat these workers simply as members of the proletariat: whether employed in manual or non-manual work, employees do not own or control capital. However, the educational

Briefing: class, work, and masculinity   **19.5**

Masculinity at work and masculinity in leisure were closely associated in Featherstone, and they were parts of a larger patriarchal structure. Dennis and his colleagues document this in what they say about the working men's clubs of the town:

> The Working Men's Clubs are predominantly male institutions. Only one of those in Featherstone admits women as members. The others absolutely forbid by rule the admittance of women into the club excepting for concerts on Saturday evening and Sunday midday and evening. . . . Whatever else members may do at the club, they spend a good deal of their time simply conversing over their beer. Conversation is notably free and easy and the men conversing have often been life-long acquaintances; having been at the same school and played together as children, they now, as adults, work at the same place and spend their leisure together in such places as the clubs. (Dennis *et al.* 1956: 142, 144)

Figure 19.10 Professional and clerical work, England and Wales, 1880–1911

Occupational category	Number of men		% increase
	1880	1911	
Clergy, ministers, priests	33,486	40,142	19.1
Barristers, solicitors	17,386	21,380	23.0
Physicians, surgeons	15,091	24,553	62.7
Dentists	3,538	7,373	108.4
Authors, journalists	5,627	12,005	113.3
Scientific	1,170	6,171	427.4
Architects	6,875	11,109	61.1
Teachers, lecturers	44,181	68,651	55.4
Civil-service administration and clerks	21,353	57,475	169.2
Local government clerks	17,993	54,257	201.5

Source: Perkin (1989: table 3.1).

credentials and intellectual skills of managerial and administrative workers have given them market advantages and opportunities that are far superior to those of even the best-paid manual workers. At the same time, their work situations within large bureaucracies typically give them authority over other employees. These are the people that Goldthorpe (1980) has described as members of a **service class**—they serve the interests of large-scale organizations by exercising delegated authority on behalf of capital and the state. They fall into categories I and II of Goldthorpe's social-class classification.

During the nineteenth century, there was a growth in the number of more routine, lower-level non-manual occupations. These did not require such a high level of technical or intellectual competence and they did not, therefore, secure such advantaged life chances. They did, nevertheless, have life chances that set them apart from manual workers. These clerks, shop assistants, supervisors, commercial travellers, and technicians were often referred to as the lower middle class in order to distinguish them from the more secure and established upper middle class of professionals and managers (Crossick 1977a; Vigne and Howkins 1977). These more routine occupations fall into category III of the Goldthorpe social-class classification.

> **➲ Connections**
> You will find a full listing of the social classes in the Goldthorpe Classification in Figure 19.4, p. 755.

A number of other occupations have also been seen as middle class. These are the entrepreneurs, shopkeepers, and self-employed artisans who combine small-scale property ownership with their own labour. They may be involved in productive or managerial work, working alongside their employees and in close contact with them, but their property ownership is the basis of their position as an employer. These people fall into Goldthorpe's social-class category IV and, like routine white-collar workers, have generally been seen as lower middle class in status.

This diversity of class and status situations is reflected in the use of the plural term 'middle classes', rather than the singular 'middle class'. Similarities in their life chances and lifestyles distinguish them from the working class below them, but, internally, they are highly diverse. They never had the kind of homogeneity that was found in the working class. This diversity is reflected, also, in uncertainty over where an upper boundary is to be drawn that separates them from a capital- and landowning upper class.

The making of the middle class

The terms 'middle class' and 'middle classes' came into use in the early nineteenth century to describe people in this diverse range of intermediate class situations. As status markers, these terms distinguished those who had no need to work with their hands from even the most respectable member of the working class. The middle classes were 'gentlemen', though not quite such superior gentlemen as those of the upper class.

The boundaries of the middle classes, like those of all social classes, were formed from patterns of mobility and interaction. The lack of clarity in their upper and lower boundaries reflects the fact that there was a small amount of short-range occupational mobility into and out of neighbouring social classes. Similarly, the internal lines of differentiation that separate the professional and managerial middle classes from the propertied middle class and all these from routine white-collar workers reflected the tendency for mobility and social interaction to flow along the lines of economic division.

The middle classes were a predominantly urban class. Through involvement in urban public life, they became the leading elements in all the main towns and cities. They held urban authority, though they deferred to the wider authority of the upper class at the national level. The cohesion of the middle classes was built through their memberships in the numerous civic bodies and voluntary associations through which they exercised this leadership.

They were members of the town council, they were magistrates, poor-law guardians, and elders of the churches and chapels, and they ran the church charities. They sat on the boards of schools and mechanics' institutes, hospitals, libraries, and savings banks, and they filled the committees of the philosophical and literary societies, sporting associations, and, above all, the political parties, clubs, and leagues (R. J. Morris 1990). These civic activities involved them in a loose network of interlocking boards and committees, around which a series of formal and informal meetings took place and in which their leisure-time interactions were forged. In a study carried out in the 1950s, Stacey (1960: ch. 5) showed how important these networks were in tying together the middle classes of the small country town of Banbury.

It was through participation in public life in the cities that the middle classes achieved a degree of cultural and political cohesion as a class. They were able to assert their autonomy with respect to the upper class, and they could exercise control over the working class. They were too diverse, however, to sustain any real class consciousness, and their unity weakened when the class grew as towns and cities expanded. The working class developed a corporate sense of their own class identity and shared fate, but the middle classes saw the world in individualistic terms. They depended on individual effort for advancement in work, and they rejected any involvement in the collective struggles of trade unionism. Middle-class collective action was limited to the defence of particular professional privileges, regulating the behaviour of the individual members of the

professions, and promoting individual opportunities and self-help.

While the diversity of the middle classes prevents any generalized account of middle-class life from being made, there are a number of common features. These can usefully be highlighted by considering the white-collar workers who filled the expanding lower levels of business bureaucracies. 'White-collar' work is discussed in Box 19.6.

The white-collar world

White-collar work has its origins in the offices of the small industrial and commercial enterprises of the early Victorian period (Lockwood 1958; G. Anderson 1976). The typical firm would employ a handful of clerks to keep up to date the ledgers and account books that recorded day-to-day business transactions. All business decisions were taken by the employer, but these decisions depended on the flow of financial information provided by clerks.

Working conditions in the Victorian office were accurately caricatured in Dickens's account of Bob Cratchit's work in Scrooge's counting house. Typically, an office

Blue-collar and white-collar work
© Alice Chadwick

● Briefing: white collar and blue collar   19.6

The white-collar worker is an office worker, so named because male office workers have traditionally been expected to wear a white shirt and tie. The term is often contrasted with the 'blue-collar' manual worker, whose designation comes from the colour of the cotton overalls that many manual workers wore. Lockwood (1958) describes the white-collar worker under the alternative name of 'black-coated worker', indicating that, in addition to a collar and tie, the clerk was expected to wear a dark suit.

would have a bookkeeper or cashier to keep the financial records and subordinate clerks to deal with the correspondence, filing, and other routine office tasks. In larger offices, a managing clerk might sit at a tall corner desk and oversee office operations, while a number of apprentice clerks might be employed to learn the trade. It was unusual for more than four clerks to be employed in any one office.

White-collar workers were propertyless, like the proletarian manual workers of the working class, but they had specific skills that gave them a superior market power. In the middle of the nineteenth century, when few manual workers were earning more than £1 a week, a routine clerk might earn up to £100 a year. A qualified and specialist clerk could be on £150 (enough to be able to employ a domestic servant at home), and a managing clerk in a large office might receive up to £400 a year. Clerks were generally given holiday and sick pay, and many could look forward to a pension on retirement.

The skills that clerks had were the ability to make quick and accurate calculations and to write clearly and legibly. Those who had a broader range of general knowledge, acquired from a training in classics, arithmetic, and English literature at secondary school, could improve their chances of getting a good clerical post. Once employed, they could acquire additional skills as they learned their work, but these were generally firm-specific and gave them little opportunity to transfer from one employer to another. On the other hand, their security of employment was very good, as were their chances of promotion.

The market and work situations of clerks were highly individualized, shaped by personal recommendations and family connections (Lockwood 1958: 22, 82). Until the end of the nineteenth century, the typical clerk was recruited through the personal contacts of an employer with the would-be clerk's relatives, teachers, and friends. In fact, the whole work situation was structured by considerations of status. Chances of promotion depended on the clerk maintaining good personal relations with his employer, who expected loyalty and conformity. Pensions and fringe benefits were not a contractual matter, but depended on the personal discretion of the employer. Because of the close personal and individual relations that they had with their employer, and because of the physical separation of the office from the works, white-collar workers enjoyed higher prestige than manual workers. Unlike skilled manual workers, they hardly had to struggle to maintain their status as respectable members of society.

The main line of division within white-collar work was that between those working in banking, insurance, and the civil service, on the one hand, and those in commercial and industrial offices, on the other. The former were, in general, better paid and lived in the better suburbs; the latter had incomes that were closer to those of skilled manual workers and they lived in the less affluent districts (Gaskell 1977). Nevertheless, even the commercial and industrial clerks differed fundamentally in their orientation, mentality, and outlook from manual workers, and they had close links through mobility and interaction with the superior clerks. Both groups had a distinctive middle-class outlook, their lifestyle and status concerns ruling out any collective solidarity or involvement with trade unions.

In 1851 clerks formed just 0.8 per cent of the British labour force, but the growth of large-scale organizations in the second half of the century produced a massive growth in numbers. By 1901, 4 per cent of the labour force were clerks, and by 1951 they formed 10.5 per cent (Lockwood 1958: 36). This expansion transformed their market and work situations. A growth in the average size of offices brought together larger numbers of clerks in a more extended division of labour and reduced their contacts with their employers. Indeed, their employers were likely to be corporate enterprises rather than individual entrepreneurs. Many of their distinctive conditions of work were eroded, although they continued to be employed in much smaller work groups than were manual workers.

Concentration and monopolization of banking and industry was relatively much greater in Germany and the United States than it was in Britain. Large firms had large offices with extensive ranks of clerical and managerial workers. They were generally very sharply distinguished from manual workers and in Germany had a distinct legal status. The middle classes became a correspondingly much more important political factor in these countries.

The continuing separation of the office from the works, and the close and, generally, cooperative relationships that clerical workers had with their managers, meant that manual workers tended to see clerks as a part of management. Nevertheless, major changes in their work situations were occurring. Office work was rapidly mechanized at the beginning of the twentieth century through the introduction of the typewriter, the calculating machine, and the telephone. Later in the century, the photocopier, the computer, the word-processor, and the fax machine brought about further transformations. Mechanization reduced the autonomy of clerical workers and made their skills of calculation and writing much less important. Across the United States and the leading European societies, office work became more routine in character, and white-collar workers had to learn to pace their work to the requirements of the office machines (Mills 1951: chapter 9; Braverman 1974).

As a result of these changes, the earnings gap between white-collar and manual work began to close. The declining demand for basic educational skills reduced the market power of those with a good basic education. At the same time, higher-level management was becoming a more technically skilled occupation, and employers required managerial recruits who had high-level educational credentials. Opportunities for the promotion of clerks into managerial grades declined, and those who entered clerical work at a young age were likely to remain there throughout their working lives.

Of fundamental importance in the first half of the twentieth century was an increase in the number of women employed in clerical work. In 1861 women comprised just over 1 per cent of British commercial clerks and 4 per cent of those in public administration (Holcombe 1973). By 1911 they comprised about 20 per cent of commercial clerks and 16 per cent of public-sector clerks (G. Anderson 1976: 2). By 1951 over a half of all clerks were female. Women were largely confined to the lowest levels of clerical work and had far fewer opportunities for promotion than did their male counterparts. Nevertheless, many male clerks felt that their own loss of income and status was a result of the influx of unmarried women who were willing to do clerical work for lower rates of pay than married men could afford to take (G. Anderson 1976: 58–9). For the most part, however, women did not directly compete with men for clerical work. They entered the completely new jobs created by the introduction of office machinery, and they faced, to the full, the mechanization of the office. This work was so highly gendered that the word 'typewriter' originally meant the woman who operated the machine, and not the machine itself. The growth of cheap female labour and the expansion of less-skilled, machine-based office work went hand in hand with each other.

The upper class

It is impossible to understand the European upper classes without understanding the importance of the values and ideas of traditional, landed society. These classes originated in land ownership and the rural world, and their development in industrial societies reflected this landed background. Traditional ideas rooted in rural and agricultural life defined a clear status hierarchy that included the aristocracy that owned the land, the farmers that worked it, the old professions that serviced them, and the agricultural labourers whose work provided their incomes. In one area of life after another, traditional status considerations were weakened as modern industry expanded. At the upper levels of the stratification system, however, traditional status ideas remained important.

The very wealthiest capitalist entrepreneurs and financiers who developed with industrial capitalism aspired to be accepted as the status equals of the landed aristocrats. If they bought land, they could begin the process of acceptance, but full acceptance might have to wait for a few generations until their new wealth had become 'old' wealth. In Britain, the economically powerful were forged

into a single social class because they accepted and deferred to the traditional social values associated with a landed aristocracy. They were a social estate as much as they were a social class. (This is discussed more fully in J. Scott 1991; see also F. M. L. Thompson 1963.) It was this class of landowners and wealthy capitalists that came to be described as an upper class. Similar trends were apparent in France and Germany, though both societies showed sharper divisions between land and industry.

The phrase 'upper class' had come into use in Britain early in the nineteenth century to describe the aristocracy, and, as wealthy industrial and commercial capitalists began to merge with this group, they, too, came to be seen as part of the upper class. By the end of the nineteenth century, the picture of Britain as a society with an upper class, a middle class, and a working class was firmly established.

At the core of the upper class was the aristocracy, and at the heart of the aristocracy was the peerage. Peers were those with titles that gave them the right to sit in the House of Lords. Below them were the gentry—the leading families in county 'Society' who dominated local affairs. The peerage and the gentry were the two main status groups within the upper class, but each was internally divided to form a complex hierarchy of status levels. Each level in this hierarchy had a distinct title or honorary designation that defined its social position.

At the top of this hierarchy were the Royal Family and the great dukes. Below them were the other ranks of the hereditary peerage (the marquesses, earls, viscounts, and barons), and the more lowly baronets, knights, esquires, and gentlemen. A whole range of other status honours further differentiated these people by their relative social standing as companions, officers, and members of the various orders of knighthood and as Companions of Honour, Deputy Lieutenants, and Justices of the Peace.

The aristocratic upper class was finely divided by its gradations of status, and these status distinctions emphasized its position as the leading element in a traditional social order. Aristocratic values were deeply embedded in the state and the church, and members of other social classes regarded the upper class as their social superiors. Farmers and farm workers were directly dependent on the power of landlords, and they had little choice but to defer to them as the leaders of rural society. Throughout the middle classes and into the working class itself, attitudes of deference to the aristocracy as the natural leaders of society were strong. Class divisions, then, were reinforced by status distinctions that both stabilized and legitimized them.

The absorption of wealthy industrialists into the upper class was a slow process. The growth in the scale of industrial activity from the middle of the nineteenth century meant that many capitalist entrepreneurs could match or surpass the wealth of those in the upper class. While many continued to define themselves—and to be defined by others—as middle class, others were rapidly becoming the economic equals of the landowners. Mobility and interaction between landowners and the large industrial and commercial capitalists increased, and by the end of the nineteenth century they had come close to becoming a single social class. They had a common dependence on property and on its use as capital to generate their privileged life chances. Aristocratic status distinctions gave this class its particular characteristics. Members of the class might take these status distinctions as the basis of their social identity and identify themselves as an upper class, but they were, in reality, a capitalist class with propertied interests in land, industry, commerce, and finance.

Landowners in the southern states of the United States played a similar role in relation to the society of the Deep South. However, industrial development was largely a northern phenomenon, and northern industrialists consolidated their power in regions without established aristocracies. The upper class of the United States, therefore, was a more exclusively industrial and financial class, though here, too, the attractions of long-established wealth ensured that 'old' families were accorded higher status than newly wealthy families.

The making of a capitalist class

Capitalist class situations generate advantaged life chances through the ownership and control of property and its use as capital. Capital takes the form of land, factories, or financial assets, and different capitalist class situations can be distinguished according to the particular type of capital involved. For much of the nineteenth century, ownership of land was one of the most important forms of capital. Landowners received income from the land that they rented out for commercial farming, and they earned a profit from the land that they farmed themselves. Many landowners also received an income from the commercial uses of their land for mining, railways, and housing. Land ownership was also an important basis of status and political authority.

The industrial and commercial entrepreneurs who built large businesses in nineteenth-century Britain had life chances that distinguished them from the middle classes and that involved them closely with landowners. They built their factories and mines on land owned by aristocrats, they invested in land on a large scale, and they invited landowners to invest in their businesses (Stone and Stone 1984). In these ways, the economic basis of a single capitalist class was established. By the turn of the twentieth century, wealthy entrepreneurs were also likely to be sending their children to the same privileged schools and to be members of the same social clubs as the aristocrats. Their sons and daughters were increasingly likely to be seen as acceptable marriage partners by the aristocrats (Davidoff and Hall 1987).

In these and other ways, mobility and interaction among those in capitalist class situations grew to the point at which separate landed and industrial classes could not be distinguished as sharply as they once could. By the 1930s, industrialists, financiers, and landowners had fully merged into a single social class. This was, however, a capitalist class that continued to follow a modified form of the lifestyle of the old upper class.

In economic terms, there were important changes to the ways in which property was held. In the nineteenth century, direct *personal* ownership of land or business was the most usual form of property ownership. As businesses expanded in size, and as land use and farming became more intensive and large scale, this direct personal form of ownership began to give way to more indirect, *corporate* forms of ownership and control. In this form of ownership, people owned companies or shares in companies, rather than owning the actual physical assets themselves.

In the large companies, financial assets rather than physical assets were the principal sources of personal wealth. Wealthy families derived their privileged life chances from the financial assets that they owned, and they were able to ensure their continuing control over the assets that generated their wealth by taking positions as directors and executives in the large companies. This was clearest in industrial and commercial businesses, but even landowners controlled their land through private companies. Wealthy capitalists diversified their sources of wealth by investing in many different companies and so acquiring business interests throughout the economy.

> ### ⊃ Connections
> We explore some of the economic aspects of these changes in ownership and control in Chapter 14, pp. 528–32. You might like to glance at that discussion before continuing with this chapter.

The capitalist social class, as it existed in the middle of the twentieth century, comprised those wealthy households who derived their privileged life chances from one of four capitalist class situations. These defined four types of capitalist:

- *Entrepreneurial capitalists* ran the business operations of large enterprises, whose shares they owned and which were, therefore, under their personal control. The businesses might have operated in industry, commerce, or land. Such businesses were often family firms run by the heirs of the original founders.

- *Rentier capitalists* had personal investments in a large number of business enterprises and were not dependent on the success of any one particular enterprise. Their original fortunes might have come from land or from a particular business, but they diversified their investments and spread them widely.

- *Executive capitalists* held top executive positions in particular enterprises. They owed their positions to their particular expertise and educational credentials and had followed a career in business.

- *Finance capitalists* had top positions in numerous enterprises. A finance capitalist was, typically, a part-time director in a large number of enterprises that operated in a wide range of industries. Their principal positions were often in banks, insurance companies, and other financial enterprises.

There was much mobility and overlap among these class situations. Executive capitalists, for example, could build up a large shareholding in the company that they ran and they could invest widely in other enterprises. Finance capitalists were often members of wealthy rentier families. Rentier capitalists were likely to be the sons or daughters of entrepreneurial capitalists, and so on. In all these ways, they formed parts of a single social class (J. Scott 1997: ch. 8).

Status factors were important in solidifying upper classes. An upper circle of 'Society' families led a round of balls, parties, and sporting events that formed the upper-class social calendar and that defined the character of the class as a whole. In Britain, the country lifestyle of hunting, shooting, and fishing, the social calendar of county Society, and the system of titles and honours cast a cloak of tradition over the new forms of economic power (M. J. Weiner 1981; Rubinstein 1993). In the United States, the upper class was similarly held together through shared sporting and leisure events (Baltzell 1958).

Of great importance in tying members of the social class together were the social networks built around common patterns of schooling and similarity of social background. Boys from capitalist class families were educated privately. In Britain this was often at the public schools that prepared them for entry to Oxford or Cambridge, and their educational background was an important source of contacts for entry into business positions or into public life. In the United States, attendance at private schools prepared upper-class boys for entry to the 'Ivy League' universities. In both societies, an 'old-boy network' combined with wider networks of kinship and friendship to bind upper-class members together (Davidoff 1973).

Ascot races: meeting place for the 'old boy network'.

© HOK Sport Architecture

Stop and reflect

Stratification in Britain since the middle of the nineteenth century can best be understood as involving a division into an upper class, the middle classes, and a working class. In this section we have shown that Marx expected this structure to become ever more polarized, and we have suggested that this has not occurred.

- A cohesive working class, consisting of manual workers and their families, was formed in the major industrial areas.

- This class had its basis in cohesive industrial communities and had a distinctive working-class culture. It did engage in the kind of political action that Marxist theory implied, but it was not a revolutionary class.

- There had been a massive expansion in clerical, managerial, and professional work over the course of the century. These intermediate class situations were the basis of the expanding middle classes.

- The capitalist class formed an upper class, defined by its traditional social status. There was a close association between aristocratic landowners and the industrial and financial capitalists.

- Do you think that it still makes sense to see the British population as divided into these three social classes?

Transforming class society

We have shown how industrial societies came to be divided into working classes, middle classes, and upper classes. Lines of internal division cross-cut these classes, making it difficult to draw their boundaries with any precision, but their broad outlines were clear. Industrial societies were class societies. Class structure was not polarized between capitalists and proletarians, as Marx had expected, as the middle classes had increased in importance. The social inequalities that we review in Chapter 18 and many other features of social life that we examine in other chapters were all organized in relation to class differences. It is for this reason that so much social research has taken class as one of its key variables.

In the second half of the twentieth century these lines of class division became less clear. Class differences in economic power persisted—and in many respects they increased—but they were now less directly reflected in differences in attitude and outlook. The language and imagery of class were, for much of the twentieth century, tied to quite specific ideas of status. Class divisions were perceived and defined in relation to ideas of respectability, gentility, accent, dress, and social background. One of the reasons for the greater invisibility of class relations has been the erosion of the traditional status values that, for so long, defined their particular character in Britain and other industrial societies. The values of the traditional social order have less of a hold on public consciousness, and so they have less of an impact on how people perceive and interpret their economic positions. The decay of these status ideas has, therefore, undermined the use of class language to describe social differences and social divisions. At the same time, many of the social conditions that, in the past, sustained a sense of class awareness have also been transformed. Working conditions and living conditions, for example, differ markedly, for many people, from those of the past. Personal and domestic consumption, encouraged by new trends in production and the mass media, have made people's productive roles less salient for their social identity. As a result, people are less likely to see their own situations in class terms. Britain remains a class society, but it has become a fragmentary class society in which people are more likely to identify themselves in non-traditional status terms or in relation to their gender and ethnicity.

Industrialism, post-industrialism, and post-modernism

Marx's failure to foresee the massive growth of the middle classes led many critics to reject his whole approach to class. The alternative they proposed held that modern societies are *industrial* societies rather than capitalist societies. This highlights the increasingly complex industrial technology and occupational division of labour found in contemporary industrial societies and holds that differences in property ownership are no longer important features of social stratification. In industrial societies, patterns of stratification reflect the prestige attached to occupations according to their functional importance in an advanced industrial economy (Kerr *et al.* 1960).

More recent theorists have held that the continuing development of industrial societies has led to a state of post-industrialism in which the growing importance of scientific knowledge and technical expertise has further reduced the salience of class relations. For some commentators, a post-industrial society is a post-modern society. In a post-modern society, class relations are completely submerged and individuals no longer see themselves as members of social classes. Social identities are diverse and fragmented and class consciousness is something of the past. We hold that post-modern theorists overstate their case, though we will show that there have, indeed, been fundamental changes in class relations and class consciousness.

Occupational change and stratification

These arguments rest on a recognition that the development of industrial technology is characterized by an **occupational transition**, a comprehensive shift in occupational structure (Payne 1987b; see also Clark 1940). New occupations are created as production expands and becomes more complex, and the need for many older occupations disappears. There is a growing need for technical and specialist occupations requiring high levels of education and training.

The idea of the occupational transition sees occupations as distributed into three economic sectors that differ in their technical requirements and education. In the **primary sector** are agricultural, mining, and quarrying occupations directly involved in the production and extraction of raw materials and basic resources. The **secondary sector** comprises manufacturing occupations that use raw materials to produce finished consumer goods and machinery. Finally, the **tertiary sector** contains the service and commercial occupations that distribute consumer goods and provide banking and insurance facilities. Over time, the relative size of these three sectors alters as the scale and complexity of technology changes. The model of the occupational transition is shown in Figure 19.11. The transition from a pre-industrial to an industrial society involved a massive growth in manufacturing capacity and so an expansion of the secondary sector. In an industrial society, the primary and the tertiary sectors are each less important than the secondary sector of manufacturing employment. This does not necessarily mean that secondary-sector occupations comprise a majority of all occupations in an industrial society. Only in Britain have secondary-sector jobs ever accounted for more than a half of the total labour force. In all other industrial societies, the size of the secondary sector stabilized at about 30 per cent of the labour force. In the United States, for example, the secondary sector accounted for 38 per cent of the labour force in 1900.

The development of industrial societies in the second half of the twentieth century produced further changes in their occupational structures. In all advanced societies the primary sector continued to decline, and there was a corresponding increase in the number of tertiary-sector occupations. By 1967, for example, 55 per cent of all jobs in the United States were service-sector jobs, compared with 24 per cent in 1900. By the 1970s, almost two-thirds of employment in the United States was in the service sector and only 4 per cent was in the primary sector. Although

Figure 19.11 The occupational transition

❷ In Chapter 8 we introduce the demographic transition and the health transition (see pp. 280–1). Look at those models and see if you can see how the model of the occupational transition relates to them. Does it involve a similar and related sequence of three stages? Do you think it is useful to use the term 'post-industrial society' to describe the current stage of social development?

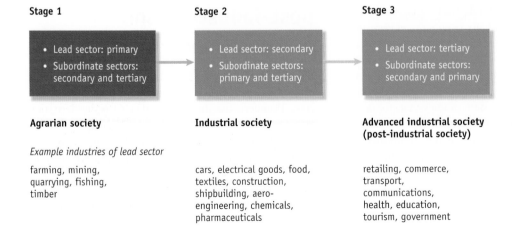

Stage 1

- Lead sector: primary
- Subordinate sectors: secondary and tertiary

Agrarian society

Example industries of lead sector

farming, mining, quarrying, fishing, timber

Stage 2

- Lead sector: secondary
- Subordinate sectors: primary and tertiary

Industrial society

cars, electrical goods, food, textiles, construction, shipbuilding, aero-engineering, chemicals, pharmaceuticals

Stage 3

- Lead sector: tertiary
- Subordinate sectors: secondary and primary

Advanced industrial society (post-industrial society)

retailing, commerce, transport, communications, health, education, tourism, government

these trends cannot be seen simply as a shift from manual to non-manual work, they are manifest in an increase in the proportion of non-manual workers in the United States from 18 per cent to 59 per cent between 1900 and 1990. It is these changes that led many to describe the United States as a post-industrial society rather than simply as an advanced industrial society.

This view of industrialism and post-industrialism sees the occupational transition as having produced a massive growth in intermediate occupations that are neither capitalist nor proletarian. The capitalist and the proletarian classes themselves have declined in size and changed in character. The decline in the primary and secondary sectors, it is argued, has led to a decline in the number of manual jobs that formed the core of the proletarian working class. The remaining manual workers are able to enjoy the income and job security that brings them closer to the middle classes. At the same time, changes in the financing of industry have made the ownership of capital far less significant than it was in the past. The small capitalist class is disappearing, to be replaced by salaried managers. It is concluded that there has been an embourgeoisement of the working class and a managerial transformation of the capitalist class.

Embourgeoisement and managerialism

Embourgeoisement is a rather awkward word that means 'becoming bourgeois' or 'becoming middle class'. It has been the cornerstone of a theory that suggests that the manual working class has merged with the middle classes. **Managerialism**, on the other hand, points to the disappearance of the capitalist class. It suggests that the growth in executive and managerial occupations has reduced the power and influence of those with capital (Dahrendorf 1957).

Advocates of embourgeoisement claim that a greater degree of equality and of affluence experienced from the 1940s and 1950s eroded the distinctive values and way of life of the working class. Wage levels improved, job security was enhanced, and people have far higher disposable incomes than their parents and grandparents. The higher incomes of manual workers have allowed them to buy the new consumer goods that became available in the post-war period. Manual workers can afford cars, televisions, and washing machines, many own their own homes, and they can afford to furnish and decorate their homes in more comfortable and stylish ways than before. They are, embourgeoisement theorists argue, adopting middle-class values and lifestyles to match their middle-class incomes (Mayer 1963; Lipset 1964).

Advocates of managerialist theory hold that a growing scale of business enterprise has vastly increased the number of shareholders, most of whom have little or no influence over business affairs and cannot really be considered as capitalists. At the same time, shareholding has become completely irrelevant when enterprises finance their

activities from accumulated resources (Parsons 1953; Bell 1961). Managerialists see the supplanting of capitalists by salaried managers who hold key positions in the expanding business bureaucracies. Managers previously had authority delegated to them by the capitalist owners. In the second half of the twentieth century, however, they held this authority in their own right. They owe their positions to the technical knowledge and expertise acquired through their education and on which the industrial system is increasingly dependent. The growing demand for managers, it is held, has expanded the middle sections of the stratification system.

Embourgeoisement and managerialism have been seen as the bases of a fundamental change in the whole shape of the stratification system. The theory of industrial society claims that the shape of the stratification system has changed from a triangle or pyramid to a diamond. The number of those in the middle increases, while the numbers of those at the bottom and the very top declines. This is illustrated in Figure 19.12. There is a single, large middle class that stretches from the topmost managers through to manual workers; only the marginal 'underclass' is excluded from it. For many, this middle-class society is seen as being, to all intents and purposes, classless—class as a source of social division is dead.

In summary, the theory of industrial society has suggested that contemporary systems of stratification can be characterized by three features (Goldthorpe 1964):

- *Reduced differentiation.* The gap between top and bottom in the stratification system declines and there is a move towards greater equality and homogeneity.

- *Increased consistency.* Occupation becomes the primary basis of social stratification, with all other inequalities being linked closely to it. Income and prestige, for example, are closely tied to one another, and property becomes irrelevant.

- *Greater mobility.* There are high levels of occupational mobility, with many opportunities for the able and talented to rise. In this open meritocracy, there are few sharp boundaries dividing one social class from another.

Figure 19.12 Embourgeoisement

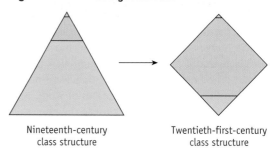

Nineteenth-century class structure → Twentieth-first-century class structure

What is the evidence for this? What has happened to the principal lines of class division? We will now look at these questions.

Manual work and class identity

Those in manual working jobs and their dependants today account for perhaps just over a half of the population in Britain. In other industrial societies the levels are slightly lower than this. Theorists of industrial society have recognized that manual work and manufacturing occupations have not completely disappeared. Members of many households still depend on manual work for their life chances. Nevertheless, these theorists hold that the differences in life chances between manual and non-manual workers are less marked than in the past. Economic change has increased the amount of mobility and interaction, and there is no longer a sharp class boundary separating a working class from the middle classes. Manual workers are no longer an inferior, exploited group in terms of their economic resources and spending power. They have undergone a process of embourgeoisement.

Affluence and the working class

The theory of embourgeoisement was an attempt to explore some of the consequences of economic growth in the post-war period. It pointed to the affluence and higher levels of consumption that the mass of the population had come to enjoy, and, at the same time, it recognized that technical change in industry was rapidly leading to the disappearance of old forms of manual work. The newly affluent manual workers were employed, for the most part, in factories using automatic or continuous-flow systems of production that required workers to monitor and supervise machinery rather than to engage in heavy or repetitive manual work. The new manual workers were technicians rather than operatives. Their work situations, as much as their market situations, were seen as having been fundamentally transformed.

Attention was also given to urban change in the years following the Second World War. City centres and industrial districts were redeveloped, larger numbers of people settled in the new suburbs and estates, and there was an expansion of dormitory towns set apart from the big industrial centres. Large numbers of people had moved away from the places in which traditional working-class culture had thrived. They now lived in areas that were not so closely tied to particular types and places of work. As a result, people were less likely to live close to their kin, they had fewer social contacts with their neighbours, and their leisure patterns were less bound to work and locality.

> **⊙ Connections**
>
> The technical changes in work and their implications were raised by Blauner (1964). We discuss his ideas in Chapter 17, pp. 656–7. Changes in urban patterns of community are discussed in Chapter 13, pp. 496–7. You might want to review what we say in those places.

Embourgeoisement theorists argued that these changes had eroded the structural basis of the working class. Manual workers were no longer confined by the restrictive cultural outlook of working-class communal solidarity. They were no longer likely to identify themselves in class terms. At the same time, these workers and their families were becoming much more sensitive to matters of status. Their affluence allowed them to consume goods that could previously be afforded only by the middle classes, and they aspired to the status associated with them. Consumer lifestyles had become the means to status advancement into the middle class (Zweig 1961; Klein 1965; see also Mayer 1963; Lipset 1964).

The most sustained criticisms of the embourgeoisement thesis have come from Goldthorpe, Lockwood, and their colleagues (Goldthorpe *et al.* 1969; see also Goldthorpe and Lockwood 1963; Lockwood 1960; Goldthorpe 1964). They have shown that, while the situation of manual workers has indeed altered, the embourgeoisement thesis must be rejected. They discussed the theory's shortcomings under the three headings of the economic, relational, and normative aspects of change.

- *Economic aspects.* While there may have been some growth in manual-worker incomes and, therefore, an increasing similarity with non-manual patterns of consumption, there are still very important differences between the work situations of manual and non-manual workers. Considered as producers, rather than as consumers, even routine non-manual workers have superior working conditions. They still enjoy greater security of employment, better pension and holiday provision, and enhanced chances of promotion.

- *Relational aspects.* There is little evidence that there has been any significant growth in either mobility or interaction across the manual/non-manual divide. This remains as an important social-class boundary.

- *Normative aspects.* Affluent manual workers have not abandoned working-class values and norms for middle-class ones. Changes in their market situation and their patterns of residence have simply led them to *adapt* their old norms to their new circumstances. There is no evidence of changing aspirations.

Not satisfied with a negative critique of the theory of embourgeoisement, Goldthorpe *et al.* (1969) undertook a study of their own (see Box 19.7). Their aim was to investigate what was really happening to manual workers. They recognized that the debate over embourgeoisement centred on what was happening to those who worked in the most advanced systems of production, and they set out to study this group. They sought workers in the technologically advanced industries who were geographically mobile, who were enjoying relatively high pay, and who had good living conditions in socially mixed areas. They settled on a study in Luton, a prosperous and expanding town, where they interviewed workers in the motor, engineering, and chemical industries.

Goldthorpe *et al.* found that the work situations of manual workers were very different from those of non-manual workers. Workers reported high levels of dissatisfaction with work that they regarded as dreary and monotonous. However, they tolerated these conditions because of the high pay. Goldthorpe *et al.* describe these workers as having an **instrumental orientation** to their work. Work is a mere means to obtain income, and not as something that is, in itself, a source of meaning and satisfaction. Pay in excess of the £20 per week received by many of the workers was achieved only as a result of overtime working. This increased the typical working week to almost 50 hours. The clerical workers in their sample earned only slightly less

than this, but they got this for a standard working week of 38.5 hours with no overtime or shift work.

Corresponding to the manual workers' instrumental view of work was a rejection of the idea of work as a source of satisfying relationships with others. They did not identify with their work, and they did not seek out workmates for friendly interaction outside the workplace. Very few manual workers were active in the sports and social clubs organized by their employers. These were mainly the province of the non-manual workers.

In their patterns of free-time interaction, manual workers drew less on workmates than did the clerical workers. In general, they drew their leisure-time partners from their extended family (where family members lived locally) and from their neighbours. This was particularly marked when entertaining in the home, as it was very rare for anyone other than family members to be invited for a meal or party. Where interaction with non-family members did occur outside the home, this was mainly with other manual workers. There was little or no leisure-time interaction between manual and non-manual workers.

For most manual workers, however, their social relations took the form of **privatism**. They were largely confined to the private sphere of the family household. The need to work long, unsocial hours, meant that leisure-time activities were, of necessity, focused on the private, domestic world of the nuclear family. The affluent manual workers were home- and family-centred.

THEORY AND METHODS   **19.7**

The affluent worker study

Goldthorpe and his colleagues drew a sample of 229 married men earning, in 1962, at least £17 per week. They also interviewed a small sample of 54 non-manual workers for comparison. Workers were employed in one of three factories: Vauxhall Motors, Skefco Ball Bearings, and Laporte Chemicals. Their sample was not a random one, but was chosen specifically to fit the needs of the research.

The research involved two long interviews. The first, with the worker himself, involved questions on work history, the nature of work, and trade unionism. The second interview, carried out at home, asked workers and their wives about their leisure, family relationships, education, politics, and images of society.

The results of the research were written up in three books: one on industrial attitudes and behaviour (Goldthorpe *et al.* 1968*a*), one on politics (Goldthorpe *et al.* 1968*b*), and a third that contained the core findings on class as a whole (Goldthorpe *et al.* 1969). The third volume is organized around the three central aspects of change that they identified: the economic aspects (Chapter 3), relational aspects (Chapter 4), and normative aspects (Chapter 5).

⟳ Connections

Goldthorpe *et al.* (1969) use what they call an action frame of reference in their study. Did you notice a similarity between their idea of the instrumental orientation to work and Weber's concept of instrumental action? See Chapter 2, p. 39, for a discussion of this.

Although the affluent workers had broader aspirations for what they hoped to achieve in their lives and in those of their children, their norms and outlook were still shaped by their class situations as manual workers. They wanted greater purchasing power as consumers, and they sought higher wages to achieve this, but this was because they wanted particular consumer goods and not because they wanted a 'middle-class' life style. Similarly, they wanted their children to have the kind of education that would improve their chances of entering non-manual jobs, but this was because of the greater security that these jobs offered and not because they were higher status, middle-class jobs.

Goldthorpe *et al.* give particular attention to the images of society that underpin the norms and values adopted by the affluent workers. Very few held to the two-class power model of 'us' and 'them' that had been central to the traditional proletarian image of society. However, there was no sign that support for the middle-class image of a continuous status hierarchy had grown. Images of society were not, in fact, sharply crystallized at all, and they showed much variation and flexibility. Most typical was a *money model* of society, an image of society as organized around differences in income, assets, and material living standards.

Workers saw society as consisting of one large, central social class that contained most manual and non-manual workers. Differences of income within this class were a matter of degree, and people moved up or down according to whatever income they were currently able to earn. This class was variously—and quite arbitrarily—described as working class, middle class, or even lower class. Workers contrasted this central mass with one or more small social classes with vastly superior spending power and that they called millionaires, high society, or the well-to-do. Sometimes they recognized a small impoverished class at the bottom of the class structure that they referred to simply as the poor or 'the dregs'.

Class and identity

The emphasis that Goldthorpe *et al.* and the original advocates of embourgeoisement placed on affluence seems rather strange today. The 1950s and 1960s were, indeed, periods of economic growth and prosperity for many manual workers, but there were long periods of recession during the following decades. As Marx had claimed, capitalist societies follow a cyclical pattern of booms followed by slumps. This cycle of affluence and recession has not produced the ever-deepening slumps that Marx anticipated. Indeed, absolute living standards seem to have shown a continuous improvement. Nevertheless, it is important to know whether recession has an effect on the pattern of change described by Goldthorpe and his colleagues.

Fiona Devine (1992) set out to investigate this through a restudy of Luton in the 1980s. She found that Luton workers still shared an experience of geographical mobility, but she suggests that this did not result in a narrow instrumentalism about work. While some workers had moved to Luton in search of higher pay than they could earn elsewhere, others had been motivated simply by the search for work of any kind. They typically came from areas of high unemployment with no job prospects at all. The relatively prosperous industries of Luton offered job opportunities, where other areas could offer only the prospect of continuing unemployment.

Geographical mobility had been seen by Goldthorpe *et al.* as underpinning the family-centred lifestyles that the workers and their families had adopted in Luton. These families were recent migrants and had few members of their extended kinship networks living in the area. They had to look to their own resources for leisure and entertainment. Devine shows that the early migrants to Luton

had, in fact, been followed by kin, friends, and neighbours who also sought jobs and better housing. They naturally chose to migrate to an area where friends or family were already to be found. Networks of kinship and friendship had, therefore, been rebuilt in Luton by the 1980s. People were less isolated than they had been in the 1960s, and they were less likely to be so dependent on the members of their immediate nuclear family.

Devine argues, therefore, that the Luton workers of the 1980s did not lead such privatized lifestyles as those of the 1960s. The three-generation family was an important source of informal support and sociability. While these kinship links were not on the scale of the kinship solidarity found in Featherstone and Bethnal Green, they were still very important. It was possible to rely on family members for babysitting and other forms of informal care and support, and they were important sources of leisure-time interaction. Over time, neighbours had also become more important in free-time interaction. With the expansion of local industries it was also more likely that work colleagues would be neighbours.

> **⊃ Connections**
>
> You will find it useful to look at our discussion of changes in the domestic divisions of labour in Chapter 12, pp. 458–61. Perhaps you might also like to look at the discussion of the decline of community in Chapter 13, pp. 496–501.
>
> Look back at our discussion of Lord Cadogan and the identification of 'the working class' at the beginning of this chapter. What do these arguments about changes in manual work tell us about the existence of a working class?

This decline in privatism and family-centredness was also manifest in work patterns. Women generally returned to the labour market after bringing up their children, and so were less exclusively concerned with domestic issues. The household division of labour remained a gendered division of labour. Husbands did not take on equal responsibility for domestic work, and neither partner saw the family household as the sole focus of their concerns. Nevertheless, household commitments did take up a large proportion of their time. By comparison with the traditional working class, there were far fewer opportunities for going to clubs and pubs or for involvement in other communal leisure activities. As in the past, however, these opportunities are gendered: opportunities for communal sociability differ between men and women. For women, childcare responsibilities are a major constraint on social activities outside the home.

A money image of society remained the most common form of class awareness. Workers compared themselves with those who were, like them, working for their living and judged their own income against the standards of living

Briefing: coal is not our life 19.8

The style of life found among traditional manual workers in Featherstone (pp. 762–4 above) was associated with their work in the mining industry and found its expression in trade unionism and Labour politics. This style of life largely disappeared with the decline of the mining industry and the collapse of the mining union. The height of power for the National Union of Mineworkers (NUM) was in the 1970s, when it took on the Conservative government of Edward Heath. The union aimed to repeat this victory in 1984–5, when it launched a strike against the Thatcher government. This time, however, economic change was working against the union: coal was rapidly being replaced by other sources of fuel, and the number of people working in the industry was in long-term decline. The number of pits fell from 170 to 13 between 1984 and 2002. Over the same period, the membership of the NUM fell from 180,000 to less than 3,000. Politically, the union retains some considerable influence, though this, too, has declined. In 1945, thirty-seven members of parliament were sponsored by the NUM, but by 2010 there were just ten.

We discuss general trends in trade unionism in 'The decline of trade unions', Chapter 17, pp. 678–80.

they saw in other working people. However, their knowledge of the true extent of income differences was limited. Feeling that others were not that much better off than themselves, they sought relatively modest improvements in their economic situation. They did, however, support policies of social justice and a desire for a fair system of income distribution.

For manual workers, then, class is not such an important way of describing their experiences of inequality as it was in the past. They see their situation in money terms, which they sometimes refer to in the language of class, but they do not *live* class in the way that was so common a generation ago. Class identity has weakened, and other identities now rival it. This makes it difficult to use the term 'working class' to describe manual workers (but see Roberts *et al.* 1977). The cohesive working class of the past has been transformed into a more fragmentary social class: it retains its inferior life chances and it is still identifiable as a social class through its patterns of mobility and interaction, but it no longer has any significant cultural or political cohesion. Working-class culture has dissolved, along with the working-class communities (see Box 19.8). Attitudes and values are more diverse, and they are more likely to concern issues of consumption than issues of work and production.

The 'underclass'

It is now possible to return to one issue that was left unresolved in Chapter 18. We show that the poor still exist and

 Controversy and debate Views on classlessness   19.9

'The class war is obsolete . . . We are all middle class now' (Harold Macmillan in 1959).

'In the world we now live in, divisions into class are meaningless. We are all working people now' (Margaret Thatcher in 1988).

'[Britain must become] a genuinely classless society in which people can rise to whatever level that their own abilities and good fortune may take them, from whatever their starting point' (John Major in 1990).

'Slowly but surely the old establishment is being replaced by a new, larger, more meritocratic middle class. . . . A middle class characterized by greater tolerance of difference, greater ambition to succeed, greater opportunities to earn a decent living. A middle class that will include millions of people who

traditionally may see themselves as working class, but whose ambitions are far broader than those of their parents and grandparents' (Tony Blair in 1999).

'My view is very simple . . . that what people are interested in is not where you come from but where you're going to, what you've got to offer' (David Cameron in 2009).

❓ What view of 'class' and mobility did each of the prime ministers take? How valid are their claims?

➲ Look at the discussion of the language of class in the work of Beverley Skeggs (1997) and consider what its implications are for the notion of classlessness.

that they experience significantly disadvantaged life chances, but we left open the question of whether they should be described as a separate social class. Now that we have completed our discussion of stratification concepts and of the contemporary situation of manual workers, we can close this issue.

The poor can be said to form an underclass only if there is a social-class boundary dividing them from other manual workers. This exists if mobility and interaction patterns separate them from other manual workers and are associated with the development of a distinct culture of poverty. The evidence that we present in Chapter 18, pp. 727–9, shows that there is, in fact, a substantial turnover among those in poverty. Many obtain employment or higher pay after a period of poverty; and many unskilled workers are likely to fall into poverty whenever their labour-market situations deteriorate. There is a considerable degree of mobility across the poverty line, and the poor are linked through kinship and friendship to other manual workers.

Poverty is a condition of serious disadvantage and deprivation, but it is an ever-present possibility for any manual worker who lacks skills or whose skills are made redundant by technical advances. People fall into poverty for a number of quite different reasons. Those in irregular forms of employment are quite distinct from those in long-term unemployment. They have far better opportunities to re-enter the world of regular employment and, therefore, to escape their poverty (L. Morris 1995).

There is, then, no separate underclass. There are those who live in truly disadvantaged situations (W. J. Wilson 1987) that involve varying forms and degrees of status exclusion and that are, in much public discussion, stigmatized as an underclass of 'undeserving' second-class citizens. But they are a part of the fragmentary class of manual workers; they are not a separate and distinct social class.

Managers, professionals, and global capital

A striking trend in the development of contemporary societies has been the massive growth in management positions in large-scale bureaucratic organizations. The total number of people today who are dependent on managerial and other forms of non-manual work amounts to around 40 per cent of the total population in most industrial societies. This growth in managerial *numbers* was seen by the supporters of the managerialist thesis as signalling a growth in managerial *power*. The rise of technically qualified managers was seen as undermining the position of the capitalist class, whose property was no longer necessary in large-scale organizations.

The capitalist class has not disappeared, although it has been transformed. In most industrial societies it amounts to less than 1 per cent of the population. It is also the case that managers are far more diverse than the managerialist writers suggested. Most managers are involved in financial administration, but they range all the way from top executive capitalists through senior financial managers and a whole hierarchy of levels to routine administrative and office workers at the lower levels of the corporate bureaucracies. The middle classes have become more diverse than ever before. In Chapter 14, pp. 533–5, we discuss the trend towards debureaucratization since the 1970s. This has eroded the power and life chances of many managers, destroying what areas of common interest they had. A capitalist class can still be distinguished from the mass of the middle classes, but the middle classes now exist as more or less completely separate entrepreneurial, professional, and administrative classes and fragments.

Management and the capitalist class

The idea of the managerial revolution was developed in the debate on ownership and control that we review in Chapter 14 and is summarized in Box 19.10. With the growth of large-scale production, joint-stock companies drew on larger pools of investment capital, and the powers of their owners were diluted. The implications of this have been hotly debated (Berle and Means 1932; Florence 1961; Zeitlin 1989; J. Scott 1997), and it is now clear that ownership has remained an important factor in the control of businesses.

There are still very wealthy and powerful propertied families whose life chances are far superior to those enjoyed by most managers. These families now work alongside and through the large banks, insurance companies, and pension funds that actually own the great bulk of company shares and that provide the capital that large organizations require. There are close economic links among the executive capitalists and finance capitalists who direct the major financial and industrial enterprises, the rentier capitalists whose savings and investments feed the financial system, and the entrepreneurial capitalists who retain a substantial personal or family stake in particular enterprises. There are also strong links among them through mobility and interaction.

The close links between ownership and control in contemporary societies have been described by Mills (1956) as resulting in a 'managerial reorganization' of the capitalist class. Business enterprises have become more closely interconnected through interlocking directorships and through the intertwining shareholdings of the big financial investors. At the same time, those who hold directorships and top executive positions in these enterprises are drawn overwhelmingly from wealthy families with inherited property. A capitalist class survives because it has combined personal wealth with participation in top-level management.

Members of this class in Britain are united through their educational background in the traditional upper-class institutions of public school and ancient university. From the beginning of the Second World War to 1970, the proportion of directors in big British banks who had been to a public school increased from two-thirds to over three-quarters. The proportion who had been to Oxford or Cambridge University increased to almost two-thirds over the same period. Those directors with multiple directorships were especially likely to have entered business through the public school and Oxbridge route. Although larger numbers are entering business with a degree from a Business School, they are still only a minority of top executive managers. Capitalists and their families interact frequently with one another, and their membership in exclusive London social clubs is, as in the past, an important basis for their informal connections and for the building of social cohesion (Useem 1984). In the United States, too, a continuing commonality of educational background is associated with attendance at Business Schools, especially such top university institutes as the Kellogg School of Management, the Booth School of Business, and the Wharton School.

While there is much continuity with upper-class cultural values and patterns of sociability, these status elements are much weaker than in the past. Traditional 'gentlemanly' norms in business were finally eroded in the 1980s, as the promotion of an enterprise culture pushed aggressive money-making values to the fore. Upper-class institutions and practices survived rather longer in the sphere of leisure, where many of the events of the traditional social calendar remain important meeting places for the wealthy. These events are now, however, dominated by the newly rich, by fashionable celebrities, and by corporate sponsorship. They have become more directly tied into business activities. The traditional lifestyle is no longer aspired to as an escape from business; it is adopted as part and parcel of the business world itself.

The extent of this change should not be overstated, but it is clear that it is no longer sensible to talk about an upper class as if it included virtually all the capitalist class. The true upper class or aristocracy is now a minority within the capitalist class, and its distinct status no longer coincides with an overall economic superiority. It is upper class in name, but not in reality. The capitalist class stands at the top of the stratification system. Its continuing fascination with titles, honours, and traditional sporting events is a minor distraction from its real concern with the making and spending of money.

The growing globalization of economic, political, and cultural relations has led some to claim that class relations have transcended the nation state and have become international. As a result, social classes have, therefore, to be understood as global social groupings. Leslie Sklair (2001) has argued that globalization has led to the formation of a transnational capitalist class. He argues that the economic interests of property-owners and company directors are now, more and more, globally linked. Big corporations raise capital in stock markets that are intertwined into a global financial system, and their shareholders may be drawn from a large number of countries. At the same time, the corporations are engaged in production and trading activities that are no longer confined to particular national economies. Purely domestic corporations, limited to an involvement in a particular national economy, are fewer in number than ever before. The directors and top managers of the transnational corporations must travel extensively and oversee activities, and they may spend long periods away from their home country. Boards are recruited from the many countries in which the corporations operate.

As a result of these tendencies, Sklair argues, there is an emerging transnational capitalist class whose members have common interests and a common outlook in business activity. Their consciousness is no longer limited by particular national concerns but is global in character. They develop cross-national political alliances with national states and business agencies, such as coordinating agencies, think tanks, and sales agencies. Their class consciousness centres on neo-liberalism and consumerism. They seek to establish unregulated global markets in which unfettered competitive forces shape corporate decision-making and determine the overall growth and development of particular economies, and they seek to expand markets through converting ever more sectors of the world's population into consumers of the products of the transnational corporations. A particularly strong form of this argument has been put by Bauman (1998), who holds that corporate owners and controllers have become so detached from any national base that they are no longer 'space-tied' and are the holders of a truly free-floating and global form of power.

> **Connections**
> You might like to read our discussion of globalization and transnational corporations in Chapter 16, pp. 623–4, and Chapter 14, pp. 543–5. Look for evidence to help you assess the claim that there is a transnational capitalist class. Does the growth of an international division of labour and the embedding of local production systems into global structures suggest that it is possible to talk of a transnational working class?

The impact of globalization on class relations should not be overstated. The internationalization of economic relations began in the nineteenth century, if not before, and was a crucial factor in the development of national capitalisms and their capitalist classes. There is, however, a far greater mobility of capital and capitalists than ever before, and there is a corresponding increase in the level of transnational economic integration. The capitalist classes found in the various national economies are more diverse in their origins and more cosmopolitan in their outlook than the capitalist classes of the first half of the twentieth century.

Professionals, entrepreneurs, and bureaucrats

The middle classes always had a low degree of class cohesion, held together by status rather than common economic interests. They comprised an open-status hierarchy stretching from the lowest clerk or shop assistant through the ranks of managers and professionals to entrepreneurs and civil servants. The development of large-scale organization brought about a fundamental transformation of clerical and managerial work.

Small-scale entrepreneurs and the professions were also transformed by the development of large-scale organization. Small businesses came under great pressure as the economy became more concentrated. Many had to adapt by becoming subcontractors and suppliers to larger businesses. Small-scale capital remains particularly important in farming, building, retailing, and services, and in such manufacturing industries as engineering and textiles (Scase and Goffee 1982). Studies of social mobility show these to have a relatively high level of self-recruitment and to remain distinct from other sections of the middle classes. Nevertheless, a significant number of small entrepreneurs do come from a managerial background, and a much smaller number have built their businesses into large-scale operations.

Professional workers have relied on their cultural capital for the educational credentials that give them entry to jobs that require specialist or technical knowledge. The old professions—medicine, the law, the church, and the universities—have experienced erosion of their working conditions and life chances as their work has become more firmly embedded in public- and private-sector bureaucracies (T. Johnson 1972).

The accountants and engineers produced in large numbers from the late nineteenth century were, from the start, bureaucratic employees rather than autonomous self-employed professionals, and a whole range of newer professions have grown and been incorporated directly into the expanding bureaucracies through the twentieth century. This bureaucratization of employment has been especially rapid since the 1950s. Teachers, social workers, medical technicians, nurses, estate agents, financial advisers, and similar occupations have increased massively in numbers. The bureaucratization of the professions destroyed traditional professional autonomy and created divisions of the kind that exist between the various levels of management.

Managers, senior and junior, owe their life chances far more to their command situations—to their authority—than to their possession of educational credentials. They have generally been promoted through the internal labour markets of the organizations for which they work, building up skills and competencies that cannot easily be transferred from one organization or industry to another and cannot be passed directly on to sons or daughters. Savage and his colleagues (1992) follow E. O. Wright (1985) in describing these skills as 'organizational assets'.

Until recently, many managers enjoyed, in effect, lifetime employment. The fact that their organizational assets (unlike property or educational qualifications) were not transferable made little difference to them as they climbed the organizational hierarchy. Since the 1970s, however, managerial work has been transformed by the restructuring of large-scale organizations. Through debureaucratization and 'downsizing', enterprises have become less bureaucratic and hierarchies have become flatter.

Managers have lost their jobs in large numbers, and this has been especially marked where computers and information-technology equipment can be introduced. Those who have remained in employment have had to become more flexible in their working patterns. Internal labour markets have declined in importance, and much

> **Connections**
> The organizational changes that have eroded the command situations of managers are discussed in Chapter 17. Look at pp. 671–6 and read our discussion of post-Fordism and the flexible firm.

managerial work has been contracted out to self-employed consultants and service firms.

The middle classes of the first part of the twentieth century were rooted in small-scale property, the exercise of authority, and the possession of the cultural capital required for entry to the professions. Each of these bases remains important. Small-scale property did not disappear with the concentration of economic activity, and it has continued to provide opportunities for many to improve their life chances. Clerical workers, as we have shown, faced declining life chances as their market and work situations deteriorated with the expansion and mechanization of office work, but managerial and administrative workers continued to enjoy superior life chances and a distinct status. Similarly, the expansion of the new professions has opened up more opportunities for those with educational credentials to improve their market chances.

The cohesion that the middle classes had in the past depended on the level of mobility and interaction among those in class situations based in property, bureaucracy, and cultural assets. Mobility occurred when people could convert one kind of asset into another. Those with capital, for example, might buy private schooling for their children and so improve their chances of obtaining the educational credentials that allowed them to enter one of the professions or to join a corporate organization and achieve a senior position. Similarly, those who had a successful career in a corporate bureaucracy might be able to save enough money to set up their children in a small business. This was what Bourdieu (1977) called the 'reconversion' of class assets.

These changes led to doubts about where and how sharply to draw the boundaries that divide the middle classes from other social classes. In Britain, Savage et al. (1992) argue, the middle classes have a relatively low level of cohesion because rates of reconversion are very limited. The professional middle class was relatively closed to those from a propertied or bureaucratic background, and very few small businesses were started by those who had been successful in management or the professions. Of particular significance, they argue, is the fact that managerial success has never depended on the achievement of a high level of technical expertise in school and university examinations.

This low level of class unity has now weakened further. Using results from the Oxford Mobility Study, Savage et al. show that the managerial and professional workers sometimes grouped together as a service class are actually very distinct from one another. They have significantly different opportunities in respect of their life chances and their lifestyles. The things that differentiate professionals from managers are more important than any similarities that there may be. Members of the professions are much better able to pass on their class situations to their children because entry to the professions depends on cultural or educational capital.

Particularly important differences in class interests are highlighted by the association between the professions and the state. Professional workers have an interest in a thriving public sector and are less likely to support cutbacks in the public sector or attacks on professional privileges (such as enhanced pensions). Managerial workers and small property-owners, on the other hand, are more likely to be committed to an expansion of the private sector and a reduction in the resources assigned to the public sector.

Many in the intermediate class situations see themselves as part of a large central class, as did the affluent workers of the 1960s, but this is not an especially salient aspect of their social identity. They are more likely to see themselves in narrower occupational terms, or in terms of their gender, ethnicity, or public-service role. Neither the traditional status hierarchy nor the imagery of class is a natural or spontaneous source of social identity.

There is, then, a fragmentation of the middle classes, dividing them along the lines of propertied assets, organizational assets, and educational assets. This fragmentation has been matched by a much reduced involvement in the public life of towns and cities. The middle classes today no longer seek out a high degree of local civic participation. In the restudy of Banbury in the late 1960s, Stacey et al. (1975) found that the much enlarged town had far less of a civic character than it had shown in the 1950s.

In his most recent work, Savage and his colleagues (2005) have explored the impact of globalization on the middle classes and the extent to which local, communal identities and solidarities can still be built. Members of the middle classes are now highly mobile, both geographically and socially, moving around the branches of globalized business enterprises in the pursuit of their careers. They are involved in differentiated and distinct networks of connection and interest in the diverse fields of work, leisure, and friendship. They necessarily develop a 'cosmopolitan' orientation rather than retaining entrenched 'local' commitments to the particular areas in which they may have been born and bred. Nevertheless, they do not construct their own identities in global terms.

Savage et al. (2005) identify a process of 'elective belonging' by which people choose to identify with a particular locality that they feel is, or can be made, congruent with their aspirations and desired lifestyles. Current place of residence remains the most important anchor in these cosmopolitan lives, and it is the means through which people can secure access to education, work, and leisure. In their narratives of everyday life they do not typically connect their immediate concerns with global issues. They see themselves as belonging to a particular locality—a village, town, or suburb—within a larger metropolitan or regional district, but they rarely see themselves in either national or global terms.

Stop and reflect

In this section we have looked at the fragmentation of the classic class society that existed until the middle of the twentieth century. We started out from a consideration of the ideas of industrialism and industrial society. We looked at the implications of the occupational transition for patterns of social stratification.

- Embourgeoisement and managerialism have fragmented all three social classes.

- Changes in the organization of manual work and the transformation of long-standing communities have undermined the solidarity and cohesion of the working class. Manual workers tend to be more privatized and less conscious of themselves as members of a working class.

- How useful are ideas of class consciousness and collective organization in understanding the attitudes and behaviour of manual workers today?

- Debureaucratization and downsizing have helped to restructure the middle classes, producing a greater separation of their entrepreneurial, professional, and bureaucratic elements.

- The capitalist class has undergone a 'managerial reorganization' and is no longer subordinate to the status values of the aristocracy.

- Why have some people claimed that 'we are all middle class now'?

Key concepts

- capitalist class (see also ruling class) 747
- caste 752
- class situation 746
- class society 751
- command situation 749
- command society 752
- embourgeoisement 773
- instrumental orientation 775
- managerialism 773

- market situation 761
- occupational transition 772
- party 751
- polarization 760
- primary sector 772
- privatism 775
- proletarianization 760
- secondary sector 772
- service class 765
- social class 751

- social estate 751
- social stratification 744
- status situation 749
- status society 752
- style of life 748
- tertiary sector 772
- working class (see also proletariat) 747
- work situation 761

Workshop 19

Study 19 Images of class

On pp. 774–6 we looked at the *Affluent Worker* project, undertaken by Goldthorpe, Lockwood, Bechhofer, and Platt (1969) in order to investigate changes in class outlook and orientations among well-paid and highly mobile workers in the new and expanding town of Luton. The study found that workers adopted distinct models or images of class, through which they defined their positions in their society and those of the people they encountered in their social relationships. The project established the idea that class imagery was the basis of social identity in contemporary societies.

Most recent studies have suggested that changes have occurred since the 1960s, when the *Affluent Worker* project was carried out. It has been argued that a complex of social changes may have undermined the tendency of people to define themselves in class terms. People are now likely to see their identities in terms of gender, ethnicity, sexuality, or consumption—or by some combination of these.

A recent project, however, has returned to the original findings of the *Affluent Worker* project and has argued that the tendency to adopt class imagery may not have been as clear as it appeared to the original researchers. Mike Savage (2005*b*) has undertaken a secondary analysis of the original questionnaire schedules used in the *Affluent Worker* project and has come to very different conclusions from those of Goldthorpe and his colleagues.

The original schedules were brought together and archived in the UK Data Archive (Qualidata) at the University of Essex, where Savage was able to consult them. Savage begins by showing that the recorded responses were actually much more sophisticated than they appear in the published reports. He also notes, however, that people tended to be ambivalent or uncertain about the idea of class. Many were nervous or apprehensive, unwilling to elaborate on their view of class—one respondent broke off the interview when the issue of class was broached. It seemed clear to Savage that many respondents felt that the researchers expected them to talk about class in 'sociological' terms: it was not an idea that came to them naturally, but was felt to be an academic idea that they were expected to try to articulate. Interviewees were uncertain and frustrated because they were not sure that they were going to give the researchers the 'right' answer.

Where people employed the language of class, it was in an attempt to differentiate themselves from an 'upper class' of wealthy 'nobs and snobs' and to depict their distinctiveness and individuality as just an 'ordinary' person. Thus, Savage concludes that popular ideas of class do not derive from the social relations of work and community but from the language through which people try to theorize their own individuality and ordinariness.

❓ How would you go about exploring class imagery today? What kinds of question do you think could be asked without leading people to answer in particular ways? You might find it useful to consider these questions in the light of our discussion of questionnaire methodology and interviewing on pp. 74–80.

Media watch 19 An Indian middle class

India has become one of the most dynamic economies in the world, rapidly industrializing and contributing to global economic growth. No longer a society underdeveloped by Western multinational companies, it has a thriving indigenous industry, and Indian businesses now take major controlling investments in Western companies. It now has huge and successful business schools that consistently produce graduates able to enter the global managerial market. However, this economic growth goes alongside continuing poverty: a quarter of the world's poorest people live in India.

There is a huge sector of administrative, professional, and clerical occupations in the mass media, retailing, and airline transport. Many people will be familiar with the Indian call centres that operate on behalf of many British and American companies. Above all, however, the expansion of such jobs has been in the computer-software and financial-services industries.

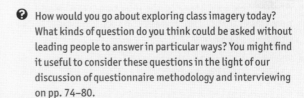

These are the people whose growing consumerism has fuelled Indian economic growth.

In an article in *Prospect* magazine, Chakravarthi Ram-Prasad identifies this as a huge middle class that embodies both the successes and the failures of Indian industrialization:

> ... commitment to their own idea of India and their central role in its economic rise makes the middle classes sure of themselves. But at the same time, their sense of citizenship is weak: they do not, on the whole, extend a sense of solidarity to the poor; they often do not acknowledge the role of the state in their own rise or its capacity to solve any of the country's problems; and they are, in general, politically apathetic.

The article suggests a lack of solidarity between the middle class and the mass of the population and relates this to the great social diversity of the country and, in particular, to its caste system. It is impossible, Ram-Prasad argues, to establish any kind of sense of common humanity across caste boundaries, and,

therefore, there can be no social or political unity of the Indian population around common ideals of citizenship. This problem is made worse, it is claimed, by the existence of a substantial Muslim minority population that has little solidarity with the Hindu majority. Thus, 'Prosperous India has not yet provided sufficient social infrastructure to make the country less brutal for those at the bottom.'

Source: Chakravarthi (2007).

❷ How useful is it to apply the term 'middle class' to a society such as India? Can the Indian middle class be regarded as having the same characteristics as one in the United States or Britain?

➲ Look at our discussion of caste on p. 752. Are these categories likely to make sense in a complex industrial society? You should read Ram-Prasad's article in full to see how he applies these terms.

❷ Would you expect to find solidarity over common citizenship between a prosperous middle class and the rural poor?

Discussion points

You will find it useful to consider the following issues.

Conceptualizing stratification

At the beginning of 'The making of a class society' we looked at the theory of capitalism and class society. In 'A fragmentary class society' we looked at the theory of industrialism and the fragmentation of class:

● What do you understand by the following terms: stratification, class situation; social class; class consciousness; status situation; style of life?

● What does it mean to talk about class and status as 'causal components' in life chances?

● Make sure that you understand the principal ideas on stratification of the following writers: Weber, Marx, Parsons, Warner.

● Considering our discussion of capitalism and class society, how would you assess Marx's ideas of polarization and proletarianization?

● Turning to our discussion of industrialism and class society, what do you understand by the idea of embourgeoisement?

Subordinate social strata

We looked at a number of issues in relation to the formation and fragmentation of a working class:

● In what sense is it useful to see the working class as consisting of manual workers?

● What do you understand by the following: market situation; work situation; instrumental orientation; privatism; money model of society?

● What are the principal social institutions and organizations that were involved in the formation of a cohesive working class? (You will find it useful to refer to other chapters when considering this question.)

● We returned to the debate over the idea of an underclass (considered in Chapter 18). Can the so-called underclass be regarded as a true social class?

Dominant and intermediate social strata

The middle classes and the upper classes are usefully considered together, as their histories are so intertwined. We looked at the formation and fragmentation of the middle classes and at their relationship to capitalist entrepreneurs and the landowning aristocracy:

● What do you understand by the following terms: intermediate class situations; service class; white-collar worker; aristocracy; peerage.

● What kinds of occupation would you include among those defining intermediate class situations?

● How would you distinguish between the following: entrepreneurial capitalist; rentier capitalist; executive capitalist; finance capitalist.

We looked at a number of features in the organization of work that have affected class situations. Remind yourself about what we say in Chapters 14 and 17, and then consider the following:

● What is meant by the idea of the managerial revolution?

● How have debureaucratization and downsizing altered the class situation of managers?

Explore further

Good general reading on the issues discussed in this chapter can be found in:

Scott, J. (1996), *Stratification and Power: Structures of Class, Status and Command* (Cambridge: Polity Press). *A broad overview of the conceptual and theoretical issues considered in the first section of this chapter.*

Dahrendorf, R. (1957), *Class and Class Conflict in an Industrial Society* (London: Routledge & Kegan Paul, 1959). *A classic attempt to present an alternative to a Marxist view of class.*

Savage, M. (2000), *Class Analysis and Social Transformation* (Buckingham: Open University Press). *An exploration of contemporary charges in class relations and class identities.*

Important empirical studies can be found in:

Devine, F. (1992), *Affluent Workers Revisited: Privatism and the Working Class* (Edinburgh: Edinburgh University Press). *An important reassessment of the Goldthorpe et al. study.*

Goldthorpe, J. H., Lockwood, D., Bechhofer, F., and Platt, J. (1969), *The Affluent Worker in the Class Structure* (Cambridge: Cambridge University Press). *The principal study of recent developments in working-class attitudes and organization. Also well worth reading for its account of Marxist theory and its problems.*

Stacey, M. (1960), *Tradition and Change: A Study of Banbury* (Oxford: Oxford University Press). *Together with its companion volume (Stacey et al. 1975), this gives a good overview of social stratification in a 'typical' town in southern England.*

Stacey, M., Batstone, E., Bell, C., and Murcott, A. (1975), *Power, Persistence and Change* (London: Routledge & Kegan Paul). *The follow-up to the original Banbury study (Stacey 1960).*

Some of the theoretical and empirical issues are taken further in:

Wright, E. O. (2005) (ed.), *Approaches to Class Analysis* (Cambridge: Cambridge University Press). *An edited collection that compares a number of different theories of class in terms of their empirical value. Each chapter is written by a specialist in the particular theoretical approach.*

Goldthorpe, J. H. (1980), *Social Mobility and Class Structure* (Oxford: Clarendon Press). *The standard account of social mobility in Britain, though limited by its focus on men.*

Wilson, W. J. (1987), *The Truly Disadvantaged* (Chicago: University of Chicago Press). *An important study of the 'underclass' in the United States. Suggests that, treated carefully, the concept may have some value in understanding ghetto poverty.*

Two films explore issues of class and stratification:

The Loneliness of the Long Distance Runner (1962). *Explores the upward social mobility of clerical workers in the 1950s and 1960s.*

The Ruling Class (1972). *A parody of the traditional upper classes in decline.*

Online resources

Visit the Online Resource Centre that accompanies this book to access more learning resources and other interesting material on stratification, class, and status at:
www.oxfordtextbooks.co.uk/orc/fulcher4e/

A useful source of information and links on social class and stratification is at the Sociosite of the University of Amsterdam:
www.sociosite.net/topics/inequality.php

For information on those at the top of the status system and on the Royal family, consult:
www.debretts.co.uk and www.royal.gov.uk

BUBL is an academic information centre run from the University of Strathclyde. Sources on slavery can be found at the BUBL site on:
http://bubl.ac.uk/link/s/slavery.htm

Supporting material on slavery can be seen at the Mersey Maritime Museum:
www.liverpoolmuseums.org.uk/maritime/slavery

There is useful background on African Americans at an exhibition set up by the Library of Congress:
http://lcweb2.loc.gov/ammem/aaohtml

The Web contains much official and Hindu information on caste. You might find it useful to look at the Dalit Freedom Network website that highlights the position and human-rights situation of 'untouchables' in contemporary India:
www.dalitnetwork.org

Power, Division, and Protest

Contents

Who is powerful?

An American magazine recently published its annual list of the world's hundred most powerful women. The top ten in this list are:

1. Angela Merkel
2. Sheila Bair
3. Indra Nooyi
4. Cynthia Carroll
5. Ho Ching
6. Irene Rosenfeld
7. Ellen Kukkman
8. Angela Braly
9. Anne Lauvergeon
10. Lynne Elsenhans

Sources: *Forbes*(2009*b*).

Although the list is headed by German Chancellor Angela Merkel, it also includes many unfamiliar names drawn from politics, business, and entertainment. A majority of the women in the top ten powerful women are chief executives of major American multinational companies: Indra Nooyi (drink manufacturer Pepsico), Irene Rosenfeld (food company Kraft), Ellen Kullman (chemicals giant Dupont), Angela Braly (health insurance company WellPoint), and Lynne Elsenhans (petrochemical concern Sunoco). Non-American chief executives in the top ten are Cynthia Carroll of the UK-based Anglo-American mining company that is a major force in the gold and diamond mining business, Anne Lauvergeon of French nuclear power company Areva, and Ho Ching of Singapore financial company Temasek. Sheila Bair, rated as number two, is Chair of the Federal Deposit Insurance Corporation, a US government regulatory agency in the financial services sector. Politicians other than Merkel come somewhat lower in the list: Cristuina Fernandez, the President of Argentina, is at number 11, Sonia Ghandi of the Indian national Congress Party is at number 13, and Christine Lagarde, the French Finance Minister, is at number 15. Queen Elizabeth II is ranked at number 42. Michelle Obama, wife of the US President, ranks number 40.

What does it mean to describe such people as those listed above as powerful? How does their power relate to and compare with that of men? How do the power and influence of business compare with those of the elected heads of government departments and their officials? Are their invisibility and anonymity a sign of their power, or a sign of a lack of power? Most importantly, perhaps, how was the list compiled and what evidence and indicators of power were used?

This kind of exercise might simply be a mass-media parlour game, but it does raise serious questions about power. Even if we reject the methodology as the basis for serious social research, we have to know what we can put in its place as an effective approach to power. What are the social structures in which power is located, and can we identify individuals as the powerful figures? Can we identify power at the top without also looking at the power mobilized by groups who oppose this power and protest against its effects?

Concepts and theories

The relationship between class and political power has been the central concern of Marxist class theory, which has stressed the opposition between working-class and ruling-class organizations and movements. Discussion of the working class has centred on the nature of working-class consciousness and political action, while discussion of the ruling class has explored the relation of dominant classes to state power. Marxists have seen the working class as developing forms of political action that challenge the established social order and, ultimately, bring about its revolutionary overthrow. The ruling class, on the other hand, has been seen as the politically organized capitalist class with control of the state machinery.

Critics of Marxism have attacked both aspects of the Marxist theory. They have shown that the working class has not become the revolutionary force that Marx expected, and have rejected the idea that the state is dominated by a capitalist class. Writers in the so-called elitist tradition of social theory replaced the Marxist concept of the ruling class with the idea of a political elite or ruling elite. They argue that those who exercise political power are drawn from a variety of classes and that political action cannot simply be reduced to class relations and class conflict.

> ⊃ *Connections*
>
> If you are unsure about class and Marxist class theory, you should look at our discussion of these topics in Chapter 19. Modern states and state policies are covered more fully in Chapter 15.

Class and power

Marx saw social classes as categories of people who share certain economic interests. He believed that, when the members of a class became conscious of their shared interests, they would form or support a political party to promote their interests. Their class consciousness and their solidarity would underpin the collective action that forges them into a **class for itself**. The members of a social class organized for political action are able to act for themselves, consciously and in their collective interests. They no longer form a mere class 'in itself', an aggregate of similar individuals. They have a unity and cohesion built around a shared programme of action.

As we show in Chapter 19, pp. 759–61, Marx saw capitalist societies becoming ever more polarized: the economic division between working class and capitalist class would become more marked and would be reflected in a polarization of class consciousness and political action. The working class was being organized into a network of trade unions, pressure groups, and political parties that together comprised a powerful and progressive social movement. This is the **labour movement**, and Marx saw socialist and communist parties playing a leading role in it (see Box 20.1). The capitalist class, on the other hand, was directly involved in the exercise of state power. Its members held all the leading positions in parliament, government, and other state bodies. They formed a ruling class, and their political power was growing with the growth of the state. The conflict between working class and capitalist class, then, had become politically organized as a struggle between the labour movement and the ruling class.

Most sociologists now accept that Marx's view of class polarization cannot be upheld in this strong form. The development of the major capitalist societies did not confirm his expectations. Nevertheless, there is still great value in his theoretical concepts, which have proved a remarkably powerful basis for understanding some of the central trends in modern societies.

Working-class politics

The development of modern industry and the factory system of production had brought workers together in ever larger numbers. Marx saw this as beginning the transformation of the working class from a mere disorganized mass into a class for itself. At first, workers developed a consciousness

---

THEORY AND METHODS   20.1

Social movements

A social movement is a broad alliance or network of individuals, groups, and organizations united by their shared goals, aspirations, and interests. A social movement may comprise trade unions, political parties, cooperatives, neighbourhood action groups, pressure groups, and any other collective organizations in so far as they share a common political purpose. Social movements may include formal organizations, but they are not themselves organizations with a formal structure of leadership and administration.

Most typically, social movements have been concerned with protest or change, rather than with defence of the existing order (A. Scott 1990). The labour movement is a social movement with its base in the working class and its organizations, and with a commitment to socialist ideals (Hobhouse 1893; Sombart 1908).

in common with those working in the same trade or industry, or those who lived in the same locality. They formed trade unions to pursue their demands for higher wages and improved conditions of work, and they formed cooperatives to eliminate their dependence on profit-making retailers. As their consciousness and confidence advanced, so they forged a broader class consciousness with other workers, regardless of trade or skill. Their consciousness took a more political character, and they became involved in political parties and parliamentary committees.

Class-conscious workers saw themselves as part of a labour movement, and Marx expected them to give electoral support to political parties that voiced their demands. Wherever workers had the right to vote, he expected them to vote for parties that identified themselves with the aims of the labour movement. These were Socialist, Social Democratic, Labour, and Communist parties. Through their contacts with the intellectuals who led these parties, manual workers would sharpen and crystallize their consciousness of shared class interests.

For Marx, then, manual workers were moving towards ever more radical forms of political action. He believed that this popular radicalism would eventually give rise to a revolution. Workers would support organizations aiming at the overthrow of capitalist society and would seek its replacement with a new and more humane social order. Some Marxists interpret **revolution** to mean the violent overthrow of the social order through mass collective action. Others see it as a long-term and peaceful process of radical structural change.

Working-class consciousness and radicalism have been sustained by the structures of working-class communities. The most important obstacle to their full development that Marx identified was the influence of the capitalist press, which he saw as indoctrinating the workers and giving them a **false consciousness** of their own situation. The working class might—in the short term—fail to recognize their real interests and adopt bourgeois ideas and attitudes. To understand working-class consciousness and action, then, it is necessary to look at the social control exercised by the ruling class (Mann 1973).

Ruling-class politics

Marx saw all societies as dominated by ruling classes. In capitalist societies, he argued, the capitalist class—the owners of capital—has control of the machinery of the

> **Connections**
>
> Look at our discussion of the effects of the mass media in 'Media influence and the audience', Chapter 10, pp. 357–60. Look, in particular, at our discussion of the media-effects model. What criticisms would you make of this as an explanation of political socialization?

state and so forms the ruling class. Government in the modern state is simply the executive committee of the bourgeoisie because the whole state apparatus—parliament and government, the police, the judiciary, the civil service and the military—operates as an instrument of class rule.

The capitalist class monopolizes access to positions of political authority in the state because of the ways in which people are recruited to these positions. Members of the top positions within the state are drawn from property-owning families involved in business. Sons and, more rarely, daughters of capitalists are able to secure careers that take them into the senior levels of the state, and there is a constant circulation of personnel between positions of political authority and the business world.

Marx recognized that some members of the middle classes held senior positions in the state. Lawyers and managers, for example, often played an important part. However, he did not see this as undermining his position. Those from the higher levels of the middle classes were considered to be the mere servants of the bourgeoisie, who held the real power. They were a subordinate service class. Members of the working class and the lower middle class, on the other hand, were excluded even from nominal involvement in exercising political power.

The Marxist view is that states in capitalist societies act in the interests of business, property, and capital. This occurs, said Marx, because capitalist interests are directly represented within the state by bourgeois families and because state departments and agencies are pressured and lobbied by organized business interests. Employers' associations, trade bodies, and chambers of commerce all have the power to put pressure on state departments and agencies and can persuade them to take business interests seriously. Manipulation and pressure are not the only ways through which a state can be made to act in the interests of capital. All states depend on taxation to finance their activities. If they are to retain a tax income, they must not damage the profitability of the business sector that provides much of its revenue. For all these reasons, Marxists see democracy as an illusion under capitalism. The outcome of competitive elections is irrelevant to the real exercise of power. The state machinery always reflects the power of the capitalist class.

Capitalist property-owners, like the working class, can develop a class consciousness and form themselves into a class for itself. Marx saw the state as central to the political organization of the capitalist class into a conscious ruling class. When capitalists are aware of their own economic interests, they are able to translate them into state policies. Marx holds, however, that their power extends beyond the state itself and into such areas as the churches, the mass media, and the educational system. These social institutions become organized around the power of the ruling

Dominant ideology

An ideology is a system of beliefs, values, and norms that expresses and legitimates the interests of a particular social group. A dominant ideology is one that expresses and legitimates the interests of a dominant social class and has become the basis of cultural socialization. Alternative ideas and forms of consciousness are difficult to establish in the face of the power behind the dominant ideology. Subordinate classes tend to accept, rather than to oppose, the existing social order. For many Marxists, this is a sign of their false consciousness: they accept the ideas of the bourgeoisie, rather than ideas that reflect their own interests.

Critics of this idea say that people are not simply socialized into a false consciousness. They have the power to develop their own ideas and values. Look at our discussion of socialization in Chapter 4 and at the critique of the Marxist view of the dominant ideology in Abercrombie *et al.* (1979). How useful do you think it is to talk about false consciousness? You might like to consider this issue in relation to our discussion of the embourgeoisement of the working class in Chapter 19, pp. 773–4.

class, and its consciousness becomes the dominant cultural force in society. The class consciousness of the dominant class becomes what later writers have called a **dominant ideology**.

The values and norms of a dominant ideology are transmitted through the mass media, the churches, and the educational system. They are the basis of socialization in families and communities. All fully socialized members of a society—capitalists and workers alike—become committed both to the underlying values of the society and to the institutions they legitimate. The power of a capitalist class, then, is especially strong where its economic dominance is matched by a political and a cultural dominance. Where a class is dominant in all spheres of society, the Italian Marxist Gramsci described it as exercising a **hegemony**. A ruling class is a hegemonic class.

Hegemony and class politics

Gramsci's purpose in writing about hegemony was to analyse its consequences for working-class consciousness and organization. If the power of a capitalist class is so all-pervasive, it is unlikely that members of the working class will organize themselves into trade unions and parties that challenge that power. Manual workers, through their socialization, are influenced by the dominant ideology, and their attitudes and values will reflect its concerns. This does not mean, however, that the working class is completely absorbed into the system. It is typically

characterized by what Gramsci called a **dual consciousness**. On the one hand, workers are subject to the hegemonic power of a dominant ideology that ties them ever more closely to the dominant bourgeois institutions. On the other hand, their practical, day-to-day experiences of exploitation and oppression lead them to develop a more autonomous and oppositional class consciousness that is rooted in the immediate day-to-day conditions of working-class life.

The politics of the working class is shaped by the tension between these two forms of consciousness. One aspect of their consciousness expresses the dominant ideology, while the other expresses their interests as an exploited class. The development of the working class into a class for itself involves a strengthening of its autonomous consciousness and, in particular, the forming of trade unions and political parties into a social movement that can exercise an effective **counter-hegemony**. That is to say, they establish forms of economic, political, and cultural consciousness and organization that allow them to challenge the hegemony of the ruling class. Through their participation in the political struggle of the labour movement, they strengthen the radical values and ideas that allow them to withstand the influence of the dominant ideology and to develop a more genuine political strategy of their own.

Empirical research on the connection between class and politics has been heavily influenced by Marxist theory. While researchers have rejected many of its specific claims, and they have certainly denied that there is any inevitability about class conflict, the broad themes and concerns of Marxist theory have set the scene for their research programmes. In particular, the mainstream of empirical research has been built around the idea that political processes can be explained in terms of the dynamics of class division and class action. It has been shown, for example, that there has been a strong and enduring link between the working class and left-wing political viewpoints. This has been seen as the basis of manual-worker support for trade unions (see Chapter 17, pp. 654–6) and for political parties. It has been assumed that there will be a close association between class situation and voting behaviour in any society in which all adults have the right to vote in local and national elections. Manual workers have been expected

➔ **Connections**

Look at our discussion of Gramsci in Chapter 10, pp. 352–3, where we show how his work, like that of Lukács and the Frankfurt school, has had a major influence on studies of the mass media. Gramsci's *Prison Notebooks*, which contain his leading ideas, were written in the 1930s, but were not widely available until the 1970s. They had a major impact on the reorientation of Marxist social theory at that time.

to show a strong tendency to vote for socialist and communist parties.

Elites and power

Not all research into politics and political power has adopted this class-based point of reference, which many critics of Marxism have seen as involving an economic determinism. Politics and culture, these critics claim, have been seen by Marxists as mere reflections of economic class relations and are allowed no autonomy from the economic base of the society. The most notable critics of Marxism on this point were the Italian political sociologists Mosca and Pareto (see Box 20.3). They developed this criticism in their rejection of Marx's concept of the ruling class. It is wrong, they argued, to see the dominant political forces in all societies as being economically determined social classes. Positions of political authority can be held by those from a variety of backgrounds, and not only by the economically powerful.

However, Pareto and Mosca shared with Marx the idea that those in authority in society would always be a minority and that the majority would have little part to play in the running of the state. The holders of political authority were described by these writers as forming an elite. An **elite** is an autonomous and independent social force that can recruit, in part, from a dominant economic class, but can also recruit from specific ethnic, religious, and other social groups. Once established, and on whatever basis, an elite can exclude the mass of the population from any effective say in political decision-making. Elections give little scope

> **Connections**
>
> This might be the point at which you should turn to Chapter 19, pp. 746–51, and look briefly at our account of Weber. There we argue that authority is the basis of a third dimension of stratification, alongside class and status, and that elites could be understood in this way. You should be able to connect that discussion with the following discussion of Mosca and Pareto.

for real popular participation by the masses, and many respond to this by choosing not to vote or by accepting that their role is simply to choose between rival sections within the elite. The elite in a society is a ruling minority—an entrenched, self-perpetuating controlling group—but it is not necessarily a ruling class (Bottomore 1993).

The ruling elite

All societies, Mosca and Pareto argued, are ruled by minorities. The idea of rule by the majority is a sham. Elections do not really determine state policies, as political leaders can manipulate the electorate and can dupe them into supporting parties that will not actually pursue their interests when in power. Parties are organized agents of sectional, minority interests, and state policies reflect these minority interests rather than majority concerns. The ruling minority—the **ruling elite**—consists of all those who occupy positions of command in the major social institutions through which power is organized in a society. The political structure of the state is one especially important cluster of social institutions, and a **political elite** lies at the heart of any ruling elite. Those who hold top positions of authority in the economy and a church, however, can also form a part of the ruling elite if these social institutions are important elements in the overall power structure.

Mosca looked at the relationship between the political elite and what he called the social forces. Social forces have specific abilities, aptitudes, or skills that give them a power base in their society. For example, the military, the clergy, economic leaders, and the intelligentsia are each organized around hierarchies of authority that lie outside the sphere of the state. A political elite, then, is one element among others in the larger ruling elite. A ruling elite is a particular coalition of social forces. One particular strand of empirical research on elites has been the investigation of membership and recruitment in those top positions of authority seen as the basis of power in a society.

The boundaries of a ruling elite can be explored in the patterns of circulation through which social institutions are connected. Circulation—the movement of individuals from one social position to another—ties social positions together into a single structure of power. This circulation can occur within the lifetime of individuals or between one generation

---

THEORY AND METHODS   **20.3**

Gaetano Mosca and Vilfredo Pareto

Gaetano Mosca and Vilfredo Pareto were contemporaries of Max Weber and Émile Durkheim. Mosca (1858–1941) published his major work on political sociology, translated as *The Ruling Class*, in 1896. Pareto (1848–1923) worked as an engineer and an economist before publishing his *Treatise in General Sociology* in 1916. It was Pareto who introduced the word 'elite' and who, therefore, achieved widespread recognition as an innovator. This was much to the annoyance of Mosca, who claimed to have introduced the idea of the elite, if not the word. Both writers remained intellectually active until the 1920s, though they were little known outside their native Italy. Their major works began to be translated into English only in the 1930s, after which elite studies and elitist theory became very important. They were especially influential among the theorists of the managerial revolution that we discussed in Chapter 14, pp. 530–1.

and another. Elite circulation is a particular form of the social mobility that we look at in Chapters 18 and 19.

One of the leading investigators of this topic was C. Wright Mills (1956), whose study of the United States during the 1950s showed that power was centred on the political, economic, and military hierarchies and that the occupants of the top command situations in these three hierarchies overlapped to such an extent that they formed a single **power elite**. Although the relative power of the three sections of the power elite might vary over time, they were united by their common social background and interests. The power elite, according to Mills, was not solely economic in character: it was not a ruling class in the Marxist sense, despite the fact that large numbers of capitalist property-owners were members of it. The political and military hierarchies were independent of the economic hierarchy, but all three were fused together in a single power elite.

Pareto saw circulation as the means through which the skills and abilities required by a state could be brought into its political elite from outside. In many circumstances, however, circulation is limited by the *exclusion* of people from certain classes or social groups. A ruling elite might, for example, limit key positions to the male descendants of its own members and so become closed in character. Women and men from non-elite backgrounds would be unable to enter the elite, even if they had qualities that might be useful to it. Closed elites, Pareto argued, are less able to adapt to changing circumstances. They are fixed and rigid and may face opposition from those who have superior skills and resources. They are liable to be overthrown by counter-elites recruited from the excluded social forces. History, then, involves a constant struggle of elites against counter-elites. There can, however, be no end to elite rule: all that can happen is the cyclical replacement of one elite by another.

Mass action and mass society

If the idea of the ruling elite can be seen as a deliberate attempt to replace the Marxist idea of the ruling class, the idea of the mass can be seen as an attempt to replace the Marxist concept of the proletariat or working class. Where the Marxist sees modern societies as organized around a conflict between ruling classes and working classes, elite theory sees them as organized around the relationship between elites and masses.

Pareto and Mosca were critics of equality and democracy. They used such terms as 'the mob', 'the herd', and 'the mass' to describe the newly empowered workers, whose collective actions they saw as dangerous sources of disorder. The masses were the so-called dangerous classes that were liable to be swayed by irrational ideas and that were a threat to the individualism and freedom that had slowly been achieved in modern society. More generally, equality itself was seen as a levelling process in which culture and lifestyles became homogeneous and bland, making it difficult to sustain the cultural achievements of the past. High culture was threatened by the growth of a popular mass culture and the creation of an anonymous, depersonalized, and alienated society.

> ⮎ *Connections*
> You might find it useful to look at our discussion of mass culture and popular culture in Chapter 10, where there is a fuller consideration of these arguments on pp. 355–6.

The masses are seen by elite theorists as incapable of critical, reflective thought. They are passive conformists, following the line of the majority and subject to manipulation by a cynical elite. Michels (1912), a close friend and associate of Mosca, paid particular attention to the ways in which the leaders of socialist parties and trade unions could become separated from their members. Despite their radical traditions, the leaders tended to form an elite that could manipulate their passive mass membership. Because they are so easily manipulated, however, the masses are seen as susceptible to charismatic leaders who can rouse them into extremist and violent politics (Kornhauser 1959; Giner 1976).

 ## *Stop and reflect*

In this section we have looked at the main theoretical positions on power and politics. These are the class and the elite models. Marxist class theory looks at the organized political struggles of the working class and the capitalist class.

- Capitalist classes dominate all areas of the state and become ruling classes. A ruling class exercises a political and cultural hegemony.

- When a working class achieves consciousness as a class for itself, it is organized into a labour movement.

- Workers tend to develop a dual consciousness. This is a consequence of their socialization and of their own day-to-day experiences.

- Do the concepts of hegemony and socialization imply that workers simply take on the ideas and values expressed in the mass media?

The elite theories of Mosca and Pareto reject economic determinism and set out an alternative to Marxism.

- All societies are dominated by a ruling elite that occupies the top positions of command. Its members are involved in a constant circulation from one section of the elite to another.

- Elitist theories are associated with the idea of mass society and mass culture.

- Does the idea of 'mass culture' rest upon a value judgement that denigrates popular culture?

The politics of class

Britain and the United States are democratic political systems. A basic feature of citizenship in these and other advanced societies has been the right to vote, and politics is organized through party competition for votes in local and national elections. Until the middle of the nineteenth century, voting and party politics in both countries were largely matters for men with property. Few employees and few women had the right to vote. In the United States, the property qualification was ended in 1850, giving all adult white males the right to vote. The abolition of slavery in 1865 and a Voting Act of 1870 meant that black males, as citizens, had the right to vote. Despite these legal changes, tax requirements and literacy tests were widely used to prevent African Americans from exercising their rights. These restrictions were not fully removed until 1966. In Britain, householders—who were mainly male—were given the right to vote in 1884, but not until 1918 was this right extended to all adult males. Only from 1920 in the United States and from 1928 in Britain did women win the right to vote in national elections. The democratic voting system is discussed in Box 20.4.

In this section we will look at whether the formal democratic structure corresponds to the realities of political power. In particular, we will look at the extent to which politics has been structured by class during the first half of the twentieth century. We will look at patterns of working-class organization and electoral behaviour and at the background and recruitment of political elites.

Briefing: elections   **20.4**

Parliamentary elections in Britain take place about every four or five years. The country is divided into a number of local constituencies. These constituencies are parts of counties and boroughs and are supposed to have similar numbers of people living in them. In 1900 there were 670 constituencies, and there were 650 in 2010. Voters in each constituency elect one member of parliament from the various candidates who stand for election.

After the election, the party that has had the most MPs elected is usually able to form a government, the party leader becoming prime minister. Because Britain has a constituency system, a party with a majority of the constituency seats may not have received a majority of the votes across the whole country. Most elections give one party or another a majority of seats, but no party since 1918 has ever won a majority of the total votes.

➔ *Try to find out about the voting systems in other countries. Some of these have systems of proportional representation such as that used in elections for the Northern Ireland Assembly. See if you can work out what this means and how it differs from the British constituency system.*

Elections and class voting

The link between class and party has long been central to British politics. The leading study of this topic concluded that 'party allegiance has followed class lines more strongly in Britain than anywhere else in the English-speaking world' (Butler and Stokes 1969: 65). A strong link between class and politics has, nevertheless, been apparent in all European countries. The influence of class has been modified by differences in religion, ethnicity, gender, and region, but class has always been the strongest influence on voting.

The class basis of politics has usually been described in terms of the difference between parties of the left and parties of the right. The terms 'left' and 'right' came into use in eighteenth-century France, where the aristocracy (who supported royal privileges) sat on the right-hand side of the parliamentary chamber. The bourgeoisie (who opposed these privileges) sat on the left-hand side. During the French Revolution, the terms came to be used more generally to describe conservative and radical opinions.

The left–right distinction implies that political parties can be arranged along a line from the most radical (at the left) to the most conservative (at the right), with 'moderate' opinion being in the centre. The terms have continued to be used as a convenient way of summarizing political differences, though there are many political parties that cannot easily be placed along such a line.

Members of the working class have been seen as most likely to support left-wing parties—typically socialist or communist parties—that advocate greater equality, a redistribution of economic resources, and high levels of social welfare. Members of the middle classes and upper classes, on the other hand, have been seen as most likely to support right-wing parties that stress individual freedom and responsibility, and the maintenance of the privileges and advantages of those who succeed in the market system.

Wherever class divisions are sharp, party differences have tended to follow this left–right pattern (Lipset and Rokkan 1967; Korpi 1983). Communist, Socialist, and Labour parties have attracted the support of manual workers across Europe, while Conservative and Liberal parties have been supported by the more advantaged classes. Class divisions have been less sharp in the United States, and left-wing parties have been weak. However, the relatively more left-wing Democratic Party has consistently gained more support from manual workers than has the more conservative Republican Party.

It was in the United States that the earliest and most influential studies of the class–party relationship were undertaken (Lazarsfeld *et al.* 1948; Campbell *et al.* 1960). These studies found that voting behaviour could be explained by differences in material interests: those with the greatest resources tended to support parties of the right, while those with fewer resources tended to vote for parties of the left. These differences were reinforced wherever social classes formed tight and relatively closed social networks of interaction. In these circumstances, shared experiences produced a greater awareness of shared interests and, therefore, a strong tendency to vote for whichever party supported and promoted those interests. In Britain and continental Europe, class cohesion was especially strong, and the tendency towards class politics was particularly marked. In the United States, on the other hand, class cohesion was much weaker—social mobility was much greater—and the structural basis for a labour movement committed to socialism was never established (Sombart 1906).

This suggests that the Marxist idea of a dominant ideology is seriously misleading. Manual workers were voting largely on the basis of class solidarity and class interests, and not on the basis of their socialization into a false consciousness. We will show, however, that these ideas can be combined using Gramsci's idea of dual consciousness.

The labour movement and labour politics

We show in Chapter 19 that a working class was formed in Britain by the early years of the twentieth century. The concentration of economic activity brought workers together in larger numbers, it increased their dependence on one another in a technical division of labour, and it made workers and their families completely dependent on their earnings from work. By concentrating workers' families in densely populated towns and cities, the development of industry and capitalism brought into being a social class that could be described in Marxist terms as a

 Briefing: the Labour Party   20.5

The Independent Labour Party (ILP) was formed under Keir Hardie in 1893. In 1900 it joined with the Fabian Society and the Social Democratic Federation (a Marxist group led by Henry Hyndman) to form the Labour Representation Committee (LRC). The aims of the LRC, under Ramsey MacDonald, were to achieve improved working conditions through increasing the representation of manual workers in parliament. In 1906 the LRC was renamed the Labour Party. In the 1906 general election, it secured the election of twenty-nine 'Labour' MPs. Until 1913 trade unions were not allowed to use their funds for political purposes. This limited their influence over Labour Party policy, although they played a major part in shaping its policies and concerns. The first Labour government was formed at the beginning of 1924, but it lasted less than a year.

Figure 20.1 Labour share of the vote, 1906–1950

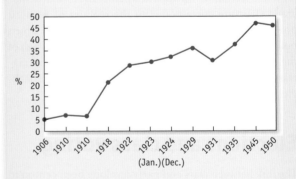

1906	1910 (Jan.)	1910 (Dec.)	1918	1922	1923	1924	1929	1931	1935	1945	1950
5.9	7.6	7.1	22.2	29.5	30.5	33.0	37.1	30.6	37.9	47.8	46.1

Source: Adapted from Butler and Butler (2000: 213–16).

'class for itself'. Skill differentials among workers diminished in importance, as did wage differentials, though a distinction between skilled and unskilled workers remained an important feature of working-class life and politics. For both sections of the working class, however, the Cooperative Societies, the trade unions, and the Labour Party were the means through which they pursued their common interests and forged a sense of class identity and class consciousness.

Working-class awareness revolved around an image of British society as divided between 'us' and 'them'. The working class—us—was seen as subordinate in terms of power to the bosses, 'gaffers', and employers—them—on whom the workers depended for their work and for their wages. 'They' were better off than 'us', and 'we' rarely saw 'them' because 'they' lived in the well-to-do districts far away from 'our' neighbourhood. This image of society saw 'them' as controlling the government, through the Conservative Party, and so having the power to determine the decisions of the state and to benefit from its policies.

Manual workers and their families were excluded from the electoral process for much of the nineteenth century. Denial of the right to organize into trade unions resulted in many urban riots and disturbances. Most notable among these was the riot at St Peter's Fields in Manchester in 1819, known to history as the battle of Peterloo. The massacre of workers by the militia at Peterloo was an event that helped to change the climate of parliamentary opinion about political rights. The threat to social and political order that the dangerous classes were thought to pose led many in the upper-class and middle-class political leadership to begin to see the granting of industrial and political rights to all men—though not yet to all women—as a way of ensuring their political loyalty. If manual workers were denied these rights any longer, it was held, they would—as Marx anticipated—become ever more revolutionary. If, on the other hand, they were made full citizens of their society, they would acquire a stake in the continuance of the political system and would seek peaceful and limited changes through the electoral mechanism.

Not until 1918 were all male manual workers able to vote in parliamentary elections. Until this time the working class had, indeed, little direct influence in national parliamentary politics. Male householders, many of whom were skilled workers, had been given the vote in 1884, and

this had been a major factor in forcing the Liberal Party to enter into closer relations with the trade unions. A number of 'labour' representatives were elected to parliament as part of the Liberal block. The formation of the Labour Party in 1906 increased the parliamentary representation of the working class, and skilled workers continued to have the most important influence over Labour policy in the first two decades of the twentieth century.

The Labour Party grew in strength at the same time as the working class was becoming more solidaristic and cohesive. Its electoral growth was largely at the expense of the Liberal Party, which has not won sufficient seats to form a government since the First World War. The Labour Party received just under a tenth of the total national vote in 1910, and its share had risen to over one-third by the middle of the 1920s and to about a half by 1950. Figure 20.1 shows that this rise, despite a setback in 1931, was virtually continuous over the whole of the first half of the century. The extension of the right to vote in 1918 increased the Labour share from 7.1 per cent to 22.2 per cent. By 1945 the Labour share had risen to 46.1 per cent. The working class had found its political voice in the Labour Party, and the Labour Party found its main electoral base in the working class.

Explaining political choice

A survey of political attitudes in the 1960s reported that only 8 per cent of electors refused to identify themselves as either working class or middle class (Butler and Stokes 1969). The vast majority of those who identified themselves as working class were manual workers or supervisors. Almost three-quarters of the people who identified themselves as working class described themselves as Labour Party supporters, and over three-quarters of those who identified themselves as middle class saw themselves as Conservatives.

Party support could be seen, in part, as involving a rational calculation of self-interest based on the perceived match between class interests and party policies. Butler and Stokes argue, however, that working-class support for the Labour Party was, more importantly, an institutionalized custom within working-class communities. Subcultural norms stressing party commitment were acquired through primary socialization in the family and were reinforced by later participation in the formal and informal social relations and activities of working-class life.

Through their early socialization within the family, children developed an interest in politics and a sense of party commitment. Parents who had a strong interest in politics and a definite attachment to a particular party were likely to bring up their children with a similar interest and commitment. Children learned that their parents had a normative commitment to a particular party, and it was natural that they grew up sharing this commitment. The strength

---

> **⊃ Connections**
>
> We discuss the civil and political rights of citizenship in Chapter 18, pp. 697–9. What other set of rights did Marshall identify in his definition of citizenship?
>
> You might like to look at our discussion of urban riots in Chapter 13, pp. 503–5. Is it useful to see riots as the actions of the 'dangerous classes'?

Figure 20.2   Class, socialization, and voting

'The appropriateness of a particular party to a particular class was for many children the main explanation as to why their parents voted as they did, especially in the working class. . . . An elector who absorbed in childhood a belief about a normative bond of class and party, and who finds this bond reinforced by many of the face-to-face associations in his adult life, may easily accept party allegiance as a natural element in his class culture quite apart from any well-defined understanding of the benefits that his party may confer upon his class or himself.' (Butler and Stokes 1969: 91)

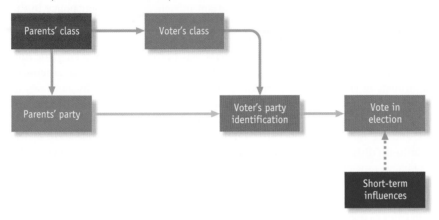

Source: Denver (1994: 48, figure 2.2).

of working-class support for the Labour Party, Butler and Stokes argue, can be explained by socialization into working-class culture. Working-class culture defined British society in terms of social class, and it encouraged the adoption of a class perspective in political action. Labour voting appeared to manual workers living in a working-class community as simply the normal or natural thing to do. This model of voting is shown in Figure 20.2.

The role of socialization in working-class support for the Labour Party has usefully been explored by Parkin (1967), who draws on Gramsci's ideas of hegemony and dual consciousness. Parkin begins by identifying what he calls the 'dominant institutional orders' of British society. These are the key institutions of power: the state, the Established Church, the public schools, the monarchy and the aristocracy, elites of all kinds, and the whole structure of private property and business enterprise. These institutions, he argues, have been tied into a single cohesive structure. They embody a set of core values that correspond closely to the ideology of Conservatism. All members of society have been exposed to these values through their socialization at school and through the mass media. The values were a major influence over their attitudes and actions, and they can be considered to have been truly hegemonic.

> **↻ Connections**
>
> Look at our discussion of primary and secondary socialization in Chapter 4, pp. 113–14, and then read our account of working-class communities in Chapter 19, pp. 761–4. These sections will give you the essential background for understanding this view of voting.

Conservative voting can be seen as what Parkin calls a 'symbolic reaffirmation' of the hegemonic values of British society. People voted for the Conservative Party because they identified with the values with which it was associated. Labour voting, on the other hand, involved a commitment to values that ran counter to the hegemonic values. It was 'a symbolic act of deviance' from the dominant values of British society (Parkin 1967: 282). Those in the lower social strata were less influenced by the dominant values because their immediate day-to-day experiences reinforced a different view of power. However, they were unlikely to show a strong tendency towards Labour voting unless they subscribed to an alternative system of values that supported their political deviance. Labour voting was likely to occur on a significant scale only if an alternative and more radical set of values could be built and so could counter the influence of the dominant values. In the absence of such a value system, people remained subject to the overwhelming influence of the dominant values.

Labour voting is most likely to be found where it is sustained by social institutions that reinforce values of collective solidarity and—in its broadest sense—socialism. Parkin sees the institutions of the labour movement and the working-class community as having been the basis of these radical, counter-hegemonic values. The trade unions, the cooperatives, and the Labour Party, together with nonconformist churches and Sunday schools, clubs, and pubs, and the workplace and street-corner solidarity of the traditional proletarian community were a fertile ground for the growth of alternative values. They also provided a structural barrier to the influence of the dominant values: those who lived in these communities and participated in the labour movement were relatively insulated from the hegemonic values and were better able to build on their own day-to-day experiences and to sustain the values that led them to vote for the Labour Party.

Conversely, manual workers who did not live in working-class communities were more likely to experience the full force of the hegemonic values and so were likely to vote Conservative. Workers in small towns dominated by small firms were likely to have relatively close contacts with their employers and managers, and they were unlikely to live in large occupational communities. These working and living conditions were the basis of the *deferential workers*, those who deferred to the authority of the traditional leaders of society (Lockwood 1966; McKenzie and Silver 1968).

The working class, then, has been divided in its political allegiance. Those living in cohesive and solidaristic working-class communities tended to vote Labour, while those living in smaller and more diverse communities tended to vote Conservative. For this reason, the extension of the franchise to all manual workers did not mean that the Labour Party was able to rely on the support of the majority of the population. The Conservatives were able to retain considerable electoral strength. Between 1886 and 1964, the Conservative Party was decisively defeated in a general election only twice (in 1906 and in 1945). Just over a quarter of those who identified themselves as working class in 1963 were Conservative voters. This striking electoral success was possible only because a significant number of manual workers voted Conservative.

Not all these working-class Conservatives, however, were deferential workers. In the early years of the twentieth century, many manual workers who lived in working-class communities were supporters of the Conservative or Liberal parties. Butler and Stokes (1969) explain this in terms of their model of political socialization. People acquire their political allegiances in childhood. Those who were young in the years before the Labour Party existed, or when it was a relatively new party, were, of course, unlikely to have had parents who were already committed to the Labour Party. These people could not be socialized into an already existing Labour-supporting subculture. It was only as the old Liberal Party collapsed during the 1920s that the Labour Party consolidated its political position and a tradition of Labour voting developed in working-class communities. Only in the post-war period have there been significant numbers of electors whose early socialization took place in families with an existing Labour Party commitment. This helps to explain the age distribution of voting preferences. Older people—socialized before the Labour Party achieved its greatest strength in working-class communities—have shown a greater tendency to vote Conservative than have younger people.

The trends in the Labour share of the vote that are shown in Figure 20.1 (p. 794) are the outcome of these processes. The rapidly growing share going to the Labour Party in the first three decades of the century corresponds to the period in which it was replacing the Liberal Party at the national level and was building its strength in the local working-class communities. Its slower growth in the following decades was a result of its success in retaining the support of the children of its early supporters. The trends in voting are a clear indication of the strength of the link between class and party affiliation.

Political elites and ruling classes

There is considerable evidence that political power in all the leading capitalist societies has been monopolized by their dominant social classes. Although this evidence is most easily available for Britain and the United States, studies of Canada, Australia, France, Germany, and Japan have all shown a similar picture (Bottomore and Brym 1989). In this section, we will look at the British and American evidence on the power of the capitalist class in the state. In a later section, we turn to political authority in the Soviet Union, where there was no capitalist class. Soviet society from 1917 to 1991 was very clearly dominated by a ruling elite that was very different in character from the political elites of capitalist societies.

Politics and power in the United States

Perhaps the most fruitful approach to the nature of class power in the United States is that of G. William Domhoff (1971, 1979, 2006). Domhoff's work is a powerful synthesis of ideas drawn from both Marxist theory and the elitist theory of Mills. He introduces the term **governing class** to describe the particular alignment of power that exists between the capitalist social class and the exercise of political authority. Not only has the capitalist class been disproportionately advantaged in terms of its income, assets, and other life chances; it has also contributed a disproportionate number of its members to top command situations in the decision-making institutions of the state.

Domhoff substantiates this claim in relation to four processes that make up the structure of decision-making. For much of the twentieth century these processes worked together to consolidate capitalist class power in the United States. These are:

- *the special-interest process* through which individuals and business enterprises are able to influence governments to satisfy their specific and narrow short-run interests;

- *the policy-formation process* through which general policies of interest to the dominant class as a whole are developed and implemented;
- *the candidate-selection process* through which dominant class members secure access to elected politicians;
- *the ideology process* that ensures the dissemination and enforcement of the assumptions, beliefs, and attitudes that underpin the formation of policies and politicians conducive to business interests.

The *special-interest process* comprises a network of lobbyists, committees, and organizations that connect business and government. This allows the flow of information, advice, pressure and—not infrequently—bribes. It comprises the visible world of pressure-group politics, together with the less visible behind-the-scenes world of informal pressure and power (Bachrach and Baratz 1962). Domhoff shows, for example, how lobbying organizations can undermine attempts to regulate industries and can minimize the effects of proposed legislation. Advisory committees can provide the information and guidance that departments and government agencies need for their decision-making. Hired lawyers can help companies to secure tax advantages. The special-interest process is that system of social relations through which individuals and organizations pressure, influence, and persuade governments to act in support of their interests.

The *policy-formation process* is concerned with larger, more general issues and policies. It allows the special interests of particular sectors, enterprises, and individuals to be forged into a wider class consciousness. It involves a network of foundations, research institutes, think tanks, and committees that interlock with corporate boards and government offices, and it is through these that the political dimension of a class consciousness is built (Useem 1984). Such organizations as the Council on Foreign Relations, the Committee for Economic Development, and the Business Council have been centrally involved in discussions of world trade, overseas aid, health, population, taxation, labour relations, and education. The results of these discussions have been disseminated through informal

Barack Obama press briefing: the heart of the lobbying and pressure system

© Getty Images/ Chip Somodevilla

lunches and meetings and through conferences, journals, and reports. Presidential Commissions and mass-media news reports all feed into this process.

Candidate-selection involves the processes through which individuals are recruited to elected governmental posts and also the processes through which, once elected, they remain responsive to capitalist interests. Financial power is central to the selection and supervision of candidates. Elections are a costly matter, and politicians in large states and the central government depend on their personal wealth or on large-scale financial contributions to fund their campaigns. Those who have the best access to the necessary funds are likely to be selected for office or to be able to exercise a strong influence over the nomination of candidates. The biggest recipient of business donations in the United States has been the Republican Party, though large donors have often sought to maintain their influence over government by giving financial support to the Democrats as well. So long as their chosen candidates continue to support business interests, the parties can be sure of a substantial flow of funds from the business world.

These processes have ensured that politicians have been disproportionately drawn from the higher levels of the class structure, and particularly from business and professional families. Politicians are, by and large, pragmatists who seek to get along with the business interests on whom they depend. Most do not have strong policy preferences of their own. They have a general commitment to business and propertied interests and are responsive to their special interests and favoured policies: 'Despite the considerable efforts of organized labor and middle-income reformers, the candidate-selection process produces a predominance of politicians who sooner or later become sympathetic to the prevailing wisdom within either the moderate or ultraconservative faction of the power elite' (Domhoff 1979: 167).

The *ideology process* is a more general process that supports and reinforces the other three processes of class domination. Domhoff holds that it is through the ideology process that public opinion is moulded and that attitudes and values conducive to the dominance of the governing class are sustained. These hegemonic values are the liberal values of individualism, free enterprise, competition, equality of opportunity, and restrictions on the role of government. To be a good American is to subscribe to these values. They are central to discussions in the policy-formation process. The organizations involved in the formulation of policies disseminate them, explicitly and implicitly, through advertising and public relations, through educational strategies, and through the mass media. They create a climate of opinion that sustains the existing political arrangements. While most people may not actively and enthusiastically endorse them, they will, at the very least, adopt an attitude of resigned acquiescence. Existing

arrangements are barely questioned. The ideology process minimizes the possibility that any autonomous and more radical consciousness will develop.

Local political power

Domhoff's view of the relationship between class and power at the national level has been supported by a number of studies of particular localities. Studies of Newburyport and Philadelphia in New England, Morris in the Midwest, and Muncie in Indiana have documented the existence of wealthy capitalist classes that dominate local politics (see Box 20.6). The Lynds' studies (Lynd and Lynd 1929, 1937) of Muncie during the 1920s and 1930s, for example, discovered a business class, centred around a particular dominant family, that had interests in local manufacturing and banking enterprises. This class monopolized positions of political power in the local administration and in the political parties.

Dahl (1961) studied the small city of New Haven in Connecticut, New England, during the middle and the late 1950s. His aim was to explore the question of whether the elected officials were, indeed, the holders of real decision-making power. In undertaking this research, Dahl wanted to set out a critique of the ruling elite and the ruling-class views of politics. Domhoff (1978) has shown, however, that Dahl's results are better seen as contributing to the broadening of a class perspective on political power.

Until the 1840s, New Haven, like many other New England cities and towns, was run by a patrician aristocracy of wealthy commercial and professional families. They were Congregationalists in religion, reflecting the Puritan inheritance of the founding families. The development of new industries in the nineteenth century forced them to

---

THEORY AND METHODS 20.6

Community power studies

Community power studies have often been published using false names for the towns studied. This is to highlight the fact that they are treated as general case studies rather than unique accounts. It also helps to protect the anonymity of the people studied. The most famous pseudonyms are 'Yankee City' (Newburyport), 'Jonesville' (Morris), and 'Middletown' (Muncie). Try to find these towns on a map of the United States. Can you also find New Haven, which we discuss below? Do you think it is valid to generalize from studies of these localities?

→ Try to think of other areas of research where there might be an ethical requirement to present data using false names. You should review our discussion of the ethics of social research in Chapter 3, pp. 103–5.

> **Connections**

If you have read Chapter 11, 'Religion, belief, and meaning', you will recognize some connections with Herberg's argument about ethnicity and migration in the United States. You might find it useful to go back and have another look at his argument, on p. 405. Perhaps you might also like to look back at our discussion on pp. 397–8 of what Weber said about Puritanism.

share their power with new entrepreneurs who had interests in manufacturing, banking, and insurance. During this period, there was also much working-class migration from Ireland, Germany, Italy, and Eastern Europe, and these European migrants became actively involved in the newly established electoral system. Party leaders who sought success in the elections had to try to attract their support, and the mobilization of ethnic-minority votes became an important feature of local politics.

Dahl saw the 1950s as marked by a shift away from a concern for the sectional advantages of particular minority groups. This political shift, argues Dahl, was not unique to New Haven but was nationwide. Mayor Lee in New Haven and President Eisenhower in Washington edged the Republicans away from the sectional matters that dominated the old 'machine politics'. The new politics was more concerned with collective benefits, and the critical area for decision-making was urban redevelopment and renewal. As a result of these changes, claims Dahl, the social notables (the descendants of the old patricians) and the economic notables (the entrepreneurs and people of business) lost their former dominance. Class power was counterbalanced by electoral power. Dahl recognized, however, that capitalist families remained an influential force in local politics:

> The Social and Economic Notables of today ... are scarcely a ruling elite.... They are, however, frequently influential on specific decisions, particularly when these directly involve business prosperity. Moreover, politicians are wary of their potential influence and avoid policies that might unite the notables in bitter opposition.

Dahl 1961: 84

In his critical discussion of Dahl's work, Domhoff (1978) re-examines the issue of urban redevelopment and shows that political action by the mayor was, in fact, preceded by a long period of business lobbying and pressure, including action at the national and state level. It was only after this preparatory period, and after federal legislation had opened up new options, that local politicians saw a political opportunity and attempted to carry this through by mobilizing popular support for it. Business leaders in New Haven were organized through the Chamber of Commerce

and other civic organizations, where local political policies were developed in relation to national programmes. They formed the central part of a local policy-formation and opinion-making process that connected to the national-level processes that Domhoff had identified in his other works. Dahl's study, by focusing on a relatively late phase in the whole process, ignored the earlier preparatory work in which business leaders had been heavily involved.

Domhoff has also shown that the economic and social notables can be seen as having a high level of class unity and that they must be seen in relation to the larger national capitalist class of which they are a part. American cities, he argues, should not be seen in isolation but as elements in a larger political economy. They are *growth machines*: engines of capital accumulation within a capitalist system that is both national and international in scope. Businesses in New Haven have been locked into this economy through links of ownership and control. Local business leaders have directorships in large multinationals, and business leaders from New York and other financial centres have connections to New Haven companies. While some small towns may be dominated by small businesses or the middle classes, Domhoff concludes that New Haven was important enough to have a significant presence of those who are indisputably members of the national capitalist class.

A British ruling class?

A series of studies have shown the links between class advantages and political power in Britain. These occur through kinship, education, and recruitment. The Conservative Party, the government, the civil service, the legal profession, and the military have all been overwhelmingly recruited from the capitalist class and have been unified through bonds of intermarriage and a common educational background (Guttsman 1963). This research showed that landed property was a fundamental element in the structure of political power through much of the twentieth century and that the old public schools and universities (most particularly, Eton and Harrow schools and Oxford and Cambridge universities) were the means through which landed and industrial interests were tied together and through which careers in the political elite could be built. Well into the twentieth century, the upper-class institutions remained central to capitalist class power. These trends are shown for various elites in Figure 20.3.

The most systematic explorations of these processes have been undertaken by Miliband (1969) and John Scott (1991), who have drawn on similar ideas to those of

> **Connections**

If you are not familiar with the idea of a capitalist class and how it developed in Britain, look at the discussion of this in Chapter 19, pp. 768–70.

Figure 20.3 Elite background and recruitment, Britain, 1939–1970

	% from private school			
	1939	1950	1960	1970
Top civil servants	90.5	59.9	65.0	61.7
Ambassadors	75.5	72.6	82.6	82.5
Top army officers	63.6	71.9	83.2	86.1
Top navy officers	19.8	14.6	20.9	37.5
Top air force officers	69.7	59.1	59.5	65.0
Top judiciary	84.4	86.8	82.5	83.5

	% from Oxford or Cambridge University			
	1939	1950	1960	1970
Top civil servants	77.4	56.3	69.5	69.3
Ambassadors	49.0	66.1	84.1	80.0
Top army officers	25	8.8	12.4	24.3
Top navy officers	—	—	—	—
Top air force officers	18.2	13.6	19.1	17.5
Top judiciary	77.8	73.6	74.6	84.6

Source: Boyd (1973: tables 4–9, 13–17).

❷ Why do you think that military officers have relatively low rates of attendance at Oxford and Cambridge? Check out the role of such specialist institutions as Sandhurst, Dartmouth, and Cranfield if you are unsure.

Domhoff (see also Miliband 1982, 1989). Their work depends upon the identification of two distinct concepts: the capitalist class and the state elite. The capitalist class, as we show in Chapter 19, consists of those who depend upon property ownership and the use of property for their advantaged life chances. It has interests in both landed and non-landed forms of property. The **state elite**, on the other hand, comprises the leading command situations in the government, parliament, the civil service, the military and para-military, and the judiciary, which together make up the state system. If people from a capitalist class background disproportionately fill the leading positions in the state elite, they can be described as a ruling class.

However, things are rarely this straightforward. A capitalist class is small in size, and the state elite must recruit people from other class backgrounds. To deal with this issue, Scott has introduced the ideas of the **power bloc** and the power elite. A power bloc is an alignment of classes that have certain shared interests and concerns and a common focus on the exercise of state power, although they may have many conflicting interests as well. The classes are aligned by the predominance of one class within the power bloc. A power elite exists wherever positions within the state elite are drawn overwhelmingly from a power bloc.

Figure 20.4 Forms of power elite

Cohesion and integration of power bloc

Class basis of power bloc	Unitary	Pluralist
Restricted	Exclusive power elite	Segmented power elite
Extended	Inclusive power elite	Fragmentary power elite

When a capitalist class holds the paramount position within such a power bloc, it can be described as a ruling class.

To develop this argument, Scott constructed a typology of power elites to highlight the distinctive features of the British situation. This typology is shown in Figure 20.4. Power elites are classified by the extent to which they are solidaristic, with a high level of group consciousness and cohesion, and the extent to which one class within the alignment holds a paramount position. The four types of power elite are defined as follows:

- An *exclusive power elite* exists wherever a power bloc is drawn from a restricted and highly uniform social background and is able to achieve a high level of social solidarity and cohesion.

- An *inclusive power elite* exists when there is a solidaristic power bloc not dominated by any particular class. The power bloc draws from a limited number of classes, but these are relatively equally balanced.

- A *segmented power elite* exists wherever a power bloc dominated by a particular class is, nevertheless, divided into a number of separate and distinct fractions and so has a relatively low level of overall cohesion.

- A *fragmented power elite* exists wherever the constituent classes of a power bloc are relatively evenly balanced and there is very little overall solidarity and cohesion.

Wherever the structure of political recruitment is more widely drawn than in these models and no power bloc exists, there will be no power elite. In these circumstances, the distribution of power within the state cannot usefully be described as involving a single elite.

Scott argues that political authority in Britain has, indeed, been dominated by a power bloc. An alignment of the capitalist class with those in entrepreneurial, professional, and managerial class situations has provided the core of those who have been recruited to top positions within the state. The capitalist class has been paramount within this alignment and it has been disproportionately represented in all the key areas of the state elite.

The solidarity of this power elite was based on the continuing significance of the old public schools and universities. Formerly the exclusive preserve of the upper class, these institutions opened up their recruitment to a wider social band during the second half of the twentieth century. The classes that make up the power bloc are precisely those that benefited from this and that have been disproportionately represented in the various branches of the state elite. These people sat on the most important boards, commissions, councils, and committees, and they met frequently at business meetings, lunches, dinners, and ceremonies. Informal interaction in the exclusive London social clubs, involvement in the same round of social activities, and connections through marriage, tied them into a strong structure of power. Using the categories of Figure 20.4, the British power elite can be described as an exclusive power elite within which the capitalist class has been paramount. For this reason, it can be said that Britain has had a ruling class.

Totalitarianism and command societies

We have looked at ruling elites and their class basis in capitalist societies, but ruling elites also exist in other types of advanced industrial society. To explore this further, we will look at elite organization in Soviet Russia. This has often been described as a system of rule based on a totalitarian political system.

The concept of **totalitarianism** was introduced to describe the politics and social stratification of Nazi Germany, Fascist Italy, and the Soviet Union. In each of these three societies, it was held, a ruling elite had total control over all aspects of social life, and so totalitarian regimes differed markedly from the liberal and democratic regimes of Britain and the United States. Throughout the period of the cold war between East and West, liberal commentators on the Soviet Union stressed its totalitarian character. Their work had an ideological character, helping to legitimate and reinforce the hostility of Western governments to the Soviet Union and the states of Eastern Europe that formed the Communist bloc (Friedrich and Brzezinski 1956; Shapiro 1972; see also Lefort 1986). In their opposition to the official Marxism of the Communist systems, totalitarian theorists also contributed to the critique of Marxist ideas in the social sciences. Totalitarian theory was, in all respects, anti-Marxist.

Despite these ideological uses of totalitarianism, it has a real sociological content and can help us to understand modern societies with highly centralized political systems. You will find it useful to read our discussion of command situations in Chapter 19, p. 749.

Totalitarianism defined

A totalitarian system is one in which no area of life falls outside the scope of the state. Everything is subordinate to the collective goals set by the ruling elite. There is no room for autonomous public opinion, and no proper constitutional system of decision-making. The state is a highly centralized system of command that allows its top bureaucrats to form a ruling elite. This bureaucracy operates, without restrictions, to set the agenda and to enforce all decisions. All actions of the state and its elite are justified in relation to its official ideology. The state is, in effect, organized as an *ecclesia*: an all-embracing system organized around an orthodox and tightly enforced system of beliefs. These kinds of regime tend to produce or to be produced by absolute rulers who can act as personal dictators. Such individuals may have charismatic qualities that enable them to rise to power and to mobilize mass support, but they must rely on ruthless terror and intimidation to maintain their rule.

Those who live under a totalitarian regime have little or no individual freedom. Their attitudes and opinions are shaped by the mass media and the educational system, which operate as agencies of indoctrination and propaganda in the service of the official ideology. People's movements are tightly controlled, both within the country and abroad, and they are subject to direct force and coercion, as well as more indirect surveillance by secret police.

Where Marxism sees economic forces as the most important determinants of social development, totalitarian theorists place greater emphasis on politics and the state. For some of these theorists, however, politics must ultimately adapt to the need to develop an advanced industrial technology. Kerr *et al.* (1960), for example, hold that centralized regimes of totalitarian political control are incompatible with the requirements of an advanced industrial technology. This technology, they hold, is compatible only with the pluralistic structures of liberal democracy. According to this view, totalitarian regimes faced a critical

> ➥ *Connections*
>
> Much of the argument about totalitarianism draws on Weber's analysis of rationality and bureaucracy. You might like to look at what we say about this in Chapter 14, pp. 518–19. In that chapter, you will also find a brief discussion of Weber's idea of charismatic authority. By this, he meant the form of authority that involves a belief in the exceptional or superhuman characteristics of the ruler.
>
> The idea of the ecclesia is defined in Chapter 11, p. 400, where you will also find a discussion of the religious character of Soviet Communism (pp. 406–7).

problem. If they took steps to develop their industrial base, they would sow the seeds of their eventual collapse; but if they tried to maintain totalitarian control, they would be unable to achieve industrial advance and economic growth. The dilemma of totalitarianism, then, was that of industrial development and political collapse versus industrial stagnation and political survival. However, industrial stagnation could not be sustained in the long term. The political collapse of totalitarianism was inevitable.

The three societies seen as exemplifying the totalitarian model are the Fascist regime of 1921–43 in Italy, the Nazi regime of 1933–45 in Germany, and the Communist regime in Russia from 1917 until the 1980s. In each case, a personal dictator (Mussolini, Hitler, Stalin) seemed able to use the centralized power of a one-party state to exercise total and arbitrary power. Benito Mussolini's Fascist Party achieved power in a period of political weakness in Italy and, from the mid-1920s, established a strong and centralized system. It entered into a military alliance with Germany once Adolf Hitler had achieved similar power there. The Communist Revolution of 1917 in Russia established the Soviet Union as an important political power under Lenin, but it was as Josef Stalin rose to power in the 1920s that the system became more centralized. The system became less overtly coercive after the death of Stalin in 1953, but most of its principal structures remained in place until the Brezhnev regime of the 1970s and 1980s.

Political command and state socialism

The most interesting society to consider in relation to the concept of totalitarianism is the Soviet Union, where centralized and autocratic political control lasted much longer. It differs from the other cases in a number of important respects. While Italy and Germany were capitalist societies and the totalitarian regimes encouraged business interests, the Soviet system grew from an explicitly anti-capitalist revolution. In both Germany and Italy, defeat in war helped to bring about the end of their totalitarian systems, while Russian totalitarianism seems to have collapsed because of its own internal problems. The Soviet Union is a useful case for assessing arguments about the incompatibility between totalitarianism and advanced industrial technology.

After the death of Lenin, Stalin used his base in the Communist Party bureaucracy to purge all actual and potential opponents to his rule. By sacking and, in later years, murdering the old revolutionaries who might have challenged him, he built a massive and centralized bureaucracy of professional administrators who were responsible solely to him. Those who did not conform suffered show trials, confinement in concentration camps (the infamous gulags), and extermination.

Ordinary people were subject to the same kinds of controls, their conformity being enforced by a network of police informers and a system of literary and political

THEORY AND METHODS **20.7**

Totalitarianism

The idea of totalitarianism has often been used by those strongly committed to elitist theories. It is seen as an extreme form of tight elite control. A useful discussion has defined it as involving:

- *one-party rule*: absence of competitive elections, lack of restrictions on leadership;
- an *official ideology* as the basis of social order and centralized power;
- *personal dictatorship* of a pre-eminent individual;
- use of *terror and force*: concentration camps and political police to maintain order and conformity;
- *centrally planned economy*, stressing production and accumulation over consumption;
- *restrictions on freedom* of movement; subordination of individual and private interests to collective goals;
- *indoctrination and propaganda* through monopoly control over mass media, education, and all cultural institutions; attempt to maintain total conformity.

Source: Adapted from Curtis (1979: 7–9).

censorship. Deviance from political orthodoxy was regarded not only as a crime, but as a sign of mental illness. The official view was that anyone who could not see the self-evident truth of Communist ideology was, quite obviously, insane. Mental hospitals were used more as prisons than as hospitals, and the totalitarian system made use of a particularly strong form of the total institution.

Under Stalin's successors—Khrushchev and Brezhnev were the most important—some of the more ruthless and arbitrary characteristics of the regime were dismantled. However, the tight structure of political control and censorship remained. The concentration camps and mental hospitals became, if anything, even more important in maintaining social control. Economic activity was given a greater degree of autonomy from the centralized planning system, but political, cultural, and personal life remained tightly controlled from the centre.

So, was the Soviet Union totalitarian? One organization (the Communist Party fused with the state) exercised massive power in all areas of social life. This control,

> ⮕ *Connections*
>
> Look at our discussion of the labelling of deviant behaviour in Chapter 7, pp. 229–33; you might also like to review what we said in 'Medicalization and the mind', pp. 291–5. You will find a discussion of the total institution in Chapter 14, p. 524.

however, was never 'total' in the sense implied by some of the more extreme proponents of the idea. Central control barely reached some of the more distant villages, especially in the non-Russian Republics incorporated into the Soviet Union. While centralized party control was tight throughout Eastern Europe after the Second World War, the regimes of East Germany, Poland, Hungary, and Czechoslovakia were far weaker than the Stalinist system of the Soviet Union itself.

For this reason, the term cannot be used without qualification. D. Lane (1976) has made the useful suggestion that the Soviet Union should be seen as a system of **state socialism**, rather than simply as totalitarian (see Box 20.8). This is an attempt to give greater attention to the relationship between economics and politics and to patterns of stratification. State socialism is a system in which the pursuit of social and economic equality is achieved through a centralized, state-directed promotion of economic development. The Soviet state, Lane argues, was concerned with mobilizing the population for industrial development. The system was a state-directed system of socialist modernization.

In state socialism, politics is related to a specific form of social stratification. The ruling elite that built the Soviet Union also built an entrenched position for itself. It eventually became the dominant force in the society. The ruling elite, sometimes described as the *nomenklatura*, came to form a self-perpetuating social stratum with privileges and life chances not available to the mass of the population (Matthews 1978). It is this structure of privilege for those in positions of political command that explains the persistence of the centralized structures described as totalitarian.

The central features of the system were geared to the maintenance of elite privileges and the suppression of all opposition to this.

The Communist regimes of Russia and Eastern Europe collapsed in a series of both peaceful and violent events from the late 1980s. This led to fundamental transformations in the whole global structure of power, some of which are discussed in Chapter 16. The collapse of Communism seemed a very sudden change, but its roots were deep within the structures of the state socialist regimes.

Under Brezhnev in the 1970s and 1980s, the Soviet economy stagnated. The industrial forces that had been developed under Stalin were held back from further development by a centralized political system that was unwilling and unable to respond to these problems. Not until Gorbachev's reforms of the mid-1980s was this problem addressed. Stagnation had made reform more acceptable to the leadership, and Gorbachev encouraged greater autonomy for market-based systems of distribution. In 1986 he launched a policy of *perestroika* or restructuring, aimed at abandoning centralized planning and administration (White 1991). This policy was rapidly extended to the political system through a policy of *glasnost* (openness or democratization). The momentum behind these changes came from the much-expanded intelligentsia of educated, professional, and non-manual employees, whose interests and consciousness differed from those of manual workers as well as from those of the *nomenklatura*, the dominant group of officials.

The attempt to resolve the economic contradictions of the system weakened its totalitarian elements and allowed the emergence of, in effect, a multi-party political system.

THEORY AND METHODS 20.8

State socialism

'It is a society distinguished by a state-owned, more or less centrally administered economy, controlled by a dominant communist party which seeks, on the basis of Marxism–Leninism and through the agency of the state, to mobilize the population to reach a classless society' (D. Lane 1996).

Two systems compared:

	Capitalism	State socialism
Public rights	'Citizenship': private property and individual freedom	'Comradeship': state property and equality
Means of economic coordination	Market competition administration	Planning and centralized
Means of political coordination	Democracy and electoral competition	Central control: party and bureaucracy
Means of social integration	Pluralistic private associations	Collectivist public associations
Basis of public order	Rule of law (legal order)	Politics (discretionary order)
Source of social identity	Leisure and consumption	Labour and production

Source: Adapted from D. Lane (1996: 52).

The Communist Party proved unable to hold on to its monopoly position, and the regime lost its legitimacy. However, the economic reforms did not produce a strong and growing economy. Instead, there was declining production, sharply rising price inflation, and massive unemployment. The Gorbachev reforms had failed in their economic goals, and Gorbachev himself lost control of the situation. The Soviet Union and the remnants of its totalitarian system disintegrated.

It appears, then, that Kerr and his colleagues were correct to point to the impossibility of combining a totalitarian command system with an advanced and growing industrial economy. The contradiction built into the very structure of state socialism ensured its eventual collapse.

 Stop and reflect

In this section we have looked at the evidence on class politics in the first half of the twentieth century. We looked, first, at the working class.

- Members of the working class in all industrial societies have shown a strong tendency to support parties of the left. Electoral support for Labour grew continuously through the first half of the twentieth century.

- Working-class support for the Labour Party in Britain developed in cohesive working-class communities that allowed the development of a strong and autonomous political consciousness.

- Working-class conservatism occurred mainly in smaller and more socially mixed communities where there was less class solidarity among manual workers.

- Why was working-class support for Labour so strongly linked to the existence of cohesive working-class communities?

We then turned to the question of whether Britain and the United States had ruling classes.

- The dominant class in the United States operated through the special-interest process, the policy-formation process, the candidate-selection process, and the ideology process.

- Local city politics was dominated by business interests linked to the national capitalist class.

- Can the politics of contemporary cities be understood in terms of a struggle balance between business and other social interests?

- The ruling class in Britain is a power elite that has been highly cohesive and restricted in its social background.

- Do you find the idea of a ruling class to be a compelling way to understand the distribution of power today?

Finally, we looked at politics in a non-capitalist society, the Soviet Union.

- The Soviet Union was a state socialist system with a totalitarian ruling elite.

Politics beyond class

We have shown that, for the first fifty or sixty years of the twentieth century, politics in capitalist societies was organized around class. In Britain, the United States, and elsewhere, political authority, political organization, and political action were structured around the patterns of social stratification that we describe in 'The making of a class society', Chapter 19, pp. 758–70. A strong and cohesive working class was organized into trade unions and a Labour Party, and it gave much electoral support to that party. The middle classes provided the backbone of electoral support for the Conservative Party, and an upper class monopolized the exercise of political power within the state.

Our argument in Chapter 19, however, is that the clear lines of division and the contours of solidarity that charac-terized stratification in the first half of the twentieth century had become increasingly more fragmentary in the second half. Class divisions persisted, but they had become less visible, and social classes became less cohesive and conscious of themselves. It is now time to investigate the implications of these changes for the structure of politics. What is the nature of politics, power, and protest in a fragmentary class society?

The end of class politics?

Many researchers have identified what they believe to be a contemporary decline in the significance of class relations for political action. In place of class as a single, unitary focus

→ *Connections*
You will find a more extended discussion of democracy in Chapter 15, pp. 560–1.

for the distribution of political power, they have identified a more diverse plurality of political groups. This pluralist view of power structures is a critical development of elitist theory that turns it into a radical theory of democracy.

The classical idea of democracy—rule by the mass of the citizens—had been seen as a mere sham by Mosca and Pareto, who held that a small minority or elite would always rule. Weber held to this same point of view, but he argued that it was important to explore the electoral controls that can be imposed on elite power in modern democracies. In a democracy, he held, people can *choose* the political elite through the ballot box. Weber recognized, of course, that things were rarely as simple as this and that there were many areas in modern societies where electoral control did not exist, but his emphasis on the electoral process and party competition laid the basis for the view that later came to be called democratic elitism. According to this point of view, democracy can be seen as the competition of elites.

This position holds that the existence of elites is compatible with the idea of democracy, so long as there is more than one elite and so long as there is effective competition among them. The political sphere of a democratic society is like the economic marketplace. It is an arena in which party-based elites must compete for the votes of the political consumers. Just as consumer demand in the economic market is supposed to guarantee consumer sovereignty, so political demands in the electoral market are held to guarantee popular democratic sovereignty. In a competitive system, politicians will supply the policies and programmes that the electors demand.

Writers who have developed the elitist theory of democracy and the more general pluralist standpoint have often overstated their case. They have, however, identified an important dimension of contemporary politics and a fundamental area in which the exercise of political power has been transformed. In the rest of this chapter we will look at the extent to which they are correct to see class politics as having been replaced by pluralistic politics.

Pluralism, issues, and power

Pluralist theory sees a whole variety of interest groups, pressure groups, and associations as joining the older parties in the competition for power. Pluralists hold that power in contemporary industrial societies has been dispersed among a large number of individuals and organizations. Political decisions are, therefore, the outcome of shifting struggles among these groups as they each seek to pursue their particular interests or to promote their particular values. The competitive struggle for the votes of an informed and politically aware electorate occurs within this larger context, and it is no longer possible to identify monopolistic centres of political power.

Elitism and pluralism present very different images of the structure of power in modern societies. Elitists, like Marxists, see power as concentrated in the hands of a single ruling group. Pluralists, on the other hand, see it as dispersed among a number of separate *veto groups*, each of which is able to counter the influence of others. This difference in viewpoint is also associated with a difference in methodology. Where elitists stress the circulation of individuals among social positions with the potential or capacity for power, pluralists stress the direct study of patterns of decision-making and the actual exercise of power. Lukes (1974) has effectively shown, however, that these should not be seen as mutually contradictory arguments. They are, rather, complementary aspects of the social distribution of power. Power exists as both a *capacity* (defined by the structural location of people and groups) and an active exercise of *agency* in individual and collective action (see also J. Scott 2001).

Pluralist views were developed most forcefully in the 1950s and 1960s, when writers such as Dahl set out their critical views on ruling-elite and ruling-class theories. In his study of New Haven, Dahl (1961) argued that elitists had merely *assumed* the existence of an all-pervasive elite, rather than actually *demonstrating* its existence with evidence. Whether an elite exists in a particular society, he held, is an empirical question. It is to be approached in an open-minded way and is not to be decided in advance on the basis of theoretical prejudice.

Dahl held that political power can best be investigated through the key decisions made in a particular society. Sociologists should see who participates in these decisions and whose preferences actually prevail as a result of them. If a ruling elite exists, Dahl says, it will be found that the same small group of people participate in all decisions and that the outcomes of these decisions correspond to their preferences and political programmes. If this cannot be demonstrated, then there is no ruling elite.

Dahl suggests, in fact, that there is little evidence that modern societies are dominated by ruling elites. Although those who actually participate in the active exercise of power may be a minority in their society, the constitutional framework of democracy ensures that they will represent and be responsive to the majority. They are open rather than closed groups. The structure of civil and political freedom in contemporary societies requires that political parties compete for the votes of the electorate. The extension of the franchise has meant that parties are responsive to the wishes and interests of all adult citizens in their societies. In order to secure power within a democratic system, parties and candidates must try to attract the support of enough voters to give them a majority in the legislative body.

In New Haven, Dahl showed that this political participation is open to all electors, though manual workers were far less active than non-manual workers. Political issues are generally raised or organized by politically active intellectuals, experts, and reformers who are able to attract the support of other professionals and politicians. Though broader political pressure may sometimes force an issue on to the agenda, most voters limit their role to voting on the issues raised by the political activists. Political parties are coalitions of activists, and their dependence on popular votes in a democratic system means that politicians have to weigh political issues in terms of a calculation of the likely electoral support that will be given by non-activists.

A similar picture is painted of political power at the national level. A government in Britain must be drawn from a majority party or from a coalition of parties that can mobilize a majority in the House of Commons. In a presidential system, on the other hand, matters are a little more complicated. In the United States, for example, the division of powers between President and Congress means that a presidential candidate must aim to secure a majority of the popular vote and must hope that his or her party will have or be able to attain a majority of seats in Congress. In either case, the competition for votes is seen as a guarantee that popular, majority concerns and interests will carry the day in political decision-making. The new party politics is a politics of issues rather than a politics of class.

From this point of view, the overall structure of contemporary political leadership has become more pluralistic. Each party may form a small minority in the population, but the competition among parties ensures democratic decision-making. At the same time, the political leadership itself is simply one powerful group among many. The power of the state is checked by the countervailing power of employers' associations, trade unions, and a whole variety of pressure groups and interest groups and associations. Such groups form around particular political preferences and choices, and the struggle of interest groups is a major force in the political process. This does not mean there is no longer a ruling class. Many of the features of the old system persist, and it is certainly not the case that all political groups are equal in power. Domhoff's most recent study (2006) demonstrates a continuity in patterns of political power in the United States, with connections between business and presidential politics remaining strong under both Clinton and Bush. The difficulties faced by Obama in securing his reforms to the health-care system show that little changed with his election. Nevertheless, there has been a greater degree of pluralism in the exercise of political power. Different sections of the population participate in different sets of decisions, and the preferences of one group may often be counter-balanced by those of others. Instead of a monolithic ruling elite, contemporary societies tend towards a greater plurality of interest groups and a fragmentation of power.

> → **Connections**
>
> If you are unsure about the points that we are making about identity, read our discussion of this whole question in Chapter 4, pp. 113–20.

Pluralist views of the end of class, the end of ideological politics, and the decentralization of power have been taken up in the post-modernist theories of the 1980s and 1990s (G. McLennan 1989). According to these theorists, societies must be seen as resulting from the competitive struggles of a plurality of specific social groups. Foucault, for example, identified decentred power relations focused in specialized organizations and agencies rather than in such overarching structures as states or social classes. Along with the pressure groups and associations identified by earlier pluralists, contemporary post-modern pluralists have identified a wider range of social groups based on consumption, lifestyle, and personal identity. Groups and group identities themselves are not fixed, but are shifting and fragmented. Individuals build up a number of identities that can vary quite significantly from one situation to another. As a result, group consciousness and large-scale collective action are abandoned for a new and radically individualized politics of difference and identity.

Pluralist and post-modernist theories, then, claim that there is a declining significance of class and class-based politics in contemporary societies. These societies show a corresponding increase in the significance of individualistic concerns about issues and identities in the political sphere. The impact of these ideas can be seen most clearly in the debates over issue voting and over the growing significance of new social movements.

Trends in party support

We have shown that British politics in the first half of the twentieth century was marked by a very close association between social class and party preference. During the last forty years, however, this link has weakened, and the stable two-party electoral system has shifted towards a more volatile three-party system. The reasons for this political shift have been much debated, and they highlight the significance of the changing patterns of social stratification that we discussed in Chapter 19.

> → **Connections**
>
> If you have not yet looked at the debate about the working class in the post-war period, read our discussion of this in Chapter 19, pp. 774–7. You will find it useful background for understanding the political changes that we look at in this chapter.

The proportion of manual workers voting for the Labour Party declined from 69 per cent to 50 per cent between 1966 and 1979. After dropping even further to 38 per cent in 1983, Labour support among manual workers stood at 45 per cent in 1992. The proportion of non-manual workers voting for the Conservative Party remained at or above 60 per cent until 1979, and then dropped slowly but inexorably to 49 per cent by 1992. This means that about two-thirds of each class still voted for their customary or natural party in 1966, while less than a half of each did so in 1992. Although manual-worker support for the Labour Party increased at the 2001 election, it feel away again by 2005 to stand at 45 per cent of unskilled workers and 43 per cent of skilled workers, reflecting a growth in Labour cross-class support. Some partial evidence from the 2010 election suggests that, among voters, 44 per cent of unskilled workers voted Labour, but just 22 per cent of skilled workers did so. Many skilled workers had either changed their party allegiance or had decided not to vote.

As we will show later, there is also much evidence to suggest that the reasons that people have for voting one way or another have altered. People are now less likely to vote principally because of socialized class preferences. There has been a weakening of class attachment to particular political parties. The main beneficiaries of this have been the Liberal Democrats and their predecessors (the Liberals and the Social Democrats), who were supported by 14 per cent of non-manual workers and 6 per cent of manual workers in 1966, but by 25 per cent of non-manual workers and 20 per cent of manual workers in 1992. The main loser, until the middle of the 1980s, was the Labour Party. Figure 20.5 shows that the share of the total vote going to the Labour Party in general elections declined between 1950 and 1983. While the share of the vote going to the Labour Party recovered slightly during a trough of Conservative unpopularity after 1987, the secure core of Labour voting remained far below the level attained in 1945. Even the Labour landslide victory of 1997 was achieved with a lower share of the vote than in 1945.

A major reason for the decline in the total *share* of the vote going to the Labour Party is the decline in the number of manual workers and a corresponding increase in the number of non-manual workers. To the extent that there is still a tendency for manual workers to vote Labour, a decline in the number of manual workers will result in a fall in the Labour vote. It has been calculated that around a half of the total fall in the Labour vote up to the 1980s can be explained in this way (Heath *et al.* 1985). Conversely, of course, about a half of the fall in the Labour vote could not be explained in these terms. Many manual workers were simply no longer willing to vote Labour in the same kind of automatic way that they had a generation earlier. The fall in the Labour vote up to the 1980s is a combined result of the declining size of the working class and a loos-

New Labour voters: will they stay loyal?
© Alice Chadwick

ening of class attachments. This has led to a greater volatility in party support, and this, in turn, has created opportunities for a growth in electoral support for the Liberal Democrats.

Figure 20.5 also shows that the Labour share of the vote has increased since the middle of the 1980s. In 1983 it was 27.6 per cent and increased to 43.1 per cent in 1997. The share of the vote fell over successive elections from this high point, and by 2010 it was, at 29.0 per cent, only just above its level of 1983. The increase in the Labour share of the vote at the end of the twentieth century may be explained, in part, by a return of manual workers to the Labour Party, though the fall in support since then shows that this does not seem to involve the kind of unqualified support that the Party received in the past. However, the decline in the number of manual workers must mean that the rise in the Labour vote was also a result of the increasing willingness of non-manual workers to vote Labour. The Labour Party is no longer the automatic party of choice for manual workers. It is a party that can attract both manual and non-manual workers, but neither of them give it unqualified long-term support.

Figure 20.5 Labour share of the vote, 1950–2010

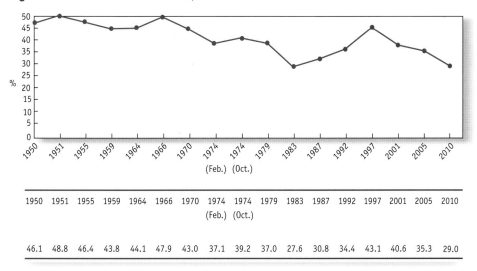

1950	1951	1955	1959	1964	1966	1970	1974 (Feb.)	1974 (Oct.)	1979	1983	1987	1992	1997	2001	2005	2010
46.1	48.8	46.4	43.8	44.1	47.9	43.0	37.1	39.2	37.0	27.6	30.8	34.4	43.1	40.6	35.3	29.0

Source: Adapted from Butler and Butler (2000: 213–16), with authors' data for 1997, 2001, 2005, and 2010.

Before we look at the reasons for this, we must examine a peculiarity of the British electoral system. As we have already shown, the governing party is the one that wins the most seats in parliament. The nature of the British constituency system is such that there is no direct relationship between the number of votes that a party receives and the number of seats that it wins. If a party's support is concentrated in particular parts of the country, it may receive a large number of votes but relatively few seats. Support for Labour, for example, was formerly very concentrated in northern working-class communities, while support for the Conservatives came from rural and more socially mixed areas. Labour could receive a large number of votes, but the concentration of these votes in particular constituencies made it difficult for it to win enough seats to win an election.

The consequences of this can be seen in Figure 20.5. In 1997 the Labour Party received 43.1 per cent of the vote and formed a government with a massive majority of 179 seats; the Conservatives received 31 per cent of the vote. In 2001, Labour received 40.6 per cent of the vote and had a majority of 166. Yet in 1970 the Labour Party had received 43.0 per cent of the vote and the Conservatives had become the governing party with a majority of 31 seats. In 1951, when its support was much more heavily concentrated in industrial constituencies, Labour received a much larger 48.8 per cent of the vote, but the Conservatives won the election with a majority of 16 seats. In 2005, Labour won 35.3 per cent of the vote, but its majority was just 66. The drop in Labour support in 2010 meant that, although the Conservatives received 36.1 per cent of the vote, they were unable to secure an overall majority and were forced into a coalition government. These figures underline the paradox that the strength of popular support for a party is not the only thing that determines its chances of forming a government. What matters is its strength relative to all other parties, and the way in which its support is spread across the country. The results of the 2010 election show that there was a much more equal pattern of voting support for the three parties—Conservatives on 36.1 per cent, Labour on 29.0 per cent, and the Liberal Democrats on 23.0 per cent—and a concentration of Labour support in Merseyside, Greater Manchester, and South Wales.

Class dealignment and issue voting

Why is there a greater willingness of people to vote for parties other than the traditional party of their class? This is a difficult question to answer. In fact, many researchers now hold that it no longer makes sense to talk about the natural party for a particular class. This belief is associated with the idea that there has been a process of **dealignment** between class and party. The concept of dealignment refers to the breaking of the automatic, socialized connection between class and party. Party support is no longer aligned with class background and class interests. This is still a rather controversial idea, but it provides a powerful explanation of electoral trends in the post-war period. Dealignment and the changing shape of the class structure have produced a fundamental transformation in the stable two-party system that existed for the first half of the century.

This trend towards dealignment is not unique to Britain. Figure 20.6 (p. 811) shows that class and politics became dealigned in all the advanced capitalist societies during the post-war period. This graph measures dealignment using the *Alford index*, a measure of association between class and party that overcomes some of the limitations of relying simply on a measure of the absolute fall in the

HAIRDRESSERS

PLEASE SIGN OUR
PETITION
AGAINST HUNTING

Younger people are increasingly turning towards new forms of political activism.

© Alice Chadwick

share of the vote going to a particular party. The decline in class voting, it can be seen, has been most marked in the United States, where the process of dealignment began much earlier, but the general pattern appears in all the advanced societies.

Voter dealignment involves two interrelated processes, which can be considered in turn. These are:

- *partisan dealignment*: a weakening of party commitment;
- *class dealignment*: a breakdown in the link between class background and political behaviour.

Partisan dealignment has generally been seen as one of the main consequences of growing political awareness. Until the 1960s, only a small minority of voters had any great awareness of political issues. Most people simply did not see politics as having any relevance for them. Political attachments were a matter of taken-for-granted commitments acquired during socialization, and they were accepted largely

unreflectively. People are now less likely to take over the political attitudes of their parents uncritically. They are more reflective about political matters and have a greater variety of sources of information available to them.

Traditional attachments, whether to Labour or the Conservatives, have been eroded by the expansion of formal education and the mass media, which supply information to people and encourage them to reflect upon political issues. Politics has become far more of a matter of choice. Manual workers, for example, are now as likely to be instrumental about their political behaviour as they are about their work and their involvement in trade unions. This does not mean, of course, that all normative and ideological commitments have disappeared: people do still have fundamental, ideologically grounded points of view. Nor does it mean that political issues are decided in a fully rational and critical way. The point is simply that ideological commitments are less strongly attached to particular political parties, and that people have a greater range of sources of information available to them in making their political choices.

Increasing numbers of voters now see themselves as uncommitted to a particular political party. They are floating voters. This is why levels of party support recorded in political opinion polls can vary so much over time and especially during the course of an election campaign. (General problems of measuring electoral support are discussed in Box 20.9, p. 812). People are pragmatic voters who make their political decisions on the basis of the perceived successes and failures of parties in relation to their policy goals. Parties are judged on their record and on their likely actions in the future.

Class dealignment is generally seen as resulting from much deeper changes. The changes in work and residential patterns among manual workers that we discuss in Chapters 13 and 19 have eroded the communal bases of solidarity that previously formed manual workers into a cohesive social class. This class solidarity had been the main structural base for working-class Labour voting. With the weakening of class solidarity, the link between manual work and Labour voting was broken.

Some commentators have linked this with the idea that consumer identities are now more salient to people than class identities. The sphere of consumption, it is argued, is now more significant to people than their involvement in work and production. In particular, a division between publicly provided services and those provided through the market creates new bases for political action. Dunleavy and Husbands (1985), for example, have contrasted the commodity-mode and the public-service-mode consumption of such things as housing, welfare, health, education, and transport.

In the past, these goods and services were closely associated with class divisions rooted in the sphere of

Figure 20.6 Class dealignment, a comparison

The Alford index

The Alford index—named after its inventor, the American sociologist Robert Alford—is the percentage of manual workers voting for left-wing parties minus the percentage of non-manual workers voting for these parties. The resulting index can vary from 0 to 100. A value of 0 occurs when voting for parties of the left is evenly spread across the population. The index rises when voting becomes more skewed. A value of 100 occurs when there is a strong association between class and party. In the unlikely event of non-manual workers showing a greater tendency than manual workers to vote for the left, the index would be negative.

This index has been criticized for using a rather crude manual/non-manual division, and alternative measures have not produced such a clear pattern. There is, however, no consensus about what a better measure should try to do. It is likely that the admittedly crude Alford index has—at the very least—shown that the class—party relationship has become less straightforward than in the past.

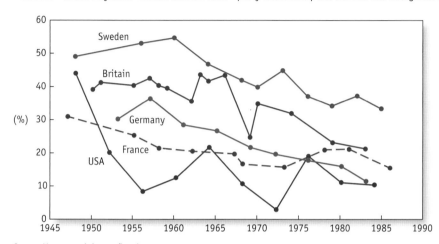

Source: Manza *et al.* (1995: fig. 1).

production. Members of the middle classes had access to private-sector housing, health, education, and transport, consuming them as commodities. Members of the working class, on the other hand, have more typically relied on public-sector provision, consuming these under bureaucratically regulated and publicly financed conditions. Increasingly, however, manual workers have come to be divided between those who remain dependent on the public sector for these goods and those who are able to acquire them in the private sector.

The attempt to cut back state expenditure and to privatize state activities has politicized these matters, and the votes of manual workers are now likely to be split according to the *consumption sector* in which they are located. Those who remain dependent on public provision will tend to support parties that defend and promote the public sector and that seek to expand public spending. Those who have easy access to private, commodified health, transport, and housing will tend to support parties that advocate restrictions on the state and an expansion of market-based provision. Affluent manual workers, it has been argued, are more likely to vote Conservative than they are to vote Labour.

According to some writers, the various consumption-sector cleavages do not coincide with one another: users of private transport may not be users of private health, and public-housing tenants may not be dependent on public-

welfare benefits. People tend to occupy a number of quite distinct consumption-sector locations, each of which gives them a distinct status situation. They are subject to the cross-cutting influences of status and class. Voting choices reflect the particular pull of these contending forces as they appear to voters in a particular election. Party support is no longer an unreflective response to shared class conditions; it is a more deliberate and calculative act of political choice in relation to considerations of status and consumption (see Box 20.10, p. 812).

It is not only consumer identities that have weakened the class–party relationship. Ascribed identities of gender, ethnicity, and sexuality have become less bound by tradition, and the growth of a more rational political culture has allowed people to re-examine the political implications of their personal identities. A growth in so-called post-materialist values, especially in the younger, post-war generation, has been seen as the basis of a concern for such issues as environmental protection, peace, citizenship rights, and the quality of life more generally (Inglehart 1990). This value shift has been linked to the growth of youth subcultures that have led many young people to abstain from voting for parties that fail to have any distinctive focus on issues relevant to them.

For all these reasons, issues have become more salient in the political sphere. Political parties have altered their

THEORY AND METHODS 20.9

Opinion polls and sampling error

In advance of each general election, and regularly through each parliament, the newspapers and the television report the results of opinion polls that claim to show the state of public support for various political parties and their leaders. These polls, like any survey, are subject to sampling error. In a survey using a random sample of about 1,000, the error is about ±3 per cent. That is, if a poll reports that Labour support in its sample stands at 37 per cent, the actual figure in the population as a whole is likely to be between 34 per cent and 40 per cent. This is as accurate as polls of this kind can be. The party lead is difficult to estimate when party support is fairly closely matched. If 33 per cent of the sample supported the Conservatives, the actual range of Conservative support would be 30 per cent to 36 per cent. So, it is just as likely that the Conservatives lead Labour by 36 per cent to 34 per cent as it is that Labour leads the Conservatives by 40 per cent to 30 per cent.

This problem with sampling error explains why polls differ from one another and why some newspapers feel that an average 'poll of polls' gives a more reliable picture. The problem is made worse if the polls are treated as predictions of the election result: questions ask about voting intentions, and, even if people tell the truth, their intentions may change between the date of the poll and the date of the election.

The calculation of the error that we have used is often used as a guideline in reporting poll results, though it is not strictly valid for non-random samples. Most polls have in the past used quota samples with face-to-face interviews. In an attempt to increase the reliability of their results, some polling organizations now use random sampling methods with telephone interviews. Computerized telephone directories or random dialling systems can be used as a sampling frame of electors, over 90 per cent of whom live in households with telephones. Random sampling helps to minimize bias and to give a precise calculation of error. Many polling organizations now use panel surveys rather than drawing a fresh sample for each survey.

Issues of bias and error are discussed in Chapter 3, pp. 92–3.

THEORY AND METHODS 20.10

Commodification and juridification

The *commodification* of services in the private sector has been contrasted with the *decommodified* or *juridified* provision of services in the public sector. These terms are used by Habermas (1973), and they are discussed more fully in Chapter 15, pp. 564–5, where we look at Esping-Andersen's work on welfare.

We go on to look at the growing importance of ascribed identities, such as those of gender and ethnicity. You might like to look at Chapters 5 and 6, where we discuss these.

These judgements are not, of course, based on a detailed consideration of the small print of election manifestos. They are, rather, shaped by the presentation of issues and the arguments of party leaders in the mass media. The central point, however, is that political behaviour is motivated by conscious attitudes and opinions about broad issues, and that people act rationally in relation to the knowledge they have about these issues (however inaccurate this knowledge might be). They are, therefore, more likely to be influenced by the discussion of issues during an election campaign and by the attempts of politicians to mobilize support around salient issues.

Rational choice and the political market

Dealignment and a growing concern for issues go a long way towards explaining the trends in Labour voting shown in Figure 20.5 (p. 809). During the 1980s, when Labour support was at its lowest, there was much talk about the need for the party to 'modernize' its image and abandon its association with class politics. The new and more politically aware voters, it was argued, would never be attracted to vote for the party unless it became more concerned with the issues that now mattered to people. A struggle ensued to change the party, and Tony Blair's New Labour was the result of the party's successful transformation from a class-based party to an issue-based party. The creation of New Labour was a rational response of the party leadership to the electoral situation that they faced.

This response can be understood in terms of the changing character of elections. Instead of involving the confrontation of rival ideologies, an election is now a competitive political market. The most powerful model for understanding this new kind of political system is that of Downs (1957). Any political party in a democratic system must compete for votes with other parties. This electoral competition means that the voter stands in the same position relative to political parties as the consumer does relative to the business enterprises that produce goods and services. Parties are the suppliers of policies and programmes,

policies and images, new parties have arisen, and politics has become much more a matter of issue voting than of class voting. Studies have shown that people are concerned about such issues as unemployment, the European Union, prices, trade unions, the National Health Service, law and order, education. The outcomes of general elections can be explained, in large part, by the changing salience of these issues and voters' perceptions of the ability of each party to deal with them effectively (Sarlvik and Crewe 1983; M. Franklin 1985).

and they must take account of the preferences of the electors. People will vote only for those parties that are able to supply them with the policies and programmes that they think will deal with the issues they judge to be the most important. From this model of the political market, Downs drew a number of interesting conclusions about party behaviour.

Voters choose between parties on the basis of their policies in relation to the issues with which they are concerned. It is, of course, unlikely that voters will have full information about the position of each party on every separate political issue. Even if they did have this kind of comprehensive information, they would be unlikely to find themselves in total agreement with one party and totally opposed to all others. Elections, however, require them to choose one party rather than another, and so voters must simplify their issue-based choices in some way. This can be achieved if each voter bases her or his voting decision on the overall image of a party as being, on balance, likely to act in a way that she or he will approve of. Downs argues that rational leaders of political parties will respond by putting together packages of policies that they believe will be attractive to the largest number of voters. These packages of policies define the images of the parties, and voters are able to make their political choice on the basis of them.

Downs shows that, where voters and parties act in the way that his model suggests, there will be a tendency for ideological differences to diminish and for parties to converge around particular policies (see also Przeworski and Sprague 1986). Specifically, he argues, party images will tend to converge towards the centre in any political system in which political views are evenly spread along a left–right spectrum. In such a system, each party attempts to maximize its votes by moving just far enough towards the centre to gain the support of a majority of the electorate. The optimum point for any party that seeks electoral victory is the mid-point in the spectrum of political opinions. Anywhere closer to the left or right than this mid-point would allow a rival party to win majority support. This argument is illustrated in Figure 20.7.

If a Labour Party with a left-wing image positions itself too far to the left—as shown in the top panel of the diagram—it will get the support of only, say, 30 per cent of the electorate. All those with views to the left of the party will vote for it, but those with views to its right are less likely to do so. This allows a rival party to position itself anywhere to its right and so gain up to 70 per cent of the votes. Rational party leaders, then, would try to position the Labour Party closer to the centre, so reducing the number of uncommitted voters. If the party moves to the position shown in the middle panel, for example, it would receive 40 per cent support. Even here, however, a rival centrist party could still gain up to 60 per cent of the votes and win the election. The only safe political position for a Labour Party that seeks to win elections, then, is the mid-point, as shown in the bottom panel. In this situation, a rival party may be able to secure an equal number of votes, but it cannot gain any more than this. Similar pressures, of course, operate on other parties, and a right-wing party, for example, would also be under pressure to move towards the centre. Downs concludes that, over time, democratic political systems will show a tendency for party images to become more and more similar as they gravitate towards the centre of the political spectrum.

Figure 20.7 Convergence to centre politics

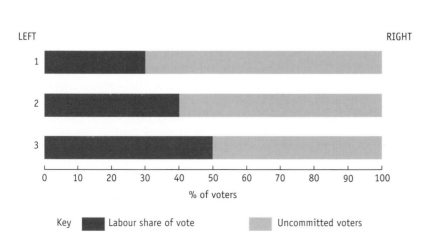

Source: *Guardian*, 12 April 1995.

This model—like any other model—can account for only a part of the political process in contemporary societies. Parties are not simply vote-maximizing machines that take the existing spread of public opinion as given and position themselves cynically wherever they can optimize their chances of electoral success. Parties are also driven by ideological considerations and by the expectations and interests of their core of committed supporters. These commitments do persist, even in a situation of dealignment, and they are important constraints on party leaders. For this reason, parties may undertake electorally risky strategies by positioning themselves in a particular ideological position in the hope that they can shift the whole climate of public opinion in their favour. As we show in Chapter 15, the Conservative Party in Britain—like its counterparts in other capitalist societies—successfully shifted public opinion towards the right during the 1980s, reflecting a wider shift of opinion that had begun during the 1970s.

Such shifts of opinion and party practice do not mean that Downs's model loses its relevance. His model still explains the electoral constraints faced by parties in a competitive system, and the idea of party convergence retains its relevance. If public opinion is predominantly oriented towards the right, parties are likely to converge towards a right-of-centre position. This, it can be argued, is exactly the situation that existed in Britain during the 1980s and 1990s. The success of 'Thatcherism' meant that a left-wing Labour Party became increasingly less likely to achieve success in general elections. Faced with the prospect of continuing defeat, there was pressure on the party leadership to relax its ideological commitments and shift towards the right. Such a strategy, of course, encounters opposition from sections within the party and from committed supporters, and the disputes that divided the Labour Party during the 1980s were focused on exactly these considerations. The successful faction in the Labour Party—the so-called modernizers—argued that public opinion was not going to swing to the left, so the party must move to the right. Any other strategy, they held, was not rational for a party that wanted to achieve electoral success.

This is, of course, a simplified model of two-party competition. Although it can explain much about politics in contemporary democratic systems (Himmelweit et al. 1985), Heath and his colleagues (1991) have shown that there is much continuity between the old class politics and the new issue politics. Neither theories of class politics nor theories of issue politics can be taken as full and comprehensive theories. It is necessary to combine the two.

The explanations of class politics proposed by Butler and Stokes (1969) and by Parkin (1967) tended to present a rather too deterministic picture. People never were simply over-socialized automatons who voted unreflectively as the bearers of deep and enduring value commitments. Working-class communities never were so custom-bound as the stronger versions of these arguments implied, and there was always a willingness to judge political issues in relation to social interests. Unless this were the case, no political change would be possible, and the Labour Party could never have established itself in the first place. The dealignment thesis, on the other hand, depicts voters as purely rational calculators who respond in a conscious and deliberate way to changes in the political marketplace. The theory ignores the continuing importance of customary and ideological commitments. People are not so cold-bloodedly rational as the stronger versions of dealignment theory imply.

Human motivation has always involved a mixture of commitment and rationality. What has changed, argue Heath and his colleagues, are the circumstances in which people find themselves and, therefore, the balance between the two types of motivation. Traditional working-class communities and patterns of work have, indeed, broken down, political awareness has increased, and the mass-media presentation of issues has become more important, but voters do still have partisan commitments that shape the pragmatic calculations that they make at election times. Labour's electoral strategy has been successful, argue Heath et al., because the party has attracted voters on the centre and the left, not because they have attracted large numbers of voters from the right. It is easier to win the votes of those who have ideological commitments that lie in the same direction as those of the party leadership than it is to win the votes of ideological opponents.

The results of the general elections since 1997 suggest that Labour successfully attracted those with traditional working-class commitments, those to the left of centre, and also a number of uncommitted and purely pragmatic voters. The scale of the Labour victories, however, was not simply a result of large numbers of former Conservative voters shifting their vote to the Labour Party. The Conservative vote fell massively, and about a quarter of former Conservative voters shifted to Labour. However, others voted for anti-European parties of the right, and many simply did not vote at all. The Labour successes were made possible, in large part, by the complete collapse in support for the Conservative Party on the part of those with ideological commitments towards the right. The emergence of the Conservatives as the dominant partners in a coalition government in 2010 reflected not a regrowth in Conservative support, but a complete collapse in Labour support. The Conservative share of the vote was actually lower than it had been in 1945, when Labour had won a post-war landslide victory.

New social movements

The class politics of the working class were expressed in a labour movement whose organizations and institutions translated economic considerations into electoral support for the Labour Party and into programmes for collective political action. The dealignment of class and politics traced in voting behaviour is associated with wider changes in patterns of collective action described as involving the rise of new social movements. By contrast with the economic and political forms of the old class-based social movements, new social movements are concerned with the promotion and change of cultural values and the construction of personal lifestyles. This has been seen as the basis of movements as diverse as those concerned with black power, women's liberation, peace and anti-war protest, and environmental protection, all of which grew rapidly in strength and radicalism from the 1950s. Politics has increasingly been defined by the issues raised in these new social movements, and writers such as Beck (1992) have argued that advanced capitalist societies have experienced a growth in 'sub-politics' outside the formal machinery of government. (See also the critical review in A. Scott 1990; and see Byrne 1997.)

A leading theorist of the new social movements has been Alain Touraine (1971, 1981, 1992), who sees them in relation to the development of a post-industrial society. Old-style class politics, he argues, reflected the conditions of an industrial society, where the basis of economic activity lay in the ownership and control of manufacturing assets. In the new post-industrial society, on the other hand, economic activity is driven by the ownership and control of knowledge-based assets. The new social movements that dominate contemporary politics have their roots in the production and consumption of knowledge and cultural values. For some, this is particularly associated with the strengthening of so-called post-material values.

Critical theory and social movements

We outline many of the problems involved in the idea of post-industrialism in Chapter 17, but it can hardly be doubted that the production and consumption of knowledge have, indeed, acquired a much greater importance in the contemporary world. This was seen early on by the critical theorists, and was given a particularly influential expression by Herbert Marcuse (1964), who is discussed in Box 20.11.

According to Marcuse, technological development had largely resolved the economic problems of capitalist production on which Marx had concentrated his attention. By making possible sustained economic growth, technological development had allowed advanced capitalist societies to generate levels of affluence that freed the majority of the

working class from material want and motivated them to acquire more and more consumer goods. They became participants in a popular, mass culture of consumption, motivated mainly by the desire to follow the consumer lifestyles promoted in the mass media. Echoing earlier ideas on mass society, Marcuse held that workers had been duped by the advertising industry and the mass media into pursuing the very consumer goods whose expanded production was the basis of capitalist growth. Their pursuit of these 'false needs', he argued, leads them to identify with the capitalist system, effectively tying them into the existing social structure and destroying any motivation that they may previously have had for opposition or protest. Class consciousness and class conflict become things of the past and the proletariat can no longer be seen as an agent of revolutionary change.

Marcuse tried to identify what new agencies of revolutionary change there might be in these new circumstances. The poor and the unemployed, he held, were excluded from the benefits and advantages of consumerism. The group that some later writers would term an 'underclass' were, therefore, a possible source of radical opposition. Their consciousness of their exploitation and oppression, he argued, would lead them to appreciate the common cause they had with the mass of exploited workers and peasants in the less developed societies of the world. Those that Frantz Fanon (1967) called 'the wretched of the earth' would replace the proletariat as the principal focus of radical change in advanced capitalism.

Marcuse did, however, identify some possible sources of change from within the structure of consumer society itself. The emptiness of mass culture, he argued, led students, whose education gave them a more critical insight into the system, to reject consumerism and to espouse an alternative culture. This was a counter-culture focused around the emotional and personal needs repressed by commercialized consumerism. Where the wretched of the earth would press for the material benefits of advanced capitalism to be spread more widely, the student movement of the 1960s had initiated a new politics of personal identity and of cultural and emotional emancipation.

These views have been extended by Habermas (1973), whose view is that the growth of state regulation over the economy has transformed purely economic divisions into politically defined divisions. Class relations are no longer experienced directly. They are latent in a more complex social structure and are experienced only through the political divisions among social categories defined by consumption-sector cleavages: divisions between taxpayers, the sick, school children, transport users, students, the elderly, and so on. At the same time, those who occupy these consumption categories have become the bases of new social movements that have replaced the labour movement as the driving force in politics. In a similar vein, Beck (1992) points to a growing 'individualization' of class relations. Class inequalities still exist, but they are no longer experienced as a shared, collective fate. Instead, class conditions are experienced in relation to individualized lifestyle differences of consumption, gender, sexuality,

ethnicity, and environmental location. These individualized differences are the bases of new social identities. The students, on whom Marcuse focused, are simply one of these consumption-sector categories drawn into opposition to the way in which society is organized. Contemporary politics is shaped by the student movement, the women's movement, the peace movement, and a whole variety of loose social groupings concerned with transport and roads, environmental matters, health and welfare, and so on.

The rise of these new social movements reflects the wider restructuring of contemporary societies. In contemporary capitalist societies, argues Habermas, economic and political activity predominate over all other spheres of social life, and all forms of action and social relationship are shaped by technical, instrumental considerations. The social relations of the family, household, and community that sustain social identities, lifestyles, and subcultures form what Habermas terms the **socio-cultural lifeworld**. They are increasingly subjected to the processes of commodification and juridification, so becoming distorted by the requirements of the economic and political systems.

New social movements: new forms of protest.

© Greenpeace/Davison

⊃ Connections

Do not worry if you find this argument difficult. Read our discussion of welfare and commodification in Chapter 15, pp. 564–5, and then return to Habermas's argument.

An example of this would be the way in which the health and welfare needs of families are now organized. Families no longer draw solely, or even mainly, on the support of wider kinship and community networks. They must rely on the often contradictory pressures of a bureaucratic system of entitlements and commercial systems of provision. In the same way, the ancient woodlands, parklands, and flood meadows of many communities are subject to contradictory pressures. They are subject to commodified market pressures for housing and road building, aimed at meeting the demands of house purchasers, private motorists, and commercial road hauliers, but they are also influenced by the bureaucratic procedures of the planning and regulatory systems.

A political culture of what Habermas calls 'civic privatism' and 'familial-vocational privatism' encourages political involvement only through the ballot box, not through direct participation, and it encourages an overriding orientation towards consumption, career, leisure, and status. The political issues on which people can vote in general elections are confined to a relatively narrow range. There is no real possibility of considering the fundamental social issues inherent in consumption-sector cleavages. The political system is insulated from any effective popular participation, despite the formal democratic constitutions that have been introduced. The formulation and expression of concerns generated within the socio-cultural lifeworld are suppressed. Nevertheless, this suppression cannot be complete, and alternative cultural and political forms do arise. These are the new social movements that emerge outside the framework of conventional politics.

These social movements are of two types:

- *defensive* social movements;
- *offensive* social movements.

A *defensive* movement emphasizes a romanticized, traditional way of life seen as being undermined by contemporary economic and political changes. This is found, Habermas argues, in conservative and fundamentalist social movements that stress the particularistic, ascriptive solidarities of gender, age, and nation. An *offensive* movement, on the other hand, aims to reassert the autonomy of the socio-cultural lifeworld by transforming it. This is found in the radical social movements that aim to liberate people from economic and political repression and to open up greater possibilities for democratic participation and the formation of autonomous identities.

For Habermas, then, the old social movements of class and interests have increasingly been replaced by new social movements. These are 'post-class' movements concerned with the politics of identity. Many of these new social movements combine both defensive and offensive responses. Feminism, for example, he sees as an offensive movement aimed at overthrowing male dominance and establishing a politics of difference. At the same time, however, it also has a defensive orientation, in so far as it roots itself in what are seen as essential female characteristics and the subordinate position of women in the nuclear family. This dual orientation, argues Habermas, underpins the many political divisions within the women's movement.

In the same way, Habermas sees the peace, anti-nuclear, and ecology movements as combining defensive and offensive orientations: they are radical movements of social change that promote greater participation in political decision-making, but they retain a concern for protecting a traditional or 'natural' environment (see A. Scott 1990: 75–8). A concern for community and environment, as we show in Chapter 16, pp. 629–35, may express a fundamentalist reaction to the central principles of economic and political rationality.

Peace, poverty, and protest

The characteristics of a new social movement have been interestingly highlighted by Roseneil (1995) in her investigation of opposition to the United States Air Force Cruise missile base at Greenham Common, near Newbury (see Box 20.12, p. 818). The defining characteristic of this opposition to the installation of nuclear weapons was that it was organized and sustained by women, who linked their anti-nuclear stance to an explicitly feminist position.

The camp began almost by chance, following a women's peace march to the airfield. The idea of a women-only camp became the focus for constructing a collective identity for the participants as they began to engage in new forms of collective action. They saw themselves as engaged in an anti-nuclear campaign, as participants in a community of women and a community of lesbians (though many participants were not lesbians), and as involved in an enjoyable, 'fun' way of life. They were tied together as participants in a way of life that was organized around autonomy, non-violence, respect for individuality and difference, care for the environment, the pursuit of pleasure, and an emphasis on emotional and spiritual concerns.

Roseneil argues that the camp would not have been possible if there had not been a transition from private to public patriarchy (Walby 1990). The legal and economic powers of husbands that had been central to private, family-based patriarchy were reduced in the years following the Second World War as more women entered the public world of employment. In so doing, however, women entered new kinds of patriarchal relations that were

THEORY AND METHODS   20.12

Research at Greenham Common

As a young participant in the peace camp set up at Greenham Common in 1981, Sasha Roseneil had first-hand experience on which to draw in her research. She combined this with interviews undertaken between four and ten years later, when she had trained in sociology and had decided to carry out systematic research on the topic. Contacting those whom she had known at the camp, she constructed a snowball sample of other participants to interview. These data were supplemented with documentary sources, such as diaries, newsletters, and newspapers.

Roseneil used a method of triangulation, but the core of her work drew on her own participation. Look at our discussion of participant observation in 'Ethnographic research', Chapter 3, pp. 81–4, and consider its implications for Roseneil's work. You can find her account in Roseneil (1995).

❓ Is personal experience of an issue or problem an advantage or a disadvantage to a researcher?

---

integral to the institutions of the market and the state. Women did, however, gain some financial autonomy by their entry into employment and from their improved access to welfare benefits. This financial autonomy was crucial in allowing them to travel to Greenham Common and spend time at the camp. Once the peace camp had been established by its founders, participation was a realistic option for those who wished to be involved. A raising of consciousness was achieved in the context of close interpersonal relations at the camp that led the participants to value other women's company much more highly than they had done before.

The collapse of the Soviet Union, on which the Cruise missiles had been targeted, led to the eventual decommissioning of the base and the closing of the peace camp in 1994. While the camp itself ended, the consciousness achieved and the social networks established continued to be highly valued by the participants. Involvement in the campaign had brought them into contact with groups and organizations concerned with other and related issues. Many of the women went on to become involved in anti-militarist, environmental, and animal-rights groups, in campaigns against sexual violence, and in a whole range of other political activities.

Experience of participation in this way of life helped women to politicize their sense of identity and, in many cases, to forge a distinctively feminist political consciousness:

> ... at Greenham many women experienced, often for the first time in their lives, a sense of real participation in decision-making and social life, a feeling that their opinions mattered, deserved expression and would be taken seriously .... For many women, reflection on this, mediated by the feminist discourses to which they became exposed at Greenham, contributed to a new consciousness of men's domination of political and social life, even within the peace movement and radical groups.

Roseneil 1995: 145

Political globalization has generated a globalization of protest. Networks of states and transnational agencies have become more important agents at the global level, and particular nation states must operate within a framework set by such bodies as the United Nations, the International Monetary Fund, the World Bank, the World Trade Organization, and many other such bodies. Since the 1970s, issues of environmental control and economic development have been discussed through a series of summits, international conferences, and commissions.

These international meetings have come to be seen by activists concerned with environmental problems as places where they need to express their views and to lobby the various transnational agencies and their sponsoring nation states. The World Trade Organization and the G8 group of advanced economies have been central to these meetings and have become the foci for global protest. Anti-globalization protesters who link globalization to international inequality and environmental damage have organized marches and campaigns at these meetings, and on such occasions as May Day. The greatest level of conflict has been apparent at the World Trade Organization meeting in Seattle in 1999 and the G8 meeting in Genoa in 2001, but violent protest and police counteraction has been apparent in London, Milan, Prague, Barcelona, and other major centres. Huge protests were organized for the July 2005 summit, to coincide with a rally and other events for the 'Make Poverty History' campaign. The mass media cover these events, but you will find more first-hand information (of varying reliability) on the alternative news media such as www.Indymedia.org. These forms of opposition are what Arrighi *et al.* (1989) have called 'antisystemic' protest movements.

Environmentalists have been involved in a number of protests against the building of new roads in areas of established countryside since the 1980s. Following the Twyford Down and Solsbury Hill protests, in which many of the Greenham Common activists were involved, the most notable in the last years of the twentieth century were at Newbury and Fairmile (near Exeter). The Fairmile protest camp was set up in an attempt to block the construction of a new trunk road in east Devon. It involved conventional camping arrangements (tents and prefabricated huts), together with a series of tree houses and a network of tunnels and underground defensive bunkers. The protests ended with bailiffs, acting for the authorities, dismantling the camps and evicting activists. The tunnels and the tunnellers proved particularly difficult to remove, and the attempts drew much publicity for the campaign. In early 1997 many of the veterans of the Newbury and Fairmile protests moved on to a new tree house and tunnel camp to protest against the proposed runway extension at Manchester airport. The protest was unsuccessful and the new runway went into use in 2001. Public-spending cuts

during the late 1990s reduced the level of the road-building programme and there have been fewer anti-road protests since then. Much recent environmental protest has been linked to concern over climate change and the impact of airports and air travel on carbon emissions. Direct action groups such as Plane Stupid have had short-term successes, most recently grounding planes at Stansted Airport after breaching perimeter security (see www.planestupid.com).

Stop and reflect

In this section we have looked at the end of class politics and the development of new forms of politics and protest. Party politics in Britain and the United States has become more pluralistic since the 1950s.

● In elections, there has been a process of dealignment: weakened party commitment and a weakened class–party link.

● Consumption divisions and issues of status now have a greater significance in politics.

● Electoral support for the Labour Party declined for much of the post-war period. Renewed electoral success was associated with the adoption of a new image.

● Pressures in contemporary electoral systems tend to result in party convergence towards the centre ground.

● Does the end of class politics mean that class is no longer an important social division? You might like to look back at our discussion in Chapter 19, pp. 771–81, when you have considered this question.

Outside the electoral system, new social movements and direct action now play a great role.

● New social movements tend to be organized around issues of consumption and personal identity, and in relation to post-material values.

● What examples of significant new social movements can you think of?

Key concepts

● class for itself 788
● counter-hegemony 790
● dealignment 809
● dominant ideology 790
● dual consciousness 790
● elite 791
● false consciousness 789

● governing class 797
● hegemony 790
● labour movement 788
● political elite 791
● power bloc 801
● power elite 792
● revolution 789

● ruling elite 791
● socio-cultural lifeworld 816
● state elite 801
● state socialism 804
● totalitarianism 802

Workshop 20

Study 20 Political discourse

Max Atkinson (1984) used the techniques of conversation analysis and the ideas of Goffman to examine politicians' speeches. His aim was to show how successful politicians had acquired techniques for building up support among those in their audience. By following particular rules of language use, politicians could ensure that their listeners applauded, laughed, and cried at appropriate times and so came to identify with the message that was being put across. Speaker and listener were drawn into a shared world of ideas and values, and politicians could, for example, reinforce people's sense of national identity and their willingness to support particular policies. These skills are particularly well developed in the great charismatic leaders who have been able to mobilize mass audiences: Lenin in Russia, Hitler in Germany, Churchill in Britain, and Martin Luther King in the United States. At more mundane levels, these techniques have become part of the stock-in-trade of all successful politicians.

The rules of language that they use are not consciously learned and applied, although, since the publication of Atkinson's book, the techniques that he describes have been taught to politicians and have allowed them to become more conscious, and more cynical, in their use of these speaking skills.

These ideas can best be seen in the techniques used for drawing applause during a speech. The standard length of a burst of applause, Atkinson shows, is eight seconds (plus or minus one second). Both audiences and speakers have internalized understandings about when it is appropriate to clap and for how long. This makes it possible for a speaker to manipulate the audience and 'milk' the applause. The fact that audiences begin to clap at points where an argument is completed, and that they come in just before the final words, allows an effective speaker to structure his or her speech in such a way as to emphasize completion points and so maximize the effects of the applause. The speaker supplies the appropriate cue for applause.

Atkinson recognizes a number of techniques for doing this, which he calls 'claptraps':

1 *Projecting a name*. This claptrap has three stages: identify the person (pause), describe him or her (pause), and announce the name. This lets the audience know who is to speak and cues them to clap when the name is announced. The claptrap may be preceded by a 'Now' or a 'However' to indicate that something special is about to happen.

2 *Lists of three*. Lists of three (rather than two or four) appear to be complete without being over-long. The third item is widely recognized as a completion point for applause. Politicians will talk of the need for 'purpose, strategy, and resolve' or shedding 'blood, sweat, and tears'. Such lists can also be combined with pauses for effect: 'We bring this before you (pause), at conference (pause), this week'. They can also be used in repetition for effect and to produce memorable soundbites. The oppositional chant 'Maggie, Maggie, Maggie—Out, Out, Out' is one example, as are the claims for 'Education, Education, Education' or to 'Spend, Spend, Spend'.

3 *Contrastive pairs*. This involves making a contrast between two statements. The speech is constructed so that the audience will agree with both parts of the contrast, and they come in with their applause at the end of the third statement. Examples are 'It is one thing to . . . , but it is quite another to . . . ', or 'It is right to . . . , but it is wrong to . . . .'

The best chances of applause, Atkinson argues, are when these various tricks are combined in a single speech or section of a speech, as each reinforces the others. They can also be combined with body language that signals the key points. The truly charismatic speakers, he argues, are the effective, if unconscious, users of these techniques.

➔ Look at the text of a political speech and see if you can spot any of these techniques. You will find these printed word-for-word on the party websites: www.conservative-party.org.uk; www.labour.org.uk; www.libdems.org.uk.

➔ Record a political speech from a television news broadcast or documentary. Search for evidence on the frequency with which the various techniques are used. Which politicians seem to be the most effective in the use of these techniques?

❓ Can you find any other examples of common 'claptraps' or rhetorical devices in political speeches?

Media watch 20 Political protest

Several thousand protesters have taken part in a demonstration in central London against the conflict in Iraq. The route took protesters along Whitehall and into Piccadilly before reaching Hyde Park for a rally. . . . Police said about 10,000 people took part, but Stop The War Coalition said up to 100,000 were protesting (http://news.bbc.co.uk/1/hi/england/london/4275542.stm).

Tens of thousands of people packed downtown Washington yesterday and marched past the White House in the largest show of antiwar sentiment in the nation's capital since the conflict in Iraq began. The demonstration drew grandmothers in wheelchairs and babies in strollers, military veterans in fatigues and protest veterans in tie-dye (www.washingtonpost.com/wp-dyn/content/article/2005/09/24/AR2005092401701.html).

Anti-war rallies in Britain, the United States, and elsewhere took place simultaneously on 24 September 2005, as protesters in a loose alliance of social movements took to the streets. Although members of various political parties were involved, the protests and demonstrations were not controlled by the major parties but were loosely coordinated by a variety of social movements. The aim of the rallies was not to contest an election or gain parliamentary power but to change the climate of public opinion and influence political leaders from outside the conventional framework of politics. Such rallies have continued in subsequent years.

Earlier in the summer of 2005, almost a quarter of a million protesters converged on Edinburgh for a march under the banner 'Make Poverty History', and many went on a few days later to protest outside the meeting of the G8 group of nations at Gleneagles (see the coalition website at **www.makepovertyhistory.org**). The protests were spearheaded by Bob Geldof but brought together many established pressure groups and new social movements, as well as thousands of people without formal political connections. It has been estimated by the BBC that around 200 separate groups were involved in the protest (**http://news.bbc.co.uk/1/hi/uk/4234811.stm**). The protest forms part of a global network of protest organizations.

❷ How influential can such protests be? Does the fact that world poverty is still a reality and foreign troops are still involved in Iraq show that such protest can never be successful? Look at the official government response to the Make Poverty History protest (http://webarchive.nationalarchives.gov.uk/+/http://www.dfid.gov.uk/news/files/mph-conditionality.asp). Are you convinced by the response? Does this show that the protest was successful?

❷ How reliable is media coverage of these protest events? Look at the unofficial news reports and comments on the Iraq anti-war protests at www.indymedia.co.uk. Would you put greater reliance on these sources than on coverage on the BBC and in national newspapers? You might like to collect newspaper cuttings on the next major political protest and to follow its course through the national media and the various unofficial websites.

Discussion points

Ruling elites and ruling classes

- What do you understand by the terms: ruling class; ruling elite; and dominant ideology?
- Was Marx correct to describe the modern state as 'the executive committee of the bourgeoisie'? What do the 'power lists' at the beginning of the chapter tell you about this?
- What forms of political power have emerged in post-Communist Russia? Can the political leadership still be described as a ruling elite? As capitalism develops in these societies, will we see the development of a ruling class?

Voting and elections

- How would you distinguish between issue politics and class politics? Has class disappeared as an important factor in politics?
- Look at Figures 20.1 (p. 794) and 20.5 (p. 809), which give data on the share of the vote going to Labour. Compile a similar graph of the share of the vote going to the Conservative Party. The results of an election are influenced by the turnout (the proportion of the total electorate who actually vote). Would you expect to find different results in a graph of the

proportion of the total electorate voting for each of the parties? You will find Butler and Butler (2000) a useful source for the information that you need.

- Collect the election addresses and manifestos of the main political parties. Can their views and policies be arranged along a line from left to right? Is there any evidence for convergence in policies?

- Are the results of local elections shaped by the same factors as national elections?

Social movements and social protest

- What do you understand by the term new social movement?

- How useful is it to distinguish between defensive and offensive social movements?

- Collect newspaper cuttings on environmental protests (for example, opposition to a new bypass or an airport extension) or on animal-welfare campaigns. What evidence do these give you on the class, age, gender, and ethnic backgrounds of participants?

- Is the labour movement a thing of the past? Is politics now becoming the politics of protest and the new social movements?

Explore further

Good introductions to the issues of power and politics that we have looked at in this chapter can be found in the following books:

Bottomore, T. B. (1993), *Elites and Society* (2nd edn, London: Routledge & Kegan Paul). *A very good summary of the main themes in elite theory. Follow this with two attempts to use elite and class concepts to explore power in the United States (Domhoff 2006) and Britain (Scott 1991).*

Domhoff, G. W. (2006), *Who Rules America? Power, Politics, and Social Change* (New York: McGraw-Hill).

Scott, J. (1991), *Who Rules Britain?* (Cambridge: Polity Press).

Denver, D. (2002), *Elections and Voters in Britain* (Basingstoke: Palgrave). *A good, up-to-date summary of data and debates.*

Scott, A. (1990), *Ideology and the New Social Movements* (London: Unwin Hyman). *A handy summary of some of the key theoretical issues raised in studies of new social movements.*

Roseneil, S. (1995), *Disarming Patriarchy: Feminism and Political Action at Greenham* (Buckingham: Open University Press). *An*

excellent piece of ethnographic work that really gives the sense of what it means to be involved in a social movement.

For more depth on some of these issues, look at the following:

Miliband, R. (1969), *The State in Capitalist Society* (London: Weidenfeld & Nicolson). *A classic early statement of the ruling-class model.*

Sarlvik, B., and Crewe, I. (1983), *Decade of Dealignment* (Cambridge: Cambridge University Press). *An influential statement of the dealignment thesis. Crewe was one of the first to appreciate its importance.*

Heath, A., Jowell, R., and Curtice, J. (1985), *How Britain Votes* (Oxford: Pergamon). *A counter argument to Sarlvik and Crewe (1983). Also very good.*

Lane, D. (1996), *The Rise and Fall of State Socialism* (Cambridge: Polity Press). *A readable account by one of the leading scholars in the area.*

Online resources

Visit the Online Resource Centre that accompanies this book to access more learning resources and other interesting material on power, division, and protest at:
www.oxfordtextbooks.co.uk/orc/fulcher4e/

The official websites of government and parliament, containing many reports and official documents, are:
www.direct.gov.uk/Homepage/fs/en

and

www.parliament.the-stationery-office.co.uk

You can find party political information at the websites of the principal parties:
www.conservative-party.org.uk

www.labour.org.uk
www.libdems.org.uk

An interesting website that contains network charts and diagrams of the American power elite is:
www.theyrule.net

Useful sources on environmental social movements can be found at Richard Kimber's site at Keele University:
http://www.politicsresources.net/area/uk/environ.htm

Glossary

Concepts in *blue italic* are entries in the glossary.

Absolute mobility The total level of social mobility, upwards or downwards, in the occupational hierarchy of a society. The raw measure of overall movement. Distinguished from *relative mobility*.

Action approach An approach to development that sees it as dependent on local initiatives.

Action frame of reference Term used by Parsons to describe the particular system of concepts that allows us to talk about human social action, rather than about physical events or biological behaviour. Used generally to describe the common elements in all action and interaction theories.

Adaptation In Parsonian theory, one of the four fundamental needs of a social system. It is the need to accumulate resources from the environment so that they are available for future actions. (See *function*.)

Addiction Occurs where people have become physiologically dependent on the use of a particular drug and so suffer serious and persistent withdrawal symptoms when its use is stopped. Addiction has a biological basis, but is shaped by social factors.

Aestheticization The greater significance of culture in the design of products, as image and appearance become more important than function.

Aesthetic labour Work that involves the embodiment of certain capacities and attitudes to do with the appearance of the employee.

Age cohort A category of people who are born at the same or similar time and who, therefore, undergo *life course* transitions at the same time.

Alienation In Marxian theory, a concept that designates the way in which the economic relations under which people work can change their labour from a creative act into a distorted and dehumanized activity.

Analytical realism The philosophical basis of Parsons's sociology. Involves a recognition that all observations are dependent on theoretical concepts but, at the same time, tells us something about what the world is actually like.

Anatomo-politics An aspect of a *disciplinary society* that involves controls over the individual body. A form of power that shapes the capabilities and skills that can be used in social action.

Anomie In Durkheim, this refers to a state of normlessness, an absence of social regulation by shared norms. In Merton it was extended to refer to a discrepancy between culturally prescribed goals and the culturally approved means for their attainment.

Assets The total stock of economic resources that a person or household has been able to accumulate. May be physical or financial assets and often generate an income.

Assimilation The process through which an ethnic minority takes on the values, norms, and ways of behaving of the dominant, mainstream group and is accepted by the latter as a full member of their society.

Authoritarian populism The generation of popular support for strong law-and-order policies by the manipulation of popular anxieties about crime and disorder.

Authority A form of organized power where those who rule or make decisions do so on the basis of a legitimate right to issue commands and to expect obedience. It is particularly characteristic of bureaucratic administration.

Awareness contexts Term used in the study of death and dying to refer to the kind and degree of understanding that patients, relatives, and medical staff have about a person's medical condition. Glaser and Strauss recognized four different awareness contexts in hospitals: closed awareness, suspected awareness, mutual-pretence awareness, and open awareness.

Back regions In Goffman, this refers to those places where people feel that they can avoid the gaze of an audience and so feel that they can relax and act in ways that may be contrary to the image that they are trying to present in public.

Bar chart A type of graph or chart in which variables are represented as horizontal or vertical bars. The lengths of the bars correspond to the totals shown in the columns or rows of a table.

Base In Marxian theory, the foundation, or substructure, of a society. Refers to the economy and class relations that are organized into a particular *mode of production* and that are the basis for the social *superstructure*.

Bias Statistical term for the discrepancy between any actual *sample* and one that would have resulted from a purely random process of selection. It results from the way in which selection is carried out. The degree of bias in a sample is difficult to measure with any precision. The extent to which an unbiased sample differs from a completely representative sample is termed 'error'. Error can be measured and controlled.

Biological determinism The idea that all aspects of human behaviour can be explained in terms of the universal and innate constitutional and genetic characteristics that people have as human beings.

Biopolitics Foucault's term for control over whole populations. A form of power that shapes demographic factors—births, deaths, and marriages—through statistical investigation, public health, and controls over migration.

Bisexuality A category of sexuality applied to those who engage in sexual acts with both men and women.

Bourgeoisie One of the two principal social classes in Marxian theory: the *capitalist class*.

Bureaucracy A type of *organization* characterized by: a division of labour based on specialist expertise; a hierarchy of officials; regulation by impersonal rules; the disciplined conduct of duties.

Capitalism An economic system in which economic activity is financed by the investment of capital in the expectation of making a profit. According to Karl Marx, its key features were the private ownership of the *means of production* and wage labour.

Capitalist class (see also *ruling classes*) In Marxian theory, the class that owns the means of production in a *capitalist society*. It is the privileged class that oppresses and exploits the *proletariat*, or *working class*, occupying the leading positions of political power.

Capitalist society A form of society in which the private ownership of the means of production is the basic driving force. The economy is organized around a system of market exchange in which there is a class division between those who own the means of production (the *capitalist class*) and those who work as wage labourers (the *working class*).

Carceral organization A term used by Michel Foucault to describe organizations that cut off their inmates from contact with the outside world and subject them to regimes of isolation and surveillance.

Career deviance A form of *deviance* in which those who engage in the deviance pursue a specific structured role that involves a typical sequence of events and experiences that is common to all in that role.

Caste A type of social stratum in a system of social stratification in which status privileges based in ideas of ritual purity and pollution separate ethnic groups from each other. This system is characteristic of traditional India, but the concept has also been used to describe the situation of African-Americans in the southern states of the United States.

Causal explanation A form of analysis in which the origin and development of a social phenomenon are the primary concern. Those prior events or conditions without which an event would not have occurred are its causes. To identify the causes of an event is to explain it. Durkheim contrasted this with *functional analysis*.

Citizenship The rights and obligations attached to full membership in a society. Generally seen as involving civil, political, and social rights stressing *equality*. Recent work in race and ethnic relations has also stressed the idea of cultural citizenship and *multiculturalism*, while work on sexuality has stressed intimate citizenship, as expressed in the politics of the gay and women's movement.

City The first cities were concentrations of population that carried out specialized religious, political, and economic functions for their surrounding areas and controlled these areas. The industrial cities that emerged first in the nineteenth century were seen as having a distinctive *urban way of life* because of their large size, high density of population, and social diversity.

Civil religion A system of beliefs in which the secular world itself is given a sacred character. Typically focused around ideas of national identity and the rituals that surround national institutions.

Class for itself A *social class* whose members have become conscious of their shared interests and whose social *solidarity* predisposes them to support a political movement that promotes their interests.

Class situation A position in the capital, product, or labour markets that forms a specific causal component in people's *life chances*. Formed through the economic relations through which control over marketable resources is organized for the attainment of income, assets, and other life chances. It also determines the interests that people have in protecting and enhancing their life chances.

Class society A form of society in which *class situations* are the most important determinants of individual *life chances*.

Client control A system of medical organization in which aristocratic or other patrons, rather than medical experts, determine the conditions under which medicine is practised.

Closed (structure of inequality) A structure of inequality in which people's chances of social mobility are tightly constrained by their social origin and where, therefore, rates of mobility are low.

Cognitive interests In the work of Habermas, this refers to the particular social interests that shape people's needs for knowledge. He recognized interests in technical control, practical understanding, and emancipation.

Cohabitation An unmarried couple living together.

Cohort Those born within a particular period of years.

Collective consumption A term used by Manuel Castells to refer to those goods and services consumed by workers that were not obtained on an individual basis but supplied by the state.

Collective representations In Durkheim's theory, these are the shared images and ideas that people hold about the moral obligations that bind them together as members of their society. They often have a sacred character.

Command situation A position in a structure of *authority* that is a specific causal component in people's *life chances*. Creates interests in the maintenance or enhancement of powers of command.

Command society A form of society in which *command situations* are the most important determinants of individual *life chances*.

Commodification The process whereby aspects of life are turned into 'things' with a monetary value that can be bought and sold on the market.

Communitarianism A movement of those who believe that welfare should be based on the mutual support provided by members of a local community through local institutions and organizations.

Community A community consists of a group of people who have some aspect of their lives in common, engage in common activities and collective action, and have a shared and distinctive sense of identity.

Conscience collective In Durkheim's theory, a French term for the symbols and ideas that sustain social life and underpin the social order. Refers to both the consciousness that is shared by the members of the society and the moral ideas that form their consciences.

Content analysis A method for analysing *documents* that involves counting the number of times that particular words or images appear. Its aim is to measure the significance of the particular ideas conveyed in words and images.

Conversation analysis A research method that examines the structure of natural conversations in order to investigate the rules and procedures that are involved in organizing communications and accounting for actions.

Corporatism The *incorporation* of the leaders of trade unions, and employers' organizations, in the process of developing and implementing government policy.

Correspondence principle The argument, put forward by Bowles and Gintis, that education provides an appropriately motivated and compliant labour force for the capitalist employer through social relationships at school which match those found in the work situation.

Counter-hegemony Forms of economic, political, and cultural consciousness that are organized into a social movement that challenges the *hegemony* of a *ruling class*. Gramsci saw counter-hegemony as being produced by a *working class* that is organized as a *class for itself*.

Covert research A research method in which a sociologist is a hidden observer or a complete participant. People are not aware that they are being observed for research purposes.

Craft crime Small-scale, skilled theft, such as that of pickpockets, cutpurses, and confidence tricksters.

Crime That form of *deviance* that involves an infraction of the criminal law.

Cult A loosely organized religious grouping without any sharp boundaries and with no exclusive system of beliefs. Cult beliefs are open and flexible. The term is often used, however, in a pejorative sense to refer to a tight and exclusive *sect* of whom the writer disapproves.

Cultural capital This concept, associated with the work of Pierre Bourdieu, refers to the cultural advantages of those who have assimilated the dominant culture of the society, advantages that lead to superior educational performance, which can be translated into occupational and financial success.

Cultural determinism A theoretical position that holds that all social phenomena are shaped by culture, and by culture alone. The contrary doctrine to *biological determinism*, which sees social phenomena as shaped exclusively by biological factors.

Cultural-deprivation theory The theory that working-class children have been disadvantaged in education by values and beliefs that hold them back rather than any financial or other material disadvantages.

Culture The beliefs of a society and their symbolic representation in creative activities. Sometimes used in a broader way to mean way of life.

Custodial parenthood The placing of responsibility for the care of children with one parent after separation or divorce.

Cyberculture A culture that has a purely electronic existence in the cyberspace created by the Internet.

Dark figure In any statistical measure, but especially in statistics of crime, this is the hidden and unmeasured level of what is being measured. Crimes reported to the police and acted upon by them—and that are measured in official statistics—form only a small proportion of the total amount of crime that actually occurs.

Dealignment A breakdown in the relationship between *social class* and *party* in voting behaviour, that was formerly produced through *socialization*. Generally seen as involving partisan dealignment (a weakening of party commitment) and class dealignment (a breakdown in the link between class background and political behaviour).

Death trajectory A socially learned set of expectations concerning how a dying patient should approach their death. A role that is expected of a dying person.

Debureaucratization The reversal of bureaucratizing tendencies by the development of non-bureaucratic organizations to perform the tasks previously carried out by bureaucracies.

Decarceration The process of shifting from the imprisonment of deviants to their treatment or punishment in the community.

Decommodification The process whereby aspects of life, typically health, education, and welfare in general, are removed from the market-place and provided by the state.

Democracy Literally rule by the people, but usually taken to mean a political system where government is carried out by the freely elected representatives of the people.

Democratization The process by which representative assemblies with political power emerge and the vote is extended to all adults.

Demographic transition A population trend associated with industrialization and involving three stages: a period of high death rates and high birth rates; a period of falling death rates; and, finally, a period of low death rates and low birth rates.

Denomination A church that is organized around voluntary rather than compulsory membership and a separation between church and state. A denomination is tolerant towards other religions and is willing to coexist with them.

Dependency theory The theory that economic domination by the developed societies prevents *development* elsewhere by keeping other societies in a relationship of economic dependence.

Deskilling Reducing the skill required to carry out work tasks, by breaking them down into simpler tasks or introducing machinery that can be operated with less skill.

Development Used sometimes to refer to the broad historical process through which modern institutions are acquired but, when used in the context of the ex-colonial societies of Africa, Asia, and Latin America, usually taken to mean economic growth.

Deviance Nonconformity with social norms or expectations. Deviant behaviour is behaviour that is seen as counter to the norms of specific social groups.

Devolution The decentralization of government by a nation state to subnational units.

Diaspora Population movements involving a global dispersion from an original homeland.

Disability A disadvantage that is caused for the physically impaired by particular forms of social organization. Distinguished from *impairment*.

Disciplinary society Foucault's term for a form of society in which there is a growing concern to secure the human base of national wealth through the introduction of new forms of social power over human biology. He identifies these forms of power as *biopolitics* and *anatomo-politics*.

Displacement of goals When the means to an end become the end itself, as when obedience to the rules becomes a goal in its own right, rather than a means of enabling an organization to achieve its goals.

Division of labour In economics, a distribution of work tasks. Durkheim broadened this into the more general idea of the differentiation of occupations and social positions of all types. Central to the social *solidarity* of modern societies.

Documents Objects that contain written texts. Documents may be hand-written, printed, or electronic.

Domestic division of labour Usually refers to the division of labour between a person primarily concerned with earning money through paid work and a person primarily concerned with housework, though it can also be used to refer to the division of household tasks between them.

Domestic labour All work concerned with the maintenance of the household, including housework and domestic production, but not including *homework*.

Dominant culture The culture of the ruling class, which enables it to dominate subordinate classes.

Dominant ideology The class consciousness of a dominant or *ruling class* when formed into a systematic set of *values* and ideas transmitted through the mass media, the churches, and the educational system. Used in a very similar way to *dominant culture*.

Double burden The notion that women in paid employment continue to carry full responsibility for housework and childcare.

Drift Movement in and out of a particular form of behaviour, generally applied to movement in and out of deviant activity. Behaviour becomes stabilized as 'deviant' when it becomes *secondary deviation*.

Dual consciousness In Gramsci's theory, a description of *working-class* consciousness. On the one hand, workers are subject to *hegemony* expressed in a *dominant ideology*. On the other hand, they develop an autonomous consciousness rooted in their everyday practical experiences.

Dynamic density In Durkheim's theory, a term referring to an increase in the number of social relationships and, therefore, in the amount of communication and interaction among members of a society.

Ecclesia A church that is organized around compulsory membership and that claims spiritual authority over all who live within a particular territory. It has a systematic dogma and is intolerant of other religions.

Education Those aspects of the socialization process that take place through formal instruction in organizations and institutions specialized in providing this instruction.

Elaborated codes A term used by Basil Bernstein to describe speech patterns that make meanings explicit by spelling out in relatively long and complex sentences what people intend to say. They are the opposite of *restricted codes*.

Elite Any social group occupying positions of *authority*, especially within states and large economic organizations.

Embourgeoisement A theory that suggests that the manual *working class* in contemporary societies has become more affluent and more 'bourgeois' in outlook and so has merged into an enlarged middle class.

Emigration The movement out of a country of people who intend to settle elsewhere.

Emotional labour The use of specific techniques to control the emotions that must be expressed as an integral part of a particular process of labour.

Emphasized femininity A term used by Connell to describe the dominant femininity. It corresponds to *hegemonic* *masculinity* but is not itself hegemonic because it is subordinate to the dominant masculinity.

Equality A condition in which all members of a society are equal to one another in one or more measurable respects. Includes *equality of opportunity*, *equality of outset*, and *equality of outcome*.

Equality of opportunity A condition in which entry to all social positions is governed by criteria of *universalism*: they are open to all on the basis of merit, rather than being limited by birth or social background.

Equality of outcome A condition in which all members of a society enjoy the same standard of living and *life chances*.

Equality of outset A condition in which all start out from similar positions in the competition for advantages, as in a competitive race.

Ethnicity A general category for describing collective identities. Ethnic groups are defined by their sense of sharing a distinct culture that can be traced back to the historical or territorial origins of the group.

Evolution Introduced into biology by Spencer and Darwin, who argued that biological species develop through a constant struggle for existence in which only those best adapted to their environment can survive. Spencer applied the idea to the development and change of societies, which he saw as surviving only if they were well adapted to their environment.

Extended family A family unit that extends beyond the *nuclear family* of parents and children.

False consciousness For Marx, this was the misunderstanding that characterizes much *working-class* thought and that results from the effects of a *dominant ideology*. People fail to understand the real conditions under which they live and act.

Family A much-debated term, often defined as a social group based on marriage, biological descent, and adoption. We have put forward the less exclusive definition of a small group of closely related people who share a distinct sense of identity and a responsibility for each other that outweighs commitments to others.

Feminism A movement to end inequalities between men and women and overthrow the male domination of society.

Fertility The actual rate of birth found in a particular society or individual. Measured through the crude birth rate or through age-standardized birth rates.

Finance capital A term used by those who argued that the control of industry passed from industrial to financial hands as banks and financial corporations became the effective owners of companies.

Fiscal crisis The notion that the increasing burden of taxation in order to finance the welfare state brought about a crisis of capitalism.

Flexible firm The term used by John Atkinson to describe companies that have adapted to greater economic uncertainty and increasing competition by using labour in a more flexible way.

Focus group A group of individuals brought together by a researcher to be interviewed as a group. Consisting usually of between four and ten individuals, the focus group is a useful way of exploring people's responses to the challenges of others and for uncovering how attitudes and opinions are arrived at through discussion with others.

Folk culture In pre-industrial societies the oral and craft culture of the people, as contrasted with the *high culture* of the elite.

Function The part played by something in relation to the overall structure and continuity of a society or social group. Functions have often been seen in relation to the presumed needs of social systems. This is a central idea in structural functionalist theory.

Functional analysis A form of analysis in which the effects or consequences of an event for a society are the primary concern. Durkheim contrasted this with *causal explanation*.

Functionalism The theoretical perspective that explains institutions in terms of the functions that they perform for the society as a whole.

Gatekeepers Those who control access to resources.

Gender Expectations of the way that men and women are expected to feel, think, and behave.

Gendering Process through which knowledge and practices are shaped by patriarchal relations that embody male power over women (or, much more rarely, the opposite). The knowledge or practices come to be associated with or to reflect the concerns of those socialized into specific *gender-roles*.

Gender order A term used by Connell to refer to the overall hierarchy of masculinities and femininities in a society.

Gender-role Specification of the way in which men and women are expected to feel, think, and behave.

Generalized other A term introduced by George Mead. It refers to the image that children build up in their minds of the attitude of people in general towards them and their behaviour. It is built up as they consider the likely reactions of others and it becomes the voice of their moral conscience.

Generation A kinship group defined by parent–child relationships, so that grandparents, parents, and children each form, with their cousins, a distinct generation.

Global city A distinct group of cities which are the headquarters of transnational corporations and global financial operations.

Globalization The spread of relationships and organizations across the world, bringing about a growing awareness of the world as a whole.

Glocalization The interpenetration of global and local processes of change.

Goal attainment In Parsonian theory, one of the four functional needs of a social system. It is the need to mobilize existing resources in relation to individual and collective goals.

Governing class A particular alignment of power between a *capitalist class* and the exercise of political *authority*. A looser form of the Marxian idea of a *ruling class*.

Health transition Parallel to the *demographic transition*, a trend in health associated with industrialization and involving three stages: a period of epidemics and high rates of acute infectious disease; a period of concentrated infectious disease and improving public health; and a period of enhanced medicine, greater longevity, and high rates of chronic degenerative disease.

Hegemonic masculinity A term introduced by Connell to refer to the dominant set of ideas about how men should behave, which establish the superiority of the male.

Hegemony Gramsci's term for the political and cultural dominance that corresponds to the economic dominance of a *capitalist class* and other *ruling classes*.

Heterosexuality A category of sexuality introduced in the nineteenth century to describe the sexual orientation of those who engaged in sexual acts with the opposite sex.

Hidden curriculum This refers not to the content of the formal school curriculum but the values, attitudes, and behaviour patterns instilled through the organization and social relationships of the school.

High culture The culture of the elite, associated with the arts. Generally contrasted with *folk culture*.

Historical materialism Term applied to Marxian theory to describe its emphasis on history as the transition from one *mode of production* to another. Sometimes seen as implying that such economic changes are the *base* upon which changes in the political and cultural *superstructure* are produced.

Homework Paid work carried out at home for an outside employer, including telework but not waged *domestic labour*.

Homosexuality A category of sexuality introduced in the nineteenth century to describe the sexual orientation of those who engaged in sexual acts with persons of the same sex.

Household A person or group of people, who share facilities, living in a particular residential unit.

Housing classes The notion, put forward by Rex and Moore, that ownership of domestic property was as important in determining class situation as the ownership of industrial property.

Human-relations school An approach to the management of labour which was based on meeting employees' non-economic needs and recognized the importance of the work group in determining productivity.

Human resource management (HRM) An approach to management that emphasized that the employees of a company were its most important resource.

Hybridity A 'mixed' *social identity*. The concept comes from post-modern theories that highlight the way that the constant reconstruction of identities combines meanings that may be logically incompatible. A social identity may, therefore, be an unstable synthesis of diverse ideas.

Hypothesis A suggested relationship between two or more factors that can be tested against evidence.

Idealist Often contrasted with *materialist*, this is the view that moral *values* and ideas are central to the formation of customs and practices in a society. Also applied to the more general philosophical position associated with this.

Ideal type Weber's term for scientific concepts, seen as logical, ideal constructions from one-sided, *value*-relevant standpoints.

Ideologies Forms of consciousness and knowledge that are shaped by the material conditions under which people live. Marx saw these as reflecting the conditions of particular *social classes*.

Illness Any perceived departure from a socially recognized condition of health and that is subject to medical treatment. It is not simply a biological or physical condition but depends on what physiological and mental states are regarded as 'normal' within a particular society.

Immigration The movement into a country of people who intend to settle there.

Impairment Exists when someone has a defective bodily part such as a limb or an organ, including the brain. Distinguished from *disability*.

Incarceration Isolation of people from the wider society, as in their confinement behind walls.

Income The flow of resources that a person or household receives in a particular period. Contrasted with *assets*.

Incorporation The process of removing opposition to a ruling class by including representatives of those who are ruled in the key institutions of a society.

Industrialism The organization of production on the basis of the concentration of labour in large workplaces, a specialized *division of labour*, and a separation of management from labour.

Industrial society A form of society that is organized around the achievement of material well-being through an expanding *division of labour* and an industrial technology of production.

Inferiority complex A sense of *self* in which people compare themselves to others and come to see themselves as inferior or as a failure.

Inflow mobility A measure of social mobility. The proportion of individuals within a particular category who have come from specific other categories. Typically applied to occupational mobility and contrasted with *outflow mobility*.

Information society A society in which knowledge is the main resource.

Insanity role A form of the *sick role*. It is performed when people act in terms of particular images of mental disorder, acting as those who label them expect them to behave.

Institutional racism Where a racialized ethnic group is systematically disadvantaged by the ways in which social institutions operate, even if these have not been built around explicit racist ideas. Racism is inscribed in the institutions and practices themselves.

Institutionalization of industrial conflict The increasing organization and regulation of industrial conflict, so that it is expressed within an institutional framework.

Institutions Established practices that regulate the various activities that make up social life, but sometimes used in the same way as *organizations*.

Instrumental orientation An orientation to work that sees it solely as a means to obtaining an income and not as a source of any intrinsic meaning or satisfaction.

Integration In Parsonian theory, one of the four functional needs of a social system. It is the need to ensure the cohesion and *solidarity* of the social system itself.

Interest group A group organized around the pursuit and promotion of specific *interests*. Examples are trades unions and political parties. Dahrendorf and other conflict theorists have stressed their origins in particular *social classes*.

Interests Those things that are advantageous to someone, given his or her social position. Individuals may not always be aware of their own interests and so may act in ways that disadvantage themselves. Marxists have stressed the importance of the interests that people have as members of *social classes*.

Internalization The process through which people learn the expectations that define particular *roles* and make them an integral element in their own personality and motivation. They become an inner source of commitment rather than an external source of constraint. Occurs through *socialization*.

Intersex Refers to those who cannot be unambiguously assigned to one sex or the other on the basis of their anatomy and biology.

Joint parenting The placing of responsibility for the care of children after separation or divorce with both parents.

Juridification The provision of welfare through legal entitlement and administrative procedures, as a result of *decommodification*.

Kinship A network of relatives (kin) who are connected by common descent or by marriage.

Labelling theory A theory of deviance that derives from *symbolic interactionism*. Holds that it is the fact of being labelled as a deviant by the members of a powerful or dominant social group that makes action deviant.

Labour movement A network of trade unions, pressure groups, and political parties that together comprise a social movement that pursues the interests of a *working class*.

Latency In Parsonian theory, one of the four functional needs of a social system. It is the need to build up a store of motivation and commitments that can be used, when required, for all the various activities of a society.

Legitimacy The recognition that the rulers of a society have authority by right rather than by power alone.

Lesbianism A label applied to women who engage in sex acts with other women but also used to refer to a sisterhood of women without any necessary implication of sexual activity.

Life chances The opportunities that a person has to acquire income, education, housing, health, and other valued resources. They are the basis of social inequalities.

Life course Sometimes referred to as the life cycle. The process through which a person or family passes through common changes in life stages, such as infancy, childhood, adulthood, and old age. The stages of life are not biologically given but are socially constructed and so can be quite variable from one society to another.

Life history A format for interviewing that follows a biographical pattern, following the key stages in a person's life. More generally, the *narrative* that a person produces to account for the events of their life and their current situation.

Line chart A graph in which trends and patterns over time are shown by a simple line that connects the points that represent the separate values.

Managerialism A theory that points to the disappearance of the *capitalist class*. It suggests that a growth in managerial and executive occupations has reduced the power of those who own the capital.

Managerial revolution The theory that the fragmentation of share ownership shifted power from those that owned companies to those that managed them.

Market situation A position that a person occupies in the capital, product, or labour markets and that is the basis of their class situation. For members of the *working class* this is their position as employees earning a wage through labour.

Marketization The process of returning publicly provided goods and services to the market-place and introducing market mechanisms to public services.

Mass culture The commercialized and standardized popular culture produced by industrialization, replacing the *folk culture* and undermining the standards of *high culture*.

Mass media Media which can reach large numbers of people, a term often used to imply that they enable the manipulation of the population by those that rule a society.

Mass society The atomized society of isolated individuals, which, according to some theorists, such as William Kornhauser, resulted from the decline of community after industrialization and urbanization. Atomization made it easy for political leaders to manipulate people.

Materialist Often contrasted with *idealist*, this is the view that the struggle over unequally distributed economic resources is central to the way of life in a society. Also applied to the more general philosophical position associated with this, including *historical materialism*.

Means of production The workplace, machinery, and raw materials that made production possible. The private ownership of the means of production was, according to Karl Marx, a key feature of *capitalism*.

Mechanical solidarity In Durkheim, this is the form of social *solidarity* characteristic of undifferentiated, communal societies. Characterized by strong integration and regulation.

Media (Plural of medium) Means of communication that mediate between those who provide information and those who receive it.

Media imperialism The continued domination of the Third World by the developed world through the *media*. Often used to refer specifically to their domination by American capitalism and associated with the Americanization of culture.

Medical gaze A term introduced by Foucault to describe the specific way of seeing and acting towards their patients adopted by trained doctors. It involves specific forms of investigation, teaching, and clinical intervention, building on an image of the sick body as an object in need of expert technical care.

Medicalization The process through which more and more areas of life become subject to the *medical gaze*. Matters that used to be seen as the responsibility of priests, social workers, or teachers, or that were left to the individual concerned, come to be seen as 'medical' matters.

Melting pot Based on the idea of *assimilation*. A view of the city as a place where different ethnic migrants mix freely and are, over time, forged into a common social identity.

Meritocracy A system in which there is a close association between individual merit and social achievement. An open educational system is the means through which occupational recruitment and mobility take place.

Model A simplified picture of a situation or process, expressed in words and/or diagrams, that shows how its various elements are connected to each other.

Mode of production The technical and human resources of production and the specific property relations and *division of labour* under which they are used. Marx saw history as a succession of modes of production: primitive, ancient, Asiatic, feudal, and capitalist.

Modernization theory The theory that *development* takes place through the diffusion of values, attitudes, and technology from developed to undeveloped societies.

Moral career The internal and personal aspects of a career. The specific sequence of learning experiences and changes in conceptions of self and identity that occur as people follow their career. Widely used in studies of *career deviance*.

Moral panic An exaggerated media reaction to deviant behaviour, which has the effect of amplifying this behaviour by drawing attention to it. This concept is particularly associated with the work of Stan Cohen.

Mortality The actual rate of death found in a particular society or individual. Measured through the crude death rate or through age-standardized death rates.

Multiculturalism The demand that the diversity of ethnic cultures within a society should be respected and equally valued in official policy and in everyday life. Recently described as cultural *citizenship*.

Narratives The biographical accounts that people construct to account for their actions as they construct and reconstruct their own biographies, drawing selectively on their memories and on the cultural stock of acceptable explanations. Narratives tend to follow a number of standardized forms.

Nation A people with a sense of identity, a common language, and a distinct culture, which may or may not correspond to a *nation state*.

Nation state A political unit based on the claim that its citizens are members of a nation that lives within defined borders.

Nationalism The belief that a *nation* has the right to self-government through its own *nation state*. Also the belief that national identity and the obligations of national citizenship should take precedence over those of any other social unit or group that a person belongs to.

Negotiated order The notion that the implementation of the rules of an *organization* is not imposed but depends on negotiation between the various parties involved.

Neo-conservatism The 'new conservatism' of the 1970s and after which reasserted traditional beliefs in morality, 'the family', and the maintenance of law and order.

Neo-liberalism The 'new liberalism' of the 1970s and after which returned to the beliefs in the freedom and responsibility of the individual and the market provision of goods and services that characterized the *dominant ideology* of early nineteenth-century Britain.

New vocationalism The 1980s movement to make education more relevant to the occupational requirements of the economy and the job needs of students.

Normalization This occurs when deviant behaviour is defined as something that is marginal to the identity of the deviator: it is treated as 'normal'. The behaviour remains a matter of *primary deviation*.

Norms Rules of behaviour. Often used in conjunction with *values*.

Nuclear family Usually defined as a family unit consisting only of parents and children, though, according to Edward Shorter, its key feature is not so much a matter of which family members are present as its separation from the wider society, its focus on domestic life, and the emotional quality of its relationships.

Observation As a research method this involves watching people and listening to them in order to collect naturally occurring data about what they do and what they say. A sociological observer can take the role of the complete participant, the participant-as-observer, or the complete observer.

Occupational mobility Movement from one occupation to another. Measured as *inflow mobility* or *outflow mobility*.

Occupational transition A trend describing stages in the process of industrialization. In the agrarian period the *primary sector* is dominant; in the industrial period the *secondary sector* is dominant; and in the advanced industrial, or post-industrial, period the *tertiary sector* is dominant. Linked to the *demographic transition* and the *health transition*.

Open (structure of inequality) A structure of inequality in which people's chances of social mobility are relatively independent of their social origin and are shaped by, for example, their education. Characterized by relatively high rates of mobility.

Operationalization The process through which a theoretical concept is converted into a more concrete and measurable indicator that can be used in empirical investigations.

Oppositional subculture A term used by Paul Willis to refer to the emergence in schools of a set of beliefs and practices that rejected the values and authority of the dominant culture.

Oral history A form of interviewing in which the aim is to uncover people's recollections of events through which they have lived and to construct a picture of their shared memories of the past.

Organic solidarity In Durkheim, this is the form of social *solidarity* characteristic of differentiated societies and produced by interdependence in a *division of labour*. Involves moderate levels of integration and regulation and a high degree of individualism.

Organization A structure for carrying out a particular activity, with a specified goal, a defined membership, rules of behaviour, and authority relationships.

Orientation to work The attitudes to work that workers bring with them to work, as opposed to attitudes formed at work.

Outflow mobility A measure of social mobility. The proportion of individuals who have moved out of the social category from which they began their lives. Typically applied to occupational mobility and contrasted with *inflow mobility*.

Overt research A research method in which a sociologist is open about the fact that ethnographic research is being undertaken and that they are trying to obtain relevant information. The researcher's role tends to be that of the participant-as-observer.

Own Goffman's term for those who share a deviant identity and so have a common understanding of stigmatization from their personal experiences. The own help people to organize a life around their deviance.

Parentocracy A term used by Phillip Brown to contrast the growing belief in the middle class that people should use their resources, through the exercise of choice, to get the best possible education for their children with the *meritocratic* belief that educational success should be a result of ability and effort.

Particularism A system that restricts opportunities to particular social groups and categories. Sometimes seen as a system based on ascription rather than achievement.

Party Any group that is united around a particular cause or interest and that claims to represent particular strata or social categories in the political sphere. Political parties are particular types of party concerned with competing for positions of power within a state.

Patriarchy Has come to mean male domination, though its original meaning was domination by the father.

Perfect mobility The level of social mobility in a completely *open* system of *meritocracy*. A statistical measure of perfect mobility is used as a yardstick to assess the extent to which actual systems are *closed* and limit mobility on the basis of a person's social origins.

Performativity A term used by Butler to refer to the bodily inscription of sexual differences through the repeated performance of gendered behaviour.

Personal identity A person's identity as a unique and distinct individual. Marked off by a personal name that individualizes someone and distinguishes them from all others who may share their *social identity*.

Phenomenology A philosophical approach that aims to describe the contents of people's subjective experiences of the world. It has inspired a number of interaction theories that explore the social construction of reality in everyday life.

Pie chart A circular graph divided into segments. If the area of the whole circle is made to represent a total figure, then the area of each segment, or slice, represents the share of the total belonging to a particular social group or category.

Polarization The sharpening division of a class structure between the two poles of wealth and poverty.

Political elite Those who hold positions of *authority* within a state. May form the core of a *ruling elite*.

Popular culture The culture and way of life of ordinary people, as contrasted with an elite *high culture*.

Positivism Comte's term for knowledge that is disciplined, empirical, and scientific, free from religious or political bias. Involves an emphasis on rational, critical thought and the use of evidence. Often misused as a term to denigrate quantitative and survey research.

Post-adolescence Stage in life when people have become relatively independent of their parents but have not yet assumed the responsibilities of adult life.

Post-Fordism A term used to describe the more flexible methods of production focused on product innovation, diversity and quality, and requiring multi-skilled and highly committed employees, that some claim have succeeded Fordist mass production.

Post-industrial society The notion, particularly associated with the work of Daniel Bell, that the shift of economic activity from the production of goods to services means that knowledge has become the prime resource in an *information society*.

Post-modern city A term used to describe the decentralized and fragmented contemporary city, where the economy is based on the production, distribution, and consumption of images.

Post-modern organization A collective term for organizations with flexible structures that contrast with the Weberian model of *bureaucracy*.

Post-modernism Theories of the post-modern see modern societies as based upon an industrial technology and a high level of structural integration. They hold that social theory should no longer focus on overarching structures, but should, instead, recognize the fragmentation and diversity in cultural and social life that comprises a distinctive post-modern condition.

Power bloc   An alignment of social classes that have certain shared interests and concerns and a common focus on the exercise of state power.

Power elite   Mills's term for a *ruling elite* defined by its dominance in the political, economic, and military hierarchies.

Primary deviation   Behaviour that runs counter to the normative expectations of a group and is recognized as deviant behaviour by its members, but which is tolerated or indulged as an allowable or permissible departure from what is normally expected.

Primary groups   Groups involving face-to-face interactions between their members, who see each other as individuals. These are usually contrasted with *secondary groups*.

Primary identities   *Social identities* built up through *primary socialization*, especially identities of personhood, gender, and ethnicity.

Primary sector   Occupational sector comprising work in agriculture, mining, and quarrying that is directly involved with the production and extraction of raw materials and basic resources.

Primary socialization   *Socialization* that takes place in infancy and childhood, typically within a family or a small household of carers.

Privatism   Involvement in social relations that are concerned exclusively with the private or domestic sphere of the home and family.

Privatization   The transfer of ownership of manufacturing or services from the public to the private sector.

Probability sampling   A method of sampling in which it is possible to calculate the probabilities of selecting any particular type of person or event. Includes simple random, systematic random, stratified random, and other forms of sampling.

Professional control   A system of medical organization in which doctors, as medical experts, are able to determine the conditions under which they practise their medicine.

Project crime   Large-scale robbery and fraud that involves the cooperation of teams of people. Includes forms of bank robbery, train robbery, and drug-trafficking.

Proletarianization   The process through which the occupants of intermediate *class situations* are transformed into wage labourers, becoming part of the *proletariat*.

Proletariat   One of the two principal social classes in Marxian theory: the *working class*.

Public sphere   A space where people can freely discuss matters of general importance to them as citizens. The theory of the public sphere is particularly associated with the work of Jürgen Habermas.

Queer theory   A theory of sexuality that rejects the commonly held idea that there are distinct and biologically determined sexual orientations.

Questionnaire   A printed list of questions used in a social survey.

Race   A purely social construct, based on the observed physical and cultural characteristics of individuals (such as skin colour). Use of the term in everyday life rests on beliefs in the significance of supposed biological differences that are seen as determining social differences.

Racialization   Process through which ethnic identities and group boundaries are defined in specifically racial terms.

Racism   Those structures and processes of disadvantage and inequality that are built around a *racist discourse*.

Racist discourse   A whole set of shared ideas about 'race' and racial difference.

Rationalization   In Weber's theory, a shift from value-rational actions to instrumentally rational actions. Refers to the cultural changes and changing social practices that this involves. Most generally, a shift from traditional and customary outlooks to rational and calculative ones.

Reconstituted families   Families brought together through the marriage or cohabitation of couples with children from previous relationships.

Relative autonomy   As used by Marxist writers, the notion that the existence of different sectional interests within capital enables the state to arbitrate between them and act in the long-term interests of capital as a whole.

Relative mobility   That part of total or *absolute mobility* that results from the degree of openness in an occupational structure. Measures of relative mobility disregard movement that is due to changes in the occupational structure and look at the mobility chances of one group compared with another. Sometimes called social fluidity.

Relative poverty   A condition where people follow a way of life that is deprived relative to the standard of living that is customary or accepted as normal in their society. They are unable to pursue the rights and obligations of *citizenship* to the full.

Reproduction of class   This refers to structures and processes that perpetuate the existing class structure and maintain the advantages and disadvantages of those in different class situations.

Reproduction of labour   This concept has been used in two different ways, to refer to the provision of the essential housing, feeding, and health care needed by workers, and to refer to the production of disciplined and obedient workers. They have in common the idea that the supply of labour to meet the requirements of the capitalist employer is not an automatic process but requires particular institutions and practices.

Research design   The planning of a research project. At its most general level this involves translating general ideas and concerns into specific and researchable questions. Decisions must be made about the methods, the purposes, the style, and the strategy of the research.

Reserve army of labour Originally applied by Karl Marx to the unemployed, who were available to expand production but also kept wages low through their availability for work, but then applied to married women, who can be seen as performing the same functions, by Veronica Beechey.

Residual rule-breaking This is deviation from rules that relate not to specific kinds of interaction and relationship, but to the very nature of social interaction itself. According to Scheff, schizophrenia is rooted in residual rule-breaking.

Respondent In a survey, the person who responds to the questions on a *questionnaire*.

Response rate The proportion of the members of a *sample* who respond to a survey.

Restricted codes A term used by Basil Bernstein to describe speech patterns in which meanings are implicit and relatively short and simple sentences, using few words, are used. They are the opposite of *elaborated codes*.

Revolution Radical political and social transformation. Sometimes seen as a violent overthrow through mass collective action, but can also include longer-term and peaceful processes of radical structural change.

Risk society Society in which there is an increase in technologically and socially generated dangers, as against purely natural disasters. This encourages the growth of a 'risk consciousness', a predisposition to express anxieties about these dangers in the language of risk.

Roles The normative expectations attached to particular social positions. These define the ways in which people are expected to behave. The normative expectations provide a 'script' for appropriate social behaviour.

Role-taking In role-learning theory, people are seen as taking on culturally given roles and acting them out in predetermined ways. *Symbolic interactionism* contrasts this with more active processes of role-making.

Ruling classes In Marxian theory, the dominant social class in a society. In *capitalist society*, it is a *capitalist class* that forms the ruling class by holding all the key positions in the leadership of the state.

Ruling elite A social group that occupies the leading positions of *authority* in all the major social institutions of a society.

Sample A selection of people drawn from the larger population that is being studied. A properly selected sample allows the researcher to generalize about the whole population and its subgroups. Although usually discussed in the context of survey research, much ethnographic and documentary research also involves sampling and selection.

Science A systematic investigation that is carried out through observational methods and guided by theory.

Scientific management A technique of management based on the subdivision of tasks, the measurement of the time taken to complete them, the training of workers in the exact movements required, and payment according to the amount they produce.

Secondary deviation *Deviance* proper. Occurs when deviations are not normalized but are stigmatized or punished in some way. Social reaction becomes a central element in the deviant's identity.

Secondary groups Large social groups where relationships are distant and impersonal, and their members interact on the basis of their specialized roles rather than individual characters. Usually contrasted with *primary groups*.

Secondary identities *Social identities* acquired during *secondary socialization*, especially identities associated with work, leisure, consumption, and politics.

Secondary sector Occupational sector comprising work in manufacturing occupations that produce finished consumer goods and machinery.

Secondary socialization *Socialization* that begins in later childhood and continues into later life. It is the process through which people build up their knowledge of a broader range of social skills and acquire a more detailed knowledge of roles outside the family.

Sect A body of people whose religious beliefs diverge from those of others within the same religion. Claims a monopoly of religious truth, but is voluntary and involves a high level of emotional commitment.

Secularization The declining significance of religion in public life. It involves a *disengagement* of religion from public institutions and a *disenchantment* or 'desacralization' of life. Religious belief becomes a purely private and personal matter, and it loses much of its spiritual character.

Segmental relationships These are relationships based on specialized roles rather than an all-round knowledge of a person.

Self A person's sense of his or her own uniqueness or individuality, built up from a person's impression or image in the eyes of others.

Self-presentation The techniques through which people represent themselves, as a particular kind of person, to others with whom they interact.

Self-provisioning Obtaining goods and services by do-it-yourself means.

Semi-structured interviews An interview in which the interviewer has a checklist of topics and questions to be explored. The way that these topics and questions are approached and the order in which they are taken depends on the flow of conversation rather than following a predetermined order.

Serial monogamy The increasingly common practice of moving through a series of marriages.

Service class Managerial, professional, and administrative workers in advantaged *market situations* and involved in the exercise of delegated *authority* in the workplace. They serve the interests of the large-scale organizations within which they work.

Sex The physical and anatomical characteristics that are held to distinguish men from women.

Sexism A complex of structures and processes of discrimination and inequality that are built around sexist ideas, ideas in which gender categories and stereotypes play a central part.

Sex-role Has the same meaning as *gender-role*, though this has tended to supplant it, because sex-role implies that the behaviour of men and women is shaped by their sex rather than by gendered expectations.

Sexuality The activity that people find physically arousing and those aspects of identity, lifestyle, and community associated with this activity.

Sick role A *role* that defines the ways in which people who are ill should behave so as to minimize the disruptive effects of their illness on ordinary social life. Through their knowledge of the sick role, people learn how to be ill in socially acceptable ways.

Significant other An interaction partner who is highly important emotionally and whose roles may be taken over and explored in, for example, play.

Slavery A system of production in which workers are treated as the property of those that employ them, and can therefore be bought and sold.

Social capital The educational and occupational advantages resulting from the membership of networks and the knowledge of how to profit from them.

Social class A type of social stratum in a system of *social stratification* in which people owe their *life chances* to the *class situations* that they occupy. Property and market divisions are central to social class division.

Social differentiation The specialization of activities into a complex structure of separate, but interlinked, spheres of activity. Typically involves the building of a *division of labour*.

Social estate A type of social stratum in a system of *social stratification* in which people owe their *life chances* to status ideas of superiority and inferiority.

Social facts Durkheim's characterization of the distinctively social level of explanation. Social facts are ways of thinking, feeling, and acting that are collective, rather than purely individual, and can be regarded as external to individuals and as constraining them.

Social identity A particular label that has been applied to someone in order to indicate the type of person that they are.

Social stratification The division of a society into strata or layers that lie one above another in a hierarchy of advantaged and disadvantaged *life chances*.

Social structure Stable and enduring patterns that exist within a social group and shape the behaviour of its members. Structural-functionalist writers see the structure of a society as a normative framework, as the institutionalized expectations that govern people's actions. Marxists and conflict theorists see the structure of a society as the actual social relations that arise from the distribution of resources and involve the inequality and domination that condition people's actions. Social structure has to be seen as comprising both institutions and relations.

Socialization The process through which someone learns how to be a member of a particular society. It is through socialization that people learn specific skills and abilities and what kinds of people they are.

Society Most commonly used to refer to the totality of social relationships within a national population, as in British society, but often used loosely to refer to any social unit, from a local group to 'global society'.

Socio-cultural lifeworld In Habermas, the social relations of family, household, and community that sustain social identities, lifestyles, and subcultures.

Sociological imagination According to C. Wright Mills and Anthony Giddens, the special quality of mind required by the sociologist.

Socioscapes Local societies where there are routine, everyday interactions between people who belong to different networks and have little in common except the fact that they live in the same area.

Sociospheres The largely separate worlds of those who interact in a *socioscape* rather than a local *community*.

Solidarity The factor of cohesion in a society that results from the integration of individuals into social groups and their regulation by shared norms. Durkheim distinguished between *mechanical solidarity* and *organic solidarity*.

Spirit of capitalism A system of beliefs that encourage the accumulation of income and assets through productive activity.

State The complex of institutions and organizations that maintain order, develop and implement policy, collect taxes, provide political representation, and manage a country's external relationships.

State elite The occupants of the leading command situations in the government, parliament, civil service, military and paramilitary, and judicial apparatuses that together make up the state system.

State socialism A system in which the pursuit of social and economic *equality* is achieved through a centralized, state-directed promotion of economic development. Often seen as a form of *totalitarianism*.

Status situation A position in a hierarchy of prestige, of superiority and inferiority, that is a specific causal component in people's *life chances*. Formed through the communal relations through which prestige is accorded to a particular lifestyle and so becomes a determinant of life chances.

Status society A form of society in which *status situations* are the most important determinants of individual life chances.

Style of life The way in which people carry out the tasks associated with their most important social positions and the customs and practices that they follow as members of particular societies.

Stylization The design of products to fit the requirements of style rather than function.

Subcultures The values, beliefs, and way of life of particular, usually subordinated, groups within society. Often contrasted with the *dominant culture*. The term is generally used to refer to youth cultures or the cultures of subordinate classes. The concept of subculture, which essentially means an 'under-culture', implies the existence of a dominant culture, a notion similar to that of *dominant ideology*, which we discussed above.

Superego A term introduced by Sigmund Freud to refer to a child's internalization of the attitudes and prohibitions of its parents. It is the basis of the 'conscience', of the child's sense of right and wrong, and becomes an important element in its control over its own behaviour.

Superstructure In Marxian theory, the political, legal, and customary social institutions that arise on the *base* of a society.

Surveillance A concept introduced by Foucault to describe some of the key mechanisms of a *disciplinary society*. It involves the collection and processing of information on individuals through censuses and surveys and through physical observation.

Sustainable development *Development* which does not damage the environment in ways that will reduce the prospects for development in the future.

Symbolic interactionism Body of theory associated, in particular, with George Mead and developed at the University of Chicago from the 1920s to the 1950s. Centres on the idea that people act on the basis of their definition of the situation and that social reality is nothing other than the social constructions built up in interaction.

Tertiary sector Occupational sector comprising work in service and commercial occupations that distribute consumer goods and that provide banking and insurance services.

Textual analysis A method for analysing documents that involves grasping the qualitative, rather than the quantitative, significance of the words and images used in a text.

Third way The notion, associated with New Labour, that an alternative should be found to the policies of both the 'old left' and the 'new right'.

Third World The notion that ex-colonial societies formed a distinct world that would find its own path to modernity, avoiding the evils of the routes taken by the capitalist 'first world' and the socialist 'second world'.

Total institutions A term popularized by Erving Goffman for *organizations* that took control of their inmates by stripping them of their identities.

Totalitarianism A system in which all aspects of life are regulated by the state and everything is subordinated to the collective goals set by a *ruling elite*. Often involves the use of terror and force, and places great restrictions on individual freedom.

Totemism A form of religion in a clan or segmental society. Each clan is identified with a particular animal or plant, which serves as its emblem or totem.

Transnational corporation (TNC) A company that produces goods and/or services in more than one country.

Triangulation The combination of diverse research methods in order to illuminate different aspects of what is being studied.

Unconscious Drives and desires that are rooted in human biology and that motivate people's actions may be denied or suppressed, causing emotional energy to build up to form an unconscious part of the mind that Freud called the 'id'. Human personality involves a struggle between the id and the conscious ego.

Underclass The truly deprived and disadvantaged, who are excluded from any effective participation in mainstream society. The term has often been used in political discourse, however, as a pejorative label that blames the victims of poverty for their own deprivation.

Underdevelopment The reduction of levels of *development* in the rest of the world by the industrial societies. This concept is particularly associated with the work of André Gundar Frank.

Understanding The inference of people's subjective meanings from observations of their actions. It involves a degree of empathy that will allow an interpretation of their actions to be built.

Underworld An urban criminal area that forms an occupational community for criminals and that has established *values* and norms of its own. Often termed a subculture of crime.

Union density A way of measuring the degree to which a labour force is unionized by calculating the proportion of employees who are members of unions.

Universalism A system that treats all people in the same way, without any consideration of their particular or unique characteristics. Often seen as a system based on achievement rather than ascription.

Urban ecology This refers to the approach to the study of the city, associated with the Chicago school of sociology, which treated it as though it were a natural environment, in which species competed for dominance.

Urbanization The growth of cities and the shift of population from rural to urban areas.

Urban way of life A term particularly associated with Louis Wirth, who argued that the distinctive features of city life, notably large and dense populations, and a highly specialized division of labour, resulted in *segmental relationships* and the formation of *secondary groups*. People lived isolated lives in the city and urban society was weakly integrated and unstable.

Values Cultural beliefs and ideas that have a normative or moral character, specifying what is good and what ought or should happen in particular societies. For sociologists such as Parsons, a value consensus is central to any society; for sociologists such as Marx, societies are more likely to be divided into class-based value systems or *ideologies*. Weber saw all sociological concepts as value-relevant, as reflecting the values of those who produced them. Often used in conjunction with *norms*, as in the 'norms and values of a society'.

Virtual communities Communities that exist in a purely electronic form through interactions on the Internet.

Wealth The opposite of poverty (*relative poverty*). Because of their *income* and *assets*, the wealthy are able to enjoy *life chances* and lifestyles that are superior to those that are recognized as normal for citizens in their society. Wealth is the basis of privilege.

Welfare pluralism The provision of welfare by many different agencies, such as charities and other voluntary bodies, rather than by the state.

Welfare state Used sometimes to mean simply welfare provided by the state, but also more specifically state welfare that is universal in character, i.e. provided for the whole population of a society.

White-collar crime Offences carried out by those in the middle classes. It includes occupational crimes of the affluent, organizational crimes, and any other crimes committed by the relatively affluent that tend to be treated more leniently than those of the less affluent.

Wise Goffman's term for people who are not involved in deviant activity but who are, nevertheless, in the know about the secret life of those who are. They are sympathetic and supportive towards the deviants, even though they are not a part of their *own* group.

Work situation Together with *market situation*, it defines the *class situation* of a person. It is a person's position within the organizational setting of a system of production, especially their involvement in the exercise of or their subjection to *authority*.

Workfare The principle that welfare policy should be designed to get people off state benefits and into paid employment.

Working class In Marxian theory, the class that in *capitalist society* is propertyless and must seek employment in the labour market in order to secure a living from their wages. They are exploited by a *capitalist class*, which benefits at their expense.

World economy Used by Immanuel Wallerstein to refer to a *world system* that has multiple political centres but is integrated economically.

World empire Used by Immanuel Wallerstein to refer to a *world system* that has a single political centre and is integrated by a bureaucratic structure.

World system Used by Immanuel Wallerstein to refer to a social unit that includes a complete range of specialized activities in a *division of labour*.

World-accommodating religion A religion that adopts an attitude of mild disapproval or of acceptance of the world as it is.

World-affirming religion A religion that embraces many of the central cultural goals and *values* of a society but claims to offer new means to achieve them.

World-rejecting religion A religion that denigrates the central values and assumptions of a society and attempts to establish an alternative way of life.

Xenophobia Extreme hatred of foreigners.

Bibliography

Aaronovitch, S. (1961), *The Ruling Class* (London: Lawrence & Wishart).

Abbott, P., and Wallace, C. (1990), *An Introduction to Sociology: Feminist Perspectives* (London: Routledge).

Abercrombie, N. (1996), *Television and Society* (Cambridge: Polity Press).

Abercrombie, N., and Warde, A. (1992) (eds), *Social Change in Contemporary Britain* (Cambridge: Polity Press).

Abercrombie, N., Turner, B. S., and Hill, S. (1979), *The Dominant Ideology Thesis* (London: George Allen & Unwin).

Aberle, D. F., Cohen, A. K., Davis, A. K., Levy, M. J., and Sutton, F. X. (1950), 'The Functional Prerequisites of a Society', *Ethics*, 60.

Acker, J. (1989), 'The Problem with Patriarchy', *Sociology*, 23/2.

ActionAid (2004), *Power Hungry*, www.actionaid.org.uk.

ActionAid (2005), UK, press release, 11 April.

Adams, D. (1980), *The Restaurant at the End of the Universe* (London: Pan Books).

Adams, W. M. (1995), 'Sustainable Development?', in Johnston *et al.* (1995).

Adler, A. (1928), *Understanding Human Nature* (London: George Allen & Unwin).

Adorno, T., and Horkheimer, W. (1986), *Dialectic of Enlightenment* (2nd edn, London: Verso).

Adorno, T., Albert, H., Dahrendorf, R., Habermas, J., Pilot, H., and Popper, K. R. (1969), *The Positivist Dispute in German Sociology* (London: Heinemann Educational Books, 1976).

Albini, J. (1971), *The American Mafia* (New York: Appleton, Crofts).

Albini, J. (1988), 'Donald Cressey's Contribution to the Study of Organized Crime', in P. J. Ryan and G. E. Rush (eds), *Understanding Organized Crime in Global Perspective* (Thousand Oaks, CA: Sage, 1997).

Albini, J., Rogers, R. E., Shabalin, V., Kutushev, V., Moiseev, V., and Anderson, J. (1997), 'Russian Organized Crime', in P. J. Ryan and G. E. Rush (eds), *Understanding Organized Crime in Global Perspective* (Thousand Oaks, CA: Sage).

Albrecht, G. L., Seelman, K. D., and Bury, M. (2001) (eds), *Handbook of Disability Studies* (Thousand Oaks, CA: Sage).

Albrow, M. C. (1970), *Bureaucracy* (London: Pall Mall).

Albrow, M. C. (1996), *The Global Age* (Cambridge: Polity Press).

Albrow, M. C. (1997), 'Travelling Beyond Local Cultures: Socioscapes in a Global City', in Eade (1997).

Albrow, M. C., Eade, J., Durrschmidt, J., and Washbourne, N. (1997), 'The Impact of Globalization on Sociological Concepts: Community, Culture, and Milieu', in Eade (1997).

Aldridge, A. (2000), *Religion in the Contemporary World* (Cambridge, Polity Press).

Alexander, C. (1996), *The Art of Being Black* (Oxford: Oxford University Press).

Alexander, J. (1985) (ed.), *Neofunctionalism* (Beverly Hills, CA: Sage).

Alexander, J. (1988), *Action and its Environments* (New York: Columbia University Press).

Allan, G. (1999) (ed.), *The Sociology of the Family* (Oxford: Blackwell).

Allan, G., and Crow, G. (2001), *Families, Households, and Society* (Basingstoke: Palgrave).

Allen, D. (2001), *The Changing Shape of Nursing Practice* (London: Routledge).

Allen, I. (2005), 'Women Doctors and their Careers: What Now?', *British Medical Journal*, 331.

Alvarado, M., Gutch, R., and Wollen, T. (1987), *Learning the Media: An Introduction to Media Teaching* (Basingstoke: Macmillan).

Anderson, B. (1991), *Imagined Communities: Reflections on the Origin and Spread of Nationalism* (2nd edn, London: Verso).

Anderson, B. (2000), *Doing the Dirty Work: The Global Politics of Domestic Labour* (London: Zed Books).

Anderson, G. (1976), *Victorian Clerks* (Manchester: Manchester University Press).

Anderson, M. (1971), *Family Structure in Nineteenth Century Lancashire* (Cambridge: Cambridge University Press).

Anderson, M. (1980), *Approaches to the History of the Western Family* (London: Macmillan).

Anderson, N. (1923), *The Hobo: The Sociology of the Homeless Man* (Chicago: University of Chicago Press).

Andreas, P. (2002), 'Transnational Crime and Economic Globalization', in M. Berdal and M. Serrano (eds), *Transnational Organized Crime and International Security* (Boulder, CO: Lynne Rienner).

Andreski, S. L. (1976) (ed.), *Herbert Spencer: Structure, Function, and Evolution* (London: Nelson).

Ang, I. (1985), *Watching Dallas: Soap Opera and the Melodramatic Imagination* (New York: Methuen & Co.).

Annandale, E. (2008), 'Liberation: A Danger to Women's Health?', *Sociology Review*, 17/4.

Anthias, F. (1992), *Ethnicity, Class, Gender and Migration* (Aldershot: Avebury).

Anthias, F., and Yuval-Davis, N. (1993), *Racialized Boundaries: Race, Nation, Gender, Colour and Classes and the Anti-Racist Struggle* (London: Routledge).

Appadurai, A. (1990), 'Disjuncture and Difference in the Global Cultural Economy', *Public Culture*, 2/2.

Apple, M., Ball, S., and Gandin, L. (2009) (ed), *The Routledge International Handbook of the Sociology of Education* London: Routledge).

Arber, S., Dale, A., and Gilbert, G. Nigel. (1986), 'The limitations of existing social class classifications for women', in A. Jacoby (ed.), *The measurement of social class* (pp. 73–93). (London: Social Research Association).

Archer, L. (2003), *Race, Masculinity, and Schooling: Muslim Boys and Education* (Maidenhead: Open University Press).

Archer, R. (2008), *Why is There No Labor Party in the United States?* (Princeton: Princeton University Press).

Ariès, P. (1962), *Centuries of Childhood: A Social History of Family Life* (New York: Alfred A. Knopf).

Armstrong, P., Glyn, A., and Harrison, J. (1984), *Capitalism since World War Two* (London: Fontana).

Arrighi, G., Hopkins, T. C., and Wallerstein, I. (1989), *Antisystemic Movements* (London: Verso).

Ashton, D. N. (1986), *Unemployment under Capitalism: The Sociology of British and American Labour Markets* (Brighton: Harvester).

Ashton, D. N., and Sung, J. (1997), 'Education, Skill Formation, and Economic Development: The Singaporean Approach', in Halsey *et al.* (1997).

Atkinson, A. B. (1983), *The Economics of Inequality* (2nd edn, Oxford: Clarendon Press).

Atkinson, J. M. (1978), *Discovering Suicide* (London: Macmillan).

Atkinson, J. M. (1984), *Our Masters' Voice* (London: Tavistock).

Atkinson, P. (1983), 'Eating Virtue', in A. Murcott (ed.), *The Sociology of Food and Eating* (Aldershot: Gower).

Audit Commission (2002), *Special Educational Needs: A Mainstream Issue* (London: Audit Commission).

Auld, J., Doorn, N., and South, N. (1986), 'Irregular Work, Irregular Pleasures: Heroin in the 1980s', in R. Matthews and J. Young (eds), *Confronting Crime* (London: Sage).

Avant, D. (2005), *The Market for Force: The Consequences of Privatizing Security* (Cambridge: Cambridge University Press).

Bachrach, P., and Baratz, M. S. (1962), 'The Two Faces of Power', *American Political Science Review*, 56.

Back, L. (1996), *New Ethnicities and Urban Culture* (London: UCL Press).

Backett-Milburn, K., and McKie, L. (2001), *Constructing Gendered Bodies* (Basingstoke: Palgrave).

Baggott, R. (1994), *Health and Health Care in Britain* (Basingstoke: Macmillan).

Bagguley, P. (1990), *Restructuring: Place, Class and Gender* (Thousand Oaks: Sage).

Bailey, J. (1988), *Pessimism* (London: Routledge & Kegan Paul).

Bales, R. F. (1950), *Interaction Process Analysis* (Cambridge, MA: Addison-Wesley).

Ball, K., and Webster, F. (2003) (eds), *The Intensification of Surveillance: Crime, Terrorism, and Warfare in the Information Age* (London: Pluto Press).

Ball, S. (1981), *Beachside Comprehensive: A Case-Study of Secondary Schooling* (Cambridge: Cambridge University Press).

Ball, S. (2003a), *Class Strategies and the Education Market: The Middle Classes and Social Advantage* (London: Routledge Farmer).

Ball, S. (2003b), 'It's Not What You Know', *Sociology Review*, 13/1.

Ball, S. (2004) (ed.), *The Routledge Farmer Reader in the Sociology of Education* (London: Routledge Farmer).

Ball, S., Bowe, R., and Gewirtz, S. (1995), 'Circuits of Schooling: A Sociological Exploration of Parental Choice of School in Social-Class Contexts', *Sociological Review*, 43.

Baltzell, E. D. (1958), *Philadelphia Gentlemen: The Making of a National Upper Class* (New York: Free Press).

Banks, J. (1954), *Prosperity and Parenthood* (London: Routledge & Kegan Paul).

Banks, O. (1981), *Faces of Feminism: A Study of Feminism as a Social Movement* (Oxford: Martin Robertson).

Banton, M. (1987), *Racial Theories* (Cambridge: Cambridge University Press; 2nd edn, 2000).

Banton, M., and Harwood, J. (1975), *The Race Concept* (Newton Abbott: David and Charles).

Barclay, P. (1995) (ed.), *Joseph Rowntree Foundation Inquiry into Income and Wealth*, i (York: Joseph Rowntree Foundation).

Barker, E. (1984), *The Making of a Moonie* (Oxford: Basil Blackwell).

Barker, E. (1989), *New Religious Movements* (London: HMSO).

Barker, M. (1981), *The New Racism* (London: Junction Books).

Barker, M. (1989), *Comics: Ideology, Power, and the Critics* (Manchester: Manchester University Press).

Barnes, C., and Mercer, G. (2003), *Disability* (Cambridge: Polity Press).

Barnett, T., and Whiteside, A. (2006), *AIDS in the Twenty-First Century: Disease and Globalization* (Houndmills: Palgrave Macmillan).

Barrett, M., and Barrett, D. (2001), *Star Trek* (Cambridge: Polity Press).

Barrett, M., and McIntosh, M. (1991), *The Anti-Social Family* (2nd edn, London: Verso).

Baudrillard, J. (1981) *Simulations* (New York: Semiotext(e), 1983).

Bauman, Z. (1989), *Modernity and the Holocaust* (Cambridge: Polity Press).

Bauman, Z. (1990), *Thinking Sociologically* (Oxford: Basil Blackwell).

Bauman, Z. (1993), *Postmodern Ethics* (Oxford: Basil Blackwell).

Bauman, Z. (1995), *Life in Fragments: Essays in Postmodern Morality* (Oxford: Basil Blackwell).

Bauman, Z. (1998), *Globalization: The Human Consequences* (Cambridge: Polity Press).

Bauman, Z. (2000), *Liquid Modernity* (Cambridge: Polity Press).

Bauman, Z., and May, T. (2001), *Thinking Sociologically* (2nd edn, Oxford: Basil Blackwell).

Beatty, C., Fothergill, S., Gore, T., and Powell, R. (2007), *The Real Level of Unemployment 2007* (Sheffield Hallam University: Centre for Regional Economic and Social Research).

Bechofer, F. and McCrone, D. (2008), 'Talking the Talk: National Identity in England and Scotland', in Park, A. *et al.* (2008).

Beck, U. (1992), *Risk Society: Towards a New Modernity* (London: Sage).

Beck, U. (2000a), *What is Globalization?* (Cambridge: Polity Press).

Beck, U. (2000b), *The Brave New World of Work* (Cambridge: Polity Press).

Beck, U., and Beck-Gernsheim, P. (1995), *The Normal Chaos of Love* (Cambridge: Polity Press).

Becker, G. S. (1976), *The Economic Approach to Human Behavior* (Chicago: University of Chicago Press).

Becker, H. S. (1953), 'Becoming a Marihuana User', in Becker (1963).

Becker, H. S. (1963), *Outsiders: Studies in the Sociology of Deviance* (New York: Free Press).

Becker, H. S. (1970), *Sociological Work* (Chicago: University of Chicago Press).

Becker, H. S. (1982), *Art Worlds* (Berkeley and Los Angeles: University of California Press).

Becker, H. S. (1998), *Tricks of the Trade* (Chicago: University of Chicago Press).

Becker, H. S., Greer, B., Hughes, E. C., and Strauss, A. L. (1961), *Boys in White* (New York: John Wiley).

Becker, H. S., Greer, B., and Hughes, E. C. (1968), *Making the Grade* (New York: John Wiley).

Beckford, J. A. (1989), *Religion and Advanced Industrial Society* (London: Unwin Hyman).

Beechey, V. (1987), *Unequal Work* (London: Verso).

Beer, D., and Burrows, R. (2007), 'Sociology and, of and in Web 2.0: Some Initial Considerations', *Sociological Research Online*, 12: 5, www.socresonline.org.uk/12/5/17.html.

Bell, D. (1961), *The End of Ideology* (New York: Collier-Macmillan).

Bell, D. (1973), *The Coming of Post-Industrial Society: A Venture in Social Forecasting* (London: Heinemann).

Bell, D. (1979), *The Cultural Contradictions of Capitalism* (London: Heinemann).

Bell, D., and Kennedy, B. (2000), *The Cybercultures Reader* (London: Routledge).

Bell, M. (2003), 'Say No to News on Tap', *Independent Review*, 16 December.

Bellah, R. N. (1967), 'Civil Religion in America', *Daedalus*, 96.

Bellah, R. N (1970), *Beyond Belief* (New York: Harper & Row).

Benedict, R. (1934), *Patterns of Culture* (London: Routledge & Kegan Paul).

Benedict, R. (1946), *The Chrysanthemum and the Sword* (Tokyo: Charles E. Tuttle).

Benedictus, L. (2005), 'London: The World in One City', *Guardian*, 1 January.

Berger, P. L. (1961*a*), *The Noise of Solemn Assemblies* (Garden City, NY: Doubleday).

Berger, P. L. (1961*b*), *The Precarious Vision* (Garden City, NY: Doubleday).

Berger, P. L. (1963), *Invitation to Sociology: A Humanistic Perspective* (Harmondsworth: Penguin).

Berger, P. L. (1967), *The Sacred Canopy: Elements of a Sociological Theory of Religion* (New York: Doubleday).

Berger, P. L. (1969), *The Social Reality of Religion* (London: Faber & Faber; UK edn of *The Sacred Canopy*).

Berger, P. L. (1987), *The Capitalist Revolution: Fifty Propositions about Prosperity, Equality, and Liberty* (Aldershot: Wildhouse House).

Berger, P. L., and Kellner, H. (1970), 'Marriage and the Construction of Reality', in H. P. Dreitzel (ed.), *Recent Sociology, Number 2* (New York: Macmillan).

Berger, P. L., and Luckmann, T. (1966), *The Social Construction of Reality: A Treatise in the Sociology of Knowledge* (New York: Doubleday; repr. Harmondsworth: Allen Lane, 1971).

Berle, A. A., and Means, G. C. (1932), *The Modern Corporation and Private Property* (London: Macmillan).

Berners-Lee, T. (with Fischetti, M.) (2000), *Weaving the Web: The Past, Present, and Future of the World Wide Web* (London: Texere).

Bernstein, A. (2002), 'Representation, Identity, and the Media', in Newbold *et al.* (2002).

Bernstein, B. (1961), 'Social Class and Linguistic Development: A Theory of Social Learning', in Halsey *et al.* (1961).

Bernstein, B. (1962), 'Linguistic Codes, Hesitation Phenomena and Intelligence', in B. Bernstein (ed.), *Classes, Codes, and Control, Volume 1* (London: Routledge and Kegan Paul, 1971).

Bernstein, B. (1970), 'Education Cannot Compensate for Society', *New Society*, 387.

Bernstein, B. (1977), 'Social Class, Language, and Socialization', in Karabel and Halsey (1977).

Bernstein, B. (1997), *Pedagogy, Symbolic Control, and Identity: Theory, Research, Critique* (London: Taylor & Francis).

Bernstein, E. (2007), *Temporarily Yours: Intimacy, Authenticity, and the Commerce of Sex* (Chicago: University of Chicago Press).

Berthoud, R. (1998), 'Defining Ethnic Groups: Origin or Identity', *Patterns of Prejudice*, 32.

Berthoud, R. (2000), 'Family Formation in Multi-Cultural Britain: Three Patterns of Diversity', Working Paper 2000–34 (University of Essex: Institute for Social and Economic Research).

Berthoud, R., and Gershuny, J. (2000), *Seven Years in the Lives of British Families* (Bristol: Policy Press).

Bhaba, H. (1994), *The Location of Culture* (London: Routledge).

Bhachu, P. (1988), '*Apni Marzi Kardhi* Home and Work: Sikh Women in Britain', in Westwood and Bhachu (1988*b*).

Bianchini, F., and Schwengel, H. (1991), 'Re-Imagining the City', in J. Corner and S. Harvey (eds), *Enterprise and Heritage* (London: Routledge).

Birrell, D. (2007), 'Devolution and Social Care: Are there Four Systems of Social Care in the United Kingdom?', paper presented at Social Policy Association Conference, University of Birmingham, July, www.sochealth.co.uk.

Black, D., Townsend, P., Davidson, N., and Whitehead, M. (1980), 'The Black Report', in P. Townsend and N. Davidson (eds), *Inequalities in Health* (Harmondsworth: Penguin, 1992).

Blackburn, C. (1991), *Poverty and Health: Working with Families* (Buckingham: Open University Press).

Blair, T. (1998), 'The Third Way: New Politics for the New Century', *Fabian Pamphlet*, 588.

Blakemore, K., and Griggs, E. (2007), *Social Policy: An Introduction* (3rd edn, Maidenhead: Open University Press).

Blanden, J., Gregg, P., and Machin, S. (2005), 'Intergenerational Mobility in Europe and North America', Centre for Economic Performance, London School of Economics.

Blau, P., and Duncan, O. D. (1967), *The American Occupational Structure* (New York: Wiley).

Blau, P. M. (1964), *Exchange and Power in Social Life* (New York: John Wiley).

Blauner, R. (1964), *Alienation and Freedom: The Factory Worker and his Industry* (Chicago: University of Chicago Press).

Blaxter, M., and Paterson, E. (1982), *Mothers and Daughters: A Three Generational Study of Health Attitudes and Behaviour* (London: Heinemann Educational Books).

Blok, A. (1974), *The Mafia of a Sicilian Village, 1860–1960* (New York: Harper & Row).

Blumer, H. (1966), 'Sociological Implications of the Thought of George Herbert Mead', in H. Blumer, *Symbolic Interactionism* (Englewood Cliffs, NJ: Prentice-Hall, 1969).

Boas, F. (1911), *The Mind of Primitive Man* (New York: Macmillan).

Bocock, R. (1974), *Ritual in Industrial Society: A Sociological Analysis of Ritualism in Modern England* (London: George Allen & Unwin).

Boissevain, J. (1974), *Friends of Friends* (Oxford: Basil Blackwell).

Bolton, S. (2001), 'Changing Faces: Nurses as Emotional Jugglers', *Sociology of Health and Illness*, 23: 1.

Bolton, S. (2005), *Emotion Management in the Workplace* (Basingstoke: Palgrave Macmillan).

Bolton, S., and Boyd, C. (2003), 'Trolley Dolly or Skilled Emotion Manager: Moving on from Hochschild's Managed Heart', *Work, Employment, and Society*, 17/2.

Booth, C. (1886), 'Occupations of the People of the United Kingdom', *Journal of the Royal Statistical Society* (June).

Booth, C. (1901–2), *Life and Labour of the People of London* (17 vols, London: Macmillan).

Booth, D. (1993), 'Development Research: From Impasse to a New Agenda', in Schuurman (1993).

Bordo, S. (1993), *Unbearable Weight: Feminism, Western Culture, and the Body* (Berkeley and Los Angeles: University of California Press).

Bottomore, T. B. (1993), *Elites and Society* (2nd edn, London: Routledge & Kegan Paul).

Bottomore, T. B., and Brym, R. J. (1989) (eds), *The Capitalist Class* (Hemel Hempstead: Harvester Wheatsheaf).

Bourdieu, P. (1977), *Reproduction in Education, Society, and Culture* (London: Sage).

Bourdieu, P. (1984), *Distinction: A Social Critique of the Judgment of Taste* (London: Routlege & Kegan Paul).

Bourdieu, P. (1988), *Homo Academicus* (Cambridge: Polity Press).

Bourgois, P. (1995), *In Search of Respect. Selling Crack in El Barrio* (Cambridge: Cambridge University Press, 2003).

Bowlby, J. (1965), *Child Care and the Growth of Love* (2nd edn, Harmondsworth: Penguin).

Bowles, S., and Gintis, H. (1976), *Schooling in Capitalist America: Educational Reform and the Contradictions of Economic Life* (London: Routledge & Kegan Paul).

Boycott, R., and Margolis, Z. (2010), 'Is this a Terrible Time to be a Feminist?', *Observer*, 7 March.

Boyce, T. (2009), 'Media, Moral Panics, and Obesity', *Sociology Review*, 18/3.

Boyd, D. (1973), *Elites and their Education* (London: National Foundation for Educational Research).

Boyd-Barrett, O. (1995), 'Conceptualizing the "Public Sphere"', in Boyd-Barrett and Newbold (1995).

Boyden, J. (1997), 'Childhood and the Policymakers: A Comparative Perspective on the Globalization of Childhood', in A. James and A. Prout (eds), *Constructing and Reconstructing Childhood: Contemporary Issues in the Sociological Study of Childhood* (London: Falmer).

Boyes, R. (2008), 'Banking Crisis Gives Added Capital to Karl Marx's Writings', *The Times*, 20 October.

Bradley, H. (1989), *Men's Work, Women's Work: A Sociological History of the Sexual Division of Labour in Employment* (Cambridge: Polity Press).

Brah, A., and Minhas, R. (1988), 'Structural Racism or Cultural Difference: Schooling for Asian Girls', in Woodhead and Mcgrath (1988).

Bramley, H. (2002), 'Diana, Princess of Wales: The Contemporary Goddess' Sociological Research Online, vol. 7, no. 1, http://www.socresonline.org.uk/7/1/bramley.html.

Braverman, H. (1974), *Labor and Monopoly Capital: The Degradation of Work in the Twentieth Century* (New York: Monthly Review Press).

Breen, R. (2004), *Social Mobility in Europe* (Oxford: Oxford University Press).

Brewer, J. D. (2000), *Ethnography* (Buckingham: Open University Press).

Brewer, S. (2001), *A Child's World: A Unique Insight into how Children Think* (London: Headline).

Broad, R., and Fleming, S. (1981) (eds), *Nella Last's War* (London: Falling Wall Press).

Broadbent, K. (2003), *Women's Employment in Japan: The Experience of Part-Time Workers* (London: Curzon).

Brown, C. (1984), *Black and White Britain* (London: Policy Studies Institute).

Brown, G., and Harris, T. (1978), *Social Origins of Depression* (London: Tavistock).

Brown, M. (1994), *Soap Opera and Women's Talk: The Pleasures of Resistance* (London: Sage).

Brown, P. (1989), 'Schooling for Inequality? Ordinary Kids in School and the Labour Market', in Cosin *et al.* (1989).

Brown, P. (1995), 'Cultural Capital and Social Exclusion: Some Observations on Recent Trends in Education, Employment, and the Labour Market', *Work, Employment, and Society*, 9.

Brown, P., and Hesketh A. (with Williams, S.) (2004), *The Mismanagement of Talent: Employability and Jobs in the Knowledge Economy* (Oxford: Oxford University Press).

Brown, P., and Lauder, H. (1997), 'Education, Globalization, and Economic Development', in Halsey *et al.* (1997).

Bruce, S. (1983), 'The Persistence of Religion: Conservative Protestantism in the United Kingdom', *Sociological Review*, 31.

Bruce, S. (1984), *Firm in the Faith* (Aldershot: Gower).

Bruce, S. (1985), 'Authority and Fission: The Protestants' Divisions', *British Journal of Sociology*, 36.

Bruce, S. (1986), 'Militants and the Margins: British Political Protestantism', *Sociological Review*, 34.

Bruce, S. (1994), *The Edge of the Union: The Ulster Loyalist Political Vision* (Oxford: Oxford University Press).

Bruce, S. (1995), *Religion in Modern Britain* (Oxford: Oxford University Press).

Bruce, S. (1999*a*), *Choice and Religion: A Critique of Rational Choice Theory* (Oxford: Oxford University Press).

Bruce, S. (1999*b*), *Sociology: A Very Short Introduction* (Oxford: Oxford University Press).

Bruce, S. (2003), *Politics and Religion* (Cambridge: Polity Press).

Bruch, H. (1973), *Eating Disorders* (New York: Basic Books).

Bruch, H. (1979), *The Golden Cage: The Enigma of Anorexia Nervosa* (New York: Vintage).

Bruner, J. (1966), *Toward a Theory of Instruction* (Cambridge, MA: Belknap Press).

Bryman, A. (1999), 'The Disneyization of Society', *Sociological Review*, 47/1.

Bryman, A. (2004), *The Disneyization of Society* (London: Sage).

Bryman, A. (2008), *Social Research Methods* (3rd edn, Oxford: Oxford University Press).

Brynin, M., and Ermisch. J. (2009) (eds), *Changing Relationships* (London: Routledge).

Bulmer, M. (1982) (ed.), *Social Research Ethics* (London: Macmillan).

Bunting, M. (2004), 'Family Fortunes', *Guardian*, 25 September.

Burawoy, M. (2004), Personal Statement to American Sociological Association.

Burchardt, T. (2005), *The Education and Employment of Disabled Young People: Frustrated Ambition* (York: Joseph Rowntree Foundation).

Burgess, R. G. (1984), *In the Field: An Introduction to Field Research* (London: George Allen & Unwin).

Burgess, R. G. (1986) (ed.), *Key Variables in Social Research* (London: Routledge & Kegan Paul).

Burgess, S., Greaves, E., Vignoles, A., and Wilson, D. (2009), 'Parental Choice of Primary School in England: What "Type" of School Do Parents Choose?', University of Bristol: Centre for Market and Public Organization.

Burghes, L. (1994), *Lone Parenthood and Family Disruption: The Outcomes for Children* (London: Family Policy Studies Centre).

Burke, Jason (2004), *Al-Qaeda: The True Story of Radical Islam* (Harmondsworth: Penguin).

Burke, Jason (2005), 'Al-Qaida is Now an Idea, not an Organization', *Guardian*, 5 August.

Burnham, J. (1941), *The Managerial Revolution* (New York: John Day).

Burns, T., and Stalker, G. M. (1961), *The Management of Innovation* (London: Tavistock).

Burt, C. (1946), *Intelligence and Fertility* (London: Eugenics Society).

Busfield, J. (1996), *Men, Women and Madness: Understanding Gender and Mental Disorder* (London: Macmillan).

Busfield, J. (2000), *Health and Health Care in Modern Britain* (Oxford: Oxford University Press).

Butler, D., and Butler, G. E. (2000), *British Political Fact* (London: Macmillan).

Butler, D., and Stokes, D. E. (1969), *Political Change in Britain: Forces Shaping Electoral Change* (London: Macmillan).

Butler, J. (1990), *Gender Trouble: Feminism and the Subversion of Identity* (2nd edn, London: Routledge).

Butler, J. (1993), *Bodies That Matter: On the Discursive Limits of 'Sex'* (London: Routledge).

Butler, T. (1996), '"People Like Us": The Gentrification of Hackney in the 1980s', in Butler and Rustin (1996).

Byrne, D. (2001), *Understanding the Urban* (Houndmills: Palgrave).

Byrne, P. (1997), *Social Movements in Britain* (London: Routledge).

Campbell, A. (1981), *Girl Delinquents* (Oxford: Basil Blackwell).

Campbell, A., Converse, P. S., Miller, W. E., and Stokes, D. E. (1960), *The American Voter* (New York: John Wiley).

Campbell, B. (1993), *Goliath: Britain's Dangerous Places* (London: Methuen).

Cantle, T. (2007), 'Race and Community Cohesion', *Sociology Review*, 16/3.

Carey, A. (1967), 'The Hawthorne Studies: A Radical Criticism', *American Sociological Review*, 32.

Carmichael, F., and Ward, R. (2001), 'Male Unemployment and Crime in England and Wales', *Economics Letters*, 73/1.

Carmichael, S., and Hamilton, C. V. (1968), *Black Power: The Politics of Liberation in America* (London: Jonathan Cape).

Carroll, R. (2008), 'Tourism Curbed in Bid to Save Galapagos Haven', *Guardian*, 12 October.

Cassen, R., and Kingdon, Geeta (2007), *Tackling Low Educational Achievement* (York: Joseph Rowntree Foundation).

Castells, M. (1977), *The Urban Question* (London: Edward Arnold).

Castells, M. (1996), *The Information Age: Economy, Society and Culture*, i: *The Rise of the Network Society* (Oxford: Basil Blackwell).

Castles, S., and Miller, M. J. (2003), *The Age of Migration: International Population Movements in the Modern World* (3rd edn, Basingstoke: Palgrave Macmillan).

Castles, S., and Miller, M. J. (2009), *The Age of Migration: International Population Movements in the Modern World* (4th edn, Basingstoke: Palgrave Macmillan).

Cavadino, M., and Dignan, J. (1997), *The Penal System: An Introduction* (2nd edn, London: Sage).

Cavadino, M., and Dignan, J. (2002), *The Penal System: An Introduction* (3rd edn, London: Sage).

Cavadino, M., and Dignan, J. (2007), *The Penal System: An Introduction* (4th edn, London: Sage).

Cawson, P., Wattam, C., Brooker, S., and Kelly, G. (2000), *Child Maltreatment in the United Kingdom: A Study of the Prevalence of Child Abuse and Neglect* (London: NSPCC).

Central Office of Information (1995), *Population* (London: HMSO).

Centre for Contemporary Cultural Studies (1982), *The Empire Strikes Back* (London: Hutchinson).

Chakravarthi, Ram-Prasad (2007), 'India's Middle Class Failure', *Prospect*, 30 September, www.prospectmagazine.co.uk/2007/09/indiasmiddleclassfailure.

Chalmers, D. M. (1987), *Hooded Americanism: The History of the Ku Klux Klan*, (3rd edn, Durham NC: Duke University Press).

Chamberlain, H. S. (1899), *Foundations of the Nineteenth Century* (London: John Lane, 1911).

Chandler, A. D., Jnr (1962), *Strategy and Structure* (Cambridge, MA: Belknap Press).

Chapman, M., and Wykes, C. (1996), *Plain Figures* (2nd edn, London: HMSO).

Chapman, T. (2004), *Gender and Domestic Life: Changing Practices in Families and Households* (Basingstoke: Palgrave Macmillan).

Charles, N. (2002), *Gender in Modern Britain* (Oxford: Oxford University Press).

Charles, N., and Davies, C. (2005), 'Studying the Particular, Illuminating the General: Community Studies and Community in Wales', *Sociological Review*, 53/4: 672–90.

Charles, N., and Kerr, M. (1988), *Women, Food and Families* (Manchester: Manchester University Press).

Charles, N., Davies, C., and Harris, C. (2008*a*), *Families in Transition: Social Change, Family Formation, and Kin Relationships* (Bristol: Policy Press).

Charles, N., Davies, C., and Harris, C. (2008*b*), 'The Family: Continuity and Change', *Sociology Review*, 18/2.

Chernin, K. (1985), *The Hungry Self: Women, Eating and Identity* (New York: Harper & Row).

Chesney, K. (1968), *The Victorian Underworld* (Harmondsworth: Penguin).

Cheung, C. (2000), 'A Home on the Web: Presentations of Self on Personal Homepages', in Gauntlett (2000*b*).

Child, J. (1984), *Organization: A Guide to Problems and Practice* (London: Harper & Row).

Chiozza-Money, L. G. (1905), *Riches and Poverty* (London: Methuen).

Chitty, C. (2009), *Education Policy in Britain* (2nd edn, Basingstoke: Palgrave Macmillan).

Chodorow, N. (1978), *The Reproduction of Mothering: Psychoanalysis and the Sociology of Gender* (Berkeley and Los Angeles: University of California Press).

Chomsky, N. (1965), *Aspects of the Theory of Syntax* (Cambridge, MA: MIT Press).

Cicourel, A. V. (1964), *Method and Measurement in Sociology* (New York: Free Press).

Clark, C. (1940), *The Conditions of Economic Progress* (London: Macmillan).

Clark, N. (2009), 'Battle of Social-Networking Sites', *Independent*, 28 May.

Clarke, J., Hall, S., Jefferson, J., and Roberts, B. (1976), 'Subcultures, Cultures, and Class: A Theoretical Overview', in Hall and Jefferson (1976).

Clarke, M. (1986), *Regulating the City* (Buckingham: Open University Press).

Clarke, M. (1990), *Business Crime: Its Nature and Control* (Cambridge: Polity Press).

Clegg, S. R. (1990), *Modern Organizations: Organization Studies in the Postmodern World* (London: Sage).

Clegg, S. R., and Dunkerley, D. (1980), *Organization, Class, and Control* (London: Routledge & Kegan Paul).

Clegg, S. R., and Hardy, C. (1999), *Studying Organization: Theory and Method* (London: Sage).

Coates, D. (1989), *The Crisis of Labour* (London: Philip Allan).

Coates, K., and Silburn, R. (1970), *Poverty: The Forgotten Englishmen* (Harmondsworth: Penguin).

Cohen, A. K. (1955), *Delinquent Boys* (Glencoe, IL: Free Press).

Cohen, R., and Kennedy, P. (2000*a*), *Global Sociology* (London: Macmillan).

Cohen, R., and Kennedy, P. (2000*b*), 'Challenging a Gendered World', in R. Cohen and P. Kennedy, *Global Sociology* (Basingstoke: Macmillan).

Cohen, S. (1972), *Folk Devils and Moral Panics: The Creation of the Mods and Rockers* (London: Macgibbon & Kee).

Cohen, S. (1985), *Visions of Social Control* (Cambridge: Polity Press).

Coleman, D., and Salt, J. (1992), *The British Population: Patterns, Trends and Processes* (Oxford: Oxford University Press).

Coleman, J. (1990), *Foundations of Social Theory* (Cambridge, MA: Belknap Press).

Colley, L. (1992), *Britons: Forging the Nation 1707–1837* (New Haven, CT: Yale University Press).

Collins, R. (1994), *Four Sociological Traditions* (Oxford: Oxford University Press).

Collison, M. (1994), 'Drug Offenders and Criminal Justice: Careers, Compulsion, Commitment and Penalty', *Crime, Law and Society*, 21.

Commission for Africa (2005), *Our Common Interest* (London: Penguin); www.commissionforafrica.info/2005-report.

Connell, R. W. (1987), *Gender and Power: Society, the Person, and Sexual Politics* (Cambridge: Polity Press).

Connell, R. W. (1995), *Masculinities* (Cambridge: Polity Press).

Cook, E. (1996), 'The Nuclear Family is Dead: Long Live the Extended Family', *Independent on Sunday*, 11 November.

Cooley, C. H. (1902), *Human Nature and the Social Order* (New York: Scribner's).

Cooley, C. H. (1909), *Social Organization* (New Brunswick, NJ: Transaction, 1983).

Coomber, R. (2006), *Pusher Myths: Re-Situating the Drug Dealer* (London: Free Association Books).

Corbin, J., and Strauss, A. L. (1985), 'Managing Chronic Illness at Home', *Qualitative Sociology*, 8.

Corby, B. (2000), *Child Abuse: Towards a Knowledge Base* (2nd edn, Buckingham: Open University Press).

Corrigan, P. (1983), 'Film Entertainment as Ideology and Pleasure: Towards a History of Audiences', in Curran and Porter (1983).

Cottle, S. (2003) (ed.), *Media Organization and Production* (London: Sage).

Coulter, J. (1973), *Approaches to Insanity* (Oxford: Martin Robertson).

Coupland, A. (1992), 'Docklands: Dream or Disaster', in Thornley (1992).

Cox, O. C. (1948), *Caste, Class, and Race: A Study in Social Dynamics* (New York: Doubleday & Co.).

Craib, I. (1984), *Modern Social Theory* (Brighton: Harvester Wheatsheaf).

Craib, I. (1997), *Classical Social Theory* (Oxford: Oxford University Press).

Cressey, D. (1969), *Theft of the Nation* (New York: Harper & Row).

Critcher, C., Bramham, P., and Tomlinson, A. (1995), *The Sociology of Leisure* (London: Chapman and Hall).

Croal, H. (1992), *White Collar Crime* (Buckingham: Open University Press).

Crompton, R. (1997), *Women and Work in Modern Britain* (Oxford: Oxford University Press).

Crompton, R., and Harris, F. (1998), 'Explaining Women's Employment Patterns: "Orientations to Work" Revisited', *British Journal of Sociology*, 49/1.

Crompton, R., and Jones, G. (1984), *White-Collar Proletariat* (London: Macmillan).

Crompton, R., and Le Feuvre, N. (1992), 'Gender and Bureaucracy: Women in Finance in Britain and France', in Savage and Witz (1992).

Crompton, R., Brockmann, M., and Lyonette, C. (2005), 'Attitudes, Women's Employment and the Domestic Division of Labour: A Cross-National Analysis in Two Waves', *Work, Employment, and Society*, 19/2.

Cronin, Audrey Kurth (2006), 'How al-Qaida Ends', *International Security*, 31/1.

Cross, G. (1990) (ed.), *Worktowners in Blackpool: Mass Observation and Popular Leisure in the 1930s* (London: Routledge).

Crossick, G. (1977a), 'The Emergence of the Lower Middle Class in Britain', in Crossick (1977b).

Crothers, C. (1987), *Robert Merton* (Chichester: Ellis Horwood).

Crow, G. (2002), *Social Solidarities: Theories, Identities, and Social Change* (Buckingham: Open University Press).

Crow, G., and Allan, G. (1994), *Community Life: An Introduction to Local Social Relations* (Hemel Hempstead: Harvester Wheatsheaf).

Cully, M., and Woodland, S. (1997), 'Trade Union Membership and Recognition', *Labour Market Trends*, 105/6 (June).

Cunningham, H. (1995), *Children and Childhood in Western Society since 1500* (London: Longman).

Cunningham, H. (2006), *The Invention of Childhood* (London: BBC Books).

Curran, J., and Seaton, J. (1991), *Power without Responsibility: The Press and Broadcasting in Britain* (4th edn, London: Routledge).

Curtis, M. (1979), *Totalitarianism* (New Brunswick, NJ: Transaction Books).

Dahl, R. (1961), *Who Governs?* (New Haven, CT: Yale University Press).

Dahrendorf, R. (1957), *Class and Class Conflict in an Industrial Society* (London: Routledge & Kegan Paul, 1959).

Dale, R. (1989), *The State and Education Policy* (Milton Keynes: Open University Press).

Daly, M. (1978), *Gyn/Ecology: The Metaethics of Radical Feminism* (London: Women's Press).

Dandeker, C. (1990), *Surveillance, Power and Modernity: Bureaucracy and Discipline from 1700 to the Present Day* (Cambridge: Polity Press).

Darwin, C. (1859), *On the Origin of Species*, edited with an introduction by G. Beer (Oxford: Oxford University Press, 1996).

Davidoff, L. (1973), *The Best Circles* (London: Croom Helm).

Davidoff, L. (1990), 'The Family in Britain', in F. M. L. Thompson (1990).

Davidoff, L., and Hall, C. (1987), *Family Fortunes* (London: Hutchinson).

Davidson, R. (1992), 'Asian Gangs and Asian Organized Crime in Chicago', in P. J. Ryan and G. E. Rush (eds), *Understanding Organized Crime in Global Perspective* (Thousand Oaks, CA: Sage, 1997).

Davie, G. (1990), '"An Ordinary God": The Paradox of Religion in Contemporary Britain', *British Journal of Sociology*, 41.

Davie, G. (1994), *Religion in Britain since 1945* (Oxford: Basil Blackwell).

Davis, A. B. (1941), *Deep South* (Chicago: University of Chicago Press).

Davis, F. (1961), 'Deviance Disavowal: The Management of Strained Interaction by the Visibly Handicapped', *Social Problems*, 9.

Davis, Kathleen (1995), *Reshaping the Female Body: The Dilemma of Cosmetic Surgery* (New York: Routledge & Kegan Paul).

Davis, Kingsley (1945), 'The World Demographic Transition', *Annals of the American Academy of Political and Social Science*, 273.

Davis, Kingsley, and Moore, W. E. (1945), 'Some Principles of Stratification', *American Sociological Review*, 10.

Davis, L. J. (1995), *Enforcing Normality: Disability, Deafness, and the Body* (London: Verso).

Day, G., and Thompson, A. (2004), *Theorizing Nationalism* (Basingstoke: Palgrave Macmillan).

Day, S. (2007) *On the Game: Women and Sex Work* (London: Pluto).

Deacon, R. (2006), *Devolution in Britain Today* (2nd edn, Manchester: Manchester University Press).

de Beauvoir, S. (1949), *The Second Sex* (London: Jonathan Cape, 1953).

Dedoussis, V., and Littler, C. (1994), 'Understanding the Transfer of Japanese Management Practices: The Australian Case', in Elger and Smith (1994).

Delamont, S. (2001), *Changing Women, Unchanged Men: Sociological Perspectives on Gender in a Post-Industrial Society* (Buckingham: Open University Press).

Delanty, G. (2003), *Community* (London: Routledge).

Delanty, G. (2009), *Community* (2nd edn, London: Routledge).

Delphy, C. (1977), *The Main Enemy* (London: Women's Research and Resources Centre).

Dench, G., Gavron, K., and Young, M. (2006), *The New East End: Kinship, Race, and Conflict* (London: Profile Books).

Dennis, N., Henriques, F., and Slaughter, C. (1956), *Coal is our Life* (London: Eyre & Spottiswoode).

Denver, D. (1994), *Elections and Voting Behaviour in Britain* (2nd edn, Hemel Hempstead: Harvester Wheatsheaf).

Denver, D. (2002), *Elections and Voters in Britain* (Basingstoke: Palgrave).

Department of Health (2002), *Delivering the NHS Plan* (London: HMSO).

de Vaus, G. (1991), *Surveys in Social Research* (London: UCL Press).

Devine, F. (1992), *Affluent Workers Revisited: Privatism and the Working Class* (Edinburgh: Edinburgh University Press).

de Waal, A. (2005), 'Paternity Rights and Parental Responsibilities', *Guardian*, 23 August.

DFES (2006), *Permanent and Fixed Period Exclusion from Schools, 2004–5*, SFR 24/2006 (London: HMSO).

Dicken, P. (1992), *Global Shift: The Internationalization of Economic Activity* (London: Paul Chapman).

Dicken, P. (2007), *Global Shift: The Internationalization of Economic Activity* (5th edn, London: Sage).

Dingwall, R., Rafferty, R. M., and Webster, C. (1988), *An Introduction to the Social History of Nursing* (London: Routledge).

Dixey, R. (1988), 'A Means to Get Out of the House: Working-Class Women, Leisure and Bingo', in J. Little, L. Peake, and P. Richardson (eds.), *Women in Cities* (London: Macmillan).

Dobratz, B. A. (2000), *The White Separatist Movement in the United States: White Power, White Pride*. (Baltimore: Johns Hopkins University Press).

Dodd, K., and Dodd, P. (1992), 'From the East End to *Eastenders*: Representations of the Working Class, 1890–1990', in Strinati and Wagg (1992).

Dollard, J. (1937), *Caste and Class in a Southern Town* (New York: Harper Brothers).

Domhoff, G. W. (1971), *The Higher Circles: The Governing Class in America* (New York: Vintage Books).

Domhoff, G. W. (1978), *Who Really Rules? New Haven and Community Power Reexamined* (New Brunswick, NJ: Transaction Books).

Domhoff, G. W. (1979), *The Powers That Be: Processes of Ruling Class Domination in America* (New York: Vintage).

Domhoff, G. W. (2006), *Who Rules America? Power, Politics, and Social Change* (New York: McGraw-Hill).

Dore, R. P. (1973), *British Factory–Japanese Factory: The Origins of National Diversity in Industrial Relations* (London: George Allen & Unwin).

Dore, R. P. (1976), *The Diploma Disease: Education, Qualification, and Development* (London: Allen and Unwin).

Dore, R. P. (1987), *Taking Japan Seriously: A Confucian Perspective on Leading Economic Issues* (London: Athlone Press).

Dorn, N., and South, N. (1987), *A Land Fit for Heroin* (London: Macmillan).

Dorn, N., Murji, K., and South, N. (1992), *Traffickers* (London: Routledge).

Douglas, J. D. (1967), *The Social Meanings of Suicide* (Princeton: Princeton University Press).

Douglas, J. W. B. (1964), *The Home and the School* (London: MacGibbon & Kee).

Douglas, J. W. B., Ross, J., and Simpson, H. (1968), *All Our Futures: A Longitudinal Study of Secondary Education* (London: Peter Davies).

Downes, D. (1966), *The Delinquent Solution: A Study in Subcultural Theory* (London: Routledge & Kegan Paul).

Downs, A. (1957), *An Economic Theory of Democracy* (New York: Harper & Brothers).

Drake, S. C., and Cayton, H. B. (1945), *Black Metropolis* (New York: Harcourt Brace).

Dube, S., and Csete, J. (2008), 'A Chance to Fix the Fight against Aids', *Guardian*, 3 August.

Du Bois, W. E. B. (1899), *The Philadelphia Negro* (Philadelphia: University of Philadelphia Press).

Du Bois, W. E. B. (1903), *The Souls of Black Folks* (Chicago: A. C. McClurg).

Dumazedier, J. (1967), *Towards a Leisure Society* (London: Collier-Macmillan).

Duncan, S., and Phillips M. (2008), 'New Families? Tradition and Change in Modern Relationships', in Park *et al.* (2008).

Duncombe, J., and Marsden, D. (1993), 'Love and Intimacy: The Gender Division of Emotion and Emotion Work', *Sociology*, 27.

Duncombe, J., and Marsden, D. (1995), 'Women's "Triple Shift": Paid Employment, Domestic Labour and "Emotion Work"', *Sociology Review*, 4/4.

Dunleavy, P., and Husbands, C. T. (1985), *British Democracy at the Crossroads* (London: George Allen & Unwin).

Dunne, G. (1999), 'A Passion for "Sameness"?: Sexuality and Gender Accountability', in Silva and Smart (1999).

Dunning, E., and Sheard, K. (2005), *Barbarians, Gentlemen, and Players: A Sociological Study of the Development of Rugby Football* (2nd edn, London: Routledge).

Durkheim, E. (1893), *The Division of Labour in Society* (London: Macmillan, 1984).

Durkheim, E. (1895), *The Rules of the Sociological Method* (London: Macmillan, 1982).

Durkheim, E. (1897), *Suicide: A Study in Sociology* (London: Routledge & Kegan Paul, 1952).

Durkheim, E. (1912), *The Elementary Forms of the Religious Life* (London: George Allen & Unwin, 1915).

Durkheim, E. (1925), *Moral Education: A Study in the Theory and Application of the Sociology of Education*, trans. E. Wilson and H. Schnurer (New York: Free Press of Glencoe, 1961).

Durkheim, E., and Mauss, M. (1903), *Primitive Classification* (London: Cohen & West, 1963).

Dworkin, A. (1983), *Right-Wing Women* (New York: Pedigree Books).

Dwyer, P. (2004), 'Creeping Conditionality in the UK: From Welfare Rights to Conditional Entitlements?', *Canadian Journal of Sociology*, 29/2.

Eade, J. (1997) (ed.), *Living the Global City: Globalization as Local Process* (London: Routledge).

Edwards, R. (2008) (ed.), *Researching Families and Communities: Social and Generational Change* (London: Routledge).

Edwards, S. (1984), *Women on Trial* (Manchester: Manchester University Press).

Edwards, T. (1997), *Men in the Mirror: Men's Fashion, Masculinity, and Consumer Society* (London: Cassell).

Ehrenreich, B., and Hochschild, A. R. (2003), *Global Women: Nannies, Maids and Sex Workers in the New Economy* (London: Granta).

Eldridge, J. (1993*a*), 'News, Truth and Power', in Eldridge (1993*b*).

Eldridge, J., Kitzinger, J., and Williams, K. (1997), *The Mass Media and Power in Modern Britain* (Oxford: Oxford University Press).

Elger, T., and Smith, C. (1994) (eds), *Global Japanization: The Transnational Transformation of the Labour Process* (London: Routledge).

Elliot, F. R. (1996), *Gender, Family, and Society* (Basingstoke: Macmillan).

Elliot, J. (1997), 'What Do Women Want? Women, Work, and the Hakim Debate', *Sociology Review*, 6/4.

Elliott, L. (2004), *The Global Politics of the Environment* (2nd edn, Basingstoke: Palgrave Macmillan).

Elliott, L., and Curtis, P. (2009), 'UK's Income Gap Widest since 60s', *Guardian*, 8 May.

Ellison, N., and Pierson, C. (2003) (eds), *Developments in British Social Policy 2* (Basingstoke: Palgrave Macmillan).

Elster, J. (1989), *The Cement of Society* (Cambridge: Cambridge University Press).

Emerson, J. (1970), 'Behaviour in Private Places: Sustaining Definitions of Reality in Gynecological Examinations', in H.-P. Dreitzel (ed.), *Recent Sociology, Number 2* (New York: Macmillan).

Emmer, P. (1993), 'Intercontinental Migrations as a World Historical Process', *European Review*, 1/1: 67–74.

Engels, F. (1845), *The Condition of the Working Class in England in 1844* (Harmondsworth: Penguin, 1987).

Epstein, S. (1994), 'A Queer Encounter: Sociology and the Study of Sexuality', *Sociological Theory*, 12/2.

Erikson, E. (1950), *Childhood and Society* (New York: W. W. Norton).

Erikson, R., and Goldthorpe, J. (1993), *The Constant Flux* (Oxford: Clarendon Press).

ESPAD (2007), *European School Survey Project on Alcohol and Other Drugs*, www.espad.org.

ESPAD (2009), *The 2007 ESPAD Report* (Stockholm Sweedish Council for Information on Alcohol and other Drugs).

Esping-Andersen, G. (1990), *The Three Worlds of Welfare Capitalism* (Cambridge: Polity Press).

Esping-Andersen, G., and Korpi, W. (1984), 'Social Policy and Class Politics in Post-War Capitalism: Scandinavia, Austria, and Germany', in Goldthorpe (1984).

Ettorre, B. (1992), *Women and Substance Use* (London: Macmillan).

Etzioni, A. (1995), *The Spirit of Community: Rights, Responsibilities, and the Communitarian Agenda* (London: Fontana).

Evans, A. D., and Falk, W. W. (1986), *Learning to be Deaf* (Berlin: Mouton de Gruyter).

Evans, K. (1997), 'Men's Towns: Women and the Urban Environment', *Sociology Review*, 6/3.

Evans, M., and Cerny, P. (2003), 'Globalization and Social Policy', in Ellison and Pierson (2003).

Evans, Y., Herbert, J., Datta, K., May J., Mcllwaine, C., and Wills, J. (2005), 'Making the City Work' (Queen Mary, University of London: Department of Geography).

Fagin, J. R., and Batur, P. (2004), 'Racism in Comparative Perspective', in G. Ritzer (ed.), *Contemporary Social Problems* (Thousand Oaks, CA: Sage).

Fallows, J. (2008). 'The Connection has been Reset', *Atlantic* (March).

Fanon, F. (1967), *The Wretched of the Earth* (Harmondsworth: Penguin).

Farrington, D. P., and Morris, A. M. (1983), 'Sex, Sentencing and Reconviction', *British Journal of Criminology*, 23.

Fausto-Sterling, A. (2000), *Sexing the Body* (New York: Basic Books).

Featherman, D. L., Jones, R. L., and Hauser, R. M. (1975), 'Assumptions of Social Mobility Research in the United States: The Case of Occupational Status', *Social Science Research*, 4.

Febvre, L., and Martin, H.-J. (1976), *The Coming of the Book: The Impact of Printing 1450–1800* (London: New Left Books).

Felstead, A., and Jewson, N. (2000), *In Work, at Home: Towards an Understanding of Homeworking* (London: Routledge).

Felstead, A., Jewson, N., and Walters, S. (2005), *Changing Places of Work* (Basingstoke: Palgrave Macmillan).

Fenton, K. A., *et al.* (2005), 'Ethnic Variations in Sexual Behaviour in Great Britain and Risk of Sexually Transmitted Infections: A Probability Survey', *Lancet*, 365 (April): 9466.

Ferguson, H. (2004), *Protecting Children in Time: Child Abuse, Child Protection, and the Consequences of Modernism* (Basingstoke: Palgrave Macmillan).

Ferguson, M. (1982), *The Aquarian Conspiracy* (London: Granada).

Ferguson, N. (2009), *Too Big to Live* (London: Centre for Policy Studies).

Festinger, L., Riecken, H. W., and Schachter, S. (1956), *When Prophecy Fails* (New York: Harper & Row).

Fielding, N. (1981), *The National Front* (London: Routledge & Kegan Paul).

Fielding, N. (1982), 'Observational Research on the British Police', in M. Bulmer (ed.), *Social Research Ethics* (London: Macmillan).

Finch, J. (1989), *Family Obligations and Social Change* (Cambridge: Polity Press).

Findlay, M. (1999), *The Globalization of Crime* (Cambridge: Cambridge University Press).

Finestone, H. (1964), 'Cats, Kicks, and Color', in H. Becter (ed.), *The Other Side* (Chicago: Free Press).

Firestone, S. (1971), *The Dialectic of Sex* (London: Jonathan Cape).

Fischer, C. S. (1975), 'Towards a Subcultural Theory of Urbanism', *American Journal of Sociology*, 80/6.

Fisk, R. (2009), 'The Demise of the Dollar', *Independent*, 6 October.

Fitzhugh, G. (1854), 'Sociology for the South', in H. Wish (ed.), *Ante-Bellum* (New York: G. P. Putnam's Sons, 1960).

Flanagan, W. (1993), *Contemporary Urban Sociology* (Cambridge: Cambridge University Press).

Fletcher, R. (1991), *Science, Ideology and the Media* (New Brunswick, NJ: Transaction Books).

Flew, T. (2007), *Understanding Global Media* (Houndmills: Palgrave Macmillan).

Florence, P. S. (1961), *Ownership, Control, and Success of Large Companies* (London: Sweet & Maxwell).

Flynn, J. R. (1980), *Race, I.Q. and Jensen* (London: Routledge & Kegan Paul).

Forbes (2009a), 'Special Report: The Celebrity 100', www.forbes.com/lists/2009/53/celebrity-09_The-Celebrity-100_EarningsPrevYear.html.

Forbes (2009b), 'The World's 100 Most Powerful Women'. 19 August, www.forbes.com/2009/08/18/worlds-most-powerful-women-forbes-woman-power-women-09-angela-merkel_land.html.%3C.

Forster, P. G. (1972), 'Secularization in the English Context: Some Conceptual and Empirical Problems', *Sociological Review*, 20.

Foster, J. (1974), *Class Struggle and the Industrial Revolution: Early Industrial Capitalism in Three English Towns* (London: Weidenfeld & Nicolson).

Foucault, M. (1961), *Madness and Civilization* (New York: Vintage Books, 1973).

Foucault, M. (1963), *The Birth of the Clinic* (New York: Vintage Books, 1975).

Foucault, M. (1971), *The Archaeology of Knowledge* (New York: Pantheon, 1972).

Foucault, M. (1975), *Discipline and Punish* (London: Allen Lane, 1977).

Foucault, M. (1976), *The History of Sexuality, i. An Introduction* (New York: Vintage Books, 1980).

Foucault, M. (1984a), *The History of Sexuality, ii. The Use of Pleasure* (New York: Vintage Books, 1986).

Foucault, M. (1984b), *The History of Sexuality, iii. The Care of the Self* (New York: Vintage Books, 1988).

Frank, A. G. (1967), *Capitalism and Underdevelopment in Latin America: Historical Studies of Chile and Brazil* (New York: Monthly Review Press).

Frank, A. G. (1998), *ReORIENT: Global Economy in the Asian Age* (Berkeley and Los Angeles: University of California Press).

Frankenberg, R. (1966), *Communities in Britain: Social Life in Town and Country* (Harmondsworth: Penguin).

Franklin, A. (2003), *Tourism: An Introduction* (London: Sage).

Franklin, B. (1994), *Packaging Politics: Political Communications in Britain's Media Democracy* (London: Edward Arnold).

Franklin, M. (1985), *The Decline of Class Voting in Britain* (Oxford: Oxford University Press).

Fraser, D. (1984), *The Evolution of the British Welfare State: A History of Social Policy since the Industrial Revolution* (2nd edn, London: Macmillan).

Fraser, D. (2009), *The Evolution of the British Welfare State* (4th edn, London: Macmillan).

Fraser, S. (1995) (ed.), *The Bell Curve Wars* (New York: Basic Books).

Frazer, E. (1987), 'Teenage Girls Reading *Jackie*', *Media, Culture, and Society*, 8.

Frazier, E. F. (1932), *The Negro Family in Chicago* (Chicago: University of Chicago Press).

Freeman, D. (1984), *Margaret Mead and the Heretic* (Harmondsworth: Penguin, 1996).

Freidson, E. (1970), *The Profession of Medicine* (New York: Dodd Mead).

Freud, S. (1900), *The Interpretation of Dreams* (London: George Allen & Unwin, 1954).

Freud, S. (1901), *The Psychopathology of Everyday Life* (Harmondsworth: Penguin, 1975).

Freud, S. (1905), 'Three Essays on Sexuality', in S. Freud, *On Sexuality* (Harmondsworth: Penguin, 1977).

Freud, S. (1915–17), *Introductory Lectures on Psychoanalysis* (London: George Allen & Unwin, 1922).

Freud, S. (1923), *The Ego and the Id* (London: Hogarth Press, 1962).

Friedan, B. (1962), *The Feminine Mystique* (New York: Dell).

Friedman, H., and Mereedeen, S. (1980), *The Dynamics of Industrial Conflict* (London: Croom Helm).

Friedrich, C. J., and Brzezinski, Z. K. (1956), *Totalitarian Dictatorship and Autocracy* (New York: Praeger).

Friedrichs, R. W. (1970), *A Sociology of Sociology* (New York: Free Press).

Frobel, F., Heinrichs J., and Kreye O. (1980), *The New International Division of Labour* (Cambridge: Cambridge University Press).

Fromm, E. (1942), *Fear of Freedom* (London: Routledge & Kegan Paul).

Fukuyama, F. (1989), 'The End of History?', *National Interest*, 16.

Fulcher, J. (1991), *Labour Movements, Employers, and the State: Conflict and Co-operation in Britain and Sweden* (Oxford: Clarendon Press).

Fulcher, J. (2004), *Capitalism: A Very Short Introduction* (Oxford: Oxford University Press).

Fuller, M. (1983), 'Qualified Criticism, Critical Qualifications', in Barton and Walker (1983).

Gabriel, Y. (1988), *Working Lives in Catering* (London: Routledge Kegan Paul).

Gagliardi, P. (1996), 'Exploring the Aesthetic Side of Organizational Life', in S. Clegg, C. Hardy, and W. Nord (eds), *Handbook of Organization Studies* (London: Sage).

Gall, G. (2004), 'Union Busting at Amazon.com in Britain', *Word Power Books*, 2 January.

Gall, G. (2006), 'Introduction', in *Union Recognition: Organising and Bargaining Outcomes* (London: Routledge).

Gall, G. (2009) (ed.), *Union Revitalisation in Advanced Economies* (Houndmills: Palgrave Macmillan).

Gallie, D. and Marsh, C. (1994), 'The Experience of Unemployment' in Gallie, D. and Vogler, C., *Social Change and the Experience of Unemployment* (Oxford: Oxford University Press).

Gallin, D. (2002), 'Labour as a Global Social Force', in J. Harrod and R. O'Brien (eds), *Global Unions?* (London: Routledge).

Galton, F. (1869), *Hereditary Genius* (London: Friedmann, 1978).

Galtung, J., and Ruge, M. (1981), 'Structuring and Selecting News', in S. Cohen and J. Young (eds), *The Manufacture of News: Deviance, Social Problems and the Mass Media* (London: Constable).

Galtung, J., and Ruge, M. (1999), 'The Structure of Foreign News', in H. Tumber (ed.), *News: A Reader* (Oxford: Oxford University Press).

Gambetta, D. (1993), *The Sicilian Mafia* (Cambridge, MA: Harvard University Press).

Gamble, A. (1994), *The Free Economy and the Strong State: The Politics of Thatcherism* (2nd edn, London: Macmillan).

Gans, H. J. (1968), *People and Plans: Essays on Urban Problems and Solutions* (New York: Basic Books).

Gans, H. J. (1995), 'Urbanism and Suburbanism as Ways of Life: A Reevaluation of Definitions', in Kasinitz (1995).

Gardner, R., Cairns, J., and Lawton, D. (2004) (eds), *Faith Schools: Consensus or Conflict* (London: Routledge Falmer).

Garfinkel, H. (1967), *Studies in Ethnomethodology* (Englewood Cliffs, NJ: Prentice-Hall).

Gaskell, M. (1977), 'Housing and the Lower Middle Class, 1870–1914', in Crossick (1977b).

Gatrell, C. (2008), 'Involved Fatherhood', *Sociology Review*, 18/1.

Gauntlett, D. (2000a), 'Web.Studies: A User's Guide', in Gauntlett (2000b).

Gauntlett, D. (2000b) (ed.), *Web.Studies: Rewiring Media Studies for the Digital Age* (London: Arnold).

Gauntlett, D. (2008), *Media, Gender and Identity: An Introduction* (2nd edn, London: Routledge).

Gavron, H. (1968), *The Captive Wife* (Harmondsworth: Penguin).

Gavron, K. (2006), 'Besieged in the East End', *Sunday Times*, 23 April.

Gelles, R. J., and Cornell, C. P. (1987) (eds), 'Elder Abuse: The Status of Current Knowledge', in R. J. Gelles, *Family Violence* (2nd edn, London: Sage).

Gelsthorpe, L. (1993) (ed.), *Minority Ethnic Groups in the Criminal Justice System* (Cambridge: Institute of Criminology).

Gentleman, A. (2009), 'Children in Care: How Britain is Failing its Most Vulnerable', *Guardian*, 20 April.

Geraghty, C. (1992), 'British Soaps in the 1980s', in Strinati and Wagg (1992).

Gergen, K. (1994), *Realities and Relationships* (Cambridge, MA: Harvard University Press).

Gergen, K., and Gergen, M. (1983), 'Narratives of the Self', in T. R. Sarbin and K. E. Scheibe (eds), *Studies in Social Identity* (New York: Praeger).

Gershuny, J. (1988), 'Time, Technology, and the Informal Economy', in Pahl (1988).

Gershuny, J. (1992), 'Change in the Domestic Division of Labour in the UK, 1975–1987: Dependent Labour versus Adaptive Partnership', in Abercrombie and Warde (1992).

Gerth, H. H., and Mills, C. W. (1953), *Character and Social Structure* (New York: Harcourt, Brace, and World).

Giallombardo, R. (1966), *Society of Women: A Study of a Women's Prison* (New York: Wiley).

Gibson, O., and Rattansi, A. (2006), 'Look East', *Guardian*, 13 November.

Giddens, A. (1971), *Capitalism and Modern Social Theory* (Cambridge: Cambridge University Press).

Giddens, A. (1976), *New Rules of the Sociological Method* (London: Hutchinson).

Giddens, A. (1981), *A Contemporary Critique of Historical Materialism*, i: *Power, Property, and the State* (London: Macmillan).

Giddens, A. (1985), *The Nation-State and Violence* (Cambridge: Polity Press).

Giddens, A. (1986), *Sociology: A Brief but Critical Introduction* (2nd edn, London: Macmillan).

Giddens, A. (1990), *The Consequences of Modernity* (Cambridge: Polity Press).

Giddens, A. (1991), *Modernity and Self-Identity* (Cambridge: Polity Press).

Giddens, A. (1994), *Beyond Left and Right: The Future of Radical Politics* (Cambridge: Polity Press).

Giddens, A. (1998), *The Third Way: The Renewal of Social Democracy* (Cambridge: Polity Press).

Giddens, A. (1999), *Runaway World: How Globalisation is Reshaping our Lives* (London: Profile Books).

Gill, M. (2000), *Commercial Robbery* (London, Blackstone Press).

Gillespie, M., and Toynbee, J. (2006) (eds), *Analysing Media Texts* (Maidenhead: Open University Press).

Gilman, C. P. (1898), *Women and Economics: A Study of the Economic Relations between Women and Men as a Factor in Social Evolution* (London: Prometheus Books, 1994).

Gilman, C. P. (1911), *The Man-Made World, or Our Androcentric Culture* (New York: Humanity Books, 2001).

Gilroy, P. (1987), *There Aint No Black in the Union Jack* (London: Hutchinson).

Gilroy, P. (1993), *The Black Atlantic: Modernity and Double Consciousness* (London: Verso).

Giner, S. (1976), *Mass Society* (London: Martin Robertson).

Ginn J., Arber, S., Brannen, J., Dale, A., Dex, S., Elias, P., Moss, P., Pahl, J., Roberts, C., and Rubery, J. (1996), 'Feminist Fallacies: A Reply to Hakim on Women's Employment', *British Journal of Sociology*, 47/1.

Gittings, J. (2002), 'Industrial Waste Will Pour into China Dam', *Guardian*, 21 January.

Gittins, D. (1993), *The Family in Question: Changing Households and Familiar Ideologies* (2nd edn, London: Macmillan).

Glaser, B. G., and Strauss, A. L. (1965), *Awareness of Dying* (Chicago: Aldine).

Glaser, B. G., and Strauss, A. L. (1968), *Time for Dying* (Chicago: Aldine).

Glasgow University Media Group (1976), *Bad News* (London: Routledge & Kegan Paul).

Glass, D. V. (1954) (ed.), *Social Mobility in Britain* (London: Routledge & Kegan Paul).

Glazer, N., and Moynihan, D. P. (1963), *Beyond the Melting Pot: The Negroes, Puerto Ricans, Jews, Italians, and Irish of New York City* (Cambridge, MA: MIT Press, 1970).

Glazer, N., and Moynihan, D. P (1970), 'New York City in 1970', in N. Glazer and D. P. Moynihan, *Beyond the Melting Pot: The Negroes, Puerto Ricans, Jews, Italians, and Irish of New York City* (Cambridge, MA: MIT Press, 1970; reprint of 1963 edn, with additional chapter).

Gleiman, H. (1995), *Psychology* (4th edn, New York: W. W. Norton).

Glennerster, H. (1995), *British Social Policy since 1945* (Oxford: Blackwell).

Glennerster, H. (2000), *British Social Policy since 1945* (2nd edn, Oxford: Blackwell).

Glennerster, H. (2001), 'United Kingdom Education 1997–2001', Centre for the Analysis of Social Exclusion, Case Paper 50.

Glennerster, H. (2006), *British Social Policy since 1945* (3rd edn, Oxford: Blackwell).

Glucksmann, M. A. (1995), 'Why "Work"? Gender and the "Total Social Organization of Labour"', *Gender, Work, and Organization*, 2/2.

Gobineau, J. A. Comte de (1853–5), *Essay on the Inequality of Human Races* (New York: Putnam, 1915).

Goffman, E. (1959), *The Presentation of Self in Everyday Life* (Harmondsworth: Penguin).

Goffman, E. (1961b), *Asylums: Essays on the Social Situation of Mental Patients and Other Inmates* (New York: Doubleday).

Goffman, E. (1963a), *Relations in Public* (New York: Free Press).

Goffman, E. (1963b), *Stigma* (Englewood Cliffs, NJ: Prentice-Hall).

Goffman, E. (1979), *Gender Advertisements* (London: Macmillan).

Goggin, G. (2000), 'Pay per Browse? The Web's Commercial Futures', in Gauntlett (2000b).

Gold, R. (1958), 'Roles in Sociological Field Observation', *Social Forces*, 36.

Goldthorpe, J. H. (1964), 'Social Stratification in Industrial Society', *Sociological Review Monograph*, 8.

Goldthorpe, J. H. (1980), *Social Mobility and Class Structure* (Oxford: Clarendon Press).

Goldthorpe, J. H. (1983), 'Women and Class Analysis: In Defence of the Conventional View', *Sociology*, 17.

Goldthorpe, J. H., and Lockwood, D. (1963), 'Affluence and the British Class Structure', *Sociological Review*, 11.

Goldthorpe, J. H., Lockwood, D., Bechhofer, F., and Platt, J. (1968a), *The Affluent Worker: Industrial Attitudes and Behaviour* (Cambridge: Cambridge University Press).

Goldthorpe, J. H., Lockwood, D., Bechhofer, F., and Platt, J. (1968b), *The Affluent Worker: Political Attitudes and Behaviour* (Cambridge: Cambridge University Press).

Goldthorpe, J. H., Lockwood, D., Bechhofer, F., and Platt, J. (1969), *The Affluent Worker in the Class Structure* (Cambridge: Cambridge University Press).

Gough, I. (1979), *The Political Economy of the Welfare State* (London: Macmillan).

Gould, A. (1993), *Capitalist Welfare Systems: A Comparison of Japan, Britain, and Sweden* (London: Longman).

Gould, S. J. (1981), *The Mismeasure of Man* (Harmondsworth: Penguin, 1984).

Gouldner, A. (1954a), *Patterns of Industrial Bureaucracy: A Case Study of Modern Factory Administration* (New York: Free Press).

Gouldner, A. (1954b), *Wildcat Strike* (New York: Antioch Press).

Gouldner, A. (1970), *The Coming Crisis of Western Sociology* (New York: Basic Books).

Graham, S., and Marvin, S. (2001), *Splintering Urbanism: Networked Infrastructures, Technological Mobilities and the Urban Condition* (London: Routledge).

Gray, A. (1992), *Video Playtime: The Gendering of a Leisure Technology* (London: Routledge).

Green, D. (2009), 'Editor's Introduction', in MacEoin (2009).

Greer, G. (1999), *The Whole Woman* (London: Doubleday).

Gregory, J. (2009), *In the Mix: Narrowing the Gap between Public and Private Housing (*London: Fabian Society).

Gregory, M., and Connolly, S. (2008), 'The Price of Reconciliation', *Economic Journal*, 118: 526.

Gregson, N., and Lowe, M. (1994), *Servicing the Middle Classes: Class, Gender, and Waged Domestic Labour in Contemporary Britain* (London: Routledge).

Grey, C., and Wilmott, H. (2005), *Critical Management Studies: A Reader* (Oxford: Oxford University Press).

Grint, K. (1999), *The Sociology of Work: An Introduction* (2nd edn, Cambridge: Polity Press).

Grint, K. (2000) (ed.), *Work and Society: A Reader* (Cambridge: Policy Press).

Grint, K. (2005), *The Sociology of Work: An Introduction* (3rd edn, Cambridge: Polity Press).

Gross, N., Mason, W. S., and McEachern, A. W. (1958), *Explorations in Role Analysis: Studies of the School Superintendency Role* (New York: John Wiley).

Guardian News Blog (2008), 'Knife Crime: What is the Truth?', 17 July, www.guardian.co.uk/news/blog/2008/jul/17/crimeisdownbutwhatabout.

Guha, S. (2000), 'All the Risks, None of the Rewards', *Telegraph Travel*, 2 September.

Gumbel, A. (2005), 'Paradise Lost', *Independent*, 18 April.

Gumplowicz, L. (1885), *Outlines of Sociology* (Philadelphia: American Academy of Political and Social Science, 1899).

Gunter, B. (2003), *News and the Net* (Mahwah, NJ: Lawrence Elbaum).

Gunter, B. (2008), 'Why Study Media Content?', *Sociology Review*, 18/2.

Gurevitch, M. (1996), 'The Globalization of Electronic Journalism', in Curran and Gurevitch (1996).

Guthrie, D. (2009), *China and Globalization: The Social, Economic and Political Transformation of Chinese Society* (rev.edn, London: Routledge).

Guttsman, W. L. (1963), *The British Political Elite* (London: MacGibbon & Kee).

Habermas, J. (1967), *On the Logic of the Social Sciences* (Cambridge: Polity Press, 1988).

Habermas, J. (1968), *Knowledge and Human Interests* (London: Heinemann, 1972).

Habermas, J. (1968–9), *Towards a Rational Society* (London: Heinemann, 1971).

Habermas, J. (1973), *Legitimation Crisis* (London: Heinemann, 1976).

Habermas, J. (1981a), *The Theory of Communicative Action*, i: *Reason and the Rationalisation of Society* (London: Heinemann, 1984).

Habermas, J. (1981b), *The Theory of Communicative Action*, ii: *The Critique of Functionalist Reason* (London: Heinemann, 1987).

Hakim, C. (1993), 'The Myth of Rising Female Employment', *Work, Employment, and Society*, 7/1.

Hakim, C. (1995), 'Five Feminist Myths about Women's Employment', *British Journal of Sociology*, 46/3.

Hakim, C. (1996), *Key Issues in Women's Work: Female Heterogeneity and the Polarization of Women's Employment* (London: Athlone Press).

Hall, C. (1982*a*), 'The Butcher, the Baker, the Candlestickmaker: The Shop and the Family in the Industrial Revolution', in Whitelegg *et al.* (1982).

Hall, C. (1982*b*), 'The Home Turned Upside Down? The Working-Class Family in Cotton Textiles 1780–1850', in Whitelegg *et al.* (1982).

Hall, C. (1998), 'The Early Formation of Victorian Domestic Ideology', in Shoemaker and Vincent (1998).

Hall, L. (1991), *Hidden Anxieties: Male Sexuality, 1900–1950* (Cambridge: Cambridge University Press).

Hall, S. (1989), 'New Ethnicities', in *Black Film, Black Cinema*, ICA Document 7 (London: Institute of Contemporary Arts).

Hall, S., and Jacques, M. (1983) (eds), *The Politics of Thatcherism* (London: Lawrence & Wishart).

Hall, S., Critcher, C., Jefferson, T., Clarke, J., and Roberts, B. (1978), *Policing the Crisis: Mugging, the State, and Law and Order* (London: Macmillan).

Hallin, D. C. (1996), 'Commercialism and Professionalism in the American News Media', in Curran and Gurevitch (1996).

Halsey, A. H. (1997), 'Trends in Access and Equity in Higher Education: Britain in International Perspective', in Halsey *et al.* (1997).

Halsey, A. H., Heath, A., and Ridge, J. (1980), *Origins and Destinations: Family, Class, and Education in Modern Britain* (Oxford: Clarendon Press).

Hamilton, P. (1983), *Talcott Parsons* (Chichester: Ellis Horwood).

Hamilton, P., and Thompson K. (2002) (eds), *The Uses of Sociology* (Oxford: Blackwell).

Harding, S. (1986), *The Science Question in Feminism* (Milton Keynes: Open University Press).

Hargreaves, D. H. (1967), *Social Relations in a Secondary School* (London: Routledge & Kegan Paul).

Hargreaves, D. H. (1982), *The Challenge for the Comprehensive School: Culture, Curriculum, and Community* (London: Routledge).

Hari, J. (2009), 'The Dark Side of Dubai', *Independent*, 7 April.

Harrington, M. (1962) *The Other America: Poverty in the United States* (New York: Macmillan).

Harris, N. (1995), *The New Untouchables: Immigration and the New World Worker* (London: I. B. Tauris).

Harrison, D. (1994), 'Tourism, Capitalism and Development in Less Developed Countries', in Sklair (1994).

Harrison, P. (1985), *Inside the Inner City: Life under the Cutting Edge* (London: Penguin).

Harrison, T. (1949), 'Little Kinsey: Mass Observation's Sex Survey of 1949', in L. Stanley (ed.), *Sex Surveyed, 1949–1994* (London: Taylor & Francis, 1995).

Hartmann, H. (1981), 'The Unhappy Marriage of Marxism and Feminism: Towards a More Progressive Union', in L. Sargent (ed.), *Women and Revolution: The Unhappy Marriage of Marxism and Feminism* (London: Pluto).

Hartsock, N. (1983), 'The Feminist Standpoint: Developing the Ground for a Specifically Feminist Historical Materialism', in S. Harding and M. Hintikka (eds), *Discovering Reality: Feminist Perspectives on Epistemology, Metaphysics, Methodology and Philosophy of Science* (Dordrecht: D. D. Reidel).

Hay, C. (1996), *Re-Stating Social and Political Change* (Buckingham: Open University Press).

Hearnshaw, L. S. (1979), *Cyril Burt: Psychologist* (London: Hodder & Stoughton).

Heath, A. (1981), *Social Mobility* (Glasgow: Fontana).

Heath, A. (1989), 'Class in the Classroom', in Cosin *et al.* (1989).

Heath, A., Jowell, R., and Curtice, J. (1985), *How Britain Votes* (Oxford: Pergamon Press).

Heath, A., Jowell, R., Curtice, J. Evans, G., Field, J., and Witherspoon, S. (1991), *Understanding Political Change: The British Voter, 1964–1987* (Oxford: Pergamon Press).

Heath, S. (2004), 'Transforming Friendship: Are Housemates the New Family?', *Sociology Review*, 14/1.

Heath, S., and Cleaver, E. (2003), *Young, Free and Single?: Twenty-Somethings and Household Change* (Basingstoke: Palgrave Macmillan).

Heaton, T., and Lawson, T. (1996), *Education and Training* (London: Macmillan).

Hebdige, D. (1979), *Subculture: The Meaning of Style* (London: Methuen).

Heelas, P. (1996), *The New Age Movement* (Oxford: Blackwell).

HEFCE (2010), *Trends in Young Participation in Higher Education: Core Results for England* (Bristol: Higher Education Funding Council for England).

Heffernan, R. (2000), *New Labour and Thatcherism: Political Change in Britain* (Houndmills; Macmillan).

Hegel, G. W. F. (1821), *Philosophy of Right* (Oxford: Oxford University Press, 1952).

Heidensohn, F. (1985), *Women and Crime* (London: Macmillan).

Held, D. (1980), *An Introduction to Critical Theory* (London: Hutchinson).

Held, D. (2006), *Models of Democracy* (3rd edn, Cambridge: Polity Press).

Held, D., and McGrew, A. (2007), *Globalization/Anti-Globalization* (2nd edn, Cambridge: Polity Press).

Held, D., McGrew, A. Goldblatt, D., and Perraton, J. (1999), *Global Transformations: Politics, Economics, and Culture* (Cambridge: Polity Press).

Hendrick, H. (1994), *Child Welfare: England 1872–1989* (London: Routledge).

Henriques, F. M. (1953), *Family and Colour in Jamaica* (London: Eyre & Spottiswoode).

Herberg, W. (1955), *Protestant, Catholic, Jew* (New York: Doubleday).

Herrnstein, R. J., and Murray, C. (1994), *The Bell Curve: Intelligence and Class Structure in American Life* (New York: Free Press).

Hesmondhalgh, D. (2007), *The Cultural Industries* (2nd edn, London: Sage).

Hickman, M. (2009), 'Suppliers Run Rings around Regulators', *Independent*, 7 October.

Higgs, E. (1996), *A Clearer Sense of the Census: The Victorian Census and Historical Research* (London: HMSO).

Hilferding, R. (1910), *Finance Capital* (London: Routledge & Kegan Paul, 1981).

Hill, M. (2003), *Understanding Social Policy* (7th edn, Oxford: Blackwell).

Hill, P. (2003), *The Japanese Mafia* (Oxford: Oxford University Press).

Hill Collins, P. (1990), *Black Feminist Thought* (London: Harper Collins).

Hills, J. (1995), *Joseph Rowntree Inquiry into Income and Wealth*, ii (York: Joseph Rowntree Foundation).

Himmelweit, H., Humphreys, P., and Jaeger, M. (1985), *How Voters Decide* (Milton Keynes: Open University Press).

Hindess, B. (1973), *The Use of Official Statistics in Sociology* (London: Macmillan).

Hinton, P. R. (1995), *Statistics Explained* (London: Routledge).

Hirst, P., and Thompson, G. (1996), *Globalization in Question: The International Economy and the Possibilities of Governance* (Cambridge: Polity Press).

Hitler, A. (1925), *Mein Kampf* (London: Hurst & Blackett, 1939).

Hoag, H. (2008), 'Brains apart', *New Scientist*, 2665.

Hobbs, D. (1988), *Doing the Business* (Oxford: Oxford University Press).

Hobbs, D. (1994), 'Professional and Organized Crime in Britain', in M. Maguire, R. Morgan, and R. Reiner (eds), *The Oxford Handbook of Criminology* (Oxford: Clarendon Press).

Hobbs, D., Lister, S., Hadfield, P., Winlow, S., and Hall, S. (2000), 'Receiving Shadows: Governance and Liminality in the Night-Time Economy', *British Journal of Sociology*, 51.

Hobbs, D., Hadfield, P., Lister, S., and Winlow, S. (2002), 'Door Lore: The Art and Economics of Intimidation', *British Journal of Criminology*, 42.

Hobhouse, L. J. (1893), *The Labour Movement* (London: T. Fisher Unwin).

Hobsbawm, E. J. (1969), *Bandits* (Harmondsworth: Penguin, 1972).

Hobsbawm, E. J. (1977), *The Age of Capital 1848–1875* (London: Sphere Books).

Hobsbawm, E. J. (1987), *The Age of Empire* (London: Weidenfeld & Nicolson).

Hochschild, A. R. (1983), *The Managed Heart: Commercialization of Human Feeling* (Berkeley and Los Angeles: University of California Press).

Hockey, J., and James, A. (2003), *Social Identities across the Life Course* (Basingstoke: Palgrave Macmillan).

Hodges, L. (2000), 'The Long, Uphill Struggle of the Academic Woman', *Independent*, 22 June.

Hodgkinson, M. (2007), 'London 2012 Must Learn from the £1bn Sydney Hangover', *Daily Telegraph*, 8 February.

Hoggart, R. (1957), *The Uses of Literacy* (London: Chatto & Windus).

Holcombe, L. (1973), *Victorian Ladies at Work* (Newton Abbot: David & Charles).

Holdaway, S. (1982), '"An Inside Job": A Case Study of Covert Research on the Police', in Bulmer (1982).

Holdaway, S. (1983), *Inside the British Police* (Oxford: Basil Blackwell).

Holleman, H., McChesney, R., Bellamy Foster, J., and Jamil Jonna, R. (2009), 'The Penal State in an Age of Crisis', *Monthly Review* (June).

Hollingshead, J. (1861), *Ragged London in 1861* (London: Dent).

Holme, A. (1985), 'Family and Homes in East London', *New Society*, 12 July.

Holmes, M. (2009), *Gender and Everyday Life* (London: Routledge).

Holt, R. (1989), *Sport and the British: A Modern History* (Oxford: Clarendon Press).

Holt, R., and Mason, T. (2000), *Sport in Britain 1945–2000* (Oxford: Blackwell).

Homan, R., and Bulmer, M. (1982), 'On the Merits of Covert Methods: A Dialogue', in Bulmer (1982).

Homans, G. C. (1961), *Social Behaviour: Its Elementary Forms* (London: Routledge & Kegan Paul).

Home Office (2001), *Community Cohesion: A Report of the Independent Review Team* (London: HMSO).

Home Office (2009). *Drug Misuse Declared: Findings from the 2009/09 British Crime Survey: England and Wales* (London: HMSO).

Horney, K. (1937), *The Neurotic Personality of Our Time* (New York: W. W. Norton).

Horney, K. (1946), *Our Inner Conflict* (London: Routledge & Kegan Paul).

Hornsby-Smith, M. P. (1987), *Roman Catholicism in England* (Cambridge: Cambridge University Press).

Hornsby-Smith, M. P. (1991), *Roman Catholic Beliefs in England* (Cambridge: Cambridge University Press).

Hornsby-Smith, M. P., Lee, R. M., and Turcan, K. A. (1982), 'A Typology of English Catholics', *Sociological Review*, 30.

Horne, J. (2006), *Sport in Consumer Culture* (Houndmills: Palgrave Macmillan).

Horne, J., Tomlinson, A., and Whannel G. (1999), *An Introduction to the Sociological and Cultural Analysis of Sport* (London: Routledge).

Howard, E. (1898), *Tomorrow: A Peaceful Path to Real Reform* (London: Sonnenschein).

Howe, S. (2005), 'Loyalism's Rage against the Fading Light of Britishness', *Guardian*, 10 October.

Huff, D. (1954), *How to Lie with Statistics* (London: Victor Gollancz).

Hughes, H. (1854), *Treatise of Sociology: Theoretical and Practical* (New York: Negro Universities Press, 1968).

Hughes, M. (2008), 'The Name's Sky, Ocean Sky', *Independent*, 29 September.

Hulme, D., and Turner, M. M. (1990), *Sociology and Development: Theories, Policies, and Practices* (New York: Harvester Wheatsheaf).

Humphreys, L. (1970), *Tearoom Trade* (London: Duckworth).

Hunt, S. (2005), *The Life Course: A Sociological Introduction* (Basingstoke: Palgrave Macmillan).

Hunt, S. A. (2009) (ed.), *Family Trends: British Families since the 1950s* (London: Family and Parenting Institute).

Huntington, S. P. (1993), 'The Clash of Civilizations', *Foreign Affairs*, 72/3.

Hutchby, I (2006), *Media Talk: Conversation Analysis and the Study of Broadcasting* (Maidenhead: Open University Press).

Ianni, F. A. J., and Reuss-Ianni, E. R. (1972), *A Family Business* (New York: Russell Sage Foundation).

Iganski, P. (2002) (ed.), *The Hate Debate: Should Hate Be Punished as a Crime?* (London: Profile Books).

Ignatieff, M. (1978), *A Just Measure of Pain: The Penitentiary in the Industrial Revolution* (New York: Columbia University Press).

Illich, I. (1973), *Deschooling Society* (Harmondsworth: Penguin).

Illich, I. (1977), *Limits to Medicine: Medical Nemesis. The Expropriation of Health* (Harmondsworth: Penguin).

Inglehart, R. (1990), *Culture Shift in Advanced Industrial Society* (Princeton: Princeton University Press).

Internet World Stats (2009), www.internetworldstats.com.

Jackson, B. (1968), *Working Class Community: Some General Notions Raised by a Series of Studies in Northern England* (London: Routledge & Kegan Paul).

Jackson, B., and Marsden, D. (1962), *Education and the Working Class* (London: Routledge & Kegan Paul).

Jackson, C. (2006), *Lads and Ladettes in School* (Buckingham: Open University Press).

Jackson, C., and Tinkler, P. (2007), '"Ladettes" and "Modern Girls": "Troublesome" Young Femininities', *Sociological Review*, 55/2.

Jacobs, J. (1961), *The Death and Life of Great American Cities* (London: Jonathan Cape).

Jacques, M. (2006), 'The Death of Doha Signals the Demise of Globalisation', *Guardian*, 13 July.

Jacques, M. (2009), *When China Rules the World: The Rise of the Middle Kingdom and the End of the Western World* (London: Allen Lane).

James, A. L., Bottomley, A. K., Liebling, A., and Clare, E. (1997), *Privatizing Prisons: Rhetoric and Reality* (London: Sage).

James, A., Jenks, C., and Prout, A. (1998), *Theorizing Childhood* (Cambridge: Polity Press).

Jameson, F. (1984), 'Postmodernism or the Cultural Logic of Late Capitalism', *New Left Review*, 146.

Jarvis, H., Cloke, J., and Kantor, P. (2009), *Cities and Gender* (Routledge).

Jawad, H. (1998), *The Rights of Women in Islam: An Authentic Approach* (London: Macmillan).

Jay, M. (1973), *The Dialectical Imagination* (London: Heinemann).

Jeffers, S., Hoggett, P., and Harrison, L. (1996), 'Race, Ethnicity, and Community in Three Localities', *New Community*, 22/1.

Jencks, C. (1972), *Inequality: A Reassessment of the Effects of Family and Schooling in America* (New York: Basic Books).

Jenkins, R. (1992), *Pierre Bourdieu* (London: Routledge).

Jenkins, R. (1996), *Social Identities* (London: Routledge).

Jenkins, R. (2002), *Foundations of Sociology* (Basingstoke: Palgrave Macmillan).

Jenkins, S. (1996), *Changing Places: Income Mobility and Poverty Dynamics in Britain* (Colchester: British Household Panel Study, University of Essex).

Jensen, A. (1969), 'Environment, Heredity, and Intelligence', *Harvard Educational Review*, 2.

Jensen, C. (2004), 'Trade Unionism: Differences and Similarities: A Comparative View on Europe, USA and Asia', paper presented at the International Industrial Relations Association Conference, Seoul.

Jessop, B. (2002), *The Future of the Capitalist State* (Cambridge: Polity Press).

Jewson, N. (1976), 'The Disappearance of the Sick Man from Medical Cosmologies', *Sociology*, 10.

Jewson, N. (1989), 'No Place like Home: Sociological Perspectives on Housing', in *Social Studies Review*, 4/4: 128.

Jewson, N. (1990), 'Inner City Riots', *Social Studies Review*, 5/5.

Johnson, A., *et al.* (2001), 'Sexual Behaviour in Britain: Partnerships, Practices, and HIV Risk Behaviours', *Lancet*, 358/9296.

Johnson, H. M. (1961), *Sociology: A Systematic Introduction* (London: Routledge & Kegan Paul).

Johnson, J., Cohen, P., Smailes, E., Kasen, S., and Brook, J. (2002), 'Television Viewing and Aggressive Behaviour during Adolescence and Adulthood', *Science*, 295 (29 March).

Johnson, T. (1972), *Professions and Power* (London: Macmillan).

Johnston, L. (1992), *The Rebirth of Private Policing* (London: Routledge).

Jones, M. (2009), 'Moral Panics', *Sociology Review*, 18/3.

Jordan, T. (1999), *Cyberspace: The Culture and Politics of Cyberspace and the Internet* (London: Routledge).

Joshi, H. (1989), *The Changing Population of Britain* (Oxford: Blackwell).

Jowell, R., Brook, L., Prior, G., and Taylor, B. (1991), *British Social Attitudes* (Aldershot: Gower).

Jowett, M. (2001), 'Is Feminism still Important', *Sociology Review*, 11/1.

Joynson, R. B. (1989), *The Burt Affair* (London: Routledge).

Kanter, R. M. (1977), *Men and Women of the Corporation* (New York: Basic Books).

Karn, V., Kemeny, J., and Williams, P. (1985), *Home Ownership in the Inner City* (Aldershot: Gower).

Kasinitz, P. (1995) (ed.), *Metropolis: Centre and Symbol of our Times* (London: Macmillan).

Keat, R., and Urry, J. (1975), *Social Theory as Science* (London: Routledge & Kegan Paul).

Keenan, W. (2004), 'Dress Code Communication in Sociological Perspective', in P. Hills (ed.), *As Others See Us* (Dereham: Peter Francis).

Kegley, C., and Wittkopf, E. (1999), *World Politics* (7th edn, Basingstoke: Macmillan).

Kerr, C., Dunlop, J. T., Harbison, F., and Myers, C. A. (1960), *Industrialism and Industrial Man* (Cambridge, MA: Harvard University Press).

Kerr, M. (1958), *The People of Ship Street* (London: Routledge & Kegan Paul).

Kersley, B., Alpin, C., Forth, J., Bryson, A., Bewley, H., Dix, J., and Oxenbridge, S. (2005), *Inside the Workplace: First Findings from the 2004 Workplace Employment Relations Survey* (London: Routledge).

Kessel, A. (2008), 'Top Women Lured to States as English Game is Left Behind', *Observer*, 5 October.

King, A. (1990), *Global Cities: Post-Imperialism and the Internationalization of London* (London: Routledge).

King, D. (1987), 'The State, Capital and Urban Change in Britain', in Smith and Feagin (1987).

King, R. (1978), *All Things Bright and Beautiful: A Sociological Study of an Infants' Classroom* (Chichester: John Wiley).

King, S. (2009), 'As Capitalism Stares into the Abyss, was Marx Right all along?', *Independent*, 2 March.

Kitzinger, J. (1997), 'Media Influence', *Sociology Review*, 6/4.

Klein, J. (1965), *Samples from English Culture* (London: Routledge & Kegan Paul).

Klein, N. (2007), *The Shock Doctrine: The Rise of Disaster Capitalism* (New York: Metropolitan Books).

Kohlberg, L. (1981), *Essays on Moral Development, Volume 1* (San Francisco: Jossey-Bass).

Korczynski, M. (2001), 'The Contradictions of Service Work: Call Centre as Customer-oriented Bureaucracy', in Sturdy *et al.* (2001).

Kornhauser, W. (1959), *The Politics of Mass Society* (New York: Free Press).

Kornhauser, W. (1960), *The Politics of Mass Society* (London: Routledge & Kegan Paul).

Korpi, W. (1983), *The Democratic Class Struggle* (London: Routledge & Kegan Paul).

Kuhn, T. S. (1962), *The Structure of Scientific Revolutions* (Chicago: University of Chicago Press).

Lacey, C. (1970), *Hightown Grammar: The School as a Social System* (Manchester: Manchester University Press).

Laing, R. D. (1960), *The Divided Self* (London: Tavistock).

Laing, R. D. (1961), *Self and Others* (London: Tavistock).

Laing, R. D., and Esterson, A. (1964), *Sanity, Madness and the Family* (Harmondsworth: Penguin).

Lane, C. (1981), *The Rites of Rulers: Ritual in Industrial Society—The Soviet Case* (Cambridge: Cambridge University Press).

Lane, D. (1976), *The Socialist Industrial State* (London: George Allen & Unwin).

Lane, D. (1996), *The Rise and Fall of State Socialism* (Cambridge: Polity Press).

Lane, T., and Roberts, K. (1971), *Strike at Pilkingtons* (London: Fontana).

Laqueur, T. (1990), *Making Sex: Body and Gender from the Greeks to Freud* (Cambridge, MA: Harvard University Press).

Lash, S., and Urry, J. (1987), *The End of Organized Capitalism* (Cambridge: Polity Press).

Lash, S., and Urry, J. (1994), *Economies of Signs and Space* (London: Sage).

Laslett, T. P. R., and Wall, R. (1972) (eds), *Household and Family in Past Time* (Cambridge: Cambridge University Press).

Laurance, J. (2009), 'Women are "Taking over the Health Service"', *Independent*, 3 June.

Lavalette, M. (1996), 'Thatcher's Working Children: Contemporary Issues of Child Labour', in Pilcher and Wagg (1996).

Lawler, S. (2000), *Mothering the Self: Mothers, Daughters, Subjects* (London: Routledge).

Lawless, P., and Brown, F. (1986), *Urban Growth and Change in Britain: An Introduction* (London: Harper & Row).

Lawrence, F. (2005), 'The Precarious Existence of the Thousands in Britain's Underclass', *Guardian*, 10 January.

Layton-Henry, Z. (1984), *The Politics of Race in Britain* (London: Allen & Unwin).

Lazarsfeld, P., Berelson, B. R., and Gauzet, H. (1948), *The People's Choice* (New York: Columbia University Press).

Lea, J., and Young, J. (1984), *What is to be Done about Law and Order* (Harmondsworth: Penguin).

Le Corbusier (1947), *City of Tomorrow and its Planning* (London: Architectural Press).

Lee, J. (1989), 'Social Class and Schooling', in Cole (1989).

Lefort, C. (1986), *The Political Forms of Modern Society* (Cambridge: Polity Press).

Legates, R. T., and Stout, F. (2007) (eds), *The City Reader* (4th edn, London: Routledge).

Legge, K. (1995), 'HRM: Rhetoric, Reality, and Hidden Agendas', in Storey (1995*b*).

Le Grand, J. (1982), *The Strategy of Equality* (London: Allen & Unwin).

Le Grand, J. (2005), 'Payment by Results Will Save our Health Service', *Guardian*, 12 October.

Leighton, T. (2009), 'Anger at Delay of Women's Summer Super League', *Guardian*, 6 April.

Lemert, E. (1967), *Human Deviance, Social Problems and Social Control* (Englewood Cliffs, NJ: Prentice-Hall).

Levi, M. (1987), *Regulating Fraud: White Collar Crime and the Criminal Process* (London: Tavistock).

Levine, D. (1971), *Georg Simmel on Individuality and Social Forms: Selected Writings* (Chicago: University of Chicago Press).

Lévi-Strauss, C. (1962), *Totemism* (London: Merlin Press).

Levitas, R. (1996), 'Fiddling while Britain Burns? The Measurement of Unemployment', in Levitas and Guy (1996).

Levitas, R. (2005), *The Inclusive Society: Social Exclusion and New Labour* (2nd edn, Basingstoke: Palgrave Macmillan).

Levitas, R., and Guy, W. (1996) (eds), *Interpreting Official Statistics* (London: Routledge).

Levy, M. J. (1966), *Modernization and the Structure of Societies* (Princeton: Princeton University Press).

Lewis, J. (2003), 'Responsibilities and Rights: Changing the Balance', in Ellison and Pierson (2003).

Lewis, O. (1961), *The Children of Sanchez* (New York: Random House).

Lewis, O. (1966), *La Vida* (New York: Random House).

Lichtenstein, B. (2002), 'AIDS as a Social Problem', in Ritzer (2004).

Lievrou, L., and Livingstone, S. (2006) (eds), *The Handbook of New Media: Updated Student Edition* (London: Sage).

Lincoln, C. E. (1973), *The Black Muslims in America* (Boston: Beacon Press).

Lincoln, S. (2004), 'Teenage Girls Bedroom Culture: Codes versus Zones', in A. Bennett and K. Harris (eds), *Beyond Subculture: Critical Commentaries on Subcultural Theory* (Palgrave: Hampshire).

Ling, T. (1968), *A History of Religion, East and West* (Houndmills: Macmillan).

Lipset, S. M. (1964), 'The Changing Class Structure of Contemporary European Politics', *Daedelus*, 63.

Lipset, S. M., and Bendix, R. (1959), *Social Mobility in an Industrial Society* (Berkeley and Los Angeles: University of California Press).

Lipset, S. M., and Rokkan, S. (1967) (eds), *Party Systems and Voter Alignment* (New York: Free Press).

Lisle-Williams, M. (1984), 'Beyond the Market: The Survival of Family Capitalism in the English Merchant Banks', *British Journal of Sociology*, 35.

Living in Britain: Preliminary Results from the 1995 General Household Survey (1996) (London: HMSO).

Lockwood, D. (1958), *The Blackcoated Worker* (Oxford: Oxford University Press, 1993).

Lockwood, D. (1960), 'The New Working Class', *European Journal of Sociology*, 1.

Lockwood, D. (1966), 'Sources of Variation in Working Class Images of Society', *Sociological Review*, 14.

Lombroso, C., and Ferrero, W. F. (1895), *The Female Offender* (London: Fisher Unwin).

Long, N. (2001), *Development Sociology: Actor Perspectives* (London: Routledge).

Love, J. F. (1986), *McDonalds behind the Arches* (Toronto: Bantam Books).

Loveday, B. (1996), 'Crime at the Core?', in Leishman *et al.* (1996).

Lowe, R. (2004), *The Welfare State in Britain since 1945* (3rd edn, London: Macmillan).

Luhmann, N. (1982), *The Differentiation of Society* (New York: Columbia University Press).

Luhmann, N. (1984), *Social Systems* (Stanford, CA: Stanford University Press).

Lukács, G. (1923), *History and Class Consciousness* (London: Merlin Press, 1971).

Lukes, S. (1967), 'Alienation and Anomie', in P. Laslett and W. G. Runciman (eds), *Politics, Philosophy and Society* (Oxford: Basil Blackwell).

Lukes, S. (1973), *Émile Durkheim: His Life and Work* (Harmondsworth: Allen Lane/The Penguin Press).

Lukes, S. (1974), *Power: A Radical View* (London: Macmillan).

Lupton, D. (1996), *Food, the Body and the Self* (London: Sage).

Lury, C. (1996), *Consumer Culture* (Cambridge: Polity Press).

Lynd, R. S., and Lynd, H. M. (1929), *Middletown* (New York: Harcourt Brace).

Lynd, R. S., and Lynd, H. M. (1937), *Middletown in Transition* (New York: Harcourt Brace).

Lyon, D. (2001), *Surveillance Society: Monitoring Everyday Life* (Buckingham: Open University Press).

Lyotard, J.-F. (1979), *The Postmodern Condition* (Manchester: Manchester University Press, 1984).

Mac An Ghaill, M. (1996), 'What About the Boys?: Schooling, Class and Crisis Masculinity', *Sociological Review*, 44/3.

McCahill, M., and Norris, C. (1999), 'Watching the Workers: Crime, CCTV, and the Workplace', in P. Davies, P. Francis, and V. Jupp (eds), *Invisible Crimes: Their Victims and their Regulation* (Houndmills: Macmillan).

McCarthy, T. (1978), *The Critical Theory of Jürgen Habermas* (London: Hutchinson).

McChesney, R. (2003), 'Corporate Media, Global Capitalism', in Cottle (2003).

MacEoin, D. (2009), *Sharia Law or 'One Law for All'*, www.civitas,org.uk.

Macgregor, S. (2003), 'Social Exclusion', in Ellison and Pierson (2003).

McIntosh, M. (1975), *The Organisation of Crime* (London: Macmillan).

Mack, Joanna, and Lansley, S. (1985), *Poor Britain* (London: George Allen & Unwin).

Mack, John (1964), 'Full Time Miscreants, Delinquent Neighbourhoods and Criminal Networks', *British Journal of Sociology*, 15.

McKeganey, N., and Barnard, M. (1996), *Sex Work on the Streets: Prostitutes and their Clients* (Buckingham: Open University Press).

McKenzie, R. T., and Silver, A. (1968), *Angels in Marble* (London: Heinemann).

McKeown, T. (1979), *The Role of Medicine* (Oxford: Blackwell).

McKibbin, R. (1990), *The Ideologies of Class: Social Relations in Britain: 1880–1950* (Oxford: Oxford University Press).

Mackintosh, N. J. (1995) (ed.), *Cyril Burt: Fraud or Framed* (Oxford: Oxford University Press).

McLellan, D. (1971), *The Thought of Karl Marx* (London: Macmillan).

McLellan, D. (1973), *Karl Marx: His Life and Thought* (London: Macmillan).

McLennan, G. (1989), *Marxism, Pluralism and Beyond* (Cambridge: Polity Press).

McPherson, A., and Willms, J. (1989), 'Comprehensive Schooling is Better and Fairer', in Cosin *et al.* (1989).

Macpherson, W. (1999), *The Stephen Lawrence Inquiry*. Cm 4262–I (London: HMSO), www.archive.official-documents.co.uk/document/cm42/4262/4262.htm.

McRobbie, A. (1991), *Feminism and Youth Culture: From Jackie to Just Seventeen* (London: Macmillan).

McRobbie, A. (1996), '*More!* New Sexualities in Girls' and Women's Magazines', in J. Curran, D. Morley, and V. Walkerdine (eds), *Cultural Studies and Communications* (London: Arnold).

McRobbie, A., and McCabe, T. (1981), *Feminism for Girls: An Adventure Story* (London: Routledge & Kegan Paul).

Maguire, J. (2002) (ed.), *Theory, Sport, and Society* (Amsterdam: JAI Press).

Maguire, M. (1994), 'Crime Statistics, Patterns, and Trends: Changing Perceptions and their Implications', in M. Maguire, R. Morgan, and

R. Reiner (eds), *The Oxford Handbook of Criminology* (Oxford: Oxford University Press).

Maguire, M., and Bennett, T. (1982), *Burglary in a Dwelling: The Offence, the Offender and the Victim* (London: Macmillan).

Malcolmson, R. W. (1988), 'Ways of Getting a Living in Eighteenth-Century England', in Pahl (1988).

Malinowski, B. (1922), *Argonauts of the Western Pacific* (London: George Routledge).

Malinowski, B. (1929), *The Sexual Life of Savages* (London: George Routledge).

Malinowski, B. (1935), *Coral Gardens and their Magic* (London: Allen & Unwin).

Maltby, R., and Craven I. (1995), *Hollywood Cinema: An Introduction* (Oxford: Blackwell).

Malthus, T. R. (1798), *An Essay on the Principle of Population* (Harmondsworth: Penguin Books, 1970).

Mandel, E. (1967), *The Formation of the Economic Thought of Karl Marx* (London: New Left Books, 1971).

Mann, M. (1973), *Consciousness and Action among the Western Working Class* (London: Macmillan).

Mann, M. (1986), *The Sources of Social Power* (Cambridge: Cambridge University Press).

Mannheim, H. (1940), *Social Aspects of Crime in England between the Wars* (London: Allen & Unwin).

Mannheim, K. (1927), 'The Problem of Generations', in K. Mannheim, *Essays in the Sociology of Knowledge* (London: Routledge & Kegan Paul, 1952).

Manza, J., Hout, M., and Brooks, C. (1995), 'Class Voting in Capitalist Democracies since World War II', *Annual Review of Sociology*, 21.

Marcuse, H. (1956), *Eros and Civilization* (London: Routledge & Kegan Paul).

Marcuse, H. (1964), *One Dimensional Man* (London: Routledge & Kegan Paul).

Mars, G. (1982), *Cheats at Work* (London: Allen & Unwin).

Marsh, C. (1986), 'Social Class and Occupation', in R. G. Burgess (ed.), *Key Variables in Social Investigation* (London: Routledge & Kegan Paul).

Marshall, G. (1982), *In Search of the Spirit of Capitalism* (London: Hutchinson).

Marshall, T. H. (1949), *Citizenship and Social Class* (London: Pluto Press, 1992).

Martin, D. A. (1962), 'The Denomination', *British Journal of Sociology*, 13.

Martin, D. A. (1967), *A Sociology of English Religion* (London: Heinemann Educational Books).

Martin, G. (2004), 'Sea Change: The Modern Terrorist Environment in Perspective', in Ritzer (2004).

Martineau, H. (1837). *Society in America*, abridged edn, ed. S. M Lipset (New York: Doubleday, 1962).

Marx, K. (1844), *Economic and Philosophical Manuscripts* (London: Lawrence & Wishart, 1959).

Marx, K. (1845–6), *The German Ideology*, extract in *Karl Marx: Selected Writings in Sociology and Social Philosophy*, ed. T. B. Bottomore, and M. Rubel (Harmondsworth: Penguin, 1963).

Marx, K. (1858), *Grundrisse* (Harmondsworth: Penguin, 1973).

Marx, K. (1864–5), *Capital*, iii (Harmondsworth: Penguin, 1981).

Marx, K. (1867), *Capital*, i (Harmondsworth: Penguin, 1976).

Marx, K., and Engels, F. (1848), *The Communist Manifesto* (Harmondsworth: Penguin, 1967).

Mason, D. (2000), *Race and Ethnicity in Modern Britain* (2nd edn, Oxford: Oxford University Press).

Mason, P. (2007), 'Kenya in Crisis', *BBC News Channel*, 8 January.

Mass Observation. (1943) *The Pub and the People: A Worktown Study* (London: Gollancz).

Massey, D. (1994), *Space, Place, and Gender* (Cambridge: Polity Press).

Massey, D., and Jess, P. (1995), *A Place in the World? Places, Cultures, and Globalization* (Oxford: Oxford University Press).

Matthews, M. (1978), *Privilege in the Soviet Union* (London: George Allen & Unwin).

Matza, D. (1964), *Delinquency and Drift* (New York: John Wiley & Sons).

Mauss, M. (1925), *The Gift* (London: Routledge & Kegan Paul, 1966).

May, T. (2001), *Social Research: Issues, Methods and Processes* (3rd edn, Buckingham: Open University Press).

Mayer, K.-U. (1963), 'The Changing Shape of the American Class Structure', *Social Research*, 30.

Mayhew, H. (1861*a*), *London Labour and the London Poor* (London: Frank Cass, 1967).

Mayhew, H. (1861*b*), *London's Underworld*, ed. P. Quennell (London: Spring Books, 1950).

Mead, G. (1927), *Mind, Self and Society* (Chicago: University of Chicago Press, 1934).

Mead, M. (1928), *Coming of Age in Samoa: A Study of Adolescence and Sex in Primitive Societies* (Harmondsworth: Penguin, 1943).

Mead, M. (1930), *Growing Up in New Guinea: A Study of Adolescence and Sex in Primitive Societies* (Harmondsworth: Penguin, 1942).

Mead, M. (1935), *Sex and Temperament in Three Primitive Societies* (London: Routledge).

Mead, M. (1950), *Male and Female* (Harmondsworth: Penguin, 1962).

Mead, M. (1953), 'National Character', in A. L. Kroeber (ed.), *Anthropology Today* (Chicago: University of Chicago Press).

Meegan, R. (1989), 'Paradise Postponed: The Growth and Decline of Merseyside's Outer Estates', in Cooke (1989).

Meetham, K. (2001), *Tourism and Global Society* (Basingstoke: Palgrave).

Mennell, S., Murcott, A., and von Otter, A. H. (1992), *The Sociology of Food: Eating, Diet and Culture* (London: Sage).

Merchant, C. (1992), *Radical Ecology* (New York: Routledge).

Merton, R. K. (1936), 'The Unanticipated Consequences of Purposive Social Action', *American Sociological Review*, 1.

Merton, R. K. (1938*a*), *Science, Technology and Society in Seventeenth Century England* (New York: Harper & Row, 1970).

Merton, R. K. (1938*b*), 'Social Structure and Anomie', *American Sociological Review*, 3.

Merton, R. K. (1940), 'Bureaucratic Structure and Personality', *Social Forces*, 18.

Merton, R. K. (1949), 'Manifest and Latent Function', in R. K. Merton, *Social Theory and Social Structure* (New York: Harper & Row).

Merton, R. K. (1957), 'The Role Set: Problems in Sociological Theory', *British Journal of Sociology*, 8.

Michels, R. (1912), *Political Parties* (London: Collins Books, 1962).

Middleton, C. (1979), 'The Sexual Division of Labour in Feudal England', *New Left Review*, 113–14.

Miles, H. (2005), *Al-Jazeera: How Arab TV News Challenged the World* (London: Abacus).

Miles, R. (1984), 'Marxism versus the Sociology of Race Relations', *Ethnic and Racial Studies*, 7.

Miles, R. (1989), *Racism* (London: Routledge).

Miles, S., and Miles, M. (2004), *Consuming Cities* (Basingstoke: Palgrave Macmillan).

Miliband, R. (1969), *The State in Capitalist Society* (London: Weidenfeld & Nicolson).

Miliband, R. (1982), *Capitalist Democracy in Britain* (Oxford: Oxford University Press).

Miliband, R. (1989), *Divided Societies* (Oxford: Oxford University Press).

Millett, K. (1970), *Sexual Politics* (New York: Doubleday).

Mills, C. W. (1951), *White Collar: The American Middle Classes* (New York: Oxford University Press).

Mills, C. W. (1956), *The Power Elite* (New York: Oxford University Press).

Mills, C. W. (1959), *The Sociological Imagination* (2nd edn, New York: Oxford University Press, 2000).

Millward, N. (1994), *The New Industrial Relations?* (London: Policy Studies Institute).

Millward, N., Bryson, A., and Forth, J. (2000), *All Change at Work? British Employment Relations 1980–98, as portrayed by the Workplace Industrial Relations Survey Series* (London: Routledge).

Minton, A. (2009), *Ground Control: Fear and Happiness in the Twenty-First Century City* (London: Penguin).

Mirza, M., Senthikumaran, A., and Ja'far, Z. (2007), *Living Apart Together: British Muslims and the Paradox of Multiculturalism* (London: Policy Exchange).

Mitter, S. (1986), *Common Fate, Common Bond: Women in the Global Economy* (London: Pluto Press).

Modood, T., Berthoud, R., Lakey, J., Nazroo, J., Smith, P., Virdee, S., and Beishan, S. (1997), *Ethnic Minorities in Britain: Diversity and Disadvantage* (London: Policy Studies Institute).

Montesquieu, Baron de Charles de Secondat (1748), *The Spirit of the Laws* (Cambridge: Cambridge University Press, 1989).

Morgan, D. (1996), *Family Connections: An Introduction to Family Studies* (Cambridge: Polity Press).

Morgan, D. (1999), 'Risk and Family Practices', in Silva and Smart (1999).

Morozov, E. (2009), 'How Dictators Watch us on the Web', *Prospect*, 165.

Morris, L. (1994), *Dangerous Classes* (London: Routledge).

Morris, L. (1995), *Social Divisions* (London: UCL Press).

Morris, P. (1969), *Put Away* (London: Routledge & Kegan Paul).

Morris, R. J. (1979), *Class and Class Consciousness in the Industrial Revolution* (London: Macmillan).

Morris, R. J. (1990), *Class, Sect and Party: The Making of the British Middle Class, Leeds 1820–1850* (Manchester: Manchester University Press).

Morris, T. (1957), *The Criminal Area* (London: Routledge & Kegan Paul).

Mort, F. (1996), *Cultures of Consumption: Masculinities and Social Space in Late Twentieth-Century Britain* (London: Routledge).

Mortimore, P. (1997), 'Can Effective Schools Compensate for Society', in Halsey *et al.* (1997).

Morton, J. (1992), *Gangland: London's Underworld* (London: Little Brown).

Mosca, G. (1896), *The Ruling Class* (New York: McGraw-Hill, 1939).

Moser, C., and Kalton, G. (1979), *Survey Methods in Social Investigation* (London: Heinemann Educational Books).

Moynihan, D. P. (1965), *The Negro Family: The Case for National Action* (Washington: US Department of Labor).

Moyo, D. (2009), *Dead Aid: Why Aid is not Working and how There is Another Way for Africa* (London: Allen Lane).

Mulholland, K. (1998), '"Survivors" versus "Movers and Shakers": The Reconstitution of Management and Careers in the Privatised Utilities', in P. Thompson and C. Warhurst (eds), *Workplaces of the Future* (Houndmills: Macmillan).

Mumford, L. (1961), *The City in History: Its Origins, its Transformation, and its Projects* (London: Secker & Warburg).

Murcott, A. (1982), 'On the Social Significance of the "Cooked Dinner" in South Wales', *Social Science Information*, 21.

Murdoch, J., and Marsden, T. (1994), *Reconstituting Rurality: Class, Community, and Power in the Development Process* (London: UCL Press).

Murdock, G. (1992), 'Embedded Persuasions: The Fall and Rise of Integrated Advertising', in Strinati and Wagg (1992).

Murdock, G., and Golding, P. (1977), 'Capitalism, Communication, and Class Relations', in Curran *et al.* (1977).

Murdock, G. P. (1949), *Social Structure* (New York: Macmillan).

Murray, C. (1984), *Losing Ground: American Social Policy 1950–1980* (New York: Basic Books).

Murray, C. (1990), *The Making of the British Underclass* (London: Institute of Economic Affairs).

Myrdal, G. (1944), *An American Dilemma* (New York: Harper).

Myrdal, G. (1962), *Challenge to Affluence* (London: Victor Gollancz).

Nairn, T. (1977), *The Break-up of Britain: Crisis and Neo-nationalism* (London: New Left Books).

Nairn, T. (2000), *After Britain: New Labour and the Return of Scotland* (London: Granta Books).

Nazroo, J. (1999), 'Uncovering Gender Differences in the Use of Marital Violence: The Effect of Methodology', in Allan (1999).

Neale, B., and Smart, C. (1997), 'Experiments with Parenthood', *Sociology*, 31/2.

Nelken, D. (1994), 'White Collar Crime', in M. Maguire, R. Morgan, and R. Reiner (eds), *The Oxford Handbook of Criminology* (Oxford: Oxford University Press).

Nellis, M. (2003), '"They Don't Even Know We're There": The Electronic Monitoring of Offenders in England and Wales', in K. Ball and F. Webster (eds), *The Intensification of Surveillance: Crime, Terrorism and Warfare in the Information Age* (London: Pluto).

Nelson, G. K. (1969), *Spiritualism and Society* (London: Routledge & Kegan Paul).

Nettleton, S. (1995), *The Sociology of Health and Illness* (Cambridge: Polity Press).

Newall, C., and Foggo, D. (2008), 'Revealed: Amazon Staff Punished for Being Ill', *Sunday Times*, 14 December.

Newbold, C., Boyd-Barrett, O., and Van den Bulck, H. (2002) (eds), *The Media Book* (London: Arnold).

Newburn, T., and Hagell, A. (1995), 'Violence on Screen', *Sociology Review*, 4/3.

Newby, H. (1977), *The Deferential Worker: A Study of Farm Workers in East Anglia* (London: Allen Lane).

NHS Information Centre (2009), report, www.ic.nhs.uk/pubs/psychiatricmorbidity07.

Nichols, W. A. T. (1996), 'Social Class: Official, Sociological and Marxist', in Levitas and Guy (1996).

Nichols, W. A. T., and Benyon, H. (1977), *Living with Capitalism* (London: Routledge & Kegan Paul).

Nickson, D., Warhurst, C., Witz, A., and Cullen, A. (2001), 'The Importance of Being Aesthetic: Work, Employment, and Service Organization', in Sturdy *et al.* (2001).

Nicolson, A. (2009), 'Boom Town', *Guardian*, 13 February.

Niebuhr, H. R. (1929), *The Social Sources of Denominationalism* (New York: Holt).

Nissel, M. (1987), *People Count: A History of the General Register Office* (London: HMSO).

Noon, M., and Blyton, P. (2007), *The Realities of Work* (3rd edn, London: Macmillan Business).

Norden, M. (1994), *The Cinema of Isolation: A History of Physical Disability in the Movies* (New Brunswick, NJ: Rutgers University Press).

North, M. (2008), 'Mob Rule', *Independent*, 29 August.

Oakley, A. (1974), *The Sociology of Housework* (Oxford: Martin Robertson).

Oakley, A. (1984), *The Captured Womb: A History of the Medical Care of Pregnant Women* (Oxford: Blackwell).

Oakley, A., Brannen, J., and Dodd, K. (1992), 'Young People, Gender and Smoking in the United Kingdom', *Health Precautions International*, 7.

O'Brien, M., and Jones, D. (1996), 'Revisiting Family and Kinship', *Sociology Review*, 5/3.

O'Connell Davidson, J. (1998), *Prostitution, Power, and Freedom* (Cambridge: Polity Press).

O'Connell Davidson, J., and Layder, D. (1994), *Methods, Sex and Madness* (London: Routledge).

O'Donnell, M., and Sharpe, S. (2004), 'The Social Construction of Youthful Masculinities', in Ball (2004).

Office for National Statistics (2004), *Living in Britain 2002* (London: Office for National Statistics).

Office for National Statistics (2006), *Annual Abstract of Statistics* (Basingstoke: Palgrave).

Office for National Statistics (2009), *Annual Survey of Hours and Earnings*, www.statistics.gov.uk/downloads/theme_labour/ASHE-2009/2009_occupation.pdf.

Office for National Statistics (2010). 'Health: Asians Have Worst Self-Reported Health', www.statistics.gov.uk/cci/nugget.asp?id=464.

O'Grady, S. (2009), 'China will Overtake America, the Only Question is When', *Independent*, 6 October.

Ohmae, K. (1990), *The Borderless World* (London: Collins).

Oliver, M. (1983), *Social Work with Disabled People* (Basingstoke: Macmillan).

Oliver, M. (1996), *Understanding Disability* (Houndmills: Macmillan).

Oppenheim, A. N. (1966), *Questionnaire Design and Attitude Measurement* (London: Heinemann Educational Books).

Oppenheim, C. (1993), *Poverty: The Facts* (rev. edn, London: Child Poverty Action Group).

Orans, M. (1996), *Not Even Wrong: Margaret Mead, Derek Freeman and the Samoans* (Novato, CA: Chandler and Sharp).

Osborne, S. (2008), 'Lessons for London', *Independent*, 9 August.

Osler, A., Street, S., Lall, M., and Vincent, K. (2002), *Not a Problem? Girls and School Exclusion* (London: National Children's Bureau).

Oxfam (2009), 'Turning the Tide: How to Best Protect Workers Employed by Gangmaseters, Five Years after Morecambe Bay' (31 July), www.oxfam.org.uk/resources/policy/trade/downloads/bp_ukpp_gla.pdf.

Packard, V. (1963), *The Hidden Persuaders* (Harmondsworth: Penguin).

Pahl, J. (1984), *Divisions of Labour* (Oxford: Blackwell).

Pahl, J. (1988) (ed.), *On Work: Historical, Theoretical and Comparative Approaches* (Oxford: Blackwell).

Pahl, J. (1989), *Money and Marriage* (London: Macmillan).

Pahl, J. (1993), 'Money, Marriage, and Ideology: Holding the Purse Strings?', *Sociology Review*, 3/1.

Pahl, R. (1965), 'Class and Community in English Commuter Villages', *Sociologia Ruralis*, 5.

Pakulski, J. (1997), 'Cultural Citizenship', in *Citizenship Studies*, 1.

Palmer, C. (2004), 'Death, Danger and the Selling of Risk in Adventure Sports', in Wheaton (2004).

Palmer, R. L. (1980), *Anorexia Nervosa* (Harmondsworth: Penguin).

Pareto, V. (1916), *The Mind and Society*.

Park, A., Curtice, J., Thomson, K., Phillips, M., Johnson, M., and Clery, E. (2008) (eds), *British Social Attitudes: The 24th Report* (London: Sage).

Park, R. E., and Burgess, E. W. (with McKenzie, R. D.) (1925), *The City* (Chicago: University of Chicago Press).

Parker, H., and Measham, F. (1994), 'Pick 'n' Mix: Changing Patterns of Illicit Drug Use amongst 1990s Adolescents', *Drugs*, 1.

Parker, S. (1976), 'Work and Leisure', in Butterworth and Weir (1976).

Parkin, F. (1967), 'Working Class Conservatives: A Theory of Political Deviance', *British Journal of Sociology*, 18.

Parkin, F. (1971), *Class Inequality and Political Order* (London: McGibbon & Kee).

Parkin, F. (1982), *Max Weber* (Chichester: Ellis Horwood).

Parsons, T. (1937), *The Structure of Social Action* (New York: McGraw-Hill).

Parsons, T. (1940), 'An Analytical Approach to the Theory of Social Stratification', in Parsons (1954).

Parsons, T. (1949), 'The Social Structure of the Family', in R. Anshen (ed.), *The Family, Its Functions and Destiny* (New York: Harper).

Parsons, T. (1951), *The Social System* (New York: Free Press).

Parsons, T. (1953), 'A Revised Analytical Approach to the Theory of Social Stratification', in Parsons (1954).

Parsons, T. (1954), *Essays in Sociological Theory* (rev. edn, New York: Free Press).

Parsons, T. (1959), 'The School Class as a Social System: Some of its Functions in American Society', *Harvard Educational Review*, 29/4; also in Parsons (1964).

Parsons, T. (1966a), 'Full Citizenship for the Negro American?', in T. Parsons (1969), *Politics and Social Structure* (New York: Free Press).

Parsons, T. (1966b), *Societies: Evolutionary and Comparative Perspectives* (Englewood Cliffs, NJ: Prentice-Hall).

Parsons, T. (1970), 'Equality and Inequality in Modern Society, or Social Stratification Revisited', *Sociological Inquiry*, 40.

Parsons, T. (1971), *The System of Modern Societies* (Englewood Cliffs, NJ: Prentice-Hall).

Parsons, T., and Bales, R. F. (1956), *Family, Socialization and Interaction Process* (London: Routledge & Kegan Paul).

Parsons, T., and Smelser, N. J. (1956), *Economy and Society* (New York: Free Press).

Pateman, C. (1989) (ed.), *The Disorder of Women* (Cambridge: Polity Press).

Paterson, O. (1967), *The Sociology of Slavery* (London: MacGibbon & Kee).

Paterson, O. (1982), *Slavery and Social Death* (Cambridge, MA: Harvard University Press).

Patterson, S. (1963), *Dark Strangers* (London: Tavistock).

Payne, G. (1987a), *Employment and Opportunity* (London: Macmillan).

Payne, G. (1987b), *Mobility and Change in Modern Society* (London: Macmillan).

Payne, G., and Roberts, J. (2002), 'Opening and Closing the Gates: Recent Developments in Male Social Mobility in Britain', *Sociological Research Online*, 6/4.

Pember-Reeves, M. (1913), *Round about a Pound a Week* (London: Virago).

Percy-Smith, J., and Hillyard, P. (1985), 'Miners in the Arms of the Law: A Statistical Analysis', *Journal of Law and Society*, 12.

Perkin, H. (1989), *The Rise of Professional Society* (London: Routledge).

Phillips, A., and Moss, P. (1988), *Who Cares for Europe's Children* (Brussels: European Commission).

Phillips, M. (2005), 'The Two Faces of Britain', *Daily Mail*, 25 May.

Phillips, T. (2005), 'After 7/7: Sleepwalking to Segregation', speech given to the Manchester Council for Community Relations, 22 September.

Philo, G. (1990), *Seeing and Believing: The Influence of Television* (London: Routledge).

Philo, G., and Berry, M. (2004), *Bad News from Israel* (London: Pluto Press).

Phizacklea, A., and Wolkowitz, C. (1995), *Homeworking Women: Gender, Racism and Class at Work* (London: Sage).

Piaget, J. (1924), *Judgment and Reasoning in the Child* (London: Routledge & Kegan Paul, 1928).

Piaget, J. (1932), *The Moral Judgement of the Child* (Harmondsworth: Penguin, 1983).

Piaget, J. (1936), *The Origins of Intelligence in the Child* (London: Routledge & Kegan Paul, 1953).

Pickering, W. F. S. (1984), *Durkheim on Religion* (London: Routledge & Kegan Paul).

Pierson, C. (1998), *Beyond the Welfare State* (2nd edn, Cambridge: Polity Press).

Pilcher, J. (1995), *Age and Generation in Modern Britain* (Oxford: Oxford University Press).

Pilcher, J. (1999), *Women in Contemporary Britain* (London: Routledge).

Pilkington, P. (2009), 'Republicans Steal Barack Obama's Campaigning Tricks', *Guardian*, 18 September.

Platt, L. (2005a), *Discovering Child Poverty: The Creation of a Policy Agenda from 1800 to the Present* (Bristol: Policy Press).

Platt, L. (2005b), 'The Intergenerational Social Mobility of Minority Ethnic Groups', *Sociology*, 39: 445.

Plummer, K. (1975), *Sexual Stigma: An Interactionist Account* (London: Routledge).

Plummer, K. (1995), *Telling Sexual Stories* (London: Routledge).

Plummer, K. (2001), *Documents of Life 2* (London: George Allen & Unwin).

Pole, C. (2001), 'Changing Education, Changing Times', *Sociology Review*, 11/1.

Pollak, O. (1950), *The Criminality of Women* (New York: A. S. Barnes, 1961).

Pollard, S. (1965), *The Genesis of Modern Management* (Harmondsworth: Penguin).

Pollert, A. (1988), 'The "Flexible Firm": Fixation or Fact', *Work, Employment, and Society*, 2/3.

Pollert, A. (1991) (ed.), *Farewell to Flexibility?* (Oxford: Blackwell).

Pollert, A. (1996), 'Gender and Class Revisited; Or the Poverty of "Patriarchy"', *Sociology*, 30/4.

Pollock, A. M. (2005), *NHS plc: The Privatization of our Health Care* (London: Verso).

Pollock, L. (1983), *Forgotten Children: Parent–Child Relations from 1500 to 1900* (Cambridge: Cambridge University Press).

Polsby, N. (1969), *Hustlers, Beats and Others* (Harmondsworth: Penguin).

Popper, K. (1959), *The Logic of Scientific Discovery* (London: Routledge & Kegan Paul).

Potts, L. (1990), *The World Labour Market: A History of Migration* (London: Zed Books).

Poulantzas, N. (1975), *Classes in Contemporary Capitalism* (London: New Left Books).

Pratt, J., and Fearnley, R. (1996), 'Stratford City Challenge', in Butler and Rustin (1996).

Priestley, M. (2003), *Disability: A Life Course Approach* (Cambridge: Polity Press).

Pringle, R. (1989), *Secretaries Talk: Sexuality, Power, and Work* (London: Verso).

Pryce, K. (1986), *Endless Pressure: A Study of West Indian Life Styles in Bristol* (2nd edn, Bristol: Bristol Classics).

Przeworski, A., and Sprague, J. (1986), *Paper Stones: A History of Electoral Socialism* (Chicago: Chicago University Press).

Pusey, M. (1987), *Jürgen Habermas* (Chichester: Ellis Horwood).

Puwar, N. (1997), 'Gender and Political Elites: Women in the House of Commons', *Sociology Review*, 7/2.

Quigley, D. (1993), *The Interpretation of Caste* (Oxford: Oxford University Press).

Radcliffe-Brown, A. R. (1922), *The Andaman Islanders* (Cambridge: Cambridge University Press).

Radcliffe-Brown, A. R (1930), 'The Social Organisation of the Australian Tribes', *Oceana*, 1.

Radcliffe-Brown, A. R (1952), *Structure and Function in Primitive Society* (London: Cohen & West).

Radkau, J. (2009) *Max Weber: A Biography* (Cambridge: Polity Press).

Rampton, A. (1981), *West Indian Children in Our Schools* (London: HMSO).

Randall, D., and Momberg, E. (2009), 'The Mystery Grows', *Independent*, 20 September.

Ransome, P. (1992), *Antonio Gramsci: A New Introduction* (New York: Harvester Wheatsheaf).

Ratcliffe, P. (1981), *Racism and Reaction* (London: Routledge).

Rattansi, A. (1988), '"Race", Education and British Society', in Dale *et al.* (1988).

Rayment, J. (2008), 'Army Faces Fight over Women on the Front Line', *Sunday Telegraph*, 28 September.

Redding, G. (1990), *The Spirit of Chinese Capitalism* (Hong Kong: Hong Kong University Press).

Rees, T. (1992), *Women and the Labour Market* (London: Routledge).

Reich, C. (1971), *The Greening of America* (Harmondsworth: Penguin).

Reich, R. B. (1997), 'Why the Rich are Getting Richer and the Poor Poorer', in Halsey *et al.* (1997).

Reid, A. J. (1992), *Social Classes and Social Relations in Britain, 1850–1914* (London: Macmillan).

Reid, I. (1977), *Social Class Differences in Britain* (London: Open Books).

Reid, I. (1996), 'Education and Inequality', *Sociology Review*, 6/2.

Reiner, R. (1992), *The Politics of the Police* (Brighton: Harvester Wheatsheaf).

Religious Trends (2001), *Religious Trends 3, 2002–2003* (London: Christian Research).

Revell, K. R. S. (1965), 'Changes in the Social Distribution of Property', *International Journal of Economic History*, 1.

Rex, J. A. (1961), *Key Problems of Sociological Theory* (London: Routledge & Kegan Paul).

Rex, J. A. (1970), *Race Relations in Sociological Theory* (London: Weidenfeld & Nicolson).

Rex, J. A., and Moore, R. (1967), *Race, Community, and Conflict: A Study of Sparkbrook* (London: Oxford University Press).

Rheingold, H. (2000), 'Community Development in the Cybersociety of the Future', in Gauntlett (2000b).

Rich, A. (1980), 'Compulsory Heterosexuality and Lesbian Existence', *Signs*, 5/4.

Richards, M. P. M., and Elliott, B. J. (1991), 'Sex and Marriage in the 1960s and 1970s', in D. Clark (ed.), *Marriage, Domestic Life, and Social Change: Writings for Jacqueline Burgoyne (1944–88)* (London: Routledge).

Richardson, D. and Robinson, V. (2007) (eds), *Introducing Gender and Women's Studies* (3rd edn, London: Palgrave Macmillan).

Riesman, D. (1961), *The Lonely Crowd* (New Haven, CT: Yale University Press).

Ritzer, G. (1996), *The McDonaldization of Society: An Investigation into the Changing Character of Social Life* (rev. edn, Thousand Oaks, CA: Pine Forge Press).

Ritzer, G. (2007), *The McDonaldization of Society: An Investigation into the Changing Character of Social Life* (5th edn; Thousand Oaks, CA: Pine Forge Press).

Roberts, E. (1984), *A Woman's Place: An Oral History of Working Class Women, 1890–1940* (Oxford: Blackwell).

Roberts, H. (1985), *The Patient Patients: Women and their Doctors* (London: Pandora Press).

Roberts, H. (1990), *Women's Health Counts* (London: Routledge).

Roberts, K., Clark, F. G., Clark, S. C., and Semeonoff, E. (1977), *The Fragmentary Class Structure* (London: Heinemann).

Roberts, R. (1973), *The Classic Slum: Salford in the First Quarter of the Century* (Harmondsworth: Penguin).

Robertson, J. (2007), 'Do they mean us?', *Sociology Review*, 17/1.

Robertson, R. (1992), *Globalization: Social Theory and Global Culture* (London: Sage).

Robinson, M., and Smith, D. (1993), *Step by Step: Focus on Stepfamilies* (Brighton: Harvester Wheatsheaf).

Robson, C. (1993), *Real World Research* (Oxford: Blackwell).

Rodger, J. J. (1996), *Family Life and Social Control* (Houndmills: Macmillan).

Roethlisberger, F. J., and Dickson, W. J. (1939), *Management and the Worker* (Cambridge, MA: Harvard University Press).

Room, G. (1990), *'New Poverty' in the European Community* (London: Macmillan).

Roopnarine, J. L., and Gielen, U. P. (2005) (eds), *Families in Global Perspective* (London: Pearson).

Rose, D., and O'Reilly, K. (1998), *The ESRC Review of Government Social Classifications* (London: Office for National Statistics and the Economic and Social Research Council).

Rose, D., and Sullivan, O. (1993), *Introductory Data Analysis for Social Scientists* (2nd edn, Milton Keynes: Open University Press).

Rose, E. J. B., Deakin, N., Cohen, B., and McNeal, J. (1969), *Colour and Citizenship: A Report on British Race Relations* (Oxford: Oxford University Press).

Rose, M. (1975), *Industrial Behaviour: Theoretical Developments since Taylor* (London: Allen Lane).

Rose, M. (2003), 'Good Deal, Bad Deal? Job Satisfaction in Occupations', *Work, Employment and Society*, 17/3.

Rosen, H. (1974), *Language and Class* (3rd edn, Bristol: Falling Wall Press).

Roseneil, S. (1995), *Disarming Patriarchy: Feminism and Political Action at Greenham* (Buckingham: Open University Press).

Rosenham, D. L. (1973), 'On Being Sane in an Insane Place', *Science*, 179.

Ross, A. M., and Hartman, P. T. (1960), *Changing Patterns of Industrial Conflict* (New York: Wiley).

Roszak, T. (1971), *The Making of a Counter Culture: Reflections on the Technocratic Society and its Youthful Opposition* (London: Faber & Faber).

Routh, G. (1987), *Occupations of the People of Great Britain, 1801–1981* (London: Macmillan).

Rowntree, S. (1901), *Poverty: A Study of Town Life* (London: Longmans Green).

Rowntree, S. (1941), *Poverty and Progress* (London: Longmans Green).

Rowntree, S., and Lavers, G. R. (1951), *Poverty and the Welfare State* (London: Longmans Green).

Royal College of Physicians (2009), *Women and Medicine: The Future: Summary of Findings* (London: Royal College of Physicians).

Royle, E. (1987), *Modern Britain: A Social History 1750–1985* (London: Edward Arnold).

Rubinstein, W. D. (1981), *Men of Property* (London: Croom Helm).

Rubinstein, W. D (1986), *Wealth and Inequality in Britain* (London: Faber & Faber).

Rubinstein, W. D (1993), *Capitalism, Culture, and Decline in Britain, 1750–1990* (London: Routledge).

Ruggiero, V., and South, N. (1995), *Eurodrugs* (London: UCL Press).

Ruggiero, V., South, N., and Taylor, I. (1998) (eds), *The New European Criminality* (London: Routledge).

Runciman, W. G. (1966), *Relative Deprivation and Social Justice* (London: Routledge & Kegan Paul).

Runciman, W. G. (1993), 'Has British Capitalism Changed since the First World War?', *British Journal of Sociology*, 44/1.

Russell, D. E. H. (1986), *The Secret Trauma: Incest in the Lives of Girls and Women* (New York: Basic Books).

Russell, D. E. H. (1990), *Rape in Marriage* (2nd edn, Bloomington: Indiana University Press).

Rutter, M. (1972), *Maternal Deprivation Reassessed* (Harmondsworth: Penguin).

Rutter, M., Maughan, B., Mortimore, P., Ouston, J., with Smith, A. (1979), *Fifteen Thousand Hours: Secondary Schools and their Effects on Children* (London: Open Books).

Sacks, H. (1965–72), *Lectures on Conversation* (Oxford: Blackwell, 1992).

Salmon, G. (2004), *E-Moderating: The Key to Teaching and Learning Online* (2nd edn, London: Taylor and Francis).

Sancho, J. (2003), *Disabling Prejudice: Attitudes towards Disability and its Portrayal on Television* (available from BBC, BSC, ITC websites).

Sarlvik, B., and Crewe, I. (1983), *Decade of Dealignment* (Cambridge: Cambridge University Press).

Sassen, S. (2001), *The Global City: New York, London, Tokyo* (2nd edn, Princeton: Princeton University Press).

Saunders, P. (1986), *Social Theory and the Urban Question* (London: Hutchinson).

Saunders, P. (1990), *A Nation of Home Owners* (London: Unwin Hyman).

Savage, M. (2000*a*), *Class Analysis and Social Transformation* (Buckingham: Open University Press).

Savage, M. (2005*b*), 'Revisiting the Affluent Worker Study', *Sociological Review*, 39/5.

Savage, M., and Miles, A. (1994), *The Remaking of the British Working Class, 1840–1940* (London: Routledge).

Savage, M., and Warde, A. (2002), *Urban Sociology, Capitalism and Modernity* (2nd edn, London: Macmillan).

Savage, M., Barlow, J., Dickens, P., and Fielding, T. (1992), *Property, Bureaucracy and Culture: Middle Class Formation in Contemporary Britain* (London: Routledge).

Savage, M., Warde, A., and Ward, K. (2003), *Urban Sociology, Capitalism and Modernity* (2nd edn, London: Palgrave Macmillan).

Savage, M., Bagnall, G., and Longhurst, B. (2005), *Globalization and Belonging* (London: Sage).

Scase, D., and Goffee, L. (1982), *The Entrepreneurial Middle Class* (London: Croom Helm).

Scase, R. (2002), *Living in the Corporate Zoo* (Oxford: Capstone).

Schaefer, R. T. (2008) (ed.), *Encyclopedia of Race, Ethnicity, and Society* (New York: Sage)

Scheff, T. J. (1966), *Becoming Mentally Ill: A Sociological Theory* (New York: Aldine, 1984).

Schiller, H. (1969), *Mass Communications and American Empire* (Boston: Beacon).

Schreiner, O. (1899), 'The Woman Question' in C. Barash (ed.), *An Olive Schreiner Reader* (London: Pandora Press, 1987).

Schreiner, O. (1911), *Women and Labour.* (London: Unwin).

Schur, E. (1971), *Labelling Deviant Behaviour: Its Sociological Implications* (New York: Harper & Row).

Schwartz, M. S., and Schwartz, C. G. (1955), 'Problems in Participant Observation', *American Journal of Sociology*, 60.

Scott, A. (1990), *Ideology and the New Social Movements* (London: Unwin Hyman).

Scott, J. (1990), *A Matter of Record: Documentary Sources in Social Research* (Cambridge: Polity Press).

Scott, J. (1991), *Who Rules Britain?* (Cambridge: Polity Press).

Scott, J. (1994), *Poverty and Wealth: Citizenship, Deprivation and Privilege* (Harlow: Longman).

Scott, J. (1995), *Sociological Theory: Contemporary Debates* (Cheltenham: Edward Elgar).

Scott, J. (1996), *Stratification and Power: Structures of Class, Status and Command* (Cambridge: Polity Press).

Scott, J. (1997), *Corporate Business and Capitalist Classes* (Oxford: Oxford University Press).

Scott, J. (2001), *Power* (Cambridge: Polity Press).

Scott, J. (2006*a*), *Social Theory: Central Issues in Sociology* (London: Sage).

Scott, J. (2006*b*), *Fifty Key Sociologists: The Formative Theorists* (London: Routledge).

Scott, J. (2006*c*), *Fifty Key Sociologists: The Contemporary Theorists* (London: Routledge).

Scott, R. A. (1969), *The Making of Blind Men* (New York: Russell Sage Foundation).

Scott, S. (2005), 'The Red, Shaking Fool: Dramaturgical Dilemmas in Shyness', *Symbolic Interaction*, 28/1.

Scott, S. (2007), *Shyness and Society* (Houndmills: Palgrave).

Scull, A. (1979), *Museums of Madness* (London: Allen Lane).

Scull, A. (1984), *Decarceration: Community Treatment and the Deviant: A Radical View* (2nd edn, Cambridge: Polity Press).

Seabrook, J. (2004), *Consuming Cultures: Globalization and Local Lives* (Oxford: New Internationalist).

Seeman, M. (1959), 'On the Meaning of Alienation', *American Sociological Review*, 24.

Segalen, M. (1983), *Love and Power in the Peasant Family* (Oxford: Blackwell).

Sennett, R. (1973), *The Uses of Disorder* (Harmondsworth: Penguin).

Seymour, W. (1998), *Remaking the Body: Rehabilitation and Change* (London: Routledge).

Shah, S. (2004), 'Planet Murdoch', *Independent*, 18 October.

Shakespeare, T. (2003), '"I Haven't Seen that in the Kama Sutra": The Sexual Stories of Disabled People', in Weeks *et al.* (2003).

Shapiro, L. (1972), *Totalitarianism* (New York: Praeger).

Sharpe, S. (1994), *Just Like a Girl: How Girls Learn to be Women* (Harmondsworth: Penguin).

Shaw, C. (1930), *The Jack Roller: A Delinquent Boy's Own Story* (Chicago: University of Chicago Press).

Shelley, M. (1818) *Frankenstein* (Harmondsworth: Penguin, 1994).

Shilling, C. (1993), *The Body in Social Theory* (London: Sage).

Shils, E., and Young, M. (1953), 'The Meaning of the Coronation', *British Journal of Sociology*, 1.

Shiva, V. (2000), 'Poverty and Globalization', BBC Reith Lectures, 2000, www.bbc.co.uk/radio4/reith2000.

Shoemaker, R. (1998), *Gender in English Society, 1650–1850: The Emergence of Separate Spheres* (London: Longman).

Shorter, E. (1976), *The Making of the Modern Family* (London: Collins).

Shover, N. (1996), *Great Pretenders: Pursuits and Careers of Persistent Thieves* (Boulder, CO: Westview Press).

Shover, N., and Decker, S. (1996), *Burglars on the Job: Streetlife and Residential Break-ins* (Boston: Northeastern University Press).

Sikka, P. (2003), 'The Role of Offshore Financial Centres in Globalization', *Accounting Forum*, 27/4.

Silva, E., and Smart, C. (1999) (eds), *The New Family?* (London: Sage).

Silver, D. (2000), 'Looking Backwards, Looking Forwards: Cyberculture Studies 1990–2000', in Gauntlett (2000*b*).

Silverstein, L. B., and Auerbach, C. F. (2005), '(Post)modern Families', in Roopnarine and Gielen (2005).

Smart, B. (2005), *The Sport Star: Modern Sport and the Cultural Economy of Sporting Celebrity* (London: Sage).

Sim, A. (1994), 'Did You See "Witness"? The Myth of Amish Separatism', *Sociology Review*, 3.

Simmel, G. (1900), *The Philosophy of Money* (London: Routledge & Kegan Paul, 1978).

Simmel, G. (1908), *Soziologie: Untersuchungen über die Formen der Vergesselschaftung* (Berlin: Dimcker & Humblot, 1968).

Simon, B. (1991), *Education and the Social Order 1940–1990* (London: Lawrence & Wishart).

Skeggs, B. (1997), *Formations of Class and Gender: Becoming Respectable* (London: Sage).

Skellington, R. (1992), *'Race' in Britain Today* (London: Sage).

Sklair, L. (1991), *Sociology of the Global System* (London: Harvester Wheatsheaf).

Sklair, L. (1994) (ed.), *Capitalism and Development* (London: Routledge).

Sklair, L. (2001), *The Transnational Capitalist Class* (Oxford: Blackwell).

Skocpol, T. (1985), 'Bringing the State Back In: Strategies of Analysis in Current Research', in Evans *et al.* (1985).

Smart, B. (2005), *The Sport Star: Modern Sport and the Cultural Economy of Sporting Celebrity* (London: Stage).

Smart, C. (1977), *Women, Crime and Criminology* (London: Routledge & Kegan Paul).

Smith, A. (1986), *The Ethnic Origins of Nations* (Oxford: Blackwell).

Smith, A. (1991), *National Identity* (Harmondsworth: Penguin).

Smith, A. (1994), 'The Origins of Nations', in Hutchinson and Smith (1994).

Smith, D. (2009), 'Mobiles Give Africa's Farmers the Chance to Set out their Stall', *Observer*, 4 January.

Smith, D., and Tomlinson, S. (1989), *The School Effect: A Study of Multi-Racial Comprehensives* (London: Policy Studies Institute).

Smith, D. E. (1987), *The Everyday World as Problematic* (Milton Keynes: Open University Press).

Smith, J. (2007), 'Ye've got to 'ave balls to play this game sir!' Boys, Peers, and Fears: The Negative Effect of School-Based "Cultural Accomplices" in Constructing Hegemonic Masculinities', *Gender and Education*, 19/2.

Smith, M., and Kollock, P. (1999) (eds), *Communities in Cyberspace* (London: Routledge).

Smith, M. P., and Feagin, J. M. (1987) (eds), *The Capitalist City: Global Restructuring and Community Politics* (Oxford: Blackwell).

Smithers, A. (1994), 'A Quiet Revolution in Post-16 Education', *Independent*, 29 September.

Sneade, A. (2001), 'Trade Union Membership 1999–2000: An Analysis of Data from the Certification Officer and the Labour Force Survey', *Labour Market Trends*, 109/9 (September).

Social Trends (various years), *Social Trends* (London: HMSO), www.statistics.co.uk.

Solomos, J. (1993), *Race and Racism in Britain* (London: Macmillan).

Solomos, J., and Back, L. (1996), *Racism and Society* (Basingstoke: Macmillan).

Sombart, W. (1906), *Why is there no Socialism in the United States* (London: Macmillan, 1976).

Sombart, W. (1908), *Socialism and the Social Movement* (London: J. M. Dent, 1909).

Spearman, C. (1904), 'General Intelligence: Objectively Determined and Measured', *American Journal of Psychology*, 15.

Spender, D. (1982), *Invisible Women: The Schooling Scandal* (London: Writers and Readers Publishing Co-operative).

Sreberny-Mohammadi, A. (1996), 'The Global and Local in International Communications', in Curran and Gurevitch (1996).

Stacey, M. (1960), *Tradition and Change: A Study of Banbury* (Oxford: Oxford University Press).

Stacey, M. (1987), 'Health, Illness and Medicine', in P. Worsley (ed.), *The New Introductory Sociology* (Harmondsworth: Penguin).

Stacey, M., Batstone, E., Bell, C., and Murcott, A. (1975), *Power, Persistence and Change* (London: Routledge & Kegan Paul).

Stanworth, M. (1983), *Gender and Schooling: A Study of Sexual Divisions in the Classroom* (London: Hutchinson).

Stanworth, M. (1987*a*), 'Reproductive Technologies and the Deconstruction of Motherhood', in M. Stanworth (ed.), *Gender, Motherhood and Medicine* (Cambridge: Polity Press).

Stanworth, M. (1987*b*) (ed.), *Gender, Motherhood and Medicine* (Cambridge: Polity Press).

Stedman Jones, G. (1971), *Outcast London* (Oxford: Oxford University Press).

Steele, J. (2009), 'Conflict Looms in Kurdistan', *Independent*, 15 July.

Steger, M. (2003), *Globalization: A Very Short Introduction* (Oxford: Oxford University Press).

Stein, A., and Plummer, K. (1994), '"I Can't Even Think Straight": Queer Theory and the Missing Sexual Revolution in Sociology', *Sociological Theory*, 12/2.

Stiglitz, J. (2002), *Globalization and its Discontents* (London: Allen Lane).

Stone, L. (1977), *The Family, Sex, and Marriage in England 1500–1800* (London: Weidenfeld & Nicolson).

Stone, L., and Stone, J. F. (1984), *An Open Elite?* (Oxford: Oxford University Press).

Stonewall (2009), 'Education for All', www.stonewall.org.uk.

Storey, J. (1995a), 'Human Resource Management: Still Marching On, or Marching Out', in Storey (1995b).

Storey, J. (1995b) (ed.), *Human Resource Management* (London: Routledge).

Straus, M. A., and Gelles, R. J. (1986), 'Societal Change and Change in Family Violence from 1975 to 1985 as Revealed by Two National Surveys', *Journal of Marriage and the Family*, 48.

Strauss, A. L. (1959), *Mirrors and Masks: The Search for Identity* (London: Martin Robertson, 1977).

Strauss, A. L., Schatzman, L., Ehrlich, D., Bucher, R., and Sabshin, M. (1963), 'The Hospital and its Negotiated Order', in E. Friedson (ed.), *The Hospital in Modern Society* (New York: Free Press).

Strinati, D. (1992), 'Post-Modernism: A Theory without Frontiers', *Sociology Review*, 1/4.

Strinati, D. (1995), *An Introduction to Theories of Popular Culture* (London: Routledge).

Strinati, D. (2000), *An Introduction to Studying Popular Culture* (London: Routledge).

Sturdy, A., Grugulis, I., and Willmott, H. (2001) (eds), *Customer Service: Empowerment and Entrapment* (Basingstoke: Palgrave).

Styhre, A. (2007), *The Innovative Bureaucracy: Bureaucracy in an Age of Fluidity* (London: Routledge).

Sullivan, H. S. (1939), *Conceptions of Modern Psychiatry* (New York: W. W. Norton, 1947).

Sullivan, O. (2000), 'The Division of Domestic Labour: Twenty Years of Change', *Sociology*, 34/3.

Sunday Telegraph (1999), 3 October, www.isteve.com/2002_How_White_Are_Blacks.htm.

Sutherland, E. H. (1937), *The Professional Thief* (Chicago: University of Chicago Press).

Sutherland, E. H. (1939), *Principles of Criminology* (Chicago: J. B. Lippincott).

Sutherland, E. H. (1949), *White Collar Crime* (New York: Holt, Rinehart & Winston).

Sutherland, H., Sefton, T., and Piachaud, D. (2003), *Poverty in Britain: The Impact of Government Policy since 1997* (London: London School of Economics for the Joseph Rowntree Foundation).

Swann, M. (1985), *Education for All* (London: HMSO).

Szasz, T. (1962), *The Myth of Mental Illness* (London: Secker & Warburg).

Szasz, T. (1970), *The Manufacture of Madness* (New York: Harper & Row).

Szreter, S. R. (1984), 'The Genesis of the Registrar-General's Social Classification of Occupations', *British Journal of Sociology*, 25.

Taylor, F. (1911), *The Principles of Scientific Management* (New York: Harper & Row).

Taylor, I., Evans, K., and Fraser, P. (1996), *A Tale of Two Cities: Global Change, Local Feeling, and Everyday Life in the North of England. A Study in Manchester and Sheffield* (London: Routledge).

The Oxford Dictionary of Sociology (2005) (3rd edn, Oxford: Oxford University Press).

Thomas, C. (1999), *Female Forms: Experiencing and Understanding Disability* (Buckingham: Open University Press).

Thomas, K. (1971), *Religion and the Decline of Magic* (London: Weidenfeld & Nicolson).

Thomas, W. I., and Znaniecki, F. (1918–19), *The Polish Peasant in Europe and America* (New York: Dover Publishing, 1958).

Thompson, E. P. (1963), *The Making of the English Working Class* (Harmondsworth: Penguin).

Thompson, F. M. L. (1963), *English Landed Society in the Nineteenth Century* (London: Routledge & Kegan Paul).

Thompson, K. (1976) (ed.), *Auguste Comte: The Foundations of Sociology* (London: Nelson).

Thompson, K. (1982), *Émile Durkheim* (Chichester: Ellis Horwood).

Thompson, K. (1992), 'Religion, Values and Ideology', in R. Bocock and K. Thompson (eds), *Social and Cultural Forms of Modernity* (Cambridge: Polity Press).

Thompson, P. (1978), *The Voice of the Past* (Oxford: Oxford University Press).

Thompson, P. (1993), 'The Labour Process: Changing Theory, Changing Practice', *Sociology Review*, 3/2.

Thompson, W. S. (1929), 'Population', *American Journal of Sociology*, 34.

Thornhill, R., and Palmer, C. T. (2000), *A Natural History of Rape: Biological Bases of Sexual Coercion* (Cambridge, MA: MIT Press).

Thorns, D. (2002), *The Transformation of Cities: Urban Theory and Urban Life* (Basingstoke: Palgrave Macmillan).

Thornton, S. (1997), 'The Social Logic of Subcultural Capital', in Gelder and Thornton (1997).

Thrasher, F. (1927), *The Gang* (Chicago: University of Chicago Press).

The Times Atlas of World History (1978) (London: Times Books).

Tocqueville, A. de (1835–40), *Democracy in America* (London: Fontana Press, 1994).

Tomlinson, S. (2005), *Education in a Post-Welfare Society* (2nd edn, (Buckingham: Open University Press).

Tonnies, F. (1887), *Community and Association* (London: Routledge & Kegan Paul, 1955).

Touraine, A. (1971), *The Post-Industrial Society—Tomorrow's Social History: Classes, Conflicts and Culture in the Programmed Society* (New York: Random House).

Touraine, A. (1981), *The Voice and the Eye: An Analysis of Social Movements* (Cambridge: Cambridge University Press).

Touraine, A. (1992), *Critique of Modernity* (Oxford: Blackwell, 1995).

Townsend, P. (1963), *The Family Life of Old People* (Harmondsworth: Penguin).

Townsend, P. (1974), 'The Concept of Poverty', in D. Wedderburn (ed.), *Poverty, Inequality and Class Structure* (Cambridge: Cambridge University Press).

Townsend, P. (1979), *Poverty in the United Kingdom* (Harmondsworth: Penguin).

Townsend, P. (1991), 'Living Standards and Health in the Inner Cities', in Macgregor and Pimlott (1991).

Townsend, P., and Gordon, D. (2002), *World Poverty: New Policies to Defeat an Old Enemy* (Bristol: Policy Press).

Townsend, P., Corrigan, P., and Kowarzik, U. (1987), *Poverty and Labour in London* (London: Low Pay Unit).

Toynbee, P. (2002), 'A Job Is Not Enough', *Guardian*, 14 June.

Toynbee, P. (2005), 'Manic Marketization is Driving the NHS into Cut-throat Chaos', *Guardian*, 7 October.

Toynbee, P. (2006), 'The Next Year Is Crucial if We Are to Make Poverty History at Home', *Guardian*, 31 March.

Toynbee, P. (2009), 'Equal Opportunity is Fantasy in any Society this Unequal', *Guardian*, 27 July.

Troeltsch, E. (1912), *The Social Teaching of the Christian Churches* (London: George Allen & Unwin, 1931).

Troyna, B., and Carrington, B. (1990), *Education, Racism, and Reform* (London: Routledge).

Trumbach, R. (1998), 'The Birth of the Queen: Sodomy and the Emergence of Gender Equality in Modern Culture, 1660–1750', in Shoemaker and Vincent (1998).

Tuchman, J. (1981), 'The Symbolic Annihilation of Women by the Mass Media', in S. Cohen and J. Young (eds), *The Manufacture of News* (London: Constable).

Tunstall, J. (1971), *Journalists at Work* (London: Constable).

Tunstall, J. (1995), 'Specialist Correspondents: Goals, Careers, Roles', in Boyd-Barrett and Newbold (1995).

Tunstall, J. (1996), *Newspaper Power: The New National Press in Britain* (Oxford: Clarendon Press).

Turk, Austin T. (2004), 'The Sociology of Terrorism', *Annual Review of Sociology*, 30.

Turkle, S. (1997), *Life on the Screen: Identity in the Age of the Internet* (New York: Simon & Schuster).

Turner, B. (1991), *Religion and Social Theory* (2nd edn, London: Routledge).

Turner, B. (1996), *The Body and Society* (2nd edn, London: Sage).

Turner, R. (1962), 'Role-Taking: Process versus Conformity', in A. Rose (ed.), *Human Behaviour and Social Processes* (London: Routledge & Kegan Paul).

Turner, T., and Liebe, S. (2002), 'Forget Community Care: Reinstitutonalisation is Here', *British Journal of Psychiatry*, 181: 253.

Twigg, J. (1983), 'Vegetarianism and the Eating of Meat', in A. Murcott (ed.), *The Sociology of Food and Eating* (Aldershot: Gower).

UNAIDS (2008), *2008 Report on the Global Aids Epidemic*, UNAIDS/08.25E/JC1510E.

UNHCR (2010), *Global Trends*, www.unhcr.org.

United Nations (2003a), *The Impact of Aids* (New York: United Nations).

United Nations (2003b), *World Fertility Report* (New York: United Nations).

United Nations (2004a), *World Population to 2300* (New York: United Nations).

United Nations (2004b), *World Urbanization Prospects: The 2003 Revision* (New York: United Nations).

United Nations Centre for Human Settlements (1996), *An Urbanizing World: Global Report on Human Settlements* (Oxford: Oxford University Press).

United Nations Department of Economic and Social Affairs (2006), *World Population Prospects: The 2006 Revision* (New York: United Nations Department of Economic and Social Affairs, Population Division).

United Nations Development Programme (1999), *Human Development Report* (Oxford: Oxford University Press).

United Nations Development Programme (2001), *Human Development Report* (Oxford: Oxford University Press).

United Nations Development Programme (2004), *Human Development Report* (Oxford: Oxford University Press).

United Nations Development Programme (2009), *Human Development Report: Overcoming Barriers: Human Mobility and Development* (http://hdr.undp.org/en).

United Nations Population Fund (1996), *The State of World Population* (New York: UNFPA).

United Nations Population Fund (2000), *State of the World Population* (New York: UNFPA).

United Nations Statistics Division (2009), *Environmental Indicators: Greenhouse Gas Emissions*, http://unstats.un.org/unsd/environment/air_co2_emissions.htm.

UPIAS (1976), *Fundamental Principles of Disability* (London: Union of the Physically Impaired Against Segregation).

Urry, J. (2000), *Sociology beyond Societies* (London: Routledge).

Urry, J. (2002), *The Tourist Gaze* (2nd edn, London: Sage).

Useem, M. (1984), *The Inner Circle* (New York: Oxford University Press).

Valentine, G. (1992), 'Women's Fear and the Design of Public Space', *Built Environment*, 16/4.

Varese, F. (2001), *The Russian Mafia* (Oxford: Oxford University Press).

Vigne, T., and Howkins, A. (1977), 'The Small Shopkeeper in Industrial and Market Towns', in Crossick (1977b).

Vincent, J. A. (1995), *Inequality and Old Age* (London: UCL Press).

Visser, J. (2006), 'Union Membership Statistics in 24 Countries', *Monthly Labour Review* (January), 38–49.

Voas, D., and Bruce, S. (2004), 'The 2001 Census and Christian Identification in Britain', *Journal of Contemporary Religion*, 19/1.

Vogler, C., and Pahl, J. (1993), 'Social and Economic Change and the Organization of Money within Marriage', *Work, Employment, and Society*, 7/1.

Vygotsky, L. (1934), *Thought and Language* (Cambridge, MA: MIT Press, 1986).

Wacquant, L. (2009), *Punishing the Poor: The Neoliberal Government of Social Insecurity* (Durham, NC: Duke University Press).

Waddington, I. (1973), 'The Role of the Hospital in the Development of Modern Medicine', *Sociology*, 7.

Waddington, P. A. J. (1996), 'Public Order Policing: Citizenship and Moral Ambiguity', in Leishman *et al.* (1996).

Wainwright, H. (2003), *Reclaim the State: Experiments in Popular Democracy* (London: Verso).

Walby, S. (1986), *Patriarchy at Work* (Cambridge: Polity Press).

Walby, S. (1990), *Theorizing Patriarchy* (Oxford: Blackwell).

Walby, S. (1997), *Gender Transformations* (London: Routledge).

Walby, S., and Allen, J. (2004), *Domestic Violence, Sexual Assault, and Stalking: Findings from the British Crime Survey*. Home Office Research Study 276 (London: HMSO).

Waller, P., Morris, R, and Simpson, D. (2008), *Understanding the Formulation and Development of Government Policy in the Context of FOI* (University College London: Constitution Unit).

Wallerstein, I. (1974), 'The Rise and Future Demise of the World Capitalist System: Concepts for Comparative Analysis', *Comparative Studies in Society and History*, 16.

Wallis, R. (1976), *The Road to Total Freedom* (London: Heinemann).

Wallis, R. (1984), *Elementary Forms of the New Religious Life* (London: Routledge Kegan Paul).

Wallis, R., and Bruce, S. (1992), 'Secularization: The Orthodox Model', in S. Bruce (ed.), *Religion and Modernization: Sociologists and Historians Debate the Secularization Thesis* (Oxford: Oxford University Press).

Wallop, H. (2009a), 'Foreign Power Firms Told to Cut UK Bills', *Daily Telegraph*, 12 February.

Wallop, H. (2009b), 'Death of the Traditional Family', *Daily Telegraph*, 16 April.

Walmsley, R. (2009), *World Prison Population List* (8th edn, Kings College London: International Centre for Prison Studies).

Walsh, D. (1986), *Heavy Business: Commercial Burglary and Robbery* (London: Routledge & Kegan Paul).

Walter, N. (1998), *The New Feminism* (London: Little Brown).

Walter, N. (2010), *Living Dolls: The Return of Sexism* (London: Virago).

Walvin, J. (1993), *Black Ivory: A History of British Slavery* (London: Fontana).

Ward, K. J. (1999a), 'The Cyber-Ethnographic (Re)Construction of Two Feminist Online Communities', *Sociological Research Online*, 4/1, www.socresonline.org.uk/socresonline/4/1/ward.html.

Ward, K. J. (1999b), 'Cyber-Ethnography and the Emergence of the Virtually New Community', *Journal of Information Technology*, 14/1: 95–105.

Warde, A. (1991), 'Gentrification as Consumption: Issues of Class and Gender', *Society and Space*, 9/2.

Warde, A., and Hetherington, K. (1993), 'A Changing Domestic Division of Labour? Issues of Measurement and Interpretation', *Work, Employment and Society*, 7/1.

Warner, W. L. (1936), 'American Class and Caste', *American Journal of Sociology*, 42.

Warner, W. L. (1953), *American Life: Dream and Reality* (Chicago: University of Chicago Press).

Warner, W. L., and Lunt, P. S. (1941), *The Social Life of a Modern Community* (New Haven, CT: Yale University Press).

Warr, P. (1983), 'Job Loss, Unemployment and Psychological Well-Being', in E. Van De Vliet and V. Allen (eds), *Role Transitions* (New York: Plenum Press).

Warren, C. A. B., and Rasmussen, P. K. (1977), 'Sex and Gender in Field Research', *Urban Life*, 6.

Waters, M. (1995), *Globalization* (London: Routledge).

Watson, S. (1992), 'Femocratic Feminisms', in Savage and Witz (1992).

Watson, S., and Gibson, K. (1995) (eds), *Postmodern Cities and Spaces* (Oxford: Blackwell).

Watts, J. (2006), 'War of the Words', *Media Guardian*, 20 February.

Webb, B., and Webb, S. (1932), *Methods of Social Study* (London: Longmans Green).

Weber, Marianne (1926), *Max Weber: A Biography* (New York: John Wiley, 1975).

Weber, Max (1904–5), *The Protestant Ethic and the Spirit of Capitalism* (London: George Allen & Unwin, 1930, and various other editions).

Weber, Max (1914), 'The Economy and the Arena of Normative and De Facto Powers', in Max Weber, *Economy and Society*, ed. G. Roth and C. Wittich (Berkeley and Los Angeles: University of California Press, 1968).

Weber, Max (1915), *The Religion of China* (New York: Macmillan, 1951).

Weber, Max (1916), *The Religion of India* (New York: Macmillan, 1958).

Weber, Max (1919), 'Politics as a Vocation', in *From Max Weber: Essays in Sociology*, ed. H. H. Gerth and C. W. Mills (London: Routledge & Kegan Paul, 1948).

Weber, Max (1920), 'Conceptual Exposition', in Max Weber, *Economy and Society*, ed. G. Roth and C. Wittich (Berkeley and Los Angeles: University of California Press, 1968).

Weber, Max (1923), *General Economic History* (New York: Collier, 1961).

Webster, D. (1995), *Why Freud Was Wrong* (London: Fontana).

Weeks, J. (1985), *Sexuality and its Discontents: Meanings, Myths and Modern Sexualities* (London: Routledge).

Weeks, J. (1989), *Sex, Politics, and Society: The Regulation of Sexuality since 1800* (2nd edn, London: Longman).

Weeks, J. Holland, J., and Waites, M. (2003) (eds), *Sexualities and Society* (Cambridge: Polity Press).

Weiner, G., Arnot, M., and David, M. (1997), 'Is the Future Female? Female Success, Male Disadvantage, and Changing Gender Patterns in Education', in Halsey *et al*. (1997).

Weiner, M. J. (1981), *English Culture and the Decline of the Entrepreneurial Spirit* (Harmondsworth: Penguin, 1985).

Wellings, K., Field, J., Johnson, A., and Wadsworth, J. (1994), *Sexual Behaviour in Britain: The National Survey of Sexual Attitudes and Lifestyles* (Harmondsworth: Penguin).

Wellings, K., *et al*. (2001), 'Sexual Behaviour in Britain: Early Heterosexual Experience', *Lancet*, 358/9296.

Wellman, B., and Gulia, M. (1999), 'Virtual Communities as Communities', in Smith and Kollock (1999).

Werbner, P. (1988), 'Taking and Giving: Working Women and Female Bonds in a Pakistani Immigrant Neighbourhood', in Westwood and Bhachu (1988*b*).

Westergaard, J. H., and Resler, H. (1975), *Class in a Capitalist Society* (London: Heinemann).

Westmarland, L. (2001), *Gender and Policing: Sex, Power and Police Culture* (Cullompton: Willan Publishing).

Westwood, S., and Williams, J. (1997) (eds), *Imagining Cities: Scripts, Signs, and Meanings* (London: Routledge).

Wheaton, B. (2004) (ed.), *Understanding Lifestyle Sports: Consumption, Identity, and Difference* (London: Routledge).

White, S. (1991), *Gorbachev and After* (Cambridge: Cambridge University Press).

WHO (1999), *World Health Report 1999: Making a Difference* (Geneva: World Health Organization), www.who.int/whr/1999/en/whr99_en.pdf.

WHO (2005), *World Health Report 2005: Make Every Mother and Child Count* (Geneva: World Health Organization), www.who.int/whr/2005/whr2005_en.pdf.

Wiener, M. (1980), *English Culture and the Decline of the Industrial Spirit 1850–1980* (Cambridge: Cambridge University Press).

Wilensky, H. (1975), *The Welfare State and Equality: Structural and Ideological Roots of Public Expenditure* (Berkeley and Los Angeles: University of California Press).

Wilkinson, I. (2001), *Anxiety in a Risk Society* (London: Routledge).

Wilkinson, S. (1992), 'Towards a New City', in P. Healey (ed.), *Rebuilding the City* (London: Spon).

Williams, C. L., and Stein, A. (2002) (eds), *Sexuality and Gender* (Oxford: Blackwell).

Williams, J. (2005), 'Education, Ethnicity, and Choice', *Sociology Review*, 14/3.

Williams, K., Mitsui, I., and Haslam, C. (1994), 'How Far from Japan? A Case Study of Japanese Press Shop Practice and Management Calculation', in Elger and Smith (1994).

Williams, M., and May, T. (1996), *An Introduction to the Philosophy of Social Research* (London: UCL Press).

Williams, P. (2002), 'Cooperation among Criminal Organizations', in M. Berdal and M. Serrano (eds), *Transnational Organized Crime and International Security* (Boulder, CO: Lynne Rienner).

Willis, P. (1977), *Learning to Labour: How Working Class Kids Get Working Class Jobs* (Farnborough: Saxon House).

Willmott, P. (1986), *Social Networks, Informal Care and Public Policy* (London: Policy Studies Institute).

Willmott, P. (1988), 'Urban Kinship Past and Present', *Social Studies Review*, 4/2.

Willmott, P., and Young, M. (1960), *Family and Class in a London Suburb* (London: Routledge & Kegan Paul).

Wilson, B. R. (1966), *Religion in Secular Society* (Harmondsworth: Penguin, 1969).

Wilson, B. R. (1976), *Contemporary Transformations of Religion* (Oxford: Oxford University Press).

Wilson, E. (1995), 'The Invisible *Flâneur*', in Watson and Gibson (1995).

Wilson, W. J. (1987), *The Truly Disadvantaged* (Chicago: University of Chicago Press).

Winlow, S., Hobbs, D., Lister, S., and Hadfield, P. (2001), 'Get Ready to Duck: Bouncers and the Realities of Ethnographic Research on Violent Groups', *British Journal of Criminology*, 42.

Winnicott, D. W. (1965), *The Family and Individual Development* (London: Tavistock).

Winship, J. (1987), *Inside Women's Magazines* (London: Pandora).

Winter, K., and Connolly, P. (1996), '"Keeping it in the Family": Thatcherism and the Children Act 1989', in Pilcher and Wagg (1996).

Wirth, L. (1938), 'Urbanism as a Way of Life', *American Journal of Sociology*, 44/1.

Witz, A. (1992), *Professions and Patriarchy* (London: Routledge).

Witz, A., and Savage, M. (1992), 'The Gender of Organizations', in Savage and Witz (1992).

Witz, A., Warhurst, C., and Nickson, D. (2002), 'The Labour of Aesthetics and the Aesthetics of Organization', *Organization*, 9/3.

Wolf, N. (1991), *The Beauty Myth: How Images of Beauty are Used against Women* (New York: Wm Morrow).

Wolff, K. H. (1950), *The Sociology of Georg Simmel* (New York: Free Press).

Wollstonecraft, M. (1792) *A Vindication of the Rights of Woman* (Harmondsworth: Penguin, 1975).

Wood, S. (1989), 'The Transformation of Work', in S. Wood (ed.), *The Transformation of Work: Skill, Flexibility and the Labour Process* (London: Unwin Hyman).

World Economic Forum (2007), *The Global Gender Gap Report 2007*, www.weforum.org/pdf/gendergap/report2007.pdf.

Wright, C. (1988), 'School Processes: An Ethnographic Study', in Dale *et al.* (1988).

Wright, C., Weekes, D., McGlaughlin, A., and Webb, D. (1998), 'Masculinised Discourses within Education and the Construction of Black, Male Identities', *British Journal of the Sociology of Education*, 19/1.

Wright, E. O. (1985), *Classes* (London: Verso).

Wright, E. O. (1997), *Class Counts* (Cambridge: Cambridge University Press).

Wright, E. O. (2005) (ed.), *Approaches to Class Analysis* (Cambridge: Cambridge University Press).

Wrong, D. (1961), 'The Oversocialized Concept of Man in Modern Sociology', *American Sociological Review*, 26.

Yablonsky, L. (1967), *The Violent Gang* (Harmondsworth: Penguin).

Yearley, S. (1991), *The Green Case: A Sociology of Environmental Issues, Arguments, and Politics* (London: Routledge).

Yearley, S. (1996), *Sociology, Environmentalism, Globalization: Reinventing the Globe* (London: Sage).

Yin, R. K. (2003), *Case Study Research: Design and Methods* (3rd edn, London: Sage).

Yoneyama, S. (1999), *The Japanese High School: Silence and Resistance* (London: Routledge).

Young, J. (1971), *The Drugtakers* (London: McGibbon & Kee).

Young, M., and Willmott, P. (1957), *Family and Kinship in East London* (London: Routledge & Kegan Paul).

Zeitlin, M. R. (1989), *The Large Corporation and the Capitalist Class* (Cambridge: Polity Press).

Zola, I. K. (1975), 'Medicine as an Institution of Social Control', in C. Cox and A. Mead (eds), *A Sociology of Medical Practice* (New York: Collier-Macmillan).

Zorbaugh, H. (1929), *The Gold Coast and the Slum* (Chicago: University of Chicago Press).

Zukin, S. (1995), *The Culture of Cities* (Oxford: Blackwell).

Zweig, F. (1948), *Men in the Pits* (London: Victor Gollancz).

Zweig, F. (1961), *The Worker in an Affluent Society* (London: Heinemann).

Index